1990 Novel & Short Story Writer's Market

1990 Novel & Short Story Writer's Market

Editor: Robin Gee

Assistant Editor: Lisa Carpenter

Cincinnati, Ohio

Distributed in Canada by Prentice-Hall of Canada Ltd., 1870 Birchmount Road, Scarborough, Ontario M1P 2J7. Also distributed in Australia by Kirby Books, Private Bag No. 19, P.O. Alexandria NSW2015.

Managing Editor, Market Books Department: Constance J. Achabal

1990 Novel & Short Story Writer's Market.

Published by F&W Publications, 1507 Dana Ave., Cincinnati, Ohio 45207. Printed and bound in the United States of America.

International Standard Serial Number ISSN 0897-9812
International Standard Book Number 0-89879-381-5

Contents

1 From the Editors

Writing Techniques

Personal Views

3 **An Interview with Margaret Atwood,** *by Roya Fahmy Swartz*
The author of A Handmaid's Tale, Cat's Eye *and other novels tells how she got started and offers advice to beginning writers.*

8 **Let's Say You Wrote Badly This Morning,** *by David Huddle*
Author Huddle tells how professional writers are like professional athletes and how writers can learn about dealing with rejection by keeping an eye on the pitcher's mound.

12 **Two Pros on Prose,** *by James Kisner and J.N. Williamson*
A double interview with two successful horror writers at different stages in their careers.

23 **The Writing Life,** *by Annie Dillard*
The author of Pilgrim at Tinker Creek *and* American Childhood *writes about her craft and its place in her life.*

29 **The Imagined Reader,** *by Eve Shelnutt*
Short story writer and Professor of English at Ohio University, Eve Shelnutt tells writers how to envision readers and how to write for those readers.

Craft and Technique

33 **The Hair of the Dog That Bit You,** *by Henriette Anne Klauser*
This writing consultant tells how using right brain/left brain techniques can help you get started writing.

38 **How Many Stories Are There in Your Story?,** *by Gordon Weaver*
Author and Professor of English at Oklahoma State, Gordon Weaver tells how to break writer's block by varying the viewpoints in your story.

43 **Character Development: Being a Thief of Souls,** *by Rita Mae Brown*
The author of Rubyfruit Jungle, Southern Discomfort *and other books tells writers how to create realistic characters by developing the power of observation.*

49 **Plotting for Suspense,** *by Stephanie Kay Bendel*
Mystery author Bendel tells how to build suspense by stacking the odds against your protagonist and your reader.

55 **The Last Stages,** *by Geoffrey Bocca*
The author of 11 novels tells how to work with editors and polish stories.

Writing for Specialized Audiences

62 **No Bones About It: How to Write Today's Horror,** *by David Taylor*
Taylor discusses what readers want and what they do not want in their horror fiction.

71 **Writing Romance Novels: Follow Your Dream,** *by Ruth Ryan Langan*
The author of 17 romance novels tells how she changed her dream to reality.

77 **Bringing Back the Western,** *by Dennis E. Showalter*
Historian Showalter explores the market for western fiction and the recent resurgence of interest in the genre.

81 **Succeeding with Popular Fiction,** *by Alice Harron Orr*
Mystery author, romance editor and agent Alice Harron Orr discusses the difference between literary and popular fiction and what sells.

Publishing

85 **Understanding the Marketplace,** *by Leonard S. Bernstein*
A poet and short story writer, the author of The Official Guide to Wine Snobbery *discusses the market for short commercial fiction and his theory on the probability of acceptance and rejection.*

89 **Writing Workshops: A Publishers' Clearinghouse,** *by David Weddle*
This writer offers a straightforward discussion of writing workshops and the functions they serve, as well as those they do not.

91 **Finding the Right Agent,** *by Donald MacCampbell*
An agent himself, MacCampbell tells how to find an agent, what to look for and how to approach one.

94 **Publishing Contract Terms: Royalties Defined,** *by Brad Bunnin*
Publishing lawyer Bunnin explains royalties and how publishers pay writers.

100 **Writer on the Road: Self-Promoting Your Book,** *by Gerry Maddren*
Tips on self promotion by the author of On the Case of the Johannisberg Riesling.

The Markets

103 How to Get the Most Out of This Book

107 The Business of Fiction Writing

116 Literary and Small Circulation Magazines

Close-ups:
123 **Thomson Littlefield,** ***The Albany Review***
The joy of discovering a well-crafted story, says this fiction editor, makes his job a pleasure.

202 **Darshan Perusek,** ***Kaleidoscope***
This editor discusses her magazine's development from a small do-it-yourself journal to a major outlet for work by and about the disabled.

320 Commercial Periodicals

Close-up:
368 **Ellen Datlow,** ***Omni***
The fiction editor of a leading science magazine tells what makes a good science fiction tale and what she looks for in a manuscript.

393 Small Press

Close-ups:
417 **Austin Wright, Writer**
Wright describes his daily routine and personal discipline as a writer.

425 **Emilie Buchwald, Milkweed Editions**
The publisher of a successful Midwest press discusses the advantages of working with a small publisher.

444 **Norma Alarcon, Third Woman Press**
Alarcon explains her reasons for starting a press featuring work by Latinas.

450 **Irene Zahava, Woman Sleuth Mystery Series**
Mysteries by women have a special viewpoint, but suspense is still the key, says this publisher.

456 **Commercial Publishers**

Close-ups:

468 **Ellen Steiber and Robin Hardy, Cloverdale Press**
These editors discuss how a packager differs from a publisher and why packagers are a good place for writers to start.

470 **Sheila Gilbert, Daw Books**
The executive editor discusses the science fiction and fantasy market and the special relationship between writers and readers of the genre.

485 **Kaye Gibbons, Writer**
Surprise was this writer's first reaction to the success of her first novel.

495 **Pat Cadigan, Writer**
Science fiction writer Cadigan discusses changes in the genre and the power of persistence.

504 **Contests and Awards**

542 **Literary Agents**

Close-up:

551 **Sandra Dijkstra, Agent**
Dijkstra tells what an agent can and cannot do for a writer.

573 **Glossary**

576 **Category Index**

599 **Markets Index**

Acknowledgments

The editor wishes to thank the following for their original contributions to the 1990 edition of *Novel and Short Story Writer's Market*:

Stephanie Kay Bendel, "Plotting for Suspense"
James Kisner and J.N. Williamson, "Two Pros on Prose"
Roya Fahmy Swartz, "An Interview with Margaret Atwood"
David Taylor, "How to Write Today's Horror"
Gordon Weaver, "How Many Stories Are There in Your Story?"

The editor of *Novel and Short Story Writer's Market* gratefully acknowledges the following publishers, authors and agents for granting permission to publish their articles and book excerpts:

Leonard S. Bernstein, "Understanding the Marketplace," from *Getting Published: The Writer in the Combat Zone*, copyright © 1986. Reprinted by permission of William Morrow & Co.

Geoffrey Bocca, "The Last Stages," from *You Can Write a Novel*, copyright © 1983. Reprinted with permission of Prentice Hall, a division of Simon Schuster.

Rita Mae Brown, "Character Development: Being a Thief of Souls," from *Starting from Scratch*, copyright © 1988 by Speakeasy Productions, Inc. Reprinted with permission of Bantam, a division of Bantam, Doubleday, Dell Publishing Group, Inc.

Brad Bunnin and Peter Beren, Pages 29-37 from *The Writer's Legal Companion*, copyright © 1988. Reprinted with permission of Addison-Wesley Publishing Co., Inc., Reading, MA.

Annie Dillard, selected excerpts from *The Writing Life*, copyright © 1989 by Annie Dillard. Reprinted by permission of Harper & Row, Publishers, Inc.

David Huddle, "Let's Say You Wrote Badly This Morning," from *The New York Times*, copyright © 1988 by The New York Times Company. Reprinted by permission.

Henriette Anne Klauser, "The Hair of the Dog That Bit You," from *Writing on Both Sides of the Brain, Breakthrough Techniques for People Who Write*, copyright © 1987 by Henriette Anne Klauser. Reprinted by permission of Harper & Row, Publishers, Inc.

Ruth Ryan Langan, "Write Romance Novels," from *Voices on Writing Fiction*, edited by Elizabeth Kane Buzzelli and Carolyn Hall. Copyright ® 1987. Reprinted with permission by Detroit Women Writers Press, Detroit, MI.

Donald MacCampbell, "Finding the Right Agent," from *The Writing Business*, copyright © 1978 by Donald MacCampbell. Reprinted by permission of Crown Publishers, Inc.

Gerry Maddren, "On the Road with the Case of the Johannisberg Riesling or Self-Promoting Your Book," originally published in the *Writers Connection* newsletter, April © 1989. Reprinted with permission.

Alice Harron Orr, "How to Write Popular Fiction That Sells," tape AHO-1 from the *How to Succeed as a Commercial Novelist* tape series (selected excerpts), copyright © 1989. Reprinted with permission by Alice Harron Orr.

Eve Shelnutt, "The Imagined Reader," from *The Writing Room*, copyright © 1989. Reprinted with permission by Longstreet Press.

Dennis E. Showalter, "Bringing Back the Western." Reprinted from the May 5, 1989 issue of *Publishers Weekly*, published by the Bowker Magazine Group of Cahners Publishing Co., a division of Reed Publishing USA. Copyright © 1989 by Reed Publishing USA. Reprinted with permission.

David Weddle, "Writing Workshops: A Publishers' Clearinghouse." Reprinted from the October 5, 1989 issue of *Rolling Stone* magazine, copyright © 1989 by Straight Arrow Publishers, Inc. All rights reserved. Reprinted by permission.

From the Editors

Welcome to the tenth edition of our annual directory for fiction writers. Looking back at earlier editions we realize how much we've changed over the years. We have a new format and a new name and, most importantly, we've more than doubled the number of markets listed—from about 800 in the 1980/81 book to more than 1,900 listings in this, the 1990 edition of *Novel & Short Story Writer's Market.*

Our book looks very different now than it did ten years ago, but some things have not changed. In our first edition, editors John Brady and Jean Fredette wrote, "We dedicate this book to *you*, the determined writer—from beginner to bestseller—with the sincere hope that our work, along with your own hard work at the typewriter, will lead you to even higher fields of writing achievement . . . ."

Fiction writers today are perhaps more likely to be found hard at work at their personal computers, but we know all the frustration and joy of this profession have remained unchanged. And our dedication to providing both beginning and experienced fiction writers with support and encouragement, as well as detailed marketing information, has not changed either.

The past decade has been one of rapid changes in the fiction market. We've experienced a wave of mergers and buy-outs, shrinking the number of commercial publishing outlets. Yet, with the help of desk top publishing technology, we've seen a growth in the number of small presses and small magazines. It's hard at this point to predict what will happen in the next ten years, but we're confident the market will remain strong.

The outlook for the coming year is bright and we know this edition will be a useful tool throughout the year. This year we met with fiction writers and asked for their input in developing the book. As a result we've increased our emphasis on popular and genre fiction, added new listings for literary magazines and expanded our business section.

Check the section titled, "How to Get the Most Out of This Book," for a sample listing followed by complete details on each listing element to help you make full use of all the information given in each listing. In the "Business of Fiction Writing" section, which incorporates "Manuscript Mechanics" featured in earlier editions, we've added cover letter samples and postage-by-the-page charts for both the U.S. and Canada.

We're most proud, however, to be able to bring you a collection of exciting and inspirational articles from some of the top fiction writers and editors. This edition includes an exclusive interview with bestselling author Margaret Atwood and excerpts from new books on writing by Annie Dillard, Rita Mae Brown and Eve Shelnutt.

Through our research we found many of our more successful readers write category and genre fiction. Mystery writer Stephanie Bendel and romance author Ruth Ryan Langan offer tips on how to write their special types of fiction. We've included a special double interview with horror writers J.N. Williamson and James Kisner, as well as David Taylor's article on why horror is so popular. Editors Ellen Datlow of *Omni* and Sheila Gilbert of Daw Books discuss in close-ups the science fiction market as does award-winning science fiction author Pat Cadigan. To round out our genre focus we've also included articles on the renewed interest in westerns and the appeal of popular fiction.

Other close-ups include interviews with the editors of *The Albany Review* and *Kaleidoscope* and we discuss new-found success with novelist Kaye Gibbons. Agent Sandra Dijkstra tells writers why small press publication is important and the editors at Cloverdale Press explain the ins and outs of book packaging.

You will notice we've changed the name of our literary section to include small circulation magazines. In the past we've had difficulty defining what exactly "little" magazine means, so we found the fairest criteria is to use circulation figures. We've moved all magazines, literary and commercial, with circulations under 10,000 to the renamed Literary and Small Circulation section. Yet you will continue to find larger circulation literary magazines in this section as well and large commercial publications in the section titled Commercial Periodicals.

You may also notice we no longer include a Special Markets section which included publishers of comic books and graphic novels. This year we're pleased to announce these listings and hundreds more will be included in our new sister publication, *Humor and Cartoon Markets*.

Poets will find several literary markets open to their work in our book, but *Poet's Market* contains listings specifically geared to poetry submissions.

Changes in all our books are a result of our research and input from our readers. In fact, we'd like to close by inviting you to write us. Let us know of new markets or information you may come across or just drop us a line on what's happening in your writing career. We'd like to know what you think of the book, but we'd also like to know more about you—what type of writing you do and what kinds of information would help you reach your writing goals. With your help we can continue our commitment to provide you with the best marketing advice for the next decade and beyond.

Robin Gee

Lisa Carpenter

Writing Techniques

An Interview with Margaret Atwood

by Roya Fahmy Swartz

In 1957 in a quiet suburb of Toronto, Ontario, a young woman sat writing in her home. She wanted more than anything to be a writer. So, very soon afterwards, she went out and purchased a *Writer's Market* and some additional magazines. She looked through the listings, saw that the highest paying magazine was *True Confessions*, shrugged her shoulders and sat down to write. But the "true confessions" didn't come so easy. She eventually gave up on *True Confessions*, but she did persevere in writing: short stories, poetry and novels.

She continued to write and in 1967, at the age of 26, she won the highest literary award in Canada: The Governor General's Award. The award honored her book of poetry, *The Circle Game*.

That young rising literary star was Margaret Atwood. Since then she has written many works of fiction, poetry and screenplays. Among them: *The Circle Game*, *The Edible Woman*, *Lady Oracle* and her most recent, *Cat's Eye*. Her 1986 novel, *The Handmaid's Tale*, is now being made into a feature film. Writer Roya Swartz, representing *Novel and Short Story Writer's Market*, spoke by phone with Ms. Atwood at her home in Toronto, Ontario.

Roya Swartz: When did you first begin to write professionally? What were your first works?
Margaret Atwood: My first published works were poetry. My first poetry book, *The Circle Game*, was published in 1966 with some other books of poetry in Canada. It was difficult to publish novels in Canada in the 1960s. However, I wrote my first novel, *The Edible Woman* in 1964 and 1965, but it was not published until 1969 in England and Canada, and 1970 in the United States.

RS: Have you written ever since you were a child? When did you start?
MA: I started writing seriously at 16 in grade 12. I had no journals, no interest in writing until that time. My eleventh-grade teacher was interviewed some years ago in a "This-is-Your-Life" type project. She was quite honest and said that she saw no particular talent in me at all.

RS: Did something happen in grade 12 to spark your interest, a monumental change?

Roya Fahmy Swartz *is an actress and writer currently living in Cincinnati, Ohio.*

MA: There must have been, but I don't remember what. There were no high-profile writers in Canada in the 1950's and a very small audience. What we studied was British literature and British curriculum: Shakespeare of course; George Elliot; and Jane Austen. I read *Pride and Prejudice* at the age of 12. It was good that I was studying women writers but they were dead women. I knew no living Canadian writers or North American writers. I did have a very good English teacher in 12th grade. My family has always been great book readers, we always had a lot of books around growing up. My brother, who is a scientist, wrote at that age as well. We both wrote, we were both good at science. He became a scientist, I became a writer.

RS: Let me ask you about your education. Where and what you studied and at which university?
MA: I studied a course called Honors English at the University of Toronto; that program of course is no longer in existence. Then I went to Radcliff Graduate School for one year, and eventually it merged with Harvard graduate school. I was there for four years.

RS: After that you went back to Canada? To writing?
MA: And then I got a job teaching in Montreal. I moved to Alberta for two years, taught at the University of Alberta, then I went to England and France, writing there. I returned to the University of Toronto as a writer-in-residence and took a teaching job there in 1972.

RS: You mentioned it was very hard to get novels published in Canada in the '60s. How did you get your work noticed and published?
MA: It was easier to get poetry published and I started with poetry. There were good things and bad things about being in Canada in the '60s. The bad thing was that it was hard to get published and the audience was small. It was not until the middle of the '60s when things started to happen. The good thing was that there weren't very many people writing, so if you were any good at all, you did get noticed. Now that there are more people writing, it is proportionately harder to make an impact. *But* there is also a lot more publication.

RS: So there were not many publishing houses?
MA: There were only five literary magazines in Canada in the early '60s. In 1960 there were five novels published in the entire year in English-speaking Canada by English-speaking writers. So that's about the scale of things. You were thought to be doing well if they knew about you, if they were aware of your work.

RS: So you just sent your manuscripts out to them?
MA: Well, of course, because the literary culture was so small. If you were a writer and showing some promise, usually people were very kind to you. In a way, that is hard to envision today. There are so many young people wanting to write, it would be impossible to discover them and take note of all of them.

RS: How do you approach editors and publishers as a beginning writer? What is your advice to beginning writers?
MA: Well, it's different for poetry and prose. There are a lot of little magazines, literary magazines and other magazines that are publishing short stories and poetry. They're still a way in. That you can do without an agent. It is almost impossible these days to have a manuscript read by a publisher without having an agent because they don't have time to read that many manuscripts.

I would recommend someone doing their first writing get to know that literary magazine world. Figure out what literary magazines publish what you want to write. Submit there first. When you have some of those publications to your credit, other people are more likely to get to see your work and an agent might look at you.

RS: And you have an agent yourself?
MA: Of course. She has been my agent since 1975. She's from the States but has lived in Canada. She's affiliated with English agents, John Farquharson Ltd.

RS: Did anything happen, a significant event, a turning point, that influenced you a great deal in your writing?
MA: There were several turning points. The first book of poetry that I published won the highest literary award in Canada. I was 26 years old. When *The Circle Game* won the Governor General's Award. It was great because I was broke. With the money I bought myself an electric typewriter. The second thing would be the publication of my second novel, *Surfacing*, in 1972. That was the crossing of the line. I was able to support myself with my writing. There is a point at which you cease to be promising and become more of a fixture. Not just potential, you've actualized potential.

RS: As far as the progression of your novels and poetry, has it been a steady, gradual progression? A raising of your feminist consciousness, awareness?
MA: What you read is as important as what you write. Remember, I started in 1956. There was no feminist movement in Canada. However, it was not as bad as people are led to believe. For instance, at my high school and my college, we were not told that the best thing for us to do was to get married. On the contrary, we were encouraged to have and pursue careers. This was Canada, not the "monolithic cheerleaders" attitude that prevailed in the U.S. Also, Betty Friedan's *Feminine Mystique* came early in the '60s as did Simone De Beauvoir's *The Second Sex*. I can remember reading them just about the time I was writing *The Edible Woman*. You cannot say there was a feminist movement, because there wasn't in Canada. However, since then, there has been a great deal written. Certainly, a great many aspects have been explored since the women's movement began. There have been some changes, although let us not pretend the changes are always either permanent or universal.

RS: When you were recently interviewed on the PBS show, "Bookmark," someone asked you if *Cats Eye* was a women's book. You responded, "What do you mean? Was *War and Peace* a women's book?"
MA: It depends on what they mean by women's books. That usually means a book that only women read. I don't think so, judging from my audience. "Women's novel" also has a derogatory implication. Any book about relationships is a women's book, any book with women in it is a women's book. This idea of "only women read women's books" is wrong. Men writers don't get that implication of being a member of a separate group. Nobody ever judges a book as a "men's book" because it was written by a man.

RS: What are you presently doing?
MA: I have just come from nine months of book tours for *Cat's Eye* in three different countries: Canada, England and the United States. When you are on a book tour, you have very little time to write. I have just also finished being a guest editor and writing the introduction for *Best American Short Stories of 1988*. It's a big job, but I did just finish a short story. You can only do little things while on a book tour.

RS: How was the book tour? Was it a blur of hotels, cities and people?
MA: Well, the nice thing about it is that I get a chance to see my friends around the world. We (my husband and I) have quite a few friends in London because we have lived there from time to time.

RS: It must be nice to set your own hours.
MA: It is nice to set your own hours; it's called freelance writing, which often means you work much more than eight hours a day, sometimes 13 or 14. And often a lot of work comes at once.

RS: Where do your ideas, your inspiration, come from?
MA: One never knows where writers get ideas. They just come and there is always more information than you can deal with. Getting the ideas is not the problem, getting the time to sit and work out the ideas is the problem.

I think a lot of novels begin as questions. For example, *Handmaid's Tale* began as a question. Really, a couple of questions: "If you were going to take over the United States, how would you do it?" "If women's place isn't the home, how are you going to get them back into the home now that they are not there?" "How are you going to make them go back when they don't want to?"

RS: For the screenplay of *Handmaid's Tale* you chose one of my favorite playwrights, Harold Pinter, to write it. Why?
MA: I would like to say it was *my* idea but it wasn't. It was the producer's idea, but I thought it was quite brilliant.

RS: Do you have a desire to write screenplays?
MA: Well, I have written screenplays since 1971. But they are not a writer's medium. Screenplays . . . how they are interpreted or end up, is not in our control. A most crucial scene could end up on the cutting room floor. Anything can happen to it between the time you write it and the time it gets shown. So the writer, whether it be a book writer or a screenwriter, has really no control in the movies. People who have the control are the director and the film editor. So, it's fun, and I enjoy doing it, but it's not the same as writing a book. With a book, the buck stops with you. You're responsible for all the words in that book. In a screenplay the buck starts with you. Then it could end up on the floor (of the editing room.)

RS: Will you participate at all in the filming?
MA: I'm making a visitation to the set and I am a consultant. These things are much more informal than they sound. And I'm sure there will be a lot of talk of "well, this wasn't like the book . . . that wasn't in the book." A movie cannot be a book. A book cannot be a movie. They are two different art forms.

RS: Do you come across any pitfalls in your writing? What are they? You mentioned time is a problem.
MA: Yes, of course, time. I was juggling jobs and did not have any money for 16 years. I think the thing to emphasize is that writing is a gambler's profession. There is no guarantee of anything. You can put in a lot of time, a lot of effort, invest a great deal of emotional energy and nothing may come out of it. There are no guarantees. So, unless one is fairly committed and willing to make that investment, don't do it.

RS: When you were teaching at the university, how did you handle your time? Did you get up at 5 a.m. and write, or write when you came home?
MA: I was teaching in Canada, and the academic year is mid-September to the end of April. I had May, June, July, August and half of September and I would save my money and live on it when I wrote. I lived frugally. I could write short stories and poetry when teaching, but not novels. Novels take a sustained amount of concentration. If you sit down to write and get interrupted, its hard to keep your train of thought.

RS: What advice in particular would you give young women writers?
MA: Read a lot and write a lot. Speak your voice. I don't think it is that different from advice you would give any writer. But, for a group that is not the dominant group or force, there are pitfalls. There is a support group, or people that will support your work because you are a woman. But, the bad thing is the same people may demand things of you because you are a woman writer.

RS: This is your time now. Is there anything that you would like to say or add?
MA: Well, I would like to say that when I was 16, and wanted to be a writer, one of the first things I did was go out and buy one of those *Writer's Market* books. But the result was quite funny because I was quite naive. I thought, "Well, if I am going to be a writer, I have to support myself with some kind of writing." So I looked to see what (kind of writing) paid money. And what paid the most money was *True Confessions*. So I went out and bought some *True Confessions* magazines. I thought, "Well these plots are pretty easy, I can write this." But, in fact, it was a lot harder than I thought. The vocabulary was very specialized.

RS: So did you ever end up selling anything to *True Confessions*?
MA: No, I couldn't finish the stories. But I used to pour over those *Writer's Market*s and writers' magazines. For example, one important thing I learned from them was to always send a self-addressed, stamped envelope. I didn't have anybody to tell me that, because we didn't have any creative writing courses at school. They taught me the nuts and bolts.

RS: It must have been exciting when you started – like being a pioneer – no boundaries?
MA: Yes, but you don't feel like a pioneer, you feel more like you are walking a tightrope with your eyes blindfolded. If I had known the odds, I probably wouldn't have become a writer, it would have discouraged me right away. Ignorance was bliss, yes; I did not see any reason why I couldn't become a world-famous writer. If some sensible adult had gotten a hold of me and said, "Who do you think you are? Here you are living in this boring suburb in Toronto, how can you possibly suppose you are going to be a writer?" I would have been flattened. I didn't know any better. And there was *Writer's Digest*, books and magazines telling me I could do it.

© Laurence Acland 1988.

'Let's Say You Wrote Badly This Morning'

by David Huddle

In September I had a novel rejected. In October of the same year, I had that rejection on my mind as I watched the American and National League baseball playoffs. I had a new television set that allowed me to see what I had never really noticed before–the facial expressions of the players. What particularly intrigued me was how batters look when they strike out and how pitchers look when they give up a home run.

In one incredible game, just after the center fielder, with two balls and two strikes on him, had hit a ninth-inning homer, the camera switched to a close-up of the reflief pitcher. I have never seen such visible anguish. The pitcher was a veteran, a man who gave the appearance of being quiet, proud and possessed of a great deal of hard-earned skill. There was in his face at that moment the sign of a crushed spirit. I wondered how he could ever make himself pitch to another batter.

Getting my novel rejected was not at all similar to what I imagine was that pitcher's experience of pitching a ninth-inning, game-winning home-run ball. My publisher, David Godine, gave me the bad news in straightforward fashion as he and I drove from a day's fishing on the Lamoille River in Vermont. In fact, the news was much worse that I expected—not only did Mr. Godine not want to publish the novel himself, he also thought it would be a dreadful mistake for me to let anyone publish it. I think I'd known for a long while that my book was weak. Consciously I'd hoped that an editor might be able to give me suggestions so that I could revise it to make it good. Unconsciously I think I wanted somebody to tell me to put the thing away.

I figure I worked on the novel for an average of about three hours a day for 10 months—let's say I had about 900 hours of writing time invested in that 307-page manuscript. That's not counting the time I spent thinking about it while driving to the grocery store or solved some difficult problem in it with my subconscious mind while I slept.

As novels go mine was written pretty efficiently. Ten years is not an outrageous amount of time for a writer to work on a book—Hannah Green, my old teacher at Columbia, gave that much of her life (say, conservatively, about 11,000 writing hours) to *The Dead of the House*. Ralph Ellison apparently has been working on his second novel for more than 20 years. But Ann Beattie is said to have done one of her novels in about a month, and one can imagine Isaac Asimov starting a book on Monday and mailing the finished manuscript to his publisher the following Monday.

In my adult life I've written something in the neighborhood of 40 or 50 short stories, of which I've published maybe 25. There are only a few stories I still have on hand—ones that haven't found a home—that I can remember with any clarity. Usually when they aren't much good, I recognize that after they've gathered a couple of rejections, and I either revise them or put them away.

When he's not watching baseball, **David Huddle** *teaches at the University of Vermont and at the Bread Loaf School of English. He is the author of* Stopping by Home, Only the Little Bone *and a collection of short stories,* The High Spirits.

But this is the first novel I've ever written, and my immediate plan for it is to put it away. My theory about these matters is that if there's anything worthwhile in that manuscript, it will stick in my mind enough to send me back to the novel in a year or two. If there isn't anything worthwhile there, I'll forget all about it and let the manuscript gather dust.

The model for my theory is the behavior of baseball players. There are *no* pitchers who do not give up home runs; there are *no* batters who do not strike out. There are *no* major league pitchers or batters who have not somehow learned to survive giving up home runs and striking out. That much is obvious.

Putting failure to use

What seems to me less obvious is how these "failures" must be digested, or put to use, in the overall experience of the player. I am not able to be precise here, because I'm simply speculating about something that is immensely complicated. A jogger once explained to me that the nerves of the ankle are so sensitive and complex that each time a runner sets his foot down, hundreds of messages are conveyed to the runner's brain about the nature of the terrain and the requirements for weight distribution, balance and muscle strength. I'm certain that a ninth-inning home run would register complexly and permanently in a pitcher's mind and body, and that the next time he faced a similar circumstance, his pitching would be informed by his awful experience. His continuing baseball career would depend to some extent on his converting that encounter into something useful for his pitching.

There are a few examples of writers who for one reason or another were stopped in their work. The Fugitive poet and critic John Crowe Ransom stopped writing original verse in his mid-30's, though he tinkered with his old poems, making little changes here and there, for the rest of his life. After the publication of *Gone With the Wind*, Margaret Mitchell devoted her writing energy to answering her fan mail. A few years ago a young man named John Kennedy Toole drove to Milledgeville, Ga., to commit suicide after his novel had been turned down a number of times; that book, *A Confederacy of Dunces*, was posthumously published to considerable acclaim. And will somebody please tell me what has happened to Harper Lee, author of nothing since her wonderful *To Kill a Mockingbird*?"

However sturdy the human body may be, it is also immensely delicate. Any little malfunction – say, for example, one ever-so-slightly damaged nerve in an ankle – can cause the apparatus to break down significantly: the unhittable 95 m.p.h. fastball can become the immensely hittable 87 m.p.h. not-so-fastball. For an athlete to perform well, he must be able to extend himself out into a territory in which he is immensley vulnerable.

Of the many ways in which athletes and artists are similar, one is that, unlike accountants or plumbers or insurance salesmen, to succeed at all they must perform at an extraordinary level of excellence. Another is that they must be willing to extend themselves irrationally in order to achieve that level of performance. A writer must be willing to make a fool of him- or herself, must attempt to mine the depths of the subconscious mind and to soar to the heights of the imagination without concern for cave-ins or crashes. You don't have to write all-out all the time, but you have to be ready to write all-out any time your story or your poem or your novel asks you to. Hold back and you produce what just about any literate citizen can produce, a "pretty good" piece of work. Like the cautious pitcher, the timid writer can spend a lifetime in the minor leagues.

And what is more likely than failure – the strikeout, the crucial home run given up, the manuscript criticized and rejected – to produce caution or timidity? An instinctive response to painful experience is to avoid the behavior that produced the pain. To function at the level of excellence required for survival, writers like athletes must go against instinct, must absorb their failures and become stronger, must endlessly repeat the behavior that produced the pain. It's not merely a matter of putting the failed work behind you and going on; what you must do is convert the energy of a failed past work into usable energy for present and future work.

Esthetic luck

Easy to say: put failure to use. How do you do it? The one notion I can offer has to do with what I'll call "esthetic luck"—a sibling of "athletic luck."

Esthetic luck is random and two-headed. No writer, no matter how accomplished, can be certain when sitting down to work that the results of his or her best efforts will be writing of high quality. One can school oneself to a high level of technical skill, construct ideal working circumstances of time and place, regularly come to the writing desk rested, alert and in good health, achieve a state of brutal self-honesty, open one's mind to every possibility of concept and language, and nevertheless write one lousy line after another. Conversely (and perversely) one may pick up a napkin in a bar to make a few notes, and suddenly find oneself writing fabulous stuff. The odds of writing well are a great deal better if the writer is well prepared, but there's never a guarantee of good writing.

If production is the first of the two heads of esthetic luck, then the second is reception: even if one has the good fortune to complete a brilliant piece of writing., there's a good chance it will go unrecognized by anyone else. Fine poems and stories and novels are rejected all the time. The story goes that *The Catcher in the Rye* was turned down by 20 publishing houses before it found a taker. A much-admired poet I know says that while the best journals accept some of her work, they usually reject what she knows to be the best poems in any group she submits to them

There's a story that someone once asked the poet Richard Wilbur how he dealt with rejection slips and he confessed that he didn't know because he'd never received one. This seems to me such an absolutely necessary anecdote that if it didn't already exist we'd have to invent it: if esthetic luck is truly random—meaning that no matter what we do we can't assure ourselves that we'll write well, and that even if we write well we can't count on anyone's recognizing our achievement—it stands to reason that somebody somewhere would have to harvest nothing but good fortune.

What I think is valuable about understanding the crazy nature of esthetic luck is that it can be just as encouraging as it is discouraging. Understanding esthetic luck is the key to serenity for a writer. Let's say you wrote badly this morning, and the mail brought you a rejection slip for a sheaf of poems and an insulting note paper-clipped to a returned short story and another note from an editorial assistant at a publishing house explaining that somehow the manuscript of your novel has been misplaced, they're sorry they've taken a year to let you know this, but the editor you sent it to in the first place has been fired, and so there's no need, really, to send them another copy. Lots of sensible people would take such a morning as a clear sign that there are better ways to spend your time than trying to write well. But our ideally serene writer will read the same evidence to make the opposite case: if your luck is bad today the odds are improved that you'll get good luck tomorrow.

Esthetic luck is the major argument in favor of working through a process of revising a piece of writing through many drafts. If you're a supremely talented artist and you hit a very lucky day, then maybe you can write a poem or story or chapter of a novel that needs no revision. If you're a regular writer with your appointed portion of esthetic luck, you'll need to come at the piece again and again. I like to think of revision as a form of self-forgiveness: you can allow yourself mistakes and shortcomings in your writing because you know you're coming back later to improve it. Revision is the way you cope with the bad luck that made your writing less than brilliant this morning. Revision is the hope you hold out for yourself to make something beautiful tomorrow though you didn't quite manage it today. Revision is democracy's literary method, the tool that allows an ordinary person to aspire to extraordinary achievement.

What writers and ballplayers know

The equivalent of revision available to an athlete is repetition: batters and pitchers usually face each other more than once in a game and many times over the course of their mutual careers. In my opinion, baseball players would be able to offer more testimony to the capriciousness of athletic luck than the players of any other game. (My most outrageous notion on this matter is that the crazy luck of baseball accounts for the vast role of spitting by its players: to spit is to change one's chemistry, to cast out the immediate past, to set oneself to face the future.) But in their thinking, batters and pitchers must proceed in a logical manner: they consider the scouting reports and the opinions of their coaches and fellow players; they consider "the last time up," along with the history they have shared in all their previous encounters; they make adjustments; they spit for luck.

In the overall balance of esthetic luck, by my calculations, the bad outweighs the good by a ratio of about 17 to 1, but the good nevertheless exists. Somebody who worked hard for years with little visible or invisible success suddenly gets a contract and publishes a fine book that is well reviewed and that almost makes it to the *New York Times* best-seller list; this somebody wins prizes and fellowships, receives invitations to lecture. For every version of this happy story, there are 17 hard-working literary citizens who have given a considerable portion of their lives to the practice of their art, every one of them with artistic gifts in various stages of development. All 17 have had the experience of writing well on a regular basis; not one of them has had much success at publishing.

Something at issue here is a peculiarly American conflict between the heroic and the actual: one of our basic misconceptions about talent is that either you have it or you don't—if you have it, performance is an effortless matter for you, and if you don't have it, you're hopeless. One of the most destructive archetypes of the American consciousness is "The Natural," the person who can do something perfectly without ever trying; a sibling of the "The Natural" is "The Discovery," a person who finds out he or she has this perfect ability or who is discovered by an expert to have it. From experience, I can tell you that the most common motivating factor for people attending the Bread Loaf Writers' Conference is to find out whether or not they "have what it takes."

And what the great American game of baseball seems to me to demonstrate most obviously is that those who "have what it takes" must nevertheless work hard at their craft all the time and that many who might have been judged not to "have what it takes" can also, through hard work at their craft, perform well. Recent years of World Series and league championship games have shown us great hitters and pitchers hitting and pitching badly while players we've never heard of perform beautifully. What veteran baseball players and writers know is that constantly working hard will produce a respectable batting or earned run average, a stack of pages of substantial literary value, an acceptance from a good journal.

I am not describing a method of achieving happiness. I am describing what seems to me a necessary and healthy way for a few people to carry out their lives; happiness has nothing to do with it. What seems to me the only legitimate goal of any would-be writer is to achieve a circumstance of ongoing work, the serenity to carry out the daily writing and revising of what poems, stories or novels are given one to write. On those occasions when one's serenity seems to collapse, I recommend that one step out into one's backyard and vigorously spit.

Two Pros on Prose

What follows is a unique set of interviews, created especially for beginning writers. J.N. Williamson and James Kisner, both professional writers, interviewed each other. Why these two? Because each writer is at a different stage in his career, and each has a different perspective to offer as to what makes for writing success.

There are similarities between the two—both have written horror fiction—but many differences as well, and these differences offer the beginning writer many insights into the creative process of writing, as well as into the marketing of fiction.

J.N. Williamson is the author of 34 published novels, including *The Black School* and *Hellstorm* from Dell, the writer of more than seventy published short stories, and a prize-winning anthologist. His fiction anthologies include *Masques* and *Masques II* (Maclay & Associates), *The Best of Masques* (Berkley Books) and *Masques III* (St. Martin's Press). He was also the editor of the Writer's Digest book *How to Write Tales of Horror, Fantasy & Science Fiction*.

It is also worthwhile noting that in his anthologies Williamson has introduced to professional publication 13 new writers, several of whom were his students during the period (1984-1988) he was an instructor for Writer's Digest School.

James Kisner has published six novels, including *Nero's Vice*, *Slice of Life*, *Strands*, and *Night Glow*, which vary in theme from supernatural horror to science fiction. His stories have appeared in many anthologies, including *Masques II* and *Masques III*, *Phantoms* (DAW Books), *Scare Care* (Tor Books), and *Urban Horrors* (Dark Harvest Books). He is a regular contributor to *Mystery Scene* magazine and has been an instructor for Writer's Digest School since 1987.

J.N. Williamson represents the views of an established pro with many credits. James Kisner is at the midpoint of his career—definitely not a beginner—but certainly well on his way to becoming established as a writer whose prose is known for its originality and unique style. The interviews begin with Kisner interviewing J.N. Williamson.

Writers James Kisner and J.N. Williamson.

James Kisner Interviews J.N. Williamson

James Kisner: You began your full-time career as a writer rather late—at 43. How has this affected your career?
J.N. Williamson: It has made a difference in my career partly because there was a relative lack of substance to the early fiction I wrote a few decades ago, and I think simply living longer and being observant over the years has enabled me to learn enough that maybe I'm a better writer.

J.K.: Was it difficult for you to get an agent when you first started?
J.W.: That was the first stroke of luck I had; sometimes I think it was the last. One half of Ellery Queen, whose name was Frederic Danney—a nice man who bought a few of my stories for *Ellery Queen's Mystery Magazine*—surprised me by spending about an hour on the telephone with me, giving me some idea of what agents were like, what needs they filled, and then introduced his own agent Larry Sterning in Wisconsin to me.

J.K.: Did you sell your first novel through an agent?
J.W.: Yes. Though it happened that Larry Sterning was about as old as the gentlemen who consisted of Ellery Queen, and he was slowing down. But he had a protogè named Ray Puechner who became my first agent.

J.K.: Do you consider having an agent essential to success?
J.W.: It depends on whether or not you're talking books or short fiction. Agents no longer particularly want to represent short stories because the amount of money an agent can make at 10 or 15 percent from an average story sale isn't worth the time to them. But, yes, it is probably essential to have an agent—from the standpoint of marketing my novels and making sure that someone more knowledgeable about contracts than I is reading them.

J.K.: Let's talk a little about the genre you work in, horror. How did you choose it?
J.W.: I could say by trial and error, Jim, but it's more the truth that the right genre found me, and I believe that may be true with most writers. I'd already tried to write detective and mystery stories. When I was still a kid, I fell in love with the idea of writing science fiction, which I didn't sell at all! I went through a long phase of imitation without realizing I *was* imitating various writers like F. Scott Fitzgerald and J.D. Salinger. So I went back to selling mystery stories and never even considered writing a novel. Until I had a nightmare one night. Being that, it was horrific. I thought it was a great idea so I outlined it sort of by instinct and then started to write it. And I thought, "God, this is what I *should* have been writing all my life," meaning not only the genre, but at novel length. It actually seemed easier to write a novel instead of short fiction!

J.K.: Well, you're deep into horror now. It remains a genre that is often not taken seriously by the critical community. Except when a horror writer becomes quite successful, then he's relabled "mainstream" so the critics can say nice things about him without embarrassment! Does that bother you, Jerry?
J.W.: Yes, it does—more than it should, probably. The whole labeling process bothers me as much as it does Richard Matheson. I interviewed him for my first *Masques* anthology, and even though it was only about five years ago I didn't fully understand what he meant by labeling. Now I do. Dick and Ray Bradbury are often called science fiction writers when they're really something else. And that "something else" is wonderful *storytellers*. I don't suppose I will have the choice any more than any other writer of horror has had to change people's minds about labeling, but I'm not at all ashamed of anything that I write—unless the writing is simply not very well done!

J.K.: Do you advise young writers to go into genre writing or to pursue mainstream writing?

J.W.: I wouldn't hesitate to recommend genre fiction. That's probably the speediest way to get your fiction into print. Within any category there are the important "classy" publications and those that are small or "unimportant." If you write what is mainstream fiction, the markets for short stories aren't as numerous. And I think you almost require some special credentials or an "in" if you're writing a so-called serious novel.

J.K.: You are known for helping other writers, while some established writers remain aloof. Why do you make the effort to help other people?
J.W.: Numerous professional writers when I was a boy and a young man helped me—Frederic Danney, August Derleth and Anthony Boucher; an Indiana pulp writer named G.T. Fleming-Roberts and, once, a talented lady mystery writer named Leslie Ford. She was actually my first contact with a professional, and she steered me to Tommy Fleming-Roberts who tolerated my sixteen-year-old stories with amazing patience. My helping is a way of continuity.

J.K.: What mistakes have you made in your career that you would advise beginning writers not to make?
J.W.: The primary one, in my case, is preaching. Even when I was a little kid my writing had a moralistic bent. To this day, I write stories that often try to teach principles that I advocate. What I've tried to do as a professional is sustain the point of view and always make it *secondary* to the story. It's a very bad idea to tell everybody what to do in real life, let alone in fiction!

J.K.: You mean like not getting up on a soapbox? If you have a moralistic point to make, make it subtly rather than preach?
J.W.: Yes. You can make your point through your characters. If you want to give advice on political themes, create a political character. A professional trick then is if you want to show an example of bad politics through fiction, make the politician a bad guy, and *because* we see him doing evil things we infer that the politics he stands for are wrong. Another piece of advice I find that beginning writers need is not to adhere too closely to factual events in their own lives or their family's and friends' lives. There's nothing wrong with borrowing from facts, but you must remember, when you're writing fiction, that the story line comes *first*.

J.K.: How do you go about structuring a novel after you have the idea and know the story you want to tell?
J.W.: Once I have the idea and I know that general story line, I carry them around in my head for two or three weeks, then outline. When I outline I generally accomplish that in about a day and a half to two days. Then I work from it and seldom veer from it because the outline ends up being at least four to five-thousand words long.

J.K.: What do you consider the strong points of your writing—the characteristics that make it successful?
J.W.: I believe it's a blend of qualities. First, there's the fact that I'm well-read by contemporary standards, and I read about many things. Not just in books but in magazines, newspapers, wherever. I let myself be moved by what I read and the emotion becomes my view, my decision, about virtually every topic. If a fiction writer reads only fiction, the work will be less informed, thinner, possibly bereft of viewpoint. All this feeds the other strong point I feel people may find in my fiction: It's original. Like it or loathe it, my stuff is always original and takes a stand. I'm no wimp as a writer, partly because *I think constantly of myself as a writer*. So I stay alert to ideas, situations, characters, which are retained in notes till I need them. These qualities combine to allow me to hear my own *voice*, so to speak, whenever I sit down to write. And I let it go. I trust it, now—but that would not have been

possible if I hadn't read, written; read, written; read, written.

J.K.: They ask writers if they work at particular times of the day. I know you've written fiction at every hour of the clock. Is it ever hard to realize people in your neighborhood are working regular work days and you sometimes begin a major story at eleven o'clock at night?
J.W.: It is. Yes. One of the things that I'd like to point out to beginning writers is that if they've been people who always felt a need to fit in, to have very close cronies around a lot, then they may need to rethink the vocation of writing. You feel like the odd man out in almost any human situation that doesn't include another professional writer.

J.K.: Are you saying that a full-time writer's life is different and leads to even greater separation from society than is generally described?
J.W.: I believe it is more difficult. A man who works in a service capacity, for example, is working with objects that are familiar to everyone, objects that can be seen. The things I'm working with are intangibles. They exist only in my mind, or in an outline. The point is that when members of my family or my friends are even kind enough to want to ask me about my work, they really haven't the foggiest notion what to ask! And that bothers me, because I'd like to have the same social interplay I had when I worked at other things.

J.K.: Have listings of new publications ever helped you sell a story or book?
J.W.: As a matter of fact, Maclay and Associates in Baltimore was listed in *Writer's Digest* magazine at a time when three of my publishers had folded in one six-month period. Maclay became interested in publishing an original anthology, which eventually became *Masques*.

J.K.: You had published more than 20 novels before you edited *Masques*. Did that make you a better or more demanding anthologist? And what role has teaching for Writer's Digest School played in your selections of material?
J.W.: To answer in reverse order, Jim, teaching for Writer's Digest probably taught me more about writing than I'd learned since I knew at the point I finished my first or second novel. Not only was there the repetition of mistakes, some of which I realized for the first time I made, but a freshness and spontaneity that seemed very worthwhile and sort of revived my flagging spirits at times. I believe that having been a novelist already made me alert to a lot of tricks that some writers tend to foist off on anthologists, and having both read and written a great deal in horror, almost more aware of trite ideas and trite means of saying things.

J.K.: When you edit a horror anthology, you say it's necessary to submit stories that scare you in some way. Once that's done, what improves an unknown writer's chances with you?
J.W.: Their basic idea should be fresh and expressed with as much originality as possible. Secondly, if a new writer would understand that many anthologists, including me, need to reserve the longer lengths for well-known pros, they'd keep the yarn under 3,000 words.

J.K.: You've said you try to balance an anthology between different styles, different themes and subject matters. I know that in the current *Masques III* there's a story that you had to fight to keep included even though you may not have agreed with the author's point of view. Did you feel a moral obligation to do that, or did you just feel that was being professional?
J.W.: I think it was taking the right professional viewpoint. There are very few themes or messages I wouldn't include in an anthology. Groundbreaking ideas obviously will, at times, touch on controversial subjects. At the same time I would recommend that new writers not try with other editors to come up with exceedingly controversial premises because, frankly, most editors won't accept them!

J.K.: Harlan Ellison's *Dangerous Visions*, which was published about 20 years ago, was

considered a ground-breaking anthology because the stories dealt with things that were taboo themes. Are you saying that things have switched back—that editors are becoming more conscious of controversy than they used to be?
J.W.: I think most editors are more resistant to taboo stories than they used to be, unless they are expressed in the style of the "new horror" being written today. To get by with being really different and saying things that are genuinely shocking, a newcomer probably has to follow some groundbreaker in a given genre—unless he or she has the courage to send out the story or novel repeatedly. If I'm the guy who gets it and it fits my anthology, I'll be delighted to see it. Modesty aside, I don't believe there are many editors who regard that the way I do.

J.K.: You mentioned to me a young guy who hopes to be a science fiction writer who told you he'd methodically tried to read *all* the science fiction stories recommended in your *How to Write Tales of Horror, Fantasy & Science Fiction*, but couldn't find some of them. Wasn't he taking what we say about being familiar with a genre and about originality too seriously?
J.W.: Yes. He was a young man we met at a workshop in another state. At the end of the first session, he came up and told me that in his efforts to write a truly original science fiction story he had read the article in the how-to book by one James Kisner, and then he went back into the list of recommended stories and novels at the back of the book and set out to read all the praised science fiction there was! I told him that I really thought he had probably read enough to familiarize himself with the genre, and go ahead and write the story now.

J.K.: When people like us speak of "marketing" our work, does that ever bother you? Is there a point at which we should begin to comment on art?
J.W.: That question came to mind at the same workshop when I realized after two days of talking to those people who wanted to be writers neither they nor I had mentioned "art." Personally, I find "marketing" my fiction a fairly disgusting idea, utterly mundane, and I would say that getting a good agent is the answer to that. Art, as a lot of other people have said, is accidental if not incidental; it just happens. Nevertheless, it does seem today that how we sell our work sometimes seems to be more important than how we write it.

J.K.: Do you prefer writing novels or short stories now?
J.W.: These days I usually prefer to write short fiction because I find it more challenging. A great many writers including more professionals than I'd care to name don't really understand that a short story is a different form entirely than a novel for reasons other than length.

J.K.: You don't agree with the old axiom that any short story can be a novel, and any novel can be a short story?
J.W.: No more than any basketball player can become a high hurdler. A short story isn't likely to cover a great period of time or have as many characters as a novel, among other things. A good novel has subplots and subtexture, while a story is basically concerned with a certain point in time and a certain outcome in a character's life, and that, when you get there, the writer gets out of it—the story's over. A novel must run 60 to 70,000 words, let's say, at least. I didn't grasp these things until about five or six years back after I'd already published many short stories. I have a God-given facility for writing at length that is now, after doing it so often, so developed I probably could write a novel on almost any subject without doing much more than sitting down and drafting it. That is very far from art, and it isn't very challenging.

J.K.: So you're saying your short stories are more "artistic" than your novels?

J.W.: Not always, but at this stage, for me, a novel lets a writer spread out and the writing of it becomes pretty facile—exhausting due to the length, but not as creatively difficult. There's much more you can do with a novel, but the doing is not necessarily as important as the perceptions within what you are saying.

J.K.: Many of your short stories have appeared in the small press. Would you advise a beginner to try to get placed there rather than go for the major markets?
J.W.: I used to think it was just fine to send your first stories or articles to *Playboy* or *Omni*, or whatever. Now I feel that unless you are truly brilliant, it's probably a waste of time. However, there are major magazines within most genres that can bring you recognition as well as a few dollars more than the very small press and I don't see any reason why you shouldn't try them. The mistake some insecure writers make is selling one or two short stories to a small readership publication, then settling for that. A writing career, like most things, should be a growth process.

J.K.: At this point in your career you've written over thirty novels and countless short stories. Where do you see your career going in the future?
J.W.: That growth process I mentioned is supposed to continue for a full-time pro too, I believe. I have the capacity now that I didn't have ten years ago for undertaking themes and human complexities that would once have been too much for me. The drawback for a pro at my particular level is the tendency either to take oneself too gravely—which I sometimes do in my short stories—or to write the same things over and over.

J.K.: If someone asked you, "Who is J.N. Williamson now?" how would you sum yourself up? Have you reached every career goal you want to reach?
J.W.: I'm largely what I want to be as a man, and in my sights now are, I believe, accessible goals as a writer. I find myself pleasantly surprised to be able to say that my heart doesn't seem to have changed in all these years in what I was after. I was never particularly in search of a fortune as much as the right to say well—in my fiction—what I want to say, for as many readers as possible. This goal to some extent has been reached. I'm hopeful of establishing a lasting body of work that will be read as long as people read. But if I reach the point that I believe I have accomplished all my goals and said everything I want to say as a writer—*have* to say— they should yank my typewriter away from me. I still aspire to greatness. This is a topic almost no author discusses in an interview, yet it's probably at the heart of why most writers begin to write at all. It's the dream, the concept, of doing something enduring, important, even immortal, and I don't think that's wrong of us. Like most ideals, it's something one goes on striving for even when there's no longer a nickel's worth of sound reason for believing it's possible. Well, I still have the nickel now and I still think it's possible.

J.N. Williamson Interviews James Kisner

J.N. Williamson: Jim, you've taught almost three years for Writer's Digest School. What do you feel is the most frequent failing new writers make?
James Kisner: The most frequent failing is an inability to generate fresh ideas. They tend to go with the simplest or easiest idea that comes into their heads, rather than work at it.

J.N.: To what do you attribute that?
J.K.: Too many students take too literally the idea that "everything's been done before," and therefore it doesn't matter if it's done again. For example, one story idea I frequently get is about the child whose imaginary friend turns out to be real. I've received this so many times, I automatically reject it, because it's been "done to death," and few editors would look at it. I realize many things *have* been done before, but if you're going to do it

again, do it in a different way. Don't write *Christine* again. I always tell them that Stephen King has done it, and they shouldn't attempt to re-do it unless they can do a much better job.

J.N.: If everything's been done, what is the writer to do?
J.K.: Beginners fail to understand that the process of writing is a synthesis. You may get an idea that was inspired by King, Matheson, or Harlan Ellison. Harlan himself, while editing *Dangerous Visions* was inspired by Theodore Sturgeon's story on Jack the Ripper to do a similar story. He was *inspired* by it; he didn't steal it. If you're inspired by King to write a vampire story that's fine, but it should be a different kind of vampire story.

J.N.: Have you ever seen an amateur's idea that you would've stolen, if you weren't honest?
J.K.: I've seen one or two, but I wouldn't ever consciously do that. I feel that if another writer comes up with an idea, then it's his or her right to develop it. If I thought of a new wrinkle for it, I'd contact the writer and ask if he minded if I did my own version. Which is what Harlan did with Sturgeon. And Sturgeon didn't mind.

J.N.: You are that rare writer who managed to sell his first novel, *Nero's Vice*, without an agent. If you were marketing your first novel today, what would you do differently?
J.K.: First, I would have spent more time on outlining the novel to give it greater cohesion. Second, because I sold it on my own, rather than through an agent, I was naive as to what I could say to an editor, and I agreed to changes in the book that I felt, upon reflection, weakened it considerably, especially when it came to marketing it. Had I known more, I wouldn't have compromised so much. The beginning writer is so eager to get published he'll make compromises, saying "Oh, sure, I'll change the werewolf into a mummy—anything—just so I'll get published." Whereas the professional knows when to stand his ground and say, "No. I'm not going to change that."

J.N.: Have you done that yourself?
J.K.: Yes. About a year ago, I had an offer from an editor based on my having to change a book substantially. I told my agent, "No. This is the way it should be. If she doesn't like it, send it to another editor." My agent backed me up on this.

J.N.: As a writer of several paperback genre novels, have you seen a marked difference between the way you're being edited now and what happened with *Nero's Vice*?
J.K.: Surprisingly, with my genre novels there has been almost no tampering with my writing—other than punctuation and a few word choices. I don't mind if an editor adds a comma here and there, so long as the meaning isn't affected. In general, I would say that I've had more freedom writing genre work than I did when I was trying to establish myself as a so-called "mainstream" writer.

J.N.: Do you feel, as writers sometimes whisper among themselves, that readers are becoming sated or simply aren't as attentive as they used to be? So should new writers make the pacing of the novel a more important matter than it's been before, or are there other ways in which a novel should be somehow simpler in order to acquire readership?
J.K.: That's pandering to the market. If you alter your writing to pander to a market trend—or supposed trend—then you're compromising your craft, number one, and number two, you're no longer a writer, you're a hack. The only concession a writer should make to the market is to maintain a contemporary style and viewpoint, since there's no market for Victorian prose. Be aware of what's going on in the world so you don't make outrageous *faux pas* about things. If you know nothing about rock 'n' roll, find out something about it. Do your research.

Returning to the subject of pacing, I think you may be referring to the supposed fact that people nowadays have shorter attention spans. That's why movies are paced like rock videos, for example, and the scenes in TV shows are very short. Supposedly, you can't hold a person's attention very long. Yet these same people to whom they are giving brief spurts of action can sit in front of a video game for hours.

J.N.: Let's discuss that a moment—the subject of movies as opposed to novels.
J.K.: Many younger writers unabashedly admit their inspiration is movies rather than any fiction they've read. They are often trying to create, say, a splatter movie in prose rather than a horror novel. I think the audience is distinctly different, and that people's attention spans vary according to the experience. You go to a movie expecting to see compressed into two hours anything from maybe a day or a week to a hundred years. So scenes have to be short; pacing is critical. Real life isn't like that, obviously. A book has to compress events to an extent, but you don't sit down expecting to finish a book in two hours; you expect the reading experience to take time. It may take several days to read the book—you're going to get involved. You don't expect to commit to a movie that way.

J.N.: But pacing is important in fiction as well.
J.K.: Yes, but a book should not be paced according to cinematic style. The pacing grows out of the subject matter of the book. If you're writing a psychological horror novel, the pacing should be slow, contemplative. If you're writing a novel about slasher killers, it should be a fast and hard-hitting pace.

J.N.: There's a big difference between writing fiction or a screenplay, simply because of what can be graphically demonstrated and what cannot. For example, the movie doesn't have to describe a woman in a certain way. She just appears on the screen.
J.K.: In fiction you have to build that woman bit by bit in the reader's mind, until finally she explodes into view—and then the reader knows what she looks like throughout the book. Some writers have been saying description is unnecessary, that you just say a woman walked into the room. I don't agree with that. Part of the experience of fiction is the craft involved in describing that woman. Because an author points out what is special about this character. In a film, it's more a matter of casting, which the screenwriter may not get involved in at all.

J.N.: What can you tell new writers about the importance of a title of a short story?
J.K.: I think a strong title is almost as important as a strong opening sentence—if for no other reason than to get attention. Beginners use the most nowhere, nondescript titles, which don't compell you to read the story. One master of titles is Harlan Ellison, with stories titled "The Beast That Shouted Love at the Heart of the World" and "I Have No Mouth and I Must Scream." You *have* to read either of those stories—any editor would too. At least the first page to see what's going on. Beginners will write a story about a mean little kid and call it "The Mean Little Kid." What's interesting about that? Usually, if the title is that bland, then the first sentence will probably be bad too.

J.N.: Do you find that many beginners really start their stories on the second page?
J.K.: Sometimes, the third or fourth page. They start a story as if they were writing a Victorian novel, and I think that's a failing of our educational system. Too many English teachers are telling our students that Nathaniel Hawthorne is a great writer—Dickens is great, Melville, etc. Sure, they *are* great, but not writers to imitate. Edgar Allan Poe was a great writer, but don't imitate him. He was writing a hundred-fifty years ago. Nowadays, his writing wouldn't work.

J.N.: Let's talk about novels. You outline your novels. How strongly do you feel about this practice, Jim?

J.K.: Well, my first novel, as I mentioned, I didn't outline enough. Now I find outlining an absolute necessity. The length varies considerably. I recently did a 32-page, 10,000 word outline for a novel. Then again, I sold another book on the strength of a six-page outline alone. But in each case, the outline was sufficient for the idea of the book and its later construction. It depends on the type of book and the complexity of the plot or concept.

J.N.: When you begin to work from that outline, how much leeway do you give yourself to make changes?
J.K.: A lot—because I know some of the problems I stated in the outline at the time I'm writing it I may not have completely resolved in my mind—such as how will I get from point A to point B in the plot. It may involve creating a new character—which I had to do in one of my novels. When I wrote the outline, I didn't know I'd need to do that, but I worked with that attitude.

J.N.: I think we should say that when we "outline" we don't mean what English teachers mean by outlines with roman numeral I and II and subsets.
J.K.: No, what we are talking about is what is known in movie terms as a "treatment." We are telling the story in abbreviated form without all the ornate detail.

J.N.: Do you find your characters tending to grow or change on you?
J.K.: The characters do take on their own lives and I find myself trying to make them do things they shouldn't do and they resist. Or I'll have them saying things and I'll think, "No, she would never say that."

J.N.: Would you recommend a talented new writer concentrate on mainstream or genre fiction?
J.K.: I would recommend any beginning writer to find, first of all, the things that he is pleased to read and see if he's good at writing them. For example, I love to read mysteries, but I'm not a very good mystery writer. I love to read science fiction and I do think I'm good at that. Try several types of writing on for size and see what feels right. You may be surprised. Using myself as an example, I never thought I would write horror.

J.N.: I never knew that.
J.K.: I never even considered it. I thought I was going to be a mainstream writer or a science fiction writer. Because the writers I admired were Philip K. Dick, Harlan Ellison, Philip Jose Farmer, Robert Silverberg and John Brunner. The reason I didn't consider horror was that I didn't know what it was. I made the mistake a lot of beginners make in thinking the genre of horror is the same thing as horror in movies. Then I started reading horror—the works of people like yourself, Peter Straub, King, Bill Nolan and Richard Matheson—and I understood the true scope of horror. I realized I could write it, and many of my ideas fit into horror better than into what is generally labeled science fiction. Beginners make the same mistake about other genres too—westerns, mysteries, etc.

J.N.: Do you think horror today may be more suited to very far out experimental ideas than science fiction is now or maybe even where science fiction was in the forties and fifties?
J.K.: I think horror is probably the most flexible genre at this point, not only in content but in style. To back up a bit, I used to think horror was what we see in the movies and that horror was a very limited formula type of fiction. Whereas it is not at all. The number of themes, the types of horror you can write, is infinite. Much modern science fiction seems to me to be a regurgitation of old science fiction—though that's not true of all of it, of course. I don't see the type of stretching in science fiction today that you see in the early work of Ellison, or Bradbury where they were breaking ground. Actually they were breaking ground for the flexibility of horror.

Again, beginning writers fail to understand that a movie is a completely different experience and most splatter films are directed at an audience that doesn't read anyhow. For that audience, they're perfect. The writer who writes fiction that's like a splatter movie will not endure. Many of them will turn out to be one-shot writers.

J.N.: At this point in your career, what separates you from your current selling level and the plateau of a familiar but not internationally well-known writer? For example, Dean Koontz was selling novels but by no means world famous around the beginning of this decade. Is his great success now something he did for himself with his own talent entirely or is it a question of the right timing, the right agent, a movie sale or something else that propels you or me to Dean's present level?
J.K.: All those things you mention can make a difference—but there's really no one magic thing that you do that will make you successful. In a writer's workshop, there's always someone who stands up and says, "If I get an agent, will I be successful? If I use the right sized envelope, will I be successful?" I think what propels Dean Koontz or King from a mediocre level to a higher level of success is there comes that point when the universe or society or whatever responds to your perseverance and recognizes you are ready to step into the major leagues and then compensates you accordingly.

J.N.: When do you think a writer has made it? Is there any particular accomplishment that makes you think you have truly arrived?
J.K.: I've always felt it would be if I sold a book to the movies. I think I would have arrived—not as an artist, or for the money, or anything like that—but for just being recognized that my work was important enough to be transferred to a medium that would reach a much wider audience than fiction does. That's my personal thing. For some people, it might be something else entirely.

J.N.: What do you think is the best way to generate ideas in order to achieve the level of originality you have in your work?
J.K.: I read outside of my genre as much as possible and to read in as many areas of nonfiction as I can. I have books in my library about every subject imaginable—from transvestism to antique tin cans. I don't know what a particular book may provide for me. One of my best horror ideas came from reading a book on true crime. Too many beginners read only one genre and think, "If I'm going to be a great horror writer I should read everything Stephen King ever wrote." I've found that many horror writers tell me they read very little horror on their own. When you read too much in one genre you're liable to become imitative. However, a beginning writer should read widely in a genre to get a feel for it. That's how I discovered I could write it. But you get to a certain point and you say I know what this is, now I can do it.

J.N.: Your education is "classical" in the traditional sense. Has that benefited you as a writer?
J.K.: Yes. Too many beginning writers are trying to write with too shallow an education. Whether they go to college or not is immaterial. I've met many self-educated people who are much better read than I am. The point is that a good writer needs a sense of the history of literature to be successful as a writer, and you need to read some Dickens, some Dostoevksy, some Melville, and other great classics—because they are part of our world consciousness, and the good writers tap into the world consciousness when they create.

J.N.: What are the most frustrating aspects of establishing oneself as a writer—aside from finances?
J.K.: Learning to deal with the time frames of publishers. There is no immediate feedback in this business. You write a book or story and it may be a year or more before you actually

see it in print. But you have to learn to live with that, because that's the way the business works.

J.N.: What do you find is the most fascinating aspect of writing—the part that gives you the most satisfaction?
J.K.: It's the creative process itself. The idea of sitting down with nothing in front of you and creating whole worlds, whole lives, characters that don't really exist, and making them come alive. I'm also fascinated by the fact that I can't figure out how I do it—or how any of us do it. And when I get into it—deeply involved—it's the most wonderful experience in the world.

J.N.: What did it feel like the first time you sat down at a signing party, and had your own readers approaching and asking you to autograph your very own novel or story?
J.K.: My first emotion was surprise. I didn't realize there were that many people out there who had read my work. I thought, gosh, maybe I am somebody and I'm the only one who doesn't know it. It's like when Laurel and Hardy took their first world tour in the thirties, they were surprised to find out that everybody loved them. They'd just been in the studio all those years and hadn't gone out to meet the public that adored them. Once I got over my surprise, I found that it was very satisfying to sign my name on my work as a kind of consummation of the creative process. It was a validation of my work. It was a wonderful feeling.

J.N.: Is there anything else about writing that touched you that way?
J.K.: Yes, the first time I walked into a store and saw many books sitting there with my name on them, and the excitement of knowing people were going to pick them up and buy them and maybe like them. It still excites me. Sometimes I feel like I want to shout, "That's me. I'm the one who did that." I have that same rush of excitement every time a book comes out. And that is one of the things that makes writing worth the effort and keeps me going.

The Writing Life

by Annie Dillard

When you write, you lay out a line of words. The line of words is a miner's pick, a woodcarver's gouge, a surgeon's probe. You wield it, and it digs a path you follow. Soon you find yourself deep in new territory. Is it a dead end, or have you located the real subject? You will know tomorrow, or this time next year.

You make the path boldly and follow it fearfully. You go where the path leads. At the end of the path, you find a box canyon. You hammer out reports, dispatch bulletins.

The writing has changed, in your hands, and in a twinkling, from an expression of your notions to an epistemological tool. The new place interests you because it is not clear. You attend. In your humility, you lay down the words carefully, watching all the angles. Now the earlier writing looks soft and careless. Process is nothing; erase your tracks. The path is not the work. I hope your tracks have grown over; I hope birds ate the crumbs; I hope you will toss it all and not look back.

The line of words is a hammer. You hammer against the walls of your house. You tap the walls, lightly, everywhere. After giving many years' attention to these things, you know what to listen for. Some of the walls are bearing walls; they have to stay, or everything will fall down. Other walls can go with impunity; you can hear the difference. Unfortunately, it is often a bearing wall that has to go. It cannot be helped. There is only one solution, which appalls you, but there it is. Knock it out. Duck.

Courage utterly opposes the bold hope that this is such fine stuff the work needs it, or the world. Courage, exhausted, stands on bare reality: This writing weakens the work. You must demolish the work and start over. You can save some of the sentences, like bricks. It will be a miracle if you can save some of the paragraphs, no matter how excellent in themselves or hard-won. You can waste a year worrying about it, or you can get it over with now. (Are you a woman or a mouse?)

The part you must jettison is not only the best written part; it is also, oddly, that part which was to have been the very point. It is the original key passage, the passage on which the rest has to hang, and from which you yourself drew the courage to begin. Henry James knew it well, and said it best. In his preface to *The Spoils of Poynton*, he pities the writer, in a comical pair of sentences that rises to a howl: "Which is the work in which he hasn't surrendered, under dire difficulty, the best thing he meant to have kept? In which indeed, before the dreadful *done*, doesn't he ask himself what has become of the thing all for the sweet sake of which it was to proceed to that extremity?"

So it is that a writer writes many books. In each book, he intended several urgent and vivid points, many of which he sacrificed as the book's form hardened. "The youth gets together his materials to build a bridge to the moon," Thoreau noted mournfully, "or perchance a palace or temple on the earth, and at length the middle-aged man concludes to build a wood-shed with them." The writer returns to these materials, these passionate subjects, as to unfinished business, for they are his life's work.

It is the beginning of a work that the writer throws away.

A painting covers its tracks. Painters work from the ground up. The latest version of a

Annie Dillard *won a Pulitzer Prize for her classic book on living with nature,* Pilgrim at Tinker Creek. *She has written eight books including* An American Childhood *and* Living by Fiction.

painting overlays earlier versions, and obliterates them. Writers, on the other hand, work from left to right. The discardable chapters are on the left. The latest version of a literary work begins somewhere in the work's middle, and hardens toward the end. The earlier version remains lumpishly on the left; the work's beginning greets the reader with the wrong hand. In those early pages and chapters anyone may find bold leaps to nowhere, read the brave beginnings of dropped themes, hear a tone since abandoned, discover blind alleys, track red herrings, and laboriously learn a setting now false.

Several delusions weaken the writer's resolve to throw away work. If he has read his pages too often, those pages will have a necessary quality, the ring of the inevitable, like poetry known by heart; they will perfectly answer their own familiar rhythms. He will retain them. He may retain those pages if they possess some virtues, such as power in themselves, though they lack the cardinal virtue, which is pertinence to, and unity with, the book's thrust. Sometimes the writer leaves his early chapters in place from gratitude; he cannot contemplate them or read them without feeling again the blessed relief that exalted him when the words first appeared – relief that he was writing anything at all. That beginning served to get him where he was going, after all; surely the reader needs it, too, as groundwork. But no.

Every year the aspiring photographer brought a stack of his best prints to an old, honored photographer, seeking his judgment. Every year the old man studied the prints and painstakingly ordered them into two piles, bad and good. Every year the old man moved a certain landscape print into the bad stack. At length he turned to the young man: "You submit this same landscape every year, and every year I put it on the bad stack. Why do you like it so much?" The young photographer said, "Because I had to climb a mountain to get it."

A cabdriver sang his songs to me, in New York. Some we sang together. He had turned the meter off; he drove around midtown, singing. One long song he sang twice; it was the only dull one. I said, You already sang that one; let's sing something else. And he said, "You don't know how long it took me to get that one together."

How many books do we read from which the writer lacked courage to tie off the umbilical cord? How many gifts do we open from which the writer neglected to remove the price tag? Is it pertinent, is it courteous, for us to learn what it cost the writer personally?

When you are stuck in a book; when you are well into writing it, and know what comes next, and yet cannot go on; when every morning for a week or a month you enter its room and turn your back on it; then the trouble is either of two things. Either the structure has forked, so the narrative, or the logic, has developed a hairline fracture that will shortly split it up the middle – or you are approaching a fatal mistake. What you had planned will not do. If you pursue your present course, the book will explode or collapse, and you do not know about it yet, quite.

In Bridgeport, Connecticut, one morning in April 1987, a six-story concrete-slab building under construction collapsed, and killed twenty-eight men. Just before it collapsed, a woman across the street leaned from her window and said to a passerby, "That building is starting to shake." "Lady," he said, according to the Hartford *Courant*, "you got rocks in your head."

You notice only this: your worker – your one and only, your prized, coddled, and driven worker – is not going out on that job. Will not budge, not even for you, boss. Has been at it long enough to know when the air smells wrong; can sense a tremor through boot soles. Nonsense, you say; it is perfectly safe. But the worker will not go. Will not even look at the site. Just developed heart trouble. Would rather starve. Sorry.

What do you do? Acknowledge, first, that you cannot do nothing. Lay out the structure you already have, x-ray it for a hairline fracture, find it, and think about it for a week or a year; solve the insoluble problem. Or subject the next part, the part at which the worker balks, to harsh tests. It harbors an unexamined and wrong premise. Something completely necessary is false or fatal. Once you find it, and if you can accept the finding, of course it will mean starting again. This is why many experienced writers urge young men and women to learn a useful trade.

Putting a book together is interesting and exhilarating. It is sufficiently difficult and complex that it engages all your intelligence. It is life at its most free. Your freedom as a writer is not freedom of expression in the sense of wild blurting; you may not let rip. It is life at its most free, if you are fortunate enough to be able to try it, because you select your materials, invent your task, and pace yourself. In the democracies, you may even write and publish anything you please about any governments or institutions, even if what you write is demonstrably false.

The obverse of this freedom, of course, is that your work is so meaningless, so fully for yourself alone, and so worthless to the world, that no one except you cares whether you do it well, or ever. You are free to make several thousand close judgment calls a day. Your freedom is a by-product of your days' triviality. A shoe salesman—who is doing others' tasks, who must answer to two or three bosses, who must do his job their way, and must put himself in their hands, at their place, during their hours—is nevertheless working usefully. Further, if the shoe salesman fails to appear one morning, someone will notice and miss him. Your manuscript, on which you lavish such care, has no needs or wishes; it knows you not. Nor does anyone need your manuscript; everyone needs shoes more. There are many manuscripts already—worthy ones, most edifying and moving ones, intelligent and powerful ones. If you believed *Paradise Lost* to be excellent, would you buy it? Why not shoot yourself, actually, rather than finish one more excellent manuscript on which to gag the world?

To find a honey tree, first catch a bee. Catch a bee when its legs are heavy with pollen; then it is ready for home. It is simple enough to catch a bee on a flower: hold a cup or glass above the bee, and when it flies up, cap the cup with a piece of cardboard. Carry the bee to a nearby open spot—best an elevated one—release it, and watch where it goes. Keep your eyes on it as long as you can see it, and hie you to that last known place. Wait there until you see another bee; catch it, release it, and watch. Bee after bee will lead toward the honey tree, until you see the final bee enter the tree. Thoreau describes this process in his journals. So a book leads its writer.

You may wonder how you start, how you catch the first one. What do you use for bait?

You have no choice. One bad winter in the Arctic, and not too long ago, an Algonquin woman and her baby were left alone after everyone else in their winter camp had starved. Ernest Thompson Seton tells it. The woman walked from the camp where everyone had died, and found at a lake a cache. The cache contained one small fishhook. It was simple to rig a line, but she had no bait, and no hope of bait. The baby cried. She took a knife and cut a strip from her own thigh. She fished with the worm of her own flesh and caught a jackfish; she fed the child and herself. Of course she saved the fish gut for bait. She lived alone at the lake, on fish, until spring, when she walked out again and found people. Seton's informant had seen the scar on her thigh.

It takes years to write a book—between two and ten years. Less is so rare as to be statistically insignificant. One American writer has written a dozen major books over six decades. He wrote one of those books, a perfect novel, in three months. He speaks of it, still, with awe, almost whispering. Who wants to offend the spirit that hands out such books?

Faulkner wrote *As I Lay Dying* in six weeks; he claimed he knocked it off in his spare time from a twelve-hour-a-day job performing manual labor. There are other examples from other continents and centuries, just as albinos, assassins, saints, big people, and little people show up from time to time in large populations. Out of a human population on earth of four and half billion, perhaps twenty people can write a book in a year. Some people lift cars, too. Some people enter week-long sled-dog races, go over Niagara Falls in barrels, fly planes through the Arc de Triomphe. Some people feel no pain in childbirth. Some people eat cars. There is no call to take human extremes as norms.

Writing a book, full time, takes between two and ten years. The long poem, John Berryman said, takes between five and ten years. Thomas Mann was a prodigy of production. Working full time, he wrote a page a day. That is 365 pages a year, for he did write every day—a good-sized book a year. At a page a day, he was one of the most prolific writers who ever lived. Flaubert wrote steadily, with only the usual, appalling, strains. For twenty-five years he finished a big book every five to seven years. My guess is that full-time writers average a book every five years: seventy-three usable pages a year, or a usable fifth of a page a day. The years that biographers and other nonfiction writers spend amassing and mastering materials are well matched by the years novelists and short-story writers spend fabricating solid worlds that answer to immaterial truths. On plenty of days the writer can write three or four pages, and on plenty of other days he concludes he must throw them away.

Octavio Paz cites the example of "Saint-Pol-Roux, who used to hang the inscription 'The poet is working' from his door while he slept."

The notion that one can write better during one season of the year than another Samuel Johnson labeled, "Imagination operating upon luxury." Another luxury for an idle imagination is the writer's own feeling about the work. There is neither a proportional relationship, nor an inverse one, between a writer's estimation of a work in progress and its actual quality. The feeling that the work is magnificent, and the feeling that it is abominable, are both mosquitoes to be repelled, ignored, or killed, but not indulged.

The reason to perfect a piece of prose as it progresses—to secure each sentence before building on it—is that original writing fashions a form. It unrolls out into nothingness. It grows cell to cell, bole to bough to twig to leaf; any careful word may suggest a route, may begin a strand of metaphor or event out of which much, or all, will develop. Perfecting the work inch by inch, writing from the first work toward the last, displays the courage and fear this method induces. The strain, like Giacometti's penciled search for precision and honesty, enlivens the work and impels it toward its truest end. A pile of decent work behind him, no matter how small, fuels the writer's hope, too; his pride emboldens and impels him. One Washington writer—Charlie Butts—so prizes momentum, and so fears self-consciousness, that he writes fiction in a rush of his own devising. He leaves his house on distracting errands, hurries in the door, and without taking off his coat, sits at a typewriter and retypes in a blur of speed all of the story he has written to date. Impetus propels him to add another sentence or two before he notices he is writing and seizes up. Then he leaves the house and repeats the process; he runs in the door and retypes the entire story, hoping to squeeze out another sentence the way some car engines turn over after the ignition is off, or the way Warner Bros.' Wile E. Coyote continues running for several yards beyond the edge of a cliff, until he notices.

The reason not to perfect a work as it progresses is that, concomitantly, original work fashions a form the true shape of which it discovers only as it proceeds, so the early strokes are useless, however fine their sheen. Only when a paragraph's role in the context of the whole work is clear can the envisioning writer direct its complexity of detail to strengthen the work's ends.

Fiction writers who toss up their arms helplessly because their characters "take over"—

powerful rascals, what is a god to do?—refer, I think, to those structural mysteries that seize any serious work, whether or not it possesses fifth-column characters who wreak havoc from within. Sometimes part of a book simply gets up and walks away. Dr. S.P. Monks describes one species, which lives on rocky Pacific shores:

"I am inclined to think that *Phataria* . . . always breaks itself, no matter what may be the impulse. They make breaks when conditions are changed, sometimes within a few hours after being placed in jars . . . Whatever may be the stimulus, the animal can and does break of itself . . . The ordinary method is for the main portion of the starfish to remain fixed and passive with the tube feet set on the side of the departing ray, and for this ray to walk slowly away at right angles to the body, to change position, twist, and do all the active labor necessary to the breakage." Marine biologist Ed Ricketts comments on this: "It would seem that in an animal that deliberately pulls itself apart we have the very acme of something or other."

The written word is weak. Many people prefer life to it. Life gets your blood going, and it smells good. Writing is mere writing, literature is mere. It appeals only to the subtlest senses—the imagination's vision, and the imagination's hearing—and the moral sense, and the intellect. This writing that you do, that so thrills you, that so rocks and exhilarates you, as if you were dancing next to the band, is barely audible to anyone else. The reader's ear must adjust down from loud life to the subtle, imaginary sounds of the written word. An ordinary reader picking up a book can't yet hear a thing; it will take half an hour to pick up the writing's modulations, its ups and downs and louds and softs.

An intriguing entomological experiment shows that a male butterfly will ignore a living female butterfly of his own species in favor of a painted cardboard one, if the cardboard one is big. If the cardboard one is bigger than he is, bigger than any female butterfly ever could be. He jumps the piece of cardboard. Over and over again, he jumps the piece of cardboard. Nearby, the real living female butterfly opens and closes her wings in vain.

Films and television stimulate the body's senses too, in big ways. A nine-foot handsome face, and its three-foot-wide smile, are irresistible. Look at the long legs on that man, as high as a wall, and coming straight toward you. The music builds. The moving, lighted screen fills your brain. You do not like filmed car chases? See if you can turn away. Try not to watch. Even knowing you are manipulated, you are still as helpless as the male butterfly drawn to painted cardboard.

That is the movies. That is their ground. The printed word cannot compete with the movies on their ground, and should not. You can describe beautiful faces, car chases, or valleys full of Indians on horseback until you run out of words, and you will not approach the movies' spectacle. Novels written with film contracts in mind have a faint but unmistakable, and ruinous, odor. I cannot name what, in the text, alerts the reader to suspect the writer of mixed motives; I cannot specify which sentences, in several books, have caused me to read on with increasing dismay, and finally close the books because I smelled a rat. Such books seem uneasy being books; they seem to fling off their disguises and jump onto screens.

Why would anyone read a book instead of watching big people move on a screen? Because a book can be literature. It is a subtle thing—a poor thing, but our own. In my view, the more literary the book—the more purely verbal, crafted sentence by sentence, the more imaginative, reasoned, and deep—the more likely people are to read it. The people who read are the people who like literature, after all, whatever that might be. They like, or require, what books alone have. If they want to see films that evening, they will find films. If they do not like to read, they will not. People who read are not too lazy to flip on the television; they prefer books. I cannot imagine a sorrier pursuit than struggling for years to write a book that attemps to appeal to people who do not read in the first place.

You climb a long ladder until you can see over the roof, or over the clouds. You are writing a book. You watch your shod feet step on each round rung, one at a time; you do not hurry and do not rest. Your feet feel the steep ladder's balance; the long muscles in your thighs check its sway. You climb steadily, doing your job in the dark. When you reach the end, there is nothing more to climb. The sun hits you. The bright wideness surprises you; you had forgotten there was an end. You look back at the ladder's two feet on the distant grass, astonished.

"The line of words is a hammer. You hammer against the walls of your house . . . Some of the walls are bearing walls . . . Unfortunately it is often the bearing wall that has to go . . . Knock it out. Duck."

—Annie Dillard

The Imagined Reader

by Eve Shelnutt

A story is not experienced by the reader as a flat surface. The deeper, more complex a story's sub-surface, the greater will be the reader's intellectual activity and, possibly, emotional and sensual engagement. He can feel as though he has entered new territory, read certain signs for direction, and visited the populace, on some occasions as a privileged guest privy to the inhabitants' thoughts, feelings, and dreams.

If the reader is viewed by the writer as an active participant in the writer's process, a component to be reckoned with, the relevant question is: Who is my imagined reader?

While some contemporary critics are uncomfortable studying literature from the viewpoint of readers' responses and prefer to look at a piece of writing as setting up its own terms apart from the readers' history with language and culture, writers nonetheless imagine a reader. At whatever level of consciousness, the action of writing presumes a receiver of the action.

I am speaking of the general reader who reads simply to enrich his life. It is not *for* him, necessarily, that the writer writes; rather, the writer imagines a tension which may be established in a piece of writing and, while establishing it in prose, envisions how the tensions may be perceived, received, taken apart and examined, or, simply, how they are felt.

If we say that a writer is his own first reader, we imply his taking the place of an imagined reader, before the work is ready for reading, for *a* reading. We know, of course, that readers differ. We also know that the writer has difficulties being his own reader because of his subjective investment and immersion during the creative act. This imagined reader is necessarily, then, an elusive character in a process of change as we as writers change. The more we write and then read, the more intricate will the imagined reader's personality become, mirroring our growing sophistication.

If we try, however, to approach the imagined reader tentatively as a component in the writing process, it may be useful to ask first: In this particular story, what would I have a reader *do* with the materials? If a story's whole is more than its parts, it is because, like fabric, it becomes whole cloth as a result of the individual threads' having been woven together. And the reader may try to take the material apart thread by thread. If he succeeds, these are the easy stories, because our finest fictions in both the story and novel forms appear indestructible, so tightly are they woven, so intricately patterned. These are the fictions we stand in awe before and contemplate again and again because they yield enough to fascinate us but not enough to destruct. Tolstoy's *War and Peace* is in this category, as well as Melville's *Moby Dick*. Of modern stories, Katherine Ann Porter's *Noon Wine* appears to withstand repeated readings. And there are many more, in all languages. But what is certain is that many more easily unraveled, flimsy works of fiction exist. The individual writer knows this as fact and is haunted by it. We know that at least some readers have read enough to measure what they read.

Writer as reader

It seems to me that the first task of a writer trying to develop his or her imagined reader is to work at curing himself of naiveté through reading. It is a task which can never be

Eve Shelnutt *is a professor of English at Ohio University. The recipient of both the* Mademoiselle *Fiction Award and the O. Henry Prize for her short fiction, she is now working on a novel.*

completed, but too many beginning writers try to avoid an apprenticeship to literature. A similar tactic by a surgeon would meet with disastrous results, as if there were no need to meet the patient, take his medical history, or keep abreast of technology.

Reading is used by the writer not only as preparation for a career. It can be vital to the ongoing development of a writer's craft and especially of an imagined reader. If I want to imagine a reader who will read my writing, I need to estimate him through my own reading, observing literature that has rewarded him in the past and considering what rewards him currently.

This does not mean, of course, that what is popular must affect what I write. To the contrary, in fact. A writer seeks a reader for his or her particular work in its uniqueness and idiosyncrasy. But part of what a writer does is estimate how his special vision can be *translated* into form, what shapes to draw out of the silence of himself. The form and language of a writer's work are not wholly predetermined, no matter how much he may feel dogged by what has been written before and what is being written now. An imagined reader is a judicious selection of an image from many images of "The Reader."

Writers need to read partly to discover the readers we *don't* want. Calmly and with self-assurance, V.S. Naipaul has stated that he does not write for the masses. When we notice a very young writer's first novel vault him into fame and fortune, enough to give him what we presume in our envy is unlimited freedom for writing, a statement such as Naipaul's seems quite radical. But we can become victimized by rumors of fame and fortune. We can forget to ask of the young writer's work: "But is it any good?"

The question is crucial, for the writer can be seduced by images of fame, perhaps now more than ever before since contemporary publishing practices and economics dictate appealing to a mass of readers rather than to readers whose backgrounds in literature make them highly discriminating. To many, being a writer now appears to be a good career *because* a number of young writers have "made it big." It is hard to imagine Poe, for example, enticing others into the writer's career by his image so fraught with anguish. But reviewers now appear to focus as much on the writer as on the writing; we are spoon-fed stories of instant fame with, at best, news that the writer spent a year in a university writing program before his teacher sent the protégé's novel off to an agent and, voilà – fame.

The writer beginning to develop a relationship with an imagined reader should be wary of the seduction in such stories. It is far too easy for a writer to begin to tailor his or her writing to the fads of the day, especially when it is so difficult for a writer to find shapes and languages for his *own* vision. Yet if he does not, his writing will be ephemeral or like fodder for the herd gathered round the fad. It is, after all, not the *reader's* job to protect a writer's potential; rather, it is the writer's job to imagine a reader he or she wants.

And the imagined reader must arise from a writer's changing estimation of his capabilities; that is, a writer needs to estimate what it is *possible* for him to do as a writer while leaving space for the estimation to grow. For example, as a southerner I grew up reading Eudora Welty's name and seeing her books. As soon as I was sophisticated as a reader, I began reading her work. I was captivated by it, especially by how intricately a sense of place is woven into the fabric of her work. I knew the locales, and I had heard the speech of her characters. When I began to write, I imagined that I too, would write such stories, and, in some recess of the brain, I imagined having for my own work *her* readers. But as I wrote and read more, as I undersood increasingly what had comprised my own personality out of my own background, I began to realize not only our radical differences as writers but the differences in the readers our work appealed to. No matter how much I admire Welty, my relationship is different, as have been my experiences with people, if, that is, it is fair to deduce Welty's experiences with people from reading her fiction. Too, I began to understand from reading that *as a writer* and not simply as a reader, my affinity is greater to Porter, to John Hawkes, Gina Berriault, James Purdy, V.S. Naipaul.

Handling influences

When we imagine a reader of our own writing, we are in part assessing our experience in the world and taking into account how it will influence the way we *can* write. For *this* writing we need readers.

But even then we should be cautious that we don't allow our imagined or actual readership to obscure our visions. In creative writing programs, students and faculty worry that their readers—fellow writers and faculty—are too much like themselves. And they know, too, that some writing programs foster experimental writing while others insist young writers ground themselves first in the traditional forms. Some programs expose students only to writing by published contemporary writers as models. Students in writing programs who are interested in protecting their personal visions, *their* writing, assess the biases of any program and compensate for them with broader viewpoints.

It is more difficult, however, to compensate for influences on one's work—especially the work of imagining a reader—when a complex of forces combine to promote a particular kind of writing. A writer whose vision is antithetical to the prevailing mode of writing can feel hapless and depressed. It is easy to assuage depression by asking, "Ought I not revise my vision and write what 'they' want, if I want to publish?" An example of this pressure on a writer is the prevalence of the "minimalist" story, which strips the story down to the basics of plot rendered in "plain" language, which in this case means not the plainness of Katherine Anne Porter's prose in *Noon Wine* or V.S. Naipaul's in *Miguel Street* but rather, colloquial language which sounds like American speech. Not only is style effaced in the minimalist story; cause and effect are too. As a result, plot is heightened, but only because of other absences since the actions of characters are often trivial, mere incidents of daily life. Meaningful dialogue is undercut as well, because, within trivial events, people appear to talk out of habit since, with cause and effect absent, they have nothing to ponder or to ask. What is left, then, are portraits of incidents in an ambience most frequently rendered through the brand-name products characters use and the television they watch. The stories are about "the way we live now," as a number of reviewers have said, and they have captivated a readership that is itself immersed in cultural changes—the changes in perceptions and realities about the family, sex, money, politics.

The developing writer, however, should be wary and self-protective in the face of this fiction, no matter its readership, even if such wariness means that finding one's readers, as well as imagining a reader whose needs are different, becomes more difficult. It is too easy for the writing in a particular era to appear, in sum, over time, so similar as to be indistinguishable, one story from another, one writer from another. Too, the broad point of view from which such work issues may bear little relationship to one's inherent viewpoint about either writing or the world. And the use of language arising from the broad viewpoint may allow a writer little, in style of language, by which to satisfy the urge to write that was an impetus to writing.

Alongside the "minimalist" fiction has arisen fiction and poetry focusing on what is termed "the working class," meaning blue-collar workers, and "the underclass," meaning groups of people whose eduction, poverty, mental stability, or intelligence keep them cut off from the mainstream of society. In this fiction, what is new is not such characters, however, since they have appeared in fiction repeatedly over time. What is new is the fiction's point of view since the narrator most often refrains from providing a perspective on the characters' conflicts but rather adopts a viewpoint and language identical with the characters. Because Russell Banks's novel *Continental Drift* contains a narrator who aggressively provides a viewpoint, his novel could be called traditional even though its style often reflects what society considers "blue-collar" ways of thinking and speaking. But his novel is an exception to the general trend in characterizing such people and their lives.

The developing writer who has himself been privy to a wide variety of class structures and strata and thus has material for transformation into fiction by virtue of knowledge and understanding, observing the popularity of his writing about middle-lower, lower, and sub-class characters, would need to ask questions about the imagined reader. These stories are read *not* by the classes they portray, again within a viewpoint mirroring the classes, but by the upper-middle classes, usually. With the narrators of this new fiction relinquishing the function of providing an outside perspective, the reader is given, by and large, what is by virtue of circumstance – the difference between the materials and the class of the reader – a voyeuristic experience. Such fiction does present portraits of characters, or course, but the restrained narrative intervention leaves unclear for what *purpose* the portraits are being presented.

I present these examples of current trends in fiction to suggest that defining an imagined reader is not simple because the reader cannot be imagined apart from his social/cultural position.

The problem of imagining a reader is two-fold, then. As writers we are aware to some degree of the material we have and know that we are to some extent bound to it. As we render it into form, we will interest particular readers by the specific nature of the material itself and by the manner in which it is presented. And we are aware that the reader is a social creature responding to a changing world, making assessments of it, however obscured by prejudice or faddishness. We must maneuver between these claims in order to imagine a reader for our work, and how adroitly we maneuver will in part determine the quality of our work.

"Reading is used by the writer not only as a preparation for a career. It can be vital to the development of a writer's craft and especially of an imagined reader."

—Eve Shelnutt

The Hair of the Dog That Bit You

by Henriette Anne Klauser

"Writing is simple, Muffy," says Jeff MacNelly's Perfesser in the comic strip *Shoe*. "First, you have to make sure you have plenty of paper . . . sharp pencils . . . typewriter ribbon. Then put your belly up to your desk . . . roll a sheet of paper into the typewriter . . . and stare at it until beads of blood appear on your forehead."

Writing need not give you a bloody brow. The plain sheet of paper, the void screen, is what is causing the anxiety, so fill it with words. The best antidote to writer's block is—to write. The hair of the dog that is biting you provides the instant cure. Remember, the key to writing fluently is to separate writing from editing. *Rapidwriting*—letting the words spill out without stopping to critique or correct or rearrange—is one dependable way to keep the two functions apart.

When you edit and write at the same time, the result is often a disaster: a disaster for you as a writer and eventually for your reader. Purple patches come from the unrestricted pen. Go back and edit later. Later is when you invite the logical sequential strength side of you to come forward and apply all the techniques of good grammar and construction that have been drilled into you since the beginning of your school days.

Rapidwriting is sometimes called *nonstop writing* or *freewriting*. As all of its names suggest, it is a method of writing in a flowing way without stopping to reread, to evaluate. It is a way of holding Caliban at bay while giving Ariel complete freedom to tap into some of your most creative ideas.

If you have ever been in a brainstorming session with a group of people, you know the power and the creative energy that come from throwing ideas on the table without fear that someone will attack or laugh at them. Often the seed of a great and workable idea is inherent in an absurd one.

The essential ingredient to brainstorming—we caught on to this years ago—is that it must be nonjudgmental. Anyone in the group is allowed to toss in even improbable and unreasonable ideas without fear of being put down or ridiculed. The free-flowing and open-ended nature of the exchange creates a climate in which good ideas are generated; in fact, some ideas are born that I guarantee would never have come to light had the group not insisted on waiting until later to figure out their ultimate worth.

So rapidwriting is like a private conference—brainstorming for one. Get all the ideas out on the table, and tell the critical judgmental member of the board (your Caliban side) to suspend comment, to keep his mouth shut and his judgments to himself, for now at least.

Give yourself permission to write some "junque" as well as whatever else comes out. You will be surprised at the quality of the good parts.

Dr. Henriette Anne Klauser, PhD., *is the founder and president of Writing Resource Workshops. A member of the National Speaker's Association, she gives workshops on writing, based on her book,* Writing on Both Sides of the Brain, *to Fortune 500 companies. She has also taught writing at universities on both coasts.*

Mulch for the mind

Giving yourself permission to write garbage is like having a compost pile in the backyard. It might smell a little and even look yucky, but it provides a fertile environment for some great stuff to grow.

A fellow in one of my classes had written only a few lines of poetry before taking my workshop. Six months later, he had written enough poetry to publish a book of poems. He sent me a copy of his collection; I was touched and amused when I read the dedication: "This book is dedicated to Henriette Anne Klauser, who first gave me permission to write garbage, none of which I trust is included here."

We put extraordinary pressure on ourselves and even on our great and famous to write perfectly all of the time. The truly greats of music and literature have disregarded our collective injunction, sometimes at the cost of much pain.

Once I went to a piano concert where a brilliant Russian pianist was playing an evening of Franz Liszt. He played the *Tarantella*, the *Don Juan Fantasy*, and *Liebestraum*. The music was celestial; it took the top off my head. When the house lights went up, I turned my attention to the program notes. I was still somewhat dazed from the power and the majesty of the music I had just heard. What I read there brought me sharply back to the mundane world.

"Liszt," the program said, "was a typical product of the Romantic Age. . . . He produced more than seven hundred works, including many that are either uneven in quality, superficially constructed, or down-right dull."

Ha! Do you see the press for perfection we put even on our great composers? We do not allow even Liszt to have mulch for his mind. Can you imagine what it would have been like had Liszt sat down and said, "I am not going to write anything at all. I am not going to write one note until I think of something grand. Until I can compose *Liebestraum* without stopping, do the *Tarantella* from top to bottom, until I can let my pen fly across the page and never cross out or write something less than celestial, I will not write at all. No way will I ever put myself in the position of having some program notes on my music dismiss the bulk of my outpourings as being dull, shallow, and uneven."

Chances are he never would have written the soaring music that thrills the heart today, 150 years later.

So when you are writing garbage, think of Liszt. You may give yourself permission (or take mine if you need it) to write at least 600 documents that are either uneven in quality, superficially constructed, or downright dull. Once you get that out of the way, you are free to do the kind of writing that will make your heart sing and move your readers.

An exercise in rapidwriting

Take a clean sheet of paper, and rather than waiting for red sweat, plunge right in and start to write. If you do not know what to say, write that. Write whatever comes to your mind, whether it is on the subject or off it. If you hear Caliban saying that what you are writing stinks, then write that down, but do not stop writing. If Caliban thinks you have chosen the wrong word, include that assessment also. Circle the word, and keep on writing. Incorporate all the negativism and critical judgment right along with the content. That is how I wrote this paragraph. Then I went back and crossed out all the static.

If your premature edit voice is particularly loud and interfering, you can take this freedom one step further by using what I call the "Invisible Ink Approach." Put a sheet of carbon between two pieces of paper, and write on the top paper with a dead ball-point pen. There will be nothing to correct, no way to reread what you wrote until you finish the page and lift the carbon.

Whether you write with this magic writing method or use conventional ink on paper, keep track as you write of what your mind is telling you about your writing. If, while you are writing, you are able to identify some kind of accompanying emotion, say so. Name it. If you feel anxious or bored or angry or energized, write that down as you go along. Locate your feeling in some part of your body. Do you feel a tightness in your hands, a constriction in your throat? Is there a flip-flop in your stomach, a set to your jaw, an itch in your nose? Do your eyes begin to smart and water? Write it down.

Include all your wandering ideas as well as those that are on target. Peter Elbow, in *Writing Without Teachers*, calls this approach *freewriting* and remarks that when you use this method to launch your work, you use up more paper but chew up fewer pencils.

The score is more than even. The words on the paper you use up will become more and more useful to you as more and more of the passages you write in this nonjudgmental fashion will be exactly what you wanted to say at the pace you wanted to say it. It is true that when you go back to edit (that is, when the Caliban Critic comes back at your invitation) you will find more in these spilled-out words than you thought was there as you were tumbling out the phrases. Sometimes it shocks me, when I am striking out the interspersed comments, to see how critical my early editing voice can be—and how often mistaken.

When that voice creeps up, we have been trained usually to stop—to bite the pencil, to ponder at length, to give up altogether. What I am asking you to do instead is to railroad right through, to keep on writing *for a minimum of ten minutes*. You will see in just a moment why that minimum is necessary. Mark where you want to stop, and keep on writing. When you look at that spot later and see the worth of what followed, you will begin to get the picture. You will begin to get the idea of how damaging and self-defeating it is to give into the judgment of editing before its time.

Our motto is this: *We do no editing before its time.* (Make a plaque of it.)

Excelsior!

Where was your marker? When you wrote nonstop for ten minutes, did you find at eight point five minutes you wanted to stop? Were you surprised to find a good idea just on the other side of that urge to quit?

Mountain climbers tell me that when they are making an ascent, whether they are novice or experienced climbers, they start out fresh and eager and then, right before the summit, they hit a wall, an almost perceptible place of wanting to quit. The novice will turn back, congratulating himself on getting even that far, unless he remembers the advice of the more experienced climber at base camp the night before. Watch out for the wall! she told him. Push on when you want to stop. The best is just around the corner. The summit is yet to come. Do not give up. Do not turn back. Excelsior! Ever upward!

Those of you who have children or have ever assisted as labor coach at the birth of a child will recognize this as the time of transition. Transition is the time in the birth process when the mother decides that this is more than she bargained for and decides to let someone else have this baby. Then the father smiles broadly because he knows that this is the sign he has waited for, the clear sign that the baby has almost arrived.

So welcome the wall. Good stuff lies just beyond. Keep on writing past the exhaustion or the emptiness, past the urge to quit, and reach the summit. Think of me, down here at base camp, shouting "Excelsior!"—goading you onward when you feel as though it is enough, as though you have nothing more to say. Excelsior! Ever upward! On to the summit!

A real-life mountain climber in one of my seminars told me that he plays a mental trick on himself when he hits the wall. He says to himself, "I know that you are tired, I know you want to stop, just keep climbing for ten more minutes. At the end of ten more minutes, if you still want to quit, then I will stop." Pushing himself that ten more minutes always gives him the "second wind" he needs to carry through to the top.

Adjust that trick to your writing wall, whether your reluctance is based on the flow of ideas ("That's it; I've run out of ideas") or actual time ("Well, it's almost midnight; I've worked on this long enough"). Set yourself a goal, "I will write until the bottom of this page," or "I will continue writing for five more minutes." Agree to quit if nothing happens. Go the extra mile, and you may find yourself covering a league before you know it.

The progress log

They say that it took Edison over a thousand tries before he perfected the filament in a light bulb so that the light bulb would stay on. One time, he was asked if that was discouraging – to try a thousand times and fail. "Never thought of it as failure," he answered. "It was only a thousand ways *not* to make an electric light bulb."

I want you to establish a notebook called the Progress Log to turn a light on in your mind and discover your personal writing pattern.

The name Progress Log (or PL) has been carefully chosen with Edison's story in mind. A log records a journey, and progress implies a moving forward. Whatever you note, whatever you learn is part of a progress, part of your journey. Every entry is a step forward. So the Progress Log is a collection, a journal, a diary that records what is happening and what has happened with you and this thing called writing. It chronicles your past history as a writer, records your present struggles and triumphs, and anticipates the future of your writing life.

This is unlike the journal some of you may keep already, where you write your daily events or play around with new forms, record ideas or conversations, or watch the pattern of your dreams or the pattern of your diet. Journals of that kind are very useful, but what I am talking about here is a specific notebook where you chart your course and your progress *as a writer*. And you make an entry every day.

"*Nulla dies sine linea*," says Pliny – "Never a day without a line." I have the motto, in Latin, as a deliberately florid plaque above my desk and writ in large letters across the front of my PL. Every day I write something, and that something often develops into the unexpected.

Somehow an energy comes just from keeping such a record, even if you do not go back and pull the information all together and make connections. I can vouch for the effectiveness personally. I used a Progress Log for many years before deciding I had moved beyond that stage. Then one day I heard myself exhorting the participants in one of my workshops to use the PL and to write in it every day and thought, "How can I tell them to do it when I'm not doing it?"

So I went back to my PL, and my writing output increased dramatically. I cannot explain it, but just keeping track of what was happening with me and my writing generated an energy. Mayor Koch of New York was known to go up to his constituents on the street and say "How'my doin'?" I guess there was a feeling of well-being in knowing that he was even asking. The PL is like that. You feel good just to know that someone is asking, and that in itself will give you the power to write. Also, you will notice patterns emerge. You will see quite clearly what keeps you from writing your best and impedes your fluency, and what primes the pump and gets the words flowing. You will notice the times you write well and the audiences you write your best for. Once you are aware of your strengths and weaknesses, you are free to create your own moments of fluency.

Your own progress log

Across the front of a brand-new notebook, write in large letters the words *Progress Log*. This notebook can be any size you wish, but it should be used exclusively for this purpose. Date your entries; it is often revealing to include the time as well. If you normally carry a small notebook, it is easy to jot down the ideas as they occur to you; either make that little notebook your PL or copy whatever you jotted down during the day into the big notebook at night.

What you are doing here is simply recording information. Let a pattern emerge gradually. Do not try to impose one or to analyze your entry psychologically. A useful pose is that of the dedicated but detached anthropologist noting and recording the tribal customs, cataloguing artifacts as you unearth them. No need to figure out what all this data means until you finish the dig; just write it down and later you can see what comes together.

What to write in this exercise? Date the entry, note the time, and then use rapidwriting to record what is happening to you so far. Where do you see yourself in your writing, and where would you like to be?

Now write down what is happening as you read this, as you do the exercises. What was the rapidwriting exercise like for you? Did it make you feel anxious? Were you surprised by the quality of what you wrote when you went back and reread it?

Other things to include in your Progress Log might be stories that will come to you about how you learned to write—the good stories and the more painful ones about how your writing was received, how it was rewarded, or what happened when it did not please the person in authority. Here are some examples:

> When I was in the fourth grade, I won the Little Hot Spot medal for the best essay on safeguarding the home against fire. I got the day off school and went to City Hall where the mayor pinned the medal on my chest while the Marine Band played.

> Prof. W. did not like what I wrote. He tore up my paper in front of the whole class. I can still feel that rip go through me and hear the class titter.

> Things are slowing down now. Maybe I need to take a break, or have I just hit the wall? Tell you what, self. Ten more minutes, and if at the end of ten minutes, you still want to stop, then you can, okay?

> With the rapidwriting, I found I was unexpectedly pleased with some of the thoughts and wording. A bit of it might even be useful in current or future writing. However I did feel a bit strained towards the end—my hand aching from the intensity—aware of others moving on to their third page—wondering if the time was up yet. In looking at it now though, I am rather pleased and I like the idea of doing this for ten minutes without stopping. I also noticed I am self-conscious about my uncertainty concerning correct punctuation and grammar. I feel it's important, but my formal background is very shaky; everyone was so busy acknowledging me as a creative whiz kid that I got away with murder. I think that's unfortunate. Perhaps it would be worth my while to actually study a grammar book or two.

The PL can help you break through writer's block. It's also a useful tool for generating ideas. Its unfettered nature seems to invite concepts that prove valuable in future writing, while its fluency encourages the sorting through of ideas valuable to any project. Several times I have gone back to reread a PL from years ago and found there a clue to my present writing.

It is better not to have any preconceived notions, however, of where the PL is leading or where it might take you. Go with the flow; I promise your effort will be amply rewarded.

These two simple techniques—rapidwriting and the Progress Log—combine to radically change the way you write. Take it from a pro who has been using both for over a decade: the more you use them, the better they get!

How Many Stories Are There in Your Story?

by Gordon Weaver

Every fiction writer has experienced—and will confront again, more than once—periods of Writer's Block. One species of this terrifying literary virus presents itself in the form of the suspicion that one has nothing left to write about; the writer has said it all, used up all the characters and events that came—or so it seemed—almost unbidden from the wells of experience and imagination that flowed so freely heretofore.

Writer's Block can feel lethal, a permanent and terminal condition, but usually disappears—having caused no lasting damage—sooner or later. Still, it is a depressing emotional experience and the prospect of eventual remission does not alleviate it. The fear of its next onset lingers, a spectre haunting the writer's consciousness, inhibiting and undercutting the satisfaction animating those marvelous periods when one's work goes well.

Like death and taxes, the possibility of Writer's Block will never go away, yet one way of coping with it lies in deliberate manipulation of point of view, that central formal and technical feature of any fiction. By self-conscious experimentation with point of view in a given story, the blocked—or near-blocked—writer can open up the fictional possibilities of any story material.

Changes in point of view can liberate a writer by dramatizing just how rich and varied are the many possible stories inherent in what seems like a single story—the one that will not seem to allow itself to be written, that difficult story that, by failing to yield to the writer's concerted effort, just might bring on another fit of the dread Block.

Consider: the nature of a given story is absolutely dependent on the character from whose point of view it is told. The writer's choice of viewpoint, like the camera's frame, directs and focuses a reader's vision of the events; point of view determines not only *what* the reader knows, it also affects *how* the reader responds to the "information" (characters, events in the narrative presented). Generally, the viewpoint character will be the story's central character, hero or heroine, the reader's main interest, if only because the reader is kept in that character's presence throughout the course of the story. A reader's reaction to events is colored—because given through the viewpoint character's consciousness and sensibility—by that character's opinions and emotions. Control of point of view enables the writer to control reader response to every character and event comprising the story at hand.

Arbitrary changes in viewpoint—self-indulgence practiced by bad or novice writers—are jarring and off-putting to a reader, rather like the effect of arbitrarily changing one's seat in the theater while the movie plays on the screen. Frequent changes in point of view will create fictional chaos and reader confusion. But a writer's choice to try a different point of view in a story that seems impossible to bring off successfully offers a fresh opportunity for success, because it literally creates a new story.

Gordon Weaver *'s latest book is* The Eight Corners of the World. *Professor of English and Director of the Graduate Creative Writing Program at Oklahoma State University, he is also the editor of the* Twayne Studies in Short Fiction *and the literary journal,* Cimarron Review.

The boy and the bicycle

Imagine a hypothetical story line. This (untitled) story will be about a ten-year-old boy. An only child, his parents are poor, unable to give him the things—clothes, toys, amusements—his more affluent friends enjoy. This boy yearns for only one thing: a new bicycle. His parents, aware of their son's desire, agree to make a great effort and sacrifice; they will deny themselves, scrimp and save, trim the family budget for a full year, and, on their son's eleventh birthday, present him with the gift of a new top-of-the-line bicycle.

As his birthday approaches, this fictional boy anticipates yet another Spartan celebration, a cake with candles perhaps, but no "big" gift. His parents are diligent in their effort, faithful to their decision, and the morning of their son's birthday, wheel a gleaming ten-speed out of its hiding place in a neighbor's garage. It is the happiest day of the boy's life.

His birthday is one of pure celebration, spent riding his new ten-speed about the neighborhood, showing it off to his friends, pedaling in a fit of exultant abandon. Only late that night, long after his usual bedtime, can his father and mother persuade him to put the bike up on the front porch and go to bed; their son sleeps the sleep of total, exhausted joy, dreaming himself, as he falls asleep, still on his wonderful bicycle, imagining himself rising early to go out once again, another day of riding the streets of his neighborhood.

He wakes early, dresses in haste, dashes past his parent's bedroom to the porch—to find his bicycle gone, stolen during the night. Unbelieving for a moment, then grief-stricken, he runs inside, wakes his father and mother; they join him in a search of the neighborhood, call the police to report the theft, all to no avail. The bicycle is gone, stolen, and is never recovered.

Granted, this is not a particularly promising story line (and certainly a simple one), but it does embody elements of anticipation, realization, disappointment, and loss, emotions every writer and reader has experienced in some context or another. Can it be a "story"? It can be several, each very distinct from the other depending on the point of view chosen by its hypothetical author. Consider some possibilities.

Told from the boy's point of view it presents the possibilities (and potential problems) of capturing his innocent yearning for something all his friends take for granted, of dramatizing the pathos of his belief that nothing will happen to satisfy that desire, of making a reader share the unbounded delight the boy experiences when the bicycle is wheeled out and given to him, his unrestrained exuberance as he rides through the day and evening, his sense of pride in showing it off to his neighborhood. *With* the boy—because his viewpoint compels it—the reader shares these innocent emotions; with the boy, a reader puts the ten-speed up on the porch and goes, reluctantly, toward a sleep of perfect satisfaction. And with the boy, the reader rushes out to the porch, is shocked at the bike's absence, runs to tell his parents, joins in the futile search, is left with the devastating fact of loss, a hard lesson of life.

Told from the boy's point of view, this is (potentially!) a story of innocence traumatized, a story of painful instruction, of the worldly wisdom that comes of great hurt. It is also, potentially, a sentimental story, perhaps too blatantly so. What story is it if told from another viewpoint?

The father's story

I suspect the sentimentality inherent in this hypothetical story could be minimized if it were told from the father's point of view. The issues central to *this* fiction are certainly more adult; compelled by the father's viewpoint to encounter an adult world, the reader is made intimate with the terms of parenthood, with the father's need to give his son a gift beyond his means, his admirable—even noble—resolve to exert himself beyond the ordinary to create an occasion for his son that has the potential to become one of the most memorable in the lifetimes of both.

From the father's point of view, this story embraces the hard facts of social reality, of status and economics and family values under strain in the context. Surely, given this viewpoint, the reader will be made privy to this father's memories of his own (perhaps also deprived?) childhood, and will share this decent man's determination to rise above circumstances to give his son something more and better than he himself ever knew. And the reader will likely be invited into the marital relationship of these parents as they agree to make their sacrifices for their son's sake. The hard facts of the situation – the father's minimal employment, his frustration as a breadwinner, his wife's cooperation and support, will be brought to the fore in this possible version of my hypothetical story.

Given the same narrative, this father's story will offer a deep and rich paternal and parental satisfaction; imagine father's and mother's fulfillment as they drift off to sleep. Come morning, the reader is *with* the father, wakened by the boy's near-hysterical announcement that the bicycle is gone! The reader shares the rollercoaster of probable emotions: confusion, disbelief, bewilderment, anger, rage, bitterness. Now, told from this viewpoint, the story's theme speaks of a grim futility, of the seeming impossibility of this good man's effort to affect the life of his son, of how deluded he was to imagine he might make a brighter day (and life!) for his son than he had ever experienced, of the world's disregard for a man's best effort to create even a single day's unmitigated joy.

Given the father's viewpoint, this (formerly) sentimental story of a boy's dashed enthusiasm can become one dramatizing the inexorable forces – social and economic – that thwart and stunt a man's hope for his progeny and posterity, for his family's future. What other stories lie within this hypothetical material?

Any number, it seems to me. Imagine this story told by the neighbor in whose garage the new bicycle is hidden until the day of the boy's birthday. Or imagine this story told by the thief, the jealous and mean-spirited neighbor boy who sneaks up on the porch in the dark hours of the late night, wheels it away, determined to have it for himself or to sell it for something *he* wants more than anything else in the world. Just imagine.

Multiple experiences, multiple stories

The process I mean to suggest here, self-consciously and deliberately adopting one or more alternative viewpoints possible in given story material, can, and will, I think, help any writer overcome the onset of a Block that, otherwise, can be a long and depressing experience. One need not take my word alone for it. Some excellent writers have done this, and the evidence of their successes is worth one's taking a careful look.

Daniel Curley has two fine stories that illustrate exactly this sort of "manipulation" of story material. In "A Ride in the Snow" (*In The Hands of Our Enemies*, University of Illinois Press, 1970), he tells a story with a first-person persona. Three University of Alabama students are driving from Massachusetts to New York through a heavy snowstorm, listening on the rented car's radio to their team play in the Rose Bowl. They stall in the drifted snow near the peak of a hill, then become involved with an older couple from another stalled car, struggling to free their vehicle. The protagonist is exhausted by efforts to move the two cars over the crest, is given whiskey by the older couple, passes out, and only wakes in time to learn Alabama has lost the big game.

It is a subtle story, about a young man's innocent effort to prove his manhood for his friends and the older couple, and of his disillusionment: he has wasted his strength, been rewarded only with money (by the couple) – his friends do not appreciate the magnitude of what the experience has meant to him. Like Alabama's effort on the gridiron, the narrator (and viewpoint character) of this Daniel Curley story has given his best in a situation in which he cannot triumph. "A Ride in the Snow" is a delicate and low-key fiction about misspent and misdirected youthful enthusiasm and energy, about the fallacy of attempting to prove one's manhood in an inappropriate context, about the difficulties of attaining to true maturity.

In a later collection (*Love in the Winter*, University of Illinois Press, 1976), Curley tells essentially the same story ("Love in the Winter") in the sense that the narrative is unchanged, the same incidents occur, but it is an entirely different story because he tells it (in third-person voice this time) from the point of view of Ross Taylor, the male half of the older couple encountered in "A Ride in the Snow." Here, Ross Taylor is a middle-aged academic giving a ride from a conference to Grace Martin, a lady dean he only recently met at the conference. This is a story of late-blooming and abortive romance, of inept and unsuccessful seduction, of the folly, not of youth, but of otherwise mature and responsible people when they are brought together in unusual circumstances.

In "Love in the Winter," Taylor's hope of seducing Grace Martin (she seems amenable) is thwarted by the snowstorm that stops their car near the top of same hill we read of in "A Ride in the Snow," and their involvement with the Alabama college boys who help free their vehicle brings Taylor face to face with the practical absurdity and moral irresponsibility of his original design of passionate seduction. The Alabama college boys, in this version, are totally subordinate to Ross and Grace; their youthful vigor, enthusiasm, and boisterous sexuality persuade both of the fact that they are too old, too careful, and too responsible to really go through with an amorous liaison.

In "A Ride in the Snow" and "Love in the Winter," Daniel Curley demonstrates that *this* story (cars stuck near a hilltop in a snowstorm) contains *at least* two distinct stories; the former is a story of youth experiencing a kind of qualified maturation, the latter a story of mature people making a pathetic stab at regaining the intensity of long-lost youth.

A single experience, many viewpoints

Other examples abound in the tradition. Joseph Conrad, who complained he could think of nothing to write about (despite his adventurous personal experience), makes a novel, *Nostromo* (1904), from the spectrum of viewpoints that consider a single action, the theft of the fictional Republic of Costaguana's national treasury during a revolution by the book's eponymous hero, to whom it has been entrusted for safekeeping. In his *Lord Jim*, Jim's initial failure of courage, and his later heroism, are viewed differently by several characters, giving the reader a rich texture of alternative interpretations, the vehicle for the novel's complicated and ambiguous theme. John Williams' National Book Award-winning epistolary novel, *Augustus* (1973), is another relevant example, and Nelson Algren worked a minor variation on this sort of manipulation in his stories, "A Bottle of Milk for Mother" and "The Captain is a Card," where the same line of dialogue ("I knew I'd never live to be twenty-one.") is made to climax two very different stories.

The operative principle embodied here is that a single experience, viewed by different observers (narrators, viewpoints) is, in fact, potentially multiple experiences.

Imagine a landscape, any vista. Now imagine how it would be described, in turn, by a farmer, a real estate developer, and a military strategist. The farmer, I submit, looks at land to evaluate its possible productivity—what sort of soil lies under the vegetation, what is the drainage, will it resist erosion, is it better suited to livestock grazing or a cash crop? A developer will see it, in his mind's eye (from his point of view!), divided into housing plots, wonder what the cost per acre to purchase will be, look to the proximity of roads, schools, and nearby dwellings. A military sensibility would, it seems reasonable, wonder what tactics might be used to assault and conquer defenders dug in there, how it might be defended from counter-attack.

It is all the same "story" (a landscape), but different (multiple) "stories," depending upon the point of view chosen.

An exercise in viewpoint

Writers who have never tried something like this with their material might benefit from a few exercises. Consider a last example, one that will hopefully suggest some strategies for writers interested in expanding the story potential of their materials:

Imagine the simplest and most basic of narrative conflicts, a fistfight between two men. How many possible stories lie implicit in this fictional matter if various viewpoints are employed?

This "story" could be told, of course, by a disembodied and wholly objective third-person persona, one that views the two combatants from "outside," simply reporting the blow-by-blow to the reader. It could also be told by an entirely omniscient third-person narrator, one capable of telling the reader what each of the fighters thinks and feels as the fight ensues, their respective motivations, what rides on the outcome of the fight for each, how it started, etc.

Now imagine this story told from the point of view (first or third-person persona) of the man who is winning the fight; imagine it told on behalf of the man losing. What was one story is now at least (potentially) four.

Try writing this story (scene, really) from the viewpoint, not of one of the fighters, but from the point of view of a bystander. It is one story if this witness is neutral or indifferent to adversaries, simply interested in watching a good fight. It is yet another story if told from the point of view of an observer who has a vested interest (a wager at stake, or is a close friend of one of the fighters). It is still another potential story if the viewpoint character has money bet on the probable winner—another if the money is riding on the apparent loser. What if this observer is the subtly scheming instigator of the fight who spread a rumor or told a lie to cause it to start?

Different writers can construct their own hypotheses in order to go through such an exercise, but what can be learned is the same in any case: story material, considered within the organizing (and interpretive) perspective of viewpoint, is rife with wide varieties of story possibilities. There are any number—it all depends on the writer's imagination—of "stories" within any single story.

And learning this can shorten and ease that most unhappy fact of life for any fiction writer, a case of the Block, just as it multiplies the possibilities of story materials at hand.

Character Development: Being a Thief of Souls

by Rita Mae Brown

All human encounters embrace a magical quality. One strives to entertain, listen, learn and wink at frailty. Even if you never see that individual again she has left an invisible fingerprint on your soul and you upon hers.

Perhaps some of you have been accustomed to looking at the world through the prism of money and power. There's nothing wrong with that; our culture encourages narrowing our focus to external realities. People and Nature have the power to widen that focus. Emotion and spirit can become stronger realities than money and power. Most Americans get a whiff of this when they fall violently, romantically in love. This hit of suprarational life is a high. It's not irrational – it's beyond rational, and there's a big difference.

Falling in love has been a central theme of literature in Western culture. Romantic love enlivens characters sterilized by rationality. It's a potent form of magical encounter. But I repeat, all encounters possess a magical quality. As a writer you want your characters to reach your reader with their magic. The encounter should be as real as, perhaps even more intense than, if the character were met in the flesh.

Creating characters is enormous fun. Noncreative people think that writers make up characters and then jerk them through the plot. They talk about us playing God. It's not like that. If anything, the character winds up controlling the writer. For genre fiction – e.g., mystery, science fiction, Gothic romance – this is not true. Those are the suburbs of literature wherein the reader is invited into what is basically a verbal puzzle; it is always solved in the final chapter. That's fine and it's necessary escapism. Everyone needs it sometimes. However, the plot is the book. That's the definition of genre fiction. True fiction takes the writer places s/he has never been and calls forth deep emotions. The people are vividly real. Marianne Moore used to say that poetry was "imaginary gardens with real toads in them." It's true for the fiction writer as well.

Real characters

Characters surround you. You will observe people much as an actor observes them. Every gesture, inflection, nuance is vital to you. You've got to pierce the exterior of people and bore into the center. You can't go about grilling strangers. You can do it to your friends but you might not keep them long. You'll have to learn to develop your powers of observation. You must become a thief of souls. Once you've "got" someone, you try to put her/him on the page.

You will rarely take one person, whole, and transfer him to fiction. Characters are almost always composites plus a touch of imagination. You distill people much as a liquor manufacturer distills grain. Let me give you two examples:

In addition to her latest book, Starting From Scratch: A Different Kind of Writer's Manual, ***Rita Mae Brown*** *is the author of several books including* High Hearts, Sudden Death *and* Rubyfruit Jungle.

Example 1: Tinker Lundstrom suffered in the hot vise of summer. He walked down Main Street wiping his brow with a red bandanna. Behind him an ancient Volvo backfired. Tinker hit the pavement and began crawling for cover.

Example 2: Tinker Lundstrom suffered in the hot vise of summer. He hated the heat. It reminded him of Viet Nam and those stinking rice paddies. Here he was, safe in Charlottesville, but he couldn't shake the fears that plagued him. He was okay until he heard any kind of loud report. He'd jump or hide and then, embarrassed, heart racing, he'd realize he wasn't in real danger.

There's nothing hideously wrong with Example 2, but Example 1 gets you into the character more quickly. The reader has been jolted by Tinker's response to a Volvo belch, just as Tinker was jolted by the event itself. As the story unfolds, you can reveal Tinker's fears and dreams. Example 2 in a flat, direct way, tells you about Tinker. You're a writer. You don't tell. You show. Example 1 shows you a character. Example 2 tells you about him. Example 1 is a distillation; Example 2 is still bran mash.

The most common mistake made by beginning writers in developing character is that they tell you too much. In fact, most of them give the background of each character as they introduce that person. The drive of the story gets stalled every time a new person walks onto the page. Dull. There's an easy way to avoid this sin. Before you ever start your novel, sit down and write out your main characters' histories. Then draw up genealogical charts so you can see, instantly as you work, who is related to whom. You'll see when characters were born and when they died. A short biography of your characters and their personality traits will also help you combine characters. A beginner's mistake in fiction is in fragmenting emotions into separate characters.

Real people have dominant traits allied with secondary traits. So do real characters. People can be contradictory and irrational. So can real characters; just be careful on the contradictions. If you do it too much it looks as if you are desperately manipulating your plot. If you have a character, however, who constantly contradicts himself, that can be funny. There, too, be careful. A character may serve the plot—indeed, s/he must—but if it is obvious, then your work will get suspiciously close to genre books, where the plot is the book and the characters merely devices. These books—e.g., Agatha Christie's mysteries—are fun to read but they aren't true novels.

A life of their own

The more you write, the more spontaneous you will become. Spontaneity is based on the knowledge we have acquired. When your characters become spontaneous—by which I mean they have a life of their own and they surprise you or even fool you—then you're doing something right. You are no longer pulling your characters through the novel. They are knocking you around at the typewriter. Don't be surprised if they wake you up at night either. This is a common occurrence, but many fiction writers won't talk about it. Our left-brain culture, top-heavy with facts and desperately low on imagination, takes such admissions as a confession of lunacy. How sad. We're losing our ability to see in Technicolor.

A black-and-white world is a nonfiction world. I read nonfiction constantly and I write it when there is no alternative. No matter how glorious nonfiction is, to me it always smacks of the term paper. Here's an easy way to see the difference between nonfiction writers and fiction writers, between left-brain people and right-brain people: They can run. We can dance.

Everyone has the capacity to use both hemispheres of the brain, but America seems quite frightened of the imaginative hemisphere (Dionysius versus Apollo again) unless sanitized. All I can tell you is, if you hear your characters, if one of them shakes you out of bed at 4:30 A.M., protect that experience with your life. And thank the Muses because you're alive!

The inner life

Character biographies and genealogies help you keep things straight and they also help you define family characteristics if that's useful to your novel. Most family members, over generations, share common traits. Different though blood relations are on the surface, underneath they are surprisingly bound together. If you wanted to be nasty you could say the family is the transmission belt of pathology. If you want to be optimistic you could say the family is the cradle of love. For instance, although adopted, I, like a duckling, was imprinted by my adoptive parents and their family. We share one vivid family trait. We all have a sharp, biting sense of humor.

There's a family here in Charlottesville that's famous for their ability to breed. No matter what generation, they throw children like litters. Such details are not central to your character but they are informative. That's why you'll save yourself a lot of trouble if you map out your characters first.

Character is destiny. You've heard it before. It's true. The resolution of any plot must come from within the character. The redemption or destruction of any character is not the result of an external event (deus ex machina) but the result of that character's motivation. The inner life of people drives and manipulates their outer lives. If you remember that, the strange events that befall your characters will no longer seem strange. Wouldn't hurt to look at your own life either. We are the architects of our own Fate.

Granted, terrible things happen over which no one has control. You've got a character, young, female, enduring the siege of Richmond. Women couldn't vote. So the horror of war is visited upon her through no political fault of her own. However, what happens to her (short of a cannonball dropping on her head) within the framework of that war is up to her.

A compass need not see north in order to feel its pull. Ideas affect people even if they are not intellectual people. Emotions, even more than ideas, pull on people like that magnetic North Pole. Consider, again, our young damsel quivering on the anvil of war. She could have left the South before this mess. She didn't. That tells you she was either unconcerned with politics or that she loved her geographical place on this earth and was willing to brave the future. The excitement around her must have rubbed off. Bad though it was, it was never boring. The young respond strongly to that. We could further explore why this woman is in Richmond, but you get the idea. Her determination is the result of things she knows and things she doesn't, that hidden pull from the magnetic North Pole.

To explain the inner life of characters, at length, is to cheat readers of their own intelligence and experience. Show them people as they would meet them if the reader were in the book. Or let them imagine what would happen to them (without ever saying it directly) if the character stepped out of the book into the reader's real life. Let your readers figure out the character. Don't do it for them. Never insult readers' intelligence nor take away the joy of discovery.

Finding the voice

Within the context of character you will find the answer to the first basic problem of writing a novel. Do I write in the first person or the third? If you're quiet your main character will tell you what to do. First novels are traditionally written in the first person. Everyone gets that one for free. After that, the choice is difficult.

To write in the first person creates an immediacy, a closeness to that character—provided the character is, on some level, likable or fascinating. The trouble is, you lose a wide perspective. You can't give that perspective to your first-person narrator. If you did, she or he would have the mind of a god. She'd know too much, see too much. *Memoirs of Hadrian* by Marguerite Yourcenar is the only first-person novel I can think of whose narrator, of vast intellect, will not offend the reader.

By using third person you gain perspective, deeper irony, and a balance of emotions. You lose immediacy and you lose, to some extent, reader identification with your main character. Obviously, Margaret Mitchell solved that problem with Scarlett. Everyone identifies with Scarlett. However, such a strong connection to a single character using third person is difficult.

Again, your characters will tell you. Trust the characters. Don't manipulate them. It doesn't work.

The first person voice reaches up and tugs at your sleeve. Go back to Tinker Lundstrom, our Viet Nam veteran. He doesn't tug at your sleeve but you're interested in him (I hope). Feel the difference?

Some questions

When I teach writing I give out a set of questions that help students understand character. They have a month to complete the assignment if it's a semester course. On those occasions when I've filled in for a week, we do this in abbreviated form.

You must find people in the following age groups: twenty to thirty, thirty to forty, forty to fifty, fifty to sixty, sixty to seventy, seventy plus. They must represent a mixture of sex, race, and class background. Your assignment is to go out and interview them, asking the following questions:

1. What person or persons had the greatest influence on your life? Why?
2. How did you find the person you married, if you married? What was it that drew you together? What kept you together or, if divorced, tore you apart?
3. When do you remember paying for things? Do you remember what a loaf of bread, a pound of butter, and a quart of milk cost when you were a child? What do you think about prices today?
4. Have you ever believed in an elected official? Why or why not? Are you politically active today?
5. What events outside your personal life stand out in your mind? (For instance, Mother remembered the news of the sinking of the *Titanic* and how the casualty lists were incomplete for days. She also remembered the *Hindenberg*.) These memories constitute what I call "generational birthmarks." My generation was shocked at the murder of John Kennedy. My mother was not. She'd seen assassinations before. Generations use events that assaulted them or uplifted them. They refer to them and are upset when a different generation does not understand the importance of the event. For instance, an older American who is black can tell you where she was when Joe Louis won the title. A younger black American might not care about Joe Louis but he might remember Muhammad Ali refusing to go to Viet Nam. Songs, books, films are also generationally marked. See if you can get your people to recall cultural events too. For some reason, people recall disasters first.
6. Where have you lived in your life? What place did you like the best?
7. If you had children, how did they change your life?
8. Can you recall expressions you used as a young person that you don't use today, such as "bee's knees," "far out," "swell"?
9. If you could tell other people something and hope they would remember it, what would you tell them?

On the appointed day the class would come in with their answers. It usually took a week to go through the material. Some students even brought in photos and tape recordings so we could hear the cadence of the people's speech. This exercise was the most popular of the chores I assigned. It forced students to develop interview skills. It got them out of themselves. Beginning fiction writers are often self-indulgent and self-obsessed. It taught them that other people know a great deal. Ultimately, I hope it taught them respect for people different from themselves.

After this material is digested, each student has to write a short story, in dialogue, between two of the people interviewed.

Irrational beings

The human animal varies from class to class, culture to culture. In one way we are consistent: We are irrational. Whenever you create a character you must allow for the existence of irrationality. I'm not saying that your characters beat their breasts before heaven because they're out of cigarettes. I'm saying: Use this fundamental of the human mind to enlarge your characters. Do you remember the scene in Tolstoy's *Resurrection* in which the judge, possibly bored, watches the defendant come into the courtroom? He decides to count the steps the accused takes and to base his decision upon whether it takes him an odd or an even number of steps to reach his seat. That's irrational and very funny.

Sometimes this is displayed by the author. In *War and Peace* there is a passage in which Tolstoy compares Napoleon to a little boy in a carriage who has been given "baby reins." The child slaps the reins around, yanks them, and thinks he is driving the carriage. Napoleon was like that child. The forces of history, not the child, hurtled the carriage forward. It's a lovely passage but highly subjective. Napoleon laid waste a great deal of Russia, burned Moscow and killed thousands and thousands of people. (Tolstoy's grandfather was in the war.) Although the Russians eventually won, it was at great price and not necessarily because of brilliant leadership. The weather proved a very effective general. Tolstoy so hates Napoleon that he can't give him credit for his contributions to history, to law and to government. So he mocks him in a vivid passage. That's irrational.

Some writers are especially attracted to deeply irrational states of being. Think of *Notes from the Underground* or *Crime and Punishment*. If you want an American author, think of Truman Capote's nonficiton.

Most of us stay within the norm of human behavior. Murder is within the norm if one is threatened enough. Mass murder is not. Almost any extreme state provoked in a human will be accepted by the reader if the causes of that extreme state are carefully stated or shown. It's much more difficult to create sympathy for psychotic or totally evil characters.

Define *normal*. Maybe normal is the average of the deviance.

Character types

Finally I'd like to consider character types. There are definite human types recognizable in most cultures. There's the busybody and gossip. There's the humorless drudge. There's the constant worrier. There's the feckless partier. There are people who need enemies to give them identity. There are people ever spinning through the turnstiles of nostalgia.

You can't reduce human behavior to a simple set of responses, but you can recognize common strategies for facing life. You could have a very complicated character who bitches. That's how he handles stress. Your reader has seen that. It's familiar. Use the familiar to draw the reader deeper into the character, into what's behind the bitching.

Think of the zodiac. In a way, the zodiac has identified the twelve basic personality types for you. Each type has a good side and a bad side. The types are arranged on a wheel, which means no one type has precedence over any other type. Each person is then a combination of the good and the bad within his or her type. Whether you choose to believe in astrology is up to you. I always read my horoscope in the paper. It gives me something to believe in between breakfast and brushing my teeth at night.

If you wish the reassurance of twentieth-century research and conventional language, take the Myers-Briggs Type Indicator test. A trained management consultant or therapist can give you the test, which is a lark because there is no right or wrong answer, only your answer. Not only do you learn about your type, you learn about the other types in the two-hour interpretation. (I took the test in October 1986, and it cost $100. I'm an INTJ, for those of you familiar with the terminology – but on a secondary level, I've got lots of "feeling.") Personality is divided into sixteen personality types. These types are a shorthand course in character for a writer. However, don't get carried away with this. Use it as a guide. Your characters still must come from inside, must be felt. A character is more received than conceived.

Please Understand Me; Character and Temperament Types, by David Keirsey and Marilyn Bates, is a popular introduction to type.[1]

Write this on a piece of paper and stick it on your bathroom mirror: "Survival alters ideology." As life buffets you and your characters, this sentence will intensify in meaning. Change, growing from within and forced from without, is the mainspring of character development, of the process of human maturation.

[1]Distributed by Prometheus Nemesis Book Company, P.O. Box 2748 Del Mar, California 92014.

Plotting for Suspense

by Stephanie Kay Bendel

"I couldn't put it down." "My heart was pounding as I read the last chapter." "I stayed up late last night to finish that book—I had to find out how it ended!"

All authors would like to hear remarks like these about their works. Reality, however, reminds us that relatively few books provide truly memorable levels of suspense. On the other hand those that do usually sell well often stay in print for years. While the life span of most short stories is less than a year, unusually suspenseful ones are reprinted regularly in anthologies and are often adapted as screenplays. Well aware of these facts, my students frequently ask me how one goes about creating a suspenseful plot. After several years trying to help them analyze their plots for suspense, I've come up with a few helpful guidelines.

Suspense defined

First of all, we do well to give a little thought to exactly what suspense is. The word can be used in several ways, at least three of which can be applied to suspenseful writing: 1) to define a state of *anxiety*; 2) to define a state of *uncertainty* or *indecision*; 3) to define a state of *interest* and *excitement* experienced during a period of *waiting*.

It is worth keeping all three definitions in mind when writing suspense fiction, since almost all stories can be reduced to a simple formula: The protagonist has a problem. How suspenseful the story will be depends upon how much the readers care whether the problem is resolved—in other words, how *anxious* we can make them. In turn, how much the readers care about the resolution of the problem depends in large part upon how much they care about the people the problem affects; therefore, suspenseful writing demands that the author emotionally involve the readers in both the events taking place in the story and the character(s) who stands to suffer if things don't turn out right.

Thus, the author must initially give the readers someone to root for and to identify with. The aim here is to get the readers so involved that they imagine they are the protagonist and experience the anxiety of being in the protagonist's dilemma. Remember to make the main problem big enough so that the person(s) the readers are rooting for will suffer a good deal if it isn't solved.

Once the initial problem is created and the readers are emotionally involved with one or more characters, the author can increase suspense in several ways, all of which produce either more anxiety, uncertainty, or excitement:

1) By creating more obstacles for the protagonist to deal with. The obstacles may be part of the problem at hand, or they may be unrelated; for example, personal problems may be intruding, making resolution of the main problem more difficult.

2) By making sure that obvious solutions to the problem don't work. Increase the protagonist's—and therefore the readers'—frustration.

3) By raising the stakes. What happens if the main problem is not resolved? Can the situation be made worse than it already is?

Mystery and suspense writer **Stephanie Kay Bendel** *teaches creative writing to both adults and children in Boulder, Colorado. She is also the author of* Making Crime Pay *and, under the name Andrea Harris,* Scream Away.

4) By isolating the protagonist. Make sure that he or she can't simply turn to someone else for help or emotional support. Make your character solve the problem alone.

5) By cultivating uncertainty. Suspense is increased whenever we don't know whom to trust or whether or not a plan will work even if we manage to carry it off.

6) By keeping up the action. As soon as the readers begin to feel that the protagonist has a problem in hand, suspense levels will fall. We can raise them again by making sure the protagonist always has an immediate problem to deal with.

7) By creating a deadline. As the time allowed for solving the problem grows shorter, tension automatically increases.

To illustrate, let's consider a sample plot: A young woman—we'll call her Rachel—is brutally murdered, and the detective assigned to take charge of the investigation will be our protagonist—we'll call him Jake. At this point, so far as the reader is concerned, the murder is just another case for Jake—his motivation to solve it is his desire to do his job well. On the other hand, if he doesn't catch the murderer, it won't be the end of the world—merely another unsolved case, a fact of life for policemen. How do we take a run-of-the mill case and turn it into a suspenseful story?

Involve the reader's emotions

The first order of business is to emotionally involve the readers by showing them that Rachel was a likeable person; we'll make her a reporter whose friends and coworkers describe her to Jake as an honest, hardworking, caring woman who believed in what she did—and she did a lot of good, perhaps exposing corruption and deceit. It will be even better if we can show that those affected by the corruption and deceit were particularly vulnerable—for instance, children, the elderly, or the handicapped. Perhaps Jake even has first-hand knowledge of her accomplishments.

Now Rachel is not just another corpse. Jake—and the readers—will think of her as a real person—a likeable person who did not deserve to die.

We'll further involve the readers by showing them that Jake is a decent fellow—someone they can identify with. We'll give him some good qualities and some faults.

It is important that we make Jake a real human being—neither a superman nor a saint, for the readers cannot be anxious about a superman who can take care of himself in any situation. Nor can they identify with a saint—none of us has ever met anyone who was perfect—and we are all too aware of our own shortcomings to identify with someone who has none.

So what will Jake be like? To be a policeman, dealing constantly with the seamy side of life, he has to be pretty tough. He must witness death, suffering and injustice without going to pieces. We want our readers to admire that strength. On the other hand, Jake can't be insensitive or completely cynical, or the readers will emotionally distance themselves from him.

Remember, it's important to *show*—not tell—the readers what kind of man Jake is. How can we do that? Let's show Jake at the murder scene. He'll see the brutality Rachel suffered before her death and he'll clinically interpret the meaning of each piece of evidence: the blow to the right side of her head may mean her attacker was left-handed; her broken fingernails will show that she fought desperately for her life; the blood on the carpet, the walls, the tablecloth and the chair will tell him that she didn't die quickly or without pain.

Though Jake is being very professional, we'll simultaneously make it clear that he suffers because of the trauma his work entails. Perhaps he has ulcers or nightmares or insomnia, or maybe he drinks more than he should. And again, we won't just tell the readers he is suffering; we'll show him popping antacid tablets as he works, or waking in a cold sweat in the middle of the night after dreaming about Rachel's death, or needing a drink to fall asleep.

Jake must impress the readers as a real human being. He'll have some faults, but they won't be failings that the readers have no patience with because they'll understand why he behaves the way he does. For example, if somewhere in the story Jake forgets his son's birthday, we'll show that his absent-mindedness is not a byproduct of insensitivity – he feels terrible when he realizes what has happened. But he's been so overwhelmed by the complexity of his case and the pressures put upon him that the readers will honestly feel as though they too might forget their child's birthday under the same circumstances. When Jake loses his temper with the amiable young officer who is trying to help him, we'll already have shown that Jake has a pounding headache, he hasn't slept for two days and he's beginning to believe that whoever murdered Rachel has a good chance of getting away with it.

If we do these things well, the readers will certainly be emotionally involved with Jake. At the same time, we've already enlarged the original problem to some extent. No longer are we watching a detective solve a routine murder – there is something special about this case. We've made the problem more important – but have we made it important enough? Could we do even more?

Enlarge the problem

One of the ways to make the protagonist's dilemma worse is to make the villain(s) more powerful. Remember, we said Rachel was an investigative reporter. Suppose she told one of her co-workers that she was onto a big story. As Jake tracks down information, he begins to suspect that Rachel had discovered something damaging about an influential person – someone of great wealth or political power, someone who has a good deal of control over many other people. Now Jake is not up against an ordinary killer. He's trying to catch someone who has the ability to thwart the investigation, to buy off policemen, destroy evidence, and silence witnesses.

Provide additional obstacles

Once we are satisfied we've made the main problem big enough, we need to look at what other obstacles Jake is encountering. Some of them may arise directly from the case itself. Because Rachel was a reporter, the media focuses more than usual attention on the murder, demanding daily to know what progress is being made, putting Jake on the spot. We'll further complicate matters by having Jake make some progress that he must keep secret to avoid tipping off the suspect(s) in the investigation. Now even though Jake is doing a good job and getting closer to solving the case, he is being perceived as failing. His superiors, worried about the negative image the department is projecting, disassociate themselves from him as much as possible, and put even more pressure on him. Most of the other detectives don't want to be connected to a case that may be political trouble. The only person Jake can depend on is his long-time partner and friend, Detective Walt Hanson.

Other obstacles may arise from personal aspects of Jake's life. Let's give Jake a wife – we'll call her Myrna. She's a fine woman – a good policeman's wife – so our readers will like her and want Jake to have a good relationship with her. It is important to remember that if we want to cause problems between Jake and Myrna, we need to do it in such a way that the readers are not alienated from either of them. If, for example, we made Myrna a shrew who made unreasonable demands on Jake, our readers wouldn't feel much conflict – they wouldn't understand why Jake would feel a need to accommodate her. Considering the problems he has at work, they'd feel he'd be justified in ignoring Myrna for the time being.

Thus, we have to show that Myrna is a decent person. She understands the strain of Jake's job and tries to be supportive of him, she puts up with the long and irregular hours he must work, and usually handles most of the day-to-day problems at home by herself so that Jake won't be further pressured when he returns from work. We need to know that she and Jake love each other very much, and that conflict between them is truly distressing.

Accordingly, we won't let Myrna become upset over relatively small problems. We must give her an important reason for needing Jake's attention at this particular time. For example, suppose her mother has just been diagnosed as terminally ill. Now Jake's wife is understandably upset and is looking to him for emotional support. Our readers will sympathize with Myrna, and will hope that Jake can comfort her. But they'll also see that he is being pulled in two directions at once, and every time Myrna needs him, a serious development at work will be taking him away. And whatever he's doing to solve Rachel's murder, part of him feels he should be with Myrna. No matter what he does, Jake will feel bad.

Eliminate obvious solutions

It is important to remember that every time we pose a problem for Jake, the readers are going to say to themselves, "If I were Jake, what would I do?", and they will try to come up with possible solutions to his problems. What we must do is stay one step ahead of the readers and show them that their solutions won't work.

At this point in the story, what might the readers think Jake should do? Take some time off to be with his wife? We'll show there's no way he can do that. Even when he tries to spend some time with her, the phone rings—he's urgently needed elsewhere. Should he get more manpower on the case so it will be solved more quickly? We've already partially blocked that possibility by having his superiors and fellow detectives wanting to disassociate themselves from the investigation of Rachel's murder, so Jake and Walt have to carry on alone.

What will the readers expect them to do now? One obvious course is to talk further with Rachel's co-workers who said she'd been working on a big story. Perhaps more information will lead to the killer. But let's show that talking with them won't help Jake and Walt anymore—why not? Suppose everyone is now reluctant to give our heroes any information. Some of them even deny what they've said earlier. Perhaps one of the informants is murdered. Thus, Jake and Walt not only have been reminded how powerful their opponent is, but they've had some of their options destroyed. The murdered informant cannot ever testify, and the others are less likely to come forward.

In this way, the first three or four methods that come to mind for reducing the stress Jake is under must be shown to be unworkable. Each time the reader realizes that a course of action is not possible, or that it won't work, tension levels in the story are elevated.

Raise the stakes

To further increase suspense, we'll raise the stakes for Jake. When we first began, failing to solve Rachel's murder would have been a personal frustration for him, but not the end of the world; all policemen have to live with unsolved cases. So far we have changed the situation so that if Jake doesn't solve the case, he'll look bad professionally, and the police department's image will suffer. His superiors will be angry with him and possibly his job will be in jeopardy. Can we make things worse? Well, let's suppose that as Jake continues to investigate, he begins to uncover evidence that points to himself! Now he's in a terrible dilemma: If he suppresses the evidence and is caught doing so, he will look very guilty, will be taken off the case, won't be able to find the real killer, will probably lose his job and very likely will be tried for a murder he didn't commit. If he doesn't suppress the evidence, the same things will still happen; his only chance is to suppress the evidence and hope he doesn't get caught before he solves the case. To make matters worse, Jake can no longer confide in Walt without involving him in an illegal activity.

Notice how neatly we've boxed Jake in. Undoubtedly it will have occurred to some readers that Jake might simply quit his job if things became too bad. After all, a policeman can always find work as a private detective or a security consultant, and if Jake did that, he would also be emotionally available for Myrna. But now that evidence has turned up pointing to him, we've cut off the possibility of Jake just walking away from the problem. If he leaves, someone else will certainly turn up the evidence against him, and he'll look guiltier than ever.

Isolate the protagonist

Another device for raising suspense levels in a story is to isolate the protagonist—prevent anyone else from helping him solve the problem. To a certain extent we've already done this: Jake's coworkers are avoiding involvement in the case, and his superiors are putting pressure on him. His informants won't help him any longer, and his wife can't comfort him because she's got her own serious problem to deal with.

How can we isolate Jake even more? Well, let's suppose Myrna's mother lives a couple of thousand miles away, and of course, now that she's so ill, Myrna wants to be with her. Now Jake will be physically alone. We can even arrange to give him another problem to deal with—he has to borrow money to pay for Myrna's trip. Furthermore, he'll feel bad that he can't accompany Myrna, but the way the murder case is going, he cannot possibly leave town.

Now there's no one at home to give Jake the emotional support that he needs more than ever, and there's only one person who can help him solve Rachel's murder: his trusted partner. To some extent, we've put distance between the two men by forcing Jake to keep an important secret from Walt. However, most readers want to feel that if push comes to shove, Walt would come through for Jake, even risking his job in the process. Can we isolate Jake even more by removing even that hope? Yes, but we must proceed very carefully, and we'll do it by means of yet another helpful trick: promoting uncertainty.

Promote uncertainty

Until now, we've worked hard to convince the readers that Jake can trust Walt. If we change the situation too quickly, our story will lose credibility and won't be at all suspenseful. What we need to do is to plant little seeds of distrust.

Suppose Jake realizes that Walt has lied to him. We'll make it a small lie, something almost trivial, and there might be a good reason why Walt tells it, but Jake can't be sure. All he knows is that he's beginning to distrust his partner.

As the story goes on, Jake will realize that the false evidence pointing to him must have been planted with the aid or knowledge of someone within the Police Department. As much as he doesn't want to, he—and the readers—will have to begin suspecting Walt.

Uncertainty can also be used to produce suspense in other ways. Suppose Jake comes to suspect that Rachel had some hard evidence against the villain(s) and that she may have hidden it. Can Jake figure out where it is? Will he recognize it when he sees it? Will it be enough to exonerate him and indict the real culprit(s)? Does anyone else know or suspect that Rachel hid some evidence? Will someone else find it and destroy it before Jake gets there?

Of course, we could go on all day piling problems up for poor Jake, but we must exercise good judgment in deciding when enough is enough. I once wrote a story about a family in which six of seven siblings had heart attacks. I took the situation from real life—that is exactly what happened in my father's family—and I hoped to convey the sense of helplessness and horror the family lived with. Instead I found I had created an emotional overload. I read the story to a small group of writers and discovered that they were giggling uncontrollably by the third or fourth heart attack.

The point to remember is that while in real life the six heart attacks occurred over a period of twenty-five years, giving the family time to adjust and accept the emotional strain of one illness before facing another, I was asking my audience to absorb the total impact in one evening! As a result, my story had no credibility even though I was describing actual events.

If, for example, Jake's mother-in-law dies and Myrna threatens to divorce him if he doesn't drop everything and travel a couple of thousand miles for the funeral, and then it becomes apparent that not only is his friend Walt somehow involved in Rachel's murder, but he is trying to frame Jake for it, and then his sister calls and informs Jake that her son has been kidnapped, a ransom note has just arrived and Jake must come right away—well, our story will be in shambles. The readers will surely throw the book down in disgust and disbelief.

There are no firm guidelines as to how much your protagonist can believably endure. A truly skillful writer can make an audience accept almost any premise, but you need to be acutely aware of your own limitations.

Create a deadline

The final thing that a suspense story needs is a clock ticking in the background. The greatest problem in the world won't create any anxiety if there's an infinite amount of time available to resolve it. On the other hand, if the reader is aware that dire consequences will follow if the problem is not solved by a certain time, suspense will continue to mount as that time draws nearer.

Let's suppose that the villain of our story is a prominent industrialist who has curried favor with local politicians for years. He is donating a large tract of forested land to the state to be used as a park and recreation area, thus affording him a large tax write-off. What Rachel discovered and Jake finds out is that the forest was used for many years as a testing ground for various pesticides and herbicides that the industrialist manufactured. The land and water are contaminated with long-lasting toxins, and the park is scheduled to be opened tomorrow. Jake must gather enough evidence to force state officials to prevent thousands of people from camping and picnicking there, and he has only a few hours left to do it!

Now, when we've made things just as bad as we feel we can while maintaining credibility, and time is running out, we'll have reached the climax of our story—suspense is as high as we can make it. The time has come to start solving our protagonist's problems in a satisfying way—but that's another topic!

The Last Stages

by Geoffrey Bocca

When you have the last draft of your novel done, the real hard work begins. Some writers insist that they do their best work in revision. But many other writers—and especially beginners—cannot bring themselves to recognize, let alone perform, the kind of surgery needed to make the novel work. In such cases, happy the writers who have good editors.

Since good revision and good line editing (or manuscript editing, so that it will not be confused with copy editing) are much the same, I shall treat them together under the general category of editing. This means that you have acquired the services of an experienced editor. And how do you do that? There are several possibilities. The most conventional way is for your editor to be provided by your publisher. And how do you find a publisher? Well . . .

It sometimes seems to me that some of my students are more concerned with learning how to find a good agent than they are with learning how to write. That is understandable. It is not easy for an unpublished author to attract a publisher's attention. But it is not as difficult as it is made out to be. Too many writers assume that they get rejection notices because their work hasn't been read by a publisher's readers. The truth is that they probably get rejections because their stuff *has* been read. Publishers have no stake in turning down a good book. Even publishers who claim they don't accept unsolicited material will always take a peek at it to see if it has promise.

I have nothing against literary agents. They are wonderful people. I dedicated my last book to my own agent. Agents know which publishing houses are looking for what. They know the personal tastes of individual editors. They will read a manuscript and think, "This won't go at Knopf. But Jimmy at Doubleday loves this kind of book. Or maybe Crown." Agents always have a shrewd idea of how much to ask for in the way of advances and royalties. They are great negotiators. They are good to have on your side. But you can live without them.

If you elect to submit your manuscript without the help of an agent, here is a tip that I know to be helpful because I got it from the editor-in-chief of a major publishing house. Always submit your manuscript to an individual editor and make sure that that editor is *not* the editor-in-chief. The editor-in-chief is always overworked, overwhelmed. He will pass the manuscript, unread, to an assistant for prescreening. It will wind up not at the top of the heap of manuscripts, but with the most junior editorial trainee who, in the charming jargon of publishing, is in charge of the "slush pile."

Thus, if you want your manuscript read by someone senior, do not simply send it to the publisher or to the fiction editor or to the editor-in-chief. Instead, go to the library and get hold of the current edition of *Literary Market Place*, the annual publication put out by R.R. Bowker Company that lists the names, titles, addresses, and telephone numbers of virtually everyone in the publishing business. Choose at random the name of a senior editor in the house of your choice and send him or her your manuscript. The fit may not be ideal; you could be dealing with someone temperamentally unsuited to your kind of writing. But you will be dealing not with an overworked tyro, but with an experienced professional who may at least have the wit to pass your submission—if it warrants it—to the right colleague. To

Prolific author **Geoffrey Bocca** *wrote 11 novels, seven biographies, four travel books, three histories and one book of literary criticism during his writing career. He taught creative writing at Pennsylvania State University before his death in 1983.*

get even that far in one of today's busy publishing houses, is as Henri IV said of being a Breton duke, no small beer.

Some specifics on submission

I am getting ahead of myself. Let's go back to the moment when you realize that you are ready to submit. Your novel is completed and needs only to be typed and mailed. We now touch on the important subject of presentation.

Let us assume that it is Friday evening and the lights are going out in the publishers' offices in New York. A publisher has two manuscripts on her desk, and she is deciding which one to take for weekend reading "out on the island" (for some reason publishers all seem to spend their weekends on the island, at the shore, or in the Hamptons). One manuscript is typed and presented in a professional way. The other is a typographical shambles. You do not have to think very hard to decide which one she will take.

I always type every page of my final draft myself. It sounds time-consuming and it is, but somehow I always find something that can be improved, polished, honed—no matter how many times I have rewritten and revised.

The typewriter should have keyboard in pica type, not the smaller elite type sometimes used by secretaries. There are several reasons for this. Pica is easier to read, especially when many thousands of words are involved. It is also an easier type for the author to work with. An average manuscript page in pica type will amount to about 250 words. A page of elite will be closer to 300 words. So each page you revise will mean 20 percent more physical labor for you, and I can tell you from painful experience on one elite typewriter that at the end of a hard day's work, it feels like much more!

I keep half a dozen typewriters. Two electric typewriters. One for town and one for country. A medium-sized typewriter waits for me in London, and an ultra-lightweight I keep in a corner for air travel. There are two more kept in reserve in case one or another breaks down. All have identical pica type so that the publisher will be given the impression of professional continuity: that the manuscript has come off one typewriter. To heighten this comfortable impression I give my typewriter ribbons a shorter life than is necessary and discard them as soon as they begin to fade even slightly. It is amazing how many professional writers neglect this small but important point. A friend of mine who has sold about three novels and several nonfiction books wrote me recently, bleating that his manuscripts were being returned to him. I could easily see why. I could hardly read his letter because his ribbon was so faint.

Publishers like wide left-hand margins to allow them space for their pencil marks. My left-hand margins are always two inches deep. Publishers need to breathe the air of white paper. At the bottom of the page I try to leave another two inches of white space, for my own convenience as well as the publisher's. I might decide upon rereading that the page needs a rewrite that will add a couple of lines.

Clean type is also important. Larry Freundlich of Wyndham Books, who published my book *Bestseller*, told me he is physically repelled by a manuscript in which the o, e, and a emerge as •, e, and a. The manuscript should probably be the conventional black type on white paper, though I have read a manuscript typed in sepia-brown that was very restful to the eye.

I was surprised to be told by several students that publishers will draw up a contract for a novel on the basis of some specimen chapters and a summary of what is to come. They had read it somewhere in some specialist magazines. This is not my experience or that of publishers to whom I have spoken on the subject. It is certainly not the practice with fiction, unless one's work is well known and admired by the publisher. Take it for granted that your novel should be completed before it is submitted.

Professional criticism and the writer

Let us say that you have submitted your complete manuscript and that it has been accepted. Now begins one of the most painful and illuminating phases of the entire writing process: the phase in which for the first time you relinquish your cherished creation into the hands of another person—probably a stranger—so that he or she can edit it.

For the sake of simplicity, I have so far been assuming that that first other person will be a member of your publisher's editorial staff, but in reality it might be your agent or your creative writing teacher. Whoever it is, the result is bound to be something of a shock to your ego. And if you permit it to be too much of a shock, if you treat each criticism as an affront rather than as a potentially valuable gift, you are probably doomed.

The first person to look at the results of my first attempt at writing fiction was a wonderfully accomplished editor, Knox Burger. I still have the preliminary comments he sent me. Here is a sampling:

> Your opening is weak. However, if you turn to page 73, second paragraph, I think you will agree that it would make a gripping start, especially if you follow it with a flashback to the sequence which begins on page 15 in the manuscript.
>
> Dorothy and Priscilla are too similar in character. I think they could be telescoped into one.
>
> P. 81. I think the sex here could be implied rather than be made explicit.
>
> Tom is a stick throughout and slows down the action whenever you bring him in. Either cut him out altogether, or think of ways you can make him more interesting.
>
> P. 181. The fight scene is GREAT!!!!!!

And so on for page after page. I followed the same technique with my students when I was a professor of creative writing.

You do not have to take all professional criticism as gospel, because professionals can be wrong too. But on the other hand, arrogance by the author has killed many a potential novel. Some years ago, a friend whom I will call Bill showed me the manuscript of his first novel. Bill was a professional magazine writer, a former newspaper reporter, and a foreign correspondent. He wrote one of those rare novels in which the theme is riveting even in a brief description. It is about a lovable slob of a newspaper reporter called Joe. He loves his mother and his girl friend. He helps old ladies cross the road, repairs his neighbors' television set, drinks beer from the can, and is an easy touch for his pals. But he is overweight, a messy eater, and seems to own only one suit. His girl friend issues an ultimatum: smarten up or else. Joe goes on a crash diet, has his suits made to measure, visits elegant hairdressers, and studies wine. At each stage of his education he becomes less lovable, meaner, and ends up as the editor of the paper and detested by everybody.

It was a variation on the old theme of whether it is better to be an old man's queen or a young man's slave. I enthusiastically promoted the book to a publisher, warning him also that it needed a lot of work, and the publisher drew up a contract. Out of friendship for Bill I went over the manuscript the way Knox Burger had gone over mine, spelling out my views line by line. I telephoned Bill to say that I had finished. He stopped by to pick up the manuscript—but left the notes behind, unread. "Hello," I said to myself, warning bells jingling in my ears.

Another fine original writer and a lawyer, whom I will call Tom, was one of my potentially most exciting students. I put him onto a publisher I felt sure would love his manuscript, but *warned* him, "Tom, you are an arguer, in love with your own words. If the publisher likes the book and suggests changes, listen. Don't argue, explain, or theorize. If you do, the publisher will say to himself, 'Oh, oh! He'll criticize the copy editing, complain of slow progress, hit the roof over the jacket, be on the telephone all the time. Not worth the trouble. Pity. It's a good book, but no thanks.' "

It is commonplace among editors to say that the way a writer responds to editing is a sure index of how professional he is. It is not the best-selling authors (some of whom need lots of help) who give their editors the most trouble; it is the too sensitive beginners. Which may be one reason why many editors think twice before taking on first novels.

Objectivity: How it can help

What is it that makes a good editor's intervention so valuable? How can an editor pretend to know more about how a particular novel should be written than the person who created it? The fact is that an editor may often bring to a manuscript only one thing that its author cannot. *Objectivity*.

The author will have been totally immersed in his novel for months or even years. He will have rewritten scenes countless times, changed characters, restructured the plot, fiddled endlessly with passages of dialogue. He will have lavished so much attention on stylistic details and bits of narrative machinery that he will—almost inevitably—have lost his ability to see how the whole book works on first reading. It is the old problem of the forest and the trees.

But the editor *is* a first-time reader. And more than that, he is a reader who, unlike most of us, is trained not just to stop at saying vaguely "I kind of lost interest toward the end," or "The Priscilla character never grabbed me, somehow." Instead, the editor tries to use all his professional skills both to identify, as explicitly as possible, the weaknesses and to propose what to do about them.

Of course, the more time an editor spends with a manuscript, the more he will distance himself from his first impressions and the more his own objectivity will erode. That is why wise authors—and editors—always should pay careful attention to the editor's first impressions.

Nor should you scorn an editor's suggestions because they seem painful to your pride, difficult to accomplish, or simply something that you have never even considered. A good remedy can work magic. I will give you two examples.

My novel *The Fourth Horseman* is about a gang of English and Irish renegades who descend on Hollywood Park racetrack and steal not only the money from the money room but every purse, pocketbook, and wallet from the 35,000 spectators. For purposes of plot, the central character Brownlow, a disgraced SAS officer, needs a financial genius. He knows just the man, Kolev, a defector from the Soviet Union living in a sleazy district of Paris:

> He pressed the bell to Kolev's flat. He had expected the natural caution from a man with so many enemies in the Soviet Union and so many solicitors of aid among impoverished Russians in the west. He expected double-locks, chains, a barking dog, or at least a muttered "Who's there?" from the other side of the door. Instead it was flung open with a crash that snowed plaster from the walls, by a man naked except for a pair of baggy drawers. Everything about him seemed to wave, wriggle and gibber. He capered first on one leg and then the other. The arms gesticulated at a rate that reminded Brownlow of a four-armed Indian dancing God. Unkempt hair flew about wild, red-rimmed eyes. The man was a giant, at least six feet four inches in height. But most disconcerting of all was a Webley automatic held aloft in his right hand, enabling Brownlow to note that it was fully loaded.
>
> "Are you José André Lacour, you pig?" the apparition yelled. "Or Prakhorenko?"
>
> "Neither."
>
> "Sure you're not Prakhorenko? You look like Prakhorenko!"
>
> Brownlow considered his past confrontations with armed adversaries. He coped. He soothed. Gently he led Kolev into the flat and took the gun from his hand . . . Kolev flung his tangled dust-smelling hair on Brownlow's shoulders, overwhelmed

him with his size, almost knocking him to the rug. Kolev sobbed. "Why do the Americans debilitate themselves to keep the Soviet Union afloat? Why don't they do the Russians a favor and let the system rot of its own putrescence?" Brownlow freed himself, took his silk handkerchief from his breast pocket and wiped away Kolev's tears. He sat the professor on a creaking settee, found a corkscrew to open the vodka bottle and two clean glasses. When Kolev's emotions subsided, Brownlow sat facing him and addressed him in carefully worded French.

"First of all, Joseph Alexandrovitch, I have a financial proposition which will appeal to you. But before I make it, I want to ask you, who is the most evil man in the world?"

"My father," said Kolev smiling. "Papa."

"Wrong."

"You never met the bugger. During the Stalin purges of the 1930's, Papa would take out the family album and ink out the face of each former comrade as he was executed. He told me and my beloved sister, Rosa, 'When you cut down the forests, the chips must fly. My time will come.' The old sod kept an attaché case containing toiletries and change of underwear, waiting for the knock on the door in the small hours . . ."

Anyone who read *The Fourth Horseman* may be excused a puzzled frown. "Out! " said my editor, James Wade, his Irish eyes unsmiling as he ran a pencil through the whole scene (which continues for several more pages). Furious arguments ensued. "Kolev is the most colorful character in the whole book," I yelled.

"I don't disagree," said Wade, "and I am sure he will be the most colorful character in your next book. But he slows down the narrative. He does not fit in with the other characters. Besides, you have already introduced the girl to whom you attribute an exceptionally high IQ. Make her the financial genius the gang needs. . . ."

Wade was right. But I have not thrown Kolev away. I have filed him, as James Wade knew I would, for my next novel. The moral is that almost no author can reliably cut his own novel. There are too many scenes and characters that he loves for the wrong reasons. The author who is asked to cut 100 pages from his novel will certainly cut the wrong 100. It is one of the facts of novel writing.

Another example, less painful because I wasn't on the receiving end: The author, Linda Wells, asked me to read her excellent novel about the War of Independence, *Patriot's Lady*, before mailing it to her publisher. I saw that here and there, through overenthusiasm, she had fallen into the error of too much direct narrative. A few suggestions on my part, I think, corrected her faults and emphasized a basic tenet of fiction writing: almost every sentence should provide a counterpoint to the previous sentence. Here is a page of Linda Wells' manuscript, with the faults underlined.

They galloped down the road at a dead run. Sarah dared to think they were safe. At the fork leading to the Jamestown road, she heard horses. Were they behind her? She couldn't tell. No, they were coming from Greensward.

Jackson pulled on his rein, the horses rearing to a halt. "They've found us out. We must bluff or make a run for it."

"Run for it!" shouted Sarah.

Jackson jerked the reins and turned the horses down the road which led away from Williamsburg and toward Jamestown. "If we escape, we can go around and take an old path I remember."

Sarah could only nod. She bumped up and down in her saddle. Unable to keep her seat with the stirrup too long for her legs, she flew into the air with every jolt. She was too frightened to feel pain.

The horsemen were gaining on them. She heard Stuart call her name. "Sarah! Stop!" She saw the flash of powder. A shot was fired. She heard the crack seconds

> later. They fired another shot. She heard Stuart cursing the man with the gun. In the black void through which they hurtled, she heard a horse scream in pain.

The page had to be edited to eliminate the constant repetition of "she heard," "she bumped," "she flew," "she saw," "she was," and so on. By use of the counterpoint to each succeeding sentence, the task was easy and made for better narrative.

> They galloped down the road at a dead run. Sarah dared to think she was safe. At the fork leading to the Jamestown road, she heard horses. Were they coming behind her? (Original: she couldn't tell.) No, they were coming from Greensward. Jackson pulled on his rein, the horse rearing to a halt. "They've found us out. We must bluff or make a run for it."
>
> "Run for it!" shouted Sarah.
>
> Jackson jerked the reins and turned the horses down the road which led away from Williamsburg and toward Jamestown. "If we escape, we can go around and take an old path I remember."
>
> Sarah could only nod. (Original: she bumped.) Every jolt of the horse sent her flying into the air (Original: she flew), her feet losing stirrups that were too long for her legs, but her fear (Original: she was too frightened) obliterated her pain.
>
> The horsemen were gaining on them. Stuart called her name. (Original: She heard Stuart call her name.) "Sarah! Stop!" Powder flashed in the darkness. (Original: she saw a flash.) The crack of the shot was heard seconds later. (Original: she heard the crack.) They fired another shot. She heard (as in original) Stuart curse (instead of "cursing" in original) the man with the gun. In the black void through which they hurtled, a horse screamed in pain. (Original: she heard a horse scream.)

These examples suggest the two main ways in which the manuscript editor can help the author. In the first example, Jim Wade's advice about deleting Kolev—like Knox Burger's earlier advice about Dorothy and Priscilla, Tom, and where the novel should begin—had to do with large structural matters. This is where the editor's fresh vision is likely to be most useful, for it is about the big picture that the writer's judgment may be most uncertain.

The second example, my advice to Linda Wells, was of a different order, more narrowly focused on technique. Not all editors are sufficiently good writers themselves to be able to give this kind of advice—which doesn't mean that they don't try. When an editor gives you detailed technical advice on your writing style, listen but be cautious. He may be right; he may be right for someone else but not for you; or he may be dead wrong.

Copyediting and the long wait

Once past the trauma—or maybe eye-opening pleasure—of manuscript editing, you will move on to the vital phase of copy editing. One day your publisher will send your manuscript back to you, its pages covered with myriad little varicolored pencilings—all apparently designed to prove to you that you know nothing of spelling, punctuation, or grammar, and that you are not even capable of remembering between page 7 and 243 the correct middle initial of your heroine's name. There is seldom much you can do with a copy-edited manuscript except to answer the copy editor's queries, but you should go over it carefully, all the same. Copy editors have been known to get misguided bees in their bonnets, such as scrupulously correcting in dialogue grammatical errors that the author had deliberately inserted to show his character's lack of education.

In one of my novels I have an Irish terrorist whom I called Erroll Flynn. My alert copy editor commented that I had misspelled the movie star's name. She was right, and I had not noticed. So rather than correct the misspelling on page after page, I turned it to a certain small advantage and inserted, "Poor Mrs. Flynn even misspelled the name of her own child, and he grew up to be extremely ugly and never forgave her."

Other phases will follow—proofreading, obtaining permissions for quoted matter, answering publicity questionnaires, approving jacket copy, and so on—each more remote than the last from the true creative writing process, and all contained within the seemingly endless waiting period between finished manuscript and printed book.

There is much to be said about the many subtle and unexpected pressures that beset an author on his way to, and following, publication, but they lie beyond the scope of what this is meant to be about: the craft of fiction writing. So I shall simply repeat a bit of advice I gave you earlier: the minute you finish your first novel, begin working on the second. If you can understand why I say this, so much the better. If not, trust me.

"You don't have to take all professional criticism as gospel, because professionals can be wrong too. But on the other hand, arrogance by the author has killed many a potential novel."

—Geoffrey Bocca

— No Bones About It: How to Write Today's Horror

by D.W. Taylor

It all began thousands of years ago in some dark and smoky cave with a tale-teller chanting to his awe-struck tribe huddled around a sputtering fire. He sang of strange beasts, angry gods, and dark magic afoot in a dangerous world. In other words, horror stories.

All known societies have a rich history of these super-natural myths and legends. Their purpose, like fairy tales for children, is to explain the threatening universe beyond the cave, to simplify a confusing world seemingly dominated by forces greater than ourselves.

But we're civilized now. No more of that "moon eating the sun" business. We know an astronomical event when we see one. Why, we don't even throw virgins into volcanoes anymore to keep them (the volcanoes) from erupting.

Yet we still love our horror tales. Today they enjoy unprecedented popularity. Critic Douglas Winter estimates that in the past fifteen years more horror novels have been published than in the entire previous history of the printed word. Stephen King has over fifty million copies of his books in print, and Dean R. Koontz is nipping at his heels.

Horror is everywhere in our post-print media, too. The genre's three archetypes—the Vampire, the Monster, and the Ghost—have been immortalized in the breakfast cereals Count Chocula, Frankenberry, and Boo Berry. On TV, horror is used to hawk everything from floor polish to charge cards. The number of horror films is staggering, multiplying themselves in sequel after sequel like some evil spawn. And don't forget that the music video which sparked the current craze, Michael Jackson's 1982 "Thriller," was nothing if not a little shop of horrors.

Horror's awe-ful appeal

The first task for a writer hoping to publish in this genre is to understand the reasons for such enormous popularity, to fathom the complex social and emotional elements which fueled the horror "boom" that began in the early 1970s and continues nearly unabated today. Like Freddie Kreuger and Jason, horror refuses to die. And to write it successfully, we need to know why.

When H.P. Lovecraft observed in the 1930s that the appeal of horror was narrow because it required imagination and detachment from life, the Rhode Island recluse couldn't have anticipated the profound threats to our imaginations and lives the last decade of this century. Can anyone doubt that we live in a horrific world? Missile silos overflow with pent-up doom. The AIDS virus stalks our globe. The "greenhouse effect" has nothing to do with fecundity. And above Antarctica there's a hole in the ozone layer that's the size of the continental United States. Someone should wake up Lovecraft and tell him that imagination and detachment have become virtual requirements for maintaining one's sanity today. Our need for horror stories parallels our sense of alienation, helplessness and fear—as common today as pollution. Horror has become an important way for us to deal with

David Taylor *'s horror tales have appeared in numerous magazines and anthologies including* Gorezone, Masques III, Scare Care *and* Weird Tales. *Associate Professor of English at Moravian College, he is also the director of the university's writing center and an instructor for Writer's Digest School.*

these emotions by letting us confront them in a make-believe world, gain a sense of control there, and bring a little of it back with us.

But a horror writer need look no further than his own backyard to find his subject matter: the misery of the ghetto-child, the degradation of women, the shame of the homeless, the unspeakable isolation of a nursing home. There's real horror in loneliness and rage, in twisted love and jealously, in the rampant greed that threatens to rot us from within. Much of today's horror is about these dark stains on our souls, the cancers of our minds.

Since Lovecraft's time we've increasingly fooled ourselves into thinking that the universe is fully explainable in terms of natural laws which are discoverable through science. Once we understand these laws, the reasoning goes, we'll be the undisputed masters of the universe and our lives in it. Yet, at the same time, we suspect and hope that there are still occult forces out there that we can never fully understand. We are driven to seek them out because our science and rationalism threaten to rid the universe of all mystery.

But there is another appeal about which we mustn't fool ourselves: the violence of our species is found in horror literature in distilled form, pure as plutonium, and is a metaphor for the everyday brutality that lies just beneath the surface of our lives. This compulsion to violence is another legacy from our early hominid ancestors, who fought off extinction on the African veldt. Eons of biologic evolution have ingrained the savage instincts of the hunter into us, yet our current lives give us little opportunity for its expression. In many ways we have become automatons regulated by the corporation's clock and must suppress our savagery—and pay the price in ulcers, heart disease, and social psychopaths.

The emotional and physical violence of horror literature act as a safety valve for our repressed animalism. What commuter doesn't cheer for King Kong as he rips the five o'clock train from its tracks? Who hasn't wished to strike out against the nameless, faceless regulation of our lives, a conformity that threatens to turn us into unthinking, unfeeling workaholics? Who doesn't see in Frankenstein's monster, who was refused the affection he craved, the expression of our own innate hostilities? Few of us in this complex, technological, alienating world have not felt at times misunderstood, unappreciated, alone, dehumanized. Horror stories have become a convenient and harmless way of striking back, of giving in to those mysterious and feral forces, allowing them to take control and wreck havoc on the stultifying regularity of our lives.

A safety valve. One which allows us to exercise, in the words of Stephen King, "those antisocial emotions which society demands we keep stoppered up . . . for society's and our own good." We can also understand why this literature appeals so strongly to adolescents in the process of rebelling against authority and social conformity. Horror literature, like rock 'n' roll, is strenuously antisocial and especially popular with teens experimenting with the extremes of their emotions.

Horror also appeals to the dark side in us. We hold an inescapable fascination with the grave and the mystery of death. At the instant of our birth, the countdown to oblivion begins as each passing moment brings us closer to death. It is said that Voltaire possessed a clock which, in addition to chiming the hour, intoned the solemn words: "One hour nearer the grave." Death is the one aspect of life that cannot be denied. And as Stephen King observed, the reading of horror and supernatural tales is a form of preparation for our own deaths, a "danse macabre" before the void, as well as a way to satisfy our curiosity about the most important event in our lives except birth.

So perhaps the ultimate appeal of horror is the affirmation that it provides. The opposite of death is life. If supernatural evil exists in this world, as many horror stories posit, so must supernatural good. Black magic is balanced by white. The Wicked Witch of the West met her match in Glenda, the Good Witch of the North. If the fallen angel Lucifer lives and is at work in our lives, so must be God.

In a starkly rational world that would banish such beings, horror literature gives them back to us: their magic, their power, the reality they once held in simpler times. As critics over the years have noted, fantasy literature works like religion in our lives. It helps to satisfy our need to believe in forces greater than ourselves, worlds different from our own. It touches that part of us that dreams of what never was and can never be. But for a brief and magic moment it is real and we believe. And are filled with awe.

What today's readers want

So the question becomes how to write awe-inspiring stories that will leave readers panting and our bank accounts swelling. What worked for M.R. James and Algernon Blackwood in the 20s, Lovecraft in the 30s, Richard Matheson and Ray Bradbury in the 50s, Robert Aickman in the 60s, Stephen King and Peter Straub in the 70s and Stephen King and Clive Barker in the 80s, won't necessarily frighten or entertain readers in the 90s. What will?

During a course in "Contemporary Horror Fiction" at Moravian College in Pennsylvania, I asked thirty-two undergraduates, who represented virtually every major from accounting to zoology, exactly that question as well as several others in a market survey of this genre's traditionally most enthusiastic audience: young adults.

I first asked, "What are the elements that make for a good horror story?" And then had them explore the flip-side: "What ruins a horror story for you?" I wanted to know if their answers would reveal any difference between the standards that critics and teachers have set for the contemporary horror story and the personal criteria that readers actually use as they stand in front of the rack at Waldenbooks and decide whether or not to reach for their wallets. Even a cursory glance at best-seller lists, especially those from decades past, reveals the striking difference between popular taste (what sells) and critical taste (what's praised). That sounds hideously commercial, and any writer who would slavishly follow the results of a market survey is bound to write only perfunctory, uninspired drivel. The one thing this genre doesn't need is more cynical, assembly-line novels penned for the sole purpose of making money and feeding off the accomplishments of serious writers. The horror story, so far at least, has managed to outlive the hacks and sleazoid publishers whose only allegiance is to the quick buck, a testimony to the power of this genre and humanity's need for it.

But there is also too much focus in school on literature written mainly for an audience of critics and teachers. That's a shame because the true glory of literature, I've come to believe, lies in its ability to hold an audience spellbound with the power of narrative, which is our oldest and still most prevalent way of understanding the world. We've always told stories to each other, especially horror and fantasy stories, as a way of mentally shaping and reshaping the inscrutable universe around us. Although one may deplore and berate TV and movies as sugar-water substitutes for the meat and potatoes of literature, these media rather democratically satisfy the human thirst for story, for narrative. And whenever a "serious" writer forsakes the obligation to tell a good story, whenever his purpose for writing is no longer to weave the magic spell of narrative but to produce "great art" and to please elitist critics, that writer will surely be replaced by movies and TV—or a better storyteller.

So I agree with J.N. Williamson, who in connection with this course appeared at our college for a lecture and public reading. This popular American novelist said to my students one day in class, "Art is accidental; it is incidental to having told our story as best we can." The fact that more than one hundred students tried to register for the thirty-two available seats in this course is evidence that horror authors like Williamson have never lost their commitment to tell a good story, to entertain, and the students knew that. Therefore, an attempt to understand the expectations of readers in this genre isn't necessarily a bad thing, indeed it is a manifestly logical and necessary thing.

The results of the survey surprised me. By the end of the semester, we had read and discussed over forty stories from contemporary commercial and small press magazines like *Grue*, *Pulphouse*, and *Noctulpa*; from literary anthologies like *Masques*; and from single-author collections like *Skeleton Crew*. Our semester of dark fantasy was brightened by the novels of several "sons": Jackson, Matheson, Williamson, Wilson; as well as by Straub, Koontz, and the King. Student reaction was as varied as our story types. Some reveled in rock horror and splatterpunk, finding the quiet literary horror tale monumentally boring. Others felt that technohorror and urban allegorical horror spoke most directly to this age of AIDS and "wildings" in Central Park. Still others couldn't get enough of the ghosts, vampires and werewolves of old. Surely, I thought after presiding over impassioned debates about the literary merits of "Blood Rape of the Lust Ghouls," there is going to be little, if any, agreement among this bunch on the elements of a good horror story. I was wrong.

Suspense: Keep 'em on the edge

One result astonished me: 97 percent of the students listed "suspense" as the primary ingredient of a good horror story. Keep in mind that this was *not* a multiple-choice survey; these students had a blank page in front of them and could have written down anything. The fact that all but one *self-selected* the element of suspense further underscores its cardinal importance to them. In effect, the results say that these readers bring to the horror story one paramount expectation: to be entertained with the element of anticipation, dread, and uncertainty; in a word, *suspense*. Virtually every student wrote something like:

> "I want to be kept on the edge of my seat."
>
> "True suspense keeps you glued to the book until it's finished, then you say 'Whew!' "
>
> "I like stories that have constant suspense and give me ideas of how to get revenge on my brother."

Hope you're not that brother.

In their comments on suspense lies a strong clue as to how to handle one of the most challenging aspects of writing in this genre: providing a satisfying ending. These students obviously preferred, when possible, for the unrelenting suspense to lead to an unexpected, even shocking ending. They wrote, "I want the suspense to lead to a good twist at the end," and, "A good ending is one you didn't expect." One even borrowed a favorite word of Stephen King's: "A suspenseful ending is one you didn't expect and leaves you scared shitless!"

Now, everyone owes thanks to Douglas E. Winter, who has engendered more respect for this genre than any other modern critic. Yet it is both interesting and instructive that in his essay, "Darkness Absolute: The Standards of Excellence in Horror Fiction," this eminent *critic* does not once mention suspense. Yet when professional *writers* like Dean Koontz and J.N. Williamson, whose hungry families depend upon them to sell books, instruct us on the craft of writing horror fiction, their primary topic is how to create and maintain suspense. So there is, at least in this instance, a difference between the viewpoint of the critic and of the reader, for whom the "bottom line" is to be entertained. No doubt a writer should aspire to standards of excellence. But in order to be read, which is surely a writer's first goal, he had first better make sure he tells a suspense-packed story that leads to a dynamite ending.

Character: Someone like me

What surprised me about the second result was how much everyone – students, writers, critics – agreed on it. Believable characters are what hold a horror story together; they are the engines of its power. In his essay "Keeping the Reader on the Edge of His Seat," Koontz, the acknowledged "Dean of Suspense," provides this maxim, "Suspense in fiction results primarily from the reader's identification with and concern about lead characters who are complex, convincing, and appealing." Douglas Winter lists characterization as his second standard of excellence and quotes another pretty good horror writer, Stephen King: " 'You have got to love the people . . . that allows horror to be possible.' "

My students agree: they listed believable, sympathetic characters as the second key to a good horror story. Typical of their comments were: "A really good horror story for me is when the author is able to make you 'feel' for the characters—their pain, fear, happiness, wanting." Others said simply, "Having believable characters is what lets me get into the story." Considering these comments, it should come as no surprise that students voted as their favorite work of the semester Robert R. McCammon's "Nightcrawlers" (*Masques*), a suspenseful story of a Vietnam vet's nightmarish guilt, a sorrow which becomes so strong that it explodes with a harrowing and deadly substantiality.

Setting: A mirror for madness

Perhaps another reason for the popularity of "Nightcrawlers" is that its vivid setting, a stormy summer night at a roadside diner in rural Alabama, fulfills a third requirement: A story of dark fantasy must be anchored solidly in a believable, realistic setting. Modern readers expect the modern horror story to take place in familiar surroundings that provide a mating ground for the natural and the supernatural. Today's readers seem to know intuitively that today's horror requires a context of normality, a true-to-life backdrop that accentuates the grotesque.

There was a close similarity between my students' comments and those of critics. In "Horrors: An Introduction to Writing Horror Fiction," T.E.D. Klein, *Twilight Zone Magazine*'s first editor, writes that before bringing the supernatural on stage, the writer must first "establish, so thoroughly that we can believe in it, the reality of the world." One student put this simply as: "I've got to believe I'm there." When another student wrote, "A good horror story needs a balance between the realistic and the bizarre," it's almost as if he had been reading Douglas Winter: "An effective horror writer embraces the ordinary so that the extraordinary will be heightened." So readers and critics agree: Use of the fantastic does not excuse the horror author from the task of conjuring up a vivid, everyday reality on the page. On the contrary, it increases the importance of that task.

Plot: Picking up the pace

Another strong preference, and one that is closely related to the need for suspense, concerns the pace of the writing and the plot. What should an aspiring horror writer make of such comments as: "The action has to keep up. Once it lets down, it's all over for me"? Or, "I like it when the tone is very fast-paced reading. It's too boring when it reads slow and feels drawn out"? Is there a key to best-sellerdom in this student's desire for "concise and coherent stories [that] are both easy to read and entertaining. When reading for entertainment, one shouldn't have to analyze a story to understand it"? Similar preferences for a quick, easy read were expressed by a majority of the students surveyed.

Why this desire for a fast-paced, action-packed story? No doubt much could be made of the shortened attention spans of this generation that has never known life without television, the 12-year decline in standardized reading scores, the increasing emphasis on immediate gratification, the murder-by-the-minute slasher films and MTV. Regardless, the single ineluctable fact is that when they pick up a horror story, these young readers expect to be entertained. They may surreptitiously admire James Joyce's dazzling experiments, they may harbor a secret craving for John Updike's perfumed sentences, they may even look to Saul Bellow for help in an existential crisis. But when they pick up a horror story, they want *fun*. And that means fast-paced and suspenseful, easy on the literary embellishment, and without a side order of metaphysical reflections on life in a Godless universe, thank you very much.

More gore: Taboo or not taboo?

The results here reaffirm the important distinction between literary horror and celluloid horror, whose "shock schlock" attempts to exploit young readers. Significantly, these students warned against too much explicitness in literature. "Too much gore, if not justified, ruins a story, although I like to see it on films to admire the special effects." Of those who expressed a preference for gore and the emotion of repugnance, each did so with important qualifiers, saying for example, "A *little* gore doesn't hurt"; and "Graphic gore to a *tasteful* point."

Explicitness is an expected part of the genre today; indeed, the job of the horror writer always has been and always will be to assault taboos, to broadcast our unspeakable urges, to show us the nauseating possibilities that we fear. But there still is a clear line separating effective from ineffective use of the genre's extreme and rebellious materials: They must be justified by the story's context, tone and theme. As sometimes–splatterpunk Robert R. McCammon (*Swan Song, The Wolf's Hour*) said in a recent interview, "I don't believe there can be any bad taste in creating a scene, only bad writing in handling it."

Explicitness can also be a double-edged sword. It's not by accident that many expressed a preference for suggestiveness in description, which we called "narrative blurring"–a phrase T.E.D. Klein uses to capture H.P. Lovecraft's dictum: "Never state an horror when it can be suggested." These students agreed. "Description should be only enough so that the reader can get a picture, but not so much that there's nothing left for the imagination." Such comments illustrate the principle that still guides even these jaded viewers of the hack-em-and-slash-em films: Our own imaginations can still scare us more than any author could ever hope to. Good horror writers merely *collaborate* with our minds.

What today's readers don't want

An important part of writing successfully in any genre is learning what *not* to do. Unfortunately, the path to publication is not straight and narrow, without blind alleys and sloughs of despair. And to avoid those pitfalls one must discover not only what a good horror story is, but also what one *isn't*.

Just as these readers were unanimous in what they wanted most from a horror story (fast-paced suspense), they were equally adamant about what ruins their fun: anything that smacks of a "literary" treatment and slows down the pace. Eighty-one percent made comments like:

> "Can't stand long, drawn-out stories which overkill with background and details about characters and about life–makes for tiresome reading."
>
> "I don't like stories that go into so much detail about everything that I lose the plot and my head spins by the time I'm through reading."
>
> "Detail upon detail, description upon description, bore upon bore!"

One student said simply: "Literary horror–yuck!" On the surface, such comments seem to contradict the need they expressed earlier for finely-drawn characters and setting. But these students are actually displaying a solid understanding of this genre and its uniqueness. As readers of horror, they expect to be entertained by a suspenseful tale of dark fantasy. Their comments imply that while theme, realistic characters and settings are important props in the entertainment, those elements must be kept secondary. Too much of a good thing blurs the boundary between the horror story (a literature of fear and the fantastic) and the "literary" story (a literature of character and theme) which they've come to associate with school. As one student begged when we were about to discuss Stephen King for the first time, "Please don't tell me he's good literature; I like him too much."

Sadly, "literature" for many young readers has become associated solely with the stories of mainstream realism chosen by authority figures for textbooks, stories which for many years students have had to analyze, take tests on and regurgitate teachers' interpretations of—a useless and demeaning experience at best. For the above student and many like him, horror—with its emphasis on plot, suspense and extremes—gives back to literature what schools have managed to strip away: its pleasure, entertainment, fun.

The guessing game

A lot of the fun in this genre comes from the important game that goes on between writer and reader, wherein the writer tries to stay always one step ahead, doling out just enough information to keep the story intriguing and coherent yet the reader still guessing and in suspense. The horror writer must walk a tightrope, balancing delicately between predictability and obscurity, telling neither too much nor too little.

Failure to avoid those extremes was the pitfall most frequently cited by these students. Eighty-eight percent complained about predictability, saying again and again: "I don't like authors who give away too much too soon." Their comments here also reaffirm the importance of the ending in this genre. Several students wrote, "An obvious ending ruins the whole story," and one even made an impassioned plea to writers: "To all horror authors: please don't give away the ending before I get there. It makes me want my money back!"

These students also grew impatient with authors who withheld too much information and left readers baffled about what really happened. Sixty-nine percent objected to "stories where everything is a confused jumble of events." Their typical reaction was not one that bodes well for repeat sales: "Too much confusion in a story and I just give up."

Some of these comments arose from our reading of several experimental stories in which authors challenged the reader by violating one or more traditional rules of narrative and attempting to let the form of the story mirror a character's confused mental state or be a comment on the illusory nature of reality. That myself and several English majors in the class were the only ones who liked such stories further underscores the expectations of the majority: A story that is entertaining does not make unusual, "literary" demands on its readers. Experimentation may be important for an artist's and a genre's growth, but it won't necessarily do well in the bookstore. The student who wrote, "A horror story that loses me is boring. If I can't understand it, I can't very well enjoy it," was also serving notice about his tolerance for literary innovation.

One man's meat

These students were traditional in another way. A majority flatly rejected gratuitous acts of sex and violence. They would agree with Ramsey Campbell, author of *The Influence*, who once said in an interview: "In the worst horror fiction, violence is a substitute for imagination and just about everything else one might look for in fiction." Campbell was drawing the same distinction between sensationalism and the legitimate use of violence as my students did:

> "Stories that have no justification for their violence bore me."
>
> "Blood and guts shouldn't be used unnecessarily, some writers don't understand this."
>
> "What ruins a story for me? Too much purposeless blood and gore."

I should add that Moravian College is church-affiliated in name only; these are typical students from a variety of religious—and non-religious—backgrounds. I think their reaction is a typical one also, and it helps to answer a question posed by many social critics and parents about how far explicitness can go in the media: Where will it end? What's the stopping point? These eighteen- to twenty-year-olds, products of the sexual revolution, suggest that explicitness contains its own antidote: boredom.

A willing suspension

These readers also strongly objected to what they called "unbelievable" writing: setting, characters, style, or story logic that failed to keep them immersed in the tale, their skepticism on hold. They wrote: "The horror has to be made believable. If not, then the story has nothing for me," and "I have to be able to believe in the setting, characters and esp. the monsters etc." My favorite remark about style was: "Writers should avoid clichés like the plague."

These comments touch on one of the real paradoxes and challenges of dark fantasy: An author must write so convincingly, so realistically that the reader achieves a "willing suspension of disbelief" in the face of that which is patently unreal. Most English professors, whose primary focus is the "slice of life" moralistic tale, would have a difficult time understanding the pitfall that these students are pointing out.

Horror fans know that, in this genre, writing believably means more than just capturing everyday reality. It means using the same qualities of prose found in the best mainstream writing to set up a quotidian reality, and then to move the reader beyond it into the realm of the fantastic—while maintaining his belief in something that just isn't so. To quote Richard Matheson, *grand pére* of the modern horror story: "Pound for pound, fantasy makes a tougher opponent for the creative person." Fans know that, even if their teachers don't.

Getting fresh

Robert Bloch, another *grand pére* who in *Psycho* staked out fresh territory for the psychological horror story, remarked in his introduction to *How to Write Tales of Horror, Fantasy and Science Fiction* that "... in order for a writer to do his or her best, he must incorporate originality, a prime ingredient for success. If the theme is old, the twist or payoff must be new." My students couldn't agree more. They derided "stories that seem to be carbon copies of others." These readers demanded that "A plot should not seem even remotely familiar," and that "If the supernatural is used, it must have a new twist."

Like Bloch, they seemed to recognize that each genre places a premium on different writing talents: the extrapolative powers of the SF author, the observational skills of the mainstream realist, the plotting finesse of the mystery writer. The students were laying down an important *caveat* for aspiring horror writers: In a genre which attempts to entertain with suspense and dark fantasy, there is a keen demand for raw imaginative power and an unorthodox daring-do of mind that can take writer and reader where others fear to tread.

In the end

It's clear that young readers have a genuine enthusiasm for this literature. Contemporary horror fiction taps an excitement for reading in them that is almost always absent from a classroom dominated by the classics and the modern darlings of English Departments. Anne Tyler, Saul Bellow, and John Fowles are fine writers, but what truly excites these students is horror. It speaks to them in a way that *Silas Marner* does not. And their response to horror ficiton reaffirms the force that literature can have in young lives when teachers allow it.

These readers have also a clear set of their own standards. While they can appreciate the graphic detail and daring assaults of contemporary splatterpunks like John Skipp and Craig Spector, David J. Schow, and Joe Lansdale, they still insist that certain boundaries be observed. They demand quality writing, especially in characterization. One of the more hotly contested questions among today's critics—whether horror should be psychologically or supernaturally based—does not seem important to them. An equal number of students wrote "A good horror story blends reality, fantasy, and the supernatural" as did those who said, "I like stories that can really happen because they scare me the most."

In the end, although the surface features of the horror tale have changed to reflect the times, today's readers still want genuine characters inside a vividly written story based on a fresh and frightening premise, pulled together by a suspenseful plot that keeps them turning the pages—rapidly. Although no formula can guarantee writing success, that one is a good place to start.

Horror Novel Checklist

Like any literary form, the horror novel has its conventions—ones which the apprentice struggles with, the professional masters and the greats soar beyond as they shatter the boundaries of genre, whether it be Elizabethan revenge tragedy (*Hamlet*) or pact-with-the-devil tales (*Faust*).

At Moravian College, as part of a workshop in writing the horror novel, we analyzed 30 mass market paperbacks from among the latest releases by Zebra, Leisure, Onyx, Pinnacle, Bart, Tor, St. Martin's and others. Not surprisingly, we found that the basic elements of fiction—an *opening* that hooks readers, *exposition* of characters and their situation, *complications*, *climax* and *resolution*—still provided the underlying structure, but these elements had been altered to fit the special conventions of a literature of fear and the bizarre. Here's the checklist we devised for writing our horror novels:

☐ *The Grabber.* Have you opened with a prologue or short chapter which provides a brief but tantalizing (and usually violent) glimpse of the secret horror which will propel the story forward?

☐ *Backfill.* Within chapters 1-5, have you introduced the main characters and their problems, and isolated them in one locale (a town, resort, swamp, etc.) along with the horror?

☐ *Turn Up the Heat.* Do your middle chapters show increasingly weird/violent events which threaten the protagonists and force them to investigate and eventually confront the horror (usually ancient or occult) that has been triggered?

☐ *Flash Slash.* If the pace slows, have you flashed to a "slash" or "mutilation" scene of minor characters to show the horror at its gruesome work?

☐ *Final Jeopardy.* Does your final climax scene contain sufficient pay-off for the reader? When things have gotten as bad as they can get for the protags, with seemingly no way out, just as they are about to be overpowered by the superior horrific force, *something* enables them to triumph—courage, ingenuity, imagination, a tool or piece of information previously planted.

☐ *It Lives.* A short final chapter or epilogue should show the main characters at peace, resuming their normal lives but changed forever by their encounter with evil. But have you also hinted that the victory is a temporary one, and that the horror has merely gone back into hiding and could rise again someday—possibly in a sequel?

Other conventions to keep in mind: *Cupid Strikes* refers to the romantic subplot in horror novels wherein the hero and heroine meet and join together (spiritually and physically) to fight the evil besetting them.

Bang for the Buck means that readers expect the horror novelist to offer well-researched information on a legend or myth, occult or psychic lore, exotic geographical location, sport, profession, etc.

Body Count and overall levels of violence vary greatly from publisher to publisher; be sure to analyze a particular house's recent releases before submitting. Doing so could save a great deal of postage, waiting and grief. More importantly, such study and preparation is the real "secret" to writing a horror novel.

—D.W. Taylor

Writing Romance Novels: Follow Your Dream

by Ruth Ryan Langan

If someone had told me five years ago that I would be quoted on the front page of the *Wall Street Journal* and interviewed on *Good Morning, America* and the *Phil Donahue Show*, I would have laughed. Why in the world would anyone be interested in a woman who married her childhood sweetheart, raised five children, and still lives a mile from her parents' home?

Five years ago, I was still dreaming about writing a book. Now, the dream has come true. But it all started a long time ago.

As a high school student who wrote for the school paper and co-edited the yearbook, I dreamed of getting a degree in English and journalism, eventually teaching on the high school or college level, and possibly writing for a local paper.

After high school, I realized that college for me would cause my family hardship, so I rejected my scholarship and found a stenographic job. I married the boy I had met in first grade and had dated all through school. A year later, I quit my job to stay home with our first baby. Four more babies followed. I put my dreams of college, teaching, and writing on the shelf, where for the next twenty years, they gathered dust. Then several years ago my daughter gave me some paperback romances for Mother's Day. We read them and enjoyed them. Later, I bought a few more. I was becoming addicted to the thrill of romance and the happy endings.

My first step on the road to becoming a writer occurred on my birthday. While enjoying a second cup of coffee, I read a newspaper column asking who people would choose if they could be anyone in history. The usual answers followed: Queen Elizabeth, Jackie Kennedy, etc. I remember feeling very smug about my life that day. I had a husband whose love for me continued to grow. Five beautiful, healthy children. I didn't want to be anyone else. But, a nagging little voice said, "Yes, but if you could be yourself and do anything?" I chose then to be a writer – a romance writer.

I gave myself a special birthday present. I would steal an hour a day from a very busy schedule and try to write a book. If I wrote a page a day, within a year I'd have 365 pages of a novel. (Bear in mind that I had no special training for such an ambitious project. But I was an avid reader.)

Each day, after my children left for school, and my husband left for work, I dragged out an old portable typewriter, set it on the kitchen table, and slipped into my fictional world. Months passed before my family caught me. When I admitted what I was doing, I expected teasing, laughter, derision. What I got was real support. "Atta girl. Go for it. Hey, Mom, neat."

Writing that book was the hardest thing I ever did. So many times I wanted to quit. There were the million and one distractions from family and friends. Many times I wondered why I was doing something so difficult, with odds so great against my effort ever being published. Evenings I typed in my bedroom, now on an electric typewriter, with typing table and chair – all the proper writing tools were gifts from my husband – listening to my family's

***Ruth Ryan Langan** is the author of 17 contemporary and historical romance novels including* Heart's Secrets, Mysteries of the Heart, Whims of Fate *and* Destiny's Daughter.

sounds of laughter from another part of the house. I wondered why I was giving up so much for a silly dream. Then I'd go on to the next chapter, telling myself to at least finish a rough draft.

While I wrote, I read everything I could about getting published. At the library, I read books and periodicals on writing. When I discovered a magazine that answered many of my questions, I bought a year's subscription. Each month, just when my enthusiasm would begin to dim, my "friend" would arrive in the mail and bolster my resolve.

That first book took well over the projected year to finish. I sent the first three chapters to Harlequin (the only publisher of romances that I knew of) and promptly started work on a second novel. I was convinced that I had just written a masterpiece, and I would soon become rich and famous.

Harlequin took nearly five months to reject my first attempt at a sale. The rejection was so painful, I took to my bed and wept. For several days I dragged around, mourning for my dream. Yet I found myself going back to my typewriter, pounding out the next chapter of my latest novel. Soon I was again convinced that this second novel would be so wonderful they would beg to publish it.

Harlequin took nearly four months to reject my second novel. By then, I was deeply into a third book. I discovered that I had learned much about writing, and without knowing it, about discipline. By now, it was nothing for me to spend several hours at a time writing, pulling the "perfect" phrase out of my mind when needed, finding new ways to describe mundane events, and becoming comfortable with dialogue. And I no longer blushed when I wrote love scenes.

What do publishers and editors want?

While learning my craft by writing, I also learned about the publishing industry, and romance publishers especially. For example, romance publishers are more than willing to read unagented manuscripts. They may be the only publishing houses that read everything submitted to them, so important to the novice writer.

Today's reader has become very discriminating. As the reader becomes more discriminating, so do editors. Today's editors demand well-written novels. They want realistic settings and believable plots, with flesh and blood American heroes and heroines. The editors demand that problems be solved in a logical way. No longer will we read of a series of misunderstandings that are resolved in the final chapter. Our hero and heroine must be informed, intelligent people, who reflect contemporary readers and their lifestyle.

Forget the 18-year-old nymph and the 42-year-old recluse. Begin with two contemporary people with whom today's reader can identify.

Remember also that perfect people are not interesting, and the reader cannot identify with them. Give your characters flaws. Real people have hang-ups, problems, tensions, quirks that make them different from everyone else. The good writer can do no less for her characters. Give them little mannerisms that set them apart from others. If they have realistic problems, keep these problems in the background. You're writing a romance, not a psychology handbook.

Must your heroine always have flaming hair and sky-blue eyes? Must your hero always be tall, dark, and handsome? Take another look around you. You'll see millions of attractive people, but few who fall into one category. Look, really look, at hair color, eye color, manner of dress. Then give your characters some individuality.

Can you plot an original story?

The romance novel must be professionally crafted. No one wants to read about two people who meet, fall in love, and get married. That does not a novel make. But if two people meet, are instantly attracted, and can't possibly get together, that makes for fun reading. Why can't they get together? The list of reasons is endless. Maybe one of them has been hurt and thrown a protective shield against future pain. One of them may have a career which takes precedence over marriage.

The key element in the romance novel is *romance*. If the writer separates her characters for any length of time, the element of romance is missing. Throughout the novel, the two people must be constantly thrown together, and they must confront their emotions.

Give your characters contemporary problems, and proceed to solve their problems in an intelligent manner. Even when these two people finally get together and are enjoying a tender romance, throw up roadblocks in their relationship. For the reader, the fun of these novels is watching the characters jump each hurdle, find the path smooth, then discover another hurdle.

What about dialogue?

If you are writing contemporary romances, keep your dialogue simple and contemporary. People tend to speak in short bursts, not long dissertations. Avoid slang and "in" phrases which will date your manuscript.

Historical romances almost demand more flowery language. The writer who mistakenly adds a contemporary phrase to her historical novel will catch the reader's eye and interrupt the flow of the story.

Avoid useless dialogue. The joy of being a writer is that we can ponder for days until we come up with the perfect retort for our hero or heroine. Every bit of dialogue should either move the story line along or give the reader new insight into our character. Dialogue enhances the novel by breaking up the narrative and making the story immediate. When two characters are speaking, the reader is there with them, completely involved in their exchange.

I suggest that any writer who is unsure of the dialogue try this simple exercise. Read the dialogue aloud. Does it sound like real people speaking? Does it suit your novel? Did it move the story along, or was it simply tacked on as a change of pace? If the story advances without it, discard it.

Afraid of writing dialogue? Try this. Write a short story, no more than eight or ten pages. The entire story must be written in dialogue. No connecting words at all. No tag lines (he said). When you have completed this exercise, you will never again be afraid to tackle dialogue.

How important is the setting?

A contemporary novel can be set anywhere because love can blossom anywhere. Even though most readers prefer to read about an exotic place they have never visited, the adage to "write about something you know" still holds true. Unless you are willing to do research, you should stick to familiar places. If you use a real city or town, make certain your facts are accurate.

Because historical romances must be historically accurate, research is vital. Make certain the manner of dress, speech, and travel is authentic. Almost everything today can be researched at a local library.

What elements make an effective romantic scene?

Hemingway spoke volumes about lovemaking in the simple phrase, "And the earth moved." Every romance novelist must come up with a new and better way to describe all the agony and ecstacy of love. It is not enough to say, "He kissed her passionately. She melted into his arms." What did he feel as his lips touched hers? Why had he waited so long? Why was it suddenly right now? What did she feel as she melted into his embrace? What kept her from giving more of herself? The reader wants to know. Make the scene immediate by allowing the reader to feel with the characters all the fears, the hesitations, the joys, the thrills.

Don't make the mistake of thinking that a string of body parts will make for sensuous reading. Romance novels must never become sex manuals. The reader of romance is interested in feelings. Intense feelings. Make your reader share all the vulnerabilities of your characters. Then the reader cares about these people. And as slowly as the heroine falls in love with the hero, so will your reader fall in love right along with her.

You must involve all the senses. Readers want to smell her special brand of cologne, his after shave; to taste the honeyed softness of their lips; to touch the rough texture of his palm against her satin skin; to see the look of love reflected in their eyes; to feel intensely the joy, the pain, the longing of these two lovers.

When you have crafted an interesting plot, peopled it with warm, believable characters, given them interesting dialogue to speak, and sprinkled your story with exciting, sensuous scenes, you have a first draft of your story.

Does your opening grab your reader?

The next step is to take an objective look at your opening. Does your book begin with action? Readers of shorter-length novels like to be hurled immediately into the action. If not action, can you begin with dialogue? The reader must immediately know who is speaking, and why, to be drawn deeper into your novel.

If you have neither action nor dialogue, is your opening scene one of description of either the hero or heroine? Remember, you need not begin with physical descriptions of your characters. Unless you do so skillfully, you will lose the reader's interest. Go back to your opening paragraphs, and start again.

When you have polished your opening chapter until it is a gem, go on to the rest of the manuscript. Every piece of dialogue, every bit of description must be polished until it is the best you can do. Then, and only then, is your manuscript ready for submission.

How can you find a publisher?

Most romance publishing houses offer Tip Sheets and How to Submit Sheets. By enclosing a self-addressed, stamped envelope along with your request, they will forward such sheets to you. If the publisher requests a complete manuscript, that's what you send. Along with a cover letter explaining the kind of novel this is (historical, contemporary), include a general word count (approx. 55,000 words, or just over 150,000 words), and the line for which you have targeted this manuscript (Silhouette Desire or Harlequin Super). If you aren't certain just where this manuscript will fit into the publisher's lineup, say so.

If the publisher has requested the first three chapters and a brief synopsis, send them. Most publishers can tell in the first chapter whether or not the manuscript makes the grade. If they like what they read, they will request the rest of the manuscript.

A synopsis is simply the entire story in capsule form. The simplest way to write a synopsis is this: Think of the editor sitting across the room. She has asked you to tell her briefly what your book is about. In present tense, tell her. If you wish to point out specific highlights in your book, do so. If you think funny or dramatic bits of dialogue will enhance your synopsis, include them. What the editor is really looking for is what the conflicts are and how you will resolve them. Remember that today's editor wants intelligent resolutions to the conflicts. Keep the synopsis brief.

Enclose with these three chapters and synopsis a cover letter telling the editor whether this is part of a complete or incomplete manuscript. If you have written only these three chapters, be prepared to have the manuscript finished if the editor should care to see the entire book.

Writing romance novels is not a get-rich-quick scheme. It requires a great deal of discipline. It is hard work. So if you are looking for a fast buck, but have never really cared for romances, don't read them, and think them beneath your talents, I urge you to look elsewhere for a lucrative market.

If you love reading romances, if you can't think of a better way to spend the rest of your life than writing wonderfully romantic, uplifting novels—then I urge you to consider writing the romance novel. The writers who succeed in this lucrative market are writers who love and respect the genre. If you are a lover of romance, welcome to the fold. I wish you all the best in this satisfying profession.

Oh, yes. That third novel? Silhouette Books bought *Just Like Yesterday* and published it in 1981. I have written eleven more for Silhouette with a contract for more.

My first historical novel, *Nevada Nights*, was bought by Pocket Books for its Tapestry Line, and I have completed three more major historicals for Pocket Books.

And the dream goes on.

A romance reading list

When asked what piece of advice they would give to writers interested in writing romance fiction, writers and publishers almost always say, "Read!" Despite the repeat successes of some romance writers, one writer says "Romance writing is not a get-rich quick scheme. It takes lots of research. You should be well-read within the field and truly enjoy romance fiction. In other words, those who have never read a romance need not apply."

Although reading is sound advice, a writer unfamiliar with the genre may be overwhelmed by the sheer volume of romance titles available. There are a number of ways to compile a reading list. Word-of-mouth is one way. Writers can also attend conferences or ask their local librarian for the most frequently borrowed books. Romance magazines such as *Romantic Times* (163 Joralemon St., Brooklyn Heights NY 11201) include reviews of the latest releases as well as inside information on the field.

We wanted, however, to be able to provide our readers with a suggested reading list. Not an all-encompassing list, but at least a place for interested writers to start. So we asked members of the Cincinnati branch of the Romance Writers of America to give us a list of their favorites. What we found was that, while there was little consensus on what were the best books, most agreed writers should start by reading classic romantic fiction and then choose a category that interests them—regency, historical, contemporary, romantic suspense or young adult romance. Despite the variety of authors mentioned, certain names came up repeatedly. These included Laura London, Laurie McBain, Christine Monson, LaVyrle Spencer and Kathleen Woodiwiss for historicals and Anya Seton, Mary Stewart and Phyllis Whitney for romantic suspense.

Cincinnati RWA member Marcy Piland wrote, "In short, I'd recommend writers find an author they like, then read everything that author wrote. Usually an author's basic story format remains consistent, but as her writing matures a reader will notice subtle changes (characterizations have more depth, sensual images seem clearer, more poignant). A novice writer will probably learn more if they follow at least one published writer through her career, then sample the best of the others." With that in mind, here is a sampling of one group's favorites:

Classic romance:

Gone With the Wind by Margaret Mitchell. This title won hands down and is mentioned consistently at romance conferences as the all-time classic romance.

Jane Eyre by Charlotte Bronte.

Wuthering Heights by Emily Bronte.

Regency Buck (or almost anything else) by Georgette Heyer.

Historical romance:

Shanna by Kathleen Woodiwiss (Avon).
Hummingbird by LaVyrle Spencer (Jove).
Stormfire by Christine Monson (Avon).
Windflower by Laura London (Dell).
A Rose in Winter by Kathleen Woodiwiss (Avon).

Romantic suspense:

The Crystal Cave by Mary Stewart (Fawcett).
The Moon Spinners (or anything else by this prolific author) by Mary Stewart (Fawcett).
Green Darkness by Anya Seton (Fawcett). This one shows up on lists of suspense and gothic romance.
Vermillion by Phyllis Whitney (Fawcett) Again, anything by Whitney.

Remember this is only a list of *suggested* titles. The group did not mention contemporary romances. In fact, there are probably other omissions, but such is the nature of lists. We welcome your suggestions for next year's list—just drop us a line.

"Today's reader has become very discriminating. As the reader becomes more discriminating, so do editors . . .. They want realistic settings and believable plots, with flesh and blood American heroes and heroines."

—Ruth Ryan Langan

Bringing Back the Western

by Dennis E. Showalter

For 20 years, academic and commercial forums have proclaimed "the death of the western." Scholars vied to demonstrate the seamy underside of the frontier. Television producers looked askance at prospective viewers—allegedly rural and elderly in a yuppie age. Film producers grumbled about "bad box office," citing cost overruns and negative balance sheets to bolster their stand.

Then a television miniseries captured America's attention and renewed appetite in the publishing world for a genre long considered passé. "There's no doubt," says G. Gregory Tobin, senior editor of Bantam Books, "that Larry McMurtry's *Lonesome Dove* did a lot to put the western back in the public consciousness. But we've got to remember that *Lonesome Dove* was also the best-loved novel of the 1980s, in my opinion. Rarely does a day go by when someone doesn't mention it to me—and this was *before* the series even went into production."

Lonesome Dove was a top bestseller in both hardcover and paperback, has sold more than three million copies to date and is still selling in its Pocket Books edition. Bantam's Stuart Applebaum sees a certain irony in *Lonesome Dove*'s importance to the western genre.

"McMurtry is antigeneric," says Applebaum. "He decries the western mythology and insists he writes antiwesterns. Yet he's embraced by those who admire the western as such." Tobin agrees that "McMurtry was not writing a 'western.' What he did was write a masterful novel of the West. He created some unforgettable characters. And those achievements encouraged readers to explore the western as a category."

Guarding the flame

"Westerns were always being written, even if they weren't always being published," says Tobin, "and even in the lean times, Bantam kept faith with its heritage of publishing high-quality western fiction. This gave us credibility with the writing community, which has helped us attract promising new names." Leslie Schnur, editorial director at Dell, also describes her firm as perceiving a continuing audience for western fiction. Dell is republishing the works of Luke Short in a new program and polishing the ongoing modern series Hangman and Arrow and Saber.

Roberta Grossman, publisher of Zebra Books, thinks western stories in print have actually benefited from the dearth of westerns in theaters and on television. Stuart Applebaum agrees: "Television in the 1950s and '60s was dominated by westerns. For years, every movie house in mid-America featured westerns, singly or as part of a double bill. Those outlets have dried to a trickle, so their fans turn to books."

Nor is optimism confined to the paperback book. Sara Ann Fried is a consulting editor with M. Evans. "I do 12 hardcover novels a year—in the series M. Evans Novels of the

Dennis E. Showalter *is a professor of history at Colorado College in Colorado Springs. A military historian, he is the co-author of* Voices From the Third Reich: An Oral History *and is working on his next book titled,* Tannenberg: Clash of Empires.

West – and I like to buy books with mass market potential, books that aren't limited in reader appeal."

Some publishing houses are reluctant to speak of a "comeback" for westerns. "They never did go away," says Tom Colgan, editor of Berkley Books. "Westerns were like a bad check or a vampire. They hung around. We had a huge backlist, including many award winners. We kept reprinting them and they always sold.

"A good western," Colgan continues, "lasts forever. This is a unique phenomenon, unfathomable in the context of even midlist category fiction, most of which is here today and gone tomorrow." Jim Frost, editor-in-chief of Warner Books, makes a similar point: "One of our sales leaders is the late Max Brand."

The Louis L'Amour phenomenon

But any discussion of contemporary western writing must focus on Louis L'Amour. "Louis L'Amour is to the western," says Stuart Applebaum, "what Agatha Christie is to the mystery novel. No single author has so dominated a literary category. Louis transcended his genre. Like John le Carré or Frederick Forsyth, he moved into the mainstream. But at the same time, he understood the importance of his base in paperback readership."

The numbers illustrating his success are indisputable. In 1975, according to Applebaum, L'Amour had 50 million copies in print. By 1989 the number had gone to over 200 million! "Louis L'Amour has had more individual million-copy bestsellers than any writer of our time. Over 90 of his titles have gone over a million. I believe he's the only author whose novels are all in print – 103 of them."

Applebaum describes L'Amour as a master of what editors call the "traditional" western. Exact definitions of this concept vary. G. Gregory Tobin understands a traditional western as "a book of between 50,000 and 65,000 words, set some time in the 19th century, usually west of the Mississippi River. It involves a hero faced with a problem that is resolved through physical action against an authentic background."

Leona Nevler, editor-in-chief of Fawcett and Ivy, suggests that "westerns, with very few exceptions, remain 'pure.' They stay true to their genre. They stick to simple stories and don't go off in as many directions as other kinds of fiction."

For Sara Ann Fried, the western is first of all a novel. "I like strong characters combined with a strong historical element – a sense of realness about time and place. Formula books are not for me; good novels are. For example, I tend to resist revenge themes and stories told in the first person, but I bought a first-person revenge novel because it was so good."

The hero image

Storytelling is, however, only one aspect of a successful "traditional" western. Another, according to Matt Sitwell, editor at New American Library, is characterization. "Our heroes are a lot like our readers," he says. "They may not possess much formal education, but they show acumen and savvy in what they do. They struggle to maintain morality in the face of savagery, to sustain standards in a society still defining itself."

Applebaum stresses a third element, authenticity: "L'Amour's backgrounds were as solid as his story lines. He was a nonstop researcher of the history, the customs and the behavior he put into his books." And L'Amour's domination of the category in recent years posed a challenge to writers and publishers. Jim Frost says that "one reason we've fallen back on familiar 'brand names' like Max Brand is that we haven't found capable younger writers. I don't know why, except that they seem to perceive the western as too limited by conventions."

Matt Sitwell suggests marketing is part of the problem. "It has been hard to establish new authors in the western field. Wholesalers simply relied so heavily on L'Amour's work that new names had only a limited chance of breaking through." NAL's response is common in current publishing: the western series. "In a sense," says Sitwell, "we're sorry a series is the only thing we can make work. The market for them is crowded. It's hard to compete for space in stores, or for sale to distribution companies. But, on the other hand, a series offers a regular program and regular delivery in the way no single author can."

Series authorship is not inevitably a collective effort. According to Leslie Schnur, Dell's Arrow and Saber and Hangman series are each done by a single author, G.A. Carrington and Craig Foley, respectively. May Ann Eckles, a Ballantine editor, says that Ballantine issues original series without even a covering title: "Robert Bell and Tim Champlain have each published seven or eight volumes featuring the same character. Richard Wheeler will be doing a new original series for us next year following that concept."

The strength of series

Berkley's Tom Colgan says that a successful western series depends essentially on a simple basic structure. "A series is spare. It centers on a person with a job to do."

Most books in any genre, he thinks, are about the *single* most significant part of a character's life. "This gives them their power."

Berkley is one of the largest publishers of westerns in general, and series westerns in particular. "Every month," says Colgan, "we publish six original series. Five appear every month; two more alternate. We reprint the novels of British western writer J.T. Edson, who is number two in worldwide sales. This March we launched Tom Early's series, Sons of Texas." It all adds up to almost 100 westerns a year, and retail sales estimated at $10 million.

By no means are all western series generated in-house. George Engel is the owner of Book Creations Inc., founded by his father Lyle, which produces mid-level "family westerns" like the Frontier series, and more formulaic "category westerns" as well.

Engel describes several advantages of working with a book producer: "The publisher is dealing with a known entity, and has no worries about the usability of the finished product. Since 1965, over 60 of the 300-odd titles we've produced have made the bestseller list." Book Creations assists promotion by putting together a complete package of mailing and promotional materials with each series.

The 'adult' western

Series westerns have been one answer to the marketing problem. Another is the development of "adult westerns." Walter Zacharius, owner of Zebra Books, offers a blunt definition: "In the adult western the hero loves the woman instead of his horse." Some publishers reject this approach out of hand. "We at Bantam wouldn't touch the sex-and-violence westerns," says Stuart Applebaum. May Ann Eckles agrees. "They're not for us at Ballantine. Their audience isn't ours."

Other industry figures, including Zacharius, Jim Frost and Tom Colgan, see the adult western as currently in decline. "The public is bored with sex and violence," declares Frost. Tom Colgan, too, says that "the thrill is gone. Part of the adults' appeal was the shock value of explicit sex in a genre that had become heavily mannered, almost choreographed. Now the nation is more conservative. Booksellers are reluctant to stock 'adults' for fear of customer hostility."

The adult western may be declining but it is far from moribund. NAL's Matt Sitwell says, "We only do adult westerns, and that means explicit sex." "Adults are still our bestselling lists," says Colgan. "Longarm, with over 120 volumes, is our best series. Jake Logan is another line with numbers into the 120s." Lone Star, a Jove series whose central characters are a frontier woman and her partner, an Oriental martial-arts master, is up to number 80.

Sex is far more important than violence in this category, says Colgan, and its readers are overwhelmingly male. But though they depict explicit behavior, their editors don't think adult westerns should be confused with pornography. "We at NAL," says Matt Sitwell, "don't see our story lines as mere transitions from sex scene to sex scene. We acknowledge our readers' interest in sex, but our primary concern is good western stories with credible characters." He offers as an example of a new series, coming in July: "Canyon O'Grady focuses on an Irishman with some education and a good sense of humor. It makes his seductions more believable." The series is being done by the same writer largely responsible for NAL's successful Trailsman, whose 90th volume is due this month. "John Sharp," says Sitwell, "can keep a series alive by himself. He writes strong stories, on a par with or better than most traditional westerns."

Tom Colgan makes a similar point: "A lot of people reject adult westerns. They see them as bastardizations of the genre. But *if* one reads them with an open mind, one will find that the stories are 'traditional' in essence, and not bad stories either."

Patience, packaging, promotion

Building reader satisfaction for western series can be a slow process, according to Leona Nevler. "A first novel may not gain readers, while later ones will, as readers grow used to a writer." Greg Tobin also stresses the importance of patience. "Category publishing takes time. An author may require 10 or 15 books to hit his stride. But once he does, once a book clicks, his backlist can be promoted even if he switches categories. A major example is Elmore Leonard."

Along with patience in marketing westerns goes packaging. "For westerns and action-adventure books generally," says Jim Frost, "the cover is important both for direct accounts and wholesalers. Wholesalers in particular can pay more attention to the cover than the copy. They notice what pops out at them."

Promotion is a third aspect of marketing westerns, according to Stuart Applebaum. "Here was one of Louis L'Amour's major contributions. He rigorously promoted his books. No author was as cherished by our marketing people."

What of those publishing firms that do not—at least as yet—have an author approximating Louis L'Amour's stature in the western genre? Sara Ann Fried says a big portion of M. Evans's hardcover market involves sales to libraries and to some specialized outlets like military bases. "The large-print market is also burgeoning," she says. "More and more large-print publishers are buying rights to westerns." For paperbacks, "Our market is largely wholesale," says NAL's Matt Sitwell. "It's heaviest in the Midwest and West; the South, on the other hand, is not very big." Mary Ann Eckles concurs, noting that Ballantine sells well both to wholesalers and in bookstores. On the other hand, G. Gregory Tobin cites "a truism in paperback publishing that the books are mostly distributed through wholesalers, not retail markets. All the same, I hate to see them ghettoized."

Ghettoization is not a problem for writers at the upper end of the market. "Publishers fear young people aren't interested in westerns," says Stuart Applebaum. "But the letters and the requests for autographs Louis L'Amour received were often from youngsters. As for a gender gap, half his fan mail came from women."

'A real growth area'

Applebaum is unabashedly bullish on westerns, seeing them as "a real growth area." Leona Nevler is more measured, but hardly pessimistic. Fawcett/Ivy plans to publish 12 new books and a dozen more reissues, as well as four more series. Ballantine also mixes originals and reprints, doing 12 books a year. So the western, whether in its traditional or adult form, hardly seems ready for a final ride into the sunset.

Succeeding with Popular Fiction

by Alice Harron Orr

Emotional involvement is the first prerequisite for writing interesting fiction, because your concern and passion for the subject matter will show through in your writing. So think in terms of what subjects you're vitally interested in, of what appeals to you emotionally.

Usually ideas come from some kind of external source. Don't concern yourself if your idea has been influenced by someone else's work, for example, by another novelist or from a news feature article or from something you read in a magazine or saw in a film. There's a difference between plagiarism and inspiration. You are, of course, never going to use, or be tempted to use, that idea in the same way it was used by the previous author. The story develops inside you and you're intimately involved in its creation and its development. The story becomes a reflection of your own character and interests.

These are the kinds of ideas that take on life, the kind of life that can draw a reader into your story and make the reader want to stay there and find out what's going to happen next. It may seem simplistic to say that ideas are all around you, but it's very true. You simply have to be open to them. Yet you usually don't see a whole story. What you see is a suggestion and you have to have your antenna up and be receptive to those ideas as they occur. Watch for those inspiring little moments in life that you could make, with the help of your imagination, into a story.

Essential to that process of course is a notebook. Always have one with you. Begin to think of your life as material from which your work will spring. Everything that happens to you, everything that you see and everything that happens to your friends becomes material. Stories must of course involve people, because that's what we're interested in reading about.

No amount of clever plotting or fast action can make up for thin characters. The key to writing characters is to know the character up front. Do a little exploration of that character before you start writing. Character motivation is the key to making your plot work. In fact, when you get a letter back from an editor who says very frustratingly, "This doesn't work for me," often she means, the motivation of the character didn't work. It isn't strong enough; it isn't believable enough; it isn't significant enough. The worst thing you can do in a story, I believe, is to write about subject matter that the reader reacts to by saying, "Who cares? This isn't important enough for me to have spent all this time reading."

You must make sure that there's a great deal at stake in your story. If your heroine or hero does not succeed and reach a goal, the more dire the circumstances that result the better. I talk about the heroine more than the hero because the truth is in the present commercial market, heroines sell. Possibly because 85% of the readership is female in both popular and literary fiction, but especially in popular fiction. I will say that with the work of authors like Tom Clancy a renaissance of the hero is in the making.

So what kind of heroine does that reader, typically a woman, want to read about? She

Alice Harron Orr *has seen the publishing field from all sides. She is the author of several books, a former mystery/suspense and romance editor for Walker and Company Books and most recently a partner in the new literary agency, Kearns and Orr Associates. A frequent lecturer at writers' conferences and workshops, she is working on a book for writers titled,* How to Stop Shooting Your Career in the Foot.

wants to read about a woman who is basically three things: intelligent, independent and determined. This is a character who acts rather than is acted upon. She gets herself into trouble; she gets herself out of it. Now maybe she'll do that with a little help from the hero, but basically she's in charge of her own life. She's the kind of person we are on our best days, that perhaps we wish we were all of the time. Keep her admirable. Keep the reader rooting for her, because when the reader is rooting for this heroine, the reader has become involved in your story. The reader has a personal stake in it and wants the outcome for your protaganist to be a favorable one.

But remember that this heroine is not you. Perhaps in writing literary fiction, it's appropriate to write your own story. And in popular fiction or in any writing, of course your own life and your own personality and feelings become involved. However, in writing the kind of heroic person I'm talking about you may not be the best model to follow. Primarily because we know too well our non-heroic side and we generally have an unclear vision of ourselves as a totality. That adds up to be a rather confused subjective presentation of character. The creation of character is, on the other hand, a creative act which involves getting outside of yourself and giving birth to a separate self.

This heroine is a strong and capable person. She's a person to be taken seriously, but she's still human and vulnerable. She's compassionate and caring and generous. Most of all she's not waiting for a man to come along and make her life worthwhile; she's making a worthwhile life for herself. She's definitely not the squealing, shy, passive heroine that Tippi Hedren played in the Alfred Hitchcock movies—in the corner, eeking and squealing, "The birds are coming, the birds are coming" waiting for some man to come and save her. The contemporary heroine saves herself and she may save him as well.

First of all, remember that she is a heroine and, therefore, must behave heroically. That means no sleazy motivations. Too many big books in recent years have been based upon motivations such as greed, power hunger, career ambition and revenge. I think that fad is passing even though those books will continue to be read. Fewer and fewer are going to be bought from new authors by editors, so I would keep that in mind.

Above all else, our heroine is ethical. She has a personal code of what is right and wrong. I don't mean that she is a goody-goody type of person. In fact, in this story situation, she should be sorely tempted to violate her personal code of ethics and this can become the source of her inner conflict, and conflict is the essence of story. We don't read to read about things going well—that's boring. We like things to go well in our lives, but in our fiction, we like trouble—the more trouble, the better. The more concern about how the heroine is going to get out of that trouble, the more interest we take in the story. Anytime you can intensify the conflict for your main character, do so.

As far as the contemporary fiction hero is concerned, he is not the traditional macho man any longer. However, be careful not to make him a wimp. Men who are too sympathetic, to the point of almost having no personality, to my way of thinking, don't really need to be there. Give your male character some kind of physical orientation where he's doing physical things as opposed to just talking and doing mental things all the time. In our culture we think that men doing physical things are sexy. We do want a man who is sexy. Show him standing up for what matters to him. Show him being clever, not just brawny. We want this kind of a character in this story because we want him to be strong enough to conflict with the strong heroine. And there is no relationship with more potential for conflict than the relationship between a man and a woman trying to get along. It's darn near impossible to do that and do it successfully.

That is why I say don't forget the romance in the story. Don't be ashamed to write romance. Everybody is incorporating a love story into their books now. Even the big guys—Ken Follett, Sydney Sheldon, John LaCarré, who is supposed to have a heart as cold as a stone but ever since *The Little Drummer Girl*, we know he does not. These authors recognize the tremendous sales potential of stories with strong relationships in them. The relationship is often that of people encountering each other for the first time because there is so much trepidation in those early stages of relationships. There is a lot more potential for conflict than with people who have known each other for awhile. But watch out for unwarranted antagonism and bantering and bickering between them. Quibbling without true reason makes them look petty and unattractive. We want to read about protagonists who are attractive to us. We want to like them.

Heroic means standing up for what is right and just, taking physical and social risks accordingly and acting on what is right. The example I like to use for our contemporary hero is the character so often played in films by Martin Sheen. He has become the epitome of the character who finds himself in a terrible situation. He doesn't really want to deal with it. He'd just as soon let it all go by and somebody else take care of it, but someone has to do it. The key to this hero is his decency.

The third most important character in popular fiction is the villain. Now why do you need a villain? Again, for the purpose of plot conflict. This gives the reader someone to hate, just like the hero and the heroine have given the reader someone to love and care about. This also gives the protaganist someone to be pitted against, so that you have a struggle going on, again increasing the conflict. You also have an individual who can create more trouble for your protagonist, hence you have the potential for more story interest.

Make this villain a formidable figure. The reason you must do this is because you have created a very powerful heroine and a very strong hero. If they're going to be put up against someone, it has to be someone who is a real match for them, a worthy opponent, or there won't be any struggle.

You must also make him believable. Be very careful to avoid cartoon villains. J.R. Ewing is an interesting and amusing character for Friday nights when we are tired and don't want to deal with anything too mentally taxing, but basically he's a cartoon. He's too evil. He's too predictable. I'm not saying you have to give your villain likable traits, but I think we have to understand why he is the way he is. I use "he," because most often the villain is male when the protagonist is female. Make him an individual rather than a force or a group, simply because individuals are easier to identify and easier to hate.

Think in terms of a villain who's guilty of everyday evil. That's a good way to avoid the cartoonish kind of villain portrayal. What are the qualities of everyday evil? Manipulativeness is one of my favorites. A character who has absolutely no compunction about using people. A character who feels superior to others, which is his rationale for treating people the way he does. Total self-centeredness is a wonderful source of evil on all levels.

Nobody else matters much to this character. Of course, the ultimate extension of that is murder, as in the mystery suspense novel—the ultimate act of disrespect is to kill someone. The opposite, in other words, to the new hero's decency is the villain's sociopathic behavior. His motivation must be very clear, strong and believable. In fact, often in a story where you have good characters pitted against a villain, whether or not that story is successful depends upon whether or not we can believe the reason the villain has for doing all those dasterdly things. His behavior has to be understandable even if not acceptable. He can be a very attractive, charming figure, and along with this comes an intelligence which is used for imagination, for evil purposes rather than good.

Now you are ready to write

Those are the initial elements of a story—an idea and the characters put into a setting; preferably a real setting. Now that you're about ready to write your story, where do you start it? You start where the excitement begins and not a sentence before. That means you're going to begin in the middle of things. You'll begin when the high pitch of the story begins, the moment when something is about to happen or is in the process of happening to your heroine. She is suddenly on the edge of a situation where she has the feeling her life as she knows it, is beginning to slip out from under her and she's got to do something.

Don't tell us about the past. Don't open up with the weather. Don't describe what she has on or the room this is taking place in. Begin with conflict.

Hook the reader into the story immediately. The sooner you hook the reader, the more chance you have of keeping the reader interested, compelled to read and to continue reading throughout your story. Don't amble into your story, explode into it. Once you have the reader hooked, don't let go.

When I'm talking about popular fiction, I'm also talking about fiction that's being submitted to a publishing house for an editor to read. The editor has to be hooked on your work first because that's how you get it published. When you deal with an editor, you're dealing with someone who has had to read a lot of material that is less than titillating, less than compelling. You have to jolt that editor out of the lethargy that can be created by reading so much of that kind of material. The nature of the editor's life is that she has far too much to do and far too little time to do it. You have to truly write something that is startling and compelling in order to capture her interest.

You begin with an opening line. The opening line must be crafted like a jewel is crafted. First of all, it should, in my opinion, be written with an economy of words and a declarative, straightforward style. This could be a brief statement of dialogue if you like or a short sentence which is intriguing—something to make the reader wonder right off what's going on in this story and what's going to happen. Make it startling, if possible, and memorable. Spend a great deal of time crafting that opening line and the paragraph that follows.

In commercial fiction and probably in all good fiction, the story is the thing. It must have impact; it must be dramatic; it must keep the reader constantly interested. Any distraction from that story diminishes the dramatic effect and impact.

What are some of these distractions? Background exposition in large chunks, for example. These are long paragraphs that fill in the back story, or what happened before this story began. You must feed this background information in a very little at a time. I use to use the analogy of scattering the crumbs to birds, but then I decided the best analogy is scattering flakes to fish, because if you keep giving fish food, they'll just keep eating it until they blow up. (They're not dreadfully bright you know.) That's the analogy we want here. You only give as much background information as is absolutely necessary for the reader to understand what is going on at the present moment in the story.

Use background information as a source of suspense. When you reveal something we didn't know about these characters, you create a plot twist. When a plot twists, suddenly we see everything in a new light. Use background information sparingly and always for the benefit of the plot.

Another distraction from the story line is flashbacks. Flashbacks make you lose the forward momentum of the story. You're telling the story, going along chronologically in time and then suddenly you flash the reader back to some previous scene and you've lost, to some extent, the hook that you had in that reader. The hook begins at the opening of the story and follows in a straight line to the end. That's why it's called the story line and you should not doubleback on that line. Changes in chronological order should be left to literary fiction. They aren't particularly successful in most popular fiction.

Avoid letting your character ruminate about the story, about his life, about his beliefs about life and so on. Basically, popular fiction is talk and action. There isn't a lot of internalizing. The author should also be careful not to comment and ruminate about the story in the same fashion. The object is to translate the story idea in as clean and concise and clear a manner as possible.

Understanding the Marketplace

by Leonard S. Bernstein

At the roulette wheel in Atlantic City a seasoned gambler is playing number 39. The wheel spins, the ball lodges in number 5, and the gambler loses. Of course he loses; there are fifty numbers on the wheel. The odds against him are fifty to one.

He decides to play again, this time betting on black. The wheel spins and the ball falls into a red slot. The gambler has lost again, and this time he is visibly annoyed. Of course he's annoyed; half the slots are red and half are black. He had a fifty-fifty chance.

The encyclopedia salesman canvasses a neighborhood. He knocks on twenty doors and is hardly listened to. Does he surrender, convinced that his efforts cannot possibly pay? Of course he doesn't; somewhere ahead of him is a door that will open and an encyclopedia set that will be sold. He has only to trust in persistence and a reasonable estimate of probabilities.

The baseball player does not expect to hit a home run every time at bat; the insurance salesman does not expect to sell a policy with each phone call. But the writer, buoyed by the most remarkable expectations, sends a short story to *Redbook* and expects it to be accepted.

In fact, these are the probabilities: During the year 1985 *Redbook* received 25,000 unsolicited short story manuscripts. Five were chosen for publication. The odds were therefore 5,000 to 1. Let us assume that of the 25,000 stories, 24,000 were mediocre and only 1,000 were really possibilities, and let us assume that our manuscript was among the 1,000. Now the odds have been reduced to 200 to 1. Why then does the writer send a story to *Redbook* and expect it to be accepted? More important, why, when it is not accepted, are we so disappointed and disillusioned that we stop writing for a year?

Exaggeration? Just a bit perhaps. But in any writing course it can be observed that perfectly competent writers take one shot at a major magazine and then give up.

Well, why shouldn't they give up? Why should they have even tried in the first place? What is the answer to such a discouraging marketplace?

There are many answers: the first is to try markets where the odds are not so overwhelming. There are smaller, less competitive magazines than *Redbook* and there are hundreds of literary journals. A recent issue of *The Writer* lists 110 markets for short stories without even including the literary journals.

The second answer is that although the odds may be staggering for a single short story, they are cut exactly in half with two short stories and improve dramatically with ten short stories. A serious writer does not market a single story (as an encyclopedia salesman does not knock on a single door). A writer writes stories and submits them to the larger marketplace. If we persist, we get published. In ten years of teaching writing courses I have never known a competent writer who continued to write and continued to submit and did not get published. And let's be clear about this: I don't mean a marvelously talented writer; I mean a competent writer. Most of the writers in any writing course are competent. On the

Businessman, writing instructor, author and poet **Leonard S. Bernstein** *is the author of both books of poetry and books on the garment business, but he has also written a travel book,* The Official Guide to Wine Snobbery.

other hand I know marvelously talented writers who sent their single short story to *Redbook* and have never been published.

The rule is this: *Understand the probabilities and don't get discouraged.* Getting published is not as easy as it seems when you send out your first story, and not as difficult as it seems after you have had five stories rejected. It is involved with probabilities—with odds—like the gambler, the salesman, the ballplayer and most other endeavors in our lives.

The Rule of Twelve

The laws of probability—the "odds"— can be arranged to work *for* writers as well as against them. If the gambler bets every number on the fifty-number roulette wheel, he has a winner with each spin. Similarly, if the writer keeps enough manuscripts in the marketplace, the formidable odds against a single submission improve dramatically. If the odds are twelve to one against a single manuscript, then with twelve manuscripts in the marketplace theoretically one must be accepted.

Obviously it doesn't work quite as neatly as that, as any writer who has suffered twenty rejections on a single story will tell you. But then for every story that gets rejected twenty times there is the story that only gets rejected four times. Thus two stories collect twenty-four rejections—an *average* of twelve rejections a story.

So certainly the writer whose story has been rejected five times should hardly be bringing his typewriter to the pawnshop. He has not even begun to experience the realities of the marketplace.

To which a writer might respond, "Who wants to experience the realities of the marketplace if those are the realities?"

Well, O.K., no one said you have to play the game. If you can't accept the rules you are always welcome to drop out. But at least drop out after you *do* understand the rules. Don't submit a story three times, to the top magazines in America, and then surrender after three rejections. First of all that's naive; second it's cowardly; and third you are not being true to your own talent. Three rejections mean absolutely nothing. If you're going to drop out after three you might as well not start.

Which brings us, via a somewhat roundabout path, to THE RULE OF TWELVE. This is the rule of probabilities and it is designed to suggest a rational approach to the marketplace. You don't dive out the window if the lottery doesn't pay off, and you don't start looking over the ledge when the story comes back—yes, with a printed rejection slip—from *The Atlantic*.

In fact, almost the opposite is true. Almost all manuscripts, competently written, are publishable. It remains for the writer to find the right strata of publications, and then to pound on enough doors.

THE RULE OF TWELVE contends that every competent (not extraordinary) story or article will be accepted after a certain number of times submitted. Let's say twelve is obviously arbitrary. It depends on the writer's talent and the strata of the magazines he submits to. Some writers will have an average times-out of seventeen. Others will have six. If the seventeen-times-out writer lowers the sights a little, the number reduces to twelve. If the six-times-out writer only aims for *Playboy* and *The Atlantic*, the number goes up to twelve.

This doesn't mean that every story or article gets accepted on the twelfth submission. It means that the average is twelve; the RULE is twelve. Some stories will get accepted on the seventh submission; some on the seventeenth.

The point is the RULE does work. The pity is that few writers follow it.

THE RULE OF TWELVE therefore means that if the writer has twelve manuscripts out in the marketplace, one of them will be accepted. It also means that if there is only one manuscript out, *it* will be accepted—but not until the twelfth time out. And if there are only six manuscripts circulating, one of those will be accepted the second time around. Twelve manuscripts presented; one manuscript accepted. That's the RULE.

A writer who has less than six pieces out should be paying less attention to the probabilities of acceptance, and more attention to writing.

There are exceptions: THE RULE OF TWELVE utilizes rational probabilities *if* the writer is tuned to the marketplace. If the same story travels to *Playboy* and *Ladies' Home Journal*, scratch one of those two chances. One of them is a no-chance.

Being tuned to the marketplace also means being aware that the articles market does not end with the top ten magazines in the front of the newsstand. If you spin *that* roulette wheel the odds go from twelve to one to perhaps twenty-four to one. There's nothing wrong with trying; there is nothing lost by shooting high except stamps and time, but you should understand the possibilities. Behind the top ten come countless excellent journals, including newspapers, national and local, city magazines, airlines magazines, religious magazines, sports magazines, and specialized magazines of every description. It is really impossible to run out of markets; it can only be done if the manuscript becomes dated, and that is not a fault of the marketplace.

I genuinely believe that THE RULE Of TWLEVE is not applicable if you are only submitting a piece or two. It is somewhat like betting a single roulette number over and over. You could sit at the wheel all night and never be a winner. As a matter of pure probability, you must hit that number one time out of however many numbers are on the wheel. But probabilities require a larger mix to work.

Indeed, it takes stamina. It takes persistence and determination. But it helps to know that somewhere down that road there are probabilities that work. I think it is the one thing that can sustain the writer in the terribly cruel world of the marketplace.

At the risk of overstating my case, I'm going to illustrate the RULE as it actually might appear in a writer's records.

Story #1, which the writer did not bury, was rejected eleven times and then accepted on the 12th submission. Par for the course.

Story #2 was not accepted within this schedule, but that does not mean it was not accepted. Barring an untimely subject, this story gets accepted on the 27th or 34th submission.

Story #3 is accepted on the 18th time out. Story #4, on the 7th.

Story #5 sneaks in on the 20th time out—just before you were about to give up. Never give up.

Article #6 is accepted on the 2nd trip. Try more articles.

Article #7—a standard RULE OF TWELVE acceptance on the 14th spin.

Article #8—another standard result—the 9th.

Article #9 is accepted on the 4th time out, which is a big surprise because you thought article # 9 was pretty mediocre and destined for the outer extreme of the chart.

Article #10 is not accepted at all. Not on the 20th submission. Not on the 40th. Who told you to write about Watergate?

There it is, a realistic picture of the probabilities. Lots of submissions; not many acceptances. THE RULE OF TWELVE is illustrated on the chart on the following page. You can look at the X's and get discouraged, but you can also look at the A's. There are eight acceptances on this chart; eight magazines or newspapers that carry your by-line. All this time you thought you would never be published, and here you are—almost a professional.

The Rule of Twelve illustrated

x = rejection
A = acceptance

Magazine#	1	2	3	4	5	6	7	8	9	10	11	12	13	14	15	16	17	18	19	20
Story #1	x	x	x	x	x	x	x	x	x	x	x	A								
Story #2	x	x	x	x	x	x	x	x	x	x	x	x	x	x	x	x	x	x	x	x
Story #3	x	x	x	x	x	x	x	x	x	x	x	x	x	x	x	x	x	A		
Story #4	x	x	x	x	x	x	A													
Story #5	x	x	x	x	x	x	x	x	x	x	x	x	x	x	x	x	x	x	x	A
Article #6	x	A																		
Article #7	x	x	x	x	x	x	x	x	x	x	x	x	x	A						
Article #8	x	x	x	x	x	x	x	x	A											
Article #9	x	x	x	A																
Article #10	x	x	x	x	x	x	x	x	x	x	x	x	x	x	x	x	x	x	x	x

THE RULE OF TWELVE states that if you submit a competent manuscript to appropriate and realistic markets, it will, *on average*, be accepted on the 12th time out.

The above chart represents the acceptance/rejection record of a competent freelance writer, possibly yourself. If you look at the X's, you will give up writing and take up stamp collecting. If you look at the A's, you will note that eight of ten manuscripts have been *accepted*.

Writing Workshops: A Publishers' Clearinghouse

by David Weddle

In 1946 only two American universities—the University of Iowa and Stanford—offered degrees in creative writing; today nearly 200 do. In addition, there are approximately 150 summer writing conferences—most sponsored by universities—that offer crash courses in fiction and poetry to the general public. Nonetheless, this incredible expansion has failed to keep pace with consumer demand. Last fall Iowa's graduate writing program—the oldest and most prestigious in the country—received over 700 applications for just 47 openings. The University of California at Irvine (UCI)—Iowa's leading rival—had over 200 applications for only 12 slots.

Creative writing is a growth industry. There are more jobs for writers—as visiting authors or writers-in-residence—than perhaps at any other time in history. And they're getting paid decent money these days. "It's not like it was thirty years ago, when it was very easy to get poets to come because they didn't have jobs," says Frank Conroy, the author of *Stop-Time* and the director of the writing program at Iowa. "Now it's hard to find writers with a body of distinguished work who don't have some kind of relationship to a university." A writer with a couple of successful (or critically acclaimed) novels under his belt can earn up to $2500 for a two-day visit to a university, during which he might give a reading or attend a class or two. Really big names, like Kurt Vonnegut, command up to $10,000 a reading, and established writers can get $20,000 per academic quarter as visiting authors. After poet Rita Dove won the Pulitzer Prize in 1987, she became the object of a bidding war among several universities. (She eventually signed on at the University of Virginia.) Hot writers who are interested in the security of a tenured position as a writer-in-residence can pull in as much as $125,000 a year. What's more, such authors often cut deals that allow them to teach only one class a semester, or every other semester, or every other year. Some teach no classes at all but simply agree to be available to counsel selected students.

Not everyone is thrilled with the campus writing boom. Some publishing figures—like Ted Solotaroff, a former editor of *American Review* who's now with Harper & Row—worry that by taking refuge in universities, too many writers have become insulated from the struggles and anxieties of everyday life and have begun writing for a narrow academic audience.

Others voice concern over the quality of the work being produced. Nearly every university writing program uses the "workshop" approach, first developed at Iowa and Stanford. A typical workshop has about twelve students and a teacher. During each class session, one student brings in a story, poem or novel excerpt, and the rest of the class and the teacher critique it, discussing its strong and weak points and possible revisions. Under the direction of a talented instructor, such as Stanford's Wallace Stegner, workshops can yield fantastic results. Stanford has produced such literary all-stars as Ken Kesey, Robert Stone and Larry McMurtry, and Iowa has produced Flannery O'Connor and John Irving, among many others. But the hundreds of workshops across the country have a less spectacular track record—and have given birth to a dreaded new genre in fiction: the workshop story.

Gwyneth Cravens—author of *Love and Work*—remembers cringing when, as a fiction

David Weddle *is a West Coast freelance writer and contributing editor for* California Magazine.

editor for *New Yorker*, she received submissions from students in graduate writing programs. The stories all tended to have the same bland, homogenized prose style and by-the-numbers plots—a direct result, Cravens believes, of the workshop approach. "You have this class of twelve people sitting around a table," she says, "and there's this tremendous urge humans have to blend and conform." Quirky, offbeat stories are invariably rewritten to suit the group's collective aesthetic. By the time all of the rough edges have been smoothed away, so has most of the story's vitality and originality.

Marti Leimbach, a former graduate student at UCI, had firsthand experience with the workshop syndrome when she presented a chapter from her novel *Dying Young* to her writing class at Irvine. "They detested it," Leimbach says. "They thought it was awful." Fortunately for Leimbach, one of her teachers, Don Heiney, intervened. Heiney, a novelist who publishes under the name MacDonald Harris, worked one-to-one with Leimbach, guiding her through the writing of a first draft. He sent the finished manuscript to his New York agent, Virginia Barber, who eventually reaped a staggering $500,000 in advances for the twenty-six-year-old author.

Leimbach's experience spotlights the biggest quantifiable benefit university programs offer aspiring writers: an entrée into the world of publishing. Writers, editors and agents who teach at or visit workshops often take a shine to star students and give them their first push on the road to publication.

Success stories abound. Bret Easton Ellis was a freshman at Bennington College, in Vermont, when he attended a course titled Nonfiction as Literature, taught by journalist Joe McGinniss, author of *Fatal Vision*. Although Ellis has doubts about the value of writing courses—"Writing," he says, "is really weird, gray, diaphanous area that can't be taught"—the class did serve another purpose. McGinniss was so impressed with Ellis's essays on L.A. youth culture that he forwarded them to his former editor, Morgan Entrekin, at Simon & Schuster. Entrekin would eventually publish Ellis's best-selling novel *Less Than Zero*. Two years ago Don Heiney championed the work of another UCI student, Michael Chabon, whose first novel, *Mysteries of Pittsburgh*, would hit the bestseller list. Novelist Joyce Carol Oates—a writer-in-residence at Princeton—helped her student Jonathan Ames pick the title for his first novel, *I Pass Like Night*, and wrote a plug for the jacket of the book, which was published in August by William Morrow. Last year three graduate students at the Iowa workshop sold books to major publishing houses before even obtaining their MFAs, and the same number of students scored at UCI.

Universities have also taken on a less commercial function. Even as the market for short stories in national magazines has withered, university literary quarterlies have proliferated. The quarterlies—and their affiliated university presses—will feature authors who appeal to audiences too small to interest the demographic-obsessed publishing conglomerates.

Frank Conroy says that bottom-line mentality has caused major publishers to lose interest in developing young writers. "In general," he says, "there's much less real text editings going on, and there's far less long-term investment in writers. In the old days, the editors in the publishing houses would work with a young writer for a long time, thinking, 'Okay, this guy might take a while, but let's do it.' That's very rare now."

Gone are the days when a young Thomas Wolfe could submit a rough, overwritten manuscript to a publisher and expect an editor like Maxwell Perkins to help him pare it down to a brilliant debut novel like *Look Homeward, Angel*. "What would happen now," says Conroy, " would be that Thomas Wolfe might work in a—strange as it sounds—writing program, and that editing and cutting down from the truck-sized manuscript would occur before it went to the publisher. The better writing programs have taken over that responsibility. They are the ones who bring the younger writers along—nurture them, mentor them, do editing for them and try to help them through the early stages of their career."

—— *Finding the Right Agent*

by Donald MacCampbell

If you are shopping for an agent it might be smart to inquire among the publishers whose product you respect and would like to emulate. Most publishers have lists of the agents they do business with, but you will find them reluctant—and for very good reasons—to recommend a particular firm. Few middlemen can maintain working relations with all publishers, and they will have closer contact with some than with others.

I have spent a lifetime peddling literary properties, and yet there are a number of fine hardcover houses I have never done business with. I daresay there are editors in New York and Boston who do not even know of my existence—just as I may not know of theirs. Because an editor has never heard of Donald MacCampbell does not mean I am *persona non grata* with that editor's firm. It may only mean I have never gotten around to taking that editor to lunch.

The right agent for you

The agent who is always in the news with blockbuster deals may be an unwise choice. Even if you should be accepted as a client, there is the possibility of your being lost in the crowd. A new writer is often better off with a younger representative who is eager for business and willing to make the extra effort required to develop a promising account. Actually the option to choose between a long-established agent and one still on the way up does not always exist, for the one with the stable of famous names may not let you get past the receptionist.

The size of an agency is something to be considered when making your bid for acceptance. Whereas the one-man or one-woman operation will be in a position to offer you personal attention, the large departmentalized agency is likely to turn you over to some young apprentice out of Vassar or Harvard who is still learning how to sell and how to judge a property's value.

It cannot be repeated too often that agents exist by selling bad books because there are not enough good ones available. Nowadays when so many projects are sold on an online basis—at least after the groundbreaker has been disposed of—it takes an experienced hand to know what to send to market. When you read that a best-selling book has a history of ten or more rejections, you can safely assume it has been mishandled somewhere along the line, quite possibly by some young reader in a large agency who has been assigned to the job of placing it.

Then there is the personality problem to be considered. Your agent should send off good vibes. Many relationships are doomed from the start for lack of compatibility. I have learned to sniff out a no-no account after a very few minutes of firsthand contact; when getting acquainted by mail it can take much longer. Call it chemical antipathy if you like, it has to be reckoned with. The stores are full of books by able writers whom I would not want to handle, even if I got the 90 percent and they got the 10 percent. You must try to meet an agent in person before you become involved, so that together you can assess the likelihood of a long-term relationship. It is very much the same as entering a marriage: you

Donald MacCampbell *has been a successful New York literary agent since the 1940s. He is credited with being the first to see the vast potential of mass market publishing and has written books for writers, including* Selling What You Write *and* Don't Step On It—It May Be a Writer.

do not have to be in love, but you had better be damn good friends.

Most agents are inclined toward a particular level of material, and for this reason too you must be sure that you are approaching the appropriate people. There are a few truly *literary* agents – I said a *few* – and these will turn up their noses at anything they regard as trash. There are a great many *commercial* agents who make a good living handling projects for the masses. Fortunately there are also both literary and commercial writers who fit nicely into agencies that share their own interests. But heaven help the literary writer who signs up with a crassly commercial representative, or vice versa!

Good agents make a point of reading everything they send out to a publisher. However there are several who lean on editors and expect them to do their first reading. There is one in particlar who, according to a well-known editor, "sends stuff out by the wheelbarrow." Once an agent gets the reputation of being irresponsible in the way he or she sends out material, then the entire clientele has to suffer. You are not likely to find that agent's name on any publisher's list of favorites.

There exists a kind of unvoiced rivalry between editors and agents, probably because the latter make considerably more money for less sweat. If editors are impressed with the shrewd business "savvy" of the leading agents, they are also inclined to test the smartness of newcomers to the field by offering them minimum terms and seeing if they can get away with it. Recently I was shown a contract by a new agent which contained terms so outlandish I could hardly believe my eyes. The lease was for world rights for the duration of copyright; the advance was half what I normally receive from the same paperback publisher, and it was payable in *four* installments. When I told this agent he was getting a rotten deal, he called the editor at once. "We sent you an unagented writer's contract by mistake," he was told apologetically. "Send it back and we'll replace it." I suspect this editor was simply trying to see if he could get away with putting a new agent and an unagented writer in the same bag!

Like a marriage

Good agents, like good marriage partners, are hard to find. If you are rebuffed in your attempt to get taken aboard by the agent of your choice, do not despair, for there is a way to go about it and I will explain. Keep mailing your work directly to the publishers who have welcome mats out and, while it takes a lot longer to manage on your own, eventually you will get an offer. Now go back to the agent who has rebuffed you and place the deal in this agent's lap. What you are doing is handing out a commission in exchange for the agent's attention, and very likely a place among his or her clientele.

Let us now assume you have landed an agent and your honeymoon begins. The question arises, should the agent be expected to handle everything you write? The answer depends entirely upon the policy of the firm. Some agents will even handle poetry by a writer who can turn out successful fiction or nonfiction books. Others will want no part of what they regard as petty business.

In the days when I had contracts with clients, I always spelled out exactly what I would and would not handle. Short stories, articles, poetry, and essays were excluded from any agreement. Later, when I discarded contracts and began working on a gentlemen's-agreement basis, I began receiving these unwanted efforts from time to time until I was obliged to set a minimum commission of $250 on anything I sold. Since much of this kind of material does not produce enough revenue to make a $250 commission feasible, writers soon stopped sending it in.

Your major problem will lie with the more ambitious projects that you may be excited about but that leave your agent cold. What then? I have lost valuable accounts by turning down things that have subsequently proved salable when sent directly to publishers. Sometimes I have managed to steer a safe course between Scylla and Charybdis by offering these marginal projects, when I consider it expedient to do so, with apologetic notes to the editors suggesting the kind of rejection letter that will not give offense when passed along but that will, at the same time, support my own conclusions.

The line between *publishable* and *unpublishable* is a hard one to draw. An editor who has a gaping hold in the new seasonal list and who is desperately seeking a way to fill it may take on a property which normally he would never accept. This may turn out to be the very property that an agent wanted no part of and returned to the client with regrets. Some agents solve the dilemma of marginal properties by agreeing to take them on to preserve harmony in the relationship and then stowing them away in the horizontal files. Perhaps at a later date – maybe on the occasion of a big killing – they can quietly return the manuscript without making waves. The horizontal files, of course, become a risky solution if the big killing does not materialize!

Agents do not always lose their disgruntled clients to other agents. In recent years a more serious threat to their biggest accounts has come from lawyers experienced in the ways of publishing. Actually, big-money writers do not have to fall out with their representatives before switching to legal representatives. Their accounts simply become too complicated for agents to handle. But legal minds are expensive, and no way will they work for 10 percent. To be handled by an attorney, a writer should have a tax problem large enough to allow a generous bite out of income. I am sure this is something you will not have to think about for awhile.

“A new writer is often better off with a younger representative who is eager for business and willing to make the extra effort . . .”

–Donald MacCampbell

— *Publishing Contract Terms: Royalties Defined*

by Brad Bunnin

A royalty is a payment based on the sale of your book, the rights to which you have licensed to your publisher by a contract. In other words, in exchange for your granting the publisher the right to publish your work, you are given certain payments. Occasionally (almost always, in the case of a poem or a magazine piece), an author sells rights to a work for a one-time payment, in which case there is no continuing right to receive a royalty. But in the strong tradition of the book publishing business, the publisher calculates the royalty and pays it as a percentage of the cover price or the publisher's income from the sales of the book.

How is a royalty computed? Publishers use a variety of formulas. Let's start with trade books (hardbacks and paperbacks sold in bookstores) and mass market books (4″ × 7″ paperbacks sold principally at newsstands and in supermarkets, drugstores, and airports, usually from wire racks).

To figure royalties under most trade and mass market contracts, multiply the author's royalty percentage by the cover price (sometimes called "suggested retail price" or "list price"). This calculation yields the author's income for each book sold. Then multiply that amount by the number of books sold to determine the dollar amount the author receives. In mathematical terms, the royalty calculation looks like this:

cover price × *royalty percentage* × *number of books sold* = *author's royalty*

As you'll see, the royalties an author actually receives are likely to differ considerably from the results of this simple, straightforward calculation because of complicated royalty schedules, the effect of books returned unsold and other factors.

One relatively minor but confusing complication is the "freight passthrough" or "freight allowance." This pricing method, used by some publishers, is designed to help booksellers recover the cost of having books shipped to their stores. It works like this: A book that normally would be priced at $14.95 is priced instead at $15.70. The difference is the freight allowance, which the bookstore keeps. You must exclude the freight amount when multiplying the cover price for royalty purposes. In other words, the author receives no royalty on the freight passthrough component of the price, only on the underlying price of the book itself, usually called "invoice price," defined as the retail price less the freight passthrough amount.

EXAMPLE 1, A TRADE BOOK—*Escargot Cooking,* a trade hardcover book, sells 4,000 copies at a retail price of $10.70, including freight passthrough. The passthrough is $.70. Your royalty rate is ten percent. Your royalty per book is ten percent of $10, or $1. Your royalty income should be $4,000.

Royalty rates

Royalty rates depend on the kind of book to which they apply, the book's format, the book's sales, and the success of your negotiations. The royalty rates for trade hardcover

Brad Bunnin *is a publishing industry lawyer practicing in Berkeley, California. About 80 percent of his clients are writers and the rest are publishers, editors and designers.*

books, for example, begin at 10 percent of cover price. As sales increase, so does the royalty rate: to 12½ percent for each copy sold over 5,000 copies, and to 15 percent for each copy sold over 10,000 copies. This pattern of increasing royalties is called "escalation."

Royalty rates for trade paperbacks are commonly lower than those for hardcover trade books. Some publishers offer as little as 6-7 percent, but many are willing to give an author 10 percent, or even more in rare cases, if they really want the book. The royalty rates escalate, but not as dramatically as for hardcover books. If the basic royalty rate is 7 percent, it might climb to 8 percent at 25,000 copies. If the basic royalty rate is 8 percent, it might reach 10 percent at 25,000 copies. Some publishers that specialize in trade paperback books offer more generous royalties, as much as 10 percent rising to 12 percent at, say, 20,000 copies. But because the margin of profit is smaller for trade paperbacks than for hardbound books, the royalty usually is, too.

Mass market paperback royalty rates begin at about 5 percent. Again, the negotiated rate depends on the book and the author. We have seen mass market contracts pay as little as 4 percent of the cover price; others, especially for mass market originals, pay 10 percent or more.

Textbook royalties are calculated on "publisher's gross (or net) receipts" from sales of the book (typically about 60-80 percent of the retail price). Because the price used to figure royalties for textbooks is considerably less than that for trade books, the basic textbook royalty rate often starts at 15 percent, climbing to 18, 20, even 25 percent as sales increase.

> EXAMPLE 2, A TEXTBOOK—*Hotel Cooking*, a textbook designed for hotel schools, sells 6,000 copies. One thousand are sold directly by the publisher at the full price of $20, for publisher's net receipts of $20,000. The rest are sold to school bookstores, distributors, and others at a discount of 20 percent off cover price, or $16, for additional publisher's net receipts of $80,000. The total publisher's net receipts are $100,000, and the author's 15 percent royalty rate is multiplied by this amount to calculate the author's royalties: $15,000.

Publishers will usually be reasonable in allowing authors larger royalties if sales are strong, because the low initial rate allows the publisher the chance to recover the initial investment in the author's advance, editing, typesetting, graphics and so on. Once those costs have been recovered, the publisher should be willing to give the author a larger share.

The many ways royalties are reduced

Basic royalty rates apply only to regular book sales. The publishing contract also creates a whole structure of royalties for other kinds of sales, and those royalties are always less than those for regular sales. In extreme cases, far fewer than half a book's total sales bring in full regular royalties. Authors and agents pay insufficient attention to these reduced royalty provisions. It's up to you to understand what each contract provision means. When you do, you can bargain to get the most destructive clauses modified.

Trade publishers assign each title a retail price, and most sell them to wholesalers and bookstores at a discount from that retail price. If, for example, a book carries a cover price of $19.95, the publisher may sell it to a bookstore at a discount of 44 percent, or $11.17. These trade discounts range from 20 pecent for very small orders (one to five books), to the more typical 40-42 percent for small orders, to as much as 46-50 percent for larger ones. Publishers allow booksellers to mix titles when they order to take advantage of the larger discount.

Discount schedules have been the subject of much experimentation in the last few years, as bookstores have demanded larger profit margins for the sake of their survival. Freight passthrough pricing, larger discounts in exchange for curtailed return privileges, and a number of other plans have had an impact on pricing. Generally, though, publisher sales to bookstores are still made at a discount of 40-50 percent from cover price.

The regular royalty rate schedule is tied to publisher's sales at these normal discounts. If the publisher sells books at a larger discount, called an "excess discount," the publisher's profit per book sold diminishes. When that happens, the author's contract usually reduces the author's royalty.

The most common excess discount sale occurs when the publisher uses a wholesaler to distribute its books to the trade. The wholesaler will resell books to stores for nearly the same discount that the publisher offers when it sells directly. The wholesaler makes money by buying books from the publisher for a larger discount. The difference is the wholesaler's income.

Other excess discount sales are those made to the buyer who buys a large quantity of books, much larger than the characteristic sale to a bookstore, as a special sale or to offer as a premium. For example, the International Society of Reptile Fanciers might buy a new dictionary of lizards and make it available at low cost to new members. The premium buyer usually negotiates a better discount on these "special sales," and, as a result, the publisher's per copy profit margin is reduced.

Some publishers treat all excess discount sales alike, reducing the author's royalty rate for all of them. Others distinguish between sales made to wholesalers and those made to premium and special buyers. Most often, the publisher's response is to reduce the royalty rate to about half the full royalty rate. The publisher will sometimes base the excess discount royalty rate on the publisher's "net receipts" from these sales instead of on the cover price of the books. You can recognize an excess-discount clause from its reduced royalty for certain defined sales. Examples of the breed look like this:

> The Author shall receive the following royalties: 5 percent of the Publisher's dollar receipts from sales of the regular edition sold in bulk quantity, at special discounts, for premiums and other special sales incentives, to professional groups and industry.

Or this:

> The Publisher agrees to pay the Author as follows: On copies sold at a discount of 50 percent or more of the catalog retail price, the prevailing royalty less one-half of 1 percent for each 1 percent discount of more than 49 percent.

The first of these clauses doesn't apply to sales through wholesalers and calculates the royalty on publisher's receipts. Measured by cover price less discount, these receipts will likely be less than half cover price. And the royalty rate is also considerably less than the regular royalty rate, which in this contract was 8 percent.

The second clause covers all excess discount sales, including those to wholesalers, and uses a formula to determine the royalty for excess discount sales. The royalty goes down by one-half percent for each full percent the discount exceeds 49 percent. If the regular royalty rate is 10 percent, a 52 percent discount reduces it by 1½ percent to 8½ percent.

Because books sold to bookstores through wholesalers reach the same ultimate buyers at the same purchase price as books the publisher sells directly to bookstores, and because the publisher saves money by not having to fulfill orders from its own warehouse with its own staff, there is a strong argument that wholesale sales shouldn't reduce royalties. Many publishers don't penalize royalties for sales through wholesalers, no matter how big the discount; they apply the clause only to premium or special sales, outside normal trade channels. Others limit the effect of the clause by applying it to a stated maximum percentage of books sold, perhaps 20 percent.

If the contract provides that you will be paid a percentage of the publisher's net receipts, make sure the term *net receipts* is defined. Make sure, too, that only direct costs of sale (for example, commissions) are deducted from the publisher's gross receipts to calculate its net. You shouldn't be paying part of your publisher's overhead by way of a deduction from your royalty base.

Consider the mythical case of *The Great Big Book of Shrimp*, a regional cookbook with modest sales until the Universal Shrimpers Association decided to make it a promotional premium given to fish markets coast-to-coast. The publisher shipped 50,000 trade paperback copies in a year, for $2 each. The author's contract carried a basic royalty rate of 8 percent, escalating to 10 percent at sales of 20,000 copies, based on a suggested retail list price of $7.95. "Whoopee," exulted the author. "It's jumbo prawns from now on!" Then he read the special-sales clause. Unfortunately for him, the royalty on special sales was fixed at 10 percent of the publisher's net receipts, for a royalty of $10,000, not the $36,570 that would have been payable for normal retail sales. The result: one more year of imitation crab.

SMALL-PRESS WARNING – If you are dealing with a small publishing house, you should review the details of any discounted royalty provision with particular care. Most publishing companies with gross sales of less than $1,000,000 or so don't have their own salespeople or commissioned reps. This means they rely heavily on wholesalers such as Bookpeople, The Distributors, Ingram, Pacific Pipeline, Book Carrier, Publisher's Group West, and many others; and they sell a high percentage of their books at a discount of more than 50 percent. So a nominal 10 percent royalty may end up being little more than half the royalty you expect. But some trade publishers, and most textbook and professional book publishers, don't base royalties on cover or invoice price. Instead, they pay royalties on the money they receive from the sale of books, which they call publisher's gross receipts, publisher's actual receipts, publisher's cash receipts, or publisher's net receipts (if certain costs of sale are deducted). Royalties based on these publisher's receipts are not paid on the cover price unless a book is sold for full price. More often, royalties are based on the wholesale price the publisher gets from a bookstore or distributor. To figure the royalty, you must multiply the aggregate amount the publisher receives by the royalty rate.

NOTE ON EXPORT SALES – If your publisher is likely to sell significant quantities of your book abroad, pay special attention to the contract provision that sets royalties for these sales. It usually sets them at about half the royalty you'd expect. The publisher faces special problems when exporting books (customs duties, for example), but some publishers nevertheless find it more profitable to export books (especially to English-reading countries) than to sell a license for publication there.

Limitation of royalties – the spreadforward

Some authors agree with their publisher to limit royalties to a stated amount each year, no matter how much their books earn, by a device called "royalty spreadforward." The ostensible reason is to prevent royalty income generated by a best-selling book from driving the author into a higher tax bracket. We should all have such problems.

No matter what your tax position, you are almost always better off taking your earnings and solving your own tax problems than allowing your publisher to hold the funds for you. When you're earning enough for this issue to matter, you'll also be able to pay for first-rate tax advice. Be sure to discuss any sort of deferred compensation deal with your tax advisor, lawyer, or accountant before agreeing to it. Our advice, in general, is to take every penny you can get, as fast as you can get it. Here's what happened to one wildly successful author who didn't. Nancy Friday agreed with her publisher to limit royalties to $25,000 a year, although her books, such as *My Mother, My Self* and *A Secret Garden*, have sold millions of copies. She brought suit to set aside that provision of her contract. In the meantime, her publisher had the use of thousands of dollars that belong to Ms. Friday, who essentially made a large, interest-free loan to her publisher.

Returns

The publishing industry has traditionally been one of the few where the manufacturer (the publisher) will take back unsold merchandise for full credit. Recently, some publishers have restricted or eliminated the right of bookstores to return merchandise, offering instead a higher discount rate. But for most publishers, some sort of return privilege is still the rule.

The publishing contract usually provides for an author's royalty payments to be figured "less returns." These two words mean that the publisher need not pay a royalty on books sold to booksellers if those copies are later returned because they failed to sell. How do returns affect payments to authors? The publisher is always afraid that if royalties are paid on the basis of books shipped, large quantities of unsold books may be returned months later. In theory, this would give the publisher the right to ask the author to return royalty payments already made, because what looked like sales turned out not to be. We say "in theory" because, not surprisingly, publishers are wary about an author's ability or willingness to reimburse overpaid royalties. To deal with this problem before it occurs, publishers withhold part of the author's royalties from the start. The withheld royalties are called a "reserve against returns." Some contracts specify the percentage the publisher may withhold, which can be as high as 35 or even 50 percent. Others allow the publisher a "reasonable reserve." The industry average on returns is about 15-25 percent of trade books shipped, somewhat higher for mass market paperbacks. Front-list books (those just published for the first time) tend to produce higher returns than back-list books with a proven sales history. It isn't wise to sign a contract with an unspecified reserve, or one much larger than industry averages, although some entirely reputable publishers won't negotiate a ceiling on the size of the reserve. Negotiations should be based on the kind of book and the rate of returns for similar books.

The reserve-against-returns provision of your contract should also restrict the reserve to a specific period of time. This is particularly sensible when you understand that most publishers allow bookstores to return books for only a limited period. The return period varies with the type of book, anywhere from a few months to a year or more. Unfortunately, if you have no language to the contrary it may take months—or even years—before the publisher is ready to pay royalties out of the reserve account. In a world where money is perennially tight, a few publishers are unwilling to release money until they absolutely must. This sort of abuse is inexcusable, but it does occur. Therefore, be sure to insist that the publisher credits you for all accumulated, unused reserves in the third accounting period after the reserved royalties were earned. That means the publisher has a year to ship the books and determine whether they stay sold, and several months more to pay you. A fair clause reads as follows:

> Publisher may establish a reserve against returns based on the returns history of the Work but not to exceed 20 percent of amounts earned through normal retail sales, and shall pay Author any royalties reserved but not applied to returns with the payment due for the third royalty accounting period after the reserved royalties have accrued.

The advance

Because publishers know that authors need money to live on while writing, they are often willing to pay authors some portion of royalties long before the manuscript is finished. These payments are called "advances." The payment of advances is usually scheduled in the contract, which means that the publisher pays them in installments. Here are two typical advance schedules:

> The advance shall be paid one-third upon signing the publishing contract, one-

third upon acceptance of the completed manuscript, and one-third upon publication.

Author shall be paid her advance one-half when this contract is signed and one-half when she delivers a satisfactory, complete manuscript of the Work to Publisher.

An experienced writer who knows that long delays—often one, two, or even three years—may occur between submission of the manuscript and publication will negotiate to get the largest possible share of the advance before publication. On the other hand, in this era of the blockbuster book and advances big enough to be front page news, publishers negotiate the payment of advances in a number of smaller portions, the last of which may not be payable until a year after publication! The larger the advance, the more likely the publisher will insist on this approach.

Advances are almost always *nonreturnable*, but they are almost always *recoupable*. Understanding the difference between these terms is crucial.

The publisher that pays a recoupable advance assumes the risk that the book (once accepted for publication) will never earn back its advance. Here's how it works. Money the author receives as an advance is his to keep no matter how many books are sold. However, the author doesn't get more money until his earnings from royalties and subsidiary rights income equal the amount of the advance. Thus, if Arthur Author writes a book for a $10,000 advance, and the royalty rate is 10 percent of the $9.95 cover price, his book must sell 10,051 copies before he is entitled to any further payment.

A large advance is almost always better than a small one. It's money in hand now, not a promise of future payment. And, in addition to relieving financial pressure on the author, it establishes the publisher's substantial investment in your book. In an age when publishers pump out too many books, editors change from company to company willy-nilly, and whole companies pass from one conglomerate to another, the fact that a publisher has made a substantial initial investment in your book can mean the difference between an active sales and promotion effort and an unsupported, sink-or-swim release of your work.

Writer on the Road or Self-Promoting Your Book

by Gerry Maddren

Rarely is an author's work accorded a $150,000 publicity campaign like Harvey Mackay's *Swim With the Sharks Without Being Eaten Alive*. Most publishers allot modest sums for advertising the majority of their titles. Small presses have almost no budget for that sort of thing. But you've written this terrific manuscript; it's about to be printed. How do you keep it from going under in the stacks of books overrunning the marketplace?

Personal contacts

First of all, you turn your energies toward the bookstores. Most bookstore owners and managers are happy to meet authors. One owner after accepting *The Case of the Johannisberg Riesling* press kit I offered, said, "If it weren't for people like you, we bookstore owners would be out of business." So put bookstores high on your book promotion list. And as soon as you receive a copy of your publisher's catalogue, get photocopies of the page that describes your book (use a highlighter if necessary to make it stand out) and call on your local bookstores. At this point, your goal is simply to make them aware of the book and establish contact.

Send your material to teachers of writing classes in adult schools and colleges and offer to speak to their students on writing the mystery novel or the biography or whatever your category is. Of course, you won't get paid, but you will be able to sell some books to your audience, and you will also get some publicity . . . because you will have written press releases to your local newspapers advising them that you, author of XYZ, will be speaking at such and such a school on a particular date. If the school will allow public admittance, so much the better. In that case, your press releases stand a greater chance of being printed in the various papers. These releases must be brief and as attention-grabbing as you can make them. By all means include an intriguing and pertinent fact or two about yourself or your book. And give your phone number in case further information is desired.

If your press releases don't work right away, don't despair. Three months after I sent one press release, I got a phone call from a reporter on the *Daily News*. He'd been going through the files and had come across my release and thought it would make a good story. Would I give him an interview? I did, and it resulted in a very nice article that included my picture.

I made photocopies of the picture and article and put them in individual press kits, which I mailed or hand-delivered to bookstores out of my area.

Organizations can do wonders for your book. I joined Mystery Writers of America when I sold my third mystery short story and Women Writers West some time later. Fellow members have been of inestimable help—veteran novelists giving me the benefit of their

Gerry Maddren *is the author of more than 50 short stories, appearing in both adult and children's magazines. A member of Mystery Writers of America, Sisters in Crime and other writers' organizations, she has just completed the second of her mystery-wine novels,* The Case of the Cabernet Crossing *and is working on a novel based on the mother-daughter detective team from her short story,* Fit for Felony.

experiences with publishing and others arranging autograph parties. Whatever organization you belong to will undoubtedly be supportive and willing to schedule a book signing for an author-member.

Reviews

Your publisher will send out some review copies to the obvious places, but a lot of review markets will be overlooked. I found it worked best to send these reviewers a cut galley (the first chapter or two depending on length and appeal), a copy of the cover blurb written by an award-winning author, some of the aforementioned newspaper clippings, the price, and the date of publication. I also included a self-addressed postcard which allowed reviewers to check whether they wanted to see the galleys in toto or a complimentary review copy. This was far cheaper than indiscriminately sending out weighty galleys of the entire manuscript. There was also more likelihood that whatever the reviewer requested would be read.

Other strategies

Try to find a tie-in that will work for you. When I learned there was to be a three-day Food & Wine Classic in Aspen, Colorado, last June, I wrote to two bookstores suggesting that since the title of my novel was *The Case of the Johannisberg Riesling* and it was a mystery set in the wine country of California, it might be both appropriate and mutually beneficial to schedule a book signing at their stores during that time. One store never answered, but the other sent back a warm letter. I not only signed books in that bookstore but in the wine-tasting tent as well. This appearance also netted me a great article in the *Snowmass Times* (which of course went into my press kit).

As an added bonus, one of the vintners from Washington state asked if I would mind if the winery ordered some of my books to sell in its winery boutique. The idea was such a good one that I decided to write and introduce my book to other wineries with gift shops.

You'll also want to maintain your initial contacts with bookstores. Keep them updated on any publicity the book is enjoying. It pays off; the local Duttons has a stack of my books next to their cash register.

And if you have occasion to go out of town, take a half-dozen press kits with you and consult the yellow pages for bookstores in that area. Keep records of every bookstore, including the names of store owners/managers/buyers. Jot down the dates of personal calls, phone calls, letters or press kits sent, etc., so that nothing is duplicated or overlooked.

Make sure the bookstores know which distributors are handling your book. Check to see that your book is on the distributor's microfiche. And if it isn't, contact your publisher so that something is done to correct the situation. A bookstore can't sell your books if they aren't on the shelf.

Keep in mind that it is to your advantage to work with your publisher. Discuss your book promotion plans with him or her. You're on the same team. You have a common goal—to sell the book. To achieve that goal, try using the same creativity to promote your book that you used to create it. With that attitude in mind, you will find the promotion both fun and rewarding.

Important Listing Information

• *Listings are* not *advertisements. Although the information herein is as accurate as possible, the listings are not endorsed or guaranteed by the editor of* Novel & Short Story Writer's Market.
• Novel & Short Story Writer's Market *reserves the right to exclude any listing that does not meet its requirements.*

Key to Symbols and Abbreviations

‡ New listing in all sections
* Subsidy publisher in Small Press and Commercial Book publishers sections
■ Book packager or producer
ms – manuscript; **mss**-manuscripts
b&w – black and white (photo)
SASE – self-addressed, stamped envelope
SAE – self-addressed envelope
IRC – International Reply Coupon, for use on reply mail in Canada and foreign markets.
FAX – a communications system used to transmit documents over the telephone lines.

(See Glossary for definitions of words and expressions used in writing/publishing.)

How to Get the Most Out of This Book

Once you've completed your novel or short story, your next step will be to begin your search for a publisher. Finding the right market for your work requires careful research and planning. This book is designed to help you with that search by providing listings of magazine and book publishers looking for fiction submissions. To make your search easier, the listings are divided into six sections: literary and small circulation magazines, commercial periodicals, small presses, commercial book publishers, contests and awards, and literary agents. Following each main section is a list of similar foreign markets (for more information on approaching foreign publishers, see the "Business of Fiction Writing").

If you are not sure what category your work fits in or if you just want to explore the possibilities, start by browsing through the sections to find a market that interests you. The browsing method will also help you get an idea of what types of fiction are most needed, payment ranges and other general information about the magazine or book publishing industry. Read the section introductions to learn more about current trends and information specific to the type of listing featured in each section.

To help narrow your search, we've also included a category index located immediately preceding the general index at the back of the book. The category index is divided into sections (i.e. literary and small circulation magazines, commercial magazines, etc.) and each section is divided by specific fiction categories or genres. For example, if you are looking for a small press publisher that accepts science fiction, look under "Small Press" in the category index and find the "Science Fiction" heading. There you will find an alphabetical list of all the small press publishers of science fiction listed in the book.

Once you've selected a listing, it is important to read it carefully. A dagger (‡) before a listing indicates a listing new to the 1990 edition. In the book publisher sections, a listing may also have an asterisk, indicating it is a subsidy publisher or a diamond indicating the listing is that of a book packager. For quick reference see the "Key to Symbols and Abbreviations." Further explanation of these and other symbols and terms can be found in the section introductions and in the glossary.

We've also ranked the magazine and book publishers with the following codes to help you select those markets most appropriate for your work.

- I *Open to beginners. Especially encourages new writers to submit fiction;*
- II *Accepts work both from beginning and established writers, depending on quality;*
- III *Prestige market, generally hard to break into, usually accepting work only by established or agented writers and a very few outstanding new writers;*
- IV *Specialized publication or press, limited to contributors from certain regions or within a specific age group or to those writing on specialized subjects or themes.*

We occasionally receive letters asking why a certain magazine, book publisher, contest or agent is not in the book. Sometimes when we contact a listing, the editor or agent does not want to be listed because they: do not use very much fiction; are overwhelmed or backlogged with submissions; are having financial difficulty or have been recently sold; use only solicited material; accept work from a select group of writers; do not have the staff or time for the many unsolicited manuscripts a listing may bring.

Some listings do not appear because we have chosen not to list them. We investigate complaints about misrepresentation by editors or agents in the information they provide us or about unethical or unprofessional activities in a publisher's dealings with writers. If we find these reports to be true, after thorough investigation, we will delete a listing. See "Important Listing Information" for more about our listing policies.

If you feel you have not been treated fairly by a market listed in our book we advise you take the following steps:

- First, try to contact the listing. Sometimes one phone call or letter can quickly clear up the matter.
- Be sure to document all your correspondence with the listing. When you write to us with a complaint, we will ask for the name of your manuscript, the date of your submission and the dates and nature of your subsequent correspondence.
- We will write to the publisher, editor or agent and ask them to resolve the problem. We will then enter your letter into our files.
- The number, frequency and severity of unresolved complaints will be considered in our decision whether or not to delete the listing from the book.

To find out what happened to listings that appeared in the 1989 edition, but not in the 1990 edition, check the list of "Other Markets" at the end of each section. This list also includes a few well-known markets that have declined a listing.

Listings appearing in *Novel & Short Story Writer's Market* are compiled from detailed questionnaires, phone interviews and information provided by editors, publishers, awards directors and agents. The publishing industry is volatile and changes of address, editor, policies and needs happen frequently. To keep up with the changes we suggest you check the monthly Markets column in *Writer's Digest* magazine.

We also rely on our readers for information on new markets and changes in the markets listed in the book. Write us if you have any new information or if you have suggestions on how to improve our listings to better suit your writing needs.

Sample listing

The following is a sample listing. Each element of the listing is numbered and numbers correspond to the explanations following the listing. For more information on specific terms, see the glossary and the introductions to each section.

(1)‡AFTER HOURS (II), A Magazine of Dark Fantasy and Horror, 21541 Oakbrook, Mission Viejo CA 92692-3044. **(2)** Editor: William G. Raley. **(3)** Magazine: 8½x11; 48-56 pages; #3 grade offset paper; #3 grade uncoated cover; about 3 illustrations per issue; photographs sometimes with interviews. **(4)** "*After Hours* features stories too weird or off-the-wall to happen during the day. Therefore, all stories *must* take place after dark! For adults and young adults." **(5)**Quarterly. **(6)** Estab. 1989. **(7)** Circ. 750.

(8) Needs: Condensed/excerpted novel, fantasy, horror, humor/satire, psychic/supernatural/occult, suspense/mystery. "No science fiction, 'typical' crime stories (where the only motive is murder, rape or robbery), political or military." **(9)** Receives 200 unsolicited mss/month. **(10)**Buys 12 mss/issue; 50 mss/year. **(11)** Publishes ms "about 6 months" after acceptance. **(12)** Recently published work by J. N. Williamson, Steve Rasnictem and Ronald Kelly. **(13)** Length: 2,500 words preferred; 6,000 words maximum. Publishes short shorts.

(14) How to Contact: Send complete ms with a cover letter. Include "where you heard about *After Hours*, *brief* list of credits. Cover letter is optional." **(15)** Reports in 2 months on mss. **(16)** SASE for ms or query. **(17)** Photocopied and reprint submissions OK. Accepts computer printout submissions. Accepts electronic submissions via disk. **(18)** Sample copy $4. Fiction guidelines for #10 SAE and 1 first class stamp.

(19) Payment: Pays $60 maximum (1 cent/word) and one contributor's copy.

(20) Terms: Pays on acceptance for first North American serial rights. Sends galleys to author.

(21) Advice: "Readers don't want to wait around for something to happen. I need action (or at least an atmosphere of dread) on page one. Good characterization is a must. As far as plots go, don't be afraid to be original. I avoid overdone plots. There are so many stories where people come back from the dead, or turn into a monster, that it's no longer entertaining. Characters should be believable, with women portrayed as equals. No excessive blood or violence. If your story has a fresh plot (or a new twist on an old one) or is just plain strange, you've probably got a sale."

(1) Symbols, names, addresses and phone numbers. One or more symbols may precede the name of the market. A dagger symbol (‡) indicates the listing is new. Other symbols include subsidy (*) or book packager (■).
(2) Contact name. Whenever possible send your query or submission to a specific person. Use the fiction editor's name, if available. If you are not sure of the gender, it is best to use the full name (e.g. Robin Jones). If no name is given in the listing, check other sources (the masthead, if it is a magazine or, for the book publishing industry, check the directory, *Literary Market Place*).
(3) Physical description. Listings for publications often include physical description—the number of pages, type of paper, binding, number of illustrations or photos. This information is provided to give you some idea of the quality and type of publication. Magazines with inexpensive paper and binding may be more open to the work of new writers.
(4) Descriptive quote. This is a quote from the publisher describing the magazine or book publisher. The statement sometimes focuses on the publisher's philosophy and often contains a description of the audience. In book publishers' listings this is followed by a description of the types of books published (e.g., hardbound originals, paperback reprints).
(5) Frequency of publication. Some literary magazines published by universities are not published in the summer; the listing will then include a line beginning with "Does not read manuscripts from . . ."
(6) Date established. New magazines are often receptive to new writers.
(7) Circulation. For the literary and small circulation magazines, circulation is under 10,000. In book publisher listings information is included on the number of titles and percentage of fiction titles published each year.
(8) Needs. This section lists the types of fiction needed. Sometimes a quote about what is most needed and what material should not be submitted.
(9) Number of manuscripts received. This can give you an idea of the competition. If a publisher receives several hundred manuscripts each week, but only publishes two or three, response time will be slow and competition high.
(10) Number of manuscripts published. See number 9.
(11) Time between publication and acceptance. This is especially important if you will not be paid until publication. Some small journals may take up to one year to publish.
(12) Recently published. Names of authors and, if the listing is an agent or book publisher, book titles will appear in this section.
(13) Length requirements. Minimum and maximum word lengths are often given. Short shorts are short pieces under 700 words, unless otherwise indicated.
(14) How to contact. This section gives details on how to contact the listing including whether it is necessary to query first or to send a complete manuscript. If sample chapters are required, send *consecutive* chapters, preferably starting with the first chapter. Cover letter and other submission requirements are listed here.
(15) Reporting time. This is a rough estimate of the time it will take for the publisher to respond to your query or submission. New publishers sometimes miscalculate the time needed to respond to the submissions generated by this book. Add three weeks to the time given, but if you have waited much longer, feel free to check the status of your submission with a letter, return postcard or a phone call.
(16) SASE. A self-addressed, stamped envelope in a size to fit your manuscript or letter is usually required.
(17) Acceptable submissions. If reprints, simultaneous or photocopied submissions are accepted, it will say so here. If not mentioned, they probably are not acceptable. When in doubt, call or write to obtain fiction guidelines. If computer disk submissions are accepted, contact the publisher to find out specifics.
(18) Sample copy and guidelines. To find out more about a publisher, it is best to obtain a sample copy, catalog or fiction guidelines.

(19) Payment. Some small and literary magazines only pay in copies, others pay excellent rates. Note whether payment is made on acceptance or on publication. For book publishers, advances are upfront payments, made in one or more installments against royalties. You will not receive royalties until the advance has been covered.
(20) Terms. This is an important section. Note what type of rights you are selling. If the publication is not copyrighted, all rights belong to the author. Often the rights will revert to the author upon publication. Both of these agreements are the same as one-time rights—the publisher acquires or buys the right to publish your piece one time only. For more information on rights, see the "Business of Fiction Writing."
(21) Advice. Read the information in this section carefully. It is here where publishers and editors have the opportunity to pass on inside information on how to approach their magazine or publishing firm.

We include in the listings as much specific information as possible, but there are some items we do not mention because they are basically the same for all listings. See "The Business of Fiction Writing" for more on the basic requirements of all fiction markets.

Remember your market research should begin with a careful study of the listing but it should not end there. Whenever possible try to obtain a sample copy or catalog. For book publishers, check *Books in Print* at the library to find a publisher's titles and take a look a some of their books. The library also has publishing industry magazines such as *Publishers Weekly* as well as magazines for writers. These can help you keep informed of new publishers and changes in the field.

The Business of Fiction Writing

Novel & Short Story Writer's Market is designed to be a marketing tool. While listings contain most of the essential details of submission, there are some "unwritten rules" of which writers, especially beginners, should be aware. We've included much of this information in this section—a compilation of information on submission, approaching markets and manuscript mechanics.

Approaching magazine markets. While it is essential for nonfiction markets, a query letter by itself is usually not needed by most magazine fiction editors. If you are approaching a magazine to find out if fiction is accepted, a query is fine, but editors looking for short fiction want to see *how* you write. Many editors don't even read queries—they want to go right to the story. A cover letter, however, can be useful as a letter of introduction, but it must be accompanied by the actual piece. Include basic information in your cover letter—name, address, a brief list of previous publications—if you have any—and two or three sentences about the piece (why you are sending it to *this* magazine or how your experience influenced your story). Keep it to one page and remember to include a self-addressed, stamped envelope for reply.

Approaching book publishers. Some book publishers do ask for queries first, but most want a query plus sample chapters or an outline or, occasionally, the complete manuscript. Again, make your letter brief. Include the essentials about yourself—name, address, phone number and publishing experience. Include only the personal information related to your story. For example, if your story takes place in Mexico City and you lived there for two years, mention it—it adds credibility. Show that you have researched the market with a few sentences about why you chose this publisher. For example, if you chose the publisher because you feel your book would fit nicely into their young adult romance line, let them know.

Book proposals. A book proposal is a package sent to a publisher that includes a cover letter and one or more of the following: sample chapters, outline, synopsis, author bio, publications list. When asked to send sample chapters, send up to three *consecutive* chapters. An outline covers the highlights of your book chapter by chapter. Be sure to include details on main characters, the plot and subplots. Outlines can run up to 30 pages, depending on the length of your novel. The object is to tell what happens in a concise, but clear, manner. A synopsis is a very brief description of what happens in the story. Keep it to two or three pages. The terms synopsis and outline are sometimes used interchangeably, so be sure to find out exactly what each publisher wants.

Agents. Agents are not usually needed for short fiction and most do not handle it unless they already have a working relationship with you. For novels, however, you may want to consider working through an agent, especially if you are interested in marketing to publishers who do not look at unsolicited submissions. For more on approaching agents see the introduction to the Literary Agents section and the article, "Finding the Right Agent," by Donald MacCampbell, starting on page 91.

Approaching foreign markets. When sending return postage to another country, do not send stamps. You must purchase International Reply Coupons (IRCs). The foreign publisher can use the IRCs to buy stamps from his/her own country. IRCs cost 95 cents each and can be purchased at the main branch of your local post office. This rule applies

4102 Hennepin Ave.
Minneapolis, MN 55410
(612) 555-9098

March 19, 1990

Mr. Todd Kraft
Editor, Great Plains Review
3007 LaSalle
Milwaukee, WI 53211

Dear Todd Kraft:

I wanted you to have a chance to see my newest story, "Breakfast at Midnight," which I'm enclosing, along with a return envelope and return postage.

The story is set in Grenada during the American military invasion in 1984. I was in Grenada at the time as a tourist; though this piece is fiction, some of the details and events are taken from my own experience during the first hours of the invasion.

My previous work has appeared in several publications, including Milkweed Chronicle, Great River Review, Loonfeather, and The Lake Street Review. My nonfiction (including two pieces on Grenada) has appeared in the St. Paul Pioneer Press. I've been writing for several years and am currently at work on my M.A. in creative writing at the University of Minnesota.

I've been reading and enjoying Great Plains Review since 1985, and always look forward to the next issue.

Sincerely,

Helen Gould

This is a cover letter for a short story sent to a magazine. Notice the letter is brief and to the point. The second paragraph includes direct personal information of relevance to the story. Paragraph three is a brief list of publishing credits. This and the following two samples are from **Manuscript Submissions by Scott Edelstein*****, published as part of the Elements of Fiction Writing series by Writer's Digest Books.***

Scott Edelstein
2706 West 43 Street, Suite 102
Minneapolis, MN 55410
(612) 929-9123

About 4500 words

COMFORT

by Scott Edelstein

Ever since I was a little boy, my mother suffered from chronic headaches. She'd usually get them in late afternoon, especially when the days were hot and muggy. She hated to take pills, and when one of her headaches would set in, she'd lie down on her bed, close her eyes, and have my father sit beside her and rub her forehead. Almost always, the headaches would go away after a few minutes of rubbing. This impressed me immensely, and probably had something to do with my becoming a massage therapist fifteen years later. From the start, however, my mother had wanted me to be a doctor.

One hot, thick summer afternoon when I was six, my mother called me up to her bedroom. My father was away in Columbus on business, and she said to me, "Bobby, would you like to try rubbing my head for me?"

"Sure," I said, delighted at the chance to do a grownup's job.

The first page of a short manuscript should include your name, address, phone number and the approximate word length.

Scott Edelstein
2706 West 43 Street, Suite 102
Minneapolis, MN 55410
(612) 929-9123

Agent:
Bobbe Siegel
41 West 83 Street
New York, NY 10024
(212) 877-4985

IT ALL HAPPENED SO FAST

A Novel by Scott Edelstein

Proposed Length: 75,000 words

A book manuscript cover sheet should include contact information for both the author and the agent (if the author has one).

Scott Edelstein *has published seven books, three specifically for writers. He has had 30 pieces of short fiction published in magazines such as* Ellery Queen's Mystery Magazine, Artlines *and* City Miner. *He is editor of the science fiction anthology,* Future Pastimes.

between countries in North America—U.S. writers sending return postage to Canadian publishers (and vice versa) must use IRCs.

Main branches of local banks will cash foreign checks, but keep in mind payment quoted in our listings by foreign publishers is usually payment in their currency. Also note reporting time is longer in most overseas markets. To save time and money, you may want to include a return postcard (with IRC) with your submission and forego asking for a manuscript to be returned.

Some mailing tips. Manuscripts under five pages long can be folded into thirds and sent in a business-sized envelope. For submissions of five pages or more, however, mail it flat in a 9x12 or 10x13 envelope. Your manuscript will look best if it is mailed in an envelope only slightly larger. For the return envelope, fold it in half, address it to yourself and add a stamp (or clip IRCs to it with a paper clip).

Mark both of your envelopes in all caps, FIRST CLASS MAIL or SPECIAL FOURTH CLASS MANUSCRIPT RATE. The second method is cheaper, but it is handled the same as Parcel Post (Third Class) and is only for manuscripts weighing more than one pound and mailed within the U.S. First Class mailing assures fastest delivery and better handling

Book Manuscripts should be mailed in a sturdy box (a ream-size typing paper box works well). Tape the box shut and tape corners to reinforce them. To ensure your manuscript's safe return, enclose a self-addressed and stamped insulated bag mailer. You may want to check with the United Postal Service (UPS) or other mailing services for rates when mailing large manuscript packages.

If you use an office or personal postage meter, do not date the return envelope—it could cause problems if the manuscript is held too long before being returned. First Class mail is forwarded or returned automatically. Mark Third or Fourth Class return envelopes with "Return Postage Guaranteed" to have them returned.

If you send a cover letter with a Fourth Class manuscript, you must indicate this on the envelope (FIRST CLASS LETTER ENCLOSED) and include First Class postage.

It is not necessary to insure or certify your submission. In fact, many publishers do not appreciate receiving unsolicited manuscripts in this manner. Your best insurance is to always keep a copy of all submissions and letters.

Manuscript mechanics. A professionally presented manuscript will not guarantee publication. Yet on the other hand, a handwritten story in pencil on the back of your shopping list will almost always be rejected no matter how well written it is. A sloppy, hard-to-read manuscript will not be read—publishers simply do not have the time. Here's a list of suggested submission techniques for polished manuscript presentation:

- Use white, 8½×11 bond paper, preferably 16 or 20 lb. weight. The paper should be heavy enough so that it will not show pages underneath it and strong enough to take handling by several people. Do not use onion skin or erasable paper.
- Type your manuscript on a typewriter with a dark ribbon. Make sure the letters are clean and crisp. You can also use a computer printer, but avoid hard-to-read dot matrix. Near-letter or letter quality is acceptable.
- Proofread carefully. Most editors will not mind an occasional white-out, but do not send a marked up manuscript or one with many typos. Also keep a dictionary, thesaurus and stylebook handy.
- Always double space and leave a 1¼ inch margin on all sides of the page. For a short story manuscript, your first page should include your name, address and phone number (single-spaced) in the upper left corner. In the upper right, indicate an approximate word count. Center the name of your story about one-third of the way down, skip two or three lines and center your byline (byline is optional). Skip three lines and begin your story.
- For subsequent pages, include your last name and a page number in the upper right hand corner.
- For book manuscripts, use a separate cover sheet. Put your name, address and phone

U.S. Postage by the Page

by Carolyn Hardesty

Mailing costs can be an appreciable part of writing expenditures. The chart below can help save money as well as time by allowing you to figure the fees for sending your manuscripts to prospective publishers. A good supply of stamps in denominations of 25¢ and 20¢ can save you many trips to the post office.

Postage rates are listed by numbers of pages (using 20 lb. paper) according to the most commonly used envelopes and their self-addressed, stamped envelopes (SASEs). While most writers prefer to send their work First Class, Third Class is becoming a choice for some. Third Class moves more slowly, but it costs less than First Class after the first 4 ounces. Also, it is permissible in Third Class to include a letter pertaining to the material inside.

First Class mail weighing more than 11 ounces is assessed according to weight plus geographical zone.

Postcards can be a bargain for writers. If the postage costs are higher than another computer printout or photocopied version of a manuscript, a postcard can be used for the editor's reply. The cost is 15¢.

For short manuscripts or long queries, use a #10 (business-size) envelope with a 25¢ stamp. Four pages is the limit if you are including a SASE. The cost is 30¢ to Canada. Another option is the 6×9 envelope. For 1-3 pages, postage is 25¢ in the U.S. and 30¢ to Canada. For 1-7 pages with SASE, cost is 45¢ in the U.S. and 52¢ to Canada.

Other services include certified mail, 85¢; return receipts, 90¢; and insurance for typing and production costs, 70¢ for $50 liability; $1.50 for $100. These services plus manuscripts accompanied by photographs, slides, cardboard inserts or other items necessitate individual weighings at a postal station.

Ounces	9×12 9×12 SASE number of pages	9×12 SASE (for return trips) number of pages	First Class Postage	Third Class Postage	Postage from U.S. to Canada
under 2	. . .	1 to 2	$ .35*	$ .45	$ .40*
2	1 to 4	3 to 8	.45	.45	.52
3	5 to 10	9 to 12	.65	.65	.74
4	11 to 16	13 to 19	.85	.85	.96
5	17 to 21	20 to 25	1.05	1.00	1.18
6	22 to 27	26 to 30	1.25	1.00	1.40
7	28 to 32	31 to 35	1.45	1.10	1.62
8	33 to 38	36 to 41	1.65	1.10	1.84
9	39 to 44	42 to 46	1.85	1.20	2.06
10	45 to 49	47 to 52	2.05	1.20	2.28
11	50 to 55	53 to 57	2.25	1.30	2.50

***This cost includes an assessment for oversized mail that is light in weight.**

Carolyn Hardesty's short fiction has appeared in Four Minute Fictions, The North American Review *and the* Montana Review. *Her essays have appeared in several collections including* The Best American Essays of 1989. *She is also editor of* Iowa Woman *magazine.*

Canadian Postage by the Page

by Barbara Murrin

The following chart is for the convenience of Canadian writers sending domestic mail and American writers sending an envelope with International Reply Coupons (IRCs) or Canadian stamps for return of a manuscript from a Canadian publisher.

For complete postage assistance, use in conjunction with the U.S. Postage by the Page. Remember that manuscripts returning from the U.S. to Canada will take a U.S. stamped envelope although the original manuscript was sent with Canadian postage. This applies to return envelopes sent by American writers to Canada, too, which must be accompanied with IRCs or Canadian postage.

In a #10 envelope, you can have up to five pages for 38¢ (on manuscripts within Canada) or 44¢ (on manuscripts going to the U.S.). If you enclose a SASE, four pages is the limit. If you use 10×13 envelopes, send one page less than indicated on the chart.

IRC's are worth 44¢ Canadian postage but cost 95¢ to buy in the U.S. (Hint to U.S. writers: If you live near the border or have a friend in Canada, stock up on Canadian stamps. Not only are they more convenient than IRCs, they are cheaper.)

Canada Post has made major changes in designation of types of mail, as follows:

Standard Letter Mail	Minimum size: 9cm × 14cm (3⅝″×5½″); Maximum size: 14cm × 24.5cm (5½″×9⅝″); Maximum thickness: 5mm (3/16″)
Oversize Letter Mail	Minimum size: 14cm × 24.5cm (5½″×9⅝″); Maximum size: 27cm ×38cm (10⅞″×15″); Maximum thickness: 2cm (13/16″)
International Letter Mail	Minimum size: 9cm × 14cm (3⅝″×5½″); Maximum size: Length + width + depth 90cm (36″) Greatest dimension must not exceed 60cm (24″)

Insurance: To U.S. and within Canada – 45¢ for each $100 coverage to a maximum coverage of $1000. International – 65¢ for each $100 coverage to a maximum coverage of $1000.
Registered Mail: $2.70 plus postage (air or surface – any destination). Legal proof of mailing and indemnity coverage of $100 included. Add 37¢ for each additional $100 coverage desired to a maximum coverage of $1000.
Certified Mail: $1.55 plus postage (within Canada, only). Signed proof of delivery is automatically returned to you.

Weight up to	9×12 envelope, 9×12 SASE number of pages*	9×12 SASE (for return trips) number of pages	Canada Standard	Canada Oversize	First Class to U.S. Standard	First Class to U.S. Oversize
30 g/1.07 oz.	. . .	1 to 3	$ .38	$ .48	$ .44	$ .54
50 g/1.78 oz.	1 to 4	4 to 7	.59	.76	.64	.98
100 g/3.5 oz.	5 to 14	8 to 18	.76	.76	. . .	.98
200 g/7.1 oz.	15 to 46	19 to 49	(1.14)	1.14		1.76
300 g/10.7 oz.	47 to 57	50 to 61	(1.52)	1.52		2.20
400 g/14.2 oz.	58 to 79	62 to 82	(1.90)	1.90		3.08
500 g/17.8 oz.	80 to 101	83 to 104	(2.28)	2.28		3.96
1.0 kg/2.2 lbs.	102 to 208	105 to 212	**	**	(air pkt.)	7.00

*Based on 20 lb. paper and 2 adhesive labels per envelope.
**For Canadian residents mailing parcels 1 kg. and over within Canada (domestic mail), rates vary according to destination. Ask your Post Master for the chart for your area.

Barbara Murrin *owns and operates a desk-top publishing business in Williams Lake, British Columbia. She teaches business subjects at a nearby community college and, when there is time, writes romance. Her entry was a semi-finalist in a recent Romance Writers of America competition.*

in the upper left corner and word count in the upper right. Some writers list their agent's name and address in the upper right (word count is then placed at the bottom of the page). Center your title and byline about half way down the page. Start your first chapter on the next page. Begin by centering the chapter number and chapter title (if there is one) about one-third of the way down the page. Be sure to include your last name and page number in the upper right of this page and each page to follow. Start each chapter with a new page.

- There are a number of ways to count the number of words in your piece. One way is to count the number of words in five lines and divide that number by five to find an average. Then count the number of lines and multiply to find the total words. For long pieces, you may want to count exactly how many words in the first three pages, divide by three and multiply by the number of pages you have.
- Always keep a copy. Manuscripts do get lost. To avoid expensive mailing costs, send only what is required. If a publisher asks for two sample chapters, only send two. If you are including artwork or photos, but you are not positive they will be used, send photocopies. Artwork is hard to replace.
- Most publishers do not expect you to provide artwork and some insist on selecting their own illustrators, but if you have suggestions, please let them know. Magazine publishers work in a very visual field and are usually open to ideas.
- If you want a reply or if you want your manuscript returned, enclose a self-addressed, stamped envelope (SASE). For most letters, a business-size (#10) envelope will do. Avoid using any envelope too small for an 8½x11 sheet of paper. For manuscripts, be sure to include enough postage and an envelope large enough to contain it. If you are requesting a magazine, send an envelope big enough to fit. When in doubt, you can send a label with your address and stamps.
- When sending electronic (disk or modem) submissions, contact the publisher first for specific information and follow the directions carefully.
- Keep accurate records. This can be done in a number of ways, but be sure to keep track of where your stories are and how long they have been "out." Write down submission dates. If you do not hear about your submission for a long time—about three weeks to one month longer than the reporting time stated in the listing—you may want to contact the publisher. When you do, you will need an accurate record for reference.

Rights. Know what rights you are selling. The Copyright Law states that writers are selling one-time rights unless they and the publisher have agreed otherwise. Below is a list of various rights. Be sure you know exactly what rights you are selling before you agree to the sale.

- All rights allow a publisher to use the manuscript anywhere and in any form, including movie and book club sales, without further payment to the writer.
- Copyright is the legal right to exclusive publication, sale or distribution of a literary work. This right is that of the writer or creator of the piece and you need simply to include your name, date and the copyright symbol on your piece in order to copyright it. You can also register your copyright with the Copyright Office, although it is not necessary. Request information and forms from the Register of Copyrights, Library of Congress, Washington DC 20559.
- First Serial Rights mean that the publisher has the right to publish your work for the first time in any periodical.
- First North American Serial Rights are the same as First Serial, but they are only for publication on the North American Continent.
- One-time rights allow a publisher to publish a story one time.
- Reprint rights are permission to print a piece that was first published somewhere else.
- Second Serial Rights allow a publisher to print a piece in another periodical after it appeared for the first time in book form or in a magazine.
- Subsidiary rights are all rights other than book publishing rights included in a book

contract such as book club rights, movie rights and paperback rights.

- Work-for-hire is work that does not belong to the creator. If you do work-for-hire, you do not own the copyright and cannot sell any rights. For example, if you write a pamphlet for your company as an employee, generally the rights to that material do not belong to you. Writers doing work-for-hire are usually paid a flat fee for the work and do not collect royalties or other payments.

Market conditions are constantly changing! If you're still using this book and it is 1991 or later, buy the newest edition of* Novel & Short Story Writer's Market *at your favorite bookstore or order directly from Writer's Digest Books.

Literary and Small Circulation Magazines

Literary journals and small circulation magazines offer new writers an excellent opportunity for publication. This year we've redefined the criteria for inclusion in this section. Some of the small magazines, whose thrust is commercial but whose size, payment methods and openness to new writers more closely resemble literary publications, are included in this section. About 15 magazines that previously appeared in the Commercial Periodicals section and whose circulations were under 10,000 were moved to this section.

This new criteria has added magazines that are highly specialized. Some are designed specifically for readers interested in a sport or readers who practice a particular religion. Be sure to read the listings to make sure your work fits the publication to which you are submitting.

This section is the largest and fastest growing section in the book. Each year we lose some publications, but we also add many. To narrow your search, check the Category Index in the back of the book to help you locate the literary and small circulation publications best suited to your work.

Types of literary and small circulation magazines

You can often tell a lot about a magazine by its title. We have found that magazines listed in this section whose titles include the word "writer" in them are most open to new writers. Many are published by a small group of writers and are open to almost any type of writing. Horror and science fiction magazines are often easily identified by their titles.

University-backed publications and magazines, using state names, are usually looking for literary material and only infrequently consider genre or popular fiction.

A growing number of magazines listed in this section can be considered micro press. These publications, commonly one-man operations, are sometimes known as 'zines. They offer experimental or avant garde (even bizarre) material mixed with a variety of graphics and clip art. These publications almost never pay writers and don't have widespread circulation but can be outlets for work that may be considered too far out for most publications. Reading 'zines can also be a lot of fun.

Check the descriptive information in the listings. A magazine printed on acid-free paper and perfect bound will often carry more prestige than one photocopied on 20 lb. bond paper. Yet, keep in mind that publications produced inexpensively are the most open to the work of new writers.

This year we've added two literary bulletin boards—perhaps a wave for the future. These computer services publish stories transmitted over a modem. They offer opportunities for readers to comment on the material displayed and often offer interactive fiction and group stories. Writers are paid either in bulletin board time or in cash. Some writers worry about copyright infringement, but works on bulletin board are protected under existing copyright laws. Keep a hard copy just in case.

The pros and cons

Many of the publications in this section do not pay writers for their work. Some pay only in contributor's copies and those that do pay often pay very little. Yet there are a number of reasons publication in literary and small circulation journals is appealing.

The opportunity to publish is perhaps the main reason most writers submit to the markets in this section. Not only do they help you build publication credits, but they also help new writers gain valuable publishing experience. Publication credits of almost any type tell commercial magazine editors and book publishers that you know the ropes.

The second reason many turn to literary journals is prestige. Publication in *The Paris Review*, *Cimarron Review* or *The North American Review* carries weight in the literary community. Many book publishers tell us they look for new talent in the pages of these prestige literary magazines.

Also with the growing interest in publishing short story collections, publication of your short stories can attract attention for a future book of your own stories. In addition some of the more prestigious literary magazines do pay writers well.

One of the major concerns for most writers submitting to small magazines is the stability factor. If a magazine has been around a long time, or has university or state funding, chances are good that the magazine will continue publishing. For new, small, independent publications, however, the chance of their folding within one year is high.

Size of staff can also be a problem. Editors often don't foresee the number of manuscripts their listing may bring. They may have said they report back to writers within one or two weeks, but are soon overwhelmed by the number of manuscripts they receive. Wait an additional three or four weeks before querying a magazine about your story. Chances are they just fell behind.

Occasionally we list a magazine that requires a subscription or a small fee for submission. This information is given in italics within a listing. If you are asked to submit a fee from a magazine whose listing does not reflect such a fee, please let us know. We want our listings to be as accurate as possible.

How to submit

Once you have obtained a sample copy and writers' guidelines and decide which magazine is best suited to your work, you will want to send the manuscript. Unless the submission guidelines or listing says otherwise, send your complete manuscript with a cover letter and a SASE for a reply. Remember, when sending to a Canadian magazine from the U.S. or vice versa, include International Reply Coupons instead of stamps.

Your cover letter should be brief—keep it to one or two pages. Avoid giving a lot of personal information unless it is directly related to your story. Your letter should spark interest in the story, but not tell the whole story.

As with commercial publications, professionalism counts. Send clean, typo-free, double-spaced material. While a clean manuscript does not secure publication, one that cannot be read will not be read.

Avoid the blanket-submission method. Many writers go through the listings alphabetically, sending to the "As" first. Not only do they miss important listings later in the section, but they also flood magazines at the beginning of the section. Take the time to explore the listings here to find those magazines most likely to be interested in your work.

If you are interested in learning more about fanzines, see the quarterly magazine, *Factsheet Five* (6 Arizona Ave., Rensselaer NY 12144-4502). For more literary magazines that feature poetry see, *Poet's Market* (Writer's Digest Books, 1507 Dana Ave., Cincinnati OH 45207) and *The International Directory of Little Magazines and Small Presses* (Dustbooks, Box 100, Paradise CA 95967).

Here's the ranking system we've used to categorize the listings in this section.

I Publication encourages beginning writers or unpublished writers to submit work for consideration and publishes new writers frequently;
II Publication accepts work by established writers and by new writers of exceptional talent;
III Publication does not encourage beginning writers; prints mostly writers with previous publication credits and a very few new writers;
IV Special-interest or regional publication, open only to writers in certain genres or on certain subjects or from certain geographical areas.

ABBEY (II), White Urp Press, 5360 Fallriver Row Court, Columbia MD 20144. Editor: David Greisman. Magazine: 8½×11; 18-26 pages; Xerox paper; illustrations. "Unassumed intelligence in a publication of finite production for the type of person who knows the pure poetry of Molson Ale." Quarterly. Estab. 1970. Circ. 200.
Needs: Literary, contemporary, prose poem, science fiction and regional (appreciation of Maryland). "Nothing political! Nothing pornographic." Accepts 3-6 mss/year. Receives approximately 5 unsolicited fiction mss each month. Does not read mss in summer. Length: 1,000-2,000 words. Sometimes recommends other markets.
How to Contact: Query with SASE. Accepts computer printout submissions. Reports in 1 month. Publishes ms 3-9 months after acceptance. Sample copy 50¢.
Payment: 1-2 free author's copies.
Terms: Acquires one-time rights.
Advice: "Plug in the typewriter. Buy stamps. Don't imitate Thomas Hardy. Drink less than Behan or Thomas. Tell stories like Frederic Raphael." Most mss are rejected because "the stories themselves aren't interesting. Also, too many writers tend to lose their narrative strengths by introducing gimmicks and tricks where they are least needed. I'll accept nothing more than 6-7 pages. Know the mag you submit to. A good 'fit' does the writer and the magazine proud."

ACM, (ANOTHER CHICAGO MAGAZINE) (II), Another Chicago Press, Box 11223, Chicago IL 60611. (312)524-1289. Editors: Lee Webster and Barry Silesky. Fiction Editor: Sharon Solwitz. Magazine: 5½×8½; 150-200 pages; "art folio each issue." Estab. 1977.
Needs: Contemporary, literary, experimental, feminist, gay/lesbian, ethnic, humor/satire, prose poem, translations and political/socio-historical. Receives 75-100 unsolicited fiction mss each month. Recently published work by Fred Nadis, Curtis White, Gary Soto; published new writers in the last year. Sometimes recommends other markets.
How to Contact: Unsolicited mss acceptable with SASE. Accepts computer printout submissions. Publishes ms 6 months to 1 year after acceptance. Sample copies are available for $8 ppd. Reports in 2 months.
Payment: Small honorarium plus contributor's copy.
Terms: Acquires first North American serial rights.
Advice: "Get used to rejection slips, and don't get discouraged. Keep query and introductory letters short. Make sure ms has name and address on every page, and that it is clean, neat and proofread. We are looking for stories with freshness and originality in subject angle and style."

ACTA VICTORIANA (I, II), 150 Charles St. West, Toronto, Ontario M5S 1K9 Canada. Editor: Emma Thom. Magazine: 9½×13; 40 pages; glossy paper; cornwall cover; illustrations and photos. "We publish the poetry, prose, drawings and photographs of university students as well as of other writers. The magazine reaches the University of Toronto community as well as students of other universities. Semiannually. Estab. 1875. Circ. 1,500+.
Needs: Contemporary, ethnic, experimental, humor/satire, literary, mainstream, prose poem. Accepts 4-5 mss/issue; 8-10 mss/year. Publishes ms 2 months after acceptance. Recently published work by Craig Stephenson, Peter McCallum and Douglas Brown; published new writers within the last year. Length: 1,500 words maximum.
How to Contact: Send complete manuscript with cover letter, which should include information about the writer's previous publishing credits and biography. Reports in 2 months on mss. SASE. Simultaneous and photocopied submissions OK. Accepts computer printout submissions. Sample copy and fiction guidelines for $3 and 9×12 SAE.
Payment: Pays contributor's copies.
Advice: "University publications such as ours offer beginning fiction writers good opportunities to get published. If your piece is innovative and exciting, yet at the same time well-crafted, you will have a good chance of getting published. Editors change yearly in this student journal, yet our editorial policy remains roughly the same."

ADARA (IV), 905 Wild Circle, Clarkston GA 30021. (404)296-8463. Editor: Elizabeth Shaw. Magazine: 8½×11; 100 pages; 60 lb cover stock; illustrations; photos. *All materials must be related to Doctor Who.* Semiannually. Estab. 1986. Circ. 100.

Needs: Adventure, fantasy, feminist, gay, historical, humor/satire, prose poem, science fiction, serialized/excerpted novel, *all* set in the universe of Doctor Who. No "Mary Sue" (authoress gets Doctor) stories; nothing sexual, obscene, or explicitly gory. Buys 5 mss/issue; 10-12 mss/year. Manuscripts usually published in next issue after acceptance. Recently published work by Janet Reedman, Ed Oram and Autumn Lee. Published new writers within the last year. Length: 7,500 words preferred. Publishes short shorts. Length: 2 pages. Sometimes critiques rejected mss and recommends other markets.

How to Contact: Send complete ms with cover letter, which should state "where else author has been published, if story is simultaneous submission, whether it has been published elsewhere." Reports in 2 weeks on queries; 1 month on mss. SASE for ms, not needed for query. Photocopied submissions OK. Accepts computer printout submissions. Accepts electronic submissions via IBM compatible computer, 5¼ disk, in RFT/DCA on Displaywriter 3. Sample copy $8. Fiction guidelines free.

Payment: Pays in contributor's copies.

Terms: Acquires one-time rights. Sends galleys to author.

Advice: "Grammar and spelling are very important. I do reject incoherent stories, which I don't consider 'modern' or 'experimental'—just incoherent. My readers are international (Canada, Great Britain and Australia as well as the USA), so few local-interest-only references should be used. No one is ever turned down for too *high* an intellectual content. Stories emphasizing character over action are preferred, especially those demonstrating that we are all, and have all felt, alien *somewhere*, and we can, nevertheless, get along."

ADRIFT(II), Writing: Irish, Irish American and . . ., #4D, 239 E. 5th St., New York NY 10003. Editor: Thomas McGonigle. Magazine: 8×11; 32 pages; 60 lb paper stock; 65 lb cover stock; illustrations; photos. "Irish-Irish American as a basis—though we are interested in advanced writing from anywhere." Semiannually. Estab. 1983. Circ. 1,000+.

Needs: Contemporary, erotica, ethnic, experimental, feminist, gay, lesbian, literary, translations. Receives 40 unsolicited mss/month. Buys 3 mss/issue. Recent issues have included work by Francis Stuart. Published new writers within the last year. Length: open. Sometimes critiques rejected mss and recommends other markets.

How to Contact: Send complete ms. Reports as soon as possible. SASE for ms. Photocopied submissions OK. Accepts computer printout submissions. Sample copy $5.

Payment: Pays $7.50-300.

Terms: Pays on publication for first rights.

Advice: "The writing should argue with, among others, James Joyce, Flann O'Brien, Juan Goytisolo, Ingeborg Bachmann, E.M. Cioran, Max Stirner, Patrick Kavanagh."

THE ADROIT EXPRESSION (I), Box 73, Courtney PA 15029. (412)379-8019. Editor: Xavier F. Aguilar. Newspaper: 8½×11; 3-5 pages; 20 lb paper and cover stock; some illustrations. For the aspiring writer, poet and graphic artist. Triannually. Estab. 1986. Circ. 75.

Needs: Adventure, contemporary, experimental, fantasy, literary, mainstream, prose poem, romance (contemporary). No erotica. Receives 10 unsolicited mss/month. Accepts 4-8 mss/issue; 12-24 mss/year. Recently published work by Becky Knight, Marsha Powers and Deborah T. Johnson. Published work by previously unpublished writers in the last year. Length: 1,000 words minimum; 3,000 words maximum.

How to Contact: Send complete ms. Reports in 1 month on mss. "Please keep copies of works submitted as none can be returned." SASE. Photocopied submissions and reprint submissions OK. Sample copy $4.

Payment: "A byline and one contributor's copy is disbursement for contributions and all rights remain with authors."

AEGEAN REVIEW (IV), Suite 2A, 220 West 19th St., New York NY 10011. Editor: Dinos Sitotis. Fiction Editor: Barbara Fields. Magazine: 7×10; 80 pages; 60 lb paper; laminated cover; illustrations and photos. "*Aegean Review* is devoted to subjects Greek, fiction, essays, poetry and art. Authors are Americans, Greeks and Greek-Americans. Our subscribers are Greek-American predominantly, but

The double dagger before a listing indicates that the listing is new in this edition. New markets are often the most receptive to freelance contributions.

we have many readers who are simply interested in literature or in Greece." Semiannually. Estab. 1986. Circ. 3,000.

Needs: Greek subjects. "Fiction must be well-written and have a tie to Greece, however tenuous." Receives 5 unsolicited mss/month. Buys 2 mss/issue; 4 mss/year. Publishes ms within one year of acceptance. Recently published work by Jorge Luis Borges, Menis Koumandareas and Truman Capote. Length: 3,000 words average.

How to Contact: Send manuscript and cover letter. Cover letter should include basic information about writer and manuscript. Reports in 9 months. SASE for ms. Simultaneous, photocopied and reprint submissions OK. Accepts computer printout submissions. Sample copy for $5.

Payment: Pays $25-100, "but if we found something we liked very much and it was more, we would pay for it."

Terms: Pays on publication for first rights or first North American serial rights. Sends galleys to author.

Advice: "Choosing fiction is largely a subjective and personal matter for us. We try to emphasize excellence in writing. We find that we receive quite a few amateurish manuscripts, almost unreadable. We solicit manuscripts from writers who we know have had either professional or personal experiences with Greece or Greek literature."

AERIAL (II), Box 25642, Washington DC 20007. (202)333-1544. Editor: Rod Smith. Magazine: 6x9; 64 pages; 75 lb paper; 10 pt. CIS cover stock; photos on cover only. Semiannually. Estab. 1984. Circ. 750.

Needs: Experimental, literary, translations. Receives 10 mss/month. Accepts 1-2 mss/issue; 3-4 mss/year. Publishes ms within 3-12 months of acceptance (average). Length: ½ page-10 pages. Sometimes critiques rejected mss.

How to Contact: Send ms—short fiction or excerpts—with or without cover letter. Reports in 1 week to 1 month. SASE. Photocopied and reprint submissions OK. Accepts computer printout submissions. Sample copy for $6.

Payment: Pays in contributor's copies.

Terms: Acquires one-time rights.

Advice: "We consider ourselves politically and aesthetically 'dissident.' Believe that it is important and necessary to explore alternative modes of conceptualization given the current dangerous global situation."

‡AFTER HOURS (II), A Magazine of Dark Fantasy and Horror, 21541 Oakbrook, Mission Viejo CA 92692-3044. Editor: William G. Raley. Magazine: 8½×11; 48-56 pages; #3 grade offset paper; #3 grade uncoated cover; about 3 illustrations per issue; photographs sometimes with interviews. "*After Hours* features stories too weird or off-the-wall to happen during the day. Therefore, all stories *must* take place after dark! For adults and young adults." Quarterly. Estab. 1989. Circ. 750.

Needs: Condensed/excerpted novel, fantasy, horror, humor/satire, psychic/supernatural/occult, suspense/mystery. "No science fiction, 'typical' crime stories (where the only motive is murder, rape, or robbery), political or military." Receives 200 unsolicited mss/month. Buys 12 mss/issue; 50 mss/year. Publishes ms "about 6 months" after acceptance. Recently published work by J.N. Williamson, Steve Rasnictem and Ronald Kelly. Length: 2,500 words preferred; 6,000 words maximum. Publishes short shorts.

How to Contact: Send complete ms with cover letter. Include "where you heard about *After Hours*, *brief* list of credits. Cover letter is optional." Reports in 2 months on mss. SASE for ms or query. Photocopied and reprint submissions OK. Accepts computer printout submissions. Accepts electronic submissions via disk. Sample copy for $4. Fiction guidelines for #10 SAE and 1 first class stamp.

Payment: Pays $60 maximum (1¢/word) and one contributor's copy.

Terms: Pays on acceptance for first North American serial rights. Sends galleys to author.

Advice: "Readers don't want to wait around for something to happen. I need action (or at least an atmosphere of dread) on page one. Good characterization is a must. As far as plots go, don't be afraid to be original. I avoid overdone plots. There are so many stories where people come back from the dead, or turn into a monster, that it's no longer entertaining. Characters should be believable, with women portrayed as equals. No excessive blood or violence. If your story has a fresh plot (or a new twist on an old one) or is just plain strange, you've probably got a sale."

AGNI (II), Creative Writing Program, Boston University, 236 Bay State Rd., Boston MA 02215. (617)354-8522. Editor-in-Chief: Askold Melnyczuk. Magazine: 5½×8½; 212-300 pages; 55 lb booktext paper; glossy cover stock; occasional illustrations and photos. "Eclectic literary magazine publishing first-rate poems and stories." Semiannually. Estab. 1972.

Needs: Stories, excerpted novels, prose poems and translations. Receives 150 unsolicited fiction mss/month. Accepts 4-7 mss/issue, 8-12 mss/year. Recently published work by Stephen Minot, Suzanne Gardinier, and Marco Papa. Rarely critiques rejected mss or recommends other markets.
How to Contact: Send complete ms with SASE and cover letter listing previous publications. Simultaneous and photocopied submissions OK. Accepts computer printout submissions. Reports in 1 month. Sample copy $5.
Payment: Pays $10/page for poetry, $40 for prose; 3 contributor's copies; extra copies 60% of retail price.
Terms: Pays on publication for first North American serial rights. Sends galleys to author. Copyright reverts to author upon publication.
Advice: "Read *Agni* carefully to understand the kinds of stories we publish. Read—everything, classics, literary journals, bestsellers."

ALABAMA LITERARY REVIEW (II), Smith 264, Troy State University, Troy AL 36082. (205)566-3000, ext. 306. Editor: Theron Montgomery. Fiction Editor: Jim Davis. Magazine: 6×11½; 100+ pages; top paper quality; some illustrations; photos. "National magazine for a broad range of the best contemporary fiction, poetry and essays and drama that we can find." Semiannually. Estab. 1987.
Needs: Condensed novel, contemporary, erotica, ethnic, experimental, fantasy, feminist, historical (general), humor/satire, literary, prose poem, regional, science fiction, serialized/excerpted novel, suspense/mystery, translations. "Serious writing." Receives 50 unsolicited fiction mss/month. Buys 2 fiction mss/issue. Publishes ms 5-6 months after acceptance. Published work by Joseph Lane, Thomas Wooten, and Mary Jane Mayo; published new writers within the last year. Length: 2,000-3,000 words average. Publishes short shorts of 1,000 words. Sometimes comments on rejected mss and recommends other markets.
How to Contact: Send complete ms with cover letter or submit through agent. Reports on queries in 2 weeks; on mss in 2-4 weeks (except in summer). SASE. Simultaneous submissions OK. Accepts computer printouts, no dot-matrix "unless Xeroxed." Sample copy $4 plus 50 postage.
Payment: Pays in contributor's copies.
Terms: First rights returned to author.
Advice: "Read our publication first. Avoid negative qualities pertaining to gimmickry and a self-centered point of view. We are interested in any kind of writing if it is *serious* and *honest* in the sense of 'the human heart in conflict with itself.' "

ALASKA QUARTERLY REVIEW (II), University of Alaska, 3211 Providence Dr., Anchorage AK 99508. (907)786-1327. Fiction Editor: Ronald Spatz. Magazine: 6x9; 146 pages; 60 lb Glatfelter paper; 10 pt. C15 black ink varnish cover stock; photos on cover only. Magazine of "contemporary literary art and criticism for a general literary audience." Semiannually. Estab. 1982.
Needs: Contemporary, experimental, literary, prose poem and translations. Receives 50 unsolicited fiction mss/month. Accepts 5-11 mss/issue, 15-22 mss/year. Does not read mss May 15-August 15. Published new writers within the last year. Publishes short shorts. Occasionally critiques rejected mss.
How to Contact: Send complete ms with SASE. Photocopied submissions OK. Reports in 2 months. Publishes ms 6 months to 1 year after acceptance. Sample copy $4.
Payment: 1 free contributor's copy and a year's subscription.
Terms: Acquires first rights.
Advice: "We have made a significant investment in fiction. The reason is quality; serious fiction *needs* a market. Try to have everything build to a singleness of effect."

THE ALBANY REVIEW (II), 4 Central Ave., Albany New York 12210. (518)436-5787. Editor-in-Chief: Theodore Bouloukos II. Fiction Editor: Thomson H. Littlefield. Magazine: 11×14; 56-72 pages; premium 50 lb white paper; 91 lb media print satin cover stock; illustrations and photographs. "We consider ourselves a monthly feast for upscale, 28-56, literate, lively and interested readers." Monthly. Estab. 1987. Circ. 15,000.
Needs: Contemporary, experimental, humor/satire, literary, mainstream, prose poem, translations. "Second-person narration, coupled with minimalist prose, is a yawn for us. As well, we like generic romance only in our private lives." Receives 90-150 unsolicited mss/month. Accepts 5 mss/month; 3 mss/issue. Publishes ms 2-3 months after acceptance. Length: 3,000-4,000 words average; 750 words minimum; 10,000 words maximum.

Read the Business of Fiction section to learn the correct way to prepare and submit a manuscript.

How to Contact: Send complete ms with cover letter. Cover letter should include "brief biography with published credits." Reports in 2 weeks on queries; 3-4 weeks on mss. SASE. Reprint submissions OK. Computer printout submissions OK. Electronic submissions via Macintosh only. Sample copy $1.50. Fiction guidelines free for #10 SASE.
Payment: Pays in contributor's copies; charges for extras.
Terms: Acquires first rights.
Advice: Looks for "good solid, exact writing, whose flow of imagery conveys more than a spiritual strength but rather a resonance in the mind and soul. Strong, powerful writing is measured by form, function and tight composition. Obviously, well-developed characters and settings that take you there are rudimentary to all finished work—so we often look for surprises. As well, what Robert Frost said about the image a poem makes is true of good fiction: 'It all begins in delight and ends in wisdom.' "

‡THE ALCHEMIST (II), Box 123, Lasalle, Quebec H8R 3T7 Canada. Editor: Marco Fraticelli. Magazine: 5½×8½; b&w illustrations and photographs. "We publish prose in most issues with no prejudices in regard to style, but we tend to favor the experimental rather than the traditional." Published irregularly. Estab. 1974. Circ. 500.
Needs: Literary, feminist, gay, lesbian and psychic/supernatural/occult. Buys 1 ms/issue.
How to Contact: Send complete ms with SASE or IRC. Accepts computer printout submissions. Accepts disk submissions compatible with Apple. Prefers hard copy with disk submission. Reports in 1 month. Publishes ms an average of 6 months after acceptance. Sample copy $2.
Payment: Free author's copies.
Terms: Rights remain with author.
Advice: "Please—no American stamps on the SASE."

ALDEBARAN (II), Roger Williams College, Ferry Rd., Bristol RI 02809. (401)253-1040. Editor: Jodi L. Kehn. Magazine: 5½×8½; 60-80 pages; illustrations; photos. Literary publication of prose and poetry for a general audience. Published annually or twice a year. Estab. 1970.
Needs: Will consider all fiction. Receives approximately 10 unsolicited fiction mss each month. Does not read mss in summer. Preferred length: 10-15 pages or shorter. Critiques rejected mss when there is time.
How to Contact: Send complete ms with SASE and cover letter, which should include "information for possible contributor's notes—but cover letters will not influence decision on publication." Accepts computer printout submissions. Reports in 1 month. Sample copy $1 with SASE.
Payment: 2 free author's copies.
Terms: Copyright reverts to author on publication.
Advice: Mss are rejected because of "incomplete stories, no live character, basic grammatical errors; usually returned with suggestions for revision and character change."

ALLEGHENY REVIEW (IV), A National Journal of Undergraduate Literature, Box 32, Allegheny College, Meadville PA 16335. (814)332-6553. Editors: Nancy Williams and Erik Schuckers. Magazine: 6×9; 100 pages; 60 lb White Wove paper; illustrations; photos. "The *Allegheny Review* is an annual journal composed *entirely* of undergraduate contributions selected from submissions from colleges across the nation. Short fiction topics are open, the only restriction being status as an undergraduate student. Volume is aimed at the undergraduate student with an aim toward providing the missing communications link between undergraduate writers in this nation." Annually. Estab. 1983. Circ. 1,000.
Needs: Confession, contemporary, experimental, humor/satire, literary with any topic, mainstream. "All mss must possess adequate literary merit to be regarded as serious literature. Topics are open. The *Review* is intended primarily as a creative outlet for the undergraduate writer, and is suitable as a creative writing text. In the past three issues we have found the content to be extremely interesting to all levels of readers." Accepts 10-15 fiction mss per volume/year. Published new writers within the last year. Length: 5,000 words average. "Length necessary to tell the tale." Also publishes short shorts. Sometimes recommends other markets.
How to Contact: Send complete manuscript with cover letter (name of school, author currently attending; some background on the evolution/creation of the piece). Reports in 2 months on mss following January 31 deadline. No response in summer. SASE for ms. Photocopied submissions OK. Accepts computer printouts. Sample copy for 8x11 SAE and 3 first class stamps.
Payment: Free subscription to magazine, contributor's copies, charge for extras.
Terms: Acquires first rights.
Advice: "Selected story judged most outstanding by editors receives $50 award. Although we are entirely student run, we expect submissions with a high level of quality. Be professional and serious—*we are*. The *Review* is ideal for the developing writer to see how and what others in peer group are creating."

Close-up

Thomson Littlefield

The Albany Review

Regardless of trends, what makes a story good has not changed much over the years, says Dr. Thomson Littlefield, fiction editor for *The Albany Review*. Before joining the staff of the monthly literary journal, Littlefield taught English at the State University of New York at Albany for 29 years. Solid storytelling, a sense of drama and universal appeal continue to be reliable criteria for determining quality in fiction, he says.

"I look for stories dealing with humankind in God's world. Obedience and rebellion, birth and death, faithfulness and betrayal, duty and pleasure, joy and anguish—these are some of the themes readers respond to. Robert Frost once said 'it all begins in delight and ends in wisdom.' He was talking about poetry, but it holds true for fiction as well."

Yet the way a writer tells a story is almost as important as the theme, Littlefield adds. Stories selected for publication in *The Albany Review* also must be well-crafted. "The writing must be sensitive and imaginative and in keeping with the matter it is written about. I don't read very far if a submission shows no feel for language. We're willing to provide copyediting, but only for writers who demonstrate a gift for words."

The independent journal was established in 1987, but in this short time has built a circulation of 15,000, a fulltime staff of 10 and a reputation for quality. This reputation is reflected not only in its circulation figures, but also in the number of unsolicited submissions the magazine receives.

Littlefield receives 50 to 75 manuscripts each month, but publishes two or three each issue. At this point he is planning for issues up to one year ahead, so manuscripts accepted now may not be published until next year. In fairness to authors, however, he will get back to them on their submissions in no more than two months.

Because of the magazine's name, Littlefield says he sometimes receives cover letters from authors who say they sent their manuscript because it deals with Albany or the region. "Actually very little of the fiction we publish has a local setting, though I feel a flash of pleasure when I find something dealing with what I consider my world."

As far as specific subjects or other requirements, the magazine is open—in fact, quality is the only criteria. "I never refuse to consider a piece for reasons of length alone, but we do publish short pieces. Most are between 2,000 and 3,500." On the other hand, he is not against running shorter or longer pieces and even novel excerpts, as long as variety is maintained.

It's hard to pinpoint what he does not want to see, says Littlefield, except to say manuscripts are rejected for bad writing or "illiteracy on the part of the writer." He talks more freely about the joy of finding a publishable manuscript. "I cherish the discovery—discovery for me, for the characters, for the writer, for the reader. I do this for pleasure and it gives me *great* pleasure."

—*Robin Gee*

ALPHA BEAT SOUP (IV), 5110 Adam St., Montréal, Québec H1V 1W8 Canada. Editor: Dave Christy. Magazine: 7½×9; 95-125 pages; illustrations. "Beat and modern literature—prose, reviews and poetry." Semiannually. Plans special fiction issue. Estab. 1987. Circ. 250.

Needs: Erotica, experimental, literary and prose poem. Published work by Charles Bukowski, Joy Walsh and Arthur Knight; published new writers within the last year. Length: 600 words minimum; 1,000 words maximum. Sometimes recommends other markets.

How to Contact: Query first. Reports on queries ASAP. SASE. Simultaneous, photocopied and reprint submissions OK. Sample copy for $4.

Payment: Pays in contributor's copies.

Terms: Rights remain with author.

Advice: "*ABS* is the finest journal of its kind available today, having, with 6 issues, published the widest range of published and unpublished writers you'll find in the small press scene."

‡ALTERNATIVE FICTION & POETRY (IV), 7783 Kensington Ln., Hanover Park IL 60103. Editor: Philip Athans. Magazine: 8½×11; 50 pages; 20 lb white paper; vellum bristol cover; illustrations and photos. "Avant-garde or especially unique material of a highly experimental nature." Irregular. Estab. 1986. Circ. 1,000.

Needs: Experimental and translations. No religious, racist/sexist, science fiction, horror, romance. "Absolutely *no* simultaneous submissions, novels, novel excerpts or previously-published material accepted." Receives 250-300 unsolicited fiction mss/month; accepts 6-10 fiction mss/issue; 12-30 mss/year. Published work by Miekal And, William S. Burroughs and Gerry Reith; published new writers within the last year. Publishes short shorts. Occasionally critiques rejected mss. Sometimes recommends other markets.

How to Contact: Send complete ms. Reports in 2-6 months. SASE. Photocopied submissions OK. Accepts computer printout submissions. Sample copy $3. No response without SASE.

Payment: Pays in contributor's copies.

Terms: Acquires one-time rights. Publication copyrighted "only by the individual contributors."

‡AMARANTH (II), Tales of the Supernatural, MKASHEF Enterprises, P.O. Box 368, Poway CA 92064-0005. Editor: Alayne Gelfand. Magazine: 8½×11; 150 pages; 60 lb paper; full-color cover; illustrations. "Any supernatural, paranormal, inexplicable situation *EXCEPT* vampires, 'devil worship'*or* 'sword and sorcery' for adult, sophisticated, educated, literary audience." Annually. Estab. 1990.

Needs: Adventure, contemporary, erotica, ethnic, experimental, fantasy, feminist, gay, historical (general), lesbian literary, prose poem, romance (contemporary), science fiction, suspense/mystery. "We are *not* looking for 'gore horror' but the emotional/spiritual/psychic side of the supernatural. Ghosts, werewolves, witches, poltergeists, wraiths, succubus as well as bizarre or inexplicable situations are only a few acceptable subjects. No vampire or 'sword and sorcery' stories. No victimization of women. No 'singles bar' settings." Receives 5-30 unsolicited mss/month. Buys 5-15 mss/issue. Does not read mss September-March. Publishes ms 1 month to 1 year after acceptance. Agented fiction 1%. Length: 2,000 words preferred; 10,000 maximum. Publishes short shorts. Sometimes critiques rejected mss and recommends other markets.

How to Contact: Query first. Send for detailed guidelines. Include a *brief* biography of writing experience. Reports in 3 weeks on queries; 4 months on mss. SASE. Accepts photocopies, computer printouts or disk submissions (IBM WordPerfect). Sample copy for $15 but none available yet. Fiction guidelines for #10 SAE and one 1st class stamp.

Payment: Pays 1¢/word and contributor's copies.

Terms: Pays on publication for first North American serial rights.

Advice: "I am looking for unique ideas told in unique, beautiful, interesting ways. A story must grab me from word one and keep me moving through it and with it to the end. A manuscript that is handled professionally, that tells an unusual story with detailed characterization, that has lyrical writing and avoids clichéd situations and word usage will stand out of the pack."

‡THE AMARANTH REVIEW (I, II), Window Publications, P.O. Box 56235, Phoenix AZ 85079. (602)527-8085. Editor: Dana L. Yost. Magazine: 8½×11; 60-80 pages; 60 lb offset paper; 90 lb cover stock; illustrations and occasional photos. "Our theme is eclectic—we are interested in poetry and short fiction which deals with the human condition in its broadest possible expression. For an educated, thinking audience of those who enjoy quality poetry and fiction." Estab. 1989. Circ. 500.

Needs: Literary and contemporary. Plan to publish special fiction issue or an anthology in the future. Receives 100+ unsolicited mss/month. Accepts 8-10 mss/issue; 20 mss/year. Publishes ms 2-6 months after acceptance. Recently published work by Genni Gunn and Richard Ploetz. Length: 2,500 words average; 3,500 words maximum. Publishes short shorts. Sometimes critiques rejected mss and recommends other markets.

How to Contact: Send complete ms with cover letter. Include how the writer heard about us–brief bio is also welcome. Reports in 2 weeks on queries; 1 month on ms. SASE. Simultaneous and photocopied submissions OK. Accepts computer printout submissions. Accepts electronic submissions (IBM Word Perfect 5.0 only). Sample copy $5.50. Writer's guidelines for #10 SAE and 1 first class stamp.
Payment: Free subscription to magazine; pays in contributor's copies; charges for extras (50% discount.)
Terms: Acquires first North American serial rights.
Advice: "The one basic requirement is that the piece be good, quality fiction. But more specifically, we look for the piece to deal with some basic condition of the human existence, and we look for the piece to hit hard and knock us into thinking–really thinking–about the issue or circumstances of the story. My advice is for the writer to be honest with the story he or she is trying to tell–and this means no compromises; if you have to re-write your story a dozen times to get it right, do so, and then once you feel it is ready read it out loud, checking for errors you missed. Write from the heart, and write every day, and have the courage to send out your manuscripts when they are ready–keeping a journal is great for building the writing habit, but there comes a time when we must finally tuck our manuscripts into an envelope and give them a chance to make it on their own."

‡AMATEUR WRITERS JOURNAL (I), Four Seasons Poetry Club Magazine, R.V. Gill Publishing Co., 3457 Monroe St., Bellaire OH 43906. (614)676-0881. Editor: Rosalind Gill. Magazine: 8½×11; 38 pages; 20 lb paper; no cover; illustrations. "Stories, articles, essays and poetry on all subjects. No avant-garde or porno-type manuscripts of any kind accepted. Poetry, when seasonal, published only in the season for which it is appropriate. Same rule applies to stories. For a family audience." Bimonthly. Estab. 1967. Circ. 700+.
Needs: Adventure, contemporary, fantasy, horror, humor/satire, mainstream, religious/inspirational, contemporary romance, science fiction, suspense/mystery, young adult/teen. Receives around 300 fiction mss/month. Accepts 8 fiction mss/issue; 48 mss/year. Publishes ms "within 3 months" after acceptance. 1,200 words average; 1,500 words maximum. Sometimes critiques rejected mss and recommends other markets.
How to Contact: Send complete ms with cover letter. State whether you are offering first rights, or, if material has been published elsewhere, the name of the publication in which your work appeared. Reports on queries in 1 month; on mss in 1 week. SASE. Photocopied submissions OK. Accepts computer printout submissions. Sample copy available for $1.25 and 3 first class stamps. Fiction guidelines for #10 SAE and 2 first class stamps.
Payment: No payment.
Terms: Acquires one-time rights.
Advice: "I believe that all fiction writers should have a showplace for their work, and my magazine readers prefer fiction to non-fiction, although I accept both."

‡AMBERGRIS (I, II), Box 29919, Cincinnati OH 45229. Editor: Mark Kissling. Magazine: 5×8; 80-90 pages; 40 lb offset paper; 60 lb offset cover; illustrations; photographs. "*Ambergris* is a semi-annual, non-profit magazine dedicated to the discovery and publication of quality art and literature." Semiannually. Estab. 1987. Circ. 500.
Needs: "Excellent short fiction showing stylistic distinction. Contemporary themes, any subject". No simultaneous submissions accepted. No strictly preschool, juvenile, romance, serialized/excerpted novel or young adult. Receives 30-40 mss/month. Accepts 4 mss/issue. Publishes ms "up to one year" after acceptance. Word length open, prefers under 5,000 words.
How to Contact: Send complete ms with cover letter which should include a three-sentence biographical sketch. One work of fiction per submission. Reports on mss in 2 months. Enclose SASE for return of mss. simultaneous, Sample copy $3. Fiction guidelines free with SAE and 1 first class stamp.
Payment: Two contributor's copies, extras available at half cover price.
Terms: Acquires first North American serial rights.
Advice: "We give special consideration to works by Ohio writers and about the Midwest in general. We attempt to foster the emerging writer, but encourage beginning writers and others unfamiliar with our format to look at a sample copy before submitting work." Sponsors annual contest with $50 cash prizes for best poem and short story; send SASE for information.

AMELIA (II), 329 E St., Bakersfield CA 93304. (805)323-4064. Editor-in-Chief: Frederick A. Raborg, Jr. Magazine: 5½×8½; 124-136 pages; perfect bound; 60 lb high quality moistrite matte paper; kromekote cover; four-color covers; original illustrations; b&w photos. "A general review using fine fiction, poetry, criticism, belles lettres, one-act plays, fine pen-and-ink sketches and line drawings, sophisticated cartoons, book reviews and translations of both fiction and poetry for general readers with catholic tastes for quality writing." Quarterly. Plans special fiction issue each July. Estab. 1984. Circ. 1,250.

Needs: Adventure, contemporary, erotica, ethnic, experimental, fantasy, feminist, gay, historical (general), humor/satire, lesbian, literary, mainstream, prose poem, regional, science fiction, senior citizen/retirement, sports, suspense/mystery, translations, western. Nothing "obviously pornographic or patently religious." Receives 160-180 unsolicited mss/month. Buys up to 9 mss/issue; 25-36 mss/year. Published 4 new writers within the last year. Recently published Judson Jerome, Jack Curtis, Eugene Dubnov and Merrill Joan Gerber. Length: 3,000 words average; 1,000 words minimum; 5,000 words maximum. Usually critiques rejected ms. Sometimes recommends other markets.
How to Contact: Send complete manuscript. Cover letter with previous credits if applicable to *Amelia* and perhaps a brief personal comment to show personality and experience. Reports in 1 week on queries; 2 weeks-3 months on mss. SASE. Photocopied submissions OK. Accepts computer printout submissions; prefers letter-quality. Sample copy for $6.50. Fiction guidelines free for #10 SAE and 1 first class stamp.
Payment: Pays $35-50 plus 2 contributor's copies; extras with 20% discount.
Terms: Pays on acceptance. Buys first North American serial rights. Sends galleys to author "when deadline permits."
Advice: "Write carefully and well, but have a strong story to relate. I look for depth of plot and uniqueness, and strong characterization. Study manuscript mechanics and submission procedures. Neatness does count. There is a sameness—a cloning process—among most magazines today that tends to dull the senses. Magazines like *Amelia* will awaken those senses while offering stories and poems of lasting value."

AMERICAN DANE (II,IV), The Danish Brotherhood in America, 3717 Harney, Box 31748, Omaha NE 68131. (402)341-5049. Editor: Pamela K. Dorau. Magazine: 8¼×11; 20-28 pages; 40 lb paper; slick cover; illustrations and photos. "The *American Dane* is the official publication of the Danish Brotherhood. Corporate purpose of the Danish Brotherhood is to promote and perpetuate Danish culture and traditions and to provide Fraternal benefits and family protection." Estab. 1916. Circ. 8,900.
Needs: Ethnic. "Danish!" Receives 4 unsolicited fiction mss/month. Accepts 1 ms/issue; 12 mss/year. Reads mss during August and September only. Publishes ms up to one year after acceptance. Length: 1,000 words average; 3,000 words maximum. Publishes short shorts.
How to Contact: Query first. SASE. Simultaneous submissions OK. Accepts computer printout submissions, including dot-matrix. Sample copy for $1 and 9×12 SAE with 54¢ postage. Fiction guidelines free for 4×9½ SAE and 1 first class stamp.
Payment: Pays $15-$50.
Terms: Pays on publication for first rights. Publication not copyrighted.
Advice: "Think Danish!"

THE AMERICAN VOICE (II), 332 W. Broadway, Louisville KY 40202. (502)562-0045. Editors: Sallie Bingham and Frederick Smock. Magazine: 6×9; 110 pages; acid-free paper; 80 lb cover; photos occasionally. "An eclectic reader, publishing work by new and established writers in the U.S., Canada and South America, for a usually—but not necessarily—college educated audience." Quarterly. Estab. 1985. Circ. 1,500.
Needs: Experimental, feminist, gay, humor/satire, lesbian, literary, serialized/excerpted novel, translations. "Nothing that is racist, sexist, homophobic or classist." Receives 400 unsolicited mss/month. Buys 5 mss/issue; 20 mss/year. Publishes ms approximately 5 months after acceptance. Agented fiction 5%. No preferred word length. Publishes short shorts. Occasionally critiques rejected mss and recommends other markets.
How to Contact: Send complete ms with cover letter, which should include the writer's publishing history. Reports in 6 weeks on mss. SASE. Simultaneous and photocopied submissions OK. Accepts computer printout submissions. Sample copy for $5.
Payment: Pays $400—prose; $150—translator of prose, and free subscription to magazine.
Terms: Pays on publication for first North American serial rights. Sometimes sends galleys to author.

‡THE AMERICAS REVIEW (II,IV) A Review of Hispanic Literature and Art of the USA, Arte Publico Press, 4800 Calhoun, University of Houston, Houston, TX 77204-2090. (713)749-4768. Editors: Dr. Julian Olivares and Evangelina Vigil-Pinon. Magazine: 5½×8½; 128 pages; illustrations and photographs. "*The Americas Review* publishes contemporary fiction written by U.S. Hispanics—Mexican Americans, Puerto Ricans, Cuban Americans, etc." Quarterly. Estab. 1972.
Needs: Contemporary, ethnic, literary, women's, hispanic literature. No novels. Receives 12-15 fiction mss/month. Accepts 2-3 mss/issue; 8-12 mss/year. Publishes mss "6 months to 1 year" after acceptance. Length: 3,000-4,500 average number of words; 1,500 words minimum; 6,000 words maximum. Publishes short shorts. Sometimes critiques rejected mss and recommends other markets.
How to Contact: Send complete manuscript. Reports in 3 months. SASE. Photocopied submission OK. Accepts computer printout submissions, no dot-matrix. Accepts electronic submissions via IBM compatible disk. Sample copy $5; $10 double issue.

Payment: $50-200; 5 contributor's copies.
Terms: Pays on acceptance for first rights, and rights to 40% of fees if story is reprinted. Sponsors award for fiction writers.
Advice: "There has been a noticeable increase in quality in U.S. Hispanic literature."

‡THE AMHERST REVIEW (II), Box 1811, Amherst College, Amherst MA 01002. (413)542-2250. Editor: Josh Jacobs. Fiction Editor: Lisa Stanton. Magazine: 7½×8½; 60-70 pages; illustrations and photographs. "We are a college literary magazine publishing work by students, faculty and professionals. We seek submissions of poetry, fiction, and essay for the college community." Annually.
Needs: Adventure, confession, contemporary, ethnic, experimental, fantasy, feminist, gay, historical (general), horror, humor/satire, lesbian, mainstream, prose poem, psychic/supernatural/occult, regional, romance, science fiction, suspense/mystery, translations, western. "No sentimentality." Receives 10-20 unsolicited mss/month. Does not read mss March-August. Length: 4,500 words; 7,200 words maximum.
How to Contact: Send complete ms with cover letter. Reports in 4 months on mss. Accepts computer printout submissions. Sample copy for $5, SAE and $1 postage.
Payment: 2 free contributor's copies; $5 charge for extras.
Terms: Acquires first rights.

THE ANGLICAN MAGAZINE (II), The Anglican Church of Canada, 600 Jarvis St., Toronto, Ontario M4Y 2J6 Canada. (416)924-9192. Editor: John Bird. Magazine: half tabloid; 48 pages; upgraded newsprint paper; glossy cover stock; b&w illustrations; b&w inside photographs; color cover. "*The Anglican Magazine* calls forth from its readers a Christian response to family and social concerns. Encourages and aids the ministry of clergy and lay people. Especially interested in human rights and justice issues. Our readers are committed Christians, especially of the Anglican Church (Episcopal). Readers want to know about Anglican and other Christian life in all areas of the world. They want to know how they can minister with people in local communities." Published seven times a year. Estab. 1889. Circ. 10,000.
Needs: Literary, contemporary and humor. "We do not require religious/inspirational stories. No sentimental writing; no moralizing please!" Buys up to 1 ms/issue. Receives approximately 10 unsolicited fiction mss/month. "We publish work by little known authors. We definitely favour Canadian writers." Length: 1,000-1,500 words.
How to Contact: Send complete ms with SAE and IRC (*not US stamps*). Reports in 1 month on ms. Publishes ms 3-6 months after acceptance. Free sample copy.
Payment: Pays honorarium.
Advice: "Don't write long letters to the editor. Make sure you study the market; read the whole magazine, not just the fiction. We receive very few good stories. If you can write simply, with insight and sensitivity, let us see your work. If it's done well, fiction can be highly effective in informing and helping the reader to understand and respond to an issue – to know what it feels like to be a certain person in a certain situation. Stories do not have to be overly 'religious' to reflect the truth about God's children." Mss are rejected because they are "too long or there is too much moralizing. We sometimes 'discover' a beginning writer who has potential."

ANTAEUS (III), The Ecco Press, 26 W. 17th St., New York NY 10011. (212)645-2214. Editor-in-Chief: Daniel Halpern. Managing and Associate Editor: Lee Ann Chearneyi. Magazine: 6½×9; 275 pages; Warren old style paper; illustrations and photographs sometimes. "Literary magazine of fiction and poetry, literary documents, and occasional essays for those seriously interested in contemporary writing." Quarterly. Estab. 1970. Circ. 5,000.
Needs: Contemporary, literary, prose poem, excerpted novel, and translations. No romance, science fiction. Receives 600 unsolicited fiction mss/month. Recently published fiction by Richard Ford, Donald Hall, Joyce Carol Oates; published new writers within the last year. Rarely critiques rejected mss.
How to Contact: Send complete ms with SASE. Photocopied submissions OK; no multiple submissions. Accepts computer printout submissions; prefers letter-quality. Reports in 6-8 weeks. Sample copy $5. Fiction guidelines free with SASE.
Payment: Pays $10/page and 2 free contributor's copies. 40% discount for extras.
Terms: Pays on publication for first North American serial rights and right to reprint in any anthology consisting of 75% or more material from *Antaeus*.
Advice: "Read the magazine before submitting. Most mss are solicited, but we do actively search the unsolicited mss for suitable material. Unless stories are extremely short (2-3 pages), send only one. Do not be angry if you get only a printed rejection note; we *have* read the manuscript. Always include an SASE. Keep cover letters short, cordial and to the point."

ANTIETAM REVIEW (II,IV), Washington County Arts Council, 82 W. Washington St., Hagerstown MD 21740. (301)791-3132. Editor: Ann B. Knox. Magazine: 8½×11; 42 pages; photos. A literary journal of short fiction, poetry and black-and-white photographs. Annually. Estab. 1982. Circ. 1,000.

Needs: Contemporary, ethnic, experimental, feminist, literary and prose poem. "We read manuscripts from our region—Maryland, Pennsylvania, Virginia, West Virginia and Washington D.C. only. We read from October 1 to March 1." Receives about 100 unsolicited mss/month; accepts 7-9 stories/year. Published work by Rachel Simon, Elisavietta Ritchie, Philip Bufithis; published new writers within the last year. Length: 3,000 words average.
How to Contact: "Send ms and SASE with a cover letter. Let us know if you have published before and where." Photocopies OK. Accepts computer printouts; prefers letter-quality. Reports in 1 to 2 months. "If we hold a story, we let the writer know. Occasionally we critique returned ms or ask for rewrites." Sample copy $4.50.
Payment: "We believe it is a matter of dignity that writers and poets be paid. We have been able to give $100 a story and $25 a poem, but this depends on funding. Also 2 copies." Prizes: "We offer a $100 annual literary award in addition to the $100, for the best story."
Terms: Acquires first North American serial rights. Sends pre-publication galleys if author requests.
Advice: "We look for well crafted work that shows attention to clarity and precision of language. We like relevant detail but want to see significant emotional movement within the course of the story—something happening to the central character. This journal was started in response to the absence of fiction markets for emerging writers. Its purpose is to give exposure to fiction writers, poets and photographers of high artistic quality who might otherwise have difficulty placing their work."

THE ANTIGONISH REVIEW, St. Francis Xavier University, Antigonish, Nova Scotia B2G 1C0 Canada. (902)867-3962. Editor: George Sanderson. Literary magazine for educated and creative readers. Quarterly. Estab. 1970. Circ. 800.
Needs: Literary, contemporary, prose poem and translations. No erotic or political material. Accepts 6 mss/issue. Receives 25 unsolicited fiction mss each month. Published work by Arnold Bloch, Richard Butts and Helen Barolini; published new writers within the last year. Length: 3,000-5,000 words. Sometimes comments briefly on rejected mss.
How to Contact: Send complete ms with cover letter. SASE or IRC. Accepts disk submissions compatible with Apple and Macintosh. Prefers hard copy with disk submission. Reports in 3 months. Publishes ms 3 months to 1 year after acceptance.
Payment: 2 free author's copies.
Terms: Acquires first rights.
Advice: "Learn the fundamentals and do not deluge an editor."

ANTIOCH REVIEW (II), Box 148, Yellow Springs OH 45387. (513)767-6389. Editor: Robert S. Fogarty. Associate Editor: Nolan Miller. Magazine: 6×9; 128 pages; 60 lb book offset paper; coated cover stock; illustrations "seldom." "Literary and cultural review of contemporary issues in politics, American and international studies, and literature for general readership." Quarterly. Published special fiction issue last year; plans another. Estab. 1941. Circ. 4,000.
Needs: Literary, contemporary, translations and experimental. No children's, science fiction or popular market. Buys 3-4 mss/issue, 10-12 mss/year. Receives approximately 175 unsolicited fiction mss each month. Approximately 1-2% of fiction agented. Length: any length the story justifies.
How to Contact: Send complete ms with SASE, preferably mailed flat. Accepts computer printout submissions, prefers letter-quality. Reports in 2 months. Publishes ms 6-9 months after acceptance. Sample copy $5; free guidelines with SASE.
Payment: $10/page; 2 free author's copies. $2.70 for extras.
Terms: Pays on publication for first and one-time rights (rights returned to author on request).
Advice: "Our best advice, always, is to *read* the *Antioch Review* to see what type of material we publish. Quality fiction requires an engagement of the reader's intellectual interest supported by mature emotional relevance, written in a style that is rich and rewarding without being freaky. The great number of stories submitted to us indicates that fiction apparently still has great appeal. We assume that if so many are writing fiction, many must be reading it."

APAEROS (I), 960 S.W. Jefferson Ave., Corvallis OR 97333. Clerks: Kathe and John Burt. Newsletter: 8½×11; 24-32 pages; photos if photocopyable. "Sex, erotica, relationships (het, lesbian, gay), turn-ons, nudism, VD and rape prevention, etc. For sharing feelings, knowledge, questions, problems, stories, drawings and fantasies. Ready-to-photocopy pages published unedited." Bimonthly. Estab. 1985. Circ. 100.
Needs: Confession, erotica, feminist, gay, lesbian, romance (contemporary, historical, young adult), comic strips, prose poem, science fiction, serialized/excerpted novel, spiritual. Published new writers within the last year. Publishes short shorts. Sometimes comments on rejected mss or recommends other markets.
How to Contact: Send $2 and SASE for sample and guidelines. SASE for mss. Simultaneous, photocopied and reprint submissions OK. Accepts computer printouts. Sample copy and guidelines for #10 envelope and 1 first class stamp. "State that you are over 18."

Payment: "Increased pages; maybe free subscription extensions."
Terms: Publication copyrighted via "common law."
Advice: "*Apaeros* is *un*edited, reader-written. The amateur press is good for learning the trade."

APPALACHIAN HERITAGE (I, II), Berea College, Hutchins Library, Berea KY 40404. (606)986-9341. Editor: Sidney Farr. Magazine: 7×9½; 80 pages; 60 lb stock; 10 pt Warrenflo cover; drawings and clip art; b&w photos. "*Appalachian Heritage* is a southern Appalachian literary magazine. We try to keep a balance of fiction, poetry, essays, scholarly works, etc., for a general audience and/or those interested in the Appalachian mountains." Quarterly. Estab. 1973. Circ. 1,100.
Needs: Regional, literary, historical. Receives 20-25 unsolicited mss/month. Accepts 2 or 3 mss/issue; 10 or more mss/year. Published work by Robert Morgan, Richard Hague and James Still; published new writers within the last year. No reading fee, but "would prefer a subscription first." Length: 2,000-2,500 word average; 3,000 words maximum. Publishes short shorts. Length: 500 words. Occasionally critiques rejected mss and recommends other markets.
How to Contact: Send complete ms with cover letter. Reports in 1-2 weeks on queries; 3-4 weeks on mss. SASE for ms. Simultaneous, photocopied submissions OK "if clear and readable." Accepts computer printout submissions, no dot-matrix. Sample copy for $4.
Payment: 3 free contributor's copies; $4 charge for extras.
Terms: Acquires one-time rights.
Advice: "Trends in fiction change frequently. Right now the trend is toward slick, modern pieces with very little regional or ethnic material appearing in print. The pendulum will swing the other way again, and there will be a space for that kind of fiction. It seems to me there is always a chance to have really good writing published, somewhere. Keep writing and keep trying the markets. Diligent writing and rewriting can perfect your art. Be sure to study the market. Do not send me a slick piece of writing set in New York City, for example, with no idea on your part of the kinds of things I am interested in seeing. It is a waste of your time and money. Get a sample copy, or subscribe to the publication, study it carefully, then send your material."

ARGONAUT (II), Box 4201, Austin TX 78765-4201. Editor: Michael Ambrose. Magazine: 5¼×8¼; 48 pages; 60 lb paper; varied cover stock; illustrations; photos. "*Argonaut* is a weird fantasy/science fiction magazine. The word 'fantasy' carries few restrictions here. *Argonaut* readers want original, literate, unusual stories." Annually. Estab. 1972. Circ. 500.
Needs: Science fiction, fantasy, horror and prose poem. Buys 5-8 mss/issue. Receives 40-50 unsolicited fiction mss each month. Published work by Charles R. Saunders, Albert J. Manachino and Dale Hammell. Length: 2,500-10,000 words. Sometimes recommends other markets.
How to Contact: Send complete ms with SASE. "It is nice to know a little something about the author." Reports in 1-2 months. Sample copy $3.
Payment: 2 or more copies. Extras at 50% discount.
Terms: Acquires first North American serial rights.
Advice: "Read *Argonaut* and other sf-fantasy magazines before submitting anything. Don't submit more than one story at a time, and keep trying when rejected. *Argonaut*'s infrequent publishing schedule compels me to be very selective of the stories I receive. It takes more than a polished style with no originality of idea, or all idea with no style on the other hand, to get me interested."

ARNAZELLA (II), Arnazella's Reading List, English Department, Bellevue Community College, Bellevue WA 98007. (206)641-2021. Advisor: Roger George. Magazine: 5×6; 104 pages, 70 lb paper; heavy coated cover; illustrations and photos. "For those interested in quality fiction." Annually. Estab. 1976. Circ. 500.
Needs: Adventure, contemporary, erotica, ethnic, experimental, fantasy, feminist, gay, historical, humor/satire, lesbian, literary, mainstream, prose poem, regional, religious/inspirational, science fiction, suspense/mystery, translations. Submit in fall and winter for issue to be published in spring. Published new writers within the last year. Publishes short shorts. *Preference may be given to local contributors.*
How to Contact: Send complete ms with cover letter. Reports on mss in spring. SASE. Photocopied submissions OK. Accepts computer printout submissions. Sample copy for $5. Fictioh guidelines for #10 SAE and 1 first class stamp.
Payment: Pays in contributor's copies.
Terms: Acquires first rights. "Best student story earns $25."
Advice: "Read this and similar magazines, reading critically and analytically."

ART BRIGADE, 3904½ Maplewood, Austin TX 78722. (512)322-0706. Editor: Ben Davis. Fiction Editors: Ben Davis and Mark Capps. Tabloid: 11×14; 24-32 pages; newsprint paper; book stock cover; illustrations and photographs. "*Art Brigade* exists for the purpose of publishing bold new fiction and poetry, covering personalities in the arts, and helping people link up with other alternative media outlets. For other writers, musicians, independent publishers and artists. Also distributed to college students and others in Texas." Bimonthly. Also publishes *Surface Tension,* quarterly art/fiction supplement with experimental/political focus. Estab. 1987. Circ. 5,000.

Needs: Contemporary, erotica, experimental, fantasy, feminist, gay, horror, humor/satire, lesbian, literary, science fiction, serialized/excerpted novel, translations, political. "No pointless pornographic nonsense, insipid or two-dimensional genre fiction, hate literature, pieces with a specialized perspective, aimless or amateurish ranting, anything incoherent, new age/pseudoscientific gobbledygook." Receives 25 unsolicited fiction mss/month. Accepts approx. 10 mss/issue; 40-50 mss/year. Publishes fiction an average of 1 month after acceptance. Length: 3,500 words averge; 4,500-5,000 words maximum. Publishes short shorts. Sometimes comments on rejected mss and recommends other markets.

How to Contact: Send complete manuscript with cover letter. Reports in 1 week on queries; 2 weeks on mss. Simultaneous, photocopied and reprint submissions OK. Computer printout submissions OK. Sample copy $1; fiction guidelines free.

Payment: Pays in contributor's copies.

Terms: Acquires one-time rights. Sends pre-publication galleys to author.

Advice: "*Art Brigade* strives to be more than a forum for challenging art and fiction. We seek to be an active part of a larger artistic community, boosting regional music and arts, linking illustrators and comic artists with writers, working with writers on special projects and in general providing a place where our contributors can grow and explore, as well. Be confident and be sure what you are doing is good and worthwhile, and be persistent and aggressive. Any good writer can find an enthusiastic readership if he tries hard enough, and works on his craft. Be original, innovative, and don't rely on the obvious, but seek to teach and reveal as well as teach or shock. Whatever else, be true to your own personal literary instincts, and persevere."

ARTEMIS (IV), An art/literary publication from the Blue Ridge Mountains, Box 8147, Roanoke VA 24014. (703)774-8440. Contact: Fiction Editors. Magazine: 6×6; 85 pages; heavy/slick paper; colored cover stock; illustrations; photos. "We publish poetry, art and fiction of the highest quality and will consider any artist/writer who lives or has lived in the Blue Ridge or Virginia. General adult audience with literary interest." Annually. Estab. 1976. Circ. 2,000.

Needs: Literary. Wants to see "the best contemporary style." Receives 40 unsolicited fiction mss/year. Accepts 3-4 mss/issue. Does not read mss Jan.-Aug. Publishes ms 4-5 months after acceptance. Published works by Rosanne Coggeshall, Jeanne Larsen, Kurt Rheinheimer; published work by new writers within the last year. Length: 1,500 words average; 2,500 words maximum.

How to Contact: Submit 2 copies of unpublished ms between Sept. 15-Nov. 15, name, address and phone on title page only. Reports in 2 months. SASE for ms. Photocopied submissions OK. Accepts computer printout. No dot-matrix unless high quality. Sample copy $6.50. "Ms not adhering to guidelines will be rejected."

Payment: 1 complimentary copy. Discount for extra copies.

Terms: Acquires first rights.

Advice: "We look for polished quality work that holds interest, has imagination, energy, voice."

ARTFUL DODGE (II), Department of English, College of Wooster, Wooster OH 44691. Editor-in-Chief: Daniel Bourne. Magazine: 100-130 pages; illustrations; photos. "There is no theme in this magazine, except literary power. We also have an ongoing interest in translations from Eastern Europe and elsewhere." Semiannually. Estab. 1979. Circ. 750.

Needs: Experimental, literary, prose poem, translations. "We judge by literary quality, not by genre. We are especially interested in fine English translations of significant contemporary prose writers." Receives 40 unsolicited fiction mss/month. Accepts 2-3 mss/issue, 5 mss/year. Recently published fiction by Edward Kleinschmidt, William S. Burroughs and Elizabeth Bartlett; published 2 new writers within the last year. Length: 10,000 words maximum; 2,500 words average. Occasionally critiques rejected mss.

How to Contact: Send complete ms with SASE. Do not send more than 30 pages at a time. Photocopied submissions OK. Reports in 2-3 months. Sample copies of older, single issues are $2.75 or five issues for $5; recent issues are double issues, available for $5.75. Free fiction guidelines for #10 SAE and 1 first class stamp.

Payment: 1 free contributor's copy (subject to change for the better).

Terms: Acquires first North American serial rights.

Advice: "If we take time to offer criticism, do not subsequently flood us with other stories no better than the first. If starting out, get as many readers, good ones, as possible. Above all, read contemporary fiction and the magazine you are trying to publish in."

ART:MAG (II), 5055 E. Charleston, F110, Las Vegas NV 89104. (702)459-9067 or (702)383-8624. Editor: Peter Magliocco. Magazine: 5½×8½; 60 pages; 20 lb bond paper; b&w pen and ink illustrations and photographs. Publishes "irreverent, literary-minded work by committed writers," for "small press, 'quasi-art-oriented' " audience. Estab. 1984. Circ. under 100.

Needs: Condensed/excerpted novel, confession, contemporary, erotica, ethnic, experimental, fantasy, feminist, gay, historical (general), horror, humor/satire, lesbian, literary, mainstream, prose poem, psychic/supernatural/occult, regional, science fiction, suspense/mystery, translations and arts. No "slick-oriented stuff published by major magazines." Receives 1 plus ms/month. Accepts 1-2 mss/issue; 4-5 mss/year. Publishes ms within 3-6 months of acceptance. Recently published "an excerpt from James Purdy's novel, *Garmets the Living Wear,* which deals with controversial matter mainstream publishers avoided. Also published work by James Stevenson and Tristan A. MacAvery."Length: 5,000 words preferred; 250 words minimum; 10,000 words maximum. Sometimes critiques rejected mss and recommends other markets.
How to Contact: Send complete ms with cover letter. Reports in 3 months. SASE for ms. Simultaneous and photocopied submissions OK. Sample copy $2.50, 6x9 SAE and 79¢ postage. Fiction guidelines for #10 SAE and first class stamp.
Payment: Pays contributor's copies.
Terms: Acquires one-time rights.
Advice: "Seeking more novel and quality-oriented work, usually from solicited authors. Magazine fiction today needs to be concerned with the issues of fiction-writing itself—not just with a desire to publish or please the largest audience. Think about things in the fine art world as well as the literary one and keep the hard core of life as an in-between, guiding ballast for good measure."

THE ASYMPTOTICAL WORLD (II), Box 1372, Williamsport PA 17703. Editor: Michael H. Gerardi. Magazine: 8½×11; 54 pages; glossy paper; illustrated cover; b&w illustrations. "*The Asymptotical World* is a *unique* collection of psychodramas, fantasies, poems and illustrations which elucidates the moods and sensations of the world created in the mind of men, for 18 year olds and older; those who enjoy work completed in style and mood similar to Poe." Annually. Estab. 1984. Circ. 1,300.
Needs: Experimental, fantasy, horror, psychic/supernatural/occult. Receives 30 unsolicited fiction mss/month; accepts 10 fiction mss/issue. Publishes ms 6 months to 1 year after acceptance. Length: 1,000 words minimum; 2,000 words maximum.
How to Contact: Query first. SASE. Reports in 1-2 months on queries; 1-2 months on mss. Simultaneous and photocopied submissions OK. Accepts computer printouts. Sample copy $6.95 with SAE and 8 first class stamps. Fiction guidelines for 4x9 SAE and 1 first class stamp.
Payment: Pays $20-50.
Terms: Pays on publication. Acquires first rights.
Advice: "*The Asymptotical World* is definitely unique. It is strongly suggested that a writer review a copy of the magazine to study the format of a psychodrama and the manner in which the plot is left 'open-ended.' The writer will need to study the atmosphere, mood and plot of published psychodramas before preparing a feature work."

ATALANTIK (II, IV), 7630 Deer Creek Drive, Worthington OH 43085. (614)885-0550. Editor: Prabhat K. Dutta. Magazine: 8½×11; approx. 80 pages; paper quality and cover stock vary; illustrations and photos. "The publication is bilingual: Indian (Bengali) and English language. This was started to keep the Indian language alive to the Indian immigrants. This contains short stories, poems, essays, sketches, book reviews, cultural news, children's pages, etc." Quarterly. Plans special fiction issue. Estab. 1980. Circ. 400.
Needs: Adventure, condensed novel, contemporary, ethnic, experimental, historical (general), humor/satire, juvenile (5-9 years), literary, mainstream, psychic/supernatural/occult, romance, science fiction, suspense/mystery, translations, travelogue, especially to India. No politics and religion. Receives 10 unsolicited fiction mss/month. Publishes about 2-4 fiction mss/issue; about 30 mss/year. Publishes ms an average of at least 6 months after acceptance. Length: 5,000 words average. Publishes short shorts. Length: 1-2 pages. Sometimes comments on rejected mss and recommends other markets.
How to Contact: Query with clips of published work or send complete ms with cover letter; "author's bio data and a synopsis of the literary piece(s)." Reports on queries in 1 month; on mss in 4 months. SASE. Photocopied submissions OK. Computer printout submissions OK. Sample copy $6; fiction guidelines for #10 SASE.
Payment: Pays in contributor's copies; charge for extras.
Terms: Acquires all rights. Sponsors contests for fiction writers.
Advice: "A short story has to be short and should have a story too. A completely imaginative short story without any real life linkage is almost impossible. The language should be lucid and characters kept to a small number. A short story is not simply the description of an incident. It goes far beyond, far deeper. It should present the crisis of a single problem. Usually a successful short story contains a singular idea which is developed to its most probable conclusion in a uniquely charted path."

‡THE ATAVACHRON AND ALL OUR YESTERDAYS (IV), U.S.S. Resolution, Box 6501, Victoria, B.C. V8P5M4 Canada. (604)721-0682. Editors: John Herbert/Monica Spencer. Magazine: 8½×11; 60-120 pages; 20 lb new paper; 20 lb/card stock cover; illustrations; photos. "For Star Trek fans of all ages."

Quarterly (The Atavachron); Annually (All Our Yesterdays). Estab. 1985. Circ. 250.
Needs: Science Fiction: Star Trek. "No gay or KS (Kirk and Spock) stories." Publishes annual special fiction issue. Receives 2 unsolicited mss/month. Accepts 3 mss/issue; 11 mss/year. Publishes ms 2-6 months after acceptance. Recently published work by John Herbert, Jim Cowling, David Gordon-MacDonald. Length: 10,000 words average; 25,000 words maximum. Publishes short shorts. Sometimes critiques rejected mss and recommends other markets.
How to Contact: Send complete manuscript and cover letter with background on author. Reports in 3 weeks. SASE. Simultaneous, photocopied and reprint submissions OK. Accepts computer printout submissions. Sample copy $2.50 for *Atavachron,* $9.00 for *All Our Yesterdays* (Canadian). Fiction guidelines for $1.
Payment: Pays in contributor's copies.
Terms: Pays for one-time rights.
Advice: "Work has to be true to the characters, (if established Trek characters are being used) and be a uniquely different idea."

ATHENA INCOGNITO MAGAZINE (II), 2555 29th Ave., San Francisco CA 94122. (415)665-0219. Editors: Ronn Rosen and Kurt Cline. Magazine: 8½×11; approximately 30-40 pages; illustrations; Xeroxed photos. "Open-format magazine with emphasis on experimental and/or any type of quality writing. Emphasis on poetry especially." Quarterly. Estab. 1980. Circ. 100.
Needs: Any subjects OK. Receives 15 unsolicited mss/month. Publishes ms usually 2-3 months after acceptance. Requires magazine subscription "to cover postage and expense of publication" of $4 (for 1 issue) before reading ms. Published new writers within the last year. Publishes short shorts. No long pieces over 2 pages. Sometimes critiques rejected mss.
How to Contact: Send complete ms with cover letter. Reports in 2 weeks to 1 month. SASE. Simultaneous, photocopied and reprint submissions OK. Accepts computer printout submissions. Sample copy for $4; fiction guidelines for SAE and 1 first class stamp.
Payment: Pays in contributor's copies.
Terms: Acquires all rights. Publication not copyrighted.
Advice: "Experiment and practice eclecticism of all kinds! Discover! Pioneer! Dada lives!"

ATLANTIS (I), Speculative Fiction Quarterly, Xyder Press, Box 5609-Station B, Victoria, British Columbia V8R 6S4 Canada. (604)477-0951. Editor: David Gordon-MacDonald. Magazine: 8½×11; 64 pages; 20 lb letter bond paper; card cover; b&w illustrations; b&w photographs. "Science fiction, fantasy, horror, some detective and suspense. Explores speculative or fantastic themes." Quarterly. Plans special fiction issue. Estab. 1984. Circ. 1,500.
Needs: Adventure, fantasy, historical (general), horror, humor/satire, science fiction, suspense/mystery. "No manuscripts promoting racial, ethnic, religious or sexual bias." Receives 50 unsolicited mss/month. Accepts 10 mss/issue; 40-50 mss/year. Publishes ms 4-8 months after acceptance. Recently published work by A. David Moncrieff; Jeffrey D. S. Taylor; Carla Luna; published new writers within the last year. Length: 5,000 words average; 500 words minimum; 7,000 words maximum. Sometimes critiques rejected mss and recommends other markets.
How to Contact: Send complete manuscript with cover letter, which should include "short bio; history of past publications (if any); story synopsis." Reports in 4-6 weeks. SASE. Simultaneous, photocopied and reprint submissions OK. Accepts computer printouts. Sample copy or fiction guidelines for SAE and 2 (loose) first class stamps.
Payment: Free subscription to magazine and contributor's copies.
Terms: Acquires one-time rights.
Advice: Looks for "originality; clear, correct diction; a strong narrative voice; engrossing plots. Don't submit D & D or other role-playing scenarios. Don't submit slightly re-written Stephen King."

‡ATLANTIS (II), A Women's Studies Journal, Institute for the Study of Women, Mt. St. Vincent University, Halifax, Nova Scotia B3M 2J6 Canada. (902)443-4450. Editors: Susan Clark, Deborah Poff. Magazine: 7½×9½; 170-200 pages; matte quality paper; glossy cover stock; b&w illustrations and photos. "Interdisciplinary women's studies journal, accepts original research and some fiction in French and English for academics and researchers interested in feminism." Semiannually. Estab. 1975. Circ. 800.
Needs: Feminist research and creative work (short stories, poetry, etc.). Receives 20 unsolicited fiction mss/month. Accepts 1-2 mss/issue; 2-4 mss/year. Publishes ms 6-12 months after acceptance. Publishes short shorts. Critiques rejected mss.
How to Contact: Send complete ms with cover letter. Photocopied submissions OK. Accepts computer printouts. Current issue for $10; back issue for $7.50 (Canadian).
Payment: Pays 1 contributor's copy.
Advice: "We welcome and have published work by previously unpublished writers."

ATROCITY (I), Publication of the Absurd Sig of Mensa, 2419 Greensburg Pike, Pittsburgh PA 15221. Editor: Hank Roll. Newsletter: 8½×11; 8 pages; offset 20 lb paper and cover; illustrations; photographs occasionally. Humor and satire for "high IQ-Mensa" members. Monthly. Estab. 1976. Circ. 250.
Needs: Humor/satire. Liar's Club, parody, jokes, funny stories, comments on the absurdity of today's world. Receives 20 unsolicited mss/month. Accepts 5 mss/issue. Publishes ms 3-6 months after acceptance. Published 10 new writers within the last year. Length: 150 words preferred; 650 words maximum.
How to Contact: Send complete ms. "No cover letter necessary if ms states what rights (e.g. first North American serial/reprint, etc.) are offered."Reports in 1 month. SASE. Simultaneous, photocopied and reprint submissions OK. Accepts computer printout submissions; no dot-matrix. Sample copy for 50¢, #10 SAE and 2 stamps.
Payment: Pays with contributor's copies.
Terms: Acquires one-time rights.
Advice: Manuscript should be single spaced, copy ready. Horizontal format to fit on one 8½×11 sheet. "Be funny."

AURA Literary/Arts Review (II), University of Alabama at Birmingham, Box 76, University Center, Birmingham AL 35294. (205)934-3216. Editor: Stefanie Truelove and Adam Pierce. Magazine: 6×9; 150 pages; b&w illustrations and photos. "We publish various types of fiction with an emphasis on short stories. Our audience is college students, the university community and literary-minded adults, the arts community." Semiannually. Estab. 1974. Circ. 1,000.
Needs: Literary, contemporary, science fiction, regional, romance, men's, women's, feminist and ethnic. No mss longer than 7,000-8,000 words. Accepts 3-4 mss/issue. Receives 15-20 unsolicited fiction mss each month. Published works by Nickell Romjue, Josephine Marshall, Rodolfo Tomes; published new writers within the last year. Length: 2,000-8,000 words. Publishes short shorts; length according to editor's decision. Critiques rejected mss when there is time.
How to Contact: Send complete ms with SASE. No simultaneous submissions; please include biographical information. Reports in 2 months. Sample copy $2.50
Payment: 2 free author's copies.
Terms: Acquires first North American serial rights.
Advice: "We welcome experimental or traditional literature on any subject."

AXE FACTORY REVIEW (III), The Axe Factory, Box 11186, Philadelphia PA 19136. (215)331-7389. Editor: Louis McKee. Fiction Editor: Joseph Farley. Magazine: 8×10; 56 pages. Published irregularly. Estab. 1986. Circ. 500.
Needs: Contemporary, erotica, humor/satire, literary. Receives 2-4 unsolicited mss each month. Does not read during the summer. Publishes short shorts. Sometimes critiques rejected mss.
How to Contact: Send complete ms with cover letter. Reports in 2 weeks on queries; 2-6 weeks on mss. SASE. Simultaneous submissions OK. Accepts computer printout submissions; no dot-matrix. Sample copy for $5.
Payment: Pays 2 contributor's copies.
Terms: Acquires first rights.

THE AZOREAN EXPRESS (I, IV), Seven Buffaloes Press, Box 249, Big Timber MT 59011. Editor: Art Cuelho. Magazine: 6¾×8¼; 32 pages; 60 lb book paper; 3-6 illustrations/issue; photos rarely. "My overall theme is rural; I also focus on working people (the sweating professions); the American Indian and Hobo; the Dustbowl era; and I am also trying to expand with non-rural material. For rural and library and professor/student, blue collar workers, etc." Semiannually. Estab. 1985. Circ. 600.
Needs: Contemporary, ethnic, experimental, humor/satire, literary, regional, western, rural, working people. Receives 10-20 unsolicited mss/month. Accepts 2-3 mss/issue; 4-6 mss/year. Publishes ms 1-6 months after acceptance. Length: 1,000-3,000 words. Also publishes short shorts 500-1,000 words. "I take what I like; length sometimes does not matter, even when longer than usual. I'm flexible." Sometimes recommends other markets.
How to Contact: "Send cover letter with ms; general information, but it can be personal, more in line with the submitted story. Not long rambling letters." Reports in 1-4 weeks on queries; 1-4 weeks on mss. SASE. Photocopied submissions OK. Accepts computer printouts. Sample copy $3. Fiction guidelines for SASE.
Payment: Contributor's copies. "Depends on the amount of support author gives my press."
Terms: Acquires first North American serial rights. "If I decide to use material in anthology form later, I have that right." Sends pre-publication galleys to the author upon request.
Advice: "There would not be magazines like mine if I was not optimistic. But literary optimism is a two-way street. Without young fiction writers supporting fiction magazines the future is bleak, because the commercial magazines allow only formula or name writers within their pages. My own publications receive no grants. Sole support is from writers, libraries and individuals."

BABY SUE (I), Box 1111, Decatur GA 30031-1111. (404)288-2073. Editor: Don W. Seven. Magazine: 8½×11; 20 pages; illustrations and photos. "*Baby Sue* is a collection of music reviews, poetry, short fiction and cartoons," for "anyone who can think and is not easily offended." Quarterly. Plans special fiction issue. Estab. 1983. Circ. 1,500.

Needs: Erotica, experimental and humor/satire. Receives 5-10 mss/month. Accepts 3-4 mss/year. Publishes ms within 3 months of acceptance. Publishes short shorts. Length: 1-2 single-spaced pages.

How to Contact: Query with clips of published work. Reports in 1 month. SASE. Accepts computer printout submissions. Sample copy for #10 SAE and first class stamp.

Payment: Pays 1 contributor's copy.

Advice: "There's more places to get work printed than ever before. The underground press circuit is *great*! If no one will print your work, start your own publication!"

BAD HAIRCUT (II), P.O. Box 6631, Kent WA 98064. Editors: Ray GoForth, Kim Goforth. Magazine: 5½×8½; 30 pages; illustrations. Published irregularly. Estab. 1987. Circ. 500.

Needs: Experimental, humor/satire, prose poem, translations, political, world-conscious. Receives 20 fiction ms/month. Accepts 1-3 mss/issue; 4-12 mss/year. Publishes short shorts. Almost always critiques rejected mss and recommends other markets.

How to Contact: Query with or without clips of published work; send complete ms with cover letter; or "send by special messenger." Reports in 1 week on queries; 2 months on mss. SASE. Simultaneous, photocopied and reprint submissions OK. Accepts computer printout submissions. Sample copy $4. Fiction guidelines for #10 SAE and 1 first class stamp.

Payment: Free subscription to magazine or contributor's copies; charge for extras. Payment "depends on our financial state."

Terms: Acquires first North American serial rights. Rights revert to author.

Advice: "Keep on trying. You reap what you sow. Love is love. Enjoy your life. Always include a nice cover letter describing who you are and why you're sending your stuff to us."

BAD NEWZ (IV), Artists & Writers Underground, c/o Sarris Bookmarketing, 125 E. 23d St.,#300, New York NY 10010. Editor: Bob Z. Magazine: 8½×11; 50-70 pages; 20 lb paper; two-color cover; illustrations throughout. "Accepts writing only from punks or those living on the fringes of society." For an audience of "anyone who can take it." Quarterly. Estab. 1986. Circ. 1,000.

Needs: Erotica, experimental, horror, humor/satire, psychic/supernatural/occult, music. "All literature must be written from the point of view of someone *outside* the mainstream." Receives 15-20 unsolicited fiction mss/month. Accepts 2-3 mss/issue; 8-12 mss/year. Publishes ms 2-3 months after acceptance. Length: 1 word minimum; 500 words (absolute) maximum. Sometimes comments on rejected mss and recommends other markets.

How to Contact: "Since we only print very short pieces, just send the piece(s). We don't reply to queries—only to mss." SASE. Simultaneous, photocopied and reprint submissions OK. Accepts computer printouts. Sample copy $3.

Payment: Pays in contributor's copies.

Terms: Acquires first North American serial rights. Publication not copyrighted.

Advice: "The market is terrible. It's no better now than it was when Franz Kafka was being ignored, and the chances that another Kafka is being ignored right now are very good. That's why we welcome the strange and offbeat as much as possible, even encourage it—we accept things that other editors won't even read."

BALL STATE UNIVERSITY FORUM (II), Ball State University, Muncie IN 47306. (317)285-8456. Editor: Frances M. Rippy; Editor-in-Chief: Bruce W. Hozeski. Magazine: 6½×9½; 80 pages; excellent paper quality; heavy paper cover. Magazine for "educated non-specialists." One issue a year devoted to fiction of all types. Quarterly. Estab. 1960. Circ. 700.

Needs: Adventure, condensed or excerpted novel (30 pages or less), contemporary, ethnic, experimental, fantasy, feminist, gothic/historical romance, historical (general), humor/satire, literary, mainstream, prose poem, psychic/supernatural, religious/inspirational, science fiction, suspense/mystery, translations and western." Receives 30 unsolicited fiction mss/month. Accepts 15 mss/year. Publishes ms "usually 18 months maximum" after acceptance. Recently published work by Thomas A. Long, Paul Grussendorf and Barbara Rodman. Published new writers in the last year. Length: 200 words minimum, 6,000 words maximum, 4,000 words average. "Only occasionally" critiques rejected mss.

How to Contact: Send complete ms with SASE. Photocopied submissions OK. Accepts computer printout submissions. "Strongly" discourages multiple submissions. Reports in 3-4 months. Sample copy $6.

Payment: 1 free contributor's copy.
Terms: "Authors may reprint own works without payment to *Forum*, simply by acknowledging previous printing."
Advice: "Send an original, polished story in a clean copy. If it is rejected, we tell you if the vote was close and suggest sending another. Read broadly, write carefully, revise painstakingly, submit mss persistently. Short stories from the *Forum* have been listed in the Houghton Mifflin edition of *Best American Short Stories*; one was reprinted in *Prize Stories O. Henry Awards*."

LA BELLA FIGURA (I,II,IV), Box 411223, San Francisco CA 94141-1223. Editor: Rose Romano. Magazine: 8½×11; 10 pages. Publishes "work by Italian-American women, mostly about us. We now publish men also." Quarterly. Estab. 1988. Circ. 150.
Needs: Ethnic, feminist, lesbian, literary, prose poem, translations and Italian-American culture and heritage. "It is the purpose of *LBF* to provide a space for a much-neglected group of people. It is our space to share ourselves with each other and to help others understand us." Receives 10-15 mss/month. Accepts 1-2 mss/issue; 4-8 mss/year. Publishes ms within 2-3 months of acceptance. Recently published work by Maria Gillan and Rina Ferrarelli. Length: about 4-10 double-spaced pages preferred. Publishes short shorts. Sometimes critiques rejected mss and recommends other markets.
How to Contact: Send complete manuscript with cover letter, which should include previous publications and any other credits. Reports within 1 month. No longer use themes. SASE. Photocopied and reprint submissions OK. Accepts computer printout submissions. Sample copy $2. Fiction guidelines for #10 SAE and first class stamp.
Payment: Pays 2 contributor's copies; charge for extras.
Terms: Acquires one-time rights.
Advice: "There's not enough work by and about Italian-American women (especially lesbians) published yet. The writer must find that space between stereotyped and assimilated."

THE BELLINGHAM REVIEW (II), 1007 Queen St., Bellingham WA 98226. Editor: Shelley Rozen. Magazine: 5½×8; 64 pages; 60 lb white paper; varied cover stock; photos. "A literary magazine featuring original short stories, novel excerpts, short plays and poetry of palpable quality." Semiannually. Estab. 1977. Circ. 700.
Needs: All genres/subjects considered. Acquires 1-2 mss/issue. Publishes short shorts. Published new writers within the last year. Length: 5,000 words or less. Critiques rejected mss when there is time.
How to Contact: Send complete ms. Reports in 2 weeks to 3 months. Publishes ms an average of 1 year after acceptance. Sample copy $2.
Payment: 1 free author's copy plus 2-issue subscription. Charges $1.50 for extras.
Terms: Acquires first North American serial and one-time rights.
Advice: Mss are rejected for various reasons, "but the most common problem is too much *telling* and not enough *showing* of crucial details and situations. We also look for something that is different or looks at life in a different way."

BELLOWING ARK (II), A Literary Tabloid, Box 45637, Seattle WA 98145. (206)545-8302. Editor: R.R. Ward. Tabloid: 11½×16; 20 pages; electro-brite paper and cover stock; illustrations; photos. "We publish material which we feel addresses the human situation in an affirmative way. We do not publish academic fiction." Bimonthly. Plans special fiction issue. Estab. 1984. Circ. 500.
Needs: Contemporary, literary, mainstream, serialized/excerpted novel. "Anything we publish will be true." Receives 100-150 unsolicited fiction mss/year. Accepts 1-2 mss/issue; 7-12 mss/year. Time varies, but publishes ms not longer than 6 months after acceptance. Recently published work by Kim Silvera Wolterbeek, Grace Cash and Catherine Marley; published new writers within the last year. Length: 3,000-5,000 words average. Publishes short shorts. Sometimes critiques rejected mss and recommends other markets.
How to Contact: No queries. Send complete ms with cover letter and short bio. "I always cringe when I see letters listing 'credits' and stating the 'rights' offered! Such delights indicate the impossible amateur. Many beginners address me by first name – few of my close friends do." Reports in 6 weeks on mss. SASE. Sample copy for $2, 9x12 SAE and 85¢ postage.
Payment: Pays in contributor's copies.
Terms: Acquires first rights.
Advice: "*Bellowing Ark* began as (and remains) an alternative to the despair and negativity of the Workshop/Academic poetry scene; we believe that life has meaning and is worth living – the work we publish reflects that belief. Learn how to tell a story before submitting. Avoid 'trick' endings – they have all been done before and better."

BELOIT FICTION JOURNAL (II), Box 11, Beloit College WI 53511. (608)365-3391. Editor: Clint McCown. Magazine: 6×9; 112 pages; 60 lb paper; 10 pt. CIS cover stock; illustrations and photos on cover. "We are interested in publishing the best contemporary fiction and are open to all themes

except those involving pornographic, religiously dogmatic or politically propagandistic representations. Our magazine is for general readership, though most of our readers will probably have a specific interest in literary magazines." Semiannually. Estab. 1985.
Needs: Contemporary, literary, mainstream, prose poem, spiritual and sports. No pornography, religious dogma, political propaganda. Receives 75 unsolicited fiction mss/month. Accepts 8-10 mss/issue; 16-20 mss/year. Replies take longer in summer. Publishes ms within 9 months after acceptance. Length: 5,000 words average; 250 words minimum; 10,000 words maximum. Sometimes critiques rejected mss and recommends other markets.
How to Contact: Send complete ms with cover letter. Reports in 1 week on queries; 1-6 weeks on mss. SASE for ms. Simultaneous and photocopied submissions OK, if identified as such. Accepts computer printouts. Sample copy $5. Fiction guidelines free for #10 envelope and 1 first class stamp.
Advice: "Many of our contributors are writers whose work we have previously rejected. Don't let one rejection slip turn you away from our—or any—magazine."

BEYOND . . . SCIENCE FICTION & FANTASY (I,II,IV), Other Worlds Books, Box 1124, Fair Lawn NJ 07410. (201)791-6721. Editor: Shirley Winston; Fiction Editor: Roberta Rogow. Magazine: 8½×11; 48 pages; illustrations. Science fiction and fantasy fiction, art and poetry. Audience is "mostly adults, some younger." Quarterly. Estab. 1985. Circ. 300.
Needs: Fantasy and science fiction. No pornography. Receives 100 unsolicited mss/month. Accepts 10 mss/issue; 40 mss/year. Publishes ms "up to 2 years after acceptance." Length: 5,000 words average; 500 words minimum; 12,000 words maximum. Publishes short shorts. Sometimes critiques rejected mss and recommends other markets.
How to Contact: Send complete ms with cover letter. Reports in 2 months. SASE. Photocopied submissions OK. Accepts computer printout submissions. Sample copy $4.50; fiction guidelines free for SASE.
Payment: ¼¢ per word and contributor's copies.
Terms: Pays on publication for first North American serial rights.

BIG TWO-HEARTED (II,IV), Mid-Peninsula Library Cooperative, 424 Stephenson Ave., Iron Mountain MI 49801. (906)774-3005. Editor: Gary Silver. Magazine: 5½×8¼; 60 pages; 20 lb bond; 60 lb stock. "Creative, wholesome and understandable stories and poems about nature and the independent human spirit." Published every 4 months. Estab. 1985. Circ. 110.
Needs: Humor/satire, literary, prose poem and regional. No profanity, morbidity or erotica. Receives 3 mss/month. Accepts 3 mss/issue. Publishes ms within 3-6 months of acceptance. Recently published work by John O'Connor and Gene Washington; published new writers within the last year. Length: 2,000 words preferred; 500 words minimum; 3,000 words maximum. Sometimes critiques rejected mss.
How to Contact: Send complete ms with cover letter, which should include a short bio. Reports in 3 months. SASE. Photocopied submissions OK. Accepts computer printout submissions. Sample copy for $1 and 6×9 SAE.
Payment: Pays in contributor's copies.
Terms: Acquires all rights (returned to author).
Advice: "Tell a good story. Send us a clean manuscript with double-checked spelling and punctuation. Use of the traditional taboo words is an automatic rejection. Our readers like upbeat stories set in the out-of-doors."

BILINGUAL REVIEW (II, IV), Hispanic Research Center, Arizona State University, Tempe AZ 85287. (602)965-3867. Editor-in-Chief: Gary D. Keller. Scholarly/literary journal of US Hispanic life: poetry, short stories, other prose and theater. Magazine: 7×10; 96 pages; 55 lb acid-free paper; coated cover stock. Published 3 times/year. Estab. 1974. Circ. 2,000.
Needs: US Hispanic creative literature. "We accept material in English or Spanish. We publish original work only—no translations." US/Hispanic themes only. Receives 50 unsolicited fiction mss/month. Accepts 3 mss/issue, 9 mss/year. Often critiques rejected mss. Recently published work by Demetria Martínez, Alicia Gaspar de Alba, Tomás Rivera; published work of new writers within the last year.
How to Contact: Send 2 copies of complete ms with SAE and loose stamps. Simultaneous and high-quality photocopied submissions OK. Reports in 1 month on mss. Publishes ms an average of 1 year after acceptance. Sample copy $7.
Payment: 2 contributor's copies. 30% discount for extras.
Terms: Acquires all rights (50% of reprint permission fee given to author as matter of policy).
Advice: "We do not publish literature about tourists in Latin America and their perceptions of the 'native culture.' "

‡BITCH (IV), The Women's Rock Mag with Bite, San Jose Face, Suite 164, 478 W. Hamilton Ave., Campbell CA 95008. Editors: Lori Twersky and S.J. McCarthy. Magazine: 8×10; 64 pages; newsprint paper; newsprint cover; illustrations and photographs. "Publication related to women in rock music

"Anyone who has experienced an Upper Peninsula winter knows that the trees in the picture will soon be a leafy, shady green; wild strawberries and raspberries will be blossoming along the road; the fields will be planted; and the houses will be alive with the outdoor sounds of people doing life," says editor Gary Silver. The illustration was chosen not only for its visual appeal, but also because it accurately depicts Michigan's Upper Peninsula in the late winter and early spring. "To us, the mood of the illustration is not bleak, but speaks to our emphasis on nature, individual self-reliance and hope." Michael Louis Sandri is the illustrator and an Upper Peninsula native.

and other music/art subcultures (avant-garde fashion, cartooning, etc). Readers are 50% women in the rock business, 50% mixed male and female fans." Monthly. Estab. 1985. Circ. 2,500.

Needs: Fiction relating to women in rock or in avant-garde scenes (from fans to musicians). "No fantasies about your fave rock stars! Aiyee! No porno stuff on 'I dig chix in black leather!' Double Aiyee!! No anti-male diatribes! We do fight sexism, but we don't hate men." Receives fiction mss "about 1 every other month. There's usually 1½ pages per issue. But we'd run more if we got stuff we liked." Publishes ms 1 to 4 months after acceptance. Length: No minimum or maximum—"if we like it and it's long, we'll run it in two parts." Publishes short shorts. Sometimes critiques rejected mss and recommends other markets.

How to Contact: Send complete ms with cover letter. Reports in 3 months. SASE. Simultaneous, photocopied and reprint submissions OK. Accepts computer printout submissions. Accepts electronic submissions via Macintosh disk. Sample copy for 9x10 SAE with 90¢ postage.

Payment: Free subscription to magazine, contributor's copies.

Terms: Rights purchased depend on circumstances. Does not send pre-publication galleys to the author "unless we're making a major change and want to okay it."

Advice: "A sense of humor is a *big* help (we run a lot of humorous essays); and we favor smart, rowdy, *bitchy* pieces by women."

‡THE BLACK HOLE LITERARY REVIEW (I), 1312 Stonemill Court, Cincinnati OH 45215. (513)821-6670. Editor: Wm. E. Allendorf. Electronic Bulletin Board. "This is an attempt to revolutionize publishing—no paper, no rejection slips, no deadlines. For any person with access to a home computer and a modem." Estab. 1989. Circ. 150

Needs: "Any or all fiction categories are acceptable. Any size, topic, or inherent bias is acceptable. The only limitation is that the writer will not mind having his piece read, and an honest critique given directly by his readership." Plans future hardcopy anthology. Publishes ms 1-2 days after acceptance. Length: 2,000-10,000 words. Publishes short shorts, poetry, essays. "Critique given if not by editor, then by reader through Email."

How to Contact: Upload as EMAIL to the editor. Cover letter should include "titles, description (abstract), copyright notice." Reports in 1-2 days. Simultaneous submissions OK. Electronic submissions are preferable, although typing will be done at extra charge to author. Fiction guidelines free.

Payment: Pays in royalties, but charges fee for initial inputting (see below).

Terms: Charges $5 minimum subscription. Submissions cost $.50+ (deducted from subscription). Inputting from paper copy is extra. Royalties are accrued each time the piece is read. Contact editor for details. Buys one-time rights.

Advice: "If the concept of the electronic magazine goes over with the public, then the market for fiction is limitless. Any piece that an author has taken the trouble to set to print is worth publishing. However, The Hole is looking for writers that want to be read—not ones that just want to write. The electronic magazine is an interactive medium, and pieces are judged on their ability to inspire a person to read them." Writers interested in submitting should: "Do it. You would be the first to be rejected by The Hole, if we did not use your piece; to make matters easier for all concerned, submit your piece as a ASCII text file via the modem. Paper submissions are going to be re-typed, and you will be charged for the typing; if you do not have access to a home computer with a modem, buy one, borrow one, steal one. This is the wave of the future for writers."

BLACK JACK (I), Seven Buffaloes Press, Box 249, Big Timber MT 59011. Editor: Art Cuelho. "Main theme: Rural. Publishes material on the American Indian, farm and ranch, American hobo, the common working man, folklore, the Southwest, Okies, Montana, humor, Central California, etc. for people who make their living off the land. The writers write about their roots, experiences and values they receive from the American soil." Annually. Estab. 1973. Circ. 750.

Needs: Literary, contemporary, western, adventure, humor, American Indian, American hobo, and parts of novels and long short stories. "Anything that strikes me as being amateurish, without depth, without craft, I refuse. Actually I'm not opposed to any kind of writing if the author is genuine and has spent his lifetime dedicated to the written word." Buys 5-10 mss/year. Receives approximately 10-15 unsolicited fiction mss/month. Length: 3,500-5,000 words (there can be exceptions).

How to Contact: Query for current theme with SASE. Reports in 1 week on queries, 2 weeks on mss. Sample copy $4.75.

Payment: Pays 1-2 author's copies.

Terms: Acquires first North American serial rights and reserves the right to reprint material in an anthology or future *Black Jack* publications. Rights revert to author after publication.

Advice: "Enthusiasm should be matched with skill as a craftsman. That's not saying that we don't continue to learn, but every writer must have enough command of the language to compete with other proven writers. Save postage by writing first to the editor to find out his needs. A small press magazine always has specific needs at any given time. I sometimes accept material from country writers that aren't all that good at punctuation and grammar but make up for it with life's experience. This is not a highbrow publication; it belongs to the salt-of-the-earth people."

BLACK RIVER REVIEW (II), 855 Mildred Ave., Lorain OH 44052. (216)244-9654. Editor: Kaye Coller. Fiction Editor: Jack Smith. Magazine: 8½×11; 60 pages, "quality stock" paper; mat card cover stock; b&w drawings. "Contemporary writing and contemporary American culture; poetry, book reviews, essays on contemporary literature, short stories." Annually. Estab. 1985. Circ. 300.

Needs: Contemporary, experimental, humor/satire and literary. No "erotica for its own sake, stories directed toward a juvenile audience." Accepts 1 ms/year. Does not read mss May 1-Dec. 31. Publishes ms no later than June of current year. Recently published work by Tim Coats and Dan Gallik. Length: up to 3,000 words maximum. Publishes short shorts. Sometimes critiques rejected mss and recommends other markets.

How to Contact: Send SASE for current year writing competition guidelines. Reports on mss about 1 month after contest deadline (May 1 to June 1). SASE. Photocopied submissions OK. Sample copy $3 back issue; $3.50 current. Fiction guidelines for #10 SAE and 1 first class stamp.

Terms: Acquires one-time rights.

Payment: Pays in contributor's copies.

Advice: "Since it is so difficult to break in, much of the new writer's creative effort is spent trying to match trends in popular fiction, in the case of the slicks, or adapting to narrow themes ('Gay and Lesbian,' 'Vietnam War,' 'Women's Issues,' etc.) of little and literary journals. An unfortunate result, from the reader's standpoint, is that each story within a given category comes out sounding like all the rest. Among positive developments of the proliferation of small presses is the opportunity for writers to decide what to write and how to write it. My advice is support a little magazine that is both open to new writers and prints fiction you like. 'Support' doesn't necessarily mean 'buy all the back issues,' but, rather, direct involvement between contributor, magazine and reader needed to rebuild the sort of audience that was there for writers like Fitzgerald and Hemingway."

‡THE BLACK SCHOLAR (II, IV), The Black World Foundation, Box 2869, Oakland CA 94609. (415)547-6633. Editor: Robert Chrisman. Magazine: 7×10; 56+ pages; newsprint paper; glossy, 24 lb cover; illustrations; b&w photos. Magazine on black culture, research and black studies for Afro-Americans, college graduates and students. "We are also widely read by teachers, professionals and intellectuals, and are required reading for many black and Third World Studies courses." Bimonthly. Estab. 1969. Circ. 10,000.

Needs: Literary, contemporary, juvenile, young adult and ethnic. No religious/inspirational, psychic, etc. Receives approximately 75 unsolicited fiction mss each month. Published new writers within the last year. Length: 2,000-5,000 words. Sometimes recommends other markets.

How to Contact: Query with clips of published work and SASE. Reports in 2 months on queries, 1 month on mss. Free sample copy with SASE.

Payment: 10 author's copies and 1 year's subscription.

Terms: Acquires all rights.

Advice: "Poetry and fiction appear almost exclusively in our annual culture issue (generally, Sept./Oct. of given year)."

BLACK WARRIOR REVIEW (II), Box 2936, Tuscaloosa AL 35487. (205)348-4518. Editor-in-Chief: Mark Dawson. Fiction Editor: Alicia Griswold. Magazine: 6×9; approx. 144 pages; illustrations and photos sometimes. "We publish contemporary fiction, poetry, reviews, essays and interviews for a literary audience." Semiannually. Estab. 1974. Circ. 1,300-2,000.

Needs: Contemporary, literary, mainstream and prose poem. No types that are clearly "types." Receives 100 unsolicited fiction mss/month. Accepts 5 mss/issue, 10 mss/year. Approximately 25% of fiction is agented. Recently published work by Scott Gould, Max Phillips and Lynda Sexson; published new writers within the last year. Length: 7,500 words maximum; 3,000-5,000 words average. Occasionally critiques rejected mss.

How to Contact: Send complete ms with SASE. Photocopied submissions OK. Reports in 2-3 months. Publishes ms 2-5 months after acceptance. Sample copy $4. Free fiction guidelines for SAE and 1 first class stamp.

Payment: $5-10/page and 2 contributor's copies.

Terms: Pays on publication.

Advice: "Become familiar with the magazine(s) being submitted to; learn the editorial biases; accept rejection slips as part of the business; keep trying. We are not a good bet for 'commercial' fiction. Each year the *Black Warrior Review* will award $500 to a fiction writer whose work has been published in either the fall or spring issue, to be announced in the fall issue. Regular submission deadlines are August 1 for fall issue, January 1 for spring issue."

BLACK WRITER MAGAZINE (II), Terrell Associates, Box 1030, Chicago IL 60690. (312)995-5195. Editor: Mable Terrell. Fiction Editor: Herman Gilbert. Magazine: 8½×11; 40 pages; glossy paper; glossy cover; illustrations. "To assist writers in publishing their work." For "all audiences, with a special emphasis on black writers." Quarterly. Estab. 1972.

Needs: Ethnic, historical, literary, religious/inspirational, prose poem. Receives 20 unsolicited mss/month. Accepts 15 mss/issue. Publishes ms on average of 6 months after acceptance. Length: 3,000 words preferred; 2,500 words average; 1,500 words minimum. Sometimes critiques rejected mss and recommends other markets.

How to Contact: Send complete ms with cover letter, which should include "writer's opinion of the work, and rights offered." Reports in 3 weeks. SASE. Simultaneous submissions OK. Does not accept dot-matrix computer submissions. Sample copy for 8½×11 SAE and 70¢ postage. Fiction guidelines for SASE.

Payment: Free subscription to magazine.

Terms: Acquires one-time rights. Sponsors awards for fiction writers. Contest deadline May 30.

Advice: "Write the organization and ask for assistance."

‡BLATANT ARTIFICE (IV), Hallwalls Annual Anthology of Short Fiction, Hallwalls Contemporary Arts Center, 700 Main St., Buffalo NY 14202. (716)854-5828. Editor: Edmund Cardoni. Magazine: 7×9; 150 pages; high quality paper; glossy 2-color cover; illustrations; photos. "Innovative contemporary short fiction by visitors to our reading series. Fiction writers may submit work to be considered for inclusion in the reading series, but all contributors to the publication must first have been readers in the series." Audience is readers of contemporary fiction, writers, artists. Annually. Plans special fiction issue. Estab. 1986. Circ. 1,000.

Needs: Contemporary, erotica, ethnic, feminist, gay, humor/satire, lesbian, literary, excerpted novel, translations only if submitted by the original author, not by the translator, political fiction. No "genre fiction, so-called 'minimalist' fiction, Iowa-style fiction, realistic fiction, yuppie fiction." Receives 2-4 unsolicited mss/month. Buys 10-30 mss/year. Length: 1,500 words preferred; 1,250 words minimum; 2,500 words maximum. Publishes short shorts. Sometimes critiques rejected mss and recommends other markets.

How to Contact: Submit a résumé, list of publications, readings, awards, etc., and samples of writing to be considered for inclusion in the reading series. All writers invited to do readings will subsequently be invited to submit work to the annual anthology. Reports in 3 months on mss. SASE. Simultaneous and photocopied submissions OK. Published work may be submitted for consideration for inclusion in the reading series. Accepts computer printout submissions. Sample copy for SAE and $10.

Payment: Pays $35. "This is the payment for publication only, but publication ensues from first doing a reading, for which there is a separate, negotiable payment."
Terms: Pays on publication for first or one-time rights. One 3-month writer's residency *for fiction writers only* is occasionally offered, depending on availability of funding in any given year.
Advice: "Be daring or forget it, which means write as only you can write, and not as you perceive others around you (or *out there*) writing; take my word for it, most of them are wrong. Submit work and a résumé to be considered for inclusion in our reading series; if invited to give reading, subsequent publication in *Blatant Artifice* is automatic. Women writers as well as black, hispanic, and other minority writers are particularly encouraged to apply for readings and residencies at Hallwalls."

THE BLOOMSBURY REVIEW (II), Owaissa Communications, Inc., Box 8928, Denver CO 80201. (303)892-0620. Editor-in-Chief: Tom Auer. Fiction Editor: John Roberts. "*The Bloomsbury Review* is a book magazine. We publish book reviews, essays, poetry and interviews with book-related persons." Bimonthly. Estab. 1980. Circ. 50,000.
Needs: Contemporary, literary and mainstream.
How to Contact: Send complete ms with SASE. Simultaneous and photocopied submissions OK. Reports in 2 months on queries and mss. Sample copy $3.50 with 8×10 SAE and 70¢ postage. Guidelines for #10 SAE and 1 first class stamp.
Payment: $5-25; $14/year subscription to magazine and 10 free contributor's copies.
Terms: Pays on publication for first rights. Rights revert to writer.
Advice: "Can be experimental or traditional. The bottom line is good quality writing."

‡THE BLUE WATER REVIEW (II), 6226 S.W. 10th St., West Miami FL 33144. (305)266-0050. Editor/Publisher: Dennis M. Ross. Magazine. 5½×7; 45 pages; 60 lb paper; standard cover stock; illustrations and photos. "No theme. We want quality writing: fiction, interviews with well known writers and critics, poetry, and photos." Semiannually. Estab. 1989. Circ. 5,000.
Needs: Adventure, contemporary, ethnic, experimental, humor/satire, literary, mainstream, regional, sports, suspense/mystery. "No pornography, no handwritten or single spaced submissions, no manuscripts without SASE." Receives 15 unsolicited mss/month. Accepts 3-4 mss/issue; 10 mss/year. Publishes ms 1-3 months after acceptance. Agented fiction 10%. Length: 3,000 words maximum. Publishes short shorts. Sometimes critiques rejected mss.
How to Contact: Send complete manuscript with cover letter. Reports in 1 month on queries; 3 months on mss. SASE. Photocopied submissions OK. Fiction guidelines for #10 SAE and 1 first class stamp.
Payment: 1 free contributor's copy; charge for extras.
Terms: Acquires one-time rights.
Advice: "Manuscripts should have classic elements of short story, such as meaningful character change. Submit your best work no matter the publication. We want quality. Use standard form as illustrated in *Writer's Digest* (short stories."

‡BLUELINE (II, IV), English Dept., SUNY, Potsdam NY 13676. Editor-in-Chief: Anthony Tyler. Magazine: 6×9; 112 pages; 70 lb white stock paper; 65 lb smooth cover stock; illustrations; photos. "*Blueline* is interested in quality writing about the Adirondacks or other places similar in geography and spirit. We publish fiction, poetry, personal essays, book reviews and oral history for those interested in the Adirondacks, nature in general, and well-crafted writing." Annually. Estab. 1979. Circ. 700.
Needs: Adventure, contemporary, humor/satire, literary, prose poem, regional, reminiscences, oral history and nature/outdoors. Receives 8-10 unsolicited fiction mss/month. Accepts 6-8 mss/issue. Does not read January-August. Recently published fiction by Jeffrey Clapp. Published new writers within the last year. Length: 500 words minimum; 3,000 words maximum; 2,500 words average. Occasionally critiques rejected mss. Sometimes recommends other markets.
How to Contact: Send complete ms with SASE and brief bio. Photocopied submissions OK. Submit mss Aug. 1-Nov. 30. Accepts computer printout submissions, prefers letter-quality. Reports in 2-10 weeks. Publishes ms 3-6 months after acceptance. Sample copy $5.75. Free fiction guidelines for 5×10 SASE with 1 first class stamp.
Payment: 1 contributor's copy. Charges $3 each for 3 or more extra copies; $4 each for less than 3.
Terms: Acquires first rights.
Advice: "We look for concise, clear, concrete prose that tells a story and touches upon a universal theme or situation. We prefer realism to romanticism but will consider nostalgia if well done. Pay attention to grammar and syntax. Avoid murky language, sentimentality, cuteness or folksiness. We would like to see more good fiction related to the Adirondacks. Please include short biography and word count. If manuscript has potential, we work with author to improve and reconsider for publication. Our readers prefer fiction to poetry (in general) or reviews. Write from your own experience, be specific and factual (within the bounds of your story) and if you write about universal features such

as love, death, change, etc., write about them in a fresh way. Triteness and mediocracy are the hallmarks of the majority of stories seen today."

BOGG (II), A Magazine of British & North American Writing, Bogg Publications, 422 N. Cleveland St., Arlington VA 22201. (703)243-6019. U.S. Editor: John Elsberg. Magazine: 8½×11; 60-64 pages; 50 lb white paper; 50 lb cover stock; line illustrations. "American and British poetry, prose poems and other experimental short "fictions," reviews, and essays on small press." Published 3 times a year. Estab. 1968. Circ. 650.
Needs: Very short experimental and prose poem. Nothing over 1 typewritten page. Receives 25 unsolicited fiction mss/month. Accepts 1-2 mss/issue; 3-6 mss/year. Published 50% new writers within the last year. Occasionally critiques rejected mss.
How to Contact: Query first or send ms (2-6 pieces) with SASE. Photocopied submissions OK. Accepts computer printout submissions. Prefers letter-quality. Reports in 1 week on queries; 2 weeks on mss. Publishes ms 3-12 months after acceptance. Length: 300 words maximum. Sample copy $3 or $4 (current issue).
Payment: 2 contributor's copies. Reduced charge for extras.
Terms: Acquires one-time rights.
Advice: "Read magazine first. We are most interested in work of experimental or wry nature to supplement poetry. No longer (with issue #60) accepts traditional narrative short stories."

‡THE BOOK OF SPELLS (I,IV), Cat and Candle Press, Hillandale Court, Box 54, Greenville SC 29609. Editor: Susan Kimzey. Magazine. "A small press magazine of science fiction, fantasy and horror short fiction and articles of interest to readers and writers in the genre."
Needs: Fantasy, horror, science fiction. "No fiction involving copyrighted media characters (Star Trek, etc.) and no D & D transcripts." Length: open ("quality decides"). Publishes short shorts. Sometimes critiques rejected mss and recommends other markets (time permitting).
How to Contact: Send complete manuscript with cover letter and SASE for return. Accepts computer printout submissions. Fiction guidelines for #10 SAE and 1 first class stamp.
Payment: Pays in contributor's copies.
Terms: Acquires first North American serial rights.
Advice: "No real constraints as to content. Just make sure the story is strong. Give your character problems to solve, and keep things happening. Don't be afraid to push it—I don't shock easily and you're welcome to try. Don't just write a scenario—*do* something with it. If the character's problems make *you* uncomfortable, that's probably a good sign. Don't pretend you are a physics professor if you're not, and don't violate the story's internal logic."

‡BOTTOMFISH MAGAZINE (II), Bottomfish Press, Language Arts Division, De Anza College, 21250 Steven Creek Blvd., Cupertino CA 95014. (408)996-4545. Editor-in-Chief: Robert E. Brock. Magazine: 7×8½; 80-100 pages; White Bristol vellum cover; b&w high contrast illustrations and photos. "Contemporary poetry, fiction, excerpts of novels, b&w graphics and photos for literary and writing community." Annually. Estab. 1976. Circ. 500.
Needs: Experimental, literary and prose poem. "Literary excellence is our only criteria. We will consider all subjects except pornography." Receives 10-20 unsolicited fiction mss/month. Accepts 2-3 mss/issue. Does not read mss in summer. Recently published work by Janet Sisk. Length: 500 words minimum; 5,000 words maximum; 2,500 words average.
How to Contact: Send complete ms with cover letter, brief bio and SASE. Photocopied submissions OK. No multiple submissions or reprints. Accepts computer printout submissions, prefers letter-quality. Reports in 8-10 weeks. Publishes ms an average of 6 months-1 year after acceptance. Current issue: $3.50; back issue: $2.50.
Payment: 2 free contributor's copies. Charges $3.50 for extra copies.
Terms: Acquires one-time rights.
Advice: "Strive for orginality and high level of craft; avoid clichéd or stereotyped characters and plots. We don't print slick, commercial fiction, regardless of quality."

BOULEVARD (III), Opojaz Inc., 2400 Chestnut St., Philadelphia PA 19103. (215)561-1723. Editor: Richard Burgin. Magazine: 5½×8½; 150-220 pages; excellent paper; high-quality cover stock; illustrations; photos. "*Boulevard* aspires to publish the best contemporary fiction, poetry and essays we can print." Published 3 times/year. Estab. 1986. Circ. about 2,500.
Needs: Contemporary, experimental, literary, prose poem. Does not want to see "anything whose first purpose is not literary." Receives over 400 mss/month. Buys about 6 mss/issue. Publishes ms less than a year after acceptance. Agented fiction ⅓-¼. Length: 5,000 words average; 10,000 words maximum. Publishes short shorts. Published work by Madison Smartt Bell, Francine Prose, Alice Adams. Sometimes critiques rejected mss and recommends other markets.

How to Contact: Send complete ms with cover letter. Reports in 2 weeks on queries; 2 months or less on mss. SASE. Simultaneous and photocopied submissions OK. Accepts computer printout submissions. Accepts electronic submissions. Sample copy for $5 and SAE with 5 first class stamps.
Payment: Pays $50-150; contributor's copies; charges for extras.
Terms: Pays on publication for first North American serial rights. Does not send galleys to author unless requested.
Advice: "Master your own piece of emotional real estate. Be patient and persistent."

‡MARION ZIMMER BRADLEY'S FANTASY MAGAZINE, Box 245-A, Berkeley CA 94701. (415)845-7250. Editor: Marion Zimmer Bradley. Magazine: 8½×11; 64 pages; 60 lb text paper; 10 lb cover stock; b&w interior and 4 color cover illustrations. "Fantasy only; strickly family oriented." Quarterly.
Needs: Adventure, contemporary, fantasy, humor/satire, psychic/supernatural/occult, suspense/mystery and young adult/teen (10-18) (all with fantasy elements). "No avant garde or romantic fantasy. No computer games!" Receives 50-60 unsolicited mss/month. Buys 8-10 mss/issue; 36-40 mss/year. Publishes 3-4 months after acceptance. Agented fiction 5%. Length: 3,000-4,000 words average; 5,000 words maximum. Publishes short shorts. Critiques rejected mss and recommends other markets.
How to Contact: Send complete ms with cover letter "including Social Security number and previous credits in the field (only) and personal info. Maximum length 500 words." Reports on queries within 2 weeks; 1 month on mss. SASE. Photocopied submissions OK. Accepts computer printout submissions; no dot matrix. Sample copy $4.50. Fiction guidelines for 9×12 SAE and 1 first class stamp.
Payment: Pays 3¢/word; contributor's copies.
Terms: Pays on acceptance. $25 kill fee "if held 12 months or more." Buys first North American serial rights. Sometimes sends galleys to author.
Advice: "If I want to finish reading it—I figure other people will too. A manuscript stands out if I care whether the characters do well, if it has a rythm. Make sure it has characters I will know *you* care about. If you don't care about them, how do you expect me to?"

‡BREAKTHROUGH! (II), Aardvark Enterprises, 204 Millbank Dr. S.W., Calgary, Alberta T2Y 2H9 Canada. (403)256-4639. Editor: J. Alvin Speers. Magazine: 5½×8½; 52 pages; bond paper; color paper cover; illustrations. "Up-beat, informative and entertaining reading for general audience—articles, short stories, poetry, fillers and cartoons. General interest—popular with writers and readers for information and entertainment." Quarterly. Estab. 1982. Circ. 100.
Needs: Adventure, historical (general), humor/satire, literary, regional, religious/inspirational, romance (contemporary, historical, young adult), suspense/mystery. "No pornography, uncouth language, crudely suggestive, gay or lesbian." Receives 25 mss/month. Accepts 8-10 mss/issue; 30-40 mss/year. "Publication time varies with available space, held for season, etc." Length: 1,500 words; 500 words minimum; 2,500 words maximum. Publishes short shorts. Sometimes critiques rejected mss.
How to Contact: Subscribe, or buy sample and submit ms. Include brief bio. Reports in 1 week on queries. SASE. Simultaneous, photocopied and reprint submissions OK. Accepts computer printouts. Sample copy for $4. Fiction guidelines for #10 SAE, IRC, Canadian 44¢ stamp, or $1 U.S. quite acceptable.
Payment: No payment at present.
Terms: Acquires one-time rights.
Advice: "We look for quality in line with editorial guidelines, clarity of presentation of story or information message. Be familiar with our style and theme—do not submit inappropriate material. We treat submittors with respect and courtesy."

BRILLIANT STAR (II), National Spiritual Assembly of the Baha'is of the U.S., 2512 Allegheny Dr., Chattanooga TN 37421. Magazine: 8½×11; 33 pages; matte paper; glossy cover; illustrations; photos. "Central objective and theme is to develop children's conscious awareness of the oneness of humanity and appreciation of diversity." For children approx. 5-12 years old. Bimonthly. Estab. 1969. Circ. 2,300.
Needs: Adventure, ethnic, fantasy, historical (general), humor/satire, juvenile (5-9 years), preschool (1-4 years), science fiction, spiritual, suspense/mystery, young adult/teen (10-18 years). "Accepts inspirational fiction if not overtly preachy or moralistic and if not directly Christian and related directly to Christian holidays." Receives 30 unsolicited mss/month. Accepts 3-4 mss/issue; 18-24 mss/year. Publishes ms no sooner than 6 months after acceptance. Recently published work by Dottie Smith and Susan Allen; published new writers within the last year. Length: 1,000 words preferred; 500 words minimum; 1,300 words maximum. Publishes short shorts. Always critiques rejected mss and may recommend other markets.
How to Contact: No queries. Send complete ms. Cover letter not essential. Reports in 6-10 weeks on mss. SASE. Simultaneous and photocopied submissions OK "but please make a notation that it is a simultaneous sub." Accepts computer submissions. Sample copy for 9×12 SAE and 5 oz postage. Fiction guidelines for #10 SAE with 1 first class stamp.

Payment: Pays in contributor's copies (single complimentary issue only); charges for extras.

Terms: "Writer can retain own copyright or grant to the National Spiritual Assembly of the Baha'is of the U.S."

Advice: "We enjoy working with beginning writers and try to develop a constructive collaborative relationship with those who show promise and sensitivity to our aims and focus. We feel that the children's market is open to a wide variety of writers: fiction, nonfiction, science, photo-essays. Our needs for appealing fiction especially for pre-schoolers and young readers make us a good market for new writers. *Please*, have a story to tell! The single main reason for rejection of manuscripts we review is lack of plot to infuse the story with energy and make the reader want to come along. Seeking writers from Afro-American, Hispanic, Asian and Native American backgrounds to increase multi-ethnic focus of our magazine."

‡BRISTLECONE (I, II), Western Nevada Community College, 2201 West Nye Lane, Carson City NV 89703. Editor: Jeff T. Wilkes. Fiction Editor: P.A. Magnuson. Magazine: 5½×8½; 40-60 pages; Sundance Felt text paper; Sundance Felt cover stock. Literature for a mature audience. Quarterly. Estab. 1988. Circ. 200.

Needs: Adventure, contemporary, ethnic, fantasy, feminist, historical (general), humor/satire, literary, regional, suspense/mystery and western. Plans to publish special fiction issue or an anthology in the future. Receives 8-20 unsolicited mss/month. Accepts 1-3 mss/issue. Publishes ms 3-9 months after acceptance. Recently published work by John Garmon. Length: 1,000 words average. Publishes short shorts. Sometimes critiques rejected mss and recommends other markets.

How to Contact: Send complete ms with cover letter. Reports in 2 months on queries; 3 months on mss. SASE. Simultaneous, photocopied and reprint submissions OK. Accepts computer printout submissions. Sample copy $3. Fiction guidelines for #10 SAE and 1 first class stamp.

Payment: Pays two contributor's copies.

Terms: Acquires one-time or possible anthology rights. Sometimes sends galleys to author.

BVI-PACIFICA NEWSLETTER (I), Tahuti/Quetzlcoatl Press, Box 45792, Seattle WA 98145-0792. (206)547-2364 or 547-2202. Editor: Yael Dragwyla. Magazine: 5½×8½; 32-36 pages; 20 lb paper; 60 lb cover; illustrations; some photographs. "Theme: Breaking new trails in the Inner Planes (world of the mind)." Quarterly. Plans special fiction issue. Estab. 1985. Circ. 200+.

Needs: Erotica, experimental, fantasy, horror, humor/satire, psychic/supernatural/occult, science fiction, serialized/excerpted novel, suspense/mystery, SubGenius. "We want fiction, humor, poetry or graphics that make the mind turn unusual or new corners—like juxtaposition of dissonant material such that it almost makes sense—like good satire, with Punkeon, SubGenius or end-of-the-world overtones. No romance, children's, New Ager or Norman Vincent Peale-type inspirational, anything saccharine." Receives 1-2 unsolicited mss/month. Accepts 6-12 mss/issue; 6-24 mss/year. Publishes ms 3 months-1 year after acceptance. Length: 450 words preferred; 100 words minimum; 1,000 words maximum. Sometimes critiques rejected mss and recommends other markets.

How to Contact: Send complete ms with cover letter. Reports in 1-4 weeks. SASE. Simultaneous, photocopied and reprint submissions OK. Accepts computer printout submissions. Sample copy for $2.50.

Payment: Pays in contributor's copies.

Terms: Acquires first North American serial rights.

Advice: "Write with your heart as well as your head. As the state of the world today is both horrifying and disgusting in many places and respects, often the most honest and gripping fiction and the best humor deals with the terror and anger this provokes, head-on. We want fiction, humor, poetry and graphics that free up and change the mind, so that the actions underlaid by mind will change, and in the changing, maybe open up new cracks in the Cosmic Egg."

BYLINE (II), Box 130596, Edmond OK 73013. (405)348-3325. Editor-in-Chief: Marcia Preston. Managing Editor: Kathryn Fanning. Monthly magazine "aimed at encouraging and motivating all writers toward success, with special information to help new writers." Estab. 1981.

Needs: Literary, suspense/mystery and general fiction. Especially like stories with a literary or writing twist. Receives 50-75 unsolicited fiction mss/month. Accepts 1 ms/issue, 11 mss/year. Recently published work by Nina Miller and Carolyn Wall. Published many new writers within the last year. Length: 4,000 words maximum; 1,000 words minimum.

How to Contact: Send complete ms with SASE. Photocopied submissions OK. "For us, no cover letter is needed." Reports in 2-6 weeks. Publishes ms an average of 3 months after acceptance. Sample copy, guidelines and contest list for $3.

Payment: $50 and 1 free contributor's copy.
Terms: Pays on acceptance for first North American rights.
Advice: "We're very open to new writers. Submit a well-written, professionally prepared ms with SASE. No erotica or rape-and-revenge; otherwise, we'll consider most any theme. Writing connection is a plus. We also sponsor short story and poetry contests."

CACHE REVIEW (II), Cache Press, Box 19794, Seattle WA 98109-6794. (206)789-2073. Editor: Steven Brady. Magazine: 8½×11; 50 pages; 20 lb bond paper; classic laid cover; cover photos and illustrations. Magazine which publishes "quality writing in all styles." Published irregularly. Estab. 1982. Circ. 200-500.
Needs: Experimental, fantasy, historical (general), horror, humor/satire, mainstream, prose poem, regional, science fiction, serialized/excerpted novel, sports, suspense/mystery and translations. Receives 10-20 unsolicited fiction mss/month. Accepts 3-6 mss/issue, 6-12 mss/year. Does not read June-August. Recently published work by Joe Lane, John Bradley, Susan Polkicoff. Length: 10,000 words maximum. Publishes short shorts.
How to Contact: Send complete ms with SASE. Photocopied submissions OK, "but we prefer the original." Accepts computer printout submissions; prefers letter-quality. Reports in 1 month on mss. Publishes ms 6-12 months after acceptance. Sample copy $3. Fiction guidelines for #10 SAE and 1 first class stamp.
Payment: 2 free contributor's copies; $1.50 charge for extras.
Terms: All rights revert to the author. "Cash awards may be presented for the best pieces of fiction and/or poetry in each issue."
Advice: "Send your best. Don't be afraid to experiment, but remember that editors have seen all the tricks."

CAESURA (I), English Dept., Auburn University, Auburn AL 36849. (205)844-4620. Editor: Lex Williford. Fiction Editor: Tess Slogan. Magazine: 6×9; 60-80 pages. Literary journal of fiction, creative non-fiction and poetry, for a college-educated audience. Annually. Estab. 1984. Circ. 600.
Needs: Contemporary, literary, mainstream. Does not want to see work by any whose goal is to fit a genre formula. Receives 10 unsolicited mss/month. Accepts 3-6 mss/issue; 12-15/year. Does not read mss in summer. Deadline for each year's issue: January 15. Publishes ms 3-9 months after acceptance. Length: 3,000 words average; 2,000 words minimum; 7,500 words maximum. Publishes short shorts. Occasionally critiques rejected ms.
How to Contact: Send mss, SASE. Reports in 1-2 months. Accepts computer printout submissions. Sample copy $3.
Payment: Free subscription to magazine and contributor's copies. Payment varies, based upon funding.
Terms: Acquires one-time rights. Holds annual contest for short stories.
Advice: "We're looking for stories with a strong sense of scene and dramatic structure—rising action, complications, and reversals—and a subtle lyricism. Surprise us."

IL CAFFÉ (II, IV), The Italian Experience, 900 Bush, #418, San Francisco CA 94109. (415)928-4886. Editor: R.T. LoVerso. Fiction Editor: Lloyd Bruno. Magazine: 8×12; 36 pages; illustrations and photos. Publishes serialized novels, short stories, interviews, politics, economy and art for American and Italian-American professional people. Bimonthly. Estab. 1981. Circ. 20,000.
Needs: Adventure, comics, condensed novel, confession, contemporary, ethnic, humor/satire, literary, mainstream, prose poem, romance (contemporary, historical, young adult), serialized/excerpted novel and translations. Receives 5 unsolicited mss/month. Accepts 1-2 mss/issue; 6-12 mss/year. Recently published work by Masini; published new writers within the last year. Length: 3,000 words average. Also publishes short shorts. Occasionally critiques rejected mss.
How to Contact: Send complete ms with SASE. Reports in 1 month. Publishes ms 2-6 months after acceptance. Simultaneous, photocopied and previously published submissions OK. Accepts computer printout submissions, prefers letter-quality. Sample copy $2.25.
Payment: Pays in contributor's copies; $1.25 charge for extras.
Terms: Acquires first rights. Buys reprints.
Advice: Fiction should reflect "international views."

CALLALOO (II, IV), A Journal of Afro-American and African Arts and Letters, Dept. of English, University of Virginia, Charlottesville VA 22903. (804)924-6637. Editor: Charles H. Rowell. Magazine: 7×10; 200 pages. Scholarly magazine. Quarterly. Plans special fiction issue in future. Estab. 1976. Circ. 1,000.
Needs: Contemporary, ethnic (black culture), feminist, historical (general), humor/satire, literary, prose poem, regional, science fiction, serialized/excerpted novel, translations. Accepts 3-5 mss/issue; 10-20 mss/year. Length: 2,500 words average.

How to Contact: Submit complete ms and cover letter with name and address. Reports on queries in 2 weeks; 2-3 months on mss. Simultaneous and photocopied submissions OK. Previously published work "occasionally" OK. Accepts computer printout submissions. Sample copy $5.
Payment: Contributor's copies.
Terms: Acquires all rights. Sends galleys to author.

CALLIOPE (II, IV), Creative Writing Program, Roger Williams College, Bristol RI 02809. (401)253-1040, ext 2217. Co-ordinating Editor: Martha Christina. Magazine: 5½×8½; 40-56 pages; 50 lb offset paper; vellum or 60 lb cover stock; occasional illustrations and photos. "We are an eclectic little magazine publishing contemporary poetry, fiction, and occasionally interviews." Semiannually. Estab. 1977. Circ. 300.
Needs: Literary, contemporary, experimental/innovative. "We try to include 2 pieces of fiction in each issue." Receives approximately 10-20 unsolicited fiction mss each month. Does not read mss mid-March to mid-August. Published new writers within the last year. Length: 3,750 words. Publishes short shorts under 15 pages. Critiques rejected mss when there is time.
How to Contact: Send complete ms with SASE. Reports immediately or up to 3 months on mss. Sample copy $1.
Payment: 2 free author's copies and one year's subscription beginning with following issue.
Terms: Rights revert to author on publication.
Advice: "We are not interested in reading anyone's very first story. If the piece is good, it will be given careful consideration. Reading a sample copy of *Calliope* is recommended. Let the characters of the story tell their own story; we're very often (painfully) aware of the writer's presence. Episodic is fine; story need not (for our publication) have traditional beginning, middle and end."

CANADIAN AUTHOR & BOOKMAN (II), Canadian Authors Association, Suite 104, 121 Avenue Rd., Toronto, Ontario M5R 2G3 Canada. (416)926-8084. Editor: Diane Kerner. Magazine: 8½×11; 32 pages; illustrations; photos. "Craft magazine for Canadian writers, publishing articles that tell how to write and where to sell. We publish half a dozen poems and one short story per issue as well as the craft articles. We aim at the beginning or newly emerging writer." Quarterly. Estab. 1921. Circ. 3,000.
Needs: Contemporary, humor/satire, literary. "Will not accept writing for children or 'young' adult market." Receives 50-100 unsolicited mss/year. Buys 8-10 mss/issue, 30-40 mss/year. Publishes ms 3-6 months after acceptance. Published new writers within the last year. Length: 2,500 words average; 2,000 words minimum; 3,000 words maximum. Occasionally recommends other markets.
How to Contact: Send complete ms with cover letter, which should include introduction and brief bio. Reports in 1-2 weeks on queries; 1-2 months on mss. SASE. Photocopied submissions OK. Accepts computer printout submissions. Sample copy $4.50, 9×12 SAE and IRC. Fiction guidelines #10 SAE and IRC.
Payment: "Our magazine publishes one short-fiction piece per issue, which receives the Okanagan Short Fiction Award of $125 Canadian funds." Contributor's copy to the author.
Terms: Pays on publication for first North American serial rights.
Advice: "We are looking for originality, flair and imaginative work. The writer's strategy is examined from the overall structure, to the rise and fall of the sentences to the placement of the punctuation. For more specific information, send $2.50 Canadian funds to the Canadian Authors Association with your request for a reprint of *The Green Glad Bag Review*, by Geoff Hancock."

CANADIAN FICTION MAGAZINE (II,IV), Box 946, Station F, Toronto, Ontario M4Y 2N9 Canada. Editor: Geoffrey Hancock. Magazine: 6×9; 148-300 pages; book paper; overweight cover stock; 16-32 page portfolio. "This magazine is a quarterly anthology devoted exclusively to the contemporary creative writing of writers and artists in Canada and Canadians living abroad. Fiction only, no poetry. The ideal reader of *CFM* is a writer or somebody interested in all the modes, manners, voices, and conventions of contemporary fiction." Quarterly. Estab. 1971. Circ. 1,800.
Needs: Literary. "Theme, style, length and subject matter are at the discretion of the author. The only requirement is that the work be of the highest possible literary standard." Buys 10 mss/issue, 35 mss/year. Publishes short shorts. Published new writers within the last year.
How to Contact: Send complete ms with SASE or IRC. Reports in 6 weeks on mss. Publishes ms up to 18 months after acceptance. "It is absolutely crucial that three or four issues be read. We sell back issues up to 1976 for $3; current issue $9.95 (postage included). Some double issues are $15." (Canadian funds.)
Payment: $10/page (Canadian) plus one-year subscription.
Terms: Pays on publication for first North American serial rights. Sends galleys to author.
Advice: "*CFM* publishes Canada's leading writers as well as those in early stages of their careers. A wide knowledge of contemporary literature (in English and in translation) plus expertise in creative writing, modern fiction theories, current Canadian literature, and the innovative short story would be of great help to a potential contributor. *CFM* is an independent journal not associated with any

academic institution. Each issue includes French-Canadian fiction in translation, interviews with well-known Canadian writers on the techniques of their fiction, forums and manifestoes on the future of fiction, as well as art work and reviews. $500 annual prize for the best story submitted in either French or English. Contributors might study anthology spin-offs, such as *Magic Realism; Illusion: Fables, Fantasies* and *Metafictions; Shoes and Shit: Stories for Pedestrians; Canadian Writers at Work: Interviews* or *Singularities: Physics and Fiction.*

THE CAPILANO REVIEW (II), 2055 Purcell Way, North Vancouver, British Columbia V7J 3H5 Canada. (604)986-1712. Editor: Pierre Coupey. Magazine: 6×9; 80-100 pages. Magazine of "fresh, innovative art and literature for literary/artistic audience." Three issues yearly. Estab. 1973. Circ. 850.

Needs: Contemporary, experimental, literary and prose poem. Receives 30 unsolicited mss/month. Accepts 1-2 mss/issue; 4 mss/year. Recently published works by K. D. Miller, Dorothy Speak and Gladys Hindmarch. Published "lots" of new writers within the last three years. Length: 2,000-6,000 words. Publishes short shorts. Occasionally recommends other markets.

How to Contact: Send complete ms. with cover letter. Simultaneous and photocopied submissions OK. Sample copy $5 (Canadian).

Payment: Pays $60 maximum ($15/page) and 2 contributor's copies.

Terms: Pays on publication.

THE CARIBBEAN WRITER (IV), The Caribbean Research Institute, RR 02, Box 10,000–Kingshill, St. Croix, Virgin Islands 00850. (809)778-0246. Magazine: 7×10; 110 pages; 60 lb paper; glossy cover stock; illustrations and photos. "*The Caribbean Writer* is an international magazine with a Caribbean focus. The Caribbean should be central to the work, or the work should reflect a Caribbean heritage, experience or perspective." Annually. Estab. 1987. Circ. 1,000.

Needs: Contemporary, historical (general), humor/satire, literary, mainstream and prose poem. Receives 300 unsolicited mss/year. Accepts 6 mss/issue. Length: 300 words minimum; 3,750 words maximum.

How to Contact: Send complete ms with cover letter. "Blind submissions only. Send name, address and title of ms on separate sheet. Title only on ms. Mss will not be considered unless this procedure is followed." Reports "once a year." SASE. Simultaneous and photocopied submissions OK. Accepts computer printout submissions. Sample copy for $7 and $2 postage. Fiction guidelines for SASE.

Payment: 1 contributor's copy.

Terms: Acquires one-time rights.

A CAROLINA LITERARY COMPANION (II), Community Council for the Arts, Box 3554, Kinston NC 28501. (919)527-2517. Editors: Nellvena Duncan Eutsler, Mike Parker. Magazine: 5½×8½; 65-75 pages; 80 lb matte paper; 80 lb card matte cover. "The original focus of the magazine was on providing a forum for NC writers, but that emphasis has been expanded to include both established and emerging writers from any geographic area. Priority is given to manuscripts submitted by writers living in or natives of the following states: Alabama, Florida, Georgia, Kentucky, Maryland, North Carolina, South Carolina, Tennessee, Virginia, West Virginia. Subscriptions are held by individuals, academic and public libraries." Annually. Estab. 1985. Circ. 500.

Needs: Adventure, contemporary, ethnic, historical, humor/satire, literary, mainstream, regional, senior citizen/retirement, suspense/mystery. No horror stories, religious material, children's/teenager's stories, erotic or specifically sexually oriented fiction. Receives 6-10 unsolicited mss/month. Accepts 5-6 mss/issue; 10-12 mss/year. "Recently published work by Ron Rash, who won a General Electric Foundation 1987 Award for Younger Writers, sponsored by The Coordinating Council of Literary Magazines". Published new writers within the last year. Publishes short-shorts.

How to Contact: Send complete ms with cover letter. Reports in 1-2 weeks on queries; 2-4 months on mss. Photocopied submissions OK. Accepts computer printout submissions. Sample copy for $4.25, 6×9 SAE and 3 first class stamps.

Payment: Pays in contributor's copies.

Advice: "Submit! Just be sure your manuscript is legible, correctly spelled and correctly punctuated (the number of illegible and/or misspelled/mispunctuated submissions we receive is appalling). Fiction published in *A Carolina Literary Companion* is limited by space requirements to short and short-short stories."

CAROLINA QUARTERLY (II), Greenlaw Hall CB #3520, University of North Carolina, Chapel Hill NC 27514-35209. (919)962-0244. Editor-in-Chief: Rebecca Barnhouse. Fiction Editor: Lisa Carl. Literary journal: 90-100 pages; illustrations; photos. "Fiction, poetry, graphics and some reviews, for that audience–whether academic or not–with an interest in the best in poetry and short fiction." Triquarterly. Estab. 1948. Circ. 1,000.

Needs: No pornography. Receives 150-200 unsolicited fiction mss/month. Buys 5-7 mss/issue, 15-20 mss/year. Publishes ms an average of 10 weeks after acceptance. Recently published work by Ian MacMillan, Jessica Weber, Rick Bass. Published new writers within the last year. Length: 7,000 words maximum; no minimum; no preferred length. Also publishes short shorts. Occasionally critiques rejected mss.

How to Contact: Send complete ms with cover letter (no synopsis of story) and SASE to fiction editor. Photocopied submissions OK. Reports in 2-4 months. Sample copy $4; Writer's guidelines for SASE and $1 postage.

Payment: $3/printed page; 2 free contributor's copies. Regular copy price for extras.

Terms: Pays on publication for first North American serial rights.

Advice: "We publish a good many unsolicited stories and yes, I love publishing a new writer for the first time; *CQ* is a market for newcomer and professional alike. Write 'Fiction Editor' on envelope of submitted manuscript. Keep story to decent length—it's hard to publish very long stories. Also—read what gets published in the journal/magazine you're interested in. Write the kind of story you would like to read. Make your packet look professional yet modest."

‡CAROUSEL LITERARY ARTS MAGAZINE (II), Room 217, University of Guelph, Guelph, Ontario N1G 2S1 Canada. Editor: Peter Knight. Fiction Editor: Sherri Telenko. Magazine: 5½×8½; 80 pages; illustrations and photographs. "For university students and serious literary people." Annually. Estab. 1985. Circ. 500.

Needs: Adventure, contemporary, ethnic, experimental, fantasy, feminist, gay, horror, humor/satire, lesbian, literary, prose poem, religious/inspirational, romance, science fiction, sports, suspense/mystery and western. Receives 5 unsolicited mss each month; accepts 5-6 mss per issue. Publishes ms 1-2 months after acceptance. Recently published work by Leon Rooke and J.J. Steinfield. Length: 3,000 words maximum. Publishes short shorts of 1,500-2,000 words.

How to Contact: Query first; include "brief biography about writer and where work has been published before." Reports in 2 weeks on queries; 2 months on mss. SASE. Simultaneous and photocopied submission OK. Accepts computer printout submissions. Sample copy $3.50 and 2 first class stamps. Fiction guidelines for SAE.

Payment: Pays in contributor's copies.

Terms: Pays for one-time rights.

Advice: "Our publication is open mainly to new, beginning writers."

CATHEDRAL OF INSANITY (II), 1216 W. Ivesbrook, Lancaster CA 93534. Editor: Julie. Magazine: 5½×8½; 120 pages; illustrations. "The theme is mainly humor with a bit of seriousness. Publishes short stories and poetry for underground intellectuals." Bimonthly. Estab. 1988. Circ. 50.

Needs: Contemporary, experimental, humor/satire, psychic/supernatural/occult, serialized/excerpted novel and strange personal experiences. "I would like something with an underground or avant-garde feel. Nothing mainstream." Accepts 1 ms/issue; 2 mss/year. Publishes ms within 1-2 months of acceptance. Publishes short shorts. Sometimes critiques rejected mss.

How to Contact: Query with clips of published work. Reports in 2 weeks. Simultaneous and reprint submissions OK. Accepts computer printout submissions. Sample copy for $1. Fiction guidelines free.

Payment: No payment.

Advice: "Send some work. My magazine is eager for material. Short-shorts are best, nothing over 3 pages. Something humorous/satirical (I am fond of word play) or unnatural (drug experiences) is a good thing to send."

CEILIDH (II), An Informal Gathering for Story & Song, Box 6367, San Mateo CA 94403. (415)591-9902. Editors: Patrick S. Sullivan and Perry Oei. Associate Editor: Denise E. Sullivan. Magazine: 5½×8½; 32-64 pages; illustrations. "We are a growing literary magazine looking for literary fiction, drama and poetry." Quarterly. Two issues annually devoted to fiction. Estab. 1981. Circ. 500.

Needs: Experimental, literary, prose poem, science fiction, serialized/excerpted novel and translations. No romance, juvenile, erotica, preschool or young adult. Receives 25 unsolicited mss/month. Accepts 5 mss/issue; 10-12 mss/year. Published work by Karlton Kelm and Anne Brashler. Published new writers within the last year. Length: 3,000 words average; 6,000 words maximum. Also publishes short shorts. Sometimes recommends other markets.

How to Contact: Send complete ms with SASE. Reports in 6-8 weeks. Photocopied submissions OK. Accepts computer printout submissions. Publishes ms 2-3 months after acceptance. Sample copy $3.50. Fiction guidelines for #10 SAE and 1 first class stamp.

Payment: 2 contributor's copies; $3 charge for extras.
Terms: "At this point we cannot pay for every piece, but we occasionally sponsor a contest." Acquires one-time rights.
Advice: "We lean toward experimental, more serious fiction, with a strong sense of voice. Send a neat manuscript with a descriptive cover letter, SASE. Fiction is a good voice for our times. Poetry is also, but people seem to enjoy a short story over a long poem."

CENTRAL PARK (II), A Journal of the Arts and Social Theory, Neword Productions, Inc. Box 1446, New York NY 10023. (212)362-9151. Editor: Stephen-Paul Martin. Magazine: 7½×10, 100 pages; glossy cover stock; illustrations; photos. Magazine of theoretical essays, poetry, fiction, photos and graphics for intellectual audience. Semiannually. Estab. 1981. Circ. 1,000.
Needs: Contemporary, erotica, ethnic, experimental, feminist, gay, historical (general), lesbian, literary, prose poem, serialized/excerpted novel and translations. Approximately 10% of fiction is agented. Receives 50 unsolicited mss/month. Publishes short shorts of 5-10 pages. Accepts 5 mss/issue; 10 mss/year. Published works by Ron Sukenick, Clarence Major, Dick Higgins. Published new writers within the last year. Usually critiques rejected mss. Sometimes recommends other markets.
How to Contact: Send complete ms and cover letter with "publication credits, relevant personal data, reasons for sending to us. We prefer submissions from people who are familiar with the magazine. We suggest that prospective contributors order a sample copy before submitting." Reports in 2 months. SASE. Simultaneous and photocopied submissions OK. Accepts computer printout submissions. Publishes ms an average of 3 months after acceptance. Sample copy $5.
Payment: 2 contributor's copies; $5 for extras.
Terms: Acquires first rights.
Advice: "We would like to publish more short fiction, especially if it is experimental, aggressively sexual and political in nature. Write what seems to be an authentic representation of how *your* feelings interact with the social world. Let your imagination have free reign in evolving the form your work takes. Be aware of, *but not harnessed by*, conventions. We like to know who our writers are: what they do, their literary background and activities. Writers should include a cover letter and expect a personal letter in response."

‡CHAKRA (I, II, IV), Box 8551, FDR Station, New York NY 11377. Editor: Liz Camps. Fiction Editor: Richard Behrens. Tabloid; 15½×23; 16 pages; newsprint paper; illustrations and half-toned or screened photographs. "Occult/mystical, experimental, speculative, science fiction/fantasy, erotic for imaginative persons with mystical leanings." Published irregularly—2 or 3 times/year. Estab. 1988. Circ. 1,000.
Needs: Condensed/excerpted novel, erotica, experimental, fantasy, feminist, gay, horror, lesbian, literary, prose poem, psychic/supernatural/occult, religious, science fiction and "Magickal." Receives 1-2 unsolicited mss/month. Accepts 3-5 mss/issue; 8-15 mss/year. Time between acceptance and publication varies. Recently published work by d steven conkle and Greg Burnham. Length: 2,000 words average; 9,000 words maximum. Publishes short shorts. Occasionally critiques rejected mss.
How to Contact: Send complete ms with cover letter. Reports in 1 month on queries. SASE. Simultaneous, photocopied and reprint submissions OK. Accepts computer printout submissions. Sample copy $1, 9×12 SAE and 3 first class stamps.
Payment: Pays in contributor's copies. Publication not copyrighted.
Advice: "Originality, seriousness of intention are good starts. *Allegorized* personal experience makes for engaging reading. Sincerity is important. Also should be polished—no first or second drafts. Don't try to make it sound strange—your personality either fits the genre or it does not."

‡CHAMINADE LITERARY REVIEW (II), Chaminade Press, 3140 Waialae Ave., Honolulu HI 96816. (808)735-4826. Editor: Loretta Petrie; Fiction Editor: James Robinson. Magazine: 6×9; 175 pages; 50# white paper; 10 pt cis cover; photographs. "Multicultural, particularly Hawaii—poetry, fiction, artwork, criticism, photos, translations for all English-speaking internationals, but primarily Hawaii." Semiannually. Estab. 1987. Circ. 350.
Needs: Excerpted novel, ethnic, experimental, humor/satire, literary, religious/inspirational, translations. "We have published a variety including translations of Japanese writers, a fishing story set in Hawaii, fantasy set along the Amazon, but the major point is they are all 'literary.' No erotica, horror, children's or young adult, confession, lesbian, gay." Receives 8 unsolicited mss/month. Accepts 5-8 mss/issue. Publishes ms 3-6 months after acceptance. "We haven't published short shorts yet, but would depending on quality." Sometimes critiques rejected ms.
How to Contact: Send complete ms with cover letter. Include short contributor's note. Reporting time depends on how long before deadlines of May 15 and December 15. SASE. Photocopied and reprint submissions OK. If clear, near letter quality computer printout submissions are accepted. Sample copy for $3.50.

Payment: Free subscription to magazine.
Terms: Acquires one-time rights.
Advice: "We look for good writing; appeal for Hawaii audience and writers everywhere. *CLR* was founded to give added exposure to Hawaii's writers, both here and on the mainland, and to juxtapose Hawaii writing, with mainland and international work."

‡CHAPTER ONE (I), For the Unpublished Writer in All of Us, JAB Publishing, Box 4086, Cary NC 27519-4086. (919)460-6668. Editor: Belinda J. Puchajda. Magazine: 5¼×8; 100-200 pages. "For short stories and poems." Bimonthly. Estab. 1989.
Needs: Adventure, confession, contemporary, erotica, ethnic, experimental, fantasy, feminst, historical (general), horror, humor/satire, juvenile (5-9 years), literary, mainstream, preschool (1-4 years), prose poem, psychic/supernatural/occult, regional, religious/inspirational, romance (contemporary, historical, young adult), science fiction, senior citizen/retirement, sports, suspense/mystery, western, young adult/teen (10-18 years). "No pornography." Publishes annual special fiction issue. Receives 20-50 unsolicited mss/month. Buys 7 mss/issue; 42 mss/year. Publishes ms 3 months after acceptance. Length: 4,500 words; 100 words minimum; 6,000 maximum. Publishes short shorts. Length: 100 words. Sometimes critiques rejected mss and recommends other markets.
How to Contact: Send complete ms with cover letter. Include biographical information. Reports in 1 month on queries; 2 months on ms. Simultaneous, photocopied, and reprint submissions OK. Accepts computer printout submissions. Sample copy for $1. Fiction guidelines for #10 SAE and 1 first class stamp.
Payment: Pays $30 maximum; free contributor's copies.
Terms: Publication not copyrighted.
Advice: "We feel that there is a lot of talent out there, and we want to see it. Whether it be a story from a housewife who never wrote anything before, or a writer who has been writing for years and has never got published. We want to get you in print."

THE CHARITON REVIEW (II), Northeast Missouri State University, Kirksville MO 63501. (816)785-4499. Editor: Jim Barnes. Magazine: 6×9; 100+ pages; 60 lb paper; 65 lb cover stock; photographs on cover. "We demand only excellence in fiction and fiction translation for a general and college readership." Semiannually. Estab. 1975. Circ. 700+.
Needs: Literary, contemporary and translations. Buys 3-5 mss/issue, 6-10 mss/year. Recently published work by Steve Heller, John Deming, Judy Ray. Published new writers within the last year. Length: 3,000-6,000 words. Critiques rejected mss when there is time. Sometimes recommends other markets.
How to Contact: Send complete ms with SASE. Reports in less than 1 month on mss. Publishes ms an average of 6 months after acceptance. Sample copy $3 with SASE.
Payment: $5/page up to $50 maximum. Free author's copy. $2.50 for extras.
Terms: Pays on publication for first North American serial rights; rights returned on request.
Advice: "Write well and study the publication you are submitting to. We are interested only in the very best fiction and fiction translation. We are not interested in slick material. We do not read photocopies or carbon copies. Know the simple mechanics of submission—SASE, no paper clips, no odd-sized SASE, etc. Know the genre (short story, novella, etc.). Know the unwritten laws."

THE CHATTAHOOCHEE REVIEW (II), DeKalb College, 2101 Womack Rd., Dunwoody GA 30338. (404)551-3166. Editor: Lamar York. Magazine: 6×9; 150 pages; 70 lb paper; 80 lb cover stock; illustrations; photographs. Quarterly. Estab. 1980. Circ. 1,250.
Needs: Contemporary, erotica, experimental, feminist, gay, humor/satire, literary, mainstream, regional and translation. No juvenile, romance, sci-fi. Receives 500 unsolicited mss/month. Accepts 5 mss/issue. Recently published work by Leon Rooke, R.T. Smith; published new writers within the last year. Length: 2,500 words average. Sometimes critiques rejected mss and recommends other markets.
How to Contact: Send complete ms with cover letter, which should include sufficient bio for notes on contributors' page. Reports in 6 months. SASE. Photocopied submissions OK. Accepts computer printout submissions. Sample copy $3.50. Fiction guidelines printed in magazine.
Payment: Pays in contributor's copies.
Terms: Acquires first rights. "We sponsor a prize awarded to the best story printed in *The Review* throughout the year. Judged by a professional writer, not the editor."
Advice: "Arrange to read magazine before you submit to it."

CHELSEA (II), Chelsea Associates, Inc. Box 5880, Grand Central Station, New York NY 10163. Editor: Sonia Raiziss. Magazine: 6×9; 185-235 pages; 60 lb white paper; glossy cover stock; artwork; occasional photos. "We have no consistent theme except for single special issues. Otherwise, we use general material of an eclectic nature: poetry, prose, artwork, etc., for a sophisticated, literate audience interested in avant-garde literature and current writing, both national and international." Annually. Estab. 1958. Circ. 1,300.

Needs: Literary, contemporary, poetry and translations. No humorous, scatological, purely confessional or child/young-adult experiences. Receives approximately 25 unsolicited fiction mss each month. Approximately 1% of fiction is agented. Recently published work by Ronald Tobias, M.D. Elevich and Christine Lehner. Length: not over 25 printed pages. Publishes short shorts of 4-6 pages. Critiques rejected mss when there is time.
How to Contact: Query with SASE and succint cover letter with previous credits. Accepts computer printout submissions. Prefers letter-quality. Reports in 3 weeks on queries, 2 months on mss. Publishes ms within a year after acceptance. Sample copy $5 plus postage.
Payment: Author's copies, $5 per printed page; annual Chelsea Award, $500 (send SASE for guidelines).
Terms: Buys first North American serial rights plus one-time non-exclusive reprint rights.
Advice: "Familiarize yourself with issues of the magazine for character of contributions. Manuscripts should be legible, clearly typed, with minimal number of typographical errors and cross-outs, sufficient return postage. Most mss are rejected because they are conventional in theme and/or style, uninspired, contrived, etc."

CHIPS OFF THE WRITER'S BLOCK (I), Box 83371, Los Angeles CA 90083. Editor: Wanda Windham. Newsletter. "Freelancer's forum, the beginner's chance to be published." Bimonthly.
Needs: "We will consider all categories of fiction, as our publication gives writers a chance to be 'critiqued' by fellow writers." No pornographic or offensive material. Published new writers within the last year. "Always" critiques rejected mss.
How to Contact: Submit complete ms. "Cover letters are not necessary. Please note the word count on the first page of the story." Reports in 3 weeks on queries; 1 month on mss. SASE. Considers simultaneous submissions; "prefers" photocopies. Accepts computer printout submissions, no dot-matrix. Sample copy $2. Fiction guidelines for #10 SAE and 1 first class stamp.
Payment: Payment is in copies.
Advice: "The editor works directly with the author if editing is necessary or if the story needs to be reworked. The writer's peer group also sends in comments, suggestions, etc., once the story is in print. The comments are discussed in later issues."

CHIRON REVIEW (I), (formerly *The Kindred Spirit*), Rt. 2, Box 111, St. John KS 67576. (316)549-3933. Editor: Michael Hathaway. Tabloid: 10×13; 24+ pages; newsprint; illustrations; photos. Publishes "all types of material, no particular theme." Estab. 1982. Circ. 1,200.
Needs: Contemporary, experimental, humor/satire, literary. Receives 6 mss/month. Accepts 1 ms/issue; 4 mss/year. Publishes ms within 6-12 months of acceptance. Length: 3,500 words preferred. Publishes short shorts. Sometimes recommends other markets to writers of rejected mss.
How to Contact: Send complete ms with cover letter. Reports in 2 weeks. SASE. Photocopied submissions OK. Accepts computer printout submissions. Sample copy for $2 ($4 overseas). Fiction guidelines for #10 SAE and 1 first class stamp.
Payment: Pays 1 contributor's copy. Charge for extra copies.
Terms: Acquires first rights.

CHOPLOGIC (I,II), 151 First Ave., Studio D, New York NY. 10003. (212)713-5754. Editor: Eric Gunnar Rochow. Magazine: 7×8½; 24 pages; 20 lb bond paper; self cover; illustrations and photographs. "We feel the title describes our content. Good writing, thought-provoking visuals, intelligence." Magazine is "distributed internationally (Europe mainly), predominantly 'East Village' in NYC, but read by variety of people, even my mother." Quarterly. Plans special fiction issue. Estab. 1988. Circ. 1,500.
Needs: Contemporary, experimental, humor/satire, prose, short stories. "I like writing that moves, is concise and doesn't drag along like some piece of wordy noise. No heavy romance/erotica." Receives 15-20 unsolicited mss/month. Accepts 3-5 mss/issue. Publishes ms 2-3 months after acceptance. Length: 250-500 words preferred.
How to Contact: Send complete ms with cover letter. Cover letter should include "short letter of introduction, orientation to the moon at time of writing." Reports in 4-6 weeks. SASE. Sample copy for $1, 7×10 SAE and 2 first class stamps.
Payment: Pays in contributor's copies.
Terms: Acquires one-time rights.
Advice: "I can be optimistic to those that write from the heart and not in a dictated style of some academic standard. Though William Safire is not a fiction writer, he is good with words. Write what you want rather than what you think will sell. If you want to prostitute yourself, join the Writer's Guild. Just be cool, be yourself, let us get to know you through your work and enjoy it rather than having to labor through the piece and shelve it."

‡CHRISTIAN OUTLOOK (I,IV), Hutton Publications, Box 1870, Hayden ID 83835. (208)772-6184. Editor: Linda Hutton. Newsletter: 8½×11; 3 pages; b&w illustrations. "Magazine nondenominational, inspirational for middle-of-the-road Christian (*not* evangelical)." Quarterly. Estab. 1988. Circ. 300.

Needs: Religious/inspirational. "Do not use present tense." Receives 50 unsolicited mss/month. Buys 2-3 mss/issue; 8-12mss/year. Publishes ms up to one year after acceptance. Recently published work by May Wareberg and Margaret Shauer. Length: 300-1,500 words; 1,000 average. Publishes short shorts. Length: 300 words. Sometimes critiques rejected mss and recommends other markets.
How to Contact: Submit complete manuscript. Reports in 3 weeks on mss. SASE. Accepts simultaneous, photocopied and reprint submissions. Accepts computer printout submissions. Sample copy free for #10 SAE and 2 first class stamps. Fiction guidelines for #10 SAE and 1 first class stamp.
Payment: ¼¢/word and contributor's copies.
Terms: Pays on acceptance for one-time rights.
Advice: "A dash of humor is always welcome; religious writers tend to take themselves too seriously and be too intense. The arrogant attitude of some religious publications, demanding that freelancers be members of their denominations, infuriated me and led me to start publishing an open, non-denominational newsletter to encourage beginning religious writers."

CHRYSALIS (II), Journal of the Swedenborg Foundation, The Swedenborg Foundation, 139 E. 23rd St., New York NY 10010. (212)673-7310. Send mss to: Rt. 1, Box 184, Dillwyn VA 23936. (804)983-3021. Editor-in-Chief: Carol S. Lawson. Fiction Editor: Phoebe Loughrey. Magazine: 7½×10; 96 pages; archival paper; coated cover stock; illustrations; photos. "A literary magazine centered around one theme per issue (e.g., 'Wise Woman: A Human Process' and 'Aspects of African Spirit' and 'Tree of Knowledge'). Publishes fiction, articles, poetry, book and film reviews for intellectually curious readers interested in spiritual topics." Triannually. "Would like to publish special fiction issues, but we need more writers!" Estab. 1985. Circ. 1,000.
Needs: Adventure, contemporary, experimental, historical (general), literary, mainstream, science fiction, spiritual, sports, suspense/mystery. No religious, juvenile, preschool. Receives 40 mss/month. Buys 2-3 mss/issue; 6-9 mss/year. Publishes ms within 9 months of acceptance. Recently published work by Virgil Livingston, A.D. McIntyre, Daniel Matokot; published new writers within the last year. Length: 1,500 words minimum; 2,500 words maximum. Publishes short shorts. Sometimes critiques rejected mss and recommends other markets. Does not accept reprinted or inpress material.
How to Contact: Query first and send SASE for guidelines. Reports in 2 weeks on queries; in 1 month on mss. SASE. Photocopied submissions OK. Accepts computer printout submissions, "prefers letter quality." Sample copy for $5. Fiction guidelines for #10 SAE and 1 first class stamp.
Payment: Pays $75-250, free subscription to magazine and 5 contributor's copies.
Terms: Pays on publication for one-time rights. Sends galleys to author.
Advice: Looking for "1. *Quality*; 2. appeal for our audience; 3. relevance to/illumination of an aspect of issue's theme."

‡CICADA (II, IV), 329 "E" St., Bakersfield CA 93304. (805)323-4064. Editor: Frederick A. Raborg, Jr. Magazine: 5½×8¼; 24 pages; Matte cover stock; illustrations and photos. "Oriental poetry and fiction related to the Orient for general readership and haiku enthusiasts." Quarterly. Estab. 1985. Circ. 600.
Needs: Adventure, contemporary, erotica, ethnic, experimental, fantasy, feminist, historical (general), horror, humor/satire, lesbian, literary, mainstream, psychic/supernatural/occult, regional, contemporary romance, historical romance, young adult romance, science fiction, senior citizen/retirement, suspense/mystery and translations *all with Oriental slant*. "We look for strong fiction with Oriental (especially Japanese) content or flavor. Stories need not have 'happy' endings, and we are open to the experimental and/or avant-garde. Erotica is fine (the Japanese love their erotica); pornography, no." Receives 30+ unsolicited mss/month. Buys 1 ms/issue; 4 mss/year. Publishes ms 6 months-1 year after acceptance. Agented fiction 5%. Recently published work by Gilbert Garand and Jim Mastro. Length: 2,000 words average; 500 words minimum; 3,000 words maximum. Critiques rejected ms when appropriate. Always recommends other markets.
How to Contact: Send complete ms with cover letter. Include Social Security number and appropriate information about the writer in relationship to the Orient. Reports in 2 weeks on queries; 3 months on mss (if seriously considered). SASE. Photocopied submissions OK. Accepts computer printout submissions. Sample copy $4. Fiction guidelines for #10 SAE and 1 first class stamp.
Payment: Pays $10-25 plus contributor's copies; charge for extras.
Terms: Pays on publication for first North American serial rights. $5 kill fee.
Advice: Looks for "excellence and appropriate storyline. Strong characterization and knowledge of the Orient are musts. Neatness counts high on my list for first impressions. A writer should demonstrate a high degree of professionalism."

CIMARRON REVIEW (II), Oklahoma State University, 205 Morrill, Stillwater OK 74078-0135. (405)744-9476. Editor: Gordon Weaver. Managing Editor: Deborah Bransford. Magazine: 6×9; 100 pages; illustrations on cover. "Poetry and fiction on contemporary themes; personal essay on contemporary issues that cope with life in the 20th century, for educated literary readers. We work hard to reflect quality." Quarterly. Estab. 1967. Circ. 500.

Needs: Literary and contemporary. No collegiate reminiscences or juvenilia. Accepts 6-7 mss/issue, 24-28 mss/year. Recently published works by Peter Makuck, Mary Lee Settle, John Timmerman; published new writers within the last year. Sometimes recommends other markets.

How to Contact: Send complete ms with SASE. "Short cover letters are appropriate but not essential, except for providing *CR* with the most recent mailing address available." Accepts computer printout submissions, prefers letter-quality. Reports in 4-6 weeks on mss. Publishes ms 6-9 months after acceptance. Free sample copy with SASE.

Payment: 3 free author's copies.

Terms: Acquires all rights on publication.

Advice: "Short fiction is a genre uniquely suited to the modern world. *CR* seeks an individual, innovative style that focuses on contemporary themes."

CLOCKWATCH REVIEW (II), A Journal of the Arts, Dept. of English, Illinois Wesleyan University, Bloomington IL 61702. (309)556-3352. Editor: James Plath. Magazine: 5½×8½; 64 pages; coated stock paper; glossy cover stock; illustrations; photos. "We publish stories which are *literary* as well as alive, colorful, enjoyable–stories which linger like shadows," for a general audience. Semiannually. Estab. 1983. Circ. 1,500.

Needs: Contemporary, experimental, humor/satire, literary, mainstream, prose poem and regional. Receives 50-60 unsolicited mss/month. Accepts 2 mss/issue; 4 mss/year. Recently published work by Ellen Hunnicutt, V.K. Gibson, J.W. Major; published new writers within the last year. Length: 2,500 words average; 1,200 words minimum; 4,000 words maximum. Occasionally critiques rejected mss if requested.

How to Contact: Send complete ms. Reports in 2 months. SASE. Photocopied submissions OK. Accepts computer printout submissions. Prefers letter-quality. Publishes ms 3-12 months after acceptance. Sample copy $3.

Payment: 2 contributor's copies and hand-crafted cut-out coin jewelry. "We also offer a cash prize for the best short story published in *CR* each year."

Terms: Acquires first serial rights.

Advice: "*Clockwatch* has always tried to expand the audience for quality contemporary poetry and fiction by publishing a highly visual magazine that is thin enough to invite reading. We've included interviews with popular musicians and artists in order to further interest a general, as well as academic, public and show the interrelationship of the arts. Give us characters with meat on their bones, colorful but not clichéd; give us natural plots, not contrived or melodramatic. Above all, give us your *best* work."

COCHRAN'S CORNER (I), Box 2036, Waldorf, MD 20601. (301)843-0485. Editor: Debra G. Tompkins. Magazine: 5½×8; 52 pages. "We publish both fiction and nonfiction and poetry. Our only requirement is no strong language." For a "family" audience. Plans a special fiction issue. Quarterly. Estab. 1986. Circ. 500.

Needs: Adventure, historical (general), horror, humor/satire, juvenile (5-9 years), preschool (1-4 years), prose poem, religious/inspirational, romance, science fiction, suspense/mystery and young adult/teen (10-18 years). "Mss must be free from language you wouldn't want your/our children to read." Receives 50 mss/month. Accepts 4 mss/issue; 8 mss/year. Publishes ms by the next issue after acceptance. Recently published work by Juni Dunkin, Ruth Cox Anderson, Becky Knight. Length: 500 words preferred; 300 words minimum; 1,000 words maximum. Sometimes critiques unsolicited mss and recommends other markets.

How to Contact: Send complete ms with cover letter. Reports in 3 weeks on queries; 3 months on mss. SASE for manuscript. Simultaneous, photocopied and reprint submissions OK. Accepts computer printout submissions. Sample copy for $3, 5×9 SAE and 90¢ postage. Fiction guidelines for #10 SAE and 1 first class stamp.

Payment: Pays in contributor's copies.

Terms: Acquires one-time rights.

Advice: "I feel the quality of fiction is getting better. The public is demanding a good read, instead of having sex or violence carry the story. I predict that fiction has a good future. We like to print the story as the writer submits it if possible. This way writers can compare their work with their peers and take the necessary steps to improve and go on to sell to bigger magazines. Stories from the heart desire a place to be published. We try to fill that need."

THE COE REVIEW (II), Student Senate of Coe College, 1220 1st St., Cedar Rapids IA 52402. Contact: Cyrus Cramer. Magazine: 8½×5½; 100-150 pages; illustrations; photos. Annual anthology of "quality experimental writing in both poetry and fiction. Especially directed to an academic or experimental literary audience that is concerned with current literature." Annually. Estab. 1972. Circ. 500.

Needs: Literary, contemporary, psychic/supernatural, science fiction, fantasy, feminist, gay/lesbian, erotica, quality ethnic, regional, serialized and condensed novels, translations. "We publish students, unsolicited professional and solicited professional mss. *The Coe Review* is growing and it is our goal to become nationally acknowledged in literary circles as a forerunner in the publication of experimental writing. We support writing workshops and invite both writing professors and student writers to submit." No "religious propaganda, gothic, romance, western, mystery or adventure." Length: 500-4,000 words.

How to Contact: Send complete ms with SASE. "Mss sent in summer will possibly not be returned until fall depending on availability of a fiction editor in summer." Accepts computer printout submissions. Sample copy $4.

Payment: $25-100 for solicitations. 1 free author's copy. $4 charge for extras.

Terms: Pays on publication for all rights "but possibly sooner with solicited mss. Upon request we will reassign rights to the author."

Advice: "We desire material that seeks to explore the vast imaginative landscape and expand the boundaries thereof. Study experimental writers such as Borges, Vonnegut, Brautigan, J. Baumbach and Manual Puig. Avoid sentimentalism. Do not be afraid to experiment or to write intelligent fiction."

COLD-DRILL MAGAZINE (IV), English Dept., Boise State University, 1910 University Dr., Boise ID 83725. (208)385-1999. Editor: Tom Trusky. Magazine: 6×9; 150 pages; Beckett text paper; illustrations; photos. Material submitted *must be by Idaho authors or deal with Idaho*. For adult audiences. Annually. Estab. 1970. Circ. 500.

Needs: Adventure, contemporary, erotica, ethnic, experimental, fantasy, feminist, gay, horror, humor/satire, lesbian, literary, mainstream, science fiction, serialized/excerpted novel, suspense/mystery, translations, western, Idaho topics. "Manuscripts are selected in December for the annual issue in March. Authors may submit any time, but they will not be notified unless they are selected; if they are, notification will be in late December, early January." No children's literature, romance, gothic, true confession, psychic, religious or inspirational. Receives 10 fiction mss/month. Accepts 5-7 mss/year. Publishes short shorts.

How to Contact: Query first. Reports in 2 weeks. SASE. Simultaneous and photocopied submissions OK. Accepts computer printouts. Sample copy $5. Fiction guidelines for #10 SAE and 1 first class stamp.

Payment: Pays in contributor's copies.

Terms: Acquires first rights.

Advice: "We publish the best in Idaho literature, regardless of the genre. Know the publication."

COLLAGES AND BRICOLAGES (II), The Journal of International Writing, Office of International Programs, 212 Founders Hall, Clarion University of Pennsylvania, Clarion PA 16214. (814)226-2340. Editor: Marie-José Fortis. Magazine: 8×11; 100-150 pages; illustrations. "The theme, if there is any, is international post-modern/avant-gardist culture. The magazine may include essays, short stories, short plays, poems that show innovative promise." Annually. Estab. 1987. Plans special fiction issue.

Needs: Contemporary, ethnic, experimental, feminist, humor/satire, literary, mainstream, philosophical, prose poem and science fiction. "Also post-modern, surrealist designs/illustrations are welcome." Receives about 10 unsolicited fiction mss/month. Publishes ms 6-9 months after acceptance. Recently published work by Alice Brand, Doug Bollines, Colin Mcleod; published new writers within the last year. Publishes short shorts. Sometimes critiques rejected ms; recommends other markets when there is time.

How to Contact: Send complete ms with cover letter. Reports in 2-3 months. SASE. Simultaneous submissions OK. Accepts computer printout submissions. Sample copy $5.

Payment: Pays two contributor's copies.

Terms: Acquires first rights.

Advice: "As far as fiction is concerned, it seems that everything has been said before. Hence, the writer's despair. This literary despair should be an asset to today's young writer. It should be his motif. The only innovation that can still be done is language innovation, playfulness, humor (with a sense of doom). We are now living in a neo-dada age, in a 'post-modern aura.' Hence, the writer's input should concentrate on these premises. Writing about the decadence of inspiration can bring us to a new age in literature. (The Dadaist despair was, after all, answered with surrealism.)We encourage experimental and literary writers that do not shy away from reading the classics."

COLORADO REVIEW (II), English Department, Colorado State University, Fort Collins CO 80523. (303)491-6428. Managing Editor: Bill Tremblay. Fiction Editor: David Milofsky. Translation Editor: Mary Crow. Literary magazine: 80-100 pages; 70 lb book weight paper; glossy cover stock. Semiannually. Estab. 1977. Circ. 1,000.

Needs: Contemporary, ethnic, experimental, literary, mainstream, translations. Receives 100 unsolicited fiction mss/month. Accepts 2-3 mss/issue. Recently published work by David Huddle, Francois Camoin, Patricia Eakins. Published new writers within the last year. Length: under 6,000 words. Does not read mss May-August. Occasionally critiques rejected mss and recommends other markets.
How to Contact: Send complete ms with SASE and brief bio and previous publications. Accepts computer printout submissions; prefers letter-quality. Reports in 3 months. Publishes ms 3-6 months after acceptance. Sample copy $5.
Payment: $5/printed page; 1 subscription to magazine; 2 free contributor's copies; $5 charge for extras.
Terms: Pays on publication for first North American serial rights. "We assign copyright to author on request." Sends galleys to author "when time permits."
Advice: "We are interested in manuscripts which show craft, imagination and a convincing voice. Character development, strong story lines and thematic insight are always desired. If a story has reached a level of technical competence, we are receptive to the fiction working on its own terms. The oldest advice is still the best: persistence. Approach every aspect of the writing process with pride, conscientiousness—from word choice to manuscript appearance."

COLORADO-NORTH REVIEW (I, II), University of Northern Colorado, Greeley CO 80639. (303)351-1350. Editor: Joel Long. Magazine: 5½×8½; 64 pages; 70 lb paper; 80 lb cover stock; illustrations; photos. Magazine of poetry, short fiction, translations, photography, interviews and graphic arts for writers or those interested in contemporary creativity. Published in winter and spring. Estab. 1968. Circ. 2,500.
Needs: Contemporary, literary and prose poem. Receives 100 unsolicited fiction mss/month. Accepts 70 mss/issue (including poetry), 140 mss/year. Published work by James Lentestey and Dennis Vannatta. Length: 1,000 words maximum. Critiques rejected mss by request.
How to Contact: Send complete ms with SASE and brief biographical info for contributor's section. Photocopied submissions OK. Reports in 3 months. Publishes ms 2-3 months after acceptance. Sample copy $3.50; free guidelines with SASE.
Terms: Pays in contributor's copies.
Advice: We print poetry, art, and short fiction, so space is limited for short fiction, averaging three to four stories an issue. Obviously we must be very selective so send your best work. We are looking for stories whose form is dictated by its content. Innovative work is welcome as long as the innovation meets its own standards for quality. Work with insight is always appreciated. Please do not send simultaneous submissions.

COLUMBIA: A MAGAZINE OF POETRY & PROSE (II), 404 Dodge Hall, Columbia University, New York NY 10027. (212)854-4391. Editors: Rotating. Magazine: 5¼×8¼; approximately 200 pages; coated cover stock; illustrations, photos. "We accept short stories, novel excerpts, translations, interviews, nonfiction and poetry." Annually.
Needs: Literary, prose poem and translations. Accepts 3-10 mss/issue. Receives approximately 125 unsolicited fiction mss each month. Does not read mss April 1 to August 31. Recently published work by Philip Lopate, Amy Hempel, Madison Smartt Bell; published 5-8 unpublished writers within the year. Length: 25 pages maximum. Publishes short shorts.
How to Contact: Send complete ms with SASE. Accepts computer printout submissions. Reports in 1-2 months. Sample copy $5.
Payment: Pays in author's copies. $3 charge for extras. Offers annual fiction awards.
Advice: "Don't overwhelm editors. Send work that's not longer than 20 pages."

COLUMBUS SINGLE SCENE (II,IV), Box 30856, Gahanna OH 43230. (614)476-8802. Editor: Jeanne Marlowe. Magazine: 8×11; 24 pages; illustrations; photos. Single living, male-female relationship topics covered for single adults. Monthly. Estab. 1985. Circ. 5,000.
Needs: Confession, contemporary, experimental, fantasy, humor/satire, mainstream, suspense/mystery. Buys 12 mss/year. Publication time varies "now that I have a backlog." Recently published work by Lori Ness, Robert Weinstein, John Birchler; published new writers within the last year. Length: 5,000 words maximum; "shorter ms more likely to be accepted." Publishes short shorts. Occasionally critiques rejected mss.
How to Contact: Send complete ms with a statement granting one time rights in exchange for copies. Reports in 1 week on queries; 2-4 weeks on mss. SASE for ms, "unless you don't want ms returned." Simultaneous, photocopied and reprint submissions OK, "if not from local publications." Accepts computer printout submissions. Sample copy $1.

Payment: Contributor's copies and advertising trade for most; $25 plus advertising trade maximum.
Terms: Pays on acceptance for one-time rights.
Advice: "My readers are primarily interested in meeting people, dating/relating to the other sex. I like to include a biographical note about my contributors' relation to singles. Although I have little space, I like to tackle tough problems and integrate fiction with editorial and personal experience. I don't shy away from the controversial, but do the superficial."

COMMON LIVES/LESBIAN LIVES (IV), A Lesbian Quarterly, Box 1553, Iowa City IA 52244. Contact: Tess Catalano and Tracy Moore. "*CL/LL* seeks to document the experiences and thoughts of lesbians for lesbian audience." Magazine: 5×8½; 112-128 pages; illustrations; photos. Quarterly.
Needs: Adventure, comics, contemporary, erotica, ethnic, experimental, fantasy, feminist, historical (general), humor/satire, juvenile, lesbian, prose poem, psychic/supernatural/occult, regional, romance, science fiction, senior citizen/retirement, suspense/mystery, western and young adult/teen. "*All pertaining to lesbian culture.*" Length: 4-10 pages. Occasionally critiques rejected mss.
How to Contact: Send complete ms with cover letter; a short bio sketch is required. Reports in 4 months. SASE. Photocopied submissions OK. Accepts computer printout submissions. Publishes ms up to 4 months after acceptance. Published "many" new writers within the last year. Sample copy $4.
Payment: 2 contributor's copies.
Advice: "Readers relate stories to their lives; fiction is an interesting and accessible way for lesbians to document their experience and express their opinions."

A COMPANION IN ZEOR (I,II,IV), 17 Ashland Ave., RR 5, R Box 82, Cardiff NJ 08232. Editor: Karen Litman. Fanzine: 8½x11; 60 pages; "letter" paper; heavy blue cover; b&w line illustrations; occasional b&w photographs. Publishes science fiction based on the various Universe creations of Jacqueline Lichtenberg. Occasional features on Star Trek, and other interests, convention reports, reviews of movies and books, recordings, etc. Published irregularly. Estab. 1978. Circ. 300.
Needs: Fantasy, humor/satire, prose poem, science fiction. "No vicious satire. Nothing X rated. Homosexuality prohibited unless *essential* in story. We run a clean publication that anyone should be able to read without fear." Occasionally receives one manuscript a month. Accepts "as much as can afford to print." Publication of an accepted ms "can take years, due to limit of finances available for publication." Occasionally critiques rejected mss and recommends other markets.
How to Contact: Query first or send complete ms with cover letter. "Prefer cover letters about any writing experience prior, or related interests toward writing aims." Reports in 1 month. SASE. Simultaneous and photocopied submissions OK. Accepts computer printout submissions. Sample copy price depends on individual circumstances. Fiction guidelines for #10 SAE and 1 first class stamp. "I write individual letters to all queries. No form letter at present." SASE preferred for guidelines, but not required (our present contact with writers is small). If volume of inquiries becomes larger, a SASE will be required.
Payment: Pays in contributor's copies.
Terms: Acquires first rights.
Advice: "We take fiction based on any and all of Jacqueline Lichtenberg's published novels. The contributor should be familiar with these works before contributing material to my fanzine. Also accepts manuscripts on cassette from visually handicapped if submitted. 'Zines also on tape for those individuals."

COMPOST NEWSLETTER (IV), Compost Coven, 729 Fifth Ave., San Francisco CA 94118. (415)751-9466. Editor: Valerie Walker. Newsletter: 8½×11; 20 pages; bond paper and cover; illustrations and scanned photographs. Publishes "humor/satire from a pagan/punk perspective." Published 8 times/year. Estab. 1981. Circ. under 100.
Needs: Experimental, fantasy, feminist, gay, humor/satire, lesbian, psychic/supernatural/occult, science fiction, serialized novel, pagan. No Christian. Publishes ms within 1 or 2 issues after acceptance. Length: 500 words minimum; 2,000 words maximum.
How to Contact: Query with clips of published work. Reports in 2 months. SASE. Simultaneous, photocopied and reprint submissions OK. Accepts dot-matrix computer printouts; accepts electronic submissions via Macintosh disk. Sample copy $2. (Make checks/MO's out to Valerie Walker; mark "for CNL".)
Payment: Pays in contributor's copies.
Terms: Acquires one-time rights. Publication not copyrighted.
Advice: "If you don't like the magazine market, go out and make one of your own. Type single space on white paper, or send a Macintosh disk in MacWrite or Microsoft Word. Don't bother to format unless it's essential for the feel of the piece. Entertain us, even if you're serious. Get strange." Publishes ms "if it is funny, bizarre, or we agree with its politics."

‡CONCHO RIVER REVIEW (I, II, IV), Fort Concho Museum Press, 213 East Avenue D, San Angelo TX 76903. (915)657-4441. Editor: Terence A. Dalrymple. Magazine: 6½×9; 100-125 pages; 60 lb Ardor offset paper; Classic Laid Color cover stock; b&w drawings. "We publish any fiction of high quality–no thematic specialties–contributors must be residents of Texas or the Southwest generally." Semiannually. Estab. 1987. Circ. 300.

Needs: Contemporary, ethnic, historical (general), humor/satire, literary, regional and western. No erotica; no science fiction. Receives 10-15 unsolicited mss/month. Accepts 3-6 mss/issue; 8-10 mss/year. Publishes ms 4 months after acceptance. Recently published work by Robert Flynn, Clay Reynolds, Roland Sodowsky. Length: 3,500 words average; 1,500 words minimum; 5,000 words maximum. Sometimes critiques rejected mss and recommends other markets.

How to Contact: Send complege ms with SASE; cover letter optional. Reports in 3 weeks on queries; 3-8 weeks on mss. SASE for ms. Simultaneous and photocopied submissions OK. Accepts computer printout submissions. Sample copy $4. Fiction guidelines for #10 SAE and 1 first class stamp.

Payment: Pays in contributor's copies; $4 charge for extras.

Terms: Acquires first rights.

Advice: "We prefer a clear sense of conflict, strong characterization and effective dialogue."

CONDITIONS: A Feminist Magazine With an Emphasis on Writings by Lesbians (II), Box 159046, Van Brunt Station, Brooklyn NY 11215-9046. Collective of editors. Magazine: 8½×11; 200 pages; good paper; color cover stock; illustrations and photographs. A magazine of work "by published and unpublished writers of many different backgrounds for women of all ages and backgrounds who feel that a commitment to other women is an integral part of their lives." Annually. Estab. 1976.

Needs: Ethnic, feminist, lesbian, literary, prose poem, translations. Wants to see mss "which reflect the experiences and viewpoints of Third World, working-class and older women." Receives 10 unsolicited fiction mss/month. Accepts 12 mss/issue. Recently published work by Shay Youngblood, Mariana Romo-Carmona, Leslea Newman; published new writers in the last year. Length: 500 words minimum, 10,000 words maximum, 5,000 words average. Occasionally critiques rejected mss.

How to Contact: Send complete ms with SASE. Photocopied submissions OK. Reports in 2 months. Sample copy $8.95.

Payment: 2 free contributor's copies.

Advice: "Buy a copy first to understand purpose of magazine. Revise, revise, revise, and keep trying."

CONFRONTATION (II), English Dept., C.W. Post of Long Island University, Greenvale NY 11548. (516)299-2391. Editor: Martin Tucker. Fiction Editor: William Fahey. Magazine: 6×9; 190-250 pages; 70 lb paper; 80 lb cover; illustrations; photos. "We like to have a 'range' of subjects, form and style in each issue and are open to all forms. Quality is our major concern. Our audience is literate, thinking college students; educated and self-educated lay persons." Semiannually. Published special fiction issue last year; plans another. Estab. 1968. Circ. 2,000.

Needs: Literary, contemporary, prose poem, regional and translations. No "proseletyzing" literature. Buys 30 mss/issue, 60 mss/year. Receives 400 unsolicited fiction mss each month. Does not read June-September. Approximately 10-15% of fiction is agented. Recently published work by Jerzy Kosinski, Irvin Faust, Mae Briskin; published new writers within the last year. Length: 500-4,000 words. Publishes short shorts. Critiques rejected mss when there is time. Sometimes recommends other markets.

How to Contact: Send complete ms with SASE. "Cover letters acceptable, not necessary. We accept simultaneous submissions but do not like it." Accepts computer printout submissions, letter-quality only. Reports in 6 weeks on mss. Publishes ms 6-12 months after acceptance. Sample copy $3.

Payment: $10-$100. 1 free author's copy. Half price for extras.

Terms: Pays on publication for all rights "with transfer on request to author."

Advice: "Keep trying."

‡THE CONSPIRACY OF SILENCE (II), 26 Hastings Ave., Toronto, Ontario M4L 2L7 Canada. (416)462-3665. Editors: Stephen Pender/Michael Holmes. Magazine: 8½×11; 50-80 pages. Estab. 1988. Circ. 300.

Needs: Adventure, contemporary, erotica, ethnic, experimental, literary, prose poem and translations (French, Arabic). Receives 5 unsolicited mss/month. Accepts 1 ms/issue; 2-3 mss/year. Publishes ms 4 months after acceptance. Length up to 1,500 words maximum. Publishes short shorts. Critiques rejected mss and recommends other markets.

How to Contact: Send complete ms with cover letter. Reports in 1 week on queries; 4-6 weeks on mss (sometimes longer in spring). SASE (IRCs). Simultaneous, photocopied and reprint submissions OK. Accepts computer printout submissions. Sample copy $4.50. Fiction guidelines for SAE.

Payment: Pays in contributor's copies.

Advice: "Be conscious of the power of the word–rhythm–the nature of the text as wholly separate from the author–intertextuality."

‡CORNFIELD REVIEW (II), The Ohio State University at Marion, 1465 Mt. Vernon Ave., Marion OH 43302. (614) 389-2361. Editor: Stuart Lishan. Fiction Editor: Martha Bartter. Magazine: 5½×8½; 64 pages; good paper quality; slick color cover stockk; b&w illustrations and photographs. Theme is "celebrating the changes and challenges of the Midwestern experience." Annually. Estab. 1975. Circ. 500.
Needs: Contemporary, ethnic, experimental, fantasy, historical, literary, regional, science fiction. No sex and violence. Receives 2-3 unsolicited mss per month; accepts 3-4 mss per issue, "depending on length." Does not read mss during the summer. Publishes ms up to 1 year after acceptance. Length: 1,500-2,500 words preferred; 3,000 words maximum. "Briefly" comments on rejected mss.
How to Contact: Send complete ms with cover letter. Reports on ms in 5 weeks. SASE for mss. Accepts computer printout submissions.
Payment: Pays in contributor's copies; charge for extras.
Terms: All rights revert to author upon written request.

‡CORONA (II), Marking the Edges of Many Circles, Department of History and Philosophy, Montana State University, Bozeman MT 59717. (406)994-5200. Magazine: 7×10; 130 pages; 60 lb "mountre matte" paper; 65 lb hammermill cover stock; illustrations; photos. "Interdisciplinary magazine—essays, poetry, fiction, imagery, science, history, recipes, humor, etc., for those educated, curious, with a profound interest in the arts and contemporary thought." Annually. Estab. 1980. Circ. 2,000.
Needs: Comics, contemporary, experimental, fantasy, feminist, gay, lesbian, humor/satire, literary, preschool, prose poem, psychic/supernatural/occult, regional, romance and senior citizen/retirement. "Our fiction ranges from the traditional Talmudic tale to fiction engendered by speculative science, from the extended joke to regional reflection—if it isn't accessible and original, please don't send it." Receives varying number of unsolicited fiction mss/month. Accepts 6 mss/issue. Publishes short shorts. Recently published work by Rhoda Lerman and Stephen Dixon; published new writers within the last year. Occasionally critiques rejected mss. Sometimes recommends other markets.
How to Contact: Send complete ms with SASE. Accepts computer printout submissions, prefers letter-quality. Reports in 4 months on mss. Sample copy $7.
Payment: Minimal honorarium; 2 free contributor's copies; discounted charge for extras.
Terms: Acquires first rights. Sends galleys to author upon request.
Advice: "Be knowledgeable of contents other than fiction in *Corona*; one must know the journal."

COSMIC LANDSCAPES (I), An Alternative Science Fiction Magazine, % Dan Petitpas, 6 Edson St., Hyde Park MA 02136. (617)361-0622. Editor: Dan Petitpas. Magazine: 7×8½; 32-56 pages; white bond paper and cover stock; illustrations; photos occasionally. "A magazine which publishes science fiction for science-fiction readers; also articles and news of interest to writers and SF fans. Occasionally prints works of horror and fantasy." Annually. Estab. 1983. Circ. 100.
Needs: Science fiction. Receives 10-15 unsolicited mss/month. Accepts 8 mss/issue. Published new writers in the last year. Length: 2,500 words average; 25 words minimum. Will consider all lengths. "Every manuscript receives a personal evaluation by the editor." Sometimes recommends other markets.
How to Contact: Send complete ms with info about the author. Reports usually in 1 week-3 months. SASE. Photocopied submissions preferred. Accepts readable computer printout submissions. Sample copy $3. Fiction guidelines free with SASE.
Payment: 2 contributor's copies; charges $1.50 for extras.
Terms: Acquires one-time rights. Publication copyrighted.
Advice: "Writers should send a cover letter; include SASE and a return address. I like to know a little about them. Please give some background, and how the story pertains to their experience. Learn manuscript formats. Get E. B. White's *Elements of Style*. Don't get all your ideas from TV shows or movies. Try to know the basics."

THE COUCH POTATO JOURNAL (I, II, IV), A Quarterly Fanzine of Fiction, Poetry, Art and Essays, 6861 Catlett Rd., St. Augustine FL 32084. (904)824-6581. Editor: T. M. Spell. Magazine: 5½×8½; 30 pages; 20 lb bond paper and cover; b&w illustrations. "Publication to entertain readers with fiction, poetry, art and essays based on science fiction and fantasy television shows. It is also our desire to provide an outlet for creative expression among fan artists and writers who have not yet achieved professional publication, but who have goals in that direction." Quarterly. Plans special fiction issue. Estab. 1988. Circ. approx. 200.
Needs: Adventure, fantasy, prose poem, romance, science fiction and suspense/mystery. Special interests: high fantasy, dark fantasy, sword and sorcery, space opera, cyberpunk, science gone mad, all related to sf/f television shows. "The shows we give the most attention to are *Beauty and the Beast*, *Friday the 13th: The Series*, *Max Headroom*, and *Werewolf*, but we will consider work based on any sf/f television show. No pornography: nothing degrading or sadistic; stories written for their gore, shock or disgust value alone, that have no independent plot; 'Mary Sue' stories (author's character 'gets'

series character) without an independent plot line of some sort." Receives 10-25 unsolicited mss/month. Buys 5-10 mss/issue; 20-40 mss/year. Publishes ms 3-6 months after acceptance. Length: 250 words minimum; 25,000 words maximum. Sometimes critiques rejected mss and recommends other markets.
How to Contact: Send complete ms with cover letter. "Tell me a little about what you're submitting (is it a story, poem(s), or essay?) and what series your work is based on." Reports in 1-3 weeks on queries; 2-8 weeks on mss. SASE. Photocopied submissions OK. Accepts computer printout submissions. Sample copy for $3. Fiction guidelines for #10 SAE and 1 first class stamp.
Payment: Pays free subscription and contributor's copies.
Terms: Acquires one-time rights.
Advice: "Know and love sf/fantasy—not just the shows and movies, but the books and magazines as well. It helps to know what's been done to death and what territory is wide open for exploration. Still, don't be afraid to tackle an idea that's been used often (alien invasion, for instance); write about it from your point of view and the chances are the resulting story will be fresh and moving. It helps to love the show you write about to the point of maniacal obsession (most fans, myself included, do). Fandom is a way of life and that devotion will rub off on your fiction, often overcoming all but the worst stylistic flaws. Something to keep in mind: most of the bestselling *Star Trek* novels were written by *Star Trek* fans, and a great many fan writers go on to be *selling*, professional writers."

COYDOG REVIEW (II, III), A Journal of Poetry, Short Fiction, Essays and Graphics, Box 2608, Aptos CA 95001. (408)761-1824. Editor: Candida Lawrence. Magazine: 7×9½; 125 pages; Xerox paper; fine press cover; b&w art and photos. "*Coydog Review* seeks honest, original work on any subject, in any style, for a literate audience that enjoys reading about everyday experiences." Annually. Estab. 1984. Circ. 200-500.
Needs: Erotic, ethnic, experimental, feminist, gay, humor/satire, lesbian, literary, mainstream, prose poem, regional, science fiction, excerpted novel and autobiographical. No obvious porn. Receives 60 unsolicited mss/month. Accepts 20 mss/issue. Recently published works by Michelle Dionetti, Robert Bly, Paul Milenski; published new writers within the last year. Length: under 10,000 words average. Also publishes short shorts. Occasionally critiques rejected mss and recommends other markets.
How to Contact: Send complete ms with SASE. Reports in 1 month on mss. Simultaneous and photocopied submissions OK. Accepts computer printout submissions. Sample copy $5.95.
Payment: 2 contributor's copies. Sometimes offers prize money for special themes.
Terms: Acquires one-time rights.
Advice: "Write about what you know, not what you think you ought to know or feel, and do not imitate a sophistication which is false. Risk reading your work out loud to yourself before sending. The editor is especially interested in work which tips toward autobiography but avoids self-indulgence. Getting published *anywhere* is a thrill for a beginning or continuing writer. The thrill translates into more devotion to craft. Avoid over-explanation of motive or character. Dramatic flashbacks are becoming *very* trite and ho-hum."

CRAB CREEK REVIEW (II), 4462 Whitman Ave. N., Seattle WA 98103. (206)633-1090. Editor: Linda Clifton. Fiction Editor: Carol Orlock. Magazine: 6×10 minitab; 32 pages; ultrabright newsprint paper; self cover; line drawings. "Magazine publishing poetry, short stories, art and essays for adult, college-educated audience interested in literary, visual and dramatic arts and in politics." Triquarterly. Estab. 1983. Circ. 350.
Needs: Contemporary, humor/satire, literary and translations. No confession, erotica, horror, juvenile, preschool, religious/inspirational, romance or young adult. Receives 20 unsolicited mss/month. Accepts 2 mss/issue; 6 mss/year. Recently published work by Carol Orlock, Rebecca Wells, Robert Neuman; published new writers within the last year. Length: 3,000 words average; 1,200 words minimum; 4,000 words maximum. Publishes short shorts. Occasionally critiques rejected mss.
How to Contact: Send complete ms with short list of credits. Reports in 2 months. SASE. Photocopied submissions OK "but no simultaneous submissions." Accepts computer printout submissions; prefers letter-quality. Sample copy $3.
Payment: 2 free contributor's copies; $2 charge for extras.
Terms: Acquires first rights. Rarely buys reprints.
Advice: "We appreciate 'sudden fictions.' Type name and address on each piece. Enclose SASE. Send no more than one story in a packet (except for short shorts—no more than 3, 10 pages total)."

CRAZYHORSE (III), Dept. of English, Univ. of Arkansas, Little Rock, AR 72204. (501)569-3160. Managing Editor: Zabelle Stodola. Fiction Editor: David Jauss. Magazine: 6×9; 140 pages; cover and front page illustrations only. "Publishes original, quality literary fiction." Biannually. Estab. 1960. Circ. 800.
Needs: Literary. No formula (science-fiction, gothic, detective, etc.) fiction. Receives 100-150 unsolicited mss/month. Buys 4-5 mss/issue; 8-10 mss/year. Does not read mss in summer. Publishes short shorts. Past contributors include Lee K. Abbott, Frederick Busch, Andre Dubus, Pam Durban, H.E.

Francis, James Hannah, Gordon Lish, Bobbie Ann Mason and Maura Stanton. Published new writers within the last year. "Rarely" critiques rejected mss.

How to Contact: Send complete ms with cover letter. Reports in 1 week on queries; 1-4 weeks on mss. SASE. Photocopied submissions OK. Accepts computer printout submissions. Sample copy $4.

Payment: Pays $10/page and contributor's copies.

Terms: Pays on publicaton for first North American serial rights. *Crazyhorse* awards $500 to the author of the best work of fiction published in a given year.

Advice: "Read a sample issue and submit work that you believe is as good as or better than the fiction we've published."

CRAZYQUILT (II), 3341 Adams Ave., San Diego CA 92116. (619)576-0104. Editor: Marsh Cassady. Magazine: 5½×8½; 92 pages; illustrations and photos. "We publish short fiction, poems, nonfiction about writing and writers, one-act plays and b&w illustrations and photos." Quarterly. Estab. 1986. Circ. 175.

Needs: Contemporary, ethnic, fantasy, gay, historical, humor/satire, literary, mainstream, science fiction, excerpted novel, suspense/mystery. "Shorter pieces are preferred." Receives 85-100 unsolicited mss/quarter. Accepts 1-3 mss/issue; 4-12 mss/year. Publishes 6-12 months after acceptance. Recently published work by Charles Brashers, Peter Telep, Cathryn Alpert; published new writers within the last year. Length: 1,500 words minimum; 5,000 words maximum. Publishes short shorts. Occasionally critiques rejected mss.

How to Contact: Send complete ms with cover letter. Reports in 3 weeks on mss. Simultaneous and photocopied submissions OK. Accepts computer printout submissions. Sample copy $4.50 ($2.50 for back issue). Fiction guidelines for SAE and 1 first class stamp.

Payment: 2 free contributor's copies.

Terms: Acquires first North American serial rights or one-time rights. Holds annual poetry and fiction contest ($100, $50 and $25 prizes) and annual chapbook contest.

Advice: "Write a story that is well constructed, develops characters and maintains interest."

CREATIVE KIDS (I, IV), GCT, Inc., Box 6448, Mobile AL 36660. (205)478-4700. Editor: Fay L. Gold. Magazine: 8½×11; 32 pages; illustrations; photos. Material by children for children. Published 8 times/year. Estab. 1980. Circ: 10,000.

Needs: "We publish work by children ages 5-18." Juvenile (5-9 years); young adult/teen (10-18 years). No sexist, racist or violent fiction. Accepts 8-10 mss/issue; 60-80 mss/year. Publishes ms up to one year after acceptance. Published new writers within the last year. Publishes short shorts.

How to Contact: Send complete ms with cover letter, which should include name, age, home address, school name and address. Reports in 2 weeks on queries; 1 month on mss. SASE. Accepts computer printout submissions, no dot-matrix. Sample copy $3.

Payment: Pays contributor's copy only.

Terms: Acquires all rights.

Advice: "Ours is a magazine to encourage young creative writers to use their imaginations, talent and writing skills. Type the manuscript—double space. Include all vital information about author. Send to one magazine at a time."

THE CREATIVE WOMAN (I,IV), Governors State University, University Park IL 60466. (312)534-5000, ext. 2524. Editor: Dr. Helen Hughes. Magazine: 8½×11; 48 pages; illustrations; photos. "Focus on a special topic each issue, presented from a feminist viewpoint." Estab. 1977. Circ. 800.

Needs: Feminist, humor/satire, prose poem, spiritual and sports. Receives 5 unsolicited fiction mss/month. Accepts 1 ms/issue; 3 mss/year. Publishes ms 3-12 months after acceptance. Recently published work by Susan Griffin. Also publishes short shorts. Occasionally critiques rejected mss and recommends other markets.

How to Contact: Send complete ms with cover letter. Reporting time varies. SASE for ms. Photocopied submissions and reprints OK. Accepts computer printouts. Sample copy $3.

Payment: Pays in contributor's copies.

Advice: "Read our magazine before submitting. Don't give up."

‡THE CRESCENT REVIEW (II), The Crescent Review, Inc., Box 15065, Winston-Salem NC 27113. (919)924-1851. Fiction Editor: Guy Nancekeville. Magazine: 6×9; 136-160 pages; 70 lb Williamsburg offset paper; 65 lb carnival white cover stock. "A fiction writer's magazine for the literate, college-educated and young at heart. We don't use essays or reviews. We have a strong bias toward unpublished Southeasterners." Semiannually. Estab. 1983. Circ. 500.

Needs: Contemporary, erotica, ethnic, experimental, fantasy, humor/satire, literary, mainstream, psychic/supernatural/occult, regional, science fiction, suspense. No "inspirational, dull or darkly introspective material." Receives 60 unsolicited mss/month. Accepts 18-20 mss/issue; 36-40 mss/year. Recently published work by Madison Smartt Bell, Tom Whalen and Michael Martone; published new writers within the last year. Length: 3,000-5,000 words average; 150 words minimum; 8,000 words maximum.

How to Contact: Send complete ms. Reports in 4 months. SASE. Photocopied submissions OK. Accepts computer printout submissions; prefers letter-quality. Sample copy $6.

Payment: 2 free contributor's copies; $6 charge for extras.

Terms: Acquires first North American serial rights.

Advice: "We started *The Crescent Review* in 1983 as a vehicle for talented young southeastern writers of short fiction. There seemed to be a great need for a magazine like ours in this part of the country. The quality of some of the submissions we've received bears out this need. We've had stories reprinted in *Best American Short Stories, 1984, Harper's* and *Pushcart Prize.*"

‡THE CRIMSON FULL MOON(I,IV): A Newsletter of the White Goddess Religion, Malkhutian Rite Temple Society, Box 3728, Augusta GA 30914. Editor: Rev. Patrick Saucer. Newsletter: 8½×11; 20 lb paper; black and white illustrations and photographs. "Publishes material on Goddess worship, paganism, feminism, astrology, etc. for pagans, feminists, liberal Jews and Christians." Monthly. Estab. 1987. Circ. 200.

Needs: Feminist, lesbian, prose poem, psychic/supernatural/occult. "We are interested in materials concerning goddess worship, paganism, feminism, Jewish mysticism, astrology, witchcraft. We do not want to see any material which is satanic." Receives 15 unsolicited mss/month. Accepts 12 mss/year. Publishes ms 1-2 months after acceptance. Length: 1,000 words; 3,000 words maximum. Publishes short shorts. Sometimes recommends other markets.

How to Contact: Send complete ms with cover letter. Reports in 1 week on queries; 1 month on mss. SASE. Simultaneous and photocopied submissions OK. Accepts computer printout submissions. Accepts electronic disk submissions. Sample copy and fiction guidelines for $1, legal-size SAE and 2 first class stamps.

Payment: Free subscription to magazine, contributor's copies.

Terms: Inquire about rights purchased. Publication not copyrighted.

Advice: "We are interested in both beginners and established writers. A beginning fiction writer should not hesitate to submit materials to us."

CROSS TIMBERS REVIEW (II), Cisco Junior College, Cisco TX 76437. (817)442-2567. Editor: Monte Lewis. Fiction Editor: Sue Doak. Magazine: 6×9½; 64 pages average; 65 lb paper; 80 lb cover stock; pen and ink illustrations. "To serve as a medium through which regional ideas and works may be presented to a broader readership, while at the same time not excluding the works of international writers, for academic and general audience." Semiannually. Estab. 1983. Circ. 250.

Needs: Adventure, ethnic, historical (general), humor/satire, literary, regional, western, southwestern material. Receives 5-10 unsolicited fiction mss/month. Accepts 2-3 mss/issue; 4-6 mss/year. Does not read mss June/July. Publishes ms 3-6 months after acceptance. Length: 3,000-4,000 words average; 1,000 words minimum; 4,000 words maximum. Sometimes critiques rejected mss.

How to Contact: Send complete ms and cover letter with name, address. Reports in 6 weeks on queries; 6 months on mss. SASE for ms. Photocopied submissions OK. Accepts computer printouts. Sample copy $3.

Payment: Pays in 3 contributor's copies, $3 charge for extras.

Terms: Acquires one-time rights. Sends galleys to author.

Advice: "We like stories with *impact*. The story must say something with preciseness and punch. The Southwest has a rich tradition of fiction; we want to encourage writers to keep the tradition alive. We attempt to showcase Texas writers."

CROSS-CANADA WRITERS' MAGAZINE (II), Box 277, Station F, Toronto, Ontario M4Y 2L7 Canada. Editor-in-Chief: Ted Plantos. Magazine: 8½×11; 32 pages; 70 lb paper; card-coated cover stock; illustrations; photos. "The Canadian literary writer's magazine." Published 3 times/year. Estab. 1978. Circ. 2,000.

Needs: Literary, prose poem and regional. "We welcome submissions of fiction from American authors. We offer American as well as Canadian writers the most comprehensive, current literary market listings published in Canada. We keep our readers in touch with the Canadian literary scene and available markets for their work." Receives 15-20 unsolicited fiction mss/month. Accepts 1-2 mss/issue, 3-6 mss/year. Recently published work by Don Bailey, Patricia Stone and Renato Trujillo; published new writers within the last year. Length: 3,000 words maximum. Publishes short shorts. Occasionally critiques rejected mss.

How to Contact: Send complete ms with SASE and bio. Photocopied submissions OK. Accepts computer printout submissions; prefers letter-quality. Reports in 2 weeks on queries; 5 weeks on mss. Publishes ms "up to one year" after acceptance. Sample copy $3.95.

Payment: Honorarium.
Terms: Acquires first rights and one-time rights.
Advice: Recommends studying an issue before submitting. Subscriptions: $14 (Canadian individuals); $16 (individuals abroad); $20 (Canadian institutions); $24 (institutions abroad)."Before submitting, a writer should read the story as though he/she is a magazine subscriber encountering it in cold print: i.e., put self in the reader's shoes. Does the story entertain, hold interest?"

CROSSCURRENTS (III), 2200 Glastonbury Rd., Westlake Village CA 91361. Editor: Linda Brown Michelson. Magazine: 6×9; 176 pages; 70 lb paper stock; laminated cover; line drawings and halftone photos. "*Crosscurrents* is a literary magazine offering another corner for today's artistry. We publish short fiction, poetry, graphic arts and nonfiction. We direct our publication toward an educated audience who appreciate good writing and good art and who enjoy a periodic sampling of current trends in these fields." Quarterly. Estab. 1980. Circ. 3,000.
Needs: Most categories except heavy erotica, juvenile, science fiction and young adult. "Good writing is what we look for and consider first. We want high quality literary fiction." Buys 7-12 mss/issue, 45 mss/year. Approximately 10% of fiction is agented. Recently published fiction by Alvin Greenberg, Joyce Carol Oates and Alice Adams; published new writers in the last year. Length: 6,000 words maximum. Critiques rejected mss when there is time.
How to Contact: Send complete ms with SASE. Reviews material June 1-Nov 30 each year. No simultaneous submissions. Accepts computer printout submissions. Prefers letter-quality. Reports in 6 weeks on mss. Publishes ms 4-6 months after acceptance. Sample copy $5.
Payment: $35 minimum. Offers 50% kill fee for assigned ms not published.
Terms: Pays on publication for first North American serial rights.
Advice: "Look at a sample issue to see what we publish. Include a short letter with your manuscript to let us know who you are. If given encouragement, submit three or four times each year, not every week. Study the awards collections and make sure your work measures up. Even small publications receive submissions from Nobel winners, and so self-monitoring will, in the long run, save postage."

CUBE LITERARY MAGAZINE (II), Box 5165, Richmond VA 23220. Editor: Eric Mathews. Magazine: 8½×11; 70+ pages; 70 lb offset paper; 63 lb gloss cover; b&w illustrations. "A serious literary magazine, seeking the unique and innovative voices of short fiction and poetry." Semi-annual. Plans special fiction issue. Estab. 1988. Circ. 1,000.
Needs: Adventure, condensed/excerpted novel, confession, contemporary, ethnic, experimental, fantasy, horror, humor/satire, literary, mainstream, prose poem, psychic/supernatural/occult, science fiction, suspense/mystery, translations. "No romance or religious and/or inspirational." Receives 20 unsolicited mss/month. Buys 10-15 mss/issue; 20-30 mss/year. Publishes ms 4 months maximum after acceptance. Recently published work by Isak Romun, Daniel Quinn, Michael Afflitto. Length: 3,000 words preferred; 100 words minimum; 5,000 words maximum. Always critiques rejected mss and often recommends other markets.
How to Contact: Send complete ms with cover letter. Cover letter should include "author's writing experience (what and where published); where and when writer heard of *CUBE Literary Magazine*." Reports in 1 month on mss. SASE. Photocopied and reprint submissions OK. Accepts computer printout submissions. Sample copy for $4. Fiction guidelines for #10 SAE and 1 first class stamp.
Payment: Pays in contributor's copies; charge for extras.
Terms: Acquires first North American serial rights.
Advice: "As do most editors, we strongly suggest that potential 'submittors' acquire and study a *recent* sample copy of our publication. We enjoy seeing experimental fiction, no matter where it crops up. Of course, this is with the understanding that 'experimental' does not connote 'indecipherable.' The biggest problem we encounter with new or unpublished writers is weak or contrived endings. Some new writers also seem to be under the impression that vague and/or confusing stories leave readers 'options' for interpretation. Balogna. All such stories are annoying. Don't copy stories we've already published, do exactly the opposite. Remember there are no real restrictions at *CUBE*. Don't, however, send us sleazy material, only quality fiction that touches the bounds of what hasn't been done before. Please, prepare your manuscripts properly. Type your name and address on all title pages, not just on your cover letters (most of which find their way to the trash, quickly). Make sure all pages are numbered and unstapled. Never, ever, forget your SASE."

CUTBANK (III), English Department, University of Montana, Missoula MT 59812. (406)243-5231. Editor-in-Chief: David Curran. Fiction Editor: Glenda Wallace. Magazine: 5½×8½; 115-130 pages. "Publishes highest quality fiction, poetry, artwork, for a general, literary audience." Two issues or one double issue/year. Estab. 1972. Circ. 450.
Needs: "No overt stylistic limitations. Only work of high quality will be considered." Receives 200 unsolicited mss/month. Accepts 6-12 mss/year. Does not read mss from February 2-August 15. Publishes ms up to 6 months after acceptance. Published new writers within the last year. Length: 3,750

words average; 1,000 words minimum; 12,500 words maximum. Occasionally critiques rejected mss and recommends other markets.
How to Contact: Send complete ms with cover letter, which should include "name, address, publications." Reports in 1 month on queries; 1-6 months on mss. SASE. Accepts computer printout submissions; no dot-matrix. Sample copy $3 (current issue $9) and 6½×9 SAE. Fiction guidelines 50¢, #10 SAE and 1 first class stamp.
Payment: Free contributor's copies, charges for extras, 10% discount for over 15 copies.
Terms: Acquires all rights. Rights returned upon writtern request.
Advice: "Tight market, improving. Strongly suggest contributors read an issue. Every submission is read several times, by several editors. We have published both numerous new and established fiction writers, including William Pitt Root, Ralph Beer, Neil McMahon, Gordon Lish, Madeline Defrees, James Welch, Rick DeMarinis, Fred Haefele, William Yellow Robe, Leonard William Robinson, etc. Send only your best work. Note: We do not return phone calls."

‡CUTTING EDGE IRREGULAR (II), Empty Mirror Press, Inc., Box 3430, Ann Arbor MI 48106. Editor-in-Chief: Richard Julius. Managing Editor: Dana Buck. Associate Editor: Elyse Rubin. Magazine: 5½×8½; 36-40 pages; 15 lb paper; 60 lb card cover stock; illustrations; rarely photographs. "We prefer the unusual and the startling. We like to be amused, offended, surprised or amazed." Quarterly. Estab. 1985. Circ. approximately 100-200.
Needs: Contemporary, experimental, fantasy, humor/satire, literary, mainstream, psychic/supernatural/occult, science fiction. No "stories about recent divorces, pornography, juvenile literature." Receives about 50 unsolicited mss/month. Accepts 3-4 mss/issue; 12-15 mss/year. Ms published about 6-12 months after acceptance. Length: 2,500 words average; no minimum; 3,000 words maximum. Sometimes critiques rejected mss; recommends other markets.
How to Contact: Send complete ms with cover letter including "brief bio and friendly note and perhaps a check with a request for a sample copy." Reports in 1-2 weeks on queries; 2-6 weeks on mss. SASE. Simultaneous and photocopied submissions OK. Accepts computer printout submissions. Accepts electronic submissions via Macintosh disk, either 400 or 800k, MacWrite or Microsoft Word 3.0 Sample copy $4; fiction guidelines free for #10 SASE.
Payment: Contributor's copies; $3.20 charge for extras.
Terms: Acquires first North American serial rights or one-time rights. Usually sends pre-publication galleys to author. Sponsors occasional contest for fiction writers. "Annual spring poetry/fiction contest, occasional winter contest. Watch for our ads in *Poets and Writers.*"

THE DALHOUSIE REVIEW (II), Room 314, Dunn Building, Dalhousie University, Halifax, Nova Scotia B3H 3J5 Canada. Editor: Dr. Alan Andrews. Magazine: 14cm×23cm; approximately 165 pages; photographs sometimes. Publishes articles, short stories and poetry. Quarterly. Circ. 1,000.
Needs: Literary. Length: 5,000 words maximum.
How to Contact: Send complete ms with cover letter. SASE (Canadian stamps). Sample copy $5.50 (Canadian dollars) plus postage.

DAN RIVER ANTHOLOGY (I), Box 123, South Thomaston ME 04858. (207)354-6550. Editor: R. S. Danbury III. Book: 5½x8½; 156 pages; 60 lb paper; gloss 65 lb full-color cover; b&w illustrations. For general/adult audience. Annually. Estab. 1984. Circ. 1,200.
Needs: Adventure, contemporary, ethnic, experimental, fantasy, historical (general), horror, humor/satire, literary, mainstream, prose poem, psychic/supernatural/occult, regional, romance (contemporary and historical), science fiction, senior citizen/retirement, suspense/mystery and western. No "evangelical Christian, pornography or sentimentality." Receives 20-30 unsolicited mss/month. Accepts about 8-10 mss/year. Reads "mostly in March." Recently published work by Geoffrey Clark; published new writers the last year. Length: 2,000-2,400 words average; 800 words minumum; 4,000 words maximum.
How to Contact: Send complete ms with SASE and $1 (cash) reading fee. Reports in April each year. Accepts computer printout submissions. Sample copy $9.95 paperback, $19.95 cloth, plus $2.50 shipping. Fiction guidelines for #10 SASE.
Payment: 10% of all sales attributable to writer's influence: readings, mailings, autograph parties, etc., plus up to 50% discount on copies, plus other discounts to make total as high as 73%.
Terms: Acquires first rights.
Advice: "Also: The CAL Anthology – Same Guidelines. Acceptance/Rejection – November."

‡darknerve (II), 276 28th St., San Francisco CA 94131. Editor: James E. Lough. Magazine: 5½×17; 32 pages; Sub. 20 white paper; Sub. 20 white cover stock; illustrations and photos. "Examination of the 'dark' sides of living, including satire, straight or satiric essay, experimental or conventional fiction as long as they deal with topics often left unturned. For both sexes, aged twenty to the grave." Quarterly. Estab. 1988. Circ. 500.

Needs: Condensed/excerpted novel, contemporary, erotica, experimental, feminist, gay, horror, humor/satire, lesbian, literary, mainstream, prose poem, psychic/supernatural/occult, science fiction, serialized novel and translations. "No romance, slice-of-life, coming-of-age *unless* accomplished with a weird, surprising, or parodic bent." Receives 5 unsolicited mss/month. Accepts 2-3 mss/issue; 8-12 mss/year. Publishes ms 1-3 months after acceptance. Recently published work by Richard Kostelanetz, Louis Ebert and John Mach. Length: 5,000-10,000 words average; 10,000 words maximum. Publishes short shorts. Occasionally critiques rejected mss and recommends other markets.
How to Contact: Send complete ms with cover letter. Reports in 1 month on queries; 2 months on mss. SASE. Simultaneous, photocopied and reprint submissions OK. Accepts computer printout submissions. Sample copy $2.50. Fiction guidelines for #10 SAE and 1 first class stamp.
Payment: Pays in contributor's copies.
Terms: Publication not copyrighted.
Advice: Looks for "originality of language, strong imaginative content, and a penchant for the demons of the unconscious . . . not to mention its angels. Keep it interesting, bite hard, but with integrity. Show them, through seduction, what they might not want to see. And above all, keep 'em laughing; keep 'em interested."

DAUGHTERS OF SARAH (II, IV), 3801 N. Keeler, Box 416790, Chicago IL 60618. (312)736-3399. Editor: Reta Finger. Magazine: 5½×8½; 40 pages; illustrations and photos. "Christian feminist publication dealing with Christian theology, history, women and social issues from a feminist point of view." Bimonthly. Estab. 1974. Circ. 7,000.
Needs: Historical, religious/inspirational, feminist and spiritual (Christian feminist). "No subjects unrelated to feminism from Christian viewpoint." Receives 6-8 unsolicited fiction mss/month. Buys 4-6 mss/year. Recently published work by Britt Johnston. Length: 1,800 words maximum. Publishes short shorts. Occasionally critiques rejected mss "if related and close to acceptance."
How to Contact: Cover letter stating why ms was written; biography of author. Query first with description of ms and SASE. Simultaneous, photocopied and previously published submissions OK "but won't pay." Accepts computer printout submissions. Prefers letter-quality. Reports in 2 weeks on queries. Publishes "most" ms 3 months to 1 year after acceptance. Sample copy for $2.50.
Payment: Pays $15/printed page; 3 free contributor's copies. Offers kill fee of one-half stated fee.
Terms: Pays upon publication for first North American serial or one-time rights.
Advice: "Make sure topic of story fits with publication. We get many stories that are either Christian stories, women's stories, Christian women's stories, but not necessarily feminist."

DAY CARE AND EARLY EDUCATION (II, IV), Human Sciences Press, 233 Spring St., New York NY 10013. (212)620-8000. Editor: Randa Roen Nachbar. Magazine: 8½×11; 48 pages; illustrations and photographs. "Articles for classroom practice with child 0-6, for teachers and administrators in early education." Quarterly. Estab. 1973. Circ. 5,000.
Needs: Juvenile, preschool (0-4 years). No "didactic" fiction. Receives 2 fiction mss/month. Accepts 0-1 ms/issue; 2-3 mss/year. Publishes ms 6 to 9 months after acceptance. Published new writers within the last year. Length: 1,000-2,000 words average. Publishes short shorts. Sometimes critiques rejected ms.
How to Contact: Send complete ms with cover letter. Reports on queries in 3 weeks; on mss in 3 months. SASE. Photocopied submissions OK. Accepts computer printout submissions. Sample copy and fiction guidelines for 8½x11 SAE.
Payment: Pays 2 contributor's copies; charge for extras ($2.40 each). Sends prepublication galleys to the author.

‡DEAD OF NIGHT MAGAZINE (II,IV), Box 682, East Longmeadow MA 01028. Editor: L. Lin Stein. Magazine: 8½×11; number of pages vary; newsprint paper; slick b&w cover; some original illustrations and some clip art. "A magazine of horror fiction for those who are interested in Vampirism in all its guises. (The Vampire as fictional character, etc.)" Estab. 1989. Circ. 100.
Needs: Fantasy, horror, psychic/supernatural/occult. "Short-short fiction which must always stress or suggest the theme of Vampirism. It is to the advantage of both writer and editor for the writer to take the time to look over a sample copy, or to at least send for guidelines before submitting work. No 'Count Dracula' stories, or stories that portray Vampires as one-dimensional, cartoonish characters." Receives 80 unsolicited mss/month. Buys 7-12 mss/issue; 48-50 mss/year. Publishes ms 2 months-1 year after acceptance. Recently published work by J.N. Williamson, John Maclay and Edward Lodi. Length: 500-1,000 words; 500 words minimum; 2,500 words maximum. Publishes short shorts. Sometimes critiques rejected mss and recommends other markets.
How to Contact: Send complete ms with cover letter. "Cover letter should contain author's name, address, past credits, if any." Reports in 4-6 weeks on mss. SASE. Photocopied submissions OK. Accepts computer printout submissions. Sample copy for $3, 9×12 SAE and 65¢ postage. Fiction guidelines for #10 SAE and 1 first class stamp.

Payment: Pays ¼¢/word-$10 maximum; 1 free contributor's copy; charge for extras.

Terms: Pays on acceptance for one-time rights.

Advice: "We look for neatness in the cover letter and ms. Besides that, is the story entertaining, frightening, unusual? Does it have a beginning, middle and ending? Has the author fully and logically developed the characters/plot, etc.? Please read a sample copy first, or, at the very least, send for guidelines. We're after stories that approach the popular horror character – The Vampire – in unique, odd, or unusual ways. Study what we've already published, be daring."

DEATHREALM (II), 3223-F Regents Park, Greensboro NC 27405. (919)288-9138. Editor: Mark Rainey. Magazine: 5½x8½; 50-60 pages; 20 lb bond paper; 8 pt glossy coated cover stock; pen & ink, screened illustrations; b&w photos. Publishes "fantasy/horror," for a "mature" audience. Quarterly. Estab. 1987. Circ. 1,200.

Needs: Experimental, fantasy, horror, psychic/supernatural/occult and science fiction. "Sci-fi tales should have a horror slant. *Do not* send tales that are not in the realm of dark fantasy. *Strongly* recommend contributor buy a sample copy of *Deathrealm* before submitting." Receives 200 mss/month. Buys 6-8 mss/issue; 30 mss/year. Publishes ms within 1 year of acceptance. Recently published work by Joe R. Lansdale, Fred Chappell, Thomas Ligotti. Length: 5,000 words average; 10,000 words maximum. Publishes short shorts. Sometimes critiques rejected mss and recommends other markets.

How to Contact: Send complete manuscript with cover letter, which should include "publishing credits, some bio info, where they heard about *Deathrealm*. Never reveal plot in cover letter." Reports in 1 week on queries; 2-6 weeks on ms. SASE. Photocopied submissions OK. Accepts computer printout submissions, *only* if high-quality. Sample copy for $3.50 and 65¢ postage. Fiction guidelines for #10 SAE and 1 first class stamp.

Payment: Pays $5 minimum; $8 maximum; contributor's copies.

Advice: "Concentrate on characterization; development of ideas; strong atmosphere, with an important setting. I frown on gratuitous sex and violence unless it is a mere side effect of a more sophisticated story line. Stay away from overdone themes – foreboding dreams come true; being a frustrated writer; using lots of profanity and having a main character so detestable you don't care what happens to him."

‡DELIRIUM (II), Route One, Box 7X, Harrison ID 83833. Editor: Judith Shannon Paine. Magazine: 6½×9; 60 pages; 50 lb paper; 65 lb. cover; illustrations; photos occasionally. "Themes will vary. The material must be lively, well-developed. For adult audience interested in contemporary, literary, avant garde." Quarterly Estab. 1989. Circ. 200.

Needs: Contemporary, experimental, horror, humor/satire, prose poem, romance (contemporary), western, young adult/teen (10-18). "No religious, political rant, juvenile, pornography, occult." Plans special fiction issue in the future. Buys 5-10 mss/issue; 30-40 mss/year. Publishes ms 3 months after acceptance. Length: 1,800 words preferred; 250 words minimum; 2,500 words maximum. Publishes short shorts. Length: 350 words. Sometimes critiques rejected mss and recommends other markets.

How to Contact: Send complete ms with cover letter and SASE sufficient for its return. Reports in 2 weeks-3 months on mss. SASE. Accepts photocopied submissions. Sample copy for $4. (Make checks payable to publisher: Frank L. Nicholson, Muggwart Press, POB 7814, Riverside CA 92503). Fiction guidelines for #10 SAE and 1 first class stamp.

Payment: Pays $1 minimum and contributor's copies.

Terms: Pays on publication for one-time rights.

Advice: "Seek pride and pleasure by doing your very very best. A manuscript must be finely crafted, lively, original, from start to finish, neat, well-spelled and syntaxically acceptable. A fresh, funny, warm, bold or gripping manuscript will get my attention. Like fine wine, it should have its very own bouquet and have time to breathe. Be your own meanest editor. Don't be afraid. I don't bite. Have fun when you write, but do not send me boneless drool, or stuff so obtuse and turgid nobody wants to read it."

DENVER QUARTERLY (II, III), University of Denver, Denver CO 80208. (303)871-2892. Editor: Donald Revell. Magazine: 6×9; 144-160 pages; occasional illustrations. "We publish fiction, articles and poetry for a generally well-educated audience, primarily interested in literature and the literary experience. They read *DQ* to find something a little different from a strictly academic quarterly or a creative writing outlet." Quarterly. Estab. 1966. Circ. 1,200.

Needs: "We are now interested in experimental fiction (minimalism, magic realism, etc.) as well as in realistic fiction."

How to Contact: Send complete ms with SASE. Does not read mss May-September 15. Do not query. Reports in 1-2 months on mss. Publishes ms within a year after acceptance. Recently published work by Joyce Carol Oates, Jay Clayton, Charles Baxter; published new writers within the last year. No simultaneous submissions. Sample copy $5 with SASE.

Payment: Pays $5/page for fiction and poetry. 2 free author's copies plus 3 tear sheets.
Terms: Acquires first North American serial rights.
Advice: "We'll be looking for serious, realistic and experimental fiction. Nothing so quickly disqualifies a manuscript as sloppy proofreading and mechanics. Read the magazine before submitting to it. Send clean copy and a *brief* cover letter. We try to remain eclectic and I think we do, but the odds for beginners are bound to be long considering the fact that we receive nearly 8,000 mss per year and publish only about 16 short stories."

DESCANT (II), Box 314, Station P, Toronto Ontario M5S 2S8 Canada. (416)927-7059. Editor: Karen Mulhallen. Magazine: 5¾×8¾; 100-300 pages; heavy paper; good cover stock; illustrations and photos. High quality poetry and prose for an intelligent audience who wants to see a broad range of literature. Published 4 times/year. Published special fiction issue last year; plans another. Estab. 1970. Circ. 1,000.
Needs: Literary, contemporary, translations. "Although most themes are acceptable, all works must have literary merit." Receives 100-200 unsolicited mss/month. Recently published work by David Carpenter, Katherine Govier, Rohinton Mistry. Publishes short shorts. Critiques rejected mss when there is time.
How to Contact: Send complete ms with cover letter. SAE, IRC. Reports in 4 months on mss. Sample copy $7.50 plus $2 for postage to U.S.
Payment: Pays a modest honorarium and 1 year subscription. Extra author's copies at discount.
Terms: Varies.
Advice: "*Descant* has plans for several special issues in the next two years. Unsolicited work is less likely to be accepted in the coming months, and will be kept on file for longer before it appears."

DESCANT (II), Department of English, Texas Christian University, Fort Worth TX 76129. (817)921-7240. Editors: Betsy Colquitt, Stanley Trachtenberg. "*Descant* uses fiction, poetry and essays. No restriction on style, content or theme. *Descant* is a 'little' literary magazine, and its readers are those who have interest in such publications." Semiannually. Estab. 1955. Circ. 500.
Needs: Literary, contemporary and regional. No genre or category fiction. Receives approximately 50 unsolicited fiction mss each month. Does not read mss in summer. Published new writers within the last year. Length: 1,500-5,000 words. Publishes short shorts. Sometimes recommends other markets.
How to Contact: Send complete ms with SASE. Accepts computer printout submissions. Prefers letter-quality. Reports usually within 6 weeks on ms. Sample copy $4.50 (old copy).
Payment: 2 free author's copies. $4.50 charge/extra copy.
Advice: "Submit good material. Even though a small publication, *Descant* receives many submissions, and acceptances are few compared to the total number of mss received." Mss are rejected because they "are badly written, careless in style and development, shallow in characterization, trite in handling and in conception." We offer a $300 annual prize for fiction—the Frank O'Connor Prize. Award is made to the story considered (by a judge not connected to the magazine) to be the best published in a given volume of the journal."

DESERT SUN, 840 Ortiz SE #1, Albuquerque NM 87108. (505)266-8905. Editor: Craig W. Chrissinger. Magazine: 7×8½; 24-40 pages; 20 lb bond paper and cover; illustrations and photographs. Theme: science fiction, fantasy and horror. Publishes fiction, articles, essays, book reviews, movie reviews, interviews. Semiannually. Estab. 1986. Circ. 120.
Needs: Science fiction, fantasy, horror, humor/satire, erotica. "Almost any element is allowed as long as it ties in with science fiction, fantasy or horror." Receives 10-15 fiction mss/month. Accepts 10-20 mss/issue. Does not read mss March-May or August-December. Publishes ms 2-4 months after acceptance. Recently published work by William Rasmussen, D.M. Vosk, Anke Kriske; published new writers within the last year. Length: 1,000-2,000 words average; 3,200 words maximum. Sometimes critiques rejected ms and recommends other markets.
How to Contact: Send complete ms with cover letter and name, source of information about magazine. Reports on queries in 1 month; 2 months on mss. SASE. Photocopied submissions OK. Accepts computer printout submissions, including dot-matrix. Sample copy $2. Make all payments to Craig Chrissinger. Fiction guidelines for #10 SAE.
Payment: Pays in contributor's copies; charge for extras.
Terms: Acquires one-time rights. Publication copyrighted.
Advice: "First off, be as original as possible and have fun with your manuscripts. Work at your writing every day. When you're ready to submit, know about the magazine's focus and send only appropriate material. Watch out for typographical errors, and spelling and punctuation mistakes."

DETECTIVE STORY MAGAZINE (I,II), Gryphon Publications, Box 209, Brooklyn NY 11228. Editor: Gary Lovisi. Magazine: digest size; over 50 pages; offset paper; card stock cover; illustrations. Publishes "stories 2,000-4,000 words where detective (in whatever guise) is central character—stories should be *fun* and enjoyable to read." Quarterly. Estab. 1988.

Needs: Some mystery, but mostly detective. No "blood for blood's sake." Receives 20 mss/month. Accepts 9-12 mss/year. Publishes ms within 3 months to a year of acceptance. Recently published work by Will Murray, Robert Sampson and C.J. Henderson; published new writers within the last year. Length: 2,000 words minimum; 4,000 words maximum. Sometimes critiques rejected mss and recommends other markets.
How to Contact: Query first or send complete ms with cover letter. Reports in 2 weeks on queries; 1 month on mss. SASE. Photocopied submissions OK. Accepts computer printout submissions. Sample copy $4.
Payment: Pays in contributor's copies.
Terms: Acquires first North American serial rights. Copyright reverts to author.

DEVIANCE, Opus II Writing Services, Box 1706, Pawtucket RI 02862. (401)722-8187 (evenings, weekends only). Editor: Lin Collette. Magazine. 8½×11; 36-48 pages; 20 lb bond paper; heavier bond cover; b&w drawings; b&w photographs on occasion. "*Deviance* is a magazine dedicated to publishing work by persons espousing views that may not be in favor of the 'majority.' This includes feminists, lesbian/gay, non-religious or religious (i.e. discussions of religious issues that are not Judeo-Christian or which may be an unorthodox view of Christianity or Judaism), political (non-republican or democrat) and so on." Published three times yearly. Plans special fiction issue. Estab. 1987. Circ. 500.
Needs: Condensed novel, contemporary, erotica, ethnic, experimental, fantasy, feminist, gay, historical (general), horror, humor/satire, lesbian, literary, prose poems, psychic/supernatural/occult, science fiction, senior citizen/retirement, serialized/excerpted novel, spiritual, suspense/mystery, translations. "Nothing homophobic, racist, sexist, violent for violence's sake." Receives 5 fiction mss/month. Accepts 1-2 mss/issue. May publish ms up to 2 years after acceptance. Recently published work by Rombakis; published new writers within the last year. Length: 2,500 words average; 25 words minimum; 2,500 words maximum. Sometimes critiques rejected ms and recommends other markets.
How to Contact: Send complete ms with cover letter, a biography including other places published, a whimsical description of author, no longer than 10 lines. Reports on queries in 2 weeks; 1 month on mss. SASE. Simultaneous, photocopied and reprint submissions OK. Accepts computer printout submissions. Sample copy $4, SAE with 85¢ postage. Fiction guidelines for #10 SAE with 1 first class stamp. *Make checks out to Lin Collette please!*
Payment: Pays in contributor's copies; $4 charge for extras.
Terms: Acquires first rights.
Advice: "Read the magazine! We have people sending in material that is so 'mainstream' (as in inspirational, children's, Harlequin-type love stories) that we know nobody's bothering to check us out. If you can't afford a back issue, at least send for guidelines. We are looking for offbeat ways of looking at the world—we publish gay, lesbian, feminist, horror, slice-of-life, *New Yorker*-style pieces, so if you've been rejected by *The New Yorker*, give us a try."

‡DHARMA COMBAT (I), A Magazine About Spirituality, Metaphysics and Reality, Box 20593, Sun Valley NV 89433. Editor: Keith. Tabloid: 44 pages; newsprint paper; black and white illustrations and photographs. "Radical, anarchistic, heretical religious/spiritual/political view points. For fringe, informed, conspiracy buffs." Quarterly. Estab. 1988.
Needs: Experimental, humor/satire, psychic/supernatural/occult. "No middle of the road, conservative, mainstream religion." Receives 20 unsolicited mss/month. Usually publishes ms in next issue. Length: 500 words. Publishes short shorts. Sometimes critiques rejected mss and recommends other markets.
How to Contact: Query first. Reports in 2-4 weeks on queries. SASE for query. Simultaneous, photocopied and reprint submissions OK. Accepts computer printout submissions. Sample copy $2.50. Free fiction guidelines.
Payment: Pays in contributor's copies.
Terms: Acquires one-time rights.
Advice: "We are mental/spiritual activists. D.C. is a form of activism, punching holes in reality world views. We look for uniqueness of viewpoint."

DREAM INTERNATIONAL/QUARTERLY (II, IV), U.S. Address: Charles I. Jones, 121 N. Ramona St. #27, Ramona CA 92065. Australia address: Dr. Les Jones, 256 Berserker St., No. Rockhampton, Queensland 4701, Australia. Editors: Les and Chuck Jones. Magazine: 5×7; 60-80 pages; Xerox paper; parchment cover stock; some illustrations and photos. Publishes fiction and nonfiction that is dream-related or clearly inspired by a dream. Quarterly. Estab. 1981. Circ. 200.
Needs: Adventure, confession, contemporary, erotica, ethnic, experimental, fantasy, historical (general), horror, humor/satire, juvenile (5-9 years), literary, mainstream, prose poem, psychic/supernatural/occult, romance, science fiction, senior citizen/retirement, serialized/excerpted novel, spiritual, suspense/mystery, translations, western, young adult/teen (10-18). Receives 20-40 unsolicited mss/month. Publishes ms 6-8 months after acceptance. Length: 1,500 words minimum; 2,000 words maxi-

mum. Published new writers within the last year. Publishes short shorts. Length: 1,000 words. Occasionally critiques rejected mss. Sometimes recommends other markets.

How to Contact: Reports in 6 weeks on queries; 3 months on mss. SASE. Photocopied and reprint submissions OK. Accepts computer printout submissions, including dot-matrix "if legible." Sample copy for $4, SAE and 2 first class stamps. Guidelines for $1, SAE and 1 first class stamp. "Accepted mss will not be returned unless requested at time of submission."

Payment: Pays in contributor's copies; sometimes offers free magazine subscription.

Terms: Acquires one-time rights.

Advice: "Use your nightly dreams to inspire you to literary flights. Avoid stereotypes and clichés. Avoid Twilight Zone type stories. When contacting editor, make all checks, money orders, and overseas drafts payable to *Charles Jones.*"

‡DREAMS & VISIONS (II), New Frontiers in Christian Fiction, Skysong Press, RR1, Washago, Ontario L0K 2B0 Canada. Editor: Steve Stanton. Fiction Editor: Wendy Stanton. Magazine: 5½×8½; 48 pages; 20 lb bond paper; cornwall coated cover; illustrations on cover. "Contemporary Christian fiction in a variety of styles for adult Christians." Quarterly. Estab. 1989. Circ. 1,000.

Needs: Contemporary, experimental, fantasy, humor/satire, literary, religious/inspirational. "All stories should portray a Christian world view or expand upon Biblical themes or ethics in an entertaining or enlightening manner." Receives 10 unsolicited mss/month. Accepts 7 mss/issue; 30 mss/year. Publishes ms 2-6 months after acceptance. Length: 2,500 words; 1,200 words minimum; 8,000 words maximum. Sometimes critiques rejected mss and recommends other markets.

How to Contact: Send complete ms with cover letter. "Bio is optional: degrees held and in what specialties, publishing credits, service in the church, etc." Reports in 2 weeks on queries; 6-8 weeks on mss. SASE. Photocopied submissions OK. Accepts computer printout submissions. Sample copy for $3. Fiction guidelines for SAE and 1 IRC.

Payment: Pays in contributor's copies; charge for extra at ⅓ discount.

Terms: Acquires first North American serial rights and one-time, non-exclusive reprint rights.

Advice: "In general we look for work that has some literary value, that is in some way unique and relevant to Christian readers today. Our first priority is technical adequacy, though we will occasionally work with a beginning writer to polish a manuscript. Ultimately, we look for stories that glorify the Lord Jesus Christ, stories that build up rather than tear down, that exalt the sanctity of life, the holiness of God, and the value of the family."

‡EAGLE'S FLIGHT (I), A Literary Magazine, 203 N. Weigle, Watonga OK 73772. (405)623-7333. Editor: Shyamkant Kulkarni. Fiction Editor: Rekha Kulkarni. Tabloid: 8½×11; 2-4 pages; bond paper; broad sheet cover.Publication prints "fiction and poetry for a general audience." Quarterly.

Needs: Literary, mainstream, romance, suspense/mystery. Plans to publish special fiction issue in future. Accepts 1-2 mss/year. Does not read mss June-December. Length: 1,500 words preferred; 1,000 words minimum; 2,000 maximum. Publishes short shorts.

How to Contact: Query first. Reports in 6 weeks on queries; 3 months on mss. Combine SASE. Photocopied submissions OK. Accepts computer printout submissions. Sample copy or fiction guidelines for $1 and 4×9½ SAE and 1 first class stamp.

Payment: Pays $5-20, free subscription to magazine, contributor's copies; charge for extras.

Terms: Pays on publication for first North American serial rights or one-time rights.

Advice: We look for form, substance and quality. Read and study what one wants to write and work at.

EARTH'S DAUGHTERS (II), A Feminist Arts Periodical, Box 41, Central Park Station, Buffalo NY 14215. (716)837-7778. Collective editorship. Business Manager: Bonnie Johnson. Magazine: usually 5½×8½; 50 pages; 60 lb paper; coated cover; 2-4 illustrations; 2-4 photos. "We publish poetry and short fiction; also graphics, art work and photos; our focus is the experience and creative expression of women." For a general/women/feminist audience. Quarterly. Published special topical issues last year; plans more this year. Estab. 1971. Circ. 1,000.

Needs: Contemporary, erotica, ethnic, experimental, fantasy, feminist, humor/satire, literary, prose poem. "Keep the fiction short." Receives 25-50 unsolicited fiction mss/month. Accepts 2-4 mss/issue; 8-12 mss/year. Recently published work by Gabrielle Burton, Mary Jane Markell, Meredith Sue Willis and Julia Alvarez; published several new writers within the last year. Length: 400 words minimum; 1,000 words maximum; 800 words average. Occasionally critiques rejected mss and recommends other markets.

How to Contact: Send complete ms. SASE. Simultaneous and photocopied submissions OK. Accepts computer printout submissions, "must be clearly legible." Reports in 3 weeks on queries; 3 weeks to 3 months on mss. Publishes ms an average of 1 year after acceptance. Sample copy for $4.

Payment: 2 free contributor's copies, additional copies half price.

Terms: Acquires first rights. Copyright reverts to author upon publication.

Advice: "We require work of technical skill and artistic intensity; we welcome submissions from unknown writers. Send SASE in April of each year for themes of upcoming issues. Please do not inquire as to the status of your work too soon or too often—the US Mail is dependable, and we have yet to lose a manuscript."

‡ECHOES (I,II), The Hudson Valley Writers Association, Box 365, Wappingers Falls NY 12590. (914)298-8556. Editor: Lambert/McIntosh. Fiction Editor: Eileen Charbonneau. Magazine: 8½×11; 44 pages; illustrations. Quarterly. Estab. 1985. Circ. 200.

Needs: "We do not categorize material—we consider material of *all* types." Receives 15-30 unsolicited mss/month. Buys or accepts 2-5 mss/issue; 8-20 mss/year. Publishes ms 6-8 weeks after acceptance. Recently published work by Eileen Charbonneau, Nancy Walker. Length: 1,500 words preferred; 750 words minimum; 3,000 words maximum. Publishes short shorts. Sometimes critiques rejected mss and recommends other markets.

How to Contact: Send complete manuscript with cover letter. Reports in 6-8 weeks on queries/mss. SASE. Simultaneous, photocopied and reprint submissions OK. Accepts computer printout submissions. Sample copy for $4.50. Fiction guidelines for SAE.

Payment: Pays in contributor's copies.

Terms: Pays for one-time rights.

Advice: "We look for good clear writing—a plot as opposed to mood piece or slice-of-life."

EIDOS: (IV), Erotic Entertainment for Women, Men & Couples, Box 96, Boston MA 02137-0096. (617)262-0096. Editor: Brenda L. Tatelbaum. Tabloid: 10×14; 48 pages; web offset printing; illustrations; photos. Magazine of erotica for women, men and couples of all sexual orientations, preferences and lifestyles. "Explicit material regarding language and behavior formed in relationships, intimacy, moment of satisfaction—sensual, sexy, honest. For an energetic, well informed, international erotica readership." Quarterly. Estab. 1984. Circ. 7,000.

Needs: Erotica. Humorous or tongue-in-cheek erotic fiction is especially wanted. Publishes at least 4 pieces of fiction/year. Published new writers within the last year. Length: 2,000 words average; 500 words minimum; 3,500 words maximum. Occasionally critiques rejected mss and recommends other markets.

How to Contact: Send complete ms with SASE. "Cover letter with history of publication or short bio is welcome." Reports in 2 months on queries; 3 months on mss. Simultaneous and photocopied submissions OK. Accepts computer printout submissions. Sample copy $5. Fiction guidelines for #10 envelope with 1 first class stamp.

Payment: Contributor's copies.

Terms: Acquires first North American serial rights.

Advice: "We receive more erotic fiction manuscripts now than in the past. Most likely because both men and women are more comfortable with the notion of submitting these manuscripts for publication as well as the desire to see alternative sexually explicit fiction in print. Therefore we can publish more erotic fiction because we have more material to choose from. There is still a lot of debate as to what erotic fiction consists of. This is a tough market to break into. Manuscripts must fit our editorial needs and it is best to order a sample issue prior to writing or submitting material. Honest, explicitly pro-sex, mutually consensual erotica is void of power, control and degradation—no rape or coercion of any kind."

‡ELDRITCH SCIENCE (II,IV), Greater Medford Science Fiction Society, 87-6 Park, Worcester MA 01605. Editor: George Phillies. Magazine: 8½×11; 30 pages; 20 lb paper; 60 lb cover; illustrations. Science fiction and fantasy for adults. Semiannually. Estab. 1988.

Needs: Adventure, fantasy, literary, science fiction. "No horror, contemporary, erotica." Receives 5-10 unsolicited mss/month. Accepts 4 mss/issue; 8 mss/year. Publishes mss 4-6 months after acceptance. Recently published work by Cabot, Moxley, Reedman. Length: 8,000 words; 5,000 words minimum; 15,000 words maximum. Sometimes critiques rejected mss and recommends other markets.

How to Contact: Send complete ms with cover letter. Reports in 2 weeks on queries; 6-8 weeks on mss. SASE for mss. Photocopied submissions OK. Accepts computer printout submissions. Accepts electronic submissions via disk. Sample copy for 8½×11 SAE and 4 first class stamps. Free fiction guidelines.

Payment: Pays in contributor's copies.
Terms: Acquires one-time rights. Publication not copyrighted.
Advice: "Clear plots, heroes who think and solve their problems, and sparkling, literary prose. Make a manuscript stand out. Read the guidelines!"

***Eldritch Science** publishes science fantasy and science fiction. Ree Young's "Adara's Tale" illustration is based on a story by R.F. Cabot, IV. Editor George Phillies says, "The heroine of the tale, Adara, is the young lady with the sword; the creature with the tentacles is one of a series of obstacles which she confronts and overcomes."*

ELDRITCH TALES (II, IV), Yith Press, 1051 Wellington Rd., Lawrence KS 66044. (913)843-4341. Editor-in-Chief: Crispin Burnham. Magazine: 5½×8; 120 pages (average); glossy cover; illustrations; "very few" photos. "The magazine concerns horror fiction in the tradition of the old *Weird Tales* magazine. We publish fiction in the tradition of H.P. Lovecraft, Robert Bloch and Stephen King, among others, for fans of this particular genre." Semiannually. Estab. 1975. Circ. 1,000.
Needs: Horror and psychic/supernatural/occult. "No mad slasher stories or similar nonsupernatural horror stories." Receives about 8 unsolicited fiction mss/month. Accepts 12 mss/issue, 24 mss/year. Published work by J.N. Williamson, William F. Wu and Charles Grant. Published new writers within the last year. Length: 50-100 words minimum; 20,000 words maximum; 10,000 words average. Occasionally critiques rejected mss. Sometimes recommends other markets.
How to Contact: Send complete ms with SASE and cover letter stating past sales. Photocopied and previously published submissions OK. Accepts computer printout submissions, prefers letter-quality. Reports in 4 months. Publication could take up to 5 years after acceptance. Sample copy $6.
Payment: ¼¢/word; 1 contributor's copy. $1 minimum payment.
Terms: Pays in royalties on publication for first rights.
Advice: "Buy a sample copy and read it thoroughly. Most rejects with my magazine are because people have not checked out what an issue is like or what type of stories I accept. Most rejected stories fall into one of two categories: non-horror fantasy (sword & sorcery, high fantasy) or non-supernatural horror (mad slasher stories, 'Halloween' clones, I call them). When I say that they should read my publication, I'm not whistling Dixie. We hope to up the magazine's frequency to a quarterly. We also plan to be putting out one or two books a year, mostly novels, but short story collections will be considered as well."

THE ELEPHANT-EAR (II, IV), Irvine Valley College, 550 Irvine Center Dr., Irvine CA 92720. (714)559-3327. Editor: Elaine Rubenstein. Magazine: 6×9; 150+ pages; matte paper and cover stock; illustrations and photos. "The journal prints the work of Orange County writers only." Annually. Estab. 1983. Circ. 2,000.
Needs: Contemporary, ethnic, experimental, feminist, humor/satire, literary, regional. Receives 100 mss/year. Accepts 5 mss/issue. "Reads only between Feb. 14 and June 1; reports thereafter." Publishes ms within 3 months of acceptance. Length: 25 pages maximum. Publishes short shorts. Sometimes critiques rejected mss.

How to Contact: Send completed ms with cover letter, which should include "the name, address and phone number of author, the title(s) of work submitted. Author's name must not appear on manuscript." SASE. Photocopied submissions OK. Accepts computer printout submissions. Sample copy for 6x9 SAE. Free fiction guidelines.

Payment: Pays in contributor's copies.

Terms: Acquires one-time rights.

EMRYS JOURNAL (II), The Emrys Foundation, Box 8813, Greenville SC 29604. (803)288-5154. Editor: Linda Julian. Magazine: 6×9; 96 pages; 60 lb paper and cover stock; calligraphy illustrations. "We publish short fiction poetry, essays and book reviews. We are particularly interested in hearing from women and other minorities. We are mindful of the southeast but not limited to it." Annually. Estab. 1984. Circ. 300.

Needs: Contemporary, feminist, literary, mainstream and regional. "We read only during September 1-February 15. During reading periods we receive around 800 manuscripts." Accepts 3-7 stories per issue. Publishes ms 2 months after acceptance. Length: 3,500 words average; 2,500 word minimum; 6,000 word maximum. Publishes short shorts. Length 1,600 words. Sometimes recommends other markets.

How To Contact: Send complete ms with cover letter. Put no identification on manuscript; include separate sheet with title, name, address and phone. "No queries." Reports in 2 months. SASE. Photocopied submissions OK. Accepts computer printout submissions. Sample copy $4 and 7×10 SAE with 4 first class stamps. Fiction guidelines for #10 SAE and 1 first class stamp.

Payment: Pays in contributor's copies.

Terms: Acquires first rights. "Send to managing editor for guidelines."

‡ENCOUNTERS MAGAZINE (I,II,IV), Black Matrix Press, Box 5737, Grants Pass OR 97527. (503)476-7039. Editor: Guy Kenyon. Magazine: 8½×11; 48 pages, 35 lb electrabrite paper; b&w illustrations. "Action/adventure and suspense, with a dash of humor welcome, sf, fantasy and horror for a general audience in a wide age group that enjoys imaginative fiction." Quarterly. Estab. 1989. Circ. 200.

Needs: Fantasy, horror, science fiction. "No erotica or experimental fiction and no poetry." Receives 30-35 unsolicited mss/month. Accepts 8-10 mss/issue; 40-60 mss/year. Publishes 3-9 months after acceptance. Recently published Margaret Mayo McGlynn, Mark Rich and Parley Cooper. Length: 5,000 words; 1,000 words minimum; 10,000 words maximum. Sometimes critiques rejected mss and recommends other markets.

How to Contact: Send complete ms with cover letter, include a short bio about the author. Reports in 2 weeks on queries; 4-6 weeks on mss. SASE. Photocopied and reprint submissions OK. Accepts computer printout submissions. Sample copy for $2.50. Fiction guidelines for #10 SAE and 1 first class stamp.

Payment: ⅛ of a cent per word on publication plus 1 copy ($2 minimum payment).

Terms: Buys first North American serial rights.

Advice: "We lean toward those stories that have characters who are believable. No matter how exotic the setting, or how unusual the situation, the character in the story must be someone the reader can relate to. A story is about people – the rest is a tapestry on which they play out their lives. Concentrate on telling a good story. Try to involve the reader in your character's lives, make them interested in how they resolve their conflicts. Remember, as a writer you are an entertainer."

EOTU (I, II), Magazine of Experimental Fiction, 1810 W. State, #115, Boise ID 83702. Editor: Larry D. Dennis. Magazine 5½×8½; 70-80 pages; 20 lb paper; 70 lb cover; illustrations. "We publish short stories that try to say or do something new in literature, in prose. New style, new story structures, new voice, whatever." Bimonthly. Estab. 1988. Circ. 500.

Needs: Experimental, prose poem. No stories whose express purpose is to advance a religious or political belief. No pornography. Receives 150-200 unsolicited fiction mss/month; accepts 10-12 mss/issue; 60-70 mss/year. Publishes ms 4-6 months after acceptance. Recently published work by Don Webb, Bruce Boston, Conger V. Beasley; published new writers within the last year. Length: 2,500 words average; 2 words minimum; 5,000 words maximum. Sometimes comments on rejected mss or recommends other markets.

How to Contact: Send complete ms. "Cover letter isn't really necessary, but it's nice to know where they heard of us." Reports on queries in 1 week; on mss in 6-8 weeks. SASE. Photocopied submissions OK. Accepts computer printouts. Sample copy for $4; fiction guidelines for #10 SAE and 1 first class stamp.

Payment: Pays $5 minimum; $25 maximum and contributor's copies.
Terms: Pays on acceptance for first North American serial rights. Sends pre-publication galleys to author "only when a story has been edited and a writer's approval of the changes is needed."
Advice: "I've got this time and money and want to invest it in something. So, do I buy a Jiffy Lube or start a new Wendy Burger place? Or do I choose to create a business that caters to my strengths, my loves and desires? Well, that's what I'm doing. I always wanted to publish a magazine, and I've always loved short stories. I urge beginning writers to keep sending stories out. You'll never sell the one in your drawer. If a story comes back with a handwritten note, if it looks like someone really read it, send that editor another. When an editor takes time to critique, it means he's interested and he's trying to help."

EPOCH MAGAZINE (II), 251 Goldwin Smith Hall, Cornell University, Ithaca NY 14853. (607)256-3385. Editor: C.S. Giscombe. Magazine: 6×9; 80-100 pages; good quality paper; good cover stock. "Top level fiction and poetry for people who are interested in and capable of being entertained by good literature." Published 3 times a year. Estab. 1947. Circ. 1,000.
Needs: Literary, contemporary and ethnic. Buys 4-5 mss/issue. Receives approximately 100 unsolicited fiction mss each month. Does not read in summer. Recently published work by Dallas Wiebe, Sherley Anne Williams, Lee K. Abbott; published new writers in the last year. Length: 10-30 typed, double-spaced pages. Critiques rejected mss when there is time. Sometimes recommends other markets.
How to Contact: Send complete ms with SASE. Accepts computer printout submissions. "No dot-matrix please." Reports in 2-8 weeks on mss. Publishes ms an average of 3 months after acceptance. Sample copy $3.50.
Terms: Pays on publication for first North American serial rights.
Advice: "Read and be interested in the journals you're sending work to."

ERGO! (II), The Bumbershoot Literary Magazine, Bumbershoot, Box 9750, Seattle WA 98109-0750. (206)622-5123. Editor: Judith Roche. Magazine: 6×9; 100 pages; 60 lb offset stock; gloss cover; illustrations; photos. "Magazine publishes articles of interest to the literary community, book reviews, and poems and prose by competition winners and invited writers who read at the Bumbershoot Festival." Annually. Circ. 1,500.
Needs: Literary. Accepts approximately 4 mss/issue. Agented fiction 4%. Publishes short shorts.
How to Contact: Query first. Reports in 2 weeks on queries; 2 months on mss. SASE for ms. Simultaneous, photocopied and reprint submissions OK. Accepts computer printout submissions. Sample copy for $5 and 9×12 SAE.
Payment: $25-75 for articles and reviews. $150 award honoraria for Bumbershoot writers; contributor's copies.
Terms: Pays on acceptance for one-time rights.
Advice: Request application for annual contest.

EROTIC FICTION QUARTERLY (I, II, IV), EFQ Publications, Box 4958, San Francisco CA 94101. Editor: Richard Hiller. Magazine: 5×8; 186 pages; perfect bound; 50 lb offset paper; 65 lb cover stock. "Small literary magazine for thoughtful people interested in a variety of highly original and creative short fiction with sexual themes."
Needs: Any style heartfelt, intelligent erotica. Also, stories not necessarily erotic whose subject is some aspect of authentic sexual experience. No standard pornography; no "men's" stories; no contrived plots or gimmicks; no broad satire, parody or obscure "literary" writing. Length: 500 words minimum; 5,000 words maximum; 1,500 words average. Occasionally critiques rejected ms.
How to Contact: Send complete ms only. Photocopied submissions, non-returnable copy OK with SASE for reply. Fiction guidelines free with SASE.
Payment: $50.
Terms: Pays on acceptance for first rights.
Advice: "I specifically encourage unpublished as well as published writers who have something to say regarding sexual attitudes, emotions, roles, etc. Story ideas should come from real life, not media; characters should be real people. There are essentially no restrictions regarding content, style, explicitness, etc.; *originality*, *clarity* and *integrity* are most important. The philosophy is this: *EFQ* publishes stories *about* sex by persons who have something, grand vision or small insight, to say. We try not to publish anything that could easily be printed somewhere else, and what we need is original viewpoints not really describable in advance."

‡EVENT (II), Douglas College, Box 2503, New Westminster, British Columbia V3L 5B2 Canada. Editor: Dale Zieroth. Fiction Editor: Maurice Hodgson. Managing Editor: Bonnie Bauder. Magazine: 6x9; 120 pages; good quality paper; good cover stock; illustrations; photos. "Primarily a literary magazine, publishing poetry, fiction, reviews, occasionally plays and graphics; for creative writers, artists, anyone interested in contemporary literature." Published 3 times/year. Estab. 1970. Circ. 1,000.

Needs: Literary, contemporary, feminist, adventure, humor, regional. No technically poor or unoriginal pieces. Buys 6-8 mss/issue. Receives approximately 50+unsolicited fiction mss/month. Recently published work by Jane Rule, H.E. Francis, Ally McKay; published new writers within the last year. Length: 5,000 words maximum. Critiques rejected mss "when there is time."
How to Contact: Send complete ms with SASE and bio (*must* be Canadian postage or IRC). Accepts computer printout submissions. Prefers letter-quality. Reports in 4 months on mss. Publishes ms an average of 6-12 months after acceptance. Sample copy $5.
Payment: Pays $10-$15 and 2 author's copies.
Terms: Pays on publication for first North American serial rights.
Advice: "A good narrative arc is hard to find."

THE EVERGREEN CHRONICLES (II), A Journal of Gay & Lesbian Writers, Box 8939, Minneapolis MN 55408. Managing Editor: Lisa Albrecht. Magazine: 5½×8½; 36 pages; linen bond paper; b&w line drawings and photos. "No one theme, other than works must have a lesbian or gay appeal. Works sensual and erotic are considered, but must be handled well and have a purpose beyond just sexuality. We look for poetry and prose, but are open to well-crafted pieces of nearly any genre." Quarterly. Estab. 1985. Circ. 300.
Needs: Adventure, confession, contemporary, ethnic, experimental, fantasy, feminist, gay, humor/satire, lesbian, literary, romance (contemporary), science fiction, serialized/excerpted novel, suspense/mystery. "We are interested in works by gay/lesbian artists in a wide variety of genres. The subject matter need not be specifically lesbian or gay-themed, but we do look for a deep sensitivity to that experience. No hardcore sex or porno; no unnecessary violence; nothing homophobic." Accepts 3-4 mss/issue; 12-15 mss/year. Publishes ms approx. 6 weeks after acceptance. Recently published work by Terri Jewel, Lev Raphael and Ruthann Robson; published new writers in the last year. Length: 3,500-4,500 words average; no minimum; 5,200 words maximum. 25 pages double-spaced maximum on prose. Publishes short shorts. Sometimes comments on rejected mss.
How to Contact: Send 4 copies of complete ms with cover letter. "It helps to have some biographical info included." Reports on queries in 3 weeks; on mss in 3-4 months. SASE. Photocopied and reprint submissions OK. Accepts computer printouts. Sample copy for $3.50, 6×9 SAE and 65¢ postage. Fiction guidelines for #10 SAE and 1 first class stamp.
Payment: Pays in contributor's copies.
Terms: Acquires one-time rights.
Advice: "Perseverance is on a par with skill at the craft."

‡EXPLORATIONS '90, University of Alaska Southeast, 11120 Glacier Highway, Juneau AK 99801. (907)789-4418. Editor: Art Petersen. Magazine: 5½×8¼; 44 pages; heavy cover stock; illustrations and photographs. "Poetry, prose and art—we strive for artistic excellence." Annually. Estab. 1980. Circ. 250.
Needs: Erotica, experimention, humor/satire. Receives 750 mss/year. Does not read mss during summer. "We accumulate manuscripts in our files and select them one month before publication in March." Length: 2,500 words maximum.
How to Contact: Send complete ms with cover letter, which should include bio. Reports in 2-3 months. SASE. Simultaneous, photocopied and reprint submissions OK. Accepts computer printout submissions, no dot-matrix. Sample copy $2.75.
Payment: Pays 2 contributor's copies.
Terms: Acquires one-time rights (rights remain with the author).

EXPLORER MAGAZINE (I), Flory Publishing Co., Box 210, Notre Dame IN 46556. (219)277-3465. Editor: Ray Flory. Magazine: 5½×8½; 20-32 pages; 20 lb paper; 60 lb or stock cover; illustrations. Magazine with "basically an inspirational theme including love stories in good taste." Christian writing audience. Semiannually. Estab. 1960. Circ. 200.
Needs: Literary, mainstream, prose poem, religious/inspirational, romance (contemporary, historical, young adult) and science fiction. No pornography. Buys 2-3 mss/issue; 5 mss/year. Length: 600 words average; 300 words minimum; 900 words maximum. Occasionally critiques rejected mss.
How to Contact: Send complete ms with SASE. Reports in 1 week. Publishes ms up to 2 years after acceptance. Photocopied submissions OK. Sample copy $3. Fiction guidelines for SAE and 1 first class stamp.
Payment: Up to $25 and 1 free contributor's copy; $3 charge for extras.
Terms: Cash prizes of $25, $20, $15 and $10 based on subscribers' votes. A plaque is also awarded to first place winner.
Advice: "See a copy of magazine first; have a good story to tell—in *good* taste! Most fiction sent in is too *long*! Be yourself! Be honest and sincere in your style. Write what you know about. Our philosophy is to reach the world with Christian literature, drawing others closer to God and nature."

‡(F.)LIP (II, IV), A Newsletter of Feminist Innovative Writing, Box 1058, Station A, Vancouver, British Columbia V6C 2PI Canada. Editors: Jeannie Lochrie, Angela Hryniuk, Erica Hendry. Newsletter: 8½×11; 24-35 pages; semigloss cover. "Publication's emphasis is on feminist international, innovative (experimental and visionary, language and content) work." Quarterly. Estab. 1987. Circ. 1,500.

Needs: Contemporary, erotica, ethnic, experimental, fantasy, feminist, humor/satire, lesbian, literary, psychic/supernatural, inspirational, science fiction, translations, woman's. "This is a *feminist* publication; therefore, the work has to be written with this consciousness in mind. No sexist, racist, traditional, homophobic." Receives 30 unsolicited mss/month. Buys up to 4 mss/issue. Publishes ms up to 6 months after acceptance. Length: 4 typeset pages average. Publishes short shorts. Sometimes critiques rejected mss and recommends other markets.

How to Contact: Send ms with cover letter, which should include "how they found out about *(f.)Lip*; short bio note." Reports up to 3 months on queries; 2 months on mss. SASE. Photocopied submissions OK. Accepts computer printout submissions. Sample copy for $4 and 10×13 SAE with $1 Canadian postage. Guidelines for #10 SAE with 1 Canadian stamp.

Payment: Pays $10, two free subscriptions to magazine and 2 contributor's copies.

Terms: Pays on publication. Copyright remains with the author. Sends galleys to author.

Advice: "There are lots of tiny literary mags out there. Lots of mags publish traditional short stories. We are creating a space for women writing in innovative, experimental forms; for women who can't find publications that will publish, or even look at their work."

F.O.C. REVIEW (I,II), Box 101, Worth IL 60482. Editor: Michael Ogorzaly. Managing Editor: William L. Roach. Magazine: 5½×8½; over 60 pages. "We publish original stories, poems, essays, one-act plays, drawings and sketches. In addition, we seek book and film reviews." Quarterly. Plans special fiction issue. Estab. 1988. Circ. 500.

Needs: Adventure, condensed/excerpted novel, contemporary, experimental, fantasy, feminist, humor/satire, literary, prose poem, science fiction, serialized novel, sports and suspense/mystery. No romance, erotica. Receives over 30 mss/month. Accepts 10-12 mss/issue; 36 mss/year. Publishes ms in next or following issue after acceptance. Recently published work by James Linn, Rama Rao, John Nerone and Gregory Burnham. Published new writers within the last year. Length: 4,000 words maximum. Publishes short shorts. Sometimes critiques rejected mss.

How to Contact: Send 2 copies of complete ms with cover letter. Reports on mss in 2 months. SASE. Simultaneous, photocopied and reprint submissions OK. Accepts computer printout submissions. Sample copy $5. Fiction guidelines for #10 SAE and 1 first class stamp.

Payment: Pays in contributor's copies.

Terms: Acquires one-time rights.

‡FAG RAG, Box 331, Kenmore Station, Boston MA 02215. (617)661-7534. Editor: Collective. Magazine of gay male liberation. Annually. Estab. 1970. Circ. 5,000.

Needs: Gay male material only: adventure, comics, confession, erotica, fantasy, historical, men's, prose poem. Receives 5 unsolicited fiction mss/month. Accepts 5 mss/issue. Length: 1-10,000 words average.

How to Contact: Query first. Reports in 2 months on queries; 3 months on mss. SASE for query. Photocopied submissions OK. Accepts computer printout submissions. Accepts disk submissions compatible with IBM-PC/Macintosh. Sample copy $5.

Payment: Pays in 2 contributor's copies.

Terms: Acquires first North American serial rights.

THE FARMER'S MARKET (II), Midwestern Farmer's Market, Inc., Box 1272, Galesburg IL 61402. Fiction Editor: John Hughes. Magazine. 5½×8½; 100-140 pages; 60 lb offset paper; 65 lb cover; b&w illustrations and photos. Magazine publishing "quality fiction, poetry, nonfiction, plays, etc., with a Midwestern theme and/or sensibility for an adult, literate audience." Semiannually. Estab. 1982. Circ. 500.

Needs: Contemporary, feminist, humor/satire, literary, regional and excerpted novel. "We prefer material of clarity, depth and strength; strong plots, good character development." No "romance, avant-garde, juvenile, teen." Accepts 6-12 mss/year. Recently published work by Donn Irving, Mary Maddox, David Williams. Published new writers within the last year. Occasionally critiques rejected mss or recommends other markets.

How to Contact: Send complete ms with SASE. Reports in 1-2 months. Photocopied submissions OK. Accepts computer printout submissions; prefers letter-quality. Publishes ms 4-8 months after acceptance. Sample copy for $3.50 and $1 postage and handling.

Payment: 1 free contributor's copy. (Other payment dependent upon grants).
Terms: Authors retain rights.
Advice: "We're always interested in regional fiction. We are trying to publish more fiction and we are looking for exceptional manuscripts. Read the magazines before submitting. If you don't want to buy it, ask your library. We receive numerous mss that are clearly unsuitable."

FAT TUESDAY (II), 8125 Jonestown Road, Harrisburg PA 17112. Editor-in-Chief: F.M. Cotolo. Editors: B. Lyle Tabor and Thom Savion. Associate Editors: Lionel Stevroid and Kristen Vonoehrke. Journal: 8½×11 or 5x8; 27-36 pages; good to excellent paper; heavy cover stock; b&w illustrations; photos. "Generally, we are an eclectic journal of fiction, poetry and visual treats. Our issues to date have featured artists like B. Lyle Tabor, Dom Cimei, Mary Lee Gowland, Patrick Kelly, Cheryl Townsend, Joi Cook, Chuck Taylor and many more who have focused on an individualistic nature with fiery elements. We are a literary mardi gras—as the title indicates—and irreverancy is as acceptable to us as profundity as long as there is fire! Our audience is anyone who can praise literature and condemn it at the same time. Anyone too serious about it on either level will not like *Fat Tuesday*." Annually. Estab. 1981. Circ. 700.
Needs: Comics, erotica, experimental, humor/satire, literary, prose poem, psychic/supernatural/occult, serialized/excerpted novel and dada. "Although we list categories, we are open to feeling out various fields if they are delivered with the mark of an individual and not just in the format of the particular field." Receives 10 unsolicited fiction mss/month. Accepts 4-5 mss/issue. Published new writers within the last year. Length: 1,000 words maximum. Publishes short shorts. Occasionally critiques rejected mss.
How to Contact: Send complete ms with SASE. Photocopied submissions OK. Accepts computer printout submissions. "No previously published material considered." Reports in 1 month. Publishes ms 3-10 months after acceptance. Sample copy $5.
Payment: 1 free contributor's copy.
Terms: Pays for one-time rights.
Advice: "Retain your enthusiasm. Never write and submit anything without it. Buy an issue and eat it up, page by page. Then, go into your guts and write something. If you're not on fire, we'll tell you so and encourage you to try again. Don't be self-critical when you have something to say that reflects how you feel. Most of all, be aware of life outside of literature, and then let life influence your writing. It is essential that a potential submitter buy a sample issue and experience the 'zine to understand what would work and get a better idea of what we're talking about and help support the continuation of this free form of expression that *FT* calls 'littéraire verité."

‡"FEMINIST BASEBALL" (I), Box Dog Press, Box 9609, Seattle WA 98109. Editor: Craig Joyce. Magazine. 5½×8½; 60 pages; 80 lb cover stock; illustrations and photos. "Film reviews, fiction, music, etc. for a diverse to general audience." Semiammually. Estab. 1985. Circ. 500.
Needs: Confession, erotica, experimental, fantasy, gay, horror, humor/satire, lesbian, literary, mainstream, romance, young adult, science fiction, young adult/teen (10-18 years). "Nothing racist, bad, long (over 5 pages)." Publishes a special fiction issue. Receives 10 unsolicited mss/month. Accepts 2 mss/issue; 4 mss/year. Publishes 3-6 months after acceptance. Agented fiction 20%. Recently published work by Peter Wick, Nancy Ostrander. Length: 1,000 words average; 250 words minimum; 4,000 words maximum. Publishes short shorts (275-825 words). Sometimes critiques rejected mss and recommends other markets.
How to Contact: Send complete manuscript with cover letter. Reports in 3 weeks on queries. Simultaneous submissions OK. Accepts electronic submissions. Sample copy for $2. Fiction guidelines free.
Payment: Pays with free subscription to magazine.
Terms: Publication is not copyrighted.

‡FICTION (II), % Dept. of English, City College, 138th St. & Convent Ave., New York NY 10031. (212)690-8170/690-8120. Editor: Mark Jay Mirsky. Fiction Editor: Douglas Century. Magazine: 6×9; 150-250 pages; illustrations and occasionally photos. "As the name implies, we publish *only* fiction; we are looking for the best new writing available, leaning toward the unconventional and off-beat. *Fiction* has traditionally attempted to make accessible the unaccessible, to bring the experimental to a broader audience." Bi-annually. Estab. 1972. Circ. 3,000.
Needs: Contemporary, experimental, feminist, humor/satire, literary and translations. No romance, science-fiction, etc. Plan to publish special fiction issue or an anthology in the future. Receives 30-50 unsolicited mss/month. Accepts 12-20 mss/issue; 24-40 mss/year. Does not read mss May-October. Publishes ms 1-6 months after acceptance. Agented fiction 10-20%. Recently published work by Joyce Carol Oates, Max Frisch and Adolfo Bioy-Casares, Harold Brodky, Camilo José Cela. Length: Open. Publishes short shorts. Sometimes critiques rejected mss and recommends other markets.

How to Contact: Send complete ms with cover letter. Reports in 5 weeks on mss. SASE. Simultaneous and photocopied submissions OK. Accepts computer printout submissions. Sample copy $6.95. Fiction guidelines free.
Payment: Pays in contributor's copies.
Terms: Acquires first rights.
Advice: Submit "something different, off-the-wall—we would favor a less-polished but stylistically adventurous piece over a more-polished formulaic piece.

FICTION INTERNATIONAL (II), English Dept., San Diego State University, San Diego CA 92182. (619)594-6220. Editors: Harold Jaffe and Larry McCaffery. Serious literary magazine of fiction, extended reviews, essays. 200 pages; illustrations; photos. "Our twin biases are progressive politics and post-modernism." Biannually. Estab. 1973. Circ. 2,500.
Needs: Literary, political and innovative forms. Receives approximately 300 unsolicited fiction mss each month. Published new writers within the last year. No length limitations but rarely use manuscripts over 25 pages. Portions of novels acceptable if self-contained enough for independent publication. Unsolicited mss will be considered only from Septemer 1 through December 15 of each year.
How to Contact: Send complete ms with SASE. Reports in 1-3 months on mss. Sample copy for $9: query Ed Gordon, managing editor.
Payment: Varies.
Terms: Pays on publication for first rights and first North American serial rights.
Advice: "Study the magazine. We're highly selective. A difficult market for unsophisticated writers."

FICTION NETWORK MAGAZINE (II), Box 5651, San Francisco CA 94101. (415)391-6610. Editor: Jay Schaefer. Magazine: 8½×11; 48 pages; newsprint paper; 70 lb coated cover stock; illustrations. "Fiction Network distributes short stories to newspapers and publishes *Fiction Network Magazine*, which circulates to agents, editors, writers and others in publishing and film." Biannually. Estab. 1983. Circ. 6,000.
Needs: "All types of stories and subjects are acceptable; novel excerpts will be considered only if they stand alone as stories." No children's or young adult. Receives 500 unsolicited mss/month. Accepts 75 mss/year. Approximately 35% of fiction is agented. Published work by Monica Wood, Joyce Carol Oates, Bharati Mukherjee. Published new writers within the last year. Length: Varies.
How to Contact: Send complete ms or submit through agent. Reports in 4 months. Publishes ms 6-9 months after acceptance. SASE. "Do not ask us to return submissions from outside U.S. Do not send a second manuscript until you receive a response to the first. Please send manuscripts unfolded." Simultaneous and photocopied submissions OK. Accepts computer printout submissions. Prefers letter-quality. Sample copy $5 US and Canada; $7 elsewhere. Fiction guidelines for SASE.
Payment: $25-500 and up.
Terms: Pays on publication.
Advice: "We're looking for quality short fiction that appeals to a wide audience. Contributors include Alice Adams, Max Apple, Ann Beattie, Ken Chowder, Andre Dubus, Bobbie Ann Mason, Lorrie Moore, Lynne Sharon Schwartz and many previously unpublished writers. Read an issue of a magazine before submitting your writing."

‡THE FIDDLEHEAD (II), University of New Brunswick, Rm. 317, Old Arts Bld., UNB., Box 4400 Fredericton, New Brunswick E3B 5A3 Canada. (506)454-3591. Editor: Michael Taylor. Fiction Editors: Anthony Boxill, William Cragg and Michael Taylor. Magazine: 6×9; 104-128 pages; ink illustrations; photos. "No criteria for publication except quality. For a general audience, including many poets and writers." Quarterly. Estab. 1945. Circ. 1,000.
Needs: Literary. No non-literary fiction. Receives 100-150 unsolicited mss/month. Buys 4-5 mss/issue; 20-40 mss/year. Publishes ms up to 4 months after acceptance. Small percent agented fiction. Recently published work by Arych Leo Stollman; published new writers within the last year. Length: 50-3,000 words average. Publishes short shorts. Occasionally critiques rejected mss.
How to Contact: Send complete ms with cover letter. SASE. "Canadian stamps or international coupons!" for mss. Photocopied and reprint submissions OK. Accepts computer printout submissions, no dot-matrix. Sample copy for $5.50 (Canadian).
Payment: Pays $10-12/published page and 1 free contributor's copy.
Terms: Pays on publication for first or one-time rights.
Advice: "Less than 5% of the material received is published."

FIGHTING WOMAN NEWS (IV), Box 1459, Grand Central Station, New York NY 10163. Editor: Valerie Eads. Fiction Editor: Margaret Welsh. Magazine: 8½×11; 16-32 pages; 60 lb offset bond paper; illustrations; photos. "Women's martial arts, self defense, combative sports. Articles, reviews, etc., related to these subjects. Well-educated adult women who are actually involved with martial arts read us because we're there and we're good." Quaterly. Estab. 1975. circ. 3,500.

Needs: Science fiction, fantasy, feminist, adventure and translations. "No material that shows women as victims, incompetents, stereotypes; no 'fight scenes' written by people who don't know anything about fighting skills." Receives very few unsolicited fiction mss. Recently published work by Phyllis Ann Karr, Lauren Wright Douglas and Janrae Frank. Length: 2,500 words.
How to Contact: Query with clips of published work with SASE. Enclose cover letter with ms. Accepts computer printout submissions. "We must know if it is a simultaneous submission." Reports as soon as possible on queries and mss. Sample copy $3.50. Specify "fiction" when asking for samples. Free guidelines with #10 SASE.
Payment: Pays author's copies and subscription or $10 honorarium.
Terms: Pays on publication for one-time rights. Publication copyrighted; will print author's copyright if desired.
Advice: "We are now getting unsolicited mss from published writers who have what we want; i.e., a good, competent story that's just a bit too martial-arts oriented for their regular markets. Our readers have expressed a strong preference for more technique and theory with a few specific complaints about too much fiction or poetry. So even with a more regular publication schedule and corredsponding increase in total pages, we are not likely to use more fiction. Read the magazine before submitting. I also think the theme of death in combat can do with a rest. We published no fiction last year."

‡FIGMENT MAGAZINE (I, II, IV), Digest of Fantasy, Horror and Science Fiction, P.O. Box 3566, Moscow ID 83843-0477. Editors: John C. Hendee, Jr., Barb Hendee, J.P. McLaughlin. Magazine: 5½×8½; 60 pages; heavy stock cover; illustrations. "Poetry/stories/vignettes in the horror/fantasy/SF genre, for adults." Quarterly. Estab. 1989.
Needs: Fantasy, horror, psychic/supernatural/occult, science fiction. "We're open to standard plotting through metafiction, as long as the story is interesting, comprehensible and always entertaining." Receives 90 unsolicited mss/month. Buys 5-10 mss/issue; 20-40/year. Publishes ms within 6 months after acceptance. Recently published work by J.N. Williamson, D. Alexander Smith. Length: 3,000 words preferred; 5,000 words maximum. Publishes short shorts. Sometimes critiques rejected mss and recommends other markets.
How to Contact: Send complete ms with cover letter; include Social Security number, bio and listing of recent works published (titles) and where and when. Reports in 2 weeks on queries; 1-2 months on mss. SASE. Photocopied and reprint submissions OK. Accepts computer printout submissions. Accepts electronic submissions via disk (ASCII format, or query for other formats). Sample copy for $3.95. Fiction guidelines for #10 SASE.
Payment: Pays ¼-2¢/word and contributor's copies.
Terms: Pays on acceptance for first North American serial rights or other rights. Sends galleys to author.
Advice: Looks for "an original idea, or an original method for dealing with an old idea. Something that makes the fantastic and unreal become 'real.' We also give an extra bit of consideration (at least in comments on a rejection) to people who submit in a professional manner. Don't tell us what the story is about in your cover letter. If we can't figure it out from the manuscript, then some more work needs to be done."

‡FINE MADNESS (II), Box 15176, Seattle WA 98115-0176. Fiction Editor: Louis Bergsagel. Magazine 5×8; 80 pages; 65 lb paper; 60 lb cover stock. Estab. 1981. Circ. 800.
Needs: Contemporary, experimental, literary, prose poem and translations.
Receives 10 unsolicited mss/month. Accepts 1-2/issue; 2-4/year. Publishes ms no more than 1 year after acceptance. Recently published work by Naomi Nye, David Downing. Length: "approx. 12 pages max." Publishes short shorts (10 pages max.).
How to Contact: Query first or send complete ms with cover letter. Reports in 3 weeks on queries; 3 months on mss. Sample copy $4. Fiction guidelines free.
Payment: Free subscription to magazine and contributor's copies.
Terms: Pays for first North American serial rights.
Advice: "We look for original and believable characters, plot and themes; powerful and vivid language; love of imagery and the English language. Crisp dialog. No gratuitous sex, violence, proselytizing, gibberish, obscenity. In short, good writing."

FIREWEED, A Feminist Quarterly, Box 279, Station B, Toronto, Ontario M5T 2W2 Canada. Editors: The Fireweed Collective. Magazine of anti-sexist and anti-racist fiction, poetry, non-fiction, scholarly articles for "feminists and all those interested in anti-sexist writing." Quarterly. Estab. 1978. Circ. 2,000.
Needs: Condensed novel, confession, contemporary, erotica, ethnic, experimental, fantasy, lesbian, working class, women-of-color content, historical (general), humor/satire, literary, prose poem, translations. No "women's formula style." Receives 60 unsolicited fiction mss/month. Accepts 4 mss/issue;

16 mss/year. Length: 1,200 words minimum; 18,000 words maximum; 6,000 words average. Occasionally critiques rejected ms.
How to Contact: Query first with SASE. Photocopied submissions OK. Reports in 6 months on queries. Sample copy $4 in Canada, $5 in U.S.
Payment: $20 and 2 free contributor's copies.
Terms: Acquires first North American serial rights.

FIRST STORIES and STORYETTE (I,II), Box 710, Santa Monica CA 90406. (213)397-4217. Editor: Davis Lott. Magazines: 10×13 print size; 32 pages each; Electrobrite paper and cover; b&w illustrations and photographs. *First Stories* is for short stories by *unpublished* writers; *Storyette* publishes short-short stories by *published* writers. Quarterly. Plans special fiction issue. Estab. 1988. Circ. 10,000.
Needs: Adventure, confession, contemporary, fantasy, historical, humor/satire, juvenile (5-9 years), literary, mainstream, romance (contemporary, historical, young adult), science fiction, senior citizen/retirement, sports, suspense/mystery, western. *"All stories limited to 1,000-1,200 words."* Receives 2-10 unsolicited fiction mss/month; accepts 10-14 mss/issue; 40-56 mss/year. Time between acceptance and publication varies. Requires magazine subscription before reading ms. Length: 1,000-1,200 words. Sometimes comments on rejected mss and recommends other markets.
How to Contact: Query first. Reports in 2 weeks. SASE. Simultaneous and photocopied submissions OK. Accepts computer printout submissions. Sample copy and fiction guidelines for $4 plus $1 postage.
Payment: Pays 2-5¢/word for *Storyette*. "In *First Stories* an unpublished author can have his or her 1,000-1,200 word short short story set in type on a single 10×13 tabloid size page for $1 per line of typewriter type and $50 for a b&w illustration, which becomes property of the author."
Terms: Pays on publication. Sends galleys to author "for a $5 charge." Publication not copyrighted.
Advice: "When a story is published in either magazine, we send 100 copies to each author plus 100 copies to agents and act as the writer's agent on a 20% fee. If he or she *has* an agent, they get 10% and we get 10%. Our magazines are designed to act as showcases for unpublished writers (*First Stories*) or lesser-known published writers (*Storyette*). Call (213)397-4217 for further details."

FIVE FINGERS REVIEW (II), 553 25th Ave., San Francisco CA 94121. (415)386-2151. Editor: "rotating." Magazine: 6×9; 125-150 pages; photographs on cover. "*Five Fingers* is dedicated to publishing well wrought poetry and prose from various aesthetic viewpoints. The magazine provides a forum from which talented writers (new and known, traditional and experimental) act as conscientious objectors, as creative witnesses to the passions and possibilities of our time." Semiannually. Estab. 1984. Circ. 1,000.
Needs: Ethnic, experimental, feminist, gay, humor/satire, lesbian, literary, regional, prose poems, prose vignettes and works that move between the genres. Receives 15-20 unsolicited mss/month. Accepts 2-5 mss/issue. Published work by Molly Giles, W.A. Smith and Peter Johnson; published new writers in the last year. Publishes short shorts.
How to Contact: Query with clips of published work. SASE. Simultaneous, photocopied and reprint submissions OK. Sample copy for $6.
Payment: Pays in contributor's copies.
Advice: "We are particularly looking for short-short stories, prose poems, prose vignettes and works of translations."

THE FLORIDA REVIEW (II), Dept. of English, University of Central Florida, Orlando FL 32816. (407)275-2038. Editor: Pat Rushin. Associate Editor: Jonathan Harrington. Magazine: 5½×8½; 128 pages. Semiannually. Plans special fiction issue. Estab. 1972. Circ. 1,000.
Needs: Contemporary, experimental and literary. "We welcome experimental fiction, so long as it doesn't make us feel lost or stupid. We aren't especially interested in genre fiction (science fiction, romance, adventure, etc.), though a good story can transcend any genre." Receives 80 mss/month. Buys 8-10 mss/issue; 16-20 mss/year. Publishes ms within 3-6 months of acceptance. Published work by Stephen Dixon, Richard Grayson and Liz Rosenberg. Publishes short shorts.
How to Contact: Send complete ms with cover letter. Reports in 2-4 months. SASE. Simultaneous and photocopied submissions OK. Accepts computer printout submissions. Sample copy $4.50; free fiction guidelines.
Payment: Pays $5/printed page and contributor's copies. Charges for extra copies.
Terms: Pays on publication. "Copyright held by U.C.F.; reverts to author after publication. (In cases of reprints, we ask that a credit line indicate that the work first appeared in the *F.R.*)"
Advice: "We publish fiction of high 'literary' quality—stories that delight, instruct, and aren't afraid to take risks."

FOLIO: A LITERARY JOURNAL (II), Literature Department, American University, Washington DC 20016. (202)885-2971. Editor changes yearly. Magazine: 6×9; 64 pages. "Fiction is published if it is well written. We look specifically for language control and skilled plot and character development." For a scholarly audience. Semiannually. Estab. 1984. Circ. 300.

Needs: Contemporary, literary, mainstream, prose poem, sports, suspense/mystery, translations, essay, b&w art or photography. No pornography. Receives 50 unsolicited mss/month. Accepts 25 mss/issue; 50 mss/year. Does not read mss during May-August or December-January. Published work by Henry Taylor, Kermit Moyer, Linda Pastan; publishes new writers. Length: 2,500 words average; 3,000 words maximum. Publishes short shorts. Length: 3 pages. Occasionally critiques rejected mss.
How to Contact: Send complete ms with cover letter, which should include a brief biography. Reports in 1-2 weeks on queries; 1-2 months on mss. SASE. Simultaneous, photocopied and reprint submissions OK. Accepts computer printout submissions. Sample copy for $4.50. Fiction guidelines for #10 SAE and 1 first class stamp.
Payment: Pays in contributor's copies.
Terms: Acquires all rights. "$75 award for best fiction/poetry. Spring issue only. Query for guidelines."

FOOTWORK (I,II), The Paterson Literary Review, Passaic County Community College, College Blvd., Paterson NJ 07509. (201)684-6555. Editor: Maria Gillan. Magazine: 8×11; 120 pages; 60 lb paper; 70 lb cover; illustrations; Photos. Plans fiction issue in future.
Needs: Contemporary, ethnic, experimental, translations. "We are interested in quality short stories, with no taboos on subject matter." Receives about 30 unsolicited mss/month. Accepts 1 ms/issue. Publishes ms about 6 months to a year after acceptance. Published new writers within the last year. Length: 2,500-3,000 words.
How to Contact: Reports in 3 months on mss. SASE for query and ms; no simultaneous submissions or reprints. Accepts computer printouts. No dot-matrix. Sample copy $5.
Payment: Pays in contributor's copies. Acquires first North American rights.
Advice: "We look for original, vital, powerful work. The short story is—when successful—a major achievement. Because we publish relatively little work, we cannot consider stories which are slight, however charming."

‡FORMATIONS MAGAZINE, 625 Colfax St., Evanston IL 60201. Editor: Jonathan Brent. "*Formations* will publish American fiction, foreign works in translation and essays. Particular interest in analyzing and criticizing the cultural/political/social bases of current art" for academic, literary, general intellectual, interdisciplinary audience. Published 3 times/year. Estab. 1984.
Needs: Fiction of high literary quality. No particular subjects. Accepts 8-12 mss/issue; 24-36 mss/year. Length: open. Occasionally critiques rejected ms.
How to Contact: Send complete ms. Reports in varying number of weeks. SASE.
Payment: $100-1,000; in some cases subscription to magazine; 5 contributor's copies; ½ price charge for extras.
Terms: Pays on publication for first North American serial rights.

FREEWAY (II), Box 632, Glen Ellyn IL 60138. (312)668-6000 (ext. 216). Editor: Billie Sue Thompson. Magazine: 8½×11; 4 pages; newsprint paper; illustrations; photos. Weekly Sunday school paper "specializing in first-person true stories about how God has worked in teens' lives," for Christian teens ages 15-21. Circ. 50,000.
Needs: Comics, humor/satire, spiritual, allegories and parables. Receives 100 unsolicited mss/month. Recently published work by Doug Peterson, Michelle Starr; published new writers within the last year. Length: 1,000 words average. Occasionally critiques rejected mss.
How to Contact: Send complete ms with SASE. Reports in 1 month. Simultaneous and photocopied submissions OK. Accepts computer printout submissions. Prefers letter-quality. Sample copy or writing guidelines available with SASE. Fiction guidelines free for SASE with 1 first class stamp.
Terms: Pays on acceptance for first rights.
Advice: "Send us humorous fiction (parables, allegories, etc.) with a clever twist and new insight on Christian principles. Do *not* send us typical teenage short stories."

FRONTIERS (II), A Journal of Women Studies, Women Studies Program, University of Colorado, Boulder CO 80300. (303)492-3205. Editor: Nancy D. Mann. Magazine: 8½×11; 92 pages; photos. "Women studies; personal essays; academic articles in all disciplines; criticism, book and film reviews; exceptional creative work (art, short fiction, photography, poetry)."
Needs: Feminist, lesbian. Receives 15 unsolicited mss/month. Accepts 1 ms/issue. Publishes ms 6 months to 1 year after acceptance. Publishes short shorts. Sometimes critiques rejected mss and recommends other markets.
How to Contact: Send complete ms with cover letter. Reports in 1 week on queries; 3 months on mss. SASE. Accepts computer printout submissions. Sample copy for $8.
Payment: Pays 2 contributor's copies.
Terms: Buys first North American serial rights.
Advice: "It is our stated purpose to publish exceptional creative work by women; we are a *feminist* journal. *FRONTIERS* aims to make scholarship in women studies, and *exceptional* creative work, accessible to a cross-disciplinary audience inside and outside the university."

GALACTIC DISCOURSE (II), Satori Press, 1111 Dartmouth, #214, Claremont CA 91711. (714)621-3112. Editor-in-Chief: Laurie Huff. Magazine: 8½×11; 200+ pages; 60 lb non-gloss paper; 80 lb non-gloss cover stock; illustrations; astronomical photos. Magazine of "*Star Trek* fiction (characterization and character interaction are emphasized), poetry, artwork; some visionary/science fiction poetry and art for *Star Trek* fans," *Note*: "This is a 'when there's time' venture!" Published irregularly—every two years or so. Estab. 1977. Circ. 2,000.

Needs: Adventure, fantasy, feminist/lesbian, gay, humor, prose poem, psychic/supernatural/occult, science fiction, suspense/mystery. All must be within the *Star Trek* universe! No pure adventure, x-rated (explicit erotica), or "Mary-Sue." Receives less than 5 unsolicited fiction mss/month. Accepts 8-12 ms/issue. Publishes short shorts under 100 double-spaced pages. Published work by Leslie Fish, Ginna La Croix, Harriett Stallings. Length: 12,000 words maximum; 5,000 words average. "We would consider publishing novellas/novels as a special issue apart from other work." Occasionally critiques rejected mss and recommends other markets.

How to Contact: Query first with SASE and cover letter with description of manuscript(s), including length. Photocopied submissions OK. Accepts computer printout submissions. Accepts disk submissions compatible with Apple II, Franklin or IBM PC. Prefers hard copy with disk submission. Reports in 6 weeks on queries; 2 months on mss. Publishes ms 6 months-2 years after acceptance. Sample copy "not offered, sorry; send SASE for purchasing info." Fiction guidelines and sample of published material for #10 SAE and 2 first class stamps.

Payment: 1 free contributor's copy; issue price charge for extras.

Terms: Acquires second serial rights. Sends galleys to author upon request.

Advice: "We are looking for more controversial topics, psychological studies and humor." Mss are rejected because "they are poorly written, have inappropriate content and lack personal appeal. The new, lower-cost print technologies seem to be spawning more small presses. And many small presses are willing to work with beginning fiction writers. Write the story you'd like to read."

THE GAMUT (II), A Journal of Ideas and Information, Cleveland State University, 1216 Rhodes Tower, Cleveland OH 44115. (216)687-4679. Editor: Louis T. Milic. Managing Editor: Susan Dumbrys. Magazine: 7×10; 96 pages; 70 lb Patina Matte paper; Patina Matte cover stock; illustrations; photos. "*The Gamut* is a general-interest magazine that mainly publishes well-researched, interesting articles; however, we like to publish one or two pieces of fiction per issue, if we find something suitable." For the college-educated audience. Triannually. Estab. 1980. Circ. 1,200.

Needs: Contemporary, experimental, feminist, humor/satire, literary, mainstream, prose poem, regional, translations, "Our only requirement is high quality fiction." No genre fiction, no fiction for specific age groups. Receives 50 unsolicited mss/month. Accepts 1-2 mss/issue; 4-6 mss/year. Publishes mss usually 3 months, certainly 1 year after acceptance. Reading fee "only when we have contest, then $5." Published work by Margot Livesey, Nancy Potter, John Gerlach; published new writers within the last year. Length: 3,000 words average; 1,000 words minimum; 6,000 words maximum. Often critiques rejected mss and recommends other markets.

How to Contact: Send complete ms with cover letter. Reports in 1 month on queries; 3 months on mss. SASE for ms. Simultaneous and photocopied submissions OK. Accepts computer printouts. Sample copy $2.50. Fiction guidelines for #10 SAE and 1 first class stamp.

Payment: Pays $25-150, depending on length; contributor's copies; charges reduced rate for extras.

Terms: Pays on publication. Acquires first North American serial rights.

Advice: "The best advice we have for writers who wish to be published in our magazine is that they should care about the quality of their writing. Further, we are interested neither in stale approaches to fictional situations nor in avant-garde experiments that have lost touch with the purpose of literature."

GARGOYLE MAGAZINE (II), 5825 Colby, Oakland CA 94618. (415)655-3949. Editor: Toby Barlow. Magazine: 5½×8½; 480 pages; standard bulk paper; slick card cover stock; illustrations; photos. Estab. 1976. Publishes 2 times/year.

Needs: Contemporary, literary, experimental, humor/satire, prose poem, sports and translations. Recently published work by Kathy Acker, Julia Alvarez, Lucia Berlin; published new writers within the last year. "We like fiction in the 2-10 typed page range, but often publish much longer works. We generally print 3-6 stories per issue." Approximately 10% of fiction is agented. "We print 1 out of every 250 stories we read these days." Does not read in August. Critiques rejected ms when there is time. Sometimes recommends other markets.

How to Contact: Submit complete ms with SASE. Photocopied submissions OK. Accepts computer printout submissions. Prefers letter-quality. Reports in 1-2 months on mss. Publishes ms 6 months to 1 year after acceptance. Sample copy for $7.95.

Payment: Free author's copy. Half the cover price for extras.

Advice: "Small magazines are deluged with mss. Writers should keep in mind that rejection doesn't mean that the story is bad, only that the magazine editor doesn't want to, or can't use it. Writers have to learn to endure. Writers should always be familiar with the market. This means reading all the short stories/fiction you can get your hands on. It is also important to keep up with movements in the contemporary fiction. We're interested in printing excerpts from unpublished novels. We're consciously seeking out the new young writers (20-30 years old and younger)."

THE GARLAND, Loyola College, 4501 N. Charles St., Baltimore MD 21210. (301)323-1010. Editor: John Handscomb. Magazine of poetry, short fiction, photography and drawing for the college community. Annually. Estab. 1972. Circ. 1,500.

Needs: Contemporary, fantasy, humor/satire. Receives 50 unsolicited fiction mss/month. Accepts 4 mss/issue, 10 mss/year. Approximately 20% of fiction is agented. Length: 900 words minimum; 3,000 words maximum; 2,100 words average.

How to Contact: Send complete ms with SASE. Simultaneous submissions OK. Reports in 1 month on ms. Publishes ms an average of 1-3 months after acceptance. Sample copy $1 and SAE.

Payment: 1 free contributor's copy.

Terms: Acquires all rights.

Advice: "The organization has undergone drastic format changes. We are now commercial; that is, we sell space for commercial advertising. Eventually, we would like to pay a fee for all contributions, even if the fee is nominal."

GARM LU (II, IV), A Canadian Celtic Arts Journal, St. Michael's College, University of Toronto, 81 St. Mary St., Toronto, Ontario M5S 1J4 Canada. (416)926-1300 (Celtic Studies Dept.). Editor: Linda Revie. Fiction Editors: Linda Revie and Mary MacDonald. Magazine: 140mm×215mm; 60 pages; bond paper; almost cardboard cover; illustrations. "A register of the concerns and interests of those involved in Celtic studies." Semiannually. Estab. 1986. Circ. 400.

Needs: Adventure, condensed novel, confession, contemporary, erotica, ethnic, feminist, gay, historical, humor/satire, lesbian, literary, regional, religious/inspirational, serialized/excerpted novel, translations, Celtic. Receives 4 unsolicited mss/month. Buys 1 or 2 mss/issue; 3 or 4 mss/year. Length: 1,000 words preferred; 250 words minimum; 2,500 words maximum. Sometimes critiques rejected mss.

How to Contact: Query with clips of published work or send complete ms with cover letter. Reports in 2 weeks on queries; 3 weeks on mss. SASE. Simultaneous, photocopied and reprint submissions OK. Accepts computer printouts. Sample copy for $3 (American).

Payment: Free contributor's copy; charge for extras.

Terms: Acquires all rights. "In future, we will have contests that will be worth about $20 (Canadian)."

Advice: "Read it over 100 times and edit it 100 times."

GAS (I, II, IV), Journal of The Gross Americans' Society, Box 397, Marina CA 93933. (408)384-2768. Editor: Jeannette M. Hopper. Magazine: digest size; 20-50 pages; 20 lb paper; non-gloss heavy cover; pen-and-ink illustrations; photos if screened. "*Gas* is dedicated to the fine art of the gross-out; accepts humorous horror, horrible humor and blends of those genres, with an emphasis on short-short horror fiction." For "people mature enough to see that this is all strictly for fun and entertainment, and not an attempt to make any real social statement." Quarterly. Estab. 1986. Circ. 250.

Needs: Adventure, confession, contemporary, erotica, experimental, fantasy, horror, humor/satire, mainstream, prose poem, psychic/supernatural/occult, science fiction, suspense/mystery, gross humor/horror. "All fiction must have some aspect of grossness, but story is of utmost importance. Characters must be someone the reader can identify with (no utterly detestable creeps as protagonists). No scatalogical or cannibal-related stories. No hard pornography. No children placed in sexual situations. No politics, racism, religion or heavy dogma." Receives 50 unsolicited mss/month. Buys 5-10 mss/issue; 40 mss/year at most. Publishes ms 3 months to 1 year after acceptance. Published work by J.N. Williamson, Bruce Boston, Cheryl Sayre; published new writers within the last year. Length: 1,500 words maximum. Publishes short shorts of 100-1,000 words. Sometimes critiques rejected mss and recommends other markets.

How to Contact: Send complete ms with cover letter, which should include brief introduction of author and previous publications. Reports in 1 week on queries; 1-2 weeks on mss. SASE. Photocopied and reprint (5 years after publication) submissions OK. Accepts computer printout submissions. Sample copy for $3.50. Fiction guidelines for #10 SASE.

Payment: Pays ¼¢/word with a $2 minimum; contributor's copies; charge for extras.

Terms: Pays on publication for one-time rights. Occasional contests announced in magazine.

Advice: "Now concentrating more on humorous *horror*, whereas we were open to almost anything sick and funny in the past. Now the emphasis will be upon the frightening and bizarre, rather than just 'funny stuff.' I receive too many submissions from people who never should have passed English proficiency exams; spelling is terrible, punctuation is a mystery, grammar is pathetic. Master your basic tools, and that means master English. Also, read, read, read to get the feel of how the pros do it. Finally: GAS is unlike any other magazine; please read a copy before submitting."

GATEWAYS (I), Quest Graphics, P.O. Box 86151, Plano TX 75086-1510. (214)736-6249. Editor: Daniel Meyer. Magazine: 8½×11; 40-80 pages; newsprint paper; 40 lb mill cover; many illustrations; some photos. "We publish anything related to science fiction or fantasy, primarily artwork and stories, for an 18-up audience." Plans special fiction issue. Estab. 1988. Circ. 500.

Needs: Adventure, erotica, experimental, fantasy, science fiction, serialized novel. No westerns, straight romance, drug related. Receives 1-4 unsolicited fiction mss/month; accepts 4-15 mss/issue. Publishes ms approx. 6 months after acceptance. Published work by Vance Garrett, Kelli Wakefield and Jan Owens. Length: 100 words minimum; 10,000 words maximum. Sometimes comments on rejected mss and recommends other markets.

How to Contact: Send complete ms with cover letter, which should include "name, address, previous published work." Reports on queries in 2 months; on mss in 1 month. SASE for queries; not needed for mss. Simultaneous and photocopied submissions OK. Accepts dot-matrix computer printouts and electronic submissions, "Wordstar data only." Sample copy $3. Fiction guidelines for #10 SAE and 1 first class stamp.

Payment: Pays in contributor's copies.

Terms: Acquires one-time rights.

Advice: "A lot of fiction I have seen lately has had excellent ideas or plots, but the author has not proofread his/her work. Please check spelling and punctuation. Do not be put off by the delays sometimes associated with small magazines; many times the editors are working with very tight budgets. We began the magazine after discovering just how much really good material never sees print. Our goal is to provide an outlet and exposure for this material."

EL GATO TUERTO (II, IV), Box 210277, San Francisco CA 94121. Editor: Carlota Caulfield. Tabloid: 11×17; 16 pages; illustrations; photos. "We welcome works dealing with Spanish, Latin American and Caribbean literatures, but we are open to any kind of fiction, poetry or literary essays as well. We publish in Spanish and English." Quarterly. Estab. 1984. Circ. 3,000.

Needs: Adventure, confession, contemporary, ethnic, fantasy, feminist, prose poem, science fiction, suspense/mystery, translations. "Spanish, Latin American and Caribbean fiction." No horror. Receives 3-7 unsolicited mss/month. Accepts 2-3 mss/issue; 10 mss/year. Does not read mss December-January. Publishes ms 2-6 months after acceptance. Recently published work by Calvert Casey, Enrique Labrador Ruiz, Rima de Vallbona; published new writers within the last year. Length: 5-7 pages. Publishes short shorts. Length: 2 pages.

How to Contact: Query first. Reports in 3 weeks on queries; 5-7 weeks on mss. SASE. Photocopied submissions OK. Accepts computer printout submissions. Sample copy for $2 and 13×10 SAE with 56¢ postage.

Payment: Pays in contributor's copies.

Terms: Pays on publication. Publication not copyrighted.

GAY CHICAGO MAGAZINE (II), Ultra Ink, Inc. 3121 N. Broadway, Chicago IL 60657-4522. (312)327-7271. Editor: Dan Dileo. Magazine: 8½x11; 80-144 pages; newsprint paper and cover stock; illustrations; photos. Entertainment guide, information for the gay community.

Needs: Erotica (but no explicit hard core), lesbian, gay and romance. Receives "a few" unsolicited mss/month. Accepts 10-15 mss/year. Published new writers within the last year. Length: 1,000-3,000 words.

How to Contact: Send complete ms with SASE. Photocopied submissions OK. Accepts computer printout submissions. Accepts disk submissions compatible with Merganthaler Crtronic 200. Must have hard copy with disk submissions. Reports in 4-6 weeks on mss. Free sample copy for 9×12 SAE and $1.45 postage.

Payment: Minimal. 5-10 free contributor's copies; no charge for extras "if within reason."

Terms: Acquires one-time rights.

Advice: "I use fiction on a space-available basis, but plan to use more because we have doubled our format size to 8½×11."

THE GEORGIA REVIEW (II,III), The University of Georgia, Athens GA 30602. (404)542-3481. Editor-in-Chief: Stanley W. Lindberg. Associate Editor: Stephen Corey. Journal: 7×10; 216 pages (average); 50 lb woven old style paper; 80 lb cover stock; illustrations; photos. "*The Georgia Review*, winner of the 1986 National Magazine Award in Fiction, is a journal of arts and letters, featuring a blend of the best in contemporary thought and literature – essays, fiction, poetry, graphics and book reviews – for the intelligent nonspecialist as well as the specialist reader. We seek material that appeals across disciplinary lines by drawing from a wide range of interests." Quarterly. Estab. 1947. Circ. 5,300.

Needs: Experimental and literary. "We're looking for the highest quality fiction – work that is capable of sustaining subsequent readings, not throw-away pulp magazine entertainment. Nothing that fits too easily into a 'category.'" Receives about 300 unsolicited fiction mss/month. Buys 3-4 mss/issue; 12-15 mss/year. Does not read ms in June, July or August. Published work by Lee K. Abbott, Jack Driscoll,

Diana Reed; published new writers within the last year. Length: open. Occasionally critiques rejected mss.
How to Contact: Send complete ms with SASE. Photocopied submissions OK; no multiple submissions. Accepts computer printout submissions. Prefers letter-quality. Reports in 2 months. Sample copy $4; free guidelines for #10 SAE with 1 first class stamp.
Payment: Minimum: $25/printed page; 1 year complimentary subscription; 1 contributor's copy, reduced charge for extra.
Terms: Pays on publication for first North American serial rights. Sends galleys to author.

‡GESTALT (I,II), Anti-matter Publishing, 516 W. Wooster, Bowling Green OH 43402. Editor: Jeff Fearnside. Magazine: 8½×11; 48 pages; glossy paper and stock; illustations; photographs. "The theme of our magazine is on newer, less traditional literature. Our audience is anyone interested in art, ideas and literature. They are college-aged to young professional (18-35 years old)." Quarterly. Estab. 1988. Circ. 2,000.
Needs: Adventure, condensed/excerpted novel, contemporary, ethnic, experimental, fantasy, feminist, historical (general), horror, humor/satire, literary, prose poem, regional, science fiction, serialized novel, suspense/mystery, translations and western. "We would like to see a wider range of subjects than we are currently receiving." Has published a special fiction issue or an anthology (with fiction). Receives 10-20 unsolicited mss/month. Accepts 1-5 mss/month, depending on length; 4-20/year depending on length. Publishes ms 2 weeks-3 months after acceptance. "Length varies. The number of words is unique to each ms." Publishes short shorts. Sometimes critiques rejected mss.
How to Contact: Send complete ms with cover letter. "Include a return address, possibly a phone number, and a brief (two to three line) autobiography." Reports in 1 week on queries; 2 months on mss. SASE. Accepts simultaneous, photocopied, reprinted and computer printed submissions. Sample copy $2.50. Fiction guidelines free.
Payment: Pays in contributor's copies.
Terms: Purchases reprint rights only; "all other rights remain with the author."
Advice: "The single most important criteria I have in choosing fiction is this: If I like it, I'll print it. I don't think there is any higher praise for a work than to have someone say, 'I like it.' First and foremost, it must be realized that the short story is a written form of what originally was a verbal art: storytelling. Thus, it is the voice of the story, the movement of the words, that make the good ones stand apart from the poor. Beginning writers, my advice to you is to destroy one of the oldest conventions of a writer: know your audience. Forget the audience; write for yourself. You don't necessarily have to write from experience, but you should write from a familiar and deep-felt emotion. Put fear aside. Don't be afraid to run up to the edge where convention and insanity meet, and to take a long look over that edge. Embrace convention when it suits your needs, and defy convention when that suits your needs."

Editor Jeff Fearnside explained this cover, which he designed. "It shows both our serious and our slightly subversive side." The artwork is serious, but the comments such as "new and improved—now 13% bigger than before," are "deliberate parodies of traditional marketing techniques," says Fearnside. Illustrator Lawrence Oberc is also a regular contributor of art, poetry and fiction.

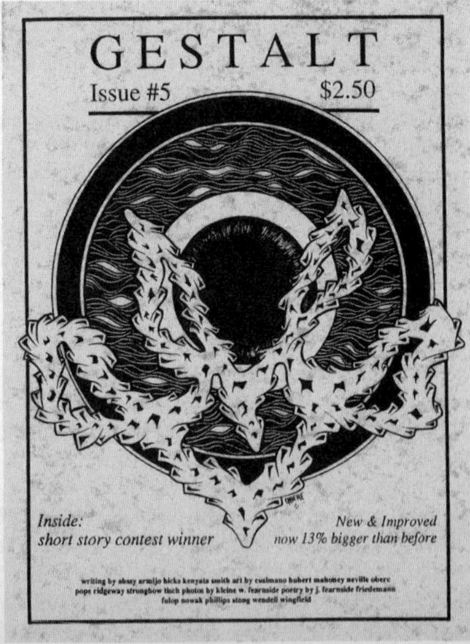

GESTALT
Issue #5
$2.50
Inside:
short story contest winner
New & Improved
now 13% bigger than before

THE GETTYSBURG REVIEW (II), Gettysburg College, Gettysburg PA 17325. (717)337-6770. Editor: Peter Stitt. Assistant Editor: Frank Graziano. Magazine: 6¾×10; approx. 200 pages; acid free paper; full color illustrations and photos. "Quality of writing is our only criterion; we publish fiction, poetry and essays." Quarterly. Estab. 1988. Circ. 1,500.

Needs: Contemporary, experimental, historical(general), humor/satire, literary, mainstream, regional and serialized novel. "We require that fiction be intelligent, and intelligently and aesthetically written." Receives approx. 25 mss/month. Buys approx. 4-6 mss/issue; 16-24 mss/year. Publishes ms within 3-6 months of acceptance. Published work by Frederick Busch, Ed Minus and Gloria Whelan. Length: 3,000 words average; 1,000 words minimum; 20,000 words maximum. Publishes short shorts. Sometimes critiques rejected mss.

How to Contact: Send complete mss with cover letter, which should include "education, credits." Reports in 3 months. SASE. Photocopied submissions OK. Accepts computer printout submissions.

Payment: Pays $20/printed page plus free subscription to magazine, contributor's copy. Charge for extra copies.

Terms: Pays on publication for first North American serial rights.

Advice: Reporting time can take three months. It is helpful to look at a sample copy of *The Gettysburg Review* to see what kinds of fiction we publish before submitting."

THE GLENS FALLS REVIEW (II), Loft Press, 42 Sherman Ave., Glens Falls NY 12801. (518)798-8110. Editor: Jean Rikhoff. Magazine: 8½×11; 48 pages; 30 lb paper; 60 lb cover; photos. Estab. 1981. Annually.

Needs: Contemporary fiction, prose poem, poetry, literary articles, some regional materials. Published work by William Kennedy, William Brock; published new writers within the last year.

How to Contact: Send complete ms with cover letter. SASE for ms. Reads from January 1 through April 15. Accepts computer printout submissions. Sample copy $5.

GOLDEN ISIS MAGAZINE (I, IV), Box 726, Salem MA 01970. Editor: Gerina Dunwich. Magazine: digest size; approx. 30-40 pages; 20 lb stock; paper cover; illustrations. "*Golden Isis* is a mystical neo-pagan literary magazine of occult fiction, Goddess-inspired poetry, artwork, Wiccan news, letters, occasional book reviews and classified ads." Quarterly. Estab. 1980. Circ. 4,000.

Needs: Psychic/supernatural/occult, bizarre fantasy and mystical Egyptian themes. "Please do not send us pornographic, religious, racist or sexist material. We will not consider stories written in present tense." Receives 40+ mss/month. Buys 2 mss/issue; 8 mss/year. Published fiction by Rod R. Vick, Cary G. Osborne and Gypsy Electra. Published many new writers within the last year. Length: 2,000 words maximum. Publishes short shorts. Occasionally critiques rejected mss and often recommends other markets.

How to Contact: Send complete ms with cover letter. Reports in 2 weeks. SASE. Simultaneous, photocopied and reprint submissions OK. Accepts computer printout submissions. Sample copy $2.95. Fiction guidelines for #10 SAE and 1 first class stamp.

Payment: Payment varies from 1 free contributor's copy to $5.

Terms: Pays on publication for first North American serial rights.

Advice: "Submit short fiction that is well-written, atmospheric and equipped with a good surprise ending. Originality is important. Quality writing is a must. Avoid clichés, poor grammar, predictable endings, unnecessary obscenity and run-on sentences, for these things will only bring you a fast rejection slip."

‡GOTTA WRITE NETWORK LITMAG (I) (I), Maren Publications, 612 Cobblestone Circle, Glenview IL 60025. Editor: Denise Fleischer. Magazine: 8½×11; 40 pages; saddle-stapled ordinary paper; matte card or lighter weight cover stock; illustrations. Magazine "serves as an open forum to discuss new markets, victories and difficulties. Gives beginning writers their first break into print." Quarterly. Estab. 1988. Circ. 75-100.

Needs: Adventure, contemporary, fantasy, historical, humor/satire, literary, mainstream, prose poem, romance, science fiction and young adult/teen. Receives 5-10 unsolicited mss per month; accepts 3-5 mss per issue; up to 20 mss a year. Mss published 1-2 months after acceptance. Recently published work by J.J. Summers, Roger Dale Trexler and Walter Lide. Length: 5 pages maximum for short stories; publishes short shorts of 1-2 pages. Critiques rejected mss and recommends other markets.

How to Contact: Send complete ms with cover letter and query letter. Include "who the writer is, type of work submitted, previous publications and the writer's focused area of writing." Reports in 2 weeks. SASE. Photocopied submissions OK; reprints considered "at times." Accepts computer printouts and electronic submissions via Apple IIC or Macintosh disks. Sample copy $2.50. Fiction guidelines free with SASE.

Payment: Contributor's copies; charge for extras.
Terms: Buys first North American serial rights.
Advice: "If I still think about the direction of the story after I've read it, I know it's good. Organize your thoughts on the plot and character development (qualities, emotions) before enduring 10 drafts. Make your characters come alive by giving them a personality and a background and then give them a little freedom. Let them take you through the story."

GRAIN (I, II), Saskatchewan Writers' Guild, Box 1154, Regina, Saskatchewan S4P 3B4 Canada. Editor: Mick Burrs. Fiction Editor: Byrna Barclay. Literary magazine: 5½×8½; 80-96 pages; Chinook offset printing; chrome-coated stock; illustrations; photos sometimes. "Fiction and poetry for people who enjoy high quality writing." Quarterly. Estab. 1973. Circ. 600-1,000.
Needs: Contemporary, experimental, literary, mainstream and prose poem. "No propaganda—only artistic/literary writing." No mss "that stay *within* the limits of conventions such as women's magazine type stories, science fiction; none that push a message." Receives 40-60 unsolicited fiction mss/month. Buys 4-7 mss/issue; 16-28 mss/year. Approximately 1% of fiction agented. Recently published two short stories by emerging writers selected for the first *Journey Prize Anthology*. Length: "No more than 20 pages." Occasionally critiques rejected mss.
How to Contact: Send complete ms with SAE, IRC and brief of one-two sentences. "Let us know if you're just beginning to send out." Reports within 6 months on ms. Publishes ms an average of 4 months after acceptance. Sample copy $5.
Payment: $30-100; 2 free contributor's copies.
Terms: Pays on publication for one-time rights. "We expect acknowledgment if the piece is republished elsewhere."
Advice: "Submit a story to us that will deepen the imaginative experience of our readers. *Grain* has established itself as a first-class magazine of serious fiction. We receive submissions from around the world. Canada is a foreign country, so we ask that you *do not* enclose US postage stamps on your return envelope. If you live outside Canada and neglect the International Reply Coupons, we *will not* read nor reply to your submission."

‡GRASSLANDS REVIEW (I), Mini-Course—University of North Texas, N.T. Box 13706, Denton TX 76203. Editor: Laura B. Kennelly. Magazine: 6×9; 55 pages. *Grasslands Review* prints creative writing of all types; poetry; fiction,essays for a general audience. Semiannually. Estab. 1989. Circ. 100.
Needs: Adventure, contemporary, ethnic, experimental, fantasy, horror, humor/satire, literary, prose poem, regional, science fiction, suspense/mystery and western. Nothing pornographic or overtly political or religious. Accepts 4-5 mss/issue. Reads only in October and March. Publishes ms 6 months after acceptance. Recently published work by Bac Eton, Tom Conlon and K. Kolodney. Length: 1,500 words average; 100-3,500 words. Publishes short shorts (100-150 words). Sometimes critiques rejected mss and recommends other markets.
How to Contact: Send complete ms with cover letter. Reports on mss in 2 months. SASE. Sample copy $1.
Payment: Pays in contributor's copies.
Terms: Acquires one-time rights. Publication not copyrighted.
Advice: "We are looking for fiction which leaves the reader with a strong feeling or impression—or a new perspective on life. The Review began as an in-class exercise to allow experienced creative writing students to learn how a little magazine is produced. We now wish to open it up to outside submissions so that our students can gain an understanding of how large the writing community is in the United States and so that they may have experience in working with other writers."

GREAT RIVER REVIEW (II), 211 W. 7th, Winona MN 55987. Fiction Editor: Onval A. Lund, Jr. Magazine: 6x8; 150 pages. Literary publication of fiction, poetry, art and book reviews. Semiannually. Estab. 1977.
Needs: "Quality fiction. No slick or sub-genre fiction." Prints 6-7 stories/issue. Receives approximately 40 unsolicited fiction mss each month. Published new writers within the last year. Length: 2,000-10,000 words.
How to Contact: Send complete ms with SASE. Photocopied submissions OK. Accepts computer printout submissions. Publishes ms 3-6 months after acceptance. Sample copy $4.50.
Advice: "Our editors seek work that reflects basic human values and that displays the care and craft at the core of good art." Priority to Midwestern writers and Midwestern settings.

GREEN MOUNTAINS REVIEW (II), Johnson State College, Box A-58, Johnson VT 05656. (802)635-2356, ext. 339. Editor: Neil Shepard. Editor: Tony Whedon. Magazine: digest size; 90-100 pages. "*GMR*'s emphasis is on quality writing. Each issue features an essay, works of fiction or suite of poems that explores an aspect of New England life." Semiannually. Estab. 1987. Circ. 1,000.

Needs: Adventure, contemporary, experimental, humor/satire, literary, mainstream, regional (New England), serialized/excerpted novel, translations. Receives 20 unsolicited mss/month. Accepts 5 mss/issue; 10 mss/year. Publishes ms 1-2 months after acceptance. Length: 25 pages maximum. Publishes short shorts. Sometimes critiques rejected mss.
How to Contact: Send complete ms with cover letter. Reports in 1 month on queries; 2 months on mss. SASE. Simultaneous and photocopied submissions OK. Accepts computer printout submissions; no dot-matrix. Sample copy for $4.
Payment: Pays in contributor's copies.
Terms: Acquires first North American serial rights. Sends galleys to author upon request.

GREEN'S MAGAZINE (II), Fiction for the Family, Green's Educational Publications, Box 3236, Regina, Saskatchewan S4P 3H1 Canada. Editor: David Green. Magazine: 5¼×8; 100 pages; 20 lb bond paper; matte cover stock; line illustrations. Publishes "solid short fiction suitable for family reading." Quarterly. Plans special fiction issue. Estab. 1972.
Needs: Adventure, fantasy, humor/satire, literary, mainstream, science fiction and suspense/mystery. No erotic or sexually explicit fiction. Receives 15-20 mss/month. Buys 10-12 mss/issue; 40-50 mss/year. Publishes ms within 3-6 months of acceptance. Agented fiction 2%. Recently published work by Solomon Pogarsky, Ann Beacham, Robert Redding. Length: 2,500 words preferred; 2,500 words minimum; 4,000 words maximum. Sometimes critiques rejected mss and recommends other markets.
How to Contact: Send complete ms. "Cover letters welcome but not necessary." Reports on mss in 2 months. SASE. "Must include international reply coupons." Photocopied submissions OK. Accepts computer printout submissions. No simultaneous submissions. Sample copy $4 (Canadian). Fiction guidelines for #10 SAE and international reply coupon.
Payment: Pays in contributor's copies.
Terms: Acquires first North American serial rights.

GREENSBORO REVIEW (II), University of North Carolina at Greensboro, Dept. of English, Greensboro NC 27412. (919)334-5459. Editor: Jim Clark. Fiction Editor: Nancy Richard. Magazine: 6×9; approximately 120 pages; 60 lb paper; 65 lb cover. Literary magazine featuring fiction and poetry for readers interested in contemporary literature. Semiannually. Circ. 500.
Needs: Contemporary and experimental. Accepts 4-8 mss/issue, 8-16 mss/year. Recently published work by Julia Alvarez, Larry Brown and Madison Smartt Bell; published new writers within the last year. Length: 7,500 words maximum.
How to Contact: Send complete ms with SASE. Unsolicited manuscripts must arrive by September 15 to be considered for the winter issue and by February 15 to be considered for the summer issue. Manuscripts arriving after those dates may be held for the next consideration. Photocopied submissions OK. Sample copy $2.50.
Payment: Pays in contributor's copies.
Terms: Acquires first North American serial rights.
Advice: "We want to see the best being written regardless of theme, subject or style. Stories from *The Greensboro Review* have been included in *The Best American Short Stories*, *Prize Stories: The O. Henry Awards*, and *Best of the West*, anthologies recognizing the finest short stories being published."

GROUNDSWELL, A Literary Review (II), The Guild Press/Hudson Valley Writers Guild, 19 Clinton Ave., Albany NY 12207. (518)449-8069. Editor: Kristen Murray. Fiction Editor: F.R. Lewis. Magazine. 5½×8½; 100 pages; 70 lb paper; occasional line drawings/graphics. "Variable themes; fiction, poetry reviews of small press publications, critical essays, focus on prominent writer with work (new) by focused-on writer. Semiannually. Estab. 1984.
Needs: Contemporary, ethnic, experimental, fantasy, feminist, gay, humor/satire, lesbian, literary, mainstream, regional, excerpted novel, suspense/mystery, translations. "We are open to any high quality, significant, honest fictions." No formula stories; stories that are racist, sexist; stories that ignore craft and clarity. Accepts up to 5 mss/issue; 4-10 mss/year. Recently published work by Elizabeth Adams, Kirpal Gordon, Beth Weatherby; published new writers within the last year. Length: 7,500 words maximum. Publishes short shorts. Length 1-6 pages. Sometimes critiques rejected ms.
How to Contact: Send complete ms with brief bio note. "We want something that can be used as a contributor's note if the story is accepted." Reports in 3 months (varies). SASE. Photocopied submissions OK. Accepts computer printout submissions, no dot-matrix. Sample copy $6 and 6×9 SAE with 6 first class stamps.
Payment: 2 contributor's copies; other payment depends on funding.
Terms: Pays for first North American serial rights. Copyright reverts to author.
Advice: "Read the magazine in which you want to publish. Polish your work. Please, please – no onion skin, no dot matrix. Send work that looks like you are proud to be sending it. Before being concerned about *where* you're going to publish it, pay attention to writing well and courageously."

GRUE MAGAZINE (II, IV), Hell's Kitchen Productions, Box 370, New York NY 10108. Editor: Peggy Nadramia. Magazine: 5½×8½; 96 pages; 60 lb paper; 10 pt. CIS film laminate cover; illustrations; photos. "Quality short fiction centered on horror and dark fantasy—new traditions in the realms of the gothic and the macabre for horror fans well read in the genre, looking for something new and different, as well as horror novices looking for a good scare." Published 3 times/year. Estab. 1985.

Needs: Horror, psychic/supernatural/occult. Receives 250 unsolicited fiction mss/month. Accepts 10 mss/issue; 25-30 mss/year. Publishes ms 1-2 years after acceptance. Published work by Thomas Ligotti, Joe R. Lansdale, Don Webb; published new writers within the last year. Length: 4,000 words average; 6,500 words maximum. Publishes short shorts of 400 words (1 printed page). Sometimes critiques rejected ms and recommends other markets.

How to Contact: Send complete ms with cover letter. "I like to hear where the writer heard about *Grue*, his most recent or prestigious sales, and maybe a word or two about himself." Reports in 3 weeks on queries; 4 months on mss. SASE for ms. Photocopied submissions OK. Accepts computer printouts. Sample copy $4.50. Fiction guidelines for #10 SAE and 1 first class stamp.

Payment: Pays in 2 contributor's copies plus ½¢ per word.

Terms: Pays on publication. Acquires first North American serial rights.

Advice: "Editors actually vie for the work of the better writers, and if your work is good, you will sell it—you just have to keep sending it out. But out of the 250 mss I read in September, maybe three of them will be by writers who cared enough to make their plots as interesting as possible, their characterizations believable, their settings unique, and who took the time to do the rewrites and polish their prose. Remember that readers of *Grue* are mainly seasoned horror fans, and *not* interested or excited by a straight vampire, werewolf or ghost story—they'll see all the signs, and guess where you're going long before you get there. Throw a new angle on what you're doing; put it in a new light. How? Well, what scares *you*? What's *your* personal phobia or anxiety? When the writer is genuinely, emotionally involved with his subject matter, and is totally honest with himself and his reader, then we can't help being involved, too, and that's where good writing begins and ends."

‡HAIGHT ASHBURY LITERARY JOURNAL (II), Box 15133, San Francisco CA 94115. (415) 221-2017. Editors: William Walker and Joanne Hotchkiss. Tabloid: 11×17; 16 pages; newsprint paper; illustrations and photographs. Annually. Estab. 1979. Circ. 2,000.

Needs: Confession, contemporary, erotica, ethnic, experimental, feminist, gay, humor/satire, lesbian, literary, mainstream and prose poem. Plans special fiction issue in the future. Receives 2 unsolicited mss/month; accepts 2-4 mss/issue; 4-8 mss/year. Publishes ms 4-6 months after acceptance. Length: 2,000 words preferred; 3,500 words maximum. Publishes short shorts of 250-300 words.

How to Contact: Send complete ms with cover letter; reports in 2 months. SASE. Photocopied submissions OK. Sample copy $1.50 with 9x12 SAE and 4 first class stamps.

Payment: Pays in contributor's copies.

‡HAPPINESS HOLDING TANK (II), Stone Press, 1790 Grand River, Okemos MI 48864. Editor: Albert Drake. Magazine: 8½×11; 30-50 pages; 20 lb bond paper; Bristol cover stock; illustrations, photos sometimes. Primarily a magazine of poetry, articles, reviews, and literary information for poets, students, teachers, other editors and laypeople. "I think a good many people read it for the literary information, much of which isn't available elsewhere." Published irregularly. Estab. 1970. Circ. 300-500.

Needs: Literary. "We publish a limited amount of fiction: very short stories, parables, prose poems, fragments and episodes. Not a good market for traditional fiction." Accepts 4-5 mss/year. Receives very few unsolicited fiction mss each month. Does not read mss in summer. Critiques rejected mss "when there is time."

How to Contact: Query. SASE. Accepts computer printout submissions. Reports in 1 week on queries, 3 weeks on mss. Publishes ms 3-5 months after acceptance. Sample copy $1 plus 68¢ postage.

Payment: 2 free author's copies.

Terms: Acquires one-time rights with automatic return of all rights to author.

Advice: "Be more careful about what you send out. Rewrite. Tighten. Compress. Read it aloud."

HARVEST MAGAZINE (I,II,IV), The Reader's Hearth, 2322 Latona Dr. NE, Salem OR 97303. Managing Editors: William Michaelian and Jay Thomas Collins. Magazine: 8½×11; 32 pages; 60 lb tahoe gloss paper; self-cover stock; illustrations; photos. Publishes "work by people 50 and over that is illustrative of their discoveries in life." Bimonthly. Estab. 1988. Circ. 3,000.

Needs: "Yarns, tales or fiction evocative of earlier times." Writers should be age 50 or older. Receives 20 fiction mss/month. Accepts 0-1 fiction mss/issue. Publishes accepted mss within 2-4 months of acceptance. Length: 2,000 words average; 200 words minimum; 7,000 words maximum. Sometimes critiques rejected mss. Sometimes recommends other markets.

How to Contact: Send complete mss with cover letter. Reports on queries in 3-5 weeks; on mss in 4-6 weeks. SASE. Photocopied submissions OK. Accepts computer printout submissions. Sample copy for $2.

Payment: Pays in contributor's copies.

Terms: Acquires one-time rights. Sometimes sends galleys to author.

Advice: "Say what you have to say in an authentic voice, both with high expectations of your reader and the result you will achieve on the page. We want to hear from you, not from an imitation of someone else."

HAUNTS (II), Tales of Unexpected Horror and the Supernatural, Nightshade Publications, Box 3342, Providence RI 02906. (401)781-9438. Editor: Joseph K. Cherkes. Magazine: 6×9 digest; 80-100 pages; 50 lb offset paper; perfect bound; pen and ink illustrations. "We are committed to publishing only the finest fiction in the genres of horror, fantasy and the supernatural from both semi-pro and established writers. We are targeted towards the 18-35 age bracket interested in tales of horror and the unknown." Quarterly. Plans special fiction issue. Estab. 1984. Circ. 1,000.

Needs: Fantasy, horror, psychic/supernatural/occult. No pure adventure, explicit sex, or blow-by-blow dismemberment. Receives 100-150 unsolicited fiction mss/month. Accepts 10-12 mss/issue; 50-75 mss/year. Publishes ms 6-9 months after acceptance. Recently published work by Mike Hurley, Kevin J. Anderson, Frank Ward; published new writers within the last year. Length: 3,500 words average; 1,000 words minimum; 8,500 words maximum. Publishes short shorts of not less than 500 words. Critiques rejected mss. Recommends other markets. Market open June 1 to December 1, inclusive.

How to Contact: Query first. "Cover letters are a nice way to introduce oneself to a new editor." Reports in 2-3 weeks on queries; 2-3 months on mss. SASE for query. Photocopied submissions OK. Accepts computer printouts. Accepts magnetic media (IBM PC-MS/DOS Ver 2.0 or higher). Sample copy $3.50 postpaid. Fiction guidelines for #10 SASE.

Payment: Pays $5-50 (subject to change). Contributor's copies, charge for extras.

Terms: Pays on publication. Acquires first North American serial rights.

Advice: "Follow writers' guidelines closely. They are a good outline of what your publisher looks for in fiction. If you think you've got the 'perfect' manuscript, go over it again – carefully. Check to make sure you've left no loose ends before sending it out. Keep your writing concise. If your story is rejected, don't give up. Try to see where the story failed. This way you can learn from your mistakes. Remember, success comes to those who persist. We plan to open to advertising on a limited basis, also plan a media campaign to increase subscriptions and distributed sales."

HAWAII PACIFIC REVIEW (II), Hawaii Pacific College, 1060 Bishop St., Honolulu HI 96813. (808)544-0259. Editor: Frederick Hohing. Magazine: 6×9; 100-150 pages; quality paper; glossy cover; illustrations and photos. "As a literary magazine located in Hawaii, we are interested in material that concerns or is set in the Pacific Rim and Asia. Categories: fiction, poetry, essays and scholarly writing." Annually. Estab. "nationwide in 1988."

Needs: Adventure, contemporary, ethnic, experimental, fantasy, humor/satire, literary, mainstream, regional, science fiction, suspense/mystery, translations. No romance, confessions, religious or juvenile. Receives approx. 25 unsolicited fiction mss/month. Accepts 4-8 mss/issue. Deadline for the Spring annual issue is January 1. Does not read in summer. Publishes ms 3-12 months after acceptance. Recently published work by Ruth Shigezawa, Marilyn Shoemaker, Susan B. Weston; published new writers within the last year. Length: 500 words minimum; 5,000 words maximum. Publishes short shorts. Sometimes critiques rejected mss or recommends other markets.

How to Contact: Send complete manuscript with cover letter, which should include a brief bio. Reports in 3 months. SASE. Simultaneous and photocopied submissions OK. Accepts computer printouts, no dot-matrix. Fiction guidelines for #10 SAE and 1 first class stamp.

Payment: Pays in contributor's copies.

Terms: Acquires first North American serial rights. Rights revert to author upon publication. "A fiction contest is in the planning stages."

Advice: "A beginning writer should take pride in his work. Professional appearance of the manuscript, therefore, is a must."

HAWAII REVIEW (II), University of Hawaii Board of Publications, 733 Donaghho Rd., Co-English Dept., Honolulu HI 96822. (808)948-8548. Editor: Elizabeth Lovell. Fiction Editor: Stewart Anderson. Magazine: 6½×9½; 100-150 pages; illustrations; photos. "We publish short stories as well as poetry and reviews by new and experienced writers. Although the *Review* reflects the concerns of writers and artists of Hawaii and the Pacific, its interests are by no means exclusively regional." For residents of Hawaii and non-residents from the continental US and abroad. Triannually. Plans special fiction issue. Estab. 1972. Circ. 4,000.

Needs: Contemporary, ethnic, experimental, horror, humor/satire, literary, prose poem, regional and translations. Receives 40-50 mss/month. Accepts no more than 10 mss/issue; 30 mss/year. Recently published work by William Pitt Root, Ursule Molinaro and Ian Macmillan; published new writers within the last year. Length: 4,000 words average; no minimum; 8,000 words maximum. Occasionally critiques mss. Recommends other markets.
How to Contact: Send complete manuscript with SASE. Reports in 3-4 months on mss. Photocopied submissions OK. Accepts computer printout submissions. Sample copy for $4. Fiction guidelines free.
Payment: "Varies depending upon funds budgeted. Last year, we paid $35-70 per story." 2 contributor's copies.
Terms: Pays on publication for all rights. Sends galleys to author upon request. After publication, copyright reverts to author upon request.

HEARTLAND JOURNAL, Box 55115, Madison WI 53705. Affiliated with the Wisconsin Academy of Sciences, Arts & Letters. (800)263-3020. Editor: Jeri McCormick, Senior Editor: Lenore M. Coberly. Quarterly. "Writers and artists must be over 60 years old."
Needs: "Uses short stories, poems, essays and articles that are carefully told." Length should suit the material. "See the magazine for guidance about what we publish." Sample copy is $5.
How to Contact: Send complete mss. and SASE. Will accept carefully written handwriting. Recently published work by Doris Kerns Quinn, Judson Jerome and Leroy Shoemaker.
Payment: Pays in contributors' copies and awards annual cash prizes.

HEAVEN BONE (IV), New Age Literary Arts, Heaven Bone Press, Box 486, Chester NY 10918. (914)469-9018. Editors: Steven Hirsch, Kirpal Gordon. Magazine: 8½×11; 49-78 pages; 20 lb standard paper; 70 lb card cover; computer clip art, graphics, line art, cartoons, halftones and photos scanned in tiff format. "New age, new consciousness, expansive, fine literary, earth and nature, spiritual path. We use current reviews, essays on new age topics, creative stories and fantasy. Also: reviews of current poetry releases and expansive literature." Readers are "spiritual seekers, healers, poets, artists, musicians, students." Semiannually. Estab. 1987. Circ. 500.
Needs: Experimental, fantasy, psychic/supernatural/occult, esoteric/scholarly, regional, religious/inspirational, spiritual, new age. "No violent, thoughtless or exploitive fiction." Receives 100-350 unsolicited mss/month. Accepts 5-15 mss/issue; 12-30 mss/year. Publishes ms 2 weeks to 6 months after acceptance. Recently published work by Richard Paul Schmonsees, Joe Richey, Jeanine Pommy-Vega; published new writers within the last year. Length: 3,500 words average; 1,800 words minimum; 7,000 words maximum. Publishes short shorts. Sometimes critiques rejected mss and may recommend other markets.
How to Contact: Send complete ms with cover letter, which should include short bio of recent activities. Reports in 2 weeks on queries; 2 weeks-6 months on mss. SASE. Reprint submissions OK. Accepts computer printout submissions, including high quality dot-matrix. Accepts electronic submissions via "Apple Mac SE versions of Macwrite, Microsoft Word v. 4.0 or Writenow v. 2.0." Sample copy $4.50. Fiction guidelines free.
Payment: Pays in contributor's copies; charges for extras.
Terms: Buys first North American serial rights. Sends galleys to author, if requested.
Advice: "Our fiction needs are tempermental, so please query first before submitting. We prefer shorter fiction. Do not send first drafts to test them on us. Please refine and polish your work before sending. Always include SASE. We are looking for the unique, unusual and excellent."

HERESIES (IV): A Feminist Publication on Art & Politics, Box 1306, Canal St. Station, New York NY 10013. (212)227-2108. Magazine: 8½×11; 96 pages; non-coated paper; b&w illustrations and photos. "We believe that what is commonly called art can have a political impact and that in the making of art and all cultural artifacts our identities as women play a distinct role . . . a place where diversity can be articulated." International and North American-wide readership; carried by many libraries, alternative bookshops, and art schools. Published two times a year. Estab. 1977. Circ. 8,000.
Needs: Feminist and lesbian. Published new writers within the last year. Publishes stories up to 10 typed pages maximum.
How to Contact: Query. Free guidelines with SASE.
Payment: Small payment post publication and several free author's copies.
Advice: "Check back issues for tone and approach. Each issue addresses a specific theme."

HIBISCUS MAGAZINE (II), Short Stories, Poetry and Art, Hibiscus Press, Box 22248, Sacramento CA 95822. Editor: Margaret Wensrich. Magazine: 8½×11; 24-28 pages; 50 lb paper; 1 ply vellum cover stock; pen-and-ink illustrations. Magazine of short stories, poetry and drawings. Estab. 1985. Published three times/year. Circ. 1,000-2,000.

Needs: Adventure, contemporary, fantasy, humor/satire, literary, mainstream, science fiction, suspense/mystery and western. Receives 500 unsolicited mss/month. Buys 3 mss/issue; 9 mss/year. Does not read mss in August or December. Published new writers within the last year. Length: 1,500-2,500 words average; 1,500 words minimum; 3,000 words maximum.

How to Contact: Send complete ms with SASE. Reports in 6-8 weeks on mss. Photocopied submissions OK. Accepts computer printout submissions; prefers letter-quality. Sample copy $4. Fiction guidelines with #10 SAE and 1 first class stamp.

Payment: $5-25; 2 free copies.

Terms: Pays on acceptance for first rights.

Advice: "We do not return many manuscripts because writers and poets are *not* including enough postage on SASE. We do not attempt to return mail without enough postage. International mail, especially from Canada, does not have sufficient postage for return of ms. Writers and poets need to go to the post office and have mail weighed and then put on correct postage."

HIGH PLAINS LITERARY REVIEW (II), 180 Adams Street, Suite 250, Denver CO 80206. (303)320-6828. Editor-in-Chief: Robert O. Greer, Jr. Magazine: 6×9; 135 pages; 70 lb paper; heavy cover stock. "The *High Plains Literary Review* publishes high quality poetry, fiction, essays, book reviews and interviews. The publication is designed to bridge the gap between high-caliber academic quarterlies and successful commercial reviews." Three times per year. Estab. 1986. Circ. 650.

Needs: Most pressing need: outstanding essays. Serious fiction, contemporary, humor/satire, literary, mainstream, regional. No true confessions, romance, pornographic, excessive violence. Receives approximately 80 unsolicited mss/month. Buys 4-6 mss/issue; 12-18 mss/year. Publishes ms usually 6 months after acceptance. Recently published work by Richard Currey, Joyce Carol Oates, Nancy Lord and Rita Dove; published new writers within the last year. Length: 4,200 words average; 1,500 words minimum; 8,000 words maximum; prefers 3,000-6,000 words. Occasionally critiques rejected mss. Sometimes recommends other markets.

How to Contact: Send complete ms with cover letter, which should include brief publishing history. Reports in 6 weeks. SASE. Simultaneous and photocopied submissions OK. Accepts computer printout submissions. Sample copy for $4.

Payment: Pays $5/page for prose and 2 contributor's copies.

Terms: Pays on publication for first North American serial rights. "Copyright reverts to author upon publication." Sends copy-edited proofs to the author.

Advice: "*HPLR* publishes *quality* writing. Send us your very best material. We will read it carefully and either accept it promptly, recommend changes or return it promptly. Do not send fragmented work. It *may* help to read a sample copy before submitting. Don't be a workshop writer."

HILL AND HOLLER: Southern Appalachian Mountains, Seven Buffaloes Press, Box 249, Big Timber MT 59011. Editor: Art Cuelho. Magazine: 5½×8½; 80 pages; 70 lb offset paper; 80 lb cover stock; illustrations; photos rarely. "I use mostly rural Appalachian material: poems and stories. Some folklore and humor. I am interested in heritage, especially in connection with the farm." Annually. Published special fiction issue. Estab. 1983. Circ. 750.

Needs: Contemporary, ethnic, humor/satire, literary, regional, rural America farm. "I don't have any prejudices in style, but I don't like sentimental slant. Deep feelings in literature are fine, but they should be portrayed with tact and skill." Receives 10 unsolicited mss/month. Accepts 4-6 mss/issue. Publishes ms 6 months to a year after acceptance. Length: 2,000-3,000 words average. Also publishes short shorts of 500-1,000 words.

How to Contact: Query first. Reports in 2 weeks on queries. SASE. Accepts computer printouts. Sample copy $4.75.

Payment: Pays in contributor's copies; charge for extras.

Terms: Acquires first North American serial rights "and permission to reprint if my press publishes a special anthology." Sometimes sends galleys to author.

Advice: "In this Southern Appalachian rural series I can be optimistic about fiction. Appalachians are very responsive to their region's literature. I have taken work by beginners that had not been previously published. Be sure to send a double-spaced clean manuscript and SASE. I have the only rural press in North America; maybe even in the world. So perhaps we have a bond in common if your roots are rural."

‡HIPPO (II), Chautauqua Press, 28834 Boniface Dr., Malibu CA 90265. (213)457-7871. Editor: Karl Heiss. Magazine: 5½×8½; 42-48 pages; #20 lb bond paper; card cover; hi-contrast b&w illustrations. "Surreal and Hyper-real writing—writing that is honest and unpretentious—has a good chance of being considered. For open-minded, artistic, optimistic, cynical, paradoxical and all encompassing minds of all ages etc." Semiannually. Estab. 1988. Circ. 150.

Needs: Adventure, confessions, contemporary, erotica, experimental, fantasy, horror, humor/satire, literary, mainstream, prose poem, psychic/supernatural/occult, regional, science fiction, western and surreality "No pure genre fiction, but love the inclusion of genre style and content elements. No pretentious stuff that could only possibly live within the confines of academia." Receives 12 unsolicited mss/month. Accepts 5-9 mss/issue; 10-18 mss/year. Publishes ms "no more than 3 months" after acceptance. Recently published work by Stephen-Paul Martin, B.Z. Niditch, Greg Boyd and Gerald Locklin. Length: 500-3,000 words average; 4,000 words maximum. Publishes short shorts. Sometimes critiques rejected mss and recommends other markets.
How to Contact: Send complete ms with cover letter. Reporting time varies. SASE. Photocopied and reprint submissions OK. Accepts computer printout submissions. Sample copy $2.50. Fiction guidlines for #10 SAE and 1 first class stamp.
Payment: Pays in contributor's copies.
Terms: Acquires first or first North American serial rights.
Advice: "Be real, be unafraid, be spontaneous, tell me whatever you want about why you like your story—or even why you don't (and that's just the cover letter). The worst I'll do is tell you I don't need the manuscript for Hippo—but I may be able to steer you to someone who would want it."

HOB-NOB (I), 994 Nissley Rd., Lancaster PA 17601. Editor/Publisher: Mildred K. Henderson. Magazine: 8½×11; 64+ pages; 20 lb bond paper; 20 lb (or heavier) cover stock; b&w illustrations; few photos. "*Hob-Nob* is a small (one-person), amateur publication currently with a literary emphasis on original prose and poetry. This publication is directed toward amateur writers and poets, but many of them would like to be professional. For some, appearance in *Hob-Nob* is simply an opportunity to be published somewhere, while others possibly see it as a springboard to bigger and better things." Semiannually. Estab. 1969. Circ. nearly 400.
Needs: Literary, adventure, contemporary, humor, fantasy, psychic/supernatural/occult, prose poem, regional, romance, religious/inspirational, science fiction, spiritual, sports, mystery, juvenile, young adult, senior citizen/retirement, very brief condensed novels, excerpts from novels. "Upbeat" subjects are preferred. "Clean only. No erotica, works with excessive swearing or blatantly sexual words, gross violence, suicide, etc." Accepts 25-35 mss/issue. Does not read new contributor's submissions March 1-December 31, to prevent a backlog; any received before January will be returned. Receives 8-10 unsolicited fiction mss each month. Recently published work by Tab France, Laura Barger, Rex Kusler; published many new writers within the last year. Length: preferably 500-2,000 words. Critiques rejected mss when there is time. Sometimes recommends other markets.
How to Contact: Send complete ms with SASE. Accepts computer printout submissions. Rejections in 2 weeks. Publishes ms at least 1½-2 years after acceptance. Sample copy for $3 or $2.50 for a back issue.
Payment: 1 free author's copy for first appearance only. $3 charge for extras. Readers' choice contest every issue—votes taken on favorite stories and poems. Small prizes.
Terms: Acquires first rights.
Advice: "Include name and address on at least the first page, and name on others. State 'original and unpublished.' I especially appreciate the 'light' touch in both fiction and nonfiction—humor, whimsy, fantasy, etc. Beginning writers: Read your work out loud! Get someone else to listen to help you spot inconsistencies, unclear passages, inappropriate word choices. Bad grammar I can correct myself, but it's best to avoid, unless it is specifically meant to be dialectical. My biggest reasons for outright rejection are: lack of space, offensive subject matter or language, excessive length, and generally poor writing. I do sometimes send a story back for a rewrite when it has possibilities but 'problems.' Currently holding for 1990."

HOBO STEW REVIEW (I, II), 2 Eliot St.#1, Somerville MA 02143. Editor: Hobo Stew. Magazine: 8½×11; photocopy paper; 65 lb card stock cover; illustrations (use black ink on white 8½x11 paper). "*H.S.R.* encourages fiction, essays, letters to editor, poetry and journalism. Quarterly. Estab. 1984. Circ. 40.
Needs: Contemporary, feminist, humor/satire, senior citizen/retirement, translations, young adult/teen (10-18). No ageist or sexist fiction, or "slices of life that are 2 dimensional." Receives 5-10 unsolicited mss/month. Accepts 3-4 mss/issue; 8-12 mss/year. Publishes short shorts. Sometimes critiques rejected mss and recommends other markets.
How to Contact: Send complete ms with cover letter. Reports in 3-4 weeks. SASE. Photocopied submissions OK. Sample copy $2. Fiction guidelines for #10 SAE with 1 first class stamp. Subscription costs $5/year.
Payment: 1 contributor's copy.
Terms: Publication not copyrighted.
Advice: "As Hobo moves about the U.S.A. (home base for *H.S.R.* has been Eugene OR; Albuquerque NM; Allston MA; and currently Sommerville MA) the publication dates differ—as do the seasons' arrival. *H.S.R.* arrives quarterly *with* the seasons. *H.S.R.* now encourages short shorts. Send a clean

copy, remember to provide return postage, if hand written make it legible—all the things taken for granted are the ones most often overlooked. Keep at it only if you can be honest."

‡HORROR, (II), The Illustrated Book of Fears, Northstar Publishing, Suite C-9 2004 E. Steger Rd., Crete IL 60417. Editor: Mort Castle. Magazine. 8½×11; 48-80 pages; newsprint; color, enamel cover. "Quality horror for a general audience." Quarterly. Estab. 1989. Circ. 10,000.

Needs: Horror, psychic/supernatural/occult. Receives 50 unsolicited mss/month. Buys 4-8 mss/issue; 30 mss/year. Recently published work by Graham Masterson, Mort Castle. Length is open. Publishes short stories. Sometimes critiques rejected mss and recommends other markets.

How to Contact: "Send no more than three single-page story proposals or one complete story in standard two-column comics-script format." Reports in 3 months on queries; 4 months on mss. SASE. Reprints submission OK. Sample copy for $4. Fiction guidelines for SAE and 45¢.

Payment: Pays $5 per page and contributor's copies.

Terms: Pays on publication, rights purchased vary.

Advice: "In the tradition of the classic *EC* comics and the Warren publications of the late 60s and early 70s, but geared to contemporary taste, *HORROR* stories range from classical foggy moor at midnight tales ('when the powers of evil are exalted') to new wave, chop-o-matic super-splatter. Artists and writers are today's and tomorrow's 'big names.' "

HOR-TASY (II, IV), Ansuda Publications, Box 158-J, Harris IA 51345. Editor/Publisher: Daniel R. Betz. Magazine: 5½×8½; 72 pages; mimeo paper; index stock cover; illustrations on cover. "*Hor-Tasy* is bringing back actual *horror* to horror lovers tired of seeing so much science fiction and SF passed off as horror. We're also very much interested in true, poetic, pure fantasy."

Needs: Fantasy and horror. "Pure fantasy: Examples are trolls, fairies and mythology. The horror we're looking for comes from the human mind—the ultimate form of horror. It must sound real—so real that in fact it could very possibly happen at any time and place. We must be able to feel the diseased mind behind the personality. No science fiction in any way, shape or form. We don't want stories in which the main character spends half his time talking to a shrink. We don't want stories that start out with: 'You're crazy,' said so and so." Accepts 6 mss/issue. Receives 15-20 unsolicited fiction mss each month. Recently published work by Charmaine Parsons, M. C. Salemme, Jude Howell; published new writers within the last year. Critiques rejected mss "unless it's way off from what we're looking for." Sometimes recommends other markets.

How to Contact: Query or send complete ms with SASE. Accepts computer printout submissions; prefers letter-quality. Reports in 1 day on queries. "If not interested (in ms), we return immediately. If interested, we may keep it as long as 6 months." Publishes ms an average of 1 year after acceptance. Sample copy $2.95. Guidelines for #10 SASE.

Payment: 2 free author's copies. Charge for extras: Cover price less special discount rates.

Terms: Acquires first North American serial rights.

Advice: "Most stories rejected are about spooks, monsters, haunted houses, spacemen, etc. Because *Hor-Tasy* is a unique publication, I suggest the potential writer get a sample copy. Only unpublished work will be considered."

HOUSEWIFE-WRITER'S FORUM (I), Drawer 1518, Lafayette CA 94549. (415)932-1143. Editor: Deborah Haeseler. Magazine: 5½×8½; 32-40 pages and 20 lb bond paper and cover stock; illustrations. "Support for the woman who juggles writing with family life. We publish short fiction, poetry, essays, nonfiction, line drawings, humor and hints. For women of all ages; house husbands who write." Quarterly. Plans special fiction issue. Estab. 1988. Circ. over 1,200.

Needs: Confession, contemporary, experimental, historical (general), humor/satire, literary, mainstream, romance (contemporary, historical), suspense/mystery. No pornographic material. Receives 50-100 mss/month. Buys 1-2 mss/issue; 4-8 mss/year. Publishes ms within 6 months to 1 year after acceptance. Recently published work by Elaine McCormick, Carol Shenold and Sherry Zanzinger. Length: 1,500 words preferred; 500 words minimum; 2,000 words maximum. Publishes short shorts. Sometimes critiques rejected mss and if possible recommends other markets.

How to Contact: Send complete ms with cover letter. Cover letter should include "the basics." Reports in 1 month on queries; 3 months on mss. SASE. Simultaneous, photocopied and reprint submissions OK. Accepts computer printout submissions. Sample copy for $4. Fiction guidelines for #10 SAE and 1 first class stamp.

Payment: Pays $1-10, plus one contributor's copy. Half price for extra copies.

Terms: Pays on publication for one-time rights. Sponsors awards for fiction writers. "We sponsor 7 contests geared to the interests of housewife-writers. First place and grand prize winners are published in an annual edition, *The Best of Housewife-Writer's Forum: The Contested Wills to Write*. Entry fees: $3 for subscribers, $4 for nonsubscribers. Prizes are based on the number of entries per category. Send #10 SAE with 1 first class stamp for guidelines and further information.

Advice: "Just write it the best you can and submit it. I'll share whatever thoughts come to mind as I read it. Play with your basic idea, try to imagine the plot unfolding in different ways. And this is something few other editors will say, but share with me any worries you have about your story as presently submitted. I read every submission as a friend would. I look for the good parts and encourage you to develop your strengths. At the same time, I try to help minimize your weaknesses (we all have them!). I think two heads are better than one, and as long as you realize that my opinion isn't perfect, we can learn from each other; and we'll both be better writers as a result. In 1990, I am launching a humor-only publication, *Housewives' Humor.* It will include humorous fiction as well as Jean Kerr/Peg Bracken/Kathleen Quinlan/Erma Bombeck-like accounts of modern womanhood—but with a dash of the sardonic."

‡HOWLING DOG (II), Box 127, Farmington MI 48332. Magazine: 6×9; 64 pages; 65 lb paper; some illustrations; some photographs. "A wild and crazy literary magazine for a diverse audience." Estab. 1985. Circ. 500.
Needs: Contemporary, experimental, humor/satire, literary and mainstream. Receives 40 unsolicited mss/month. Accepts 2 mss/issue. Publishes ms 6 months after acceptance. Recently published work by M.L. Liebler and Gregory Burnham. Length: 1,000 words average; 300 words minimum; 1,500 words maximum. Publishes short shorts. Sometimes critiques rejected mss and recommends other markets.
How to Contact: Send complete ms with cover letter. Reports in 1 year. Sample copy $4.
Payment: Pays in contributor copies; discount charge for extras.
Terms: Acquires one-time rights.
Advice: "We look for crazy, *provocative*, quick, detailed, memorable, smooth reading, emotional or otherwise interesting. Keep it *less than* 1,500 words."

HOWLING
DOG
A Journal of Letters, Words, and Lines
VOLUME: 3
NUMBER: 2
EDITOR: MARK DONOVAN
ISSN: 0888-3521

Howling Dog is a journal of poetry, fiction, graphics and found art, according to editor Mark Donovan. John Kinkowitz's illustration for this off-the-wall publication adds an appropriate canine touch.

ICE RIVER (IV), A Magazine of Speculative Writing, Fantastic Art and Contemporary Music, 953 N. Gale, Union OR 97883. Magazine: 8½×11; 40 pages. "Fiction with an element of the fantastic (i.e. speculative fiction, SF, magical realism, modern fantasy and surrealism), mainly for a crossover audience between mainstream and literary SF." Triannually. Estab. 1987. Circ. 300-500.
Needs: Experimental, modern fantasy, literary, psychic/supernatural/occult, speculative prose poem, science fiction, surrealist. "We are not looking for sword-and-sorcery fantasy, Star Wars SF or stereotypical stories. This is a market for the literature of the fantastic—stories that are literary." Receives about 20 unsolicted mss/month. Accepts 4-5 mss/per issue. Publishes ms an average of 6 months after acceptance. Recently published work by Mary Ann Cain, Mark Laidlaw, Don Webb. Length: 2,000-3,000 words average; 500 words minimum; 5,000 words maximum. Publishes short shorts. Sometimes critiques rejected mss and may recommend other markets.

How to Contact: Send complete ms with cover letter, which should include a brief bio and list of some previous publications. Reports in 2-3 months on mss. SASE. Simultaneous (if notified immediately) and photocopied submissions OK. Accepts computer printout submissions, if legible, letter quality or near letter quality. Subscriptions: $9 for 3 issues. Sample copy for $2.50. Fiction guidelines for #10 SAE and 1 first class stamp. Overseas orders should add $1 for postage.
Payment: Pays $15 plus 2 contributor's copies.
Terms: Pays on publication for first North American serial rights.

IMPULSE MAGAZINE (II), 16 Skey Lane, Toronto, Ontario M6J 3S4 Canada. (416)537-9551. Editors: Eldon Garnet, Judith Doyle, Carolyn White and Brian Boigon. Magazine: 8¼×10¾; 60 pages; 4-color glossy cover; illustrations and photos. "Theme is art and culture with an emphasis on experimental/innovative fiction, interviews, political and cultural analysis and artwork." Quarterly. Estab. 1971. Circ. 5,000.
Needs: "Experimental, innovative writing. We are also a visual publication and would appreciate any accompanying images, illustrations, etc." Accepts 4-5 mss/issue, 15-20 mss/year. Receives approximately 30 unsolicited fiction mss/month. Published new writers within the last year. Length: 250-2,000 words. Critiques rejected mss when there is time.
How to Contact: Send complete ms with SAE and IRCs. Accepts computer printout submissions. Reports in 4-6 months on mss. Sample copy $5.
Terms: Acquires first rights. "We now have a greater commitment than previously to paying all contributors."
Advice: "Keep trying. Avoid too lengthy a manuscript. Most manuscripts are either poorly conceived or simply too conventional in style and content and do not exhibit suitable awareness of the idiosyncracies of *Impulse*. We are interested in more experimental pieces of fiction."

IN-BETWEEN (I), Art & Entertainment Between the Lakes, Six Lakes Arts Communication, Inc., 43 Chapel St., Seneca Falls NY 13148. (315)568-4265. Editor: Stephen Beals. Magazine: 8½×11; 32 pages minimum; 60 lb offset paper; glossy cover; illustrations; photos. "Art and entertainment. Music, theatre, short stories, poetry. Exclusive to Finger Lakes region of New York State, for upscale arts enthusiasts." Bimonthly. Estab. 1987. 1,500 copies distributed to members, arts groups and media.
Needs: Historical (general), humor/satire, juvenile (5-9 years), prose poem, senior citizen/retirement, suspense/mystery, music, theatre. Finger Lakes writers given preference. "We are a new magazine for the Finger Lakes. We are interested in art and entertainment with a very broad view of what constitutes art. We have a rural flavor and a 'family' audience. Work must be reflective of Finger Lakes region." No erotica, sci fi, psychic, religious, romance, gay/lesbian. Accepts 1-2 mss/issue. Publishes ms 1-3 months after acceptance. Recently published work by Richard Cicarelli, Barbara Mater and David Downey. Length: 800 words average; 500 words minimum; 3,500 words maximum. Will consider longer pieces in serial form. Publishes short shorts.
How to Contact: Send complete ms with cover letter. Reports in 2-4 weeks on queries; 4-6 weeks on mss. SASE. Simultaneous, photocopied and reprint submissions OK. Accepts computer printout submissions. Accepts electronic submissions via Apple Macintosh. Sample copy and fiction guidelines free.
Payment: Pays in contributor's copies. "Some payment for special projects; query."
Advice: Most of our writers are first-timers. Keep in mind our audience is rural by choice and shouldn't be talked down to. Consideration is being given to publishing short stories in book form."

THE INDEPENDENT REVIEW (I), Box 113, Kingsville MO 64061. Editor: Shirley Janner. Magazine: 6½×8½; approx. 80 pages; chromecoat cover; cover photos. Quarterly. Estab. 1987.
Needs: Adventure, contemporary, experimental, fantasy, feminist, horror, humor/satire, mainstream, prose poem, science fiction. No porn, family tales. Receives 10-20 unsolicited mss/month. Accepts 1-4 mss/issue. Publishes ms 1-5 months after acceptance. Published new writers within the last year. Length: 1,200 words maximum. Publishes short shorts. Sometimes comments on rejected mss and recommends other markets.
How to Contact: Send complete ms. Reports in 3 months on mss. SASE. Simultaneous and photocopied submissions OK. Accepts computer printout submissions. Sample copy for $4. Fiction guidelines free for #10 SAE.
Payment: Contributor's copies.
Terms: Acquires one-time rights.
Advice: "Much fiction is lacking one or more elements of a story (beginning, middle, end!). We especially want to see beginners! Be neat and concise. SASE a must. No erasable paper. Humor gets special attention."

INDIANA REVIEW (II), 316 N. Jordan Ave., Bloomington IN 47405. (812)855-3439. Editor: Jon Tribble. Associate Editor: Russell Roby. Magazine: 6×9; 128 pages; 60 lb paper; Glatfelter cover stock. "Magazine of contemporary fiction and poetry in which there is a zest for language, some relationship between form and content, and some awareness of the world. For fiction writers/readers, followers of lively contemporary poetry." Triannually. Estab. 1976. Circ. 500.

Needs: Literary, contemporary, experimental, mainstream. "We are interested in innovation, logic, unity, a social context, a sense of humanity. All genres that meet some of these criteria are welcome." Accepts 6-8 mss/issue. Recently published work by Charles Baxter, Wright Morris, H.E. Francis; published new writers within the last year. Length: 1-35 magazine pages.

How to Contact: Send complete ms with cover letter. "Don't describe or summarize the story." SASE. Accepts computer printout submissions, prefers letter-quality. Reports in 3 weeks-3 months. Publishes ms an average of 2-10 months after acceptance. Sample copy $4.

Payment: $25/story.

Terms: Buys North American serial rights.

Advice: "Be daring, love the language. Don't imitate anyone. Refrain from the chatty cover letter. Send one story at a time (unless they're really short), and no simultaneous submissions."

‡INDIGO (II), 32 Lachalade, Lorraine, Quebec J6Z 1W4 Canada. Editor: Toni Linecker. Magazine: 8×11; 45-60 pages; 45 lb premium paper quality; glossy cover stock; illustrations and photographs. Semiannually. Estab. 1989. Circ. 1,500-2,500.

Needs: Contemporary, experimental, horror, humor/satire, literary, mainstream, psychic/supernatural/occult and serious science fiction. No juvenile, preschool, religious or silly science fiction. Plans special fiction issue. Receives 20 unsolicited mss per month; accepts 6-10 mss per issue; 12-20 mss per year. Agented fiction less than 5%. Length: 2,800-3,500 words average; 1,200 words minimum; 7,000 words maximum. Comments on rejected mss and recommends other markets.

How to Contact: Send complete ms with cover letter; bio if possible. Reports within 2 months. SASE. Photocopied, reprint and computer printout submissions OK. Sample copy $2 (Canadian) and SAE with IRCs. Fiction guidelines free with SASE.

Payment: Pays contributor's copies.

Terms: Pays for first North American serial rights.

Advice: "Rewrite your manuscript until you know it's the best you can write. Why stop with a rough precious stone if you could produce a polished gem?"

INLET (II), Virginia Wesleyan College, Norfolk VA 23502. Editor: Joseph Harkey. Magazine: 7×8½; 32-38 pages. "Poetry and short fiction for people of all ages." Annually. Estab. 1970. Circ. 700.

Needs: Literary, contemporary, mainstream, fantasy and humor. "Our main interest is well written fiction." Accepts 2-5 mss/issue. Receives 10-20 unsolicited fiction mss each month. Does not read in summer. Recently published work by Myron Taube and L.S. Bingham. Length: 500-1,500 words but "will consider up to 3,000." Sometimes recommends other markets.

How to Contact: "Manuscripts are read September through March only." Send complete ms to fiction editor with SASE. Reports in 2 months. Sample copy for 75¢ postage (Do not send personal checks.)

Payment: Free author's copies.

Advice: "Write carefully and present a neatly typed manuscript with SASE. Send an example of your best work; short shorts preferred. Some rejected manuscripts are poorly written. Some lack imaginative treatments of the problems they raise."

INNISFREE (I, II), Box 277, Manhattan Beach CA 90266. (213)545-2607. FAX (213)546-5862. Editor: Rex Winn. Magazine: 8½×11; 44 pages; 90 lb cover stock; illustrations and photos. Publishes "fiction, poetry, essays—open forum." Bimonthly. Estab. 1981. Circ. 200.

Needs: Adventure, contemporary, ethnic, fantasy, literary, mainstream, regional, science fiction and suspense/mystery. No political or religious sensationalism. Accepts 10-12 mss/issue; approx. 80 mss/year. Publishes ms within 6 months of acceptance. Recently published work by Ron Fleshman, Peter McGinn, Clem Portman and Anne Swann. Length: 3,500 words average. Publishes short shorts. Sometimes critiques rejected mss.

How to Contact: Send complete mss with cover letter. Reports in 1 month. SASE. Simultaneous, photocopied and reprint submissions OK. Accepts electronic submissions via IBM disk. Sample copy for $1. Free fiction guidelines.

Payment: No payment. Prizes offered.

Terms: Acquires one-time rights. Sponsors awards for fiction writers. "$50 for best short story, $20 for best poem."

Advice: "Fiction market is on the decline. This is an attempt to publish new writers who take pride in their work and have some talent."

INSIDE JOKE (I, II), A Newsletter of Comedy and Creativity, Box 1609, Madison Square Station, New York NY 10159. Editor: Elayne Wechsler. Newsletter: 8½×11; 32 pages; 16 or 20 lb cover/stock; illustrations. "We have no theme per se—we're more defined by what we don't publish then by what we do." Readers consist of "alternative media (non-mainstream) and mutants." Bimonthly. Estab. 1980. Circ. 250.

Needs: Experimental, fantasy, humor/satire, psychic/supernatural/occult, science fiction, serialized/excerpted story. No erotica, confessional, mainstream. Publishes ms no longer than 2 months after acceptance. Length: 500-600 words average; 1,900 words maximum. Occasionally critiques rejected mss. Sometimes recommends other markets.

How to Contact: Send for sample copy and/or writer's guidelines. SASE. Photocopied submissions OK. Accepts computer printout submissions. "I don't care if it's scrawled in blood." Sample copy $1.50. Checks *must* be made payable to "Elayne Wechsler." Fiction guidelines for #10 SAE and 1 first class stamp.

Payment: "Only staff writers receive free copies; other contributors get a discount (65¢ stamp instead of $1.50 subscription price)."

Advice: "To presume that a person who writes for pleasure without receiving payment is not a professional writer makes me sick. I sincerely hope mainstream presses someday come around to the realization that small independent publications have as much validity (if not more) as anything else listed in these pages."

INTERIM (II), Dept. of English, University of Nevada, Las Vegas NV 89154. (702)739-3471. Editor and Founder: A. Wilber Stevens. Associate Editors: James Hazen, Arlen Collier, Joe McCullough. Magazine: 6×9; 48 pages; heavy paper; glossy cover; cover illustrations. Publishes "poetry and short fiction for a serious, sophisticated, educated audience." Semiannually. Estab. 1944. Circ. 700.

Needs: Contemporary and literary. Accepts 1-2 mss/issue. Publishes ms within 6 months to 1 year of acceptance. Recently published work by Gladys Swan, James B. Hall. Length: 4,000 words preferred; 1,000 words minimum; 8,000 words maximum.

How to Contact: Send complete ms with cover letter. Reports on mss in 6 weeks. SASE. Photocopied submissions OK. Accepts computer printout submissions. Sample copy for $3.

Payment: Pays in contributor's copies and free subscription to magazine.

Advice: Looks for "quality, but would not be likely to accept anything over 20 printed pages. Emphasis traditionally has been on poetry."

‡IOWA WOMAN, Box 680, Iowa City IA 52244. Contact: Editor. Nonprofit magazine "dedicated to encouraging and publishing women writers and artists internationally." Quarterly. Estab. 1979. Circ. 2,500.

Needs: Historical, literary, women's. Receives 5-10 unsolicited mss/month. Accepts 2 mss/issue; 8 mss/year. Length: 5,000 words maximum.

How to Contact: Send complete ms. Reports in 3 months. SASE. Sample copy for $4 and SAE with 80 postage. Fiction guidelines for SAE with 1 first class stamp.

Payment: 2 free contributor's copies; $2 charge for extras.

Terms: Acquires all rights. Publication copyrighted.

JABBERWOCKY (I, II), The Magazine of Speculative Writing, 7701 SW 7th Pl., Gainesville FL 32607. (904)332-6586. Editors: Duane Bray, Jeff Vander Meer and Penelope Miller. Magazine: 5½×8½; 72 pages; coated matte paper; two-color gloss cover; 5-10 illustrations; 2-5 photographs. "An eclectic mix of styles within the bounds of fantasy, horror and science fiction (experimental, commercial, literary)." Semiannually. Estab. 1989. Circ. 1,000.

Needs: Experimental, fantasy, horror, humor/satire, literary, psychic/supernatural/occult, science fiction, serialized novel, translations. "No overtly religious. No Tolkien rehashes. (We will accept even extremely offensive work if scene(s) are essential to story.)" Receives 375 unsolicited mss/month. Buys 4-10 mss/issue; 8-20 mss/year. Publishes ms no more than 6 months after acceptance. "Will soon publish S.P. Somtow, Steve Rasnic Tem, Kathe Koja and Wayne Allen Sallee, among others." Published new writers in the last year. Length: 3,000 words preferred; 7,500 words maximum. Sometimes critiques rejected mss, "always comments (if guidelines have been observed):" Sometimes recommends other markets.

How to Contact: Send complete manuscript with cover letter, which should include "where writer saw *Jabberwocky* listed, publication credits (for bio listing if work is accepted) "plus a tearsheet of one published piece." Reports in 1-3 weeks. SASE. "Foreign submitters should send IRCs." Accepts computer printout submissions. Sample copy for $5. Fiction guidelines for #10 SAE and 1 first class stamp.

Payment: Pays $10-50. Free contributor's copy.

Terms: Pays on acceptance for first rights. Sends galleys to author.

Advice: "Style is paramount, especially for fantasy. Obviously, characterization and setting must be fully fleshed-out (though characterization may not be essential for certain stories). Writers who are unsure whether their work qualifies as speculative fiction should simply send it. Our own influences are as diverse as Harlan Ellison, Peter Beagle, Robert Heinlein, and Clive Barker (also Ursula LeGuin and, of course, Lewis Carroll). A problem some beginners face once they've made 2 or 3 sales is focusing on the writing rather than the market. Don't get too hung up with trying to be published—especially if you're young (you've got time). We appreciate exotic settings and hate the mundane."

JACARANDA REVIEW (II), Dept. of English, UCLA, Los Angeles CA 90024. (213) 825-4173. Editor: Bruce Kijewski. Fiction Editor: Katherine Swiggart. Magazine: 5½×8; 200 pages; high quality paper; Archer cover stock; cover illustrations. "We publish anything that we think is high quality, for serious readers of fiction and poetry." Semiannually. Estab. 1984. Circ. 1,000.

Needs: Condensed/excerpted novel, contemporary, experimental, literary, mainstream, prose poem and translations. "We're not particularly interested in what people call 'genre' fiction. We're interested in fiction that reflects contemporary sensibilities about contemporary life." Receives 25 mss/month. Accepts 3 mss/issue; 6 mss/year. Publishes ms within 1-2 months of acceptance. Recently published work by Jorge Luis Borges, Ed Minus and Charles Bukowski; published new writers within the last year. Length: 2,500-5,000 words preferred; 500 words minimum; 10,000 words maximum. Sometimes critiques rejected mss and recommends other markets.

How to Contact: Send complete mss with cover letter. Cover letter should include "contributor's note." Reports on queries in 2 weeks; on mss in 2 months. SASE. Simultaneous and photocopied submissions OK. Accepts computer printout submissions. Sample copy for $3.50, 6x9 SAE and 3 first class stamps.

Payment: Pays in contributor's copies. Discount for extra copies.

Terms: Acquires one-time rights.

Advice: Sees "too much *unexamined* minimalist fiction; that is, fiction that dwells in passivity and is almost ashamed of passion. Not enough fiction inspired by Garcià Marquez or Kundera. Lately we tend to like fiction that avoids minimalist mannerisms (though we do publish work in the Robison-F. Barthelme mode), that has an energetic sense of humor, and which aspires to be psychologically fearless. We're interested in good experimental fiction, too, if we can find some, and fiction about and by women. A lot of the fiction we receive seems inspired in conception but underdeveloped and unrealized in execution. Care—deeply—about the reader, and care deeply about your work."

JAM TO-DAY (II), 372 Dunstable Rd., Tyngsboro MA 01879. Fiction Editor: Judith Stanford. Co-editor: Don Stanford. Magazine: 5½×8½; 80 pages; illustrations; occasional photos. "Forum for serious nonacademic poetry and fiction by unknown and little-known contemporary writers." Annually. Published special fiction issue. Estab. 1973. Circ. 400.

Needs: Literary, contemporary, science fiction and feminist. No light fiction, word-play fiction, highly allusive or allegorical fiction. Buys 3-5 mss/year. Receives approximately 35 unsolicited fiction mss each month. Published new writers within the last year. Length: 1,500-7,500. Publishes "good quality short shorts of 300-750 words." Critiques rejected mss when there is time. Sometimes recommends other markets.

How to Contact: Send complete ms with SASE. Accepts computer printout submissions; prefers letter quality. Reports in 6 weeks on mss. Publishes ms up to 1 year after acceptance. Sample copy $4.

Payment: $5/printed page.

Terms: Pays on publication for first rights.

Advice: "We are publishing more short stories now." Reasons for rejections: "(1) poorly conceived: trite, uninteresting, poorly written, too academic; and (2) better suited to another market: well written and holds interest but better suited to mass-market magazine, or extraordinarily obscure but not obviously foolish and ought to go to experimental literary magazine."

JAPANOPHILE (II, IV), Box 223, Okemos MI 48864. (517)349-1795. Editor-in-Chief: Earl Snodgrass. Magazine: 5¼×8½; 50 pages; illustrations; photos. Magazine of "articles, photos, poetry, humor, short stories about Japanese culture, not necessarily set in Japan, for an adult audience, most with college background; travelers." Quarterly. Published special fiction issue last year; plans another. Estab. 1974. Circ. 600.

Needs: Adventure, historical (general), humor/satire, literary, mainstream, and suspense/mystery. Receives 40-100 unsolicited fiction mss/month. Buys 1 ms/issue, 4-10 mss/year. Recently published work by Gerald Dorset, Bobbi Crudup, Joan Van De Moortel; published new writers within the last year. Length: 2,000 words minimum; 9,000 words maximum; 4,000 words average. Sometimes recommends other markets.

How to Contact: Send complete ms with SASE and cover letter with author bio and information about story. Photocopied and previously published submissions OK. Accepts computer printout submissions. Reports in 2 months on mss. Sample copy $4; guidelines for #10 SAE and 1 first class stamp.

Payment: Pays $20 on publication.
Terms: Pays on publication for all rights, first North American serial rights or one-time rights (depends on situation).
Advice: "Short stories usually involve Japanese and 'foreign' (non-Japanese) characters in a way that contributes to understanding of Japanese culture and the Japanese people. However, a *good* story dealing with Japan or Japanese cultural aspects anywhere in the world will be considered, even if it does not involve this encounter or meeting of Japanese and foreign characters. Some stories may also be published in an anthology." Annual contest pays $100 plus publication for the best short story. Deadline December 31. Entry fee is $5.

‡JAZZIMINDS MAGAZINE, Box 237, Cold Spring Harbor NY 11724. (516)427-6636. Editor: Joan H. Callahan. Fiction Editor: Jiliann Coran. Magazine: 8½×11; 20-30 pages; bond paper; heavy cover stock. "We like to emphasize the 'dark' and wild sides of life for an adult audience." Annually with quarterly supplemental issues. Estab. 1987.
Needs: Condensed/excerpted novel, contemporary, experimental, literary, prose poem and translations. Plan to publish special fiction issue or anthology in the future. Accepts 6 mss/issue; 24-30 mss/year. Publishes ms 3 months-1 year after acceptance. Recently published work by Albert Rosso and L. Taesczch. Length: 1,000-2,000 words; 1,000-1,500 average. Publishes short shorts. Sometimes critiques rejected mss and recommends other markets.
How to Contact: Query first. Query with clips of published work or send complete ms with cover letter. Include brief auto-bio data. (Please send work vertically, not folded preferred.) Reports in 3 weeks on queries; 2 months on mss. SASE. Photocopied and reprint submissions OK. Accepts computer printout submissions. Sample copy $6 (make checks and mo's payable to: J. Callahan.) Fiction guidelines for SASE.
Payment: Acquires first or first North American serial rights.
Advice: "If someone has written about the 'dark' smokey wild side of life on the fringes, classic jazz, speakeasy, Billy Holliday or the bohemic life from which jazz was born, we are very interested. We suggest you get a sample copy, and take in your market. Aim high!"

JEOPARDY (II), Literary Arts Magazine, CH 132, Western Washington University, Bellingham WA 98225. (206)676-3118. Contact: Editors. Magazine: 6×9; 108 pages; 70 lb paper; Springhill 215 cover stock; illustrations and photographs. Material published: fiction, nonfiction, poetry, photographed artwork (slide form) for "all inclusive" audience. Annually. Estab. 1965. Circ. 3,000-4,000.
Needs: Adventure, contemporary, ethnic, experimental, fantasy, feminist, humor/satire, literary, mainstream, prose poem, regional, contemporary romance, science fiction and translations. No long stories. Accepts 7-10 mss/year. Length: 4 pages (average 800-1,000 words).
How to Contact: Send complete ms. SASE. Simultaneous and previously published submissions OK. Accepts computer printout submissions. Sample copy $2.
Payment: Two contributor's copies. "Sometimes *Jeopardy* awards cash prizes or special recognition to winners in various categories."
Advice: "We are a student-funded university literary publication. We are happy to look at any fiction. Sometimes, if staff is large enough, at writer's request we will comment on the work."

‡JEST (I), Humor and Variety for the Discerning Mind, 115 Hallum Dr., Auburndale FL 33823. Editor: Todd Pierce. Magazine: 8½×11; 20 pages; glossy cover; black and white illustrations. "We accept a variety of articles, many with a humorous slant. We're interested in humor that deals with social issues and pokes fun at hypocrisy. The magazine is meant to appeal more to the literary, intellectual crowd and socially conscious people looking for an alternative publication." Quarterly. Estab. 1988. Circ. 1,000.
Needs: Ethnic, experimental, fantasy, historical (general), horror, humor/satire, literary, prose poem, psychic/supernatural/occult, science fiction, translations. "We prefer stories with photographs or artwork. Also, cartoon or photo parodies." Accepts up to 5 mss/issue; up to 20 mss/year. Length: 1,000 word average; 100 words minimum; 4,000 words maximum. Publishes short shorts. Length: 250. Sometimes recommends other markets.
How to Contact: Send complete ms with cover letter. Reports in 3 months on mss. SASE for ms. Simultaneous, photocopied and reprint submissions OK. Accepts computer printout submissions. Sample copy for $2.50. Fiction guidelines for 1 first class stamp.
Payment: Pays in contributor's copies.
Terms: Acquires one-time rights.
Advice: "We would like to see unusual, unique stories which have a philosophical message or address a social issue of our time."

JEWISH CURRENTS MAGAZINE (IV), 22 E. 17th St., New York NY 10003. (212)924-5740. Editor-in-Chief: Morris U. Schappes. Magazine: 5½×8½; 48 pages. "We are a progressive monthly, broad in our interests, printing feature articles on political and cultural aspects of Jewish life in the US and elsewhere, reviews of books and film, poetry and fiction, Yiddish translations; regular columns on Israel, US Jewish community, current events, Jewish women today, secular Jewish life. Monthly themes include Holocaust and Resistance, Black-Jewish relations, Jewish Book Month, Jewish Music Month, etc. National audience, literate and politically left, well educated." Monthly. Estab. 1946. Circ. 4,000.

Needs: Contemporary, ethnic, feminist, historical (general), humor/satire, literary, senior citizen/retirement, translations. "We are interested in *authentic* experience and readable prose; Jewish themes; humanistic orientation. No religious, political sectarian; no porn or hard sex, no escapist stuff. Go easy on experimentation, but we're interested." Receives 6-10 unsolicited fiction mss/month. Accepts 0-1 ms/issue, 8-10 mss/year. Recently published work by Lou Wax, Haim Zilberman; published new writers within the last year. Length: 1,000 words minimum; 3,000 words maximum; 1,800 words average.

How to Contact: Send complete ms with cover letter. "Writers should include brief biographical information, especially their publishing histories." SASE. Reports in 2 months on mss. Publishes ms an average of 2 months to 2 years after acceptance. Sample copy $1.50 with SAE and 3 first class stamps.

Payment: 1 complimentary one-year subscription; 6 free contributor's copies.

Terms: "We readily give reprint permission at no charge." Sends galleys to author.

Advice: "Family themes are good, but avoid sentimentality; keep the prose tight, not sprawling; matters of character and moral dilemma, maturing into pain and joy, dealing with Jewish conflicts OK. Space is increasingly a problem. Tell the truth, as sparely as possible."

THE JOURNAL (II), Creative Writing Program, Ohio State University, 164 W. 17th St., Columbus OH 43210. (614)422-4076. Editor: David Citino. Magazine: 6×9; 80 pages; illustrations; photos. "We are open to all forms of quality fiction." For an educated, general adult audience. Semiannually. Estab. 1973. Circ. 1,000.

Needs: Contemporary, erotica, ethnic, experimental, feminist, gay, literary, prose poem and regional. No romance or religious/devotional. Accepts 2-12 mss/issue. Receives approximately 100 unsolicited fiction mss each month. Publishes ms within 6 months of acceptance. Agented fiction 10%. Recently published work by Anne Brashler and Kent Meyers; published new writers within the last year. Length: 4,000 words maximum. Critiques rejected mss when there is time. Sometimes recommends other markets.

How to Contact: Send complete ms with cover letter, which should list previous publications. Reports in 2 weeks on queries; 3 months on mss. SASE. Photocopied submissions OK. "No simultaneous submissions please." Accepts computer printout submissions. Prefers letter-quality. Publishes ms 1-12 months after acceptance. Sample copy $3; fiction guidelines for SASE.

Payment: Pays $25 stipend when funds are available. Free author's copies. $3 charge for extras.

Terms: Acquires First North American serial rights. Sends galleys to author. "All contributors are automatically eligible for the President's Award ($100 annual award)."

Advice: Mss are rejected because of "lack of understanding of the short story form, shallow plots, undeveloped characters. Cure: read as much well-written fiction as possible. Our readers prefer 'psychological' fiction rather than stories with intricate plots. Take care to present a clean, well-typed submission."

JOURNAL OF POLYMORPHOUS PERVERSITY (II), Wry-Bred Press, Inc., 10 Waterside Plaza, Suite 20-B, New York NY 10010. (212)689-5473. Editor: Glenn Ellenbogen. Magazine: 6¾×10; 24 pages; 60 lb paper; antique india cover stock; illustrations with some articles. "*JPP* is a humorous and satirical journal of psychology, psychiatry, and the closely allied mental health disciplines." For "psychologists, psychiatrists, social workers, psychiatric nurses, *and* the psychologically sophisticated layman." Semiannally. Plans special fiction issue. Estab. January, 1984.

Needs: Humor/satire. "We only consider materials that are 1) funny, 2) relate to psychology *or* behavior." Receives 10 unsolicited mss/month. Accepts 8 mss/issue; 16 mss/year. Recently published work by Kathleen Donald, Ph.D. Most writers published last year were previously unpublished writers. Length: 1,500 words average; 4,000 words maximum. Comments on rejected ms.

How to Contact: Send complete ms *in triplicate*. Reports in 1-3 months on mss. SASE. Simultaneous and photocopied submissions OK. Accepts computer printout submissions; prefers letter-quality. Accepts disk submissions compatible with Morrow MD-11. Prefers hard copy with a disk submission. Sample copy $5. Fiction guidelines free for #10 SAE and 1 first class stamp.

Payment: 2 contributor's copies; charge for extras: $5.

Advice: "We will *not* look at poetry or short stories. We only want to see intelligent spoofs of scholarly psychology and psychiatry articles written in scholarly scientific languages. Take a look at *real* journals of psychology and try to lampoon their *style* as much as their content. Avoid writing in first person; rather use more quasi-scientific style. There are few places to showcase satire of the social sciences, thus we provide one vehicle for injecting a dose of humor into this often too serious area."

JOURNAL OF QUANTUM 'PATAPHYSICS (I,II), Box 29756, Los Angeles CA 90029. (213)662-4569. Editor: Nigey Lennon. Fiction Editor: Lionel Rolfe. Magazine: 3½×4¼; 32 pages; bond paper; self cover; illustrations; photos. "We are "pataphysical' in nature ('pataphysics being the tongue-in-cheek pseudo-science invented by French author Alfred Jarry in the 1890s). We publish a variety of fiction, essays, articles and comics along 'pataphysical lines." For readers "reasonably intellectual and open-minded, interested in the arts and current events, not afraid of strong viewpoints." Quarterly. Estab. 1987. Circ. 3,000.

Needs: "We have published a wide variety of styles and subjects. Our only real guideline is that manuscripts fit the basically irreverent style of the magazine. Each issue is loosely organized around a particular theme, so contributors should ask about future themes." Receives 5-10 mss/month. Accepts 1-5 mss/issue; 4-10 mss/year. Publishes ms within 3 months of acceptance. Recently published work by Julia Stein, Lionel Rolfe, Nigey Lennon; published new writers within the last year. Length: 500-600 words preferred; 1,000 words maximum. Publishes short shorts. Sometimes critiques rejected mss and recommends other markets.

How to Contact: Send complete mss with cover letter. Reports on queries in 1-2 weeks; on mss in 1 month. SASE. Simultaneous, photocopied and reprint submissions OK. Accepts computer printout submissions. Sample copy for $2.

Payment: Pays in contributor's copies.

Terms: Acquires one-time rights.

Advice: "Before you waste a manuscript and an SASE, be sure you understand the *JQ'P*. Although we publish a wide variety of fiction, essays, speculative writing, etc., we are only looking for material in the spirit of the publication – that is to say, irreverent, witty, controversial, and above all, personal. If you've never seen the *JQ'P*, request a sample copy ($1.50). Feel free to send a query letter describing your manuscript – all mail is answered."

JOURNAL OF REGIONAL CRITICISM (II), Arjuna Library Press, 1025 Garner St., Box 18, Colorado Springs CO 80905. Editor: Joseph A. Uphoff, Jr. Pamphlet: size variable; number of pages variable; Xerox paper; Bristol cover stock; b&w illustrations and photos. "Surrealist and dreamlike prose poetry and very short surrealist stories to illustrate accompanying mathematical, theoretical material in the fine arts for a wide ranging audience interested in philosophical sophistication and erudite language." Variable frequency. Estab. 1979.

Needs: Adventure, contemporary, ethnic, experimental, fantasy, historical (general), horror, humor/satire, literary, mainstream, prose poem, psychic/supernatural/occult, regional, religious/inspirational, contemporary romance, science fiction. Receives 1 or fewer unsolicited fiction ms/month. Accepts 1-5 mss/issue. Publishes ms 1 month-1 year after acceptance. Recently published work by Gayle Teller, Ron Ellis and Randall Brock. Short short stories preferred. Sometimes critiques rejected mss and recommends other markets.

How to Contact: Send complete ms with cover letter. Manuscript will *not* be returned. Cover letter should include goals, behind-the-scenes explanation, and biographical material or résumé, date of birth, degrees, awards, offices and publications. Reports in 2 months on mss. SASE for query. Simultaneous, photocopied and reprint submissions OK. Accepts computer printouts. Sample copy, if and when available, for $1 postage.

Payment: By contract after profit; contributor's copies.

Terms: Acquires "prototype presentation rights." Publication copyrighted – limited edition procedure copyrights.

Advice: "Reality is, itself, a kind of fiction, but we seldom have personal control over our lives like we can have over our writings. Language can convey beautiful stories, crisis, tragedy, or merely form. That which does not exist can be made to exist in fiction. In writings, we can, through image, violate the natural laws of the universe to make fantasy. This technique is often applied to cartoons and comedy. Writings can also be made to influence the course of events rather than relating unreal situations. The news is often the basis of a good, fictional adventure. Those who do not know what surrealism is are urged to read *Nadja* by Andre Breton and the literature of Amos Tutuola."

‡JOYEUX EROTIQUE, A Journal of Literate, Happy Sex, Limelight Publishing Company, P.O. Box 11618, Denver CO 80211. Editor: Paul H. Wigton. Fiction Editor: Harry Lime. Magazine: 8×11; 60-80 pages; 30 lb bond paper; 100 lb card cover stock; occasional pen and ink illustrations. "A literate journal of happy sexual encounter." Quarterly. Estab. 1989. Circ. under 100.

Needs: "Erotica fiction only. Fiction can be presented in sci/fi, fantasy, western, contemporary, mystery, straight, lesbian, gay or gray. Eroticism must be part of and essential to the supporting story." No S&M or confession. Receives 5 mss/month; accepts 5-8 mss/issue. Publishes ms 1-6 months after acceptance. Length: 400-3,500 words preferred. "Will publish under 500 words if ms meets other criteria."

How to Contact: "Do not send ms without first sending #10 SASE for guidelines! Then send ms that conforms to the guidelines." Reports on ms in less that 1 month. SASE. Accepts any typed, clearly legible, clean copy. No simultaneous submissions. Sample copy $3.95. Fiction guidelines for #10 SAE and 1 first class stamp.

Payment: Contributor's copies. Annual award of $100 for best story of the year.

Terms: Pays for one-time rights. Publication not copyrighted.

Advice: "We find that many people in recent years do not read novels. They have not developed the habit and do not wish to take the time. They prefer short fiction. Writing for this genre, erotica, is no different than any other literary effort. Proper use of language is the framework that supports your story. Without that the story is not acceptable. Do not write for shock effect; do let yourself go, turn the readers on and leave them with a tear, a smile or laugh, a fond reminiscence and possibly a change of outlook."

K (II), 351 Dalhousie St., Brantford, Ontario N3S 3V9 Canada. Editor: G.J. McFarlane. Magazine: 7×8½; 50 pages. Has an "open theme that provides a forum for writers whose contemporary ideas establish a voice for turbulent times." Published as funds permit. Estab. 1985.

Needs: Condensed novel, confession, contemporary, erotica, experimental, feminist, humor/satire, literary, mainstream, science fiction, serialized/excerpted novel. Receives 15 unsolicited mss/month. Accepts mss "as quality and space permit." Mss published an undetermined time after acceptance. Publishes short shorts. Occasionally critiques rejected mss and recommends other markets.

How to Contact: Send complete ms with cover letter. Reports in 1 month on queries. SASE. Simultaneous, photocopied and reprint submissions OK. Accepts computer printout submissions. Sample copy $4.

Payment: Pays in contributor's copies.

‡KABBALAH YICHUD (I,IV), A Magazine for the Advancement of World Jewry, Malkhutian Rite Temple Society, Box 3728, Augusta GA 30914. Editor: Patrick Saucer. Magazine: 5½×8; 8-12 pages; 20 lb paper; 60 lb cover; black and white illustrations. "Judaism and Jewish interest for Jewish readers." Published irregularly. Estab. 1989. Circ. varies.

Needs: Contemporary, ethnic, feminist, historical (general), lesbian, literary, mainstream, prose poem, psychic/supernatural/occult, religious/inspirational, translations. "We are interested in any materials dealing with Jews and Judaism." Receives 10 unsolicited mss/month. Accepts 2-3 mss/issue; 24-36 mss/year. Publishes ms 1-3 months after acceptance. Length: 3,000 words maximum. Publishes short shorts. Sometimes recommends other markets.

How to Contact: Send complete ms with cover letter. Reports in 1 week on queries; 2 months on mss. SASE. Simultaneous and photocopied submissions OK. Accepts computer printout submissions. Accepts electronic submissions via disk. Sample copy for $1.75. Fiction guidelines for $1, #10 SAE and 1 first class stamp.

Payment: Pays in contributor's copies.

Terms: "Inquire about rights purchased."

Advice: "The purpose of the *Kabbalah Yichud* is to present the Jewish aspect of Malkhutianism which is a branch of reform Judaism. The *Kabbalah Yichud* is an official publication of the Malkhutian Rite Temple Society."

KAIROS (II), A Journal of Contemporary Thought & Criticism, Box 199, Hartsdale NY 10530. Editor: Alan Mandell. Magazine: 5½×8½; 130-150 pages; 70 lb paper; 65 lb cover stock; illustrations; photos. "We have attempted to combine literary/artistic work with social and cultural criticism. Thus, *K* includes analytic essays as well as translations, poems, interviews, reviews and, we continue to hope, fiction as well. *K* has specific themes that are typically announced in forthcoming notice of each issue." Semiannually. Estab. 1981. Circ. 500.

Needs: Experimental, feminist, literary, translations. Receives 3-4 unsolicited fiction mss/month. Recently published work by Michael Stephens. Length: 2,500 words average. Publishes short shorts. "Short short stories would be most appropriate for *K* (given size/diversity of work presented, etc.)." Sometimes critiques rejected mss and recommends other markets.

How to Contact: Query with clips of published work or send complete ms with cover letter. Reports in 6-8 weeks on mss. SASE. Photocopied submissions OK. Accepts computer printouts. Sample copy for $6.

Payment: "We provide 3 copies of that issue and extras at discount rate."

Advice: "Short stories serve, for us, as another kind of occasion to present a *diversity* of forms—of expressions—that we seek. We will always be able to include only a very small selection of fiction, but such an inclusion is important to us."

KALEIDOSCOPE (II, IV), International Magazine of Literature, Fine Arts, and Disability, 326 Locust St., Akron OH 44302. (216)762-9755, ext. 27. Editor-in-Chief: Darshan Perusek, Ph.D. Magazine: 8½×11; 56-64 pages; non-coated paper; coated cover stock; illustrations (all media); photos. Semiannually. Estab. 1979. Circ. 1,500.

Needs: Personal experience, drama, fiction, essay, humor/satire, prose poem. Receives 20-25 unsolicited fiction mss/month. Accepts 10 mss/year. Approximately 1% of fiction is agented. Recently published work by Ellen Hunnicutt, Anne Finger, Athol Fugard; published new writers within the last year. Length: 3,000 words minimum; 5,000 words maximum.

How to Contact: Query first or send complete ms and cover letter, which should include author's educational and writing background; if author has a disablity, how the disability has influenced the writing. SASE. Accepts computer printout submissions. Reports in 1 month on queries; 6 months on mss. Sample copy $2. Guidelines for #10 SAE and 1 first class stamp.

Payment: Cash payment. 2 free contributor's copies; charge for extras: $4.50.

Terms: Pays on publication for first rights. Reprints are permitted with credit given to original publication.

Advice: "Read the magazine and get fiction guidelines. Writers with disablities may write on any topic; non-disabled writers must limit themselves to the theme of disability. We seek fresh and original perspectives on disability. No bias as to style, but adamantly hostile to the sentimental and the trite. The criteria for good fiction apply in every case: thought-provoking subject matter, fresh language and imagery, effective handling of technique. Minor editing to be expected."

KALLIOPE (II), A Journal of Women's Art, Florida Community College at Jacksonville, 11901 Beach Blvd., Jacksonville FL 32216. (904)646-2346. Editor: Mary Sue Koeppel. Magazine: 7¼×8¼; 76-88 pages; 70 lb coated matte paper; Bristol cover; 16-18 halftones per issue. "A literary and visual arts journal for women, *Kalliope* celebrates women in the arts by publishing their work and by providing a forum for their ideas and opinions." Short stories, poems, plays, essays, reviews and visual art. Published 3 times/year. Estab. 1978. Circ. 1,000.

Needs: "Quality short fiction by women writers." Accepts 2-4 mss/issue. Receives approximately 25 unsolicited fiction mss each month. Recently published work by Layle Silbert, Robin Merle, Robert Gentry; published new writers within the last year. Preferred length: 750-3,000 words, but occasionally publishes longer (and shorter) pieces. Critiques rejected mss "when there is time and if requested."

How to Contact: Send complete ms with SASE and short contributor's note. Reports in 2-3 months on ms. Publishes ms an average of 1-6 months after acceptance. Sample copy $7 for current issue; $4 for issues from '78-'88.

Payment: 3 free author's copies or year's subscription. $7 charge for extras, discount for large orders.

Terms: Acquires first rights. "We accept only unpublished work. Copyright returned to author upon request."

Advice: "Read our magazine. The work we consider for publication will be well written and the characters and dialogue will be convincing and have strength and movement. We like a fresh approach and are interested in new or unusual forms. Make us believe your characters; give readers an insight which they might not have had if they had not read you. We would like to publish more work by minority writers." Manuscripts are rejected because "1) nothing *happens*!, 2) it is thinly disguised autobiography (richly disguised autobiography is OK), and 3) ending is either too pat or else just trails off."

KANA (II), Box 36091, Towson MD 21286. (301)828-6123. Editor: Laurie Rockefeller. Magazine: 5½×8½; 32 pages; 60 lb paper; 70 lb cover; illustrations. "Any material as long as it makes sense," for a "college educated and above" audience. Semiannually. Estab. 1988. Circ. 200.

Needs: Adventure, confession, contemporary, ethnic, experimental, fantasy, feminist, gay, historical (general), humor/satire, lesbian, literary, mainstream, regional, senior citizen/retirement, translations. Does not want to see "the type of fiction that drags on without saying anything; confusing material." Receives 2-3 unsolicited mss/month. Accepts 1-2 mss/issue; 2-4 mss/year. Publishes ms 1-6 months after acceptance. Length: 500-750 words preferred; 2,000 words maximum. Publishes short shorts. Sometimes critiques rejected mss.

How to Contact: Send complete ms with cover letter. Cover letter should include "a bio, return address (on work, too), writer's philosophy on writing and/or life." Reports in 2 months. SASE. Simultaneous and photocopied submissions OK "when noted as such." Accepts computer printout submissions. Sample copy for 5½×8½ SAE and 2 first class stamps. Fiction guidelines for #10 SAE and 1 first class stamp.

Payment: Pays in contributor's copies.

Terms: All rights remain with author.

Advice: "I gear my magazine towards the public instead of the literary private sectors. I believe that the hairdresser down the street enjoys reading just as much as the professor at the university, but the material in literary magazines is often too deep for non-literature majors (or otherwise), so I keep

Close-up

Darshan Perusek

Kaleidoscope

Perhaps the most remarkable thing about *Kaleidoscope* is its transformation from a class project to an award-winning national publication. The magazine began in 1979 as a creative outlet for the members of an adult learning class sponsored by the Akron, Ohio, branch of United Cerebral Palsy. Since that time, *Kaleidoscope* has become a national forum for the discussion of the role of disability in society as well as an outlet for art and literature dealing with the subject.

Dr. Darshan Perusek became involved with the magazine when her daughter joined the staff as an editorial assistant. When the editor left, Perusek, then a professor of English literature at Kent State University, was offered the position.

"When I came to the magazine in 1985, what I found was very eclectic," says Perusek, who now teaches at the University of Wisconsin. "The only unifying factor was the contributors were all disabled. It was a kind of showcase to show what disabled people could do, but it did not take the art seriously. The focus was on the disability, rather than the art."

The turning point came with Perusek's decision to change the focus from the disability of the individual contributor to the subject of disability. "Disability became thematic rather than biographic. Each issue now has a theme such as 'Disability and Children's Literature' or 'Women and Disability.' This has opened the magazine up to nondisabled writers as well as disabled."

The magazine also has undergone physical changes. Perusek established a permanent logo and design; increased funding has led to better paper and printing quality; and the artwork selected is more professional. While the artwork is striking, it enhances the content, not the other way around, she says. "Visually, my philosophy is to select the dramatic, not the melodramatic."

While she now accepts work with the theme of disability from nondisabled writers and artists, the magazine remains an outlet for all types of work from disabled individuals. It's important to keep the magazine open to the creative work of disabled people, she says, whether or not they choose to write about disability.

Perusek receives about 40 fiction submissions for every two or three stories she publishes in the biannual journal. In addition to a well-crafted piece, she looks for a unique approach to the subject – sometimes even humor. "When I took over I also found humor absent – in fact, the magazine was deadly grim. Sometimes solemnity is bad. Most serious subjects require a lightness of hand. Anything heavy-handed can sink on its own weight."

Although the magazine has a specific theme each issue, there is room for fiction on a variety of topics. "One lesson I've learned as an editor, teacher and reader is that there is no topic not suitable for a story," Perusek says. "Anything can make a good story – a brief moment or a long period of time.

"Ultimately, it comes down to how the story is done. It's not only the experience you are talking about, but the form you put it in – that's where the art comes in."

–Robin Gee

Kana simple, understandable, and free to whomever wants to read it or submit to it. I believe that Steinbeck and William Carlos Williams grasped best the contemporary short story (American, anyway)."

KANSAS QUARTERLY (I, II), Kansas Quarterly Association, 122 Denison Hall, English Dept., Kansas State University, Manhattan KS 66506. (913)532-6716. Editors: Harold Schneider, Ben Nyberg, W.R. Moses and John Rees. Magazine: 6×9; 104-356 pages; 70 lb offset paper; Frankcote 8 pt. coated cover stock; illustrations occasionally; unsolicited photos rarely. "A literary and cultural arts magazine publishing fiction and poetry. Special material on selected, announced topics in literary criticism, art history, folklore and regional history. For well-read, general and academic audiences." Quarterly. Published double and single fiction issues last year; plans repeat. Estab. 1968. Circ. 1,300.

Needs: "We consider most categories as long as the fiction is of sufficient literary quality to merit inclusion, though we have no interest in children's literature. We resist translations and parts of novels, but do not absolutely refuse them." Accepts 30-50 mss/year. Limited reading done in summer. Approximately 1% of fiction is agented. Recently published work by Rick Bass, Stephen Dixon and H. E. Francis. Published new writers within the last year. Length: 350-12,000 words. Sometimes recommends other markets.

How to Contact: Send complete ms with SASE. Reports in 3 months+ on mss. Publishes ms an average of 18-24 months after acceptance. Sample copy $6.

Payment: 2 free author's copies and annual awards to the best of the stories published.

Terms: Acquires all rights. Sends galleys to author. "We reassign rights on request at time of republication." Sponsors awards: *KQ*/KAC (national); Seaton awards (for Kansas natives or residents). Each offers 6-10 awards from $25-$250.

Advice: "Always check a sample copy of the magazine to which you send your stories—note its editors' likes and interests. Send your story with SASE—do not appear to devalue them by asking they be discarded rather than returned."

KARAMU (II), English Dept., Eastern Illinois University, Charleston IL 61920. (217)581-5614. Editor: Peggy L. Brayfield. Magazine: 5×8; 60 pages; cover illustrations. "We like fiction that builds around real experiences, real images and real characters, that shows an awareness of current fiction and the types of experiments that are going on in it, and that avoids abstraction, sentimentality, overphilosophizing and fuzzy pontifications. For a literate, college-educated audience." Annually. Estab. 1967. Circ. 500.

Needs: Literary, contemporary. Receives approximately 20-30 unsolicited fiction mss/month. Recently published work by J. Carol Goodman, Nickell Romjue and Bonnie McGara. Accepts 4-5 mss/issue. Published new writers within the last year. Length: 2,000-7,000 words. Critiques rejected mss when there is time.

How to Contact: Send complete ms with SASE. Accepts computer printout submissions, prefers letter-quality. Reports in 2-3 months on mss. Publishes ms an average of 1 year after acceptance. Sample copy $2.

Payment: 1 free author's copy. Half price charge for extras.

Advice: "Send for a sample copy, read it, and send a complete ms if your stories seem to match our taste. Please be patient—we sometimes get behind in our reading, especially between May and September. Mss submitted between January and June have the best chance. We feel that much of the best writing today is being done in short fiction."

‡KENNEBEC (II, IV), A Portfolio of Maine Writing, University of Maine at Augusta, University Heights, Augusta ME 04330. (207)622-7131. Editors: Carol Kontos, Terry Plunkett. Tabloid: 11x14; 36-40 pages; newsprint; illustrations and photos. We publish mostly Maine-related stories and poetry for a Maine and New England audience." Annually. Estab. 1975. Circ. 5,000.

Needs: Condensed novel, contemporary, experimental, fantasy, humor/satire, literary, regional, serialized/excerpted novel. Reads mss Sept. 15-Dec. 15. Published new writers within the last year. Length: 1,500-3,000 words. Publishes short shorts. "Rarely" critiques rejected mss.

How to Contact: Send complete ms with cover letter; which should include information about writer's connection with Maine. SASE. Simultaneous submissions OK. Accepts computer printout submissions. Sample copy free.

Payment: Pays in contributor's copies.

Advice: "We have limited paper available, so long manuscripts are generally not suitable."

‡THE KENYON REVIEW (II), Kenyon College, Gambier OH 43022. (614)427-3339. Editor: T.R. Hummer. "Fiction, poetry, essays, book reviews for primarily academic audience." Quarterly. Estab. 1939. Circ. 4,000.

Needs: Condensed/excerpted novel, contemporary, ethnic, experimental, fantasy, feminist, gay, historical, humor/satire, lesbian literary, mainstream, prose poem, senior citizen/retirement, translations. Receives 150-200 unsolicited fiction mss/month. Accepts up to 3 mss/issue; up to 12 mss/year. Does not read mss June-August. Publishes ms 12-18 months after acceptance. 50% of fiction is agented. Length: 3-15 (typeset) pages preferred. Rarely publishes short shorts. Sometimes comments on rejected ms.

How to Contact: Send complete ms with cover letters. Reports on mss in 1 month. SASE. Simultaneous and photocopied submissions OK. Does not accept dot-matrix computer printouts. Sample copy $6.50.

Payment: $10/page for fiction.

Terms: Pays on publication for one-time rights and option on anthology rights. Sends copy-edited version to author for approval.

Advice: "Read several issues of our publication."

KINGFISHER (II), Box 9783, N. Berkeley CA 94709. Editors: Ruthie Singer, Barbara Schultz, Lorraine Hilton-Gray, Andrea Beach. Magazine: 6×9; 120 pages; 60 lb paper; 80 lb cover; illustrations; photos. "*Kingfisher* sports no particular political or intellectual doctrine. We are interested in innovative short fiction primarily, but we will also consider poetry and translations." Biannually. Estab. 1987.

Needs: Contemporary, experimental, literary, serialized/excerpted novel and translations. No science fiction. Receives 100 unsolicited fiction mss/month. Accepts up to 20 mss/issue; up to 40 mss/year. Recently published work by John Bennett, Wendy Dutton, Chris Mazza; published new writers within the last year. Length: 3,000 words average; 12,000 words maximum. Publishes short shorts. Sometimes comments on rejected mss and recommends other markets.

How to Contact: Send complete ms with cover letter, which should include short bio and list of publication credits. Reports on queries in 1 month; on mss in 2 months. SASE. Simultaneous and photocopied submissions OK. Accepts computer printout submissions. Sample copy: $5.

Payment: Pays in contributor's copies.

Terms: Acquires one-time rights.

Advice: "We will continue to publish short works of fiction as long as we can find ones of the quality we require. The writer should please mention if he or she would like to receive specific reaction to his/her work. We are more than happy to help in that way."

KIOSK (II), English Department, S.U.N.Y. at Buffalo, 302 Clemens Hall, Buffalo NY 14260. (716)636-2570. Editors: Ted Pelton, Patrick Walters. Magazine: 5½×8½; 100 pages; card stock cover. "We seek innovative, non-formula fiction and poetry." Plans special fiction issue. Annually. Estab. 1986. Circ. 750.

Needs: Excerpted novel, erotica, experimental, feminist, gay, humor/satire, lesbian, prose poem and translations. "No genre or formula fiction; we seek fiction that defies categorization—lush, quirky, flippant, subversive, etc." Receives 15 mss/month. Accepts 6 mss/issue. Publishes ms within 6 months of acceptance. Published work by Ray Federman, Carol Berge, Tom Whalen. Length: 3,000 words preferred; 7,500 words maximum. Publishes short shorts. Sometimes critiques rejected mss; rarely recommends other markets.

How to Contact: Send complete mss with cover letter during October-February reading period. Reports in 2-3 weeks on queries; 2-3 months on mss. "Most sooner; if we keep it longer, we're considering it seriously." SASE. Simultaneous, photocopied and reprint submissions OK. Accepts computer printout submissions. Sample copy for 9x6 or larger SAE and 2 first class stamps.

Payment: Pays in contributor's copies.

Terms: Acquires one-time rights.

Advice: "*Kiosk* was started because it seemed to us that most little mags were publishing the same type of stuff—slick, literary, polished fluff that writing programs churn out like hot dogs. If you've got a different vision of writing than others seem to be buying, then maybe this mag is for you. Literary magazine writing is exciting when editors take chances and offer a place for writers who find other avenues closed." Looks for "a writer's unique vision and care for the language. Striking, unexpected images. New forms, new thinking. A certain level of technical accomplishment."

‡KOLA (IV), A Black Literary Magazine, Box 1602, Place Bonaventure, Montreal Quebec H5A 1H6 Canada. Editor: Dr. Horace I. Goddard. Magazine: 6×9; 40 pages; black and white illustrations. "Manuscripts that focus on the black experience in Africa and the African diaspora for a general audience." Estab. 1987. Circ. 300.

Needs: Contemporary, ethnic, feminist, literary, black. Accepts 3 mss/issue. Publishs ms 2 months after acceptance. Recently published work by Dr. Nigel Thomas, Randolph Homer and Yvonne Anderson. Length: 3,000-5,000 words; 2,000 words minimum; 6,000 words maximum. Sometimes critiques rejected mss.

How to Contact: Send complete manuscript with cover letter. Include bio-vita, previous publications. Reports in 3 months on mss. SASE for ms, not needed for query. Photocopied submissions OK. Accepts computer printout submissions. Sample copy for $4 and 6×9 SAE.
Payment: Two free contributor's copies.
Terms: Acquires first rights.
Advice: "The fiction must relate to the black experience. It must be of a high standard in structure: theme, plot, characterization, etc. Make sure you can follow grammar rules, use a dictionary, accept criticism, and keep on writing even though the rejection slips get you down."

LACTUCA (II), Box 621, Suffern NY 10901. Editor: Mike Selender. Magazine: folded 8½×14; 40-60 pages; 24 lb bond; soft cover; illustrations. Publishes "poetry, short fiction and b&w art, for a general literary audience." Published 3 times/year. Estab. 1986. Circ. 400.
Needs: Adventure, condensed/excerpted novel, confession, contemporary, erotica, literary, mainstream, prose poem and regional. No "self-indulgent writing or fiction about writing fiction." Receives 30 or more mss/month. Accepts 3-4 mss/issue; 10-12 mss/year. Publishes ms within 2-6 months of acceptance. Recently published work by Douglas Mendini, Tom Gidwitz, Ruthann Robson; published new writers within the last year. Length: around 12-14 typewritten double-spaced pages. Publishes short shorts. Often critiques rejected mss and recommends other markets.
How to Contact: Query first or send complete ms with cover letter. Cover letter should include "just a few brief notes about yourself. Please no long 'literary' résumés or bios. The work will speak for itself." Reports in 2 weeks on queries; 6-8 weeks on mss. SASE. Photocopied submissions OK. No simultaneous or previously published work. Accepts computer printouts. Accepts electronic submissions via "MS DOS or Macintosh formatted disk. We can convert most word-processing formats." Sample copy for $3.50. Fiction guidelines for #10 SAE and 1 first class stamp.
Payment: Pays 2-5 contributor's copies, depending on the length of the work published.
Terms: Acquires first North American serial rights. Sends galleys to author if requested. Copyrights revert to authors.
Advice: "Too much of the poetry and fiction I have been reading over the past two years has been obsessed with the act of writing or life as a writer. We're not interested in this kind of writing. I place a strong emphasis on the readability of fiction. The dialogue should be clear, and the characters speaking readily discernible. It is worth making the extra revisions necessary to obtain this level of quality. We strongly suggest that writers send a SASE for our guidelines before submitting any fiction."

LAKE EFFECT (II), Lake County Writers Group, Oswego Art Guild, Box 315, Oswego NY 13126. (315)342-3579. Editor: Jean O'Connor Fuller, M.E. Tabloid: 11½×17; 32 pages; newsprint paper and cover; illustrations; photos. "We publish short fiction, poetry, humor, reviews, b&w art and photographs and one nonfiction piece of interest to the area each issue. Our circulation is principally upstate NY." Quarterly. Estab. 1986. Circ. 10,000.
Needs: Contemporary, fantasy, historical (general), humor/satire, literary, mainstream, regional. "We want previously unpublished, honest stories." Accepts 2-3 mss/issue. Does not read mss in August. Publishes ms within 6 months after acceptance. Recently published work by David Shields, Gary Fincke; published new writers within the last year. Length: 5,000 words maximum. Publishes short shorts. Occasionally critiques rejected mss and recommends other markets.
How to Contact: Send complete ms with cover letter, which should include biographical information on author. Reports in 2 months. SASE for ms. Photocopied submissions OK. No simultaneous submissions. Accepts computer printout submissions; "dot-matrix must be readable." Sample copy for $2. Fiction guidelines for #10 SAE and 1 first class stamp.
Payment: $25 and 3 free contributor's copies; charge for extras.
Terms: Acquires first North American serial rights.
Advice: "We exist primarily to give outlet to the writers of this region, but also will use good work from outside if we like it. Send us stories about human beings we can believe in, in neat, professional style. We prefer upbeat to downbeat work, but deplore sentimentality. Do not send us your death stories."

LAKE STREET REVIEW (II), Box 7188, Powderhorn Station, Minneapolis MN 55407. Editor: Kevin FitzPatrick. Magazine: 7×8½; 40 pages; good quality paper and cover stock; illustrations; photos occasionally. "An annual literary publication focusing on the writing of poets and fiction writers, both developing and established." Annually. Estab. 1976. Circ. 600.
Needs: Contemporary, ethnic, experimental, humor/satire, literary, mainstream, prose poem, science fiction. Receives 10 fiction mss/month. Accepts 5-7 mss/issue. Deadline is September 15 of each year. Publishes ms within 1 year of acceptance. Published work by Joe Paddock, Anne Farrer Scott, Jonathan Borden; published new writers within the last last year. Length: 4,000 words average; 500 words minimum; 4,500 words maximum. Sometimes critiques rejected mss.

How to Contact: Send complete ms. Reports on queries in 1 week; on ms "no later than 2 months after the September 15 deadline." SASE. Photocopied submissions OK. Accepts computer printout submissions, no dot-matrix. Sample copy $2. Fiction guidelines for #10 SAE and 1 first class stamp.
Payment: Pays in contributor's copies (2).
Terms: Acquires first North American serial rights.

‡LANGUAGE BRIDGES QUARTERLY (II,IV), Polish-English Literary Magazine, Box 850792, Richardson TX 75085-0792. (214)530-2782. Editor: Eva Ziem. Fiction Editor: Zofia Przebindowska-Tousty. Magazine: 8½×11; 20+ pages; 60 lb paper; 65 lb cover; illustrations. "Today's Poland and Polish spirit are the main subject; a picture of life in Poland, with emphasis on the recent Polish emigration wave problems, however topics of general nature are being accepted. For both English and Polish speaking readers." Quarterly. Estab. 1989. Circ. 300.
Needs: Condensed/excerpted novel, fantasy, historical (general), humor/satire, literary, prose poem, religious/inspirational, translations, young adult/teen (10-18 years). "No horror, no vulgar language." Receives 1 unsolicited ms/month. Accepts one fiction ms every second issue. Publishes ms 3-6 months after acceptance. "Length does not matter. The longer works are broken into parts." Publishes short shorts. Sometimes critiques rejected mss and recommends other markets.
How to Contact: Send complete ms with cover letter. Reports in 2-3 months on mss. Simultaneous, photocopied and reprint submissions OK. Accepts computer printouts. Accepts electronic submissions via disk. Free sample copy and fiction guidelines.
Payment: Pays contributor's copies.
Terms: Pays for one-time rights. Sends galleys to author.
Advice: "Fiction has to be original and meaningful for us. We wish to introduce English speaking readers to Polish culture and to the current problems of Poles in Poland and abroad."

‡LAUREL REVIEW (II), Northwest Missouri State University, Dept. of English, Maryville MO 64468. (816)562-1559. Editor: Craig Goad. Fiction Readers: William Trowbridge, David Slater, Jim Simmerman, Randy Freisinger, Parker Johnson. Magazine: 6×9; 124-128 pages; good quality paper. "We publish poetry and fiction of high quality, from the traditional to the avant-garde. We are eclectic, open and flexible. Good writing is all we seek." Biannually. Estab. 1960. Circ. 500.
Needs: Literary and contemporary. Accepts 3-5 mss/issue, 6-10 mss/year. Receives approximately 25 unsolicited fiction mss each month. Approximately 1% of fiction is agented. Length: 2,000-10,000 words. Critiques rejected mss "when there is time." Reads September to May.
How to Contact: Send complete ms with SASE. Accepts computer printout submissions. Reports in 4 months on mss. "Sometimes slow!" Publishes ms an average of 1-12 months after acceptance. Sample copy $4.50.
Payment: 2 free author's copies, 1 year free subscription.
Terms: Acquires first rights. Copyright reverts to author upon request.
Advice: Send $4.50 for a back copy of the magazine. "Send no long-winded cover letters."

‡THE LEADING EDGE (II,IV), Magazine of Science Fiction and Fantasy, 3163 JKHB, Provo UT 84604. Editor: Russell W. Asplund. Fiction Editor: Stephanie Asplund. Magazine: 5×8; 100-120 pages; 20 lb bond paper; 40 lb card stock; 15-20 illustrations. "We are a magazine dedicated to the new and upcoming author, poet, and artist involved in the field of science fiction and fantasy. We are for the upcoming professional." Published 3 times/year. Circ. 400.
Needs: Adventure, experimental, fantasy, humor/satire, prose poem, science fiction. "We are very interested in experimental sf and humorous stories, but all pieces should fall within the category of sf and fiction. No graphic sex, violence, dismemberment, etc. No outrageous religious commentary. No fannish/media stories; i.e., no Star Wars, Star Trek, Dr. Who, etc." Receives 40 unsolicited mss/month. Buys 6-8 mss/issue; 20-30 mss/year. Publishes ms 1-4 months after acceptance. Recently published work by Michael R. Collings, Thomas Easton and L.E. Carroll. Length: 5,000 words; 500 words minimum; 17,000 words maximum. Publishes short shorts. Sometimes critiques rejected mss.
How to Contact: Send complete ms with cover letter. Include name and address, phone number, title of story and classification of story (leave name off manuscript—put it on cover letter only). Reports in 1-2 months on mss. SASE. Simultaneous and photocopied submissions OK. Accepts computer printout submissions. Sample copy for $2.50. Fiction guidelines #10 SAE and 1 first class stamp.
Payment: Pays $5-75 plus contributor's copies.
Terms: Pays on publication for first North American serial rights. Sends galleys to author.
Advice: "All fiction must be original, innovative and interesting. We are very familiar with the body of sf and fiction work, and look for new stories. Too many writers of sf and fiction rely on existing cliché and convention. Humor, hard science, and experimental fantasy have the best chance for publication. Accurate science, vivid imagery, and strong characterization will impress the editors. We want stories about people with problems; the setting is there to illustrate the problem, not vice versa. Proofread!!! Please send clean, proofread copy. Just because we're small doesn't mean we're sloppy. Research! Be

accurate. Our readers are *very* aware of science and history. We do not publish graphic violence or sex. Violence is okay if it is necessary to the story."

LEFT CURVE (II), Box 472, Oakland CA 94604. (415)763-7193. Editor: Csaba Polony. Magazine: 8½×11; 96 pages; 60 lb paper; 100 pt. CIS Durosheen cover; illustrations; photos. "*Left Curve* is an artist-produced journal addressing the problem(s) of cultural forms emerging from the crises of modernity that strive to be independent from the control of dominant institutions, based on the recognition of the destructiveness of commodity (capitalist) systems to all life." Published irregularly. Estab. 1974. Circ. 1,000.
Needs: Contemporary, ethnic, experimental, historical, humor/satire, literary, prose poem, regional, science fiction, translations, political. Receives approx. 1 unsolicited fiction ms/month. Accepts approx. 1 ms/issue. Publishes ms a maximum of 6 months after acceptance. Length: 1,200 words average; 500 words minimum; 2,500 words maximum. Publishes short shorts. Sometimes comments on rejected mss or recommends other markets.
How to Contact: Send complete ms with cover letter, which should include "statement on writer's intent, brief bio., why submitting to *Left Curve*." Reports on queries in 1 month; on mss in 3 months. SASE. Accepts computer printouts. Sample copy for $5, 9×12 SAE and 90¢ postage. Fiction guidelines for 2 first class stamps.
Payment: Pays in contributor's copies.
Terms: Acquires first rights.
Advice: "Be honest, realistic and gorge out the truth you wish to say. Understand yourself and the world. Have writing be a means to achieve or realize what is real."

‡LEFT-FOOTED WOMBAT (II), Literary Eccentricity, Vishnu-Ala Dav Press, 615 Ratone Ln., Manhattan KS 66502. (913)539-9273. Editor: David McGhee. Magazine: 5½×8½; 20-24 pages; bond paper; illustrations and photographs. "Unusual theme and/or writing style for an eccentric audience." Published 3 times a year. Estab. 1988.
Needs: Adventure, contemporary, erotica, ethnic, experimental, fantasy, feminist, gay, horror, humor/satire, lesbian, prose poem, psychic/supernatural/occult, regional, religious/inspirational, science fiction, senior citizen/retirement, suspense/mystery, translations. "No sap, bad science fiction, fantasies or same old stories." Receives 8 unsolicited mss/month. Accepts 1 ms/issue; 3 mss/year. Publishes ms 2-3 weeks after acceptance. Length: 2,000 words; 1,000 words minimum; 3,000 words maximum. Sometimes critiques rejected mss.
How to Contact: Send complete ms. Reports in 1 week on queries; 3-4 months on mss. SASE. Simultaneous, photocopied and reprint submissions OK. Sample copy for $1. Fiction guidelines for #10 SAE and 1 first class stamp.
Payment: Pays in contributor's copies; charges for extras.
Terms: "Author retains rights."
Advice: Looking for "writing that evokes an emotional response in a clever, subtle manner; original thoughts, plots, characters, and/or writing style; eccentric topics, themes, plots, characters; but especially written well, flowing, graceful. Keep writing as long as you enjoy. If you're writing for money, forget it. The Big Bucks are rare to find. It is about the love of the word, communicating a personal emotion, not cash. Practice and wading through dry spells are important, which is why enjoying it is a necessity."

‡LEGEND (I, II, IV), A "Robin of Sherwood" Fanzine, 1036 Hampshire Rd., Victoria, British Columbia V85 4S9 Canada. (604)598-2197. Editor: Janet P. Reedman. Magazine: size varies; 120+ pages; bond paper; cover varies; illustrations. "Fantasy: Based on TV series 'Robin of Sherwood.' Retold myths/legends; Celtic preferred. Some historical, if set in pre-1600 Europe." Semiannually. Estab. 1987. Circ. 200+.
Needs: Adventure, fantasy, historical, retold myths/legends. "Nothing excessively violent/sexual. Nothing sticky-sweet and saccharine, either!" Receives 2-3 unsolicited mss/month. Accepts 4-9 mss/issue; 4-9 mss/year. Publishes ms 4-18 months after acceptance. Length: 2,000 words preferred; 150 words minimum; 20,000 words maximum. Sometimes critiques rejected mss and recommends other markets.
How to Contact: Query first. (I'll accept mss without queries, but it might be wise to write and ask if we're still open, overstocked, etc.). Reports in 2-3 weeks on queries; 5-6 weeks on mss. SASE. "Will accept loose stamps or IRCs, as I can use stamps from other countries." Photocopied and reprint submissions OK. Accepts computer printout submissions. Sample copy $10. Fiction guidelines for #10 SAE and 1 loose first class stamp.

Payment: Pays in contributor's copies for material over 3 pages long.
Terms: Acquires first North American serial rights.
Advice: "Please support small publications, so they can *survive* to publish your work! *Read* a sample copy, so you don't waste postage and the editor's time! We have handwritten mss, juveniles, no SASE, satires, experimental fiction, 5 stories crammed in one envelope . . . *despite explicit* guidelines!"

PABLO LENNIS (I, IV), The Magazine of Science Fiction, Fantasy and Fact, Halcyon Press, Fandom House, 30 North 19th St., Lafayette IN 47904. Editor: John Thiel. Magazine: 8½×11; 30 pages; standard stock; illustrations and "occasional" photos. "Science fiction, fantasy, science, research and mystic for scientists and science fiction and fantasy appreciators." Published 4-5 times/year.
Needs: Fantasy, psychic/supernatural/occult, science fiction, spiritual. Receives 25 unsolicited mss/year. Accepts 3 mss/issue; 15 mss/year. Publishes ms 6 months after acceptance. Published work by Eugene Flinn, Archie Taylor, Martha Collins; published new writers within the last year. Length: 1,500 words average; 300 words minimum; 3,000 words maximum. Occasionally critiques rejected mss and recommends other markets.
How to Contact: "Method of submission is author's choice but he might prefer to query. No self-statement is necessary." Reports in 2 weeks. Does not accept computer printouts.
Payment: Pays in contributor's copies.
Terms: Publication not copyrighted.
Advice: "*Novel and Short Story Writer's Market* has brought in many new manuscripts, so my rate of publication has slowed down, but I don't reject frequently and then with good reasons. If you want to write a really good story, stick to materially perceived reality in setting scenes and saying something the reader would like to hear. Always have an understandable framework from which to depart imaginatively."

LETTERS MAGAZINE (II, III), Maine Writers Workshop and Mainespring Press, Box 905, RFD 1, Stonington ME 04681. (207)367-2484. Editor: Helen Nash. Magazine: 8½×11; 4+ pages; best paper. "Accepts only high quality material in all ethical fields of literature." Quarterly. Estab. 1969. Circ. 7,500.
Needs: Literary, short stories, science fiction, poetry and mystery. "No porno, confessions, etc." Buys 5-10 mss/year. Receives 150 unsolicited fiction mss each month. Published work by Richard Eberhart, G. F. Bush and Jack Matthews; published new writers within the last year. Length: 500-1,000 words. Critiques rejected mss "when justified."
How to Contact: Query "with large SASE (US postage) or send one chapter with large SASE (US postage). No returns if insufficient postage." Accepts computer printout submissions; letter-quality only. Reports in 1 month on queries. Publishes ms an average of 1 year after acceptance. Sample copy for $5 with SAE and US postage. Evaluates full-length mss at usual rate.
Payment: Varies. All cash; no copies. Usual royalties for any books published.
Terms: Pays on publication for all rights.

LIGHTHOUSE (II), Box 1377, Auburn WA 98071-1377. Editor: Tim Clinton. Magazine: 5½×8½; 56 pages; illustrations. "Timeless stories and poems for family reading—G rated." Bimonthly. Estab. 1986. Circ. 500.
Needs: Adventure, contemporary, historical, humor/satire, juvenile (5-9 years), mainstream, preschool (1-4 years), prose poem, regional, romance (contemporary, historical and young adult), senior citizen/retirement, sports, suspense/mystery, western, young adult/teen (10-18 years). Receives 300 mss/month. Accepts 15 mss/issue; 90 mss/year. Publishes ms within 2 years of acceptance. Recently published work by Birdie L. Etchison, Marguerite McClain, Scott B. Laughlin; published new writers within the last year. Length: 5,000 words maximum. Publishes short shorts.
How to Contact: Send complete mss, include Social Security number. No queries, please. Reports in 2 months on mss. SASE. Photocopied submissions OK. Accepts computer printout submissions. Sample copy for $2 (includes guidelines). Fiction guidelines for #10 SAE and 1 first class stamp.
Payment: Pays up to $50 for stories; up to $5 for poetry.
Terms: Author copies discounted at $1.50 each. Payment on publication for first rights and first North American serial rights.
Advice: "If there is a message in the story, we prefer it to be subtly hidden in the action. We feel there is a market for quality fiction stories that are entertaining and have standards of decency as well."

LILITH MAGAZINE (I, II, IV), The Jewish Women's Magazine, Suite 2432, 250 W 57th St., New York NY 10107. (212)757-0818. Editor: Susan Weidman Schneider. Fiction Editor: Julia Wolf Mazow. Magazine: 8½×11; 32 pages; 80 lb cover; b&w illustrations; b&w and color photos. Publishes work relating to Jewish feminism, for Jewish feminists, feminists and Jewish households. Quarterly. Estab. 1975. Circ. 10,000.

Needs: Ethnic, feminist, lesbian, literary, prose poem, psychic/supernatural/occult, religious/inspirational, senior citizen/retirement, spiritual, translation, young adult. Nothing that does not in any way relate to Jews, women or Jewish women." Receives 15 unsolicited mss/month. Accepts 1 ms/issue; 3 mss/year. Publishes ms 2-6 months after acceptance. Recently published work by Leslea Newman and Fredelle Maynard. Publishes short shorts.

How to Contact: Send complete ms with cover letter, which should include a 2-line bio. Reports in 2 months on queries; 2-6 months on mss. SASE. Simultaneous, photocopied and reprint submissions OK. Accepts computer printout submissions. Sample copy for $4.50 and 4 first class stamps. Fiction guidelines for #10 SAE and 1 first class stamp.

Payment: Pays in contributor's copies only.

Terms: Acquires first rights.

‡LIME GREEN BULLDOZERS (and other related species) (I), Oyster Publications, 723 N Highland Ave., Arlington Heights IL 60004. (312)871-7505. Editor: Lainie (the oyster). Newsletter: 8½×11; 20-24 pages; 20lb. white paper; 60lb. Astrobrite cover; illustrations; photos. Quarterly. Estab. 1986. Circ. 300.

Needs: "No specific theme except all communication – anything is published." Plans to publish special fiction issue or anthology in the future. Receives 1-2 unsolicited mss/month. Publishes ms 2 months after acceptance. Recently published work by John Porcellino, Eric Cook and Chris Caggiaro. Length: One (or less) typed page. Publishes short shorts.

How to Contact: Query first. Reports in 1 month. SASE. Simultaneous, photocopied and reprint submissions OK. Accepts computer printout submissions. Sample copy $2. Fiction guidelines free.

Payment: Free subscription to magazine.

Terms: Acquires one-time rights. Publication not copyrighted.

Advice: "There is no criteria – everything is accepted as long as the author keeps in touch."

LIMESTONE: A LITERARY JOURNAL (II), University of Kentucky, Dept. of English, 1215 Patterson Office Tower, Lexington KY 40506-0027. Editor: Stephen R. Whited. Fiction Editor: Rob Merritt. Magazine: 6×9; 40-70 pages; standard text paper and cover; illustrations; photos. "We publish a variety of styles and attitudes, and we're looking to expand our offering." Annually. Estab. 1981. Circ. 1,000.

Needs: Confession, contemporary, experimental, feminist, humor/satire, literary, mainstream, prose poem, regional. "We are a wee bit tired of stories about teenagers." Receives 25-50 mss/year. Accepts 5-12 mss/issue. Does not read mss June – August. Publishes ms an average of 6 months after acceptance. Recently published work by Guy Davenport, Wendell Berry, James Baker Hall; published new writers within the last year. Length: 3,000-5,000 words preferred; 5,000 words maximum. Publishes short shorts. Sometimes critiques rejected mss.

How to Contact: Send complete ms with cover letter, which should include "publishing record and brief bio." Reports in 1-2 weeks on queries; 8-10 weeks on mss. SASE. Simultaneous and photocopied submissions OK. Accepts computer printout submissions; no dot-matrix. Electronic submissions OK via IBM compatible disks. Sample copy for $3.

Payment: Pays 2 contributor's copies.

Terms: Rights revert to author.

Advice: "We encourage all interested writers, but we also want to provide a forum for creative writing students looking to publish for the first time."

LININGTON LINEUP (IV), Elizabeth Linington Society, 1223 Glen Terrace, Glassboro NJ 08028. Editor: Rinehart S. Potts. Newsletter: 8½×11; 16 pages; bond paper and cover stock; illustrations and photographs. "For those interested in the publications of Elizabeth Linington (a/k/a Lesley Egan, Egan O'Neill, Anne Blaisdell, Dell Shannon) – historical fiction and detective mysteries – therefore material must relate in some way thereto." Quarterly. Plans special fiction issue. Estab. 1984. Circ. 400.

Needs: Historical (general), literary, suspense/mystery. Receives 3-4 fiction mss/month. Accepts 1 ms/issue; 4 mss/year. Publishes ms 3 months after acceptance. *Charges reading fee of $1. Requires magazine subscription of $12 before reading.* Publishes short shorts. Sometimes comments on rejected mss.

How to Contact: Query first. Reports in 1 month. SASE. Photocopied and reprint submissions OK. Accepts computer printout submissions. Sample copy $3.

Payment: Free subscription to magazine.

Terms: Acquires first rights.

Advice: "Become familiar with Miss Linington's books and continuing characters. We have been receiving material which completely disregards the information cited above."

THE LITERARY REVIEW, An International Journal of Contemporary Writing, Fairleigh Dickinson University, 285 Madison Ave., Madison NJ 07940. (201)593-8564. Editor-in-Chief: Walter Cummins. Magazine: 6×9; 128-152 pages; illustrations; photos. "Literary magazine specializing in fiction, poetry, and essays with an international focus." Quarterly. Estab. 1957. Circ. 1,800.

Needs: Works of high literary quality only. Receives 30-40 unsolicited fiction mss/month. Approximately 1-2% of fiction is agented. Published Anne Brashler, Thomas E. Kennedy, Steve Yarbrough; published new writers within the last year. Accepts 10-12 mss/year. Occasionally critiques rejected mss. Sometimes recommends other markets.

How to Contact: Send complete ms with SASE. "Cover letter should include publication credits." Photocopied submissions OK. Accepts computer printout submissions. Reports in 10 weeks on mss. Publishes ms an average of 1-1½ years after acceptance. Sample copy $5; free guidelines with SASE.

Payment: 2 free contributor's copies; 25% discount for extras.

Terms: Acquires first rights.

Advice: "Too much of what we are seeing today is openly derivative in subject, plot and prose style. We pride ourselves on spotting new writers with fresh insight and the ability to express it."

LITTLE BALKANS REVIEW (II, IV), A Southeast Kansas Literary & Graphics Quarterly, Little Balkans Press, Inc., 601 Grandview Heights Terrace, Pittsburg KS 66762. Editor: Gene DeGruson. Fiction Editor: Shelby Horn. "Kansas is our theme, historical and contemporary, in poetry, fiction, nonfiction and art." General and academic audience. Quarterly. Estab. 1980. Circ. 1,200.

Needs: Adventure, contemporary, ethnic, experimental, fantasy, feminist, historical, horror, prose poem, spiritual, sports, humor/satire, literary, mainstream, psychic/supernatural/occult, regional, science fiction, suspense/mystery, translations, western and young adult/teen. Receives 200 unsolicited mss each month. Accepts 2 mss/issue; 8 mss/year. Length: 2,500 words average; 200 words minimum; 7,000 words maximum. Occasionally critiques rejected mss.

How to Contact: Send complete ms with cover letter. "It is desirable to know something of the personal history of the writer, since we do concentrate on this region (Southeast Kansasas), and we like to include such information in our publication." SASE. Sample copy $2.50.

Payment: 3 contributor's copies.

Terms: Acquires first rights.

Advice: "Attempt to publish in small publications, such as ours, in order to build credibility as a writer."

LLAMAS MAGAZINE (IV), The International Camelid Journal, Clay Press Inc., Box 100, Herald CA 95638. (916)448-1668. Editor: Cheryl Dal Porto. Magazine: 8½×11; 112+ pages; glossy paper; 80 lb glossy cover stock; illustrations and pictures. For llama owners and lovers. 8 issues/year. Estab. 1979. Circ. 5,500.

Needs: Adventure, historical, humor/satire. Receives 15-25 unsolicited fiction mss/month. Accepts 1-6 mss/issue; 12-24 mss/year. Publishes ms usually 3-4 months after acceptance. 15% of fiction is agented. Length: 2,000-3,000 words average. Publishes short shorts 300-1,000 words in length. Sometimes critiques rejected mss.

How to Contact: Send query to: Susan Ley, *Llamas* Asst. Editor, Box 1038, Dublin OH 43017. Reports in 1 month. Reprint submissions OK. Accepts computer printout submissions. Accepts electronic submissions via Apple 2 disk. Fiction guidelines free.

Payment: $25-500, free subscription to magazine and contributor's copies.

Terms: Pays on publication for first rights, first North American serial rights and one-time rights. Sends pre-publication galleys to author if requested.

LONE STAR (II), A Magazine of Humor, Suite 103, Box 29000, San Antonio TX 78229. Editor: Lauren Barnett. "Humor publication for the general public, comedy connoisseur and professional humorist. Audience: all ages, well-educated, well-read." Published 4-6 times a year. Estab. 1983. Circ. 1,200+.

Needs: Comics and humor/satire. "Do not want to see stories that are three pages long and take three pages before getting to the first laugh." Receives 200-500 unsolicited mss/month. Buys 1-2 mss/issue; 6-12 mss/year. Length: 800 words average; 300 words minimum; 1,000 words maximum. Occasionally critiques rejected mss.

The double dagger before a listing indicates that the listing is new in this edition. New markets are often the most receptive to freelance contributions.

How to Contact: Send SASE for guidelines first; then send complete ms. Reports in 2 to 3 months on queries; 3 to 4 months on mss. Publishes ms an average of 6 months after acceptance. SASE. Photocopied and "sometimes" previously published submissions OK. Inquire about prices for sample issues. Fiction guidelines for #10 SAE and 1 first class stamp.
Payment: $5-20 and 1 free contributor's copy; variable charge for extras.
Terms: "Policy is payment on publication, but we try to pay before." Buys first rights, first North American serial rights or one-time rights; some reprints.
Advice: "Read the guidelines, read our publications and don't give up after one rejection. We do publish more humorous fiction now. Although we publish various styles/subjects, in general, we stay away from anything prevalent in other publications. Anything submitted to *Lone Star* is automatically considered for publication in all appropriate *Lone Star* publications."

LONG SHOT, Box 6231, Hoboken NJ 07030. Editors: Danny Shot, Caren Lee Michaelson, Jack Wiler. Magazine: 5½×8½; 128 pages; 60 lb paper; 10 pt. CIS cover; illustrations; photos. Estab. 1982. Circ. 1,500.
Needs: Adventure, confession, contemporary, erotica, ethnic, experimental, fantasy, feminist, gay, horror, humor/satire, lesbian, political, prose poem, psychic/supernatural/occult, science fiction, suspense/mystery, western. Receives 100 unsolicited mss/month. Accepts 4-5 mss/issue. Does not read mss in August. Publishes ms 6 months at longest after acceptance. Recently published work by Sean Penn, Charles Bukowski, Robert Press; published new writers within the last year. Publishes short shorts. Sometimes recommends other markets.
How to Contact: Send complete ms. Reports in 4-6 weeks. SASE. Simultaneous and photocopied submissions OK. Sample copy for $5 plus $1 postage.
Payment: Pays in contributor's copies.
Terms: Acquires one-time rights.

THE LONG STORY (II), 11 Kingston St., North Andover MA 01845. (508)686-7638. Editor: R.P. Burnham. Magazine: 5½×8½; 150-200 pages; 60 lb paper; 65 lb cover stock; illustrations (b&w graphics). For serious, educated, literary people. No science fiction, adventure, romance, etc. "We publish high literary quality of any kind, but especially look for committed fiction; working class settings, left-wing themes, etc." Annually. Estab. 1983. Circ. 500.
Needs: Contemporary, ethnic, feminist and literary. Receives 30-40 unsolicited mss/month. Buys 6-7 mss/issue. Length: 8,000 words minimum; 20,000 words maximum. ("To accept 20,000 word story it would have to be right down our alley—about poor, oppressed people, i.e., committed fiction.") Sometimes recommends other markets.
How to Contact: Send complete ms with a brief cover letter. Reports in 2+ months. Publishes ms an average of 3 months to 1 year after acceptance. SASE. Photocopied submissions OK. Accepts computer printout submissions, prefers letter-quality. Sample copy for $4.
Payment: Pays in 2 free contributor's copies; $4 charge for extras.
Terms: Acquires first rights.
Advice: "Read us first and make sure submitted material is the kind we're interested in. Send clear, legible manuscripts. We're not interested in commercial success; rather we want to provide a place for long stories, the most difficult literary form to publish in our country."

LOONFEATHER (II), Bemidji Arts Center, 426 Bemidji Ave., Bemidji MN 56601. (218)751-4869. Editors: Betty Rossi and Jeane Sliney. Magazine: 6×9; 48 pages; 60 lb Hammermill Cream woven paper; 65 lb vellum cover stock; illustrations; occasional photos. A literary journal of short prose, poetry and graphics. Mostly a market for Northern Minnesota, Minnesota and Midwest writers. Semiannually. Estab. 1979. Circ. 300.
Needs: Literary, contemporary, prose poem and regional. Accepts 2-3 mss/issue, 4-6 mss/year. Recently published work by Richard Jewell, Gary Erickson, James C. Manolis. Published new writers within the last year. Length: 600-1,500 words (prefers 1,500).
How to Contact: Send complete ms with SASE, and short autobiographical sketch. Reports in 3 months. Sample copy $2 back issues; $4.95 current issue.
Payment: Free author's copies.
Terms: Acquires one-time rights.
Advice: "Send carefully crafted and literary fiction. Because of increase in size of magazine, we can include more, slightly longer fiction.The writer should familiarize himself/herself with the type of fiction published in literary magazines as opposed to family magazines, religious magazines, etc."

LOST AND FOUND TIMES (II), Luna Bisonte Prods, 137 Leland Ave., Columbus OH 43214. (614)846-4126. Editor: John M. Bennett. Magazine: 5½×8½; 40 pages; good quality paper; good cover stock; illustrations; photos. Theme: experimental, avant-garde and folk literature, art. Published irregularly. Estab. 1975. Circ. 300.

Needs: Literary, contemporary, experimental, prose poem. Prefers short pieces. Accepts approximately 2 mss/issue. Published work by Joachim Frank, Al Ackerman, Jack Saunders. Published new writers within the last year. Sometimes recommends other markets.

How to Contact: Query with clips of published work. SASE. Accepts computer printout submissions. Reports in 1 week on queries, 2 weeks on mss. Sample copy $3.

Payment: 1 free author's copy.

Terms: Rights revert to authors.

LOUISIANA LITERATURE (II), A Review of Literature and Humanities, Southeastern Louisiana University, Box 792, Hammond LA 70402. (504)549-5022. Editor: Tim Gautreaux. Magazine: 6¾×9¾; 84 pages; 70 lb paper; card cover; illustrations; photos. "We publish literary quality fiction and essays by anyone. Essays should be about Louisiana material, but creative work can be set anywhere." Semiannually. Estab. 1984. Circ. 400 paid; 1,000 printed.

Needs: Literary, mainstream, regional. No sloppy ungrammatical manuscripts. Receives 10 unsolicited mss/month. Accepts 3 mss/issue; 6 mss/year. Does not read mss June-July. Publishes ms 6 months maximum after acceptance. Published work by William Caverlee and Ingrid Smith; published new writers within the last year. Length: 2,500 words preferred; 1,000 words minimum; 6,000 words maximum. Publishes short shorts. Sometimes comments on rejected mss.

How to Contact: Send complete ms. Reports in 1-2 months on mss. SASE. Photocopied submissions OK. Accepts computer printout submissions. Sample copy $4.

Payment: Pays up to $25 and contributor's copies.

Terms: Pays on publication for one-time rights.

Advice: "Cut out everything that is not a functioning part of the story. Make sure everything is spelled correctly. Use relevant specific detail in every scene."

THE LOUISVILLE REVIEW (II), Department of English, University of Louisville, Louisville KY 40292. (502)588-6801. Editor: Sena Naslund. Magazine: 6×8¾; 100 pages; Warren's Old Style paper; cover photographs. Semiannually. Estab. 1976. Circ. 750.

Needs: Contemporary, experimental, literary, prose poem. Receives 30-40 unsolicited mss/month. Accepts 6-10 mss/issue; 12-20 mss/year. Publishes ms 2-3 months after acceptance. Recently published work by Maura Stanton, Patricia Goedicke, Michael Cadnum; Length: 50 pages maximum. Publishes short shorts.

How to Contact: Send complete ms with cover letter. Reports on queries in 2-3 weeks; 2-3 months on mss. SASE. Photocopied submissions OK. Accepts computer printout submissions, including dot-matrix, "if readable." Sample copy for $3. Fiction guidelines for #10 SAE and 1 first class stamp.

Payment: Pays in contributor's copies.

Terms: Acquires first North American serial rights.

Advice: Looks for "original concepts, fresh ideas, good storyline, engaging characters, a story that works."

LYRA (II), Journal of Poetry and Fiction, Lyra Society of the Arts, Inc., Box 3188, Guttenberg NJ 07093. (201)861-1941. Editors: L. Gil, I. Iturralde. Fiction Editor: Lourdes Gil. Magazine: 8½×11¼; approx. 32 pages; 70 lb paper; illustrations; photos. "Theme related to literature, art and films. Preference for French and Spanish literatures." Quarterly. Plans special fiction issue. Estab. 1987. Circ. 1,000.

Needs: Experimental, literary, prose poem, science fiction, translations, film, French and Spanish literature. Receives approx. 20 unsolicited mss/month. Accepts 3-4 mss/issue; approx. 12 mss/year. Publishes ms 3 months after acceptance. Recently published work by Carolyn Moore, Robert Lima, Elizabeth Macklin; published new writers within the last year. Length: 3,000 words average; 1,000 words minimum; 4,000 words maximum. Publishes short shorts.

How to Contact: Send complete ms with cover letter, which should include "some biographical information or short résumé. It saves time if we decide to publish it." Reports in 2 months. SASE. Photocopied submissions OK. Accepts computer printout submissions. Sample copy for $4; double issue, $6. Fiction guidelines for #10 SAE with 1 first class stamp.

Payment: Pays in contributor's copies.

Terms: Acquires one-time rights. Sponsors awards for fiction writers. "Send a SASE for guidelines."

Advice: "Read a sample copy and become familiar with our preferences and style. And send us several samples of your work; we like to read new authors!"

‡m needle m. (II) Box 225, Hoboken NJ 07030. (201)714-9473. Editors: jackson iz and M. Butler. Magazine: 8½×11; 30-40 pages; illustrations; photos. "New semi-annual featuring fiction, poetry, cartoon art, opinions and anything else that we like." Estab. 1989.

Needs: Open. Receives 5-10 unsolicited mss/month. Accepts 2-3 mss/issue; 8-12 mss/year. Publishes ms 6-9 months after acceptance. Length: 2,000 words maximum. Publishes short shorts. Rarely critiques rejected mss.

How to Contact: Send complete ms. "No cover letter unless you can write one that isn't boring." Reports in 2 weeks on queries; 2 months on mss. SASE. Simultaneous and photocopied submissions OK. Accepts computer printout submissions. Sample copy for 9×12 SAE and $1 postage. Fiction guidelines for #10 SAE and 1 first class stamp.

Payment: Pays in contributor's copies.

Terms: Acquires one-time rights. "Look at the title: *m needle m.* Does it mean anything to you? If it does, don't send any work. We're a comio-seric absolute effin ray of scrawled-upon napkins from the seedy cocktail lounges of life (with cool tunes on the jukebox). That's about it."

THE MACGUFFIN (II), Schoolcraft College, Department of English, 18600 Haggerty Rd., Livonia MI 48152. (313)591-6400, ext. 449. Editor: Arthur J. Lindenberg. Fiction Editor: Elizabeth Hebron. Magazine: 5½×8½; 128 pages; 60 lb paper; 110 lb cover; b&w illustrations and photos. "*The MacGuffin* is a literary magazine which publishes a range of material including poetry, nonfiction and fiction. Material ranges from traditional to experimental. We hope our periodical attracts a variety of people with many different interests." Published 3 times per year. Plans special fiction issue. Estab. 1984. Circ. 500.

Needs: Adventure, contemporary, ethnic, experimental, fantasy, historical (general), humor/satire, literary, mainstream, prose poem, psychic/supernatural/occult, science fiction, translations. No religious, inspirational, confession, romance, horror, pornography. Receives 25-40 unsolicited mss/month. Accepts 5-10 mss/issue; 10-30 mss/year. Does not read mss between July 1 and August 15. Publishes 6 months to 2 years after acceptance. Agented fiction: 10-15%. Recently published work by Richard Kostelantz, Gayle Boss, Ann Knox; published new writers within the last year. Length: 2,000-2,500 words average; 400 words minimum; 4,000 words maximum. Publishes short shorts. Length: 400 words. Occasionally critiques rejected mss and recommends other markets.

How to Contact: Send complete ms with cover letter, which should include: "1. *Brief* biographical information; 2. Note that this *is not* a simultaneous submission." Reports in 6-8 weeks. SASE. Photocopied and reprint submissions OK. Accepts computer printout submissions; including dot-matrix "if readable." Sample copy for $3. Fiction guidelines free.

Payment: Pays in 2 contributor's copies.

Terms: Acquires one-time rights.

Advice: "Be persistent. If a story is rejected, try to send it somewhere else. When we reject a story, we may accept the next one which you send us. When we make suggestions for a rewrite, we may accept the revision. There seem to be a great number of good authors of fiction, but there are far too few places for publication. However, I think this is changing. Make your characters come to life. Even the most ordinary people become fascinating if they live for your readers."

THE MADISON REVIEW (II), Department of English, Helen C. White Hall, 600 N. Park St., University of Wisconsin, Madison WI 53706. Contact: Fiction Editor. Magazine: 6×9; 180 pages. "Magazine of fiction and poetry with special emphasis on literary stories and some emphasis on midwestern writers." Published semiannually. Estab. 1978. Circ. 500.

Needs: Experimental and literary stories, prose poems and excerpts from novels. Receives 50 unsolicited fiction mss/month. Accepts 7-12 mss/issue. Published work by Richard Cohen, Fred Chappell and Janet Shaw. Published new writers within the last year. Length: no preference.

How to Contact: Send complete ms with cover letter and SASE. "The letters should give one or two sentences of relevant information about the writer—just enough to provide a context for the work." Reports in 2 months on mss. Publishes ms an average of 4 months after acceptance. "We often do not report on mss during the summer." Sample copy $4.

Payment: 2 free contributor's copies; $2.50 charge for extras.

Terms: Pays for first North American serial rights.

Advice: "We are now willing to accept chapters of novels in progress and short short fiction. Write with surgical precision—then revise. Often the label 'experimental' is used to avoid reworking a piece. If anything, the more adventurous a piece of fiction is, the more it needs to undergo revision."

Read the Business of Fiction section to learn the correct way to prepare and submit a manuscript.

THE MAGE (II, IV), A Journal of Fantasy and Science Fiction, Colgate University Student Association, Hamilton NY 13346. Editor: Richard Davis. Magazine: 8½11; about 64 pages; good-quality paper stock and cover; b&w illustrations. "Fiction, essays, poetry, artwork and commentary within the genre of science fiction and fantasy. Emphasis is on a balance of poetry, fiction and nonfiction. We do serialize longer works of exceptional quality." Semiannually. Estab. 1984. Circ. 700, to be raised to 1,000 by 1989.

Needs: Experimental, fantasy, horror, science fiction. No sword-and-sorcery adventure or stories based on Dungeons and Dragons and its ilk; no erotica. Receives 15-25 unsolicited fiction mss/month. Accepts 6-10 mss/issue; 12-20 mss/year. Does not read mss June through August. Generally publishes ms within 3 months of acceptance. Recently published work by Patricia Anthony, Eric Davin and David Lunde. Published new writers within the last year. Length: 3,500-4,500 words average; 1,000 words minimum. Usually critiques rejected mss.

How to Contact: Query first or send complete ms and cover letter with list of previous works published. Reports in 2 weeks on queries; 3-5 weeks on mss (report time is longer if submitted just before or during the summer). SASE for ms. Simultaneous and photocopied submissions OK. Accepts computer printouts. Sample copy $3.

Payment: Pays in contributor's copies.

Terms: Acquires first North American serial rights or one-time rights. Sometimes sends galleys to author.

Advice: "We are interested in writers who have practiced enough (even if nothing has been published) to develop a refined writing style. We are interested in presenting good writing first, but we do publish capsule reviews of new fiction. Submitting several of these to us will help a new writer develop some recognition of *The Mage*'s standards, which might help him/her when submitting a first manuscript to us."

MAGIC CHANGES (II), Celestial Otter Press, 2 S. 424 Emerald Grn. Dr., #F, Warrenville IL 60555-9269. (312)393-7856. Editor: John Sennett. Magazine: 8½×11; 110 pages; 60 lb paper; construction paper cover; illustrations; photos. "Theme: transformation by art. Material: poetry, songs, fiction, stories, reviews, art, essays, etc. For the entertainment and enlightenment of all ages." Annually. Estab. 1979. Circ. 500.

Needs: Literary, prose poem, science fiction, sports fiction, fantasy and erotica. "Fiction should have a magical slant." Accepts 8-12 mss/year. Receives approximately 15 unsolicited fiction mss each month. Published work by J. Weintraub, David Goodrum, Anne F. Robertson; published new writers within the last year. Length: 3,000 words maximum.

How to Contact: Send complete ms with SASE. Accepts computer printout submissions, prefers letter-quality. Accepts disk submissions compatible with IBM or Macintosh. Prefers hard copy with disk submissions. Reports in 1 month. Publishes ms an average of 5 months after acceptance. Sample copy $5. Make check payable to John Sennett.

Payment: 1-2 free author's copies. $5 charge for extras.

Terms: Acquires first North American serial rights.

Advice: "Write about something fantastic in a natural way, or something natural in a fantastic way. We need good stories—like epic Greek poems translated into prose."

THE MALAHAT REVIEW (II), University of Victoria, Box 1700, Victoria, British Columbia V8W 2Y2 Canada. (604)721-8524. Editor: Constance Rooke. Magazine: 6×9; 132 pages; photographs occasionally. Publishes fiction, poetry and reviews. Quarterly. Estab. 1967. Circ. 1,800.

Needs: Receives 100 unsolicited mss/month. Buys approximately 6 mss/issue; 25 mss/year. Publishes short shorts. Occasionally critiques rejected mss.

How to Contact: Send complete ms with cover letter. SASE (Canadian postage or IRCs). Photocopied submissions OK. Accepts computer printout submissions. Sample copy $6. Fiction guidelines free.

Payment: Pays $40 per 1,000 words; and contributor's copies.

Terms: Acquires first rights.

Advice: "If it's good, we publish it. *The Malahat Review* is a "generalist" literary magazine, which is to say that it is open to all schools of writing and does not espouse any particular ideology or aesthetic. We believe that new writers should have the opportunity of appearing with celebrated writers, and we find that a mix of unknown and famous names results very naturally from our choice of the best work we receive."

‡MANOA (III), A Pacific Journal of International Writing, University of Hawaii Press, 2840 Kolawalu/Journals Dept., Honolulu HI 96822. (808)948-8833. Editor: Robert Shapard. Fiction Editors: Roger Whitlock and Jeff Carroll. Magazine: 7×10; 200 pages. "East-West and international. An American literary magazine, emphasis on top US fiction and poetry, but each issue has a major guest-edited translated feature of recent writings from an Asian/Pacific country." Semiannually. Estab. 1989.

Needs: Excerpted novel, contemporary, literary, mainstream and translation (from nations in or bordering on the pacific). "Part of our purpose is to present top U.S. fiction, from throughout the U.S., to readers in Asian and Pacific countries. Thus we are not limited to stories related to or set in the Pacific—in fact, we do not want exotic or adventure stories set in the Pacific, but good U.S. literary fiction of any locale." Plans to publish special fiction issue or an anthology in the future. Accepts 10-12 mss/issue; 20-24/year. Publishes ms 6 months-1 year after acceptance. Agented fiction 50%. Recently published work by Anne Beattie, Ron Carlson and Francois Camoin. Publishes short shorts.
How to Contact: Send complete ms with cover letter or through agent. Reports in 1-6 weeks. SASE. Simultaneous and photocopied submissions OK. Sample copy $7.
Payment: "Highly competitive rates paid so far." Pays in contributor copies.
Terms: Pays for first North American serial, one-time or one-time reprint rights. Sends galleys to author.
Advice: "We don't have any special formulas other than we think about whether it's appropriate for what we've begun or have in mind for upcoming issues. We don't anticipate running theme issues as such, but do like to relate various writings in an issue."

MARK (II), A Journal of Scholarship, Opinion, and Literature, University of Toledo, 2801 W. Bancroft SU2514, Toledo OH 43606. (419)537-4463. Editor: Gary F. Madrzykowski. Magazine: 6×9; 72 pages; acid-free paper; some illustrations; photographs. "General theme is exploration of humanity and man's effort to understand the world around him." Annually. Estab. 1967. Circ. 3,500.
Needs: Contemporary, ethnic, humor/satire, literary, regional and science fiction. "We do not have the staff to do rewrites or heavy copyediting—send clean, legible mss only." No "typical MFA first-person narrative—we like stories, not reportage." Receives 20-25 unsolicited fiction mss/month. Accepts 7-10 mss/year. Does not read June to September. Publishes ms 6 months after acceptance. Publishes short shorts.
How to Contact: Send complete ms with cover letter, name, address and phone. Reports in January each year. Photocopied submissions OK. Accepts computer printouts. Sample copy $3 plus 7x10 SAE with 72¢ postage.
Payment: Pays two contributor's copies.
Terms: Acquires one-time rights.
Advice: "Beginning fiction writers should write in a style that is natural, not taught to them by others. More importantly, they should write about subjects they are familiar with. Be prepared for rejection, but good writing will always find a home."

THE MARYLAND REVIEW, Department of English, University of Maryland Eastern Shore, Princess Anne MD 21853. (301)651-2200, ext. 262. Editor: Chester M Hedgepeth. Magazine: 6×9; 100-150 pages; good quality paper stock; heavy cover; illustrations; photos "possibly." "We have a special interest in black literature, but we welcome all sorts of submissions. Our audience is literary, educated, well-read." Annually. Estab. 1986. Circ. 500.
Needs: Contemporary, humor/satire, literary, mainstream, black. No genre stories; no religious, political or juvenile material. Accepts approx. 12-15 mss/issue. Publishes ms "within 1 year" after acceptance. Published work by John K. Crane, David Jauss. Published new writers within the last year. Publishes short shorts. "Length is open, but we do like to include some pieces 1,500 words and under." Occasionally critiques rejected mss.
How to Contact: Send complete ms with cover letter, which should include a brief autobiography. Reports "as soon as possible." SASE. Photocopied submissions acceptable. No simultaneous submissions. Accepts computer printout submissions. Sample copy for $6.
Payment: Pays in contributor's copies.
Terms: Acquires all rights.
Advice: "Think primarily about your *characters* in fiction, about their beliefs and how they may change. Create characters and situations that are utterly new. We will give your material a careful and considerate reading. Any fiction that is flawed by grammatical errors, misspellings, etc. will not have a chance. We're seeing a lot of fine fiction these days, and we approach each story with fresh and eager eyes. Ezra Pound's battle-cry about poetry refers to fiction as well: 'Make it New!' "

‡MATI, Ommation Press, 5548 N. Sawyer, Chicago IL 60625. Editor: Effie Mihopoulos. "Primarily a poetry magazine, but we do occasional special fiction and science fiction issues." Quarterly. Estab. 1975. Circ. 1,000.
Needs: Literary, contemporary, science fiction, feminist, translations. No mystery, gothic, western, religious. Receives approximately 20 unsolicited fiction ms each month. Length: 1-2 pages. Occasionally sends ms on to editors of other publications. Sometimes recommends other markets.

How to Contact: Send complete ms with SASE. Reports in 1 week-2 months. Sample copy $1.50 with 9×12 SASE (preferred) plus 90¢ postage.

Payment: 1 free author's copy. Special contributor's rates available for extras.

Terms: Acquires first North American serial rights. "Rights revert to authors but *Mati* retains reprint rights."

Advice: "We want to see good quality writing and a neat ms with sufficient return postage; same size return as outside envelope and intelligent cover letter. Editor to be addressed as 'Dear Sir/Ms' instead of 'Dear Sir' when it's a woman editor."

MEAL, READY-TO-EAT (I), 910 Three Degree Road, Butler PA 16001. Editor: Richard Sater. Magazine: 5½×8½; 12 (12-16 pages); Xerox paper and cover; illustrations and photographs. "Theme varies with each issue depending on material published." Monthly. Estab. 1987. Circ. 100.

Needs: Adventure, contemporary, experimental, horror, humor/satire, poetry, literary, mainstream, prose poem, sports, suspense/mystery, western. Receives few unsolicited mss/month. Accepts one or two mss/issue. Published work by Patricia Henley, Marianne Boruch, Brooke Horvath. Publishes short shorts. Length: up to 4 double-spaced typed pages maximum.

How to Contact: Send complete ms with cover letter. Reports in 6 weeks on mss. SASE for ms return. Photocopied submissions OK. Accepts computer printout submissions. Sample copy for 50¢, SAE and 2 first class stamps.

Payment: Pays in contributor's copies.

Terms: Acquires one-time rights. "Post office/registered mail copyright."

Advice: "Most magazines take themselves too seriously. This one doesn't. *Meal, Ready-To-Eat* is prepared on my word processor. I do my own editing/layout/graphics. It is Xeroxed at a local copy shop and distributed by mail to interested readers. My budget is limited, but I'm attempting to put out an interesting/entertaining issue each month."

MERLYN'S PEN (IV), The National Magazine of Student Writing, Box 1058, East Greenwich RI 02818. (401)885-5175. Editor: R. Jim Stahl. Magazine 8⅛×10⅞; 36 pages; 50 lb paper; 70 lb gloss cover stock; illustrations; photos. Student writing only—grades 7 through 10, for libraries, homes and English classrooms. Bimonthly (September-April). Estab. 1985. Circ. 16,000.

Needs: Adventure, experimental, fantasy, historical (general), horror, humor/satire, literary, mainstream, regional, romance, science fiction, suspense/mystery, western, young adult/teen, editorial reviews, puzzles, word games, poetry. Must be written by students in grades 7-10. Receives 300 unsolicited fiction mss/month. Accepts 50 mss/issue; 250 mss/year. Publishes ms 3 months to 1 year after acceptance. Length: 1,500 words average; 25 words minimum; 4,000 words maximum. Publishes short shorts. Responds to rejected mss.

How to Contact: Send complete ms and cover letter with name, grade and principal's name, age, home and school address, home and school telephone number, supervising teacher's name. Reports in 10-12 weeks. SASE for ms. Accepts computer printouts. Sample copy $3.

Payment: Three contributor's copies, charge for extras. Each author published receives a free copy of *The Elements of Style*.

Terms: Author retains own copyright.

Advice: "Write what you *know*; write where you are."

MICHIGAN QUARTERLY REVIEW, University of Michigan, 3032 Rackham, Ann Arbor MI 48109. (313)764-9265. Editor: Laurence Goldstein. "An interdisciplinary journal which publishes mainly essays and reviews, with some high-quality fiction and poetry, for an intellectual, widely read audience." Quarterly. Estab. 1962. Circ. 1,500.

Needs: Literary. No "genre" fiction written for a "market." Receives 200 unsolicited fiction mss/month. Buys 2 mss/issue; 8 mss/year. Published work by Lynne Sharon Schwartz, Gloria Whelan, Ron Hansen; published new writers within the last year. Length: 1,500 words minimum; 7,000 words maximum; 5,000 words average.

How to Contact: Send complete ms with cover letter. "I like to know if a writer is at the beginning, or further along, in his or her career. Don't offer plot summaries of the enclosed story, though a background comment is welcome." SASE. Photocopied submissions OK. Accepts computer printout submissions. Prefers letter quality. Sample copy for $2 and 2 first class stamps.

Payment: Pays $8-10/printed page.

Terms: Pays on acceptance for first rights. Awards the Lawrence Foundation Prize of $500 for best story in *MQR* previous year.

Advice: "Read back issues to get a sense of tone; level of writing. *MQR* is very selective; only send the very finest, best-plotted, most-revised fiction."

THE MICKLE STREET REVIEW (IV), The Walt Whitman Association, 328 Mickle Blvd., Camden NJ 08103. (609)757-6431. Editor: Geoffrey M. Sill. Magazine: 5×7; 150-200 pages; cover illustrations; limited photographs. "Articles and essays on Walt Whitman, his life, works, recent studies and poetry in the Whitman influence." Audience is largely academic, but also about 40% general. Annually. Estab. 1979. Circ. 200.

Needs: Historical, literary. "We would only consider fiction with a bend toward exemplifying Whitman influences." Receives less than 5 mss/year. Publishes ms 1 year after acceptance. Rarely critiques rejected mss. Sometimes recommends other markets.

How to Contact: Query with clips of published works. Reports in 2 months. SASE. Photocopied and reprint submissions OK. Sample copy $5 and SAE with 4 first class stamps.

Payment: Pays in contributor's copies; $2 charge for extras for any amount over 2.

MICROCOSM (I), New Writings in Imaginative Fiction, Quixsilver Press, Box 644, Biglerville PA 17307-0644. Editor: Bob Medcalf, Jr. Magazine: 5½×8½; 24 pages; offset paper; vellum cover stock; illustrations. Short shorts with imaginative themes and treatment, for well-read readers of imaginative fiction. Annually. Plans special fiction issue. Estab. 1981. Circ. 100.

Needs: Adventure, experimental, fantasy, horror, psychic/supernatural/occult, science fiction. Receives 10 unsolicited fiction mss/month. Accepts 12 mss/issue. Publishes ms 2 to 3 years after acceptance. Length: 600 words average; 100 words minimum; 1,000 words maximum. Sometimes critiques rejected mss and recommends other markets.

How to Contact: Send complete ms and cover letter with brief publication highlights stating reading interests in the field of imaginative fiction. Reports in 4 months. SASE for ms. Simultaneous, photocopied and reprint submissions OK. Accepts computer printouts. Sample copy $3.

Payment: Free subscription to magazine, contributor's copies, charge for extras.

Terms: Acquires one-time rights.

Advice: "The beginning fiction writer can fulfill the journeyman requirements in the small press magazines if he/she diligently searches out editors willing to work with him/her on his/her beginning work. Supporting the publications that serve him or her—through subscriptions and reading fees is a requirement of this process. Send your best work. Be eager and willing to revise or rewrite new work guided by comments. Submit to other suggested markets."

MID-AMERICAN REVIEW (II), Department of English, Bowling Green State University, Bowling Green OH 43403. (419)372-2725. Contact: Robert Early, editor-in-chief. Magazine: 5½×8½; 200 pages; 60 lb bond paper; coated cover stock. "We publish serious fiction and poetry, as well as critical studies in modern literature, translations and book reviews." Published biannually. Estab. 1981.

Needs: Experimental, traditional, literary, prose poem, excerpted novel and translations. Receives about 50 unsolicited fiction mss/month. Buys 5-6 mss/issue. Does not read June-August. Approximately 5% of fiction is agented. Published work by Peter Bricklebank, Joe Ashby Porter, Tricia Tunstall; published new writers within the last year. Occasionally critiques rejected mss. Sometimes recommends other markets.

How to Contact: Send complete ms with SASE. Reports in about 2 months. Publishes ms an average of 3 months after acceptance. Sample copy $4.50.

Payment: $5/page up to $50; 2 free contributor's copies; $2 charge for extras.

Terms: Pays on publication for one-time rights.

Advice: "We just want *quality* work of whatever vision and/or style. We are now looking for more translated fiction."

MIDDLE EASTERN DANCER (II), The International Monthly Magazine of Middle Eastern Dance & Culture, Box 181572, Casselberry FL 32718-1572. (407)831-3402. Editor: Karen Kuzsel. Fiction Editor: Tracie Harris. Magazine: 8½×11; 36 pages; 60 lb stock; enamel cover; illustrations; photos. "Our theme is Middle Eastern dance and culture. We run seminar listings, professional directory, astrology geared to dancers, history, interviews, poetry, recipes, reviews of movies, clubs, shows, records, video, costuming, personal beauty care, exercise and dance choreography." Monthly. Estab. 1979. Circ. 2,500.

Needs: No fiction that does not relate to Middle-Eastern dance or culture. Receives 5 unsolicited ms/month. Publishes ms within 4 months after acceptance. Recently published work by Alan Fisher, Jeanette Larson and Sid Hoskins; published new writers within the last year. *Charges $10 if comments are desired*. Occasionally critiques rejected mss. Recommends other markets.

How to Contact: Send complete ms with cover letter, which should include "background in Middle Eastern dance or culture, why they came to write this story and how they know of the magazine." Reports in 1 month on queries. SASE. Photocopied and reprint submissions OK "if not to other Middle Eastern Dance and culture publication." Accepts computer printout submissions. Sample copy for $1 or send 9x12 SAE and 75¢ postage.

Payment: Pays $10-25 and 2 contributor's copies.
Terms: Pays on acceptance for one-time rights.
Advice: "Stick strictly to Middle Eastern dance/culture."

MIDLAND REVIEW (II), An Annual Journal of Contemporary Lit, Lit. Crit. & Art, Oklahoma State University, English Dept., Morrill Hall, Stillwater OK 74078. (405)744-9474. Editor-in-Chief: Nuala Archer. Magazine: 6½x9½; 100 pages; 80 lb paper; perfect bond cover stock; illustrations; photos. "A mixed bag of quality work." For "anyone who likes to read and for those that want news that folks in Oklahoma are alive. Publishes 30-40% OSU student material." Annually. Estab. 1985. Circ. 500.
Needs: Ethnic, experimental, feminist, historical (general), horror, literary, prose poem, psychic/supernatural/occult, regional, science fiction, translations. Receives 15 unsolicited fiction mss/month. Accepts 4 mss/issue. Publishes ms 2-6 months after acceptance. Published work by Jene Friedemann, Steffie Corcoran, Bruce Michael Gans; published new writers within the last year. Length: 4-10 pages double-spaced, typed. Publishes short shorts of 2-4 pages.
How to Contact: Send complete manuscript with cover letter. Reports in 6-8 weeks on queries. SASE for ms. Simultaneous and photocopied submissions OK. Accepts computer printouts. Sample copy for $5, 90¢ postage and 9×12 SAE. Fiction guidelines for #10 SAE and 1 first class stamp.
Payment: 1 free contributor's copy.
Terms: Copyright reverts to author.
Advice: "We want to encourage good student stories by giving them an audience with more established writers."

MINAS TIRITH EVENING-STAR (IV), W.W. Publications, Box 373, Highland MI 48031-0373. (313)887-4703. Editor: Philip Helms. Magazine: 8½×11; 40+ pages; typewriter paper; black ink illustrations; photos. Magazine of J.R.R. Tolkien and fantasy—fiction, poetry, reviews, etc. for general audience. Quarterly. Published special fiction issue; plans another. Estab. 1967. Circ. 500.
Needs: "Fantasy and Tolkien." Receives 5 unsolicited mss/month. Accepts 1 ms/issue; 5 mss/year. Published new writers within the last year. Length: 1,000-1,200 words preferred; 5,000 words maximum. Also publishes short shorts. Occasionally critiques rejected ms.
How to Contact: Send complete ms and bio. Reports in 1 week on queries; 2 weeks on mss. SASE. Photocopied and previously published submissions OK. Accepts computer printout submissions, prefers letter-quality. Sample copy $1.
Terms: Acquires first rights.
Advice: Goal is "to expand knowledge and enjoyment of J.R.R. Tolkien's and his son Christopher Tolkien's works and their worlds."

MIND IN MOTION (II), A Magazine of Poetry and Short Prose, Box 1118, Apple Valley CA 92307. (619)248-6512. Editor: Céleste Goyer. Magazine: 5½×8½; 54 pages; 20 lb paper; 50 lb cover. "We prefer to publish works of substantial brilliance that engage and encourage the readers' mind." Quarterly. Estab. 1985. Circ. 350.
Needs: Experimental, fantasy, humor/satire, literary, prose poem, science fiction. No "mainstream, romance, nostalgia, un-poetic prose; anything with a slow pace or that won't stand up to re-reading." Receives 50 unsolicited mss/month. Buys 5 mss/issue; 40 mss/year. Publishes ms 2 weeks to 3 months after acceptance. Published work by Robert E. Brimhall, Warren C. Miller, Michael K. White. Length: 2,000 words preferred; 250 words minimum; 3,500 words maximum. Sometimes critiques rejected mss and occasionally recommends other markets.
How to Contact: Send complete ms. "Cover letter or bio not necessary." SASE. Simultaneous (if notified) and photocopied submissions OK. Accepts computer printout submissions. Sample copy for $3.50. Fiction guidelines for #10 SAE and 1 first class stamp.
Payment: One contributor's copy when financially possible; charge for extras.
Terms: Acquires first North American serial rights.
Advice: "We look for fiction with no wasted words that demands re-reading, and startles us continually with the knowledge that such genius exists. Send works of cosmic pressure written poetically."

THE MIND'S EYE (I, II), Fiction and Poetry Quarterly, Box 656, Glenview IL 60025. Editor: Gene Foreman. Magazine: 5×8; 35-45 pages; 15 lb paper; vellum cover; illustrations; photographs. Semiannually. Estab. 1986. Circ. 500.
Needs: Adventure, condensed/excerpted novel, confession, contemporary, erotica, ethnic, experimental, fantasy, feminist, gay, historical (general), horror, humor/satire, lesbian, literary, mainstream, prose poem, psychic/supernatural/occult, regional, romance (contemporary, historical, young adult), science fiction, sports, suspense/mystery, translations. Receives 50 unsolicited mss/month. Accepts 6 mss/issue; 12-24 mss/year. Publishes ms 3 months-1 year after acceptance. Length: 2,000 words average; 100 words minimum; 3,000 words maximum. Publishes short shorts. Rarely critiques rejected mss.

How to Contact: Send complete ms with cover letter. Reports in 1-2 weeks on queries; 2-4 weeks on mss. SASE. Simultaneous and photocopied submissions OK. Accepts computer printout submissions. Sample copy for $3.50. Fiction guidelines free with SAE and 1 first class stamp.
Payment: Pays in contributor's copies; charge for extras.
Terms: Acquires first rights. Sponsors annual fiction and poetry contest for subscribers.
Advice: "Read at least one past issue."

MINNESOTA INK (II), Box 9148, N. St. Paul MN 55109. (612)433-3626. Managing Editor: Valerie Hockert. Variable number of pages; 40 lb paper; illustrations and photographs. "A bimonthly publication designed to provide guidance and advice as well as inspiration for writers and other people interested in writing (e.g., the college student, the business person)." Monthly. Estab. 1987.
Needs: Adventure, contemporary, experimental, fantasy, humor/satire, mainstream, regional, romance (contemporary, historical), science fiction, senior citizen/retirement, suspense/mystery, western, young adult/teen (12-18 years). Receives about 100 unsolicited mss/month. Publishes mss "usually a couple months" after acceptance. Length: 500 words minimum; 1,500 words maximum. Sometimes critiques rejected mss.
How to Contact: Send complete ms with cover letter and biographical sketch. Reports in 1-2 months. SASE. Photocopied submissions OK. Sample copy for $3. Fiction guidelines for SASE.
Payment: Pays in contributor's copies or subscription.
Terms: Acquires first rights. Sponsors contests and awards for fiction writers. "Contest announcements are published in publication."

THE MINNESOTA REVIEW (II), A Journal of Committed Writing, English Dept., SUNY-Stony Brook, Stony Brook NY 11794. (516)632-7400. Editors: Helen Cooper, William J. Harris, Marlon Ross, Michael Sprinker, Susan Squier. Fiction Editor: Fred Pfeil. Magazine: 5¼×8; approximately 160 pages; some illustrations; occasional photos. "We emphasize political writing, favoring especially socialist and feminist work." Semiannually. Estab. 1960. Circ. 1,000.
Needs: Experimental, fantasy, feminist, gay, historical (general), lesbian, literary, science fiction. Receives 20 mss/month. Accepts 3-4 mss/issue; 6-8 mss/year. Publishes ms within 6 months to 1 year after acceptance. Published work by Enid Dame, Ellen Gruber Garvey, John Berger. Length: 5,000-6,000 words preferred. Publishes short shorts. Sometimes critiques rejected mss and recommends other markets.
How to Contact: Send complete ms with cover letter (cover letter optional). Reports in 2-3 weeks on queries; 2-3 months on mss. SASE. Accepts computer printout submissions. Sample copy for $4. Fiction guidelines are free.
Payment: Pays in contributor's copies. Charge for extra copies.
Terms: Acquires first rights.
Advice: "Write good stories with explicit political themes. Read back issues of *MR* for a sense of our collective taste."

MIORITA, A JOURNAL OF ROMANIAN STUDIES (IV), The Dept. FLLL, Dewey 482, University of Rochester, Rochester NY 14627. (716)275-4258 or (716)275-4251. Co-Editors: Charles Carlton and Norman Simms. Magazine: 5½×8½; Xerox paper; occasional illustrations. Magazine of "essays, reviews, notes and translations on all aspects of Romanian history, culture, language and so on," for academic audience. Annually. Estab. 1973. Circ. 200.
Needs: Ethnic, historical, literary, regional and translations. "All categories contingent upon relationship to Romania." Receives "handful of mss per year." Accepts "no more than one per issue." Length: 2,000 words maximum. Occasionally critiques rejected mss.
How to Contact: Send complete ms. SASE preferred. Previously published work OK (depending on quality). Accepts computer printout submissions.
Payment: "We do not pay."

THE MIRACULOUS MEDAL, The Central Association of the Miraculous Medal, 475 E. Chelten Ave., Philadelphia PA 19144. (215)848-1010. Editor: Rev. Robert P. Cawley, C.M. Magazine. Quarterly.
Needs: Religious/inspirational. Receives 25 unsolicited fiction mss/month; accepts 2 mss/issue; 8 mss/year. Publishes ms up to two years or more after acceptance.
How to Contact: Query first with SASE. Sample copy and fiction guidelines free.
Payment: Pays 2¢/word minimum.
Terms: Pays on acceptance for first rights.

THE MIRROR-NORTHERN REPORT (I,IV), Box 269, 4732-53 Ave., High Prairie, Alberta T0G 1E0 Canada. (403)523-3706. Editor: Albert Burger. Magazine: 8½×11; 32-48 pages; newsprint paper; b&w illustrations; b&w photos. Publishes for a "rural–small town–native–farm" audience. Monthly. Estab. 1986. Circ. 2,000.

Needs: Adventure, contemporary, ethnic, fantasy, feminist, historical, humor, literary, mainstream, prose poem, psychic/supernatural/occult, regional, romance, science fiction, senior citizen, sports, suspense, translations, western. Receives 10 mss/month. Accepts 1 ms/issue. Publishes ms within 2-3 months of acceptance. Length: 1,000-1,500 words preferred; 2,500 words maximum. Publishes short shorts.

How to Contact: Send complete mss with cover letter. Reports in 2-3 months. SASE. Simultaneous, photocopied and reprint submissions OK. Accepts computer printout submissions. Sample copy $2.

Payment: Pays 1¢/word.

Terms: Pays on publication for one-time rights. Publication not copyrighted.

‡THE MISS LUCY WESTENRA SOCIETY OF THE UNDEAD, 125 Taylor Street, Jackson TN 38301. (901)427-7714. Editor: Lewis Sanders. Newsletter: "Vampires/Dracula, modern/classic, very, very short fiction." Estab. 1989.

Needs: Horror and vampires. "Very, very short fiction on vampires, Gothic, modern, erotic, but no porno or sleaze. Must be sent camera ready with a proper SASE." Length: 500 words average. Publishes short shorts of 500 words or less.

How to Contact: Send complete ms with cover letter. Reports on queries "as soon as possible." SASE. Simultaneous and reprint submissions OK. Sample copy $2.50, #10 SAE and 2 first class stamps. Fiction guidelines for #10 SAE and 2 first class stamps.

Payment: Pays 1 contributor's copy.

Terms: Acquires one-time rights. Publication not copyrighted.

MISSISSIPPI REVIEW (I, II), University of Southern Mississippi, Southern Station, Box 5144, Hattiesburg MS 39406. (601)266-4321. Editor: Rick Barthelme. "Literary publication for those interested in contemporary literature—writers, editors who read to be in touch with current modes." Semiannually. Estab. 1972. Circ. 1,500.

Needs: Literary, contemporary, fantasy, humor, translations, experimental, avant-garde and "art" fiction. No juvenile. Buys varied amount of mss/issue. Does not read mss in summer. Length: 100 pages maximum.

How to Contact: Send complete ms with SASE including a short cover letter. Accepts computer printout submissions. Sample copy $5.50.

Payment: Pays in author's copies. Charges cover price for extras.

Terms: Acquires first North American serial rights.

MISSISSIPPI VALLEY REVIEW (III), Western Illinois University, Dept. of English, Simpkins Hall, Macomb IL 61455. Editor: Forrest Robinson. Fiction Editor: Loren Logsdon. Magazine: 64 pages; original art on cover. "A small magazine, *MVR* has won 17 Illinois Arts Council awards in poetry and fiction. We publish stories, poems and reviews." Biannually. Estab. 1971. Circ. 400.

Needs: Literary, contemporary. Does not read mss in summer. Published work by Jack Matthews, Joseph Queenan and Rochelle Distelheim; published new writers within the last year.

How to Contact: Send complete ms with SASE. Reports in 3 months. Sample copy $3. "Do not ask for guidelines. Refer to an issue of *MVR*."

Payment: 2 free author's copies.

Terms: Individual author retains rights.

Advice: "We prefer to receive one story at a time. Getting one's work published has always been difficult. Commitment to one's art, as well as persistence, can sustain."

THE MISSOURI REVIEW (II), 107 Tate Hall, English Dept., University of Missouri, Columbia MO 65211. (314)882-6421. Editor: Greg Michalson. Magazine: 6×9; 256 pages. Theme: fiction, poetry, essays, reviews, interviews, cartoons. "All with a distinctly contemporary orientation. For writers, and the general reader with broad literary interests. We present non-established as well as established writers of excellence. The *Review* frequently runs feature sections or special issues dedicated to particular topics frequently related to fiction." Published 3 times/academic year. Estab. 1977. Circ. 2,400.

Needs: Literary, contemporary; open to all categories except juvenile, young adult. Buys 6-8 mss/issue, 18-25 mss/year. Receives approximately 300 unsolicited fiction mss each month. Published new writers within the last year. No preferred length. Critiques rejected mss "when there is time."

How to Contact: Send complete ms with SASE. Reports in 10 weeks. Sample copy $5.

Payment: $10/page minimum.

Terms: Pays on publication for all rights.

Advice: Awards William Peden Prize in fiction; $1,000 to best story published in *Missouri Review* in a given year.

MODERN LITURGY (IV), Resource Publications, Inc., Suite 290, 160 E. Virginia St., San Jose CA 95112. Fiction Editor: Ken Guentert. Magazine: 8½×11; 48 pages; 60 lb glossy paper and cover stock; illustrations and photographs. "*Modern Liturgy* is focused on the liturgical arts—music, visual art, architecture, drama, dance and storytelling. We use short pieces that lend themselves to religious education or preaching. Readers are professionals and volunteers who plan and organize worship for Roman Catholic churches." 10 issues/year. Estab. 1973.

Needs: Liturgical. "Storytelling should be creative. Short pieces that tell you you how so-and-so came to a personal relationship with Jesus don't make it here." Receives 10 unsolicited fiction mss/month. Accepts 1 ms/issue; 9 mss/year. Length: 1,500 words average; 600 words minimum; 2,500 words maximum. Publishes short shorts.

How to Contact: Send complete ms with cover letter. Reports in 6 weeks. Sample copy $4 with 9x12 SAE and 3 first class stamps. Fiction guidelines for #10 SAE and 1 first class stamp.

Payment: Free subscription and 5 contributor's copies; charge for extras.

Terms: Acquires first rights plus right to grant non-commercial reprint permission to customers.

Advice: "We don't publish 'short stories' in the classic literary sense, but we do publish much fictional material (stories, plays, skits, humor) that is of use to worship leaders and planners."

THE MOUNTAIN LAUREL, Monthly Journal of Mountain Life, Foundation Inc., P.O. Box 562, Wytheville VA 24382. (703)228-7282. Editor: Susan M. Thigpen. Tabloid: 28 pages; newsprint, illustrations and photographs. "Everyday details about life in the Blue Ridge Mountains of yesterday, for people of all ages interested in folk history." Monthly. Estab. 1983. Circ. 20,000.

Needs: Historical, humor, regional. "Stories must fit our format—we accept seasonal stories. There is always a shortage of good Christmas stories. A copy of our publication will be your best guidelines as to what we want. We will not even consider stories containing bad language, sex, gore, horror." Receives approximately 40 unsolicited fiction mss/month. Accepts up to 5 mss/issue; 60 mss/year. Publishes ms 2 to 6 months after acceptance. Length: 500-600 words average; no minimum; 1,000 words maximum. Publishes short shorts. Length 300 words. Sometimes critiques rejected mss. Recommends other markets.

How to Contact: Send complete ms with cover letter, which should include "an introduction to the writer as though he/she were meeting us in person." Reports in 1 month. SASE. Simultaneous and photocopied submissions OK. Accepts computer printout submissions. Sample copy for 9x12 SAE and 5 first class stamps. Fiction guidelines for #10 SAE and 1 first class stamp.

Payment: Pays in contributor's copies.

Terms: Pays for one-time rights.

Advice: "Tell a good story. Everything else is secondary. A tightly written story is much better than one that rambles. Short stories have no room to take off on tangents. *The Mountain Laurel* has published the work of many first-time writers as well as works by James Still and John Parris. First publication ever awarded the Blue Ridge Heritage Award."

MUSE'S MILL (I,II), Box 2117, Ashland KY 41105. (614)894-3723 (evening); (614)532-2357 (day). Editors: Carol Henshaw, Kay Ebicks and Zerry Clarke. Magazine: 8½×11; 36-60 pages. Publishes "short stories primarily; all types. Some articles, poems, graphics." For "nonacademic, eclectic reader." Quarterly. Estab. 1988. Circ. 500.

Needs: Adventure, condensed/excerpted novel, contemporary, ethnic, experimental, fantasy, horror, humor/satire, literary, mainstream, prose poem, psychic/supernatural/occult, romance (contemporary, historical), science fiction, serialized novel, sports, suspense/mystery, western, young adult/teen (10-18). No "graphic gratuitous sex or violence; racist or xenophobic" fiction. Receives 40 mss/month. Buys 14 mss/issue; 56 mss/year. Publishes ms within 3-6 months of acceptance. Published work by C.O. Lamp; Starr Lyn Butterfield, James Gish. Length: 1,500-3,000 words preferred; 50 words minimum; 5,000 words maximum. Sometimes critiques rejected mss and recommends other markets.

How to Contact: Send complete ms with cover letter, which should state previous credits. Reports on queries in 2 weeks; on mss in 9 weeks. SASE. Simultaneous, photocopied and reprint submissions OK. Accepts computer printout submissions. Accepts electronic submissions via disk. Sample copy for $5. Fiction guidelines free for SAE.

Payment: Pays $10-100 and 1 contributor's copy.

Terms: Pays on publication for one-time rights. Offers 25% kill fee. Sponsors awards for fiction writers.

Advice: "Many manuscripts we receive are grammatically correct but creatively barren. Read short fiction—good fiction, from Hemingway to Ellison and beyond. Don't watch TV so much. Write to acquire skills, then write with inspiration—listen to your muse. Make something happen in your stories, something or someone undergo change, growth, decline, etc. Expect it to be difficult and slow progress, but extremely satisfying."

MUSICWORKS (IV), A Triannual Magazine With Sound, Music Gallery, 1087 Queen St. W., Toronto, Ontario M6J 1H3 Canada. (416)533-0192. Editor: G. Young. Magazine and cassette: 48 pages; bond paper; b&w illustrations and photographs. "All aspects of contemporary sonic arts—interviews, articles, scores, visuals, sound and music on cassette." For musicians, composers, students, artists, administrators, etc. Triannually. Estab. 1978. Circ. 1,500.

Needs: Ethnic, experimental, prose poem and music-sound. No mainstream, commercial, popular fiction. Accepts less than 1 ms/issue; 1-3 mss/year, maximum. Published work by Paul Haines. Length: 2,000 words average; 5,000 words maximum. Occasionally critiques rejected mss.

How to Contact: Send proposal or query with clips of published work. Reports in 6 weeks. SASE or SAE and IRC for query and ms. Simultaneous, photocopied and previously published submissions OK. Accepts computer printout submissions, prefers letter-quality. Sample $3.25; with cassette $8.75.

Payment: Pays $200 maximum and 2-3 contributor's copies; charge for extras $2-$3.

Terms: Buys one time rights on publication.

Advice: "Our emphasis is on music, and we occasionally publish fiction related to experimental music."

‡MYSTERY NOTEBOOK (II, IV), Box 1341, F.D.R. Station, New York NY 10150. Editor: Stephen Wright. Journal and Newsletter: 8½×11; 10-16 pages; photocopied; self cover; illustrations and photos sometimes. "Mystery books, news, information; reviews and essays. Separate section covers books of merit that are not mysteries." For mystery readers and writers. Quarterly. Estab. 1984. Circ. (approx.) 1,000.

Needs: Excerpted novel (suspense/mystery). Receives few unsolicited mss. Length: brief. Short shorts considered. Occasionally comments on rejected ms.

How to Contact: Query first or query with clips of published work (preferably on mystery). Reports in 2 weeks on queries; 3 weeks on mss. SASE for ms. Photocopied and previously published submissions OK (if query first). All submissions must be letter-quality. Sample copies or back issues $10.

Payment: None. "If author is a regular contributor, he or she will receive complimentary subscription. Usually contributor receives copy of the issue in which contribution appears."

Advice: "Mystery magazines use all kinds of stories in various settings. This is also true of mystery books except that clever spy stories are still much in demand. Mystery fiction books have increased in demand—*but* the competetion is more keen than ever. So only those with real talent *and* a good knowledge of mystery-writing craft have any chance for publication. It also helps if you know and understand the market."

MYSTERY TIME (I), An Anthology of Short Stories, Box 1870, Hayden ID 83835. (208)772-6184. Editor: Linda Hutton. Booklet: 5½×8½; 44 pages; bond paper; illustrations. "Annual collection of short stories with a suspense or mystery theme for mystery buffs." Estab. 1983.

Needs: Suspense/mystery only. Receives 10-15 unsolicited fiction mss/month. Accepts 10-12 mss/year. Published work by Elizabeth Lucknell, Loretta Sallman Jackson, Vickie Britton. Published new writers within the last year. Length: 1,500 words maximum. Occasionally critiques rejected mss and recommends other markets.

How to Contact: Send complete ms with SASE. "No cover letters."Simultaneous, photocopied and previously published submissions OK. Accepts computer printout submissions. Prefers letter-quality. Reports in 1 month on mss. Publishes ms an average of 6-8 months after acceptance. Sample copy for $3.50. Fiction guidelines for #10 SAE and 22¢ postage.

Payment: ¼¢/word minimum; 1¢/word maximum. 1 free contributor's copy; $2.50 charge for extras

Terms: Acquires one-time rights. Buys reprints. Sponsors annual short story contest.

Advice: "Study a sample copy and the guidelines. Too many amateurs mark themselves as amateurs by submitting blind."

THE MYTHIC CIRCLE (I), The Mythopoeic Society, Box 6707, Altadena CA 91001. Co-Editors: Lynn Maudlin and Christine Lowentrout. Magazine: 8½×11; 50 pages; high quality photocopy paper; illustrations. "A tri-quarterly fantasy-fiction magazine. We function as a 'writer's forum,' depending heavily on letters of comment from readers. We have an occasional section called 'Mythopoeic Youth' in which we publish stories written by writers still in high school/junior high school. We have several 'theme' issues (poetry, American fantasy) and plan more of these in the future." Tri-quarterly. Estab. 1987. Circ. 150.

Needs: Short fantasy and prose poetry. "No erotica, no graphic horror, no 'hard' science fiction." Receives 25+ unsolicited ms/month. Accepts 19-20 mss/issue. Publishes ms 2-8 months after acceptance. Published work by Charles de Lint, Gwyneth Hood, Angelee Sailer Anderson; published new writers within the last year. Length: 3,000 words average. Publishes short shorts. Length: 8,000 words maximum. Always critiques rejected mss; may recommend other markets."

How to Contact: Send complete ms with cover letter. "We like to know if the person is very young—we give each ms a personal response. We get many letters that try to impress us with other places they've appeared in print—that doesn't matter much to us." Reports in 2-8 weeks. SASE. Photocopied submissions OK. Accepts computer printout submissions and IBM or MAC floppies. Sample copy $4; fiction guidelines for #10 SASE.

Payment: Contributor's copies; charges for extras.

Terms: Acquires one-time rights.

Advice: "There are very few places a fantasy writer can send to these days. *Mythic Circle* was started up because of this; also, the writers were not getting any kind of feedback when (after nine or ten months) their mss were rejected. We give the writers personalized attention—critiques, suggestions—and we rely on our readers to send us letters of comment on the stories we publish, so that the writers can see a response. Don't be discouraged by rejections, especially if personal comments/suggestions are offered."

NAKED MAN (II), c/o Mike Smetzer, Dept. of English, NW Missouri State University, Maryville, MO 64468. Editor: Mike Smetzer. Magazine: 5½×8½; 36-48 pages; offset paper; ivory bristol board cover stock; illustrations on cover. "I have eclectic tastes but generally dislike work that is only clever or spontaneous work without discipline. Since *Naked Man* reflects my personal interests and tastes, writers should examine a copy before submitting." Published irregularly. Estab. 1982.

Needs: Comics, contemporary, experimental, humor/satire, literary, mainstream, prose poem and regional. Publishes ms an average of 6 months after acceptance. Recently published work by Tim Coats, Michael Pritchett. Length: no minimum; 15,000 words maximum. Occasionally critiques rejected mss "as time permits."

How to Contact: Send complete ms with SASE. Photocopied submissions OK. Accepts letter-quality computer printout submissions. Sample copy $2.25. Subscriptions are $9 for 4 issues in U.S. and Mexico; $10.50 for other countries.

Payment: Pays in 2 contributor's copies.

Terms: Acquires first rights. Sends galleys to author.

Advice: "Most issues of *Naked Man* will now be chapbooks. Chapbook submissions may be short stories, short novelettes, mixtures of prose and poetry, or poetry; but they should have some overall unity. No unsolicited translations. Prose length about 3,000-14,000 words. Individual pieces in collections may have previous magazine publication. The author will receive 25 of 300-500 copies printed. Copyright will be to the author. *For non-subscribers there is a chapbook reading fee of $5.*"

NEBO (I), A Literary Journal, Arkansas Tech University, Dept. of English, Russellville AR 72801. (501)968-0256. Contact: Editor. Literary, fiction and poetry magazine: 5×8; 50-60 pages. For a general, academic audience. Semiannually. Estab. 1983. Circ. 500.

Needs: Experimental, literary, mainstream, reviews. Receives 20-30 unsolicited fiction mss/month. Accepts 2 mss/issue; 6-10 mss/year. Does not read mss May 31-Aug 1. Published new writers within the last year. Length: 3,000 words maximum. Occasionally critiques rejected mss.

How to Contact: Send complete ms with SASE and cover letter with bio. Simultaneous and photocopied submissions OK. Accepts computer printout submissions, prefers letter-quality. Reports in 3 months on mss. Publishes ms an average of 6 months after acceptance. Sample copy for $1.

Payment: 2 free contributor's copies.

Terms: Acquires one-time rights. "Rarely" buys reprints.

Advice: "A writer should carefully edit his short story before submitting it. Write from the heart and put everything on the line. Don't write from a phony or fake perspective. Frankly, many of the manuscripts we receive should be publishable with a little polishing. Manuscripts should *never* be submitted with misspelled words or on 'onion skin' or colored paper."

THE NEBRASKA REVIEW (II), University of Nebraska at Omaha, ASH 212, Omaha NE 68182. (402)554-2771. Fiction Editor: Richard Duggin. Magazine: 5½×8½; 72 pages; 60 lb text paper; chrome coat cover stock. "*TNR* attempts to publish the finest available contemporary fiction and poetry for college and literary types." Publishes 2 issues/year. Estab. 1973. Circ. 500.

Needs: Contemporary, humor/satire, literary and mainstream. Receives 20 unsolicited fiction mss/month. Accepts 3-5 mss/issue, 8 mss/year. Does not read April 1-September 1. Recently published work by Elizabeth Evans, Stephen Dixon and Peter Leach; published new writers within the last year. Length: 5,000-6,000 words average.

How to Contact: Send complete ms with SASE. Photocopied submissions OK. Reports in 1-2 months. Publishes ms an average of 4-6 months after acceptance. Sample copy $2.50.
Payment: 2 free contributor's copies plus 1 year subscription; $2 charge for extras.
Terms: Acquires first North American serial rights.
Advice: "Don't consider us as the last place to submit your mss. Write 'honest' stories in which the lives of your characters are the primary reason for writing and techniques of craft serve to illuminate, not overshadow, the textures of those lives. Sponsors a $300 award/year—write for rules."

NEGATIVE CAPABILITY (II), A Literary Quarterly, 62 Ridgelawn Dr. E., Mobile AL 36608. (205)661-9114. Editor-in-Chief: Sue Walker. Managing Editor: Richard G. Beyer. Magazine: 5½×8½; 160 pages; 70 lb offset paper; 2 color/varnish cover stock; illustrations; photos. Magazine of short fiction, prose poems, poetry, criticism, commentaries, journals and translations for those interested in contemporary trends, innovations in literature. Published tri-quarterly. Estab. 1981. Circ. 1,000.
Needs: Adventure, contemporary, ethnic, experimental, fantasy, feminist, gothic/historical romance, historical (general), literary, prose poem, psychic/supernatural/occult, regional, romance (contemporary), science fiction, senior citizen/retirement, suspense/mystery, translations. Accepts 2-3 mss/issue, 6-10 mss/year. Does not read July-Sept. Publishes short shorts. Published work by A.W. Landwehr, Gerald Flaherty and Richard Moore; published new writers within the last year. Length: 1,000 words minimum. Sometimes recommends other markets.
How to Contact: Query or send complete ms. SASE. Reports in 2 weeks on queries; 6 weeks on mss. Publishes ms an average of 6 months after acceptance. Sample copy $5.
Payment: 2 free contributor's copies.
Terms: Acquires first rights, first North American serial rights and one-time rights. Sends galleys to author.
Advice: "We consider all manuscripts and often work with new authors to encourage and support. We believe fiction answers a certain need that is not filled by poetry or nonfiction." Annual fiction competition. Deadline Dec. 1.

NEW BLOOD MAGAZINE (I,II), 1843 E. Venton St., Covina CA 91724. Editor: Chris Lacher. Magazine: 8½×11; 70-100 pages; 20 lb paper; color cover; b&w illustrations. "Of course, story counts, but *New Blood* publishes fiction considered too strong or gory to appear in today's periodicals; note, emphasis does not have to be on gore or grue—I just want a story that knocks me out! Fans of Clive Barker and *Fangoria* magazine, for example, will appreciate *New Blood*." Quarterly. Estab. 1986. Circ. 5,000.
Needs: Horror, gore, psychic/supernatural/occult, dark fantasy, experimental, erotica with gore or horror slant, excerpted novel, suspense/mystery, translations. "I can't use sword and sorcery, unless characters and settings are contemporary. I will consider techno-horror, science gone mad, botanical horror, science fiction with a horror slant." Receives 200 unsolicited mss/month. Accepts 10-20 mss/issue; 45-90 mss/ year. Publishes ms 3-9 months after acceptance. Agented fiction 1%, Recently published work by Clive Barker, Gary Brandner, Dean R. Koontz; published new writers within the last year. Length: 2,500 words average; 5,000 words maximum. Always critiques rejected mss. Sometimes recommends other markets.
How to Contact: Send complete ms with cover letter, which should include a brief bio. Reports on queries and mss "within 3 weeks." SASE. Simultaneous, photocopied and reprint submissions OK. Sample copy $4.
Payment: Pays 1-5¢/word.
Terms: Rights revert to author on publication.
Advice: "I see too many stories with senseless gore; involve me, show me something new. Becoming familiar with the unique type of fiction I publish by purchasing a subscription is a contributor's key to a quick sale. *New Blood* is unlike any magazine to ever appear on the newsstands, and I believe one must read *New Blood* regularly, be aware of our consistent growth, to write for us."

THE NEW CRUCIBLE (I), A Magazine About Man and His Environment, Box 7252, Spencer IA 51301. Editor: Garry De Young. Magazine: 8½×11; variable number of pages; 20 lb paper; soft cover; illustrations and photographs. Publishes "environmental material—includes the total human environment." Monthly. Plans special fiction issue. Estab. 1988.
Needs: Atheist. "Keep material concise, use clear line drawings. Environmentalists must be Materialists because the environment deals with matter. Thus also evolutionists. Keep this in mind. Manuscripts not returned. Will not accept religious or other racist or sexist material." *Charges $1/page reading fee.* Length: concise preferred. Publishes short shorts. Sometimes critiques rejected mss. Publishes original cartoons.
How to Contact: Send complete ms with cover letter. Cover letter should include "biographical sketch of author." SASE. Simultaneous, photocopied and reprint submissions OK. Accepts computer printout submissions. Sample copy for $2, 8½x11 SAE and 4 first class stamps.

Payment: Pays in contributor's copies.
Terms: "Will discuss rights with author."
Advice: "Be gutsy! Don't be afraid to attack superstitionists. Attack those good people who remain so silent—people such as newspaper editors, so-called scientists who embrace superstition such as the Jesus myth or the Virgin Mary nonsense."

NEW DELTA REVIEW (II), English Dept./Louisiana State University, Baton Rouge LA 70803. (504)388-4079. Editor: Kathleen Fitzpatrick. Fiction Editor: David Racine. Magazine: 6×9; 75-125 pages; high quality paper; glossy card cover; illustrations; photographs possible. "No theme or style biases. Poetry, fiction primarily; also creative essays and reviews." Semi-annually. Estab. 1984.
Needs: Contemporary, erotica, experimental, humor/satire, literary, mainstream, prose poem, translations. Receives 75 unsolicited mss/ month. Accepts 4-8 mss/issue. Recently published work by Rod Kessler, Thomas E. Kennedy, Thomas Fox Averill; published new writers within the last year. Length: 2,500 words average; 250 words minimum; 5,000 words maximum. Publishes short shorts. Sometimes critiques rejected mss.
How to Contact: Send complete ms with cover letter. Cover letter should include "credits, if any; no synopses, please." Reports on mss in 6-8 weeks. SASE. Mss deadlines September 15 for fall; April 15 for spring. Prefers photocopied submissions. No dot-matrix. Sample copy for $4.
Payment: Pays in contributor's copies. Charge for extras.
Terms: Acquires first North American serial rights. Sponsors award for fiction writers. Eyster Prize-$50 plus notice in magazine.
Advice: "Each submission is read by 4-7 staff members. Editors have final decision, though obviously any piece well-received by the staff has a chance for publication. We are continually asked what *kind* of fiction we like. All we can say is this: the good kind. Be brave. Explore your voice. Make sparks fly off your typewriter. And don't forget the SASE if you want a response."

NEW ENGLAND REVIEW AND BREAD LOAF QUARTERLY (III), NER/BLQ, Middlebury College, Middlebury VT 05753. (802)388-3711, ext. 5075. Editors: T.R. Hummer, Maura High. Magazine: 6×9; 140 pages; 70 lb paper; coated cover stock; illustrations; photos. A literary quarterly publishing fiction, poetry and essays on life and the craft of writing. For general readers and professional writers. Quarterly. Estab. 1977. Circ. 2,000.
Needs: Literary. Receives 250 unsolicited fiction mss/month. Accepts 5 mss/issue; 20 mss/year. Does not read ms June-August. Recently published work by Jeanne Schinto, Robert Minkoff, Kathryn Davis; published new writers within the last year. Publishes ms 3-9 months after acceptance. Agented fiction: less than 5%. Publishes short shorts. Sometimes critiques rejected mss.
How to Contact: Send complete ms with cover letter. "Cover letters that demonstrate that the writer knows the magazine, and is not submitting simultaneously elsewhere, are the ones we want to read. We don't want hype, or hard-sell, or summaries of the author's intentions." Reports in 6-8 weeks on mss. SASE. Photocopied submissions OK. Accepts computer printouts. Sample copy $4. Send #10 SAE with any inquiries.
Payment: Pays $5 per page; $10 minimum; free subscription to magazine, offprints; contributor's copies; charge for extras.
Terms: Pays on publication. Acquires first rights and reprint rights on *NER/BLQ* and Middlebury College. Sends galleys to author.
Advice: "We look for work that combines intelligence with craft and visceral appeal. To break into the prestige or literary market, writers should avoid formulae and clichés and assume that the reader is at least as intelligent and well informed as they are."

NEW FRONTIER (IV), 46 North Front, Philadelphia PA 19106. (215)627-5683. Editor: Sw. Virato. Magazine: 8×10; 48-60 pages; pulp paper stock; illustrations and photos. "We seek new age writers who have imagination yet authenticity." Monthly. Estab. 1981. Circ. 60,000.
Needs: New age. "A new style of writing is needed with a transformation theme." Receives 10-20 unsolicited mss/month. Accepts 1-2 mss/issue. Publishes ms 3 months after acceptance. Agented fiction "less than 5%." Published work by John White, Laura Anderson. Published work by new writers within the last year. Length: 1,000 words average; 750 words minimum; 2,000 words maximum. Publishes short shorts. Length: 150-500 words. Occasionally critiques rejected mss and recommends other markets.
How to Contact: Send complete ms with cover letter, which should include author's bio and credits. Reports in 2 months on mss. SASE for ms. Simultaneous, photocopied and reprint submissions OK. Accepts computer printout submissions. Sample copy for $2. Fiction guidelines for #10 SAE and 1 first class stamp.
Terms: Acquires first North American serial rights and one-time rights.
Advice: "The new age market is ready for a special kind of fiction and we are here to serve it. Don't try to get an A on your term paper. Be sincere, aware and experimental. Old ideas that are senile don't work for us. Be fully alive and aware—tune in to our new age audience/readership."

NEW LAUREL REVIEW (II), 828 Lesseps St., New Orleans LA 70117. (504)947-6001. Editor: Lee M. Grue. Assistant Editor: George Cleveland. Magazine: 6×9; 120 pages; 60 lb book paper; Sun Felt cover; illustrations; photo essays. Journal of poetry, fiction, critical articles and reviews. "We have published such internationally known writers as Martha McFerren, Tomris Uyar and Yevgeny Yevtushenko." Readership: "Literate, adult audiences as well as anyone interested in writing with significance, human interest, vitality, subtlety, etc." Annually. Estab. 1970. Circ. 500.

Needs: Literary, contemporary, fantasy and translations. No "dogmatic, excessively inspirational or political" material. Accepts 1-2 fiction mss/issue. Receives approximately 50 unsolicited fiction mss each month. Length: about 10 printed pages. Critiques rejected mss when there is time.

How to Contact: Send complete ms with SASE. Reports in 3 months. Sample copy $6.

Payment: 2 free author's copies.

Terms: Acquires first rights.

Advice: "We are interested in international issues pointing to libraries around the world. Write fresh, alive 'moving' work. Not interested in egocentric work without any importance to others. Be sure to watch simple details such as putting one's name and address on ms and clipping all pages together. Caution: Don't use overfancy or trite language."

NEW LETTERS MAGAZINE (I, II), University of Missouri-Kansas City, 5100 Rockhill Rd., Kansas City MO 64110. (816)276-1168. Editor: James McKinley. Magazine: 14 lb cream paper; illustrations. Quarterly. Estab. 1971 (continuation of *University Review*, founded 1935). Circ. 2,500.

Needs: Contemporary, ethnic, experimental, humor/satire, literary, mainstream, translations. No "bad fiction in any genre." Published work by Richard Rhodes, Jascha Kessler, Josephine Jacobsen; published work by new writers within the last year. Agented fiction: 10%. Also publishes short shorts. Occasionally critiques rejected mss.

How to Contact: Send complete ms with cover letter. Does not read mss May 15-October 15. Reports in 3 weeks on queries; 6 weeks on mss. SASE for ms. Photocopied submissions OK. Accepts computer printouts. Sample copy: $8.50 for issues older than 5 years; $5.50 for 5 years or less.

Payment: Honorarium – depends on grant/award money; 2 contributor's copies. Sends galleys to author.

Advice: "Seek publication of representative chapters in high-quality magazines as a way to the book contract. Try literary magazines first."

NEW METHODS (IV), The Journal of Animal Health Technology, Box 22605, San Francisco CA 94122-0605. (415)664-3469. Editor: Ronald S. Lippert, AHT. Newsletter ("could become magazine again"): 8½×11; 4-6 pages; 20 lb paper; illustrations; photos "rarely." Network service in the animal field educating services for mostly professionals in the animal field; e.g. animal health technicians. Monthly. Estab. 1976. Circ. 5,608.

Needs: Animals: adventure, condensed novel, contemporary, experimental, historical, mainstream, regional, science fiction and western. No stories unrelated to animals. Receives 4 unsolicited fiction mss/month. Buys one ms/issue; 12 mss/year. Length: open. "Rarely" publishes short shorts. Occasionally critiques rejected mss. Recommends other markets.

How to Contact: Query first with theme, length, expected time of completion, photos/illustrations, if any, biographical sketch of author, all necessary credits or send complete ms. Report time varies. SASE for query and ms. Simultaneous and photocopied submissions OK. Accepts computer printouts. Sample copy $2 for *NSSWM* readers with #10 SAE and 2 first class stamps. Fiction guidelines free for #10 SAE and 2 first class stamps.

Payment: Varies.

Terms: Pays on publication for one-time rights.

Advice: Contests: theme changes but is generally the biggest topics of the year in the animal field. "Emotion, personal experience – make the person feel it. We are growing."

NEW MEXICO HUMANITIES REVIEW (II), Humanities Dept., New Mexico Tech, Box A, Socorro NM 87801. (505)835-5445. Editors: John Rothfork and Jerry Bradley. Magazine: 5½×9½; 150 pages; 60 lb lakewood paper; 482 ppi cover stock; illustrations; photos. Review of poetry, essays and prose of Southwest. Readership: academic but not specialized. Published 3 times/year. Estab. 1978. Circ. 650.

Needs: Literary and regional. "No formula." Accepts 40-50 mss/year. Receives approximately 50 unsolicited fiction mss/month. Recently published work by John Deming, Fred Chappell; published new writers within the last year. Length: 6,000 words maximum. Publishes short shorts. Critiques rejected mss "when there is time." Sometimes recommends other markets.

How to Contact: Send complete ms with SASE. Accepts computer printout submissions. Reports in 2 months. Publishes ms an average of 6 months after acceptance. Sample copy $5.
Payment: 1 year subscription.
Terms: Sends galleys to author.
Advice: Mss are rejected because they are "unimaginative, predictable and technically flawed. Don't be afraid to take literary chances—be daring, experiment."

NEW MOON, A Journal of Science Fiction and Critical Feminism, Box 2056, Madison WI 53701. (608)251-3854. Editor: Janice Bogstad. "Speculative fiction, fantastic feminist fiction, reviews and criticism of such works. Copies found in university libraries, feminist and literary collections, women's studies programs." Semiannually. Estab. 1981. Circ. 600.
Needs: Experimental, fantasy, feminist, literary, prose poem, science fiction, translations. Receives 3-5 unsolicited fiction mss/month. Accepts 2-4 mss/issue; 15 mss/year. Published new writers within the last year. Length: 1,000-1,500 words average; 1,000 words minimum; 3,000 words maximum. Occasionally critiques rejected mss.
How to Contact: Query first. Cover letter should include "other interests, other publications of your work." Reports in 2 months on queries; 4 months on mss. SASE. Simultaneous, photocopied submissions and previously published work OK. "No originals." Accepts computer printout submissions. Prefers letter-quality. Sample copy $4. Fiction guidelines free for #10 SAE and 1 first class stamp.
Payment: Pays 1 contributor's copy; 60% of cover price charge for extras.
Terms: Acquires one-time rights.
Advice: "Send photocopies only. Send clean, clear copy and advise as to turnaround time expected."

NEW ORLEANS REVIEW (II), Box 195, Loyola University, New Orleans LA 70118. (504)865-2294. Editor: John Mosier. Magazine: 8½×11; 100 pages; 60 lb Scott offset paper; 12+ King James C15 cover stock; photos. "Publishes poetry, fiction, translations, photographs, nonfiction on literature and film. Readership: those interested in current culture, literature." Published 4 times/year. Estab. 1968. Circ. 1,000.
Needs: Literary, contemporary, translations. Buys 9-12 mss/year. Length: under 40 pages.
How to Contact: Send complete ms with SASE. Does not accept simultaneous submissions. Accepts computer printout submissions. Accepts disk submissions; inquire about system compatibility. Prefers hard copy with disk submission. Reports in 3 months. Sample copy $9.
Payment: "Inquire."
Terms: Pays on publication for first North American serial rights. Sends galleys to author.

‡NEW PATHWAYS (II), into Science Fiction and Fantasy, MGA Services, Box 863994, Plano TX 75086-3994. Editor: Michael G. Adkisson. Fiction Editor: Chris Kelly. Magazine: 8×10¾; 60-70 pages; uncoated stock; enamel 2-color cover; 13-20 illustrations per issue. "We like literary quality SF and fantasy. We want a nice blend of traditional and avant-garde work for sophisticated readers of SF with a sense of humor and adventure. We also run film reviews with photos." Quarterly. Estab. 1986. Circ. 1,200.
Needs: Experimental, fantasy, literary, mainstream "if it's off the wall," science fiction, translations. No "lousy fiction, Dick and Jane fiction." No more than one submission at a time. Receives 30-50 unsolicited mss/month. Buys 4-5 mss/issue; approximately 20 mss/year. Publishes ms generally within the next 4 issues. Length: 2,000-5,000 words average; 5,000 words maximum. Publishes short shorts. Length: 800-1,500 words. Occasionally critiques rejected mss or recommends other markets.
How to Contact: Send complete ms with cover letter. "The cover letter is very important! I like to have publishing history, biographical note, a note on the story if appropriate, comments on own work or on the magazine." Reports in 2 weeks on queries; 4-6 weeks on mss. SASE. Photocopied submissions OK. Accepts computer printout submissions. Query for electronic submission info. Sample copy for $4, SAE and $1 postage. Fiction guidelines for #10 SAE and 1 first class stamp.
Payment: Pays $20 and contributor's copies.
Terms: Pays on publication for one-time rights.
Advice: "I like experimental writing. I like traditional SF and avant-garde work. I like thick, rich writing and well rounded characters. We are the conscience of science fiction with a big grin. We publish intelligent, thought-provocative stories and provide an assortment of humor, art, photos, comix, and reviews.

THE NEW PRESS (II), 75-28 66 Drive, Middle Village NY 11379. (718)326-4127. Editor: Bob Abramson. Magazine: 8½×11; 20 pages; medium bond paper and cover stock; illustrations and photographs. "Poems, short stories, commentary, personal journalism. Original and entertaining." Quarterly. Estab. 1984.

Needs: Adventure, confession, ethnic, experimental, fantasy, humor/satire, literary, mainstream, prose poem, serialized/excerpted novel, spiritual, sports, translations. No violence. Receives 10 unsolicited mss/month. Accepts 2 mss/issue; 8 mss/year. Publishes ms 6 months after acceptance. Published new writers within the last year. Length: 3,000 words maximum; 100 words minimum. Sometimes critiques rejected mss and recommends other markets.
How to Contact: Send complete ms with cover letter. Reports in 2 months. SASE. Simultaneous, photocopied and reprint submissions OK. Accepts computer printout submissions. Sample copy $2; fiction guidelines free.
Payment: Pays in contributor's copies.
Terms: Pays for one-time rights.

THE NEW QUARTERLY (II, IV), New Directions in Canadian Writing, ELPP, University of Waterloo, Waterloo, Ontario N2L 3G1 Canada. (519)885-1212, ext. 2837. Managing Editor: Mary Merikle. Fiction Editors: Peter Hinchcliffe, Kim Jernigan. Magazine: 6×9; 80-120 pages; perfect bound cover, b&w cover photograph; photos with special issues. "We publish poetry, short fiction, excerpts from novels, interviews. We are particularly interested in writing which stretches the bounds of realism. Our audience includes those interested in Canadian literature." Quarterly. Published recent special issues on magic realism in Canadian writing and family fiction. Upcoming issue on Canadian Mennonite writing.
Needs: "I suppose we could be described as a 'literary' magazine. We look for writing which is fresh, innovative, well crafted. We promote beginning writers alongside more established ones. Ours is a humanist magazine—no gratuitous violence, though we are not afraid of material which is irreverent or unconventional. Our interest is more in the quality than the content of the fiction we see." Receives approx. 40 unsolicited mss/month. Buys 5-6 mss/issue; 20-24 mss/year. Publishes ms usually within 6 months after acceptance. Recently published work by Sandra Birdsell, Joan Fern Shaw and Diana Kiesners; published new writers within the last year. Length: up to 20 pages. Publishes short shorts. Sometimes recommends other markets.
How to Contact: Send complete ms with cover letter, which should include a short biographical note. Reports in 1-2 weeks on queries; approx. 3 months on mss. SASE for ms. Photocopied submissions OK. Accepts computer printout submissions, no dot-matrix. Sample copy for $3.50.
Payment: Pays $100 and contributor's copies.
Terms: Pays on publication for first North American serial rights.
Advice: "Send only one well polished manuscript at a time. Persevere. Find your own voice. The primary purpose of little literary magazines like ours is to introduce new writers to the reading public. However, because we want them to appear at their best, we apply the same standards when judging novice work as when judging that of more established writers."

NEW VIRGINIA REVIEW (II), An anthology of literary work by and important to Virginians, 1306 East Cary St., 2A, Richmond VA 23219. (804)782-1043. Rotating guest editors. Editor 1989-90: Dave Smith. Magazine: 6½×10; 300+ pages; high quality paper; coated, color cover stock. "Approximately one half of the contributors have Virginia connections; the other authors are serious writers of contemporary fiction. Occasionally guest editors set a specific theme for an issue, e.g. 1986 Young Southern Writers." Annually. Estab. 1978. Circ. 2,000.
Needs: Contemporary, experimental, literary, mainstream, serialized/excerpted novel. No blue, sci-fi, romance, children's. Receives 50-100 unsolcited fiction mss/month. Accepts an average of 15 mss/issue. Does not read from April 1 to September 1. Publishes ms an average of 6-9 months after acceptance. Length: 5,000-6,500 words average; no minimum; 8,000 words maximum. Sometimes critiques rejected mss.
How to Contact: Send complete ms with cover letter, name, address, telephone number, brief biographical comment. Reports in 6 weeks on queries; up to 6 months on mss. "Will answer questions on status of ms." SASE. Photocopied submissions OK. Accepts computer printout submissions. Sample copy $13.50 and 9x12 SAE with 5 first-class stamps.
Payment: $10/printed page; contributor's copies; charge for extras, ½ cover price.
Terms: Pays on publication for first North American serial rights. Sponsors contests and awards for Virginia writers only.
Advice: "Since we publish a wide range of styles of writing depending on the tastes of our guest editors, all we can say is—try to write good strong fiction, stick to it, and try again with another editor."

NeWEST REVIEW (II, IV), Box 394, Sub P.O. 6 Saskatoon, Saskatchewan S7N 0W0 Canada. Editorial Committee: Paul Denham, Jim Sutherland, Gail McConnell, Brett Fairbairn. Fiction Editor: Lewis Horne. Magazine: 56-72 pages; book stock; self cover; illustrations; photos. Magazine devoted to western Canada regional issues; "fiction, reviews, poetry for middle- to high-brow audience." Bimonthly (6 issues per year). Estab. 1975. Circ. 1,000.

Needs: "We want fiction of high literary quality, whatever its form and content. But we do have a heavy regional emphasis." Receives 15-20 unsolicited mss/month. Buys 1 ms/issue; 10 mss/year. Length: 2,500 words average; 1,500 words minimum; 5,000 words maximum. Sometimes recommends other markets.
How to Contact: "We like *brief* cover letters. Reports very promptly in a short letter. SAE, IRCs or Canadian postage. Photocopied submissions OK. No multiple submissions. Accepts computer printout submissions. Sample copy $1.50.
Payment: Pays $100 maximum.
Terms: Pays on publication for one-time rights.
Advice: "Polish your writing. Develop your story line. Give your characters presence. If we, the readers, are to care about the people you create, you too must take them seriously."

NIGHT SLIVERS (I,IV), A Journal of Nocturnal Pain, P.O. Box 389, Mt. Prospect IL 60056. (312)364-5746. Editor: Patricia Locis. Publisher: Kevin Kocis. Magazine: 5½×8½; 60-80 pages; 20 lb paper; 60 lb cover; few illustrations. Publishes "short-short stories of horror and pain, like a sliver evokes pain—thus, the title." Semiannually. Estab. 1988. Circ. 200.
Needs: Experimental, horror, literary, psychic/supernatural/occult. "Our main interest is horror; therefore, any other fiction category must centralize around a horrific theme. We are also in literary and experimental horror, though these are difficult to write. No slasher, cannibalism, child situations, blatant religious (including satanism) and racism." Receives 30-60 unsolicited mss/month. Buys 15-20 mss/issue; 45-60 mss/year. Publishes ms 6 months-1 year after acceptance. Length: 800 words preferred; 100 words minimum; 1,000 words maximum. Publishes short shorts. Sometimes critiques rejected mss and recommends other markets.
How to Contact: Send complete ms with cover letter. Cover letter should include "informal bio, credits, interests (personal and literary)." Reports in 2 weeks on queries; 1 month on mss. SASE. Photocopied submissions OK. Sample copy for $4.50 postpaid. Fiction guidelines for #10 SAE and 1 first class stamp.
Payment: Pays $5 minimum; $10 maximum. Two free contributor's copies; charge for extras.
Terms: Pays on publication for first North American serial rights.
Advice: "Read all the literary greats—Hemingway, Updike, Steinbeck, along with the great writers of short horror—Bradbury, Etchison, Matheson, Barker, King. Since there isn't a lot of time or space to produce strong characterization in a short-short, mood and feeling are important. Think about that before you write. Be brief, neat and professional."

NIMROD (II), International Literary Journal, Arts & Humanities Council of Tulsa, 2210 S. Main, Tulsa OK 74114. Editor-in-Chief: Francine Ringold. Magazine: 6×9; 160 pages; 60 lb white paper; illustrations; photos. "We publish one thematic issue and one awards issue each year. A recent theme was Oklahoma Indian Markings." We seek vigorous, imaginative, quality writing." Published semiannually. Estab. 1956. Circ. 2,000+.
Needs: "We accept contemporary poetry and/or prose. May submit adventure, ethnic, experimental, prose poem, science fiction or translations." Receives 120 unsolicited fiction mss/month. Published work by Gish Gen and Alvin Greenberg; published new writers within the last year. Length: 7,500 words maximum.
How to Contact: Reports in 3 weeks-3 months. Sample copy: "to see what *Nimrod* is all about, send $5.50 plus $1.50 postage. Be sure to request an awards issue."
Payment: 3 free contributor's copies.
Terms: Acquires one-time rights.
Advice: "Read the magazine. Write well. Be courageous. No superfluous words. No clichés. Keep it tight but let your imagination flow. Read the magazine. Strongly encourage writers to send #10 SASE for brochure. Rules are fairly explicit. Disqualification a possiblility if procedures not followed." Annual literary contest. Send #10 (business-size) SASE for full contest details.

NO IDEA MAGAZINE (I), Droog Productions, 3925 S.W. 3rd Ave., Gainesville FL 32607. Editor: Var Thëlin. Magazine: 8½×11; 64 pages; 37 lb newsprint; illustrations and photographs. Each issue comes with a hard-vinyl 7-inch record. "Mostly underground/punk/hardcore music and interviews, but we like delving into other art forms as well. We publish what we feel is good—be it silly or moving." Sporadically. Estab. 1985.
Needs: Adventure, contemporary, experimental, fantasy, horror, humor/satire, science fiction, suspense/mystery. "Humor of a strange, odd manner is nice. We're very open." Receives 5-10 mss/month. Publishes ms up to 6 months after acceptance. Publishes mostly short shorts. Length: 1-6 pages typed.

How to Contact: Send complete manuscript with cover letter. Photocopied submissions OK. Accepts computer printout submissions. Sample copy $2.50.
Payment: Pays in contributor's copies.
Terms: Acquires one-time rights.
Advice: "A query with $2.50 will get you a sample of our latest issue and answers to any questions asked. Just because we haven't included a writer's style of work before doesn't mean we won't print their work. Perhaps we've never been exposed to their style before."

THE NOCTURNAL LYRIC (I), Box 2602, Pasadena CA 91102-2602. (818)796-4801. Editor: Susan Ackerman. Digest: 5½×8½; 22 pages; illustrations. "We are a non-profit literary journal, dedicated to printing fiction by new writers for the sole purpose of getting read by people who otherwise might have never seen their work." Bimonthly. Estab. 1987. Circ. 150.
Needs: Experimental, fantasy, horror, humor/satire, psychic/supernatural/occult, science fiction, poetry, suspense/mystery. "We will give priority to unusual, creative pieces." Receives approx. 50 unsolicited mss/month. Publishes ms 4-8 months after acceptance. Publishes short shorts. Length: no more than 8 double-spaced typed pages.
How to Contact: Send complete ms with cover letter. Cover letter should include "something about the author, what areas of fiction he/she is interested in." Reports in 1 week on queries; 4-6 weeks on mss. SASE. Simultaneous, photocopied and reprint submissions OK. Accepts computer printout submissions. Sample copy for $1.25 (checks made out to Susan Ackerman, editor). Fiction guidelines for #10 SAE and 1 first class stamp.
Terms: Publication not copyrighted.
Advice: "We are not really impressed by the stories found in current fiction magazines. They seem to be too mainstream—too ordinary. We are saddened that writers who write from their soul are frequently rejected because their material is too controversial—or not too 'commercial.' Be as original and creative as you can be—search the depths of your being for an unusual way of expressing a story that has meaning for you. This will truly impress us."

THE NORTH AMERICAN REVIEW, University of Northern Iowa, Cedar Falls IA 50614. Editor: Robley Wilson. Publishes quality fiction. Quarterly. Estab. 1815. Circ. 4,500.
Needs: "We print quality fiction of any length and/or subject matter. Excellence is the only criterion." Reads fiction *only* from Jan. 1 to March 31. Published new writers (about 25%) within the last year. No preferred length.
How to Contact: Send complete ms with SASE. Reports in 2-3 months. Sample copy $3.
Payment: Approximately $10/printed page. 2 free author's copies. $2.50 charge for extras.
Terms: Pays on acceptance for first North American serial rights.
Advice: "We stress literary excellence and read 3,000 manuscripts a year to find an average of 35 stories that we publish. Please *read* the magazine first."

THE NORTH AMERICAN VOICE OF FATIMA (II), Barnabite Fathers, 1023 Swan Rd., Youngstown NY 14174-0167. (716)754-7489. Editor: Rev. Paul M. Keeling, C.R.S.P. Marian Magazine fostering devotion to Mary, the Mother of God. Bimonthly. Estab. 1961. Circ. 3,000.
Needs: Religious/inspirational. Recently published work by Starlette L. Howard. Length: 1,000 words average.
How to Contact: Send complete ms with SASE. Reports in 1 month on ms. Sample copy free.
Payment: 2¢/word.
Terms: Pays on publication.

NORTH DAKOTA QUARTERLY (II), University of North Dakota, Box 8237, University Station, Grand Forks ND 58202. (701)777-3321. Editor: Robert W. Lewis. Fiction Editor: William Borden. Magazine: 6×9; 200 pages; bond paper; illustrations; photos. Magazine publishing "essays in humanities; some short stories; some poetry." University audience. Quarterly. Estab. 1910. Circ. 600.
Needs: Contemporary, ethnic, experimental, feminist, historical (general), humor/satire and literary. Receives 15-20 unsolicited mss/month. Accepts 2 mss/issue; 8 mss/year. Recently published work by Jerry Bumpus, Dusty Sklar, Daniel Curley; published new writers within the last year. Length: 3,000-4,000 words average. Sometimes critiques rejected mss.
How to Contact: Send complete ms with cover letter. "But they need not be much more than hello; please read this story; I've published (if so, best examples) . . ." SASE. Reports in 3 months. Publishes ms an average of 6-8 months after acceptance. Sample copy $4.
Payment: 5 contributor's copies; 20% discount for extras; year's subscription.
Terms: Acquires one-time rights.
Advice: "We may publish a higher average number of stories in the future—3 rather than 2. Read widely. Write, write; revise, revise."

NORTHEAST JOURNAL (I, II), Box 217, Kingston RI 02881. (401)783-2356. Co-editors: Tina Letcher and Indu Suryanarayan. "A journal concerned with publishing a diverse selection of contemporary literature. The primary focus is on poetry and prose. Sometimes special issues are published, e.g., women's, Rhode Island poets." Annual. Estab. 1969 (under name of *Harbinger*). Circ. 600.
Needs: "Quality." Published new writers within the last year. Length: 1,000-3,000 words.
How to Contact: Send complete ms with SASE. Reports in 6 months. Sample copy with 10x12 SAE and $1 postage.
Payment: 1 free author's copy.
Advice: Amount of fiction published has "shrunk, along with our budget. Keep it short."

THE NORTHERN NEW ENGLAND REVIEW (IV), Box 825, Franklin Pierce College, Rindge NH 03461. (603)899-5111. Editor: April Richmond. Magazine: 8½×11; 90 pages; good paper; heavy cover; illustrations and photos. "The *Review* only publishes material from northern New England residents (Maine, New Hampshire and Vermont) or from people with strong ties in the region. We publish quality fiction, poetry, articles and book reviews. For people who identify with the northern New England lifestyle. Also, for those who are deeply interested in humanities. A copy is sent to every college library in New England." Annually. Estab. 1973. Circ. 600.
Needs: Confession, contemporary, erotica, ethnic, experimental, fantasy, feminist, historical (general), humor/satire, literary, mainstream, prose, regional, romance, science fiction, translations. "Submissions should have that 'New England' flavor to fit in with the magazine's format. No gay or lesbian fiction or hard-core erotica." Receives 5-10 unsolicited mss/month. Accepts 3 or 4 mss/issue. Published work by Barry Kaplan. Length: 5,000 words minimum; 9,000 words maximum. Occasionally comments on rejected mss.
How to Contact: Send complete ms. Reports in several weeks on queries; several months on mss. SASE for ms. Photocopied submissions OK. Accepts computer printout submissions. Prefers letter-quality. Sample copy $3.50.
Payment: Pays 2 contributor's copies; $3.50 charge for extras.
Terms: Acquires for first rights.
Advice: "Saturate the market with your work. Today's magazine fiction has more pronounced emphasis on the psychological element, chiefly how man reacts to this confusing, changing world. Characters observe society and then undergo intense self-examination. As long as the submission is well written and ties in with our northern New England format in a subtle way, we will consider it. Submissions dealing with the world of academia will also be considered."

THE NORTHERN REVIEW (II, IV), University of Wisconsin-Stevens Point, 018 LRC, Stevens Point WI 54481. (715)346-3568. Editor: Richard Behm. Fiction Editor: Lawrence Watson. Magazine: 7×8½; 48 pages; b&w photos. Semiannually. Estab. 1987. Circ. 1,000.
Needs: Essays, literary, regional. Receives 25 unsolicited fiction mss/month. Accepts 4 mss/issue; 2 mss/year. Publishes ms 6-18 months after acceptance. Recently published work by Jack Driscoll, Nancy Lord, Dinty Moore. Length: 2,000 words average. Publishes short shorts. Sometimes critiques rejected mss.
How to Contact: Send complete ms with cover letter. Reports in 1 month. SASE. Accepts computer printouts. Sample copy $4.
Payment: Pays in contributor's copies.

NORTHLAND QUARTERLY (II,IV), Northland Quarterly Publications, Inc. Suite 412, 51 E. 4th St., Winona MN 55987. (507)452-3686. Editor: Jody Wallace. Magazine: 5×8; approx. 100-125 pages; 60 lb offset paper; 10 pt cover stock; b&w illustrations; line drawings; cover photos. "Contemporary writing for discriminating reader. Short fiction, poetry, commentary and reviews. International publication, with emphasis on writers in upper-tier states and Canada. *Quarterly* features politically oriented writings, as well as regional writers and contemporary fiction from throughout US." Quarterly. Estab. 1987.
Needs: Condensed/excerpted novel, contemporary, feminist, literary, mainstream, regional, romance, serialized novel, progressive issues, political fiction. No religious, young romance. Receives 20-40 mss/month. Accepts 3-5 mss/issue. Publishes ms within 3-6 months of acceptance. Published work by Robert Flaum, Marcella Taylor, Robert Funge. Length: 1,500 words minimum; 4,000 words maximum. Publishes short shorts. Length: 300 words minimum. Sometimes critiques rejected mss and recommends other markets.
How to Contact: Query first, query with clips of published work or send complete ms with cover letter, which should include "general description of work, genre. Other places submitted, if any." Reports on queries in 2-3 weeks; in 3-4 weeks on mss. SASE. Simultaneous, photocopied and some reprint submissions OK. Accepts computer printout submissions. Accepts electronic submissions via disk. Sample copy for $4, 5×8 SAE and 4 first class stamps. Fiction guidelines for #10 SAE and 1 first class stamp.

Payment: Pays in contributor's copies.
Terms: Sends galleys to author if requested. Sponsors awards for fiction and poetry writers. "Write for information."
Advice: Looks for "contemporary, adult fiction of high quality. We adopt an unprejudiced, open attitude for all manuscripts submitted, and have published world-class writers as well as beginners."

"We felt that this illustration was well-suited to the thematic content of this issue of the* Northland Quarterly, *one that was devoted to relationships," says editor Jody Wallace of the cover illustration, titled "Pas de Deux." Award-winning artist James Namio is the illustrator.

The Northland Quarterly
poetry, prose, and commentary
"Pas de Deux"
The Relationship Dance

NORTHWEST REVIEW (II), 369 PLC, University of Oregon, Eugene OR 97403. (503)686-3957. Editor: John Witte. Fiction Editor: Cecelia Hagen.Magazine: 6×9; 140-160 pages; coated paper; high quality cover stock; illustrations; photos. "A general literary review featuring poems, stories, essays and reviews, circulated nationally and internationally. For a literate audience in avant-garde as well as traditional literary forms; interested in the important younger writers who have not yet achieved their readership." Published 3 times/year. Estab. 1957. Circ. 1,200.
Needs: Literary, contemporary, feminist, translations and experimental. Accepts 5-10 mss/issue, 20-30 mss/year. Receives approximately 80-100 unsolicited fiction mss each month. Recently published work by Jerry Bumpus, Susan Stark, Charles Marvin. Published new writers within the last year. Length: "Mss longer than 40 pages are at a disadvantage." Critiques rejected mss when there is time. Sometimes recommends other markets.
How to Contact: Send complete ms with SASE. "No simultaneous submissions are considered." Accepts computer printout submissions; prefers letter-quality. Reports in 3-4 months. Sample copy $3.
Payment: 3 free author's copies. 40% discount.
Terms: Acquires first rights.
Advice: "Persist. Copy should be clean, double-spaced, with generous margins. Careful proofing for spelling and grammar errors will reduce slowing of editorial process." Mss are rejected because of "unconvincing characters, overblown language, melodramatic plot, poor execution."

NOTEBOOK: A LITTLE MAGAZINE (II, IV), Esoterica Press, Box 170, Barstow CA 92312-0170. Editor: Ms. Yoly Zentella. Magazine: 5½×8½; 100 pages; bond paper; 90 lb cover stock; illustrations. "Accepting fiction and nonfiction. *Notebook*'s emphasis is on history, culture, art and literary critique and travel pieces. For ages 25-50, educated, some academia." Semiannually. Publishes special ethnic issues, e.g. Native American, Pacific, Asian. Estab. 1985. Circ. 100, "including many libraries."
Needs: Ethnic, (focusing especially on Chicano and Latino American pieces in English and Spanish), historical (Latino American, European and Muslim), humor/satire, literary, regional. "One yearly issue featured exclusively Chicano and Latino American writers, and we need black-American writers." Absolutely no explicit sex or obscenities accepted. Receives approximately 20-25 unsolicited fiction mss/month. Published work by Carmen M. Pursifull, Gabriela Cerda, Barbara Sheen; published

new writers within the last year. Length: 2,000 words average; 2,500 words maximum. Sometimes critiques rejected mss.
How to Contact: Send complete ms with cover letter and short biography. Reports in 2 weeks on queries; 1-2 months on mss. Always SASE for ms and correspondence. Accepts computer printouts. Sample copy $5. Make checks payable to Yoly Zentella. Fiction guidelines for #10 SAE and 1 first class stamp.
Payment: 1 free contributor's copy, charges for extras.
Terms: Acquires first North American serial rights. "Rights revert to author upon publication."
Advice: "We are now planning more fiction in our issues and less poetry. We are also considering novellas for publication, appearing exclusively in one issue." Planning an issue dealing exclusively with the African influence on the American (North and South) continents.

NOW & THEN (IV), Center for Appalachian Studies and Services, East Tennessee State University, Box 19180A, Johnson City TN 37614-0002. (615)929-5348. Editor: Pat Arnow. Magazine: 8½×11; 36-52 pages; coated paper and cover stock; illustrations; photographs. Publication focuses on Appalachian culture, present and past. Readers are mostly people in the region involved with Appalachian issues, literature, education." 3 issues/year. Estab. 1984. Circ. 880.
Needs: Ethnic, literary, regional, serialized/excerpted novel, prose poem, spiritual and sports. "Absolutely has to relate to Appalachian theme. Can be about adjustment to new environment, themes of leaving and returning, for instance. Nothing unrelated to region." Accepts 2-3 mss/issue. Publishes ms 3-4 months after acceptance. Recently published work by Gurney Norman, Lance Olsen, George Ella Lyon; published new writers within the last year. Length: 3,000 words maximum. Publishes short shorts.
How to Contact: Send complete ms with cover letter. Reports in 1 month. Include "information we can use for contributer's note." SASE. Simultaneous and photocopied submissions OK. Accepts computer printout submissions. Sample copy $3.50.
Payment: Pays up to $50 per story, contributor's copies, one year subscription.
Terms: Buys first-time rights.
Advice: "We're emphasizing Appalachian culture, which is not often appreciated because analysts are so busy looking at the trouble of the region. We're doing theme issues. Beware of stereotypes. In a regional publication like this one we get lots of them, both good guys and bad guys: salt of the earth to poor white trash. Sometimes we get letters that offer to let us polish up the story. We prefer the author does that him/herself." Send for list of upcoming themes.

NRG (II), Skydog Press, 6735 SE 78th, Portland OR 97206. Editor: Dan Raphael. Magazine/tabloid: 11×17; 20 pages; electrobrite paper; illustrations; photos. For the "educated, creative, curious." Theme is "open-ended, energized, non-linear emphasis on language and sounds"; material is "spacial, abstract, experimental." Semiannually. Estab. 1976. Circ. 1,000.
Needs: Contemporary, experimental, literary and prose poem. Receives 8 unsolicited mss/month. Accepts 6 mss/issue; 11 mss/year. Recently published work by Carles Brownson, Willie Smith, Virginia Lewis. Length: 1,000 words average; 3,000 words maximum. Occasionally critiques rejected mss.
How to Contact: Send complete ms with SASE and cover letter stating where you learned of magazine; list of 3-5 previous publications. See copy of magazine. Reports in 1 month on mss. Simultaneous and photocopied submissions OK. Accepts computer printout submissions. Publishes ms an average of 1 year after acceptance. Sample copy $1.50. "Best guideline is sample copy."
Payment: Pays in free contributor's copies only, ½ cover price charge for extras.
Terms: Acquires one-time rights.
Advice: "I'm trying to get more fiction, but am strict in my editorial bias. I don't want it to add up or be purely representational. Energy must abound in the language, or the spaces conjured. Forget what you were taught. Let the story tell you."

‡NUCLEAR FICTION (II,V), Suite 104-722, 5521 Greenville Ave., Dallas TX 75206. (214)368-5123. Editor: Brian Martin. Magazine. "An online monthly sci-fi, fantasy, horror magazine available free of charge to anyone with a computer and a modem. A printed version is available to subscribers." Estab. 1988.
Needs: Fantasy, horror and science fiction. Length: 500 words preferred.
How to Contact: Send complete ms with cover letter or upload in plain ASCII text files. Reports in 1 month if submissions mailed, 2 weeks if uploaded. Sample copy $2.
Payment: ½¢/word.
Terms: Pays on acceptance.

OAK SQUARE (II), The Short Fiction Quarterly, Oak Square Publications, Box 1238, Allston MA 02134. (617)782-5669. Publisher: Philip Borenstein. Fiction Editor: Anne E. Pluto. Magazine: 7×8½; 32-76 pages; 60 lb offset paper; card cover stock; illustrations and photographs. "*Oak Square* is a magazine of short fiction. We look for original well crafted stories by new and emerging writers. We also publish interviews, essays (non-academic, non-political), and a *small* amount of poetry." Quarterly. Estab. 1985. Circ. 500.

Needs: Contemporary, erotica, ethnic, experimental, humor/satire, literary, mainstream, prose poem, regional, serialized/excerpted novel, translations, western. No religious/inspirational, children's stories, mysteries, romances. Receives 50 unsolicited fiction mss/month. Accepts 4-10 mss/issue; 16-24 mss/year. Reads fiction January-June. Publishes ms an average of 6 months to 1 year after acceptance. Length: 2,500 words average; 4,500 words maximum. Publishes short shorts. Sometimes critiques rejected mss; recommends other markets.

How to Contact: Send complete ms with cover letter, including "publication history if any. General comments. Send us your current phone number and address—update us when you move." Reports in 2 week on queries; 3 months on mss. SASE. "We read fiction from January-June." Simultaneous submissions OK. Accepts computer printout submissions. Accepts electronic submissions via "Macintosh 3½ disk—MacWrite or Text only." Sample copy $3.50; fiction guidelines free.

Payment: Pays contributor's copies.

Terms: Acquires one-time rights. Sends pre-publication galleys to author when possible.

Advice: "Although we all hold regular '9 to 5' jobs, we are all involved in fiction, either as readers or writers. We are always looking to see 'what else is out there.' We are particularly interested in the work of other '9 to 5'ers. Write about what you know—start within yourself and work outward. Don't be pretentious. Respect your readers."

OBSIDIAN II: BLACK LITERATURE IN REVIEW (II, IV), Dept. of English, North Carolina State University, Raleigh NC 27695-8105. (919)737-3870. Editor: Gerald Barrax. Fiction Editor: Linda Beatrice Brown. Magazine: 6×9; approx. 130 pages. "Creative works in English by Black writers, scholarly critical studies by all writers on Black literature in English." Published 3 times/year (spring, summer and winter). Estab. 1975. Circ. 500.

Needs: Ethnic (pan-African), feminist. No poetry, fiction or drama mss not written by Black writers. Accepts 7-9 mss/year. Published new writers within the last year. Length: 1,500-10,000 words.

How to Contact: Send complete ms in duplicate with SASE. Reports in 3 months. Publishes ms an average of 4-6 months after acceptance. Sample copy $5.

Payment: Pays in contributor's copies.

Terms: Acquires one-time rights. Sponsors contests occasionally; guidelines published in magazine.

THE OHIO REVIEW (II), 209C Ellis Hall, Ohio University, Athens OH 45701-2979. (614)593-1900. Editor: Wayne Dodd. Magazine: 6×9; 144 pages; illustrations on cover. "We attempt to publish the best poetry and fiction written today. For a mainly literary audience." Triannually. Estab. 1971. Circ. 2,000.

Needs: Contemporary, experimental, literary. "We lean toward contemporary on all subjects." Receives 150-200 unsolicited fiction mss/month. Accepts 3 mss/issue. Does not read mss June 1-August 31. Publishes ms 6 months after acceptance. Agented fiction: 1%. Sometimes critiques rejected mss and/or recommends other markets.

How to Contact: Query first or send complete ms with cover letter. Reports in 6 weeks. SASE. Photocopied submissions OK. Accepts computer printouts. Sample copy $4.25. Fiction guidelines free for #10 SASE.

Payment: Pays $5/page, free subscription to magazine, 2 contributor's copies.

Terms: Pays on publication for first North American serial rights. Sends galleys to author.

Advice: "We feel the short story is an important part of the contemporary writing field and value it highly. Read a copy of our publication to see if your fiction is of the same quality. So often people send us work that simply doesn't fit our needs."

OLD HICKORY REVIEW (II), Jackson Writers Group, Box 1178, Jackson TN 38302. (901)424-3277. Editor: Edna Lackie. Fiction editor: Dorothy Stanfill. Magazine: 8½×11; approx. 90 pages. "Usually two short stories and 75-80 poems—nothing obscene or in poor taste. For a family audience." Semiannually. Plans special fiction issue. Estab. 1969. Circ. 300.

Needs: Contemporary, experimental, fantasy, literary, mainstream. Receives 4-5 unsolicited fiction mss/month. Accepts 2 mss/issue; 4 mss/year. Publishes ms no more than 3-4 months after acceptance. Length: 2,500-3,000 words. Publishes short shorts. Sometimes critiques rejected mss and recommends other markets.

How to Contact: Send complete ms with cover letter, which should include "credits." Reports on queries in 2-3 weeks; on mss in 1-2 months. SASE. Photocopied submissions OK. Accepts computer printouts. Sample copy $1 plus 90¢ postage. Fiction guidelines free for SAE.

Payment: Pays in contributor's copies; charge for extras. Sponsors contests for fiction writers, "advertised in literary magazine and with flyers."
Advice: "We are tired of war, nursing homes, abused children, etc. We are looking for things which are more entertaining. No pornographic fiction, no vile language. Our publication goes into schools, libraries, etc."

THE OLD RED KIMONO (II), Box 1864, Rome GA 30163. (404)295-6312. Editors: Jo Anne Starnes and Jonathan Hershey. Magazine: 8×11; 65-70 pages; white offset paper; 10 pt. board cover stock. Annually. Estab. 1974. Circ. 1,000.
Needs: Literary. "We will consider good fiction regardless of category." Receives 20-30 mss/month. Buys 2-4 mss/issue. Does not read mss April-September. "Issue out in May every year." Published work by Christopher Woods, Hubert Whitlow, Jeanne Cunningham. Length: 4,000-5,000 words preferred; 7,000 words maximum. Publishes short shorts. "We prefer short fiction."
How to Contact: Send complete ms with cover letter. Reports in 2 weeks on queries; 4-5 weeks on mss. SASE. Photocopied submissions OK. Accepts computer printout submissions. Sample copy for $2, 8×11 SAE and 4 first class stamps. Fiction guidelines for #10 SAE and 1 first class stamp.
Payment: Pays in contributor's copies.
Terms: Acquires first rights.

ON THE EDGE, 29 Concord Ave., No. 603, Cambridge MA 02138. Editor: Cathryn McIntyre.
Needs: Short-short fiction (500-2,500 words), micro-fiction (100 words or less). Subject matter can vary but should have some contemporary relevance. Also poetry, essays, interviews and art.
How to Contact: Send complete ms. "Cover letters are not necessary and those packed with credentials are discouraged. We're only interested in whether or not the work submitted is right for *On the Edge*."
Payment: Pays 2 contributor's copies.
Terms: All rights revert to author.
Advice: "*On the Edge* is open minded. We are open to all subjects that are presented in a creative, imaginative and intelligent way and show some relevance to contemporary life. Feel free to experiment, but don't overdo it. We're 'On' the Edge, not 'Over' it. Comments on rejections are rare. We are not comfortable assessing literary merits and therefore don't do it. A rejection from *On the Edge* means only that your work is not right for us, nothing more. New writers are greatly encouraged!"

OPEN MAGAZINE (II), Suite 21, 215 North Ave. W., Westfield NJ 07090. (201)249-0280. Editor: Greg Ruggiero. Fiction Editors: Editorial Board of three. Magazine: 8½×11; 50 pages; quality gloss paper; 60 lb cover stock; many illustrations and photographs. "*Open Magazine* works with uninhibited forms of writing, artwork and photography that inspire change—be they targeted at social processes or the consciousness of the individual. We are constantly restructuring, constantly trying out new ways to connect with our readers, writers and other counter-consensus publications. Verve, innovation, reader confrontation, and socio-political statement are the strengths of material we most joyfully accept." Semiannually. Estab. 1984. Circ. 1,000.
Needs: Experimental. "We are fast to accept work that pioneers form, questions the given, and risks discussing the intimate or proposing the radical. Confrontational or subtle, experimental or direct, we want intelligent work that above all else communicates to people, not to cryptitians and the telepathic. Work exploring feminisim, lesbian/gay experience, minority and third world culture, alternative politics and translations are always welcome." Receives 9-30 unsolicited fiction mss/month. Accepts approx. 6 mss/issue; approx. 12 mss/year. Published work by Barbara Ucko, Richard Royal, Greg Boyd; published new writers within the last year. Length: 200 words minimum; 5,000 words maximum. Publishes short shorts. Recommends other markets.
How to Contact: Send complete ms with cover letter, "details up to you." Reports in 1 week on queries; 1 month on mss. SASE. Simultaneous and photocopied submissions OK. Accepts computer printout submissions, no dot-matrix. Sample copy $5 and #10 SAE with 6 first class stamps. Fiction guidelines for SASE.
Payment: $50: "dependent on grant money"; contributor's copies; charge for extras.
Terms: Acquires one-time rights.
Advice: "*Open Magazine* publishes as an exploratory process directly involved with new modes of openness, perception and resistance. We encourage experimentation, but want to see more work drawing from common symbols and ordinary experience. We are devoted to readers and writers who believe that 'the real issue is not whether two and two make four or whether two and two make five, but whether life advances by people who love words or by people who love living.' "

OREGON EAST (II, IV), Hoke College Center, EOSC, La Grande OR 97850. (503)963-1787. Editor: Angela Dierdorff. Magazine: 6×9; 80 pages; illustrations and photographs. "*Oregon East* prefers fiction about the Northwest. The majority of our issues go to the students of Eastern Oregon State

College; staff, faculty and community members receive them also, and numerous high school and college libraries." Annually. Estab. 1950. Circ. 900.

Needs: Humor/satire, literary, prose poem, regional, translations. No juvenile/children's fiction. Receives 20 unsolicited mss/month. Accepts 3-6 mss/issue. Does not read April to August. Publishes ms an average of 5 months after acceptance. Recently published work by Ursula LeGuin, Madeline de Trees and George Venn. Published new writers within the last year. Length: 2,000 words average; 3,000 words maximum. Publishes short shorts. Sometimes critiques rejected mss.

How to Contact: Send complete ms with cover letter which should include name, address, brief bio. Reports in 1 week on queries; 3 months on mss. SASE. Photocopied submissions OK. Accepts computer printout submissions, no dot-matrix. Sample copy $5; fiction guidelines for #10 SASE.

Payment: 2 contributor's copies.

Terms: Rights revert to author.

Advice: "Follow our guidelines please! Keep trying: we have limited space because we must publish 50% on-campus material. *Oregon East* has been around for almost 40 years, and it has always strived to represent the Northwest's great writers and artists, as well as several from around the world."

OTHER VOICES (II), 820 Ridge Rd., Highland Park IL 60035. (312)831-4684. Editors: Dolores Weinberg and Lois Hauselman. Magazine: 5⅞×9; 168-205 pages; 60 lb paper; coated cover stock; occasional photos. "Original, fresh, diverse stories and novel excerpts" for literate adults. Semiannually. Estab. 1985. Circ. 1,500.

Needs: Contemporary, experimental, humor/satire, literary, excerpted novel. No taboos, except ineptitude and murkiness. No fantasy, horror, juvenile, psychic/occult. Receives 45 unsolicited fiction mss/month. Accepts 20-23 mss/issue. Publishes ms approx. 3-6 months after acceptance. Agented fiction: 40%. Published work by Barbara Lefcowitz, Susan B. Weston; published new writers within the last year. Length: 4,000 words average; 5,000 words maximum. Also publishes short shorts "if paired together" of 1,000 words. Only occasionally critiques rejected mss or recommends other markets.

How to Contact: Send mss with SASE or submit through agent. Cover letters "should be brief and list previous publications. Also, list title of submission. Most beginners' letters try to 'explain' the story—a big mistake." Reports in 10-12 weeks on mss. SASE. Photocopied submissions OK; no simultaneous submissions or reprints. Accepts computer printouts. Sample copy $5.90 (includes postage). Fiction guidelines for #10 SAE and 1 first class stamp.

Payment: Pays in contributor's copies and modest cash gratuity.

Terms: Acquires one-time rights.

Advice: "There are so *few* markets for *quality* fiction! We—by publishing 40-45 stories a year—provide new and established writers a forum for their work. Send us your best voice, your best work, your best best. Don't expect to earn a living at it—no matter how talented."

OTHER WORLDS (II), Science Fiction-Science Fantasy, Gryphon Publications, Box 209, Brooklyn NY 11228. Editor: Gary Lovisi. Magazine: 5×8; 40-60 pages; offset paper; card/color cover; illustrations and photographs. "Adventure—or action-oriented SF—stories that are fun to read." Annually. Estab. 1988. Circ. 300.

Needs: Science fiction. No high fantasy, sword and sorcery. Receives 10 unsolicited mss/month. Buys 4-8 mss/issue. Publishes ms 1-1½ years (usually) after acceptance. Length: 3,000 words preferred; 2,000 words minimum; 5,000 words maximum. Publishes short shorts. Length: 500-1,000 words. Sometimes critiques rejected mss and recommends other markets.

How to Contact: Send complete ms with cover letter. Reports in 2 weeks on queries; 1 month on mss. SASE. Photocopied submissions OK. Accepts computer printout submissions. Sample copy for $4. Free fiction guidelines.

Payment: Pays in contributor's copies.

Terms: Acquires first North American serial rights. Copyright reverts to author.

OUROBOROS (II), 3912 24th St., Rock Island IL 61201-6223. Editor and Publisher: Erskine Carter. Magazine: 6×9; 76 pages; 60 lb offset paper; 80 lb cover; b&w illustrations. "We publish fiction (short stories), poetry and art for thoughtful readers." Semiannually. Estab. 1985. Circ. 400.

Needs: Adventure, contemporary, experimental, fantasy, historical (general), horror, humor/satire, literary, mainstream, psychic/supernatural/occult, science fiction, suspense/mystery. "We are mainly interested in stories about people, in situations of conflict or struggle. We want to see *real* characters at odds with others, themselves, their universe. No racist/right-wing/anti-minority material." Receives 40-50 unsolicited mss/month. Accepts 8-10 mss/issue; 32-40 mss/year. Publishes ms 3 months to 1 year after acceptance. Recently published work by T.B. Ward, W. Sheidley, T. Angle; published new writers within the last year. Length: 2,500 words average; 3,500 words maximum. Publishes short shorts. Length: 500 words. Sometimes critiques rejected mss and recommends other markets.

How to Contact: Request guidelines and a sample copy. Reports in 2 weeks. SASE. Photocopied and reprint submissions OK. Accepts computer printout submissions. Sample copy of current issue for $4.50. Back issues available.
Payment: Pays in contributor's copies.
Terms: Rights revert to author. Sends galleys to author. "Cash prizes are awarded on basis of reader's poll."
Advice: "The beginning writer *can* break in here and learn valuable lessons about writing and publishing. Purchase a sample copy, write something you think will grab us, then submit. Get to know the markets. Don't waste time, energy and postage without researching."

OWLFLIGHT (I, IV), Magazine of Science Fiction and Fantasy, Unique Graphics, 1025 55th St., Oakland CA 94608. (415)655-3024. Editor: Millea Kenin. Magazine: 8½×11; 64-80 pages; 60 lb stock; b&w, line and half tone illustrations, and b&w photos. Magazine publishes "the full range of the science fiction/fantasy genre, for readers familiar with sf/fantasy." Irregularly published. Estab. 1980. Circ. 1,500.
Needs: Fantasy, science fiction. No horror. "We do not want to see anything *not* sf or fantasy, or anything racist, sexist or pro-war." Receives 100-200 unsolicited mss/month. Buys at least 10 mss/issue. Publishes ms up to 2 years after acceptance. Recently published work by Janet Fox, Ardath Mayhar, Eric M. Heidemann; published new writers within the last year. Length: 6,000 words average; 2,500 words minimum; 8,000 words maximum (10 to 32 double-spaced pages—nothing that falls outside these limits will be considered, as different word-counting methods produce different copy-fitting results). Usually briefly critiques rejected mss. Sometimes recommends other markets.
How to Contact: "Never submit mss without querying (with SASE) for guidelines, which tell what categories are open or overstocked. Cover letter should include a brief background of the writer, but not a long credit list nor a description of an enclosed story." Reports in 1 week on requested guidelines; 2-6 weeks on mss. SASE. Simultaneous, photocopied and reprint submissions OK. State whether ms is simultaneous submission. Accepts computer printout submissions, dot-matrix only if truly near letter quality. Sample copy $2.50; check must be payable to Unique Graphics. Fiction guidelines free with sample order; otherwise for #10 SAE and 45¢ postage.
Payment: Pays 1¢/word plus 3 free contributor's copies, charge for extras—½ cover price.
Terms: Pays on acceptance for first North American serial rights or one-time rights. If total at 1¢/word is under $10, it is paid on acceptance; if over $10, a $10 deposit is paid on acceptance with the balance paid on publication.
Advice: "I recommend the top-down method: Send a story first to the biggest circulation, highest paying publication that is a relevant market. If it doesn't get picked out of the slush pile, send it to the relevant newsstand magazines, or original anthologies stated for commercial publicaton. If it still hasn't been accepted, send it to the small press. That's better than sticking it in a drawer. We'd love to see experimental work that stretches the limits of the genre, but not work that is outside it or work to which the sf elements are irrelevant."

OXFORD MAGAZINE (II), Bachelor Hall, Miami University, Oxford OH 45056. (513)529-5269. Editors: Michelle Fredette and Karen Mockler. Magazine: 6×9; 85-100 pages; illustrations. Biannually. Estab. 1985. Circ. 500-1,000.
Needs: Ethnic, experimental, feminist, gay, humor/satire, lesbian, literary, translations. Receives 50-60 unsolicited mss/month. Does not read mss May through August. Publishes ms about 3 months after acceptance. Recently published work by Alberto Ríos, Diane Wakoski and James Purdy; published new writers within the last year. Length: 2,000-3,000 words average; 4,000 words maximum. Publishes short shorts.
How to Contact: Send complete ms with cover letter, which should include a short bio or interesting information. Reports in 3-4 months on mss. SASE. Photocopied submissions OK. Accepts computer printout submissions. Sample copy for $4, 10×12 SAE and 4 first class stamps.
Payment: Pays in contributor's copies and a small honorarium.
Terms: Acquires one-time rights.
Advice: "We look for writing that makes sense: fiction that makes you put down your spoon and reread the page until your soup goes cold, poems that speak to the reader and send us hugging our dog."

‡OYEZ REVIEW (I, II), 430 S. Michigan Ave., Chicago IL 60605. (312)341-2017. Editor: Patty Magierski. Magazine: 5½×8½; 91 pages; b&w camera ready illustrations and photos. Looking for "what is fresh and good" for Chicago audience. Annually. Estab. 1967. Circ. 500.

Needs: Contemporary, experimental, feminist, literary, poetry and regional. Accepts 2-5 mss/issue. Length: "about 10 pages, double-spaced."
How to Contact: Send complete ms with SASE. Reports in 3 months on ms. Photocopied submissions OK. Sample copy $4.
Payment: 5 contributor's copies.
Terms: Acquires one-time rights.
Advice: "*Oyez* encourages imaginative fiction, good dialogue, good characterization. Because our magazine is small and we have more poetry than fiction, we need/want *good*, but short fiction. We are interested in seeing what all writers can do – not just previously published writers. Since our staff changes from year to year, so does the philosophy of the publication – this year we are trying to delve into the collective American unconscious!"

P.I. MAGAZINE (II), Fact and Fiction about the world of private investigators, 755 Bronx, Toledo OH 43609. (419)382-0967. Editor: Bob Mackowiak. Magazine: 8½×11; about 50 pages; coated white paper and cover; illustrations and photographs. "All about private eyes: personality profiles and stories about professional investigators; original fiction; books, movie, video, games, etc. Audience includes private eye and mystery fans." Quarterly. Estab. 1988. Circ. 500
Needs: Adventure, humor/satire, suspense/mystery. "Principal character must be a private detective – not a police detective, spy or school teacher who solves murders on the side. No explicit sex." Buys 4-6 mss/issue. Publishes ms 2-3 months after acceptance. Recently published work by Curtis Fischer; column by Bill Palmer. Length: 2,500 words preferred; 500 words minimum; 5,000 words maximum. Publishes short shorts. Sometimes critiques rejected ms and recommends other markets if possible.
How to Contact: Send complete ms with cover letter. Reports in 4 months. SASE. Simultaneous and photocopied submissions OK. Accepts computer printout submissions. Single copy for $3.75."
Payment: Pays $15 minimum; $25 for fiction; contributor's copies; charge for extras.
Terms: Pays on publication. Acquires one-time rights.
Advice: "Private eye stories do not need to be murder mysteries, and they do not need to start with a client walking into the detective's run-down office."

THE P.U.N. (PLAY ON WORDS) (II), The Silly Club and Michael Rayner, Box 536-583, Orlando FL 32853. (407)898-0463. Editor: Danno Sullivan. Newsletter: 8 pages; cartoons. "All polite humor. Polite, meaning no foul language, sex, etc. As a joke, something like 'Child Abuse with Dr. Seuss' is OK. We have an intelligent readership. They don't mind puzzling a bit to get the joke, but they also enjoy plain silliness." Published bimonthly. Estab. 1982. Circ. 400.
Needs: Humor/satire. Receives 20 unsolicited fiction mss/month. Accepts 1-3 mss/issue; 10-20 mss/year. Publishes ms "usually next issue" after acceptance. Length: short shorts, 1 page or less. Sometimes critiques rejected mss.
How to Contact: Send complete ms with cover letter. Reports in 2-3 weeks. SASE. Simultaneous, photocopied and reprint submissions OK. Accepts computer printouts. Sample copy for #10 SASE and $1.
Payment: Pays $1 minimum, $15 maximum; contributor's copies.
Terms: Pays on acceptance for one-time rights.
Advice: "Keep it short. Keep it obviously (even if it's subtle) funny. Above all, don't write like Erma Bombeck. We get a lot of 'cute' material – *Readers Digest*-style, which is not for us. We like short *articles*, as opposed to stories. Fiction presented as fact."

‡PACIFIC REVIEW (II), Dept. of English and Comparative Lit., San Diego State University, San Diego CA 92182-0295. Contact: Editor. Magazine: 6×9; 100-150 pages; book stock paper; paper back, extra heavy cover stock; illustrations, photos. "There is no designated theme. We publish high-quality fiction, poetry, and familiar essays: academic work meant for, but not restricted to, an academic audience." Biannually. Estab. 1973. Circ. 1,000.
Needs: "We do not restrict or limit our fiction in any way other than quality. We are interested in all fiction, from the very traditional to the highly experimental. Acceptance is determined by the quality of submissions." Does not read June-August. Published new writers within the last year. Publishes short shorts. Length: 4,000 words max.
How to Contact: Send original ms with SASE. Reports in 2-4 months on mss. Sample copy $6.
Payment: 1 author's copy.
Terms: "First serial rights are *Pacific Review's*. All other rights revert to author."

PAINTED BRIDE QUARTERLY (II), Painted Bride Art Center, 230 Vine St., Philadelphia PA 19106. (215)925-9914. Literary magazine: 6×9; 96-100 pages; illustrations; photos. Quarterly. Estab. 1975. Circ. 1,000.

Needs: Contemporary, ethnic, experimental, feminist, gay, lesbian, literary, prose poem and translations. Receives 10 unsolicited mss/week. Accepts 2 mss/issue; 8 mss/year. Published new writers within the last year. Length: 3,000 words average; 5,000 words maximum. Publishes short shorts. Occasionally critiques rejected mss.
How to Contact: Send complete ms. Reports in 3 weeks-3 months. SASE. Accepts computer printout submissions. Prefers letter-quality. Sample copy $5.
Payment: 2 contributor's copies, 1 year free subscription, 50% off additional copies.
Terms: Acquires first North American serial rights.
Advice: "We want quality in whatever—we hold experimental work to as strict standards as anything else. Many of our readers write fiction; most of them enjoy a good reading. We hope to be an outlet for quality. A good story gives, first, enjoyment to the reader. We've seen a good many of them lately, and we've published the best of them."

PANDORA (I), 2844 Grayson, Ferndale MI 48220. Editor: Meg Mac Donald. Magazine: 5½×8½; 48+ pages; offset paper; heavyweight offset cover stock; b&w illustrations. Magazine for science fiction and fantasy readers. Published 4 times/year. Estab. 1978. Circ. 500.
Needs: Fantasy, science fiction and sword and sorcery. "Nothing X-rated; no horror; no gratuitous violence or sex. Unless the author created the universe, she/he should not send us stories in that universe." Receives 200 unsolicited fiction mss/month. Buys 4-6 mss/issue, 20 mss/year. Publishes ms 6 months-1 year after acceptance. Recently published work by Heather Gladney, T. Jackson King, Ted Reynolds; published many new writers within the last year. Length: 3,000 words average; 4,000 words maximum (occasional stories may be longer). Always critiques rejected mss. Sometimes recommends other markets.
How to Contact: Send complete ms with cover letter, which should include relevant publication history. Reports in 2 weeks on queries; 2-3 months on mss. Photocopied and previously published submissions OK. Accepts computer printout submissions. Prefers letter-quality. Sample copy $3.50. Free fiction guidelines with SASE.
Payment: 1-2¢/word and 1 contributor's copy.
Terms: Pays on publication for first North American serial rights, second rights or one-time rights on previously published mss.
Advice: "Plan to increase amount of fiction published; steering away from horror and fantasy set in mundane or contemporary society. Know your market! Read and study fiction everywhere, but know a given market well before trying to crack it. Write what your heart leads you to write, what moves you, excites you, frightens you. Above all use your gift for words as wisely as you can—don't write to hurt—write to enlighten! Good luck!"

‡THE PANHANDLER (II), A Magazine of Poetry and Fiction, The University of West Florida, English Dept, Pensacola FL 32514. (904)474-2923. Eidtors: Michael Yots and Stanton Millet. Magazine: 6×9; 64 pages; 40 lb paper; 70 lb cover stock. Semiannually. Estab. 1976. Circ. 500.
Needs: Contemporary, ethnic, experimental, humor/satire, literary and mainstream. No Sci Fi, horror, erotica. Plans to publish special fiction or anthology issue in the future. Receives 10 unsolicited mss/month. Accepts 2-4 mss/issue; 8-10 mss/year.Publishes ms 3-8 months after acceptance. Length: 1,500-3,000 words; 2,500 average. Sometimes critiques rejected mss and recommends other markets.
How to Contact: Send complete ms with cover letter. Including writing experience, publications. Reports in 1-4 months. SASE. Simultaneous submissions OK. Sample copy $2. Fiction guidelines for #10 SAE and 1 first class stamp.
Payment: Pays in contributor's copies.
Terms: Acquires first rights.
Advice: "We look for engaging narrative voice. Characters whose concerns are of interest to readers. Real, everyday problems, dilemmas. Clear, efficient narrative style. Manuscript must lead the reader through the story and make him feel on completion that it was worth the trip."

‡THE PAPER BAG (I, II), Box 268805, Chicago IL 60626-8805. (312)285-7972. Editor: Michael H. Brownstein. Magazine: 5½×8½; 25-40 pages; cardboard cover stock; illustrations. Quarterly. Estab. 1988. Circ. 300.
Needs: Adventure contemporary, erotica, ethnic, experimental, fantasy, feminist, horror, literary, mainstream, prose poem, suspense/mystery and western. Plans to publish special fiction or anthology issue in the future. Receives 10 unsolicited mss/month. Accepts 2-4 mss/issue; 36-60 mss/year. Publishes mss 3 months to 1 year after acceptance. Under 500 words preferred; 500 words maximum. "Has to be under 500 words." Sometimes critiques rejected mss and recommends other markets.
How to Contact: Send complete ms with cover letter. "Include brief bio for our contributor's page." Reports in 1 week on queries; 1 week to 3 months on mss. SASE. Photocopied submission OK. Sample copy $2.50. Fiction guidelines for SAE and 1 first class stamp.

Payment: Pays in contributor's copies.
Terms: Acquires first rights. Sometimes sends pre-publication galleys to the author.

PAPER RADIO (I,II), Loose Milk Review, Box 85302, Seattle WA 98145. Editors: N.S. Kvern and Dagmar Howard. Magazine: 8½×11; 28-36 pages; photocopied paper and cover; illustrations; high contrast b&w photographs. "We're open to anything, but it has to be short—usually less than 2,500 words, and only one or two per issue." Readers are "mostly people who are interested in avant garde, mail art, Xerox art, political, bizarre, surrealism, punk, literary/experimental writing and computers." Published 3 times/year. Estab. 1986. Circ. 500.
Needs: Erotica, experimental, fantasy, literary, prose poem, science fiction. Receives 10 unsolicited fiction mss/month. Accepts 4-5 mss/issue; 12-15 mss/year. Publishes ms an average of 2-3 months after acceptance. Length: 2,000 words average; 3,500 words maximum. Publishes short shorts. Sometimes critiques rejected mss.
How to Contact: Send complete ms with cover letter. "some autobiographical information is helpful—one or two paragraphs—and I like to know where they hear about our magazine." Reports in 3 weeks. SASE. Simultaneous or photocopied submissions OK. Accepts computer printout submissions. Sample copy $3.
Payment: Contributor's copies.
Terms: Acquires first rights, "artist can publish material elsewhere simultaneously."
Advice: "We are devoted to the cause of experimentation and literature and we like a wide variety of fiction. Best to see a sample copy. Our publication is orderly in its chaos, wild and untameable in its order."

THE PARIS REVIEW (II), 541 E. 72nd St., New York NY 10021. (718)539-7085. Editor: George A. Plimpton. Managing Editor: James Linville. Magazine: 5¼×8½; about 240 pages; 50 lb paper; 10 pt Cls cover stock; illustrations and photographs. "Fiction and poetry of superlative quality, whatever the genre, style or mode. Our contributors include prominent, as well as little-known and previously unpublished writers. Recent issues have included the work of Raymond Carver, Elizabeth Tallent, Rick Bass, John Koethe, Sharon Olds, Derek Walcott, Carolyn Kizer, Tess Gallagher, Peter Handke, Denis Johnson, Bobbie Ann Mason, Harold Brodkey, Joseph Brodsky, John Updike, Andre Dubus, Galway Kinnell, E.L. Doctorow and Philip Levine. 'The Art of Fiction' interview series includes important contemporary writers discussing their own work and the craft of writing." Quarterly.
Needs: Committed work of boldness and originality, combining excellence of form and voice. Receives several hundred unsolicited fiction mss each month. Published new writers within the last year. No preferred length. Also publishes short shorts.
How to Contact: Send complete ms with SASE. Reports in 6-8 weeks on mss. Sample copy $6.90.
Payment: $100-$500. 2 free author's copies. Regular charge for extras.
Terms: Pays on publication for first North American serial rights. Sends galleys to author.
Advice: "*The Paris Review* has the widest circulation of all the small presses. We are devoted to helping talented, original writers find larger audiences."

PARTING GIFTS (II), 3006 Stonecutter Terrace, Greensboro NC 27405. Editor: Robert Bixby. Magazine: 5×8; 40 pages. "High quality insightful fiction, very brief and on any theme." Semiannual. Plans special fiction issue. Estab. 1988.
Needs: "Brevity is the second most important criterion behind literary quality." Publishes ms within one year of acceptance. Length: 250 words minimum; 1,000 words maximum. Sometimes critiques rejected mss.
How to Contact: Send complete ms with cover letter. Reports in 1 day on queries; in 1-7 days on mss. SASE. Accepts computer printout submissions.
Payment: Pays in contributor's copies.
Terms: Acquires one-time rights.
Advice: Magazine fiction today "seems to celebrate drabness and disconnection. Read the works of Amy Hempel, Jim Harrison, C.K. Williams and Janet Kauffman, all excellent writers who epitomize the writing *Parting Gifts* strives to promote."

PARTISAN REVIEW (II), 236 Bay State Rd., Boston MA 02215. (617)353-4260. Editor: William Phillips. Executive Editor: Edith Kurzweil. Magazine: 6×9; 160 pages; 40 lb paper; 60 lb cover stock. Theme is of world literature and contemporary culture: fiction, essays and poetry with emphasis on the arts and political and social commentary, for the general intellectual public; scholars. Quarterly. Estab. 1934. Circ. 8,000.
Needs: Contemporary, experimental, literary, prose poem, regional and translations. Receives 100 unsolicited fiction mss/month. Buys 2 mss/issue; 8 mss/year. Recently published work by José Donoso, Isaac Bashevis Singer, Doris Lessing; published new writers within the last year. Length: open. Publishes short shorts.

How to Contact: Send complete ms with SASE and cover letter listing past credits. Photocopied submissions OK. Accepts computer printout submissions; prefers letter-quality. Reports in 4 months on mss. Sample copy for $5 and $1 postage.
Payment: Pays $25-200; 1 free contributor's copy.
Terms: Pays on publication for first rights.
Advice: "Please, research the type of fiction we publish. Often we receive manuscripts which are entirely inappropriate for our journal. Sample copies are available and this is a good way to determine audience."

‡PAVOR NOCTURNUS (I, IV), Starbuck Publishing, Suite N, 412 Maverick Dr., Palestine TX 75801. Editor: S.K. King. Magazine: 8½×11; 24-30 pages; 20 lb. paper; "heavy" cover stock; b&w illustrations. "Publishes dark fantasy, horror and psychic/supernatural/occult." Semiannually. Estab. 1989. Circ. about 150.
Needs: Experimental, fantasy, horror, psychic/supernatural/occult and science fiction. No *Star Trek* or *Star Wars* clones. Plans to publish a special fiction issue or an anthology in the future. Receives 12-15 unsolicited mss/month. Accepts 6 mss/issue; 12 mss/year. Publishes ms up to 6 months after acceptance. Recently published work by John Yarbrough, Denise Xavier. Length: 2,000 words average; 100 words minimum; 3,500 words maximum. Publishes short shorts. Length: 100-150 words. Sometimes critiques rejected mss and sometimes recommends other markets.
How to Contact: Send complete ms. Include brief bio. Reports in 2 months on mss. SASE. Simultaneous, photocopied, and reprint submissions OK. Accepts computer printout submissions. Accepts electronic submissions via disk or modem. Sample copy $3.95 and 2 first class stamps. Fiction guidelines for SAE and 1 first class stamp.
Payment: Pays in contributor's copies.
Terms: Acquires first rights or one-time rights. Sends galleys to author. Publication not copyrighted.
Advice: Looks for "something that really sticks in my mind and haunts me for a few days. Characterization is important. I look for something that borders on insanity, yet maintains an anchor in the real world—something to tie it with everyday people in everyday situations. Even a retelling of old tales can fit this category. I am a beginning writer myself and I know what you're going through. I also know that there was a first time for folks such as Kin and Straub."

THE PEGASUS REVIEW (I, IV), Box 134, Flanders NJ 07836. (201)927-0749. Editor: Art Bounds. Magazine: 5½×8½; 6-8 pages; illustrations. "Our magazine is a bimonthly, done entirely in calligraphy, illustrated. Each issue is based on a specific theme for those who appreciate quality in both writing and presentation." Plans expanded issues in 1990. Estab. 1980. Circ. 200.
Needs: Humor/satire, literary, prose poem and religious/inspirational. Themes for 1989: January/February-The 12 months; March/April-Ignorance; May/June-Patriotism; July/August-The sea; September/October-Ghosts; November/December-time. Send "your best and approach themes from any direction except the most obvious." Receives 50 unsolicited mss/month. Accepts 60 mss/year. Recently published work by Nan Sherman, Joan Payne Kincaid, Jeanpaul Ferro; published new writers within the last year. Publishes short shorts 3-3½ pages; 500 words. Themes are subject to change, so query if in doubt. Critiques rejected mss and sometimes recommends other markets.
How to Contact: Send complete ms. SASE "a must." Cover letter with author's background and full name—no initials. Photocopied submissions OK. Accepts computer printout submissions. Simultaneous submissions acceptable, if so advised. Sample copy $1.50. Fiction guidelines for SAE.
Payment: 2 contributor's copies. Occasional book awards.
Terms: Acquires one-time rights.
Advice: "Not only find time to write but make time to write. Continue to read other writers, old and new. Study your markets. Make use of your local public library. Say the usual in a different manner. Be brief. Above all, persevere."

PEMBROKE MAGAZINE (I, II), Box 60, Pembroke State University, Pembroke NC 28372. (919)521-4214, ext. 433. Editor: Shelby Stephenson. Fiction Editor: Stephen Smith. Magazine: 9×10; 225 pages; illustrations; photos. Magazine of poems and stories plus literary essays. Annually. Estab. 1969. Circ. 500.
Needs: Open. Receives 40 unsolicited mss/month. Publishes short shorts. Published work by Fred Chappell, Robert Morgan; published new writers within the last year. Length: open. Occasionally critiques rejected mss and recommends other markets.
How to Contact: Send complete ms. Reports immediately to 3 months. SASE. Accepts computer printout submissions. Prefers letter-quality. Sample copy $3 and 9×10 SAE.
Payment: 1 contributor's copy.
Advice: "Write with an end for *writing*, not publication."

‡PENCIL PRESS QUARTERLY (II), The Southern Writer's Connection, Arrowwood Desktop Publishing, Suite 627, 4524 Curry Ford Rd., Orlando FL 32825. (407)380-7428. Contact: Editor. Magazine: 8½×11; 36-42 pages; glossy paper; 80 lb gloss cover stock. Quarterly. Estab. 1986. Circ. 5,000.

Needs: Humor/satire, literary and mainstream. No horror, erotica. Plan to publish a special fiction or anthology issue in the future. Buys 3 mss/issue; 12-15 mss/year. Publishes ms 3-6 months after acceptance. 2,000-3,000 words; 2,500 averge. Occasionally publishes short shorts. Sometimes critiques rejected mss and recommends other markets.

How to Contact: Query with clips of published work or send complete ms with cover letter. Include Social Security number. Reports in 1 month on queries; 2 months on mss. SASE. Photocopies and reprint submissions OK. Accepts computer printout submissions. Accepts electronic submissions. Sample copy $3.50. Fiction guidelines for 4×9½ SAE and 1 first class stamp.

Payment: Pays $10-50 and contributor's copies.

Terms: Pays on acceptance. Purchases first rights.

PENNSYLVANIA ENGLISH (II), English Department, Penn State University—Erie, Humanities Division, Erie PA 16412. Editor: Dean Baldwin. Fiction Editor: Chris Dubbs. Magazine: 7×8½; 100 pages; 20 lb bond paper; 65 lb matte cover. For "teachers of English in Pennsylvania at the high school and college level." Semiannually. Estab. 1985. Circ. 300.

Needs: Literary, contemporary mainstream. Does not read mss from May to August. Publishes ms an average of 6 months after acceptance. Length: 5,000 words maximum. Publishes short shorts. Sometimes critiques rejected mss.

How to Contact: Send 2 copies of complete ms with cover letter. Reports in 2 months. SASE. Simultaneous and photocopied submissions OK. Accepts dot-matrix computer printouts.

Payment: Pays in contributor's copies.

Terms: Acquires first North American serial rights.

PENNSYLVANIA REVIEW, University of Pittsburgh, 526 C.L./English Dept., Pittsburgh PA 15260. (412)624-0026. Managing Editor: Deborah Pursifull. Magazine: 7×10; 70-100 pages. Magazine of fiction, poetry, nonfiction, interviews, reviews, novel excerpts, long poems for literate audience. Semiannually. Estab. 1985. Circ. 1,000.

Needs: Ethnic, experimental, feminist, gay, humor/satire, lesbian, literary, prose poem, regional, translations. "High quality!" Receives 75 unsolicited fiction mss/month. Accepts 3-5 mss/issue; 6-10 mss/year. Deadlines: Dec. 1 and March 1. Mss not read in summer months. Recently published work by Cynthia Kadohata and Carol Lee Lorenzo; published new writers within the last year. Length: 5,000 maximum words for prose. Comments on rejected mss "rarely and only if we've had some interest."

How to Contact: Send complete ms. Reports in 1 week on queries; 6-8 weeks on ms. SASE for ms. Photocopied submissions OK. Accepts computer printout submissions. Prefers letter-quality. Sample copy $5. Fiction guidelines for #10 SAE and 1 first class stamp.

Payment: $5/page for prose; 1 contributor's copy.

Terms: Pays on publication for first North American serial rights.

Advice: "Don't be discouraged when your work is returned to you. Returns are not necessarily a comment on the quality of the writing. Keep trying."

‡PEOPLENET (IV), "Where People Meet People", Box 897, Levittown NY 11756. (516)579-4043. Editor: Robert Mauro. Newsletter: 8½×11; 12 pages; 20 lb paper; 20 lb cover stock. "Romance stories featuring disabled characters." Quarterly. Estab. 1987. Circ. 200.

Needs: Romance, contemporary and disabled. Main character must be disabled. Accepts 1-2 mss/issue; 4-8 mss/year. Publishes ms up to 2 years after acceptance. Length: 500-1,000 words; 800-1,000 average. Publishes short shorts.

How to Contact: Send complete ms and SASE. Reports in 1 week "*only* if SASE there." Accepts computer printout submissions. Fiction guidelines for #10 SAE and 1 first class stamp.

Payment: Tear sheet.

Terms: Acquires first rights.

Advice: "We are looking for stories of under 1,000 words on romance with a disabled man or woman as the main character. No sob stories or 'super crip' stories. Just realistic romance. No porn. Love, respect, trust, understanding and acceptance are what I want."

PERCEPTIONS (I), 1945 S. 4th W., Missoula MT 59801. (406)543-5875. Editor: Temi Rose. Magazine: 4×5; 20 pages. Publishes "primarily women's perceptions," for readers of "all ages, both sexes." Published 3 times/year. Plans special fiction issue. Estab. 1983. Circ. 100.

Needs: Adventure, condensed/excerpted novel, confession contemporary, experimental, fantasy, feminist, prose poem, psychic/supernatural/occult, religions/inspirational, science fiction, suspense/mystery. Accepts 1 ms/issue. Length: four pages tops. Publishes short shorts. Critiques rejected mss "only if requested."
How to Contact: Query first. Reports in 2-3 weeks on queries; in 1 month on mss. SASE. Simultaneous, photocopied and reprint submissions OK. Accepts computer printout submissions. Accepts electronic submissions via disk or modem. Sample copy for $3. Fiction guidelines free for SAE and 1 first class stamp.
Payment: Pays in contributor's copies. Sponsors awards for fiction writers "only occasionally."

PEREGRINE (II), The Journal of Amherst Writers and Artists, Amherst Writers and Artists, Box 1076, Amherst MA 01004. (413)253-3307. Editor: Gene Zeiger. Magazine: 5×7; 90 pages; sturdy matte white paper; heavier cover stock; perfect bound; illustrations occasionally. "Poetry and prose—short stories, short short stories, and occasionally prose fantasies or reflections that are fiction yet are not stories." Annually.
Needs: "Most accepted pieces tend to be strong on human experience. No specific 'category' requirements. Humor is much appreciated, but it's not necessarily the focus. We don't publish children's/juvenile/'young adult' fiction, and we're not enthusiastic about gory violence, gratuitous sexism or extreme smugness." Receives more than 100 unsolicited fiction mss/month. Accepts 4-8 mss/issue. Publishes ms an average of 3-6 months after acceptance. Recently published work by Doug Anderson, Jean Anderson, Jim Eagan; published new writers within the last year. Length: 1,000-2,500 words preferred. Publishes short shorts. "Short pieces have a better chance of publication." Sometimes critiques rejected mss.
How to Contact: Send complete ms with cover letter, which should include brief biographical note and list of previous publications. Reports in 3-6 months. SASE. Simultaneous and photocopied submissions OK. Accepts computer printout submissions. Sample copy $4.
Payment: Contributor's copies.
Terms: All rights return to writer upon publication. Sponsors contests and awards for fiction writers. "Fiction contests are announced in issues of *Peregrine.* Cash prizes of $50-100 offered. Write for details."
Advice: "*Peregrine* is potentially an excellent place for a beginning fiction writer to send manuscripts. When we have time, we try to respond with at least one sentence of specific comment or encouragement—although we don't always have the time. We publish on a very fine stock, have a cover by a well established artist, and include pieces by experienced, previously published writers. Experiments with very indirect time sequence are often lost on us. We'd rather read a more conventionally narrated story. But this is not a fixed rule at all, and originality counts for a great deal. We advise simultaneous submission of manuscripts because small journals cannot be fast in responding and the writer's predicament is very clear to us. We too, offer our work and wait."

PERMAFROST (II), A Literary Journal, English Dept., University of Alaska, Fairbanks AK 99775. (907)474-7913. Contact: editors. Magazine: 5½×8; 110 pages; good quality paper; b&w illustrations and photos. Magazine of "quality, contemporary fiction, poetry, essays for intelligent readers, small press audiences, writers, educators." Published semiannually. Estab. 1976. Circ. 500.
Needs: Contemporary, ethnic, experimental, feminist, gay, humor/satire, lesbian, literary, prose poem, science fiction. No "commercial, formula writing." Receives 20-30 unsolicited mss/month. Accepts 3-4 mss/issue; 6-8 mss/year. Does not read between April 15 and August 15. Recently published work by Karen Minton; published new writers within the last year. Length: 2,500-5,000 words average; 5,000 words maximum. Also publishes short shorts of 2-10 pages. Rarely critiques rejected mss.
How to Contact: Send complete ms with cover letter. "Prefer simple letter." Reports in 2 months. SASE. Photocopied submissions OK. Accepts computer printout submissions; prefers letter-quality. Sample copy $4.
Payment: Pays 2 contributor's copies.
Terms: All rights to author. Send SASE for guidelines.
Advice: "*Permafrost* is a literary journal; we expect and hope to see your best work. If you write about Alaska, be sure your message is universal in scope and you are comfortable with the setting of your story. We welcome good fiction of all types."

PHOEBE (II), The George Mason Review, George Mason University, 4400 University Dr., Fairfax VA 22030. (703)323-3730. Editor: Ramola Dharmaraj. Fiction Editors: John Hopkins, Steve Amick. Magazine: 6×9; 72 pages; 80 lb quality paper; 0-5 illustrations per issue; 0-10 photographs per issue. "We publish fiction, poetry, photographs, illustrations and some reviews." Quarterly. Estab. 1972. Circ. 3,500.

Needs: Experimental, literary, mainstream, prose poem, regional, serialized/excerpted novel, translations. No romance, western, juvenile, erotica. Receives 20 mss/month. Accepts 5-7 mss/issue; 20-28 mss/year. Does not read mss June-July. Publishes ms 3-6 months after acceptance. Recently published work by Alan Cheuse, Richard Bausch, Paul Milensky. Length: 4,500 words average; 8,000 words maximum. Publishes short shorts. Sometimes comments on rejected mss.
How to Contact: Send complete ms with cover letter. Include "name, address, phone; if and where you've published previously. Brief bio." Reports in 1 week on queries; 6 weeks on mss. SASE. Photocopied submissions OK. Sample copy $3.25. Fiction guidelines for #10 SAE with 1 first class stamp.
Payment: Pays in 4 contributor's copies.
Terms: Acquires one-time rights.
Advice: "*Phoebe* is committed to furthering the arts and particularly to helping new writers of poetry and fiction. Many of our staff are associated with the M.F.A. program in writing at George Mason University. While we are receptive to all kinds of good writing, we particularly appreciate stories that tell stories: clean, honest prose. Studying a recent issue would be helpful."

PIG IRON (II), Box 237, Youngstown OH 44501. (216)783-1269. Editor: Jim Villani. Fiction Editor: Nate Leslie. Magazine. 8½×11; 96 pages; 60 lb offset paper; 85 pt coated cover stock; b&w illustrations; b&w 120 line photographs. "Contemporary literature by new and experimental writers." Annually. Estab. 1975. Circ. 1,000.
Needs: Literary, psychological and labor. No mainstream. Buys 1-15 mss/issue; 2-30 mss/year. Receives approximately 50 unsolicited fiction mss each month. Recently published work by Randall Silvis, Robert Fox and Gerald Haslam. Length: 8,000 words maximum.
How to Contact: Send complete ms with SASE. No simultaneous submissions. Accepts computer printout submissions. Reports in 3 months. Sample copy $3.
Payment: $5/printed page. 2 free author's copies. $3 charge for extras.
Terms: Pays on publication for first North American serial rights.
Advice: "Looking for works that do not ignore psychological development in character and plot/action." Mss are rejected because of "lack of new ideas and approaches. Writers need to work out interesting plot/action and setting/set. Read a lot; read for stylistic innovation. Send SASE for current themes list."

THE PIG PAPER (I, II), Pig Productions, 70 Cotton Dr., Mississauga, Ontario L5G 1Z9 Canada. (416)278-6594. Editor: Gary Pig Gold. Newsletter: 8½×11; 2 pages; 20 lb paper; illustrations and photos. "A study of the 'pop culture,' its past, present and future; its reflection of—and effect on—society." Bimonthly. Estab. 1975. Circ. 1,000.
Needs: Adventure, confession, contemporary, erotica, experimental, fantasy, humor/satire, prose poem, psychic/supernatural/occult, science fiction, spiritual music. "I prefer material of a short (i.e. column) length (due to severe space restrictions), on subjects—or points of view—you'd be unlikely to read about elsewhere. Receives 10 unsolicited fiction mss/month. Accepts 5 mss/issue; 25 mss/year. Published work by Ace Backwords, Rev. Kenneth K. Burke, James Lord; published new writers within the last year. Length: 1,500 words average; 100 words minimum; 10,000 words maximum. Publishes short shorts. "I can serialize a longer piece over several consecutive issues." Sometimes critiques rejected mss or recommends other markets.
How to Contact: Send complete ms with cover letter, which should include "a bit about the writer (i.e. age, surroundings), and *why* they've contacted *The Pig Paper*." Reports in 3 weeks. Simultaneous, photocopied and reprint submissions OK. Accepts computer printouts. Sample copy for 4×9 envelope and 2 first class stamps.
Payment: Pays in contributor's copies.
Terms: Acquires one-time rights. Sends pre-publication galleys to author.
Advice: Optimistic about status of magazine fiction today "because of the ever-growing size of, interaction within, and networking capabilities surrounding the (for lack of a better term) 'small press scene.' With a little research, it'd be next to impossible *not* to find a publication somewhere that would be interested in one's material. And of course, if you simply can't uncover a suitable publication somewhere, you can always start your own. Over the years, I've (proudly) earned the reputation for a being the editor who'll publish anything—eventually. If a writer takes the time, care and trouble to write material, be it fiction or otherwise, and send it to me, odds are I'll get around to publishing it sooner or later, if only out of a sense of appreciation and obligation."

THE PIKESTAFF FORUM (II), Box 127, Normal IL 61761. (309)452-4831. Editors: Robert D. Sutherland, James Scrimgeour, James McGowan and Curtis White. Tabloid: 11½×17½; 40 pages; newsprint paper; illustrations; photos. "*The Pikestaff Forum* is a general literary magazine publishing poetry, prose fiction, drama." Readership: "General literary with a wide circulation in the small press world. Readers are educated (but not academic) and have a taste for excellent serious fiction." Published

irregularly—"whenever we have sufficient quality material to warrant an issue." Estab. 1977. Circ. 1,000.
Needs: Literary and contemporary with a continuing need for good short stories or novel excerpts. "We welcome traditional and experimental works from established and non-established writers. We look for writing that is clear, concise and to the point; contains vivid imagery and sufficient concrete detail; is grounded in lived human experience; contains memorable characters and situations. No confessional self-pity or puffery; self-indulgent first or second drafts; sterile intellectual word games or five-finger exercises or slick formula writing, genre-pieces that do not go beyond their form (westerns, mysteries, gothic, horror, science fiction, swords-and-sorcery fantasy), commercially oriented mass-market stuff, violence for its own sake, racist or sexist material or pornography (sexploitation)." Accepts 1-4 mss/issue. Receives approximately 15-20 unsolicited fiction mss each month. Recently published work by Constance Pierce, Linnea Johnson; published new writers within the last year. Length: from 1 paragraph to 4,000 or 5,000 words. Critiques rejected mss when there is time.
How to Contact: Query. Send complete ms. SASE. Accepts computer printout submissions. Prefers letter-quality. Reports in 3 weeks on queries, 3 months on mss. Publishes ms up to 1 year after acceptance. Sample copy $2.
Payment: 3 free author's copies. Cover price less 50% discount for extras.
Terms: Acquires first rights. Copyright remains with author.
Advice: "We are highly selective, publishing only 3% of the stories that are submitted for consideration. Read other authors with an appreciative and critical eye; don't send out work prematurely; develop keen powers of observation and a good visual memory; get to know your characters thoroughly; don't let others (editors, friends, etc.) define or 'determine' your sense of self-worth; be willing to learn; outgrow self-indulgence. Develop discipline. Show, don't tell; and leave some work for the reader to do. Write for the fun of it (that way there's a sure return for the investment of time and effort). Always write to achieve the best quality you can; be honest with yourself, your potential readers, and your story. Learn to become your own best editor: know when you've done well, and when you haven't done as well as you can. Remember: there's a lot of competition for the available publication slots, and editorial bias is always a factor in what gets accepted for publication. Develop a sense of humor about the enterprise."

THE PIPE SMOKER'S EPHEMERIS (I, II, IV), The Universal Coterie of Pipe Smokers, 20-37 120 St., College Point NY 11356. Editor: Tom Dunn. Magazine: 8½×11; 54-66 pages; offset paper and cover; illustrations; photos. Pipe smoking and tobacco theme for general and professional audience. Irregular quarterly. Estab. 1964.
Needs: Historical (general), humor/satire, literary, pipe smoking related. Publishes ms up to 1 year after acceptance. Length: 2,500 words average; 5,000 words maximum. Also publishes short shorts. Occasionally critiques rejected mss.
How to Contact: Send complete ms with cover letter. Reports in 2 weeks on mss. Simultaneous, photocopied submissions and reprints OK. Accepts computer printouts. Sample copy for 8½x11 SAE and 6 first class stamps.
Terms: Acquires one-time rights.

PLÉIADES MAGAZINE/PHILAE MAGAZINE (I), Box 357, Suite D, 6677 W. Colfax, Lakewood CO 80214. (303)237-3398. John Moravec, Editor of Pléiades Magazine; Cyril Osmond, editor of Philae Magazine. Magazine: 8½×11; 30-50 pages; 30 lb paper; illustrations; b&w photographs. "We want well thought out material; no sex stories, and good poetry and prose. We want articles about national issues." Pléiades published twice a year; Philae is published quarterly. Estab. 1984. Circ. 10,000.
Needs: Fantasy, historical (general), horror, literary, senior citizen/retirement, serialized/excerpted novel, suspense/mystery, western. "No sex or hippie material." Receives 50-70 unsolicited mss/month. Accepts 3 mss/issue. Publishes ms three months or less after acceptance. Length: 1,200-1,500 words average; 500-800 words minimum. Occasionally critiques rejected mss and recommends other markets.
How to Contact: Send complete ms with cover letter. Reports in 1 week on queries; 2 weeks on mss. SASE. Simultaneous submissions OK. Sample copy $1.75. Fiction guidelines for #10 SAE and 1 first class stamp.
Payment: Pays in contributor's copies.
Terms: Rights remain with author. Offers awards and trophies for best work.
Advice: "Today's magazine fiction stinks. We want authors who can write non-stereotype material, and who are not brainwashed by a bureaucratic society. Learn to write, and take lessons on punctuation. We want shorter good fiction and articles."

PLOUGHSHARES (II), Box 529, Cambridge MA 02139. (617)926-9875. Editor: DeWitt Henry. "Our theme is new writing (poetry, fiction, criticism) that addresses contemporary adult readers who look to fiction and poetry for help in making sense of themselves and of each other." Quarterly. Estab. 1971. Circ. 3,500.

Needs: Literary, prose poem. "No genre (science fiction, detective, gothic, adventure, etc.), popular formula or commercial fiction whose purpose is to entertain rather than to illuminate." Buys 20+ mss/year. Receives approximately 400-600 unsolicited fiction mss each month. Recently published work by Rick Bass, Alice Hoffman, Theodore Weesner; published new writers within the last year. Length: 2,000-6,000 words.

How to Contact: "Query for guidelines and examine a sample issue. Reading periods and needs vary." Cover letter should include "previous pubs." SASE. Reports in 5 months on mss. Sample copy $5. (Please specify fiction issue sample.)

Payment: $10/page to $50 maximum, plus copies. Offers 50% kill fee for assigned ms not published.

Terms: Pays on publication for first North American serial rights.

Advice: "Be familiar with our fiction issues, fiction by our writers and by our various editors (e.g., Rosellen Brown, Tim O'Brien, Jay Neugeboren, Jayne Anne Phillips, James Allen McPherson) and more generally acquaint yourself with the best short fiction currently appearing in the literary quarterlies, and the annual prize anthologies (*Pushcart Prize, O'Henry Awards, Best American Short Stories*). Also realistically consider whether the work you are submitting is as good as or better than—in your own opinion—the work appearing in the magazine you're sending to. What is the level of competition? And what is its volume? (In our case, we accept about 1 ms in 200.) Never send 'blindly' to a magazine, or without carefully weighing your prospect there against those elsewhere. Always keep a copy of work you submit."

‡THE PLOWMAN (II), Box 414, Whitby Ontario L1N 5S4 Canada. Editor: Tony Scavetta. Tabloid: 112 pages; illustrations and photos. Monthly. Estab. 1988. Circ. 10,000.

Needs: Adventure, confession contemporary, ethnic, historical (general), juvenile (5-9 years), literary, mainstream, preschool (1-4 years), prose poem, regional, religious/inspirational, romance, senior citizen/retirement, translations, western and young adult/teen (10-18). Plans to publish special fiction issue or an anthology in the future. Publishes ms 3 months after acceptance. Length: 1 typewritten page. Sometimes critiques rejected mss and recommends other markets.

How to Contact: Send complete ms with cover letter. Reports in 1 week. Enclose IRCs. Simultaneous, photocopied and reprint submissions OK. Accepts computer printout submissions.Sample copy and fiction guidelines for $2 and large SAE.

Payment: Pays in contributor's copies; charges for extras.

Terms: Acquires one-time rights. Sends galleys to author.

‡POETIC LIBERTY (II), PL Press, 3301 John Muir Ct., Plano TX 75023. (214)424-1015. Editor: Charles Corry. Fiction Editor: Tony Howard. Magazine: digest; 60 pages; 20 lb photocopy paper; 110 bl cardstock cover. "Primary interest is on poetry and poetry review. Some fiction and essays. Audience is 50% college teachers; 50% part-time writers and those interested in creative writing." Quarterly. Estab. 1988. Circ. 250.

Needs: Contemporary, historical (general), humor/satire, literary, mainstream and prose and poems. "No religious; science fiction, pornography." Receives 10-15 unsolicited mss/month. Accepts 2-3 mss/issue; 10-15 mss/year. Publishes ms within 1 year after acceptance. Recently published work by Gerald Locklin and Arnold Lipkind. Length: 200-3,000 words; 2,500 average. Publishes short shorts.

How to Contact: Send complete manuscript with cover letter. Include brief bio. Reports in 3 months. SASE. Simultaneous, photocopied, and reprint submissions OK. Accepts computer printouts. Sample copy $2.50. Fiction guidelines free.

Payment: Pays in contributor copies (up to five if requested).

Terms: Buys one-time rights. Sends galleys to author.

Advice: "Literary quality that is tight and concise, that at least hints of more than a surface meaning; that exercises the use (or the knowledge of) good grammer and structure; I'm still waiting to receive the work of a budding Eudora Welty or Thomas Wolfe or Hart Crane—and I'll know it when I see. Read! Read! Read. Read the good college journals and recent college anthologies."

POETRY HALIFAX DARTMOUTH (I, II), BS Poetry Society, Box 7074 North, Halifax Nova Scotia B3K 5J4 Canada. Editors: Joe Blades, Eleonore Schonmaier. Magazine: 7×8½; 24 pages; bond paper; card stock cover. Bimonthly. Estab. 1986. Circ. 300.

Needs: Experimental, humor/satire, literary and prose poem. Receives 1 or 2 unsolicited mss/month; accepts 3-4 mss/year. Publishes ms 3-6 months after acceptance. Puslishes short shorts. Sometimes critiques rejected mss.

How to Contact: Send complete ms with cover letter and short bio. Reports in 3 months on queries. SASE. Photocopied submissions OK. Accepts computer printout submissions. Sample copy $2. Fiction guidelines for #10 SAE and 1 first class stamp (IRC).

Payment: $5 (Canadian).

Terms: Pays on publication for first North American serial rights.

POETRY MAGIC (I), 1630 Lake Dr., Haslett, MI 48840. (517)339-8754. Editor: Lisa Roose-Church. Magazine: 8½×11; over 20 pages; b&w illustrations. "Publish poetry and articles relating to poetry. Have used other themes. We will consider just about anything of high quality." Quarterly. Estab. 1988.
Needs: Contemporary, humor, prose poem. No pornography, science fiction, horror, fantasy. Receives over 100 mss/month. Accepts 2 mss/issue. Publishes ms within 6 months of acceptance. Recently published work by Scott Sonders. Length: 50-500 words preferred; 50 words minimum; 500 words maximum. Sometimes critiques rejected mss and recommends other markets.
How to Contact: Query first, query with clips of published work or send complete ms with cover letter. Reports in 2-4 weeks. SASE. Simultaneous (if stated), photocopied and reprint submissions OK. Accepts computer printout submissions. Sample copy for $4.50. Fiction guidelines for #10 SAE and 30¢ postage.
Payment: Pays in contributor's copies.
Terms: Acquires first rights or one-time rights.
Advice: "Correct usage of grammar, punctuation, etc. is important. We prefer fiction that is quality reading, which entices the reader for more from that author. Because we get less fiction than poetry, we are selective because our readers want to be enticed, enthralled and overwhelmed with a story. If it doesn't do this for the editor she will not accept it. Experiment and create your own style."

THE PORTABLE WALL (II), Basement Press, 215 Burlington, Billings MT 59101. (406)256-3588. Editor: Daniel Struckman. Fiction Editor: Gray Harris. Magazine: 6¼×9¼; 40 pages; cotton rag paper; best quality cover; line engravings; illustrations. "We consider all kinds of material. Bias toward humor." Twice annually. Estab. 1977. Circ. 400.
Needs: Adventure, contemporary, ethnic, experimental, feminist, historical, humor/satire, literary, mainstream, prose poem, regional, science fiction, senior citizen, sports, translations. "We hand set all type; therefore, we favor short pieces and poetry." Receives less than 1 unsolicited ms/month. Accepts one or two mss/issue; one or two mss/year. Publishes ms 6 months to a year after acceptance. Published works by Gray Harris, Wilbur Wood. Length: 2,000 words preferred. Publishes short shorts. Sometimes critiques rejected mss.
How to Contact: Send complete ms with cover letter. Reports in 2 weeks on mss. SASE. Accepts computer printout submissions. Sample copy for $5.
Payment: Free subscription to magazine.
Terms: Acquires one-time rights.
Advice: "We like language that evokes believable pictures in our minds and that tells an enjoyable story."

PORTENTS (II), 12 Fir Place, Hazlet NJ 07730. (201)888-0535. Editor: Deborah Rasmussen. Magazine: 60+ pages; illustrations; photos. "Contemporary horror, dark fantasy, movie and book reviews, crossword puzzles for an adult audience." Three issues annually. Every issue has 8-10 short stories. Estab. 1986.
Needs: Horror. No poetry or science fiction. Receives 10-15 unsolicited mss/week. Accepts 9-10 mss/issue. Publishes ms 9-10 months after acceptance. Published new writers within the last year. Length: up to 3,000 words. Publishes short shorts. Critiques every rejected mss. Recommends other markets.
How to Contact: Send complete ms with cover letter. Reports in 2 weeks on queries. SASE. Photocopied submissions OK. Accepts computer printout submissions. Sample copy $3.50. Fiction guidelines for #10 SAE and 1 first class stamp.
Payment: Pays ¼¢/word.
Advice: "Keep it short, to the point and original."

PORTLAND REVIEW (I, II), Portland State University, Box 751, Portland OR 97207. (503)725-4468. Editor: Nancy Row. "The *Review* is looking for fiction, poetry and essays that linger in the mind's eye with frightful clarity after the magazine has been put aside and the business of life resumed." Publishes three times yearly. Estab. 1955. Circ. 1,500.
Needs: "More good fiction and less bad poetry." Length: 6,000 words maximum.
How to Contact: Submit complete ms with personal biographical note, SASE. Photocopied submissions OK. Reports in 6 weeks. Sample copy for $5.
Payment: 1 free contributor's copy.
Terms: Acquires one-time rights.
Advice: "We want to increase the ratio of fiction to poetry. Stick with a few magazines and let them really get to know your work."

‡THE POST (II), Publishers Syndication International, Suite 856, 1377 K St., Washington DC 20005. Editor: A.P. Samuels. Newspaper: 8½×11; 32 pages. Monthly. Estab. 1988.
Needs: Adventure, romance and suspense/mystery. "No explicit sex, gore, extreme violence or bad language." Receives 75 unsolicited mss/month. Buys 1 ms/issue; 12 mss/year. Time between acceptance and publication varies. Agented fiction 10%. Length: 10,000 words average.

How to Contact: Send complete manuscript with cover letter. Reports on mss in 5 weeks. Accepts computer printout submissions. Fiction guidelines for #10 SAE and 1 first class stamp.
Payment: ½¢ to 4¢/word.
Terms: Pays on acceptance for all rights.

‡POTATO EYES (II), Appalachian Voices, Nightshad, Box 76, Troy ME 07987. (207)948-3427. Editors: Carolyn Page and Roy Zarucchi. Magazine: 6×9; 80 pages; 60 lb Quality Natural text paper; 80 lb Curtis flannel cover. "We tend to showcase Appalachian talent from Alabama to Quebec, and in doing so, we hope to dispel hackneyed stereotypes and political borders. Our subscribers have included: boat builder, teacher, dairy farmer, college prof, doctor, lawyer, world traveler, lumberman . . . and that was just in last week's batch."
Estab. 1989. Circ. 800.
Needs: Contemporary, humor/satire, literary, mainstream, regional, and rural themes. Receives 20 unsolicited mss/month. Accepts 3-4 mss/issue; 6-8 mss/year. Publishes ms 6 months-1 year after acceptance. Recently published work by Ed Davis, TomVerde and Carl Perrin. Length: 3,000 words maximum; 2,000 average. Publishes short shorts. Length: 450 words. Sometimes critiques rejected mss and recommends other markets.
How to Contact: Send complete ms with cover letter. Reports in 2 weeks-2 months on mss. SASE. Accepts computer printouts, no dot matrix. Sample copy $4.75, including postage. Fiction guidelines with #10 SAE.
Payment: Contributor's copies.
Terms: Acquires first North American serial rights.
Advice: "We care about the larger issues, including pollution, ecology, bio-regionalism, uncontrolled progress and "condominia," as well as the rights of the individual, particularly the elderly. We care about television, the great sewer pipe of America, and what it is doing to America's youth. We are exploring these issues with writers who have originality, a reordered perspective, and submit to us generous sprinklings of humor and satire. Although we do occasionally comment on valid fiction, we have walked away unscathed from the world of academia and refuse to correct manuscripts. We respect our contributors and treat them as professionals, however, and write personal responses to every submission if given an SASE. We expect the same treatment—clean copy without multi folds or corrections. We like brief non-Narcissistic cover letters containing the straight scoop. We suggest that beginning fiction writers spend the money they have set aside for creative writing courses or conferences and spend it instead on subscriptions to good little literary magazines."

THE POTTERSFIELD PORTFOLIO (II,IV), New Writing From Atlantic Canada, Crazy Quilt Press, 19 Oakhill Dr., Halifax Nova Scotia B3M 2V3 Canada. (902)443-9600. Editors: Donalee Moulton-Barrett, Barb Cottrell, Peggy Amirault. Magazine: 8½×11; 52 pages; good quality paper; coated cover stock; illustrations. "All material in *The Portfolio* is written by Atlantic Canadians or those with a connection—significant—to the region." Semi-annually. Estab. 1979.
Needs: Contemporary, ethnic, experimental, fantasy, feminist, gay, humor/satire, lesbian, literary, mainstream, prose poem, regional, science fiction. Receives 30-50 fiction mss/month. Buys 8-10 mss/issue. Published work by Lesley Choyce, Spider Robinson, Silver Donald Cameron; published new writers within the last year. Publishes short shorts. Sometimes comments on rejected mss and recommends other markets.
How to Contact: Send complete ms with cover letter and enough information for short bio in journal. Reports in 2 months. SASE. Simultaneous and photocopied submissions OK. Accepts computer printout submissions. Sample copy $5 (US).
Payment: Pays $25 and contributor's copies.
Terms: Pays on publication for first Canadian English-language serial rights.
Advice: "Still believe the marketplace is open to beginning writers. Tailor your fiction to a particular market—it helps to break in more quickly and avoids unnecessary rejections from publications that are not buying the type of work you're producing."

POULTRY (II, IV), A Magazine of Voice, Box 4413, Springfield MA 01101. Editors: Jack Flavin, Brendan Galvin and George Garrett. Tabloid of fiction and poetry: 8-12 pages; newspaper quality; cover photos; cartoons. Parodies contemporary poems, styles, lit-biz, contribution notes, contests, prizes, etc; for writers and readers of contemporary literature. Three or four annually. Estab. 1979. Circ. 1,000.
Needs: Humor/satire. "We want fiction that satirizes contemporary writing's foibles, pretensions, politics, etc. Make it brief and pungent. No serious fiction." Receives 10-20 unsolicited fiction mss/month. Accepts 3-4 mss/issue; 10-20 mss/year. Occasionally critiques rejected ms. Published work by R. H. W. Dillard, David R. Slavitt, R. S. Gwynn and Fred Chapell; published new writers within the last year. Publishes short shorts.

How to Contact: Send complete ms with SASE. Accepts computer printout submissions. Prefers letter-quality. Reports in 1 month. Sample copy for $2.
Payment: 10 free contributor's copies.
Terms: Acquires one-time rights.
Advice: "Read us; send us parodies of the things in contemporary writing and its scene that bug you the most! Make it new and funny, preferably brief. Nothing serious."

PRAIRIE FIRE (II), Prairie Fire Press Inc., Room 423, 100 Arthur St., Winnipeg, Manitoba R3B 1H3 Canada. (204)943-9066. Managing Editor: Andris Taskans. Magazine: 6×9; 96 pages; offset bond paper; sturdy cover stock; illustrations; photos. "Essays, critical reviews, short fiction and poetry. For writers and readers interested in Canadian literature." Published 4 times/year. Estab. 1978. Circ. 1,500.
Needs: Literary, contemporary, experimental, prose poem, reviews. "We will consider work on any topic of artistic merit, including short chapters from novels-in-progress. We wish to avoid gothic, confession, religious, romance and pornography." Buys 2-3 mss/issue, 8-10 mss/year. Does not read mss in summer. Recently published work by Sandra Birdsell, George Bowering, Robert Kroetsch; published new writers within the last year. Receives 18-20 unsolicited fiction mss each month. Publishes short shorts. Length: 5,000 maximum; no minimum; 2,000 words average. Critiques rejected mss "if requested and when there is time." Sometimes recommmends other markets.
How to Contact: Send complete ms with SASE and short bio. Reports in 2-3 months. Sample copy for $6 (Canadian).
Payment: $60 for the first page, $30 for each additional page. 1 free author's copy. $4 charge for extras.
Terms: Pays on publication for first North American serial rights. Rights revert to author on publication.
Advice: "We are publishing more fiction, and we are commissioning illustrations. Read our publication before submitting. We prefer Canadian material. Most mss are not ready for publication. Be neat, double space. Be the best writer you can be."

THE PRAIRIE JOURNAL OF CANADIAN LITERATURE (I, II, IV), Prairie Journal Press, Box 997, Station G, Calgary, Alberta T3A 3G2 Canada. Editor: A.E. Burke. Journal: 7×8½; 50-60 pages; white bond paper; Cadillac cover stock; cover illustrations. Journal of creative writing and scholarly essays, reviews for literary audience. Semiannually. Published special fiction issue last year. Estab. 1983.
Needs: Contemporary, literary, prose poem, regional, excerpted novel, novella, typed single space on camera-ready copy. Canadian authors given preference. No romance, erotica, pulp. Receives 20-40 unsolicited mss each month. Accepts 10-15 ms/issue; 20-30 mss/year. *Charges reading fee of up to $1/ page "if help requested."* Suggests sample issue before submitting ms. Recently published work by Nancy Ellen Russell, Carla Mobley, Patrick Quinn; published new writers within the last year. Length: 2,500 words average; 100 words minimum; 3,000 words maximum. Sometimes critiques rejected mss and recommends other markets.
How to Contact: Send complete ms. Reports in 1 month. SASE or SAE and IRC. Photocopied submissions OK. Accepts computer printout if letter quality, no dot-matrix. Sample copy $3 (Canadian) and SAE with $1.10 for postage or IRC. Include cover letter of past credits—a friendly introduction to a new acquaintance. Reply to queries for SAE with 48¢ for postage or IRC. No American stamps.
Payment: Contributor's copies.
Terms: Acquires first North American serial rights. In Canada author retains copyright.
Advice: Interested in "innovational work of quality. Beginning writers welcome. I have chosen to publish fiction simply because many magazines do not. Those who do in Canada are, for the most part, seeking formulaic writing. There is no point in simply republishing known authors or conventional, predictable plots. Of the genres we receive fiction is most often of the highest calibre. It is a very competitive field. Be proud of what you send. You're worth it."

PRAIRIE SCHOONER (II), University of Nebraska, English Department, 201 Andrews Hall, Lincoln NE 68588-0334. (402)472-3191. Magazine: 6×9; 144 pages; good stock paper; heavy cover stock. "A general literary quarterly of stories, poems, essays and reviews for a general educated audience that reads for pleasure." Quarterly. Estab. 1927. Circ. 2,000.
Needs: Good fiction. Accepts 4-5 mss/issue. Receives approximately 150 unsolicited fiction mss each month. Recently published work by Robley Wilson, David Huddle, Jane Ann Mullen; published new writers within the last year. Length: varies.

How to Contact: Send complete ms with SASE and cover letter listing previous publications—where, when. Reports in 3 months. Sample copy for $2.
Payment: 3 free author's copies.
Terms: Acquires all rights. Will reassign rights upon request after publication. Annual prize of $500 for best fiction, $500 for best new writer (poetry or fiction), $500 for best poetry; additional prizes, $250-1,000.
Advice: "*Prairie Schooner* is eager to see fiction from beginning and established writers. Be tenacious. Accept rejection as a temporary setback and send out rejected stories to other magazines."

"We had the opportunity to select prints from a show of Julia Dean's work and chose this image," explains* Prairie Schooner *editor Hilda Raz. Dean documents her travels through Europe, Guatemala, Mexico and the United States with essays as well as photographs.

PRIMAVERA (II, IV), University of Chicago, 1212 E. 59th St., Chicago IL 60637. (312)324-5920. Editorial Board. Magazine: 5½×8½; 100 pages; 60 lb paper; glossy cover; illustrations; photos. Literature and graphics reflecting the experiences of women: poetry, short stories, photos, drawings. Readership: "an audience interested in women's ideas and experiences." Annually. Estab. 1975. Circ. 1,000.
Needs: Literary, contemporary, science fiction, fantasy, feminist, gay/lesbian and humor. "We dislike slick stories packaged for more traditional women's magazines. We publish only work reflecting the experiences of women, but also publish mss by men." Accepts 6-10 mss/issue. Receives approximately 40 unsolicited fiction mss each month. Recently published work by Ann Harleman, Janet Sisk; published new writers within the last year. Length: 25 pages maximum. Critiques rejected mss when there is time. Often gives suggestions for revisions and invites re-submission of revised ms. Occasionally recommends other markets
How to Contact: Send complete ms with SASE. Cover letter not necessary. Accepts computer printout submissions, "if assured it is not a multiple submission." Prefers letter-quality. Reports in 1 week—5 months on mss. Publishes ms up to 1 year after acceptance. Sample copy $5; $6 for recent issues. Guidelines for #14 SASE.
Payment: 2 free author's copies.
Terms: Acquires first rights.

PRISM INTERNATIONAL (II), E462-1866 Main Mall, University of British Columbia, Vancouver, British Columbia V6T 1W5 Canada. (604)228-2514. Editor: Debbie Howlett. Magazine: 6×9; 72-80 pages; Zephyr book paper; Cornwall, coated one side cover; photos on cover. "A journal of contemporary writing—fiction, poetry, drama, creative non-fiction and translation. *Prism*'s audience is world-wide, as are our contributors." Readership: "Public and university libraries, individual subscriptions, bookstores—an audience concerned with the contemporary in literature." Published 4 times/year. Estab. 1959. Circ. 1,200.
Needs: Literary, contemporary, prose poem or translations. "Most any category as long as it is *fresh*. No overtly religious, overtly theme-heavy material or anything more message- or category-oriented than self-contained." Buys approximately 70 mss/year. Receives 50 unsolicited fiction mss each month.

Published new writers within the last year. Length: 5,000 words maximum "though flexible for outstanding work." Publishes short shorts. Critiques rejected mss when there is time. Occasionally recommends other markets.

How to Contact: Send complete ms with SASE or SAE, IRC and cover letter with bio, information and publications list. "Keep it simple. US contributors take note: US stamps are not valid in Canada and your ms will not likely be returned if it contains US stamps. Send International Reply Coupons instead." Accepts computer printout submissions. Prefers letter-quality. Reports in 3 months. Sample copy $4 (Canadian).

Payment: $30/printed page, 1 free year's subscription.

Terms: Pays on publication for first North American serial rights.

Advice: "Too many derivative, self-indulgent pieces; sloppy construction and imprecise word usage. There's not enough attention to voice and not enough invention. We are committed to publishing outstanding literary work in all genres."

PRISONERS OF THE NIGHT (II), An Adult Anthology of Erotica, Fright, Allure and . . . Vampirism, MKASHEF Enterprises, Box 368, Poway CA 92064. Editor: Alayne Gelfand. Magazine: 8½×11; 150-200 pages; 20 lb paper; slick cover; illustrations. "An adult, erotic vampire anthology of original character stories and poetry. Heterosexual and homosexual situations included." Annually. Estab. 1987. Circ. approx. 3,000.

Needs: Adventure, contemporary, erotica, experimental, fantasy, feminist, gay, horror, lesbian, literary, prose poem, psychic/supernatural/occult, science fiction, suspense/mystery, western. "All stories must be vampire stories, with unique characters, unusual situations." No fiction that deals with anyone else's creations, i.e. no "Dracula" stories. Receives 20-40 unsolicited fiction mss/month. Accepts 14-20 mss/issue. Publishes ms 1-11 months after acceptance. Recently published work by Wendy Rathbone, Leo Bigley, Della Van Hise; published new writers within the last year. Length: open. Publishes short shorts. Sometimes critiques rejected mss. Recommends other markets.

How to Contact: Send complete ms with cover letter. "A short introduction of author to the editor; name, address, *some* past credits if available." Reports in 1 week on queries; 2 months on mss. Reads *only* September-March. SASE. Photocopied submissions OK. Accepts computer printout submissions. Accepts electronic submissions via IBM Word Perfect, disk—files no longer than 18 pages each. Sample copy $15. Fiction guidelines for #10 SAE and 1 first class stamp.

Payment: Pays 1¢/word for fiction.

Terms: Pays on publication for first North American serial rights.

Advice: "Do not send me pornography. While graphic erotica is fine, I do not want to see cheap or tawdry sex for shock value alone. I'm looking for the sensuous as well as sensual aspects of the vampire. Don't use trite or over done plots. Be original, stretch your imagination!"

PROCESSED WORLD (II), #1829, 41 Sutter St., San Francisco CA 94104. (415)495-6823. Editors: Collective. Magazine: 8½×11; 44-48 pages; 20 lb bond paper; glossy cover stock; illustrations; photos. Magazine about work, office work, computers and hi-tech (satire). Triannually. May publish special fiction issue. Estab. 1981. Circ. 4,000.

Needs: Comics, confession, contemporary, fantasy, humor/satire, literary, science fiction. Accepts 1-2 mss/issue; 3-6 mss/year. Recently published work by James Pollack. Published new writers within the last year. Length: 1,250 words average; 100 words minimum; 1,500 words maximum. Occasionally critiques rejected ms.

How to Contact: Send complete ms. Reports in 4 months. SASE. Simultaneous and photocopied submissions OK. Accepts computer printout submissions. Prefers letter-quality. Sample copy $4.

Payment: Subscription to magazine.

Terms: Acquires one-time rights.

Advice: "Make it real. Make it critical of the status quo. Read the magazine before you send us a story."

‡PROEM CANADA (I,IV), A Youthful, Useful Guide to the Love of Language, Proem Canada Projects, P.O.Box 416, Peterborough, Ontario K9J 6Z3 Canada. (705) 749-5686. Editor: Chris Magwood. Magazine: 8½×11; 60 pages; book stock paper; coated card cover stock. For Canadian writers between ages 16-26. Semiannually. Estab. 1989. Circ. 3,000.

Needs: Open. Receives 100 unsolicited mss each month; accepts 6-8 mss per issue; 12-16 mss per year. Publishes ms 1-5 months after acceptance. Length: 4,000 words maximum. Publishes short shorts. Comments on rejected mss and recommends other markets.

How to Contact: Send complete ms with cover letter. Reports on queries in 1 month; reports on mss in 1-5 months. SASE. Photocopied and computer printout submissions OK. Sample copy $5. Fiction guidelines for SAE and 1 first class stamp.

Payment: $50 minimum, free subscription and contributor's copies.

Terms: Pays on publication for first rights.

Advice: "Stories about self-indulgent and 'insane' modern urban disillusioned types too frequent. Real characters with some motion and drams have always made the best stories."

PROOF ROCK (II), Literary Arts Journal, Proof Rock Press, Box 607, Halifax VA 24558. Editor: Don R. Conner. Magazine: standard size; 40-60 pages; heavy paper; heavy cover stock; illustrations; photos. "We publish the best of what is submitted in a given period. No taboos if well done." For all segments of the literary readership. Semiannually. Published special fiction issue last year. Estab. 1982. Circ. 300.

Needs: Adventure, contemporary, erotica, experimental, fantasy, humor/satire, literary, mainstream, prose poem, psychic/supernatural, romance, translations. "Excessive sentimentality is frowned upon." Receives 8-10 unsolicited fiction mss/month. Accepts 2-4 mss/issue; 4-8 mss/year. Approximately 1% of fiction is agented. Published new writers within the last year. Length: 2,500 words maximum; 2,000 words average. Occasionally critiques rejected mss and recommends other markets.

How to Contact: Send complete ms with SASE. Simultaneous, photocopied and previously published submissions OK. Accepts computer printout submissions. Prefers letter-quality. Reports in 3 months. Publishes ms an average of 1-6 months after acceptance. Sample copy $2.50. Fiction guidelines free with #10 SAE and 1 first class stamp.

Payment: 1 free contributor's copy; $2.50 charge for extras.

Terms: Acquires one-time rights.

Advice: "Our audience is passive. We need something to stir them up. Dare to be different but not obtuse. Try something new under the sun without leaving the solar system. In other words, be original, but let your originality capture the reader rather than turn him off."

PSI (II), Suite 856, 1377 K Street NW, Washington DC 20005. Editor: A.P. Samuels. Magazine: 8½×11; 32 pages; bond paper; self cover. "Mystery and romance for an adult audience." Bimonthly. Estab. 1987.

Needs: Romance (contemporary, historical, young adult), suspense/mystery. Receives 35 unsolicited mss/month. Buys 1-2 mss/issue. Published work by Sharon K. Garner, Michael Riedel; published new writers within the last year. Length: 10,000 words average. Publishes short shorts. Critiques rejected mss "only on a rare occasion."

How to Contact: Send complete ms with cover letter. Reports in 2 weeks on queries; 4 weeks on mss. SASE. Accepts computer printout submissions. Accepts electronic submissions via disk.

Payment: Pays 1-4¢/word plus royalty.

Terms: Pays on acceptance for first North American serial rights.

Advice: "Manuscripts must be for a general audience. Just good plain story telling (make it compelling). No explicit sex or ghoulish violence."

PTOLEMY/THE BROWNS MILLS REVIEW (II), Box 908, Browns Mills NJ 08015. Editor-in-Chief: David C. Vajda. Magazine: 5×8½; 8-24 pages; good quality paper; illustrations. Published annually. Estab. 1980. Circ. 250.

Needs: Contemporary, erotica, experimental, historical, humor/satire, mainstream and translations. No "plagiarized material, racist–sexist–per se." Length: 50 words minimum; 10,000 words maximum; 400-2,400 words average. Occasionally critiques rejected mss. Recommends markets.

How to Contact: Query first with unpublished samples with SASE. Reports in 1 month. Publishes ms an average of 3 months to 1 year after acceptance.

Payment: 5 contributor's copies per page.

THE PUB (I, II), Ansuda Publications, Box 158J, Harris IA 51345. Editor/Publisher: Daniel R. Betz. Magazine: 5½×8½; 72 pages; mimeo paper; heavy stock cover; illustrations on cover. "We prefer stories to have some sort of social impact within them, no matter how slight, so our fiction is different from what's published in most magazines. We aren't afraid to be different or publish something that might be objectionable to current thought. *Pub* is directed toward those people, from all walks of life, who are themselves 'different' and unique, who are interested in new ideas and forms of reasoning. Our readers enjoy *Pub* and believe in what we are doing." Published 2 times/year. Estab. 1979. Circ. 350.

Needs: Literary, psychic/supernatural/occult, fantasy, horror, mystery, adventure, serialized and condensed novels. "We are looking for honest, straightforward stories. No love stories or stories that ramble on for pages about nothing in particular." Buys reprints. Accepts 4-6 mss/issue. Receives approximately 35-40 unsolicited fiction mss each month. Published new writers within the last year. Length: 8,000 words maximum. Sometimes recommends other markets.

How to Contact: Send complete ms with SASE. Accepts computer printout submissions. Prefers letter-quality. Reports in 1 month. Publishes ms an average of 6 months after acceptance. Sample copy $2.50. Guidelines for #10 SASE.
Payment: 2 free author's copies. Cover price less special bulk discount for extras.
Terms: Acquires first North American serial rights and second serial rights on reprints.
Advice: "Read the magazine—that is *very* important. If you send a story close to what we're looking for, we'll try to help guide you to exactly what we want. We appreciate neat copy, and if photocopies are sent, we like to be able to read all of the story. Fiction seems to work for us—we are a literary magazine and have better luck with fiction than articles or poems."

PUERTO DEL SOL (I), New Mexico State University, Box 3E, Las Cruces NM 88003. (505)646-3931. Editor-in-Chief: Kevin McIlvoy. Poetry Editor: Joe Somoza. Magazine: 6×9; 200 pages; 60 lb paper; 70 lb cover stock; photos sometimes. "We publish quality material from anyone. Poetry, fiction, art, photos, interviews, reviews, parts-of-novels, long poems." Semiannually. Estab. 1961. Circ. 1,000.
Needs: Contemporary, ethnic, experimental, literary, mainstream, prose poem, excerpted novel and translations. Receives varied number of unsolicited fiction mss/month. Accepts 8-10 mss/issue; 12-15 mss/year. Does not read mss May-August. Published work by Ken Kuhlken, Susan Thornton; published new writers within the last year. Occasionally critiques rejected mss.
How to Contact: Send complete ms with SASE. Simultaneous and photocopied submissions OK. Accepts computer printout submissions. Reports in 2 months. Sample copy $4.
Payment: 3 contributor's copies.
Terms: Acquires one-time rights (rights revert to author).
Advice: "We are open to all forms of fiction, from the conventional to the wildly experimental, as long as they have integrity and are well written. Too often we receive very impressively 'polished' mss that will dazzle readers with their sheen but offer no character/reader experience of lasting value."

PULPHOUSE (II), The Hardback Magazine of Dangerous Fiction, Box 1227, Eugene OR 97440. Editor: Kristine Kathryn Rusch. Magazine: 200-250 pages; 70 lb paper; hard cover. Quarterly. Estab. 1988. Circ. 1,250 (1,000 cloth-bound trade editions; 250 leather-bound editions).
Needs: Fantasy, horror, science fiction, speculative fiction. Requirements for fall: all horror; for winter: all speculative fiction; for spring: all fantasy; for summer: all science fiction. Recently published work by Harlan Ellison, Kate Wilhelm, Michael Bishop; published new writers within the last year. Length: 7,500 words maximum.
How to Contact: Send complete ms with cover letter "that gives publication history, work history, or any other information relevant to the magazine." SASE. Sample copy for $20 (cloth); $60 (leather). Fiction guidelines for #10 SAE and 1 first class stamp.
Payment: Pays 3-6¢/word.
Terms: Pays on acceptance for one-time anthology rights.
Advice: "*Pulphouse* is subtitled The Hardback Magazine of Dangerous Fiction. By 'dangerous,' we mean fiction that takes risks, that presents viewpoints not commonly held in the field. Although such fiction can include experimental writing, it is usually best served by clean, clear prose. We are looking for strong characterization, fast-moving plot, and intriguing settings."

QUARRY (II), Quarry Press, Box 1061, Kingston, Ontario K7L 4Y5 Canada. (613)548-8429. Editor-in-Chief: Bob Hilderley. Magazine: 5½×8½; 120 pages; #1 book 120 paper; 160 lb Curtis Tweed cover stock; illustrations; photos. "Quarterly anthology of new Canadian poetry, prose. Also includes graphics, photographs and book reviews. We seek readers interested in vigorous, disciplined, new Canadian writing." Published special fiction issue; plans another. Estab. 1952. Circ. 1,100.
Needs: Experimental, fantasy, literary, science fiction, serialized/excerpted novel and translations. "We do not want highly derivative or clichéd style." Receives 60-80 unsolicited fiction mss/month. Buys 4-5 mss/issue; 20 mss/year. Does not read in July. Less than 5% of fiction is agented. Recently published work by Diane Schoemperlen, David Helwig, Joan Fern Shaw. Published new writers within the last year. Length: 3,000 words average. Publishes short shorts. Usually critiques rejected mss and recommends other markets.
How to Contact: Send complete ms with SAE, IRC and brief bio. Photocopied submissions OK. Accepts computer printout submissions; prefers letter-quality. Publishes ms an average of 3-6 months after acceptance. Sample copy $5 with 4×7 SAE and 50¢ Canadian postage or IRC.
Payment: $10/page; 1 year subscription to magazine and 1 contributor's copy.
Terms: Pays on publication for first North American serial rights.
Advice: "Read previous *Quarry* to see standard we seek. Read Canadian fiction to see Canadian trends. We seek aggressive experimentation which is coupled with competence (form, style) and stimulating subject matter. We also like traditional forms. Our annual prose issue (spring) is always a sellout. Many of our selections have been anthologized. Don't send US stamps or SASE. Use IRC. Submit with brief bio."

QUARRY WEST (II), Porter College, UCSC, Santa Cruz CA 95064. (408)429-2951. Editor: Kenneth Weisner. Fiction Editors: Kathy Chetkovich and Thad Nodine. Magazine: 6¾×8¼; 120 pages; 60 lb stock opaque paper; cover stock varies with cover art; illustrations sometimes; photos. Magazine of fiction, poetry, general nonfiction, art, graphics for a general audience. Semiannually. Estab. 1971. Circ. 750.

Needs: Traditional, experimental. Accepts 2-5 mss/issue; 4-10 mss/year. Length: 6,000 words maximum. Occasionally critiques rejected ms.

How to Contact: Send complete ms with SASE. Photocopied submissions OK. Reports in 6 weeks on mss. Publishes ms an average of 1-3 months after acceptance. Does not read mss July and August. Sample copy $3.50.

Payment: 2 free contributor's copies.

Terms: Acquires first North American serial rights. Sponsors fiction contest.

Advice: "We're interested in good writing—we've published first-time writers and experienced professionals. Don't submit material you are unsure of or perhaps don't like just for the sake of publication—only show your *best* work—read the magazine for a feeling of the kind of fiction we've published. Type double-spaced and legibly."

QUARTERLY WEST (II), University of Utah, 317 Olpin Union, Salt Lake City UT 84112. (801)581-3938. Editors: C.F. Pinkerton, Tom Schmid. Fiction Editor: Dave Stevenson. Magazine: 6×9; 150+ pages; 60 lb paper; 5-color cover stock; illustrations and photographs rarely. "We try to publish a variety of fiction by writers from all over the country. Our publication is aimed primarily at an educated audience which is interested in contemporary literature and criticism." Semiannually. "We sponsor biennual novella competition." Estab. 1976. Circ. 1,000.

Needs: Literary, contemporary, translations. Buys 4-6 mss/issue, 10-12 mss/year. Receives approximately 100 unsolicited fiction mss each month. Recently published work by Andre Dubus and Chuck Rosenthal; published new writers within the last year. No preferred length. Critiques rejected mss when there is time. Sometimes recommends other markets.

How to Contact: Send complete ms. Cover letters welcome. SASE. Accepts computer printout submissions; prefers letter-quality. Reports in 2 months; "sooner, if possible." Sample copy for $4.50.

Payment: $15-$300.

Terms: Pays on publication for first North American serial rights.

Advice: "Write a clear and unified story which does not rely on tricks or gimmicks for its effects." Mss are rejected because of "poor style, formula writing, clichés, weak characterization. We solicit quite frequently, but tend more toward the surprises—unsolicited. Don't send more than one story per submission, but submit as often as you like."

‡QUEEN OF ALL HEARTS (II), Queen Magazine, Montfort Missionaries, 26 S. Saxon Ave., Bay Shore NY 11706. (516)665-0726. Managing Editor: Roger M. Charest, S.M.M. Magazine: 7¾×10¾; 48 pages; self cover stock; illustrations; photos. Magazine of "stories, articles and features on the Mother of God by explaining the Scriptural basis and traditional teaching of the Catholic Church concerning the Mother of Jesus, her influence in fields of history, literature, art, music, poetry, etc." Bimonthly. Estab. 1950. Circ. 6,000.

Needs: Religious/inspirational. "No mss not about Our Lady, the Mother of God, the Mother of Jesus." Receives 3 unsolicited fiction mss/month. Buys 3-4 mss/issue; 24 mss/year. Length: 1,500-2,000 words. Sometimes recommends other markets.

How to Contact: Send complete ms with SASE. Photocopied submissions OK. Reports in 1 month on mss. Publishes ms 6 months to one year after acceptance. Sample copy $1.75 with 9×12 SAE.

Payment: Varies. 6 free contributor's copies.

Advice: "We are publishing stories with a Marian theme."

QUEEN'S QUARTERLY: A Canadian Review (II), John Watson Hall, Queen's University, Kingston, Ontario K7L 3N6 Canada. (613)545-2667. Editors: Ms. Martha Bailey and Dr. Clive Thomson. Magazine: 6×9; 996 pages/year 50 lb Zephyr antique paper; 65 lb Mayfair antique britewhite cover stock; illustrations. "A general interest intellectual review, featuring articles on science, politics, humanities, arts and letters. Book reviews, poetry and fiction." Published quarterly. Estab. 1893. Circ. 1,700.

Needs: Adventure, contemporary, experimental, fantasy, historical (general), humor/satire, literary, mainstream, science fiction and women's. "Special emphasis on work by Canadian writers." Buys 2 mss/issue; 8 mss/year. Recently published work by Janette Turner Hospital; published new writers within the last year. Length: 5,000 words maximum.

How to Contact: "Send complete ms—only one at a time—with SASE." Photocopied submissions OK if not part of multiple submission. Accepts computer printout submissions. Prefers letter-quality. Reports within 3 months. Sample copy $5.

Payment: $100-300 for fiction, 2 contributor's copies and 1-year subscription. $5 charge for extras.

Terms: Pays on publication for first North American serial rights. Sends galleys to author.

QUIMBY (I,IV), Box 281, Astor Station, Boston MA 02123. (617)723-5360. Editors: S. Thomas Svymbersky/Gerry Kaczolowski. Fiction Editor: S. Thomas Svymbersky. Magazine: 8½×11; 60 pages; 60 lb paper; 65 lb card cover; illustrations; photos. "*Quimby* is primarily a magazine of visual arts which includes interviews and articles of interest to artists. All art and writing printed must be by authors or artists living in the Boston area." Quarterly. Estab. 1985. Circ. 1,000.
Needs: Condensed/excerpted novel, contemporary, erotica, ethnic, experimental, feminist, gay, humor/satire, mainstream, prose poem, psychic/supernatural/occult, regional, suspense/mystery. "Looking for experimental fiction on any theme." Receives 10-15 mss/month. Accepts 2-3 mss/issue; 10-12 mss/year. Publishes ms within 2-4 months of acceptance. Length: 250 words minimum; 5,000 words maximum. Sometimes critiques rejected mss and recommends other markets.
How to Contact: Send complete mss with or without cover letter. Reports in 4-6 weeks on mss. SASE. Simultaneous and photocopied submissions OK. Accepts computer printout submissions. Sample copy for $3; fiction guidelines free.
Payment: Pays in contributor's copies.
Terms: Acquires one-time rights.
Advice: "Although *Quimby* is primarily a magazine that prints visual art, we also print a few stories each issue, and the fiction does not have to have anything to do with art. We lean toward more experimental and surrealistic themes and styles, but the main criteria is that the writing be good and the story entertaining. Authors must be from the Boston area before we will consider them, and we often ask writers to appear and read their work aloud at special events. We welcome submissions from any writers in the Boston area, but we will only print work that shows a solid grasp of the language. Besides short stories we have also printed plays and prose poems and welcome writing that is not easily categorized."

QUINTESSENTIAL SPACE DEBRIS (I, IV), Box 42, Worthington OH 43085. Editor: Kathleen Gallagher. Newsletter: 8½×11; illustrations and photographs. "Humorous articles, anecdotes, parodies of book reviews or movie reviews, serious articles about the use of humor in science-fiction books and movies. For fans and readers of science fiction and fantasy, comic books and media." Semiannually. Plans special fiction issue. Estab. 1987. Circ. 500.
Needs: Fantasy, humor/satire, science fiction. No "Star Trek, Star Trek: The Next Generation or Dr. Who pastiches using established television and movie characters." Receives "not many" unsolicited mss/month. Publishes ms 6 months-1 year after acceptance. Publishes short shorts. Sometimes critiques rejected mss.
How to Contact: Query first or send complete ms with cover letter. Reports in 2 months on queries; 3 months on mss. SASE for query, not needed for ms. Simultaneous, photocopied and reprint submissions OK. Accepts computer printout submissions. Sample copy for 9×12 SAE and 4 first class stamps. Fiction guidelines for #10 SAE and 1 first class stamp.
Payment: Free subscription to magazine and contributor's copies.
Terms: All rights revert on publication.

THE RADDLE MOON (II), 9060 Ardmore Dr., Sidney, British Columbia V8L 3S1 Canada. (604)656-4045. Editor: Susan Clark. Magazine: 6×9; 140 pages; good white paper. "Publishes language-centered and 'new lyric' poetry; fiction; essays; statements concerning new poetics; nonfiction; photos and graphics." Semiannually. Estab. 1985. Circ. 700.
Needs: Experimental, literary, prose poem, translations. No adventure, romance or any other purely action-oriented writing. Receives 20 unsolicited fiction mss/month. Recently published work by Joseph Simas, Steve Benson. No preferred length. Publishes short shorts. Sometimes critiques rejected mss.
How to Contact: Send complete ms with cover letter, which should include "some indication that the writer has read the magazine." Reports in 2 months. SASE. IRC with out-of-country submissions. Photocopied submissions OK. Accepts computer printouts. Sample copy $4.
Payment: One year subscription.

RAG MAG (II), Box 12, Goodhue MN 55027. (612)923-4590. Editor: Beverly Voldseth. Magazine: 5½×8½; 60 pages; varied paper quality; illustrations; photos. "We are eager to print poetry, prose and art work. We are open to all styles." Semiannually. Estab. 1982. Circ. 200.
Needs: Adventure, comics, contemporary, erotica, ethnic, experimental, fantasy, feminist, literary, mainstream, prose poem, regional. "Anything well written is a possibility. No extremely violent or pornographic writing." Receives 5 unsolicited mss each month. Accepts 1-2 mss/issue. Published work by Mark Bowers, Joseph Ugoretz, Graham Young; published new writers within the last year. Length: 1,000 words average; 2,200 words maximum. Occasionally critiques rejected mss. Sometimes recommends other markets.
How to Contact: Send complete ms. Reports in 2 months. SASE. Simultaneous, photocopied and previously published submissions OK. Accepts computer printout submissions. Prefers letter-quality. Single copy $4.50.

Payment: 1 contributor's copy; $4.50 charge for extras.

Terms: Acquires one-time rights.

Advice: "Submit clean copy on regular typing paper (no tissue-thin stuff). We want fresh images, sparse language, words that will lift us out of our chairs. I like the short story form. I think it's powerful and has a definite place in the literary magazine."

‡RAINBOW CITY EXPRESS (I,II,IV), Box 8447, Berkeley CA 94707-8447. Editor: Helen B. Harvey. Magazine: 8½×11; 60-80 pages; 20 lb bond paper; illustrations. "We are only interested in topics pertaining to spiritual awakening and evolution of consciousness. For highly educated, well-read, psychologically sophisticated, spiritually evolving and ecologically conscious free-thinkers." Feminist orientation. Quarterly. Estab. 1988. Circ. 1,000.

Needs: Feminist, literary, prose poem, religious/inspirational and spirituality. "We only accept *short fiction* and absolutely no novels or long fiction. No immature, romantic, violent, sexist material." Receives 10-20 unsolicited mss/month. Buys 1-2 mss/issue; 4-8 mss/year. Publishes ms 3-6 months after acceptance. Will publish in the coming year work by David Warner, Helen B. Harvey and Eugene Miller. Length: 200-1,000 words; 500-800 average. Almost always critiques rejected mss and sometimes recommends other markets.

How to Contact: "Order a sample copy and *read it first!* Then send a complete manuscript with cover letter." Reports on queries in 2-4 weeks; 3-6 months on mss. All submissions must contain SASE! Sample copy $5.50. Writer's guidelines for #10 SASE and 1 first class stamp.

Payment: "Payment is arranged on individual basis. Some cash 'honorariums' and every contributor always receives a copy of issue containing her or his work." Pays $5-50.

Terms: Pays on publication. Buys one-time rights.

Advice: Looks for "intelligent, lively, well-written material, with a substantial and plausible plot and characters. Topics must be related to our Spirituality/Consciousness slant. *Read* 1-2 copies of *RCE* first! We prefer *true* (nonfiction) stories related to spiritual awakening."

RAMBUNCTIOUS REVIEW (II), Rambunctious Press, Inc., 1221 W. Pratt Blvd., Chicago IL 60626. Editors: Mary Dellutri, Richard Goldman, Beth Hausler and Nancy Lennon. Magazine: 7½×10; 48 pages; b&w illustrations and photos. "Quality literary magazine publishing short dramatic works, poetry and short stories for general audience." Annually. Estab. 1984. Circ. 500.

Needs: Adventure, contemporary, erotica, ethnic, experimental, feminist, historical, humor/satire, literary, mainstream, prose poem and contemporary romance. No murder mysteries. Receives 10-20 unsolicited mss/month. Accepts 6 mss/year. Does not read June 1-August 31. Recently published work by Neal Lulofs, Rod Kessler, Ronald Levitsky; published new writers within the last year. Length: 15 page maximum. Publishes short shorts. Occasionally comments on rejected mss.

How to Contact: Send complete ms. Reports in 2 months on mss. SASE. Simultaneous and photocopied submissions OK. Accepts computer printout submissions. Prefers letter-quality. Sample copy $4.

Payment: 2 contributor's copies.

Terms: Acquires first rights.

Advice: "We sponsor a yearly fiction contest in the fall. Send SASE for details. Fiction lives—if you can grasp the essentials of fiction, you can recreate a bit of life."

THE RAMPANT GUINEA PIG (II), A Magazine of Fantasy & Subcreative Fiction, 20500 Enadia Way, Canoga Park CA 91306. Editor-in-Chief: Mary Ann Hodge. Magazine: 8½×11; 30 pages; 20 lb stock; illustrations. "Though we emphasize fantasy fiction, we also publish some poetry and material relating to the life and works of Donald K. Grundy. Our readers are literate and well read in fantasy. Many have an interest in children's literature." Published biannually. Estab. 1978. Circ. 100.

Needs: Fantasy, science fantasy and religious fantasy (Christian or otherwise). "Humorous, satire, parody and pastiche okay. All stories should be rated G or PG. No sword and sorcery/barbarian fiction, no *Star Trek* or *Star Wars* stories. No thinly disguised sermons or religious bigotry. I'm particularly looking for mythopoeic and subcreative fantasy, high fantasy, and stories that convey a sense of wonder and the proximity of faerie." Receives 4-8 unsolicited fiction mss/month. Prefers letter-quality or legible dot-matrix. Accepts 5-7 mss/issue; 10-14 mss/year. Recently published work by Lawrence D. Myers, Barbara Rosen; published new writers within the last year. Length: 8,000 words maximum; 5,000 words average (serials may be longer); also publishes short shorts. Occasionally critiques rejected mss. Sometimes recommends other markets.

How to Contact: Send complete ms with SASE. Photocopied submissions OK. Accepts computer printout submissions. Accepts disk submissions compatible with Macintosh Plus. Reports in 6 weeks on mss. Sample copy $3, checks payable to Mary Ann Hodge. Fiction guidelines with #10 SAE and 1 first class stamp.

Payment: 2 contributor's copies. $3 charge for extras.
Terms: Pays for first North American serial rights.
Advice: "I'm publishing more fiction per issue. Read as much fantasy as you can. But don't try to clone Tolkien. Remember that tight plotting and believable characterization and dialogue are essential in fantasy. And read one or more issues of *The Rampant Guinea Pig* before submitting so you'll know the niche we occupy in the genre. At least send for the fiction guidelines. I'm always looking for humorous stories to balance the more serious ones."

‡RE ARTS & LETTERS [REAL] (II), "A Liberal Arts Forum," Stephen F. Austin State University, P.O. Box 13007, Nacogdoches TX 75962. (409)568-2101. Editor: Lee Schultz. Academic Journal, 6×10 perfect bound, 100-130 pages; "top" stock. "65-75% of pages composed of fiction (2-4 stories per issue), poetry (20-40 per issue), an occasional play, book reviews (assigned after query), and interviews. Other 25-35% comprised of articles in scholarly format. Work is reviewed based on the intrinsic merit of the scholarship and creative work and its appeal to a sophisticated international readership." Semiannual. Estab. 1969. Circ. 400+.
Needs: Adventure, contemporary, genre, feminist, science fiction, historical, experimental, regional. No beginners. Receives 15-30 unsolicited mss per month. Accepts 2-5 mss/issue. Publishes 1-6 months after acceptance; one year for special issues. Recently published work by Jenna Fedock, Joe R. Lansdale, Lewis Shiner. Length 1,000-7,000 words. Occasionally critiques rejected mss and conditionally accepts on basis of critiques and changes. Recommends other markets.
How to Contact: Send complete ms with cover letter. Reports in 2 weeks on queries; 3-4 weeks on mss. SASE. Accepts "letter quality" computer submissions. Sample copy and Writer's Guidelines for $4. Guidelines for SASE.
Payment: Pays two contributors' copies; charges for extras.
Terms: Rights then revert to author.
Advice: "Please study an issue. Have your work checked by a well published writer—who is not a good friend."

READ ME (II), 1118 Hoyt Ave., Everett WA 98201. (206)259-0804. Editor: Ron Fleshman. Fiction Editors: Sally Taylor and Kay Nelson. Tabloid: 11×17; 24 pages; newsprint paper and cover; illustrations. "Entertainment and ideas in an accessible format. Fiction, articles, essays, poetry, reviews, puzzles, cartoons." For "grassroots middle America." Quarterly. Estab. 1988. Circ. 1,000.
Needs: Adventure, confession, contemporary, ethnic, fantasy, feminist, historical (general), horror, humor/satire, mainstream, romance (contemporary and historical), science fiction, excerpted novel, suspense/mystery, translations, western. Receives approximately 500 mss/month. Buys 20 mss/issue; 100 mss/year. Publishes ms within 18 months of acceptance. Length: 1,500 words average; 2,500 words maximum. Length: "Less is more—if well made." Sometimes critiques rejected mss and recommends other markets.
How to Contact: Send complete ms. Reports in 3 months. SASE. "No queries on fiction." Accepts computer printout submissions. Sample copy for $1.50. Fiction guidelines for #10 SAE and 1 first class stamp.
Payment: Pays $1-20 and contributor's copies. Charge for extra copies.
Terms: Pays on publication for first North American serial rights. Every issue contains contests; none require fee.
Advice: "Magazine fiction reflects editor's best guess of readers' tastes and interests. Writers are the prophets, poets, saints and madmen of society and through their work, redefine and reshape the world. To clip their work to fit available space and target specific reader may be hard to accept—but that's how it works. Write for *our* readers. Be as honest as you can with yourself and fake the remainder. Don't tell the reader a story—enlist him and allow him to share the storymaking with you. Cut every word not required."

THE REAPER (II), Story Line Press, Three Oaks Farm, Brownsville OR 97327-9718. (503)466-5352. "All fiction correspondence should be sent to Tom Wilhelmus, English Department, University of Southern Indiana, Evansville IN 47712." Editors: Robert McDowell and Mark Jarman. Fiction Editor: Tom Wilhelmus. Magazine: 5½×8½; 64-90 pages; 50 lb paper; enamel/80 lb cover; occasional illustrations. "Primarily interested in narrative poetry and essays about poetry, but prints fiction." Estab. 1981. Circ. 700.
Needs: Contemporary, erotica, ethnic, experimental, feminist, gay, humor/satire, lesbian, literary. Receives 25 mss/month. Accepts 1 mss/issue; 3 mss/year. Publishes ms within 1 year of acceptance. Agented fiction 5%. Recently published work by Barbara Haas, Gail Harper. No preferred word length. Publishes short shorts. Sometimes critiques rejected mss and recommends other markets.
How to Contact: Query first. Reports on queries in 2 weeks; on mss in 1 month. SASE. Photocopied submissions OK. No dot-matrix. Sample copy for $5, 6×9 SAE and 90¢ postage. Fiction guidelines for #10 SAE and 1 first class stamp.

Payment: Pays in contributor's copies.
Terms: Acquires one-time rights. Sometimes sends galleys to authors. Occasionally sponsors contests for fiction writers. "Read the magazine for guidelines."

RECONSTRUCTIONIST (II), Federation of Reconstructionist Congregations & Havurot, Church Rd. and Greenwood Ave., Wyncote PA 19095. (215)887-1988. Editor: Joy Levitt. Magazine: 8½×11; 32 pages; illustrations; photos. Review of Jewish culture—essays, fiction, poetry of Jewish interest for American Jews. Published 6 times/year. Estab. 1935. Circ. 9,000.
Needs: Send mss only to Joy Levitt, Box 1336, Roslyn Heights NY 11577. All other material should be sent to the Pennsylvania address. Ethnic. Receives 10 unsolicited mss/month; buys 15 mss/year. Publishes ms 1-2 years after acceptance. Recently published work by Myron Taube, Lev Raphael. Published new writers within the last year. Length: 2,500 words average; 3,000 words maximum. Publishes short shorts. Recommends other markets.
How to Contact: Send complete ms with cover letter. Reports in 6-8 weeks. SASE for mss. Photocopied submissions OK. Accepts computer printouts. Sample copy free.
Terms: Pays on publication for first rights. Publication copyrighted.

RED BASS (I, II), Red Bass Productions, 2425 Burgundy St, New Orleans LA 70117. Editor: Jay Murphy. Magazine: 8½×11; 72 pages; 60 lb offset paper; illustrations and photos. "Strongly progressive arts publication—interviews, fiction, poetry, reviews, essays that further social struggle." Irregularly. Estab. 1981. Circ. 3,000.
Needs: "We publish a variety of fiction, translations and excerpts from novels in progress—all committed to social change in one sense or another." Receives 3-5 unsolicited fiction mss/month. Accepts 1 ms/issue; 4-5 mss/year. Publishes ms in variable time after acceptance. Recently published work by Kathy Acker, James Purdy, Lucian Truscott; published new writers within the last year. Length: 1,500 words average; 500 words minimum; 3,000 words maximum. Also publishes short shorts. Sometimes critiques rejected mss and recommends other markets.
How to Contact: Send complete manuscript with cover letter. Reports in 4 weeks or more on queries; 2 months on mss. SASE for ms. Simultaneous submissions OK. Accepts computer printouts. Sample copy $5.
Payment: Free contributor's copies; sometimes cash as funds allow.
Terms: Acquires first North American serial rights.
Advice: "We plan to publish more fiction in special contexts and thematic issues, such as 'From Haiti' or 'Conspiracy Charges.' We appreciate vigorous, innovative work with integrity that also helps further critical understanding and awareness of the surrounding social, cultural, political realities."

RED CEDAR REVIEW (II), Dept. of English, Morrill Hall, Michigan State University, East Lansing MI 48825. (517)355-7570. Contact: Fiction Editor. Magazine: 5½×8½; 60-80 pages; quality b&w illustrations; good b&w photos. Theme: "literary—poetry, fiction, book reviews, one-act plays, interviews, graphics." Biannually. Estab. 1963. Circ. 400+.
Needs: Literary, feminist, regional and humorous. Accepts 3-4 mss/issue, 6-10 mss/year. Does not read mss in summer. Published new writers within the last year. Length: 500-7,000 words.
How to Contact: Send complete ms with SASE. Reports in 2 months on mss. Publishes ms up to 4 months after acceptance. Sample copy $2.
Payment: 2 free author's copies. $2.50 charge for extras.
Terms: Acquires first rights.
Advice: "Read the magazine and good literary fiction. There are many good writers out there who need a place to publish, and we try to provide them with that chance for publication. We prefer short stories that are experimental and take risks. Make your style unique—don't get lost in the mainstream work of the genre."

THE REDNECK REVIEW OF LITERATURE (II, IV), Box 730, Twin Falls ID 83301. (208)734-6653. Editor: Penelope Reedy. Magazine: 7×10; 80 pages; offset paper; cover varies from semi-glossy to felt illustrations; photos. "I consider *Redneck* to be one of the few—perhaps the only—magazines in the West seeking to bridge the gap between literate divisions. My aim is to provide literature from and to the diverse people in the western region. *Redneck* is not a political publication and takes no sides on such issues. Readership is extremely eclectic including ranchers, farmers, university professors, writers, poets, activists, civil engineers, BLM conservation officers, farm wives, attorneys, judges, truck drivers." Semiannually. Estab. 1975. Circ. 500.
Needs: "Publishes poetry, fiction, plays, essays, book reviews and folk pieces. *Redneck* deals strictly with a contemporary viewpoint/perspective, though the past can be evoked to show the reader how we got here. Nothing too academic or sentimental reminiscences. I am not interested in old-time wild west gunfighter stories." Receives 10 "or so" unsolicited mss/month. Receives 4-5 mss/issue. Recently

published work by Rafael Zepeda, Clay Reynolds and Gerald Haslam; published new writers within the last year. Length: 1,500 words minimum; 2,500 words maximum.
How to Contact: Send complete ms. SASE. No simultaneous submissions. Reprint submissions from established writers OK. Sample copy for $6 with $1 postage.
Payment: Contributor's copies.
Terms: Rights returned to author on publication.
Advice: "Use strong sense of place. Give characters action, voices. Tell the truth rather than sentimentalize."

THE REFORMED JOURNAL (II), William B. Eerdmans Publishing Co., 255 Jefferson Ave. S.E., Grand Rapids MI 49503. (616)459-4591. Editor: Mr. Jon Pott. Magazine: 8½×10⅜; 32 pages; good quality offset paper; self cover. "The *R.J.* is a religious magazine of opinion in which the contributors comment on church and society from the perspective of Reformed (Calvinistic) Protestantism. Publishes personal reflection, scholarly discussions of current issues, reviews, poems, short stories. For a well-educated readership—both clergy and laity—among evangelical and mainline Christians." Monthly. Estab. 1951. Circ. 3,000.
Needs: Religious. Receives 20 mss/month. Accepts 5 mss/issue; 60 mss/year. Recently published work by Lawrence Dorr and Virginia Stem Owens. Publishes short shorts. Sometimes critiques rejected mss and occasionally recommends other markets.
How to Contact: Send complete mss with cover letter. Reports in 1 month on queries; in 2-6 weeks on mss. Photocopied submissions OK. Accepts computer printout submissions. Free sample copy.
Payment: No payment.

RENAISSANCE FAN (I, II, IV), 2214 SE 53rd, Portland OR 97215. (503)235-0668. Magazine: 8½×11; 15-30 pages; illustrations and photos. "This is an amateur fanzine (fan magazine) related to science fiction and fantasy. Each issue has a theme." Readers are "science fiction and fantasy fans." Quarterly. Estab. 1988. Circ. 150.
Needs: Fantasy, science fiction. "We do not promote abuse and violence." Receives 3 unsolicited mss/month. Accepts up to 4 mss/issue. Publishes ms in next issue that relates to theme. Published work by Eleanor Malin, Dennis Hoggatt; published new writers within the last year. Length: 5,000 words preferred; 600 words minimum; 15,000 words maximum. Publishes short shorts. Sometimes critiques rejected mss and recommends other markets.
How to Contact: "It is best to query, but if not, find out what the themes are—a phone call is OK—no calls after 8:00 PST." SASE for ms. Simultaneous and photocopied submissions OK "must know where and when." Accepts computer printout submissions and electronic submission in ASCII, Kaypro CP/M or IBM PC. Sample copy for 9×12 SAE and 85¢. Fiction guidelines free.
Payment: Free subscription to magazine.
Terms: Acquires one-time rights.
Advice: "Readers are not mind readers. A tree is not just a tree. It is a birch or an elm or a maple. A car is an Olds, a Ford, a Chevy, a Mustang, a Pinto, etc. Be visual—use colors, sounds, smells, tastes. Appeal to the senses. Write an active story, not just a passive one. Practice. Rewrite. Submit. Listen to what you have written. Read it aloud. Know your subject. Look at what is happening around you. An everyday activity can be turned into a fantasy or science fiction story. Do not use two words where one will do—edit, edit, edit. Become a storyteller."

‡RENEGADE (II), Box 314, Bloomfield MI 48303. (313)972-5580. Editor: Michael E. Nowicki. Magazine: 5½×8½; 32 pages; 4-5 illustrations. "We are open to all forms except erotica and we publish whatever we find good." Estab. 1988. Circ. 100.
Needs: Adventure, condensed/excerpted novel, contemporary, experimental, fantasy, feminist, historical (general), horror, humor/satire, literary, mainstream, prose poem, psychic/supernatural/occult, religious/inspirational, romance, science fiction, suspense/mystery, translations and western. Receives 40-50 unsolicited mss/month. Accepts 2 mss/issue; 4 mss/year. Publishes ms 6 months after acceptance. Recently published work by Sam Astrachan. Length: 400-4,000 words; 3,000 average. Publishes short shorts. Length: 400 words. Sometimes critiques rejected mss and recommends other markets.
How to Contact: Send complete ms with cover letter. Reports in 2 weeks to 1 month on queries; 3 weeks to 2 months on mss. SASE. Sample copy $2. Fiction guidelines for #10 SAE and 1 first class stamp.
Payment: Pays in contributor's copies.
Terms: All rights revert to author. Publication not copyrighted.
Advice: "We look for characters which appear to be real and deal with life in a real way. The use of plot to forefront the clash of personalities and the theme of the work. Take advice cautiously and apply what works. Then submit it. We are always happy to critique work we read."

‡RESONANCE (IV), The Journal of Creative Self Discovery, Box 215, Beacon NY 12508. Editor: Evan Pritchard. Fiction Editor: Valeria Giannini. Magazine: 8½×11; 52 pages; offset paper; color, glossy cover stock; illustrations; photographs. "*Theme* is finding wisdom and enlightenment through living life and going within yourself—and expressed through creative activity. We lean toward New Age, self-help and spiritual readers."
Needs: Fantasy, humor/satire, juvenile (5-9 years), religious/inspirational, science fiction and visionary. "We do not publish political or sexually oriented material, religious or dogmatic material, negative self indulgent or depressing, or rose-colored utopian writing. We are looking for balance and integrity." Number of unsolicited mss received each month varies. Accepts 2-3 mss/issue. Recently published work by Susan Hanniford Crowley, Bob Rehm and Estelle Espino. Length: 600-1,200 words; 1,200 average. Publishes short shorts. Sometimes critiques rejected mss and recommends other markets.
How to Contact: Query with clips of published work. "Include where you heard about *Resonance*, what your background is as a writer." Reports in 3 months. SASE. Simultaneous, photocopied and reprint submissions OK. Accepts computer printout submissions. Sample copy $2.50 (includes postage) and 9×12 SAE.
Payment: Pays in contributor's copies.
Terms: Acquires one-time rights. Publication is not copyrighted.
Advice: "Each is considered on its own merits. We look for writers with vision, but who are well grounded in everyday life, and appreciate the craft of writing and the music of words. We look for writing that inspires us and helps us in some way; and which is enjoyable to read."

RESPONSE (II, IV), A Contemporary Jewish Review, Queens College Press, 27 W. 20th St., 9th Floor, New York NY 10011. (212)675-1168. Editor: Bennett Graff. Magazine: 6×9; 96 pages; 70 lb paper; 10 pt. CIS cover; illustrations; photos. Fiction, poetry and essays with a Jewish theme, for Jewish students and young adults. Quarterly. Estab. 1967. Circ. 2,500.
Needs: Contemporary, ethnic, experimental, feminist, historical (general), humor/satire, literary, prose poem, regional, religious/inspirational, spirituals, translations. "Nothing without some specific Jewish content." Receives 10-12 unsolicited mss/month. Accepts 5 mss/issue; 20 mss/year. Publishes ms 7-12 months after acceptance. Length: 15-20 pages (double spaced). Publishes short shorts. Sometimes critiques rejected mss and recommends other markets.
How to Contact: Send complete ms with cover letter; include brief biography of author. Reports in 6 weeks on mss. SASE. Photocopied submissions are OK. Accepts computer prinout submissions; no dot-matrix. Free sample copy.
Payment: Pays in contributor's copies.

‡RFD (II), Rt. 1, Box 127 E, Bakersville NC 28705. Contact: Fiction Editor. Magazine: 8½×11; 96 pages average; 50 lb paper; 65 lb cover stock; illustrations; photos. "Published by and for gay men who share a rural or spiritual consciousness. We seek fiction, poetry and articles dealing with gay men living in a non-urban environment and with the transpersonal dimension of gay men's lives." Quarterly. Plans special fiction issue. Estab. 1974. Circ. 2,000.
Needs: Gay-oriented, non-sexist, non-racist material dealing with gay men who share a non-urban consciousness. Receives 1 unsolicited fiction ms each month. Published new writers within the last year. Critiques rejected mss "when there is time." Sometimes recommends other markets.
How to Contact: Send complete ms with SASE. Accepts computer printout submissions. Reports in 3 months on mss. Publishes ms generally 3-6 months after acceptance. Sample copy $4. Free guidelines.
Payment: 2 free author's copies. $2 charge for extras.
Terms: Acquires simultaneous rights.
Advice: "Write for guidelines or read some back issues." Most mss are rejected because of inappropriate subject matter. "We are a country journal with radical faire beji—for gay men everywhere."

RIVER CITY Memphis State Review, (see River City) (formerly *Memphis State Review*), Dept. of English, Memphis State University, Memphis TN 38152. (901)678-8888. Editor: Sharon Bryan. Magazine: 6×9; 100 pages. National review of poetry, fiction and nonfiction. Semiannually. Estab. 1980. Circ. 1,200. Recently published work by Fred Busch. Published new writers within the last year.
How to Contact: Send complete ms with SASE. Sample copy $4.
Payment: Annual $100 prize for best poem or best short story and 2 free contributor's copies. "We pay if grant monies are available."
Terms: Acquires first North American serial rights.
Advice: "We're soliciting work from writers with a national reputation, and are occasionally able to pay, depending on grants received. I would prefer no cover letter. *River City* Writing Awards in Fiction: $2,000 1st prize, $500 2nd page, $300 3rd prize. See magazine for details."

‡RIVER STYX (II), Big River Association, 14 S. Euclid, St. Louis MO 63108. (314)361-0043. Editor: Jennifer Atkinson. Magazine: 6×8; 90 pages; visual art (b&w). "No theme restrictions, high quality, inteliigent work." Triannual. Estab. 1975.

Needs: Excerpted novel chapter, contemporary, ethnic, experimental, feminist, gay, satire, lesbian, literary, mainstream, prose poem, translations. "Avoid 'and then I woke up' stories." Receives 15 unsolicited mss/month. Buys 1-3 mss/issue; 3-8 mss/year. Reads only in September and October. Recently published work by Bonita Friedman, Leslie Becker, Fred Viebahn. Length: no more than 20-30 manuscript pages. Publishes short shorts. Sometimes critiques rejected mss and recommends other markets. Send complete manuscript with name and address on every page. Reports in 2 months on mss. Photocopied and reprint submissions OK. Accepts computer printout submissions. Sample copy $5. Fiction guidelines for #10 SAE and 1 first class stamp.
Payment: Pays $8/page maximum, free subscription to magazine and contributor's copies.
Terms: Pays on publication for first North American serial rights.
Advice: Looks for "writer's attention to the language and the sentence. Responsible, controlled narrative."

‡RIVERSIDE QUARTERLY (II,IV), Box 464, Waco TX 76703. (817)756-4749. Editor: Leland Sapiro. Fiction Editor: Redd Boggs. Magazine: 5½×8½; 64 pages; illustrations. Quarterly. Estab. 1964. Circ. 1,100.
Needs: Fantasy and science fiction. Accepts 1 mss/issue; 4 mss/year. Publishes ms 6 months after acceptance. Length: 3,500 words maximum; 3,000 words average. Publishes short shorts. Sometimes critiques rejected mss.
How to Contact: *Send directly to fiction editor, Redd Bogg, Box 1111, Berkeley, CA 94701.* Send complete ms with cover letter. Reports in 2 weeks. SASE. Simultaneous submissions OK. Accepts electronic submissions. Sample copy $2.
Payment: Pays in contributor's copies.
Terms: Acquires one-time rights. Sends galleys to author.
Advice: "Would-be contributors are urged to first inspect a copy or two of the magazine (available at any major college or public library) to see the *kind* of story we print."

RIVERWIND (II,IV), General Studies/Hocking Technical College, Nelsonville OH 45764. (614)753-3591 (ext. 2375). Editor: Audrey Naffziger. Associate Editor: C. A. Dubclak. Magazine: 6×9; 60 lb paper; cover illustrations. "College press, small literary magazine." Annually. Estab. 1975.
Needs: Adventure, contemporary, erotica, ethnic, feminist, historical (general), horror, humor/satire, literary, mainstream, prose poem, spiritual, sports, regional, translations, western. No juvenile/teen fiction. Receives 30 mss/month. Published work by Lee Martin, Roy Bentley, Kate Hancock; published new writers within the last year. Sometimes critiques rejected mss.
How to Contact: Send complete mss with cover letter. Reports on mss in 1-4 months. SASE. Photocopied submissions OK.
Payment: Pays in contributor's copies.
Advice: "Your work must be strong, entertaining. It helps if you are an Ohio/West Virginia writer. We hope to print more fiction."

ROANOKE REVIEW (II), Roanoke College, English Department, Salem VA 24153. (703)375-2500. Editor: Robert R. Walter. Magazine: 6×9; 40-60 pages. Semiannually. Estab. 1967. Circ. 300.
Needs: Receives 30-40 unsolicited mss/month. Accepts 2-3 mss/issue; 4-6 mss/year. Publishes ms 6 months after acceptance. Length: 2,500 words minimum; 7,500 words maximum. Publishes short shorts. Occasionally critiques rejected mss.
How to Contact: Send complete ms with cover letter. Reports in 1-2 weeks on queries; 8-10 weeks on mss. SASE for query. Photocopied submissions OK. Accepts computer printout submissions. Sample copy for $1.50.
Payment: Pays in contributor's copies.

‡THE ROCKFORD REVIEW (II), The Rockford Writers Guild, Box 858, Rockford IL 61103. (815)962-2552. Fiction Editor: Olivia Diamond. Magazine: 8½×11; 60 pages; b&w illustrations; b&w photos. "Eclectic in approach, we look for poetry with control of poetic line and devices with a fresh approach to old themes or new insights into the human condition whether in prose or poetry." Annually. Estab. 1971. Circ. 1,000.
Needs: Ethnic, experimental, fantasy, feminist, historical (general), humor/satire, literary and regional. No erotica, gay/lesbian. Accepts 5-6 mss/issue. Publishes ms 6-9 months after acceptance. Recently published work by Christine Swanberg, Dwight E. Humphries and Rachael Burchard. Length: 2,000-4,000 words; 2,500 average. "Would like a 2,500 word novel excerpt for a future issue." Sometimes critiques rejected mss and recommends other markets.
How to Contact: Send complete ms. "Include a short biographical note – no more than four sentences." Reports in 4-6 weeks on mss. SASE. Accepts simultaneous and photocopied submissions, reprints (as long as acknowledgement included) and computer printouts. Sample copy $5. Fiction guidelines for SAE.

Payment: Pays contributor's copies.
Terms: Acquires first North American serial rights. *Charges reading fee of $5 for poems and $5 for prose works.*
Advice: "Any subject or theme goes as long as it enhances our understanding of our humanity. We want strongly plotted stories where the action takes place in other settings besides the character's head. Experiment with point-of-view. Make sure you've got it right for your story. We would like to see a lot more short stories than we receive."

This cover portrays illustrator Wanie Reeverts' perceptions of a busy intersection outside her studio in Rockford, Illinois. "The drawing manifests the power of place and the necessity also for imaginative vision and metaphor in the art of writing," says editor Olivia Diamond. Diamond adds that though the artist's eye catches downtown Rockford, "it could be downtown anywhere—midsize to big city USA."

ROHWEDDER (II, IV), International Journal of Literature & Art, Rough Weather Press, Box 29490, Los Angeles CA 90029. Editor: Hans-Jurgen Schacht. Fiction Editors: Nancy Locke, Robert Dassanowsky-Harris and Nancy Antell. Magazine: 8½×11; 50+ pages; 20 lb paper; 90 lb cover; illustrations; photos. "Multilingual/cultural poetry and short stories. Graphic art and photography." Published irregularly. Estab. 1986.
Needs: Contemporary, ethnic, experimental, feminist, literary, regional, translations (with rights). No fillers. Receives 20-50 unsolicited mss/month. Accepts 1-3 mss/issue; 6 mss/year. Publishes ms 1 month after acceptance. Length: 1,500-2,500 words average; 200 words minimum; 2,500 words maximum. Publishes short shorts. Sometimes critiques rejected mss and recommends other markets.
How to Contact: Include bio with submission. Reports in 2 weeks on queries; 2 months on mss. SASE. Photocopied submissions OK. Accepts computer printout submissions. Sample copy for $4.50.
Payment: Pays in contributor's copies, charges for extras.
Terms: Acquires one-time right.
Advice: "Go out as far as you have to but remember the basics: clear, concise style and form. Always enclose SASE."

ROOM OF ONE'S OWN (II), Growing Room Collective, Box 46160, Station G, Vancouver, British Columbia V6R 4G5 Canada. Editors: Editorial Collective. Magazine: 5×6; 100 pages; bond paper; bond cover stock; illustrations; photos. Feminist literary: fiction, poetry, criticism, reviews. Readership: general, nonscholarly. Quarterly. Estab. 1975. Circ. 1,200.
Needs: Literary, feminist and lesbian. No "sexist or macho material." Buys 6 mss/issue. Receives approximately 40 unsolicited fiction mss each month. Approximately 2% of fiction is agented. Recently published work by Janette Turner Hospital, Anne E. Norman, Judith Monroe; published new writers within the last year. Length: 3,000 words preferred. "No critiques except unusual circumstances."
How to Contact: Send complete ms with SASE or SAE and IRC. "Please include cover letter. State whether multiple submission or not (we don't consider multiple submissions) and whether previously published." Reports in 3 months. Publishes ms an average of 1-3 months after acceptance. Sample copy $5 with SASE or SAE and IRC.

Payment: $50 plus 2 free author's copies. $2 charge for extras.
Terms: Pays on publication for first rights.
Advice: "Write well and unpretentiously." Mss are rejected because they are "unimaginative."

THE ROSE ARTS MAGAZINE (II), 336 SE 32nd Ave., Portland OR 97214. (503)231-0644. Editor: Terry Hammond. Magazine: 8½×10¾; 40+ pages; illustrations; photos. "*The Rose Arts Magazine* is dedicated to the promotion of arts and artists, gives attention also to broad cultural themes, and offers a platform for feature articles, creative writing, essays, fiction and historical perspectives." Bimonthly. Estab. 1986. Circ. 10,000.
Needs: Adventure, contemporary, ethnic, experimental, fantasy, feminist, gay, historical (general), humor/satire, lesbian, literary, psychic/supernatural/occult, regional, romance (contemporary, historical), science fiction, suspense/mystery and translations. No murders or lugubrious contents. Receives 20 unsolicited mss/month. Buys 1 ms/issue; 6 mss/year. Publishes ms 1-4 months after acceptance. Recently published work by Don Modie, Curt Fischer and Charles Richard Laing; published new writers within the last year. Length: 2,000-2,500 words average; 1,000 words minimim; 3,000 words maximum. Sometimes critiques rejected mss.
How to Contact: Send complete ms with cover letter, which should include brief, informal introduction of author and piece. Reports in 1-2 weeks on queries; 2-6 weeks on mss. SASE. Photocopied submissions OK. Accepts computer printout submissions. Sample copy for $1. Fiction guidelines free with SASE.
Payment: Pays 2½¢/word (generous number of copies provided for cost of postage only).
Terms: Pays on publication for one-time rights.
Advice: "I welcome submissions by beginning writers and am willing to work on a piece with an author by making suggestions for a second draft if necessary according to our standards of quality."

THE ROUND TABLE (II), A Journal of Poetry and Fiction, 375 Oakdale Dr., Rochester NY 14618. Editors: Alan and Barbara Lupack. Magazine: 6×9; 64 pages. "We publish serious poetry and fiction." Annually. Estab. 1984. Circ. 150.
Needs: Experimental, literary, mainstream. "The quality of the fiction is the most important criterion. We would consider work in other categories if it were especially well written." Accepts 7-10 mss/year. Does not read ms July 1-September 30. Published new writers within the last year. Publishes ms 9 months after acceptance. Publishes short shorts.
How to Contact: Send complete ms with cover letter. Reports usually in 2-3 months, but stories under consideration may be held longer. SASE for ms. Simultaneous submissions OK—if notified immediately upon acceptance elsewhere; photocopied submissions OK. Sample copy $4 (specify fiction issue). Fiction guidelines for SAE and 1 first class stamp.
Payment: Contributor's copy, reduced charge for extras.

‡SALOME: A JOURNAL OF THE PERFORMING ARTS (I, II, IV), Ommation Press, 5548 N. Sawyer, Chicago IL 60625. Editor: Effie Mihopoulos. "*Salome* seeks to cover the performing arts in a thoughtful and incisive way." Quarterly. Estab. 1976. Circ. 1,000.
Needs: Literary, contemporary, science fiction, fantasy, women's, feminist, gothic, romance, mystery, adventure, humor, serialized novels, prose poems, translations. "We seek good quality mss that relate to the performing arts or fiction with strong characters that somehow move the reader." Receives approximately 25 unsolicited fiction mss each month; accepts 40 mss/year. No preferred length. Sometimes sends mss on to editors of other publications and recommends other markets.
How to Contact: Send complete ms with SASE. Reports in 1 month. Sample copy $4, 9×12 SASE with 90¢ (book-rate) postage preferred.
Payment: 1 free author's copy. Contributor's rates for extras upon request.
Terms: Acquires first North American serial rights. "Rights revert to author, but we retain reprint rights."
Advice: "Write a well-written story or prose poem." Rejected mss are "usually badly written—improve style, grammar, etc.—too often writers send out mss before they're ready. See a sample copy. Specify fiction interest."

SALT LICK PRESS (II), Salt Lick Foundation, 1804 E. 38½ St., Austin TX 78722. Editor: James Haining. Magazine: 8½×11; 64 pages; 60 lb offset stock; 80 lb text cover; illustrations and photos. Irregular. Estab. 1969.
Needs: Contemporary, erotica, ethnic, experimental, feminist, gay, lesbian, literary. Receives 15 unsolicited mss each month. Accepts 2 mss/issue. Length: open. Occasionally critiques rejected mss.
How to Contact: Send complete ms with cover letter. Reports in 2 weeks on queries; 4 weeks on mss. SASE. Simultaneous, photocopied and reprint submissions OK. Accepts computer printout submissions. Sample copy $5, 9×12 SAE and 3 first class stamps.

Payment: Free contributor's copies.
Terms: Acquires first North American serial rights. Sends galleys to author.

SAMISDAT (II), Box 129, Richford VT 05476. (514)263-4439. Editor: Merritt Clifton. Magazine: 5½×8½; 60-80 pages; offset bond paper; vellum bristol cover stock; illustrations; photos. Publication is "environmentalist, anti-war, anti-nuke, emphatically non-leftist—basically anarchist." Publishes essays, reviews, poetry and original artwork in approximately equal proportions. Audience consists of "people constructively and conscientiously engaged in changing the world." Subscribers include many secretaries, journalists, blue-collar workers and housewives "but very few bureaucrats." Quarterly. Estab. 1973. Circ. 400+.
Needs: Adventure, contemporary, erotica, ethnic, experimental, fantasy, feminist, gay, historical (general), humor/satire, lesbian, literary, mainstream, prose poem, regional, science fiction, serialized/excerpted novel, sports, suspense/mystery, translations, western. "We're pretty damned eclectic if something is done well. Formula hackwork and basic ineptitude, though, won't ever hack it here. No whimsy; no self-indulgent whines about the difficulty of being a sensitive writer/artist." Receives approximately 10-100 unsolicited mss/month. Accepts 2-5 mss/issue. "We'd like to use a lot more than we're getting." Publishes ms 2-5 months after acceptance. Recently published work by Miriam Sagan, Thomas Michael McDade, Robert Swisher; published new writers within the last year. Length: 1,500-5,000 words. Publishes short shorts. Length: up to 1,000 words. Sometimes recommends other markets or critiques rejected mss.
How to Contact: Send complete ms with cover letter. "I like to know how old the author is, what he/she does for a living, and get a ballpark idea of writing experiences, but I do not want to see mere lists of credits. I also like to know why a writer is submitting here in particular." Reports in 1 week on queries and mss. SASE. Reprint submissions OK. "Does not read photocopies or multiple submissions of any kind." Accepts computer printout submissions. Sample copy $2.50.
Payment: Pays in contributor's copies.
Terms: Acquires one-time rights.
Advice: "I'm editor, publisher, printer, distributor, and therefore I do as I damned well please. Over the past 17 years I've found enough other people who agree with me that short stories are worthwhile that my magazine manages to support itself, more or less in the tradition of the old-time radical magazines that published the now-classical short story writers. Know the factual background to your material, e.g., if writing a historical piece, get the details right."

SAN GABRIEL VALLEY MAGAZINE (IV), Miller Books, 2908 W. Valley Blvd., Alhambra CA 91803. (213)284-7607. Editor: Joseph Miller. Magazine: 5¼×7¼; 48 pages; 60 lb book paper; vellum bristol cover stock; illustrations; photos. "Regional magazine for the Valley featuring local entertainment, dining, sports and events. We also carry articles about successful people from the area. For upper-middle class people who enjoy going out a lot." Bimonthly. Published special fiction issue last year; plans another. Estab. 1976. Circ. 3,000.
Needs: Contemporary, inspirational, psychic/supernatural/occult, western, adventure and humor. No articles on sex or ERA. Receives approximately 10 unsolicited fiction mss/month. Buys 2 mss/issue; 20 mss/year. Length: 500-2,500 words. Also publishes short shorts. Recommends other markets.
How to Contact: Send complete ms with SASE. Accepts computer printout submissions. Reports in 2 weeks on mss. Sample copy $1 with 9×12 SASE.
Payment: 5¢/word; 2 free author's copies.
Terms: Payment on acceptance for one-time rights.

SAN JOSE STUDIES (II), San Jose State University, One Washington Square, San Jose CA 95152. Editor: Fauneil J. Rinn. Magazine: digest size; 112-144 pages; good paper and cover; occasional illustrations and photos. "A journal for the general, educated reader. Covers a wide variety of materials: fiction, poetry, interviews, interdisciplinary essays. Aimed toward the college-educated common reader with an interest in the broad scope of materials." Triannually. Estab. 1975. Circ. 500.
Needs: Literary, contemporary, humor, ethnic and regional. Accepts 1-2 mss/issue, 3-6 mss/year. Receives approximately 12 unsolicited fiction mss each month. Published work by Barbara La Porte, William Kanouse. Length: 2,500-5,000+ words. Critiques rejected mss when there is time. Sometimes recommends other markets.
How to Contact: Send complete ms with SASE. Accepts computer printout submissions. Prefers letter-quality. Reports in 2 months. Publishes ms an average of 6 months to 1 year after acceptance. Sample copy for $4.
Payment: 2 free author's copies. Annual $100 award for best story, essay or poem.
Terms: Acquires first rights. Sends galleys to author.
Advice: "Name should appear *only* on cover sheet. We seldom print beginning writers of fiction. Proofread with great care."

‡SANTA MONICA REVIEW (III), Santa Monica College, 1900 Pico Blvd., Santa Monica CA 90405. (213)450-5150. Editor: James Krusoe. Magazine: 5½×8; 140 pages, rag paper. Semiannually. Estab. 1988. Circ. 1,000.

Needs: Contemporary, literary. Accepts 5 mss/issue; 10 mss/year. Publishes mss varying amount of time after publication. Recently published work by Ann Beattie, Arturo Vivante and Guy Davenport.

How to Contact: Send complete ms with cover letter. Reports in 3 months on mss. SASE. Simultaneous and photocopied submissions OK. Sample copy for $6.

Payment: Free subscription to magazine, contributor's copies.

Terms: Acquires one-time rights.

Advice: "We are *not* actively soliciting beginning work. We want to combine high quality West Coast, especially Los Angeles, writing with that from the rest of the country."

SCIENCE FICTION RANDOMLY (I, IV), Box 12705, Gainesville FL 32604. Editors: Hawk, Steve Antczak. Magazine: 8½x11; 32-48 pages; illustrations. "*SFRan* is a science fiction fanzine written by fans and intended for fans." Published "randomly"—4-6 issues per year. Plan special fiction issues/anthologies. Estab. 1987. Circ. 500.

Needs: Fantasy, horror, humor/satire, science fiction. "We publish all forms of SF, from psychological to cyberpunk. Avoid overused themes and 'tricky' endings. We would prefer instead to see more stories with well-developed characters. We are not interested in established-universe media fiction, except as parody—DO NOT send us any *Star Trek*, etc. fiction." Receives 15-20 unsolicited mss/month. Buys 4 mss/issue; 16-24 mss/year. Publishes ms average of 1-2 months after acceptance. Length: 3,500 words preferred; 10,000 maximum. Publishes short shorts. Length: 500-1,500 words. Always critiques rejected mss and sometimes recommends other markets.

How to Contact: Send complete ms with cover letter. Cover letter should include "short bio, publishing history, or anything the author feels may be of interest." Reports in 2-3 weeks. SASE. Simultaneous, photocopied and reprint submissions OK. Accepts computer printout submissions. Accepts electronic submissions on 5¼" or 3½" disks in IBM format. Sample copy for $1. Fiction guidelines for SAE.

Payment: Pays in contributor's copies.

Terms: Acquires one-time rights. Fiction rights revert on publication.

Advice: "Science Fiction is the easiest field for a new writer to break into, and the way to start is through fanzines. Fanzines give writers a forum for their work and an opportunity for criticism while still perfecting their style. Many of today's best-known pros started out in fanzines, and many of them *still* write for fanzines. Read science fiction. Know the market—SFanzines, particularly *SFRan*, are very different from the typical small-press magazine. Don't send us media-based stories unless they're parodies, and DON'T send us stories with trick endings—I promise to be very, very mean to the next person who sends me a story about two space travellers who are marooned on Earth and who turn out to be Adam and Eve."

‡SCIFANT (I), Box 398, Suisun CA 94585. Editor: Paul Doerr. Magazine: 8½×11; 98 pages (microfiche only); illustrations and photos. "We publish science fiction, fantasy, horror, space fiction and space high technology." Monthly.

Needs: Adventure, experimental, fantasy, historical (general), horror, humor/satire, romance, science fiction, serialized/excerpted novel, suspense/mystery. Receives 50+ unsolicited mss/month. Buys 30+ mss/issue. Publishes ms 2 months-2 years after acceptance. Publishes short shorts of a half page and up. Occasionally critiques rejected mss and recommends other markets.

How to Contact: Send complete ms with cover letter. Ms must be single spaced with margins no greater than a half inch and proofread (camera ready). Reports in 1 month. SASE. Simultaneous, photocopied and reprint submissions OK. Prefers letter quality computer printout submissions. Accepts electronic submissions via Apple II. Fiction guidelines for #10 SASE. Sample copy $3. (Copy in microfiche.)

Payment: Payment schedule on spec sheet.

Terms: Pays percentage of sales profit.

Advice: "Send me something! Would like to see more fiction on topics of WW II and space colonization."

SCREAM MAGAZINE (II), Fiction in a Fantastic Vein, Alternating Crimes (AC) Publishing, Box 10363, Raleigh NC 27605. (919)834-7542. Editor: Russell Boone. Assistant Editor: Katie Boone. 8¼×10½; 64 pages; 24 lb bond/60 lb offset paper; 80 lb uncoated cover; illustrations and photographs. "We publish a full range of fiction from traditional to avant garde. Readers are academics and professionals interested in the underground arts movement." Quarterly. Estab. 1985. Circ. 1,500.

Needs: Adventure, contemporary, erotica, experimental, fantasy, feminist, gay, historical (general), horror, humor/satire, lesbian, literary, psychic/supernatural/occult, regional, science fiction, serialized/excerpted novel, suspense/mystery. No religious fiction. Receives 15-25 unsolicited mss/month. Accepts 5-8 mss/issue; 12-20 mss/year. Does not read mss in December. Publishes ms 3-6 months after acceptance. Length: 2,500 words preferred; 900 words minimum; 4,000 words maximum. Sometimes critiques rejected mss and recommends other markets.

How to Contact: Send complete ms with cover letter. Reports in 3 weeks on queries; 8 weeks on mss. SASE. Photocopied submissions OK. Accepts computer printout submissions. Sample copy for $5. Free fiction guidelines. No simultaneous submissions.

Payment: Pays in contributor's copes.

Terms: Acquires first North American serial rights.

Advice: "I believe there is a 'fiction revival' on the way via the underground/small press express. The audience, the readers are out there but they can't get their fix at the general public newsstands. For the last decade (1976-1988) these discerning readers of American fiction have had to go to 'alternative bookstores' or make their discovery by word of mouth. But all this is changing. The news agencies and booksellers have already begun picking up on this and new titles are beginning to appear at newsstands around the country. In turn, I think the mainstream publications wil begin picking up on this new mood and in the next few years open up their fiction markets. Get a recent issue of *Scream*, study it and query if there are any questions."

SCRIVENER (II), 853 Sherbrooke St. W., Montreal, Quebec H3A 2T6 Canada. Editors: Julie Crawford and Ernest Alston. Magazine: 8½×11; 40 pages; glossy paper; illustrations; b&w photos. "*Scrivener* is a creative journal publishing fiction, poetry, graphics, photography, reviews, interviews and scholarly articles. We publish the best of new and established writers. We examine how current trends in North American writing are rooted in a pervasive creative dynamic; our audience is mostly scholarly and in the writing field." Annually. Estab. 1980. Circ. 800.

Needs: Good writing. Receives 40 unsolicited mss/month. Accepts 20 mss/year. Does not read mss May 1-Sept 1. Publishes ms up to 6 months after acceptance. Recently published work by James Conway, Colin Wright, Louis Phillips; published new writers within the last year. Length: 25 pages maximum. Occasionally publishes short shorts. Often critiques rejected mss. Sometimes recommends other markets.

How to Contact: Query first. Order sample copy ($2); send complete ms with cover letter with "critical statements; where we can reach you; biographical data; education; previous publications." Reports in 4 months on queries and mss. SASE/IRC preferred but not required. Simultaneous, photocopied submissions and reprints OK. Accepts computer printouts. Sample copy $3 (US in USA; Canadian in Canada). Fiction guidelines for SAE/IRC.

Payment: Sometimes pays $3-25; provides contributor's copies; charges for extras.

Terms: Pays on publication.

Advice: "Send us your best stuff. Don't be deterred by rejections. Sometimes a magazine just isn't looking for your *kind* of writing. Don't neglect the neatness of your presentation."

THE SEATTLE REVIEW (II), Padelford Hall GN-30, University of Washington, Seattle WA 98195. (206)543-9865. Editor: Donna Gerstenberger. Fiction Editor: David Bosworth. Magazine: 6×9. "Includes general fiction, poetry, craft essays on writing, and one interview per issue with a Northwest writer." Semiannually. Published special fiction issue. Estab. 1978. Circ. 1,000.

Needs: Contemporary, ethnic, experimental, fantasy, feminist, gay, historical, horror, humor/satire, lesbian, literary, mainstream, prose poem, psychic/supernatural/occult, regional, science fiction, excerpted novel, suspense/mystery, translations, western. "We also publish a series called Writers and their Craft, which deals with aspects of writing fiction (also poetry)—point of view, characterization, etc., rather than literary criticism, each issue." Does not want to see "anything in bad taste (porn, racist, etc.)." Receives about 50 unsolicited mss/month. Accepts about 3-6 mss/issue; about 4-10 mss/year. Reads mss all year but "slow to respond in summer." 25% of fiction is agented. Recently published work by David Milofsky, Lawson Fusao Inada and Liz Rosenberg; published new writers within the last year. Length: 3,500 words average; 500 words minimum; 10,000 words maximum. Publishes short shorts. Sometimes critiques rejected mss. Occasionally recommends other markets.

How to Contact: Send complete ms. "If included, cover letter should list recent publications or mss we'd seen and liked, but been unable to publish." Reports in 3 months. SASE. Accepts computer printout submissions. Sample copy "half-price if older than one year."

Payment: Pays 0-$100, free subscription to magazine, 2 contributor's copies; charge for extras.

Terms: Pays on publication for first North American serial rights. Copyright reverts to writer on publication; "please request release of rights and cite *SR* in reprint publications." Sends galleys to author.

Advice: "Beginners do well in our magazine if they send clean, well-written manuscripts. We've published a lot of 'first stories' from all over the country and take pleasure in discovery."

SEEMS (II), Lakeland College, Sheboygan WI 53081. (414)565-3871. Editor: Karl Elder. Magazine: 7×8½; 40 pages. "We publish fiction and poetry for an audience which tends to be highly literate. People read the publication, I suspect, for the sake of reading it." Published irregularly. Estab. 1971. Circ. 300.

Needs: Literary. Accepts 4 mss/issue. Receives approximately 12 unsolicited fiction mss each month. Recently published work by John Birchler; published new writers within the last year. Length: 5,000 words maximum. Also publishes short shorts. Critiques rejected mss when there is time.

How to Contact: Send complete ms with SASE. Accepts computer printout submissions. Prefers letter-quality. Reports in 2 months on mss. Publishes ms an average of 1-2 years after acceptance. Sample copy $3.

Payment: 1 free author's copy; $3 charge for extras.

Terms: Rights revert to author.

Advice: "Send clear, clean copies. Read the magazine in order to help determine the taste of the editor." Mss are rejected because of "lack of economical expression, or saying with many words what could be said in only a few. Good fiction contains all of the essential elements of poetry; study poetry and apply those elements to fiction. Our interest is shifting to story poems, the grey area between genres."

‡SENSATIONS (I,II), 2 Radio Ave., A5, Secaucus NJ 07094. Founder: David Messineo. Magazine: 8½×11; 48 pages; 20 lb inside paper, 67 lb cover paper; vellum cover; black ink line illustrations. "We publish short stories and poetry, no specific theme, for a liberal, worldly audience who reads for pleasure." Annually. Estab. 1987. Circ. 120.

Needs: Adventure, contemporary, fantasy, gay, historical, horror, humor/satire, lesbian, literary, mainstream, prose poem, regional, romance (historical), science fiction, suspense/mystery. "We're not into gratuitous profanity, pornography, or violence. Sometimes these are needed to properly tell the tale. We'll read anything unusual, providing it is submitted in accordance with our submission policies. No abstract works only the writer can understand." Receives approx. 20 unsolicited mss/issue. Accepts 4 mss/issue. Publishes ms 2 months after acceptance. Recently published work by Patricia Flinn, Karl Luntta and Ed Condon. "No more than 14 pages double-spaced." Publishes short shorts. Always critiques rejected mss; sometimes recommends other markets.

How to Contact: "Send name, address, a paragraph of background information about yourself, a paragraph about what inspired the story. We'll send submission guidelines when we are ready to judge material." Reports in 1-2 weeks on queries; 4-6 weeks on mss. SASE. Simultaneous and photocopied submissions OK. Accepts computer printout submissions. Accepts electronic submissions (Macintosh only). *Must first purchase* sample copy $5 (first issue). Check payable to "David Messineo."

Payment: No payment.

Terms: Acquired one-time rights.

Advice: "Each story must have a strong beginning that grabs the reader's attention in the first two sentences. The reader must want to read further. The characters have to be realistic and well-described. Readers must like, hate, or have some emotional response to the characters other than boredom. Setting, plot, construction, attention to detail—all are important. We work with writers to help them improve in these areas, but the better stories are written before they come to us, the greater the chance for publication. Purchase sample copy first and read the stories."

SEQUOIA, Stanford Literary Magazine, Storke Publications Bldg., Stanford CA 94305. Editor: Annie Finch. Fiction Editor: Marion Rust. "Literary Journal ranges from traditional to avant-garde for college students to retired people." Semiannually. Estab. 1887. Circ. 500.

Needs: "Literary excellence is the primary criterion. We'll consider anything but prefer literary, ethnic, avant-garde, experimental, translations and satire." Receives 50 mss/month. Accepts 2-3 mss/issue; 24-30 mss/year. Publishes ms 2 weeks to 2 months after acceptance. Length: 8,000 words or 20 pages maximum.

How to Contact: Send complete ms with SASE. Tries to report in 3 months "during academic year." Sample copy $6.

Payment: 1-2 free author's copies. Contributor's rates on request.

Terms: Author retains rights.

SERENDIPITY (I,II), The Magazine of Everything, 4295 Silver Lake Rd., Pinson AL 35126-3307. (205)681-2259. Magazine: digest size; 32 pages; Mando paper; heavy cover stock; illustrations. "SF/Fantasy/Horror, with articles on anything of interest to fans of those genres." Bimonthly. Estab. 1986. Circ. 10,000.

Needs: Condensed novel, experimental, fantasy, historical (general) horror, humor/satire, mainstream, prose poem, psychic/supernatural/occult, science fiction, serialized/excerpted novel, suspense/mystery, young adult/teen, gaming. "It's got to be *good*." Receives 40 mss/month. Accepts 6 mss/issue; 36 mss/year. Publishes ms within 4 months of acceptance. Recently published work by Ada Cochran,

Randy Williams, Janet P. Reedman; published new writers within the last year. Length: 1,500 words preferred; 500 words minimum; 3,500 words maximum. Sometimes critiques rejected mss and recommends other markets.
How to Contact: Send complete ms with cover letter. Cover letter should include "the address, previous credits list, a brief story description." Reports on queries in 1 month; in 2 months on mss. Photocopied submissions OK. Accepts computer printout submissions. Sample copy for $2. Fiction guidelines for #10 SAE and 1 first class stamp.
Payment: Pays 1-5¢/word. Acquires first North American serial rights.
Advice: "There is an incredible market for magazine fiction in the area of the small press, of which *Serendipity* is but one example. A beginning writer has an opportunity to be published, reviewed and read by other writers. It's a great bargain. Write from the heart, and make the piece something *you* would like to read."

THE SEWANEE REVIEW (III), University of the South, Sewanee TN 37375. (615)598-1245. Editor: George Core. Magazine: 6x9; 192 pages. "A literary quarterly, publishing original fiction, poetry, essays on literary and related subjects, book reviews and book notices for well-educated readers who appreciate good American and English literature." Quarterly. Estab. 1892. Circ. 3,500.
Needs: Literary, contemporary. No translations, juvenile, gay/lesbian, erotica. Buys 10-15 mss/year. Receives approximately 100 unsolicited fiction mss each month. Does not read mss June 1-August 31. Published work by Andre Dubus, Helen Bell, Merrill Joan Gerber. Published new writers within the last year. Length: 6,000-7,500 words. Critiques rejected mss "when there is time." Sometimes recommends other markets.
How to Contact: Send complete ms with SASE and cover letter stating previous publications, if any. Accepts computer printout submissions. Reports in 1 month on mss. Sample copy $6 plus 50¢ postage.
Payment: $10-12/printed page. 2 free author's copies. $3.50 charge for extras.
Terms: Pays on publication for first North American serial rights and second serial rights by agreement.
Advice: "Send only one story at a time, with a serious and sensible cover letter. We think fiction is of greater general interest than any other literary mode."

SHATTERED WIG REVIEW (I, II), Shattered Wig Productions, 3322 Greenmount Ave., Baltimore MD 21218. (301)467-4344. Editor: Collective. Magazine: 40-50 pages; "average" paper; cardstock cover; illustrations and photos. "Open forum for the discussion of the political aspects of everyday life. Fiction, poetry, graphics, essays, photos." Semiannually. Estab. 1988. Circ. 300.
Needs: Confession, contemporary, erotica, ethnic, experimental, feminist, gay, humor/satire, juvenile (5-9 years), lesbian, literary, preschool (1-4 years), prose poem, psychic/supernatural/occult, regional, senior citizen/retirement, serialized/excerpted novel, translations, young adult/teen (10-18), meat, music, film, art, pickles, revolutionary practice." Does not want "anything by Ann Beattie or John Irving." Receives 15-20 unsolicited mss/month. Publishes ms 2-4 months after acceptance. Recently published work by Al Ackerman, Jake Berry, Bella Donna; published new writers within the last year. Publishes short shorts. Sometimes critiques rejected mss and recommends other markets.
How to Contact: Send complete ms with cover letter or "visit us in Baltimore." Reports in 1 month. SASE for ms. Simultaneous, photocopied and reprint submissions OK. Accepts computer printout submissions. Sample copy for $3 and SAE.
Payment: Pays in contributor's copies.
Terms: Acquires one-time rights.
Advice: "The arts have been reduced to imploding pus with the only material rewards reserved for vapid stylists and collegiate pod suckers. The only writing that counts has no barriers between imagination and reality, thought and action. We publish any writing that addresses vital issues. Send us at least 3 pieces so we have a choice."

SHAWNEE SILHOUETTE (II), Shawnee State University, 940 Second St., Portsmouth OH 45662. (614)354-3205. Fiction Editor: Tamela Carmichael. Magazine: 5×7; 40 pages; illustrations and photos. Quarterly.
Needs: Adventure, contemporary, historical, humor/satire, literary, mainstream, regional, romance, science fiction, suspense/mystery. Receives 3 unsolicted mss/month. Accepts 3 mss/issue. Does not read mss in summer. Publishes ms an average of 3-6 months after acceptance. Published new writers within the last year. Length: 800 words average; 400 words minimum; 1,000 words maximum. Publishes short shorts. Occasionally critiques rejected mss.
How to Contact: Send complete ms with cover letter. Reports in 3 weeks on queries. SASE. Photocopied submissions OK. Accepts computer printout submissions. Sample copy $2, 5×7 SAE and 6¢ postage.
Payment: Free contributor's copies.
Terms: Acquires one-time rights.

‡SHENANDOAH: THE WASHINGTON AND LEE UNIVERSITY REVIEW (II), Box 722, Lexington VA 24450. (703)463-8765. Editor: Dabney Stuart. Managing Editor: Lynn Williams. Magazine: 6×9; 100 pages. "A quarterly literary review publishing fiction, poetry, essays and interviews." Estab. 1950. Circ. 1,000.

Needs: Quality fiction, essays, poetry.

How to Contact: Send complete ms with SASE.

Payment: $20/page for prose. One-year subscription. 1 free author's copies.

SHOE TREE (I), The Literary Magazine by and for Young Writers, National Association for Young Writers, Inc., 215 Valle del Sol Dr., Sante Fe NM 87501. (505)982-8596. Editor: Sheila Cowing. Magazine: 6×9; 64 pages; 70 lb vellum/white stock; 10 pt. cover; illustrations (photos occasionally). "*Shoe Tree* is a nationwide publication dedicated to nurturing young talent. All stories, poems and artwork are done by children between the ages of 6 and 14." Published 3 times a year. Estab. 1985. Circ. 1,000.

Needs: Adventure, contemporary, fantasy, historical, horror, humor/satire, literary, mainstream, science fiction, suspense/mystery. "No formulas or classroom assignments." Receives 100-150 unsolicited mss/month. Accepts 6 fiction mss/issue; 18 mss/year. Publishes ms 3-6 months after acceptance. Published new writers within the last year. Length: 2,000 words average; 150 words minimum; 5,000 words maximum. Occasionally critiques rejected mss. Recommends other markets sometimes.

How to Contact: Send complete ms with cover letter, which should include name, address, age, school and name of teacher. Reports in 2-4 weeks on queries; 10-12 weeks on mss. SASE. Photocopied submissions OK. Accepts computer printout submissions. Sample copy $5. Fiction guidelines for #10 SAE.

Payment: 2 free contributer's copies.

Terms: Acquires all rights. "The National Association for Young Writers sponsors three annual *Shoe Tree* contests. The contests are open to all children between the ages of 6 and 14. Categories: fiction, nonfiction and poetry. First prize in each category: $25. Deadlines: Jan. 1 (fiction); April 1 (poetry); June 1 (nonfiction). When writing for contest rules, please provide SASE."

Advice: "Because the purpose of our magazine is to nurture talented young writers, to encourage them to explore their world in words, and to help them improve their writing skills, we are very 'optimistic' toward beginning fiction writers. We look for freshness and originality. Draw on your own experiences whenever possible. Avoid formulas and stories assigned in the classroom."

SHOOTING STAR REVIEW (II, IV), 7123 Race St., Pittsburgh PA 15208. (412)731-7039. Editor: Sandra Gould Ford. Magazine: 8½×11; 32 pages; 60 lb white paper; 80 lb enamel glossy cover; heavily-illustrated; photos. "Dedicated to the African-American (Black) experience." Quarterly. Estab. 1987. Circ. 1,500.

Needs: Adventure, contemporary, experimental, literary, mainstream, regional, romance (contemporary, historical), science fiction, suspense/mystery, translations. Each issue has a different theme: "Behind Bars" (deadline March 1); "Marching to a Different Beat" (deadline June 1); "A Salute to African-American Male Writers" (deadline September 1); "Mothers and Daughters" (deadline November 15). Writers should send a SASE for guidelines. No juvenile, preschool, young adult fiction. Receives 10-20 unsolicited mss/month. Publishes 1-2 mss/issue. Publishes ms 4-6 months after acceptance. Length: 1,800 words preferred; 3,500 words maximum. Publishes short shorts. Length: 1,000 words or less. Sometimes critiques rejected mss and recommends other markets.

How to Contact: Send complete ms with cover letter. "We like to promote the writer as well as their work and would appreciate understanding who the writer is and why they write." Reports in 2 weeks on queries; 6-8 weeks on mss. SASE. Simultaneous, photocopied and reprint submissions OK. Accepts computer printout submissions. Accepts electronic submissions via "IBM compatible, 5¼" double sided/double density disk, ASCII non-formated modem 300 baud." Sample copy for $3. Fiction guidelines for #10 SAE and 1 first class stamp.

Payment: Pays $50 maximum or contributor's copies; charge for extras.

Terms: Pays on publication for first North American serial rights. Sends galleys to author upon request, if time permits.

Advice: "*Shooting Star Review* was started specifically to provide a forum for short fiction that explores the black experience. We are committed to this art form and will make space for work that satisfies our guidelines. We welcome works on white thought on black experience and issues."

SIGN OF THE TIMES (II), A Chronicle of Decadence in the Atomic Age, Studio 403, Box 70672, Seattle WA 98107-0672. (206)323-6779. Editor: Mark Souder. Tabloid: 8×10; 32 pages; book paper; 120 lb cover stock; illustrations; photos. "Decadence in all forms for those seeking literary amusement." Semiannually. Published special fiction issue last year; plans another. Estab. 1980. Circ. 750.

Needs: Comics, erotica, experimental, gay, lesbian. No religious or western manuscripts. Receives 6 unsolicited mss/month. Buys 10 mss/issue; 20 mss/year. Published work by Gary Smith, Willie Smith, Ben Satterfield. Length: 3,000 words average; 500 words minimum, 5,000 words maximum. Publishes short shorts. Sometimes comments on rejected mss and recommends other markets.
How to Contact: Send complete ms with cover letter and bio. Reports in 6 weeks on mss. SASE. Photocopied submissions OK. Accepts computer printout submissions. Prefers letter-quality. Sample copy $3.50. Fiction guidelines for #10 SASE.
Payment: Up to $20, subscription to magazine, 2 contributor's copies; 1 time cover price charge for extras.
Terms: Pays on publication for first rights plus anthology in the future.

‡THE SIGNAL (II), Network International, Box 67, Emmett ID 83617. Editors: Joan Silva and David Chorlton. Magazine: 8½×11; 68 pages; good paper; some art; photos. "Wide open. Not restricted to 'literature.' Poetry, essays, reviews, comment, interviews, speculative thought." Semiannually. Estab. 1987.
Needs: Literary, translations. No "religious dogma, journeys of self-discovery in a '57 Chevrolet, catalogues of family members." Receives few unsolicited mss/month. Accepts "perhaps 1" ms/issue. Publishes ms 6 months to 1 year after acceptance. Length: 3,000 words maximum. Publishes short shorts.
How to Contact: "Just send us the story. Cover letter optional." Reports in 10 weeks on mss. SASE. Photocopied submissions OK. Accepts computer printout submissions. Sample copy for $3. Fiction guidelines for #10 SAE and 1 first class stamp.
Payment: Pays in contributor's copies.
Terms: Acquires first rights.
Advice: "We want to remain open to all writing. Although unable to publish very much fiction, we do look for ideas expressed in any form."

SILVERFISH REVIEW (IV), Silverfish Press, Box 3541, Eugene OR 97403. (503)344-5060. Editor: Rodger Moody. High quality literary material for a general audience. Published irregularly. Estab. 1979. Circ. 500.
Needs: Literary. Accepts 1-2 mss/issue.
How to Contact: Send complete ms with SASE. Reports in 1 month on mss. Sample copy $3 and $1 for postage.
Payment: 5 free author's copies.
Terms: Rights revert to author.
Advice: "We publish primarily poetry; we will, however, publish good quality fiction."

SING HEAVENLY MUSE! (II), Box 13299, Minneapolis MN 55414. Editor: Sue Ann Martinson. Magazine: 6x9; 125 pages; 55 lb acid-free paper; 10 pt. glossy cover stock; illustrations; photos. Women's poetry, prose and artwork. Semiannually. Estab. 1977.
Needs: Literary, contemporary, fantasy, feminist, mystery, humor, prose poem and ethnic/minority. Receives approximately 30 unsolicited fiction mss each month. "Accepts mss for consideration only in April and September." Published work by Helene Cappuccio, Erika Duncan, Martha Roth. Publishes short shorts. Sometimes recommends other markets.
How to Contact: Query for information on theme issues or variations in schedule. Include cover letter with "brief writing background and publications." Accepts computer printout submissions. Reports in 1-3 months on queries and mss. Publishes ms an average of 1 year after acceptance. Sample copy $3.50.
Payment: Honorarium; 2 free copies.
Terms: Pays on publication for first rights.
Advice: "Try to avoid preaching. Look for friends also interested in writing and form a mutual support-and-criticism group."

SINISTER WISDOM (IV), Box 3252, Berkeley CA 94703. Editor: Elana Dykewomon. Magazine: 5½×8½; 128-144 pages; 55 lb stock; 10 pt CIS cover; illustrations; photos. Lesbian-feminist journal, providing fiction, poetry, drama, essays, journals and artwork. Quarterly. 1989 issues were on lesbian theory, relationships and disability. Estab. 1976. Circ. 3,000.
Needs: Adventure, contemporary, erotica, ethnic, experimental, fantasy, feminist, historical, humor/satire, lesbian, literary, prose poem, psychic, regional, science fiction, sports, translations. No heterosexual or male-oriented fiction; nothing that stereotypes or degrades women. Receives 50 unsolicited mss/month. Accepts 25 mss/issue; 75-100 mss/year. Publishes ms 1 month to 1 year after acceptance. Recently published work by Melanie Kaye/Kantrowitz, Adrienne Rich, Terri L. Jewell and Gloria Anzaldúa; published new writers within the last year. Length: 2,000 words average; 500 words mini-

mum; 4,000 words maximum. Publishes short shorts. Occasionally critiques rejected mss. Sometimes recommends other markets.

How to Contact: Send 2 copies of complete ms with cover letter, which should include a brief author's bio to be published when the work is published. Reports in 2 months on queries; 6 months on mss. SASE. Photocopied submissions OK. Accepts computer printout submissions. Sample copy $6.25; subscription $17.

Payment: Pays in contributor's copies.

Terms: Rights retained by author.

Advice: The philosophy behind *Sinister Wisdom* is "to reflect and encourage the lesbian movements for social change, especially change in the ways we use language."

SKYLARK (I), Purdue University, 2233 171st St., Hammond IN 46323. (219)844-0520. Editor: Marcia F. Jaron. Magazine: 8½×11; 100 pages; illustrations; photos. Fine arts magazine – short stories, poems and graphics for adults and children. Annually. Estab. 1971. Circ. 500.

Needs: Contemporary, ethnic, experimental, fantasy, feminist, humor/satire, juvenile, literary, mainstream, prose poem, regional, science fiction, serialized/excerpted novel, spiritual, sports, suspense/mystery and western. Receives 20 mss/month. Accepts 6-7 mss/issue. Published work by A. R. Ammons, Gerald Oosterveen and Lyn Lifshin. Published new writers within the last year. Length: 1-15 double-spaced pages.

How to Contact: Send complete ms. SASE for ms. Photocopied submissions OK. Accepts computer printout submissions. Prefers letter-quality. Sample copy $6; back issue $4.

Payment: 1 contributor's copy.

Terms: Acquires first rights. Copyright reverts to author.

Advice: "Encourage submissions from children 6-18. The goal of *Skylark* is to encourage *creativity* and give beginning and published authors showcase for their work. Check for spelling errors or typos."

SLIPSTREAM (II, IV), Box 2071, New Market Station, Niagara Falls NY 14301. (716)282-2616. Editor: Dan Sicoli. Fiction Editors: R. Borgatti, D. Sicoli and Livio Farallo. Magazine: 7×8½; 80-120 pages; high quality paper and cover; illustrations; photos. "We use poetry and short fiction with a contemporary urban feel." Estab. 1981. Circ. 400.

Needs: Reading through June 1990 for an issue on "The Working Stiff." A general issue will follow. Contemporary, erotica, ethnic, experimental, fantasy, feminist, gay, humor/satire, lesbian, literary, mainstream, prose poem and science fiction. No religious, juvenile, young adult or romance. Receives over 75 unsolicited mss/month. Accepts 2-8 mss/issue; 6-12 mss/year. Publishes short shorts under 18 pages. Recently published work by Gary Earl Ross, Kurt Nimmo and Neil Landau. Rarely critiques rejected mss. Sometimes recommends other markets.

How to Contact: Send complete ms. Reports within 2 months. SASE. Accepts computer printout submissions. Sample copy $4. Fiction guidelines for #10 SASE.

Payment: 2 contributor's copies.

Terms: Acquires one-time rights on publication.

Advice: "Writing should be honest, fresh; develop your own style. Check out a sample issue first. Don't write for the sake of writing, write from the gut as if it were a biological need. Write from experience and mean what you say, but say it in the fewest number of words."

THE SMALL POND MAGAZINE (II), Box 664, Stratford CT 06497. (203)378-4066. Editor: Napoleon St. Cyr. Magazine: 5½×8½; 42 pages; 60 lb offset paper; 65 lb cover stock; illustrations (art). "Features contemporary poetry, the salt of the earth, peppered with short prose pieces of various kinds. The college educated and erudite read it for good poetry, prose and pleasure." Triannually. Estab. 1964. Circ. 300.

Needs: "Rarely use science fiction or formula stories you'd find in *Cosmo*, *Redbook*, *Ladies Home Journal*, etc." Buys 10-12 mss/year. Longer response time in July and August. Receives approximately 50 unsolicited fiction mss each month. Length: 200-2,500 words. Critiques rejected mss when there is time. Sometimes recommends other markets.

How to Contact: Send complete ms with SASE and short vita with publishing credits. Accepts good copy computer printout submissions. Prefers letter-quality. Reports in 2 weeks-1 month. Publishes ms an average of 2 months to 1 year after acceptance. Sample copy $2.50.

Payment: 2 free author's copies. $2/copy charge for extras.

Terms: Pays for all rights.

Advice: "Send for a sample copy first. All mss must be typed. Name and address and story title on front page, name of story on succeeding pages and paginated." Mss are rejected because of "tired plots and poor grammar; also over-long – 2,500 words maximum. Don't send any writing conference ms unless it got an A or better."

SMILE (IV), Box 3502, Madison WI 53704. (608)258-1305. Magazine: 8½×11; 28 pages; colored cover; illustrations; photos. Publishes material on "non-mainstream politics; political theory and practice." Semiannually. Plans special fiction issue. Estab. 1987. Circ. 1,500.
Needs: "Anarchist or communist topics that deal with the psychosocial liberation from the oppressive society." Receives 2 unsolicited fiction mss/month. Length: 200 words minimum; 800 words maximum. Sometimes critiques rejected mss.
How to Contact: Query with clips of published work or send complete mss with cover letter. Simultaneous, photocopied and reprint submissions OK. Accepts computer printout submissions. Accepts electronic submissions via disk or modem. Sample copy for SAE and 6 first class stamps.
Payment: Pays in 2 contributor's copies.
Terms: "Everything printed is free to be copied by anyone." Publication is not copyrighted.

THE SNEAK PREVIEW (I), Box 639, Grants Pass OR 97526. (503)474-3044. Editor: Curtis Hayden. Fiction Editor: Matt Hegarty. Tabloid; 9¾×14; 24-32 pages; newsprint paper; newsprint cover; illustrations; photos. "News and arts biweekly of local events, with one page reserved for writers and poets to submit stories and poems." Biweekly. Estab. 1986. Circ. 12,500.
Needs: Adventure, condensed/excerpted novel, contemporary, experimental, historical (general), humor/satire (especially), juvenile (5-9 years), literary, mainstream, prose poem, regional, romance (contemporary, historical, young adult), science fiction, senior citizen/retirement, sports, suspense/mystery, western, young adult/teen (10-18 years). "Nothing that would offend the scruples of a small town in southern Oregon." Receives 2 unsolicted mss/month. Buys 1 ms/issue; 26 mss/year. Publishes ms within 2 weeks-6 months of acceptance. Recently published work by Leo Curzen, Cher Manuel, Garfield Price. Length: 250 words average; 200 words minimum; 300 words maximum. Sometimes critiques rejected mss and recommends other markets.
How to Contact: Query first. Reports in 2 weeks. SASE (65¢ postage is a must). Simultaneous, photocopied and reprint submissions OK. Accepts computer printout submissions. Accepts electronic submissions via disk or modem. Guidelines for SASE.
Payment: Pays $10-20 and contributor's copies.
Terms: Pays on publication for all rights. Publication not copyrighted.
Advice: "We need more people like Hunter Thompson. Everybody thinks the New-York-City-let's-get-serious-about-life-and-our-'art' is where it's at."

‡SOJOURNER, A Women's Forum (II, IV), 143 Albany St., Cambridge MA 02139. (617)661-3567. Editor-in-Chief: Karen Kahn. Magazine: 11×17; 48 pages; newsprint paper; illustrations; photos. "Feminist journal publishing interviews, nonfiction features, news, viewpoints, poetry, reviews (music, cinema, books) and fiction for women." Published monthly. Estab. 1975. Circ. 45,000.
Needs: Contemporary, ethnic, experimental, fantasy, feminist, lesbian, humor/satire, literary, prose poem and women's. Receives 20 unsolicited fiction mss/month. Accepts 10 mss/year. Approximately 10% of fiction is agented. Published new writers within the last year. Length: 1,000 words minimum; 4,000 words maximum; 2,500 words average. Recommends other markets.
How to Contact: Send complete ms with SASE and cover letter with description of previous publications; current works. Photocopied submissions OK. Publishes ms an average of 6 months after acceptance. Sample copy $2 with 10×13 SASE and 86¢ postage. Free fiction guidelines with SASE.
Payment: Subscription to magazine and 2 contributor's copies. No extra charge up to 5; $1 charge each thereafter.
Terms: First rights only.
Advice: "Pay attention to appearance of manuscript! Very difficult to wade through sloppily presented fiction, however good. Do write a cover letter. If not cute, it can't hurt and may help. Mention previous publication(s)."

‡SOLID COPY (II), Peak Output Unlimited, 122 S. Broad St., Stacyville IA 50476. (515)737-2269. Editor: Mary M. Blake. Fiction Editor: Jacquelyn D. Scheneman. Digest: 5½×8½; 60 lb. offset paper; text cover. "We publish fiction shorts for a family audience." Quarterly. Estab. 1989.
Needs: Adventure, contemporary, ethnic, experimental, fantasy, historical (general), horror, humor/satire, literary, mainstream, prose poem, psychic/supernatural/occult, regional, religious/inspirational, science fiction, senior citizen/retirement, sports, suspense/mystery, western. "No erotica, romance, preachy religious material." Accepts 10-20 mss/issue. Publishes mss within 3-6 months, average; sometimes 1-2 years. Recently published work by Colleen Drippé, Christopher Woods and Donna Bocian. Length: 500-3,600 words; some exceptions. Publishes occasional short shorts. Length: 300 words. Sometimes critiques rejected mss and recommends other markets.
How to Contact: Send complete ms with cover letter. Include recent credits and brief bio. Reports in 4-6 weeks on mss. SASE needed for reply; additional SASE for ms return. Photocopied and reprint submissions OK. Accepts computer printout submissions. Sample copy for $5. Fiction guidelines for #10 SAE and 1 first class stamp.

Payment: Free contributor's copy plus small cash stipend.
Terms: Acquires first North American serial rights, one-time rights or reprint rights.
Advice: "We like our stories to be tight—nothing superfluous. Good character development and realism go a long way. Skip the frills."

SONORA REVIEW (II), University of Arizona, Department of English, Tucson AZ 85721. (602)621-8077. Editors: Martha Ostheimer and Layne Schorr. Fiction Editors: Ellen Devos, Robert Schirmer. Magazine: 6×9; 150 pages; 16 lb paper; 20 lb cover stock; photos seldom. *The Sonora Review* publishes short fiction and poetry of high literary quality. Semiannually. Estab. 1980. Circ. 500.
Needs: Literary. "We are open to a wide range of stories with accessibility and vitality being important in any case. We're not interested in genre fiction, formula work." Buys 4-6 mss/issue. Approximately 10% of fiction is agented. Recently published work by Nancy Lord, Robyn Oughton, Ron Hansen. Length: open, though prefers work under 25 pages. Sometimes recommends other markets.
How to Contact: Send complete ms with SASE and cover letter with previous publications. Accepts computer printout submissions. Prefers letter-quality. Reports in 2 months on mss, longer for work received during summer (May-August). Publishes ms an average of 2-6 months after acceptance. Sample copy $4.
Payment: 2 free author's copies. $2 charge for extras. Annual cash prizes.
Terms: Acquires first North American serial rights. Fall issue features fiction contest winnter: 1st prize, $150; 2nd prize $75. Submit by October 1.
Advice: "We have increased the size of the magazine at 50% and are developing more special features connecting special themes and regions. Let the story sit for several months, then review it to see if you still like it. If you're unsure, keep working on it *before* sending it out. All mss are read carefully, and we try to make brief comments if time permits. Our hope is that an author will keep us interested in his or her treatment of a subject by using fresh details and writing with an authority that is absorbing." Mss are rejected because "1) we only have space for 6-8 manuscripts out of several hundred submissions annually, and 2) most of the manuscripts we receive have some merit but are not of publishable quality. It would be helpful to receive a cover letter with all manuscripts."

SOUNDINGS EAST (II), English Dept., Salem State College, Salem MA 01970. (617)741-6270. Advisory Editor: Rod Kessler. Magazine: 5½×8½; 64 pages; illustrations; photos. "Mainly a college audience, but we also distribute to libraries throughout the country." Biannually. Estab. 1973. Circ. 2,000.
Needs: Literary, contemporary, prose poem. No juvenile. Publishes 4-5 stories/issue. Receives 30 unsolicited fiction mss each month. Does not read April-August. Published work by James Brady, Terry Farish and Christina Shea. Published new writers within the last year. Length: 250-5,000 words. "We are open to short pieces as well as to long works."
How to Contact: Send complete ms with SASE between September and March. Accepts computer printout submissions. Prefers letter-quality. Reports in 2 months on mss. Sample copy $3.
Payment: 2 free author's copies.
Terms: All publication rights revert to authors.
Advice: "We're impressed by an excitement—coupled with craft—in the use of the language. It also helps to reach in and grab the reader by the heart."

SOUTH CAROLINA REVIEW (II), Clemson University, Clemson SC 29634-1503. (803)656-3229. Editors: R.J. Calhoun, Frank Day and Carol Johnston. Managing Editor: Mark Winchell. Magazine: 6×9; 132 pages; 60 lb cream white vellum paper; 65 lb cream white vellum cover stock; illustrations and photos rarely. Semiannually. Estab. 1967. Circ. 700.
Needs: Literary, contemporary, humor and ethnic. Receives approximately 50-60 unsolicited fiction mss each month. Does not read mss June-August. Recently published work by Joyce Carol Oates, Rosanne Coggeshall, Stephen Dixon; published new writers within the last year. Critiques rejected mss when there is time.
How to Contact: Send complete ms with SASE. Accepts computer printout submissions. Reports in 2 months on mss. Sample copy $3.
Payment: Pays in contributor's copies.
Advice: Mss are rejected because of "poorly structured stories, or stories without vividness or intensity. The most celebrated function of a little magazine is to take a chance on writers not yet able to get into the larger magazines—the little magazine can encourage promising writers at a time when encouragement is vitally needed. (We also publish 'name' writers, like Joyce Carol Oates, Stephen Dixon, George Garrett.) Read the masters extensively. Write and write more, with a *schedule*. Listen to editorial advice when offered. Don't get discouraged with rejections. Read what writers say about writing (e.g. *The Paris Review* Interviews with George Plimpton, gen. ed.; Welty's *One Writer's Beginnings*,etc). Take courses in writing and listen to, even if you do not follow, the advice."

SOUTH DAKOTA REVIEW (II), University of South Dakota, Box 111, University Exchange, Vermillion SD 57069. (605)677-5966. Editor: John R. Milton. Magazine: 6×9; 150+ pages; book paper; glossy cover stock; illustrations sometimes; photos on cover. Literary magazine for university and college audiences and their equivalent. Emphasis is often on the West and its writers, but will accept mss from anywhere. Issues are generally fiction and poetry with some literary essays. Quarterly. Estab. 1963. Circ. 500.
Needs: Literary, contemporary, ethnic, experimental, excerpted novel, regional and translations. "We like very well-written stories. Contemporary western American setting appeals, but not necessary. No formula stories, sports or adolescent 'I' narrator." Receives 30 unsolicited fiction mss/month. Accepts about 10-20 mss/year, more or less. Assistant editor accepts mss in June-July, sometimes August. Approximately 5% of fiction is agented. Publishes short shorts of 5 pages double-spaced typescript. Published work by Ed Loomis, Max Evans, Dennis Lynds; published new writers the last year. Length: 1,300 words minimum; 6,000 words maximum. (Has made exceptions, up to novella length.) Sometimes recommends other markets.
How to Contact: Send complete ms with SASE. "We like cover letters that are not boastful and do not attempt to sell the stories but rather provide some personal information about the writer." Photocopied submissions OK if not multiple submission. Reports in 1 month. Publishes ms an average of 1-6 months after acceptance. Sample copy $3.
Payment: 2-4 free author's copies, depending on length of ms. $2 charge for extras.
Terms: Acquires first rights and second serial rights.
Advice: Rejects mss because of "careless writing; often careless typing; stories too personal ('I' confessional), adolescent; working manuscript, not polished; subject matter that editor finds trivial. We are trying to use more fiction and more variety. We would like to see more sophisticated stories. Do not try to outguess editors and give them what you think they want. Write honestly. Be yourself."

SOUTHERN CALIFORNIA ANTHOLOGY (II), Master of Professional Writing Program—USC, MPW-WPH 404 USC, Los Angeles CA 90089-4034. (213)743-8255. Contact: Editors. Magazine: 5½×8½; 142 pages; semi-glossy cover stock. "The *Southern California Anthology* is a literary review that is an eclectic collection of previously unpublished quality contemporary fiction, poetry and interviews with established literary people, published for adults of all professions; of particular interest to those interested in serious contemporary literature." Annually. Estab. 1983. Circ. 1,500.
Needs: Contemporary, ethnic, experimental, feminist, historical (general), humor/satire, literary, mainstream, regional, serialized/excerpted novel. No juvenile, religious, confession, romance, science fiction. Receives 30 unsolicited fiction mss each month. Accepts 10-12 mss/issue. Does not read February-September. Publishes ms 4 months after acceptance. Length: 10-15 pages average; 2 pages minimum; 25 pages maximum. Publishes short shorts.
How to Contact: Send complete ms with cover letter or submit through agent. Cover letter should include list of previous publications. Reports on queries in 1 month; on mss in 4 months. SASE. Photocopied submissions OK. Accepts computer printout submissions, no dot-matrix. Sample copy $2.95. Fiction guidelines for #10 SAE and 1 first class stamp.
Payment: Pays in contributor's copies.
Terms: Acquires first rights.
Advice: "The *Anthology* pays particular attention to craft and style in its selection of narrative writing."

SOUTHERN HUMANITIES REVIEW (II, IV), Auburn University, 9088 Haley Center, Auburn University AL 36849. Co-Editors: Thomas L. Wright and Dan R. Latimer. Magazine: 6×9; 96 pages; 60 lb neutral pH, natural paper, 65 lb neutral pH med. coated cover stock; occasional illustrations and photos. "We publish essays, poetry, fiction and reviews. Our fiction has ranged from very traditional in form and content to very experimental. Literate, college-educated audience. We hope they read our journal for both enlightenment and pleasure." Quarterly. Estab. 1967. Circ. 800.
Needs: Serious fiction, fantasy, feminist, humor and regional. Receives approximately 8-10 unsolicited fiction mss each month. Accepts and prints 1-2 mss/issue, 4-6 mss/year. Slower reading time in summer. Published work by Anne Brashler, Heimito von Doderer and Ivo Andric; published new writers within the last year. Length: 3,500-5,000 words. Critiques rejected mss when there is time. Sometimes recommends other markets.
How to Contact: Send complete ms with SASE and cover letter with an explanation of topic chosen—special, certain book, etc., a little about author if they have never submitted. Accepts computer printout submissions. Prefers letter-quality. Reports in 90 days. Sample copy $4.
Payment: 1 copy; $4 charge for extras.
Terms: Acquires first rights. Sends galleys to author.
Advice: "Send us the ms with SASE. If we like it, we'll take it or we'll recommend changes. If we don't like it, we'll send it back as promptly as possible. Read the journal. Send a typewritten, clean copy carefully proofread. We also award annually the Hoepfner Prize of $100 for the best published essay or short story of the year. Let someone whose opinion you respect read your story and give you

an honest appraisal. Rewrite, if necessary, to get the most from your story."

THE SOUTHERN REVIEW (II), Louisiana State University, 43 Allen Hall, Baton Rouge LA 70803. (504)388-5108. Editor: James Olney. Magazine: 6¾×10; 240 pages; 50 lb Warren Oldstyle paper; 65 lb #1 grade cover stock; occasional photos. A literary quarterly publishing critical essays, poetry and fiction for a highly intellectual audience. Quarterly. Published special fiction issue. Estab. 1935. Circ. 3,000.
Needs: Literary and contemporary. "We emphasize style and substantial content. No mystery, fantasy or religious mss." Buys 7-8 mss/issue. Receives approximately 100 unsolicited fiction mss each month. Approximately 5% of fiction is agented. Recently published work by William Hoffman, Rick Bass, Maclin Bocock. Published new writers within the last year. Length: 2,000-10,000 words. Sometimes recommends other markets.
How to Contact: Send complete ms with cover letter and SASE. "Prefer brief letters giving information on author concerning where he/she has been published before. Biographical info and what he/she is doing now." Accepts computer printout submissions. Prefers letter-quality. Reports in 2 months on mss. Publishes ms an average of 1-2 years after acceptance. Sample copy $5.
Payment: Pays $12/printed page. 2 free author's copies.
Terms: Pays on publication for first American serial rights. "We transfer copyright to author on request." Sends galleys to author.
Advice: "Develop a careful style with characters in depth." Sponsors annual contest for best first collection of short stories published during the calendar year.

SOUTHWEST REVIEW (II), 6410 Airline, Southern Methodist University, Dallas TX 75275. (214)373-7440. Editor: Willard Spiegelman. Magazine: 6×9; 144 pages. "The majority of our readers are college-educated adults who wish to stay abreast of the latest and best in contemporary fiction, poetry, literary criticism and books in all but the most specialized disciplines." Quarterly. Estab. 1915. Circ. 1,600.
Needs: "High literary quality; no specific requirements as to subject matter, but cannot use sentimental, religious, western, poor science fiction, pornographic, true confession, mystery, juvenile or serialized or condensed novels." Receives approximately 200 unsolicited fiction mss each month. Recently published work by Meredith Steinbach, Ellen Akins, Rick Bass and Millicent Dillar. Length: prefers 3,000-5,000 words. Occasionally critiques rejected mss. Sometimes recommends other markets.
How to Contact: Send complete ms with SASE. Accepts computer printout submissions. Prefers letter-quality. Reports in 3 months on mss. Publishes ms 6 months to 1 year after acceptance. Sample copy $5. Free guidelines with SASE.
Payment: Payment varies; writers receive 3 free author's copies.
Terms: Pays on publication for first North American serial rights. Sends galleys to author.
Advice: "We have become less regional. A lot of time would be saved for us and for the writer if he looked at a copy of the *Southwest Review* before submitting. We like to receive a cover letter because it is some reassurance that the author has taken the time to check a current directory for the editor's name. When there isn't a cover letter, we wonder whether the same story is on 20 other desks around the country."

SOU'WESTER (II), English Dept., Southern Illinois University-Edwardsville, Edwardsville IL 62026-1438. (618)692-2289. Editor-in-Chief: Dickie A. Spurgeon. Magazine: 6×9; 88 pages; Warren's Olde style paper; 60 lb cover. General magazine of poetry and fiction. Published three times/year. Estab. 1960. Circ. 300.
Needs: Contemporary, erotica, ethnic, experimental, fantasy, feminist/lesbian, gay, literary, mainstream, regional and translations. Receives 40-50 unsolicited fiction mss/month. Accepts 3 mss/issue, 9 mss/year. Recently published work by Robert Wexelblatt, Robert Solomon; published new writers within the last year. Length: 5,000 words minimum; 10,000 words maximum. Occasionally critiques rejected mss.
How to Contact: Send complete ms with SASE. Simultaneous and photocopied submissions OK. Accepts computer printout submissions. Reports in 1 month. Publishes ms an average of 2 months after acceptance. Sample copy $1.50.
Payment: 2 contributor's copies. $1.50 charge for extras.
Terms: Acquires all rights.

SPACE AND TIME (II, IV), 138 W. 70th St., New York NY 10023. Editor-in-Chief: Gordon Linzner. Magazine: 5½×8½; 120 pages; 20 lb paper; index cover stock; illustrations. Magazine of "fantasy fiction of all types and sub-genres (including science fiction) – the less categorizable, the better. *S&T* tends to feature new writers and odd pieces for which there are few if any other markets. Some poetry (overstocked through 1989). *S&T* attracts readers who cannot get enough of this material or who want something new and different. Because it is small, *S&T* can take chances on stories that are either too

traditional or too experimental, and prides itself on its variety of styles and story types. Also well illustrated." Published semiannually. Estab. 1966. Circ. 400.
Needs: Adventure, fantasy, horror, humor/satire, psychic/supernatural/occult and science fiction. "Actually, will consider almost any type of fiction as long as it has a fantastic slant. No media clones—no tales involving characters/situations that are not your creation (*Star Trek*, et al) except for certain types of satire. No stories based on Von Daniken, etc., type cults." Receives 75-100 unsolicited fiction mss/month. Accepts 10 mss/issue, 20 mss/year. Published work by Phyllis Ann Karr, Mickey Zucker Reichert, Doug Beason; published new writers within the last year. Length: 12,000 words maximum. Occasionally critiques rejected mss. Sometimes recommends other markets.
How to Contact: Query first. *No unsolicited mss*. Photocopied submissions OK. Accepts computer printout submissions. Prefers letter-quality. Reports in 2 months. Publishes ms an average of 1-2 years after acceptance. Sample copy $5.
Payment: ½¢/word and 2 contributor's copies. Charges cover price less 40% contributor discount for extras.
Terms: Pays on acceptance for first North American serial rights.
Advice: "For purposes of inventory re-assessment, we are not looking at any manuscripts after 12/31/88—at the moment we cannot tell when we will be an open market again—potential contributors should inquire."

SPECTRUM (II), Box 14800, University of California, Santa Barbara CA 93107. Editor: Joshua N. Schneyer. Magazine: 6x9; 100-150 pages; illustrations and photos. "Interested in quality work. Poetry, fiction and essay." Annually. Estab. 1957. Circ. 750.
Needs: Literary. No science fiction. Does not read mss February-August. Publishes short shorts. Sometimes critiques rejected mss.
How to Contact: Send complete ms. SASE. Simultaneous submissions OK. Accepts computer printout submissions. Sample copy $4 and 7x10 SAE. Fiction guidelines for #10 SASE.
Payment: Contributor's copies.
Terms: Sponsors contests and awards for fiction writers.

SPECTRUM (II), Anna Maria College, Box 72-C, Sunset Lane, Paxton MA 01612. (617)757-4586. Editor: Robert H. Goepfert. Fiction Editor: Joseph Wilson. Magazine: 6×9; 64 pages; illustrations and photos. "An interdisciplinary publication publishing fiction as well as poetry, scholarly articles, reviews, art and photography. Submissions are especially encouraged from those affiliated with liberal arts colleges." Semiannually. Estab. 1985. Circ. 1,000.
Needs: Contemporary, experimental, historical, literary, mainstream. No western, mystery, erotica, science fiction. Receives an average of 15 unsolicited fiction ms/month. Accepts 4-6 mss/issue. Publishes ms approx. 6 months after acceptance. Length: 2,000-5,0000 words preferred; 3,000 words average; 10,000 words maximum. Publishes short shorts. Sometimes critiques rejected mss and recommends other markets.
How to Contact: Send complete ms with cover letter. Reports in 6 weeks. SASE for ms. Photocopied submissions OK. Accepts computer printouts, no dot-matrix. Sample copy for $3. Fiction guidelines free with SASE.
Payment: Pays $20 and 2 contributor's copies.
Terms: Pays on publication for first North American serial rights. Sends pre-publication galleys to author. Publication not copyrighted.
Advice: "Our chief aim is diversity."

SPINDRIFT (II), Shoreline Community College, 16101 Greenwood Ave. North, Seattle WA 98133. (206)546-4785. Editor: Carol Orlock, adviser. Magazine: 140 pages; excellent quality paper; photographs; b&w artwork. "We look for fresh, original work that is not forced or 'straining' to be literary." Annually. Estab. around 1967. Circ. 500.
Needs: Contemporary, ethnic, experimental, historical (general), prose poem, regional, science fiction, serialized/excerpted novel, translations. No romance, religious/inspirational. Receives up to 150 mss/year. Accepts up to 20 mss/issue. Does not read during spring/summer. Publishes ms 3-4 months after acceptance. Recently published work by David Halpern, Jana Harris; published new writers within the last year. Length: 250 words minimum; 3,500-4,500 words maximum. Publishes short shorts.
How to Contact: Send complete ms, and "bio, name, address, phone and list of titles submitted." Reports in 2 weeks on queries; 3 months on mss. SASE for nonfiction; mss not returned. Photocopied submissions OK. Accepts computer printout submissions. Sample copy for $6, 8×10 SAE and $1 postage.
Payment: Pays in contributor's copies; charge for extras.
Terms: Acquires first rights. Publication not copyrighted.
Advice: "The tighter the story the better. The more lyric values in the narrative the better. Read the magazine, keep working on craft. Submit several pieces by February 1."

THE SPIRIT THAT MOVES US (II), Box 820-W, Jackson Heights NY 11372-0820. (718)426-8788. Editor: Morty Sklar. Publishes fiction, poetry and artwork. "We want feeling and imagination, work coming from the human experience." Semiannually. Estab. 1975. Circ. 1,500-2,000.

Needs: "SASE first to find out what our needs are." Literary and contemporary, feminist, gay/lesbian, humor, ethnic, prose poem, spiritual, sports and translations. No sensational. Buys 5-6 mss/issue and about 15 mss for special fiction issues. Receives approximately 90 unsolicited fiction mss each month. Recently published work by Andrea Carlisle, Les Standiford, Richard Grayson; published new writers within the last year. Length: 10,000 words maximum. Critiques rejected mss when there is time.

How to Contact: Send SASE first for theme and plans. "A cover letter sort of makes the exchange more personal." Accepts computer printout submissions. Prefers letter-quality. Reports in 1 week-1 month on mss. Publishes ms an average of 6 months after acceptance. Sample copy $5 for *The Spirit That Moves Us Reader*; $3 for an issue of our choice.

Payment: Free cloth copy, 40% discount for paperbacks; 25% on all other publications.

Terms: Pays for first rights. Buys reprints for anthology issue.

Advice: "Query first for theme with SASE. We're small but good and well-reviewed. Send the work you love best. Write from yourself and not from what you feel is the fashion or what the editor wants. This editor wants what you want if it has heart, imagination and skill. Aside from the obvious reason for rejection, poor writing, the main reason for rejection is lack of human concerns—that is, the writer seems to be concerned with style more than content. Read a copy of the magazine you'll be submitting work to. Don't rely on your writing for money unless you're in it for the money. Have time to write, as much time as you can get (be anti-social if necessary)."

‡SPITBALL (I), 6224 Collegevue Pl., Cincinnati OH 45224. Editor: Mike Shannon. Magazine: 5½×8½; 52 pages; 20 lb white paper; 65-67 lb cover stock; illustrations; photos. Magazine publishing "fiction and poetry about *baseball* exclusively for an educated, literary segment of the baseball fan population." Quarterly. Estab. 1981. Circ. 1,000.

Needs: Confession, contemporary, experimental, historical, literary, mainstream and suspense. "Our only requirement concerning the type of fiction written is that the story be *primarily* about baseball." Receives "100 or so" unsolicited fiction mss/year. Accepts 7-8 mss/year. Recently published work by Dallas Wiebe, Michael Gilmartin, Rick Wilber. Published new writers within the last year. Length: no limit. The longer it is, the better it has to be. Will critique rejected mss if asked.

How to Contact: Send complete ms with SASE, and cover letter with brief bio about author. Photocopied and previously published submissions OK. Reporting time varies. Publishes ms an average of 3 months after acceptance. Sample copy $5.

Payment: "No monetary payment at present. We may offer nominal payment in the near future." 2 free contributor's copies per issue in which work appears.

Terms: Acquires first North American serial rights. Buys reprints "if the work is good enough and it hasn't had major exposure already."

Advice: "Our audience is mostly college educated and knowledgeable about baseball. The stories we have published so far have been very well written and displayed a firm grasp of the baseball world and its people. In short, audience response has been great because the stories are simply good as stories. Thus, mere use of baseball as subject is no guarantee of acceptance. We are always seeking submissions. Unlike many literary magazines, we have no backlog of accepted material. Consult *The Best of Spitball* (1988) by Pocket Books, Div. of Simon & Schuster. Still in print even if not in local bookstore. Fiction is a natural genre for our exclusive subject, baseball. There are great opportunities for writing in certain areas of fiction, baseball being one of them. Baseball has become the 'in' spectator sport among intellectuals, the general media and the 'yuppie' crowd. Consequently, as subject matter for adult fiction it has gained a much wider acceptance than it once enjoyed."

SPOOFING! (I, IV), Yarns and Such, Creative With Words Publications, Box 223226, Carmel CA 93922. (408)649-5627. Editor: Brigitta Geltrich. Booklet: 5½×8½; approx. 60 pages; bond paper; illustrations. Folklore. Semiannually. Estab. 1975. Circ. varies.

Needs: Ethnic, humor/satire, juvenile (5-9 years), preschool (1-4 years), regional, young adult/teen (10-18 years), folklore. "Once a year we publish an anthology of the writings of young writers, titled: *We are Writers Too!*" No erotica, religious fiction. Receives 50-100 unsolicited fiction mss/month. Does not read mss July-August. Publishes ms 2-6 months after acceptance. Published new writers within the last year. Length: 1,000 words average. Critiques rejected mss "when requested, *then we charge $20/prose, up to 1,000 words.*"

How to Contact: Query first or send complete ms with cover letter. "Reference has to be made to which project the manuscript is being submitted." Reports in 1 week on queries; 2 months on mss; longer on specific seasonal anthologies. SASE. Photocopied submissions OK. Accepts computer printout submissions, no dot-matrix. Accepts electronic submissions via Radio Shack Model 4/6 disk. Sample copy price varies. Fiction guidelines for #10 SAE with 2 first class stamps.

Payment: Charge for contributor's copies; 20% reduction on each copy ordered.
Terms: Acquires one-time rights.

SPSM&H (II, IV), *Amelia* Magazine, 329 "E" St., Bakersfield CA 93304. (805)323-4064. Editor: Frederick A. Raborg, Jr. Magazine: 5½×8¼; 24 pages; Matte cover stock; illustrations and photos. "*SPSM&H* publishes sonnets, sonnet sequences and fiction, articles and reviews related to the form (fiction may be romantic or Gothic) for a general readership and sonnet enthusiasts." Quarterly. Estab. 1985. Circ. 600.
Needs: Adventure, confession, contemporary, erotica, ethnic experimental, fantasy, feminist, gay, historical (general), horror, humor/satire, lesbian, literary, mainstream, regional, contemporary and historical romance, science fiction, senior citizen/retirement, suspense/mystery, translations and western. All should have romantic element. "We look for strong fiction with romantic or Gothic content, or both. Stories need not have 'happy' endings, and we are open to the experimental and/or avant-garde. Erotica is fine; pornography, no." Receives 30+ unsolicited mss/month. Buys 1 ms/issue; 4 mss/year. Publishes ms 6 months-1 year after acceptance. Agented fiction 5%. Recently published work by Mary Louise R. O'Hara and Clara Castelar Bjorlie. Length: 2,000 words average; 500 words minimum; 3,000 words maximum. When appropriate critiques rejected ms; Recommends other markets.
How to Contact: Send complete ms with cover letter. Should include Social Security number. Reports in 2 weeks. SASE. Photocopied submissions OK. Accepts computer printout submissions. Sample copy $4. Fiction guidelines for #10 SAE and 1 first class stamp.
Payment: Pays $10-25; contributor's copies; charge for extras.
Terms: Pays on publication for first North American serial rights.
Advice: "A good story line (plot) and strong characterization are vital. I want to know the writer has done his homework and is striving to become professional."

SQUARE ONE (I, II), A Magazine of Fiction, Box 11921, Milwaukee WI 53211. Editor: William D. Gagliani. Magazine: 7×8½; 75-90 pages; 20 lb white bond paper; 80 lb colored linen cover; illustrations; pen and ink drawings or any black on white. "There is no specific theme at *Square One*, but we publish only fiction and illustrations. Aimed at a general literate audience—people who *enjoy* reading fiction." Annually (currently). Estab. 1984. Circ. 250.
Needs: Open to all categories. "We like exciting stories in which things happen and characters *exist*." Receives 40-50 unsolicited fiction mss/month. Does not read mss between May and September. Accepts 6-12 mss/issue, depending on lengths; 6-12 mss/year. Publishes ms generally 1-11 months after acceptance. Recently published work by Kent Glenzer, Cheryl Sayre, Susan Taylor-Boyd; published new writers within the last year. Length: 3,000 words average; 7,500 words maximum. Publishes short shorts but not vignettes. "It is editorial policy to comment on at least 85% of submissions rejected, but please be patient—we have a very small staff."
How to Contact: Send complete ms with cover letter. "Too many letters explain or describe the story. Let the fiction stand on its own. If it doesn't, the letter won't help. We like a brief bio and a few credits, but some writers get carried away. Use restraint and plain language—don't try to impress (it usually backfires)." Reports in 1-11 months on mss. SASE for ms. Simultaneous (if so labeled), photocopied and reprint submissions OK. Accepts computer printouts. Can accept electronic submissions via disk, but "We can accept DS/DD disks for Kaypro 2X (CP/M), Wordstar, and 3½" Atari Mega Disks (using only Wordwriter St). Hard copy should accompany any electronic submissions." Sample copy $3.50, 9×12 SAE, and 6 first class stamps (recent issue). Fiction guidelines for #10 SAE and 1 first class stamp. Please make checks payable to William D. Gagliani.
Payment: Two contributor's copies.
Terms: Pays for one-time rights.
Advice: "*Square One* is not a journal for beginners, despite what the name may imply. Rather, the name refers to the back-to-basics approach that we take—fiction must first and foremost be compelling. We want to see stories that elicit a response from the reader. We will give slight preference to Wisconsin writers, but will gladly consider submissions from anywhere. We must stress that, since we are an almost annual publication, contributors should expect long response lags. Our staff is small and *Square One* is a part-time endeavor. Patience is the best advice we can offer. Also, we oppose the absurdity of asking that writers subscribe to every magazine they would like to write for, especially given most writers' financial state. Check local public and college libraries and bookstores to see what's going on in the small press and literary markets, and—as a matter of dignity—consider carefully before submitting to magazines that routinely charge reading fees."

STAMP AXE (I), Upper Ground Press, Société de Diffusion; Stamp Axe, 4484 Ave. Coloniale, Montréal, Québec H2W 2C7 Canada. (514)281-6644. Editor: Pier Lefe Bure. Magazine: size varies; 50-100 pages; plainfield 140(m) paper; silkscreened cover; illustrations and photographs. Quarterly. Plans special fiction issue. Estab. 1986.

Needs: Adventure, condensed novel, confession, contemporary, erotica, ethnic, experimental, fantasy, historical (general), horror, humor/satire, psychic/supernatural/occult, science fiction. "No conventional type of writing." Receives one or two unsolicited mss/month. Length: 1 page preferred. Sometimes critiques rejected mss and recommends other markets.
How to Contact: Query with clips of published work or submit sample and portfolio. Reports in 2 weeks on queries; 2 months on mss. SASE. Simultaneous, photocopied and reprint submissions OK. Accepts computer printout submissions.
Payment: Pays $3 minimum; $35 maximum; contributor's copies.
Terms: Copyright reverts to the author.
Advice: "Just go to the nearest post office and send us what you have, but please keep original manuscript. If you can submit graphic artwork that goes with it, it would be great. And in case you like to express yourself (orally), you can send a cassette, for audio compilation on cassette or even for a radio broadcast. You can also insert some music in the background. You can submit a photocopy of your short stories, but you must put a 'hand touch' on each before sending it. If you are not familiar with this, don't be shy to ask—it would be a pleasure for me to reply."

STAR ROUTE JOURNAL (II), Box 1451, Redway CA 95560. (707)923-3256. Editor: May Siler Anderson. Magazine: 10¾×14½; 24 pages usually; newsprint paper and cover; b&w illustrations and photos. "Counter-culture—still think of ourselves as hippies—interested in environment, politics, philosophy, exploring ideas and changing consciousness. For people who are dissatisfied with pop culture and looking for new meaning." Monthly. Plans special fiction issue. Estab. 1978. Circ. 700.
Needs: Erotica, ethnic, experimental, feminist, gay, humor/satire, lesbian, literary, prose poem, science fiction, translations. Special interest: fiction having to do with hippies/1960s. Nothing "supportive of right-wing politics, racist views, militarism, mainstream conformist culture, consumerism." Receives 4-5 unsolicited fiction mss/month. "Would like to publish 1 short story/month. Plan to devote December issue to fiction and poetry." Publishes ms 1-4 months after acceptance. Published work by Paul Encimer, David Mohrmann and Jeff Spuck; published new writers within the last year. Length: 1,700 words average; 1,000 words minimum; 2,500 words maximum. Publishes short shorts. Sometimes comments on rejected mss and recommends other markets.
How to Contact: Send complete ms. Reports in 3-4 weeks. SASE. Simultaneous, photocopied and reprint submissions OK. Accepts computer printouts. Sample copy $1. Fiction guidelines for #10 SAE and 1 first class stamp.
Payment: Pays in contributor's copies, free subscription to magazine. Charge for extras.
Terms: Acquires first rights. Publication not copyrighted "at present." Sponsors contests for fiction writers. "We publish a fiction/poetry issue every December with first, second and third prizes. We have essay contests 2 or 3 times a year."
Advice: "Usually everything is read by three of us and our decisions are highly subjective; either we like it or we don't. We like pieces with humor, insight, heart and imagination."

‡STARRY NIGHTS, Merry Men Press, 274 Roanoke Road, ElCajon CA 92020. (619) 442-5541. Editor: Robin Hood. Magazine: 8½×11; 200 pages; 20 lb paper; 90 lb cover stock. Erotic science fiction/fantasy, poetry, art "for a mature audience." Estab. 1990.
Needs: Erotica. "See guidelines for definition of erotica. There's a big difference between *E* and *pornography*." Has published special fiction issue in the past. Receives 7 unsolicited mss per month; buys up to 15 mss per issue. Publishes ms 1-11 months after acceptance. Publishes short shorts. Comments on rejected mss and recommends other markets.
How to Contact: Reports in 1 week on queries; 1 month on mss. SASE. Photocopied and computer printout submissions OK. Accepts electronic submissions, "hard copy must be included." Fiction guidelines for SAE and 1 first class stamp.
Payment: .01/word and 1 contributor's copy.
Terms: Pays on publication for first North American serial rights.

‡STARSHORE (I,II,IV), A Magazine For the SF Reader, McAlpine Publishing, Suite 116, 800 Seahawk Circle, Virginia Beach VA 23452. (804)468-2969. Editor: Richard Rowand. Magazine: 8½×11; approx. 60 pages; 60 lb coated paper; 100 lb coated cover. "We publish science fiction with some fantasy for the well-educated adult, primarily male, 20-45." Quarterly. Estab. 1990.
Needs: Science fiction, experimental, fantasy. "No shared world stories and rehashes of television shows (Battlestar Galactica, etc.)." Accepts 7-12 mss/issue; 28-48 mss/year. Publishes ms 3-4 months after acceptance. Length: 5,000 words; 2,500 words minimum; 10,000 words maximum. Publishes short shorts. Occasionally critiques rejected ms and recommends other markets.
How to Contact: Send complete ms with cover letter explaining previous writing experience or credits. Reports in 2-3 weeks on queries; 1-2 months on mss. SASE. Simultaneous and photocopied submissions OK. Accepts computer printout submissions. Fiction guidelines for #10 SAE and 1 first class stamp.

Payment: Pays 1¢/word minimum and contributor's copies.
Terms: Pays on publication for first North American serial rights. Sends galleys to author "when time allows."

STARSONG (I, II), A Magazine of Fantasy, Science Fiction and Horror, Box 260B, St. Matthews SC 29135. Editor: Larry D. Kirby III. Magazine: 8½×11; 90 pages; Xeroxed paper; heavy cover stock; illustrations and photos. Quarterly. Estab. 1987. Circ. 400.
Needs: Fantasy, horror, humor/satire, prose poem, psychic/supernatural/occult, science fiction. Receives 60 unsolicited fiction mss/month. Accepts 8-12 mss/issue; 32-48 mss/year. Publishes ms 3-6 months after acceptance. Recently published work by Russell Lynch, Wade Tarzia, Kathleen Jurgens; published new writers within the last year. No preferred word length. Publishes short shorts. Sometimes critiques rejected mss.
How to Contact: Send complete ms with cover letter, which should include "bio." SASE. Photocopied submissions OK. Accepts computer printouts. Sample copy for $5; fiction guidelines for #10 SAE and 1 first class stamp.
Payment: Pays in contributor's copies.
Terms: Acquires one-time rights.
Advice: "Larger mags won't experiment with style or subject matter. I like new ideas and particularly like new authors. Try new ideas. Experiment. Be willing to rewrite. Pay attention to your dreams. Read small press mags. By the time you change your style to match what's in the big mags, the style will change. Don't send cyberpunk. It's boring."

STARWIND (I), Starwind Press, Box 98, Ripley OH 45167. (513)392-4549. Editor: David F. Powell. Magazine: 8½×11; 64 pages; 60 lb offset paper and cover; b&w illustrations; line shot photos. "Science fiction and fantasy for young adults (teen to 25 or so) with interest in science, technology, science fiction and fantasy." Quarterly. Estab. 1974. Circ. 2,000.
Needs: Fantasy, humor/satire, science fiction. "We like SF that shows hope for the future and protagonists who interact with their environment rather than let themselves be manipulated by it." No horror, pastiches of other authors, stories featuring characters created by others (i.e. Captain Kirk and crew, Dr. Who, etc.). Receives 50+ unsolicited mss/month. Buys 4-6 mss/issue; 16-24 mss/year. Publishes ms between 4 months-2 years after acceptance. Published work by Barbara Myers, Allen Byerle, Kurt Hyatt; published new writers within the last year. Length: 3,000-8,000 words average; 2,000 words minimum; 10,000 words maximum. Occasionally critiques rejected mss.
How to Contact: Send complete ms. Reports in 6-8 weeks. SASE for ms. Photocopied submissions OK. Accepts computer printouts. Accepts electronic submissions via disk for the IBM PC or PC compatible; MacIntosh; word processors: Multimate, WordStar, MacWrite, or ASCII. Sample copy $3.50; issue #2-4 $2.50. Fiction guidelines free for #10 SAE and 1 first class stamp.
Payment: Pays 1-4¢/word and contributor's copies.
Terms: Pays 25% on acceptance; 75% on publication. "25% payment is kill fee if we decide not to publish story." Rights negotiable. Sends galleys to the author.
Advice: "I certainly think a beginning writer can be successful if he/she studies the publication *before* submitting, and matches the submission with the magazine's needs. Get our guidelines and study them *before* submitting. Don't submit something *way over* or *way under* our word length requirements. Be understanding of editors; they can get swamped very easily, *especially* if there's only one editor handling all submissions. You don't need to write a synopsis of your story in your cover letter – the story should be able to stand on its own.

‡THE STERLING WEB (II), Arachnid Publishing, Box 38383, Tallahassee FL 32315. Editors: Ann Kennedy and Amy Mann. Magazine: 8½×11; 80-100 pages; 20 lb paper; glossy cover; b&w illustrations and photographs. "Speculative fiction for those that seek to be challenged – all ages." Quarterly. Estab. 1989.
Needs: Experimental, fantasy, horror, humor/satire, psychic/supernatural/occult, science fiction. "No slash n' gore, no predictable endings." Publishes annual special fiction issue. Receives 30-40 unsolicited mss/month. Accepts 8-12 mss/issue. Publishes ms 3-9 months after acceptance. Length: 2,500 words; 5,000 words maximum. Publishes short shorts. Sometimes critiques on rejected ms and recommends other markets.
How to Contact: "Get guidelines, or better yet, a copy of our magazine, and then submit." Reports in 1-2 weeks on queries; 1 month on mss. SASE. Photocopied submissions OK. Accepts computer printout submissions. Accepts electronic submissions. Sample copy for $4.75 plus 75¢ postage and handling. Fiction guidelines for #10 SAE and 1 first class stamp.

Payment: 2 contributor's copies. Discount to writers for additional copies.
Terms: Acquires first North American serial rights.
Advice: "The kind of work I look for is a piece that will stay with me long after I've finished reading it. It must paint pictures in my mind that are not easily erased. Read a copy of our magazine, at least—get our Writer's Guidelines. Also, read *Dangerous Visions*—edited by Harlan Ellison. That's the flavor we're looking for."

‡STONE DRUM (II), An International Magazine of the Arts, Box 233, Valley View TX 76272. (817)665-1145. Editor: Joseph Colin Murphey. Fiction Editor: Dwight Fullingim. Magazine: 6×9; 64-108 pages; 60 lb paper; slick 80 lb cover; graphics 8-10 illustrations; photographs. "We have no stated theme: the best writing to be found in poetry, fiction, articles on the craft of the arts and book reviews for adults generally educated in the humanities." Annually. Estab. 1972. Circ. 300.
Needs: Excerpted novel, contemporary, fantasy, humor/satire, literary, mainstream, psychic/supernatural/occult. "No erotica, no pornography, no all-out, no-holds-barred adult language." Receives 3-10 unsolicited mss/month. Accepts 3-6 ms/issue,except for specials. Publishes ms 6 months after acceptance. Recently published work by Elizabeth/Paul Bartlett, Joseph Bruchac and Jonathan London. Length: 2,000 words; 4,000 words maximum. Publishes short shorts. Sometimes critiques rejected ms and recommends other markets.
How to Contact: Send complete ms with cover letter. Reports in 3 weeks on mss. SASE. Photocopied submissions OK. Accepts computer printout submissions. Accepts electronic submissions. Sample copy for $4. Fiction guidelines for #10 SAE and 1 first class stamp.
Payment: Pays in contributor's copies.
Terms: Acquires one-time rights.
Advice: "Craft and experience, seem rather simultaneous, but I look for a good story line and dialogue that is believable, fitting to the context with people talking like people talk—regional or national—the way people talk in our time. Read some good market magazine that explains what editors expect. It wouldn't hurt to know something about manuscript form and the expectation of as near a perfect presentation as possible."

STONE SOUP (I), The Magazine By Children, Children's Art Foundation, Box 83, Santa Cruz CA 95063. (408)426-5557. Editor: Gerry Mandel. Magazine: 6×8¾; 48 pages; high quality paper; Sequoia matte cover stock; illustrations; photos. Stories, poems, book reviews and art by children up to age 13. Readership: children, librarians, educators. Published 5 times/year. Estab. 1973. Circ. 11,000.
Needs: Fiction by children on themes based on their own experiences, observations or special interests. No clichés, no formulas, no writing exercises; original work only. Receives approximately 500 unsolicited fiction mss each month. Accepts approx. 15 mss/issue. Published new writers within the last year. Length: 150-2,500 words. Critiques rejected mss upon request.
How to Contact: Send complete ms with cover letter. "We like to learn a little about our young writers, why they like to write, and how they came to write the story they are submitting." SASE. Accepts computer printout submissions. Prefers letter-quality. Reports in 1 month on mss. Publishes ms an average of 1-6 months after acceptance. Sample copy $4. Free guidelines with SASE.
Payment: 2 free author's copies; $2 charge for extras.
Terms: Acquires all rights.
Advice: Mss are rejected because they are "derivatives of movies, TV, comic books; or classroom assignments or other formulas."

STORIES (II), 14 Beacon St., Boston MA 02108. Editor-in-Chief: Amy R. Kaufman. "*Stories* is a short story magazine that publishes short fiction exclusively. It is designed to encourage the writing of stories that evoke an emotional response." Quarterly. Estab. 1982.
Needs: Contemporary, ethnic, historical (general), humor/satire and literary. "Translations and sharply perceptive humor interest us; romance, mystery, fantasy, science fiction and political pieces generally do not. We will not exclude any story on the basis of genre; we wish only that the piece be the best of its genre." Buys 5-6 mss/issue. Length: 750 words minimum; 13,000 words maximum; 4,000-7,000 words average. "Editor will make every effort to assist in revising stories she feels have merit."
How to Contact: Send complete ms with SASE. Cannot answer queries. Photocopies preferred. Simultaneous submissions OK "if marked as such." Reports in 8-10 weeks on mss. Sample issue $4; 2 for $7. Free fiction guidelines with SASE.
Payment: $150 average.
Terms: *Charges $5 administrative fee for ms submitted* (brief comment will be given). Pays within one week of publication for first North American serial rights.
Advice: "Simplicity is achieved after a struggle, and universality is possible only to a degree, but we feel that these are the qualities most likely to evoke readers' sympathy and concern. Timelessness is another ideal we pursue, by avoiding language and subjects that are fashionable. Most writers submit

half-finished work—they haven't taken themselves seriously enough. Study Strunk & White's *Elements of Style*, and emulate your favorite authors. You can't aim too high."

‡STORY (II), F&W Publications, 1507 Dana Ave., Cincinnati OH 45207. (513)531-2222. Editor: Lois Rosenthal. Magazine: 6¼×9½; 128 pages; uncoated, acid-free paper; uncoated index stock. "We publish finest quality short stories. Will consider unpublished novel excerpts if they are self-inclusive." Quarterly. Estab. 1931.
Needs: Condensed/excerpted novel, contemporary, experimental, humor/satire, literary, mainstream, translations. No genre fiction—science fiction, detective, young adult, confession, romance, etc. Buys 10 mss/issue. Agented fiction 50-60%. Recently published work by Norman Mailer, Robert Olmstead and Richard Currey. Length: 5,000 words; 1,000 words minimum; 10,000 words maximum. Publishes short shorts of 500-1,500 words. Occasionally offers helpful comments on rejected mss (if it is outstanding in some way).
How to Contact: Send complete ms with or without cover letter, or submit through agent. Reports in one month or less on mss. SASE for ms. Photocopied submissions OK. Accepts computer printout submissions. Sample copy for $5, 9×12 SAE and $2.40 postage. Fiction guidelines for #10 SAE and 1 first class stamp.
Payment: Pays $100 plus 5 contributor's copies.
Terms: Pays on acceptance for first North American serial rights. Sends galleys to author.
Advice: "We look for fine writing. We publish the best stories we can find. We want to bring excellent short fiction to a wide audience, both to provide a deserved mass forum for new (and established) voices, and to help rekindle the spark for the uniquely American literary form—short fiction."

STORYQUARTERLY (II), Box 1416, Northbrook IL 60065. (312)433-0741. Co-Editors: Anne Brashler and Diane Williams. Magazine: approximately 6×9; 130 pages; good quality paper; illustrations; photos. A magazine devoted to the short story and committed to a full range of styles and forms. Published twice yearly. Estab. 1975. Circ. 3,000.
Needs: Accepts 12-15 mss/issue, 20-30 mss/year. Receives 100 unsolicited fiction mss/month. Published new writers within the last year.
How to Contact: Send complete ms with SASE. Reports in 3 months on mss. Sample copy $4.
Payment: 3 free author's copies.
Terms: Acquires one-time rights. Copyright reverts to author after publication.
Advice: "Send one manuscript at a time, subscribe to the magazine, send SASE."

‡STRANGE PLASMA (II,IV), Science Fiction and Fantasy, Edgewood Press, Box 264, Cambridge MA 02238. Editor: Stephen Pasechnick. Magazine: 8½×11; 32 pages; b&w illustrations. "Literate, unusual science fiction and fantasy for an audience interested in discovering new writers." Quarterly. Estab. 1989. Circ. 500.
Needs: Experimental, fantasy, science fiction. Receives 100 unsolicited mss/month. Buys 6-8 mss/issue; 24-32 mss/year. Publishes ms 5 months after acceptance. Recently published work by Gene Wolfe, R.A. Lafferty and Eric Brown. Length: 10,000 words. Publishes short shorts. Sometimes critiques rejected mss and recommends other markets.
How to Contact: Send complete ms with cover letter. Reports in 2 weeks on queries; 2 months on mss. SASE. Photocopied submissions. Sample copy $3. Fiction guidelines free.
Payment: Pays 2½¢/word.
Terms: Pays on acceptance for first North American serial rights.
Advice: "The fiction must be well written with particular emphasis on style, ideas, character, setting, theme, ideas, plot."

‡STROKER MAGAZINE (II), 129 2nd Ave. +3, New York NY 10003. Editor: Irving Stettner. Magazine: 5½×8½; average 52 pages; medium paper; 80 lb good cover stock; illustrations; photos. "*An un-literary* literary review interested in sincerity, verve, anger, humor and beauty. For an intelligent audience—non-academic, non-media dazed in the US and throughout the world." Published 3-4 times/year. Estab. 1974, 43 issues to date. Circ. 600.
Needs: Literary, contemporary. No academic material. Length: "3-5 pages preferred but not essential."
How to Contact: Send complete ms with SASE. Reports in 6 weeks. Sample copy $2.50.
Payment: 2 free author's copies. $1 charge for extras.
Terms: Acquires one-time rights.
Advice: "We are interested in fiction. Be sure your name and address are on the manuscript." Published new writers within the last year.

STRUGGLE (IV), A Magazine of Proletarian Revolutionary Literature, Marxist-Leninist Party USA, Detroit Branch, Box 13261, Harper Station, Detroit MI 48213-0261. Editor: Tim Hall. Magazine: 5½×8½; 24-48 pages; 20 lb white bond paper; colored cover; illustrations; occasional photographs. Publishes material related to "the struggle of the working class and all progressive people against the rule of the rich—including their war policies, racism, exploitation of the workers, oppression of women, etc." Quarterly. Estab. 1985.

Needs: Contemporary, ethnic, experimental, feminist, historical (general), humor/satire, literary, prose poem, regional, science fiction, senior citizen/retirement, suspense/mystery, translations, young adult/teen (10-18). "The theme can be approached in many ways, including plenty of categories not listed here." No romance, psychic, western, erotica, religious. Receives 1-2 unsolicited fiction mss/month. "Has published three stories in past three issues. Would like more." Publishes ms 3 months or less after acceptance. Recently published work by Leo Paulson, Greg Roberts, Peter Poyas; published new writers within the last year. Length: 1,000-3,000 words average; 5,000 words maximum. Publishes short shorts. Frequently critiques rejected mss.

How to Contact: Send complete ms; cover letter optional but helpful. "Tries to" report in 3 months. SASE. Simultaneous, photocopied and reprint submissions OK. Accepts computer printout submissions. Sample copy for $1.50.

Payment: Pays 2 contributor's copies.

Terms: No rights acquired. Publication not copyrighted.

Advice: "Write about the oppression of the working people, the poor, the minorities, women, and their rebellion against it—we are not interested in anything which accepts the status quo. We are not too worried about plot and advanced technique (fine if we get them!)—we would probably accept things others would call sketches, provided they sizzle with life and struggle. Just describe for us a situation in which some real people confront some problem of oppression, however seemingly minor. Observe and put down the real facts. Tidy it up later. We have increased our fiction portion of our content. We get poetry and songs all the time. We want more fiction."

‡STUDIA MYSTICA (II), Texas A&M University, College Station TX 77843-4227. Editor: Robert Boenig. Magazine: 5½×8½; 80 pages; glossy cover stock; illustrations; photos. Magazine featuring "mystical experience for an artistic, scholarly, religious audience." Quarterly. Estab. 1978. Circ. 400.

Needs: Literary and religious/inspirational. No occult stories. Receives 4 unsolicited fiction mss/month. Accepts 2 mss/year. Published new writers within the last year. Publishes short shorts of 3-5 pages. Length: 3,500 words minimum. Occasionally critiques rejected mss. Sometimes recommends other markets.

How to Contact: Send complete ms with SASE. Cover letter with author bio; places of publication. Simultaneous submissions OK. Reports in 1 month on mss. Publishes ms an average of 12-16 months after acceptance. Sample copy $4.

Terms: Acquires first rights. Sends galleys to author.

Advice: "Read the journal ahead of time so that we do not receive stories whose themes are not appropriate to our concerns. Our concern is with the expression of mystical experience through all the arts. Although poetry is the literary form preferred by mystics, some do turn to fiction. We don't care about the 'track record' of a writer so much as the quality of the writing and whether it expresses mystical (not occult) experience."

‡SUB-TERRAIN (I,IV), Anvil Press, Box 1575, Stn. A, Vancouver BC V6C 2P7 Canada. (604)876-8700. Editor: B. Kaufman, J.L. McCarthy and P. Petrie. Newspaper: 7×10; 16-20 pages; good-offset printed paper; 60 lb. cover stock; illustrations; photos. "We intend to function as a literary magazine with a social conscience. *Sub-Terrain* will provide a forum for work that pushes the boundaries in form or content." Estab. 1988.

Needs: Erotica, experimental, humor/satire and literary. Receives 6-10 unsolicited mss/month. Accepts 3-4 mss/issue. Publishes ms 1-4 months after acceptance. Length: 200-3,000 words; 400-500 average. Publishes short shorts. Length: 200 words. Sometimes critiques rejected mss and "at times" recommends other markets.

How to Contact: Send complete ms with cover letter. Reports in 3-4 weeks on queries; 6-8 weeks on mss. SASE. Sample copy $2.50.

Payment: Pays in contributor's copies. Acquires one-time rights.

Advice: "We look for something special in the voice or style. Not simply something that is a well-written story. A new twist, a unique sense or vision of the world. The stuff that every mag is hoping to find. Write about things that are important to you: issues that *must* be talked about; issues that frighten, anger you. The world has all the cute, well-made stories it needs. Give words power, empower yourself and make a difference."

sub-TERRAIN ***editor J. Lawrence McCarthy says this cover "suggests to us the split personality that women feel: men notice their exterior—the hair and make-up—rather than the personality. The picture shows the underlying sadness of not being seen as a person. The title of the picture—'Red Nails'—emphasizes this." The artist, Leslie Poole, "probes his own psyche in search of the Collective Unconscious," claims his agent.***

THE SUN (II), The Sun Publishing Company, Inc., 107 N. Roberson St., Chapel Hill NC 27516. (919)942-5282. Editor: Sy Safransky. Magazine: 8½x11; 40 pages; offset paper; glossy cover stock; illustrations; photos. "*The Sun* is a magazine of ideas. We publish all kinds of writing—fiction, articles, poetry. Our only criteria are that the writing make sense and enrich our common space. We direct *The Sun* toward interests which move us, and we trust our readers will respond." Monthly. Estab. 1974. Circ. 10,000.
Needs: Open to all fiction. Accepts 1 ms/issue. Receives approximately 100 unsolicited fiction mss each month. Published work by Tillie Olsen, Susan Watkins, James Carlos Blake; published new writers within the last year. Length: 10,000 words maximum.
How to Contact: Send complete ms with SASE. Reports in 2 months. Publishes ms an average of 1-3 months after acceptance. Sample copy $3.
Payment: Up to $100 on publication, plus 2 free author's copies and a complimentary subscription.
Terms: Acquires one-time rights. Publishes reprints.

SUN DOG: THE SOUTHEAST REVIEW (II), English Department, 406 Williams, Florida State University, Tallahassee FL 32306. (904)644-4230. Editors: Craig Stroupe, Bucky McMahon and Jamie Granger. Magazine: 6×9; 60-100 pages; 70 lb paper; 10 pt. Krome Kote cover; illustrations; photos. Published biannually. Estab. 1979. Circ. 2,000.
Needs: "We want stories which are well written, beautifully written, with striking images, incidents and characters. We are interested more in quality than in style or genre." Accepts 20 mss/year. Receives approximately 60 unsolicited fiction mss each month. Reads less frequently during summer. Critiques rejected mss when there is time. Occasionally recommends other markets.
How to Contact: Send complete ms with SASE. Typed, double-spaced, on good bond. Clean photocopy acceptable. "Short bio or cover letter would be appreciated." Publishes ms an average of 2-6 months after acceptance. Sample copy $4.
Payment: 2 free author's copies. $2 charge for extras.
Terms: Acquires first North American serial rights which then revert to author.
Advice: "Avoid trendy experimentation for its own sake (present-tense narration, observation that isn't also revelation). Fresh stories, moving, interesting characters and a sensitivity to language are still fiction mainstays. Also publishes winner and runners up of the World's Best Short Short Story Contest sponsored by the Florida State University English Department. Entries should be 250 words or less, typed double-spaced on one sheet of paper, and submitted with SASE to the World's Best Short Short Story Contest at the above address. Deadline for the contest is in mid-February."

SWIFT KICK (II), 1711 Amherst St., Buffalo NY 14214. (716)837-7778. Editor: Robin Kay Willoughby. Magazine: size, number of pages, paper quality, cover stock vary; illustrations; photos, b&w line art, xerographs. Specializes in unusual formats, hard-to-classify works, visual poetry, found art, etc. for " 'pataphysical, rarified audience." Published special fiction issue; plans another. Estab. 1981. Circ. 100.

Needs: Open. "If it doesn't seem to fit a regular category, it's probably what we'd like! No boring, slipshod, everyday stuff like in mass-market magazines." Receives 5 unsolicited fiction mss/month. Accepts 1-2 mss/issue. Does not read just before Christmas. Publishes ms depending on finances (6 months-1 year) after acceptance. Publishes short shorts of 1,000 words (or 1 picture). Sometimes recommends other markets.

How to Contact: Query first for longer works or send complete ms with cover letter with short work. Reports in 2 months to 1 year. SASE ("or include reply card with OK to toss enclosed work"). Simultaneous and photocopied submissions OK. Will consider reprints of astoundingly good work (out of print). Accepts computer printouts. Sample copy for $7; "sample purchase recommended to best understand magazine's needs."

Payment: Pays in contributor's copies; half price for extras.

Terms: Acquires one-time rights. Rights revert to artists/authors. Sends galleys to author if requested.

Advice: "We always get less fiction than poetry—if a story is good, it has a good chance of publication in little mags. Editorially, I'm a snob, so don't write like anyone else; be *so* literate your writing transcends literature and (almost) literacy. Don't submit over 10 pages first time. Submit a 'grabber' that makes an editor ask for more. Don't neglect the stories in your own life for someone else's castles-in-the-air."

‡SWORD OF SHAHRAZAD (I), Amazon Publications, Box 152844, Arlington TX 76015-2844. (817) 465-3354. Editor: Kimberli Dorris. Magazine: 5½×8½; approx. 42 pages; 20 lb paper; 65 lb cover stock; illustrations. "Sword is the fiction writer's workshop-in-a-magazine. We publish fiction, feedback on published pieces, articles on writing, subscriber profiles, a markets column and many other features." Bimonthly. Estab. 1988.

Needs: Adventure, condensed/excerpted novel, contemporary, erotica, ethnic, experimental, fantasy, historical, horror, humor/satire, literary, mainstream, prose poem, psychic/supernatural/occult, regional, romance, science fiction, serialized novel, sports, suspense/mystery, translations and western. No juvenile and young adult. Has published special fiction issue and plans one for the future. Receives 30 unsolicited mss per month; accepts 5-6 mss/issue; 35-40 per year. Publishes ms 2 weeks-4 months after acceptance. Length: 8,000 words maximum. Publishes short shorts. Comments on rejected mss and recommends other markets.

How to Contact: Send complete ms with cover letter. Reports on queries in 1-2 weeks; on mss in 2-6 weeks. SASE. Simultaneous, photocopied and reprint submissions OK. Accepts computer printout and electronic submissions. Sample copy $3. Fiction guidelines for #10 SAE and 1 first class stamp.

Payment: Pays in contributor's copies.

Terms: Acquires one-time rights; sends pre-publication galleys to author.

Advice: "I'll help a writer with a strong premise whose work isn't as polished as I'd like, but the possibility of finding exceptional writing - the kind that's almost invisible and never distracts the reader from the story - well, that's what keeps me reading my stack of manuscripts! Send a *perfect* manuscript. Your story only gets one chance, so make it count. Do your proofreading *before* you mail it out. Editors don't have time to figure out what you meant to say!"

SYCAMORE REVIEW (II), Department of English, Purdue University, West Lafayette IN 47907. (317)494-3783. Editor: Henry J. Hughes. Fiction Editor: Elizabeth Stuckey-French. Magazine: 5½×8½; 1,000 pages; heavy, textured, uncoated paper; heavy matte uncoated cover; no unsolicited art. "Journal devoted to contemporary literature. We publish both traditional and experimental fiction, personal essay and poetry." Semiannually. Estab. 1989. Circ. 1,000.

Needs: Contemporary, experimental, historical (general), humor/satire, literary, mainstream, regional, sports, translations. "We generally avoid genre literature, but maintain no formal restrictions on style or subject matter. No science fiction, romance, children's." Publishes ms 3 months-1 year after acceptance. Length: 3,750 words preferred; 250 words minimum. Sometimes critiques rejected mss and recommends other markets.

How to Contact: Send complete ms with cover letter. Cover letter should include previous publications, address changes. Reports in 3 months. SASE. Simultaneous and photocopied submissions OK. Accepts computer printout submissions. Sample copy for $4. Fiction guidelines for #10 SAE and 1 first class stamp.

Payment: Pays in contributor's copies; charge for extras.
Terms: Acquires one-time rights.
Advice: "We especially recommend readers to digest work from magazines like *The Indiana Review*, *Missouri Review* and *Sewanee Review* to help shape ideas concerning the status of quality magazine fiction today. The fiction writer must read voraciously. Read stories published in *The New Yorker* and read stories appearing in your community or university magazine. When you are ready to write (you are always ready) begin writing from actual experience."

T.W.I. (I, II), A Journal of Politics and Literature, The T.W.I. (Typing While Intoxicated) Collective, Box 19441, Washington DC 20036. (202)234-9029. Editor: Curtis Olson. Magazine: 8½×11; 60 pages; 20 lb paper; illustrations. "*T.W.I.* publishes new and unique fiction and nonfiction from the lower fringes of society and culture." Published 3-4 times per year. Plans special fiction issue. Estab. 1987. Circ. 100.
Needs: Contemporary, erotica, experimental, humor/satire, literary, prose poem. "No formula fiction. Nothing written to make money." Receives 2-4 unsolicited mss/month. Accepts 6-8 mss/year. Publishes ms 3-4 months after acceptance. Recently published work by John Calvit, Carl Zimmer, Al Poe; published new writers within the last year. Length: 5,000 words maximum. Publishes short shorts. Sometimes critiques rejected mss.
How to Contact: Query first or send complete ms with cover letter. "I like a cover letter that introduces the author, tells me a bit about them, where he/she has been published, and a bit about what is unique about the submission and what it is trying to accomplish." Reports in 2 weeks on queries; 1-2 months on mss. SASE for ms. Photocopied submissions OK. Accepts computer printout submissions, no dot-matrix. Sample copy for $4.
Payment: Pays in 3 contributor's copies.
Terms: Acquires first North American serial rights.
Advice: "Most academic and magazine fiction and poetry bores me. It doesn't speak to people or to the world. I've been called an 'undergound' publisher. I guess it's true. It's in underground publications that people talk to people. That is where the future of writing is, I think (or at least, I hope). You've gotta *feel* it; and don't take yourself too seriously (but take your writing *very* seriously). *T.W.I.* is growing and changing with each issue, so our needs are constantly changing. It would probably be helpful to a contributor to write first and get our current guidelines or a copy of the latest issue."

‡TABULA RASA (I, II), A new page in fiction and poetry, Box 1920, Stn 'B', London Ontario N6A 5J4 Canada. (519)432-3488. Editor: Paul Laxon/Gord Harrison/John Kirnan. Magazine: 6×9; 70 pages; 40 lb paper; 80 lb cover stock; illustrations. "We have no specific genre of fiction in mind, though most of our submissions are contemporary—character development and plot are what we look for." Bimonthly. Estab. 1989. Circ. 500.
Needs: Contemporary, experimental, fantasy, horror, humor/satire, literary, mainstream, prose poem, science fiction, serialized novel and suspense/mystery. "We'll consider anything, though erotica and religious fiction without a good plot or characterization won't get published in *Tabula Rasa*." Receives 15-20 unsolicited fiction mss/month. Accepts 6-10 fiction mss/issue; 40-50 mss/year. Publishes ms 1-2 months after acceptance. Length: 2,000 words average; 300 words minimum; 3,500 words maximum. Publishes short shorts of 300-500 words. Sometimes critiques rejected mss and recommends other markets.
How to Contact: Send complete ms with cover letter that includes short bio and whether the manuscript has been published elsewhere, or is being considered elsewhere. Reports in 2 weeks on queries; 1-2 months on mss. SASE. Simultaneous, photocopied and reprint submissions OK. Accepts computer printout submissions. Accepts electronic submissions via disk (IBM format) or over the CompuServe network. Sample copy $3.50. Fiction guidelines for #10 SAE and IRCs.
Payment: Pays 2 contributor's copies.
Terms: Acquires one-time rights. Sends galleys to author if there are any revisions we think are necessary.
Advice: "We're looking for stories that will entertain us and make us think at the same time. Science fiction, mystery, mainstream: genre doesn't matter, interesting characters and plots do."

THE TAMPA REVIEW (III), Humanities Division, Box 135F, University of Tampa, Tampa FL 33606. (813)253-3333, ext. 424. Editor: Richard Matthews. Fiction Editor: Andy Solomon. Magazine: 8×10; over 100 pages; bond paper; illustrations; photos. "Interested in fiction of distinctive literary quality." Annually. Estab. 1988.
Needs: Contemporary, ethnic, experimental, fantasy, historical, humor/satire, literary, mainstream, prose poem, translations. "We are far more interested in quality than in genre. No sentimental as opposed to genuinely moving, nor self-conscious style at the expense of human truth." Buys 3-7 mss/issue. Publishes ms within 2 months-1 year of acceptance. Agented fiction 60%. Recently published work by Lee K. Abbott, Lorrie Moore, Tim O'Connor. Length: 1,000 words minimum; 6,000 words

maximum. Publishes short shorts "if the story is good enough." Sometimes critiques rejected mss and recommends other markets.
How to Contact: Send complete mss with cover letter, which should include brief bio and publishing record. Include Social Security number. Reports in one month. SASE. Simultaneous and photocopied submissions OK. Accepts computer printout submissions. "Letter quality preferred." Sample copy for $6, 9×12 SAE and 5 first class stamps. Fiction guidelines for #10 SAE and 1 first class stamp.
Payment: Pays $10 per printed page.
Terms: Pays on publication for first North American serial rights. Sends galleys to author.
Advice: "There are more good writers publishing in magazines today than there have been in many decades. Unfortunately, there are even more bad ones. In T. Gertler's *Elbowing the Seducer*, an editor advises a young writer that he wants to hear her voice completely, to tell (he means 'show') him in a story the truest thing she knows. We concur. Rather than a trendy workshop story or a minimalism that actually stems from not having much to say, we would like to see stories that make us believe they mattered to the writer and, more importantly, will matter to a reader. Trim until only the essential is left, and don't give up belief in yourself. And it might help to attend a good writers conference, e.g. Wesleyan or Bennington."

‡TANDAVA (II), 22453 Melrose Ct., East Detroit MI 48021. (313)779-9349. Editor: Tom Blessing. Magazine: 5½×8 or 8×11; 16-50 pages; illustrations. Frequency varies. Estab. 1982. Circ. 100.
Needs: Excerpted novel, contemporary, experimental, fantasy, literary, prose poem, science fiction. Plans special fiction issue. Receives 1 or less unsolicited mss/month. Accepts 2 mss/issue; 5 mss/year. Publishes ms 1½ years after acceptance. Length: 5,000 words maximum. Publishes short shorts. Length: Up to 2 pages. Sometimes critiques rejected mss and recommends other markets.
How to Contact: Send complete ms with cover letter. "Include introduction—where you heard of Tandava, goals, projects." Reports in 2 weeks. SASE. Simultaneous and photocopied submissions OK. Accepts computer printout submissions. Sample copy for $1.50.
Payment: Pays in contributor's copies.
Terms: Publication not copyrighted.

TAPESTRY (I), Rte. 3, Box 272-D, Ripley MS 38663. (601)837-1125. Publisher: Joan Cissom. Magazine: 8½×11"; 50-60 pages; illustrations and photographs. Monthly. Estab. 1988.
Needs: Fantasy, horror. "Publishes poems, fiction, articles on writing, interviews with pros in field market/contest news." Recently published work by David Valentino, D. M. Vosk. Length: 3,000 words maximum. Publishes short shorts.
How to Contact: Send complete ms with cover letter. SASE. Sample copy for $6.
Payment: Pays ½¢/word for fiction and 1 contributor's copy.
Terms: Pays on acceptance. Purchases one-time rights. Sponsors contest for fiction and poetry writers. Send SASE for details.
Advice: "TAPESTRY has been expanded to accomodate a more extensive market/contest section and the new feature 'Amateur's Showcase.' Talented but unknown writers and artists are featured with examples of their work. Each newcomer featured receives a free one-year subscription to TAPESTRY."

TENTRA ARTNET BBS, Garage Music Co., Box 63 Rockaway Park, New York NY 11694. Editor: Andy Anderson. Electronic bulletin board.
Needs: Adventure, contemporary, erotica, ethnic, experimental, fantasy, feminist, historical (left-wing Labor), humor/satire, literary, mainstream, prose poem, regional, science fiction, senior citizen/retirement, serialized novel, sports, suspense/mystery, translations, western, young adult/teen (10-18 years). Length: 500-5,000 words.
How to Contact: Send complete ms with cover letter or telephone voice line (718)945-115 or BBS data line (718)945-1127—8 bit word, no parity, 1 stop bit.
Terms: Pays $5-25 on acceptance for all rights.
Advice: "We invite writers to log onto our system without charge to find what we're all about."

TERROR TIME AGAIN (I), Nocturnal Publications, 1591 Taylor Street #4, St. Paul MN 55104. Editor: Donald L. Miller. Magazine: 5×8; 53-60 pages; 20 lb paper; 67 lb cover stock; illustrations. "*Terror Time Again*'s objective is to produce terror in the reader." Annually. Estab. 1987. Circ. 300.
Needs: Horror. No science fiction or sword and sorcery. Receives 20 unsolicited fiction mss/month. Accepts 10-19 mss/issue. Does not read September 1 to December 31. Publishes ms in October of year accepted. Recently published work by Allen Koszowski, Marilyn K. Martin and Dona; published new writers within the last year. Length: 1,000 words average; 200 words minimum; 2,000 words maximum. Publishes short shorts. Length: 200-500 words. Sometimes critiques rejected mss; recommends other markets.

How to Contact: Send complete ms with cover letter containing information about the author. Reports in 2 weeks on queries; 1 month on mss. SASE. Simultaneous, photocopied and reprint submissions OK. Accepts computer printout submissions, no dot-matrix. Sample copy $5; fiction guidelines free.
Payment: ¼-½¢/word; contributor's copies.
Terms: Pays on publication for one-time rights. Sponsors contests and awards for fiction writers. "*Terror Time Again* has a cover contest via *The Nightmare Express*. A cover illustration is used by an author to derive upon a story using the artwork. Interested authors need to write to me so they can find out what cover it will be. *TNE* is published every other month and it is a newsletter for horror writers."
Advice: "A writer can be whatever he/she chooses, and his/her characters reveal the truth underneath. We will work with new authors. I want the readers of *Terror Time Again* to come away from a story too scared to forget the experience."

THE TEXAS REVIEW (II), Sam Houston State University Press, Huntsville TX 77341. (713)294-1423. Editor: Paul Ruffin. Magazine: 6×9; 148-190 pages; best quality paper; 70 lb cover stock; illustrations; photos. "We publish top quality poetry, fiction, articles, interviews and reviews for a general audience." Semiannually. Estab. 1976. Circ. 700.
Needs: Literary and contemporary fiction. "We are eager enough to consider fiction of quality, no matter what its theme or subject matter. No juvenile fiction." Accepts 4 mss/issue. Receives approximately 40-60 unsolicited fiction mss each month. Published work by Richard Elman, Peter S. Scherman, Margaret Kingery; published new writers within the last year. Length: 500-10,000 words. Critiques rejected mss "when there is time." Recommends other markets.
How to Contact: Send complete ms with cover letter. SASE. Reports in 3 months on mss. Sample copy $3.
Payment: Free author's copies plus one year subscription.
Terms: Acquires all rights. Sends galleys to author.

THEMA (II,IV), Bothomos Enterprises, Box 74109, Metairie LA 70033-4109. Editor: Virginia Howard. Magazine: 5½×8½; 200 pages; good paper; Grandee Strathmore cover stock; b&w illustrations. "Different specified theme for each issue—short stories, poems, b&w artwork must relate to that theme." Quarterly. Estab. 1988.
Needs: Adventure, contemporary, experimental, humor/satire, literary, mainstream, prose poem, psychic/supernatural/occult, regional, science fiction, sports, suspense/mystery, western. "Each issue is based on a specified premise—a different unique theme for each issue. Many types of fiction acceptable, but must fit the premise. No pornographic, scatologic, erotic fiction." Publishes ms within 3-4 months of acceptance. Recently published work by Guida Jackson, Ellen Herbert, Terry Heller. Length: 4,500 words preferred; 2,700 words minimum; 6,000 words maximum. Publishes short shorts "if very clever." Length: 300-500 words. Sometimes critiques rejected mss and recommends other markets.
How to Contact: Send complete ms with cover letter, which should include "name and address, brief introduction, specifying the intended target issue for the mss." Reports on queries in 1 week; on mss in 4-6 weeks after deadline for specified issue. SASE. Photocopied submissions OK. No dot-matrix computer printouts. Sample copy for $5. Free fiction guidelines.
Payment: Pays $25.
Terms: Pays on acceptance. Purchases one-time rights.
Advice: "Do not submit a manuscript unless you have written it for a specified premise. If you don't know the upcoming themes, send for guidelines first, before sending a story. We need more stories told in the Mark Twain/O. Henry tradition in magazine fiction." Upcoming themes: The Thursday Night League (deadline May 1, 1990); Nothing ever happened to him but weather (deadline August 1, 1990).

THIN ICE (II), 379 Lincoln Ave., Council Bluffs IA 51503. (712)322-9125. Editor/Publisher: Kathleen Jurgens. Magazine: digest size; 95-110 pages; 16-20 lb paper; enamel cover; b&w, pen and ink illustrations. "Horror and dark fantasy—short stories, poetry, interviews, art." Triannually. Estab. 1987. Circ. 250.
Needs: Experimental, fantasy (dark), horror, black humor/satire, poetry, psychic/supernatural/occult. No "racist, preachy, straight porn for shock value." Receives 80-120 unsolicited mss/month. Buys approx. 10 mss/issue; approx. 40 mss/year. Publishes ms 1-2 years after acceptance. Recently published work by Bentley Little, J. N. Williamson, Colleen Drippe, Jeannette Hopper. Length: 1,000-4,000 words preferred. Critiques rejected mss.
How to Contact: Send complete ms with cover letter. Cover letter should include "a personal introduction, mention a few prior 'sales' if desired (though not necessary), where the writers heard of *Thin Ice*." Reports in 1 week on queries; 1-2 months on mss. SASE. Photocopied submissions preferred.

Accepts computer printout submissions, including dot-matrix (but prefer not to). Sample copy for $4.50 to Kathleen Jurgens ($6 outside of the U.S.). Fiction guidelines free with #10 SASE.
Payment: Pays in contributor's copies.
Terms: Acquires first North American serial rights.
Advice: "Invest in a copy of our magazine and read it from cover to cover. Get a 'feel' for the overall mood, tone, and subject matter. Don't apologize for misspellings or coffee stains on the manuscript—retype it. While we prefer informal query letters, we become quite irate when potential contributors treat us unprofessionally. We respond to all submissions personally, frequently offering editorial commentary. Always include an SASE with the correct amount of postage. Give us the full 8 weeks to repond. Absolutely no simultaneous or multiple submissions considered. Please, do not summarize the story in your cover letter."

THIRD WOMAN (II,IV), Chicano Studies Dept., Dwinelle Hall, University of California, Berkeley CA 94720. (415)642-0708 or 642-0240. Editor: Norma Alarcón. Magazine: 5½×8½; 100-150 pages; standard good quality paper; glossy color cover; illustrations; photos. "Literature and the arts focusing on the work by/about U.S. Latinas, Hispanic World and Third World Women in general: poetry, narrative, drama, reviews, interviews, etc." Semiannually. Estab. 1981. Circ. 1,500.
Needs: Ethnic, feminist, translations. Receives 4 mss/month. Accepts 10 mss/year. Publishes ms within 6 months-2 years of acceptance. Published work by Sandra Cisneros, Luz María Umpierre. Length: 5,000-10,000 words preferred. Publishes short shorts.
How to Contact: Send complete ms with cover letter. Reports on queries in 6-8 weeks; on mss in 6 months. SASE. Simultaneous and photocopied submissions OK. Accepts computer printout submissions. Free sample copy.
Payment: Pays in contributor's copies.
Terms: Acquires first rights. Sends galleys to author. Sponsors contests for fiction writers. "Contests are occasional; please write and inquire of editor."

‡THUMBPRINTS (I, IV), Thumb Area Writer's Club, Box 27, Sandusky MI 48471. Editor: Janet Ihle. Newsletter: 8½×11; 6 pages; line drawing illustrations. Material is "primarily on writing and writers." Estab. 1983. Circ. 30.
Needs: Adventure, historical (general), humor/satire, mainstream, prose poem, regional, romance (contemporary, historical and young adult), senior citizen/retirement and sports. Accepts 1ms/issue; 10-12 mss/year. Publishes ms 3-4 months after acceptance. Length: 750 words maximum; 500 average. Publishes short shorts. Length: 250-400 words. Sometimes critiques rejected mss.
How to Contact: Send complete ms only. Reports in 1 month on queries; 2 months on mss. SASE. Photocopied submissions OK. Accepts computer printout submissions. Sample copy 50¢, #10 SASE. Guidelines for SASE.
Payment: Pays in contributor's copies; charges for extras.
Terms: Acquires first or one-time rights. Publication not copyrighted.

‡TIDEWATER (II), TeeDub Press, 5517-5th NW, Seattle WA 98107. (206)784-5835. Editor: Scott Hartwich. Magazine: 7×8½; 40 pages. "Theme is open; I publish prose, poetry and essays relating to literature." Quarterly. Estab. 1987.
Needs: Excerpted novel, contemporary, ethnic, experimental, feminist, gay, humor/satire, lesbian, literary, prose poem. "No religious or romance fiction. Plans special fiction issue. Accepts 8-12 mss/year (these numbers can increase if submissions increase). Publishes ms 2 weeks-3 months after acceptance. Length: Preferred 3,000 words; 100 words minimum; 6,000 words maximum. Sometimes critiques rejected mss and recommends other markets.
How to Contact: Send complete ms with cover letter, 3-5 line bio and previous publication credits. Reports in 2 weeks on queries; 6-8 weeks on mss. SASE. Simultaneous and photocopied submissions OK. Accepts computer printout submissions. Sample copy for $2, 9×12 SAE and 4 first class stamps. Fiction guidelines for #10 SAE and 1 first class stamp.
Payment: Pays with free subscription and contributor's copies.
Terms: Acquires first rights. Sends galleys to author (if requested).
Advice: "I like to see Universal themes approached with fresh eyes, and viewpoints developed by an examination of one's own perspective on the world, rather than a condensing of the world's countless viewpoints into a kind-of vicarious, artificial 'opinion.' I think spotless, grammatically correct manuscripts with no misspelled words attract my attention, because they reflect a true caring on the author's part; sloppy writing with poor mechanics seems to be making it onto shelves more and more frequently. Anyone can have noble, insightful, original ideas, but the presentation of these ideas, the translation of ideas onto paper, is not just an afterthought—it is the key element."

TIMBUKTU (II), Box 469, Charlottesville VA 22902. Editor: Molly Turner. Magazine: 8½×11; 80-100 pages; vellum paper; heavy, glossy card cover stock; illustrations; photos. "*Timbuktu* is nationally distributed and has a diverse audience." Semiannually. Estab. 1987. Circ. 800.

Needs: Literary, poetry. "No genre stuff, no writing program formula stories—just fresh, innovative, well-written manuscripts." Receives 300-400 mss/month. Accepts 3-5 mss/issue; 8-10 mss/year. Publishes ms within 6 months of acceptance. Recently published work by John Casey, Douglas Day, Marin Sorescu. No preferred length. Publishes short shorts. Sometimes critiques rejected mss and recommends other markets.
How to Contact: Send complete ms. Reports in 1 week on queries; in 6-8 weeks on mss. SASE. Accepts computer printout submissions. Sample copy for $5. Fiction guidelines for SAE and 1 first class stamp.
Payment: Pays $25-200 story, $5-50 poem and free subscription to magazine; contributor's copies.
Terms: Acquires one-time rights.
Advice: "Cover letters generally don't contribute much—I'm only interested if the writer knows the magazine for some reason and has something interesting to say about why they chose to submit to us rather than someone else."

‡TOAD HIWAY (II), Box 44, Universal IN 47884. (317)832-8918. Editor: Doug Martin. Fiction Editor: John Colvin. Magazine: 5½×8½; 20 pages; ink drawing illustrations; b&w photos. "We are especially interested in avant-garde material, but quality mainstream fiction also will be considered." Quarterly. Estab. 1989. Circ. 200.
Needs: Condensed/excerpted novel, contemporary, erotica, experimental, humor/satire, prose poem, science fiction and translations. "We especially enjoy fiction which challenges or offends people, but this doesn't mean we want a ms filled with obscenities for no particular reason (unless perhaps it is a dada piece). We are looking for *intelligent* material that offends the average person." Plans to publish special fiction or anthology issue in the future. Receives 10 unsolicited mss/month. Accepts 1-2 mss/issue; 4-8 mss/year. Publishes ms 3-6 months after acceptance. Length: 30,000 words maximum; 5,000 average. Publishes short shorts. Sometimes critiques rejected mss and recommends other markets.
How to Contact: Send complete ms with cover letter. "If you've been published before, be specific about magazines and dates." Reports in 6 weeks on queries; 3 months on mss. SASE. Simultaneous submissions OK. Sample copy $2. Fiction guidelines for #10 SAE.
Payment: Pays in contributor's copies.
Terms: Acquires one-time rights.
Advice: "Far too much of what we receive appears to have been mailed in after receiving a *B+* from Professor Doodle. Keep rewriting until your story seems comparable to some of the professional writers being published today. Set your story aside, then reread and revise it again. If you take this much trouble in your writing, you will already have a jump on most of the mss we receive."

TRADESWOMEN (I,IV), A Quarterly Magazine for Women in Blue-Collar Work, Tradeswomen, Inc., P.O. Box 40664, San Francisco CA 94140. (415) 821-7334. Editors: Molly Martin and Helen Vozenilek. Magazine: 8½×11; 40 pages; b&w photographs. Quarterly. Estab. 1981. Circ. 1,500.
Needs: "Looking for fiction about women in blue-collar employment; on-the-job stories, 'what it's like' stories by women and men." Receives 1-2 unsolicited mss/month; accepts 1-2 mss/issue. Publishes ms 3-6 months after acceptance. Length: 2,000 words average; 3,000 words maximum. Publishes short shorts. Recommends other markets for rejected mss.
How to Contact: Send complete ms with cover letter. Reports on queries in 1 month; on ms in 2 months. SASE. Simultaneous, photocopied and reprint submissions OK. Accepts computer printout submissions. Sample copy $2. Fiction guidelines free.

TRAJECTORIES (II), The Journal of Science Fiction of the Southwest, Box 49249, Austin TX 78765. (512)444-1861. Publisher: Richard Shannon. Managing Editor: Susan Sneller. Tabloid: 11×14½; 32+ pages; newsprint paper and cover; b&w illustrations and photos, some color. "Speculative fiction, especially science fiction and nonfiction coverage of related subculture. Includes interviews, listings of events, articles and news on science. For science fiction/fantasy fans, writers and artists within the field and breaking into the field. Heavy college student readership." Quarterly. Estab. 1987. Circ. over 5,000.
Needs: Science fiction, some fantasy, humor/satire (of SF/fantasy nature), prose poem, spiritual (if SF/fantasy in nature), serialized/excerpted novel. Does not want to see "macabre 'real life' horror, slasher stories, etc. No stories involving licensed media characters. We have made a decision to not use overly violent stories, or stories where violence and/or war are glorified or otherwise shown in a positive manner." Receives 8-12 mss/month. Buys 2-3 mss/issue; 15-20 mss/year. Publishes ms within 3-9 months of acceptance. Recently published work by Lewis Shiner, and Steve Selich; published new writers within the last year. Length: 2,000-5,000 words preferred; 15,000 words maximum. Publishes short shorts. Sometimes critiques rejected mss and recommends other markets.
How to Contact: Send complete ms with cover letter. Query on pieces over 15,000 words. Reports in 4-6 weeks on queries; within 2 months on mss. SASE. Simultaneous, photocopied and reprint submissions OK. Accepts computer printout submissions. Accepts electronic submission via disk or

modem (with advance notice). "3½ inch disk, Macintosh MacWrite, MacPaint, Superpaint, Microsoft Word. 5½ inch disk–IBM word-processing programs." Sample copy for $2, 9×12 SAE and 4 first class stamps. Fiction guidelines for #10 SASE, also sent with sample copy if requested.
Payment: Pays $20-125 (more on longer pieces) and contributor's copies.
Terms: Pays on publication for first North American serial rights and one-time rights. Sends galleys to author on request.
Advice: "Though there seems to be more professional magazine markets in science fiction/fantasy than other genres, the number is still limited. They are, however, where most new SF/fantasy writers 'break in' the market. These cutting edge publications (such as *Asimov's*, *Analog* and *Omni*), are important vehicles for establishing new talent. Breaking these markets are tough, but can be done.

TRAMP (I, II), (formerly *Ransom*),Box 1386, Columbia SC 29202. Editor: Alan Howard. Magazine: 5½×8; 32 pages; some illustrations. "contemporary poetry and prose." Quarterly. Estab. 1987. Circ. 200.
Needs: Contemporary, erotica, ethnic, experimental, fantasy, gay, humor/satire, lesbian, prose poem. "Fiction for *Tramp* must be very short, very tight, and a little off-beat. Also interested in short incidental pieces such as journal or letter excerpts." Receives 5-10 unsolicited mss/month. Buys 1-3 mss/issue; 4-12 mss/year. Publishes ms 6 months maximum after acceptance. Recently published work by Cliff Burns, Willie Smith, Bennie Lee Sinclair. Length: 400 words maximum. Sometimes critiques rejected mss.
How to Contact: Send complete ms with cover letter. Reports in 1-2 months. SASE. Accepts computer printout submissions. Sample copy for $3. Fiction guidelines for #10 SAE and 1 first class stamp.
Payment: Pays in contributor's copies.
Terms: Acquires one-time rights.
Advice: "We prefer experimental fiction, but it should be accessible."

TRANSLATION (II), The Translation Center, Columbia University, 412 Dodge, New York NY 10027. (212)854-2305. Executive Director: Diane G.H. Cook. Magazine: 6×9; 200-300 pages; coated cover stock; photos. Semiannually. Estab. 1972. Circ. 1,500.
Needs: Literary translations only. Accepts varying number of mss/year. Receives approximately 20-30 unsolicited fiction mss each month. Length: very short or excerpts; not in excess of 15 mss pages. Critiques rejected mss "rarely, because of time involved."
How to Contact: Send complete translation ms accompanied by original language text, 10-line autobiography, 10-line author's biography and SASE. Note required stating copyright clearance has been obtained. Reports in 3-6 months on mss. Single copy $9. Subscription $17.
Payment: 2 complimentary translator copies.
Terms: Acquires first North American serial rights for that volume publication only.
Advice: "We are particularly interested in translations from the lesser-known languages. Annual awards of $1,000 for outstanding translation of a substantial part of a book-length literary work. Translator must have letter of intent to publish from a publisher. Write for description and application for awards program."

TREETOP PANORAMA (I), Rt 1, Box 160 Payson IL 62360. Editor: Jared Scarborough. Magazine: 8¾×11½; 16 pages; many illustrations. Publication is "environmental/rural, international/peace, public policy/poetic (in other words, multi-faceted)." Triannually. Estab. 1983. Circ. 500-1,000.
Needs: Receives 1 unsolicited ms/month. Buys 1 ms/issue; 2 mss/year. Publishes ms 6-18 months after acceptance. Recently published work by Phyllis E. Ring, J. Kenneth Sieben. Length: 1,000 words average; 250 words minimum; 1,500 words maximum. Occasionally critiques rejected mss. Sometimes recommends other markets.
How to Contact: Send complete ms with cover letter. Reports in 2-3 weeks on mss. SASE. Simultaneous and photocopied submissions OK. Accepts computer printout submissions. Sample copy for $2.
Payment: Pays $10 plus contributor's copies.
Terms: Pays on publication for one-time rights. Sends galleys to author if piece has been edited.
Advice: "Fiction is not my publication's major concern. Read a sample copy first, to ensure integration. Use compact, semi-poetic expression to shorten material. For a publication like mine, cover letters are crucial. Not only are submissions with cover letters more likely to receive personal comments in return, but a personal touch tips me off immediately to whether or not a writer is willing to invest the necessary time when it comes to the give and take of revision (a common process with beginning and even with veteran writers)."

TRIQUARTERLY (II), Northwestern University, 2020 Ridge Ave., Evanston IL 60208. (312)491-7614. Fiction Editors: Reginald Gibbons and Susan Hahn. Magazine: 6×9¼; 240+ pages; 60 lb paper; heavy cover stock; illustration; photos. "A general literary quarterly especially devoted to fiction. We publish short stories, novellas or excerpts from novels, by American and foreign writers. Genre or style is not a primary consideration. We aim for the general but serious and sophisticated reader. Many of our readers are also writers." Published 3 times/year. Estab. 1964. Circ. 5,000.

Needs: Literary, contemporary and translations. "No prejudices or preconceptions against anything *except* genre fiction (sci fi, romances, etc.)." Buys 10 mss/issue, 30 mss/year. Receives approximately 500 unsolicited fiction mss each month. Does not read May 1-Sept. 30. Approximately 10% of fiction is agented. Recently published work by Angela Jackson, Carol Bly, Leon Rooke; published new writers within the last year. Length: no requirement. Publishes short shorts.

How to Contact: Send complete ms with SASE. Reports in 3-4 months on mss. Publishes ms an average of 6 months to 1 year after acceptance. Sample copy $4.

Payment: $100-500, 2 free author's copies. Cover price less 40% discount for extras.

Terms: Pays on publication for first North American serial rights. Sends galleys to author.

TUCUMCARI LITERARY REVIEW (I), 3108 W. Bellevue Ave., Los Angeles CA 90026. Editor: Troxey Kemper. Magazine: 5½×8½; 32 pages; 20 lb bond paper; 110 lb cover; few illustrations; Xerox photographs. "Old-fashioned fiction that can be read and reread for pleasure; no weird, strange pipe dreams." Bimonthly. Estab. 1988. Circ. small.

Needs: Adventure, condensed/excerpted novel, contemporary, ethnic, historical (general), humor/satire, literary, mainstream, regional, (SW USA), senior citizen/retirement, suspense/mystery, western. No science fiction, sedition, blasphemy, fetishism, drugs/acid rock, pornography, horror, martial arts. Accepts 2 or 3 mss/issue; 12-18 mss/year. Publishes ms 2 to 4 months after acceptance. Length: 400-1,200 words preferred. Sometimes critiques rejected mss and recommends other markets.

How to Contact: Send complete ms with or without cover letter. Cover letter should include "anything pertinent to the submission." Reports in 2 weeks. SASE. Simultaneous, photocopied and reprint submissions OK. Accepts computer printout submissions. Sample copy for $1.50 plus 50¢ postage. Fiction guidelines for #10 SAE and 1 first class stamp.

Payment: Pays in contributor's copies.

Terms: Acquires one-time rights. Publication not copyrighted.

Advice: "Does the work 'say something' or is it a hodgepodge of sentence fragments and paragraphs, not tied together into a story? No 'it was all a dream' endings."

TURNSTILE (II), Suite 2348, 175 Fifth Ave., New York NY 10010. Editor: Amit Shah. Magazine: 6×9; 128 pages; 55 lb paper; 10 pt cover; illustrations; photos. "Publishing work by new writers." Biannually. Estab. 1988. Circ. 1,500.

Needs: Contemporary, experimental, humor/satire, literary, regional. No genre fiction. Receives approx. 40 unsolicited fiction mss/month. Publishes approx. 8 short story mss/issue. Publishes ms 3-4 months after acceptance. Recently published work by Fenton Johnson, Richard Russo, Barbara Leith; published new writers within the last year. Length: 2,000 words average; 4,000 words maximum. Publishes short shorts. Sometimes comments on rejected mss or recommends other markets.

How to Contact: Query first or send complete ms with cover letter. Reports on queries in 1-2 weeks; on mss in 4-6 weeks. SASE. Simultaneous and photocopied submissions OK. Accepts computer printouts. Sample copy for $6.50 and 9×12 SAE; fiction guidelines for #10 SAE and 1 first class stamp.

Payment: Pays in contributor's copies; charge for extras.

Terms: Acquires one-time rights.

Advice: "Also publishes essays and subjective nonfiction. Also interviews with writers."

TV-TS TAPESTRY JOURNAL (II), International Foundation for Gender Education, Inc., Box 367, Wayland MA 01778. Editor: Merissa S. Lynn. Magazine: 8½×11; 160-180 pages; coated paper; 80 lb coated cover; illustrations; photos. "Transvestism/transsexualism fiction, nonfiction (how-to, biography, etc.), editorial and opinion, etc. For *all* persons interested in transvestism and transsexualism." Quarterly. Estab. 1978. Circ. 10,000.

Needs: Condensed novel, contemporary, historical (general), humor/satire, TVism and TSism psychology. True-to-life, tasteful, non-sexual, positive stories. "No unbelievable fantasy, fetishistic, negatives." Receives 2-5 unsolicited fiction mss/month. Accepts 1-2 mss/issue; 4-8 mss/year. Length: 3,000 words average; 5,000 words maximum. Also publishes short shorts. Occasionally critiques rejected mss and recommends other markets.

How to Contact: Send complete ms with cover letter. SASE. Simultaneous, photocopied submissions and reprints OK. Accepts computer printouts. Accepts electronic submissions via IBM compatible disk, MS DOS 1.1 and 2.1. Sample copy $5.

Payment: Pays in contributor's copies.

Advice: "Submissions must be non-sexual and relevant to the cross-dressing/transsexual theme. We are more interested in what the writer has to say than the quality of the writing. If the writer has a valuable message to our readers, we will help the writer with editing and rewriting. *Tapestry* is a nonprofit tax exempt journal designed to provide education and support. Submitted items should be positive and informative."

TWISTED, 22071 Pineview Dr., Antioch IL 60002. (312)395-3085. Editor: Christine Hoard. Magazine: 8½×11; 152 pages; 60 lb paper; 67 lb cover; illustrations; photos. "Emphasis on contemporary horror and fantasy, anything on the dark side of reality." For readers of horror, "weird," fantasy, etc. Published irregularly. Estab. 1985. Circ. 150.

Needs: Fantasy, horror, prose poem, psychic/supernatural/occult, science fiction. "No hard science fiction, no sword and sorcery. Graphic horror or sex scenes OK if tastefully done. Sexist-racist writing turns me off." Receives approx. 12 unsolicited fiction mss/month. Accepts 10 mss/issue. Publishes ms 2 months to 2 years after acceptance. Recently published work by David Bruce, Joe Faust, Kathleen Jurgens; published new writers within the last year. Length: 2,000 words average; 200 words minimum; 5,000 words maximum. Sometimes critiques rejected mss and recommends other markets.

How to Contact: Reporting time varies. Cover letters not necessary but appreciated. Photocopied submissions OK. Accepts computer printouts. Sample copy $6. Fiction guidelines for #10 SAE and 1 first class stamp.

Payment: Pays in contributor's copies.

Terms: Acquires first rights.

Advice: "Right now we are in the market for a *limited* number of stories, as we are almost overstocked. Try to be original and avoid rehashing formula stories. Look into smaller press magazines. They are open to more experimental work and work by new writers."

2 AM MAGAZINE (I, II, IV), Box 6754, Rockford IL 61125-1754. (815)397-5901. Editor: Gretta M. Anderson. Magazine: 8½×11; 60 or more pages; 60 lb offset paper; 70 lb offset cover; illustrations; photos occasionally. "Horror, science fiction, fantasy stories, poetry, articles and art for a sophisticated adult audience." Quarterly. Summer fiction issue planned. Estab. 1986. Circ. 1,000.

Needs: Experimental, fantasy, horror, humor/satire, prose poem, psychic/supernatural/occult, science fiction, suspense/mystery. No juvenile. Receives 400 unsolicited mss/month. Buys 12-14 mss/issue; 50 mss/year. Publishes ms an average of 6-9 months after acceptance. Published work by J. N. Williamson, Elizabeth Engstrom, Leonard Carpenter; published new writers within the last year. Length: 1,800 words average; 500 words minimum; 5,000 words maximum. Publishes short shorts. Sometimes critiques rejected mss and recommends other markets.

How to Contact: Send complete ms with cover letter (cover letter optional). Reports in 1 month on queries; 6-10 weeks on mss. SASE. Simultaneous, photocopied and reprint submissions OK. Accepts computer printout submissions, no dot-matrix. Sample copy $4.95 and $1 postage. Fiction guidelines for #10 SASE.

Payment: ½¢/word minimum, negotiable maximum; 1 contributor's copy; 40% discount on additional copies.

Terms: Pays on acceptance for one-time rights with non-exclusive anthology option. Sends prepublication galleys to author.

Advice: "Publishing more pages of fiction, more sf, some sword and sorcery and mystery, as well as horror. Put name and address on manuscript, double-space, use standard ms format. Pseudonym should appear under title on first manuscript page. True name and address should appear on upper left on first ms page."

‡TWO-TON SANTA (II), Box 1332, Portsmouth NH 03801. (603)427-0631. Editor: Guy Capecelatro III. Fiction Editor: Dan Leone. Magazine: 5¾×8¼; 4 pages. "Because of its size, only four pages, the material must be fairly short. Most tend to be stories and poems about real people dealing with somehow, ironic situations. Weekly. Estab. 1988. Circ. 200.

Needs: Condensed/excerpted novel, contemporary, erotica, experimental, feminist, gay, horror, humor/satire, juvenile (5-9 years), lesbian, preschool (1-4 years), prose poem, religious/inspirational and senior citizen/retirement. "We do not encourage writing styles that tend to alienate people. The language should not detract from or overwhelm the story itself." Publishes annual fiction issue. Receives 400 unsolicited mss/month. Accepts 2 mss/month; 112 mss/year. Publishes ms 2-4 weeks after acceptance. Recently published work by Ray Halliday, Nancy Krygowsky and Pagan Kennedy. Length: 3-700 words; 100-300 average. Sometimes critiques rejected mss and recommends other markets.

How to Contact: Query first. Reports in 2-3 weeks. Simultaneous, photocopied and reprint submissions OK. Accepts computer printout submissions.

Payment: Pays in contributor's copies.

Terms: Acquires one-time rights.

Advice: "The stories that stand out are ones that provide a glimpse into real life. They are imaginative in their presentation of how we exist. Stories don't necessarily follow a logical progression, but should invoke some sort of feeling within the reader. Each scene should work at being a part of the whole, if only in setting or voice. The language should not hinder an idea but be used merely as a presentation."

TYRO MAGAZINE (I), For Discriminating Readers and Developing Writers, 194 Carlbert Street, Sault Ste. Marie, Ontario P6A 5E1 Canada. (705)253-6402. Editor: Stan Gordon. Magazine: 5½×8½; approx. 110 pages; bond paper; firm card cover; some illustrations; photographs. Published "to provide a forum and practice medium for writers to try out almost any type of short fiction. We also publish some poetry and nonfiction, and how-to articles on writing." Special fiction issue planned. Bimonthly. Estab. 1984. Circ. 500.

Needs: Adventure, condensed novel, confession, contemporary, ethnic, experimental, fantasy, historical (general), horror, humor/satire, juvenile (5-9 years), literary, mainstream, preschool (0-4 years), prose poem, psychic/supernatural, regional, religious/inspirational, romance (contemporary, historical, young adult), science fiction, senior citizen/retirement, serialized/excerpted novel, spiritual, sports, suspense/mystery, young adult/teen (10-18 years). No "wildly experimental or legally dangerous" material. Receives about 40 unsolicited mss/month. Accepts 8-12 mss/issue; 60-80 mss/year. Publishes ms 2 months after acceptance. Published work by David Sandstad, Stephen Flocks and Robert Peterson. Published new writers within the last year. Length: 500 words minimum; 5,000 words maximum. Publishes short shorts. Usually critiques rejected mss. Sometimes recommends other markets.

How to Contact: Send complete ms with cover letter. Reports in 2 weeks on queries; 3-4 weeks on mss. SASE for ms. Simultaneous and photocopied submissions OK. Accepts computer printout submissions. Sample copy $5. Free fiction guidelines.

Payment: Offers awards of over 10¢/word for the best fiction in each issue.

Terms: Writers retain all rights.

Advice: "Short fiction must be trim and active; everything must advance the story."

‡UNION STREET REVIEW (II), Box 19078, Alexandria VA 22320. (703)836-4549. Editor: Ellen Stone. Magazine: 5½×8½; 110-150 pages; 65 lb paper; 65 lb cover stock; few illustrations and photos. Literary magazine publishing high quality fiction, poetry, memoirs. Semiannually. Estab. 1988. Circ. 500.

Needs: Condensed/excerpted novel, ethnic, humor/satire, literary, translations and significant memoirs. Receives 50 unsolicited mss/month. Accepts 10 mss/issue. Publishes ms within one year after acceptance. Length: over 5,000 words average.

How to Contact: Send complete ms. Reports in 2 weeks on queries; 3-4 months on mss. SASE. Simultaneous and photocopied submissions OK. Sample copy $5.50.

Payment: Two free contributor's copies; $3 charge for extras.

Terms: Acquires one-time rights.

Advice: "Stories usually run over 15 double-spaced typed pages. Beside long short stories, will publish novel excerpts and well-written memoirs."

UNIVERSITY OF PORTLAND REVIEW (II), University of Portland, 5000 N. Willamette Blvd., Portland OR 97203. (503)283-7144. Editor-in-Chief: Thompson M. Faller. Magazine: 5×8; 40-55 pages. "Magazine for the college-educated layman of liberal arts background. Its purpose is to comment on the human condition and to present information in different fields with relevance to the contemporary scene." Published semiannually. Established 1948. Circ. 1,000.

Needs: "Only fiction that makes a significant statement about the contemporary scene will be employed." Receives 4 unsolicited mss/month. Accepts 2-3 mss/issue, 4-6 mss/year. Published new writers within the last year. Length: 1,500 words minimum; 3,500 words maximum; 2,000 words average. Sometimes recommends other markets.

How to Contact: Send complete ms with SASE. Reports in 3 weeks on queries; 6 months on mss. Publishes ms up to 1 year after acceptance. Sample copy 50¢.

Payment: 5 contributor's copies. 50¢ charge for extras.

Terms: Pays for all rights.

UNKNOWNS (I, II), Abri Publications, Suite 1, 1900 Century Blvd., Atlanta GA 30345. (404)636-3145. Publisher: Julia B. Davidson. Editor: Christine Puckett. Magazine: 11×8; 70-100 pages; good quality paper; excellent cover stock; few illustrations. Quarterly collection of short fiction and poems. Estab. 1973. Circ. 500.

Needs: Short fiction and poems that combine simplicity and beauty of language with dramatizations of ageless truth. "Please write for an audience whose tastes are traditional and for whose reading time there is much competition." Also offers criticism service; write for free information. Published work by Carl Freeman, Walter Matthew Duenning, Eva Blake; published new writers within the last year. Length: 2,700-2,800 words. Sometimes recommends other markets.

How to Contact: Send complete ms with cover letter. SASE. Reports as soon as possible. Publishes ms an average of 1 year after acceptance. Sample copy $5; postage $1.
Payment: 1 contributor's copy.
Terms: Acquires first rights (all rights revert to author).
Advice: "Become craftsmen in private before trying to become artists in public. Learn all you can about publishing in general. Write for the enjoyment and benefit of readers, and think about how your work can affect civilization."

UNMUZZLED OX (III), Unmuzzled Ox Foundation Ltd., 105 Hudson St., New York NY 10013. Editor: Michael Andre. Tabloid. "Magazine about life for an intelligent audience." Quarterly. Estab. 1971. Circ. 20,000.
Needs: Contemporary, literary, prose poem and translations. No commercial material. Receives 10-15 unsolicited mss/month. Buys 1-5 mss/issue. Occasionally critiques rejected mss.
How to Contact: "Cover letter is significant." Reports in 1 month. SASE. Sample copy $7.50.
Payment: Contributor's copies.

THE UNSPEAKABLE VISIONS OF THE INDIVIDUAL (III, IV), Box 439, California PA 15419. (412)938-8956. Editors: Arthur and Kit Knight. Magazine: Specializes in beat generation-oriented fiction for "well educated—above average literacy." Annually. Estab. 1971. Circ. 2,000.
Needs: Confession, contemporary, erotica, literary, prose poem, excerpted novel, autobiographical fiction, e.g., Jack Kerouac. Receives 10-15 unsolicited mss/month. Buys 2 mss/issue. Length: 2,000-3,000 words average. Occasionally comments on rejected ms.
How to Contact: Send complete ms. Reports in 3 months maximum. SASE. Photocopied submissions OK. Accepts computer printout submissions. Sample copy $3.50.
Payment: 2 copies plus $10.
Terms: Pays on publication for first rights.

US1 WORKSHEETS (II), US1 Poets' Cooperative, 21 Lake Dr., Roosevelt NJ 08555. (609)448-5096. Editor: Rotating board. Magazine: 8½×11; 60 pages; good paper. Publishes poetry and fiction. Annually. Estab. 1973.
Needs: "No restrictions on subject matter or style. Good story telling or character deliniation appreciated. Audience does not include children." Publishes ms within 3 months of acceptance. Recently published work by J.A. Perkins, Cynthia Goodling, Judith McNally. Publishes short shorts. Sometimes critiques rejected mss.
How to Contact: Query first. Reports on queries in 1 week. SASE. Photocopied submissions OK. Sample copy for $3.
Payment: Pays in contributor's copies.
Terms: Acquires one-time rights. Copyright "reverts to author."

VALLEY GRAPEVINE (I, IV), Seven Buffaloes Press, Box 249, Big Timber MT 59011. Editor/Publisher: Art Cuelho. Theme: "poems, stories, history, folklore, photographs, ink drawings or anything native to the Great Central Valley of California, which includes the San Joaquin and Sacramento valleys. Focus is on land and people and the oil fields, farms, orchards, Okies, small town life, hobos." Readership: "Rural and small town audience, the common man with a rural background, salt-of-the-earth. The working man reads *Valley Grapevine* because it's his personal history recorded." Annually. Estab. 1978. Circ. 500.
Needs: Literary, contemporary, western and ethnic (Okie, Arkie). No academic, religious (unless natural to theme), gay/lesbian or supernatural material. Receives approximately 4-5 unsolicited fiction mss each month. Length: 2,500-10,000 (prefers 5,000) words.
How to Contact: Query. SASE for query, ms. Reports in 1 week. Sample copy available to writers for $4.75.
Payment: 1-2 author's copies.
Terms: Acquires first North American serial rights. Returns rights to author after publication, but reserves the right to reprint in an anthology or any future special collection of Seven Buffaloes Press.
Advice: "Buy a copy to get a feel of the professional quality of the writing. Know the theme of a particular issue. Some contributors have 30 years experience as writers; most 15 years. Age does not matter; quality does."

VALLEY WOMEN'S VOICE (II,IV), Feminist Newsjournal, 321 Student Union, University of Massachusetts, Amherst MA 01002. (413)545-2436. Newspaper: 16 pages. "Feminist analysis, feminist poetry, stories, health articles, revolution-visionary-action oriented." For women readers. Monthly. Estab. 1979. Circ. 5,000.

Needs: Ethnic, feminist, lesbian, prose poem, spiritual, women's sports. Any subject "as long as it is feminist." Receives 3-10 mss/month. Recently published work by Roni D. Ginsberg; published new writers within the last year. Length: no more than five pages.
How to Contact: Send complete ms with cover letter. "Cover letter should include short biographical statement which provides a context for work submitted." SASE. Simultaneous, photocopied and reprint submissions OK. Accepts computer printout submissions. Sample copy for $1.
Payment: No payment.

VAR TUFA (I,II), Box 697, Cotati CA 94931. (707)795-3079 or (415)863-2961. Editor: William Batchelor. Associate Editor: Justin Gorman. Tabloid: 32 pages; newsprint paper; illustrations; photos. Published "as a vehicle for promoting our erratic lifestyle and way of thinking. *Var Tufa* is limited to an alternative audience and tends to attract a lot of the freak types." Quarterly. Estab. 1986. Circ. 3,500.
Needs: Horror, humor/satire, psychic/supernatural/occult. "Basically anything that is good. We have very high standards." Accepts 1-3 mss/year "from tribe members." Publishes short shorts.
How to Contact: Send complete ms with cover letter. "Talk to us; we are pretty easy to deal with." SASE. Photocopied submissions OK. No dot-matrix computer printout submissions. Free sample copy and fiction guidelines.
Payment: "We pay with magazines and T shirts."
Terms: Publication not copyrighted.
Advice: "We will *not* print poetry. We're looking for something that can't be classified. Don't expect much of a payment, for we are very poor students and publish *Var Tufa* with our own funds. To make a living and write solely what you want to write are two fine notions that do not equate. We have an established netework, we have a reputation. Don't expect money—write to have others comment on your work. Reader reactions, whether good or bad, always make the writer feel as if he/she has accomplished something. Best of luck."

VERDICT MAGAZINE (I, IV), Journal of the Southern California Defense Counsel, 1055 Wilshire Blvd., 19th Floor, Los Angeles CA 90017. (213)580-1449. Editor: Sharon Muir. Magazine: 8½×11; 48 pages; slick paper; 70 lb Tahoe cover; clip art illustrations. "The magazine is geared to lawyers who specialize in insurance defense law. It is a trade publication that focuses on their work, legal cases and lifestyles." Quarterly. Estab. 1973. Circ. 5,000.
Needs: Law. Receives 10 unsolicited mss/month. Buys 2 mss/issue. Publishes ms 6 months-1 year after acceptance. Length: 2,000 words average. Publishes short shorts. Occasionally critiques rejected mss. Recommends other markets.
How to Contact: Send complete ms and cover letter with brief description of submitted ms. SASE. Simultaneous and photocopied submissions OK. Accepts computer printout submissions. Sample copy for $5 or 11×14 SAE and 10 first class stamps.
Payment: Pays $10.
Terms: Pays on publication for one-time rights.

‡A VERY SMALL MAGAZINE (I), (Perfect for Pocket or Purse), % Blevins, 1000 Sixth St. SW, #813, Washington DC 20024. Editor: Beth Blevins. Magazine: 4×5; 24 pages; illustrations. "We usually publish parodies and humorous pieces—also 'theme' issues—myth, travel, etc. For people who like pocket-sized magazines." Frequency varies. Estab. 1989. Circ. 200.
Needs: Adventure, confession (not true stories stuff), erotica, experimental, feminist, humor/satire, serialized novel (very small novel). "Open to anything interesting, concise and well-written. No romance, bad science fiction, stupid erotica." Receives 10-15 unsolicited mss/month. Accepts 1-2 mss/issue. Publishes ms 3 months-1 year after acceptance. Recently published work by Barry Greer; David Perelman-Hall. Length: 500 words preferred; 2,000 words maximum. Publishes short shorts. Length: 250-500 words. Sometimes critiques rejected mss (especially if writer requests) and recommends other markets.
How to Contact: Send complete ms with cover letter. Reports in 2 months on queries; 1-6 months on mss. SASE. Simultaneous, photocopied and reprint submissions OK. Accepts computer printout submissions. Sample copy for $1.
Payment: Pays free subscription to magazine or contributor's copies.
Terms: Publication is not copyrighted. (Copyright statement in each issue though.)
Advice: Looks for material "that's concise, well-written and refreshingly original (or funny). Go ahead—maybe better to send a query and read a sample issue to see what you're getting into."

‡VIDEOMANIA (I,II), The Video Collectors Newspaper, LegsOfStone Publishing Co., Box 47, Princeton WI 54968. (414)295-6813. Editor: Bob Katerzynske. Tabloid; 10½×16; 32+ pages; newsprint paper; ground wood cover; b&w/color illustrations and photographs. "Slanted towards the home entertainment buff, individuals with a *real* interest in home video and entertainment. Publishes *any-*

thing we feel is of interest to our readers—fiction and non-fiction. Audience is mostly male (90%), but female readership is always increasing." Bimonthly. Estab. 1982. Circ. 5-6,000.

Needs: Experimental, fantasy, feminist, horror, humor/satire, lesbian, mainstream, video/film. Receives 3-4 unsolicited mss/month. Buys 1-2 mss/issue; 6-9 mss/year. Publishes ms 2-6 months after acceptance. Length: 1,000 words; 750 words minimum; 1,200 words maximum. Publishes short shorts. Length: 500 words. Sometimes critiques rejected mss and recommends other markets.

How to Contact: Send complete ms with cover letter. Reports in 2-4 weeks. SASE. Computer printout submissions are acceptable. Sample copy for $2.50, 9×12 SAE and $1 postage. Fiction guidelines for #10 SAE and 1 first class stamp.

Payment: Pays $2.50 token payment in certain cases; contributor's copies.

Terms: Pays on publication for all rights or as writer prefers.

Advice: "If the editor likes it, it's in. A good manuscript should not be too heavy; a *touch* of humor goes a long way with us. Don't expect to get rich off of us. On the other hand, we're more willing than other publications to look at the first-time, non-published writer. We've published established writers in the past that wanted to use our publication as sort of a sounding board for something experimental."

THE VILLAGE IDIOT (II), An Irregular Periodical, Mother of Ashes Press, Box 66, Harrison ID 83833. Editor: Judith Shannon Paine. Magazine: Format varies; illustrations; photos. *The Village Idiot* publishes poetry, pictures and stories. "Well-written stories are preferred, but that criteria can be overlooked if the fiction 'breathes.' " For literate audience. Published: irregularly. Estab. 1970. Circ. 100.

Needs: Adventure, confession, contemporary, erotica, ethnic, experimental, fantasy, feminist, gay, historical (general), humor/satire, lesbian, literary, mainstream, prose poem, romance (contemporary and historical), science fiction, senior citizen/retirement, suspense/mystery, translations, western. "Subject matter is not so important as style. The magazine has a bias in favor of a literal method of story telling; no stream-of-consciousness and none of this writing that seems to work at obscuring the story's action and/or intent. Most important is that the fiction 'breathe.' " No novels, preteen, occult, religious. Publishes ms up to 1 year after acceptance. Recently published work by Ruth Jespersen, Walt Franklin, William Harrel; published new writers within the last year. Length: 2,000-2,500 words average; 100 words minimum; 3,000 words maximum. Occasionally critiques rejected mss.

How to Contact: Send complete ms with SASE. Reports 3 months maximum. Photocopied submissions OK. Accepts computer printouts. Sample copy $4.

Payment: Nominal cash payment "at the whim of the press" and contributor's copies (2 if the second one is requested).

Terms: Acquires one-time rights (copyright for author).

Advice: "Be the most critical, mean editor on the block before you submit copy for consideration."

VINTAGE NORTHWEST (I, IV), Northshore Senior Center (Sponsor), Box 193, Bothell WA 98041. (206)487-1201. Editors: Volunteer editorial board. Magazine: 7×8½; 64 pages; illustrations. "We are a senior literary magazine, published by and for seniors. All work done by volunteers except printing." For "all ages who are interested in our seniors' experiences." Winter and summer. Estab. 1980. Circ. 500.

Needs: Adventure, comedy, condensed novel (1,000 words maximum), fantasy, historical, humor/satire, inspirational, poetry, senior citizen/retirement, suspense/mystery. No religious or political mss. Receives 2-3 unsolicited mss/month. Accepts 2 mss/issue. Published work by Virginia Vahey, Jean W. Immerwahr; published new writers within the last year. Length: 1,000 words maximum. Occasionally critiques rejected mss.

How to Contact: Send complete ms. SASE. Simultaneous, photocopied and previously published submissions OK. Accepts computer printout submissions. Sample copy for $2. Fiction guidelines with SASE.

Payment: Pays 1 free contributor's copy.

Advice: "Our only requirement is that the author be over 50 when submission is written."

VIRGIN MEAT FANZINE (I), 5247 W. L10, Quartz Hill CA 93536. (805)943-5604. Editor: Steve Blum. Digest: 5×8½; 26 pages. Published "about once every 3 months." Estab. 1987. Circ. 350.

Needs: "Mild erotic vampire tales. Lesbian and straight ok, no gay. Poetry should be dark and depressing." Receives 3-4 mss/day. Length: 1,000 words maximum.

How to Contact: Send complete ms with cover letter. Reports in 1 week. Simultaneous, photocopied and reprint submissions OK. Accepts computer printout submissions. Sample copy $1.

Payment: Pays in contributor's copies.

Terms: Acquires one-time rights. Publication not copyrighted.

VIRGINIA QUARTERLY REVIEW (III), 1 W. Range, Charlottesville VA 22903. (804)924-3124. Editor: Staige Blackford. "A national magazine of literature and discussion. A lay, intellectual audience, people who are not out-and-out scholars but who are interested in ideas and literature." Quarterly. Estab. 1925. Circ. 4,500.

Needs: Literary, contemporary, feminist, romance, adventure, humor, ethnic, serialized novels (excerpts) and translations. "No gay/lesbian or pornography." Buys 3 mss/issue, 20 mss/year. Length: 3,000-7,000 words.

How to Contact: Query or send complete ms. SASE. Reports in 2 weeks on queries, 2 months on mss. Sample copy $5.

Payment: $10/printed page. Offers Emily Clark Balch Award for best published short story of the year.

Terms: Pays on publication for all rights. "Will transfer upon request."

Advice: "Because of the competition, it's difficult for a nonpublished writer to break in."

VISIBILITIES (IV), Box 1258, Peter Stuyvesant Station, New York NY 10009-1258. (212)473-4635. Editor: Susan T. Chasin. Magazine: 8×11; 32+ pages; coated paper; heavy coated cover stock; illustrations and photographs. "We are an international magazine by and for lesbians." Bimonthly. Estab. 1987. Circ. 5,000.

Needs: Lesbian. No "violence, sexist, racist, agist, etc." Accepts 1 ms/issue. Length: 1,300 words average; 1,000 words minimum; 1,500 words maximum. Publishes short shorts. Sometimes critiques rejected mss.

How to Contact: Send complete ms with cover letter, which should include "just basics; name, address, telephone and how you heard about us." Reports in 2 weeks on queries; 2 months on mss. SASE. Accepts computer printout submissions, no dot-matrix. Sample copy $2.25; fiction guidelines for #10 SASE.

Payment: Contributor's copies; $5 charge for extras.

Terms: Acquires first North American serial rights.

Advice: "We are looking for life-affirming fiction—which tells us how people can live healthy, productive lives as lesbians. This does not preclude stories about painful experiences—but tell us how your characters survive and keep going."

‡WASCANA REVIEW (II), University of Regina, Regina, Saskatchewan S4S 0A2 Canada. Editor: Joan Givner. "Literary criticism, fiction and poetry for readers of serious fiction." Semiannually. Estab. 1966. Circ. 500.

Needs: Literary and humor. Buys 6 mss/year. Receives approximately 20 unsolicited fiction mss/month. Approximately 5% of fiction is agented. Length: no requirement. Occasionally recommends other markets.

How to Contact: Send complete ms with SASE. Accepts computer printout submissions. Prefers letter-quality. Reports in 2 months on mss. Publishes ms an average of 1 year after acceptance. Sample copy $4. Free guidelines with SAE, IRC.

Payment: $3/page for prose; $10/page for poetry. 2 free author's copies.

Terms: Pays on publication for all rights.

Advice: "Stories are often technically incompetent or deal with trite subjects. Usually stories are longer than necessary by about one-third. Be more ruthless in cutting back on unnecessary verbiage."

WASHINGTON REVIEW (II, IV), Friends of the Washington Review of the Arts, Box 50132, Washington DC 20004. (202)638-0515. Fiction Editor: Jeff Richards. "We publish fiction, poetry, articles and reviews on all areas of the arts. We have a particular interest in the interrelationships of the arts and emphasize the cultural life of the DC area." Readership: "Artists, writers and those interested in cultural life in this area." Bimonthly. Estab. 1975. Circ. 10,000.

Needs: Literary. Accepts 1-2 mss/issue. Receives approximately 50-100 unsolicited fiction mss each month. Length: Prefers 2,000 words or less. Critiques rejected mss when there is time.

How to Contact: Send complete ms with SASE. Reports in 2 months. Publishes ms an average of 6 months after acceptance. Copy for tabloid-sized SASE and $2.50.

Payment: Author's copies plus small payment whenever possible.

Terms: Pays on publication for first North American serial rights.

Advice: "Edit your writing for redundant adjectives. Make sure everything makes sense: the plot, character, motivation. Try to avoid clichés."

‡WAYSIDE (I, II), Box 225, Hoboken NJ 07030. (201)256-2230. Editors: Mark Butler and Gail DeGirolamo. Magazine: 8½×11; 30-40 pages; illustrations; photos. "New quarterly featuring fiction, poetry, cartoon art, essays and anything else that we like." Estab. 1989.

Needs: Adventure, contemporary, erotica, ethnic, experimental, fantasy, feminist, gay, historical (general), horror, humor/satire, lesbian, literary, prose poem, science fiction, sports, suspense/mystery and western. Receives 5-10 unsolicited mss/month. Accepts 2-3 mss/issue; 8-12/year. Publishes ms 6-9 months after acceptance. Length: 2,000 words maximum. Publishes short shorts. Sometimes critiques rejected mss and recommends other markets.
How to Contact: Send complete ms with cover letter. Reports on queries in 2 weeks; 2 months on mss. SASE. Simultaneous, photocopied submissions OK. Accepts computer printout submissions. Sample copy for 9×12 SAE; $1 postage. Fiction guidelines for #10 SAE and 1 first class stamp.
Payment: Pays in contributor's copies.
Terms: Acquires one-time rights. Publication not copyrighted.
Advice: "Look at the title: *Wayside*. We like off-beat, fresh, experimental work. But don't use this criteria as a rationale for submitting work that is structurally unsound, or worse, work that has no structure at all. Be willing to try *any* idea, but we want the entire lamp, not just the light bult."

WEIRDBOOK (II), Box 149, Amherst Branch, Buffalo NY 14226. Editor: W. Paul Ganley. Magazine: 8½×11; 64 pages; self cover; illustrations. "Latter day 'pulp magazine' along the lines of the old pulp magazine *Weird Tales*. We tend to use established writers. We look for an audience of fairly literate people who like good writing and good characterization in their fantasy and horror fiction, but are tired of the clichés in the field." Annually. Estab. 1968. Circ. 1,000.
Needs: *Presently overstocked.* Psychic/supernatural, fantasy, horror and gothic (not modern). No psychological horror; mystery fiction; physical horror (blood); traditional ghost stories (unless original theme); science fiction; swords and sorcery without a supernatural element; or reincarnation stories that conclude with 'And the doctor patted him on . . . THE END!' " Buys 8-12 mss/issue. Length: 15,000 words maximum. Sometimes recommends other markets.
How to Contact: Send complete ms with SASE. Reports in 3 months on mss. Sample copy $5.75. Guidelines for #10 SASE.
Payment: 1¢ word minimum and 1 free author's copy.
Terms: Pays on publication ("part on acceptance only for solicited mss") for first North American serial rights plus right to reprint the entire issue.
Advice: *Currently overstocked.* "Read a copy and then some of the best anthologies in the field (such as DAW's 'Best Horror of the Year,' Arkham House anthologies, etc.) Occasionally we keep mss longer than planned. When sending a SASE marked 'book rate' (or anything not first class) the writer should add 'Forwarding Postage Guaranteed.' "

WEST BRANCH (II), Bucknell Hall, Bucknell University, Lewisburg PA 17837. Editors: K. Patten and R. Taylor. Magazine: 5½×8½; 96-120 pages; good quality paper; illustrations; photos. Fiction and poetry for readers of contemporary literature. Biannually. Estab. 1977. Circ. 500.
Needs: Literary, contemporary, prose poems and translations. No science fiction. Accepts 3-6 mss/issue. Recently published work by Betty Clare, David Milofsky, Layle Silbert; published new writers within the last year. No preferred length.
How to Contact: Send complete ms with cover letter, "with information about writer's background, previous publications, etc." SASE. Reports in 6 weeks on mss. Sample copy $2.
Payment: 2 free author's copies and one-year subscription; cover price less 20% discount charge for extras.
Terms: Acquires first rights.
Advice: "Narrative art fulfills a basic human need—our dreams attest to this—and storytelling is therefore a high calling in any age. Find your own voice and vision. Make a story that speaks to your own mysteries. Cultivate simplicity in form, complexity in theme. Look and listen through your characters."

WEST COAST REVIEW (II), West Coast Review Publishing Society, % English Dept., Simon Fraser University, Burnaby, British Columbia V5A 1S6 Canada. (604)291-4287. Magazine: 6×9; 80 pages, focusing on "contemporary poetry, short fiction, drama and reviews." Triannually. Estab. 1966. Circ. 700.
Needs: Contemporary, experimental, literary, prose poem, serialized/excerpted novel (possibly) and translations (possible if translator arranges for all necessary permissions). Receives 10-20 unsolicited fiction mss/month. Accepts 2-3 mss/issue, 8-10 mss/year. Less than 10% of fiction is agented. Recently published work by George Bowering, Anselm Hollo, John Mills; published new writers within the last year. Length: 250 words minimum; 5,000 words maximum.
How to Contact: Send complete ms with SAE, IRC. "Photocopies acceptable with assurances that they are not under consideration elsewhere." Accepts computer printout submissions. Prefers letter-quality. Include a short biographical note. Reports in 2-3 months on mss. Publishes ms an average of 1-12 months after acceptance. Sample copy $4 (Canadian) with 8x11 SAE and 68¢ postage (IRC).

Payment: Approx. $4-5/page and 1-year subscription.
Terms: Pays on acceptance for first rights.
Advice: "Read several issues before submitting. Send standard, professional submissions."

‡THE WEST TEXAS SUN (IV), NJN Inc., Box 61541, San Angelo TX 76906. (915)944-8918. Editor: Soren Nielsen. Magazine; 24-32 pages; newsprint paper and cover; b&w illustrations and photos. "Stories focusing on West Texans and the region for people interested in West Texas." Monthly. Estab. 1989. Circ. 2,000.
Needs: Adventure, condensed/excerpted novel, contemporary, historical (general), humor/satire, literary, mainstream, regional, religious/inspirational, sports and western (ranching, horses). No erotica. Receives 2-3 unsolicited mss/month. Buys 1 ms/issue; 18-20 mss/year. Publishes ms 1-3 months after acceptance. Recently published work by Elmer Kelton, Robert Flynn and Sean Warner; published new writers within the last year. Length: 2,500 words; 500 words minimum; 4,000 words maximum. Publishes short shorts. Length: 50-200 words. Sometimes critiques rejected mss and recommends other markets.
How to Contact: Query first. Include social security number. Reports in 2-3 weeks. SASE. Simultaneous, photocopied and reprint submissions OK. Computer printout submissions are acceptable. Sample copy for 75¢ and SAE. Fiction guidelines are free.
Payment: Pays $5-400; charge for extras.
Terms: Pays on publication for first rights.

WHAT (II), Box 338, Station J, Toronto, Ontario M4J 4Y8 Canada. Editor: Jason Sherman. Tabloid: 11×17; 16 pages; newsprint; illustrations and photos. "To create new audiences for established and beginning/lesser-known writers of poetry, fiction, drama and criticism by making such writing available on a free basis and in large quantity, and by inviting the participation of readers through a letters/commentary section." Bimonthly. Estab. 1985. Circ. 10,000.
Needs: "Submissions are judged on the basis of the quality of the writing, regardless of the nature of the content/subject matter." Receives 10 unsolicited mss/month; accepts 1 ms/issue; 6 mss/year. Publishes ms 2-4 months after acceptance. Recently published work by Günter Grass, Liliana Heker, Julio Cortazar; published new writers within the last year. Length: 2,000 words average; no minimum; 3,000 words maximum, but will serialize if longer. Publishes short shorts. Comments on most rejected mss and sometimes recommends other markets.
How to Contact: Send complete ms with cover letter, which should include "where the reader heard of or saw the magazine; whether the reader has read the magazine (and thus feels his or her work is suitable for it); list of prior and/or forthcoming publications." Reports on queries in 2 weeks; on mss in 2 months on average. SASE or IRC. Simultaneous, photocopied and reprint submissions OK. Accepts computer printout submissions. Accepts electronic submissions "but query first." Sample copy $2 (Canadian).
Payment: Pays $100 for short story; $25-$50 for short shorts.
Terms: Buys first North American serial rights or one-time rights.
Advice: "Much of what we see is written to fill a specific formula, which means it is devoid of any passion the author might have otherwise put into the work. Guidelines and generalizations are fine as they go, but taken too seriously they hurt the material. Read us before you send us your work."

WHETSTONE (II), English Dept., University of Lethbridge, Lethbridge, Alberta T1K 3M4 Canada. (403)329-2490. Contact: Editor. Magazine: approximately 6×9; 48-64 pages; superbond paper; pen or pencil sketches; photos. Magazine publishing "poetry, prose, drama, prints, photographs and occasional music compositions for a university audience." Twice yearly. Estab. 1971. Circ. 200.
Needs: Experimental, literary and mainstream. "Interested in works by native writers/artists. Interested in multi-media works by individuals or collaborators. Yearly writing contest with cash prizes." Receives 1 unsolicited fiction ms/month. Accepts 1-2 ms/issue, 3-4 mss/year. Does not read May through August. Published new writers within the last year. Length: 12 double-spaced pages maximum.
How to Contact: Send complete ms with SASE, or SAE with IRC and cover letter with author's background and experience. Simultaneous and photocopied submissions OK. Accepts computer printout submissions. Prefers letter-quality. Reports in 5 months on mss. Publishes ms an average of 3-4 months after acceptance. Sample copy $3 (Canadian) and 7½×10½ or larger SAE and 2 Canadian first class stamps or IRCs.
Payment: 1 free contributor's copy and $10 honorarium.
Terms: Acquires no rights.
Advice: "We seek most styles of quality writing. Avoid moralizing."

The double dagger before a listing indicates that the listing is new in this edition. New markets are often the most receptive to freelance contributions.

WHISKEY ISLAND MAGAZINE, University Center 7, Cleveland State University, Cleveland OH 44115. (216)687-2056. Editor: Jeff Erdie. Magazine with no specific theme of fiction, poetry, photography. Published two times/year. Estab. 1978. Circ. 2,500.
Needs: Receives 20-30 unsolicited fiction mss/month. Acquires 3-4 mss/issue. Length: 5,000 words maximum; 2,000-3,000 words average.
How to Contact: Send complete ms with SASE. No simultaneous or previously published submissions. Reports in 2 months on mss. Sample copy $3.
Payment: 2 free contributor's copies.
Terms: Acquires one-time rights.
Advice: "Please include brief bio."

‡WHISPERING WIND MAGAZINE (I, II, IV), American Indian: Past & Present, Written Heritage, 8009 Wales St., New Orleans LA 70126. (504)241-5866. Editor: Jack B. Heriard. Magazine: 8½×11; 32 pages; 60 lb paper; 70 lb cover stock; color cover, b&w illustrations; b&w photos. "American Indian theme; material culture, illustrated craft articles. Articles are welcome that reflect our American Indian culture, both past and present." Audience: 52% Indian, 16+ years of age. Bimonthly. Estab. 1967. Circ. 6,000.
Needs: Special interest: American Indian. "Fiction must be American Indian related (theme) and yet historically accurate. Accuracy must also include material culture. Stories must not be stereotyped." Publishes ms up to one year after acceptance. Length: 1,500 words average. Publishes short shorts. Critiques rejected mss. Recommends other markets.
How to Contact: Send complete ms with cover letter with reasons for submission and illustration requirements. Reports in 3 months on queries. SASE for ms. Simultaneous submissions OK. Accepts computer printouts. Sample copy $4. Fiction guidelines free.
Payment: Free subscription to magazine, 6 contributor's copies, charge for extras.
Terms: Acquires first rights.
Advice: "There is a need for quality fiction about the American Indian. We publish fiction at least 4 times/year. The story must be accurate in every detail, i.e. tribal location, dress, material culture, historical perspectives, except that of the characters and basic storyline. Although fiction, it will be better received if the story is believable. Do not stereotype the characters."

THE WHITE WALL REVIEW, 63 Gould St., Toronto, Ontario M5B 1E9 Canada. Editor: Changes annually. Magazine: 5¾×8¾; 150 pages; Zephyr Antique paper; soft cover, glossy; two-tone illustrations; b&w photographs. Book of poetry, prose, art, plays, music and photography. Publishes both Ryerson Polytechnical Institute and professional writers. For Toronto and/or university audience. Annually. Estab. 1976. Circ. 500.
Needs: "No content 'requirements.' " Must be reasonably short. Nothing "spawning hate, prejudice or obscenity." Accepts 100+ mss/book. Recently published work by Gaetan Charlebois, Tony Cosier, Laurie Kruk; published new writers within the last year.
How to Contact: Send complete ms with cover letter. "The cover letter should contain important information about why the writer is submitting to our publication, where he/she saw our information and some biographical information." Reports on mss "when accepted." SASE or SAE and IRC for ms. Simultaneous and photocopied submissions OK. Accepts computer printout submissions; prefers letter-quality. Sample copy $5 and SAE (8½×11), plus $1 for postage and handling.
Payment: Pays 1 contributor's copy.
Terms: Acquires first or one-time rights.
Advice: "Keep it *short*. We look for creativity but not to the point of obscurity."

THE WICAZO SA REVIEW (IV), A Journal of American Indian Studies, Eastern Washington University, Indian Studies, MS25-188, Cheney WA 99004. (509)359-2871. Editor: Elizabeth Cook-Lynn. Magazine: 8½×11; 50 pages. Publishes material relating to "Indian studies—all types, including scholarly research and reviews, for an academic audience." Plans special fiction issue. Estab. 1985. Circ. 300-500.
Needs: American Indian. "We wish to publish the creative works of American Indian writers. This is an academic journal devoted to the development of Indian studies topics. We want fiction *by* American Indians, not *about* American Indians." Recently published work by Simon Ortiz, Earle Thompson and Ralph Salisbury. Publishes short shorts.
How to Contact: Send complete ms with cover letter. Reports in 3 months. SASE. Sample copy $4.
Payment: No payment.
Terms: Acquires first rights.
Advice: "Very little of magazine fiction today appeals to the ethnicity and the cultural diversity of America in any realistic way. Know the body of work which is now called Contemporary American Indian Fiction—the N. Scott Momaday, Simon Ortiz, Leslie Silko work, the criticism which is emerging from this development, the journals and collections which publish in this field."

WIDE OPEN MAGAZINE (II), Wide Open Press, 116 Lincoln St., Santa Rosa CA 95401. (707)545-3821. Editors: Clif and Lynn Simms. Magazine: 8½×11; 48 pages; 60 lb paper and cover. "Magazine is concerned with providing support and encouragement to writers." Quarterly. Estab. 1984. Circ. 500.
Needs: Adventure, contemporary, ethnic, experimental, fantasy, feminist, gay, historical (general), horror, humor/satire, lesbian, mainstream, psychic/supernatural/occult, science fiction, senior citizen/retirement, suspense/mystery, western. No "religious, children's, vignettes or character studies without plot." Receives 40 unsolicited mss/month. Buys 3 mss/issue; 12 mss/year. Publishes ms 1-3 months after acceptance. *A $5 reading fee should accompany each prose submission.* This fee will be refunded for all works that we accept for publication. Recently published work by Ed Griffin, Robert R. Ramsey, Eric Steinman; published new writers within the last year. Length: 2,500 words maximum. Publishes short shorts. Sometimes critiques rejected mss and recommends other markets.
How to Contact: Send complete ms. "We want no clips or bios, please. Let the work stand on its own." Reports in 3 months. SASE. Photocopied and reprint submissions OK. Accepts computer printout submissions. Sample copy $7. Fiction guidelines for #10 SASE and 1 first class stamp.
Payment: Charges $5 reading fee (*see above*). Pays $5-$25; 1 contributor copy; charges $7 for extras.
Terms: Pays on publication for one-time rights.
Advice: "We find most magazine fiction today of very poor quality. It is too often esoteric and unfeeling, leaving the reader with the reaction 'who cares?' We love stories about real people in real situations. We believe publications are dropping fiction because their editors select low-quality fiction that they cannot sell to readers."

THE WIDENER REVIEW (III), Widener University, 14th and Chesnut Sts., Chester PA 19013. (215)499-4341. Fiction editor: Michael Clark. Magazine: 5¼×8½; 80 pages. Fiction, poetry, book reviews for general audience. Annually. Estab. 1984. Circ. 250.
Needs: Contemporary, experimental, literary, mainstream, regional, serialized/excerpted novel. Receives 15 unsolicited mss/month. Publishes 3-4 mss/issue. Does not read mss in summer. Publishes ms 3-9 months after acceptance. Length: 1,000 words minimum; 5,000 words maximum. Occasionally critiques rejected mss.
How to Contact: Send complete ms with cover letter. Reports in 3 months on mss. SASE for ms. No simultaneous or photocopied submissions or reprints. Accepts computer printouts. Sample copy $3. Fiction guidelines for #10 SAE and 1 first class stamp.
Payment: Pays in contributor's copies; charge for extras.
Terms: Acquires first serial rights.

‡WILD EAST (I,II), The Alternative Atlantic Arts and Culture Magazine, Suite 201, 467 Waterloo Row, Fredericton, New Brunswick E3B 1Z6 Canada. Editor: Margaret McLeod. Magazine: 8½×11; 28-32 pages; plainsfield paper; illustrations and photographs. Publishes work by Atlantic artists and writers. Quarterly. Estab. 1988. Circ. 750.
Needs: Contemporary, ethnic, experimental, feminist, humor/satire, literary, psychic/supernatural/occult. "Atlantic writers and artists preferred!" "No classist, racist, homophobic, or sexist material." Plans special fiction issue. Receives 10-15 unsolicited mss/month. Accepts 2-3 mss/issue. Publishes ms 6-9 months after acceptance. Length: 2,000 words. Publishes short shorts. Sometimes critiques rejected mss.
How to Contact: Send complete ms with cover letter. Include some bio introduction. Reports in 6 months. SASE. Photocopied and computer printout submissions OK. Sample copy $3. Fiction guidelines for #10 SAE.
Payment: Pays in contributor's copies, sometimes cash.
Terms: Acquires first North American serial rights.

WILLOW SPRINGS (II, III), Box 1062, Eastern Washington University, Cheney WA 99004. (509)458-6424. Editor: Gillian Conoley. Semiannually. Estab. 1977. Circ. 900.
Needs: Parts of novels, short stories, literary, prose poems and translations. Receives 50 unsolicited mss/month. Accepts 3-4 mss/issue; 6-8 mss/year. Recently published work by David Russell Young, William Van Wert, Susan Wheeler; published new writers within the last year. Length: 5,000 words maximum. Rarely critiques rejected mss.
How to Contact: Send complete ms with SASE. Photocopied submissions OK. No simultanious submissions. Reports in 2-3 months on mss. Publishes ms an average of 1-6 months after acceptance. Sample copy for $4.

Payment: 2 contributor's copies.
Terms: Acquires first North American rights.
Advice: "We hope to attract good fiction writers to our magazine, and we've made a commitment to publish 4 stories per issue. We like fiction that exhibits a fresh approach to language. Our most recent issues, we feel, indicate the quality and level of our commitment."

WIND MAGAZINE, Rt. 1, Box 809K, Pikeville KY 41501. (606)631-1129. Editor: Quentin R. Howard. Magazine: 5½×8½; 86+ pages. "Literary journal with stories, poems, book reviews from the small presses and some university presses. Readership is students, literary people, professors, housewives and others." Published irregularly. Estab. 1971. Circ. 500.
Needs: Literary and regional. "No restriction on form, content or subject." Recently published work by Anabel Thomas, Peter LaSalle and Mary Clearman Bleu; published new writers within the last year. Length: no minimum; 5,000 words maximum. Critiques rejected mss when there is time.
How to Contact: Send complete ms with SASE. Photocopied submissions OK. Accepts computer printout submissions; prefers letter-quality. Reports in 1 month. Publishes ms an average of 1 year after acceptance. Sample copy $2.50.
Payment: Free author's copies. $1.50 charge for extras.
Terms: Acquires first rights. Publication not copyrighted.
Advice: "We're constantly looking for beginning fiction writers. Diversity is one of our major editorial goals. No multiple submissions please. We have no taboos, but set our own standards on reading each ms."

WISCONSIN ACADEMY REVIEW (II, IV), Wisconsin Academy of Sciences, Arts & Letters, 1922 University Ave., Madison WI 53705. (608)263-1692. Editor-in-Chief: Patricia Powell. Magazine: 8½×11; 64-80 pages; 75 lb coated paper; coated cover stock; illustrations; photos. "The *Review* reflects the focus of the sponsoring institution with its editorial emphasis on Wisconsin's intellectual, cultural, social and physical environment. It features short fiction, poetry, essays and Wisconsin-related book reviews for well-educated, well-traveled people interested in furthering regional arts and literature and disseminating information about sciences." Quarterly. Publishes annual fiction issue. Estab. 1954. Circ. 2,000.
Needs: Experimental, historical (general), humor/satire, literary, mainstream, prose poem. "Author must have lived or be living in Wisconsin or fiction must be set in Wisconsin." Receives 5-6 unsolicited fiction mss/month. Accepts 1-2 mss/issue; 8-10 mss/year. Published new writers within the last year. Length: 1,000 words minimum; 4,000 words maximum; 3,000 words average.
How to Contact: Send complete ms with SAE and state author's connection to Wisconsin, the prerequisite. Photocopied submissions OK. Accepts computer printout submissions. Prefers letter-quality. Publishes ms an average of 6 months after acceptance. Sample copy $2. Fiction guidelines for SAE and 1 first class stamp.
Payment: 5 contributor's copies.
Terms: Pays on publication for first rights.

THE WISCONSIN RESTAURATEUR (I, II), Wisconsin Restaurant Association, 125 W. Doty, Madison WI 53703. (608)251-3663. Editor: Jan LaRue. Magazine: 8½×11; 80 pages; 80 lb enamel cover stock; illustrations; photos. Published for foodservice operators in the state of Wisconsin and for suppliers of those operations. Theme is the promotion, protection and improvement of the foodservice industry for foodservice workers, students, operators and suppliers. Monthly except December/January combined. Estab. 1933. Circ. 4,200.
Needs: Literary, contemporary, feminist, science fiction, regional, western, mystery, adventure, humor, juvenile and young adult. "Only exceptional fiction material used. No stories accepted that put down persons in the foodservice business or poke fun at any group of people. No off-color material. No religious, no political." Buys 1-2 mss/issue, 12-24 mss/year. Receives 15-20 unsolicited fiction mss/month. Length: 500-2,500 words. Critiques rejected mss "when there is time."
How to Contact: Send complete ms with SASE. Accepts computer printout submissions. Reports in 1 month. Free sample copy with 8½×11 SASE. Free guidelines with SASE.
Payment: $2.50-$20. Free author's copy. 50¢ charge for extra copy.
Terms: Pays on acceptance for first rights and first North American serial rights.
Advice: "Make sure there is some kind of lesson to be learned, a humorous aspect, or some kind of moral to your story." Mss are rejected because they are not written for the restaurateur/reader.

Read the Business of Fiction section to learn the correct way to prepare and submit a manuscript.

WISCONSIN REVIEW (II), Box 158, Radford Hall, University of Wisconsin, Oshkosh WI 45901. (414)424-2267. Editor: Michael J. Beirne. Magazine: 6×9; 60-100 pages; illustrations. Literary prose and poetry. Triquarterly. Estab. 1966. Circ. 2,000.

Needs: Literary and experimental. Receives 30 unsolicited fiction mss each month. Published new writers within the last year. Length: up to 5,000 words. Publishes short shorts. Critiques rejected mss when there is time. Occasionally recommends other markets.

How to Contact: Send complete ms with SASE and cover letter with bio notes. Reports in 1-2 months. Publishes ms an average of 1-2 months after acceptance. Sample copy $2.

Payment: Pays in contributor's copies.

Terms: Acquires first rights.

Advice: "We look for well-crafted work with well developed characters and plots and meaningful situations."

‡WITNESS (II), Suite 200, 31000 Northwestern Hwy., Farmington Hills MI 48018. (313)626-1110. Editor: Peter Stine. Magazine: 6×9; 160 pages; 60 lb white paper; perfect bound; often illustrations and photos. "Fiction, poetry, essays that highlight the role of the modern writer as witness to the times." Quarterly. Estab. 1987. Circ. 3,000.

Needs: Condensed/excerpted novel, contemporary, experimental, fantasy, feminist, literary and sports. "Alternate special or thematic issues: consult back issues or write for themes." Plans to publish a special fiction issue or an anthology in the future. Receives 150 unsolicited mss/month. Buys 10 mss/issue; 40 mss/year. Publishes ms 3 months-1 year after acceptance. Agented fiction 20%. Recently published work by Joyce Carol Oates, Amy Hempel and Richard Currey. Length: 3,500 words average. Publishes short shorts–500 words. Sometimes critiques rejected mss.

How to Contact: Send complete ms with cover letter. Reports in 3 months on mss. SASE. Simultaneous and photocopied submissions OK. Accepts computer printout submissions. Accepts electronic submissions. Sample copy $5. Fiction guidelines for #10 SAE and 1 first class stamp.

Payment: Pays $6/page minimum and contributor's copies.

Terms: Pays on publication for first North American serial rights.

Advice: Looks for "intelligence, compassion, lucidity, original voice. *Witness* blends features of literary and issue-oriented magazine and highlights the writer as witness. Alternate special issues (*Holocaust*, *Writings from Prison*, *Sixties*, etc.)"

WITNESS (I), (formerly *Witness to the Bizarre*), Box 278, Ronks PA 17572-0278. Editor: Melinda Jaeb. Magazine: digest size; 48 pages; 20 lb paper; heavy cover stock; illustrations on cover. "Horror, fantasy, sci/fi, gothic. For persons who are bored with the spaceman stories." Quarterly. Estab. 1988. Circ. 200+.

Needs: Fantasy, horror, psychic/supernatural/occult, science fiction, suspense/mystery. "Nothing murderous, sexual, fantasy with mumbo-jumbo names, galactica, fantasy set in a futuristic world." Receives 175 unsolicited mss/month. Accepts 15 mss/issue; 40 mss/year. Publishes ms 4-8 months after acceptance. Published new writers within the last year. Length: 1,500 words preferred; 500 words minimum; 3,000 words maximum. Publishes short shorts. Always comments on rejected mss; sometimes recommends other markets.

How to Contact: Send complete ms with cover letter, "no listing of credits: your work is what is meritable. Interesting cover letters that are personalized are enjoyed." Reports in 3 weeks on queries; 2 weeks on mss. SASE. No simultaneous submissions. Photocopied submissions OK. Sample copy for $5 (Payable to Melinda Jaeb). Fiction guidelines for #10 SAE and 1 first class stamp.

Payment: Pays in 2 contributor's copies.

Terms: Acquires first North American serial rights. Sponsors awards for fiction writers. "At end of year, a survey is conducted for all regular readers for the most memorable and bizarre story. The prize is $50."

Advice: "I want material that overrides *The Twilight Zone*, and the dime-a-dozen galactica and alien-orientated magazines. I want things that are really impossible possibilities. The coined phrase of 'you must know someone' to get a story published isn't true as far as *Witness* is concerned. I *always* comment on mss, or recommend other markets. No writer will *ever* be frustrated by *Witness*'s rejection slips, because we are encouraging and personal. As writers, we know what it's like out there! Do not submit without buying a sample–you have no idea what you are submitting to until you see it."

‡WOMAN OF POWER (II, IV), A Magazine of Feminism, Spirituality, and Politics, Box 827, Cambridge MA 02238. (617)625-7885. Editor: Char McKee. Magazine: 8½×11; 88-96 pages; 60 lb offset stock; 60 lb glossy cover; illustrations and photos. "Upcoming themes include: 'Humor,' 'Women's Bodies,' 'Magic,' 'The Living Earth,' and 'Women in Community.' Our magazine is read by women." Quarterly. Estab. 1984. Circ. 15,000.

Needs: Ethnic, experimental, fantasy, feminist, humor/satire, lesbian, literary, psychic/supernatural/occult, religious/inspirational, science fiction, senior citizen/retirement, women's, young adult/teen. "We print works by women only." Receives 20 unsolicited mss/month. Accepts 1 or 2 mss/issue. Publishes ms 3-6 months after acceptance. Published new writers within the last year. Length: 1,000 words minimum; 3,500 words maximum. Publishes short shorts. Sometimes critiques rejected mss. Sometimes recommends other markets.
How to Contact: Send complete ms with cover letter, which should include "a short biography and reasons for submitting." Reports in 2 weeks on queries; 3 months on mss. SASE. Simultaneous, photocopied and reprint submissions OK. Computer printout submissions acceptable. Sample copy $7. Fiction guidelines for #10 SAE and 1 first class stamp.
Payment: Pays in 2 contributor's copies.
Terms: Acquires one-time rights. Sends galleys to author on request. Rights revert to authors.
Advice: "It is imperative that women read our magazine before submitting. We have a very *specific* focus which is related to women's spirituality and is best understood by studying past issues. And all materials must directly relate to one of our themes. We print high quality photographs and artwork by women."

THE WORCESTER REVIEW, Worcester Country Poetry Association, Inc., 6 Chatham St., Worcester MA 01609. Editor: Rodger Martin. Magazine: 6×9; 60-100 pages; 60 lb white offset paper; 10 pt C15 cover stock; illustrations and photos. "We like high quality, creative poetry, artwork and fiction. Critical articles should be connected to New England." Semiannually. Estab. 1972. Circ. 1,000.
Needs: Literary, prose poem. "We encourage New England writers in the hopes we will publish at least 30% New England but want the other 70% to show the best of writing from across the US." Receives 10-20 unsolicited fiction mss/month. Accepts 2-4 mss/issue. Publishes ms an average of 6 months to 1 year after acceptance. Less than 10% of fiction is agented. Recently published work by Debra Friedman, Carol Glickfeld. Length: 2,000 words average; 1,000 words minimum; 4,000 words maximum. Publishes short shorts. Sometimes critiques rejected mss and recommends other markets.
How to Contact: Send complete ms with cover letter. Reports in 2 weeks on queries; 4-5 months on mss. SASE. Simultaneous submissions OK if other markets are clearly identified. Accepts computer printout submissions. Sample copy $4; fiction guidelines free.
Payment: 2 contributor's copies and honorarium if possible.
Terms: Acquires one-time rights.
Advice: "Send only one short story—reading editors do not like to read two by the same author at the same time. We will use only one. We generally look for creative work with a blend of craftsmanship, insight and empathy. This does not exclude humor. We won't print work that is shoddy in any of these areas."

WORD & IMAGE (I), The Illustrated Journal, 3811 Priest Lake Dr., Nashville TN 37217. (615)361-4733. Editor: Joanna Long. Magazine: 7×8½; 48-64 pages; 22 lb paper; 60 lb cover; illustrations and photographs. "Strongly visual—usually up-beat material—well-crafted but not obscure or 'arty.' General interest stories and poetry, some nonfiction. No sensational or 'porn.' " Semiannually. Estab. 1986. Circ. 800.
Needs: Condensed/excerpted novel, contemporary, fantasy (occasionally), historical (general—"We feature a history topic in each issue,") humor/satire, literary prose poem, regional, religious/inspirational, romance (historical), senior citizen/retirement. "*Word & Image* is a nonprofit press committed to helping senior citizens and other worthy causes." Receives 10 unsolicited mss/month. Accepts 3-4 mss/issue; 6-8 mss/year. Length: 1,500-2,500 words preferred; 600-700 words minimum; 3,500 words maximum. Publishes short shorts. Sometimes critiques rejected mss and recommends other markets.
How to Contact: Send complete ms with cover letter. Cover letter should include "brief bio info." Reports in 2-3 weeks. SASE. Photocopied and reprint submissions OK. Accepts computer printout submissions. Sample copy for $3. Fiction guidelines for #10 SAE and 1 first class stamp.
Payment: 1 contributor's copy; charge for extras: $3 each.
Terms: Acquires one-time rights. Publication copyrighted.
Advice: "Study a sample copy."

‡WORKING CLASSICS (I,II,IV), Red Wheelbarrow Press, 298 Ninth Ave., San Francisco CA 94118. (415)387-3412. Editor: David Joseph. Magazine: 8½×11; 24 pages; 70 lb cover stock; illustrations; photos. Magazine of "creative work, fiction, nonfiction, poetry, interviews, reviews, comics, by and for working people—especially the organized, trade unionists (both rank and file and leadership), artists, leftists, progressives." Semiannually. Plans special fiction issue. Estab. 1982. Circ. 1,000.
Needs: Comics, contemporary, ethnic, experimental, feminist, gay, historical, humor/satire, lesbian, literary, prose poem and regional. No psychic/supernatural/occult, religious/inspirational. Receives 12 unsolicited mss/month. Accepts 2 mss/issue; 4 mss/year. Recently published the works of Paul Casey and Carrie Jenkins; published new writers within the past year. Length: 2,400 words average; 250

words minimum; 18,000 words maximum. Occasionally critiques rejected mss. Recommends other markets.
How to Contact: Send complete ms. "We're interested in the concrete process involved in your actual conditions. We like to know why you believe your story is for our audience of working people and working writers." Reports in 3 months. SASE. Simultaneous, photocopied and previously published submissions OK. Accepts computer printout submissions; prefers letter-quality. Accepts disk submissions for IBM or compatible. Prefers hard copy with disk submission. Sample copy for $3.
Payment: 1 free contributor's copy; reduced charge for extras.
Terms: Acquires one-time rights.
Advice: "The recent expansion in the short fiction market seems to have come to a halt. I think it will remain open with room for new developments in fiction. Dirty realism is not the last word in fiction. Yet realism often may be necessary for focusing details taken from observation. The combination of imagination and observation creates the dynamics of short fiction."

WRIT MAGAZINE (II), 2 Sussex Ave., Toronto, Ontario M5S 1J5 Canada. (416)978-4871. Editor: Roger Greenwald. Assoc. Editor: Richard Lush. Magazine: 6×9; 96 pages; Zephyr laid paper; cover stock varies; cover illustrations. "Literary magazine for literate readers interested in the work of new writers." Annually. Publishes occasional special fiction issues. Estab. 1970. Circ. 700.
Needs: Literary, short stories, short shorts, parts of novels, translations. Accepts 10-15 mss/year. Does not read mss in summer. Recently published fiction by David Galef, Vitaliano Brancati, Dacia Maraini, Ivar Lo-Johansson; published new writers in the last year. Length: 300-20,000 words. Critiques rejected mss "when there is time. Sometimes recommends other markets."
How to Contact: Send complete ms with SASE (Canadian stamps or IRCs) and brief biographical note on author and/or translator, and a phone number. Translators must send copy of original text. Accepts computer printout submissions if letter quality. Reports in 2-3 months. Sample copy $6.
Payment: 2 free author's copies. Negotiates charge for extras.
Terms: Acquires first North American serial rights. Copyright reverts to author.
Advice: "Look at your target magazine before submitting."

THE WRITERS' BAR-B-Q (II), Sangamon Writers, Inc., 924 Bryn Mawr, Springfield IL 62703. (217)525-6987. Fiction Editors: Tim Osburn, Becky Bradway, Gary Smith, Gael Cox Carnes, Marcia Womack. Magazine: 8½×11; 80-110 pages; slick cover stock with full-page photo; illustrations and photos. "*The Writers' Bar-B-Q* is a fiction magazine that is looking for unpretentious, fun, exciting writing. A good story with purpose and well-drawn characters is more important to us than clever phrasing. We want writing that shows the author cares, and has something to say." Semiannually. Estab. 1987. Circ. 1,000.
Needs: Adventure, contemporary, erotica, ethnic, experimental, fantasy, feminist, gay, historical (general), horror, humor/satire, lesbian, literary, mainstream, psychic/supernatural/occult, regional, science fiction, serialized/excerpted novel, suspense/mystery, translations. "Display a strong personal voice, a unique view of the world, and a sense of commitment and caring toward the characters and subject. Contemporary, thoughtful sci-fi, horror and detective are encouraged, along with more mainstream, contemporary work. We publish novel excerpts and long stories, as well as shorter pieces. We are looking for inventiveness, humor and insight. No formulas—whether they be genre formulas or academic formulas. Work that is sexist, racist or homophobic should not be mailed!" Receives 50-100 unsolicited fiction mss/month. Accepts 15-20 mss/issue; 30-40 mss/year. Publishes ms 6 months to 1 year after acceptance. Recently published work by Lowry Pei, Nolan Porterfield, Dan Curley, Sandra Kolonkiewicz, Karen Peterson; published new writers within the last year. Length: 500-15,000 words. Sometimes critiques rejected mss.
How to Contact: Send complete ms with cover letter, which should include "a sense of who the writer is—a list of publications is fine, but personality is more fun." Reports in 6-12 weeks on mss. SASE. Simultaneous and photocopied submissions OK. Accepts computer printout submissions. Accepts electronic submissions via disk. "We have an Epson MS-DOS." Sample copy $5.
Payment: 3 contributor's copies.
Terms: Acquires first rights. Rights revert upon publication.
Advice: "The editors of the *Bar-B-Q* come from a maligned area of the country—the Midwest—which is filled with talented authors who suffer under the cliché of Midwesterners as backwoods, illiterate hicks. We want to provide a place where wonderful, unconventional, supposedly unmarketable writing can be found. We want Midwestern and other silenced stories to be discovered."

WRITERS' FORUM (II), University of Colorado at Colorado Springs, Colorado Springs CO 80933-7150. Editor: Dr. Alex Blackburn. "Ten to fifteen short stories or self-contained novel excerpts published once a year along with 25-35 poems. Funded by grants from National Endowment for the Arts, Coordinating Council for Literary Magazines, University of Colorado, McGraw Hill and others. Highest literary quality only: mainstream, avant-garde, with preference to western themes. For small press enthusiasts, teachers and students of creative writing, commercial agents/publishers, university

libraries and departments interested in contemporary American literature." Estab. 1974.
Needs: Literary, contemporary, ethnic (Native American, Chicano, not excluding others) and regional (West). No "sentimental, over-plotted, pornographic, anecdotal, polemical, trendy, disguised autobiographical, fantasy (sexual, extra-terrestrial), pseudo-philosophical, passionless, placeless, undramatized, etc. material." Accepts 10-12 mss/issue. Receives approximately 40 unsolicited fiction mss each month and will publish new as well as experienced authors. Recently published fiction by Thomas E. Kennedy, Charles Baxter, Gladys Swan; published many new writers within the last year. Length: 1,500-10,000 words. Critiques rejected mss "when there is time and perceived merit."
How to Contact: Send complete ms and letter with relevant career information with SASE. Accepts computer printout submissions; prefers letter-quality. Reports in 3-5 weeks on mss. Publishes ms an average of 6 months after acceptance. Sample back copy $5.95 to *NSSWM* readers. Current copy $5.95.
Payment: 1 free author's copy. Cover price less 60% discount for extras.
Terms: Acquires one-time rights. Rights revert to author.
Advice: "Read our publication. Be prepared for constructive criticism. We especially seek submissions that show immersion in place (trans-Mississippi West) and development of credible characters. Turned off by slick 'decadent' New York-ish content. Probably the TV-influenced fiction is the most quickly rejected. Our format – a 5½×8½ professionally edited and printed paperback book – lends credibility to authors published in our imprint."

WRITERS NEWSLETTER (I), Writers Studio, 1530 7th St., Rock Island IL 61201. (309)788-3980. Editor: Betty Mowery. Newsletter: 8½×11; 8-9 pages. "Anything of help to writers." Bimonthly. Estab. 1968. Circ. 385.
Needs: Adventure, contemporary, experimental, historical (general), humor/satire, mainstream, prose poem, regional, religious/inspiration, romance, spiritual, suspense/mystery. "Also, articles, fiction, nonfiction and poetry manuscripts from young authors K-12, for young author page. Please state age on manuscript." No erotica. Receives about 12 mss/month. Buys or accepts up to 6 mss/issue. Publishes ms within 3 months of acceptance. Recently published work by David R. Collins, Evelyn Witter, Chris Walkowicz; published new writers within the last year. Length: 500 words maximum. Publishes short shorts. Length: 200 words.
How to Contact: Send complete ms. Reports in 1 week. SASE. Simultaneous, photocopied and reprint submissions OK. Accepts computer printout submissions. Sample copy for $1.
Payment: Pays in contributor's copies.
Terms: Acquires first rights.
Advice: "Just send a manuscript, but first read a copy of our publication to get an idea of what type of material we take. Please send SASE. If not, manuscripts *will not* be returned. Be sure name and address is on the manuscript."

WRITERS' RENDEZVOUS (I), 3954 Mississippi St., Suite 8, San Diego CA 92104. (619)296-2758. Editor: Karen Campbell. Newsletter: 8½×11; approx. 24 pages; bond paper; no cover; line drawings. "Writer-oriented, publish only work relating to freelance writing and penpalling." Quarterly. Plans special fiction issue. Estab. 1986. Circ. 100.
Needs: No fiction "not related to writing/penpalling." Receives approx. 10 unsolicited fiction mss/month. Publishes approx. 2 mss/issue; approx. 10 mss/year. Publishes ms 6 weeks-1 year after acceptance. Recently published work by Bettye Griffin, Jan McDaniel, Linda Hutton; published new writers within the last year. Length: 750 words average; 1,500 words maximum. Publishes short shorts. Sometimes comments on rejected mss and recommends other markets. "No erotica!!"
How to Contact: Send complete ms with cover letter. Reports in 2-4 weeks. SASE. Simultaneous, photocopied and reprint submissions OK. Accepts computer printouts, including dot-matrix "with true descenders only." Sample copy for $3, #10 SAE and 3 first class stamps; fiction guidelines for #10 SAE and 1 first class stamp.
Payment: Pays in contributor's copies.
Terms: Acquires one-time rights. Publication not copyrighted. Sponsors contests for fiction writers. "SASE for guidelines; $2 entry fee. Cash prize."
Advice: "Proofread. Then proofread again. Then ask a friend or teacher to proofread. Use your dictionary – both for spelling and meaning. Read the guidelines carefully. And, if you want cash for your work, be sure you aren't submitting to markets which pay copies. (I've had several acceptances fall through when I advised the author of our non-payment policy)."

WRITING PURSUITS (I), 1863 Bitterroot Dr., Twin Falls ID 83301. (208)734-0746 (evenings). Editor: Bill White. Newsletter: 8×11; 3-5 pages; illustrations. Newsletter for writers. Monthly except July and August. Estab. 1986. Circ. approximately 200.
Needs: Literary, regional, suspense/mystery, humor/satire and western. No erotica, gay, lesbian, religious or occult fiction. Accepts 1 ms/issue; 10 mss/year. Publishes ms within 1-2 months of acceptance. Length: 500 words maximum. Sometimes critiques rejected mss and recommends other markets.

How to Contact: Query first. Reports in 1-2 weeks. SASE. Photocopied submissions OK. Accepts computer printout submissions; also electronic submissions via disk or modem. Sample copy for 50¢ or #10 SAE and 1 first class stamp. Fiction guidelines for 10 SAE and 1 first class stamp.
Payment: Pays in contributor's copies.
Terms: Acquires first rights.
Advice: "Be persistent. Study a sample of our publication. Make your story exciting. Our name may change soon. Contact above address for information."

WYOMING, THE HUB OF THE WHEEL (II), A Journal for Universal Spokesmen, Willow Bee Publishing House, Box 9, Saratoga WY 82331. (307)326-5214. Editor: Lenore A. Senior. Fiction Editor: Dawn Senior. Magazine: 6×9; 100 pages average; 60 lb paper; 10 pt CIS cover; illustrations; photographs. "Themes: Peace (from International Peace to Personal Peace), The Human Race, Positive Relationships (Between People, Youth & Age, People & Nature), The Human Spirit and all its Possibilities." Semiannually. Estab. 1985. Circ. 300.
Needs: Contemporary, ethnic, experimental, literary, prose poem, regional, translations. "No violence, sex, religious materials or writing in any way racist or sexist." Receives 15 unsolicited fiction mss/month. Publishes 2-6 mss/issue. Publishes mss 6-18 months after acceptance. Recently published work by Rochelle Lynn Holt, Elizabeth Follin-Jones. Length: 2,500 words maximum. Publishes short shorts. Sometimes comments on rejected mss or recommends other markets.
How to Contact: Send complete ms with cover letter, which should include a short bio. Reports on queries in 4-6 weeks; on mss in 6-8 weeks. SASE. Simultaneous and photocopied submissions OK. Accepts computer printouts. Sample copy for $5. Fiction guidelines for #10 SAE and 45¢ postage.
Payment: Pays 1 contributor's copy. Contributor discounts also available.
Terms: Acquires one-time rights.
Advice: "We look for fiction of emotional and psychological depth and clear, understandable, yet subtle language that is sensitive to the reader's intelligence, imagination and sense of the exquisite mystery of existence. Beginners' best hope of achieving excellence is to look deeply into their own experience and honestly draw from those elements of it that best contain the universal within the unique and particular."

XAVIER REVIEW (I, II), Xavier University, Box 110C, New Orleans LA 70125. (504)486-7411, ext. 7481. Editor: Thomas Bonner, Jr. Magazine of "poetry/fiction/nonfiction/reviews (contemporary literature) for professional writers/libraries/colleges/universities." Published semiannually. Estab. 1980. Circ. 500.
Needs: Contemporary, ethnic, experimental, historical (general), literary, Latin-American, prose poem, Southern, religious, serialized/excerpted novel, translations. Receives 30 unsolicited fiction mss/month. Buys 2 mss/issue; 4 mss/year. Length: 10-15 pages. Occasionally critiques rejected mss.
How to Contact: Send complete ms. SASE. Sample copy $3.
Payment: 2 contributor's copies.

‡YAK (II), A Journal of Art & Literature, 738 Manning Ave. Toronto, Ontario M6G 2W4 Canada. (416)530-0890. Editor: Michael Redhill. Fiction Editors: Penny Manios and Alana Richman. Magazine: 5½×8½; 42 pages; Plainfield 70 lb paper; Mayfair cover stock; photos. "We are, simply, interested in polished energetic writing. No thematic or stylistic restrictions." Semiannually. Estab. 1987. Circ. 500.
Needs: Excerpted novel, contemporary, erotica, ethnic, experimental, feminist, gay, humor/satire, lesbian, literary and prose poem. No romance, racism, documentary, diary entries. Plans to publish special fiction or anthology issue in the future. Receives 10-15 unsolicited mss/month. Accepts 2-3 ms/issue; 5-6 mss/year. Publishes ms 1-2 months after acceptance. Length: 3,000 words maximum; 2,500 average. Publishes short shorts. Sometimes critiques rejected mss.
How to Contact: Send complete ms with cover letter. Reports in 3-5 months on mss. SASE. Photocopied submissions OK. Accepts computer printout submissions. Sample copy $2.50. Fiction guidelines for #10 SAE and 44¢ Canadian or IRC.
Payment: Pays in contributor's copies.
Terms: Acquires one-time rights.
Advice: "*Read. Revise. Wait.* Don't send until being rejected won't hurt. If you're that close to your work, don't risk ruining your relationship to it by sending it off. Get perspective first. We wish to be a conduit between beginning and established writers. We began with that in mind and continue. Aside from that, we want to maintain a level of excellence, shunning the boring and the bourgeois."

THE YALE REVIEW (II), Yale University Press, 1902A Yale Station, New Haven CT 06520. (203)432-0499. Editor: Penelope Laurans. Managing Editor: Wendy Wipprecht. "A general interest quarterly; publishes literary criticism, original fiction and poetry, cultural commentary, book reviews for an informed general audience." Quarterly. Estab. 1911. Circ. 6,000.

Needs: Literary and contemporary. Buys 4-8 mss/year. Less than 1% of fiction is agented. Length: 3,000-5,000 words.
How to Contact: Send complete ms with SASE. Reports in 2 months. Publishes ms up to 1 year after acceptance. Sample copy $7.
Payment: Approximately $100. 1 free author's copy; $3 charge for extras.
Terms: Makes assignments on a work-for-hire basis. Pays on publication for first North American serial rights.

YELLOW SILK (II): Journal of Erotic Arts, Verygraphics, Box 6374, Albany CA 94706. Editor/Publisher: Lily Pond. Magazine: 8⅜×10⅞; 52 pages; matte coated stock; glossy cover stock; 4-color illustrations; photos. "We are interested in nonpornographic erotic literature: joyous, mad, musical, elegant, passionate and beautiful. 'All persuasions; no brutality' is our editorial policy. Literary excellence is a priority; innovative forms are welcomed, as well as traditional ones." Published quarterly. Estab. 1981. Circ. 16,000.
Needs: Comics, erotica, ethnic, experimental, fantasy, feminist/lesbian, gay, humor/satire, literary, prose poem, science fiction and translations. No "blow-by-blow" descriptions; no hackneyed writing except when used for satirical purposes. Nothing containing brutality. Buys 4-5 mss/issue; 16-20 mss/year. Recently published work by William Kotzwinkle, Gary Soto. Published new writers within the last year. Length: no preference. Occasionally critiques rejected ms.
How to Contact: Send complete ms with SASE and include short, *personal* bio notes. No queries. No pre-published material. No simultaneous submissions. Name, address and phone number on each page. Photocopied submissions OK. Accepts computer printout submissions; prefers letter-quality. Reports in 3 months on mss. Publishes ms up to 3 years after acceptance. Sample copy $6.
Payment: 3 contributor's copies plus minimum of $10 per prose item.
Terms: Pays on publication for all periodical and anthology rights for one year following publication, at which time rights revert back to author; and non-exclusive reprint and anthology rights for the duration of the copyright.
Advice: "Read, read, read! Including our magazine—plus Nabokov, Ntozake Shange, Rimbaud, Virginia Woolf, William Kotzwinkle, James Joyce. Then send in your story! Trust that the magazine/editor will not rip you off—they don't. As they say, 'find your own voice,' then trust it. Most manuscripts I reject appear to be written by people without great amounts of writing experience. It takes years (frequently) to develop your work to publishable quality; it can take many re-writes on each individual piece. I also see many approaches to sexuality (for my magazine) that are trite and not fresh. The use of language is not original, and the people do not seem real. However, the gems come too, and what a wonderful moment that is. Please don't send me anything with blue eye shadow."

YOUNG JUDAEAN (IV), Hadassah Zionist Youth Commission, 50 W. 58th St., New York NY 10019. (212)355-7900, ext. 452. Editor: Mordecai Newman. Magazine: 8½×11; 16 pages; illustrations. "*Young Judaean* is for members of the Young Judaea Zionist youth movement, ages 9-12." Quarterly. Estab. 1910. Circ. 4,000.
Needs: Children's fiction including adventure, ethnic, fantasy, historical, humor/satire, juvenile, prose poem, religious, science fiction, suspense/mystery and translations. "All stories must have Jewish relevance." Receives 10-15 unsolicited fiction mss/month. Publishes ms up to 2 years after acceptance. Buys 1-2 mss/issue; 10-20 mss/year. Length: 500 words minimum; 1,500 words maximum; 1,000 words average.
How to Contact: Send complete ms with SASE. Photocopied submissions OK. Reports in 3 months on mss. Sample copy for 75¢. Free fiction guidelines.
Payment: Pays 5¢/word up to $50; 2 free contributor's copies; 75¢ charge for extras.
Terms: Pays on publication for first rights.
Advice: "Stories must be of Jewish interest—lively and accessible to children without being condescending."

‡YOUNG VOICES MAGAZINE (I, II, IV), The Magazine of Young People's Creative Work, Box 2321, Olympia WA 98507. (206)357-4863. Editor: Steve Charak. Magazine: "All materials are by elementary and middle school students for children and adults interested in children's work." Bimonthly. Estab. 1988. Circ. 1,000.
Needs: Adventure, experimental, historical (general), humor/satire, juvenile (5-14), literary, mainstream, prose poem, and science fiction. "Everything must be written by elementary or middle school students. (8th grade is the limit)" No excessive violence or sexual content. Plans a special fiction issue or an anthology in the future. Receives 50 unsolicited mss/month. Buys 30 mss/issue; 160-200 mss/year. Publishes ms 2-4 months after acceptance. Recently published work by Amanda Trause and Lani Olson. Length: 500 words average. Publishes short shorts. Always critiques rejected mss and recommends other markets.

How to Contact: Send complete ms with cover letter. Make sure age, grade and school are in the letter. Simultaneous, photocopied and reprint submissions OK. Accepts computer printout submissions. Sample copy $3. Fiction guidelines free.
Payment: Pays $3-5 and contributor's copies.
Terms: Pays on acceptance for one-time rights.

Z MISCELLANEOUS (II), Again & Again Press, Box 20041, Cherokee Station, New York NY 10028. Editor: Charles Fabrizio. Magazine: 8½×11; 90 pages; 70 lb paper; 80 lb cover stock; illustrations. "Publishes work that enables the reader to reassess the familiar, discover the new, and learn about the different." Quarterly. Estab. 1987. Circ. 300.
Needs: Contemporary, ethnic, fantasy, horror, humor/satire, literary, mainstream, science fiction. "We welcome original, well-crafted stories that present clearly defined characters, a logical progression of events, and a coherent plot." No confessions, romance, religious, political or pornography. Receives approx. 50-75 unsolicited fiction mss/month. Accepts 10-15 mss/issue; 60-75 mss/year. Publishes ms an average of 2-4 months after acceptance. Recently published work by Norman German, Dale A. White, Bruce Boston; published new writers within the last year. Length: 2,000 words maximum. Publishes short shorts. Sometimes critiques rejected mss.
How to Contact: Send complete ms with cover letter. (Cover letter optional.) Reports in 6 weeks. SASE. Photocopied submissions OK. "No simultaneous submissions." Accepts computer printout submissions, no dot-matrix. Sample copy $4; fiction guidelines for #10 SASE.
Payment: $10 maximum; tearsheets of work.
Terms: Pays on acceptance for first rights. "An Achievement Award In Fiction, chosen by the magazine's staff, is selected from the stories published in each issue and carries a payment of $10. The works so cited are eligible for the Annual Achievement In Fiction Award, which is determined by the magazine's subscribers and carries a payment of $50."
Advice: "Editorial comments/suggestions are meant to help a writer achieve the full potential of their work. You may, and have every right to disagree with the editor's opinion. But editors and writers should be allies, not adversaries."

‡ZERO HOUR (I, II, IV), "Where Culture Meets Crime," Box 766, Seattle WA 98111. (206)621-8829. Editor: Jim Jones. Tabloid: 11×16; 36 pages; newsprint paper; illustrations and photos. "We are interested in fringe culture. We publish fiction, poetry, essays, confessions, photos, illustrations, interviews, for young, politically left audience interested in current affairs, non-mainstream music, art, culture." Semiannually. Estab. 1988. Circ. 3,000.
Needs: Confessions, erotica, ethnic, experimental, feminist, gay, humor/satire, psychic/supernatural/occult and translations. "Each issue revolves around an issue in contemporary culture: cults and fanaticism, addiction, pornography, etc." No romance, inspirational, juvenile/young, sports. Receives 5 unsolicited mss/month. Accepts 3 mss/issue; 9 mss/year. Publishes ms 2-3 months after acceptance. Recently published work by Jesse Bernstein and Mike Allmayer. Length: 1,200 words average; 400 words minimum; 1,500 words maximum. Publishes short shorts. Length: 400 words. Sometimes critiques rejected mss.
How to Contact: Query first. Reports in 2 weeks on queries; 1 month on mss. SASE. Simultaneous and photocopied submissions OK. Accepts computer printout submissions. Sample copy $3, 9×12 SAE and 5 first class stamps. Fiction guidelines free.
Payment: Pays in contributor's copies.
Terms: Acquires one-time rights. Sends galleys to author.
Advice: "Does it fit our theme? Is it well written, from an unusual point of view or on an unexplored/underexplored topic?"

ZOIKS! (I, II, IV), Curdling the Cream of the Mind, 2509 M Avent Ferry Rd., Raleigh NC 27606. (919)821-2196. Editor: Skip Elsheimer. Fiction Editor: Joe Corey. Magazine: illustrations and photos. "*Zoiks!* is interested in new ideas and new ways of thinking. Or at least using old ideas in a new way. Exploring the world through cynicism." Plans special fiction issue. Estab. 1986.
Needs: Experimental, humor/satire, psychic/supernatural/occult, translations, underground literature, conspiracy-oriented fiction. "I'm interested in anything that will make you question your surroundings. No fiction that is pretentious, lacking humor." Receives 2-3 unsolicited mss/month. Accepts 1-2 mss/issue; 6-12 mss/year. Recently published work by Joe Corey, Skip Elsheimer, Karen Bartlett; published new writers within the last year. Publishes short shorts. Sometimes critiques rejected mss or recommends other markets.
How to Contact: Query first with clips of published work or send complete ms with cover letter, which should include address. Should tell something about the author. Reports in 3 weeks. Simultaneous, photocopied and reprint submissions OK. Accepts computer submissions. Accepts electronic submissions via Macintosh 800K. Sample copy for $1.

Payment: Pays in contributor's copies; charges for extras at cost.
Terms: Publication not copyrighted. Work belongs to the author.
Advice: "I feel that magazine fiction is too industry oriented. Everyone should have a shot at getting published. Express *yourself*! Not the style of another famous author."

‡ZYMERGY (II), (Literary Review), Box 1746, Place du Parc, Montreal, Quebec H2W 2R7 Canada. Editor: Sonja A. Skarstedt. Magazine: 6×9; 160 pages; buff paper; Cornwall/laminated cover stock; illustrations; photos. "We publish poetry, fiction and interviews, articles: all attempting to focus on and come to grips with what is happening in today's literary movements, splayed though they might happen to be." Semiannually. Estab. 1987. Circ. 500.
Needs: "Good short stories," excerpted novel, feminist, literary and prose poem. "We are particularly interested in the new, previously-unpublished writers whose writing takes a risk. Nothing gratuitous, manipulative, predictable (pornography and violence, e.g.)." Plan to publish fiction issue or anthology in the future. Receives 20-100 unsolicited mss/month. Accepts 1-5 mss/issue. Publishes ms 6 months after acceptance. Length: 1200 words/average. Briefly comments on rejected mss and sometimes recommends other markets.
How to Contact: Send complete ms with cover letter. Include biographical information to be used in "Contributor's Column." Reports in 3 weeks on mss. SASE. Photocopied submissions OK. Accepts computer printout submissions. (No simultaneous submissions.) Sample copy $5 (Canadian). Checks payable to S. Skarstedt.
Payment: Pays in contributor's copies.
Terms: Acquires first rights and the right, should the story be reprinted/anthologized, to be acknowledged.
Advice: "We look for originality. The ability to 'pull' the reader inside the story's/characters' environment. Non-stylized writing. If you don't enjoy writing—don't write!"

ZYZZYVA (II, IV), The Last Word: West Coast Writers and Artists, Suite 1400, 41 Sutter St., San Francisco CA 94104. (415)982-3440. Editor: Howard Junker. Magazine: 6×9; 136 pages; Starwhite Vicksburg smooth paper; graphics; photos. "Literate" magazine. Quarterly. Estab. 1985. Circ. 3,000.
Needs: Contemporary, experimental, literary, prose poem. West Coast writers only. Receives 200 unsolicited mss/month. Buys 5 fiction mss/issue; 20 mss/year. Agented fiction: 10%. Recent issues have included Salvatore La Puma, Gina Berriault, Juan Felipe Herrera; published new writers within the last year. Length: varies.
How to Contact: Send complete ms. "Cover letters are of minimal importance." Reports in 2 weeks on mss. SASE. No simultaneous submissions or reprints. Accepts computer printouts. Sample copy $8. Fiction guidelines on masthead page.
Payment: Pays $25-100.
Terms: Pays on acceptance for first North American serial rights.
Advice: "Keep the faith."

Foreign Literary and Small Circulation Magazines

The following is a list of literary and small circulation publications from countries outside the U.S. and Canada that accept or buy short fiction in English (or in the universal languages of Esperanto or Ido) by North American writers.

Before sending a manuscript to a foreign publication with which you are unfamiliar, it's a good idea to query first for information on the magazine's needs and methods of submission. Send for sample copies, or try visiting the main branch of your local library, a nearby college library or bookstore to find a copy.

All correspondence to foreign countries must include International Reply Coupons, if you want a reply or material returned. You may find it less expensive to send copies of your manuscript for the publisher to keep and just enclose a return postcard with one IRC for a reply. Keep in mind response time is slow for many foreign publishers, but don't hesitate to send a reply postcard with IRC to check the status of your submission.

ACUMEN, 6, The Mount, Furzeham, Brixham, Devon TQ5 8QY England. Fiction Editor: Patricia Oxley. Circ. 500. "Literary magazine with an emphasis on poetry. I use 2-4 short stories/year (2 issues) which are around 1,500 words, have a clear statement and are written in a literary style. Writers paid in extra copies of *Acumen*. Writers receive copies of the issue containing their work. Send sufficient IRCs to cover return postage. Make sure name and address are on manuscript (not just covering letter or, worse still, on outside of envelope.)"

‡AMBIT, 17 Priory Gardens, London N6 5QY England. Fiction Editor: J. G. Ballard. Circ. 2,000. Publishes 12 stories/year. "Fantasy, science fiction stories where quotidian events are seen from an extraordinary viewpoint." Pays 2 complimentary copies and £5 per page. "*Ambit* is a good place for North American writers to send work. We regularly publish U.S. writers. Writers should screen each magazine first to see whether it has an open, adventurous editorial policy. Closed parochial magazines and journals should be shunned and allowed to shrivel in their own time."

AMMONITE, Suite 5, Somdor House, Station Road, Gillingham Dorset SP8 4QA England. Publishes 6 stories/year. Publishes science fiction, fantasy and mythical fiction. Pays in copies. "Buy a sample copy." ($2.50 including postage.)

‡AN SEANRVD, 25 Newtown Ave., Blackrock, Dublin 882575 Ireland. Fiction Editor: Rudi Holzapfel. Circulation varies. Accepts Catholic and patriotic material and anything well written considered." Pays 3 contributor's copies. "Have humility and patience."

‡ANTIGRUPPO, Coop. Antigruppo Siciliano, via Argenteria Km4, Trapani, Sicily 91026 Italy. Editor: Nat Scammacca. Fiction Editor: Gianni Diecidue. Needs literary, contemporary, humor, translations, history (local, Sicilian, Scots, Greek, English, Yugoslavian, Israel, Hungarian and French). "Send previously published material so we can then ask for the material we want. Ask for our 21 points of the Antigruppo, which is a pluralistic guide and encouragement to write as one speaks. Don't copy anyone but oneself and write the way the language is spoken at home in your own region, not imitating others. Material must interest the Sicilian reader."

AQUARIUS, Flat 10, Room-A, 116 Sutherland Ave., Maida-Vale, London W9 England. Fiction Editor: Sean Glackin. Circ. 5,000. Publishes five stories/issue. Interested in humor/satire, literary, prose poem and serialized/excerpted novels. "We publish prose and poetry and reviews." Payment is by agreement. "We only suggest changes. Most stories are taken on merit." Price in UK £2 50p. plus postage and packing; in US $12 plus $3 postage.

AUGURIES, 48 Anglesey Road, Alverstoke, Gosport, Hampshire P012 2EQ England. Editor: Nik Morton. Circ. 300. Averages 30-40 stories/year. "Science fiction and fantasy, maximum length 4,000 words." Pays £2 per 1,000 words plus complimentary copy. "Buy back issues, then try me!" Sample copy $3. Subscription $10 (4 issues).

BRAVE NEW WORD, Box 88, Clifton Hill, Victoria 3068 Australia. Fiction Editor: Helen Murnane. Circ. 300-1,500. Publishes 60 mss/year. "We publish contemporary Australian short stories and poetry. We would consider a small amount of international writing." Writers receive either 2 copies or a small payment. Enclose SASE.

CENCRASTUS, 34 Queen Street, Edinburgh EH2 1JY Scotland. Fiction Editor: Ray Ross. Circ. 2,000. Publishes 1 or more short stories per issue. "Scottish literature arts and affairs magazine with international bias. Produced quarterly." Writers are paid for published fiction and receive contributor's copies. "We look at all copy submitted. SAE."

CENTRAL COAST COURIER, Box 44, Oxford, Tasmania 7190 Australia. Fiction Editor: J.C. Read. Circ. 1,000. Local newspaper publishing general fiction and poetry on a bimonthly basis. Pays nominal fee; sends contributor's copy where possible. Maximum word length for short stories: 1,500 words. Also uses summaries of novels.

CONTRAST, Box 3841, Cape Town 8000 South Africa. Editor: Geoffrey Hareshape. Circ. 1,000. Averages 6-8 short stories/year. "A literary journal of Southern Africa; emphasis on publishing short stories (max 6,500 words), poetry and literary articles." No payment – contributor's copies sent. "Include self-addressed envelope."

CREATIVE FORUM, Bahri Publications Pvt Limited., 57 Santnagar, Box 7023, New Delhi 110065 India. Fiction Editor: U.S. Bahri. Circ. 1,800. Publishes 8-12 stories annually. "We accept short stories only for our journal, *Creative Forum*. Novels/novellas accepted if suitable subsidy is forthcoming from the author." Pays in copies. Manuscripts should be "neatly typed and not beyond 200 A4 size sheets."

DADA DANCE MAGAZINE, %Fligel, 35 Falkland St., Glasgow G12, Scotland. Editor: Dee Rimbaud. "We are Scotland's alternative literature magazine; and are looking for work that is unusual, bizarre, underground, poetic, erratic, suicidal or ecstatic—anything that is born of genius or madness." No payment. All mss submitted must include IRC. Sample copy £4 (sterling) or $10 (dollars).

DILIMAN REVIEW, University of the Philippines, Diliman, Quezon City 3004 Philippines. Editor: Eddie Ercultura.

‡edge magazine, 1933-8 Hazama-cho, Hachioji-shi, Tokyo 193 Japan. Fiction Editor: Michael O'Rourke. Circ. 500. Publishes 15-20 stories/year. "*edge* is a non-profit literary magazine providing a forum in English for writers of all nationalities in Japan. We also aim to make the work of writers in English-speaking countries more widely available in Japan. Submissions are chosen based only on literary merit—*edge* is open to all styles and genres, 'sudden fiction,' short stories and novel excerpts. Particularly interested in translations of contemporary writers, at the moment, especially from Japanese and other Asian languages." Pays 2 contributor's copies. Maximum length 5,000 words. "Please include sufficient postage with SASE—this means at least *two* IRC's for airmail letter, more for ms."

‡FOOLSCAP, 78 Friars Road, East Ham, London E6 1LL England. Fiction and Poetry Editor: Judi Benson. Publishes 6 items/year. "We are primarily poetry though can handle short fiction of up to 5 pages. This could include a scene from a novel. We are looking for strong quality work but will give careful consideration to all submissions. Any subject considered, also nonfiction." Pays 2 contributor's copies. "Do not send work exceeding 5 typed pages as the magazine does not have the space. Send manuscript in typed form with SASE for return (IRCs)."

FORESIGHT (IV), 44 Brockhurst Rd., Hodge Hill, Birmingham B36 8JB England. Editor: John Barklam. Fiction Editor: Judy Barklam. Magazine including "new age material, world peace, psychic phenomena, research, occultism, spiritualism, mysticism, UFOs, philosophy, etc. Shorter articles required on a specific theme related to the subject matter of *Foresight* magazine." Sample copy for 30p and 25p postage.

FORUM FABULATORUM, Cort Adelersgade 5, 2.tv., DK-1053 Copenhagen K Denmark. Fiction Editor: Morten Sorensen. Circ. 250. Publishes 60,000-80,000 words of fiction annually. "*Forum Fabulatorum* is a fiction magazine devoted to 'fantastic literature,' by which is meant fantasy, horror and science fiction, although other kinds of non-naturalist prose and poetry are welcomed. Prints both 'name' authors and beginners, and both conventional and avant-garde material. Typically, *Forum Fabulatorum* pays around Danish kroner 150 for a story with first Danish rights; all contributors receive at least two free copies of the issue where they appear. Concentrate on psychological, philosophical and perhaps supernatural content; avoid hard science fiction, pulp and formula fiction. Stylistic innovation encouraged." English language submissions welcomed.

FRANK, An International Journal of Contemporary Writing and Art (II), B.P. 29 94301 Vincennes, Cedex France. Editor: David Applefield. "Eclectic, serious fiction—all styles, voices—and translations, novel extracts" for literary international audience. "Send your best work, consult a copy of the journal before submitting." Recently published work by Hubert Selby, Raymond Carver, Robert Coover and Rita Dove. Sample copy $8.

‡THE FRED, F11D Park Hall, Martell Road, London SE21 England. Editor: David Huggins. Circ. 20,000. "*The Fred* is committed to printing new writing, mainly short stories between 1,500 and 4,000 words in length. This is no hard and fast rule. Each piece considered on merit, of whatever length." Pays one contributor's copy.

‡GLOBAL TAPESTRY JOURNAL (II), BB Books, 1 Spring Bank, Longsight Rd., Salesbury, Blackburn, Lancashire BB1 9EU England. Editor: Dave Cunliffe. "Post-underground with avant-garde, experimental, alternative, counterculture, psychedelic, mystical, anarchist, etc. fiction for a bohemian and counterculture audience." Recently published fiction by Andrew Darlington, H.R. Felgenhauer, Chris Challis; published work by new writers within the last year. Sample copy $2.

GOING DOWN SWINGING, Box 64, Coburg Victoria 3058 Australia. Fiction Editor: Kevin Brophy. Circ. 500. Publishes approx. 80 pages of fiction/year. "We publish short stories, prose poetry, poetry and prose reviews. We try to encourage young or new writers as well as established writers. Interested in experimental writing. Writers not paid as we can't afford it. Writers receive a copy of the issue they are published in. Send ms, International Reply Coupons and a short biographical note."

HECATE, Box 99, St. Lucia Q4037 Australia. Fiction Editor: Carole Ferrier. Circ. 2,000. Publishes 5-6 stories annually. "Socialist feminist; we like political stories (broadly defined)." Writers receive $6/page and 5 copies. "We only rarely publish non-Australian writers of fiction."

‡THE HONEST ULSTERMAN, 102 Elm Park Mansions, Park Walk, London SW10 OAP U.K. Fiction Editor: Robert Johnstone. Circ. 1,000. Publishes 3-4 stories/year. "Mainly poetry, book review, socio-political comment, short stories, novel extracts, etc. Main interest is Ireland/Northern Ireland." Writers receive small payment and two contributor's copies.

HRAFNHOH, 32 Strŷd Ebeneser, Pontypridd Mid Glamorgan CF37 5PB Wales. Fiction Editor: Joseph Biddulph. Circ. 200-500. "Only poetry published to date, mostly connected with Biddulph surname studies, with a little explicitly Christian literature. I could use the following, however: 1. short story with strong historical base in pottery industry, Trenton, New Jersey, particularly about immigrants from North Staffordshire, England; 2. fictionalised incident in Primitive Methodist history. No payment made, but as many free copies as needed. Free copy of any of my other (mostly linguistic) publications if wanted. Be brief, use a lot of local colour and nature description: write in a controlled, resonant prose, perhaps a rather old-fashioned, Victorian style if possible, avoiding modern North American idiom. Please provide sources in footnotes."

IKARIE XB, Jaroslav Olša, Jr., Anhaltova 41/987, 169 00, Prague 6 Czechoslovakia. Editors: Ivan Adamovič and Jaroslav Olša, Jr. Circ. 700. Averages 30 short stories/year. "We are interested in good quality SF—no fantasy please. *IKARIE XB* is a semi-professional magazine published 3 times yearly, each issue publishing more than 75,000 words." Authors receive copies of their publications.

‡ILLUMINATIONS, An International Magazine of Contemporary Writing, I.S.T., Box 2651, Dar Es Salaam Tanzania. Circ. 500. Publishes 2-3 stories/year. "Devoted to contemporary poetry from around the world. Stories (up to three) used when appropriate. Will consider excerpted novel, prose poetry and translations." Payment is in contributor's copies and free subscription.

‡INDIAN LITERATURE, Sahitya Akademi, National Academy of Letters, Rabindra Bhavan, 35 Ferozeshah Rd., New Delhi 110 001 India. Fiction Editor: Dr. D.S. Rao. Circ. 2,500. Publishes 6 issues/year; 144-240 pages/issue. "Carries translations of creative work from 22 Indian literatures including Indian English." Sample copy $7.

IRON MAGAZINE (II), Iron Press, 5 Marden Ter., Cullercoats, North Shields, Tyne & Wear NE30 4PD England. Editor: Peter Mortimer. Circ. 800. Publishes 14 stories/year. "Literary magazine of contemporary fiction, poetry, articles and graphics." Pays approx. £10/page. No simultaneous submissions. Five poems, two stories per submission maximum. Sample copy for $5 (no bills-no checks). "Please see magazine before submitting and don't submit to it before you're ready!"

LA KANCERKLINIKO (IV), 162 rue Paradis, 13006 Marseille France. Phone: 91-3752-15. Fiction Editor: Laurent Septier. Circ. 300. Publishes 40 pages of fiction annually. "An esperanto magazine which appears 4 times annually. Each issue contains 32 pages. *La Kancerkliniko* is a political and cultural magazine. General fiction, science fiction, etc. Short stories or very short novels. The short story (or the very short novel) must be written only in esperanto, either original or translation from any other language."

LANDFALL/CAXTON PRESS, P.O. Box 25-088, Christchurch New Zealand. Fiction Editor: Iain Sharp. Publishes 20 stories/year. "We are willing to consider any type of serious fiction, whether the style is regarded as conservative or avant-garde." Length: maximum 15,000 words. Pays NZ $30-60, depending on length of story. "In New Zealand we follow English spelling conventions. Without wishing to be unduly nationalist, we would normally give first preference to stories which contain some kind of North American-New Zealand connection."

‡THE MAGPIE'S NEST, 176 Stoney Lane, Sparkhill, Birmingham B12 8AN, England, U.K. Fiction Editor: Bal Saini. Circ. 700. No payment due to high cost of postage to the US; contributor's copies are not sent, unless return postage is included (about $3 US). "The magazine only comes out when I can afford to pay for the printing—so writers must not accept quick results. The editor would love to receive mss from anywhere and does read them all. If American contributors have friends in U.K., it would be best if they mail their submissions to their friends and ask them to mail them to various magazines, a lot of money on postage could be saved."

‡MARANG, Dept. of English, University of Botswana, P/B 0022, Gaborone Botswana. Editor: A.N. Mensah. Circ. 200. "Departmental journal featuring poems, short stories and critical articles from colleagues in the Southern African region." Writers are not paid for work used; writers receive copies of the publication in which work appears.

MARGIN, a quarterly magazine for imaginative writing and ideas, 20 Brook Green, London W6 7BL England. Fiction Editor: Robin Magowan. Circ. 2,000. Publishes 8-12 short stories or extracts from novels/year. "Arts quarterly including politics, fine arts, literature, architecture, etc. Fiction should be adventurous in its approach both to writing and content." Writers receive 4 free copies plus $25/page. "Read two or three issues of *margin* before submitting. We are also interested in good obsessive prose."

MEANJIN, University of Melbourne, Parkville, Victoria 3052 Australia. Fiction Editors: Jenny Lee and Gerald Murnane. Circ. 3,000. "*Meanjin*'s emphasis is on publishing a wide range of writing by new and established writers. Our primary orientation is toward Australian writers, but material from overseas sources is also published." Writer receives approx. $50 per 1,000 words and 2 copies. "Please submit typed manuscript and enclose return addressed envelope with IRCs."

MOMENTUM, % Pamela Goodwin, Almere Farm, Rossett, Wrexham, Clwyd LL12 0BY Wales. Fiction Editor: Jeff Bell. Circ. 350. Publishes an average of 18 stories annually. "*Momentum:* A 'middle-of-the-road' general interest mag with some verse, specializing in new writers—within those parameters anything goes, but no way-out extremes of fantasy or cult stuff, etc. Fiction only. Published 3 times a year (50 page edition)." Writers receive 1 contributor's copy. "Type fairly legibly, 2500 words maximum and a rough word count is welcome, one side of a sheet please. Address (and name) on copy. Politics *not* barred."

‡THE MUSE, A Literary Journal of the English Association at Nsukka, Dept. of English, University of Nigeria, Nsukka, Nigeria. Fiction Editor: Emmanuel Chukwuanukwu. Publishes 4-5 fiction pieces/year depending on the year's space allocation. "*The Muse* is a literary journal celebrating its silver jubilee this year—designed to offer students of the department and a few lecturers or writers an opportunity to express themselves in the literary classes of short stories, poems, book reviews, literary criticisms and essays." Pays contributor's copies. "Work should be interesting, of a high literary quality, typed, double-line spacing in three or four full scale sheets—should bear the name, profession and address of its author—and be directed to the editor."

NEW HOPE INTERNATIONAL, 20 Werneth Ave., Hyde, SK14 5NL England. Fiction Editor: Gerald England. Circ. 500. Publishes 1-4 stories annually. Publishes "mainly poetry. Fiction used must be essentially literary but not pretentious. Only short fiction used (max 2,000 words). Would use more fiction but the standard submitted (in comparison to the poetry) has been rather poor." Payment: 1 complimentary copy. Guidelines available for IRC. Sample copy: $3.

NIEUWE KOEKRAND, Box 14767, 1001 LG Amsterdam Holland. Fiction Editor: Johan Van Leeuwen. Circ. 2,000. Publishes 2-3 pages of fiction/issue. "*Nieuwe Koekrand* is basically considered a hardcore/punk magazine but often goes beyond that. It also includes articles on writers/fiction/movies/politics/art/comics/horror. Fiction we use is horror and political satire. Writers don't get paid. I put in 50% of the money to get the magazine published. Others put in their efforts and energy. Don't expect too much response on getting stuff published. In case you send in something, make sure it's not over 5,000 words (approximately)."

NINTH DECADE, 12 Stevenage Rd., London SW6 6ES England. Editor: Ian Robinson. Circ. 600. Averages 3 fiction titles/year. "*Ninth Decade* is an avant-garde literary magazine publishing poetry, fiction, reviews, essays. Most material is solicited. Fiction should be innovative, avant-garde. No surrealism." Pays in copies.

NORTHERN PERSPECTIVE, Box 40146, Casuarina 0811 Australia. Fiction Editor: Dr. Lyn Riddett. Circ. 1,000. Publishes about 200 pages of fiction annually. "Publishes short stories, poems, book reviews. *Northern Perspective* is a liberal arts/literary magazine." Writers are paid and receive contributor's copies. "Strive for 'form' and style in short story; image in poetry."

OKIKE, An African Journal of New Writing, Box 53, Nsukka, Anambra, Nigeria. Founding Editor/Publisher: Chinua Achebe. Editor: Ossie Enekwe. "Literature of contemporary commitment by Africans and others for an academic/literary/general audience." Published biannually. Estab. 1971. Circ. 6,000. Needs: ethnic, experimental, literary, prose poem, serialized/excerpted novel, translations, women's. Accepts 3-4 mss/issue, 9-12 mss/year. Pays 1 free contributor's copy.

‡OPOSSUM, Waldecker Str. 19, 6000 Frankfurt 50, W. Germany. Fiction Editor: Sebastian Moll. Circ. 600. Publishes 3 or 4 issues/year. "*Opossum* is a young literary magazine, that is singular in its approach: published by a group of West German students, its main concept is multitude, multitude of style and language. Ever since the first publication in May 1988, the editors have been collecting short stories, poems and essays in German, French, English and Spanish but also comics, drawings and photography by young artists. The editors are seeking contact to American, French and Hispanic authors who are willing to contribute texts." Pays in contributor's copies.

OUTRIDER, Journal of Multicultural Literare, P.O. Box 210, Indooroopilly, Queensland 4068, Australia. Fiction Editor: Manfred Jurgensen. Circ. 1,000. Publishes approx. 20 short stories plus other prose features annually. "*Outrider* aims to extend the concept of Australian literature. It publishes literary prose, poetry and articles dealing wth literature in Australia. Translated works are welcome." Pays $10/1,000 words. "We expect a professional presentation of manuscripts (enclose self-addressed stamped envelope!). There are no restrictions on what we publish, provided it is good writing."

PANURGE (I), 22 Belle Grove West, Newcastle-on-Tyne NE2 4LT England. Fiction Editor: David Almond. Circ. 1,000. Published twice/year. Perfectbound, 120 pages. "Dedicated to short fiction by new and up-and-coming names. Each issue features several previously unpublished names. Several *Panurge* writers have been included in major anthologies, approached by agents, offered contracts by publishers. We seek work that shows vitality of language, command of form, an individual approach. We pay 1 month after publication and send 1 contributor's copy. Overseas subscription £7. Sample copy £3.50."

PEACE AND FREEDOM, 17 Farrow Rd., Whaplode Drove, Spalding, Lincs. PE12 OTS England. Fiction Editor: Paul Rance. Circ. 500+. Publishes around a dozen short stories annually. "A mixture of poetry, art, short stories, music and general features. *P and F* has a general humanism slant, as the title suggests, but good literature is judged purely as literature. Anything which is inventive, compelling, compassionate and literate will stand a chance of acceptance. Any racist, sexist, American-Russian tirades will be instantly returned." Pays in copies. "A sample copy of *P and F* costs $2 (75p SAE UK) and is advisable." Subscription—$7 (£3 UK) for 4 issues. "If we have a lot of work to read, of equal merit, then the work sent in by subscribers will be chosen first. No stories over 1,000 words, please. U.S. payment should be by I.M.O.'s—$14 (£6 UK). For that you get 8 issues and a 30 word advert free, plus other freebies, and info on the small press scene. Writers selling their work can advertise at $5 (£2 UK) for a 50 word ad, special offer to writers only."

‡PHLOGISTON (II,IV), Burning Tiger Press, Box 11-708 Manners St., Wellington, Aotearoa, New Zealand. Fiction Editor: Alex Heatley. Circ. 100. Publishes 8 stories/year. "Specializes in 'science fiction, fantasy, humor/satire,' but also considers general material." Pays in contributor's copies. "Try a copy to get our flavor, take an Alka Seltzer, then send us your best and most unusual work."

‡PROBE, SFSA, Box 79179, Senderwood, 2145, South Africa. Fiction Editor: Neil van Niekerk. Circ. 130. Publishes 8-10 stories/year. "A subscription only clubzine for South African SF fans. Very limited distribution. The clubzine is a quarterly digest-sized booklet (60-80 pages)." 8,000 words max.

PROSPICE, (formerly *The Moorlands Review*), Prospice Publishing Ltd., Box 18, Buxton, Derbyshire SK17 6YP England. Editors: J.C.R. Green and Roger Elkin. "We require good short fiction of any style, particularly literary, but not 'twee' or 'sentimental.' We are a quality literary magazine and publish work of the best quality from both established and unknown writers. Recent fiction from Ian Robinson, Gerrit Achterberg, Helga Novak, Philip Gross, Laurence Lerner, etc."

RASHI, Box 1198, Hamilton New Zealand. Editor: Norman Simms. Circ. 100. Averages 3 or 4 short stories/year. "Jewish Studies and Culture. All kinds of short fiction—usually 200-1,500 words." Pays in copies. "Remember limitations of space, and special thematic concerns." Now published as The Literary Supplement to *The New Zealand Jewish Chronicle.*

‡SCRIPSI, Ormond College, University of Melbourne, Parkville, Victoria 3052 Australia. Fiction Editor: Peter Craven. Circ. 2,500. Publishes 4-8 stories/year. *Scripsi* publishes Australian and international fiction, poetry and criticism. Pays in contributor's copies. Payment nominal.

SLOW DANCER (II), Flat 4, 1 Park Valley, The Park, Nottingham NG7 1BS England. Fiction Editors: John Harvey and Jennifer Bailey. Circ. 500. Twice yearly. Reading period November 1-April 30. Averages 1-2 short stories per issue. Pays 2 contributor's copies. Back numbers from Alan Brooks, Box 3010, RFD 1, Lubec, ME 04652 for $4. Submissions must be sent to UK.

SOCIAL ALTERNATIVES, % Dept. of Government, University of Queensland, St. Lucia, Queensland 4067 Australia. Fiction Editor: Reba Gostand. Circ. 3,000. Publishes 2-3 stories in each quarterly issue. "The journal is socio-political, but stories of any theme or style will be considered. The criterion is excellence." Pays writers "if we have money—we usually don't." Writers receive one contributor's copy. Send "3 copies of story, immaculately presented so no sub-editing is necessary. SASE for return."

STAND MAGAZINE, 179 Wingrove Rd., Newcastle Upon Tyne, NE4 9DA England. Fiction Editor: Lorna Tracy. Circ. 4,500. Averages 16-20 stories/year. "*Stand* is an international quarterly publishing poetry, short stories, reviews, criticism and translations." Payment: £30 per 1,000 words of prose on publication; contributor's copies. "Read copies of the magazine before submitting. Enclose sufficient IRCs for return of mss/reply. No more than 6 poems or 2 short stories at any one time." Sponsors biennial short competition: First prize, $1,500. Send 2 IRCs for information.

STUDIO: A JOURNAL OF CHRISTIANS WRITING (II), 727 Peel St., Albury 2640 Australia. Fiction Editor: Paul Grover. Circ. 300. Averages 20-30 stories/year. "*Studio* publishes prose and poetry of literary merit, offers a venue for new and aspiring writers, and seeks to create a sense of community among Christians writing." Pays in copies. Sample copy $8. Subscription $37 for four issues (one year). International draft in Australian dollars.

‡TAK TAK TAK, 46 Bailey St., Old Basford, Nottingham NG6 0HA England. Fiction Editors: Andrew and Tim Brown. Circ. 300. "1 or 2 magazines containing about 3 pieces of fiction each. Also 1 or 2 books each year. *Tak Tak Tak* is a paperback magazine with cassette for music and the spoken word. We use all sorts of fiction, but for reasons of space it can't be too long. (2,500 words maximum)." Pays one contributor's copy. "Send a letter explaining what you want."

TEARS IN THE FENCE (II), 38 Hod View, Stourpaine, Nr. Blandford Forum, Dorset DT11 8TN England. Editor: David Caddy. A magazine of poetry, fiction and graphics, "blended with a conservation section to develop the concepts of ecology and conservation beyond their present narrow usage." Pays £7.50 per story plus complimentary copy of the magazine. Sample copy $4.

‡THINK FOR YOURSELF/FLOWER POT PRESS, 8 Lindsay Road (2f4), Leith, Edinburgh EH6 4DT Scotland. Fiction Editor: Paul Rutherford. Circ. 500. Publishes 6-7 stories/year. "*Think For Yourself* is a small D.I.Y. (Do It Yourself) magazine covering bands, politics, fiction and humor. Published three or so times a year. Most of the stuff is about why friendships and people can't work, etc., etc. Flower Pot Press is looking for stuff to publish; anything is considered." Pays in contributor's copies.

‡TOGETHER, For all concerned with Christian Education, The National Society, Church House, Great Smith St., London SW1P 3NZ England. Editor-in-Chief: Mrs. P. Egan. Magazine of forward-looking Christian education for children under 12. Short stories, plays, services, projects, etc. Also songs, carols, occasional poems. Readers are primary school and Sunday school teachers, clergy.

VERANDAH, Victoria College, %TAS 336, Glentferrie Rd., Hawthorn, Victoria 3144 Australia. Circ. 1,000. Publishes 6-8 stories annually. "*Verandah* is an annual publication published by TAS (Toorak Assocation of Students and Victoria College). *Verandah* is edited by students of Victoria College who are majoring in writing and literature. We publish contemporary fiction (no science fiction), poetry and nonfiction and graphics. No pay for published fiction. Writers and artists receive 2 copies of each issue. Mss should be " typed, presented on A4-sized paper, double-spaced and, if author wants ms returned, a stamped, self-addressed envelope with sufficient postage must be included. We accept submissions from late February to mid-July, and *Verandah* is published in October."

VIGIL (II), (formerly *Period Piece & Paperback*), Vigil Publications, Suite 5, Somdor House Station Rd., Gillingham, Dorset SP8 4QA England. Editor: John Howard. Magazine: 5½×8½; 44 pages; illustrations. "Simply the enjoyment of varied forms of poetry and literature with an informed view of poetic technique." Plans special fiction issue. Estab. 1979. Circ. 250. Needs: experimental, literary, regional. Length: 1,500 words. Pays in contributor's copies. Contributor guidelines available for IRC. "Most of the stories we receive are banal or lacking in honesty. Well structured, vibrantly expressed work is a delight when it arrives. Freshness and originality must always find an audience."

WESTERLY, c/o University of Western Australia, Nedlands, Western Australia 6009 Australia. A quarterly of poetry, prose and articles of a literary and cultural kind, giving special attention to Australia and Southeast Asia.

WORKS, 12 Blakestones Rd., Slaithwaite, Huddersfield HD7 5UQ England. Fiction Editors: D. Hughes and A. Stewart. Circ. 1,000+. 70%+ of content is fiction. "52 pages speculative and imaginative fiction (SF) with poetry, illustrated. Published quarterly. Price: Enclose IRC. $5 *cash only* for 1 issue, $20 *cash only* for 4 issues. Member of the New Science Fiction Alliance. Pays in copies. "All manuscripts should be accompanied by a SASE (in the UK). Usual maximum is 4,500 words."

THE WRITERS' ROSTRUM (I), 14 Ardbeg Rd., Rothesay, Bute PA20 0NJ Scotland. Fiction Editor: Jenny Chaplin. Circ. 1,000. Publishes approx. 15 short stories annually. "My magazine *The Writers' Rostrum* has been described as 'cosy' and being like 'tea and cream buns on a Sunday afternoon.' From this, you will gather that I refuse to publish anything that is in any way controversial, political or obscene. Short stories are on such topics as family life, friendship, telepathy and other aspects of the supernatural. Also seasonal topics: beauties of nature, etc. Writers in Britain receive cheque (£1-£3) on publication, together with a copy of the particular issue in which their work appears. Writers abroad receive complimentary copy. Keep to the required wordage, 900 words maximum. If at all possible, study the magazine. Always send SASE and/or IRC. Where possible, I will suggest other UK markets, since my main aim is to help handicapped/beginners/retired people get started on the craft of writing and see their work published."

‡WRITING (I), 87 Brookhouse Road, Farnborough, Hants GU14 OBU England. Editor: Barbara Horsfall. Circ. 400. Publishes 12 stories/year. "Writing is for freelance writers, authors or poets. Content: articles, book reviews, short stories, verse, plus information and services for writers. Our aim is to inform and entertain." Small payment in UK: overseas writers receive contributor's copies. Offensive suggestions and lurid dialogue goes into trash can. Stories should not exceed 1,500 words. Human interest, humour, mystery, seasonal, non-political. Always interested when lifestyle of own country/area/traditions woven into story. I.R.C.'s *must* be enclosed if you would like a reply or critique.

Other literary and small circulation magazines

The following literary magazines appeared in the 1989 edition of *Novel and Short Story Writer's Market* but are not in the 1990 edition. Those publications whose editors did not respond to our request for an update of their listings may not have done so for a variety of reasons—they may be out of business, for example, or they may be overstocked with submissions. These "no responses" are listed with no additional explanation below. If an explanation was given, it appears in parenthesis next to the listing name. Note that literary magazines from outside the U.S. and Canada appear at the end of this list.

Abyss Magazine Action Time
Aethlon
Alpha Adventures SF&F
Alpha Literary Magazine
American Fiction '89
American Screamer (moved; no forwarding address)
Another Point Of View
L'Apache (asked to be left out this year)
Apalachee Quarterly
Apple Blossom Connection (no longer publishing)
Arba Sicula
Arrastra (asked to be deleted)
Backbone Magazine
Belladonna
Berkeley Fiction Review
Black Dog
Blizzard Rambler
Blonde On Blonde Magazine (no longer publishing)
Blue Sky Journal (asked to be deleted)
Book Of Contemporary Myth
Breakfast Without Meat (asked to be left out this year)
Bronte Street
Broomstick
Burning Toddlers
Calapooya Collage
California Quarterly
Calli's Tales (asked to be left out this year)
Calyx (asked to be left out this year)
Castle (asked to be deleted)
Celibate Woman
Chicago Review
Chiricu
Chronoscope (out of business)
Clifton Magazine
Compassion Magazine (no longer publishing)
Conjunctions
Connecticut Writer (submit thru contest only)
Cotton Boll/Atlanta Review
Cream City Review
Creative Spirit (no longer doing fiction)
Crystal Rainbow (asked to be left out this year)
Dark Starr (out of business)
Dark Visions (out of business)
Dekalb Literary Journal (out of business)
Dementia
Door Country Almanak
Dreamshore
DV-8 (moved; no forwarding address)
Edges
Ellipsis
emPo Magazine
Enfantaisie (asked to be left out this year)
Exit
Exquisite Corpse
Fantasy and Terror
Felicity
Feminist Studies
Fennel Stalk
Festivals (no longer publishing)
Fiction Review
Flipside
Four Quarters
Freelancer's Report (out of business)
Fright Depot
Generation
Gingerbread Diary
Goofus Office Gazette
Grand Street (contacted, no response)
Helicon Nine (out of business)
Hoofstrikes Newsletter
Horror Show
Icelandic Canadian
In Transit (out of business)
Iowa Review
Irish and American Review
Jefferson Review (out of business)
Kallisti (out of business)
Kids Lib News
Kid Times (moved; no forwarding address)
Lapis
Lime (moved; no forwarding address)
Live Letters Magazine

Mad Engineer
Magical Blend
Massachusetts Review
McGuffey Writer
Mill Hunk Herald Magazine (moved; no forwarding address)
Monocacy Valley Review
Montana Review
Monthly Independent Tribune Times Journal Post Gazette News Chronicle Bulletin
Mount Thrushmore Monument
Moving Out
the new renaissance (asked to be left out this year)
Nightmares of Reason (no longer publishing)
Nightsun
Nostoc Magazine
Ogre Magazine (asked to be deleted)
Open Wide (out of business)
Ouija Madness
Outerbridge
Pangloss Papers (out of business)
Passages North
Passages Travel Magazine (moved; no forwarding address)
Piedmont Literary Review
Pig in a Pamphlet
Plainswoman (asked to be left out this year)
Plough: North Coast Review (out of business)
P.M.
Primordial Eye
Pulpsmith (out of business)
The Quarterly (contacted, will consider next year)
RaJah
Real Fiction
ReflectionsRight Here
Ripples Magazine
Scribbler
Searching Souls Magazine (moved; no forwarding address)
II Chronicles Magazine (out of business)
Short Story Review (out of business)
Slate and Style
Snowy Egret
Sonoma Mandala
Sore Dove
Star-Web Paper
Stellanova
Stories and Letters Digest (out of business)
Streamlines (asked to be deleted)
Sub Rosa
Summerfield Journal
Tales of the Old West (moved; no forwarding address)
Tara's Literary Arts Journal (out of business)
Threepenny Review
Touchstone
Uncommon Reader (out of business)
University of Windsor Review
Voices in the Wilderness
Washington D.C. Periodical
Webster Review (out of business)
James White Review
White Walls (asked to be deleted)
William and Mary Review
Wooster Review (out of business)
World Humor and Irony Membership Serial Yearbook (no longer publishing)
Writer's Bloc (out of business)
Writer's Exchange (asked to be deleted)
Writer's Gazette (no longer publishing)
Writer's Haven Journal
Writer's in Waiting Newsletter (out of business)
Written Word (out of business)
Zone (moved; no forwarding address)

Other foreign literary and small circulation magazines

Argo
Back Brain Recluse
Boundary
Corpus Journal
Critical Quarterly
Crosscurrent (out of business)
Dark Horizons
Edinburgh Review
Fickje
Granta
Gypsy (incomplete information)
Harry's Hand (out of business)
Ido-Vivo
Inkshed
Linq
Luna
Matrix (out of business)
Nnidnid Surreality
Ore (no longer taking fiction)
Printed Matter
Scarp
Sepia
Smoke
Starkindler (moved, no forwarding address)
Stride
The World of English

Commercial Periodicals

Fiction demands for commercial periodicals generally differ from those of literary. Commercial periodicals tend to cater more to those who read mainstream popular fiction.

The majority of the magazines listed in this section do not use fiction as their primary source of text. Quite the contrary, some of the smaller specialty magazines such as *Horse Illustrated* and *Volleyball Monthly* do not publish fiction in every issue. When they do publish fiction, it is usually a short piece dealing with the specific category.

We have added over 30 new markets to this section. These markets partially consist of regional (*Maine*, *Arizona Coast*, *Ann Arbor*, *Bostonia*) as well as specialty (*Balloon Life*, *American Atheist*, *Chess Life*, *Tattoo Advocate*) publications. Major new listings this year include *Mother Jones*, which is including limited fiction as part of its new format; and *Special Report: Fiction*. Unfortunately, a variety of circumstances has also caused the loss of a few markets. *Essence*, *American Trucker* and *L.A. West* no longer publish fiction. In addition, *Southern Magazine* and *Rod Serling's The Twilight Zone Magazine* no longer publish anything—they're out of business.

This year we re-evaluated the criteria for a listing in this section. In keeping with the attitude that *commercial* means *cash*, magazines that do not offer financial compensation are no longer in this section. Also, publications with under 10,000 circulation are no longer included. Thus, 15 magazines previously listed in this section have been moved to the Literary/Small Circulation section.

Finally, keep in mind several magazines appearing in this directory in 1989 are now currently overstocked with fiction manuscripts or no longer accept unsolicited manuscripts and therefore have opted against a listing.

Essential steps for the aspiring author

In order to have a manuscript accepted as a result of using this book, it is imperative the first step be carried out: READ THE LISTINGS! The category index in the back of this book is meant to be a guide—not a sole source for submitting. Just because a particular publication is listed under a certain category does not mean everything pertaining to that category is appropriate for that publication. Numerous editors still complain about the high volume of inappropriate submissions they receive. Do *not* submit a story about a football player to *Balloon Life*, *Beckett Baseball Card Monthly* or *Bowbender*. Or, do not send a Mickey Spillane-type mystery to a feminist publication seeking suspenseful fiction. Chances are, that's not the type of suspense they're seeking. Jill Herzig of *Cosmopolitan* writes, "We would suggest that writers familiarize themselves with the publication *before* they submit, so they can determine in advance if their work is suitable for the magazine's market."

Most of the editors contacted expressed in one way or another the need for writers to *read* the magazine before actually submitting to it. Granted, it can be costly for a writer to buy a copy of every magazine he/she is interested in submitting to, but being familiar with a magazine's needs and contents may be worth the extra cost if an editor recognizes the writer's knowledge of the magazine. *Weird Tales* editor John Betancourt writes, "We receive far too many inappropriate submissions. People who want to write for us really should check out the magazine before submitting anything. Why waste your postage and our time?"

Seventeen fiction editor Adrian Nicole LeBlanc has the same simple sentiment: "It's nothing new, but read the magazine."

Make sure to pay particular attention to the "How to Contact" part of each listing, for editors' requirements differ. For example, some editors want cover letters mailed with the manuscript; some do not. Of those who want cover letters, some only want basic and biographical information and not a "selling" or "re-telling" of the story. Others appreciate a brief synopsis. "Most inquiry letters are far too long. If you can't sell me an idea in a brief paragraph, you're not going to sell the reader on reading your finished article or story," says John Gilbert, former editor of *Mature Years*. Past published credits are required by some editors before they will even look at an author's submission, but most editors we contacted said they judge a story by the story alone, regardless of who the author is.

It should go without saying how the actual submitted manuscript should appear. A professional-looking manuscript, neatly typed and double-spaced, is a must. Spelling and grammatical mistakes are a real turn-off to editors. After all, if the writer doesn't even care how the manuscript looks, why should the editor? Considering the high volume of submissions commercial periodicals receive, a professional-looking manuscript will not guarantee acceptance, but an ill-prepared one full of typos and other mistakes is a sure bet for the unread slush pile.

All editors, regardless of what type of fiction they handle, look for realistic dialogue, well-developed plots and solid characterization. They also seek subjects that are original and appropriate for the audience.

Continuing and upcoming trends

With today's Baby Boomers having children of their own, children's stories are in great demand and continue to be an area of growth. *Jack and Jill*, *Humpty Dumpty's Magazine* and *Children's Digest* are all seeking health-related material presented in an interesting manner. Children's publications such as *Seek*, *Wee Wisdom* and *On The Line* are religiously-oriented, but don't desire material "too preachy." Editors for children's literature warn that too often submitted material tends not to be worded appropriately for the particular age group of the target market. Stories for children should not be worded elaborately, but avoid "talking down" to the audience also.

More magazines for senior citizens are beginning to show up in the marketplace. Thanks to today's technology, people are living longer. As is evident by magazines such as *Mature Years*, *Arthritis Today* and *Meridian*, the potential of the over-60 market is just beginning to be realized and promises to be an area of growth for the future.

Many of our listings consist of regional publications, such as *Ann Arbor*, *Bostonia*, *Arizona Coast*, *Maine*, *Milwaukee*, *Northeast* and *Northwest*. Of course, when submitting fiction to magazines like these, it is important that the story possess a specific flavor for the particular region. Because of this requirement (being familiar with the region), those who do know the area have something of a "home court advantage."

Watch newsstands and the markets column in *Writer's Digest* for recent market trends.

To find markets in this section for particular categories of fiction, check the fiction subject index located just before the Markets Index at the back of the book.

Here's the ranking system we've used to categorize the listings in this section.

I Periodical encourages beginning or unpublished writers to submit work for consideration and publishes new writers frequently;

II Periodical publishes work by established writers and occasionally by new writers of exceptional talent;

III Magazine does not encourage beginning writers; prints mostly writers with substantial previous publication credits and a very few new writers;

IV Special-interest or regional magazine, open only to writers on certain topics or from certain geographical areas.

ABORIGINAL SCIENCE FICTION (II, IV), Box 2449, Woburn MA 01888-0849. Editor: Charles C. Ryan. 8½×11; 68 pages; 45 lb glossy paper; 100 lb cover; 4-color illustrations; photos. "*Aboriginal Science Fiction* is looking for good science fiction stories. While 'hard' science fiction will get the most favorable attention, *Aboriginal Science Fiction* also wants good action-adventure stories, *good* space opera, humor and science fantasy for adult science fiction readers." Bimonthly. Estab. 1986. Circ. 31,000-45,000.

Needs: Science fiction. Original, previously unpublished work only. "No fantasy, sword and sorcery, horror, or Twilight-Zone type stories." Receives 120-140 unsolicited mss/week. Buys 5-7 mss/issue; 30-42 mss/year. Publishes ms 6 months to 1 year after acceptance. Agented fiction 5%. Recently published work by Larry Niven, David Brin and Walter Jon Williams; published new writers within the last year. Length: 2,500 words minimum; 4,500 words maximum. Publishes short shorts "no shorter than 1,500-2,000 words for fiction. Jokes may be 50-150 words." Sometimes comments on rejected mss.

How to Contact: Send complete ms. Reports on mss in 4-10 weeks. SASE. Good quality photocopied submissions OK. Accepts computer printout submissions. Sample copy for $3.50 plus 50¢ postage and handling. Fiction guidelines for #10 SAE and 1 first class stamp.

Payment: Pays "$250 flat" and 2 contributor's copies.

Terms: Pays on publication for first North American serial rights and non-exclusive reprint and foreign options.

Advice: "Stories with the best chance of acceptance will make unique use of science ideas, have lively, convincing characters, an ingenious plot, a powerful and well integrated theme, and use an imaginative setting. We recommend you read *Aboriginal Science Fiction* to obtain an idea of the type of stories we publish, and we also recommend you read other Science Fiction publications. Watching science fiction on television or at the movies will not provide adequate experience or background to write a good science fiction story."

AIM MAGAZINE (I, II), 7308 S. Eberhart Ave., Chicago IL 60619. (312)874-6184. Editor: Ruth Apilado. Fiction Editor: Mark Boone. Newspaper: 8½×11; 48 pages; slick paper; photos and illustrations. "Material of social significance: down-to-earth gut. Personal experience, inspirational." For "high school, college and general public." Quarterly. Published special fiction issue last year; plans another. Estab. 1973. Circ. 10,000.

Needs: Open. No "religious" mss. Receives 25 unsolicited mss/month. Buys 15 mss/issue; 60 mss/year. Recently published work by Jan Brown, Alta Waddell, Jacqueline Sharpe; published new writers within the last year. Length: 800-1,000 words average. Publishes short shorts. Sometimes comments on rejected mss.

How to Contact: Send complete ms. SASE with a cover letter and author's photograph. Simultaneous submissions OK. Accepts computer printout submissions. Sample copy for $3.50 with SAE (9×12) and $1 postage. Fiction guidelines for #10 envelope and 1 first class stamp.

Payment: Pays $15-25.

Terms: Pays on publication for first rights.

Advice: "Search for those in your community who are making unselfish contributions to their community and write about them. Write from the heart."

alive now! (I, II), The Upper Room, Box 189, Nashville TN 37202-0189. (615)340-7218. Editor: Mary Ruth Coffman. Magazine of devotional writing and visuals for young adults. Bimonthly. Estab. 1971. Circ. 75,000.

Needs: Religious/inspirational. Buys 4 mss/issue; 12 mss/year. Length: 10 words minimum; 300 words maximum.

How to Contact: Send complete mss with SASE. Photocopied and previously published submissions OK. Accepts computer printout submissions. Prefers letter-quality. Reports in 3 months on mss. Sample copy free. Fiction guidelines free. Enclose SASE.

Payment: Pays $5-25; 12 contributor's copies.

Terms: Pays on publication for first rights, one-time rights, newspaper and periodical rights. Occasionally buys reprints.

ALOHA, The Magazine of Hawaii and the Pacific (IV), Davick Publishing Co., 49 South Hotel St., Suite 309, Honolulu HI 96813. (808)523-9871. Editor: Cheryl Tsutsumi. Magazine about the 50th state. Upscale demographics. Bimonthly. Estab. 1979. Circ. 65,000.

Needs: "Only fiction that illuminates the Hawaiian experience. No stories about tourists in Waikiki or beachboys or contrived pidgin dialogue." Receives 3-4 unsolicited mss/month. Length: 2,000 words average.

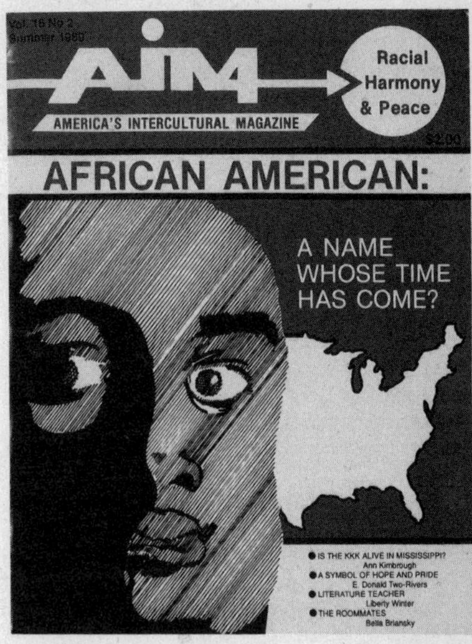

Staff artist Bill Jackson created this cover promoting Rev. Edward D. Braxton's article, "African American—A Name Whose Time Has Come?" According to editor Ruth Apilado, Aim's objective is to "promote racial harmony and peace through the written word."

How to Contact: Send complete ms. Reports in 2 months. Publishes ms up to 1 year after acceptance. SASE. Photocopied submissions OK. Accepts computer printout submissions. Letter-quality only. Sample copy $2.95.
Payment: 10¢/word minimum.
Terms: Pays on publication for all rights.
Advice: "Submit only fiction that is truly local in character. Do not try to write anything about Hawaii if you have not experienced this culturally different part of America."

AMERICAN ACCENT SHORT STORY MAGAZINE (I), Box 80270, Las Vegas NV 89180. (702)648-2669. Publisher/Editor: Marvin Gelbart. Editor: Carol Colina. Magazine: 5⅛×7¼; 176 pages; newsprint paper; 70 lb coated cover; some illustrations. "A forum for introducing new authors to the reading public—all genres." Monthly. Estab. 1988.
Needs: Adventure, contemporary, fantasy, historical, humor/satire, literary, mainstream, romance (contemporary), science fiction and suspense/mystery. Buys approx. 10 mss/issue. Recently published work by James C. McLaughlin, Earl McNevin and Harrison R. Thompson; published new writers within the last year. Length: 4,000 words preferred; 1,000 words minimum; 5,000 words maximum.
How to Contact: Send complete ms with cover letter. Reports in 16 weeks. SASE. Simultaneous and photocopied submissions OK. Sample copy for $2.25; fiction guidelines free with a #10 SASE.
Payment: Pays $50-250; contributor's copies.
Terms: Pays on publication for first North American serial rights or other rights.
Advice: "The ability to see inside every character's mind, in a given story, only confuses the reader. Writers should accept the discipline of telling a story from a single viewpoint."

AMERICAN ATHEIST (II, IV), A Journal of Atheist News and Thought, American Atheist Press, Box 140195, Austin TX 78714-0195. (512)458-1244. Editor: R. Murray-O'Hair. Magazine: 8½×11; 56 pages; 40 lb offset paper; 80 lb glossy cover; illustrations and photographs. "The *American Atheist* is devoted to the history and lifestyle of atheism, as well as critiques of religion. It attempts to promote an understanding of atheism, while staying aware of religious intrusions into modern life. Most of its articles are aimed at a general—but atheistic—readership. Most readers are college or self-educated." Monthly. Estab. 1958. Circ. 30,000.
Needs: Contemporary, feminist, historical (general), humor/satire, atheist, anti-religious. "All material should have something of particular interest to atheists." No religious fiction. Receives 0-6 mss/month. "We would like to publish 1 story per issue; we do *not* receive enough quality mss to do so." Publishes ms "1-3 months" after acceptance. Length: 2,000-3,000 words preferred; 800 words minimum; 5,000 words maximum. Sometimes critiques rejected mss.

How to Contact: Send complete ms with cover letter and biographical material. Reports in 8 weeks. SASE. Photocopied submissions OK. Accepts computer printout submissions. Accepts electronic submissions, "Word Perfect compatible or in ASCII. Should be accompanied by printout." Sample copy 9×12 SAE or label. Fiction guidelines for #10 SASE.
Payment: $15/thousand words, free subscription to the magazine and contributor's copies.
Terms: Pays on acceptance for one-time rights.
Advice: "Our magazine has a preponderance of serious 'heavy' reading matter. Sometimes our readers need a break from it. There's so little atheist fiction, we would like to encourage it."

‡THE AMERICAN CITIZEN ITALIAN PRESS, 13681 "V" St., Omaha NE 68137. Editor: Diana C. Failla. Magazine. Quarterly (soon to be monthly).
Needs: Ethnic, historical (general), humor/satire, mainstream and translations. Receives 4-5 unsolicited mss/month. Buys 1-2 mss/issue. Length: 80 words minimum; 1,200 words maximum. Publishes short shorts.
How to Contact: Send complete ms with cover letter. Reports in 1 month on queries. Simultaneous and photocopied submissions OK. Accepts computer printout submissions. Sample copy and fiction guidelines for 9×12 SAE.
Payment: Pays $15-20.
Terms: Pays on publication for one-time rights.

AMERICAN DANE (II, IV), The Danish Brotherhood in America, 3717 Harney, Box 31748, Omaha NE 68131. (402)341-5049. Editor: Pamela K. Dorau. Magazine: 8¼×11; 20-28 pages; 40 lb paper; slick cover; illustrations and photos. "The *American Dane* is the official publication of the Danish Brotherhood. Corporate purpose of the Danish Brotherhood is to promote and perpetuate Danish culture and tradition and to provide Fraternal benefits and family protection." Estab. 1916. Circ. 8,900.
Needs: "Danish!" Receives 4 unsolicited fiction mss/month. Accepts 1 ms up to one year after acceptance. Length: 1,000 words average; 3,000 words maximum. Publishes short shorts.
How to Contact: Query first. SASE. Simultaneous submissions OK. Accepts computer printout submissions. Sample copy for $1 and 9×12 SAE with 54¢ postage. Fiction guidelines free for 4×9½ SAE and 1 first class stamp.
Payment: Pays $15-50.
Terms: Pays on publication for first rights. Publication not copyrighted.
Advice: "Think Danish!"

THE AMERICAN NEWSPAPER CARRIER (II), Box 15300, Winston-Salem NC 27113. (919)760-0769. Editor: Marilyn H. Rollins. Newsletter: 9×12; 4 pages; slick paper; b&w illustrations and photos. "A motivational newsletter publishing upbeat articles—mystery, humor, adventure and inspirational material for newspaper carriers (younger teenagers, male and female)." Monthly. Estab. 1927.
Needs: Adventure, comics, humor/satire, inspirational, suspense/mystery and young adult/teen. No erotica, fantasy, feminist, gay, juvenile, lesbian, preschool, psychic/supernatural or serialized/excerpted novel. Receives approximately 12 unsolicited mss/month. Buys 1 ms/issue; 12 mss/year. "About all" of fiction is agented. Published new writers within the last year. Length: approximately 1,000 words average; 800 words minimum; 1,200 words maximum. Publishes short shorts of 1,000 words. Rarely critiques rejected mss.
How to Contact: Send complete ms. Reports in 1 month. Publishes ms 3-6 months after acceptance. SASE. Accepts computer printout submissions. Free sample copy and fiction guidelines with #10 SAE and 1 first class stamp for each.
Payment: Pays $25.
Terms: Pays on acceptance for all rights.
Advice: "We prefer that stories concern or refer to newspaper carriers. Well-written upbeat stories—happy and humorous—are rare."

The double dagger before a listing indicates that the listing is new in this edition. New markets are often the most receptive to freelance contributions.

Market categories: (I) Beginning; (II) General; (III) Prestige; (IV) Specialized.

AMERICAN SQUAREDANCE (IV), Burdick Enterprises, Box 488, Huron OH 44839. (419)433-2188. Editors: Stan and Cathie Burdick. Magazine: 5×8½; 100 pages; 50 lb offset paper; glossy 60 lb cover stock; illustrations; photos. Magazine about square dancing. Monthly. Estab. 1945. Circ. 20,000.
Needs: Adventure, fantasy, historical, humor/satire, romance, science fiction and western. Must have square dance theme. Recently published work by John Heisey, Marilyn Dove, David Stone. Buys 2+ mss/year. Length: 2,500 words average. Publishes short stories of 1,000 words average.
How to Contact: Send complete ms with SASE and cover letter with bio. Reports in 2 weeks on queries. Publishes ms within 6 months after acceptance. Free sample copy. Free fiction guidelines.
Payment: Pays $2/column inch minimum; free magazine subscription or free contributor's copies.
Terms: Pays on publication for all rights.

ANALOG SCIENCE FICTION/SCIENCE FACT (II), Davis Publications, Inc., 380 Lexington Ave., New York NY 10017. (212)557-9100. Editor: Stanley Schmidt. Magazine: 5$^{3}/_{16}$×7⅜; 192 pages; illustrations (drawings); photos. "Well written science fiction based on speculative ideas and fact articles on topics on the present and future frontiers of research. Our readership includes intelligent laymen and/or those professionally active in science and technology." Thirteen times yearly. Estab. 1930. Circ. 100,000.
Needs: Science fiction and serialized novels. "No stories which are not truly science fiction in the sense of having a plausible speculative idea *integral to the story*." Buys 4-8 mss/issue. Receives 300-500 unsolicited fiction mss/month. Publishes short shorts. Approximately 30% of fiction is agented. Recently published work by Isaac Asimov, Ben Bova and Michael F. Flynn; published new writers within the last year. Length: 2,000-80,000 words. Critiques rejected mss "when there is time." Sometimes recommends other markets.
How to Contact: Send complete ms with SASE. Cover letter with "anything that I need to know before reading the story, e.g. that it's a rewrite I suggested or that it incorporates copyrighted material. Otherwise, no cover letter is needed." Query with SASE only on serials. Accepts computer printout submissions. Prefers letter-quality. Reports in 1 month on both query and ms. Free guidelines with SASE. Sample copy for $2.50.
Payment: 5¢-8¢/word.
Terms: Pays on acceptance for first North American serial rights and nonexclusive foreign rights. Sends galleys to author.
Advice: Mss are rejected because of "inaccurate science; poor plotting, characterization or writing in general. We literally only have room for 1-2% of what we get. Many stories are rejected not because of anything conspicuously *wrong*, but because they lack anything sufficiently *special*. What we buy must stand out from the crowd. Fresh, thought-provoking ideas are important. Familiarize yourself with the magazine—but don't try to imitate what we've already published."

‡ANN ARBOR (IV), Serving Ann Arbor, Miotke Media & Marketing Inc. 477 N. Dixie, Monroe MI 48161. (313)242-8788. Editor: Mike Tunison. Magazine: 8½×11; 44-50 pages; 70 lb glossy paper; 80 lb cover stock; illustrations and photos. Regional writers about region in title. Monthly.
Needs: Historical (general) and regional. Receives 25 unsolicited mss/month. Buys 1 ms/issue; 10 mss/year. Publishes ms 2-3 months after acceptance. Length: 4,000 words minimum; 4,000 words maximum; 1,000 words average.
How to Contact: Query first. Reports in 3 weeks on queries; 5 weeks on mss. SASE. Simultaneous, photocopied and reprint submissions OK. Accepts computer printout submissions. Sample copy for 9×12 SAE and 4 first class stamps. Fiction guidelines for #10 SAE and 1 first class stamp.
Payment: Up to $25, free subscription and contributor's copies.
Terms: Pays on publication for one-time rights.

ARETE (I,II), Forum for Thought, 405 W. Washington St., Suite 418, San Diego CA 92103. (619)237-0074. Fiction/Poetry Editor: Erica Lowe. Magazine. Published 6 times/year. Estab. 1988. Circ. 40,000.
Needs: Condensed/excerpted novel, contemporary, ethnic, literary, mainstream and translations. Recently published work by David Leavitt, Rita Mae Brown, Wendell Berry. Receives 500 unsolicited fiction mss/month. Buys 1-2 fiction mss/issue; 12 fiction mss/year. Publishes ms 2-5 months after acceptance. Agented fiction 10%. Length: 2,500 words preferred; 1,000 words minimum; 4,000 words maximum.
How to Contact: Editors highly suggest contributors read the magazine before submitting. Send complete ms with cover letter. Reports in 6-8 weeks on mss. SASE required. Accepts photocopied and simultaneous submissions, "as long as we know." Accepts dot-matrix computer printout submissions. Sample copy for $2.95. Fiction guidelines for SASE.
Payment: Pays $300-2,000.
Terms: Pays before publication for one-time rights. Sends pre-publication galleys to author "if requested."

‡ARIZONA COAST (II), Hale Conmmunications, Inc., 912 Joshua, Parker AZ 85344. (602)669-6464. Editor: Jerry Hale. Magazine: 5½×8½; 40 pages; gloss 70#; illustrations; photos. Publication prints stories about tourism, old West, lifestyle for young travel oriented family audiences, showbirds and senior citizens. Bimonthly. Estab. 1988. Circ. 15,000.
Needs: Condensed/excerpted novel, historical (general), senior citizen/retirement, serialized novel, western. Receives 1 unsolicited mss/month. Accepts 1 ms/issue; 6 mss/year. Publishes ms within 6 months after acceptance. Publishes short shorts. Sometimes critiques rejected mss and recommends other markets.
How to Contact: Send complete ms with cover letter. Reports in 2 months. Simultaneous submissions OK. Computer printout submissions are acceptable. Accepts electronic submissions. Sample copy free.
Payment: Free subscription to magazine. Buys one-time rights.

ART TIMES (II), A Cultural and Creative Journal, CSS Publications, Inc., 7484 Fite Rd., Saugerties NY 12477. (914)246-6944. Editor: Raymond J. Steiner. Magazine: 12×15; 20 pages; Jet paper and cover; illustrations; photos. "Arts magazine covering the disciplines for an over 40, affluent, arts-conscious and literate audience." Monthly. Estab. 1984. Circ. 15,000.
Needs: Adventure, contemporary, ethnic, fantasy, feminist, gay, historical, humor/satire, lesbian, literary, mainstream and science fiction. "We seek quality literary pieces. No violence, sexist, erotic, juvenile, racist, romantic, political, etc." Receives 25-30 mss/month. Buys 1 ms/issue; 11 mss/year. Publishes ms within 14-16 months of acceptance. Length: 1,500 words maximum. Publishes short shorts.
How to Contact: Send complete ms with cover letter. Reports in 6 months. SASE. Simultaneous and photocopied submissions OK. Accepts computer printout submissions; also electronic submissions via disk. Sample copy for $1.75, 9×12 SAE and 3 first class stamps. Fiction guidelines for #10 SAE and 1 first class stamp.
Payment: Pays $15, free subscription to magazine (one year); six contributor's copies.
Terms: Pays on publication for first North American serial rights.

ARTHRITIS TODAY (II), Publication of the Arthritis Foundation, Arthritis Foundation, 1314 Spring St. NW, Atlanta GA 30309. (404)872-7100. Editor: Cindy T. McDaniel. Magazine: 60+ pages; 45 lb coated paper; 70 lb coated cover; color illustrations and photos. Publishes material relating to "better living with arthritis; general health and the older years." Estab. 1987. Circ. 700,000.
Needs: Adventure, historical, humor/satire, senior citizen/retirement, health/arthritis. "Fiction should appeal to an older audience; direct reference to arthritis is not required, but might increase chances of acceptance." Receives 12-15 unsolicited mss/month. Buys 1 ms/issue; 4-5 mss/year. Publishes ms up to 1 year after acceptance. Recently published work by Charles Nicholson, Lorraine Jolian Cazin, Ray Lipay. Length: 1,000-2,500 words preferred. Publishes 250-500 word short shorts. Sometimes critiques rejected mss and recommends other markets.
How to Contact: Query with clips of published work or submit complete ms with cover letter. Reports in 6 weeks. SASE preferred. Simultaneous, photocopied and reprint submissions OK. Accepts dot-matrix computer printouts. Sample copy and fiction guidelines free.
Payment: Pays $250 minimum; $900 maximum; contributor's copies.
Terms: Pays on acceptance for one-time rights, plus unlimited reprint rights in any Arthritis Foundation publication. Offers 25% kill fee.
Advice: "Become familiar with the book—know the type article we print. Don't send articles that are clearly irrelevant or aimed at the wrong audience."

ISAAC ASIMOV'S SCIENCE FICTION MAGAZINE (II), Davis Publications, Inc., 380 Lexington Ave., New York NY 10017. Editor: Gardner Dozois. Magazine: 5³⁄₁₆×7⅜ (trim size); 192 pages; 29 lb newspaper; 70 lb to 8 pt CIS cover stock; illustrations; rarely photos. Magazine consists of science fiction and fantasy stories for adults and young adults. 13 issues a year. Estab. 1977. Circ. 120,000.
Needs: Science fiction and fantasy. No horror or psychic/supernatural. Buys 10 mss/issue. Publishes short shorts. Receives approximately 800 unsolicited fiction mss each month. Approximately 30% of fiction is agented. Recently published work by George Alec Effinger, Walter Jon Williams, Gregory Benford and Judith Moffett; published new writers in the last year. Length: up to 20,000 words. Critiques rejected mss "when there is time." Sometimes recommends other markets.
How to Contact: Send complete ms with SASE. Photocopied submissions OK. Accepts letter-quality computer printout submissions only. Reports in 1-2 months on mss. Publishes ms 6-12 months after acceptance. Free fiction guidelines with #10 SASE. Sample copy $2.

Read the Business of Fiction section to learn the correct way to prepare and submit a manuscript.

Payment: 6¢-8¢/word for stories up to 7,500 words; 5¢/word for stories over 12,500; $450 for stories between those limits.
Terms: Pays on acceptance for first North American serial rights plus specified foreign rights, as explained in contract. Very rarely buys reprints. Sends galleys to author.
Advice: We are "looking for character stories rather than those emphasizing technology or science. New writers will do best with a story under 10,000 words. Every new science fiction or fantasy film seems to 'inspire' writers—and this is not a desirable trend. We consider every submission. We published several first stories last year. Be sure to be familiar with our magazine and the type of story we like; workshops and lots of practice help."

THE ASSOCIATE REFORMED PRESBYTERIAN (II), The Associate Reformed Presbyterian, Inc., 1 Cleveland St., Greenville SC 29601. (803)232-8297. Editor: Ben Johnston. Magazine: 8½×11; 32-48 pages; 50 lb offset paper; illustrations; photos. "We are the official magazine of our denomination. Articles generally relate to activities within the denomination—conferences, department work, etc., with a few special articles that would be of general interest to readers." Monthly. Estab. 1976. Circ. 7,000.
Needs: Contemporary, juvenile, religious/inspirational, spiritual and young adult/teen. "Stories should portray Christian values. No retelling of Bible stories or 'talking animal' stories. Stories for youth should deal with resolving real issues for young people." Receives 30-40 unsolicited fiction mss/month. Buys 1 ms/some months; 10-12 mss/year. Publishes ms within 1 year after acceptance. Recently published work by Martha Washam, William Crenshaw, Sara McDonald, published new writers within the last year. Length: 300-750 words (children); 1,250 words maximum (youth). Sometimes critiques rejected mss. Occasionally recommends other markets.
How to Contact: Query and cover letter preferred. Reports in 6 weeks on queries and mss. Simultaneous submissions OK. Sample copy $1.50; fiction guidelines for #10 SAE and 1 first class stamp.
Payment: Pays $20-50 and contributor's copies.
Terms: Buys first rights.

ATLANTA SINGLES MAGAZINE, Sigma Publications, 3423 Piedmont Dr. NE, Suite 320, Atlanta GA 30305. (404)239-0642. Editor: Margaret Anthony. Magazine: 8½×11; 80 pages; 50 lb paper; 80 lb cover; illustrations; photographs. "Magazine for singles; publishes mostly nonfiction work by local writers. Occasional fiction, but not often." Bimonthly. Estab. 1977. Circ. 15,000.
Needs: Contemporary, humor/satire, single life. No sci-fi or erotica. Receives 20-25 unsolicited mss/month. Accepts up to 3-5 mss/year. Publishes ms 3-6 months after acceptance. Length: 1,500 words average; 1,000 words minimum; 2,500 words maximum. Sometimes critiques rejected mss and recommends other markets.
How to Contact: Query first or send complete ms with cover letter. "Include a short bio and areas of interest in cover letter." Reports in 1 month. SASE. Simultaneous, photocopied and reprint submissions OK. Accepts computer printout submissions, including dot-matrix. Sample copy for $2. Fiction guidelines free.
Payment: Pays $100-300.
Terms: Pays on publication for one-time rights.

THE ATLANTIC ADVOCATE (I, II, IV), University Press of New Brunswick Ltd., Box 3370, Fredericton, New Brunswick E3B 5A2 Canada. (506)452-6671. Editor: Marilee Little. Magazine: 8¼×10⅞; 64 pages; coated offset paper and cover; illustrations; photos. Magazine of the Atlantic Provinces of Canada—Nova Scotia, New Brunswick, Prince Edward Island and Newfoundland. For "audience 25 years and over." Monthly. Estab. 1956. Circ. 30,000.
Needs: Historical (general), humor/satire and regional. Nothing "offensive or in poor taste." Recently published work by Elda Cadogan, Eric Cameron and Muriel Miller. Receives 5 unsolicited mss/month. Buys 20 mss/year. "I plan to publish more short stories—at least one piece of fiction per issue." Length: 1,000-1,200 words average; 1,500 words maximum. Occasionally comments on rejected mss.
How to Contact: Send in mss. Reports in 3-4 weeks. Accepts computer printout submissions. Prefers letter-quality. Fiction guidelines free.
Payment: Pays 8¢-10¢/word and contributor's copies; charge for extras.
Terms: Pays on publication for first North American serial rights.

ATLANTIC MONTHLY (II), 745 Boylston St., Boston MA 02116. (617)536-9500. Editor: William Whitworth. Senior Editor: Michael Curtis. General magazine for the college educated with broad cultural interests. Monthly. Estab. 1857. Circ. 500,000.
Needs: Literary and contemporary. "Seeks fiction that is clear, tightly written with strong sense of 'story' and well-defined characters." Buys 15-18 stories/year. Receives approximately 1,000 unsolicited fiction mss each month. Recently published work by Alice Munro, E.S. Goldman, Charles Baxter and T.C. Boyle; published new writers within the last year. Preferred length: 2,000-6,000 words.

How to Contact: Send cover letter and complete ms with SASE. "Grudgingly" accepts dot-matrix submissions. Prefers letter-quality. Reports in 2 months on mss.
Payment: $2,500/story.
Terms: Pays on acceptance for first North American serial rights.
Advice: When making first contact, "cover letters are sometimes helpful, particularly if they cite prior publications or involvement in writing programs. Common mistakes: excessive cuteness, too lengthy a list of prior publications."

ATLANTIC SALMON JOURNAL (IV), The Atlantic Salmon Federation, 1435 St. Alexandre #1030, Montreal, Quebec H3A 2G4 Canada. (514)842-8059. Editor: Terry Davis. Magazine: 8½×11; 48-56 pages; 140 lb stock; 140 lb cover; illustrations; photographs. Conservation of Atlantic salmon: History, research, angling, science and management articles for conservationists, biologists, anglers and politicians. Quarterly. Estab. 1952. Circ. 20,000.
Needs: Historical (general), humor/satire. Receives 2-3 unsolicited mss/month. Buys 2 mss/issue. Publishes ms 2-6 months after acceptance. Length: 2,000-3,000 words average; 1,500 words minimum; 3,000 words maximum. Publishes short shorts.
How to Contact: Query with clips of published work or send complete manuscript with cover letter. Reports in 4-6 weeks on queries; 6-8 weeks on mss. SASE. Simultaneous submissions OK. Accepts computer printout submissions, no dot-matrix. Accepts electronic submissions via IBM floppy diskette, Wordstar or Word-Perfect. Sample copy for 9×12 SAE and 51¢ postage. Fiction guidelines for #8 or #10 SAE and 39¢ postage.
Payment: Pays $50-350 and contributor's copies.
Terms: Pays on publication for first rights or first North American serial rights.

‡BALLOON LIFE, The Magazine for Hot Air Ballooning (II,IV), 3381 Pony Express Dr., Sacramento CA 95834. (916)922-9648. Editor: Glen Moyer. Magazine: 8½×11; 48+ pages; 80 lb Tahoe Gloss; color, b&w photos. "Sport of hot air ballooning. Readers participate in hot air ballooning as pilots, crew, official observers at events and spectators."
Needs: Humor/satire, sports and hot air ballooning. "Manuscripts should involve the sport of hot air ballooning in any aspect." Buys 4-6 mss/year. Publishes ms within 3-4 months after acceptance. Recently published work by Carl Kohler and Lorna Powers; published new writers within the last year. Length: 800 words minimum; 1,500 words maximum; 1,200 words average. Publishes 400-500 word short shorts. Length: 400-500 words. Sometimes critiques rejected mss and recommends other markets.
How to Contact: Send complete ms with cover letter that includes Social Security number. Reports in 3 weeks on queries; 2 weeks on mss. SASE. Simultaneous, photocopied and reprint submissions OK. Accepts computer printout submissions. Sample copy for 9×12 SAE and $1.65 postage. Fiction guidelines for #10 SAE and 1 first class stamp.
Payment: Pays $25-75 and contributor's copies.
Terms: Pays on publication for first North American serial, one-time or other rights. 50-100% kill fee.
Advice: "Generally the magazine looks for humor pieces that can provide a light-hearted change of pace from the technical and current event articles. An example of a work we used was titled 'Balloon Astrology' and dealt with the character of a hot air balloon based on what sign it was born (made) under."

BALTIMORE JEWISH TIMES (II, IV), 2104 N. Charles St., Baltimore MD 21218. (301)752-3504. Magazine: 160 pages a week, average; illustrations; photos. Magazine with subjects of interest to Jewish readers. Weekly. Estab. 1918. Circ. 19,000.
Needs: Contemporary Jewish themes only. Receives 7-10 unsolicited fiction mss/month. Buys 10-15 mss/year. Length: 3,500 words maximum (or 6-15 typed pages). Occasionally critiques rejected mss.
How to Contact: Send complete ms. Simultaneous, photocopied and previously published submissions OK "on occasion." Accepts computer printout submissions; prefers letter-quality. Reports in 2 months on mss. Sample copy $2 and legal-size envelope.
Payment: Pays $35-150.
Terms: Pays on publication.

‡BEAR (IV), Masculinity . . . without the trappings, COA, 2215 R Market St. #148, San Francisco CA 94114. (415)552-1506. Editor: Richard H. Bulger. Magazine: 60-120 pages; Vista paper; 70 lb gloss cover stock; illustrations and photos. "Bear is about the average American working man—who happens to be gay. For gay men 25-55." Bimonthly. Estab. 1987. Circ. 20,000.
Needs: Confession, erotica, gay, humor/satire and serialized novel. "Must be sex-positive. Don't make a big deal about an individual's sexual preference. Use masculine American archetypes. No youth-oriented fiction; sex-negative or self-hating pieces; leather sex." Plans to publish special fiction issue or anthology in the future. Receives 10-15 unsolicited mss/month. Buys 1-2 mss/issue. Publishes ms 3-6 months after acceptance. Recently published work by Jay Shaffer, Furr and Ed Bishop. Length: 500

words minimum; 3,000 words average. Publishes short stories. Sometimes critiques rejected mss and recommends other markets.
How to Contact: Send complete ms with cover letter that includes Social Security number. Reports in 2-3 weeks on queries; 1-2 months on mss. SASE. Simultaneous, photocopied and reprint submissions OK. Accepts computer printout submissions. Prefers electronic submissions via disk or modem. Sample copy $6. Fiction guidelines for #10 SAE and 1 first class stamp.
Payment: Pays $25-150 and three contributor's copies for all rights (prefer), first North American serial and first rights.
Terms: Pays half on acceptance, half on publication. 50% kill fee.

BECKETT BASEBALL CARD MONTHLY (IV), Statabase, 4887 Alpha Rd., Suite 200, Dallas TX 75244. (214)991-6657. Editor: Dr. James Beckett. Fiction Editor: Fred Reed. Magazine: 8½×11; 96 pages; coated glossy paper; 8 pt. Sterling cover; 12 illustrations; 100+ photographs. "Collecting baseball cards is a leisure-time avocation. It's wholesome and something the entire family can do together. We emphasize its positive aspects. For card collectors and sports enthusiasts, 6-60." Monthly. Estab. 1984. Circ. 465,000 paid.
Needs: Humor/satire, juvenile (5-9 years), sports, young adult/teen (10-18 years). "Sports hero worship; historical fiction involving real baseball figures; fictionalizing specific franchises of national interest such as the Yankees, Dodgers or Mets." No fiction that is "unrealistic sportswise." Publishes ms 4-6 months after acceptance. Length: 1,500 words average; 2,500 words maximum. Publishes short shorts. Sometimes comments on rejected mss or recommends other markets "if we feel we can help the reader close the gap between rejection and acceptance."
How to Contact: Send complete ms with cover letter. Include Social Security number. Reports in 6 weeks. SASE. Will consider reprints "if prior publication is in a very obscure or very prestigious publication." Accepts dot-matrix computer printouts; accepts electronic submissions via IBM ASCII files. Sample copy $3. Fiction guidelines free.
Payment: Pays $80-400.
Terms: Pays on acceptance for first rights.
Advice: "Fiction must be baseball oriented and accessible to both pre-teenagers and adults; fiction must stress redeeming social values; fictionalization must involve the heroes of the game (past or present) or a major-league baseball franchise with significant national following. The writer must have a healthy regard for standard English usage. A prospective writer must examine several issues of our publication prior to submission. Our publication is extremely successful in our genre, and our writers must respect the sensivities of our readers. We are different from other sports publications and a prospective writer must understand our distinctiveness to make a sale here."

BIKE REPORT (I, IV), Bikecentennial, Box 8308, Missoula MT 59807. (406)721-1776. Editor: Daniel D'Ambrosio. Magazine on bicycle touring: 8½×11; 24 pages; coated paper; self cover; illustrations and b&w photos. 9 times yearly. Estab. 1974. Circ. 15,000.
Needs: Adventure, fantasy, historical (general), humor/satire, regional and senior citizen/retirement with a bicycling theme. Buys variable number mss/year. Published new writers within the last year. Length: 2,000 words average; 1,000 words minimum; 2,500 words maximum. Publishes short shorts. Occasionally comments on a rejected ms.
How to Contact: Send complete ms with SASE. Reports in 6 weeks on mss. Simultaneous, photocopied and previously published submissions OK. Accepts computer printout submissions. Prefers letter-quality. Prefers hard copy with disk submission. Sample copy for $1, 9×12 SAE and 60¢ postage. Fiction guidelines free for #10 SAE and 1 first class stamp.
Payment: Pays 3¢/word.
Terms: Pays on publication for first North American serial rights.

BLACK BELT (II), Rainbow Publications, Inc., 1813 Victory Place, Burbank CA 91504. (818)843-4444. Executive Editor: Jim Coleman. Magazine: 106 pages. Emphasizes "martial arts for both practitioner and layman." Monthly. Circ. 100,000.
Needs: Martial arts-related, historical and modern-day. Buys 1-2 fiction mss/year. Publishes ms 3 months to one year after acceptance. Recently published work by Glenn Yancey.
How to Contact: Query first. Reports in 1 month. Photocopied submissions OK. Accepts computer printout submissions, "prefers letter quality."
Payment: Pays $100-175.
Terms: Pays on publication for first North American serial rights, retains right to republish.

THE B'NAI B'RITH INTERNATIONAL JEWISH MONTHLY (IV), 1640 Rhode Island Ave. NW, Washington DC 20036. (202)857-6645. Editor: Jeff Rubin. Magazine: 8⅛×10⅞; 48-56 pages; coated stock; illustrations; photos. Subjects of Jewish interest—politics, culture, lifestyle, religion—for a Jewish family audience. 10 times annually. Estab. 1886.

Needs: Contemporary, ethnic, historical (general), humor/satire. No immigrant memoirs; holocaust memoirs. Receives 2 unsolicited mss/month. Buys 2 mss/year. Publishes ms 6 months to 1 year after acceptance. Length: 2,500 words average; 1,000 words minimum; 5,000 words maximum. Occasionally critiques rejected mss. Recommends other markets.

How to Contact: Reports in 1 month on queries; 6 weeks on mss. Include cover letter and SASE. Accepts computer printout submissions. Accepts electronic submissions via disk or modem. Sample copy $1.

Payment: Pays $100-$750.

Terms: Pays on publication for first North American serial rights. Sends galleys to author.

Advice: "A writer who submits a manuscript without a cover letter doesn't seem to have an awareness of interest in our publication. Cover letters should include a sentence or two of biographical information (publishing credits) and an introduction to the story."

BOSTON REVIEW (II), Boston Critic Inc., 33 Harrison Ave., Boston MA 02111. Publisher/Editor: Margaret Ann Roth. "A bimonthly magazine of the arts and culture." Tabloid: 11×17; 24-32 pages; jet paper. Estab. 1975. Circ. 10,000.

Needs: Contemporary, ethnic, experimental, humor/satire, literary, mainstream, prose poem, regional, serialized/excerpted novel, sports and translations. Receives 100+ unsolicited fiction mss/month. Buys 4-6 mss/year. Recently published work by Joyce Carol Oates, Yasunari Kawabata, Christopher Coe. Length: 3,000 words maximum; 2,000 words average. Publishes short shorts. Occasionally critiques rejected ms.

How to Contact: Send complete ms with cover letter and SASE. "You can almost always tell professional writers by the very thought-out way they present themselves in cover letters. But even a beginning writer should find some link between the work (its style, subject, etc.) and the publication—some reason why the editor should consider publishing it." Simultaneous and photocopied mss OK. Accepts computer printout submissions. Reports in 2-3 months on mss. Publishes ms an average of 4 months after acceptance. Sample copy $3.

Payment: $50-200 and 2 contributor's copies.

Terms: Pays on publication for first rights. Publication copyrighted.

Advice: "We believe that original fiction is an important part of our culture—and that this should be represented by the *Boston Review*. We have embarked on a more vigorous fiction program—including a special effort to work with new writers."

‡BOSTONIA MAGAZINE (IV), The magazine of culture and ideas, Boston University, 10 Lenox St., Brookline MA 02146. (617)353-3081/2917. Editor: Lori Calabro. Fiction Editor: Kathleen Cahill. Magazine: 8½×11; 72-80 pages; 60 lb paper; 80 lb cover stock. "Thoughtful provocative prose for audience mostly in New England." Bimonthly. Estab. 1900. Circ. 140,000.

Needs: Adventure, condensed/excerpted novel, contemporary, ethnic, experimental, horror, humor/satire, literary, mainstream, regional, serialized novel and suspense/mystery. "Writer either must live in New England or story must be set in New England." Plans to publish special fiction issue or anthology in the future. Receives 5-10 unsolicited mss each month. Buys 1 ms/issue; 6 mss/year. Recently published work by Sebastian Junger, Kitty Burns Florey and Jonathan Webster. Length: 3,000 words average; 1,500 words minimum; 4,000-5,000 words maximum.

How to Contact: Send complete ms with cover letter. Reporting time varies. SASE. Sample copy $2.50. Free fiction guidelines.

Payment: Pays $400-700, contributor's copies, charges for extras.

Terms: Pays on acceptance for first North American serial rights.

BOWBENDER (II, IV), Canada's Archery Magazine, Box 912, Carstairs, Alberta T0M 0N0 Canada. (403)337-3023. Editor: Kathleen Windsor. Magazine: 8¼×10⅞; 48 pages; 60 lb gloss stock; 100 lb gloss cover; illustrations; photos. "We publish material dealing with hunting, wildlife, conservation, equipment, nature and Olympic team coverage etc., for outdoorsmen, especially hunters and competitive archers." Published 5 times/year. Estab. 1984. Circ. 45,000.

Needs: Adventure, sports and western. "*Might* publish fiction if it concerns (bow) hunting, archery or traveling in the Canadian outdoors." Does not want to see anything veering off the topic of archery in Canada. Publishes ms within 1 year after acceptance. Length: 2,000 words average; 500 words minimum; 3,000 words maximum.

How to Contact: Query first or send complete manuscript with cover letter, which should include a brief autobiography (archery) to be included in the magazine. Reports in 1 week on queries; 2 weeks on mss. SASE for ms. Photocopied submissions OK. Accepts computer printout submissions. Sample copy for $2.95 (Canadian), 9×12 SAE and $1.12 (Canadian postage). Editorial/Photography guidelines for #10 SAE and 38¢ (Canadian), 25¢ (U.S.) postage.

Payment: Pays $300 maximum. (Roughly 10¢/word depending on regularity of submission, quality photo complement, etc.) Free contributor's copies; charge for extras.
Terms: Pays on publication for first North American serial rights, or first Canadian if requested and acceptable.
Advice: "Fiction remains a 'big' maybe. Write for guidelines and review a sample copy first."

BOWHUNTER MAGAZINE (IV), The Magazine for the Hunting Archer, Cowles Magazines, Inc., 2245 Kohn Rd., Box 8200, Harrisburg, PA 17105. (717)657-9555. Editor: M.R. James. Executive Editor: Dave Canfield. Magazine. 8¼×10¾; 150 pages; 75 lb glossy paper; 150 lb glossy cover stock; illustrations and photographs. "We are a special interest publication for people who hunt with the bow and arrow. We publish hunting adventure and how-to stories. Our audience is predominantly male, 30-50, middle income." Bimonthly. Circ. 230,000.
Needs: Bowhunting, outdoor adventure. "Writers must expect a very limited market. We buy only one or two fiction pieces a year. Writers must know the market—bowhunting—and let that be the theme of their work. No 'me and my dog' types of stories; no stories by people who have obviously never held a bow in their hands." Receives 1-2 unsolicited fiction mss/month. Buys 1-2 mss/year. Publishes ms 3 months to 2 years after acceptance. Length: 2,000 words average; 500 words minimum; 3,000 words maximum. Publishes short shorts. Length: 500. Sometimes critiques rejected mss and recommends other markets.
How to Contact: Query first or send complete ms with cover letter. Reports in 2 weeks on queries; 6 weeks on mss. Accepts computer printout submissions. Sample copy for $2 and 8½×11 SAE with appropriate postage. Fiction guidelines for #10 SAE and 1 first class stamp.
Payment: $25-250; free subscription to the magazine, if requested; contributor's copies, if requested up to 6; charge for extras, half price over 6.
Terms: Pays on acceptance for first North American serial rights.
Advice: "We have a resident humorist who supplies us with most of the 'fiction' we need. But if a story comes through the door which captures the essence of bowhunting and we feel it will reach out to our readers, we will buy it. Despite our macho outdoor magazine status, we are a bunch of English majors who love to read. You can't bull your way around real outdoor people—they can spot a phony at 20 paces. If you've never camped out under the stars and listened to an elk bugle and try to relate that experience without really experiencing it, someone's going to know. We are very specialized; we don't want stories about shooting apples off people's heads or of Cupid's arrow finding its mark. James Dickey's *Deliverance* used bowhunting metaphorically, very effectively . . . while we don't expect that type of writing from everyone, that's the kind of feeling that characterizes a good piece of outdoor fiction."

BOYS' LIFE (III), For All Boys, Boy Scouts of America, Magazine Division, 1325 Walnut Hill Lane, Box 152079, Irving TX 75015-2079. (214)580-2000. Editor-in-Chief: William B. McMorris. Fiction Editor: William E. Butterworth IV. Magazine: 8×11; 68 pages; slick cover stock; illustrations; photos. "*Boys' Life* covers Boy Scout activities and general interest subjects for ages 8 to 18, Boy Scouts, Cub Scouts and others of that age group." Monthly. Estab. 1911. Circ. 1,500,000.
Needs: Adventure, humor/satire, science fiction, suspense/mystery, western and sports. "We publish short stories aimed at a young adult audience and frequently written from the viewpoint of a 10- to 16-year-old boy protagonist." Receives approximately 100 unsolicited mss/month. Buys 12-18 mss/year. Recently published work by Donald J. Sobol, Maureen Crane Wartski, Raboo Rodgers; published new writers within the last year. Length: 500 words minimum; 2,500 words maximum; 2,000 words average. "Very rarely" critiques rejected ms.
How to Contact: Send complete ms with SASE. "We'd much rather see manuscripts than queries." Simultaneous and photocopied submissions OK. Prefers letter-quality type. Reports in 2 weeks on mss. For sample copy "check your local library." Writer's guidelines available; send SASE.
Payment: Pays $500 and up, "depending on length and writer's experience with us."
Terms: Pays on acceptance for one-time rights.
Advice: "*Boys' Life* writers understand the reader. They treat them as intelligent human beings with a thirst for knowledge and entertainment. We tend to use many of the same authors repeatedly because their characters, themes, etc., develop a following among our readers."

BREAD (II), Church of the Nazarene, 6401 The Paseo, Kansas City MO 64131. (816)333-7000. Editor: Karen De Sollar. Magazine: 8½×11; 34 pages; illustrations; photos. Christian leisure reading magazine for junior and senior high students. Monthly.
Needs: Adventure and how-to stories on Christian living. Themes should be school and church oriented. Adventure stories wanted, but without sermonizing. Buys 25 mss/year. Does not read in summer. Recently published work by Alan Cliburn and Betty Steele Everett; published new writers within the last year.

How to Contact: Send complete ms with SASE. Reports in 6 weeks on mss. Free sample copy and guidelines for SASE.
Payment: Pays 3½¢/word for first rights and 3¢/word for second rights.
Terms: Pays on acceptance for first rights and second serial rights. Accepts simultaneous submissions. Byline given.
Advice: "Our readers clamor for fiction."

BUFFALO SPREE MAGAZINE (II, IV), Spree Publishing Co., Inc., 4511 Harlem Rd., Buffalo NY 14226. (716)839-3405. Editor: Johanna V. Shotell. Fiction Editor: Gary L. Goss. "City magazine for professional, educated and above-average income people." Quarterly. Estab. 1967. Circ. 21,000.
Needs: Literary, contemporary, feminist, mystery, adventure, humor and ethnic. No pornographic or religious. Buys 10 mss/issue, 40 mss/year. Length: 1,800 words maximum.
How to Contact: Send complete ms with SASE. Reports within 3 to 6 months on ms. Sample copy for $2 with 9×12 SASE and $2.40 postage.
Payment: $50-125; 1 free author's copy.
Terms: Pays on publication for first rights.

BUGLE (II), The Quarterly Journal of the Rocky Mountain Elk Foundation, Box 8249, Missoula MT 59807. Editor: Lance Schelvan. Magazine: 8½×11; 92-156 pages; 70 lb gloss paper; 80 lb gloss cover; illustrations; 4-color photos. Publishes material on "elk and the future of elk across the North American continent, for elk hunters, hunters in general and conservationists." Quarterly. Estab. 1984. Circ. 120,000.
Needs: Adventure, condensed novel, experimental, historical, humor/satire, western. Receives 40-50 unsolicited fiction mss/month. Publishes ms 3-6 months after acceptance. Recently published work by John Haviland, M. Andrew Taylor; published new writers within the last year. Length: 2,000 words average; 1,500 words minimum; 3,000 words maximum. Publishes short shorts. Sometimes recommends other markets.
How to Contact: Send complete ms with cover letter, which should include short biographical sketch of author. Reports in 2-3 weeks. Simultaneous, photocopied and reprint submissions OK. Accepts computer printouts. Sample copy for $4; fiction guidelines free.
Payment: Free subscription to magazine and contributor's copies.
Advice: "Stay away from 'formula' outdoor writing."

CAMPUS LIFE MAGAZINE (II), Christianity Today, Inc., 465 Gundersen Drive, Carol Stream IL 60188. (312)260-6200. Managing Editor: James Long. Senior Editor: Christopher Lutes. Magazine: 8¼×11¼; 100 pages; 4-color and b&w illustrations; 4-color and b&w photos. "General interest magazine with a religious twist. Not limited strictly to Christian content." Articles "vary from serious to humorous to current trends and issues, for high school and college age readers." Monthly. Plans special fiction issue. Estab. 1942. Circ. 130,000.
Needs: Condensed novel, fantasy, humor/satire, prose poem, science fiction, serialized/excerpted novel and young adult. Prefers "realistic situations. We are a Christian magazine but are *not* interested in sappy, formulaic, sentimentally religious stories. We *are* interested in well crafted stories that portray life realistically, stories high school and college youth relate to. Nothing contradictory of Christian values. If you don't understand our market and style, don't submit." Receives 30 unsolicited fiction mss/month. Buys 5 mss/year. Reading and response time slower in summer. Recently published work by Barbara Durkin. Length: 1,000-3,000 words average, "possibly longer." Publishes short shorts.
How to Contact: Query with short synopsis of work, published samples and SASE. Simultaneous, photocopied and previously published submissions OK. Reports in 4-6 weeks on queries. Sample copy $2 and 9½×11 envelope.
Payment: Pays "generally" $250-400; 2 contributor's copies.
Terms: Pays on acceptance for one-time rights.
Advice: "We print finely crafted fiction that carries a contemporary teen (older teen) theme. First person fiction often works best. Ask us for sample copy with fiction story. Fiction communicates to our reader. We want to encourage fiction writers who have something to say to or about young people without getting propagandistic."

CANADIAN MESSENGER (IV), Apostleship of Prayer, 661 Greenwood Ave., Toronto, Ontario M4J 4B3 Canada. (416)466-1195. Editors: Rev. F.J. Power, S.J.; Alfred De Manche. Magazine: 7×10; 32 pages; glossy paper; self cover; illustrations; photos. Publishes material with a "religious theme or a moral about people, adventure, heroism and humor, for Roman Catholic adults." Monthly. Estab. 1891. Circ. 17,000.

Needs: Religious/inspirational. Receives 10 mss/month. Buys 1 ms/issue. Publishes ms within 1-1½ years of acceptance. Length: 500 words minimum; 1,500 words maximum.
How to Contact: Send complete ms with cover letter. Reports on mss in "a few" weeks. SASE. Accepts computer printout submissions. Sample copy for $1. Fiction guidelines for $1 and 7½×10½ SAE.
Payment: Pays 4¢/word.
Terms: Pays on acceptance for first North American rights.

CAPPER'S (II), Stauffer Communications, Inc., 616 Jefferson, Topeka KS 66607. (913)295-1108. Editor: Nancy Peavler. Magazine: 24-48 pages; newsprint paper and cover stock; photos. A "clean, uplifting and nonsensational newspaper for families from children to grandparents." Biweekly. Estab. 1879. Circ. 400,000.
Needs: Serialized novels. "We accept only novel-length stories for serialization. No fiction containing violence or obscenity." Buys 2-3 stories/year. Receives 2-3 unsolicited fiction mss each month. Recently published work by Cleoral Lovell, Ellie Watson McMasters, Betty Jarmusch; published new writers within the last year. Sometimes recommends other markets.
How to Contact: Send complete ms with SASE. Cover letter and/or synopsis helpful. Reports in 5-6 months on ms. Sample copy 75¢.
Payment: $150-200 for one-time serialization. Free author's copies (1-2 copies as needed for copyright).
Terms: Pays on acceptance for second serial (reprint) rights and one-time rights.
Advice: "Be patient. Send SASE. Copy your work before sending–mss do get lost!"

CAT FANCY (IV), Fancy Publications, Box 6050, Mission Viejo CA 92690. (714)855-8822. Editor-in-Chief: K.E. Segnar. General cat and kitten magazine, consumer oriented for cat and kitten lovers. Published monthly. Circ. 321,000.
Needs: Cat-related themes only. Receives approximately 60 unsolicited fiction mss/month. Accepts 12 mss/year. Approximately 10% of fiction agented. Recently published work by Barbara L. Diamond, Edward W. Clarke and Sandi Fisher. Published new writers within the last year. Length: 3,000 words maximum. Sometimes recommends other markets.
How to Contact: Send complete ms with SASE. Simultaneous and photocopied submissions OK. Reports in 2 months. Publishes ms 2-10 months after acceptance. Sample copy $3.50. Free fiction guidelines with SASE.
Payment: 5¢/word and 2 contributor's copies. $3.50 charge for extras.
Terms: Rarely buys reprints.
Advice: "Stories should focus on a cat or cats, not just be about people who happen to have a cat. No anthropomorphism. Carefully review the publication, especially the short stories we have published before, and study our writer's guidelines."

CATHOLIC FORESTER (I, II, III), Catholic Order of Foresters, 425 W. Shuman Blvd., Box 3012, Naperville IL 60566-7012. (708)983-4920. Editor: Barbara Cunningham. Magazine: 8¼×10¾; 40 pages; 45 lb paper and 60 lb cover stock; illustrations; photos. "No special theme but we want interesting, lively stories and articles. No true confessions type, no dumb romances. People who have not bothered to study the art of writing need not apply." Bimonthly. Estab. 1884. Circ. 160,000.
Needs: Adventure, contemporary, ethnic, feminist, humor/satire, mainstream, regional, senior citizen/retirement, sports and suspense/mystery. Receives 200 unsolicited fiction mss/month. Buys approximately 4 mss/issue; 25 mss/year. "Publication may be immediate or not for 4-5 months." Agented fiction: 5%. Recently published work by John Keefauver. Length: 2,000 words average; 3,000 words maximum. Also publishes short shorts. Occasionally critiques rejected mss. Sometimes recommends other markets.
How to Contact: Send complete ms. "Cover letters extolling the virtue of the story do not help–manuscripts stand or fall on their own merit. I do not accept queries anymore–too many problems in authors misunderstanding 'speculation.'" SASE for ms. Simultaneous, photocopied submissions and reprints OK. Sample copy for 8½×11 SAE and 73¢ postage. Fiction guidelines for #10 SASE.
Payment: Pays 5¢ minimum; and one contributor's copy. Author may request more copies–no charge.
Advice: "I enjoy a short, friendly cover letter but do not appreciate a long letter telling me the author's personal history, past credits, a complicated synopsis of the story enclosed, and his/her opinion of it. The only thing that counts is the quality and suitability of the story itself. I do make short comments occasionally on rejection slips but cannot go into great detail. Before submitting a story, act out some of your scenes to see if they make sense–speak your dialogue aloud to assure that it is realistic. Ask yourself 'is this how people really talk to each other?' Also, every rejection doesn't mean that the editor thinks the story is bad. It may just simply not fit the publication's readers, or that our space is limited."

CAVALIER MAGAZINE (II), Dugent Publishing Corp., 2355 Salzedo St., Coral Gables FL 33134. (305)443-2378. Editor: Douglas Allen. Fiction Editor: M. DeWalt. Magazine: 8½×11; 103 pages; 60 lb paper; laminated cover stock; illustrations; photos. Sexually oriented, sophisticated magazine for single men aged 18-35. Published special fiction issue last year; plans another. Monthly. Estab. 1952. Circ. 250,000.

Needs: Adventure, horror and erotica. No material on children, religious subjects or anything that might be libelous. Buys 3 mss/issue. Receives approximately 200 unsolicited fiction mss each month. Recently published work by Janris Manley, Dillon McGrath, Wayne Rogers; published new writers within the last year. Length: 1,500-3,000 words. Critiques rejected mss "when there is time." Sometimes recommends other markets.

How to Contact: Send complete ms with SASE. A cover letter is not necessary except if ms is a multiple submission or there's special information. Accepts computer printout submissions. Prefers letter-quality. Reports in 3-6 weeks on mss. Sample copy for $3. Free fiction guidelines with SASE.

Payment: $200-300. Offers 50% kill fee for assigned mss not published.

Terms: Pays on publication for first North American serial rights.

Advice: Mss are rejected because writers "either don't know our market or the manuscripts are too long or too short. Length and erotic content are crucial (erotica in *every* story). Fiction is often much sexier and more imaginative than photos. If you are a poor speller, grammarian or typist, have your work proofread. Ask for our guidelines and follow them. Occasionally sponsors contests . . . watch publication."

CHANGES, For Adult Children, U.S. Journal Inc., 3201 SW 15th St., Deerfield Beach FL 33442. (305)360-0909. Associate Editor: Andrew Meacham. Managing Editor: Jeffrey Laign. Magazine: 8½×11; 80 pages; slick paper; glossy cover; illustrations; photos. "Fiction often deals with recovery from dysfunctional families. Readers are children of alcoholics and other dysfunctional families." Bimonthly. Estab. 1986. Circ. 60,000.

Needs: "Quality, professional fiction, typed, double-spaced." Receives 30 mss/month. Buys 1-3 mss/issue. Publishes ms within several months of acceptance. Agented fiction 5%. Recently published work by Lloyd Skloot, Elizabeth Benedict. Length: 2,000 words maximum. Publishes short shorts. Sometimes critiques rejected mss and recommends other markets.

How to Contact: Query with clips of published work or send complete ms with cover letter which should include Social Security number and "a short professional bio." Reports in 6 weeks. SASE. Simultaneous submissions OK. Accepts computer printout submissions. Sample copy for SAE. Fiction guidelines for #10 SAE and 1 first class stamp.

Payment: Pays 15¢/word.

Terms: Pays on publication for first North American serial rights. Publication copyrighted.

Advice: "Too much of the fiction we read is superficial and imitative. We're looking for bold new writers who have something to say. A too-subtle message is better than a predictable one."

CHESAPEAKE BAY MAGAZINE (II, IV), Chesapeake Bay Communications, Inc., 1819 Bay Ridge Ave., Annapolis MD 21403. (301)263-2662. Editor: Jean Waller. Magazine: 8½×11½; 88 pages; coated stock paper; coated cover stock; illustrations; photos. "*Chesapeake Bay Magazine* is a regional publication for those who enjoy reading about the Bay and its tributaries. Most of our articles are boating-related. Our readers are yachtsmen, boating families, fishermen, ecologists, anyone who is part of Chesapeake Bay life." Monthly. Estab. 1971. Circ. 32,000.

Needs: Fantasy, mystery, adventure, humor and historical. "Any fiction piece *must* concern the Chesapeake Bay. Only stories done by authors who are familiar with the area are accepted. No general type stories with the Chesapeake Bay superimposed in an attempt to make a sale." Buys 4 short stories/year. Receives approximately 3 unsolicited fiction mss each month. Recently published work by Gilbert Byron and Arline Chase. Published new writers within the last year. Length: 1,250-3,000 words. Publishes short shorts.

How to Contact: Query or send ms, including cover letter with bio information to indicate familiarity with our publication. SASE always. Reports in 1 month on queries, 2 months on mss. Publishes ms an average of 12-14 months after acceptance. Sample copy $2. Free fiction guidelines with SASE.

Payment: Pays $85-125. 2 free author's copies.

Terms: Pays on publication for all rights or first North American serial rights.

Advice: "Make sure you have knowledge of the area. Send only material that is related to our market. All manuscripts must be typed, double-spaced, in duplicate. Our readers are interested in any and all material about the Chesapeake Bay area. Thus we use a limited amount of fiction as well as factual material. Work must be fairly short, or have clear break-points for serialization."

CHESS LIFE (IV), U.S. Chess Federation, 186 Route 9W, New Windsor NY 12550. (914)562-8350. Editor: Julie Anne Desch. Magazine: 8¼×10¾; 68 pages; slick paper; illustrations and photos. "Chess: news, theory, human interest, for chess players (mostly male)." Monthly. Circ. 58,000.

Needs: "Chess must be central to story." Receives 3 unsolicited mss/month. Accepts 2 mss/year. Publishes short shorts. Occasionally critiques rejected mss.
How to Contact: Query first. Sample copy and fiction guidelines free.

CHIC (II), Larry Flynt Publications, 9171 Wilshire Blvd., Suite 300, Beverly Hills CA 90210. Executive Editor: Allan MacDonell. Magazine: 100 pages; illustrations; photos. "Men's magazine, for men and women." Monthly. Estab. 1976. Circ. 100,000.
Needs: Erotica. Receives 20-30 unsolicited mss/month. Buys 1 ms/issue; 12 mss/year. Publishes ms 1-6 months after acceptance. Published new writers within the last year. Length: 3,500 words average; 3,000 words minimum; 4,000 words maximum. Occasionally critiques rejected mss. Recommends other markets.
How to Contact: Send complete manuscript with cover letter, which should include "writer's name, address, telephone number and whether the manuscript has been or is being offered elsewhere." Reports in 4-6 weeks. SASE for ms. Photocopied submissions OK. Accepts computer printout submissions. Fiction guidelines free for SASE.
Payment: Pays $500.
Terms: Pays on acceptance for all rights.
Advice: "Readers have indicated a desire to read well written erotic fiction, which we classify as a good story with a sexual undercurrent. The writer should read several published short stories to see the general tone and style that we're looking for. The writer should keep in mind that the first requirement is that the story be a well written piece of fiction, and secondarily that it deal with sex; we are not interested in 'clinically descriptive' sex accounts."

CHICKADEE (II), The Magazine for Young Children from OWL, Young Naturalist Foundation, 56 The Esplanade, Suite 306, Toronto, Ontario M5E 1A7 Canada. (416)868-6001. FAX (416)868-6009. Editor-in-Chief: Sylvia Funston. Magazine: 8½×11¾; 32 pages; glossy paper and cover stock; illustrations and photographs. "*Chickadee* is created to give children under nine a lively, fun-filled look at the world around them. Each issue has a mix of activities, puzzles, games and read-aloud stories." Monthly except July and August. Estab. 1979. Circ. 130,000.
Needs: Juvenile. No fantasy, religious or anthropomorphic material. Buys 1 ms/issue; 10 mss/year. Recently published work by Harriet Webster, Patti Farmer and Sue Pace; published new writers within the last year. Length: 200 words minimum; 800 words maximum; 500 words average. Recommends other markets.
How to Contact: Send complete ms and cover letter with $1 to cover postage and handling. Reports in 2 months. Publishes ms an average of 1 year after acceptance. Sample copy for $3.25. Free fiction guidelines for SAE.
Payment: Pays $25-350; 1 free contributor's copy.
Terms: Pays on publication for all rights. Occasionally buys reprints.
Advice: "We are looking for shorter stories that contain a puzzle, mystery, twist or tie-in to a puzzle that follows on the next spread. Make sure the story has a beginning, middle and an end. This seems simple, but it is often a problem for new writers."

CHILD LIFE, The Benjamin Franklin Literary & Medical Society, Inc., Box 567, 1100 Waterway Blvd., Indianapolis IN 46206. (317)636-8881. Editor: Steve Charles. Juvenile magazine for youngsters ages 8-11. Looking for adventure, humor, contemporary situations, folk and fairy tales and stories that deal with an aspect of health, nutrition, exercise (sports) or safety.
Needs: Juvenile. No adult or adolescent fiction. Recently published work by Nancy Sweetland, Ben Westfried, Toby Speed and Carole Forman. Published new writers within the last year. Length: 1,200 words maximum.
How to Contact: Send complete ms with SASE. Reports in 8-10 weeks. Sample copy 75¢. Free writer's guidelines with SASE.
Payment: Approximately 8¢/word for all rights.
Terms: Pays on publication.
Advice: "Always keep in mind your audience's attention span and interests: grab their attention quickly, be imaginative, and try to make your dialogue free and as natural as possible."

CHILDREN'S DIGEST (II), Children's Better Health Institute, Box 567, 1100 Waterway Blvd., Indianapolis IN 46206. Editor: Elizabeth A. Rinck. Magazine: 6½×9; 48 pages; reflective and preseparated illustrations; color and b&w photos. Magazine with special emphasis on health, nutrition, exercise and safety for pre-teens.
Needs: "Realistic stories, short plays, adventure and mysteries. We would like to see more stories that reflect today's society: concern for the environment, single-parent families and children from diverse backgrounds. Humorous stories are highly desirable. We especially need stories that *subtly* encourage readers to develop better health or safety habits. Stories should not exceed 1,500 words."

Receives 40-50 unsolicited fiction mss each month. Recently published work by Charles Ghigna, Frances Gorman Risser and Julia Lieser; published new writers within the last year.
How to Contact: Send complete ms with SASE. A cover letter isn't necessary unless an author wishes to include publishing credits and special knowledge of the subject matter. Sample copy 75¢. Queries not needed. Reports in 10 weeks. Free guidelines with SASE.
Payment: Pays approximately 8¢/word with up to 10 free author's copies.
Terms: Pays on publication for all rights.
Advice: "We try to present our health-related material in a positive—not a negative—light, and we try to incorporate humor and a light approach wherever possible without minimizing the seriousness of what we are saying. Fiction stories that deal with a health theme need not have health as the primary subject but should include it in some way in the course of events. Most rejected health-related manuscripts are too preachy or they lack substance. Children's magazines are not training grounds where authors learn to write 'real' material for 'real' readers. Because our readers frequently have limited attention spans, it is very important that we offer them well written stories."

CHILDREN'S PLAYMATE, The Benjamin Franklin Literary & Medical Society, Inc., Box 567, 1100 Waterway Blvd., Indianapolis IN 46206. (317)636-8881. Editor: Elizabeth A. Rinck. Magazine: 6½×9; 48 pages; preseparated and reflective art; b&w and color illustrations. Juvenile magazine for children ages 6-8 years.
Needs: Juvenile with special emphasis on health, nutrition, safety and exercise. "Our present needs are for short, entertaining stories with a subtle health angle. Seasonal material is also always welcome." No adult or adolescent fiction. Receives approximately 150 unsolicited fiction mss each month. Recently published work by Nancy Gotter Gates, Kathleen Nekich, Jean Leedale Hobson and Marge O'Harra; published new writers within the last year. Length: 700 words or less. Indicate word count on material.
How to Contact: Send complete ms with SASE. Accepts computer printout submissions. Prefers letter-quality. Reports in 8-10 weeks. Sample copy for 75¢.
Payment: Approximately 8¢/word and up to 10 free author's copies.
Terms: Pays on publication for all rights.
Advice: "Stories should be kept simple and entertaining. Study past issues of the magazine—be aware of vocabulary limitations of the readers."

CHRISTIAN LIVING FOR SENIOR HIGHS (IV), David C. Cook Publishing Co., 850 N. Grove, Elgin IL 60120. (312)741-2400. Editor: Douglas Schmidt. A take-home Sunday school paper: 8½×11; 4 pages; Penegra paper and cover; full color illustrations and photos. For senior high classes. Weekly.
Needs: Christian spiritual. Writers work mostly on assignment. "Each piece must present some aspect of the Christian life without being preachy. No closing sermons and no pat answers. Any topic appropriate to senior high is acceptable." Buys 5-10 mss/year. Length: 900-1,200 words.
How to Contact: Send complete ms with SASE. No queries please. Cover letter with brief bio, religious credentials and experience with senior highs. Reports in 2 months on mss. Free guidelines with SASE.
Payment: Pays $100-125.
Terms: Pays on acceptance for all rights.
Advice: "You've got to know kids and be aware of the struggles Christian kids are facing today. Don't write about how things were when you were a teenager—kids don't want to hear it."

CHRISTMAS (IV), The Annual of Christmas Literature and Art, Augsburg Fortress, 426 S. 5th St., Box 1209, Minneapolis MN 55440. (612)330-3300. Editor: Gloria Bengtson. Fiction Editor: Jennifer Huber. Magazine: 10⅜×13¾; 64 pages; illustrations and photographs. "Christmas—its history, celebration, traditions, music, customs, literature. For anyone who observes Christmas, especially its religious significance." Annually. Estab. 1931.
Needs: Ethnic, historical (general), literary, mainstream, prose poem, religious/inspirational, Christmas. No romance, horror, gay, lesbian. Receives 40 unsolicited mss/month. Buys 2-3 mss/issue. Publishes ms 1-3 years after acceptance. Length: 5,000 words preferred.
How to Contact: Send complete ms with cover letter. Reports in 2 weeks on queries; 2-10 weeks on mss. SASE. Simultaneous and reprint submissions OK. Sample copy for $7.95. Fiction guidelines for #10 SAE and 1 first class stamp.
Payment: Pays $150-300. Free contributor's copies; charge for extras. Pays on acceptance. Purchases all rights, first rights and one-time rights.

THE CHURCH HERALD (II), 6157 28th St. SE, Grand Rapids MI 49546-6999. (616)957-1351. Editor: John Stapert. Managing Editor: Jeffrey Japinga. Magazine: 8½×11; 48 pages. "We deal with religious themes and other reflections of a faith in God for a general audience, most members of the Reformed Church in America." Monthly. Estab. 1944. Circ. 47,000.

Needs: Prose poem, religious/inspirational, spiritual. Length: 1,200-1,800. Sometimes critiques rejected mss and may recommend other markets. Recently published work by Louis Lotz, James Schaap.
How to Contact: Send query with story synopsis and anticipated length. Reports in 6 weeks on queries. SASE. Accepts computer printout submissions.
Payment: Pay varies according to length.
Terms: Pays on acceptance for all rights, first rights, first North American serial rights and one-time rights.

THE CHURCH MUSICIAN (IV), The Sunday School Board of the Southern Baptist Convention, 127 9th Ave. N., Nashville TN 37234. (615)251-2961. Editor: William M. Anderson Jr. "*The Church Musician* is for church music leaders in local churches—music directors, pastors, organists, pianists, choir coordinators, and members of music councils and/or other planning committees or groups. Music leaders read the magazine for spiritual enrichment, testimonials, human interest stories and other materials related to music programs in local churches." Monthly. Estab. 1950. Circ. 20,000.
Needs: Categories related to church music. Receives 1-2 unsolicited fiction mss each month. Length: 750-2,000 words.
How to Contact: Send complete ms with SAE. Reports in 2 months on ms. Free sample copy with SAE and 30¢ postage. No simultaneous submissions.
Payment: Maximum 5¢ per word.
Terms: Pays on acceptance for all rights. Publication copyrighted.
Advice: "Avoid mushy sentiment when writing. It must be believable and, of course, practical." Many mss are rejected because they are "too long, too general, too sweet and sentimental, shallow."

CLUBHOUSE (II), Your Story Hour, Box 15, Berrien Springs MI 49103. (616)471-3701. Editor-in-Chief: Elaine Trumbo. Magazine: 6×9; 32 pages; 60 lb offset paper; self cover stock; illustrations and some photos. "A Christian magazine designed to help young people feel good about themselves. Our primary goal is to let them know there is a God and that He loves kids. Stories are non-moralistic in tone and full of adventure." Readers are "children 9-14 years old. Stories are selected for the upper end of the age range. Primary audience—kids without church affiliation." Published 6 times/year. Estab. 1951 under former name *The Good Deeder*. Circ. 15,000.
Needs: Adventure, contemporary, historical (general), religious, young adult/teen. No Christmas stories that refer to Santa, elves, reindeer, etc. No Halloween/occult stories. Receives 250+ unsolicited fiction mss/month. Buys 6 mss/issue, 40 mss/year. Reads mss in March-April only. Published new writers within the last year. Length: 1,000-1,200 words. Occasionally critiques rejected mss. Occasionally recommends other markets.
How to Contact: Send complete ms, starting in April. SASE always. Simultaneous and photocopied submissions and previously published work OK. Accepts computer printout submissions; prefers letter-quality. Reports in 2 months on queries and mss. Publishes ms 6-18 months after acceptance. Free sample copy with 6×9 SAE and 3 first class stamps. Free fiction guidelines with #10 SAE and 1 first class stamp.
Payment: Pays $25-35 and contributor's copies.
Terms: Pays on acceptance for any rights offered. Buys reprints.
Advice: "Especially interested in stories in which children are responsible, heroic, kind, etc., not stories in which children are pushed into admitting that a parent, sibling, friend, etc., was right all along. I want upbeat, fun, exciting stories. Do not mention church, Sunday School, etc., just because this is a Christian magazine. General tone of the magazine is warmth, not criticism. Remember that a story should follow a plot sequence and be properly wrapped up at the end. Most stories I reject involve kids who have regrettable turns of behavior which they finally change, appeal to a too-young age group, are preachy, are the wrong length or lack sparkle. Fiction can be more exact than truths, because details can be fashioned to complete the plot which might by necessity be omitted if the account were strictly factual."

‡COASTAL CRUISING, New World Publishing Group, Inc. 814 Arendell St., Morehead City NC 28557. (919)247-4183. Editor: Ted Jones. Magazine: 8½×11; 64 pages; 60 lb hard finish paper; slides, prints, b&w. "Pleasure cruising in boats in North American coastal waters for all ages, relatively affluent." Monthly. Estab. 1986.
Needs: Adventure, humor/satire and sports (boating). "We have a very limited interest in fiction which must relate to 'coastal cruising.' Recent titles published: 'Ashley's Big Fish,' 'The Winking Urns,' 'A Burning Experience.'" Receives 1 unsolicited ms/month. Buys 3-6 mss/year. Publishes ms 3-6 months after acceptance. Recently published work by John A. Norris and Jan Murphy. Length: 6,000 words maximum. Publishes short shorts. Sometimes critiques rejected mss.

How to Contact: Query first. Reports in 2 weeks on queries; 6 weeks on mss. Photocopied and reprint submissions OK. Accepts computer printout submissions. Sample copy free.
Payment: Pays $75-300 and contributor's copies.
Terms: Pays on acceptance or publication for first North American serial or one-time rights.

COBBLESTONE: The History Magazine for Young People (IV), Cobblestone Publishing, Inc., 30 Grove St., Peterborough NH 03458. (603)924-7209. Editor-in-Chief: Carolyn P. Yoder. History magazine for children (ages 8-14): 7×9; 48 pages; 4-color covers; illustrations; b&w photos. Monthly with a national distribution.
Needs: Adventure, historical, regional and biographical fiction, reminiscences, plays and retold folk tales. *Must* relate to month's theme. Published new writers within the last year. Length: 500-1,500 words.
How to Contact: Simultaneous and previously published submissions OK. Accepts computer printout submissions. Publishes ms an average of 6 weeks after acceptance. Sample copy $3.95, enclose 7½×10½ (or larger) SASE. Free guidelines with SASE.
Payment: Pays 10-15¢/word.
Terms: Pays on publication. Buys all rights. Buys reprints. Makes work-for-hire assignments.
Advice: "Request an editorial guideline sheet that explains the upcoming issue themes and gives query deadlines. Prefer queries to unsolicited manuscripts. We publish fiction (usually one story per issue) as it pertains to the issue's theme. Write as much as possible. Don't give up. Be true to your own style; don't try to write like other writers. Look to other writers for inspiration."

COMPUTOREDGE (IV), San Diego's MicroComputer Magazine, The Byte Buyer, Inc., Box 83086, San Diego CA 92138. (619)573-0315. Editors: Tina Berke and Wally Wang. Magazine: 8½×11; 100 pages; newsprint paper; 50 lb bookwrap cover; illustrations and photos. Publishes material relating to "personal computers from a human point of view. For new users/shoppers." Biweekly. Estab. 1983. Circ. 75,000+.
Needs: Confession, feminist, humor/satire, science fiction, computers. "*Really* has to speak to our audience/readership; new computer user/first-time shopper; new and enthusiastic about computing." Receives up to 3 unsolicited fiction mss/month. Buys 3 fiction mss/year. Publishes ms 1-9 months after acceptance. Length: 800 words minimum; 1,500 words maximum.
How to Contact: Send complete ms with cover letter. Include Social Security number and phone number. Reports in 1 month. SASE. Photocopied and reprint submissions OK. Accepts dot-matrix computer printouts if near-letter quality. Electronic submission of *accepted* mss encouraged. Sample copy for 9x12 SAE and $1.50 postage; writer's guidelines for #10 SAE and 1 first class stamp.
Payment: Pays 10¢/word.
Terms: Pays on publication for first rights or first North American serial rights. Offers $15 kill fee.
Advice: Magazine fiction today is "too trendy. Reader should be able to come away from article moved, enlightened, edified."

‡CONTACT ADVERTISING, Box 3431, Ft. Pierce FL 34948. (407)464-5447. Editor: Jerome Phillips. Fiction Editor: Diamond Delaney. Magazines and newspapers. Publications vary in size, 40-56 pages. "Group of 14 erotica, soft core publications for swingers, single males, married males." Bimonthly, quarterly and monthly. Estab. 1975. Circ. combined is 60,000.
Needs: Erotica, fantasy, feminist, gay and lesbian. Receives 8-10 unsolicited mss/month. Buys 1-2 mss/issue; 40-50 mss/year. Publishes ms 1-3 months after acceptance. Length: 2,000 words minimum; 3,500 words maximum; 2,500-3,500 words average. Sometimes critiques rejected mss and recommends other markets.
How to Contact: Query first, query with clips of published work or send complete ms with cover letter. Reports in 1-2 weeks on queries; 3-4 weeks on mss. SASE. Simultaneous, photocopied and reprint submissions OK. Accepts computer printout submissions. Sample copy for $6. Fiction guidelines free.
Payment: Pays $25-75, free subscription to magazine and three contributor's copies.
Terms: Pays on publication for all rights or first rights. Sends galleys to author if requested.
Advice: "Content must be of an adult nature but well within guidelines of the law. Fantasy, unusual sexual encounters, swinging stories or editorials of a sexual bend are acceptable."

COSMOPOLITAN MAGAZINE (III), The Hearst Corp., 224 W. 57th St., New York NY 10019. (212)649-2000. Editor: Helen Gurley Brown. Fiction Editor: Betty Kelly. Associate Fiction Editor: Gail Greiner. Most stories include male-female relationships, traditional plots, characterizations. Single career women (ages 18-34). Monthly. Circ. just under 3 million.
Needs: Contemporary, romance, mystery and adventure. "Stories should include a romantic relationship and usually a female protagonist. The characters should be in their 20s or 30s (i.e., same ages as our readers). No highly experimental pieces. Upbeat endings." Buys 1 short story plus a novel or book

excerpt/issue. Approximately 98% of fiction is agented. Recently published excerpts by Danielle Steel, Pat Booth and Belva Plain; published new writers within the last year. Length: short shorts (1,500 words); longer (2,000-4,000 words). Occasionally recommends other markets.
How to Contact: Send complete ms with SASE. Accepts computer printout submissions. Free guidelines with legal-sized SASE. Publishes ms 6-18 months after acceptance.
Payment: Pays $750-2,000.
Terms: Pays on acceptance for first North American serial rights. Buys reprints.
Advice: "It is rare that unsolicited mss are accepted. We tend to use agented, professional writers. The majority of unsolicited short stories we receive are inappropriate for *Cosmo* in terms of characters used and situations presented, or they just are not well written."

COUNTRY WOMAN (IV), Reiman Publications, Box 643, Milwaukee WI 53201. (414)423-0100. Editor: Ann Kaiser. Managing Editor: Kathleen Pohl. Magazine: 8½×11; 68 pages; excellent quality paper; excellent cover stock; illustrations and photographs. "Articles should have a rural theme and be of specific interest to women who live on a farm or ranch, or in a small town or country home, and/or are simply interested in country-oriented topics." Bimonthly. Estab. 1971. Circ. 650,000.
Needs: Fiction must be upbeat, heartwarming and focus on a country woman as central character. "Many of our stories and articles are written by our readers!" Recently published work by Rob Goubeaux, Kate Thiel and Donna Scofield; published new writers within last year. Payment for fiction: $90-125. Publishes 1 fiction story per issue and 6-8 profiles per issue. Payment is on acceptance. All articles/stories – 750-1,000 words.
How to Contact: Query first. Reports in 2-3 months. Include cover letter and SASE. Simultaneous, photocopied and reprint submissions OK. Accepts computer printout submissions. Sample copy and writer's guidelines for $2 and SASE. Guidelines for #10 SASE.
Terms: Pays on acceptance for one-time rights.

CRICKET MAGAZINE (II), Carus Corporation, Box 300, Peru IL 61354. (815)223-1500. Publisher/Editor-in-Chief: Marianne Carus. Magazine: 7×9; 64 pages; groundwood paper; #1 enamel cover stock; illustrations; photos. Magazine for children, ages 6-12. Monthly. Estab. 1973. Circ. 110,000.
Needs: Juvenile, including literary, contemporary, science fiction, historic fiction, fantasy, western, mystery, adventure, humor, ethnic and translations. No adult articles. Buys 10-20 mss/year. Receives approximately 500 unsolicited fiction mss each month. Approximately 1-2% of fiction is agented. Length: 500-1,500 words.
How to Contact: Do not query first. Send complete ms with SASE. List previous publications. Reports in 3 months on mss. Publishes ms 6-24 months after acceptance. Sample copy $2. Free guidelines with SASE.
Payment: Up to 25¢/word; 2 free author's copies. $1.25 charge for extras.
Terms: Pays on publication for first North American serial rights and one-time rights. Sends edited mss for approval. Buys reprints.
Advice: "Do not write *down* to children. Write about subjects you are familiar with which have been well researched. Children *need* fiction and fantasy. Carefully study several issues of *Cricket* before you submit your manuscript." Published new writers within the last year. Sponsors contests for children, ages 6-12.

CRUSADER MAGAZINE (II), Calvinist Cadet Corps, Box 7259, Grand Rapids MI 49510. (616)241-5616. Editor: G. Richard Broene. Magazine: 8½×11; 24 pages; 50 lb white paper and cover stock; illustrations; photos. Magazine to help boys ages 9-14 discover how God is at work in their lives and in the world around them. 7 issues/year. Estab. 1958. Circ. 12,000.
Needs: Adventure, comics, confession, ethnic, juvenile, religious/inspirational, science fiction, spiritual and sports. Receives 60 unsolicited fiction mss/month. Buys 3 mss/issue; 18 mss/year. Recently published work by Sigmund Brouwer, Alan Cliburn and Betty Steele Everett. Length: 800 words minimum; 1,500 words maximum; 1,200 words average. Publishes short shorts.
How to Contact: Send complete ms and SASE with cover letter including theme of story. Simultaneous, photocopied and previously published submissions OK. Accepts computer printout submissions. Prefers letter-quality. Reports in 3 weeks on mss. Publishes ms 4-11 months after acceptance. Free sample copy with a 9×12 SAE and 3 first class stamps. Free fiction guidelines with #10 SAE and 1 first class stamp.
Payment: Pays 2-5¢/word; 1 free contributor's copy.
Terms: Pays on acceptance for one-time rights. Buys reprints.
Advice: "On a cover sheet list the point your story is trying to make. Our magazine has a theme for each issue, and we try to fit the fiction to the theme."

‡DETROIT JEWISH NEWS, 27676 Franklin Rd., Southfield MI 48034. (313)354-6060. Associate Editor: Alan Hitsky. Newspaper: 120+ pages; illustrations and photos. Jewish news. Weekly. Estab. 1942. Circ. 20,000.

Needs: "For fiction, we prefer articles on any subject with a Jewish flavor." Receives 3-4 unsolicited mss/month. Buys 6 mss/year. Publishes ms 2-3 months after acceptance. Length: 1,000-2,000 words averge. Publishes short shorts. Sometimes critiques rejected mss.
How to Contact: Send complete ms with cover letter that includes Social Security number. Reports in 1 week on queries; 1 month on mss. SASE. Simultaneous, photocopied and reprint submissions OK. Accepts computer printout submissions. Sample copy for $1. Fiction guidelines for SAE.
Payment: Pays $40-100 and contributor's copies; charge for extras.
Terms: Pays on publication for one-time rights. Offers kill fee.

DIALOGUE (I, II), The Magazine for the Visually Impaired, Dialogue Publications, Inc., 3100 Oak Park Ave., Berwyn IL 60402. (312)749-1908. Editor-in-Chief: Bonnie Miller. Magazine: 9×11; 235 pages; matte stock; glossy cover; illustrations. Publishes information on blind-related technology and human interest articles for blind, deaf-blind and visually impaired adults. Quarterly. Estab. 1961. Circ. 50,000.
Needs: Adventure, contemporary, humor/satire, literary, mainstream, regional, senior citizen/retirement and suspense/mystery. No erotica, religion, confessional or experimental. Receives approximately 10 unsolicited fiction mss/month. Buys 3 mss/issue, 12 mss/year. Publishes ms an average of 6 months after acceptance. Recently published work by Patrick Quinn, Marieanna Pape and John Dasney; published new writers within the last year. Length: 1,500 words average; 500 words minimum; 2,000 words maximum. Publishes short shorts. Occasionally critiques rejected mss. Sometimes recommends other markets. "We give top priority to blind or visually impaired (legally blind) authors."
How to Contact: Query first or send complete ms with SASE. Also send statement of visual handicap. Reports in 2 weeks on queries; 6 weeks on mss. Photocopied and reprint submissions OK. Accepts computer printout submissions. Sample copy for $5 and #10 SAE with 1 first class stamp; free to visually impaired. Fiction guidelines free.
Payment: Pays $5-35 and contributor's copy.
Terms: Pays on acceptance for first rights. "All fiction published in *Dialogue* automatically enters the Victorin Memorial Award Contest held annually. One winner per year.
Advice: "Study the magazine. This is a very specialized field. Remember the SASE!"

DISCOVERIES (II), Nazarene Publishing House, 6401 The Paseo, Kansas City MO 64131. Editor: Molly Mitchell. Story paper. 5½×8¼; 8 pages; illustrations; color photos. "Committed to reinforce the Bible concept taught in Sunday School curriculum, for ages 8 to 12 (grades 3 to 6)." Weekly.
Needs: Religious, puzzles. Buys 1-2 stories and 1-2 puzzles/issue. Publishes ms 1-2 years after acceptance. Length: 400-800 words. Publishes short shorts.
How to Contact: Send complete ms with cover letter and SASE. Send for free sample copy and fiction guidelines with SASE.
Payment: 3.5¢/word.
Terms: Pays on acceptance for first rights.
Advice: "Stories should vividly portray definite Christian emphasis or character building values, without being preachy. Stories need to be shorter because size of story paper is smaller."

DOG FANCY, Fancy Publications, Box 6050, Mission Viejo CA 92690. (714)855-8822. Editor: Kim Thornton. General dog and puppy magazine, consumer oriented, "for dog and puppy lovers." Monthly. Circ. 150,000.
Needs: Dog-centered theme. Receives approximately 40 unsolicited fiction mss/month. Buys 12 mss/year. Length: 3,000 words maximum.
How to Contact: Query first or send complete ms. SASE always. Photocopied submissions OK. Reports in 1 month on queries, 2 months on mss. Publishes ms an average of 6 months after acceptance. Sample copy $3. Free fiction guidelines with SASE.
Payment: 5¢/word and 2 contributor's copies. $3 charge for extras.
Terms: Buys reprints.
Advice: "Must be about dogs (and people), candid; first person is preferable. Include *brief* cover letter. Write to style of publication so that no re-write is necessary. Please no stories written 'by the dog' or talking dogs. Dog and dog's experiences must be focus of article; dog shouldn't be incidental character in a 'people' story. We are always especially interested in Christmas fiction – something heartwarming for the season, though not necessarily specifically Christmassy in theme."

DRAGON MAGAZINE (IV), The Monthly Adventure Role-Playing Aid, Dragon Publishing, Box 111, Lake Geneva WI 53147. (414)248-3625. Editor: Roger E. Moore. Fiction Editor: Barbara G. Young. Magazine: 8½×11; 104 pages; 50 penn. plus paper; 80 lb northcote cover stock; illustrations; rarely photos. "*Dragon* contains primarily nonfiction – articles and essays on various aspects of the hobby of fantasy and science fiction role-playing games. One short fantasy story is published per issue. Readers are mature teens and young adults; over half our readers are under 18 years of age." Monthly.

Estab. 1976. Circ. 85,000. "We are looking for all types of fantasy (not horror) stories.
Needs: "We are *not* interested in fictionalized accounts of actual role-playing sessions." Receives 50-60 unsolicited fiction mss/month. Buys 8-10 mss/year. Recently published work by eluki bes shahar, Steve Rasnic Tem, Mickey Zucker Reichert and Mary Frances Zambreno; published new writers within the last year. Length: 1,500 words minimum; 8,000 words maximum; 3,000-4,000 words average. Occasionally critiques rejected mss.
How to Contact: Send complete ms, estimated word length, SASE. List only credits of professionally published materials. Prefers letter-quality. Reports in 2-3 weeks. Publishes ms 6-12 months after acceptance. Sample copy for $4.50. Free fiction guidelines for #10 SAE and 1 first class stamp.
Payment: Pays 5-8¢/word; 2 free contributor's copies; $2 charge for extras.
Terms: Pays on acceptance for fiction only for first Worldwide English language rights.

DRUMMER (II, IV), Desmodus, Inc., Box 11314, San Francisco CA 94101. (415)978-5377. Editor: A.F. DeBlase. Magazine: 8½×11; 100 pages; 80 lb ultrabrite paper; glossy full-color cover; illustrations and photos. "Gay male erotica, fantasy and mystery with a leather, SM or other fetish twist." Monthly. Estab. 1975. Circ. 23,000.
Needs: Adventure, erotica, fantasy, gay, horror, humor/satire, science fiction, suspense/mystery and western. "Fiction must have an appeal to gay men." Receives 20-30 unsolicited fiction mss/month. Accepts 3 mss/issue. Publishes ms 3-4 months after acceptance. Agented fiction 10%. Publishes short shorts.
How to Contact: Send complete ms with cover letter. SASE. Photocopied submissions OK; reprints OK "only if previously in foreign or very local publications." Accepts computer printouts. Accepts electronic submissions compatible with IBM PC. Sample copy for $5. Fiction guidelines for #10 SAE and 2 first class stamps.
Payment: Pays $50-200 and free contributor's copies.
Terms: Pays on publication for first North American serial rights. Sponsors annual fiction contest.

ELLERY QUEEN'S MYSTERY MAGAZINE (II), Davis Publications, Inc., 380 Lexington Ave., New York NY 10017. (212)557-9100. Editor: Eleanor Sullivan. Magazine: digest sized; 160 pages. Magazine for lovers of mystery fiction. Published 13 times/year. Estab. 1941. Circ. 350,000.
Needs: "We accept only mystery, crime and detective fiction." Buys 10-15 mss/issue. Receives approximately 250 unsolicited fiction mss each month. Approximately 50% of fiction is agented. Recently published work by Clark Howard, Robert Barnard and Ruth Rendell; published new writers within the last year. Length: up to 9,000 words. Critiques rejected mss "only when a story might be a possibility for us if revised." Sometimes recommends other markets.
How to Contact: Send complete ms with SASE. Cover letter should include publishing credits and brief biographical sketch. Reports in 1 month or sooner on mss. Publishes 6 months to 1 year after acceptance. Free fiction guidelines with SASE. Sample copy for $2.
Payment: 3¢ per word and up.
Terms: Pays on acceptance for first North American serial rights. Occasionally buys reprints.
Advice: "We usually publish at least one first story an issue—i.e., the author's first published fiction. We select stories that are fresh and of the kind our readers have expressed a liking for. In writing a detective story, you must play fair with the reader re clues and necessary information. Otherwise you have a better chance of publishing if you avoid writing to formula."

EQUILIBRIUM 10, Everyone's Entertainment (II), The Magazine of Balance, Eagle Publishing Productions, Box 162, Golden CO 80401. Editor: Gary Eagle. Magazine: 4¼×8½; 100 pages; bond and glossy paper; semi-hard cover; many illustrations and photos. *Equilibrium* deals with the subject of balance and "having fun with opposites. It is an entertainment magazine for everyone." Quarterly. Plans special issue. Estab. 1984. Circ. 15,000.
Needs: Adventure, condensed novel, confession, contemporary, erotica, ethnic, experimental, fantasy, feminist, historical (general), horror, humor/satire, juvenile (5-9 years), literary, mainstream, preschool (0-4 years), psychic/supernatural/occult, regional, religious/inspirational, romance (contemporary, historical, young adult), senior citizen/retirement, serialized/excerpted novel, suspense/mystery, translations, western, young adult/teen (10-18). "The article doesn't necessarily have to be on opposites or balance because we sometimes pair two articles of two authors up with each other for a balance effect. Even for opposition." Receives 150 unsolicited mss/month. Accepts 30 mss/issue; 1,100 mss/year. Length: 1,200 words maximum. Publishes short shorts.
How to Contact: "We are not responsible for any unsolicited material. Tell a little about the article quickly. Unsolicited submissions sent with query are welcomed, but include sufficient return postage. Keep a copy for your files." Reports in 10 weeks on queries; 3 months on mss minimum. SASE. Simultaneous, photocopied and reprint submissions OK. Accepts computer printout submissions, no dot-matrix. "We offer serious inquiries a special package as an investment on their behalf. Includes: a sample copy of *Equilibrium*, Generic Word Search, author's guidelines, author's topic index, The

Pyramid Edition (mini-newspaper), business opportunities and Cheepstake Sweepstakes Contest 24 entry coupons. Send $15 plus a 9×14 SASE.
Payment: Pays $20-500. Pays in contributor's copies; charges for extras.
Terms: Pays on publication for one time and second serial rights. Publication copyrighted. Sponsors awards for fiction writers. "Just send in your article (should be on opposites or balance) and indicate that you'd like to enter the Writer's Sweepstakes (a contest that is optional but helpful). Letters are intended for publication and will be used for such. Queries may and will be published 'as is.' We offer serious queries a special package including a copy of *Equilibrium*, our *Pyramid Edition* mini-newspaper, *Generic Word Search Magazine*, *Business Opportunities* at our firm and other material for $15."
Advice: "Writers should write an article on opposites (extremes) or even do a very short one. Sketches are very nice to have. Humorous ones are good! We also need submissions for 'Contest 24.' Send $3 and SASE for current contest information. We look for association, link and synonyms or antonynms."

‡EQUINEWS: SERVING THE HORSE INDUSTRY (II, IV), All Breeds-All Disciplines, Whitehouse Publishing, Box 1778, Vernon, BC V1T 8C3 Canada. (604)545-9896. Editor: B.J. White. Tabloid: 10¼×12½; 24-28 pages; Electrabrite paper; illustrations and 85 screen photos. "For horsepersons." Estab. 1979. Circ. 17,492.
Needs: Adventure, juvenile (5-9 years), sports (horses) and young adult/teen (10-18). Receives 1-2 unsolicited mss/month. Buys 6-9 mss/year. Publishes ms 1-3 months after acceptance.
How to Contact: Send complete ms with cover letter. Reports in 1 month on queries. SASE. Sample copy for $1, 8×10 SAE. Fiction guidelines for #10 SAE.
Payment: Pay varies.
Terms: Pays on publication for first rights.

EVANGEL, Dept. of Christian Education, Free Methodist Headquarters, 901 College Ave., Winona Lake IN 46590. (219)267-7161. Editor: Vera Bethel. Sunday school take-home paper for distribution to young adults who attend church. Fiction involves young couples and singles coping with everyday crises, making decisions that show growth; ages 25-35. Magazine: 5½×8½; 8 pages; 2-color illustrations; b&w photos. Weekly. Estab. 1896. Circ. 35,000.
Needs: Religious/inspirational. "No fiction without any semblance of Christian message or where the message clobbers the reader." Buys 1 ms/issue, 52 mss/year. Receives approximately 75 unsolicited fiction mss each month. Length: 1,000-1,200 words.
How to Contact: Send complete ms with SASE. Reports in 1 month on ms. Free sample copy and free fiction guidelines with 6×9 SASE.
Payment: $45; 2 free author's copies; charge for extras.
Terms: Pays on publication for simultaneous, first, second serial (reprint), first North American serial and one-time rights.
Advice: "Choose a contemporary situation or conflict and create a good mix for the characters (not all-good or all-bad heroes and villains). Don't spell out everything in detail; let the reader fill in some blanks in the story. Keep him guessing." Rejects mss because of "unbelievable characters and predictable events in the story."

FACES (II,IV), The Magazine About People, Cobblestone Publishing, Inc. 30 Grove St., Peterborough NH 03458. (603)924-7209. Editor-in-Chief: Carolyn P. Yoder. Magazine covering world cultures for 8- to 14-year-olds; 7×9; 40 pages; 4-color covers; illustrations; b&w photos. 10 times/year.
Needs: Each issue deals with a specific theme. Editors consider "retold legends, folktales, stories from around the world relating to the theme." Length: 1,500 words maximum.
How to Contact: Query first. "Send ideas/suggestions in outline form." SASE. Sample copy $3.75; enclose 7½×10½ (or larger) SASE. Guidelines provide list of upcoming themes; free with SASE.
Payment: Pays 10-15¢/word.
Advice: "All manuscripts are reviewed by the American Museum of Natural History in New York before being accepted. Writers are encouraged to study recent back issues for content and style."

‡THE FAMILY (II, IV), Daughters of St. Paul, 50 St. Paul's Ave., Boston MA 02130. (617)522-8911. Editor: Sr. Janet Peter Figurant, FSP. Magazine: 8½×11; 40 pages; glossy paper; self-cover; illustrations and photos. Family life—themes include parenting issues, human and spiritual development, marital situations for teen-adult, popular audience predominantly Catholic. Monthly, except July-Aug. Estab. 1953. Circ. 10,000.
Needs: Religious/inspirational. "We favor upbeat stories with some sort of practical or moral message." No sex, romance, science fiction, horror, western. Receives about 100 unsolicited mss/month. Buys 3-4 mss/issue; 30-40 mss/year. Publishes ms 4-6 months after acceptance. Length: 1,000 words minimum; 1,500 words maximum; 1,200 words average. $15 fee for critique. Sometimes recommends other markets.

How to Contact: Send complete ms with cover letter that includes Social Security number and list of previously published works. Reports in 2 months on mss. SASE. Reprint submissions OK. Sample copy $1.50, 9×12 SAE and 5 first class stamps. Guidelines for #10 SAE and 1 first class stamp.
Payment: 8-10¢/word—up to $150.
Terms: Pays on publication for first North American serial or one-time rights (reprints). Sends galleys to author "only if substantive editing was required."
Advice: "We look for 1) message; 2) clarity of writing; 3) realism of plot and character development. If seasonal material, send at least 7 months in advance. We're eager to receive submissions on family topics. And we love stories that include humor."

FAMILY MAGAZINE (II), The Magazine for Military Wives, Box 4993, Walnut Creek CA 94596. (415)284-9093. Editor: Janet A. Venturino. Magazine: 80 pages; glossy paper; 80 lb glossy cover stock; illustrations; photos. Magazine with stories of interest to military wives. Audience: high school-educated, married women. Published 10 times/year. Estab. 1958. Circ. 550,000 worldwide.
Needs: Contemporary. No "singles" stories. Receives 100 unsolicited mss/month. Buys 12-20 mss/year. Published new writers within the last year. Length: 1,000-3,000 words.
How to Contact: Send complete ms. Reports in 2 months. SASE. Simultaneous and photocopied submissions OK. Accepts computer printout submissions. Prefers letter-quality. Publishes ms an average of 1 year after acceptance. Sample copy $1.25. Fiction guidelines for SASE.
Payment: Pays $75-300; 1 contributor's copy; $1.25 charge for extras.
Terms: Pays on publication for first rights.
Advice: "Good quality still jumps out as a pearl among swine."

‡FIRST (II), For Women, Heinrich Bauer North America Inc., 270 Sylvan Ave., Edgewood Cliffs NJ 07632. (201)569-6699. Editor: Dennis Neeld. Fiction Editor: Bibi Wein. Magazine: 150 pages; slick paper; illustrations and photos. "Women's service magazine for women age 18 up—no upper limit—middle American audience." Monthly. Estab. 1989. Circ. 4 million.
Needs: Contemporary, humor, literary, mainstream and regional. "No experimental, romance, formula fiction, fantasy, sci-fi, or stories with foreign settings." Receives 200 unsolicited mss/month. Buys 1 ms/issue; 12 mss/year. Time between acceptance and publication varies. Agented fiction 33⅓%. Recently published work by Chuck Wachtel, Tima Smith and Paulette Bates Alden. Length: 2,500 words minimum; 4,500 words maximum; 3,500-4,000 words average. "No short shorts." Sometimes critiques rejected mss.
How to Contact: Send complete ms with cover letter. "Cover letter should be brief, mention previous publications and agent if any, and tell us if material is seasonal. No queries please." Reports in 8-10 weeks on mss. SASE for ms. Photocopied and reprint submissions OK. Accepts computer printout submissions. Fiction guidelines for #10 SAE and 1 first class stamp. Send seasonal material 6 months in advance.
Payment: Pays $1,250-2,000 (less for reprinted material).
Terms: Pays on acceptance for first North American serial rights.
Advice: "We especially like a fresh sensibility and a sensitive handling of themes of interest to contemporary women. Read at least 3 issues of the magazine. Send us the story you had to write for yourself, not one you concocted 'especially for *First*.'"

FIRST HAND (II, IV), Experiences for Loving Men, First Hand Ltd., Box 1314, Teaneck NJ 07666. (201)836-9177. Editor: Lou Thomas. Magazine: digest size; 130 pages; illustrations. "Half of the magazine is made up of our readers' own gay sexual experiences. Rest is fiction and columns devoted to health, travel, books, etc." Monthly. Estab. 1980. Circ. 60,000.
Needs: Erotica, gay. "Should be written in first person." No science fiction or fantasy. Erotica should detail experiences based in reality. Receives 75-100 unsolicited mss/month. Buys 6 mss/issue; 72 mss/year. Publishes ms 9-18 months after acceptance. Recently published work by John Hoff, Robert Allison, Julian Biddle; published new writers within the last year. Length: 3,000 words preferred; 2,000 words minimum; 3,750 words maximum. Sometimes critiques rejected mss.
How to Contact: Send complete ms with cover letter. Reports in 4-6 weeks on mss. SASE. Accepts computer printout submissions; no dot-matrix. Sample copy for $4. Fiction guidelines for #10 SAE and 1 first class stamp.
Payment: Pays $100-150.
Terms: Pays on publication for all rights or first North American serial rights.
Advice: "Cover letters are a must. Should include writer's name, address, telephone and Social Security number and should advise on use of pseudonym if any. Also whether he is selling all rights or first North American serial rights. Avoid the hackneyed situations. Be original. We like strong plots."

FIRST for Women *targets middle-American women over the age of 18. Fiction editor Bibi Wein likes "strong narrative drive with original, believable characters and a satisfying ending." Wein assures all submissions are read and claims "we are happy to publish new writers." Cover photographer is Charles William Bush. Model is Audrey Klebahn.*

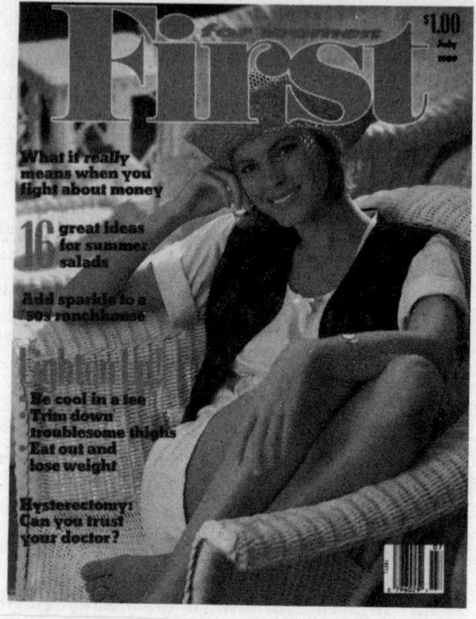

FLING (II), Relim Publishing Co., Inc., 550 Miller Ave., Mill Valley CA 94941. (415)383-5464. Editor: Arv Miller. Magazine: 8½×11; 84 pages; slick paper and cover; color illustrations; mostly color photos. "Sex-type publication for young males 18-34 who like photos of very busty young models. They also like to read sex-type stories of bosomy heroines." Bimonthly. Estab. 1957. Circ. 100,000.
Needs: Erotica, fantasy. "Much of the text material in *Fling* deals with sex in combination of busty females." No historicals, mysteries, westerns, plotless stories. Receives 2 dozen unsolicited mss/month. Buys 2-3 mss/issue; 12-15 mss/year. Publishes 2-12 months after acceptance. Published new writers within the last year. Length: 4,000 average; 2,000 words maximum. Occasionally critiques rejected mss.
How to Contact: Send complete ms with cover letter. Reports in 2-6 weeks. SASE for ms. No electronic or photocopied submissions. Sample copy $5. Fiction guidelines for SAE and 1 first class stamp.
Payment: Pays $135-200.
Terms: Pays on acceptance for first rights. Publication copyrighted.
Advice: "Read a copy of *Fling*, plus study the fiction requirement sheet. Fiction gives *Fling* a special department we feel is necessary. There is a new aspect of sensuality that can be explored by readers. Know exactly what *Fling* wants in the way of story. Or, in some cases, query editor about story ideas. *Fling* has very specific requirements in fiction that must be clearly understood by potential author. While the men's sophisticate market is big, *Fling* needs stories that are tailor-made, not the usual 'sex-mag' submissions. Most authors forget *Fling* needs a lot of emphasis on descriptions of female characters, particularly 'big-bosom' descriptions."

THE FLYFISHER (IV), Federation of Flyfishers, 1387 Cambridge Dr., Idaho Falls ID 83401. (208)523-7300. Editor: Dennis Bitton. Magazine: 8½×11; 64 pages; 70 lb glossy stock; self cover; b&w; illustrations; color and b/w photos. Magazine for fly fishermen. "We only publish material directly related to fly fishing." Quarterly. Estab. 1967. Circ. 10,000.
Needs: Fiction related to fly fishing only. Accepts 2 ms/issue, 8 mss/year. Published new writers within the last year. Length: 750 words minimum; 2,500 words maximum; 1,500 words average (preferred).
How to Contact: Query first with SASE. Reports in 1 month on queries and mss. Sample copy $3 with 9×12 SAE and 10 first class stamps. Free fiction guidelines with #10 SAE and 1 first class stamp.
Payment: $50-250.
Terms: Pays on publication for first North American serial rights and one-time rights.

FLYFISHING NEWS, VIEWS AND REVIEWS (II,IV), Bitton Inc., 1387 Cambridge, Idaho Falls, ID 83401. (208)523-7300. Editor: Dennis G. Bitton. Newspaper tabloid: 16 pages; good newsprint; b&w illustrations; b&w photos. Publishes information on flyfishing and all related subjects, flyfishermen and women. Bimonthly. Estab. 1986. Circ. 5,000.

Needs: Adventure, condensed novel, confession, historical, humor, regional. "All as flyfishing topics." Receives 20 unsolicited mss/month. Accepts 2 mss/month; 12 mss/year. Length: 1,500-2,000 words average; 250 words minimum; 4,000 words maximum. Occasionally critiques rejected mss. Recommends other markets.
How to Contact: Query first. Reports in 2 weeks. SASE.
Payment: Pays $50-250 and 5 contributor's copies. Charge for extras.
Terms: Pays 2-3 weeks after publication for one-time rights. Publication copyrighted.
Advice: "I want to see all good flyfishing fiction. Write like you talk."

THE FRIEND MAGAZINE (II), The Church of Jesus Christ of Latter-day Saints, 50 E. North Temple, Salt Lake City UT 84150. (801)531-2210. Editor: Vivian Paulsen. Magazine: 8½×10½; 50 pages; 40 lb coated paper; 70 lb coated cover stock; illustrations, photos. Publishes for 3-11 year-olds. Monthly. Estab. 1971. Circ. 220,000.
Needs: Adventure, ethnic, some historical, humor, mainstream, religious/inspirational, nature. Length: 1,000 words maximum. Publishes short shorts. Length: 250 words.
How to Contact: Send complete ms. "No query letters please." Reports in 6-8 weeks. SASE. Photocopied submissions OK. Accepts computer printout submissions. Sample copy for 9½×11 SAE and 85¢ postage.
Payment: Pays 8-11¢ a word.
Terms: Pays on acceptance for all rights.
Advice: "The *Friend* is particularly interested in stories with substance for tiny tots. Stories should focus on character-building qualities and should be wholesome without moralizing or preaching. Boys and girls resolving conflicts is a theme of particular merit. Since the magazine is circulated worldwide, the *Friend* is interested in stories and articles with universal settings, conflicts, and character. Other suggestions include rebus, picture, holiday, sports, and photo stories, or manuscripts that portray various cultures. Very short pieces (up to 250 words) are desired for younger readers and preschool children. Appropriate humor is a constant need."

‡FUTURIFIC MAGAZINE (I, II, IV), Foundation for Optimism, 280 Madison Ave., New York NY 10016. (212)684-4913. Editor: B. Szent-Miklosy. News Magazine: 8½×11; 32 pages; glossy paper; illustrations and photos. "News indicating what the future will be for a general audience." Monthly.
Needs: The future. "Do not send material unrelated to current events." Receives 2 unsolicited mss/month. Buys 1 ms/issue. Publishes ms 1-2 months after acceptance. Length: Open. Publishes short shorts. Sometimes critiques rejected mss.
How to Contact: Send complete ms with cover letter. Reports in 1 week. SASE. Simultaneous, photocopied and reprint submissions OK. Accepts computer printout submissions. Accepts electronic submissions. Sample copy for $3; 9×12 SAE and 4 first class stamps. Fiction guidelines for #10 SAE and 1 first class stamp.
Payment: Negotiated.
Terms: Pays on publication for one-time rights.

GALLERY MAGAZINE, Montcalm Publishing Corporation, 401 Park Avenue South, New York NY 10016. (212)779-8900. Editor: Marc Lichter. Fiction Editor: John Bowers. Magazine. 112 pages; illustrations and photographs. Magazine for men, 18-34. Monthly. Estab. 1972. Circ. 425,000.
Needs: Adventure, erotica, humor/satire, literary, mainstream, suspense/mystery. Receives 100 unsolicited fiction mss/month. Accepts 1 mss/issue. Publishes ms 2-3 months after acceptance. Less than 10% of fiction is agented. Length: 1,500-3,000 words average; 1,000 words minimum; 3,500 words maximum. Publishes short shorts. Sometimes critiques rejected mss and recommends other markets.
How to Contact: Send complete ms. Reports in 2 months. SASE. Photocopied submissions OK. Accepts computer printout submissions. Sample copy $5. Fiction guidelines for #10 SAE and 1 first class stamp.
Payment: $400-1,000, contributor's copies.
Terms: Pays 50% on acceptance/50% on publication. Buys first North American serial rights. Publication copyrighted.

GENT (II), Dugent Publishing Corp., Suite 204, 2355 Salzedo St., Coral Gables FL 33134. (305)443-2378. Editor: Bruce Arthur. "Men's magazine designed to have erotic appeal for the reader. Our publications are directed to a male audience, but we do have a certain percentage of female readers. For the most part, our audience is interested in erotically stimulating material, but not exclusively." Monthly. Estab. 1959. Circ. 175,000.
Needs: Contemporary, science fiction, horror, erotica, mystery, adventure and humor. *Gent* specializes in "D-Cup cheesecake," and fiction should be slanted accordingly. "Most of the fiction published includes several sex scenes. No fiction that concerns children, religious subjects or anything that might be libelous." Buys 2 mss/issue, 24 mss/year. Receives approximately 30-50 unsolicited fiction mss/

month. Approximately 10% of fiction is agented. Length: 2,000-3,500 words. Critiques rejected mss "when there is time."
How to Contact: Send complete ms with SASE. Reports in 1 month on mss. Publishes ms an average of 6 weeks after acceptance. Sample copy $5. Free fiction guidelines with legal-sized SASE.
Payment: $125-200. Free author's copy.
Terms: Pays on publication for first North American serial rights.
Advice: "Since *Gent* magazine is the 'Home of the D-Cups,' stories and articles containing either characters or themes with a major emphasis on large breasts will have the best chance for consideration. Study a sample copy first." Mss are rejected because "there are not enough or ineffective erotic sequences, plot is not plausible, wrong length, or not slanted specifically for us."

GENTLEMAN'S COMPANION (I), Gentleman's Companion, Inc., Box 447, Voorhees NJ 08003. (212)564-0112. Editor: J.H. Hartley. Magazine: 8½×11; 96 pages; 50 lb coated paper; 80 lb cover stock; illustrations; photos. Men's magazine, sexually oriented material of a heavily erotic nature, geared to swinging concepts. Monthly. Published special fiction issue. Estab. 1976. Circ. 175,000.
Needs: Erotica, fantasy. No non-erotic fiction. Receives 20 unsolicited fiction mss/month; accepts 2 fiction mss/issue. Publishes ms 6 weeks to 6 months after acceptance. Length: 1,000-2,500 words.
Payment: Payment is negotiable.
How to Contact: Send complete ms with cover letter. SASE. Reports in 1 month on queries. Sample copy $3.95 and 8½×11 SAE with 2 first class stamps. Fiction guidelines for $3.95 and 8½×11 SAE with 2 first class stamps.
Terms: Pays on publication. Acquires all rights.

GOLF JOURNAL (II), United States Golf Assoc., Golf House, Far Hills NJ 07931. (201)234-2300. Editor: Robert Sommers. Managing Editor: George Eberl. Magazine: 40-48 pages; good paper; self cover stock; illustrations and photos. "The magazine's subject is golf–its history, lore, rules, equipment and general information. The focus is on amateur golf and those things applying to the millions of American golfers. Our audience is generally professional, highly literate and knowledgeable; presumably they read *Golf Journal* because of an interest in the game, its traditions, and its noncommercial aspects." Published 8 times/year. Estab. 1949. Circ. 175,000.
Needs: Humor. "Fiction is very limited. *Golf Journal* has had an occasional humorous story, topical in nature. Generally speaking, short stories are not used. Golf jokes will not be used." Buys 10-12 mss/year. Published new writers within the last year. Length: 1,000-2,000 words. Recommends other markets. Critiques rejected mss "when there is time."
How to Contact: Send complete ms with SASE. Reports in 2 months on mss. Free sample copy with SASE.
Payment: $500-1,000. 1-10 free author's copies.
Terms: Pays on acceptance.
Advice: "Know your subject (golf); familiarize yourself first with the publication." Rejects mss because "fiction usually does not serve the function of *Golf Journal*, which, as the official magazine of the United States Golf Association, deals chiefly with nonfiction subjects."

GOOD HOUSEKEEPING (II), 959 Eighth Ave., New York NY 10019. Editor: John Mack Carter. Fiction Editor: Naome Lewis. Magazine: 8×10; approximately 250 pages; slick paper; thick, high-gloss cover; 4-color illustrations, b&w and color photos. Homemaking magazine of informational articles, how-to's for homemakers of all ages. Monthly. Circ. 20 million.
Needs: Contemporary, romance and mother-child stories. Buys 2 short stories/issue. Approximately 75% of fiction is agented. Length: 1,000-4,000 words.
How to Contact: Query or send complete ms. SASE always. Accepts computer printout submissions. Prefers letter-quality. Reports in 6-8 weeks on both queries and mss. Publishes ms an average of 6 months after acceptance.
Payment: Pays standard magazine rates.
Terms: Pays on acceptance for first North American serial rights.
Advice: Most fiction is solicited. "The old standard needs restating: Know the market to which you are submitting."

THE GUIDE (II,IV), to the Gay Northeast, Box 593, Boston MA 02199. (617)266-8557. Editor: French Wall. Magazine: 8×10; 124-156; newsprint; 70 lb cover stock; photos. "Gay liberation and sex positive information, articles and columns; radical political and radical religious philosophies welcome. Audience is primarily gay men, some lesbians, bar crowd and grassroots politicos." Monthly. Estab. 1981. Circ. 22,000.
Needs: Adventure, erotica, ethnic, experimental, fantasy, feminist, gay, historical (general), humor/satire, lesbian, regional, religious/inspirational romance (contemporary, historical and young adult), science fiction, senior citizen, spiritual, sports, suspense/mystery. "Focus on empowerment–avoid-

ance of 'victim' philosophy appreciated." Receives 4 mss/month. Publishes ms within 3 months to 1 year after acceptance. Published new writers within the last year. Length: 1,800 words average; 500 words minimum; 5,000 words maximum. Publishes short shorts. Sometimes critiques rejected mss.
How to Contact: Query first. Reports in 2-4 weeks. SASE; include cover letter and phone number. Simultaneous and photocopied submissions OK. Accepts computer printout submissions. Sample copy for 9×13 SAE and 8 first class stamps.
Payment: Pays $30-120.
Terms: Pays on acceptance for all rights or first rights.
Advice: "Gay fiction writers have few (if any) places to be published in the US Northeast and Eastern Canada. *The Guide*'s format and extensive distribution in this area makes it an excellent vehicle for writers anxious to be read. *The Guide* has multiplied its press run fourfold in the past years and is committed to continued growth in this region."

GUIDE MAGAZINE, International Northwest Edition, One in Ten Publishing, Box 23070, Seattle WA 98102. (206)323-7374. Contact: Editor. "We publish humor pieces, fiction, poetry, feature stories and interpretive essays examining personalities, politics, science fiction, current events, the arts and indeed the whole of culture as it relates to gay life." Monthly. Estab. 1986. Circ. 11,000.
Needs: Adventure, condensed novels, ethnic, experimental, historical, horror, humor, mainstream, romance, science fiction, serialized novel, mystery/suspense, western. "All fiction must relate to experience of gay people. No erotica nor porn." Buys 7 fiction mss/year. Length: 800 words minimum; 3,000 words maximum.
How to Contact: Send complete ms. SASE. Simultaneous, photocopied and reprint submissions OK. Accepts computer printout submissions. Accepts electronic submissions via 5¼" disks formatted with MS/DOS files stored in ASCII or WordPerfect. Send hard copy with electronic submissions. Sample copy for 9×12 SAE and $1 postage. Writer's guidelines for #10 SAE and 1 first class stamp.
Payment: Pays up to $30.
Terms: Pays on publication for first North American serial rights, second serial (reprint) rights, simultaneous rights, or makes work-for-hire assignments. Publication copyrighted.
Advice: "Well researched and intellectually challenging pieces get top priority."

GUYS, First Hand Ltd., Box 1314, Teaneck NJ 07666. (201)836-9177. Editor: Lou Thomas. Magazine: digest size; 160 pages; illustrations; photos. "Fiction and nonfiction for today's gay man. Fiction is of an erotic nature, and we especially need short shorts and novella-length stories." Published 8 times a year. Estab. 1988.
Needs: Should be written in first person. No science fiction or fantasy. Erotica should be based on reality. Buys 7 mss/issue; 56 mss/year. Publishes ms 9-18 months after acceptance. Length: 3,000 words average; 2,000 words minimum; 3,750 words maximum. For novellas: 7,500-8,600 words. Publishes short shorts. Length: 750-1,250 words. Sometimes critiques rejected mss and recommends other markets.
How to Contact: Send complete ms with cover letter; should include writer's name, address, telephone and Social Security number and whether he is selling all rights or First North American Serial Rights. Reports in 6-8 weeks on mss. SASE. Accepts computer printout submissions, no dot-matrix. Sample copy for $5. Fiction guidelines for #10 SAE and 1 first class stamp.
Payment: Pays $100-150. $75 for short shorts (all rights); $250 for novellas (all rights).
Terms: Pays on publication or in 240 days, whichever comes first, for all rights or first North American serial rights.

HADASSAH MAGAZINE (IV), 50 W. 58th St., New York NY 10019. Executive Editor: Alan M. Tigay. Senior Editor: Zelda Shluker. General interest magazine: 8½×11; 48-70 pages; coated and uncoated paper; slick, medium weight coated cover; drawings and cartoons; photos. Primarily concerned with Israel, the American Jewish community, Jewish communities around the world and American current affairs. Monthly except combined June/July and August/September issues. Circ. 375,000.
Needs: Ethnic (Jewish). Receives 20-25 unsolicited fiction mss each month. Recently published fiction by Annie Roiphe and Dina Elenbogen; published new writers within the last year. Length: 3,000 words maximum. Also publishes short stories 1,500-2,000 words.
How to Contact: Send complete ms with SASE. Accepts computer printout submissions. Reports in 6 weeks on mss. "Not interested in multiple submissions or previously published articles."
Payment: Pays $300 minimum. Offers $100 kill fee for assigned mss not published.
Terms: Pays on publication for U.S. publication rights.
Advice: "Stories on a Jewish theme should be neither self-hating nor schmaltzy."

HARPER'S MAGAZINE (II, III), 666 Broadway, 11th Floor, New York NY 10012. (212)614-6500. Editor: Lewis H. Lapham. Magazine: 8×10¾; 80 pages; illustrations. Magazine for well educated, widely read and socially concerned readers, college-aged and older, those active in political and community affairs. Monthly. Circ. 190,000.

Needs: Contemporary and humor. Stories on contemporary life and its problems. Receives approximately 300 unsolicited fiction mss/month. Published new writers within the last year. Length: 1,000-5,000 words.
How to Contact: Query to managing editor, or through agent. Reports in 6 weeks on queries.
Payment: Pays $500-1,000. Negotiable kill fee.
Terms: Pays on acceptance for rights, which vary on each author and material. Sends galleys to author.
Advice: Buys very little fiction but *Harper's* has published short stories traditionally.

HARVEY FOR LOVING PEOPLE, Harvey Shapiro Inc., Box 2070, Cherry Hill NJ 08003. (212)564-0112. Editor: Harvey Shapiro. Managing Editor: Jack Hartley. Magazine dedicated to the enrichment of loving relationships between couples, offering sexually informative material in graphically erotic manner about swingers' lifestyles. "Our readership consists of people interested in highly informative sex-related information." Monthly. Estab. 1979. Circ. 200,000.
Needs: Lesbian and heterosexual erotica. No material accepted that is not sexually oriented. Buys 2-3 mss/issue. Length: 1,000-2,000 words.
How to Contact: Send mss with SASE. Reports in 1 month.
Payment: $50-200.
Terms: Pays on publication for all rights.
Advice: "We reserve the right to edit. Stay within the Meese Commission guidelines."

HI-CALL (II), Gospel Publishing House, 1445 Boonville Ave., Springfield MO 65802-1894. (417)862-2781. Editor: Deanna S. Harris. Take-home Sunday school paper for teenagers (ages 12-17). Weekly. Estab. 1936. Circ. 95,000.
Needs: Religious/inspirational, mystery/suspense, adventure, humor, spiritual and young adult, with a strong but not preachy Biblical emphasis. Receives approximately 100 unsolicited fiction mss/month. Recently published work by Betty Steele Everett, Alan Cliburn and Michelle Starr. Published new writers within the last year. Length: up to 1,500 words.
How to Contact: Send complete ms with SASE. Simultaneous and previously published submissions OK. Accepts computer printout submissions. Prefers letter-quality. Reports in 1-3 months on mss. Free sample copy and guidelines.
Payment: Pays 2-3¢/word.
Terms: Pays on acceptance for one-time rights.
Advice: "Most manuscripts are rejected because of shallow characters, shallow or predictable plots, and/or a lack of spiritual emphasis. Send seasonal material approximately one year in advance."

HIGH TIMES (II), Trans High Corp., 211 E. 43rd St., New York NY 10017. (212)972-8484. Editor: Steven Hager. Magazine: 8½×11; 100 pages; glossy paper; illustrations; photos. Publishes "drug-related" material for "counter-culture" readers. Monthly. Plans special fiction issue. Circ. 250,000.
Needs: Adventure, experimental, fantasy, science fiction, serialized/excerpted novel. No stories about "my drug bust." Receives 16 unsolicited mss/month. Buys 5 mss/year. Publishes ms 6-8 months after acceptance. Published new writers within the last year. Length: 2,000-4,000 preferred. Publishes short shorts.
How to Contact: Send complete ms with cover letter. Reports in 1 month on queries; 6 weeks on mss. SASE. Simultaneous, photocopied and reprint submissions OK. Accepts computer printout submissions. "Call John Holmstrom for modem information." Sample copy for $5. Fiction guidelines free.
Payment: Pays $200-600 and contributor's copies.
Terms: Pays on publication. Purchases negotiable rights.

HIGHLIGHTS FOR CHILDREN, 803 Church St., Honesdale PA 18431. (717)253-1080. Editor-in-Chief: Walter B. Barbe, Ph.D. Address fiction to: Kent L. Brown, Jr., Editor. Magazine: 8½×11; 42 pages; newsprint paper; coated cover stock; illustrations; photos. Published 11 times/year. Circ. 1.9 million.
Needs: Juvenile (ages 2-12). Unusual stories appealing to both girls and boys; stories with good characterization, strong emotional appeal, vivid, full of action. "Begin with action rather than description, have strong plot, believable setting, suspense from start to finish." Length: 900 words maximum. "We also need easy stories for very young readers (600 words)." No war, crime or violence. Buys 6-7 mss/issue. Receives 600-800 unsolicited fiction mss/month. Also publishes rebus (picture) stories of 150 words or under for the 3-4 year old child. Critiques rejected mss occasionally, "especially when editors see possibilities in story."
How to Contact: Send complete ms with SASE and include a rough word count and cover letter "with any previous acceptances by our magazine; any other published work anywhere." Accepts computer printout submissions. Prefers letter-quality. Reports in 2 months on mss. Free guidelines with SASE.

Payment: Pays 8¢ and up per word.
Terms: Pays on acceptance for all rights. Sends galleys to author.
Advice: "We accept a story on its merit whether written by an unpublished or an experienced writer. Mss are rejected because of poor writing, lack of plot, trite or worn-out plot, or poor characterization. Children *like* stories and learn about life from stories. Children learn to become lifelong fiction readers by enjoying stories." Sponsors occasional contests. Write for information.

ALFRED HITCHCOCK'S MYSTERY MAGAZINE (I, II), Davis Publications, Inc., 380 Lexington Ave., New York NY 10017. (212)557-9100. Editor: Cathleen Jordan. Mystery fiction magazine: 5$\frac{1}{16}$×7$\frac{3}{8}$; 160 pages; 28 lb newsprint paper; 60 lb machine-/coated cover stock; illustrations; photos. Published 13 times/year. Estab. 1956. Circ. 225,000.
Needs: Mystery and detection. No sensationalism. Number of mss/issue varies with length of mss. Length: up to 14,000 words. Also publishes short shorts.
How to Contact: Send complete ms and SASE. Accepts computer printout submissions. Reports in 2 months. Free guideline sheet for SASE.
Payment: 5¢/word on acceptance.

THE HOME ALTAR (II), Meditations for Families with Children, Box 590179, San Francisco, CA 94159-0179. Editor: M. Elaine Dunham. Magazine: 5¼×7¼; 64 pages; newsprint paper; coated 4-color cover stock; 2-color illustrations and photos. "*The Home Altar* is a magazine of daily devotions. For each day, there is a designated Bible reading, a short story (fiction or nonfiction) which reflects the central message of the biblical passage, and a concluding prayer." Readers are "primarily Lutheran (ELCA) families—with children between 6 and 14 years of age." Quarterly. Estab. 1940. Circ. 82,000.
Needs: Juvenile (5-9 years) and religious/inspirational. "No unsolicited manuscripts are accepted for publication in *The Home Altar*. All writing is done on assignment, to reflect specific Bible readings and themes." Accepts up to 90 mss/issue; approximately 200 mss/year. Publishes ms an average of 6 months to 1 year after acceptance. Length: 150 words average; 125 words minimum; 170 words maximum. Publishes short shorts. Length: 150 words. Sometimes critiques rejected mss.
How to Contact: Query with clips of published or unpublished work. Reports on queries in 3 months; on mss in 2 weeks. Photocopied submissions OK. Accepts computer printout submissions. Sample copy and fiction guidelines free.
Payment: $10 per "story"; contributor's copies.
Terms: Pays on acceptance for all rights.
Advice: "We're trying to serve a diverse group of readers—children of all ages as well as adults. A well written story often has several levels of meaning and will touch people of different ages and experiences in different ways. Write stories in which children are the protagonists. Keep your sentences short. Use inclusive language when referring to human beings or to God."

HOME LIFE (II), The Sunday School Board of the Southern Baptist Convention, 127 9th Ave. N., Nashville TN 37234. (615)251-2271. Editor: Charlie Warren. A Christian family magazine: 8⅛×11; 66 pages; coated paper; separate cover stock; illustrations; photos. "Top priorities are strengthening and enriching marriage; parenthood; family concerns and problems; and spiritual and personal growth. Most of our readers are married couples and parents between the ages of 25-50. They read it out of denominational loyalty and desire for Christian growth and discipleship." Monthly. Estab. 1947. Circ. 725,000.
Needs: Contemporary, prose poem, religious/inspirational, spiritual, humor and young adult. "We do not want distasteful, risqué or raunchy fiction. Nor should it be too fanciful or far-fetched." Buys 1-2 mss/issue, 12-24 mss/year. Receives approximately 100-200 unsolicited fiction mss/month. Recently published work by Grace Gray Sample, Alan Cliburn and Clare Mishica; published new writers within the last year. Length: 750-2,500 words. Publishes short shorts of 500+ words. Recommends other markets.
How to Contact: Query or send complete ms. SASE always. Simultaneous submissions OK. Accepts computer printout submissions; prefers letter-quality. Reports in 1 month on queries, 2 months on mss. Publishes ms 1 year to 20 months after acceptance. Sample copy for $1.
Payment: Up to 5¢/word for unsolicited mss. 3 free author's copies.
Terms: Pays on acceptance for all rights, first rights and first North American serial rights. Rarely buys reprints.

HOOF BEATS (IV), World's Largest Standardbred Publication, U.S. Trotting Association, 750 Michigan Ave., Columbus OH 43215. (614)224-2291. Executive Editor: Dean A. Hoffman. Magazine: 150 pages; illustrations and photographs. "All material must pertain to racing or breeding of harness horses." Audience is owners, breeders, trainers of harness horses. Monthly. Circ. 26,000.

Needs: Receives 2 unsolicited fiction mss/month. Accepts 4 mss/year. Publishes ms an average of 6 months after acceptance. Publishes short shorts. Sometimes critiques rejected ms; recommends other markets.
How to Contact: Query first with "story ideas and background of author." Reports in 1 week on queries; 2 weeks on mss. Photocopied and reprint submissions OK. Accepts computer printout submissions. Sample copy free.
Payment: $100-300.
Terms: Pays on publication for first rights.
Advice: "Don't write on speculation; query editors first."

HORSE ILLUSTRATED, Fancy Publications, Box 6050, Mission Viejo CA 92690. (714)855-8822. Editor: Jill-Marie Jones. "General all-breed horse magazine for horse lovers of all ages but mainly women riding for show and pleasure. All material is centered around horses; both English and Western riding styles are profiled." Monthly. Estab. 1982. Circ. 110,000.
Needs: Adventure, humor and suspense/mystery. "Must concern horses. Liberal—nothing unsuitable to a younger audience, although we do not want mss aimed directly at young readers." Receives 3-5 unsolicited mss/month. Buys 5-6 mss/year. Recently published work by Cooky McClung, Kit Sloane and Carol Perkins. published new writers within the last year. Length: 1,500-2,000 words average; 1,000 words minimum; 2,500 words maximum. Occasionally critiques rejected mss.
How to Contact: Query first or send complete ms. Reports in 2 months on queries; 3 months on mss. SASE. Photocopied submissions OK. Accepts computer printout submissions. Prefers letter-quality. Publishes ms 4-10 months after acceptance. Sample copy $3.25. Free fiction guidelines. SASE.
Payment: $50-150; 2 contributor's copies; $2 charge for extras ("free if request is for a reasonable number of copies").
Terms: Pays on publication for one-time rights.
Advice: "Write about adult women—*no* little girl and wild stallion or cowboy and Indian stories, please."

HUMPTY DUMPTY'S MAGAZINE (II), Children's Better Health Institute, Benjamin Franklin Literary & Medical Society, Inc., 1100 Waterway Blvd., Box 567, Indianapolis IN 46206. Editor: Christine French Clark. Magazine: 6½×9⅛; 48 pages; 35 lb paper; coated cover; color, 2-color, or b&w illustrations; rarely photos. Children's magazine stressing health, nutrition, hygiene, exercise and safety for children ages 4-6. Bimonthly, except monthly September-December.
Needs: Juvenile health-related material and material of a more general nature. No inanimate talking objects. Rhyming stories should flow easily with no contrived rhymes. Buys 3-5 mss/issue. Receives 250-300 unsolicited fiction mss/month. Length: 600 words maximum.
How to Contact: Send complete ms with SASE. Reports in 8-10 weeks. Sample copy 75¢. Editorial guidelines with SASE. No queries.
Payment: Pays minimum 8¢/word for stories plus 2 author's copies (more upon request).
Terms: Pays on publication for all rights. (One-time book rights returned when requested for specific publication.)
Advice: "In contemporary stories, characters should be up-to-date, with realistic dialogue. We're looking for health-related stories with unusual twists or surprise endings. We want to avoid stories and poems that 'preach.' We try to present the health material in a positive way, utilizing a light humorous approach wherever possible." Most rejected mss "are too wordy. Cover letters should be included only if they give pertinent information—list of credits, bibliography, or mention of any special training or qualifications that make author an authority."

HUSTLER (IV), Larry Flynt Publications, Suite 300, 9171 Wilshire Blvd., Beverly Hills CA 90210. (213)858-7100. Editor: Lonn Friend. Fiction Editor: Allan MacDonnell. Magazine: 100 pages; illustrations; photos. "Men's magazine, for men and women." Monthly. Estab. 1976. Circ. 1 million.
Needs: Erotica. Receives 20-30 unsolicited mss/month. Buys 1 ms/issue; 12 mss/year. Publishes ms 1-6 months after acceptance. Published new writers last year. Length: 3,500 words average; 3,000 words minimum; 4,000 words maximum. Occasionally critiques rejected mss. Recommends other markets.
How to Contact: Send complete ms with cover letter which should include "writer's name, address, telephone number, and whether the manuscript has been or is being offered elsewhere." Reports in 4-6 weeks on ms. SASE for ms. Photocopied submissions OK. Accepts computer printout submissions. Sample copy and fiction guidelines free.
Payment: $500.
Terms: Pays on acceptance for all rights.
Advice: "Readers have indicated a desire to read well written erotic fiction, which we classify as a good story with sexual undercurrent. The writer should keep in mind that the first requirement is that the story be a well written piece of fiction, and secondarily that it deal with sex; we are not interested in 'clinically descriptive' sex accounts."

IDEALS MAGAZINE (II), Ideals Publishing Corp., Nelson Place at Elm Hill Pike, Nashville TN 37214. (615)885-8270. Vice President of Publishing: Patricia Pingry. Magazine: 8⁷⁄₁₆×10⅞; 80 pages; 60 lb Cougarpaper; 12 pt CI-S cover; illustrations; photos. "*Ideals* is a family-oriented magazine with issues corresponding to seasons and based on traditional values." Published 8 times a year. Estab. 1944.
Needs: Seasonal, inspirational, spiritual, or humorous short, short fiction or prose poem. Beginning new policy of one short story per issue. Length: 2,000 words maximum.
How to Contact: Send complete ms with SASE. Reports in 8-12 weeks on mss.
Payment: Varies.
Terms: Pays on publication for one-time rights.
Advice: "We publish fiction that is appropriate to the theme of the issue and to our audience."

IN TOUCH (II, IV), Wesley Press, Box 50434 Indianapolis IN 46250-0434. (317)576-8144. Editor: Rebecca Higgins. Magazine: 8½×11; 32 pages; offset paper and cover stock; illustrations; photos. Publication for teens, ages 13-18. Monthly in weekly parts.
Needs: *True* experiences and Christian testimonies told in fiction style, humorous fiction, C.S. Lewis-type allegories and spiritual. Receives 100 unsolicited fiction mss/month. Length: 500-1,200 words.
How to Contact: Send complete ms with SASE. "Queries are not encouraged." Accepts computer printout submissions; prefers letter-quality. Reports in 3-6 weeks on mss. Publishes ms 6-9 months after acceptance.
Payment: Pays 4¢/word, 2¢/word on reprints.
Terms: Pays on acceptance. Byline given and brief autobiographical sketch. Buys reprints.
Advice: "Send SASE for writer's guide before submitting. We are only using true events written in fiction style, humor and allegories. Most religious fiction is unrealistic."

IN TOUCH FOR MEN (IV), 7216 Varna St., North Hollywood CA 91605. (818)764-2288. Editor: Bob Stanford. Magazine: 8×10¾; 100 pages; glossy paper; coated cover; illustrations and photographs. "*In Touch* is a magazine for gay men. It features five nude male centerfolds in each issue, but is erotic rather than pornographic. We include fiction, articles, interviews, humor, cartoons, media comment." Monthly. Estab. 1973. Circ. 70,000.
Needs: Adventure, confession, contemporary, erotica, ethnic, experimental, fantasy, gay, historical, horror, humor, literary, regional, romance (contemporary, historical, young adult), science fiction, suspense/mystery, translations, western. All characters must be over 18 years old. Stories must have an explicit erotic content. No heterosexual or internalized homophobic fiction. Buys 3 mss/month; 36 mss/year. Publishes ms 3 months after acceptance. Length: 2,500 words average; no minimum; 3,500 words maximum. Sometimes critiques rejected mss and recommends other markets.
How to Contact: Send complete ms with cover letter, name, address and Social Security number. Reports in 1 week on queries; 2 months on mss. SASE. Simultaneous, photocopied and reprint submissions, if from local publication, OK. Accepts computer printout submissions. Sample copy $4.95. Fiction guidelines free.
Payment: $25-75 (except on rare occasions for a longer piece).
Terms: Pays on acceptance for one-time rights. Publication copyrighted.
Advice: "Fiction is one of the most popular features of our magazine."

‡INDIA CURRENTS (II,IV), San Francisco Bay Area's Guide to Indian Arts, Entertainment and Dining, Box 21285, San Jose CA 95151. (408)274-6966. Editor: Arvind Kumar. Magazine: 8½×11; 72 pages; newsprint paper; illustrations and photographs. "The arts and culture of India as seen in America for Indians and non-Indians with a common interest in India." Monthly. Estab. 1987. Circ. 14,000.
Needs: All Indian content: contemporary, ethnic, feminist, historical (general), humor/satire, literary, mainstream, prose poem, psychic/supernatural/occult, regional, religious/inspirational, romance, translations (from Indian languages). "We seek material with insight into Indian culture, American culture and the crossing from one to another." Receives 12 unsolicited mss/month. Buys 6 ms/issue; 72 mss/year. Publishes ms 2-6 months after acceptance. Recently published work by Javaid Qazi, Tom Jones and Jayathi Murthy. Length: 2,000 words average; 1,500 words minimum; 4,000 words maximum. Publishes short shorts. Length: 500 words. Sometimes critiques rejected mss and recommends other markets.
How to Contact: Send complete ms with cover letter and clips of published work. Reports in 1 month on queries; 2 months on mss. SASE. Simultaneous, photocopied and reprint submissions OK. Computer printout submissions are acceptable. Accepts electronic submissions. Sample copy $2.
Payment: Pays $20/1,000 words.
Terms: Pays on publication for one-time rights.
Advice: "Story must be related to India and subcontinent in some meaningful way. The best stories are those which document some deep transformation as a result of an Indian experience, or those which show the humanity of Indians as the world's most ancient citizens."

INDIAN LIFE MAGAZINE (II, IV), Intertribal Christian Communications, Box 3765, Station B, Winnipeg, Manitoba RAW 3R6 Canada. (204)661-9333. Editor: Jim Uttley. Magazine: 8½×11; 24 pages; newsprint paper and cover stock; illustrations; photos. A nondenominational Christian magazine written and read mostly by North American Indians. Bimonthly. Estab. 1979. Circ. 63,000.

Needs: Adventure, confession, ethnic (Indian), historical (general), juvenile, men's, religious/inspirational, women's and young adult/teen. Receives 2-3 unsolicited mss/month. Buys 1 ms/issue; 4-5 mss/year. Recently published work by Margaret Primrose and Ann Dunn. Published new writers within the last year. Length: 1,000-1,200 words average. Publishes short shorts of 600-900 words. Occasionally comments on rejected mss.

How to Contact: Query first, send complete manuscript (with cover letter, bio and published clips), or query with clips of published work. Reports in 1 month on queries; in 2 months on mss. IRC or SASE ("US stamps no good up here"). Accepts computer printout submissions. Prefers letter-quality. Sample copy $1 and 8½×11 SAE. Fiction guidelines for $1 and #10 SAE.

Payment: 4¢/word and 5 contributor's copies; 50¢ charge for extras.

Terms: Pays on publication for first rights.

Advice: "Keep it simple with an Indian viewpoint at about a 5th grade reading level. Read story out loud. Have someone else read it to you. If it doesn't come across smoothly and naturally, it needs work."

INSIDE (II), The Magazine of the Jewish Exponent, Jewish Federation, 226 S. 16th St., Philadelphia PA 19102. (215)893-5700. Editor-in-Chief: Jane Biberman. Magazine: 175-225 pages; glossy paper; illustrations; photos. Aimed at middle- and upper-middle-class audience, Jewish-oriented articles and fiction. Quarterly. Estab. 1980. Circ. 80,000.

Needs: Contemporary, ethnic, humor/satire, literary and translations. No erotica. Receives approximately 10 unsolicited fiction mss/month. Buys 1-2 mss/issue, 4-8 mss/year. Published new writers within the last year. Length: 1,500 words minimum; 3,000 words maximum; 2,000 words average. Occasionally critiques rejected mss.

How to Contact: Query first with clips of published work. Reports on queries in 3 weeks. SASE. Accepts computer printouts, no dot-matrix. Simultaneous and photocopied submissions OK. Sample copy $3. Free fiction guidelines with SASE.

Payment: $100-600.

Terms: Pays on acceptance for first rights. Sometimes buys reprints. Sends galleys to author. Publication copyrighted.

Advice: "We're looking for original, avant-garde, stylish writing."

INSIDE TEXAS RUNNING (II, IV), The Tabloid Magazine That Runs Texas, 9514 Bristlebrook, Houston TX 77083. (713)498-3208. Publisher/Editor: Joanne Schmidt. Specialized tabloid for Texas joggers/runners—novice to marathoner, bicycling, aerobics and general fitness. Monthly. Estab. 1977. Circ. 10,000; overall readers 30,000.

Needs: Historical (general), humor/satire, literary, and serialized/excerpted books on running and general fitness. "Nothing sexually explicit—we're family-oriented." Texas-oriented mss preferred. Buys 1 ms/issue. Length: 500 words minimum; 2,000 words maximum. Occasionally critiques rejected mss.

How to Contact: *Query only.* "We're overrun with too much to read. Not accepting manuscripts at this time." Simultaneous, photocopied and previously published submissions OK. Reports in 1 month on mss. Sample copy $1.50. Free fiction guidelines with SASE.

Payment: $25-75.

Terms: Pays on acceptance for one-time rights. Publication copyrighted.

Advice: "If a writer has something useful and original to convey, editors will want to buy his work. Period. A writer should ask himself if he, as a reader, would find the story worth reading. Too many writers can't look beyond their own experiences and relate every boring detail of some personal incident, which they disguise as fiction."

INSIGHTS (II, IV), NRA News for Young Shooters, National Rifle Association of America, 1600 Rhode Island Ave. NW, Washington DC 20036. (202)828-6059. Editor: Brenda K. Dalessandro. Magazine: 8⅛×10⅞; 24 pages; 60 lb Midset paper and cover; illustrations and photos. "*InSights* publishes educational yet entertaining articles, teaching young hunters and shooters ways to improve their performance. For boys and girls ages eight to 20." Monthly. Estab. 1981. Circ. 40,000.

Needs: Hunting or competition shooting. No "anti-hunting, anti-firearms." Receives 5-10 unsolicited mss/month. Accepts 1 ms/issue; 12 mss/year. Publishes ms an average of 1 month to 1 year after acceptance. Recently published work by Buck Taylor and Todd Woodard. Published new writers within the last year. Length: 1,000 words minimum; 1,500 words maximum. Publishes short shorts. Sometimes critiques rejected ms; occasionally recommends other markets.

How to Contact: Query with clips of published work and cover letter. Reports in 1 month on query; 6-8 weeks on mss. SASE. Photocopied submissions OK. Accepts computer printout submissions. Sample copy and fiction guidelines free.
Payment: Up to $150.
Terms: Pays on acceptance.
Advice: "Writing is an art but publishing is a business—a big business. Any writer who understands his market place has an edge over a writer who isn't familiar with the publications that want his kind of writing. We have become more discriminating in the fiction that we buy. Story has to have a strong plot and must present a lesson, whether it is gun safety, ethics or hunting knowledge."

JACK AND JILL, The Benjamin Franklin Literary & Medical Society, Inc., 1100 Waterway Blvd., Box 567, Indianapolis IN 46206. (317)636-8881. Editor: Steve Charles. Children's magazine of articles, stories and activities many with a health, safety, exercise or nutritional-oriented theme, ages 6-8 years. Monthly except February/March, April/May, June/July, August/September. Estab. 1938.
Needs: Science fiction, mystery, sports, adventure, historical fiction and humor. Health-related stories with a subtle lesson. No religious subjects. Recently published work by Peter Fernandez, Adriana Devoy and Myra Schomberg; published new writers within the last year. Length: 500-1,500 words.
How to Contact: Send complete ms with SASE. Reports in 10 weeks on mss. Sample copy 75¢. Free fiction guidelines with SASE.
Payment: 8¢/word.
Terms: Pays on publication for all rights.
Advice: "Try to present health material in a positive—not a negative—light. Use humor and a light approach wherever possible without minimizing the seriousness of the subject. We need more humor and adventure stories."

JIVE, BLACK CONFESSIONS, BLACK ROMANCE, BRONZE THRILLS (I, II), Sterling's Magazines/Lexington Library, 355 Lexington Ave., New York NY 10017. (212)949-6850. Editor: D. Boyd. Magazine: 8½×11; 72 pages; newsprint paper; glossy cover; 8×10 photographs. "We publish stories that are ultra romantic and have romantic lovemaking scenes in them. Our audience is basically young and in high school and college. However, we have a significant audience base of divorcees and housewives. The age range is from 18-49." Bimonthly (*Jive* and *Black Romance* in odd-numbered months; *Black Confessions* and *Bronze Thrills* in even-numbered months). Estab. 1962. Circ. 100,000.
Needs: Confession, romance (contemporary, young adult). No "stories that are stereotypical to black people, ones that do not follow the basic rules of writing, or ones that are too graphic in content and lack a romantic element." Receives 200 or more unsolicited fiction mss/month. Buys 6 mss/issue (2 issues/month); 144 mss/year. Publishes ms an average of 3-6 months after acceptance. Recently published work by Francis Ray, Nancy Bulk; published new writers within the last year. Length: 15-19 pages. Always critiques rejected mss; recommends other markets.
How to Contact: Query with clips of published work or send complete ms with cover letter. A cover letter should include an author's bio and what he or she proposes to do. Of course, address and phone number." Reports in 3-6 months. SASE. Simultaneous and photocopied submissions OK. "Please contact me if simultaneously submitted work has been accepted elsewhere." Accepts computer printout submissions. Sample copy for 9×12 SAE and 5 first class stamps; fiction guidelines for #10 SAE and 2 first class stamps.
Payment: $75-100.
Terms: Pays on publication for first rights or one-time rights.
Advice: "Our four magazines are a great starting point for new writers. We accept work from beginners as well as established writers. Please study and research black culture and lifestyles if you are not a black writer. Stereotypical stories are not acceptable. Set the stories all over the world and all over the USA—not just down south. We are not looking for 'the runaway who gets turned out by a sweet-talking pimp' stories. We are looking for stories about all types of female characters. Any writer should not be afraid to communicate with us if he or she is having some difficulty with writing a story. We are available to help at any stage of the submission process. Also, writers should practice patience. If we do not contact the writer, that means that the story is being read or is being held on file for future publication. If we get in touch with the writer, it usually means a request for revision and resubmission. Do the best work possible and don't let rejection slips send you off 'the deep end.' Don't take everything that is said about your work so personally. We are buying all of our work from freelance writers.

JUGGLER'S WORLD (IV), International Juggler's Association, Box 443, Davidson NC 28036. (704)892-1296. Editor: Bill Giduz. Fiction Editor: Ken Letko. Magazine: 8½×11; 44 pages; 70 lb paper and cover stock; illustrations and photos. For and about jugglers and juggling. Quarterly.
Needs: Historical (general), humor/satire, science fiction. No stories "that don't include juggling as a central theme." Receives "very few" unsolicited mss/month. Accepts 2 mss/year. Publishes ms an average of 6 months to 1 year after acceptance. Length: 1,000 words average; 500 words minimum;

2,000 words maximum. Publishes short shorts. Sometimes critiques rejected mss.
How to Contact: Query first. Reports in 1 week. Simultaneous and photocopied submissions OK. Accepts computer printout submissions. Accepts electronic submissions via IBM compatible disk. Sample copy $2.
Payment: $25-50, free subscription to magazine and 5 contributor's copies.
Terms: Pays on acceptance for first rights.

Editor Bill Giduz photographed top world-class juggler Kris Kremo for the Summer 1989 cover, conveying juggling as "a happy, upbeat activity." In addition to being editor since 1978, Giduz has also served as a writer and photographer for the magazine.

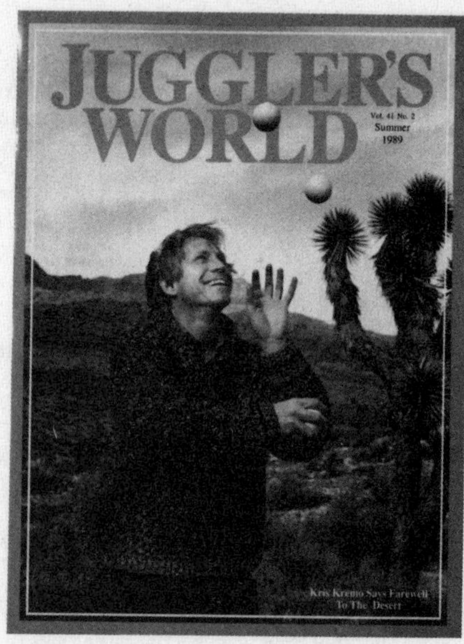

Cover photo copyright ©1989 by Bill Giduz.

KID CITY (II), Children's Television Workshop, 1 Lincoln Plaza, New York NY 10023. (212)595-3456. Editor: Maureen Hunter-Bone. Magazine: 8½x11; 32 pages; glossy cover; illustrations; photos. General interest for children 6-10 "devoted to sparking kids' interest in reading and writing about the world around them." Published 10 times/year. Estab. 1974. Circ. 260,000.
Needs: Adventure, mystery, juvenile (6-10 years), science fiction. Publishes ms 6 months "at least" after acceptance. Length: 600-750 words average; 1,000 words maximum.
How to Contact: Send complete ms with cover letter. Reports in 1-2 months on mss. SASE. Photocopied submissions OK. Accepts computer printout submissions. Sample copy $1.50 and 9×12 SAE with 75¢ postage. Writers' guidelines free for 9×12 SAE with 75¢ postage.
Payment: Pays $200-400 and contributor's copies.
Terms: Pays on acceptance for all rights (some negotiable).
Advice: "We look for bright and sparkling prose. Don't talk down. Don't stereotype. Don't use cutesy names, animals or plots. No heavy moralizing or pat dilemmas."

KINDERGARTEN LISTEN (IV), Beacon Hill Press, Box 419527, Kansas City MO 64141. (816)931-1900 or (816)333-7000 (editorial). Editor: Jan Sawyer. Fiction Editor: Lisa Ham. Tabloid: 4 page story paper; 8½×11; newsprint; newsprint cover; b&w and 4 color illustrations; 4 color photos. "Stories cover a 2-year topic cycle available upon request. Readers are kindergarten 4s, 5s and early 6s." Weekly. Estab. 1981. Circ. 45,000.
Needs: Contemporary, prose poem, religious/inspirational, spiritual, Christian topic themes. Recently published work by Barbara Kraus, Donna Colwell Rosser, V. J. Luckery. Length: 200 words minimum; 400 words maximum. Sometimes critiques rejected mss and recommends other markets.
How to Contact: Query first "if unfamiliar with 2-year topic cycle" or send complete mss. Writers must include SASE for each submission. Reports in 3 weeks on queries; in 1 month on mss. SASE. Photocopied submissions OK. Accepts computer printout submissions. Accepts electronic submissions via disk or modem in ASCII text only. Sample copy and fiction guidelines for 8½×11 SAE and 1 first class stamp.

Payment: Pays $10-17, with contributor's copies (4 each purchase). Charge for extra copies.
Terms: Pays on acceptance for all rights, first rights or one-time rights (as specified by author).
Advice: "A majority of submissions we've received lately are of poor quality. Dialogue and actions of main child characters are unrealistic to the young age group our magazine ministers to. Actions and dialogue of parent characters is often too unrealistic as well. They're either too good to be true or very stilted in actions and speech. Because today's children are growing up in a rough world, we seek to help them deal with a variety of situations from divorce to the simple worries of a young child, like being left with a new babysitter. We seek to portray fictional children finding real solutions in the love and guidance of Christ, assisted by parent and other adult figures. Too many submissions appear to come from writers who don't take the children's market seriously or view it as an easy area to write prose for. In fact, children's stories require research and realism, and much effort in writing and rewriting. Writers have to know the audience well, not just guess or try to recall what it was like to be a Pre-K kid. Few writers can relate well enough to produce good manuscripts without these efforts." Criteria used in choosing fiction: "(1) Does it relate to our theme titles for the 2-year cycle (2) Is the story interesting to children (3) Does it assist them in understanding some vital area of the Christian life, God's love, etc. (4) Is it realistic in portrayal of all characters (5) Does it flow naturally and make for good reading (6) Does the story line progress logically (7) Does it include any inappropriate references to parent behavior, an accepted practice or doctrine of the Church of the Nazarene. Ex: We've had a hair-raising number of writers portraying scenes where children are left unattended in shopping malls or some other public place—which is highly inappropriate parental behavior considering the abduction situation that has terrorized our country's parents and families. The portrayal shows little insight on the writer's part."

LADIES' HOME JOURNAL (III), (Published by Meredith Corporation), 100 Park Ave., New York NY 10017. Editor-in-Chief: Myrna Blyth. Fiction/Books Editor: Mary Lou Mullen. Magazine: 190 pages; 34-38 lb coated paper; 65 lb coated cover; illustrations and photos.
Needs: Book mss and short stories, *accepted only through an agent*. Return of unsolicited material cannot be guaranteed. Recently published work by Anne Tyler, Bobbie Ann Mason and Joyce Carol Oates. Length: approximately 3,500 words.
How to Contact: Cover letter with ms (credits). Publishes ms 4 months to 1 year after acceptance.
Terms: Buys First North American rights.
Advice: "Our readers like stories, especially those that have emotional impact. We are using fiction every month, whether it's an excerpt from a novel or a short story. Stories about relationships between people—husband/wife—mother/son—seem to be subjects that can be explored effectively in short stories. Our reader's mail and surveys attest to this fact: Readers enjoy our fiction, and are most keenly tuned to stories dealing with children. Fiction today is stronger than ever. Beginners can be optimistic; if they have talent, I do believe that talent will be discovered."

LADYS CIRCLE (II), Lopez Publications, 111 East 35th St., New York NY 10016. (212)689-3933. Fiction Editor: Mary Bemis. Magazine. "A lot of our readers are in Midwestern states." Monthly. Estab. 1963. Circ. 300,000.
Needs: Confession, ethnic, historical, humor/satire, juvenile, mainstream, religious/inspirational, romance (contemporary, historical, young adult), senior citizen/retirement, young adult/teen. Receives 100 unsolicited fiction mss/month. Buys 3-4 fiction mss/issue; about 6-7 fiction mss/year. Time between acceptance and publication "varies, usually works 2 months ahead." Length: 3,000 words preferred; 1,000 words minimum; 3,000 words maximum. Accepts short shorts "for fillers." Sometimes critiques rejected ms.
How to Contact: Query first. Reports in up to 3 months on queries. SASE. Simultaneous, photocopied and reprint submissions OK. Accepts electronic submissions via disk or modem. Sample copy for $1.95; fiction guidelines for SAE.
Payment: Pay varies, depending on ms.
Terms: Pays on publication for first North American serial rights.

LATTER-DAY WOMAN MAGAZINE (II), Box 126, Sandy UT 84070. (801)255-5239. Fiction Editor: Marsha Newman. Magazine: 5⅜×8⅜; 48-64 pages; slick 60 lb paper; 70 lb cover; mostly b&w illustrations; approx 4 color photos per issue, 1 or 2 b&w photos. "Our purpose is to offer inspiration and support to help women cope with challenges. We explore today's issues with an uplifting, reassuring perspective. Theme: to help overcome feelings of isolation and discouragement for Christian women, mainstream women, mostly mothers juggling many roles. Age range 20-up. Largest concentration between age 35-60." Bimonthly. Estab. 1986. Circ. 15,000.
Needs: Condensed novel, humor/satire, literary, mainstream, religious/inspirational. "We want stories dealing with women and their problems, written in a convincing, realistic fashion. They must leave the reader with a sense of warmth or comfort or humorous identification." Receives approx. 5 unsolicited fiction mss/month. Accepts 2 mss/issue; 12 mss/year. Length: 500 words average; 750 words maximum.

Publishes short shorts. Sometimes critiques rejected mss and may recommend other markets.
How to Contact: Send complete ms—no cover letter required. Reports in 3 months. SASE. Simultaneous, photocopied and reprint submissions OK. Accepts computer printout submissions. Sample copy free. Fiction guidelines for #10 SASE.
Payment: 5¢/word.
Terms: Pays on publication for first rights. Sends pre-publication galleys to author.
Advice: "Our readers love fiction. We don't receive nearly enough of it. We quickly print any fiction of exceptional quality and short length that comes our way. Many insights can be shared in a non-preachy way thru fiction and feedback from our readers assures us of their enthusiasm for a good story. We prefer that stories make a point, give a fresh insight, leave a feeling of completion."

LIGHTED PATHWAY (II), Church of God Publishing House (Pathway Press), 922 Montgomery Ave., Cleveland TN 37311. (615)476-4512. Editor: Marcus V. Hand. Magazine: 8½×11; 28 pages; b&w photos. Christian, evangelical, youth inspiration magazine (ages 15-25) with at least two fiction short stories per issue. Monthly. Estab. 1929. Circ. 26,000.
Needs: Adventure, contemporary, feminist, historical (general), humor/satire, juvenile, religious/inspirational and young adult. "Real life problems, no profanity." Receives 1-24 unsolicited fiction mss/month. Buys 2 (minimum) mss/issue; 24 (minimum) mss/year. Published new writers within the last year. Length: 800-1,200 words preferred; 1,500 words maximum. Occasionally critiques rejected mss.
How to Contact: Query first or send complete ms. SASE always. Simultaneous and previously published submissions OK sometimes. Accepts computer printout submissions; prefers letter-quality. Reports in 3 weeks on queries and mss. Free sample copy and fiction guidelines with SASE.
Payment: 2-5¢/word; 3 contributor's copies. 75¢ charge for extras.
Terms: Pays on acceptance for first North American serial rights and one-time rights.
Advice: "Study a sample. Make story exciting."

LIGUORIAN (I, IV), "A Leading Catholic Magazine", Liguori Publications, 1 Liguori Dr., Liguori MO 63057. (314)464-2500. Editor-in-Chief: Norman J. Muckerman, CSS.R. Managing Editor: Francine M. O'Connor. Magazine: 5×8½; 64 pages; b&w illustrations and photographs. "*Liguorian* is a Catholic magazine aimed at helping our readers to live a full Christian life. We publish articles for families, young people, children, religious and singles—all with the same aim." Monthly. Estab. 1913. Circ. 500,000.
Needs: Religious/inspirational, young adult and senior citizen/retirement (with moral Christian thrust), spiritual. "Stories submitted to *Liguorian* must have as their goal the lifting up of the reader to a higher Christian view of values and goals. We are not interested in contemporary works that lack purpose or are of questionable moral value." Receives approximately 25 unsolicited fiction mss/month. Buys 4-5 mss/year. Recently published work by Mitch Finley, Sharon Helgens and Louis G. Miller, CSS.R. Published new writers within the last year. Length: 1,500-2,000 words preferred. Also publishes short shorts. Occasionally critiques rejected mss "if we feel the author is capable of giving us something we need even though this story did not suit us." Occasionally recommends other markets.
How to Contact: Send complete ms with SASE. Accepts computer printout submissions; prefers letter-quality. Accepts disk submissions compatible with TRS-80 Model III. Prefers hard copy with disk submission. Reports in 6 weeks on mss. Sample copy for $1.25; free fiction guidelines..
Payment: 7-10¢/word and 6 contributor's copies. Offers 50% kill fee for assigned mss not published.
Terms: Pays on acceptance for all rights. Publication copyrighted.
Advice: "First read several issues containing short stories. We look for originality and creative input in each story we read. Since most editors must wade through mounds of manuscripts each month, consideration for the editor requires that the market be studied, the manuscript be carefully presented and polished before submitting. Our publication uses only one story a month. Compare this with the 25 or more we receive over the transom each month. Also, many fiction mss are written without a specific goal or thrust, i.e., an interesting incident that goes nowhere is *not a story*. We believe fiction is a highly effective mode for transmitting the Christian message and also provides a good balance in an unusually heavy issue."

LIVE, Assemblies of God, 1445 Boonville, Springfield MO 65802. (417)862-2781. Editor: John Maempa. A Sunday school take-home paper for adults containing stories and articles of believable characters working out their problems according to Bible principles. Weekly. Circ. 192,000.
Needs: Religious/inspirational, prose poem and spiritual. No controversial stories about such subjects as feminism, war or capital punishment. Buys 2 mss/issue. Recently published work by Maxine F. Dennis, E. Ruth Glover and Todd Lee; published new writers within the last year. Length: 1,000-2,000 words.

How to Contact: Send complete ms with SASE. Social Security number and word count must be included. Free sample copy and fiction guidelines only with SASE.
Payment: 3¢/word (first rights); 2¢/word (second rights).
Terms: Pays on acceptance for one-time rights.
Advice: "Closely study needs of a given publisher (what he has published) and match with the story in question."

LIVING WITH TEENAGERS (II), Baptist Sunday School Board, 127 9th Ave. North, Nashville TN 37234. (615)251-2273. Editor: Jimmy Hester. Magazine: 10⅜×8⅛; 50 pages; illustrations; photos. Magazine especially designed "to enrich the parent-teen relationship, with reading material from a Christian perspective" for Southern Baptist parents of teenagers. Quarterly. Estab. 1978. Circ. 50,000.
Needs: Religious/inspirational, spiritual and parent-teen relationships. Nothing not related to parent-teen relationships or not from a Christian perspective. Buys 2 mss/issue. Receives approximately 50 unsolicited fiction mss/month. Length: 600-1,200 words (short shorts).
How to Contact: Cover letter with reason for writing article; credentials for writing. Query with clips of published work or send complete ms. SASE always. Reports in 2 months on both queries and mss. Free sample copy with 9×12 SAE and proper postage.
Payment: 5¢/published word. 3 free author's copies.
Terms: Pays on acceptance for all and first rights.
Advice: "Sometimes a fictitious story can communicate a principle in the parent-youth relationship quite well."

LOLLIPOPS MAGAZINE (II), (formerly *Lollipops, Ladybugs and Lucky Stars*), Good Apple, Inc., Box 299, Carthage IL 62321. (217)357-3981. Editor: Jerry Aten. Magazine: 8½×11; 64 pages; illustrations. "Preschool-2nd grade publication for teachers and their students. All educational material. Short stories, poems, activities, math, gameboards." 5 times/year. Circ. 18,000.
Needs: Preschool-grade 2. Submissions cover all areas of the curriculum. Seasonal materials considered. Receives 40-50 unsolicited mss/month. Number of fiction mss bought varies per issue. Occasionally accepts short stories (500-750 words). Published new writers within the last year.
How to Contact: Query first or write for guidelines and a free sample copy. Reports in 1 week on queries. SASE for ms. Accepts computer printouts. Send for free sample copies and guidelines.
Payment: Depends on story.
Terms: Pays on publication for all rights.

THE LOOKOUT (II), Standard Publishing, 8121 Hamilton Ave., Cincinnati OH 45231. (513)931-4050. Editor: Mark A. Taylor. Magazine: 8½×11; 16 pages; newsprint paper; newsprint cover stock; illustrations; photos. "Conservative Christian magazine for adults and young adults." Weekly. Estab. 1894. Circ. 125,000.
Needs: Religious/inspirational. No predictable, preachy material. Taboos are blatant sex, swear words and drinking alcohol. Receives 50 unsolicited mss/month. Buys 1 ms/issue; buys 45-50 mss/year. Length: 1,200-2,000 words.
How to Contact: Send complete ms with SASE. Accepts computer printout submissions. Prefers letter-quality. Reports in 2 months on ms. Simultaneous, photocopied and reprint submissions OK. Publishes ms 2 months to 1 year after acceptance. Sample copy 50¢. Free guidelines with #10 SASE.
Payment: 5-6¢/word for first rights. 4-5¢/word for other rights. Free author's copies.
Terms: Pays on acceptance for one-time rights. Buys reprints.
Advice: "No queries please. Send us a believable story which is inspirational and helpful but down to earth."

THE LUTHERAN JOURNAL, Outlook Publications, Inc., 7317 Cahill Rd., Minneapolis MN 55435. (612)941-6830. Editor: Rev. A.U. Deye. A family magazine providing wholesome and inspirational reading material for the enjoyment and enrichment of Lutherans. Quarterly. Estab. 1936. Circ. 136,000.
Needs: Literary, contemporary, religious/inspirational, romance (historical), senior citizen/retirement and young adult. Must be appropriate for distribution in the churches. Buys 2-4 mss/issue. Length: 1,000-2,500 words.
How to Contact: Send complete ms with SASE. Accepts computer printout submissions. Free sample copy with SASE (59¢ postage).
Payment: $10-25 and 6 free author's copies.
Terms: Pays on publication for all and first rights.

M.A. TRAINING, Rainbow Publications, 1813 Victory Place, Burbank CA 91504. (818)843-4444. Editor: William Groak. Magazine: 88 pages; illustrations. "*M.A. Training* is a magazine limited to self-training aspects of martial arts." Quarterly. Estab. 1973. Circ. 75,000.

Needs: Self-training techniques, some fiction pertaining to the arts, workout routines, history. No erotica, and anything else that does not pertain to our focus." Receives 5-10 unsolicited mss/month. Buys 2-3 ms/issue; 6 mss/year. Length: 1,500+ words. Occasionally critiques rejected mss. Recommends other markets.
How to Contact: Query first or call 1-800-423-2874. Reports in 2-4 weeks on queries and mss. SASE for query and ms. Simultaneous and photocopied submissions OK. Accepts computer printouts. Sample copy free with SASE. Fiction guidelines free.
Payment: Pays $75-150.
Terms: Pays on publication for first North American serial rights. Publication copyrighted.
Advice: "As a martial arts magazine, we need stories that will satisfy our core readership, but also some that could interest non-martial artists. Fiction not only gives the reader a break, but also provides a change in terms of what issues can be addressed and how they can be presented."

McCALL'S (II), The New York Times Company, 230 Park Ave., New York NY 10169. Editor: Anne Mollegen Smith. Fiction Editor: Helen DelMonte. General women's magazine that explores the complex challenges facing women in the 1990s. Monthly. Estab. 1876. Circ. 5,000,000.
Needs: "We are looking for well written, thoughtful, provocative stories that will offer readers fresh insight into their own lives. Stories may be about any subject as long as it is made compelling. Slight preference for stories about women and classic women's experiences, but interesting and empathic portrayals of men's and children's lives also are welcome. Reader identification important but open to the occasional idiosyncratic story, as well as the story that reveals a new world to the reader. Stories must be generally accessible to a broad audience. Stories should have structure, an emotionally involving central conflict, strong narrative flow and a meaningful resolution. Not interested in vignettes or stories that are highly oblique. Light stories welcome as long as they are written with artistry and craft."
How to Contact: Send complete ms with SASE. Reports in 1-2 months on ms. Free guidelines with SASE. Cover letter should list previous publishing credits.
Payment: $2,500-5,000. ($2,500 for first story published in a national magazine.) $2,200 for short shorts. Length: 2,500-3,000 words. 2,000 and less for short shorts.
Terms: Pays on acceptance for first North American serial rights.
Advice: "Read the stories in the magazine, not to imitate but to get a sense of the kinds of stories we publish. Pay close attention to characterization. If the characters don't engage our interest and sympathy, the story will never work. Remember that a story must *tell* a story."

MADEMOISELLE MAGAZINE, Condé Nast Publications, Inc., 350 Madison Ave., New York NY 10017. (212)880-8690. Fiction Editor: Eileen Schnurr. Fashion magazine for women from ages 18-34 with articles of interest to women; beauty and health tips, features, home and food, fiction. Audience interested in self-improvement, curious about trends, interested in updating lifestyle and pursuing a career. Monthly. Estab. 1935. Circ. 1.1 million.
Needs: Literary and contemporary short stories. Publishes 1-2 ms/issue, 12-20 mss/year. Recently published work by Maxine Kawui, Mary Gordon, Kelly Cheny; published new writers within the last year. Length: 7-25 pages.
How to Contact: Send complete ms with SASE. Reports in 3 months. Publishes ms up to a year after acceptance. Free fiction guidelines with SASE.
Payment: $1,000 minimum for short shorts; $1,500 for short stories.
Terms: Pays on acceptance for first North American serial rights.
Advice: "We are particularly interested in stories of relevance to young single women, and we continue in the *Mademoiselle* tradition of publishing fiction of literary quality. Be sure to see the listing in Contest and Awards section for guidelines for *Mademoiselle's* Fiction Writers Contest."

THE MAGAZINE FOR CHRISTIAN YOUTH! (II), The United Methodist Publishing House, 201 8th Avenue S., Nashville TN 37202. (615)749-6463. Editor: Christopher B. Hughes. Magazine: 8½×11; 52 pages; slick, matte finish paper. "*The Magazine for Christian Youth!* tries to help teenagers develop Christian identity and live their faith in contemporary culture. Fiction and nonfiction which contributes to this purpose are welcome." Monthly. Estab. 1985. Circ. 45,000.
Needs: Adventure, contemporary, ethnic, fantasy, humor/satire, prose poem, religious/inspirational, science fiction, spiritual, suspense/mystery, translations, young adult/teen (10-18 years). "Don't preach; but story should have a message to help teenagers in some way or to make them think more deeply about an issue. No Sunday school lessons, like those found in curriculum." Receives 50-75 unsolicited mss/month. Buys 1-2 mss/issue; 12-24 mss/year. Publishes ms 9-12 months after acceptance. Length: 700-2,000 words. Publishes short shorts.
How to Contact: Send complete ms with cover letter. Reports in 3-6 months. SASE. Simultaneous and reprint submissions OK. Accepts computer printouts. Sample copy and fiction guidelines free for #10 SASE.

Payment: Pays $1.50 minimum, 4¢/word.
Terms: Pays on acceptance for first North American serial rights or one-time rights.
Advice: "Get a feel for our magazine first. Don't send in the types of fiction that would appear in Sunday school curriculum just because it's a Christian publication. Reflect the real world of teens in contemporary fiction."

MAGAZINE OF FANTASY AND SCIENCE FICTION (II), Box 56, Cornwall CT 06753. (203)672-6376. Publisher/Editor: Edward L. Ferman. Magazine: illustrations on cover only. Publishes "science fiction and fantasy. Our readers are age 13 and up who are interested in science fiction and fantasy." Monthly. Plans special fiction issue. Estab. 1949.
Needs: Fantasy and science fiction. Receives "hundreds" of unsolicited fiction submissions/month. Buys 8 fiction mss/issue ("on average"). Time between acceptance and publication varies. Length: 10,000 words maximum. Publishes short shorts. Critiques rejected ms, "if quality warrants it." Sometimes recommends other markets.
How to Contact: Send complete ms with cover letter. Reports in 6-8 weeks. SASE. Simultaneous, photocopied and reprint submissions OK. Accepts computer printout submissions; prefers letter-quality. Sample copy for $3 or $5 for 2. Fiction guidelines for SAE.
Payment: Pays 5-7¢/word.
Terms: Pays on acceptance for first North American serial rights; foreign, option on anthology if requested. Publication copyrighted.

‡MAINE, New England Publishing Co., Inc., One Auburn Center, Auburn ME 04210. (207)777-1777. Publisher: David B. Cross. Editor-in-Chief: James W. Flanagan. Magazine: 8⅜×10⅞; 48-96 pages; glossy stock; varied cover stock; full color and b&w photos and illustrations. "The statement that accompanies the title of *MAINE.* is 'for people who love it.' This is the overriding theme of the magazine. Each issue contains departmentalized features in categories that include fiction and creative writing, environment, business, sports, the arts, politics, food, health, education, outdoors and lodging, all of which pertain directly to Maine and are written by people who have had some contact with the state." Published 6 time per year. Established 1989. Circ. 30,000.
Needs: "Well written, creative stories that directly relate to Maine, or whose main characters directly relate to Maine." Length: approx. 2,500 words. Considers short shorts. "Stories exhibiting the Maine brand of humor are also welcome, as well as anecdotal material." Buys several mss/year. Receives several mss each month.
How to Contact: Send complete ms with SASE. Include cover letter discussing background and how writer/story relates to Maine. Reports ASAP with writer guidelines. Free magazine provided on request with SASE only.
Payment: Varies with each article. Writer will be contacted upon acceptance.
Terms: Pays within 30 days of publication.
Advice: "Research your article enough so that you are close to capturing the true spirit of Maine in whatever concept you are trying to convey—whether it be the people, the part of the state and its relation to the rest of the state, activities, etc. Also, 'What I did on my summer vacation' pieces don't stand much of a chance unless the circumstances were extraordinary."

MANSCAPE (II, IV), First Hand Ltd., Box 1314, Teaneck NJ 07666. (201)836-9177. Editor: Lou Thomas. Magazine: digest sized; 130 pages; illustrations. "Magazine is devoted to gay male sexual fetishes; publishes fiction and readers' letters devoted to this theme." Monthly. Estab. 1985. Circ. 60,000.
Needs: Erotica, gay. Should be written in first person. No science fiction or fantasy. Erotica must be based on real life. Receives 25 unsolicited fiction mss/month. Accepts 7 mss/issue; 84 mss/year. Publishes ms an average of 9-18 months after acceptance. Length: 3,000 words average; 2,000 words minimum; 3,750 words maximum. Sometimes critiques rejected ms.
How to Contact: Send complete ms with cover letter. SASE. Accepts computer printout submissions, no dot-matrix. Sample copy $5.00; fiction guidelines for #10 SASE.
Payment: $100-150.
Terms: Pays on publication or in 240 days, whichever comes first, for all rights or first North American serial rights.

MATURE LIVING (II), Sunday School Board of the Southern Baptist Conv., MSN 140, 127 Ninth Ave. N., Nashville TN 37234. (615)251-2191. Editor: Randy Apon. Magazine: 8½×11; 48 pages; non-glare paper; slick cover stock; illustrations; photos. "Our magazine is Christian in content and the material required is what would appeal to 60+ age group (mainly Southern Baptists): inspirational, instructional, nostalgic, humorous. Our magazine is distributed mainly through churches (especially Southern Baptist churches) that buy the magazine in bulk and distribute it to members in this age group." Monthly. Estab. 1977. Circ. 350,000.

Needs: Contemporary, religious/inspirational, humor, gardening tips, prose poem, spiritual and senior citizen/retirement. Avoid all types of pornography, drugs, liquor, horror, science fiction and stories demeaning to the elderly. Buys 1 ms/issue. Recently published work by Burndean N. Sheffy, Pearl E. Trigg, Joyce M. Sixberry; published new writers within the last year. Length: 425-1,475 words (prefers 900). "Also, please use 42-characters per line."
How to Contact: Send complete ms with SASE. Reports in 6 weeks on mss. Publishes ms an average of 1 year after acceptance. Sample copy $1. Free guidelines with SASE.
Payment: $21-73; 3 free author's copies. 85¢ charge for extras.
Terms: Pays on acceptance. First rights 15% less than all rights, reprint rights 25% less. Rarely buys reprints.
Advice: Mss are rejected because they are too long or subject matter unsuitable. "Our readers seem to enjoy an occasional short piece of fiction. It must be believable, however, and present senior adults in a favorable light."

MATURE YEARS (II), United Methodist Publishing House, 201 Eighth Ave. S., Nashville TN 37202. (615)749-6468. Editor: Donn C. Downall. Magazine: 8½×11; 112 pages; good paper; illustrations and photos. Magazine "helps persons in and nearing retirement to appropriate the resources of the Christian faith as they seek to face the problems and opportunities related to aging." Quarterly. Estab. 1953.
Needs: Religious/inspirational, nostalgia, prose poem, spiritual (for older adults). "We don't want anything poking fun at old age, saccharine stories or anything not for older adults." Buys 3-4 mss/issue, 12-16 mss/year. Needs at least one unsolicited fiction ms each month. Recently published work by Sylvia Bright Green, Jean Zadnichek and Mignon Morgan. Published new writers within the last year. Length: 1,000-1,800 words.
How to Contact: Send complete ms with SASE and Social Security number. Reports in 2 months on mss. Usually publishes ms 1 year to 18 months after acceptance. Free sample copy with 10½×11 SAE and $2.50 postage.
Payment: 4¢/word.
Terms: Pays on acceptance for all and first rights.
Advice: "Practice writing dialogue! Listen to people talk; take notes; master dialogue writing! Not easy, but well worth it! Most inquiry letters are far too long. If you can't sell me an idea in a brief paragraph, you're not going to sell the reader on reading your finished article or story."

MERIDIAN MAGAZINE (IV), Canada's Magazine for the 55 Plus, Troika Publishing Inc., Box 13337, Kanata, Ontario K2K 1X5 Canada. (613)592-5623. Magazine: 8½×11; 24-32 pages; glossy 100 lb paper; 120 lb cover stock; illustrations and photos. "*Meridian* promotes a positive view of aging and publishes information and entertainment articles for people 55 years old and older." Bimonthly. Estab. 1985. Circ. 25,000.
Needs: Humor/satire, senior citizen/retirement. Receives 10 unsolicited fiction mss/month. Accepts 2-3 mss/year. Publishes ms an average of 6 months to 1 year after acceptance. Recently published work by R.M. Thompson and Eliza Moorhouse. Length: 700 words average; 200 words minimum; 1,000 words maximum.
How to Contact: Send complete ms with cover letter. Reports in 1 month on queries; 10 weeks on mss. SASE. Simultaneous and photocopied submissions OK. Accepts computer printout submissions. Sample copy for $3 or 8½×11 SAE and 3 IRCs. Fiction guidelines for #10 SAE and IRC.
Payment: $10-30 Canadian funds; charge for extra copies.
Terms: Pays on publication for first rights.

MESSENGER OF THE SACRED HEART (II), Apostleship of Prayer, 661 Greenwood Ave., Toronto, Ontario M4J 4B3 Canada. (416)466-1195. Editors: Rev. F.J. Power, S.J., and Alfred DeManche. Magazine: 7×10; 32 pages; coated paper; selfcover; illustrations; photos. Magazine for "Canadian and U.S. Catholics interested in developing a life of prayer and spirituality; stresses the great value of our ordinary actions and lives." Monthly. Estab. 1891. Circ. 17,000.
Needs: Religious/inspirational. Stories about people, adventure, heroism, humor, drama. No poetry. Buys 1 ms/issue. Recently published work by Wilhelmena Raisbeck, Ida Mae Kempel and Helen Weldon Anderson; published new writers within the last year. Length: 750-1,500 words. Recommends other markets.

How to Contact: Send complete ms with SAE or IRC. Rarely buys reprints. Reports in 1 month on mss. Sample copy $1.50.
Payment: 4¢/word, 3 free author's copies.
Terms: Pays on acceptance for first North American serial rights.
Advice: "Develop a story that sustains interest to the end. Do not preach, but use plot and characters to convey the message or theme. Aim to move the heart as well as the mind. If you can, add a light touch or a sense of humor to the story. Your ending should have impact, leaving a moral or faith message for the reader."

METRO SINGLES LIFESTYLES (II), Metro Publications, Box 28203, Kansas City MO 64118. (816)436-8424. Editor: Robert L. Huffstutter. Fiction Editor: Earl R. Stonebridge. Tabloid: 36 pages; 30 lb newspaper stock; 30 lb cover; illustrations; photos. "Positive, uplifting, original, semi-literary material for all singles: widowed, divorced, never-married, of all ages 18 and over." Bimonthly. Estab. 1984. Circ. 25,000.
Needs: Humor/satire, literary, prose poem, religious/inspirational, romance (contemporary), special interest, spiritual, single parents. No erotic, political, moralistic fiction. Receives 2-3 unsolicited mss/month. Buys 1-2 mss/issue; 12-18 mss/year. Publishes ms 2 months after acceptance. Length: 1,500 words average; 1,200 words minimum; 4,000 words maximum. Publishes short shorts. Recently published work by Joan Cacciatore Mazza, Corinne M. Lengel and Joan Webster Anderson; published new writers within the last year. Length: 1,200. Occasionally critiques rejected mss. Recommends other markets.
How to Contact: Send complete ms with cover letter. Include short paragraph/bio listing credits (if any), current profession or job. Reports in 3 weeks on queries. SASE. Accepts computer printout submissions. Sample copy $2.
Payment: Pays $25-50, free subscription to magazine and contributor's copies.
Terms: Payment on publication.
Advice: "A question I ask myself about my own writing is: will the reader feel the time spent reading the story or article was worth the effort? Personally, I enjoy stories and articles which will create a particular emotion, build suspense, or offer excitement or entertainment. Features accompanied by photos receive special attention."

MIDSTREAM (II,IV), A Monthly Jewish Review, Theodor Herzl Foundation, 515 Park Ave., New York NY 10022. (212)752-0600. Editor: Murray Zuckoff. Magazine: 8½×11; 64 pages; 50 lb paper; 65 lb white smooth cover stock. "We are a Zionist journal; we publish material with Jewish themes or that would appeal to a Jewish readership." Monthly. Estab. 1955. Circ. 10,000.
Needs: Historical (general), humor/satire, literary, mainstream, translations. Receives 15-20 unsolicited mss/month. Accepts 1 mss/issue; 10 mss/year. Publishes ms 6-18 months after acceptance. 10% of fiction is agented. Recently published work by I. B. Singer, Anita Jackson, Enid Shomer. Length: 2,500 words average; 1,500 words minimum; 3,000 words maximum. Sometimes critiques rejected mss.
How to Contact: Send complete ms with cover letter, which should include "address, telephone, identification or affiliation of author; state that the ms is fiction." Reports in 1-2 weeks. SASE. Photocopied submissions OK. Accepts computer printout submissions; no dot-matrix. Sample copy for 9×12 SAE. Fiction guidelines for #10 SASE.
Payment: Pays 5¢/word and contributor's copies.
Terms: Pays on publication for first rights. Sends prepublication galleys to author.
Advice "Always include a cover letter and double space."

MILITARY LIFESTYLE (II), Downey Communications, Inc., 1732 Wisconsin Ave. NW, Washington DC 20007. (202)944-4000. Editor: Hope M. Daniels. Magazine: 8½×11; 80-100 pages; coated paper; illustrations and photos. Monthly magazine for military families worldwide. Ten issues per year. Estab. 1969. Circ. 520,000.
Needs: Contemporary. "Fiction must deal with lifestyle or issues of particular concern to our specific military families audience." Receives 50 unsolicited mss/month. Buys 1-2 mss/issue; 10-15 mss/year. Publishes ms 2-6 months after acceptance. Recently published work by Pamela Kennedy and Robert Robeson; published new writers within the last year. Length: 1,800 words average. Generally critiques rejected mss. Recommends other markets if applicable.
How to Contact: Send complete ms with cover letter, which should include info on writer and writing credits and history. Reports in 6-8 weeks on mss. SASE. Photocopied submissions OK. Accepts computer printout submissions. Sample copy for $1.50, 9×12 SAE and 4 first class stamps. Fiction guidelines for #10 SASE and 1 first class stamp.

Payment: Pays $400 minimum and 2 free copies.
Terms: Pays generally on publication unless held more than 6 months; then on acceptance for first North American serial rights.
Advice: "Fiction is slice-of-life reading for our audience. Primarily written by military wives or military members themselves, the stories deal with subjects very close to our readers: prolonged absences by spouses, the necessity of handling child-raising alone, the fear of accidents while spouses are on maneuvers or in dangerous situations, etc. The important point: Target the material to our audience—military families—and make the characters real, empathetic and believable. Read your copy over as an objective reader rather than as its author before submission. Better yet, read it aloud!"

MILWAUKEE MAGAZINE (IV), Quad/Graphics, 312 E. Buffalo St., Milwaukee WI 53202. (414)273-1101. Editor: Judith Woodburn. Magazine: 8x11; 150-250 pages; glossy cover stock; illustrations; photos. "Regional material/issues related to Milwaukee business, arts, entertainment and personalities" for 46 yr. median age; college-plus education and $45,000 income. Monthly. Circ. 50,000.
Needs: Contemporary, feminist, literary, mainstream, regional. "We use only Wisconsin writers." No overt romances, no thinly-veiled historical treatises, no quaint reminiscences. "*All* must have regional Wisconsin flavor, or be linked to this city or region in integral way—such as being written by a Wisconsin author. Publishes fiction (solicited mss only) on a quarterly basis (approximately). Buys 1 fiction mss/year. Publishes ms 3 months after acceptance. Recently published work by Jane Hamilton and Greg Monday. Published new writers within the last year. Length: 5,000 words. Very rarely critiques rejected ms.
How to Contact: Simultaneous and photocopied submissions OK. Accepts computer printouts. Sample copy $3.25.
Payment: Pays $500.
Terms: Pays on publication for one-time rights. Sends galleys to authors.

MODERN SHORT STORIES (I), Entertaining Stories for Fiction Lovers, Claggk Inc., 500B Bicounty Blvd., Farmingdale NY 11762. (516)293-3751. Editor: Glen Steckler. Magazine: Digest-sized; supercalendered paper; 60 lb cover stock; illustrations; photographs. Publishes "a variety of fiction for audiences of all ages." Bimonthly. Estab. 1988.
Needs: Adventure, confession, contemporary, erotica, experimental, fantasy, historical, horror, humor/satire, mainstream, psychic/supernatural/occult, regional, religious/inspirational, romance (contemporary, historical, young adult), science fiction, sports, suspense/mystery, western. Receives 500-1,000 unsolicited fiction mss/month. Buys 12-15 fiction mss/issue. Publishes mss 4 months to 1 year after acceptance. Length: 1,000-5,000 words preferred. Publishes short shorts "on rare occasions." Sometimes critiques rejected ms.
How to Contact: Send complete mss with cover letter. Reports in 1-3 weeks. SASE required. Photocopied submissions OK. Accepts computer printouts. Sample copy $2; fiction guidelines free.
Payment: Pays $10-50.
Terms: Pays on acceptance for first rights and first anthology rights.
Advice: "There is not enough space devoted to fiction today—TV has tended to replace it. However, we feel the demand is there and that is our reason for publishing *Modern Short Stories*."

THE MODERN WOODMEN (II), Modern Woodmen of America, Mississippi River at 17th St., Rock Island IL 61201. (309)786-6481. Editor: Gloria Bergh. Fiction Editor: Sandy Howell. Magazine: 8½×11; 24 pages; 50 lb paper; self cover; illustrations and photos. "We want articles that appeal to families, emphasize family interaction, for the family audience including all age groups from children to the elderly." Quarterly. Circ. 350,000.
Needs: Adventure, contemporary, historical (general), juvenile (5-9 years), mainstream, senior citizen/retirement, young adult/teen (10-18 years). Receives approx. 35 unsolicited fiction mss/month. Accepts 1-2 mss/month; 12-24 mss/year. Length: 1,200 words preferred. Sometimes critiques rejected mss, "but very seldom."
How to Contact: Send complete ms with cover letter. Reports in up to 2 months. SASE. Simultaneous, photocopied and reprint submissions OK. Accepts computer printout submissions. Sample copy for 8½×11 SAE with 2 first class stamps. Fiction guidelines for #10 SASE.
Payment: $50 and up.
Terms: Pays on acceptance for one-time rights.
Advice: "A well written short story is a drawing card to interest our readers."

MOMENT MAGAZINE (II, IV), 3000 Connecticut Ave. NW, Suite 300, Washington DC 20008. (202)387-8888. Publisher/Editor: Hershel Shanks. Managing Editor: Charlotte Anker. Magazine: 8½×11; 64 pages; 60 lb coated paper; 80 lb cover stock; illustrations and photos. Modern, historical magazine publishing material on intellectual, cultural and political issues of interest to the Jewish

community. Audience is college-educated, liberal, concerned with Jewish affairs. Monthly. Estab. 1975. Circ. 30,000.
Needs: Contemporary, ethnic, historical, religious, excerpted novel and translations. "All fiction should have Jewish content. No sentimental stories about 'Grandma' etc. Do not encourage Holocaust themes." Receives 60-80 unsolicited fiction mss/month. Buys 2-3 mss/year. Published new writers in the past year. Length: 2,000 words minimum; 4,000 words maximum; 3,000 words average. Publishes short shorts. Occasionally recommends other markets.
How to Contact: Cover letter with bio. Query first or send complete ms. SASE always. Photocopied submissions OK. No multiple submissions. Accepts computer printout submissions; prefers letter-quality. Reports in 1 month on queries; 1-2 months on mss. Publishes ms 1-12 months after acceptance. Sample copy $2.95. Free fiction guidelines for #10 SAE and 1 first class stamp.
Payment: Varies.
Terms: Pays on publication for first rights.
Advice: "We caution against over-sentimentalized writing which we get way too much of all the time. Query first is helpful; reading stories we've published a must."

‡MONROE (IV), For the People of Monroe, Miotke Media & Marketing Inc., 477 N. Dixie, Monroe MI 48161. (313)242-8788. Editor: Dave Meagher. Magazine: 8½×11; 44-50 pages; 70lb glossy; 80lb cover stock; illustrations and photographs. "Regional writers about region in title." Monthly.
Needs: Historical (general), regional. Receives 5 unsolicited mss/month. Buys 1 ms/issue; 12 mss/year. Publishes ms 2-3 months after acceptance. Length: 1,000 words average; 4,000 words maximum. Sometimes recommends rejected ms to other markets.
How to Contact: Query first. Reports in 1 week on queries; 3 weeks on mss. SASE. Simultaneous, photocopied and reprint submissions OK. Computer printout submissions are acceptable. Sample copy free with 8½×11 SAE and 4 first class stamps. Fiction guidelines free with #10 SAE and 1 first class stamp.
Payment: Pays up to $25; free subscription and contributor's copies.
Terms: Pays on publication for one-time rights.

MONTANA SENIOR CITIZENS NEWS (II,IV), Barrett-Whitman Co., Box 3363, Great Falls MT 59403. (406)761-0305. Editor: Jack Love. Tabloid: 11×17; 40-50 pages; newsprint paper and cover; illustrations; photos. Publishes "everything of interest to seniors, except most day-to-day political items like social security and topics covered in the daily news. Personal profiles of seniors, their lives, times and reminiscences." Bimonthly. Estab. 1984. Circ. 16,000.
Needs: Historical, senior citizen/retirement, western (historical or contemporary). No fiction "unrelated to experiences to which seniors can relate." Buys 1 or fewer mss/issue; 4-5 mss/year. Publishes ms within 4 months of acceptance. Published work by Anne Norris, Helen Clark, Juni Dunklin. Length: 500-700 words preferred. Publishes short shorts. Length: under 500 words.
How to Contact: Send complete ms with cover letter. Reports on mss in 1 month. SASE. Simultaneous, photocopied and reprint submissions OK. Accepts computer printout submissions. Accepts electronic submission via disk or modem. Sample copy for 9×12 SAE and $2 postage and handling.
Payment: Pays $10 minimum; 4¢/word maximum.
Terms: Pays on publication. Acquires first rights or one-time rights.

‡MOTHER JONES MAGAZINE (II,IV), Foundation for National Progress, 1663 Mission St., San Francisco CA 94103. (415)558-8881. Editor: Douglas Foster. Fiction Editor: Peggy Orenstein. Magazine: 64 pages; illustrations and photographs. "Political—left of center." Monthly. Estab. 1976. Circ. 200,000.
Needs: Feminist, gay, lesbian and political. Receives 20 unsolicited mss/month. Accepts 1-2 mss/year. Agented fiction 95%. Recently published work by Michael Dorris, Amy Hempel and Alice Walker. Length: 2,500 words average; 700 words minimum; 3,000 words maximum. Publishes short shorts. Sometimes critiques rejected mss.
How to Contact: Send complete ms with cover letter. Reports in 6-8 weeks on mss. SASE "only if they want manuscript returned." Simultaneous submissions OK. Computer printout submissions are acceptable. Sample copy for $3.
Payment: Negotiated.
Terms: Pays on acceptance for first North American serial rights.

MY FRIEND (II), The Catholic Magazine for Kids, Daughters of St. Paul, 50 St. Paul's Ave., Boston MA 02130. (617)522-8911. Editor: Sister Anne Joan. Magazine: 8½×11; 32 pages; smooth, glossy paper; smooth, glossy cover stock; illustrations; photos. Magazine of "religious truths and positive values for children in a format which is enjoyable and attractive. Each issue contains Bible stories, lives of saints and famous people, short stories, science corner, contests, projects, etc." Monthly during school year (September-June). Estab. 1979. Circ. 10,000.

"Women's issues and the media are two subjects of particular interest to the magazine," explains Richard Reynolds, communications manager for* Mother Jones*. The June 1989 cover story "focuses on what it's like to be a woman working in a male-dominated field and how the corporate takeover of network television has affected the news." New York-based portrait photographer William Coupon did the cover shot.

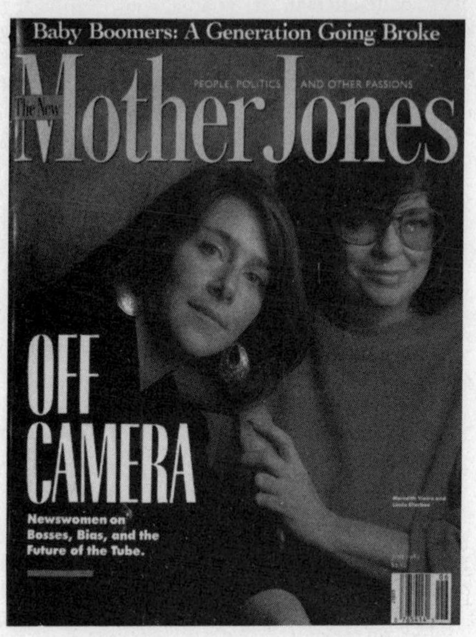

Baby Boomers: A Generation Going Broke
PEOPLE, POLITICS AND OTHER PASSIONS
The New
Mother Jones
OFF
CAMERA
Newswomen on Bosses, Bias, and the Future of the Tube.

Needs: Juvenile, prose poem, religious/inspirational, spiritual (children), sports (children). Receives 30 unsolicited fiction mss/month. Accepts 3-4 mss/issue; 30-40 mss/year. Recently published work by Virginia L. Kroll, Eileen Barr and Kay Gibson; published new writers within the past year. Length: 200 words minimum; 900 words maximum; 600 words average.
How to Contact: Send complete ms with SASE. Accepts computer printout submissions. Reports in 1-2 months on mss. Publishes ms an average of 1 year after acceptance. Free sample copy for 10×14 SAE and 60¢ postage.
Payment: 3-7¢ per word.
Advice: "We prefer child-centered stories in a real-world setting. Children enjoy fiction. They can relate to the characters and learn lessons that they might not derive from a more 'preachy' article. We accept only stories that teach wholesome, positive values. We are particularly interested in material for boys aged 8-10."

NA'AMAT WOMAN, Magazine of Na'amat USA, The Women's Labor Zionist Organization of America, 200 Madison Ave., New York NY 10016. (212)725-8010. Editor: Judith A. Sokoloff. Magazine covering a wide variety of subjects of interest to the Jewish community—including political and social issues, arts, profiles; many articles about Israel; and women's issues. Fiction must have a Jewish theme. Readers are the American Jewish community. Published 5 times/year. Estab. 1926. Circ. 30,000.
Needs: Contemporary, literary, feminist. Receives 10 unsolicited fiction mss/month. Buys 3-5 fiction mss/year. Length: 1,500 words minimum; 3,000 words maximum. Also buys nonfiction.
How to Contact: Query first or send complete ms with SASE. Photocopied submissions OK. Accepts computer printout submissions. Prefers letter-quality. Reports in 3 months on mss. Free sample copy for 9×11½ SAE and 71¢ postage.
Payment: Pays 8¢/word; 2 free contributor's copies. Offers kill fee of 25%.
Terms: Pays on publication for first North American serial rights; assignments on work-for-hire basis.
Advice: "No maudlin nostalgia or romance; no hackneyed Jewish humor and *no poetry.*"

NATIONAL LAMPOON (II), 155 Avenue of the Americas, New York NY 10013. (212)645-5040. Editor: Larry Sloman. Magazine. "We publish humor and satire." Bimonthly. Estab. 1970. Circ. 250,000.
Needs: Receives 200 unsolicited fiction mss/month. Buys 2 mss/issue. Publishes ms 2-3 months after acceptance. Length: 1,000 words preferred; 500 words minimum; 2,000 words maximum. Publishes short shorts.
How to Contact: Query first. Reports in 1-2 months. SASE preferred. Simultaneous and photocopied submissions OK. Accepts electronic submissions via disk or modem. Fiction guidelines free.
Payment: Payment is negotiated.
Terms: Pays on publication for first North American serial rights and anthology rights. Offers varying kill fee.

THE NEW YORKER (III), The New Yorker, Inc., 25 W. 43rd St., New York NY 10036. (212)840-3800. Fiction Department. A quality magazine of interesting, well written stories, articles, essays and poems for a literate audience. Weekly. Estab. 1925.

How to Contact: Send complete ms with SASE. Reports in 6-8 weeks on mss. Publishes 2 mss/issue.

Payment: Varies.

Terms: Pays on acceptance.

Advice: "Be lively, original, not overly literary. Write what you want to write, not what you think the editor would like."

NOAH'S ARK (II, IV), A Newspaper for Jewish Children, Suite 250, 8323 Southwest Freeway, Houston TX 77074. (713)771-7143. Editors: Debbie Israel Dubin and Linda Freedman Block. Tabloid: 4 pages; newsprint paper; illustrations; photos. "All material must be on some Jewish theme. Seasonal material relating to Jewish holidays is used as well as articles and stories relating to Jewish culture (charity, Soviet Jewry, ecology), etc." for Jewish children, ages 6-12. Monthly Sept.-June. Estab. 1979. Circ. 450,000.

Needs: Juvenile (6-12 years); religious/inspirational; young adult/teen (10-12 years); ages 6-12 Jewish children. "Newspaper is not only included as a supplement to numerous Jewish newspapers and sent to individual subscribers but is also distributed in bulk quantities to religious schools; therefore all stories and articles should have educational value as well as being entertaining and interesting to children." Receives 10 unsolicited mss/month. Buys "few mss but we'd probably use more if more appropriate mss were submitted." Published new writers within the last year. Length: 600 words maximum.

How to Contact: Send complete ms with SASE. "The cover letter is not necessary; the submission will be accepted or rejected on its own merits." Simultaneous, photocopied submissions and reprints OK. Accepts computer printouts. Sample copy for #10 envelope and 1 first class stamp. "The best guideline is a copy of our publication."

Payment: Varies; contributor's copies.

Terms: Pays on acceptance for one-time rights.

Advice: "Our newspaper was created by two writers looking for a place to have our work published. It has grown in only 10 years to nearly 1 million readers throughout the world. Beginners with determination can accomplish the impossible."

‡NORTH SHORE MAGAZINE (I,II), Rhapsody Productions, Inc., 509 E. 4th St., North Vancouver, British Columbia V7L 1J7 Canada. (604)988-7199. Editor: Marina Polovic. Magazine: 8×10½; 40 pages; electrabrite paper and cover; illustrations and photographs. Family and community oriented. For the family unit—kids to seniors living on the North Shore. Bimonthly. Estab. 1988. Circ. 48,000.

Needs: Adventure, contemporary, experimental, historical (general), humor/satire, literary, mainstream, regional, science fiction, suspense/mystery. "No stories about writers, stories with weak endings. There has to be something *said*—a point made in the story." Publishes annual special fiction issue. Receives 15 unsolicited mss/month. Buys 1 ms/issue; 6 mss/year. Publishes ms 2 months after acceptance. Length: 1,000 words average; 650 words minimum; 1,300 words maximum. Publishes short shorts. Length: 500 words of humor. Sometimes comments on rejected mss and recommends other markets.

How to Contact: Send complete ms with cover letter. Reports in 2 months. SASE. Simultaneous, photocopied and reprint submissions OK. Computer printout submissions are acceptable. Electronic submissions are acceptable. Sample copy for $2.25 and 8½×11 SAE. Fiction guidelines free for any size SAE.

Payment: Pays $50-75 and contributor's copies.

Terms: Pays on publication. Offers 30% kill fee. Buys first rights, first North American serial rights, one-time rights or other rights.

Advice: "Write a story on a topic you feel passion for. Engage your heart—not just your technique."

NORTHCOAST VIEW (II), Blarney Publishing, Box 1374, Eureka CA 95502. (707)443-4887. Editors: Scott K. Ryan and Damon Maguire. Magazine: 11×14½; 56 pages; electrabrite, 38 lb paper and cover; illustrations; photos. "Entertainment, recreation, arts and news magazine, open to all kinds of fiction." For Humboldt County, ages 18-75 and others. Monthly. Plans anthology in future. Estab. 1982. Circ. 22,500.

Needs: Open to most subjects. Adventure, condensed novel, contemporary, erotica, ethnic, experimental, fantasy, historical (local, general), horror, humor/satire, literary, psychic/supernatural/occult, regional, science fiction, suspense/mystery, translations. No romances. Receives 30-50 unsolicited mss/month. Buys 1-2 mss/issue; 12-20 mss/year. Publishes ms 1-3 months after acceptance. Length: 2,500 words average; 250 words minimum; 5,000 words maximum.

How to Contact: Send complete ms with cover letter (background info or bio if published). Reports in 3-6 months on mss. SASE. Simultaneous, photocopied submissions and reprints (sometimes) OK. Accepts computer printouts. No dot-matrix. Sample copy $1. Fiction guidelines for #10 SAE and 1 first class stamp.
Payment: Pays $5-150.
Terms: Pays on publication for all rights.

NORTHEAST, the Sunday Magazine of the Hartford Courant, 285 Broad St., Hartford CT 06115. (203)241-3700. Editor: Lary Bloom. Magazine: 10×11½; 32-100 pages; illustrations; photos. "A regional (New England, specifically Connecticut) magazine, we publish stories of varied subjects of interest to our Connecticut audience" for a general audience. Weekly. Published special fiction issue and a special college writing issue for fiction and poetry. Estab. 1981. Circ. 300,000.
Needs: Contemporary and regional. No children's stories or stories with distinct setting outside Connecticut. Receives 60 unsolicited mss/month. Buys 1 ms/issue. Publishes short shorts. Length: 750 words minimum; 3,500 words maximum.
How to Contact: Send complete ms with SASE. Reports in 3 weeks. Simultaneous and photocopied submissions OK. No reprints or previously published work. Accepts computer printout submissions. Prefers letter-quality. Free sample copy and fiction guidelines with 10×12 or larger SASE.
Payment: $250-600.
Terms: Pays on acceptance for one-time rights.

NORTHWEST MAGAZINE (I, II, IV), The Sunday Oregonian Magazine, 1320 SW Broadway, Portland OR 97210. (503)221-8228. Editor: Jack Hart. Magazine: 10¼×11½; 24-36 pages; illustrations; photos. Weekly. Circ. 400,000.
Needs: Contemporary, experimental fantasy, humor/satire, literary mainstream, prose poem, young adult and science fiction. Receives 20-30 mss/month. Buys 30-40 mss/year. "We don't run fiction every week. Publishes ms within 1-3 months of acceptance. Agented fiction 5%. Published new writers within the last year. Length: 2,000 words maximum. Publishes short shorts. Sometimes critiques rejected mss and recommends other markets.
How to Contact: Send complete mss with cover letter. Reports in 1 week. SASE. Photocopied submissions OK. Accepts computer printout submissions. Accepts electronic submission via disk or modem. Sample copy and fiction guidelines for SAE.
Payment: Pays $150-300 and contributor's copies.
Terms: Pays on acceptance for one-time rights. Offers kill fee. Sends galleys to author.

NUGGET (II), Dugent Publishing Corp., Suite 204, 2355 Salzedo St., Coral Gables FL 33134. (305)443-2378. Editor: Jerome Slaughter. A newsstand magazine designed to have erotic appeal for a fetish-oriented audience. Bimonthly. Estab. 1956. Circ. 100,000.
Needs: Offbeat, fetish-oriented material should encompass a variety of subjects. Most of fiction includes several sex scenes. No fiction that concerns children or religious subjects. Buys 3 mss/issue. Approximately 5% of fiction is agented. Length: 2,000-3,500 words.
How to Contact: Send complete ms with SASE. Reports in 1 month on ms. Sample copy $5. Free guidelines with legal-sized SASE.
Payment: $125-200. Free author's copy.
Terms: Pays on publication for first rights.
Advice: "Keep in mind the nature of the publication, which is fetish erotica. Subject matter can vary, but we prefer fetish themes."

OMNI (II), Penthouse International, 1965 Broadway, New York NY 10023. Fiction Editor: Ellen Datlow. Magazine: 8½×11; 114-182 pages; 40-50 lb stock paper; 100 lb Mead off cover stock; illustrations; photos. Magazine of science and science fiction with an interest in near future; stories of what science holds, what life and lifestyles will be like in areas affected by science for a young, bright and well-educated audience between ages 18-45. Monthly. Estab. 1978. Circ. 1,000,000.
Needs: Science fiction, contemporary, fantasy and technological horror. No sword and sorcery or space opera. Buys 30 mss/year. Receives approximately 400 unsolicited fiction mss/month. Approximately 5% of fiction is agented. Recently published work by T. Coraghessan Boyle, Pat Cadigan and Michael Swanwick. Published new writers within the last year. Length: 2,000 words minimum, 12,000 words maximum. Critiques rejected mss that interest me "when there is time." Sometimes recommends other markets.

How to Contact: Send complete ms with SASE. Accepts computer printout submissions, prefers letter-quality. Reports within 3 weeks on mss. Publishes ms 3 months to two years after acceptance.
Payment: Pays $1,250-2,000; 2 free author's copies.
Terms: Pays on acceptance for first North American serial rights with exclusive worldwide English language periodical rights and nonexclusive anthology rights.
Advice: "Beginning writers should read a lot of the best science fiction short stories today. We are looking for strong, well written stories dealing with the next 100 years. Don't give up on a market just because you've been rejected several times. If you're good, you'll get published eventually. Don't ever call an editor on the phone and ask why he/she rejected a story. You'll either find out in a personal rejection letter (which means the editor liked it or thought enough of your writing to comment) or you won't find out at all (most likely the editor won't remember a form-rejected story). Recent award winners and nominees: 'Schrodinger's Kitten' by George Alec Effinger won the Nebula award for novelette and is up for a Hugo award. 'Life of Buddha' by Lucius Shepard is up for the World Fantasy Award."

ON OUR BACKS (II,IV), Entertainment for the Adventurous Lesbian, Blush Productions, 526 Castro St., San Francisco CA 94114. (415)861-4723. Editor: Susie Bright. Magazine: 8½×11; 50 pages; slick paper; illustrations; photos. "Lesbian erotica, short stories, nonfiction, commentary, news clips, photos." Quarterly. Estab. 1984. Circ. 15,000.
Needs: Erotica, fantasy, humor/satire, lesbian. No "non-erotic, heterosexual" fiction. Receives 20 mss/month. Buys 2-3 mss/issue. Publishes ms within 1 year of acceptance. Published new writers within the last year. Length: 3,500 words preferred; 2,500 words minimum; 5,000 words maximum.
How to Contact: Query with clips of published work or send complete ms with cover letter. Include Social Security number. Reports in 6 weeks. SASE. No simultaneous submissions. Accepts computer printout submissions. Accepts electronic submissions via disk. Sample copy for $5. Fiction guidelines for #10 SAE and 1 first class stamp.
Payment: Pays $20-100 and contributor's copies.
Terms: Pays on publication for first North American serial rights.
Advice: "Ask yourself—does it turn me on? Ask a friend to read it—does it turn her on as well? Is it as well-written as any well-crafted non-erotic story? We love to read things that we don't see all the time—originality is definitely a plus!" Sponsors awards for fiction writers.

ON THE LINE (II), Mennonite Publishing House, 616 Walnut Ave., Scottdale PA 15683-1999. (412)887-8500. Editor: Mary Meyer. Magazine: 7×10; 8 pages; illustrations; b&w photos. "A religious take-home paper with the goal of helping children grow in their understanding and appreciation of God, the created world, themselves and other people." For children ages 10-14. Weekly. Estab. 1970. Circ. 11,000.
Needs: Adventure and religious/inspirational for older children and young teens (10-14 years). Receives 50-100 unsolicited mss/month. Buys 1 ms/issue; 52 mss/year. Length: 750-1,000 words.
How to Contact: Send complete ms with cover letter noting whether author is offering first-time or reprint rights. Reports in 1 month. SASE. Simultaneous, photocopied and previously published work OK. Accepts computer printout submissions. Prefers letter-quality. Sample copy and fiction guidelines free.
Payment: Pays on acceptance for one-time rights.
Advice: "We believe in the power of story to entertain, inspire and challenge the reader to new growth. Know children and their thoughts, feelings and interests. Be realistic with characters and events in the fiction. Stories do not need to be true, but need to *feel* true."

‡OPTIONS (I, II), The *Bi*-Monthly, AJA Publishing, Box 470, Port Chester NY 10573. Associate Editor: Diana Sheridan. Magazine: digest sized; 114 pages; newsprint paper; glossy cover stock; illustrations and photos. Sexually explicit magazine for and about bi-sexuals. 10 issues/year. Estab. 1982. Circ. 100,000.
Needs: Erotica, gay, lesbian. "First person as-if-true experiences." Accepts 5 unsolicited fiction mss/month. "Very little" of fiction is agented. Length: 2,000-3,000 words average; 2,000 words minimum. Sometimes critiques rejected mss.
How to Contact: Send complete ms with cover letter. Reports in approx 3 weeks. SASE. Photocopied submissions OK, if clearly marked "not a simultaneous submission." Accepts computer printout submissions. Sample copy $2.95 and 6×9 SAE with 5 first class stamps. Fiction guidelines for SASE.
Payment: $100. ("Letters" pay $15 each.)
Terms: Pays on publication for all rights.
Advice: "Read a copy of *Options* carefully and look at our spec sheet, before writing anything for us. We only buy 2 bi-woman/lesbian pieces per issue; need is greater for bi/gay male mss. Though we're a bi rather than gay magazine, the emphasis is on same-sex relationships. If the readers want to read about a male/female couple, they'll buy another magazine. Gay male stories sent to *Options* will also

Close-up

Ellen Datlow
Fiction Editor
Omni

© Randy Mayor.

Breaking into a large, well-known publication can be tough, but writers should not be intimidated by a big name, says *Omni* Fiction Editor Ellen Datlow. "Go ahead and try for the bigger paying markets first. It's better to let the editor decide (if your piece is publishable)."

On the other hand, even though the magazine receives from 50 to 100 manuscripts every week, *Omni* publishes only a handful of unsolicited manuscripts each year, she says, and even fewer are first stories. "We aren't looking for a lot of publishing credits, but people who have been published before gain from that experience."

Although Datlow commissions short-short pieces on certain themes, writers submitting stories for *Omni* should send longer work – manuscripts of 5,000 to 6,000 words are most needed. Send the complete manuscript, but do not include a cover letter unless you want to list some publishing credits. Never give the synopsis of your story in a letter, she says. Send neat manuscripts with large margins; make the manuscript as easy to read as possible.

One way to beat the odds is to research the market first to find out what type of stories a magazine publishes, she says. For example, *Omni* is a leading science magazine and primarily publishes science fiction. "We do not accept poetry. We have published some horror, but we are not a horror outlet."

For *Omni*, it also pays to be familiar with trends and changes within the science fiction field. The best way, of course, is to read the work of today's science fiction authors. Datlow keeps current by editing science fiction anthologies and reading science fiction book manuscripts on a freelance basis. "I like to keep my hand in science fiction book publishing," she says.

Another way to learn more about the field is to attend writer's conferences and conventions, commonly called "cons" in the field. "Cons are a good place to meet writers," she says. "Every time I go I get manuscripts. I try to participate on panels, because they offer an opportunity for editors and writers to talk.

"Conferences are a good way for writers to get to know the editors – to get a feel for their tastes. But, on the other hand, a personal relationship with an editor is not necessary. In fact, editors are probably harder on their friends, but it doesn't hurt to meet an editor."

Datlow's tastes run toward science fiction that involves the use of hard science. "I've seen a lot of anthropological science, alternate universes and a lot of going back into the past. I'm not looking for 'famous people' stories."

She looks for stories with depth of character that also use future technology. "There is a lot of interest in the future, but it seems writers have not taken hold of it yet. It is tough to keep up with technology, but a good writer knows when he can fudge a bit.

"Of course, the science must be well integrated into the story. Tell a good story first. A good story has more than one layer, a resonance. There must be something going on underneath."

– Robin Gee

be considered for publication in *Beau*, our gay male magazine. Prefer 3,000-3,500 words in length for *Beau*. *Most important: We only* publish stories that feature "safe sex" practices unless the story is clearly something that took place pre-AIDS."

THE OTHER SIDE (III), 300 W. Apsley St., Philadelphia PA 19144. (215)849-2178. Editor: Mark Olson. Fiction Editor: Barbara Moorman. Magazine of justice rooted in discipleship for Christians with a strong interest in peace, social and economic justice. Monthly. Estab. 1965. Circ. 14,000.

Needs: Contemporary, ethnic, experimental, feminist, humor/satire, literary, mainstream, spiritual and suspense/mystery. Receives 30 unsolicited fiction mss/month. Buys 6 mss/year. Recently published work by Laurie Skiba, Wilton Miller and Shirley Pendlebury. Length: 1,500 words minimum; 5,000 words maximum; 3,500 words average.

How to Contact: Send complete ms with SASE. Photocopied submissions OK. "Simultaneous submissions and pre-published material *strongly* discouraged." Accepts computer printout submissions. Accepts disk submissions compatible with IBM PC. Reports in 6-8 weeks on mss. Publishes ms 3-9 months after acceptance. Sample copy for $4.

Payment: Pays $50-250; free subscription to magazine; 5 free contributor's copies.

Terms: Pays on acceptance for all or first rights; assignments on work-for-hire basis.

OUI MAGAZINE (II), 6th Floor, 300 W. 43rd St., New York NY 10036. (212)397-5200. Editor: Richard Kidd. Magazine: 8×11; 112 pages; illustrations; photos. Magazine for college-age males and older. Monthly. Estab. 1972. Circ. 1 million.

Needs: Contemporary, fantasy, lesbian, men's, mystery and humor. Buys 1 ms/issue; 12 mss/year. Receives 200-300 unsolicited fiction mss/month. Published new writers within the last year. Length: 1,500-3,000 words.

How to Contact: Cover letter with author background, previous publications, etc. Send complete ms with SASE. Accepts computer printout submissions. Prefers letter-quality. Reports in 6-8 weeks on mss.

Payment: Pays $250 and up.

Terms: Pays on publication for first rights.

Advice: "Many mss are rejected because writers have not studied the market or the magazine. We want writers to take chances and offer us something out of the ordinary. Look at several recent issues to see what direction our fiction is headed."

OUTLAW BIKER (II, IV), Outlaw Biker Enterprises, 450 7th Ave. #2305, New York NY 10123. (212)564-0112. Publisher/Editor: Casey Exton. Magazine: 8½×11; 96 pages; 50 lb color paper; 80 lb cover stock; illustrations; photos. Publication for hard-core bikers, their partners and for tattoo enthusiasts. Monthly. Special issue 4 times/year, *Tattoo Review*. Estab. 1984. Circ. 225,000.

Needs: Biker fiction and humor. Receives 20 unsolicited mss/month. Accepts 3 fiction mss/issue. Publishes ms 4 months after acceptance. Length: 1,000 words minimum; 2,500 words maximum.

How to Contact: Send complete ms with cover letter. SASE very important. Reports on queries in 1 month. Sample copy $3.50.

Payment: Pays $50-180.

Terms: Pays on publication for all rights.

Advice: "Timely biker events with photos used constantly. Photos do not have to be professionally taken. Clear snapshots of events with the short story usually accepted. Send to: Casey Exton, Attention."

PALOUSE JOURNAL (II, IV), North Country Book Express, Box 9632, Moscow ID 83843. (208)882-0888. Editor: Tim Steury. Tabloid: 11×17; 24-40 pages; 34 lb stock; illustrations; photos. "We are a regional general interest magazine, for an educated, literate audience." Bimonthly. Estab. 1981.

Needs: Regional. "We will consider good writing of any sort, mostly with some 'hook' to our region." Buys 1 ms/issue at most; 2-6 mss/year. Published new writers within the last year. Length: 2,500 words maximum. Will consider short shorts as columns, up to 1,000 words. Occasionally critiques rejected mss. Occasionally recommends other markets.

How to Contact: Send complete ms with cover letter. Reports in 2-3 months on mss. SASE. Photocopied submissions OK. Accepts computer printout submissions. Accepts MS DOS WordStar submissions. Sample copy $2. Writers' guidelines for SASE.

Payment: Pays $25 for a short shorts, $100 for a full feature story.

Terms: Pays on publication for first North American serial rights.

Advice: "We look for good clean writing, a regional hook and relevance. Manuscripts are often rejected because writer is obviously not familiar with the magazine and story lacks regional flavor."

PENNYWHISTLE PRESS (II), Gannett Co., Inc., Box 500-P, Washington DC 20044. Editor: Anita Sama. Magazine: tabloid size; 8 pages; newsprint paper; illustrations; photos. Education and information for children ages 7-14. Weekly. Estab. 1981. Circ. 2.5 million.
Needs: Juvenile (7-9 years), (long) prose poem, young adult/teen (10-14 years). No talking animals. Receives "hundreds" of unsolicited fiction mss/month. Accepts 20 mss/year. Length: 450 words for 7-10 year olds; 850 words for older children.
How to Contact: Send complete ms with cover letter with SASE. *No* queries. No simultaneous submissions accepted. "We do not accept previously published manuscripts." Sample copy 50¢.
Payment: Varies.
Terms: Pays on acceptance.

PILLOW TALK (II), 801 2nd Ave., New York NY 10017. Editor: Sue Kossoy. Magazine: digest-sized; 98 pages; photos. Bi-monthly erotic letters magazine.
Needs: "We use approximately 20 short letters of no more than five manuscript pages per issue, and five long letters of between seven and nine manuscript pages." Published new writers within the last year. Recommends other markets.
How to Contact: "We encourage unsolicited manuscripts. Writers who have proven reliable will receive assignments."
Terms: *Pillow Talk* pays $5 per page for short letters and a $75 flat rate for long letters and articles. Pays on acceptance.
Advice: "Keep it short and sensual. We buy many more short letters than long ones. This is a 'couples-oriented' book; the sex should be a natural outgrowth of a relationship, the characters should be believable, and both male and female characters should be treated with respect. No S&M, bondage, male homosexuality, incest, underage characters or anal sex—not even in dialog, not even in implication. No language that even implies sexual violence—not even in metaphor. No ejaculation on any part of a person's body. Romance is a big plus."

‡THE PLAIN DEALER MAGAZINE (II), 1801 Superior Ave., Cleveland OH 44114. (216)344-4546. Contact: Editor. Magazine: 10×11½; 20-64 pages; color and b&w illustrations and photos. Regional magazine, Sunday supplement to The Plain Dealer newspaper for our readers (Cleveland and state). Weekly. Circ. 575,000.
Needs: Adventure, contemporary, ethnic, historical (general), humor/satire, literary, mainstream, psychic/supernatural/occult, regional, science fiction, sports, suspense/mystery. "Regional preferred." Publishes annual special summer fiction issue. Receives 10-20 unsolicited mss/month. Number of mss accepted per issue "depends on quality." Publishes ms 2-3 months after acceptance. Length: 2,000 words maximum. Occasionally comments on rejected mss.
How to Contact: Send complete ms with cover letter, include Social Security number. Reports in 1 month on mss. SASE for ms, not needed for query. Sample copy $1 and 7½×10½ SAE.
Payment: Pays $500 maximum; 2 contributor's copies.
Terms: Pays on publication for one-time rights.

PLAYBOY MAGAZINE (III), Playboy Enterprises, Inc., 919 N. Michigan Ave., Chicago IL 60611. (312)751-8000. Fiction Editor: Alice K. Turner. Magazine: 8½×11; 250 pages; glossy cover stock; illustrations; photos. Entertainment magazine for a male audience. Monthly. Estab. 1953. Circ. 4,250,342.
Needs: Literary, contemporary, science fiction, fantasy, horror, sports, western, mystery, adventure and humor. No pornography or fiction geared to a female audience. Buys 1-3 mss/issue; 25 mss/year. Receives approximately 1,200 unsolicited fiction mss each month. Recently published work by Mickey Spillane, Joyce Carol Oates, and Robert Coover. Published new writers within the last year. Length: 1,000-10,000 (average 6,000) words. Also publishes short shorts of 1,000 words. Critiques rejected mss "when there is time." Recommends other markets "sometimes."
How to Contact: Send complete ms with SASE and cover letter with prior publication information. Reports in 6-8 weeks on mss. Free guidelines with SASE.
Payment: $5,000 minimum; $2,000 minimum for short shorts.
Terms: Pays on acceptance for all rights.

PLAYGIRL MAGAZINE (II), 801 Second Ave., New York NY 10017. (212)986-5100. Fiction Editor: Mary Ellen Strote. Magazine: 8×10; 120 pages; 40 lb paper; 60 lb cover stock; illustrations; photos. Magazine for today's young women ages 18-40, average age 26, featuring entertainment, fiction, beauty and fashion, current events, sex and health. Monthly. Estab. 1973. Circ. 800,000.
Needs: Contemporary stories about relationships. "No gay, juvenile, murder, mystery or graphic sex." Receives approximately 150 unsolicited fiction mss/month. Buys 1 ms/issue. Approximately 10% of fiction is agented. Recently published work by Sharon Solwitz, Mimi Albert and Edra Ziesk; published

new writers within the last year. Length: 1,000 words minimum; 5,000 words maximum; 3,500 words average. Publishes short shorts. Occasionally critiques rejected mss.
How to Contact: Send complete ms with SASE. Simultaneous, photocopied and previously published submissions OK. Accepts computer printout submissions. Prefers letter-quality. Reports in 6-8 weeks on mss. Publishes ms an average of 3-6 months after acceptance. Sample copy from Customer Service Department; $6 includes postage and handling.
Payment: $500 minimum and 1-2 contributor's copies.
Terms: Pays on acceptance for one-time magazine rights in the English language. Occasionally buys reprints.

POCKETS (II), Devotional Magazine for Children, The Upper Room, Box 189, 1908 Grand Ave., Nashville TN 37202. (615)340-7333. Editor-in-Chief: Janet M. Bugg. Magazine: 7×9; 32 pages; 50 lb white econowrite paper; 80 lb white coated, heavy cover stock; color and 2-color illustrations; some photos. Magazine for children ages 6-12, with articles specifically geared for ages 8 to 11. "The magazine offers stories, activities, prayers, poems—all geared to giving children a better understanding of themselves as children of God." Published monthly except for January. Estab. 1981. Estimated circ. 65,000.
Needs: Adventure, contemporary, ethnic, fantasy, historical (general), juvenile, religious/inspirational and suspense/mystery. "All submissions should address the broad theme of the magazine. Each issue will be built around several themes with material which can be used by children in a variety of ways. Scripture stories, fiction, poetry, prayers, art, graphics, puzzles and activities will all be included. Submissions do not need to be overtly religious. They should help children experience a Christian lifestyle that is not always a neatly wrapped moral package, but is open to the continuing revelation of God's will. Seasonal material, both secular and liturgical, is desired. No violence, horror, sexual and racial stereotyping or fiction containing heavy moralizing." Receives approximately 120 unsolicited fiction mss/month. Buys 2-3 mss/issue; 22-33 mss/year. Publishes short shorts. A peace-with-justice theme will run throughout the magazine. Approximately 50% of fiction is agented. Published new writers last year. Recently published work by Peggy King Anderson, Angela Gibson and John Steptoe. Length: 600 words minimum; 1,500 words maximum; 1,200 words average.
How to Contact: Send complete ms with SASE. Photocopied and previously published submissions OK, but no simultaneous submissions. Accepts computer printout submissions. Reports in 2 months on mss. Publishes ms 1 year to 18 months after acceptance. Sample copy $1.70. Free fiction guidelines and themes with SASE. "Strongly advise sending for themes before submitting."
Payment: 7¢/word and up and 2-5 contributor's copies. $1.70 charge for extras; 25¢ each for 10 or more.
Terms: Pays on acceptance for newspaper and periodical rights. Buys reprints.
Advice: "Do not write *down* to children." Rejects mss because "we receive far more submissions than we can use. If all were of high quality, we still would purchase only a few. The most common problems are overworked story lines and flat, unrealistic characters. Most stories simply do not 'ring true', and children know that. Each issue is theme-related. Please send for list of themes. Include SASE."

PORTLAND MAGAZINE (II), 578 Congress St., Portland ME 04101. (207)773-5250. Editor: Colin Sargent. Managing Editor: W. Kirk Reynolds. Magazine: 68 pages; 60 lb paper; 80 lb cover stock; illustrations and photographs. "City lifestyle magazine—style, business, real estate, controversy, fashion, cuisine, interviews, art." Estab. 1986. Circ. 22,000.
Needs: Contemporary, historical, literary, mainstream, regional, suspense/mystery. Receives 20 unsolicited fiction mss/month. Buys 1 mss/issue; 12 mss/year. Publishes short shorts. Recently published work by Frederick Barthelme, Diane Lefer, Dan Domench. Length: 3 double-spaced typed pages.
How to Contact: Send complete ms with cover letter. Reports in 3 months. SASE. Accepts computer printout and electronic submissions. Sample copy $2.
Terms: Pays on publication for first North American serial rights.
Advice: "We publish ambitious short fiction featuring everyone from Frederick Barthelme to newly discovered fiction by Edna St. Vincent Millay."

PRIME TIMES (II), National Association for Retired Credit Union People, Inc., (NARCUP), Editorial Offices: Suite 120, 2802 International Ln., Madison WI 53704. (608)241-1557. Executive Editor: Joan Donovan. Magazine: medium sized; 40 pages; illustrations and photos. Editorial slant is toward redefining the mid-life transition and promoting a dynamic vision of the prime-life years. Each edition

The double dagger before a listing indicates that the listing is new in this edition. New markets are often the most receptive to freelance contributions.

revolves loosely around a theme—for example, stress management and preventive health help, second careers, unique problems of the midlife or "bridge" generation. The short story may sketch relational conflicts and resolutions between prime-life men and women, or with their children, parents, etc., or place them in situations that try their spirits and revalidate them. Fiction that is not targeted to this group but of excellent quality and broad general appeal is also very welcome. Staff will review adventure, ethnic, science fiction, fantasy, mainstream and humorous fiction as well. No sentimental romances or nostalgia pieces, please. Quarterly. Estab. 1979. Circ. 75,000.
Needs: Literary, contemporary, romance, adventure, humor, ethnic, travel. Buys 2 mss/year. Approximately 10% of fiction is agented. Recently published work by Ethan Canin. Length: 2,500-4,000 words. Shorter lengths preferred.
How to Contact: Send complete ms. SASE always. Accepts computer printout submissions. Prefers letter-quality. Reports in 4-6 weeks on queries and mss. Publishes ms 6-12 months after acceptance. Free sample copy with 9×12 SASE (5 first class stamps). Free guidelines with SASE.
Payment: $150-750. 3 free author's copies; $1 charge for each extra.
Terms: Pays on publication for first North American serial rights and for second serial (reprint) rights.
Advice: "We may feature fiction only once or twice yearly, now, instead of regularly. Quality is *everything*. Readers favor the short stories we've featured on positive human relationships. We are very happy to feature second-serial work as long as it hasn't appeared in another *national* 'maturity market' publication. *Always* request a publication's writer's guidelines before submitting. Write with emotional integrity and imagination."

PRIVATE LETTERS (I, II), 801 2nd Ave., New York NY 10017. Editor: Mario Almonte. Magazine: digest-sized; 98 pages; illustrations; photographs. Bi-monthly letters magazine.
Needs: Erotica, written in letter form. No S&M, incest, homosexuality, anal sex or sex-crazed women and macho, women-conquering studs. "We use approximately 40 short letters per issue of no more than four double-spaced manuscript pages and five long letters of about 10 double-spaced manuscript pages." Recently published work by Diana Shamblin, Frank Lee and Shirley LeRoy; published new writers last year. Recommends other markets.
How to Contact: Send complete mss. "The majority of the material is assigned to people whose writing has proven consistently top-notch. They usually reach this level by sending us unsolicited material which impresses us. We invite them to send us some more on spec, and we're impressed again. Then a long and fruitful relationship is hopefully established. We greatly encourage unsolicited submissions. We are now printing two additional issues each year, so naturally the demand for stories is higher."
Payment: Pays $5 per page for short letters; $75 for long (7-10 page) letters.
Terms: Pays on acceptance.
Advice: "If you base your writing on erotic magazines other than our own, then we'll probably find your material too gross. We want good characterization, believable plots, a little romance, with sex being a natural outgrowth of a relationship. (Yes, it can be done. Read our magazine.) Portray sex as an emotionally-charged, romantic experience—not an animalistic ritual. *Never* give up, except if you die. In which case, if you haven't succeeded as a writer yet, you probably never will. (Though there have been exceptions.) Potential writers should be advised that each issue has certain themes and topics we try to adhere to. It would be greatly to one's benefit to write to ask for a copy of the writer's guidelines *and* a list of themes and topics for upcoming issues. Also, while the longer stories of more than 7 pages pay more, there are only about five of them accepted for each issue. We buy far more 4-6 page mss."

PURPOSE (II), Mennonite Publishing House, 616 Walnut Ave., Scottdale PA 15683-1999. (412)887-8500. Editor: James E. Horsch. Magazine: 5⅜×8⅜; 8 pages; illustrations; photos. "Magazine discipleship—how to be a faithful Christian in the midst of tough everday life complexities. Use story form to present models and examples for Christians interested in exploring faithful discipleship." Weekly. Estab. 1969. Circ. 19,250.
Needs: Historical, religious/inspirational. No militaristic/narrow patriotism or racism. Receives 100 unsolicited mss/month. Buys 3 mss/issue; 40 mss/year. Publishes short shorts. Recently published work by Agnes Kempton, Christine Gould and Anne Lorimer. Length: 800 words average; 350 words minimum; 1,200 words maximum. Occasionally comments on rejected ms.
How to Contact: Prefer full manuscript. Will respond to query. Reports in 6 weeks on queries and mss. Simultaneous, photocopied and previously published work OK. Accepts computer printout submissions. Prefers letter-quality. Sample copy free with 6×9 SAE and 2 first class stamps. Writer's guidelines free with sample copy only.

Payment: Up to 5¢/word for stories and up to $1 per line for poetry and 2 contributor's copies.
Terms: Pays on acceptance for one-time rights.
Advice: Many stories are "situational—how to respond to dilemmas. Write crisp, action moving, personal style, focused upon an individual, a group of people, or an organization. The story form is an excellent literary device to use in exploring discipleship issues. There are many issues to explore. Each writer brings a unique solution. Let's hear them. The first two paragraphs are crucial in establishing the mood/issue to be resolved in the story. Work hard on this."

R-A-D-A-R (II), Standard Publishing, 8121 Hamilton Ave., Cincinnati OH 45231. (513)931-4050. Editor: Margaret Williams. Magazine: 12 pages; newsprint; illustrations; a few photos. "*R-A-D-A-R* is a take-home paper, distributed in Sunday school classes for children in grades 3-6. The stories and other features reinforce the Bible lesson taught in class. Boys and girls who attend Sunday school make up the audience. The fiction stories, Bible picture stories and other special features appeal to their interests." Weekly. Estab. 1978.
Needs: Fiction—The hero of the story should be an 11- or 12-year-old in a situation involving one or more of the following: history, mystery, animals (preferably horses or dogs), prose poem, spiritual, sports, adventure, school, travel, relationships with parents, friends and others. Stories should have believable plots and be wholesome, Christian character-building, but not "preachy." No science fiction. Receives approximately 75-100 unsolicited mss/month. Recently published work by Betty Lou Mell, Betty Steele Everett and Alan Cliburn; published new writers within the last year. Length: 900-1,000 words average; 400 words minimum; 1,200 words maximum. Publishes short shorts.
How to Contact: Send complete ms. Reports in 2 weeks on queries; 6-8 weeks on mss. SASE for ms. No simultaneous submissions; photocopied and reprint submissions OK. Accepts computer printout submissions; no dot-matrix. Reports in 6-8 weeks. Free sample copy and guidelines.
Payment: 3¢ a word. Free contributor's copy.
Terms: Pays on acceptance for first rights.
Advice: "Send for sample copy, guidesheet, and theme list. Follow the specifics of guidelines. Keep your writing current with the times and happenings of our world."

RADIANCE (II), The Magazine for Large Women, Box 31703, Oakland CA 94604. (415)482-0680. Editor: Alice Ansfield. Fiction Editors: Alice Ansfield and Carol Squires. Magazine: 8½×11; 48-52 pages; glossy/coated paper; 70 lb cover stock; illustrations; photos. "Theme is to encourage women to live fully now, whatever their body size. To stop waiting to live or feel good about themselves until they lose weight. Health, emotional well-being, cultural views of body size, poetry/art, profiles, book reviews, lots of ads for services/products for large women, etc." Audience is "large women (size 16 and over) from all walks of life, all ages, ethnic groups, education levels and lifestyles. Feminist, fashion, emotionally supportive magazine." Quarterly. Estab. 1984. Circ. 35,000.
Needs: Adventure, contemporary, erotica, ethnic, fantasy, feminist, historical, humor/satire, mainstream, preschool, prose poem, science fiction, spiritual, sports, suspense, young adult/teen. "Would prefer fiction to have in it a larger-bodied character; living in a positive, upbeat way. Our goal is to empower women." Receives 30-50 mss/month. Buys 4 mss/year. Publishes ms within 1 year of acceptance. Recently published work by Jean Gonick. Length: 1,800 words preferred; 800 words minimum; 2,500 words maximum. Publishes short shorts. Sometimes critiques rejected mss and recommends other markets.
How to Contact: Query with clips of published work and send complete mss with cover letter. Reports in 1-2 months. SASE. Simultaneous, photocopied and reprint submissions OK. Accepts computer printout submissions. Sample copy for $2.50. Fiction guidelines for #10 SASE.
Payment: Pays $50-100 and contributor's copies.
Terms: Pays on publication for one-time rights. Sends galleys to the author if requested.
Advice: "Read our magazine before sending anything to us. Know what our philosophy and points of view are before sending a manuscript. Look around within your community for inspiring, successful and unique large women doing things worth writing about. We will do more fiction in the future, as we grow and have more space for it. At this time, prefer fiction having to do with a larger woman (man, child). Read our magazine. Know our point of view."

RANGER RICK MAGAZINE (II), National Wildlife Federation, 1412 16th St. NW, Washington DC 20036-2266. (703)790-4278. Editor: Gerald Bishop. Fiction Editor: Deborah Churchman. Magazine: 8×10; 48 pages; glossy paper; 60 lb cover stock; illustrations; photos. "*Ranger Rick* emphasizes conservation and the enjoyment of nature through full-color photos and art, fiction and nonfiction articles, games and puzzles, and special columns. Our audience ranges in ages from 6-12, with the greatest number in the 7 to 10 group. We aim for a fourth grade reading level. They read for fun and information." Monthly. Estab. 1967. Circ. 800,000+.

Needs: Fantasy, mystery, adventure, science fiction and humor. "Interesting stories for kids focusing directly on nature or related subjects. Fiction that carries a conservation message is always needed, as are adventure stories involving kids with nature or the outdoors. Moralistic 'lessons' taught children by parents or teachers are not accepted. Human qualities are attributed to animals only in our regular feature, 'Adventures of Ranger Rick.'" Receives about 75 unsolicited fiction mss each month. Buys about 6 mss/year. Recently published fiction by Judy Braus. Length: 900 words maximum. Critiques rejected mss "when there is time."
How to Contact: Query with sample lead and any clips of published work with SASE. Reports in 3 weeks on queries, 2 months on mss. Publishes ms 8 months to 1 year after acceptance, but sometimes longer. Free sample copy. Free guidelines with legal-sized SASE.
Payment: $500 maximum/full-length ms.
Terms: Pays on acceptance for all rights. Very rarely buys reprints. Sends galleys to author.
Advice: "For our magazine, the writer needs to understand kids and that aspect of nature he or she is writing about—a difficult combination! Mss are rejected because they are "contrived and/or condescending—often overwritten. Some mss are anthropomorphic, others are above our readers' level. We find that fiction stories help children understand the natural world and the environmental problems it faces. Beginning writers have a chance equal to that of established authors *provided* the quality is there. We are dealing more directly with nature now."

REDBOOK (II), The Hearst Corporation, 224 W. 57th St., New York NY 10019. Editor: Annette Capone. Fiction Editor: Deborah Purcell. Magazine: 8×10¾; 150-250 pages; 34 lb paper; 70 lb cover; illustrations; photos. "*Redbook's* readership consists of American women, ages 25-44. Most are well-educated, married, have children and also work outside the home. Monthly. Estab. 1903. Circ. 4,100,000.
Needs: "*Redbook* generally publishes three to four short stories per issue. We are looking for fiction that will appeal to active, thinking, contemporary women. Stories need not be about women exclusively; we also look for fiction reflecting the broad range of human experience. We are interested in new voices and buy up to a quarter of our stories from unsolicited submissions. Standards are high: Stories must be fresh, felt and intelligent; no straight formula fiction, pat endings, highly oblique or symbolic stories without conclusions." Receives up to 3,000 unsolicited fiction mss each month; published new writers within the last year. Length: up to 22 ms pages for short stories, up to 9 pages for short shorts.
How to Contact: Send complete ms with 8×11 SASE. No queries, please. Reports in 8-10 weeks. Free guidelines for submission available on request with SASE.
Terms: Pays on acceptance. Buys first North American serial rights.
Advice: "We are looking for intelligently humorous stories (not anecdotes); stories of mystery or psychological suspense with particular attention paid to strong characterizations; topical stories; stories featuring a male protagonist and/or told from the male point of view; stories about women in uniquely challenging situations. Whatever the theme, superior craftsmanship is of paramount importance: Pay keen attention to plotting, character development and a strong and engaging storyline; character sketches and mood or slice-of-life pieces are better suited to other markets. Submit seasonal material nine to 12 months before the appropriate issue." Sponsors Short Story Contest for unpublished writers 18 years of age and up. See March issue of *Redbook* for complete rules.

REFORM JUDAISM (II), Union of American Hebrew Congregations, 838 5th Ave., New York NY 10021. (212)249-0100, ext. 400. Editor: Aron Hirt-Manheimer. Managing Editor: Joy Weinberg. Fiction Editor: Steven Schnur. Magazine: 8½×11; 32 or 48 pages; illustrations; photos. "We cover subjects of Jewish interest in general and Reform Jewish in particular, for members of Reform Jewish congregations in the United States and Canada." Quarterly. Estab. 1972. Circ. 280,000.
Needs: Humor/satire, religious/inspirational. Receives 30 unsolicited mss/month. Buys 3 mss/year. Publishes ms 3 months after acceptance. Length: 1,000 words average; 700 words minimum; 2,000 words maximum. Sometimes recommends other markets.
How to Contact: Send complete ms with cover letter. Reports in 3 weeks. SASE for ms. Simultaneous and photocopied submissions OK. Accepts computer printout submissions. Sample copy for $1 and SAE. Fiction guidelines for SAE.
Payment: Pays 10¢/word.
Terms: Pays on publication for first North American serial rights.

RELIX MAGAZINE (IV), Music for the Mind, Box 94, Brooklyn NY 11229. Editor: Toni A. Brown. Magazine: 54 pages; coated paper; 70 lb cover stock; illustrations; photos. "Classic rock publication focusing on psychedelic '60s—Grateful Dead, etc. Have other fiction project in works focusing on rock

Read the Business of Fiction section to learn the correct way to prepare and submit a manuscript.

fiction-futuristic. For 18-40 year old audience." Bimonthly. Estab. 1974. Circ. 25,000.
Needs: Music–Rock 'n Roll. "Want fiction–futuristic rock or fantasy–music related a must." Receives 5 mss/month. Buys 3 mss/year. Length: 2,000 words preferred. Publishes short shorts. Length: 250 words. Sometimes critiques rejected mss.
How to Contact: Send complete ms with cover letter. Reports in 1 year. SASE. Simultaneous submissions OK. Accepts computer printout submissions. Sample copy for $3. Fiction guidelines for #10 SAE and 1 first class stamp.
Payment: Pays $1.75/column inch.
Terms: Pays on publication for all rights.

ROAD KING MAGAZINE (I), William A. Coop, Inc., Box 250, Park Forest IL 60466. (312)481-9240. Magazine: 5¾×8; 48-88 pages; 60 lb enamel paper; 60 lb enamel cover stock; illustrations; photos. "Bi-monthly leisure-reading magazine for long-haul, over-the-road professional truckers. Contains short articles, short fiction, some product news, games, puzzles and industry news. Truck drivers read it while eating, fueling, during layovers and at other similar times while they are en route."
Needs: Truck-related, western, mystery, adventure and humor. "Remember that our magazine gets into the home and that some truckers tend to be Bible belt types. No erotica or violence." Buys 1 ms/issue; 6 mss/year. Receives 200 unsolicited fiction mss each year. Recently published work by Forrest Grove and Dan Anderson. Length: 1,200 words, maximum.
How to Contact: Send complete ms with SASE. Reports in 3-6 months on mss. Publishes ms 1-2 months after acceptance. Sample copy with 6×9 SASE.
Payment: $400 maximum.
Terms: Pays on acceptance for all rights.
Advice: "Don't phone. Don't send mss by registered or insured mail or they will be returned unopened by post office. Don't try to get us involved in lengthy correspondence. Be patient. We have a small staff and we are slow." Mss are rejected because "most don't fit our format . . . they are too long; they do not have enough knowledge of trucking; there is too much violence. Our readers like fiction. We are a leisure reading publication with a wide variety of themes and articles in each issue. Truckers can read a bit over coffee, in the washroom, etc., then save the rest of the magazine for the next stop. Know the trucker market. We are not interested in stereotypical image of truckers as macho, beer guzzling, women-chasing cowboys."

ST. ANTHONY MESSENGER (II), St. Anthony Messenger, 1615 Republic St., Cincinnati OH 45210. Editor: Norman Perry, O.F.M. Magazine: 8×10¾; 56 pages; illustrations; photos. "*St. Anthony Messenger* is a Catholic family magazine which aims to help its readers lead more fully human and Christian lives. We publish articles which report on a changing church and world, opinion pieces written from the perspective of Christian faith and values, personality profiles, and fiction which entertains and informs." Monthly. Estab. 1893. Circ. 380,000.
Needs: Contemporary, religious/inspirational, romance, senior citizen/retirement and spiritual. "We do not want mawkishly sentimental or preachy fiction. Stories are most often rejected for poor plotting and characterization; bad dialogue–listen to how people talk; inadequate motivation. Many stories say nothing, are 'happenings' rather than stories." No fetal journals, no rewritten Bible stories. Receives 50-60 unsolicited fiction mss/month. Buys 1 ms/issue; 12 mss/year. Recently published work by Hardy Wright, Joseph Pici and Margaret Van Valkenburg. Length: 2,000-2,500 words. Critiques rejected mss "when there is time." Sometimes recommends other markets.
How to Contact: Send complete ms with SASE. Accepts computer printout submissions. Prefers letter-quality. Reports in 6 to 8 weeks on mss. Publishes ms up to 1 year after acceptance. Free sample copy and guidelines with #10 SASE.
Payment: 14¢/word maximum; 2 free author's copies; $1 charge for extras.
Terms: Pays on acceptance for first North American serial rights.
Advice: "We publish one story a month and we get 500 or 600 a year. Too many offer simplistic 'solutions' or answers. Pay attention to endings. Easy, simplistic, deus ex machina endings don't work. People have to feel characters in the stories are real and have a reason to care about them and what happens to them. Fiction entertains but can also convey a point in a very telling way just as the Bible uses stories to teach."

ST. JOSEPH'S MESSENGER AND ADVOCATE OF THE BLIND (II), Sisters of St. Joseph of Peace, 541 Pavonia Ave., Jersey City NJ 07306. (201)798-4141. Magazine: 8½×11; 16 pages; illustrations; photos. For Catholics generally but not exclusively. Theme is "religious–relevant–real." Quarterly. Estab. 1903. Circ. 30,000.
Needs: Contemporary, humor/satire, mainstream, religious/inspirational, romance, and senior citizen/retirement. Receives 30-40 unsolicited fiction mss/month. Buys 3 mss/issue; 20 mss/year. Recently published work by Eileen W. Strauch. Published new writers within the last year. Length: 800 words minimum; 1,800 words maximum; 1,500 words average. Occasionally critiques rejected mss.

How to Contact: Send complete ms with SASE. Simultaneous, photocopied and previously published submissions OK. Publishes ms an average of 1 year after acceptance. Free sample copy with #10 SAE and 1 first class stamp. Free fiction guidelines with SASE.
Payment: $10-25 and 2 contributor's copies.
Terms: Pays on acceptance for one-time rights.
Advice: Rejects mss because of "vague focus or theme. Write to be read—keep material current and of interest. *Do not preach*—the story will tell the message. Keep the ending from being too obvious. Fiction is the greatest area of interest to our particular reading public."

‡SASSY MAGAZINE (II), Matilda Publications, 1 Times Square, New York NY 10036. (212)764-4860. Editor: Jane Pratt. Fiction Editor: Catherine Gysin. Magazine; 9½×11; 100-130 pages; glossy 40 lb. stock paper and cover; illustrations and photographs. "Lifestyle magazine for girls, ages 14-19, covering entertainment, fashion as well as serious subjects." Monthly. Estab. 1988. Circ. 500,000.
Needs: Contemporary, ethnic, experimental, feminist, gay, humor/satire, literary, mainstream, prose poem, regional, young adult/teen (10-18 years). "No typical teenage romance." Publishes annual special fiction issue. Receives 300 unsolicited mss/month. Buys 1 ms/issue; 12 mss/year. Publishes ms 3-6 months after publication. Recently published Christina Kelly, John Elder, Elizabeth Mosier. Length: 2,500 words; 1,000 words minimum; 3,500 words maximum. Sometimes critiques rejected mss and recommends other markets.
How to Contact: Send complete manuscript with cover letter. Include social security number and address, brief background, perhaps one sentence on what story is about or like. Reports in 3 months. SASE. Simultaneous and photocopied submissions OK. Computer printout submissions are acceptable. Sample copy for $2. Fiction guidelines are free.
Payment: Pays $1,000 and contributor's copies.
Terms: Pays on acceptance. Offers 20% kill fee. Buys all rights or first North American serial righs. Send galleys to author (if requested).
Advice: "We look for unusual new ways to write for teenagers. It helps if the story has a quirky, vernacular style that we use throughout the magazine. Generally our stories have to have a teenage protagonist but they are not typical teen fiction. In the end, our only real criterion is that a story is original, intelligent, well-crafted and moves us."

SCHOLASTIC SCOPE (II), Scholastic, Inc., 730 Broadway, New York NY 10003. Magazine: 8½×11; 22-28 pages; pulp paper stock; glossy cover; illustrations and photos. National publication on subjects of general and human interest; profiles of teenagers who have overcome obstacles or done something unusual; short stories and plays for teens. Weekly. Circ. 700,000.
Needs: Stories about the problems of teens (drugs, prejudice, runaways, failure in school, family problems, etc.); relationships between people in family; job and school situations. No crime stories. Recently published work by M.E. Kerr and Paul Zindel. Published new writers within the last year. Length: 400-2,000 words.
How to Contact: Send complete ms with SASE. Sample copy for $1.75.
Payment: Pays $125 minimum.
Terms: Acquires all rights (negotiable).
Advice: "Strive for directness, realism and action in dialogue rather than narrative. Characters should have depth. Avoid too many coincidences and random happenings."

SEACOAST LIFE (II, IV), American Marketing Systems/AMS Publishing Ltd., Box 594, North Hampton NH 03862. (603)778-1010. Fiction Editor: John A. Meng. Magazine: 8½×11; 126 pages; coated freesheet paper; 65 lb coated cover stock; 4-color illustrations, 50/issue; 4-color photographs, 75/issue. "Lifestyle, reflecting southern Maine, seacoast New Hampshire and northeast Massachusetts. We publish fiction each issue plus regional events, investigative journalism, recipes, business, health, fashion and people articles for an upscale, well-educated audience 25-50." Bi-monthly. Estab. 1985. Circ. 20,000.
Needs: Adventure, condensed novel, contemporary, fantasy, humor/satire, literary, mainstream, regional, science fiction, senior citizen/retirement, serialized/excerpted novel, suspense/mystery and translations. No radical fiction, i.e. homosexual, pornographic, etc. Receives 8-10 unsolicited fiction mss/month. Accepts 1 mss/issue; 6 mss/year (including a holiday issue). Publishes ms 3-6 months after acceptance. Recently published work by Jules Archer, Sharon Helgens and Robert Baldwin; published new writers within the last year. Length: 1,500-3,000 words average. Sometimes critiques rejected ms.
How to Contact: "Must be regional in order to submit—northern Massachusetts, coastal New Hampshire, southern Maine." Send complete ms with cover letter, writer's bio. Reports in 1 month. SASE. Simultaneous and photocopied submissions OK. Accepts computer printout submissions. Sample copy $2.50 and 9×12 SAE with $2.40 postage. Fiction guidelines for #10 SAE and 40¢ postage.

Payment: Varies; charge for copies.
Terms: Pays 30 days after publication. Rights purchased negotiated with each individual writer.
Advice: "Our readership is highly educated, critical of shabby work and loves good fiction. Our readers love to read. We will read all submissions and reply to all writers."

SEEK (II), Standard Publishing, 8121 Hamilton Ave., Cincinnati OH 45231. Editor: Eileen H. Wilmoth. Magazine: 5½×8½; 8 pages; newsprint paper; art and photos in each issue. "Inspirational stories of faith-in-action for Christian young adults; a Sunday School take-home paper." Weekly. Published special fiction issue last year; plans another. Estab. 1970. Circ. 75,000.
Needs: Religious/inspirational. Buys 150 mss/year. Published new writers within the last year. Length: 500-1,200 words.
How to Contact: Send complete ms with SASE. Accepts computer printout submissions. Prefers letter-quality. Reports in 4-6 weeks on mss. Publishes ms an average of 1 year after acceptance. Free sample copy and guidelines.
Payment: 2½-3¢/word.
Terms: Pays on acceptance. Buys reprints.
Advice: "Write a credible story with Christian slant – no preachments; avoid overworked themes such as joy in suffering, generation gaps, etc. Most mss are rejected by us because of irrelevant topic or message; unrealistic story; or poor character and/or plot development. We use fiction stories that are believable."

SENIOR LIFE MAGAZINE (IV), 1420 E. Cooley Dr., Suite 200L, Colton CA 92324. (714)824-6681. Editor: Bobbi Mason. Magazine: 8½×10¾; 48 pages; 47 lb paper; 50 lb cover; illustrations and photos. "For readers age 50+; subjects vary widely." Monthly. Estab. 1979. Circ. 30,000.
Needs: Adventure, condensed novel, historical, humor/satire, literary, inspirational, senior citizen/retirement, sports, suspense/mystery, western, nostalgia, holidays, family scenarios/reunions, RV camping, moving/relocating, trains (collectors or small steamers). No erotica, food, travel, health, political, gay/lesbian/feminist, psychic. Receives "too many" unsolicited fiction mss/month. Buys 6 fiction mss/year. Length: 400-800 words preferred. "The shorter the better; space is tight."
How to Contact: Query first; "please state 'up front' required/requested fee." Reporting time "depends on load." SASE. Simultaneous, photocopied (if clear) and reprint submissions OK. No dot-matrix computer printouts. Accepts electronic submissions via disk or modem; query for details. Sample copy $2.50.
Payment: Pays $10-$50 (with art and photos); 1 contributor's copy. Free subscription to magazine on request.
Terms: Pays on publication.
Advice: "Write tight. Space is limited. Prefer name, address and phone on all pieces sent, i.e. each page of manuscript, each sketch, graph or photo."

SEVENTEEN (II), News America, Inc., 850 3rd Ave., New York NY 10022. (212)759-8100. Fiction Editor: Adrian Nicole LeBlanc. Magazine: 8½×11; 125-400 pages; 40 lb coated paper; 80 lb coated cover stock; illustrations; photos. A service magazine with fashion, beauty care, pertinent topics such as trends in dating, attitudes, experiences and concerns during the teenage years. Monthly. Estab. 1944. Circ. 1.7 million.
Needs: High-quality literary fiction on topics of interest to teenage girls. The editors look for fresh themes and well paced plots. Buys 1 ms/issue. Receives 300 unsolicited fiction mss/month. Approximately 50% of fiction is agented. Recently published work by Margaret Atwood, David Lipsky and Particia MacInnes. Published new writers within the last year. Length: approximately 1,500-3,500 words. Also publishes short shorts.
How to Contact: Send complete ms with SASE and cover letter with relevant credits. Reports in 2 months on mss. Free guidelines when requested with SASE.
Payment: Pays $700-2,000.
Terms: Pays on acceptance for one-time rights.
Advice: "Respect the intelligence and sophistication of today's teenage reader. *Seventeen* remains open to the surprise of new voices. Our commitment to publishing the work of new writers remains strong; we continue to read every submission we receive. We believe that good fiction can move the reader toward thoughtful examination of her own life as well as the lives of others – providing her ultimately with a fuller appreciation of what it means to be human. While stories which focus on female teenage experience continue to be of interest, the less obvious possibilities are equally welcome. We encourage writers to submit literary short stories concerning subjects that may not be immediately identifiable as 'teenage,' with narrative styles that are experimental and challenging. Too often, unsolicited submissions possess voices and themes condescending and unsophisticated. Also, writers hesitate to send stories to *Seventeen* which they think too violent or risqué. Good writing holds the imaginable and then some, and if it doesn't find its home here, I'm always grateful for the introduction to a

writer's work." Co-sponsors annual teen fiction contest. Rules are announced each year in a fall issue.

SHOFAR (I, II, IV), For Jewish Kids On The Move, Senior Publications, Ltd., 43 Northcote Dr., Melville NY 11747. (914)634-9423. Editor: Gerald H. Grayson, PhD. Magazine: 8½×11; 32-48 pages; 60 lb paper; 80 lb cover; illustration; photos. Audience: Jewish children in fourth through eighth grades. Monthly (October-May). Estab. 1984. Circ. 10,000.
Needs: Adventure, contemporary, ethnic, fantasy, humor, juvenile (5-9 years), prose poem, religious/inspirational, spiritual, sports, suspense/mystery, translations, young adult/teen (10-18 years) and Jewish. Receives 12-24 unsolicited mss/month. Buys 3-5 mss/issue; 24-40 mss/year. Recently published work by Caryn Huberman, Diane Claerbout and Rabbi Sheldon Lewis. Length: 750-1,000 words. Occasionally critiques rejected mss. Recommends other markets.
How to Contact: Send complete ms with cover letter. Reports in 6-8 weeks on ms. SASE. Simultaneous, photocopied and reprint submissions OK. Accepts computer printout submissions. Sample copy for 9×12 SAE and 5 first class stamps. Fiction guidelines for 3½×6½ SAE and 1 first class stamp.
Payment: Pays 7¢/word.
Terms: Pays on publication for first North American serial rights.
Advice: "Know the magazine and the religious-education needs of Jewish elementary school age children. If you are a Jewish educator, what has worked for you in the classroom? Write it out; send it on to me; I'll help you develop the idea into a short piece of fiction. A beginning fiction writer eager to break into *Shofar* will find an eager editor willing to help."

THE SINGLE PARENT (IV), Journal of Parents Without Partners, Parents Without Partners, Inc., 8807 Colesville Rd., Silver Spring MD 20910. (301)588-9354. Editor: Allan Glennon. Magazine: 8½×11; 48 pages; 40 lb glossy paper; illustrations; photos. Publication for divorced, separated, widowed or never-married parents and their children. Published 6 times/year. Estab. 1965. Circ. 120,000.
Needs: Short stories for *children only*, not adults. Stories should deal with issues that children from one-parent families might face. Buys 2 ms/issue. Recently published work by L.N. Smith, Joan Andrews and Alan Cliburn. Published new writers within the last year. Length: 1,500 words maximum.
How to Contact: Send complete ms with SASE. Sample copy $1 or 10×12 manila SASE with 65¢ postage. Reports within 2 months.
Payment: Pays up to $75; 2 free contributor's copies.
Terms: Pays on publication.
Advice: "Upbeat, problem-solving themes preferred. Steer clear of talking, furry animals acting like humans; give us 'real' children facing real situations."

SINGLELIFE MAGAZINE (II), Single Life Enterprises, Inc., 606 W. Wisconsin Ave., Suite 706, Milwaukee WI 53203. (414)271-9700. Editor: Leifa Butrick. Magazine: 8×11; 82 pages; slick paper; illustrations; photos. "Material deals with concerns of single persons of 24-60 age group." Primarily a nonfiction magazine. Bimonthly. Estab. 1982. Circ. 25,000.
Needs: Humor/satire, literary, travel, relationships, self-help, seasonal food and entertaining. Receives 50 unsolicited mss/month. Recently published work by Larry Stolte, Hilton Anderson, Norma Jean Lutz and Jacquelyn Guidry. Publishes ms 2-4 months after acceptance. Length: 1,000 words minimum; 3,500 words maximum. Also publishes short shorts. Occasionally critiques rejected mss.
How to Contact: Send complete ms. Reports in 1 week, "depends on production schedule." SASE for ms. Simultaneous, photocopied and reprint submissions OK. Accepts computer printouts. Accepts electronic submissions via disc or modem. Sample copy $3.50. Fiction guidelines for SAE and 1 first class stamp.
Payment: Pays $50-150 and contributor's copies.
Terms: Pays on publication for one-time rights.

‡SPECIAL REPORT: FICTION (II), Whittle Communications, 505 Market St., Knoxville TN 37902. (615)595-5800. Editor: Elise Nakhnikian. Magazine; 11×15; 68 pages; glossy paper; high-gloss cover; illustrations and photographs. Each issue has a different theme. Write for guidelines. For mass market, primarily women 25-40, who have or are starting families. Quarterly. Estab. 1988. Circ. approximately 5 million.
Needs: Excerpted novel, or short story. Topic depends on upcoming themes. "No inspirational, experimental, young adult, juvenile, science fiction." Receives 100 unsolicited mss/month. Buys 6-7 mss/issue; 25 mss/year. Publishes ms 6 months after acceptance. Agented fiction 33⅓%-50%. Recently published work by John Updike, John Hersey, Kaye Gibbons. Length: 3,000 words; 4,500 words maximum. Publishes short shorts ("In fact, we're always looking for them.") "As short as you can make it work." Sometimes critiques rejected mss.
How to Contact: Send complete ms with cover letter or submit through agent. "Mention where other fiction has been published if anywhere, and prizes or awards." Reports in 2-6 months. SASE for ms, not needed for query. Photocopied submissions OK. Computer printout submissions are acceptable. Sample copy $3.50. Fiction guidelines free with #10 SAE.

Payment: Pays $1,500 and up for first serial.
Terms: Pays on acceptance (depends on situation). Buys first North American serial rights. Sends galleys to author.
Advice: "We look first for an authentic and gifted voice, for writing that sings. We also want stories that make a reader think, laugh or feel; not those inconclusive stories that make you wonder what the point of all that was. We avoid formulaic characters and plots. Write first for guidelines and at least one sample copy."

"Each issue of* Special Reports Fiction *has a different theme," says managing editor Elise Naknikian. "About one in every three or four is a 'genre,' as is this one," she says, referring to the August-October 1989 issue's focus on supernatural and horror stories. The majority of the fiction issues usually center on softer themes, such as family relationships or growing up female. Well-known artist Rene Magritte, painted the illustration.

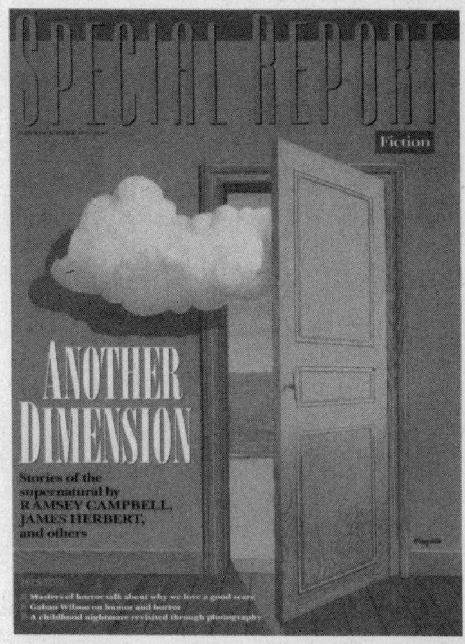

Le Poison by Rene Magritte, courtesy of Christie's and *Special Report: Fiction*

SPORTS AFIELD (II, IV), Hearst Magazine, 250 W. 55th St., New York 10019. (212)262-8835. Editor: Tom Paugh. Magazine: 8×11; 128 pages minimum; "the best paper"; 70 lb cover stock; illustrations; photos. "This is an outdoor magazine: hunting, fishing, camping, boating, conservation, etc." for men and women who take an active interest in their sport. Monthly. Estab. 1887. Circ. 542,000.
Needs: Adventure, humor/satire when related to hunting and fishing, sports (fishing, hunting, camping). No old-fashioned me-and-Joe yarns. Receives 20 unsolicited mss/week. Buys a few mss each year. Publishes ms up to 2 years after acceptance. Agented fiction: 5%. Length: 2,500 words or less. Also publishes short shorts of 200-250 words.
How to Contact: Query first; include name, address, a little background and credits, *brief* synopsis of story. Reports in 1 month on queries and mss. SASE for query. Accepts computer printouts.
Payment: Pays $850.
Terms: Pays on acceptance for first rights.
Advice: "Fiction is a very tough market—and not just in the outdoor field. Know the market."

STANDARD (II, IV), Nazarene International Headquarters, 6401 The Paseo, Kansas City MO 64131. (816)333-7000. Editor: Beth A. Watkins. Magazine: 8½×11; 8 pages; illustrations; photos. Inspirational reading for adults. Weekly. Estab. 1936. Circ. 177,000.
Needs: Religious/inspirational, spiritual. Receives 350 unsolicited mss/month (both fiction and nonfiction). Accepts 60 mss/year. Publishes ms 9-24 months after acceptance. Recently published work by Todd Lee, Floyd Allen, Jeanne Hill and Mark Littleton; published new writers within the last year. Length: 1,000 words average; 300 words minimum; 1,500 words maximum. Also publishes short shorts of 300-350 words.
How to Contact: Send complete ms with name, address and phone number. Reports in 1-2 months on mss. SASE. Simultaneous submissions OK but will pay only reprint rates. Accepts computer printouts. Sample copy and guidelines for SAE and 1 first class stamp.
Payment: Pays 3.5¢/word; 2¢/word (reprint); contributor's copies.
Terms: Pays on acceptance for one-time rights.
Advice: "Too much is superficial; containing the same story lines. Give me something original, humorous, yet helpful. I'm also looking for more stories on current social issues. Make plot, characters realistic. Contrived articles are quick to spot and reject."

STORY FRIENDS (II), Mennonite Publishing House, 616 Walnut Ave., Scottdale PA 15683. (412)887-8500. Editor: Marjorie Waybill. Sunday school publication which portrays Jesus as a friend and helper. Nonfiction and fiction for children 4-9 years of age. Weekly.

Needs: Juvenile. Stories of everyday experiences at home, in church, in school or at play, which provide models of Christian values. Length: 300-800 words.

How to Contact: Send complete ms with SASE. Seasonal or holiday material should be submitted 6 months in advance. Free sample copy.

Payment: Pays 3-5¢/word.

Terms: Pays on acceptance for one-time rights. Buys reprints. Not copyrighted.

Advice: "It is important to include relationships, patterns of forgiveness, respect, honesty, trust and caring. Prefer exciting yet plausible short stories which offer different settings, introduce children to wide ranges of friends and demonstrate joys, fears, temptations and successes of the readers."

STRAIGHT (II), Standard Publishing Co., 8121 Hamilton Ave., Cincinnati OH 45231. (513)931-4050. Editor: Carla Crane. Publication helping and encouraging teens to live a victorious, fulfilling Christian life. Distributed through churches and some private subscriptions. Magazine: 6½×7½; 12 pages; newsprint paper and cover; illustrations (color); photos. Quarterly in weekly parts. Estab. 1951. Circ. 75,000.

Needs: Contemporary, religious/inspirational, romance, spiritual, mystery, adventure and humor—all with Christian emphasis. "Stories dealing with teens and teen life, with a positive message or theme. Topics that interest teenagers include school, family life, recreation, friends, church, part-time jobs, dating and music. Main character should be a 15- or 16-year old boy or girl, a Christian and regular churchgoer, who faces situations using Bible principles." Buys 1-2 mss/issue; 75-100 mss/year. Receives approximately 100 unsolicited fiction mss/month. Less than 1% of fiction is agented. Recently published work by Alan Cliburn, Marian Bray, Teresa Cleary; published new writers within the last year. Length: 800-1,200 words. Recommends other markets.

How to Contact: Send complete ms with SASE and cover letter (experience with teens especially preferred from new writers). Accepts computer printout submissions. Reports in 1 month on mss. Publishes ms an average of 1 year after acceptance. Free sample copy and guidelines with SASE.

Payment: 2-3½¢/word.

Terms: Pays on acceptance for first and one-time rights. Buys reprints.

Advice: "Get to know us before submitting, through guidelines and sample issues (free with an SASE). And get to know teenagers. A writer must know what today's teens are like, and what kinds of conflicts they experience. In writing a short fiction piece for the teen reader, don't try to accomplish too much. If your character is dealing with the problem of prejudice, don't also deal with his/her fights with sister, desire for a bicycle, or anything else that is not absolutely essential to the reader's understanding of the major conflict."

THE STUDENT (I, II), A Christian Collegiate Magazine, Student Ministry Department of the Baptist Sunday School Board, 127 Ninth Ave., North, Nashville TN 37234. (615)251-2788. Editor: Milt Hughes. Magazine: 8¼×11; 50 pages; uncoated paper; coated cover stock; illustrations; photos. Magazine for Christians and non-Christians about life and work with Christian students on campus and related articles on living in dorm setting, dating life, missions activities, Bible study, and church ministry to students. Monthly. Estab. 1922. Circ. 40,000.

Needs: Adventure, humor, comics, confession, contemporary, ethnic, and religious/inspirational. Does not want to see mss "without purpose or without moral tone." Receives approximately 25 unsolicited fiction mss/month. Buys 1-2 mss/issue; 12-24 mss/year. Length: 300 words minimum (or less, depending on treatment); 1,000 words maximum; 750 words average.

How to Contact: Cover letter with bio and description of published works. Query first with SASE. Simultaneous, photocopied and previously published submissions OK. Reports in 3 weeks on queries; 6 weeks on mss. Sample copy 61¢. Free fiction guidelines with SASE.

Payment: 5¢/word and 3 contributor's copies.

Terms: Pays on publication for all rights, first rights, one-time rights, and assignments for work-for-hire basis.

Advice: "Fit writing to format and concept of the piece. View many issues of the magazine before you write. Our readers demand fiction which conveys our message in an interesting way."

STUDENT LAWYER (II, IV), American Bar Association, 750 N. Lake Shore Dr., Chicago IL 60611. (312)988-6048. Editor: Sarah Hoban. Managing Editor: Miriam Krasno. Magazine: 8½×10¾; 48 pages; glossy paper and cover; illustrations; photos. "Magazine for law students as part of their Law Student Division/ABA membership. Features legal aspects, trends in the law, social/legal issues, and lawyer profiles." Monthly (September-May). Circ. 35,000.

Needs: "All stories have to have a legal/law/lawyer/law-school element to them. No science fiction." Buys 1 full-length or 2-3 short humorous pieces/year. Length: 1,000-3,000 words. Sometimes recommends other markets.

How to Contact: Send complete ms with SASE. Accepts computer printout submissions. Reports in 1 month on mss. Publishes ms 1-6 months after acceptance. Sample copy $3; contact Order Fulfillment at above address.

Payment: $75-500.

Terms: Pays on acceptance for first rights. Buys very few reprints.

Advice: Rejects mss because "usually, the stories are of mediocre quality. Because we favor nonfiction pieces, the fiction we do publish has to be outstanding or at least very original. Keep trying—and *know* the magazine you're submitting to."

SUNDAY JOURNAL MAGAZINE, *The Providence Journal-Bulletin*, 75 Fountain St., Providence RI 02902. (401)277-7349. Editor: Elliot Krieger. Magazine: 10×11½; 28 pages; coated newsprint paper; illustrations; photos. "Magazine which has appeared weekly for 40 years in the *Providence Sunday Journal*." Circ. 280,000.

Needs: Regional. Recently published fiction by Paul Watkins and Ann Hood; published new writers within the last year.

How to Contact: Query with clips of published work and brief cover letter. SASE.

Payment: $175 minimum; $400 maximum.

Terms: Buys one-time rights. Sponsors short-story contest for New England writers. Deadline: June 1, 1989.

Advice: New England, especially Rhode Island, fiction only.

SUNSHINE MAGAZINE (II), Henrichs Publications, Box 40, Sunshine Park, Litchfield IL 62056. Magazine. 5¼×7¼; 48 pages; matte paper and cover stock; illustrations. "To promote good will for the betterment of our society. We publish short, non-denominational, inspirational material." Monthly. Estab. 1924. Circ. 60,000.

Needs: Adventure, historical (general), humor, juvenile (5-9 years), preschool (0-4 years), senior citizen/retirement. No fiction that is lengthy, fantasy, sexual, specifically religious, violent or dealing with death, drugs, divorce or alcohol. Receives 500 unsolicited fiction mss/month. Buys 12 mss/issue; 140 mss/year. Publishes ms within a year of acceptance. Recently published work by Robert Tefertillar, Gail Geddes, Joanna Captain; published new writers within the last year. Length: 750 words average; 100 words minimum; 1,250 words maximum. Publishes short shorts. Sometimes critiques rejected ms and recommends other markets.

How to Contact: Send complete ms with SASE and cover letter with name, address, rights offered. Reports in 2 months on mss. SASE. Photocopied submissions OK. Accepts computer printout submissions, including dot-matrix. Sample copy 50¢ or 6×8 SAE with 2 first class stamps. Fiction guidelines with #10 SASE.

Payment: $10-100, contributor's copies; charge for extras.

Terms: Pays on acceptance for first North American serial rights. Publication copyrighted.

Advice: "Beginning writers are more than welcome to submit to *Sunshine*. Don't get discouraged—just keep trying. We can use only about 5% of what we receive."

SWANK MAGAZINE (II, IV), Broadway Publishing Company, 888 7th Ave., New York NY 10106. Editor: Michael Wilde. Magazine: 8½×11; 116 pages; 20 lb paper; 60 lb coated stock; illustrations; photos. "Men's sophisticate format. Sexually-oriented material. Presumably our reader is after erotic material." Monthly. Estab. 1952. Circ. 350,000.

Needs: High-caliber erotica. "Fiction always has an erotic or other male-oriented theme; also eligible would be mystery or suspense with a very erotic scene. Writers should try to avoid the cliches of the genre." Buys 1 ms/issue, 12 mss/year. Receives approximately 80 unsolicited fiction mss each month. Length: 1,500-2,750 words.

How to Contact: Send complete ms with SASE and cover letter, which should list previous publishing credits. No simultaneous submissions. Accepts high-quality computer printout submissions. Reports in 6 weeks on mss. Sample copy $5 with SASE.

Payment: $250-400. Offers 25% kill fee for assigned ms not published.

Terms: Buys first North American serial rights.

Advice: "Research the men's magazine market." Mss are rejected because of "typical, overly simple storylines and poor execution. We're looking for interesting stories—whether erotic in theme or not—that break the mold of the usual men's magazine fiction. We're not only just considering strict erotica. Mystery, adventure, etc. with erotica passages will be considered."

‡TATTOO ADVOCATE JOURNAL (II), 380 Belmont Ave., Haledon NJ 07508. (201)790-0429. Editor: Kathy Weber. Fiction Editor: Shotsie Gorman. Journal: 8½×11; 90 pages; 10 pt. coated two cover; illustrations and photographs. "Tattoo art, fiction, poetry, humor, profiles, historical, anthropology for the general reader of ethnographic material and arts." Semiannually.
Needs: Condensed/excerpted novel, contemporary, ethnic, fantasy, feminist, gay, historical (general), horror, humor/satire, lesbian, literary, mainstream, prose poem, psychic/supernatural/occult, regional, religious/inspirational, romance (contemporary, historical), science fiction, serialized novel and suspense/mystery. "Articles that relate to Rock & Roll and Tattoos and all related subjects. Not interested in Motorcycle lifestyle material or blatantly sexual material. Fiction that uses tattoo as a reference point or as a major metaphor." Receives 4 unsolicited mss/month. Buys 2-3 mss/issue; 4-6 mss/year. Publishes ms 6 months to a year after acceptance. Agented fiction 1%. Recently published work by William Barrett, Jack Dann and Marian Engel. Length: 2,000; 500 words minimum; 6,000 words maximum. Publishes short shorts. Length: 500 words. Sometimes critiques rejected ms and recommends other markets.
How to Contact: Query with clips of published work or send complete ms with cover letter. Reports in 6 weeks on queries; 3 months on mss. SASE for ms, not needed for query. Photocopied and reprint submissions OK. Computer printout submissions are acceptable. Electronic submissions are acceptable. Sample copy for $5.50. Fiction guidelines free.
Payment: Pays $50-500 and contributor's copies; charge for extras.
Terms: Pays on acceptance. Offers 10% kill fee. Buys all rights, first rights, first North American serial rights or one-time rights.
Advice: Looks for "creative story line, unique thoughts and non-typical plots."

'TEEN MAGAZINE (II), Petersen Publishing Co., 8490 Sunset Blvd., Los Angeles CA 90069. Editor: Roxanne Camron. Magazine: 100-150 pages; 34 lb paper; 60 lb cover; illustrations and photos. "The magazine contains fashion, beauty and features for the young teenage girl. The median age of our readers is 16. Our success stems from our dealing with relevant issues teens face, printing recent entertainment news and showing the latest fashions and beauty looks." Monthly. Estab. 1957. Circ. 1 million.
Needs: Romance, adventure, mystery, humor and young adult. Every story, whether romance, mystery, humor, etc., must be aimed for teenage girls. The protagonist should be a teenager, preferably female. No experimental, science fiction, fantasy or horror. Buys 1 ms/issue; 12 mss/year. Publishes short shorts. Recently published work by Janet Dagon, Ralph Vaughan and Teri Christopherson; published new writers within the last year. Length: 2,500-4,000 words.
How to Contact: Send complete ms and short cover letter with SASE. Reports in 10 weeks on mss. Generally publishes ms 3-5 months after acceptance. Sample copy for $2.50. Free guidelines with SASE.
Payment: Pays $100.
Terms: Pays on acceptance for all rights.
Advice: "Try to find themes that suit the modern teen. We need innovative ways of looking at the age-old problems of young love, parental pressures, making friends, being left out, etc. '*TEEN* would prefer to have romance balanced with a plot, re: a girl's inner development and search for self. Handwritten mss will not be read."

TEEN POWER, Scripture Press Publications, Inc., Box 632, Glen Ellyn IL 60138. (312)668-6000. Editor: Amy Swanson. Magazine: 5⅜×8⅜; 8 pages; non-glossy paper and cover; illustrations and photographs. "Teen Power publishes mostly fiction with a conservative Christian slant—must have some sort of spiritual emphasis for young teens (11-14 years); many small town and rural; includes large readerships in Canada, England and other countries in addition to U.S." Estab. 1966. Circ. 80,000.
Needs: Adventure, humor/satire, religious/inspirational, young adult/teen (10-18 years). "All must have spiritual emphasis of some sort." Receives approx. 50-75 unsolicited mss/month. Buys 1 ms/issue; about 50 mss/year. Publishes ms at least one year after acceptance. Recently published work by Alan Cliburn, Betty Steele Everett and Chris Lutes. Length: 1,000 words preferred; 250 words minimum; 1,100 words maximum. Publishes short shorts. Length: 300-500 words. Sometimes critiques rejected mss and recommends other markets.
How to Contact: Send complete ms with cover letter. Reports in 1 month. SASE. Simultaneous, photocopied and reprint submissions OK. Accepts computer printouts. Sample copy and fiction guidelines for #10 SAE and 1 first class stamp.
Payment: Pays $20 minimum; $120 maximum; contributor's copies.
Terms: Pays on acceptance. Purchases first rights and one-time rights.
Advice: "We look for spiritual emphasis (strong but not preachy); writing style; age appropriateness; creativity in topic choice and presentation. A writer for *Teen Power* must know something about young teens and what is important to them, plus have a working knowledge of basic Christian doctrine, and be able to weave the two together."

TEENS TODAY (II), Church of the Nazarene, 6401 The Paseo, Kansas City MO 64131. (816)333-7000. Editor: Karen DeSollar. Sunday school take-home paper: 8½×11; 8 pages; illustrations; photos. For junior and senior high students involved with the Church of the Nazarene who find it interesting and helpful to their areas of life. Weekly. Circ. 60,000.

Needs: Contemporary, religious/inspirational, romance, humor, juvenile, young adult and ethnic. "Nothing that puts teens down or endorses lifestyles not in keeping with the denomination's beliefs and standards." Buys 1-2 mss/issue. Published new writers within the last year. Length: 1,000-1,500 words.

How to Contact: Send complete ms with SASE. Reports in 6 weeks on mss. Publishes ms 8-10 months after acceptance. Free sample copy and guidelines with SASE.

Payment: Pays 3½¢/word and 3¢/word on second reprint.

Terms: Pays on acceptance for first and second serial rights. Buys reprints.

Advice: "Don't be too juvenile."

TEXAS CONNECTION MAGAZINE (IV), Box 541805, Dallas TX 75220. (214)241-8350. Editor: Alan Miles. Magazine: 8½×11; 132 pages; book offset paper; 100 lb enamel cover; illustrations and photographs. "Adult erotica, for adults only." Monthly. Estab. 1985. Circ. 10,000.

Needs: Erotica, erotic cartooning, sexual fantasy, feminist, gay, humor/satire and lesbian. Receives 20-30 unsolicited mss/month. Buys 2-3 mss/issue. Publishes ms 2-3 months after acceptance. Length: 1,750 words preferred; 1,000 words minimum; 2,500 words maximum.

How to Contact: Send complete ms with cover letter. Cover letter must state writer/author's age (18 yrs. minimum). Reports in 3 weeks. SASE for ms, not needed for query. Simultaneous, photocopied and reprint submissions OK. Accepts computer printout submissions. Sample copy for $7.50. Free fiction guidelines.

Payment: Pays $25 minimum; $200 maximum. Free subscription to magazine. Free contributor's copies.

Terms: Pays on publication. Purchases all rights on some, first rights on most.

Advice: "We publish an adult, alternative lifestyle magazine that is (uniquely) distributed both in the adult store market and mass-market outlets (convenience stores) throughout 5 states: Texas (main), Oklahoma, Arkansas, Louisiana, New Mexico. We are, of course, interested in fresh, erotic fiction only."

TIKKUN (III), A Bimonthly Jewish Critique of Politics, Culture and Society, Institute for Labor and Mental Health, 5100 Leona St., Oakland CA 94619. (415)482-0805. Editor: Michael Lerner. Fiction Editors: Rosellen Brown and Marvin Hoffman. Magazine: 8×11; 96 pages; high quality paper. "*Tikkun* was created two years ago as the liberal alternative to *Commentary Magazine* and the voices of Jewish conservatism, but is not aimed just at a Jewish audience. Readers are intellectuals, political activists, Washington policy circles, writers, poets." Bimonthly.

Needs: Condensed/excerpted novel, contemporary, feminist, gay, historical (general), humor/satire, lesbian, literary, mainstream, translations, Jewish political. "No narrowly Jewish fiction. At least half of our readers are not Jewish. Or anything that is not of highest quality." Receives 150 unsolicited mss/month. Buys 1 ms/issue. Publishes ms 6-9 months after acceptance. Agented fiction 50%. Recently published work by Amos Oz, Lynne Sharon Schwartz, E.M. Broner. Length: 4,000 words preferred. Publishes short shorts. Almost always critiques rejected mss.

How to Contact: Send complete ms with cover letter. Reports in 2-3 months. SASE. Accepts computer printout submissions. Sample copy for $7.

Payment: Pays $100-250.

Terms: Pays on publication for first rights.

Advice: Looks for creativity, sensitivity, intelligence, originality, profundity of insight. "Read *Tikkun*, at least 3-4 issues worth, understand the kinds of issues that interest our readers, and then imagine yourself trying to write fiction that delights, surprises and intrigues this kind of an audience. Do not write what you think will feel sweet or appealing to this audience – but rather that which will provoke, bring to life and engage them."

TOUCH (II), Calvinettes, Box 7259, Grand Rapids MI 49510. (616)241-5616. Editor: Joanne Ilbrink. Magazine: 8½×11; 24 pages; 50 lb paper; 50 lb cover stock; illustrations and photos. "Our purpose is to lead girls into a living relationship with Jesus Christ. Puzzles, poetry, crafts, stories, articles, and club input for girls ages 9-14." Monthly. Circ. 15,000.

Needs: Adventure, ethnic, juvenile and religious/inspirational. "Articles must help girls discover how God is at work in their world and the world around them." Receives 50 unsolicited fiction mss/month. Buys 3 mss/issue; 30 mss/year. Usually does not read during February, March, September and October. Recently published work by Ida Mae Petsock. Published new writers within the last year. Length: 900 words minimum; 1,200 words maximum; 1,000 words average.

How to Contact: Send complete ms with 8×10 SASE. Prefers no cover letter. Simultaneous, photocopied and previously published submissions OK. Reports in 1 month on mss. Free sample copy for 8×10 SASE. Free guidelines.
Payment: Pays 3¢/word.
Terms: Pays on acceptance for simultaneous, first or second serial rights.
Advice: "Write for guidelines and theme update and submit manuscripts in advance of deadline. In fiction often the truths we choose to convey can be done with short stories."

TQ (TEENQUEST) (II), Good News Broadcasting Co., Box 82808, Lincoln NE 68501. (402)474-4567. Managing Editor: Karen Christianson. Magazine: 8½×11; 48 pages; illustrations; photos. "*TQ* is designed to aid the spiritual growth of young teen Christian readers by presenting Biblical principles." 11 issues/year. Estab. 1946. Circ. 70,000.
Needs: Religious/inspirational, regional, romance, adventure, fantasy, science fiction and mystery. "Stories must be grounded in Biblical Christianity and should feature teens in the 14-17 year range." Buys 3-4 mss/issue; 35-40 mss/year. Receives 50-60 unsolicited fiction mss/month. Recently published work by Nancy Rue, Stephen Bly, Marian Bray, Scott Pinzon; published new writers within the last year. Length: up to 2,000 words.
How to Contact: Send complete ms with SASE and cover letter. Accepts computer printout submissions. Prefers letter-quality. Reports in 2 months. Publishes ms 6 months to 2 years after acceptance. Free sample copy and guidelines for 9×12 SASE.
Payment: 4-7¢/word for unassigned fiction. More for assignments. 3¢/word for reprints.
Terms: Pays on acceptance for first or reprint rights. Buys reprints.
Advice: "The most common problem is that writers don't understand the limitations of stories under 2,500 words and try to cram a 6,000-word plot into 2,000 words at the expense of characterization, pacing, and mood. We feel that fiction communicates well to our teenage readers. They consistently rank fiction as their favorite part of the magazine. We get hundreds of stories on 'big issues' (death, drugs, etc). Choose less dramatic subjects, that are important to teenagers and give us a new storyline that has a Biblical emphasis, but isn't preachy. Although our magazine is based on Christian principles, we do not want fiction where the lesson learned is blatantly obvious. We're looking for subtlety. Before you try to write for teens, get to know some—talk to them, watch their TV shows, read their magazines. You'll get ideas for stories and you'll be able to write for our audience with accurate and up-to-date knowledge." Teen fiction writers under age 20 may enter annual contest.

TRAILER BOATS MAGAZINE (II, IV), Poole Publications Inc., 20700 Belshaw Ave., Box 5427, Carson CA.(902)749-5427. Editor-in-Chief: Chuck Coyne. Magazine: 100 pages; high paper quality; 80 lb cover stock. "Our magazine covers boats of 26 feet and shorter, (trailerable size limits) and related activities; skiing, fishing, cruising, travel, racing, etc. We publish how-to articles on boat and trailer maintenance, travel, skiing, boat tests and evaluations of new products." Audience: owners and prospective owners of trailerable-size boats. Monthly. Estab. 1971. Circ. 78,000.
Needs: Adventure, contemporary, fantasy, humor/satire, science fiction, and suspense/mystery. "Must meet general guidelines of the magazine regarding boats and related activities." Receives very few unsolicited fiction mss/month. Buys 1-3 mss/year. Length: 200 words minimum; 1,000 words maximum. Publishes short shorts of 500 words. Occasionally critiques rejected mss. Sometimes recommends other markets.
How to Contact: Query first with SASE. Accepts computer printout submissions. Prefers letter-quality. Reports in 1 month on queries; 4-6 weeks on mss. Publishes ms 1-6 months after acceptance. Free general guidelines. Sample copy $1.50.
Payment: 7-10¢/word.
Terms: Pays on publication for all rights.
Advice: "In our case, knowing the audience is of prime importance. Our readership and experience with fiction is limited. We are a consumer magazine with an audience of dedicated boaters. My suggestion is to know the audience and write for it specifically."

‡TURN-ON LETTERS (I, II), AJA Publishing, Box 470, Port Chester NY 10573. Editor: Julie Silver. Magazine: digest-size; 114 pages; newsprint paper; glossy cover; illustrations; photos. "Sexually explicit. Publishing first person 'letters' written as if true." Published 8 times/year. Estab. 1982. Circ. 100,000.
Needs: Erotica. Buys approx. 60 "letters"/issue; 400 "letters"/year. Publishes ms 4-8 months after acceptance. Agented fiction 50% or more. Length: 2-3 typed, double-spaced pages average. Sometimes critiques rejected mss and occasionally recommends other markets.
How to Contact: Send complete ms with or without cover letter. Reports in an average of 3 weeks on mss. SASE. Photocopied submissions if clearly marked "not simultaneous submissions" OK. Accepts computer printout submissions. Sample copy for $2.50 and 6×9 SAE with 4 first class stamps. Fiction guidelines for #10 SAE with 1 first class stamp.

Payment: Pays $15.
Terms: Pays on publication for all rights.
Advice: "Letters must be hot and must 'read real.' Material accepted by *Turn-On Letters* may be published in *Uncensored Letters* and vice-versa. We are very overstocked at present and buying relatively little material."

TURTLE MAGAZINE FOR PRESCHOOL KIDS (I, II), Children's Better Health Institute, Benjamin Franklin Literary & Medical Society, Inc., 1100 Waterway Blvd., Box 567, Indianapolis IN 46206. Editorial Director: Beth Wood Thomas. Magazine of picture stories and articles for preschool children 2-5 years old.
Needs: Juvenile (preschool). Receives approximately 75 unsolicited fiction mss/month. Length: 8-24 lines for picture stories; 500 words for bedtime or naptime stories. Special emphasis on health, nutrition, exercise and safety. Also has need for humorous and anthropomorphic animal stories.
How to Contact: Send complete ms with SASE. Reports in 8-10 weeks on mss. No queries. Send SASE for Editorial Guidelines. Sample copy 75¢.
Payment: 8¢/word (approximate). Payment varies for poetry and activities.
Terms: Pays on publication for all rights.
Advice: "Keep it simple and easy to read. Vocabulary must be below first grade level. Be familiar with past issues of the magazine."

‡UNCENSORED LETTERS (I, II), Sportomatic Publishing, Box 470, Port Chester NY 10573. Editor: Tammy Simmons. Magazine: full size; 82 pages; newsprint paper; glossy cover; illustrations; photos. "Sexually explicit. Publishing first person 'letters' written as if true." Published 7 times/year. Estab. 1984. Circ. 100,000.
Needs: Erotica. Buys 64 "letters"/issue; 448/year. Publishes ms 4-8 months after acceptance. Agented fiction 50% or more. Length: 2-3 typed, double-spaced pages. Often critiques rejected mss and occasionally recommends other markets.
How to Contact: Send complete ms with or without cover letter. Reports in an average of 3 weeks on mss. SASE. Photocopied submissions if clearly marked "not a simultaneous submission" OK. Accepts computer printout submissions. Sample copy for $2.95 and 9×12 SAE with 5 first class stamps. Fiction guidelines for #10 SAE with 1 first class stamp.
Payment: Pays $15.
Terms: Pays on publication for all rights.
Advice: "Make it different but believable . . . and *hot*! Material accepted by *Uncensored Letters* may be published in *Turn-On Letters* and vice-versa."

VIRTUE (II), The Christian Magazine for Women, Virtue Ministries, Inc., Box 850, Sisters OR 97759. (503)549-8261. Editor: Becky Durost Fish. Magazine: 8⅛×10⅞ 80 pages; illustrations; photos. Christian women's magazine featuring food, fashion, family, etc., aimed primarily at homemakers—"real women with everyday problems, etc." Published 6 times/year. Estab. 1978. Circ. 150,000.
Needs: Condensed novel, contemporary, humor, religious/inspirational and romance. "Must have Christian slant." Buys 1 ms/issue; 6 mss/year (maximum). Publishes short shorts. Length: 1,200 words minimum; 2,500 words maximum; 2,000 words average.
How to Contact: Accepts computer printout submissions. Prefers letter-quality. Reports in 6-8 weeks on ms. Sample copy $3 with 9×13 SAE and 90¢ postage. Free fiction guidelines with SASE.
Payment: 10-20¢/published word.
Terms: Pays on publication for first rights or reprint rights.
Advice: "Send us descriptive, colorful writing with good style. *Please*—no simplistic, unrealistic pat endings. There are three main reasons *Virtue* rejects fiction: 1) The stories are not believable, 2) writing is dull, and 3) the story does not convey a Christian message."

VISION (II,IV), Box 7259, Grand Rapids MI 45910. (616)241-5616. Editor: Dale Dieleman. Magazine: 8½×11; 16-20 pages; 60 lb paper; 60 lb cover; photos. *Vision*'s readers are young adults in their 20s in the U.S. and Canada. Bimonthly. Circ. 3,500.
Needs: Stories exploring values, lifestyles, relationships as young adults in workplace, campus, social settings—cultural, ethnic variety a plus. Christian perspective but no preachy, pious platitudes. Length: 1,500 words maximum.
How to Contact: Send ms plus SASE for return. Reports in 1 month on mss. Simultaneous submissions OK (specify other submission periodicals). Sample copy for 9×12 and 56¢ postage.
Payment: Pays $35-75.
Terms: Pays on acceptance.

VISTA (II), Wesley Press, Box 50434, Indianapolis IN 46953. (317)842-0444. Editor: Becky Higgins. Magazine: 8½×11; 8 pages; offset paper and cover; illustrations and photos. "*Vista* is our adult take-home paper and is published in conjunction with the Enduring Word Series adult Sunday school lesson." Weekly. Estab. 1906. Circ. 50,000.

Needs: Humor/satire, religious/inspirational, senior citizen/retirement, young adult/teen. "We are not looking for "Sunday Soap Opera," romance, stories with pat or easy outs, or incidents that wouldn't feasibly happen to members of your own church." Receives 100 unsolicited mss/month. Buys 1 mss/issue; 50 mss/year. Publishes ms 10 months after acceptance. Length: 500 words minimum; 1,300 words maximum. Sometimes critiques rejected mss.

How to Contact: Send complete ms with cover letter. Reports in 2 weeks. SASE. Simultaneous, photocopied and reprint submissions OK. Accepts computer printout submissions. Sample copy for 9×12 SAE.

Payment: Pays $10-60.

Terms: Pays on acceptance for one-time rights.

Advice: "Use the official password: John Wesley. Manuscripts for all publications must be in keeping with early Methodist teachings that people have a free will to personally accept or reject Christ. Wesleyanism also stresses a transformed life, holiness of heart and social responsibility."

THE WASHINGTONIAN (IV), Washington Magazine Co., Suite 200, 1828 L St. NW, Washington DC 20036. (202)296-3600. Editor: John A. Limpert. General interest, regional magazine. Magazine: 8¼×10⅞; 300 pages; 40 lb paper; 80 lb cover; illustrations; photos. Monthly. Estab. 1965. Circ. 161,192.

Needs: Short pieces that must be set in Washington. Receives 8-10 unsolicited fiction mss/month. Buys 3 fiction mss/year. Length: 1,000 words minimum; 10,000 words maximum. Occasionally critiques rejected mss.

How to Contact: Send complete ms with SASE. Simultaneous and photocopied submissions OK. Reports in 2 months on mss. Sample copy for $3.

Payment: $100-2,000. Negotiates kill fee for assigned mss not published.

Terms: Pays on publication for first North American rights.

WEE WISDOM MAGAZINE (II), Unity School of Christianity, Unity Villiage MO 64065. (816)524-3550-ext 397. Editor: Judy Gehrlein. Magazine: 48 pages; 45 lb pentair suede stock; 80 lb Mountie matte cover; illustrations; photos (very seldom). "We publish material designed to meet needs of today's children in an entertaining, positive way. For children through 12. 10 issues per year. Estab. 1893. Circ. 125,000.

Needs: Adventure, contemporary, fantasy, juvenile (5-9 years), preschool, (up to 4 years), young adult/teen (10-13). No violence or religious denominational. Receives 150 unsolicited mss/month. Buys 6 mss/issue; 60 mss/year. Publishes ms 6 months to 1 year after acceptance. Recently published work by Bette Killion, Shirley Mozelle, Barbara Gaal Lutz and Diane Goodman. "Many of our writers are previously unpublished." Length: 500-800 words.

How to Contact: Send complete ms with SASE and "short, informative" cover letter. Reports in 8-10 weeks on mss. Photocopied submissions OK. No simultaneous submissions or queries. Accepts computer printout submissions, no dot-matrix. Sample copy and fiction guidelines free.

Payment: Pays 4¢ per word.

Terms: Pays on acceptance for first rights.

Advice: "Grab the readers in the first few lines. Write with verbs—not adjectives. Help the child see the wisdom within himself and help him see how to use it."

WEIRD TALES (I,IV), The Unique Magazine, Terminus Publishing Company, Inc., Box 13418, Philadelphia PA 19101. Editors: George Scithers, Darrell Schweitzer and John Betancourt. Magazine: 6½×9½; 148 pages; acid-free book paper; pen and ink illustrations. "This is a professional fantasy-fiction and horror-fiction magazine." Quarterly. Estab. 1923. Circ. 11,000+.

Needs: Fantasy, horror, psychic/supernatural/occult. "Writers should be familiar with the fantasy/horror genres; the three editors are well read in the field and want fresh ideas rather than tired old retreads. To paraphrase Ursula K. LeGuin, 'If you want to write it, you gotta read it!' " Receives 400-500 unsolicited fiction mss/month. Buys 12-20 fiction mss/issue; 48-80 mss/year. Publishes ms usually less than 1 year after acceptance. Agented fiction 15%. Recently published work by Gene Wolf, Ramsey Campbell and Nancy Springer. Published new writers last year. Length: 20,000 words maximum. Publishes short shorts. Always comments on rejected mss.

How to Contact: Send complete ms with cover letter, which should include the date and return address. Reports within 1 month. SASE. Accepts photocopied submissions. Accepts dot-matrix computer printouts "if as good as typewritten pages." Sample copy $4.50. Fiction guidelines for #10 SAE and 1 first class stamp.

Payment: Pays 3¢-7¢/word, depending on length of story, plus 3 contributor's copies.
Terms: Pays on acceptance for first North American serial rights. Sends galleys to author.
Advice: *Weird Tales* is a revival of a famous old 'pulp' magazine, published in the original format, but with new fiction by many top writers and talented newcomers to the field. Basically, we're trying to make this *Weird Tales* as it would be today had it continued uninterrupted to the present. Know the field. Know manuscript format. Be familiar with the magazine, its contents and its markets. With the death of *Twilight Zone Magazine* and *The Horror Show, Weird Tales* has become the only professional horror and dark fantasy magazine in the U.S. So competition is fierce. Send only your best work."

WESTERN PEOPLE (II), Western Producer Publications, Box 2500, Saskatoon, Saskatchewan S7K 2C4 Canada. (306)665-3500. Editor: Keith Dryden. Managing Editor: Liz Delahey. Magazine: 8½×11; 16 pages; newsprint paper and cover stock; illustrations and photos. "*Western People* is for and about western Canadians, a supplement of the region's foremost weekly agricultural newspaper. Includes fiction, nonfiction (contemporary and history) and poetry. Readership is mainly rural and western Canadian." Weekly. Published special fiction issue last year; plans another. Estab. 1978. Circ. 130,000.
Needs: Contemporary, adventure and humor. Buys 20 mss/year. Publishes short shorts. Published new writers within the last year. Length: 750-2,000 words.
How to Contact: Send complete ms with SAE, IRC (or $1 without IRC). Reports in 3 weeks on mss. Free sample copy with 9×12 SAE, IRC. Free general guidelines with legal-sized SAE, IRC.
Payment: $150 maximum (more for serials).
Terms: Pays on acceptance for first North American rights.
Advice: "The story should be lively, not long, related in some way to the experience of rural western Canadians. We believe our readers enjoy a good story, particularly when it has some relevance to their own lives. Although most of the stories in *Western People* are nonfictional, we offer variety to our readers, including fiction and poetry. Write about what could happen, not what did happen. We find that beginning writers try to fictionalize actual events with a result that is neither fish nor fowl."

WIGWAG (II), 73 Spring St., New York NY 10012. (212)941-7177. Editor: Alexander Kaplen. Fiction Editor: Nancy Holyoke. Magazine: 8×10; 80-100 pages; illustrations. "General interest magazine looking for the best fiction available." Published 10 times/year. Estab. 1989. Circ. 60,000.
Needs: "Serious literary fiction of any kind." Also short children's bedtime stories. Buys 1 mss/issue. Time between acceptance and publication varies. Recently published work by Jane Smiley, Richard Bausch. Length: up to 10,000. Comments on rejected manuscripts.
How to Contact: Send a complete ms. with a cover letter. Reporting time varies. SASE. Photocopied, reprinted and computer printout submissions are acceptable.
Payment: Payment is open; "competitive with other major magazines." Pays on publication.
Terms: Rights purchased vary.

WITH MAGAZINE (II, IV), Faith & Life Press and Mennonite Publishing House, Box 347, Newton KS 67114. (316)283-5100. Editor: Susan Janzen. Magazine: 8½×11; 24 pages; 60 lb uncoated paper and cover; illustrations and photos. "Our purpose is to help teenagers understand the issues that impact them and to help them make choices that reflect Mennonite-Anabaptist understandings of living by the Spirit of Christ. We publish all types of material – fiction, nonfiction, poetry, prose poem, spiritual, sports, features, 'think' pieces, etc." Monthly. Estab. 1968. Circ. 6,500.
Needs: Contemporary, ethnic, humor/satire, literary, mainstream, religious, translations, young adult/teen (13-18 years). "We accept issue-oriented pieces as well as religious pieces. No religious fiction that gives 'pat' answers to serious situations." Receives about 50 unsolicited mss/month. Buys 1-2 mss/issue; 18-20 mss/year. Publishes ms up to 1 year after acceptance. Published work by Alan Cliburn, Marilyn Anderson and Sharon Roberts; published new writers within the last year. Length: 1,500 words preferred; 1,000 words minimum; 2,000 words maximum. Publishes short shorts. Length: 800-1,000 words. Sometimes critiques rejected mss and recommends other markets.
How to Contact: Send complete ms with cover letter, which should include short summary of author's credits and what rights they are selling. Reports in 2-3 weeks on queries; 3 months on mss. SASE. Simultaneous, photocopied and reprint submissions OK. Accepts computer printout submissions. Accepts electronic submissions via DOS (IBM compatible) disk, preferably in Wordstar. Sample copy for $1.25 with 9×12 SAE and 85¢ postage. Fiction guidelines for #10 SAE and 1 first class stamp.
Payment: Pays 2¢/word for reprints; 4¢/word for first rights. Supplies contributor's copies; charge for extras.
Terms: Pays on acceptance for first or one-time rights.
Advice: "Write with a teenage audience in mind, but don't talk down to them. Treat the audience with respect. Don't expect to make a sale with the usual 'I've-got-a-problem-give-it-all-to-Jesus-and-everything-will-turn-out-fine' story. Real life isn't always like that and teens will perceive the story as unbelievable. Do include ethnic minorities in your stories; our audience is both rural and urban."

WOMAN'S DAY (II), 1515 Broadway, New York NY 10036. (212)719-6492. Editor-in-Chief: Ellen R. Levine. Fiction Editor: Eileen Herbert Jordan. A strong service magazine geared to women, with a wide variety of well written subjects (foods, crafts, beauty, medical, etc.). Publishes 15 issues/year. Estab. 1939. Circ. 7½ million; readership 17 million.

Needs: Literary, contemporary, fantasy, women's. No violence, crime or totally male-oriented stories. *Woman's Day* does not accept any unsolicited short fiction. Length: 2,000-3,000 words average.

How to Contact: Send complete ms with SASE. Free guidelines with SASE.

Payment: Pays top rates.

Terms: Pays on acceptance for first North American serial rights. Occasionally buys reprints.

Advice: "Read the magazine and keep trying."

‡WOMEN'S AMERICAN ORT REPORTER (II,IV), Women's American ORT, 315 Park Ave. S., New York NY 10010. (212)505-7700. Editor: Eve Jacobson. Tabloid; 11×15; 20 pages; newsprint paper; photographs. "Jewish women's issues; education, for membership." Quarterly. Estab. 1968. Circ. 130,000.

Needs: Condensed/excerpted novel, ethnic, feminist, humor/satire and literary. Receives 2 unsolicited mss/month. Buys 2 mss/year. Publishes ms 3 months after acceptance. Agented fiction 50%. Length: 2,500 words. Recently published work by A.B. Yehoshua. Possibly publishes short shorts. Sometimes critiques rejected ms and recommends other markets.

How to Contact: Send complete ms with cover letter. Include Social Security number. Reports in 3 weeks. SASE. Photocopied submissions OK. Computer printout submissions are acceptable. Sample copy is free.

Payment: Pays 15¢/word.

Terms: Pays on publication for first North American serial rights.

WONDER TIME (II), Beacon Hill, Press of Kansas City, 6401 Paseo, Kansas City MO 64131. (816)333-7000. Editor: Evelyn Beals. Magazine: 8¼×11; 4 pages; self cover; color illustrations; photos. Hand-out story paper published through the Church of the Nazarene Sunday school; stories should follow outline of Sunday school lesson for 6-7 year olds. Weekly. Circ. 45,000.

Needs: Religious/inspirational and juvenile. Stories must have controlled vocabulary and be easy to read. No fairy tales or science fiction. Buys 1 ms/issue. Receives 50-75 unsolicited fiction mss/month. Approximately 25% of fiction is agented. Length: 300-550 words. Also publishes short shorts. Recommends other markets.

How to Contact: Send complete ms with SASE. Reports in 6 weeks on mss. Publishes ms an average of 1 year after acceptance. Free sample copy and curriculum guide with SASE.

Payment: Pays 3½¢/word.

Terms: Pays on acceptance for first rights. Buys reprints.

Advice: "Control vocabulary. Study children to know what children are interested in; stories should deal with children's problems of today and must be tastefully handled." Mss may be rejected because they "do not correlate with the Sunday school lessons."

YANKEE MAGAZINE (II, III), Yankee, Inc., Dublin NH 03444. Editor: Judson D. Hale. Fiction Editor: Edie Clark. Magazine: 6×9; 176+ pages; glossy paper; 4-color glossy cover stock; illustrations; 4-color photos. Entertaining and informative New England regional on current issues, people, history, antiques and crafts for general reading audience. Monthly. Estab. 1935. Circ. 1,000,000.

Needs: Literary. Fiction is to be set in New England or compatible with the area. No religious/inspirational, formula fiction or stereotypical dialect, novels or novellas. Buys 1 ms/issue; 12 mss/year. Recently published work by Andre Dubus, H. L. Mountzovres and Fred Bonnie; published new writers within the last year. Length: 2,000-4,000 words. Publishes short shorts up to 1,500 words. Recommends other markets.

How to Contact: Send complete ms with SASE and previous publications. "Cover letters are important if they provide relevant information: previous publications or awards; special courses taken; special references (e.g. 'William Shakespeare suggested I send this to you . . . .')" Reports in 3-6 weeks on mss.

Payment: $1,000.

Terms: Pays on acceptance; rights negotiable. Sends galleys to author.

Advice: "Read previous 10 stories in *Yankee* for style and content. Fiction must be realistic and reflect life as it is—complexities and ambiguities inherent. Our fiction adds to the 'complete menu'—the magazine includes many categories—humor, profiles, straight journalism, essays, etc. Listen to the advice of any editor who takes the time to write a personal letter. Go to workshops; get advice and other readings before sending story out cold." Fiction prize of $600 awarded to best story published in *Yankee* each year.

Each month, Yankee entertains and informs its readers by portraying as many different aspects of the New England experience as pages allow. "The art on the cover of every issue sets the tone for the entire contents," says Ann Grow, the magazine's editorial business manager. "This particular cover told the readers at least, 'New England, summer, Maine Coast, sailing, fun,' all images they found reinforced inside the magazine." Artist John Atwater painted this cover.

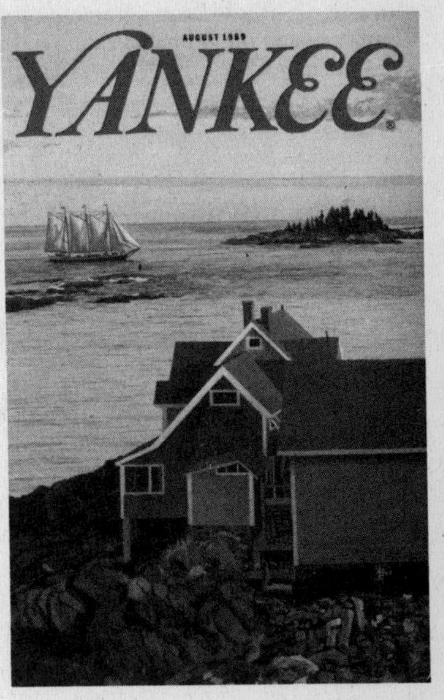

Cover painting by John Atwater. Cover ©1989 Yankee Publishing Inc., Dublin, NH. Reprinted with permission.

YOUNG AMERICAN (II), America's Newspaper for Kids, Box 12409, Portland OR 97212. (503)230-1895. Editor: Kristina T. Linden. Magazine: 10½×13. 16-32 pages; newsprint paper and cover; illustrations and photos. "Our focus is on children, and they are taken seriously. Articles are intended to inform and entertain. We are particularly interested in stories about newsworthy kids." Biweekly. Plans special fiction issue. Estab. 1983. Circ. 5.1 million in 1990.
Needs: Short (1,000 words) fiction pieces—fantasy, humor, mystery, prose poem and sports. No sex, violence, gore or religion. Receives more than 50 mss/month. Buys 4-6 mss/issue, 120 mss/year. Length: Up to 1,000 words.
How to Contact: Queries, clips, cover letters discouraged. Finished work encouraged. Reports within 4 months. No simultaneous submissions. SASE with mss. Sample copy available for $1.50. Guidelines available with SASE.
Payment: Minimum 7¢/word.
Terms: Pays on publication for first North American rights. May also purchase reprint rights of articles published in *Young American*.
Advice: "Speak to the kids, not down to them. Read some of the books that are popular with the younger set. You may be surprised of the level of sophistication of kids today. Now looking at longer fiction for serialization. Treat writing like a job, not a hobby."

THE YOUNG CRUSADER, National Woman's Christian Temperance Union, 1730 Chicago Ave., Evanston IL 60201. (312)864-1396. Editor-in-Chief: Mrs. Rachel Bubar Kelly. Managing Editor: Michael C. Vitucci. "Character building material showing high morals and sound values; inspirational, informational nature articles and stories for 6-12 year olds." Monthly. Estab. 1887. Circ. 10,000.
Needs: Juvenile. Stories should be naturally written pieces, not saccharine or preachy. Buys 3-4 mss/issue; 60 mss/year. Length: 600-800 words.
How to Contact: Send complete ms with SASE. Reports in 6 months or longer on mss. Free sample copy with SASE.
Payment: Pays ½¢/word and free author's copy.
Terms: Pays on publication. "If I like the story and use it, I'm very lenient and allow the author to use it elsewhere."

YOUNG SALVATIONIST/YOUNG SOLDIER (II, IV), The Salvation Army, 799 Bloomfield Ave., Verona NJ 07044. (201)239-0606. Editor: Capt. Robert Hostetler. Magazine: 8×11; 16 pages (*Young Salvationist*), 8 pages (*Young Soldier*); illustrations and photos. Christian emphasis articles for youth members of the Salvation Army. Monthly. Estab. 1984. Circ. 50,000.

Needs: Religious/inspirational, young adult/teen. Receives 150 unsolicited mss/month. Buys 9-10 ms/issue; 90-100 mss/year. Publishes ms 3-4 months after acceptance. Length: 1,000 words preferred; 750 words minimum; 1,200 words maximum. Publishes short shorts. Sometimes critiques rejected mss and recommends other markets.
How to Contact: Send complete ms. Reports in 1-2 weeks on queries; 2-4 weeks on mss. SASE. Simultaneous, photocopied and reprint submissions OK. Accepts computer printout submissions. Sample copy free with 8½×11 SAE and 3 first class stamps. Fiction guidelines for #10 SAE with 1 first class stamp.
Payment: Pays 3-5¢/word.
Terms: Pays on acceptance for all rights, first rights, first North American serial rights and one-time rights.

Foreign Commercial Periodicals

The following commercial magazines located in the United Kingdom, Europe, Australia and Africa are paying markets for short fiction in English by North American writers. Query first for guidelines. Always enclose a return envelope with International Reply Coupons for a reply or for return of your manuscript. You might find it less expensive, when sending manuscripts, to send copies that do not need to be returned along with a self-addressed reply postcard and one IRC. IRCs are available at the main branch of your local post office.

‡COMMANDO, D. C. Thomson Co., Ltd., Albert Square, Dundee DD1 9QJ Scotland. Publishes 96 stories/year. "War stories (WW II) in pictures. Scripts wanted – send synopsis first." Pays for published fiction and provides contributor's copies. "Write to us for information sheet."

FANTASY TALES, The Paperback Magazine of Fantasy and Terror, Robinson Publishing/Carroll & Graff, 194 Station Rd., Kings Heath, Birmingham, B14 7TE England. Fiction Editor: David A. Sutton. Circ. 30,000. Publishes 20-40 stories (quarterly). "*Fantasy Tales* is a digest-size pulp magazine that publishes fantasy, horror and some science fiction. Authors inlcude Clive Barker, Ramsey Campbell, Charles L. Grant, Robert Bloch, etc. We are looking for well-written contemporary urban horror and stories in the *Weird Tales* tradition." Writers are paid and receive a complimentary copy. "We are not interested in run-of-the-mill plotting. If you expect a reply, ensure you enclose self-addressed envelope and three IRCs. (US stamps *don't* work in Britain)."

‡FEAR, Newsfield Publications, 47 Gravel Hill, Ludlow, Shropshire S48 1QS England. Fiction Editor: David Western. Publishes fantasy, horror, science fiction and video film fiction. Pays minimum $100 for published fiction.

‡FORUM, Northern and Shell Building, Box 381, Mill Harbour, London E14 9TW England. Fiction Editor: Elizabeth Coldwell. Circ. 30,000. Publishes 13 stories/year. "Forum is the international magazine of human relations, dealing with all aspects of relationships, sexuality and sexual health. Fiction pieces are erotic short stories. No other type of fiction is accepted. Writers' fees are by arrangement with the editor. Writers are always sent one complimentary copy containing their story." Length: 2,000 words.

INTERZONE: Science fiction and fantasy, 124 Osborne Rd., Brighton BN1 6LU England. Editor: David Pringle. Circ. 14,000. Publishes 5-6 stories per issue; publishes 6 times/year. Will move to monthly schedule during 1990. "We're looking for intelligent science fiction in the 2,000-7,000 word range." Pays £30 per 1,000 words on publication and 2 free copies of magazine. "Please read our magazine before submitting."

‡IRELAND'S OWN, 1 North Main St., Wexford Ireland. Fiction Editor: Austin Channing. Circ. 56,000. Publishes 300 stories annually. "*Ireland's Own* is a homely family oriented weekly magazine with a story emphasis on the traditional values of Irish society. The short stories published reflect the thinking of ordinary, everyday people. We favour the good yarn well told." Payment £20-25 on publication. Length: 2,500-3,000 words. "Stories must have an Irish orientation."

ISRAEL-AL, 17 Borgrashov St., Tel Aviv, Israel. Fiction Editor: Orna Fraser. Circ. 250,000. Publishes fiction related to tourism. Pays 15¢/word.

‡JACKIE, D.C. Thomson & Co., Ltd., Albert Square, Dundee, Tayside, DD1 9QJ Scotland. Fiction Editor: Tracy Thow. Circ. 225,000. Publishes 50+ stories and photo series/year. "*Jackie* contains fiction, features, fashion, beauty and pop aimed at 12-16 year-old girls, with the emphasis on romance." Pays $46-50 for published fiction.

LONDON REVIEW OF BOOKS, Tavistock House S., Tavistock House Sth., London England. Fiction Editor: Susannah Clapp. Circ. 16,000. Publishes 3-6 stories annually. Publishes "book reviews with long essay-length reviews. Also publishes the occasional short story." Pays £150 per story and 5 contributor's copies.

‡MANUSHI, C-202 Lajpat Nagar-I, New Delhi-110024, India. Publishes 6 stories annually. "A bi-monthly, focusing on women's lives, work, struggles in the Indian subcontinent. Human rights perspective, with an emphasis on women's rights. Fiction should deal with Indian/Asian women's lives/concerns, and be of high literary quality." We also publish translations from Indian regional languages. Pays 1 contributor copy.

MY WEEKLY, 80 Kingsway East, Dundee DD4 8SL Scotland. Editor: Sandy Monks. "*My Weekly* is a widely read magazine aimed at 'young' women of all ages. We are read by busy young mothers, active middle-aged wives and elderly retired ladies." Fiction (romance and humor) "should deal with real, down-to-earth themes that relate to the lives of our readers. Our rates compare favourably with other British magazines. Complete stories can be of any length from 1,500 to 4,000 words. Serials from 3 to 10 installments."

NOVA SF, Perseo Libri srl, Box 1240, I-40100 Bologna Italy. Fiction Editor: Ugo Malaguti. Circ. 5,000. "Science fiction and fantasy short stories and short novels." Pays $100-600 depending on length. "No formalities required, we read all submissions and give an answer in about 6 weeks. Buys first Italian serial rights on stories."

OVERSEAS! (II), Kolpingstr. 1, Leimen 6906 West Germany. Editorial Director: Charles L. Kaufman. "*Overseas!* is published for the US military personnel stationed in Europe. It is the leading military magazine in Europe, specifically directed to males ages 18-35." Needs very short tourist, travel-in-Europe, or military-related humor for Back Talk humor page. Also need cartoons.

R&R ENTERTAINMENT DIGEST (IV), R&R Werbe GmbH, Kolpingstrasse 1, 6906 Leimen West Germany. Editor: Tory Billard. Monthly entertainment guide for military and government employees and their families stationed in Europe "specializing in travel in Europe, audio/video/photo, music and the homemaker scene. Generally we do not publish any fiction. However, best chances are with first-person stories with a tie to travel in Europe (with specifics on what to see, where to eat, shop and stay, etc.) or, better yet, celebrating American holidays in Europe." Sample copy for IRC.

REALITY MAGAZINE, Z75 Orwell Rd., Rathgar, Dublin 6 Ireland. Fiction Editor: Fr. Kevin H. Donlon. Circ. 30,000. Publishes an average of 11 short stories annually. Pays £25/piece. "Be clear, brief, to the point and practical."

SCHOOL MAGAZINE, Box A242, Sydney South NSW 2000 Australia. Fiction Editor: Anna Fienberg. Circ. 350,000. Publishes 80 stories/year. "Literary magazine for 8-11 year olds (much like *Cricket*). All types of stories—real life, fantasy, sci-fi, folk tales." Pays $112/1,000 words on acceptance—one use only. Two free copies.

‡TODAY'S GUIDE, 17-19 Buckingham Palace Rd., London SW1W OPT England. Editor: Diana Wallace. Circ. 25,000. Publishes 12 short stories annually. "Magazine aimed at girls aged 10-14. The official magazine for the Girl Guides Association. Stories need to be 1,000-1,500 words long with a Guiding background." Payment is £26-60 per 1,000 words plus contributor copy. "The story must have relevance to a Girl Guide. I prefer stories with a modern realistic background and with some recognition that not every girl has a perfect, nuclear family background for support. I would be interested in stories with a North American Guiding background."

WOMAN'S REALM, IPC Magazines, King's Reach Tower, Stamford St., London SE1 9LS England. Fiction Editor: Sally Bowden. Circ. 610,000. Publishes 50-60 stories and 12-15 short serials/year. Appeals to practical, intelligent, family family-minded women, age 23 upwards. High standard of writing required. Originality important. Writers paid for published work. "Nearest US equivalent to our kind of fiction is probably *Redbook*. Length should be 1,200-4,000 words."

‡**WOMAN'S WEEKLY**, IPC Magazines, King's Reach, Stamford St., London SE1 9LS England. Fiction Editor: Gaynor Davies. Circ. 1.3 million. Publishes 2 serials and at least one short story per week. Fees individually negotiated. Complimentary copies given. "Short stories can be on any theme, but must have love as the central core of the plot, whether in a specific romantic context, within the family or mankind in general. Serials need not be written in installments. They are submitted as complete manuscripts and we split them up." To contact send first installment (8,000 words) and synopsis of the rest.

Other commercial periodicals

Most of the following commercial magazines appeared in the 1989 edition of *Novel and Short Story Writer's Market* but are not in the 1990 edition. Those publications whose editors did not respond this year to our request for an update may have done so for a variety of reasons—they may be out of business, they are no longer taking fiction or they may be overstocked with submissions. Those publications are listed below without further explanation.

If we received information about why a publication would not appear, we included the explanation next to their name below. The list also includes a few well-known publications that declined to be listed.

Action
Amazing Stories (asked to be removed for one year)
American Trucker (no longer accepting fiction)
Amé'ricas
Angus Journal
Animal Press (asked to be removed for one year)
Bakersfield Lifestyle Magazine (asked to be deleted)
Bay & Delta Yachtsman (no longer accepting fiction)
Bird Talk
Canadian Biker Magazine
Cape Cod Compass (asked to be removed for one year)
Career Focus, College Preview, Journey, Visions
City Paper (no longer accepting fiction)
Companion of St. Francis and St. Anthony
Corvette Fever
The Disciple (asked to be deleted)
Easyriders
The Ensign (no longer accepting fiction)
Esquire (declined invitation to list)
Essence (no longer accepting fiction)
Five Great Romances, World's Greatest Love Stories
Gem
The Gem (asked to be removed for one year)
Guide Magazine
Hang Gliding
High Adventure
Hot Shots
Hustler Letters (no longer published)
In Touch Talks
Inside Kung Fu
Jewish Monthly (see instead listing for *B'nai B'rith*)
Jock Magazine
Junior Trails
Lefthander Magazine (no longer accepting fiction)
Lutheran Woman
Maine Life (out of business)
Manscape 2
Michigan Magazine (asked to be deleted)
The Mountain
National Racquetball
New Alaskan (asked to be removed for one year)
New England Senior Citizen/Senior American News (out of business)
New York Running News
Ocean Sports International
Oh! Idaho (asked to be removed for one year)
Our Family (no longer accepting fiction)
Pen Syndicate
Pennsylvania Sportsman (asked to be deleted)
Penthouse (no longer accepting unsolicited short fiction)
Prime Time Sports & Fitness
Saturday Evening Post (asked to be deleted)
Score (no longer accepting fiction)
Screw Magazine
Rod Serling's The Twilight Zone Magazine (no longer published)
Skyline
Southern Magazine (no longer published)
Splash (moved, unable to locate)
Surfing Magazine
Torso
Tristate Magazine (out of business)
Volleyball Monthly
Wag (asked to be removed)
Wave Press (complaints)
Woman's World
Wyoming Rural Electric News

Other foreign commercial periodicals

Animal World
Australian Playboy
Fair Lady
Horse and Pony Magazine
Just Seventeen
Knave
Patches
People's Friend
Personality
Simple Living
True Romances
Woman's Own
Woman's Story

Small Press

The 1980s were the years of mergers, takeovers and buy outs in the book publishing industry. The number of commercial publishing outlets has been dramatically reduced and, as a result, less fiction is being published, especially by new writers. Yet, during this same period, small press publishing has been thriving—thanks to changes in technology and a growing respect for the small press within the industry.

New technology, especially desk-top publishing, has enabled very small publishers, even those staffed by one or two people, to compete effectively with some larger houses. Fifteen years ago few small presses had the capacity to produce camera-ready copy. Much of the physical preparation for the book was sent out to typesetters, printers and other vendors, increasing the cost and limiting the number of titles the publisher could produce. Today most small press publishers can do all their pre-press preparation themselves at a fraction of the cost and time. In addition, expanded production capabilities have also meant more attractive, professional-looking books.

The small press industry has also discovered the power of numbers. Many have banded together to help each other with marketing and distribution. This has given rise to several wholesalers and distributors, such as Bookpeople, Kampmann and Company and Inland Books, specializing in handling small press titles. With improved distribution and sales networks, increased marketing savvy and better quality products, the future for small press publishing looks bright.

The small press alternative

Writers whose work might be considered too new, experimental or otherwise risky for a commercial publisher may do well to try a small press. While the advances, if they are offered, are small, publishing with a small press can be a profitable alternative. Successful small press publishers, for example, tend to keep their titles in bookstores longer than their commercial counterparts. This can actually mean more profits for the writer in the long run.

Yet money is not the main reason most writers turn to small publishers. Writers who have worked with a small press usually list a good, stable editor/writer relationship as the greatest advantage. Editors at smaller publishers tend to stay longer, because they seem to have more stake in the business—in fact, many are also the publisher and many small press publishers are writers themselves.

Small press publishers, especially those that specialize in a particular type of writing, tend to know their readership well and this can lead to increased sales. In a recent article in *Publishers Weekly* Eric Kampmann, president of Kampmann and Company said, "The small publishers often have an excellent eye for what people want and how to produce it. They have the time to spend on it and they're not diverted by all kinds of corporate matters."

Working with small presses

Writers who publish with small presses are expected to do more marketing of their own books. In fact, these publishers rely heavily on leads from their writers. Among the many ways writers can help promote their books are speaking at conferences, giving interviews to local newspapers and radio stations, giving readings and visiting bookstores, schools and libraries.

Courage and creativity are the keys to successful self-promotion. "Authors in general seem to overlook their own sources: relatives, friends, associates are all valuable promotion contacts," says Dawn Conti, marketing assistant for Haypenny Press. "With imagination and a little courage, authors can drum up quite admirable sales for themselves."

Dan O'Connell, marketing director for Allyson Publications agrees authors cannot be shy when it comes to promoting their books. "Authors' contacts with the media can be especially helpful, but most important is the willingness to hawk their books at every opportunity," he says.

For more ideas on self-promotion, see Gerry Maddren's "Writer on the Road" starting on page 100.

Submitting to small presses

While most small presses accept unsolicited submissions, many editors say literary magazines are the first place they look for new talent. Publication, even in a small journal, gives the writer experience and demonstrates to editors that the writer is familiar with the editing and publishing process.

Since many small presses are highly specialized, it is important to research the market completely before submitting. This means checking the library, sending for catalogs and for submission guidelines. For publishers listed in this book, check the small press category index located before the Markets Index and read each listing carefully.

Another way to locate publishers suited to your work is to check the *Small Press Record of Books in Print*, published by Dustbooks, in your local library. The book contains titles of books from more than 2,000 small book publishers, indexed by subject, publisher, author and title. Look for presses that have published books similar to your own.

Even though most small presses are run by only a handful of people and the atmosphere is somewhat less formal than that of larger houses, it is still important to submit professional-looking manuscripts. Submissions should be typed, double-spaced and relatively free of typos and cross-outs. Be sure to include a self-addressed stamped envelope in an appropriate size for all correspondence with a small press publisher.

Here are the codes we've used to classify the small presses listed in this book:

- *I Publisher encourages beginning or unpublished writers to submit work for consideration and publishes new writers frequently;*
- *II Publisher accepts work by established writers and by occasional new writers of unusual talent;*
- *III Publisher does not encourage beginning, unagented writers; publishes mainly writers with extensive previous publication credits and a very few new writers;*
- *IV Special-interest or regional publisher open only to writers on certain subjects or from certain geographic areas.*

ADVOCACY PRESS (IV), Box 236, Santa Barbara CA 93102. Publisher: Mindy Bingham. Estab. 1983. Small publisher with 3-5 titles/year. Hardcover and paperback originals. Books: perfect or Smythe-sewn binding; illustrations; average print order: 10,000 copies; first novel print order: 10,000. Plans 2 first novels this year; 2 fiction titles/year.

Needs: Juvenile (5-9 years); preschool/picture book. New series: 32 page picturebook of stories of little known influential women in history. Wants only feminist/nontraditional messages to boys or girls—picture books. Recently published *Father Gander Nursery Rhymes*, by Dr. Doug Harch (picture book); *Berta Benz and the Motorwagon*, by Mindy Bingham (picture book).

How to Contact: No unsolicited mss; will not return them. Submit complete manuscript with SASE. Reports in 10 weeks on queries. Simultaneous submissions OK. No photocopies. Accepts computer printouts. Request editorial policy.

Terms: Pays in royalties of 5% minimum; 10% maximum. Sends pre-publication galleys to the author. Book catalog free on request.
Advice: "We are looking for fictional stories for children 4-8 years old that give messages of self sufficiency for little girls; little boys can nurture and little girls can be anything they want to be, etc. Looking for talented writers/artists."

‡*AEGINA PRESS, INC. (I,II), 59 Oak Lane, Spring Valley, Huntington WV 25704. (304)429-7204. Imprints are University Editions, Inc. Managing Editor: Ira Herman. Estab. 1984. Independent small press. Publishes paperback originals and reprints. Books: 50 lb white text/10 point high gloss covers; photo-offset printing; perfect binding, illustrations; average print order: 500-1,000. Published new writers within the last year. Plans 4-5 first novels this year. Averages 20 total titles, 10 fiction titles each year. Sometimes comments on rejected ms.
Needs: Adventure, contemporary, experimental, faction, fantasy, historical, horror, literary, mainstream, regional, science fiction, short story collections, suspense/mystery. No racist, sexist, or obscene materials. Recently published *The Town is Aaron*, by Yereth Knowles (literary); *The Cliffs of Aries*, by Thom Nickels (science fiction); and *Overcoming Blue Eyes*, by Mando Sevillano (autobiographical fiction).
How to Contact: Accepts unsolicited mss. Query first, send outline/synopsis and 3 sample chapters or complete ms with cover letter. SASE. Agented fiction 5%. Reports in 3 weeks on queries; 1-2 months on mss. Simultaneous and photocopied submissions OK. Accepts computer printout submissions.
Terms: Pays 15% royalties. "If the manuscript meets our quality standards but is financially high risk, self-publishing through the University Editions imprint is offered. All sales proceeds go to the author until the subsidy is repaid. The author receives a 40% royalty thereafter. Remaining unsold copies belong to the author." Subsidy publishes 40%. Sends galleys to author. Publishes ms 6 months after acceptance. Writer's guidelines for #10 SASE. Book catalog for 9×12 SASE, 4 first class stamps and $2.

‡*ALASKA NATURE PRESS-PUBLISHERS (I,IV), Box 632, Eagle River AK 99577. (907)688-3082. Fiction Editor: B.R. Guild. Estab. 1978. Publishes hardcover and paperback originals. Books: offset printing; perfect binding; illustrations "when warranted"; average print order, 2,000-4,000; first novel print order: 2,000. Plans 2-4 first novels this year. Averages 2-4 total titles, 1-2 fiction titles each year. Occasionally critiques rejected ms for fee: $1/page for long novels; $25 for short works. "*Only Alaska material, please.*"
Needs: Adventure, historical, humor/satire, juvenile (animal, historical, sports, spy/adventure), mainstream, regional, science fiction, short story collections, suspense/mystery and young adult teen (easy-to-read/teen, fantasy/science fiction, historical, sports, spy/adventure). Published *Shelihof*, by Homer Kisor and *The Man Who Shot Dan McGrew*, by Emil Rasmussen.
How to Contact: Accepts unsolicited mss. Query, or submit outline/synopsis and 3 sample chapters or complete ms. SASE for query, ms. Reports in 1 month on queries, 3 months or more on mss. Simultaneous and photocopied submissions OK.
Terms: Pays in royalties of 10%; no advance at this time. *Does some subsidy publishing.* Individual arrangement with author depending on the book.
Advice: "Do not send us anything not related to Alaska. We consider first novels a real gamble in a regional market."

ALYSON PUBLICATIONS, INC. (II), 40 Plympton St., Boston MA 02118. (617)542-5679. Subsidiary is Carrier Pigeon Distributors. Fiction Editor: Sasha Alyson. Estab. 1977. Medium-sized publisher specializing in lesbian- and gay-related material. Publishes paperback originals and reprints. Books: paper and printing varies; trade paper, perfect bound binding; average print order: 8,000; first novel print order: 6,000. Published new writers within the last year; plans 4 first novels this year. Averages 15 total titles, 8 fiction titles each year. Average first novel print order 6,000 copies.
Needs: "We are interested in all categories; *all* materials must be geared toward lesbian and/or gay readers." Recently published *The Buccaneer*, by M. S. Hunter; *Behind the Mask*, by Kim Larabee; *A Mistress Moderately Fair*, by Katherine Sturtevant.

The asterisk indicates a publisher who sometimes offers subsidy arrangements. Authors are asked to subsidize part of the cost of book production. See the introduction to Commercial Publishers for more information.

How to Contact: Query first with SASE. Reports in 3 weeks on queries; 2 months on mss. Photocopied submissions OK but not preferable. Prefers letter-quality.
Terms: "We prefer to discuss terms with the author." Sends galleys to author. Book catalog for SAE and 45¢ postage.

AMERICAN ATHEIST PRESS (IV), Gustav Broukal Press, Box 140195, Austin TX 78714-0195. (512)458-1244. Editor: Robin Murray-O'Hair, Estab. 1960. Paperback originals and reprints. Books: bond and other paper; offset printing; perfect binding; illustrations "if pertinent." Averages 6 total titles/year. Occasionally critiques or comments on rejected mss.
Needs: Contemporary, humor/satire, literary, science fiction. No "religious/spiritual/occult."
How to Contact: Query with sample chapters and outline. SASE. Reports in 6 weeks on queries; 2 months on mss. Simultaneous and photocopied submissions OK. Accepts computer printout submissions. Accepts electronic submissions via IBM-PC/Word-Perfect on disk.
Terms: Pays 6-11% royalties and subscription to magazine. Writers guidelines free for #9 SASE and 1 first class stamp. Book catalog free on request.
Advice: "We only publish fiction which relates to Atheism; we receive many queries for general interest fiction, which we do not publish."

ANNICK PRESS LTD. (IV), 15 Patricia Ave., Willowdale, Ontario M2M 1H9 Canada. (416)221-4802. Publisher of children's books. Publishes hardcover and paperback originals. Books: offset paper; full-color offset printing; perfect and library binding; full-color illustrations; average print order: 9,000; first novel print order: 7,000. Plans 18 first picture books this year. Averages approximately 20 titles each year, all fiction. Average first picture book print order 2,000 cloth, 9,000 paper copies. Occasionally critiques rejected ms.
Needs: Children's books only.
How to Contact: "Annick Press publishes only work by Canadian citizens or residents." Does not accept unsolicited mss. Query with SASE. Free book catalog.
Terms: Sends galleys to author.
Advice: "Publishing more fiction this year, because our company is growing. But our publishing program is currently full."

ANOTHER CHICAGO PRESS (II), Box 11223, Chicago IL 60611. Senior Editor: Barry Silesky. Fiction Editor: Sharon Solwitz. Estab 1976. Small literary press, non-profit. Books: offset printing; perfect binding, occasional illustrations; average print order 2,000. Averages 2 total titles, 1 fiction title each year. Occasionally critiques or comments on rejected ms.
Needs: Literary. No inspirational religious fiction. Recently published *There is a Tree More Ancient Than Eden*, by Leon Forest (novel); *Margaret's Book*, by James Walton (novel); *The Blood Worth Orphan*, by Leon Forest (novel); published fiction by previously unpublished writers within the last year.
How to Contact: Does not accept or return unsolicited mss. Query first for books, then submit outline/synopsis and sample chapters. SASE. Agented fiction 10%. Reports in 3-6 weeks on queries; 8-12 weeks on mss. Simultaneous and photocopied submissions OK. Accepts computer printout submissions, but prefers letter.
Terms: Advance: $100 negotiable; honorarium depends on grant/award money. Sends galleys to author.
Advice: "Our main enterprise is the publication, bi-annually, of *ACM (Another Chicago Magazine)*. We publish novels and collections of short stories and poetry as our funds and time permit—and then probably only by solicitation."

ANOTHER WAY (IV), 400 East Las Palmas Dr., Fullerton CA 92635. (714)969-2346. President: Carrie Teasdale. Estab. 1985. Small, 2-person publisher. Publishes paperback originals. Plans 4 first novels this year. Averages about 4 total titles, 2 fiction titles each year.
Needs: Looking for practical new age fiction. Published new writers within the last year.
How to Contact: Does not accept or return unsolicited mss. Query first. SASE. Reports on queries in 1 month. Sends pre-publication galleys to author.
Advice: "Query only publishers with an expressed interest in your type of fiction. We get too many inappropriate submissions. We are *not* interested in descriptive, experiential works—we're looking for solutions, how-to's, *practical* writings."

The double dagger before a listing indicates that the listing is new in this edition. New markets are often the most receptive to freelance contributions.

ANSUDA PUBLICATIONS (II), Box 158J, Harris IA 51345. Fiction Editor: Daniel Betz. Estab. 1978. One-man operation on part-time basis, "planning to someday expand into a full-time business." Publishes paperback originals. Books: mimeo paper; mimeo printing; index stock covers with square spine binding; illustrations on cover; average print order varies. Plans 1-2 first novels this year. Averages 3-5 total titles, 1 fiction title each year. Occasionally critiques rejected mss.
Needs: Fantasy, horror, literary, mainstream, psychic/supernatural, short story collections and suspense/mystery. "Interested mostly in fantasy, horror, psychic and supernatural. No romance, juvenile, experimental, translations or science fiction." Published *Motherland*, by Martin DiCarlantonio.
How to Contact: Query first or submit outline/synopsis and 1-2 sample chapters. SASE always. Photocopied submissions OK. Accepts computer printout submissions, prefers letter-quality. Reports in 1 day on queries, 1-8 weeks on mss. Publishes ms an average of 1 year after acceptance.
Terms: Pays in royalties by arrangement and 5 author's copies. Writer's guidelines and book catalog for #10 SASE.
Advice: "We appreciate neat copy. If photocopies are sent, we like to be able to read dark letters and to read all of the story. We try to work closely with the author through the period from first submission to publication."

APPLEZABA PRESS, Box 4134, Long Beach CA 90804. Editorial Director: Shelley Hellen. Estab. 1977. "We are a family-operated publishing house, working on a part-time basis. We plan to expand over the years." Publishes paperback originals. Averages 1 fiction title each year.
Needs: Contemporary, literary, experimental, feminist, gay, lesbian, fantasy, humor/satire, translations, and short story collections. No gothic, romance, confession, inspirational, satirical, black humor or slapstick. Recently published *The Gold Rush and Other Stories*, by Gerald Locklin.
How to Contact: Accepts unsolicited mss. Submit complete ms with SASE. No simultaneous submissions; photocopied submissions OK. Accepts computer printout submissions, prefers letter-quality. Reports in 2 months. Publishes ms 2-3 years after acceptance.
Terms: Pays in author's copies and 8-15% royalties; no advance. Free book catalog.
Advice: "Cover letter with previous publications, etc. is OK. Each book, first or twentieth, has to stand on its own. If a first-time novelist has had shorter works published in magazines, it makes it somewhat easier for us to market the book. We publish only book-length material."

ARIADNE PRESS (I), 4817 Tallahassee Ave., Rockville MD 20853. (301)949-2514. President: Carol Hoover. Estab. 1976. Shoestring operation—corporation with 4 directors who also act as editors. Publishes hardcover and paperback originals (may enter paperback field). Books: 50 lb alkaline paper; offset printing; Smyth-sewn binding. Average print order 1,000; average first novel print order 1,000. Plans 1 first novel this year. Averages 1 total title each year; only fiction. Sometimes critiques rejected mss. "We comment on selected mss of superior writing quality, even when rejected."
Needs: Adventure, contemporary, fantasy, feminist, historical, humor/satire, literary, mainstream, suspense/mystery, war, Looking for "literary-mainstream" fiction. No short stories, no science fiction or horror. Published *The Lattice*, by Henry Alley (mainstream/literary).
How to Contact: Accepts unsolicited mss. Query first. SASE. 5% of fiction is agented. Reports in 1 month on queries; 2 months on mss. Simultaneous and photocopied submissions OK. Accepts computer printout submissions, no dot-matrix.
Terms: Pays royalties of 10%. No advance. Sends pre-publication galleys to author. Writer's guidelines not available. List of books in stock for #10 SASE.
Advice: "We exist primarily for non-established writers. Try large, commercial presses first."

ARSENAL PULP PRESS (II), 1150 Homer St., Vancouver, British Columbia V6B 2X6 Canada. (604)687-4233. Imprints include Tillacum Library, Pulp Press, Arsenal Editions. Editors: Stephen Osborne, Linda Field. Estab. 1972. Small, co-operative publisher. Publishes hardcover and paperback originals. Books: 60 lb deluxe book paper; offset printing; perfect binding; occasional illustrations; average print order: 500-1,000; first novel print order: 500-1,000. Plans 1 first novel this year. Averages 8 total titles, 3 fiction titles each year. Average first novel print order 1,000-2,000 copies. Occasionally critiques rejected ms.
Needs: Contemporary, experimental, literary, short story collections, translations. "We are an open-minded organization always on the lookout for new, fresh works." No romance, supernatural/occult or religious. Published *The Promise*, by W. Campbell (short stories); *The Lost Tribe*, By Don Austin (short stories); *Momentum*, by Marc Diamond (contemporary); *Hardwired Angel*, by Nora Abercrombie and Cannas Jane Dorsey (contemporary). Published new writers within the last year.

How to Contact: Accepts unsolicited mss. Submit outline/synopsis and sample chapters or complete ms with SASE or SAE and IRC. Simultaneous and photocopied submissions OK. Accepts computer printout submissions; prefers letter-quality.
Terms: Pays in royalties of 10% minimum, 15% maximum; offers $30 average advance. Sends galleys to author. "Approximately 20-30% of our titles are funded or partially funded by grants."
Advice: "Publishing of first novels depends entirely on quality of work. Publishing more fiction this year as an objective, being a literary house. We are looking for new, fresh talent. We have a 3-day novel contest, held annually on Labor Day weekend and actively encourage new writers."

ARTE PUBLICO PRESS (II, IV), University of Houston, Houston TX 77004. (713)749-4768. Publisher: Dr. Nicolas Kanellos. Estab. 1979. Small press devoted to the publication of contemporary U.S. Hispanic literature. Publishes paperback originals and occasionally reprints. Average print order 2,000-5,000; first novel print order 2,500-5,000. Sometimes critiques rejected mss.
Needs: Contemporary, ethnic, feminist, literary, short story collections. Published *A Shroud in the Family*, by Lionel Garcia (satire); *This Migrant Earth*, by Rolando Hinojosa; and *Taking Control*, by Mary Helen Ponce (short stories).
How to Contact: Accepts unsolicted mss. Submit outline/synopsis and sample chapters or complete ms with cover letter. 1% of fiction is agented. Accepts computer printout submissions.
Terms: $1,000 average advance; 20 author's copies. Sends pre-publication galleys to author. Book catalog free on request.
Tips: "All fiction, all paperback."

BANNED BOOKS (I, II), Subsidiary of Edward-William Publishing Co., Box 33280, #292, Austin TX 78764. Senior Editor: Tom Hayes. Estab. 1985. Small press with plans to expand. Publishes paperback originals. Books: 60 lb acid-free paper; sheet-fed offset printing; perfect binding; illustrations; average print order: 2,000; first novel print order: 2,000. Plans 10 first novels this year. Averages 12 total titles, 10 fiction titles each year.
Needs: Erotica, fantasy, gay, humor/satire, lesbian, science fiction, short story collections. Looking for "all forms of fiction and nonfiction for the gay/lesbian market with the exception of poetry collections." Recently published *Diary of a New York Queen*, by William Barber; *The Contactees Die Young*, by Antoinette Azolakov; *Lovers: Love and Sex Stories*, by Tee Corinne.
How to Contact: Accepts unsolicited mss. Submit sample chapters with cover letter. SASE. Reports in 3 weeks on queries; 3 months on mss. Simultaneous and photocopied submissions OK. Accepts computer printout submissions.
Terms: Pays in royalties of 10% minimum; 15% maximum; 10 author's copies. Sends galleys to author. Writer's guidelines free for SASE.
Advice: "Study the market before submitting. Much time and expense could be avoided if the author really read the entries in Novel & Short Story Writer's Market before sending it out."

BARLOW PRESS (I,II), Box 5403, Helena MT 59604. (406)449-7310. Fiction Editor: Russell B. Hill. Estab. 1987. One-person publishing/printing company which produces titles both by offset and letterpress (hand-set) printing. Publishes hardcover and paperback originals and reprints. Books: acid-free letterpress stock (i.e. Mohawk, Superfine); usually letterpress printing, occasionally offset, hand-sewn binding with end papers, heavier cover stock, sometimes leather; woodcuts, line-art plates or one-color artwork. Average print order: 500-1,000 letterpress; 2,000-3,000 offset. Publishes 2 total titles/year; plans 0-1 first fiction title this year. Sometimes critiques rejected mss.
Needs: Adventure, contemporary, historical, humor/satire, literary, mainstream, regional, short story.
How to Contact: Query first. Accepts unsolicited mss. Send complete mss with cover letter and SASE. Reports in 2 months. Simultaneous and photocopied submissions OK. Accepts computer printouts and electronic disk submissions.
Terms: Payment by individual arrangement, depending on the book. Publishes ms 6 months-2 years after acceptance. Rarely subsidy, but "publication by Barlow Press usually involves a joint effort—Barlow Press contributes the time and expenses, author contributes mss, with particular terms of reimbursement subject to negotiation."
Advice: "Frankly, a publisher like Barlow Press can't compete with larger publishers for manuscripts they want, and we encourage authors to submit material to potentially lucrative publishers first. But we are convinced too many manuscripts deserve one more reading, one more potential outlet. We don't publish most manuscripts we read, but we have never regretted reading a manuscript. And because Barlow Press handles every publication by individual arrangement with the author, we aren't shy about proposing to edit manuscripts to fit our needs."

Read the Business of Fiction section to learn the correct way to prepare and submit a manuscript.

FREDERIC C. BEIL, PUBLISHER, INC. (II), 414 Tattnall St., Savannah GA 31401. Imprints include The Sandstone Press. President: Frederic C. Beil III. Estab. 1983. General trade publisher. Publishes hardcover originals and reprints. Books: acid-free paper; letterpress and offset printing; Smyth-sewn, hardcover binding; illustrations; average print order: 2,000; first novel print order: 2,000. Plans 2 first novels this year. Averages 10 total titles, 2 fiction titles each year.
Needs: Historical, literary, regional, short story collections, translations. Recently published *A Woman of Means*, by Peter Taylor.
How to Contact: Does not accept unsolicited mss. Query first. Reports in 1 week on queries. Accepts computer printout submissions.
Terms: Payment "all negotiable." Sends galleys to author. Book catalog free on request.

BILINGUAL PRESS/EDITORIAL BILINGÜE (II, IV), Hispanic Research Center, Arizona State University, Tempe AZ 85287. (602)965-3867. Editor: Gary Keller. Estab. 1973. "University affiliated." Publishes hardcover and paperback originals, hardcover and paperback reprints. Books: 60 lb acid free paper; single sheet or web press printing; casebound and perfect bound; illustrations sometimes; average print order: 4,000 copies (1,000 case bound, 3,000 soft cover). Published new writers within the last year. Plans 2 first novels this year. Averages 12 total titles, 6 fiction each year. Sometimes comments on rejected ms.
Needs: Ethnic, literary, short story collections and translations. "We are always on the lookout for Chicano, Puerto Rican, Cuban-American or other U.S. Hispanic themes with strong and serious literary qualities and distinctive and intellectually important themes. We have been receiving a lot of fiction set in Latin America (usually Mexico or Central America) where the main charcter is either an ingenue to the culture or spy, adventurer, or mercenary. We don't publish this sort of 'Look, I'm in an exotic land' type of thing. Also, novels about the Aztecs or other pre-Columbians are very iffy." Recently published *The Ultraviolet Sky*, by Alma Luz Villanueva (serious Chicana novel), *The Day the Cisco Kid Shot John Wayne*, by Nash Candelaria (Hispanic experience in the U.S.); *Death of an Anglo*, by Alejandro Morales.
How to Contact: Query first. SASE. Include Social Security number with submission. Reports in 3 weeks on queries, 2 months on mss. Simultaneous and photocopied submissions OK. Accepts computer printout submissions.
Terms: Pays royalties of 10%. Average advance $300. Provides 10 author's copies. Sends galleys to author. Publishes ms 1 year after acceptance. Writer's guidelines not available. Book catalog free.
Advice: "Writers should take the utmost care in assuring that their manuscripts are clean, grammatically impecabble, and have perfect spelling. This is true not only of the English but the Spanish as well. All accent marks need to be in place as well as diacritical marks. When these are missing it's an immediate first indication that the author does not really know Hispanic culture and is not equipped to write about it. We are interested in publishing creative literature that treats the U.S. Hispanic experience in a distinctive, creative, revealing way. The kinds of books that we publish we keep in print for a very long time (certainly into the next century) irrespective of sales. We are busy establishing and preserving a U.S. Hispanic canon of creative literature.

BkMk PRESS (I, II), UMKC, 107 Cockefair Hall, 5216 Rockhill Rd., #204, Kansas City MO 64110. (816)276-2558. Fiction Editor: Dan Jaffe. Estab. 1971. Publishes hardback and paperback originals. Books: standard paper; offset printing; perfect and case bound binding; average print order: 1,000; Averages 6 total titles; 1 fiction title each year.
Needs: Contemporary, ethnic, experimental, historical, literary, and translations. "We are new to fiction publishing but we plan to print one collection or anthology of short stories per year." Recently published *Paper Crown*, by Tom Hawkins.
How to Contact: Query first with SASE. Reports in 3-4 months on queries.
Terms: Pays in royalties (approximately 10%, in copies and $50 adjustable by contract). Sends galleys to author. Free book catalog.

‡BLACK MOSS PRESS (II), Box 143 Station A, Windsor ON N9V-6L7 Canada. (519)252-2551. Editorial Contact Person: Kristina Russelo. Fiction Editor: Marty Gervais. Estab. 1969. "Small independent publisher assisted by government grants." Publishes paperback originals. Books: Zephyr paper; offset printing; perfect binding; 4-color cover, b&w interior illustrations; average print order: 500. Averages 10-14 total titles, 7 fiction titles each year. Sometimes comments on rejected mss.
Needs: Humor/satire, juvenile (5-9 years, including easy-to-read, contemporary), literary, preschool/picture book, short story collections. "Usually open to children's material. Nothing religious, moralistic, romance." Recently published *Crossing the Snow Line*, by Elizabeth Hay (short story collection).
How to Contact: Acceps unsolicited mss. Submit outline/synopsis and 2 sample chapters. SASE. Reports in 1-3 months. Simultaneous and photocopied submissions OK. Accepts computer printout submissions.

Terms: Pays for children's in royalties; literary in author's copies. Sends galleys to author. Publishes ms 1 year after acceptance. Book catalog for SASE.

Advice: "Generally, originality, well developed plots, strong, multi-dimensional characters and some unusual element catch my interest. It's rare that we publish new authors' works, but when we do, that's what we want. (We do publish short story collections of authors who have had some stories in lit mags.)"

‡BLACK TIE PRESS (I, II), Box 440004, 12655 Whittington Dr., Houston TX 77244. (713)789-5119. Publisher/Editor: Peter Gravis. Estab. 1986. "We are a tiny press interested in contemporary poetry and short fiction." Publishes hardcover and paperback originals. Books: Mohawk vellum, Glatfelter paper; combination offset and letter press printing; Smythe sewn; illustrations; average print order: varies from 2,000 to 2,500. Publishes "two fiction anthologies each year."

Needs: Contemporary and experimental. "Our current aim is to publish an anthology of short fiction (4-6,000 words). No science fiction, romance, spiritual, religious, juvenile, historical."

How to Contact: Query or submit complete ms (with proper postage) with cover letter. SASE necessary for returns. Reports in 3-6 months on queries. Photocopied submission OK. Accepts computer printout submissions if letter quality.

Terms: Pays in royalties. "Payment will be determined on individual basis." Publishes ms one to two years after acceptance. Writer's guidelines free for SASE or IRC.

BLOOD & GUTS PRESS, 2076 Westwood Blvd., Los Angeles CA 90025. (213)475-2700. Owners/editorial contact: Patricia and Craig Graham. Publishes hardcover originals. Books: average print order 250-1,000; also publishes signed, numbered hardcover editions. Publishes 3-5 fiction titles/year.

Needs: Mainstream fiction, science fiction, suspense/mystery. Publishes novels and short story collections. Recently published *Killer Inside Me*, by Jim Thompson (mystery); *Ray Bradbury Reviewed*, by Ray Bradbury and William F. Nolan.

How to Contact: Query first with SASE. Accepts unsolicited manuscripts. Reports in 1-6 months on queries. Simultaneous and photocopied submissions OK. Accepts computer printout submissions.

Terms: Pays negotiable advance. Sends prepublication galleys to author. Publishes ms up to 1 year after acceptance.

Advice: "Because we also own the Vagabond Books bookstore, we have a lot of authors in to sign their works. We tend to seek out authors who we know can write what we're looking for. Occasionally, I'll get a query that grabs me and I'll follow it up."

BOOKMAKERS GUILD INC. (IV), 9655 W. Colfax Ave., Lakewood CO 80215. (303)235-0203. Publisher: Barbara J. Ciletti. Estab. 1981. "We publish fiction and nonfiction for children and young adults (particularly high-quality, educational material in the language arts and natural sciences); books on social issues for adults. Publishes hardcover and paperback originals. Books: 60-80 lb matte paper; web offset printing. Smythe-sewn or perfect binding; b&w and full-color illustrations; average print order: 5,000-7,000. Averages 10 total titles/year; 2-4 fiction titles/year.

Needs: Adventure, juvenile including easy-to-read, literary, short story collections, young adult/teen (10-18 years) including historical and problem novels. "We look for material containing classic mythopoeic elements, allegory, etc. No thrillers, romance, pre-school fantasy or picture books. No fiction for adults unless uniquely literary."

How to Contact: Accepts unsolicited mss. Query first. Submit outline/synopsis and 3 sample chapters. Reports in 1 month on queries; 2 months on mss. Simultaneous submissions OK. Accepts computer printout submissions.

Terms: Pays 8-15% royalties; $1,000 average advance, negotiable (only for exceptional works); 20 author's copies. Sends galleys to author. Writers guidelines for SASE; book catalog free on request.

Advice: "We believe that fiction requires a strong central message and a comprehensive understanding of the English language."

BOOKS FOR ALL TIMES, INC., Box 2, Alexandria VA 22313. Publisher/Editor: Joe David. Estab. 1981. One-man operation. Publishes hardcover and paperback originals. Books: 60 lb paper; offset printing; perfect binding; average print order: 1,000. "No plans for new writers at present." Has published 1 fiction title to date. Occasionally critiques rejected mss.

Needs: Contemporary, literary and short story collections. "No novels at the moment; hopeful, though, of someday soon publishing a collection of quality short stories. No popular fiction or material easily published by the major or minor houses specializing in mindless entertainment. Only interested in stories of the Victor Hugo or Sinclair Lewis quality." Published *The Fire Within*, by Joe David (literary); *Glad You Asked!*, by Joe David (non-fiction).

How to Contact: Query first with SASE. Simultaneous and photocopied submission OK. Reports in 1 month on queries.
Terms: Pays negotiable advance. "Publishing/payment arrangement will depend on plans for the book." Book catalog free on request.
Advice: Interested in "controversial, honest books which satisfy the reader's curiosity to know. Read Victor Hugo, Fyodor Dostoyevsky and Sinclair Lewis, for example."

‡BOREALIS PRESS (IV), 9 Ashburn Dr., Ottawa, Ontario K2E 6N4 Canada. Imprint includes *Journal of Canadian Poetry*. Editor: Frank Tierney. Fiction Editor: Glenn Clever. Estab. 1970. Publishes hardcover and paperback originals and reprints. Books: standard book-quality paper; offset printing; perfect and cloth binding; average print order: 1,000. Buys juvenile mss with b&w illustrations. Average number of titles: 4.
Needs: Contemporary, literary, adventure, historical, juvenile and young adult. "Must have a Canadian content or author; otherwise query first." Accepts short stories. Published *Sandy*, by Nancy Freeman; *Trouble with Heroes*, by Guy Vanderhaeghe (short stories); and *Windflower: Selected Poems of Bliss Carmans*, ed. by Richmand Souster.
How to Contact: Submit complete ms with SASE (Canadian postage) or IRCs. No simultaneous submissions; photocopied submissions OK. Reports in 2 weeks on queries, 3-4 months on mss. Publishes ms 1-2 years after acceptance.
Terms: Pays 10% royalties and 3 free author's copies; no advance. Sends galleys to author. Free book catalog with SASE or IRC.
Advice: " Have your work professionally edited. We generally publish only material with a Canadian content or by a Canadian writer."

BOTTOM DOG PRESS (IV), Firelands College, Huron OH 44839. (419)433-5560. Editor/Publisher: Dr. Larry Smith. Estab. 1984. Four-person part-time operation assisted by grants from Ohio Arts Council. Publishes paperback originals. Books: fine paper; saddle or perfect binding; cover art illustrations; average print order: 1,500 fiction. Averages 3 total titles, 1-2 fiction titles each year. Always critiques or comments on rejected mss.
Needs: Literary, mainstream. Published *Best Ohio Fiction* collection (160 pages) with work by Jack Matthews, Robert Flanagan, Philip F. O'Conner, Robert Fox. Published new writers within the last year.
How to Contact: Accepts unsolicited mss. Query first. Submit complete ms with cover letter. SASE. Reports on queries in 2 weeks; 2 months on mss. Accepts computer printout submissions, no dot-matrix.
Terms: Pays royalties of 10-15% minimum and 20 author's copies. Sends galleys to author. Has done 2 books co-operatively—50/50. Book catalog free on request.
Advice: "We do an 'Ohio Writers series' specializing in chapbook collection of stories or novellas—emphasis on sense of place and strong human characters." All submissions must fall within the 35,000 word limit.

‡BREITENBUSH BOOKS, INC. (II,III), Box 82157, Portland OR 97282. Managing Editor: Thomas Booth. Estab. 1977. Independent trade publisher with national distribution. Publishes hardcover and paperback originals and paperback reprints. Averages 12-15 total titles, 4-6 fiction titles each year.
Needs: Contemporary, ethnic, experimental, historical, literary, regional, short story collections. Recently published *Umbrella of Glass*, by Henry Alley; *Rainbow Rhapsody*, by Rick Borsten; and *DeFord*, by David Shetzline (reprint).
How to Contact: Accepts unsolicited mss. Prefers published writers. Send outline/synopsis and 2 sample chapters. SASE for query. Agented fiction 20%. Reports in 1 month on queries; 6-8 weeks on mss. Simultaneous and photocopied submissions OK.
Terms: Pays in royalties and author's copies. Offers advance. Sends galleys to author. Publishes ms 9 months to 1 year after acceptance. Book catalog for 4 first class stamps (we provide envelope).

BRIGHT RING PUBLISHING (IV), Box 5768-F, Bellingham WA 98227. (206)734-1601. Editor: Mary Ann F. Kohl. Estab. 1985. One-person, full-time, plans to expand to children's fiction. Publishes paperback originals. Books: offset printing; perfect binding; b&w illustrations; average print order: 3,000-5,000. Averages 1 title each year. Sometimes critiques rejected mss.
Needs: Juvenile (5-9 yrs.), easy-to-read, preschool/picture book (also 2-9 years). "Should encourage independent/creative thinking. Possibly with a theme of 'art.' No real requirements—looking at all children's books. Nothing trendy or commercial, no scary monsters or anything too 'sappy.' "
How to Contact: Accepts unsolicited ms. Submit complete ms with cover letter. SASE. Reports in 2 weeks on queries; 6 weeks on mss. Simultaneous submissions and photocopied submissions OK. Accepts computer printout submissions.
Terms: Pays royalties of 10-15% or in author's copies. Book catalog for #10 SASE or IRC.

■**BRYANS & BRYANS (I) (Book Packager and Editorial Consultant),** Box 121, Fairfield CT 06430. (203)454-2051. President: John B. Bryans. Fiction Editor: James A. Bryans. Arranges publication of paperback originals (packages). Books: paperback/mass market. *Critiques mss: $100 charge* "for 2-page evaluation only when this has been agreed upon in advance. Often I will offer comments and criticism at no charge where we, based on a query, have encouraged submission."
Needs: Adventure, contemporary, historical, horror, humor/satire, literary, mainstream, romance (contemporary, historical). Titles (1990) include: *The Hucksters of Holiness*, by Ron Gorton (contemporary social thriller); *Cincinnati* (historical with romance elements); *Baton Rouge* (historical with romance elements); and *Portland*, by Lee Davis Willoughby.
How to Contact: Does not accept unsolicited mss. Query first. SASE. Agented fiction 80-90%. Reports in 3 weeks on queries; 2 months on mss. Electronic submissions OK via Microsoft Word on Macintosh disk.
Terms: Pays in royalties of 6% minimum; 10% maximum. Negotiable advance.
Advice: "Send us a letter, maximum 2 pages, describing the project and giving pertinent background info on yourself. Include an SASE and we will reply to let you know if we find the idea intriguing enough to see 3 sample chapters (the *first* three) and a detailed synopsis."

BURNING BOOKS (IV), 690 Market St., Suite 1501, San Francisco CA 94104. (415)788-7480. Publisher: Kathleen Burch, Michael Sumner, Melody Sumner. Estab. 1979. Three-person part-time operation. Publishes paperback originals. Books: acid-free paper; offset and letterpress printing; spiral or signature sewn binding; illustrations; average print order: 1,000-3,000. Averages 1 title/year; 1 fiction title every 2 years. *Will provide detailed critique of ms for $100.*
Needs: Literary. No "commercially inspired" fiction. Recently published *Indicia . . . A Romance*, by Kathleen Burch.
How to Contact: Does not accept unsolicited mss. Query first. Reports on queries in 6 weeks.
Terms: Pays in author's copies. Sends galleys to author. Book catalog free on request.

CADMUS EDITIONS (III), Box 687, Tiburon CA 94920. (707)431-8527. Editor: Jeffrey Miller. Estab. 1979. Emphasis on quality literature. Publishes hardcover originals and paperback originals. Books: Approximately 50% letterpress; 50% offset printing; perfect and case binding; average print order: 2,000; first novel print order: 2,000. Averages 3-5 total titles, 3 fiction titles each year.
Needs: Literary. Published *The Wandering Fool*, by Yunus Emre, translated by Edovard Roditi and Guzin Dino; *The Hungry Girls*, by Patricia Eakins; *Zig-Zag*, by Richard Thornley.
How to Contact: Does not accept or return unsolicited mss. Query first. SASE. Photocopied submissions OK.
Terms: Royalties negotiated per book. Sends galleys to author.

‡**CALYX BOOKS (II,IV),** Box B, Corvallis OR 97339. (503)753-9384. Editor: M. Donnelly. Estab. 1986. "We publish fine literature and art by women." Publishes hardcover and paperback originals. Books: offset printing; paper & cloth binding; average print order: 5,000-10,000 copies; first novel print order: 5,000. Published new writers within the last year. Plans 2 first novels this year. Averages 2-4 totals, 2 fiction, this year.
Needs: Contemporary, ethnic, experimental, feminist, lesbian, literary, short story collections and translations. Recently published *The Riverhouse Stories*, by Andrea Carlisle (literary); *The Forbidden Stitch*, by Shirley Geok-Lim, editor (anthology); and *Florilegia*, by Margarita Donnelly, editor (anthology).
How to Contact: Does not accept unsolicited mss. Query first or submit outline/synopsis and 3 sample chapters. Include SASE (IRC). *Note: Accepts mss only between January 15 and March 15 each year.* Reports in 1 month on queries; 6 months on mss. Photocopied submissions OK. Accepts computer printout submissions.
Terms: Pays royalties of 8% minimum, author's copies, (depends on grant/award money). Sends galleys to author. Publishes ms 1-2 years after acceptance. Writer's guidelines for #10 SASE or IRC and 1 first class stamp. Book catalog free on request.

CANADIAN STAGE & ARTS PUBLICATIONS (I, IV), 263 Adelaide St. W, 5th Floor, Toronto, Ontario M5H 1Y2 Canada. Editor: Patricia Michael. Estab. 1966. "Small press, slowly expanding. Canadian themes mostly—centered on the arts at present." Books: 50 or 60 lb stock (matte) or art paper; offset

Listings marked with a solid box [■] are book packagers. See the introduction to Commercial Publishers for more information.

web printing; perfect bound or saddle-stitched binding; illustrations in children's line; average print order: 1,000-5,000. Averages 1-2 total titles.
Needs: Humor/satire, literary. "Emphasis on Canadian authors. To date almost all titles have been nonfiction (exception is children's line). These themes have priority, but always interested in a good story if fiction. No strong American themes. Would *encourage* art (performing or visual) subjects though." Recently published *Image in the Mind: CBC radio drama 1944-1954*, by N. Alice Frick (docu-account of radio drama days at the Canadian Broadcasting Corp.); *Inuit Dolls: Reminders of a Heritage*.
How to Contact: Submit outline/synopsis and 1 sample chapter. SASE. Reports in 4 weeks on queries; 6 weeks on mss. Simultaneous and photocopied submissions OK.
Terms: Pays 10% royalties, depends on grant/award money. Sends prepublication galleys to author. Publishes ms up to 1 year (depends on editing process) after acceptance. "Many books have been subsidy published. Also, with Canadian content, government grants may be available. A few authors have had pre-arranged purchase orders or investment capital for the project."
Advice: "Would appreciate writers who query us with works suitable to small press budgets and marketing schemes—also those somehow tied into Canadian themes. Artistic subjects receive most attention, but we are also planning biographies and other nonfiction for the future. Most writers have been known by us in some capacity. Most unsolicited manuscripts have been totally inappropriate. A solid storyline, honest approach and dedication to subject as a literary work will catch our interest. Nothing *too* esoteric though (must have market appeal)."

CARLTON BOOKS (IV), Box 5052, Evanston IL 60204. (312)328-0400. Contact: Graham Carlton. Estab. 1985. Midsize independent publisher with plans to expand. Publishes hardcover and paperback originals and reprints.
Needs: Erotica, suspense/mystery.
How to Contact: Does not accept or return unsolicited ms. Query first. SASE.

‡*CAROLINA WREN PRESS (II,IV), Box 277, Carrboro NC 27510. (919)560-2738. Imprints are Lillipop Power Books. Editor-in-chief: Judy Hogan. Fiction Editor: Sharlene Baker. "Small non-profit independent publishing company which specializes in women's minority work and non-sexist, multi-racial children's books mainly from North Carolina." Publishes paperback originals. Books: off-set printing; perfect and saddle-stitching binding; illustrations mainly in children's; average print order: 1,000 adult, 3,000 children; first novel print order: 1,000. Published new writers within the last year. Plans 2 first novels this year. Averages 2-3 total titles each year. Sometimes comments on rejected mss (if Judy Hogan does it, $50 for 12 pages).
Needs: Contemporary, ethnic, experimental, feminist, gay, juvenile (east-to-read, fantasy, contemporary), lesbian, literary, preschool/picture book, regional, short story collections, translations. No standard clichéd stuff, romances, etc. No animals (children's books). Recently published *Love, Or a Reasonable Facsimile*, by Gloree Rogers (ethnic); *Brother and Keeper, Sister's Child*, by Margaret Stephens (literary).
How to Contact: Accepts unsolicited mss. Submit outline/synopsis and 1 or 2 sample chapters. SASE. Reports in 6 months. Photocopied submissions OK. Computer printout submissions are acceptable.
Terms: Pays in copies (10% of print run for adults. 5% for children's books). Pays cash advance and royalties if grants are available. Sends galleys to author. Publishes ms 2-3 years after acceptance. Writer's guidelines for #10 SAE and 1 first class stamp (for children's authors only). Book catalog for #10 SAE and 2 first class stamps.
Advice: "We would like to see work from more black women writers. We also have a minority editor—Alisa Johnson, who reads for all genres."

CARPENTER PRESS (I, II), Box 14387, Columbus OH 43214. Editorial Director: Robert Fox. Estab. 1973. One-man operation on part-time basis. Publishes paperback originals. Books: alkaline paper; offset printing; perfect or saddle stapled binding; illustrations sometimes; average print order: 500-2,500; first novel print order: 1,000.
Needs: Contemporary, literary, experimental, science fiction, and fantasy. "Literary rather than genre science fiction and fantasy." Published *Song for Three Voices*, by Curt Johnson (novel); and the 10th anniversary first novel contest winner, *The Three-Week Trance Diet*, by Jane Pirto. "Do not plan to publish more than one book/year including chapbooks, and this depends upon funding, which is erratic. Contemplating future competitions in the novel and short story."
How to Contact: Accepts unsolicited mss. Query. SASE. Simultaneous and photocopied submissions OK. Accepts computer printout submissions. Letter-quality only. Reports promptly.
Terms: Pays in author's copies or 10% royalties. "Terms vary according to contract." No cash advance. Free book catalog with #10 SASE.
Advice: "Don't try to impress us with whom you've studied or where you've published. Read as much as you can so you're not unwittingly repeating what's already been done. I look for freshness and originality. I wouldn't say that I favor experimental over traditional writing. Rather, I'm interested in

seeing how recent experimentation is tying tradition to the future and to the work of writers in other countries. Our books should be read before submitting. We encourage first novelists."

***CATBIRD PRESS (II)**, 44 N. 6th Ave., Highland Park NJ 08904. Publisher: Robert Wechsler. Estab. 1987. Small independent trade publisher. Publishes hardcover and paperback originals and reprints. Books: acid-free paper; offset printing; cloth/paper binding; illustrations (where relevant). Average print order: 4,000; first novel print order: 3,000. Averages 5 total titles, 1-2 fiction titles each year.
Needs: Contemporary, humor/satire (specialty); literary, mainstream, translations (specialty Czech, French and German read in-house). Recently published *Catapult*, by Vladimír Páral, translated by William E. Harkins (Czech, literary but popular).
How to Contact: Accepts unsolicited mss. Submit outline/synopsis with sample chapters. SASE. Reports in 2 weeks on queries; 4-6 weeks on mss. Simultaneous and photocopied submissions OK.
Terms: Pays royalties of 7½% minimum; 15% maximum. Average advance: $1,000; offers negotiable advance. Pays in 10 author's copies. Sends prepublication galleys to author. Publishes ms approx. 1 year after acceptance. *Some subsidy publishing;* terms depend on particular book. Writer's guidelines for #10 SAE with 1 first class stamp.
Advice: "We are a new publisher interested in quality fiction particularly of a humorous nature. We are definitely interested in unpublished novelists who combine a sense of humor with a true knowledge of and love for literature, a lack of ideology, care for craft, and self-criticism (falling out of love with one's words)."

CAVE BOOKS (IV), Subsidiary of Cave Research Foundation, 756 Harvard Ave., St. Louis MO 63130. (314)862-7646. Editor: Richard A. Watson. Estab. 1957. Small press. Publishes hardcover and paperback originals and reprints. Books: acid free paper; various methods printing; binding sewn in signatures; illustrations; average print order: 1,500; first novel print order: 1,500. Averages 4 total titles. Number of fiction titles varies each year. Critiques or comments on rejected ms.
Needs: Adventure (cave exploration). Needs any realistic novel with caves as central theme. "No gothics, romance, fantasy or science fiction. Mystery and detective OK if the action in the cave is central and realistic. (What I mean by 'realistic' is that the author must know what he or she is talking about.)"
How to Contact: Accepts unsolicited mss. Submit complete ms with cover letter. Reports in 1 week on queries; 1 month on mss. Simultaneous and photocopied submissions OK. Accepts computer printouts.
Terms: Pays in royalties of 10%. Sends galleys to author. Book catalog free on request.
Advice: Encourages first novelists. "We would like to publish more fiction, but we get very few submissions. Why doesn't someone write a historical novel about Mammoth Cave . . .?"

CHELSEA GREEN PUBLISHING CO., Route 113, P.O. Box 130, Post Mills VT 05058. (802)333-9073. Editor: Ian Baldwin. Estab. 1985. "Small independent trade publisher with plans to expand." Publishes hardcover and paperback originals. Averages 8-10 total titles, 1-2 fiction titles each year.
Needs: Serious fiction only . . . no genre fiction (ie. romance, spy, sci fi) or mainstream." Published *The Automotive History of Lucky Kellerman*, by Steve Heller (literary); *The Eight Corners of the World*, by Gordon Weaver (lit/comedy).
How to Contact: Query first. Prefers no unsolicited submissions. SASE.
Terms: Royalties to trade standards; small advances on royalties negotiable.

CHILD WELFARE LEAGUE OF AMERICA (IV), 440 First St. NW, Suite 310, Washington DC 20001. (202)638-2952. Director of Publications: Susan Brite. Estab. 1920. Nonprofit association with publishing arm. Publishes hardcover and paperback originals. Books: average print order 3,000. Publishes 1 or 2 fiction titles/year.
Needs: Published *Floating*, by Mark Krueger, PhD (stories about youth-care workers in residential homes for children).
How to Contact: Query first with SASE.
Terms: Payment varies. Book catalog free.

***CHINA BOOKS (IV)**, 2929 24th St., San Francisco CA 94110. (415)282-2994. Senior Editor: Bob Schildgen. Estab. 1959. "Publishes books about China or things Chinese." Publishes hardcover and paperback originals. Books: letterpress, offset printing; perfect binding; b&w illustrations; average print order: 5,000. Published new writers within the past year. Plans 1 first novel this year. Averages 12 total titles, 3 fiction titles each year. Sometimes critiques rejected mss.
Needs: Ethnic, subjects relating to China and translations from Chinese. Recently published *The Piano Tuner*, by Cheng Naishan; *6 Tanyin Alley*, by Liu Zongren; *Old Well*, by Zheng Yi.
How to Contact: Query first or submit outline/synopsis and 2 sample chapters. No agented fiction. Reports in 2 weeks on queries; in 1 month on mss. Simultaneous and photocopied submissions OK.
Terms: Pays royalties 5% minimum; 8% maximum. Sends galleys to author. Publishes ms 1 year after acceptance. Subsidy publishes 1%/year. Writer's guidelines and book catalog free on request.

CLARITY PRESS (I, II, IV), Suite 469, 3277 Roswell Rd NE, Atlanta GA 30505. Contact: Editorial Committee, Fiction. Estab. 1984. Small press publishing fiction and nonfiction on political, social, minority issues and human rights. Books: 120 M paper; offset printing; perfect binding; illustrations where necessary or enhancing; average print order: 2,000; first novel print order: 1,000. Plans 1 first novel this year. Averages 3 total titles/year. Occasionally critiques or comments on rejected ms.

Needs: Minority, literary, social commentary. Short stories for anthology. Published *The Invisible Women of Washington*, by Diana G. Collier, (social issues).

How to Contact: Accepts unsolicited mss. Query is a necessity. SASE. Reports in 6 weeks. Simultaneous and photocopied submissions OK. Accepts computer printout submissions.

Terms: Authors paid by individual arrangement.

Advice: "We are interested only in novels concerning political, minority or human rights issues. Mss not preceded by query letter will be returned."

CLEIS PRESS (I,II,IV), Box 14684, San Francisco CA 94114. Co-editor: Frédérique Delacoste. "Mid-size independent women's press. Publishes paperback originals and reprints." Books: offset 50 lb paper; offset printing; perfect binding; illustrations in some books; average print order: 3,000-5,000; first novel print order: 3,500. Published new writers within the past year. Averages 4 total titles, 1 fiction title each year. Sometimes critiques rejected mss.

Needs: Feminist, lesbian, literary, translations. "Particularly interested in translations of women's fiction. No mainstream, genre fiction." Recently published *Unholy Alliances*, edited by Louise Rafkin (fiction collection).

How to Contact: Submit outline and 1 chapter. SASE. Reports on queries in 1 month; on mss in 3 months. Simultaneous and photocopied submissions OK "with letter of explanation." Accepts computer printout submissions, including dot-matrix "only if NLQ."

Terms: Pays negotiable royalties. Sends pre-publication galleys to author. Publishes 6-12 months after acceptance. Writer's guidelines and book catalog for #10 SAE and 2 first class stamps.

Advice: Publishing more fiction than in the past. "We encourage new women writers."

CLIFFHANGER PRESS (II), Box 29527, Oakland CA 94604-9527. (415)763-3510. Editor: Nancy Chirich. Estab. 1986. Publishes hardcover originals. Books: 60 lb text stock paper; offset printing; case binding; average print order: 3,000; first novel print order: 3,000. Published new writers within the last year; goal is 10 novels a year.

Needs: Suspense/mystery. "Need mystery/suspense (75,000 words approximately); heavy on the American regional or foreign background. No grossly hardboiled detectives and no spies." (Send SASE for guidelines for specific needs.) Recently published *The Case of the Johannisberg Riesling*, by Gerry Maddren; *The Druge Document*, by Gregory Fitzgerald and John Dillon; *Three to get Ready*, by Hans Ostrom.

How to Contact: Please first send for writer's guidelines and book catalog, free on request for SASE. We prefer query first with outline/synopsis and 2-3 sample chapters. SASE. If sample appears to be our style, we will request complete ms. Reports in 2 weeks on queries; approx. 8 weeks on requested mss. Simultaneous and photocopied submissions OK, but please let us know. Accepts computer printout submissions, but no justified type.

Terms: No advances. Pays royalties of 10% minimum; 15% maximum. Sends galleys to author.

Advice: "Author must be able to accept editorial suggestions with grace. Our motto is 'we can work it out.' If manuscript is accepted, there is something there, so no *drastic* substantive changes would be anticipated."

***CLOTHESPIN FEVER PRESS (I)**, 5529 N. Figueroa, Los Angeles CA 90042. (213)254-1373. Publisher: Jenny Wrenn. Estab. 1986. Small two-person operation with plans to expand. Books: offset printing; perfect binding, comb or saddlestitched binding; graphics of 2 or 3 colors, photos etc., average print order: 2,000 copies. Averages 2 total titles, 0-1 fiction title each year.

Needs: Experimental, feminist, lesbian, literary, short story collections. "Looking for literary work by lesbian writers. No male stories by male writers." Recently published *Shitkickers and Other Texas Stories*, by Carolyn Weathers; *In A Different Light: An Anthology of Lesbian Writers*, by Jenny Wrenn and Carolyn Weathers; *Crazy*, by Carolyn Weathers (novel); published fiction by previously unpublished writers within the last year. "We will be publishing an anthology of prose and poetry by predominately unpublished lesbian writers this year."

How to Contact: Accepts unsolicited mss. Query first with cover letter that includes summary or topic plus sample short story or chapter. SASE. Reports in 3 weeks on queries; 3 months on mss. Simultaneous and photocopied submissions OK. Accepts computer printout submissions.

Terms: Payment is negotiable. Sends galleys to author. *"We would consider subsidy publishing."* Writer's guidelines free for SASE. Book catalog on request.

Advice: "A writer should be open to rewrite suggestions that a publisher might suggest without taking offense. Spelling and correct grammar should be strived for above all. Keep writing and rewriting but don't despair if you think your work is unmarketable. Keep in mind that the right publisher for you may be hard to find."

CONFLUENCE PRESS INC. (II), Spalding Hall, Lewis-Clark State College, Lewiston ID 83501. (208)799-2336. Imprint is Blue Moon Press. Fiction Editor: James R. Hepworth. Estab. 1976. Small trade publisher. Publishes hardcover originals and reprints; paperback originals and reprints. Books: 60 lb paper; photo offset printing; Smythe-sewn binding; average print order: 1,500-5,000 copies. Published new writers this year. Averages 10 total titles/year. Critiques rejected mss for $25/hour.

Needs: Contemporary, historical, literary, mainstream, short story collections, translations. "Our needs favor serious fiction, 1 novel and 1 short fiction collection a year, with preference going to work set in the contemporary western United States." Published *A Charge of Angels*, by L.D. Clark (fiction); and *The Other Side of the Story*, by Richard Shelton (short fiction).

How to Contact: Query first. SASE for query and ms. Agented fiction 50%. Reports in 6-8 weeks on queries and mss. Simultaneous and photocopied submissions OK. Accepts computer printouts; letter-quality only.

Terms: Pays in royalties of 10%; advance is negotiable; 10 author's copies; payment depends on grant/award money. Sends galleys to author. Book catalog for 6x9 SASE.

Advice: "We are very interested in seeing first novels from promising writers emerging from writers' workshops who wish to break into serious print. We are also particularly keen to publish the best short story writers we can find."

CORKSCREW PRESS (IV), 2815 Fenimore Rd., Silver Spring MD 20902. (301)933-0407. President: Richard Lippman. Estab. 1988. "Just getting started with first book, but plan to expand *rapidly*." Publishes paperback originals. Published new writers within the past year. Plans 2 first novels this year. Averages 3 total titles each year. Sometimes comments on rejected mss.

Needs: Humor only.

How to Contact: Does not accept unsolicited mss. Submit outline/synopsis with 2 sample chapters. SASE. Reports in 2 months. Simultaneous and photocopied submissions OK. Accepts computer printout submissions, no dot matrix.

Terms: Pays negotiable royalties. Offers negotiable advance. Provides 25 author's copies. Sends galleys to author. Book catalog for #10 SAE and 1 first class stamp.

COTEAU BOOKS (IV), Thunder Creek Publishing Co-operative Ltd., 401-2206 Dewdney Ave., Regina, Saskatchewan S4R 1H3 Canada. (306)352-5346. Managing Editor: Shelley Sopher. Estab. 1975. Small, independent publisher; focus on first-time published works. Publishes hardcover and paperback originals. Books: #2 offset or 60 lb hi-bulk paper; offset printing; perfect and smythe-sewn binding; 4 color illustrations; average print order: 1,500-3,000; first novel print order: approx. 1,500. Plans 1 first novel this year. Publishes 9-11 total titles, 5-6 fiction titles each year. Sometimes comments on rejected mss.

Needs: "We do first novels of unpublished writers, or writers who have published in another genre; dealing with Canadian/prairie issues by Canadian, and preferably western writers." No science fiction. Recently published *The Last India Overland*, by Craig Grant; *Duets*, by Per Brask and George Szanto; *Women of Influence*, by Bonnie Burhard; published fiction by previously unpublished writers within the last year.

How to Contact: Query first, then submit complete ms with cover letter. SASE. Agented fiction 10%. Reports on queries in 2 weeks; on mss in 3 months. Photocopied submissions OK. Accepts computer printout submissions "if they are in good shape."

Terms: "We're a co-operative who receives subsidies from the Canadian, provincial and local governments. We do not accept payments from authors to publish their works." Sends galleys to author. Publishes ms 1-2 years after acceptance. Book catalog free.

Advice: "We publish short-story collections, novels and poetry collections, as well as literary interviews and children's books. This is part of our mandate."

COUNCIL FOR INDIAN EDUCATION (I,IV), 517 Rimrock Rd., Billings MT 59102. (406)252-7451. Editor: Hap Gilliland. Estab. 1963. Small, non-profit organization publishing Native American materials for schools. Publishes hardcover and paperback originals. Books: offset printing; perfect bound or saddle stitched binding; b&w illustrations; average print order: 1,500; first novel print order: 1,500. Published new writers within the last year; plans 3 first novels this year. Averages 5 total titles, 4 fiction titles each year. Usually critiques rejected ms.

Needs: Adventure, ethnic, historical, juvenile (historical, adventure and others), preschool/picture book, regional, western, young adult/teen (easy-to-read, and historical). Especially needs "short novels, and short stories accurately portraying American Indian life past or present—fast moving with high interest." No sex emphasis. Recently published *Sacajawea—A Native American Heroin*, by Martha F. Bryant; *Red Power on the Rio Grande* by Franklin Folsom; *Chief Stephen's Party*, by Ann Chandonnet.
How to Contact: Accepts unsolicited mss. Submit complete ms with SASE. Reports in 3 months. Simultaneous and photocopied submissions OK. Accepts computer printout submissions.
Terms: 10% of wholesale price or 1½¢/word. Sends galleys to author. Free writer's guidelines and book catalog.
Advice: Mostly publishes original fiction in paperback. "Be sure material is culturally authentic and good for the self-concept of the group about whom it is written. If you write about minorities, make sure they are true to the culture and way of life, and that you don't downgrade any group."

CREATIVE ARTS BOOK CO. (II), 833 Bancroft Way, Berkeley CA 94710. (415)848-4777. Imprint: Black Lizard. Editorial Production Manager: Peg O'Donnell. Estab. 1975. Small independent trade publisher. Publishes hardcover originals and paperback originals and reprints. Average print order: 2,500-10,000; average first novel print order: 2,500-10,000. Published new writers within the last year. Plans 3 first novels this year. Averages 30-40 total titles; 20 fiction titles each year.
Needs: Contemporary, erotica (literary), feminist, historical, literary, regional, short story collections, suspense/mystery (Black Lizard Crime Fiction), translations, western. Recently published *Russia*, by Nikos Kazantzakis (first English translation, travel journal/literature); *A Butterfly Net And A Kingdom and other stories*, by Blair Fuller; *Death Puppet*, by Jim Nisbet (A Black Lizard Book).
How to Contact: Accepts unsolicited ms. Submit outline/synopsis and 3 sample chapters (approx. 50 pages). SASE (IRC). 50% of fiction is agented. Reports in 2 weeks on queries; 1 month on mss. Simultaneous and photocopied submissions OK. Accepts computer printout submissions.
Terms: Pays royalties of 6-10%; average advance of $500-1,000; 10 author's copies. Sends galleys to author. Writers guidelines and book catalog for SASE or IRC.

CREATIVE WITH WORDS PUBLICATIONS (II, III), Box 223226, Carmel CA 93922. Editor-in-Chief: Brigitta Geltrich. Estab. 1975. One-woman operation on part-time basis. Books: bond and stock paper; mimeographed printing; saddle stitch binding; illustrations; average print order varies. Publishes paperback anthologies of new and established writers. Averages 2 anthologies each year. *Critiques rejected mss; $10 for short stories; $20 for longer stories, folklore items, $5 for poetry.*
Needs: Humor/satire, juvenile (animal, easy-to-read, fantasy). "Editorial needs center on folkloristic items (according to themes): tall tales and such for biannual anthologies." Needs seasonal short stories appealing to general public; "tales" of folklore nature, appealing to all ages, poetry and prose written by children. Recently published anthologies, "Rural America," "Native Americans" and "The Slavic People." Prose not to exceed 1,000 words.
How to Contact: Accepts unsolicited mss. Query first; submit complete ms with SASE and cover letter. Photocopied submissions OK. Accepts computer printout submissions, prefers letter-quality. Reports in 1 month on queries; 2 months on mss. Publishes ms 1-6 months after acceptance. Writer's guidelines and catalog sheet (2 oz.) for SASE. No simultaneous submissions.
Terms: Pays in 20% reduced author copies.
Advice: Our fiction appeals to general public: children-senior citizens. Follow guidelines and rules of Creative with Words publications and not those the writer feels we should have. We only consider fiction along the lines of folklore or seasonal genres. Be brief, sincere, well-informed and proficient!

CREATIVITY UNLIMITED PRESS (II), 30819 Casilina, Rancho Palos Verdes CA 90274. (213)377-7908. Contact: Rochelle Stockwell. Estab. 1980. One-person operation with plans to expand. Publishes paperback originals and self-hypnosis cassette tapes. Books: perfect binding; illustrations; average print order: 1,000. Averages 1 title (fiction) each year. Average first novel print order 1,000 copies.
Needs: Recently published *Insides Out*, by Shelley Stockwell (plain talk poetry); *Sex and Other Touchy Subjects*, (poetry and short stories).
Advice: Write for more information.

‡CROSS-CULTURAL COMMUNICATIONS (IV), 239 Wynsum Ave., Merrick NY 11566-4725.. (516)868-5635. Editorial Director: Stanley H. Barkan. Estab. 1971. "Small/alternative literary arts publisher focusing on the traditionally neglected languages and cultures in bilingual and multimedia format." Publishes chapbooks, magazines, anthologies, novels, audio cassettes (talking books) and video cassettes (video books, video mags); hardcover and paperback originals. Number of titles in '89: 35. Publishes new women writers series, Holocaust series, Israeli writers series, Dutch writers series, Asian-American writers series.

Needs: Contemporary, literary, experimental, ethnic, humor/satire, juvenile and young adult folktales, and translations. "Main interests: bilingual short stories and children's folktales, parts of novels of authors of other cultures, translations; some American fiction. No fiction that is not directed toward other cultures. For an annual anthology of authors writing in other languages (primarily), we will be seeking very short stories with original-language copy (other than Latin script should be print quality 10/12) on good paper. Title: *Cross Cultural Review Anthology: International Fiction 1.* We expect to extend our *CCR* series to include 10 fiction issues: *Five Contemporary* (Dutch, Swedish, Yiddish, Norwegian, Danish, Yugoslav, Sicilian, Greek, Israeli, etc.) *Fiction Writers.*" Recently published *Sicilian Origin of the Odyssey*, by L.G. Pocock (bilingual English-Italian translations by Nat Scamacca) and *Sikano Americano!* by Nat Scammacca.

How to Contact: Accepts unsolicited mss. Query with SAE with 63¢ postage to include book catalog. "Note: Original language ms should accompany translations." Simultaneous and photocopied submissions "of good quality" OK. Accepts computer printout submissions. Prefers letter-quality. Reports in 1 month.

Terms: Pays "sometimes" 10-25% in royalties and "occasionally" by outright purchase, in author's copies – "10% of run for chapbook series," and "by arrangement for other publications." No advance.

Advice: "Write because you want to or you must; satisfy yourself. If you've done the best you can, then you've succeeded. You will find a publisher and an audience eventually. Generally, we have a greater interest in nonfiction novels and translations. Short stories and excerpts from novels written in one of the traditional neglected languages are preferred – with the original version (i.e., bilingual). Our kinderbook series will soon be in production with a similar bilingual emphasis, especially for folktales, fairy tales, and fables."

THE CROSSING PRESS (II), Box 1048, Freedom CA 95019. Editor: Elaine Gill. Editor, Gay Literature and Literature: John Gill. Publishes paperback and hardcover originals. Books: 50-55 lb offset paper; offset printing; perfect and hardbound binding; illustrations sometimes; average print order: 5,000; first novel print order: 3,500-5,000. Published new writers last year. Estab. 1966.

Needs: Literary, contemporary, cookbooks, feminist, gay/lesbian, herbal books, women's health.

How to Contact: Query with SASE.

Terms: Standard royalty contracts.

Advice: "We are publishing more fiction and more paperbacks. Don't submit first work before showing to very critical friends. Do the necessary research to see which publisher would possibly be interested in your work."

‡HARRY CUFF PUBLICATIONS LTD. (IV), 94 LeMarchant Rd., St. John's, Newfoundland A1C 2H2 Canada. (709)726-6590. Managing Editor: Douglas Cuff. Estab. 1981. "Small regional publisher specializing in Newfoundland." Publishes paperback originals. Books: offset printing; perfect binding; average print order: 1,000; first novel print order: 800. Averages 12 total titles, 1 fiction each year.

Needs: "Either about Newfoundland, or by a Newfoundlander, or both. No mainstream or erotica." Published *The Strange Things of the World*, by Alan Fisk (historical) and *A Fresh Breeze from Pigeon Inlet*, by Ted Russell (humorous short stories).

How to Contact: Accepts unsolicited mss. Submit outline/synopsis and 3 sample chapters. SASE (IRC) necessary for return of ms. Reports in 1 month on queries; 3-5 months on mss. Photocopied submissions OK. Accepts computer printout submissions. Accepts electronic submissions via disk (query first).

Terms: Pays royalties of 10% minimum. Sends galleys to author. Publishes ms 6-18 months after acceptance. Writer's guidelines and book catalog free.

Advice: "I would like to see more good fiction, period, but it *has* to be about Newfoundland or by a Newfoundlander (note that these are entirely discrete categories) I don't want any more mss about the Vietnam War or running a radio station in Kansas City or the like! Our readers will not buy that from us."

‡CURBSTONE PRESS (III), 321 Jackson St., Willimantic CT 06226. Co-Directors: Judy Doyle, Alexander Taylor. Estab. 1975. Number of titles: 6 in 1989. Average first novel print order 3,000 copies. Some editions published simultaneously in paperback and hardcover.

Needs: Contemporary, literary, fiction of social significance, women's, feminist, gay, lesbian, ethnic, and translations. Recently published *Ashes of Izaleo*, by Claribel Alegria and Darwin J. Flakoll; *Anna (I) Anna*, by Klaus Rifbjerg (Danish-novel); and *Beasts*, by Harold Jaffe (short story collection).

How to Contact: Prefers contact through agent; accepts unsolicited mss from writers who have published widely in magazines and literary journals or submit outline/synopsis and sample chapters with SASE. Simultaneous submissions allowable; clear photocopied submissions OK. Accepts letter-quality computer printout submissions. Allow up to 6 months for reports on mss.

Terms: Royalty payment of 12% of net; no advance. Free book catalog.
Advice: "We are looking for good first novels by serious writers. Our authors have usually established a reputation in magazines. We are especially interested in socially engaged work, feminist works or works expressing the struggle for equality and human rights. We also publish translations of contemporary world authors."

DAN RIVER PRESS (I,II), Conservatory of American Letters, Box 88, Thomaston ME 04861. (207)354-6550. President: Robert Olmsted. Fiction Editor: R.S. Danbury III. Estab. 1976. Publishes hardcover and paperback originals. Books: 60 lb offset paper; offset printing; perfect (paperback); hand-sewn (cloth) binding; illustrations; average print order: 1,000; first novel print order: 1,000. Published new writers within the past year. Averages 13-17 total titles; 3 fiction titles each year.
Needs: Adventure, contemporary, experimental, fantasy, historical, horror, humor/satire, literary, mainstream, military/war, psychic/supernatural/occult, regional, science fiction, short story collections, western. "We want good fiction that can't find a home in the big press world. No mindless stuff written flawlessly." Recently published *Looking for the Worm*, by Diana Azar (short stories); *Passengers and Kings*, by Joe Fuoco (short stories).
How to Contact: Accepts unsolicited mss. Reports in 2 weeks. Simultaneous and photocopied submissions OK, plain paper only. Accepts computer printout submissions.
Terms: Pays royalties of 10%. Sends galleys to author. After acceptance, publication "depends on many things (funding, etc.). Probably in six months once funding is achieved." Writer's guidelines for #10 SAE and 2 first class stamps. Book catalog for 6x9 SAE and 2 first class stamps.
Advice: "Submit to us (and any other small press) only when you have exhausted all hope for big press publication. Then, do not expect the small press to be a big press. We lack the resources to do things like 'promotion,' 'author's tours.' These things either go undone or are done by the author. When you give up on marketability of any novel submitted to small press, adopt a different attitude. Become humble, as you get to work on your second/next novel, grow, correct mistakes and develop an audience."

JOHN DANIEL AND COMPANY, PUBLISHERS (I, II), Box 21922, Santa Barbara CA 93121. (805)962-1780. Fiction Editor: John Daniel. Estab. 1980/reestablished 1985. Small publisher with plans to expand. Publishes paperback originals. Books: 55-65 lb book text paper; offset printing; perfect bound paperbacks; illustrations sometimes; average print order: 2,000; first novel print order: 2,000. Plans 2 first novels this year. Averages 10 total titles, 3-4 fiction titles each year. Critiques rejected ms.
Needs: "I'm open to all subjects (including nonfiction)." Literary, mainstream, short story collections. No pornographic, exploitive, illegal, or badly written fiction. Recently published *A Problem of Plumbing and Other Stories*, by James M. Bellarosa; *Lightning in July*, by Ann L. McLaughlin; *The Best of Intentions and Other Stories*, by Artie Shaw; published new writers within the last year.
How to Contact: Accepts unsolicited mss. Query first. SASE. Submit outline/synopsis and 2 sample chapters. Reports in 3 weeks on queries; 2 months on mss. Simultaneous and photocopied submissions OK. Accepts computer printouts.
Terms: Pays in royalties of 10% of net minimum. Sends galleys to author.
Advice: Encourages first novelists. "As an acquiring editor, I would never sign a book unless I were willing to publish it in its present state. Once the book is signed, though, I, as a developmental editor, would do hard labor to make the book everything it could become. Read a lot, write a lot, and stay in contact with other artists so you won't burn out from this, the loneliest profession in the world."

***MAY DAVENPORT PUBLISHERS (I, II, IV)**, 26313 Purissima Rd., Los Altos Hills CA 94022. (415)948-6499. Editor/Publisher: May Davenport. Estab. 1975. One-person operation with independent subcontractors. Publishes hardcover and paperback originals. Books: 65-80 lb paper; off-set printing; perfect binding/saddle stitch/plastic spirals; line drawing illustrations; average print order 500-3,000; average first novel print order: 3,000. Plans 1-3 first novels this year. Averages 3-5 total titles/year (including coloring books/reprints); 2-5 fiction titles/year. Sometimes critiques rejected mss.
Needs: "Overstocked with picture book mss. Prefer drama for junior and senior high students. Don't preach. Entertain!" Recently published *Comic Tale #1*, anthology, May Davenport, editor (short plays and poetry); *Darby's Rainbow*, by James C. McCoy (with short plays and poetry.); *Willy, Zilly and The Little Bantams*, by Grace Collins.
How to Contact: Query first with SASE. 2% of fiction is agented. Reports in 2-3 weeks.
Terms: Pays royalties of 10-15%; no advance. Sends galleys to author. "Partial subsidy whenever possible in advance sales of 3,000 copies, which usually covers the printing and binding costs only. The authors are usually teachers in school districts who have a special book of fiction or textbook relating to literature." Writer's guidelines free with your SASE.
Advice: "If you are print-oriented, remember the TV-oriented are not literate. They prefer visuals and verbalizing to writing. Personal tip: Combat illiteracy by creating material which will motivate children/young adults to enjoy words and actions. Write a play for this junior/senior high age. They

will read anything which they think they can participate in dramatically for themselves."

DAWNWOOD PRESS (II, IV), Fifth Floor, 387 Park Ave. South, New York NY 10016-8810. (212)532-7160. FAX: (212)213-2495. President: Kathryn Drayton. Fiction Editor: John Welch. Estab. 1984. Publishes hardcover originals. Books: 60 lb Lakewood-white paper; offset litho printing; adhesive case binding; average print order: 5,000. Averages 1 fiction title each year.

Needs: Contemporary. "Our needs are taken care of for the next 2 years." No experimental. Recently published *History's Trickiest Questions*, by Paul Kuttner (history); *Tough Questions . . . Amazing Answers*, by Paul Kuttner (non-trivia about science, sports, entertainment, places, literature, art, music); *Forget the Dog! (Beware of Owner!)*, by Paul Kuttner (satire).

How to Contact: Does not accept unsolicited mss. Submit through agent only. Reports in 2 weeks on queries; 2 weeks on mss. Simultaneous and photocopied submissions OK.

Terms: Advance negotiable. Sends galleys to author.

Advice: "Same advice since Dickens's days: Tell a story from the opening sentence in easily understood English, and if you must philosophize do so through action and colloquial dialogue."

‡*DAYSPRING PRESS, INC. (I,II), Box 135, Golden CO 80401. (303)279-2462. Editor: John C. Brainerd. Estab. 1984. "One-person 'little literary' and 'religious' operation on part-time basis; 3 periodicals, tracts and paperbacks." Books: 20# Cascade Bond Xerographic; Photo offset printing; staple, spiral, perfect bound; b&w illustrations; average print order: 1,000; first novel print order: 500. Published new writers within the last year. Plans 2 first novels this year. Plans 3-4 fiction titles this year. Sometimes critiques rejected ms. "I would not reject any material categorically. Purposefully violent, scandalous and pejorative material would have to have very definite counter values.

Needs: Sci-fi, period, and contemporary genre. Recently published *The Final Love Story*, by Bea Halperin; *The Faerie Way*, by Josie Lightman and *The Incorrupti*, by Amanda Crannech.

How to Contact: Accepts unsolicited mss. Submit complete ms with cover letter. Include SASE and Social Security number with submission. Reports in 1 month. Photocopied submissions OK. Accepts computer printout submissions.

Terms: Usually payment, may negotiate. Subsidy publishes 30% of books. Sends galleys to author (books only). Publishes ms 90 days after acceptance. Writer's guidelines for #10 SAE and 1 first class stamp. Book catalog free for 6×9 SAE and 2 first class stamps.

Advice: "I would like to see more poignant trading in the hardcore human issues and less detraction in the trivial."

‡*DEVONSHIRE PUBLISHING CO. (II), Box 85, Elgin IL 60121-0085. (312)242-3846. FAX: (708)879-0308. Vice President: Don Reynolds. Fiction Editor: Robert C. Carr. Estab. 1985. "Publisher of trade paperbacks (5½×8½) with 7 full-time employees, publishes one to two books a year." Publishes paperback originals. Books: 60 or 70 lb bookprint paper; offset printing; perfect binding; photo or pen & ink illustrations; average print order: 5,000; and first novel print order: 5,000. Published 2 new writers within the last year. Plans 1 first novel this year. Averages 2 or 3 titles, 1 fiction title each year. Sometimes comments on rejected ms.

Needs: Contemporary, historical, horror, humor/satire, literary, mainstream, psychic/supernatural/occult, regional, historical romance, science fiction and suspense/mystery. "We would like to do a mystery novel next, then perhaps a horror story." No gay fiction. Published *The Making of Bernie Trumble*, by Bob Wetherall (adult humor); *Narrow Passages*, by Lulu O'Toole (erotica/humor); *Dew of Hermon*, by Janis Fedor (romance/historical/Christian).

How to Contact: Accepts unsolicited mss (*if* accompanied by SASE). Query first, then submit outline/synopsis and 3 sample chapters. SASE. Agented fiction 25%. Reports in 1 month on queries; 2 months on mss. Simultaneous and photocopied submissions OK. Accepts computer printout submissions.

Terms: Pays royalties of 5% minimum; 10-12% maximum. Advance is negotiable. *Subsidy publishes about 20%*. "We have a 'co-op' publishing plan for mss we like but doubt its profitability. If author chooses, we split approximately half the costs for the book's production (1,000 copies) to test the market. If successful, we print more at our expense – usual royalties apply." Sends galleys to author. Publishes ms 1 year after acceptance. Writer's guidelines and catalog for #10 SASE or IRC.

Advice: "Half of our books are by first-timers. The other half is by someone doing their second book after having modest success with some other small publishing company." Writers interested in submitting work should "explain in the query letter why someone will buy the book, what other books exist that are similar, and what the author will do on his/her own to promote the book. We'd like to see more personal computer disks. After accepting a ms, it is infinitely easier for our editors to work on a compatible disk than it is on paper. We would like to see less spelling and grammatical errors. Nothing turns off one of our editors like fundamental errors, or an attitude by the author that our copy editors can make whatever corrections are necessary. It gives the impression of laziness."

DOUBLE M PRESS (II), 16455 Tuba St., Sepulveda CA 91343. (818)360-3166. Publisher: Charlotte M. Stein. Estab. 1975. Small independent press with plans to expand. Publishes hardcover and trade paperback originals. Buys juvenile mss with illustrations. Books: 60 lb white or ivory paper; web press printing; perfect binding; graphics and photographs; average first novel print order 1,000 copies.
Needs: Juvenile (fantasy, historical, contemporary), preschool, inspirational, and young adult (fantasy, historical, problem novels). "We are interested in work that deals with the problems of growth and solving contemporary situations in a 'positive' manner. No degradation, violence, or exploitation of the characters. Strong in imagination."
How to Contact: Accepts unsolicited mss. Query first with outline/synopsis and 2 sample chapters. Reports in 2 weeks on queries; 2 months, if possible, on mss. Photocopied submissions OK. Publishes ms usually within 1 year after acceptance.
Terms: Pays in royalties of 8% minimum. "We do not pay advances."
Advice: "We are gearing up to publish at least 6 titles in 1990."

***DRAGON'S DEN PUBLISHING (II, IV),** 11659 Doverwood Drive, Riverside CA 92505. Imprints include Little Dragon and Double Dragon. President: G. Michael Short. Estab. 1988. Small, full-time press. Publishes hardcover and paperback originals. Books: usually hardcover binding; cover artwork only; average print order 1,000; first novel print order 500-1,000. Plans 1 first novel this year. Sometimes comments on rejected mss; *charges $5.*
Needs: Fantasy, historical, horror, psychic/supernatural/occult, science fiction, short story collections, spiritual, suspense/mystery, young adult (fantasy/science fiction). Needs "novels dealing with the paranormal, extraordinary, etc.; also fantasy (especially sword and sorcery); historical novels dealing with the war periods; realistic horror (e.g. dealing with devil worshippers, witchcraft, voodoo, etc.)." No "fiction giving ESP a bad name; make-overs of Conan; unbelievable horror (such as *Nightmare on Elm Street* or *Friday the 13th*)."
How to Contact: Accepts unsolicited mss. Submit outline/synopsis and 3 sample chapters with SASE. Agented fiction 10%. Reports in 3-4 weeks on queries; 6-9 months on mss. Photocopied submissions OK.
Terms: Pays in royalties of 10-20%. Publishes ms 9 months to 1 year after acceptance. *Subsidy publishes* "only at author's request upon receipt of rejection. Author pays 100% of production cost." Writer's guidelines free for #10 SASE.
Advice: "A cover letter is a must! We need to know the author's background. A résumé is not necessary for fiction. We encourage agented work. Keep cover letters short (no more than a page if possible) but sweet. Do not include your synopsis in your cover letter; keep it separate."

THE ECCO PRESS (II), 26 W. 17th St., New York NY 10011. (212)645-2214. Managing Editor: Lee Ann Chearneyi. Editor: Daniel Halpern. Estab. 1970. Small publisher. Publishes hardcover and paperback originals and reprints. Books: acid-free paper; offset printing; Smythe-sewn binding; occasional illustrations. Averages 25 total titles, 10 fiction titles each year. Average first novel print order 3,000 copies.
Needs: Literary and short story collections. "We can publish possibly one or two original novels a year." No science fiction, romantic novels, western (cowboy). Published: *The Assignation*, by Joyce Carol Oates (stories); *In the Music Library*, by Ellen Hunnicutt; *A Distant Episode*, by Paul Bonles.
How to Contact: Accepts unsolicited mss. Query first especially on novels with SASE. Photocopied submissions OK. Accepts computer printout submissions, prefers letter-quality. Reports in 2 to 3 months, depending on the season.
Terms: Pays in royalties. Advance is negotiable. Writer's guidelines for SASE. Book catalog free on request.
Advice: "We are always interested in first novels and feel it's important that they be brought to the attention of the reading public."

THE EIGHTH MT. PRESS (II), 624 SE 29th Ave., Portland OR 97214. (503)233-3936. Puslisher: Ruth Gundle. Estab. 1984. One-person operation on full-time basis. Publishes paperback originals. Books: acid-free paper, perfect binding; average print order: 5,000. Averages 2 total titles, 1 fiction title, each year.
Needs: Ethnic, feminist, gay, lesbian, literary, short story collections. Published *Cows and Horses*, by Barbara Wilson (feminist/literary).
How to Contact: Accepts unsolicited mss. Query first. SASE. Reports on queries in 2 weeks; on mss in 3 weeks.
Terms: Pays royalties of 8% minimum; 10% maximum. Sends galleys to author. Publishes ms within 1 year of acceptance.

ESOTERICA PRESS (I, II, IV), Also publishes *Notebook: A Little Magazine*, Box 170, Barstow CA 92312-0170. Editor: Ms. Yoly Zentella. Estab. 1983. Two-person operation on a part-time basis. Publishes paperback originals. Books: 50 lb white/neutral paper; offset printing; saddle stitch binding; black and white illustrations and photos; average print order: 200-300; first novel print order: 150-200. Plans more than 1 first novel this year. Averages 1-2 total titles each year. Sometimes comments on rejected ms.

Needs: Contemporary, ethnic (especially Chicano), historical, juvenile (5-9, including: historical), literary, short story collections, translations (Spanish-English/English-Spanish), young adult/teen (10-18 years, including: historical); women's issues. Looking for "fiction, nonfiction based on Latino-American experience, Black-American, Arab-American. No erotic, mystery, frivolity."

How to Contact: Accepts unsolicited mss with SASE. Submit complete ms with cover letter. SASE (IRC) necessary for return of ms. Agented fiction 1%. Reports in 2-3 months on mss. Simultaneous and photocopied submissions OK. Accepts computer printout submissions.

Terms: Provides author's copies. Contract is negotiable. Profits of book are split author/publisher. Sends pre-publication galleys to author. Publishes ms 6 months to 1 year after acceptance. Writer's guidelines and book catalog for #10 SAE and 1 first class stamp.

FABER AND FABER, INC. (I, II), 50 Cross St., Winchester MA 01890. Editor: Betsy Uhrig. Small trade house which publishes literary fiction and collections. Averages 5-10 total titles each year. Recently published *Voices on The Brink*, by Tom Marshall; *Birds of the Innocent Wood*, by Diedre Madden; *Hobson's Island*, by Stefan Themerson.

How to Contact: "Prefer query and one or two sample chapters with SASE for reply. Require synopsis/description – cannot consider ms without this. Many beginning writers make the mistake of submitting entire ms without even a cover letter."

Advice: Looking for "more fiction, more paperbacks due to increasing popularity/acceptance of paperback originals. Use a word processor if at all possible."

FASA CORPORATION (II, IV), 1026 West Van Buren, Chicago IL 60607. Editor: L. Ross Babcock III. "Company responsible for science fiction, adventure games, to include adventures, scenarios, game designs and novels, for an audience high school age and up." Published new writers within the last year.

Needs: Adventure, science fiction. Publishes ms an average of 9 months to 1 year after acceptance. Occasionally critiques or comments on rejected ms. Recommends other markets.

How to Contact: Query first. Reports in 2-6 weeks. Simultaneous and photocopied submissions OK. Accepts computer printout submissions. Accepts electronic submissions via IBM ASCII or MacIntosh disks.

Terms: Pays on publication for all rights. Sends galleys to author.

Advice: "Be familiar with our product and always ask about suitability before plunging into a big piece of work that I may not be able to use."

THE FEMINIST PRESS AT THE CITY UNIVERSITY OF NEW YORK, 311 East 94 St., New York NY 10128. (212)360-5790. Publisher: Florence Howe. Estab. 1970. "Nonprofit, tax-exempt, education organization interested in changing the curriculum, the classroom and consciousness." Publishes hardcover and paperback reprints. "We use a fine quality paper, perfect bind our books, four color covers; and some cloth for library sales if the book has been out of print for some time; we shoot from the original text when possible. We always include a scholarly and literary afterword, since we are introducing a text to a new audience; average print run: 4,000." Publishes no original fiction. Averages 12 total titles/year; 4-6 fiction titles/year (reprints of feminist classics only).

Needs: Contemporary, ethnic, experimental, feminist, gay, historical, lesbian, literary, regional, science fiction, short story collections, translations, women's.

How to Contact: Accepts unsolicited mss. Query first. Submit outline/synopsis and 1 sample chapter. SASE (IRC). Reports in 2 weeks on queries; 2 months on mss. Simultaneous and photocopied submissions OK. Accepts computer printout submissions.

Terms: Pays royalties of 10% of net sales; $100 advance; 10 author's copies. Sends galleys to author. Book catalog free on request.

FIREBRAND BOOKS (II), 141 The Commons, Ithaca NY 14850. (607)272-0000. Contact: Nancy K. Bereano. Estab. 1985. Publishes quality trade paperback originals and reprints. Plans 2 first novels in 1989. Averages 6-8 total titles each year.

Needs: Feminist, lesbian. Recently published *Trash* by Dorothy Allison (short stories); *The Other Sappho*, by Ellen Frye (novel).

How to Contact: Accepts unsolicited mss. Submit outline/synopsis and sample chapters or send complete ms with cover letter. SASE. Reports in 2 weeks on queries; 2 months on mss. Simultaneous and photocopied submissions OK with notification. Accepts computer printouts.

Terms: Pays royalties.

FOUR WALLS EIGHT WINDOWS, Box 548, Village Station, New York NY 10014. (212)226-4998. Co-Publishers: John Oakes/Dan Simon. Estab. 1986. "We are a small independent publisher." Publishes hardcover and paperback originals and paperback reprints. Books: quality paper; paper or cloth binding; illustrations sometimes; average print order: 3,000-5,000; first novel print order: 3,000-5,000. Averages 9 total titles/year; approximately 3-4 fiction titles/year.
Needs: Contemporary, experimental, literary, short story collections, translations. Recently published *And We Sold the Rain: Contemporary Fiction from Central America*, edited by Rosario Santos; *Dyad*, by Michael Brodsky; *A Stone of the Heart*, by Tom Grimes.
How to Contact: "Query letter accompanied by sample chapter and SASE is best. Useful to know if writer has published elsewhere, and if so, where." Accepts unsolicited mss. Submit outline/synopsis and 1 sample chapter. SASE (IRC). 30% of fiction is agented. Reports in 2 months on mss. Simultaneous and photocopied submissions OK. Accepts computer printout submissions.
Terms: Pays standard royalties; advance varies. Sends galleys to author. Book catalog free on request.

‡THE GALILEO PRESS, LTD. (I, II), Subsidiaries or imprints include Sunspot Books. 15201 Wheeler Lane, Sparks MD 21152. (301)771-4544. Publisher: Julia Wendell. Fiction Editor: Jack Stephens. Estab. 1980. "Small independent publisher of poetry, fiction, nonfiction and juvenile with plans to expand." Publishes hardcover and paperback originals. Books: acid free paper; offset printing; Smyth-sewn and perfect binding; 4-color illustrations; average print order: 1,200; first novel print order: 1,200. Published new writers within the last year. Plans 1 first novel this year. Averages 3 total titles, 1 fiction title each year. Occasionally comments on rejected ms; *$10 submission fee*.
Needs: Experimental, literary and short story collections. Recently published *Life in the Middle of the Century*, by John Dranow (two novellas).
How to Contact: Accepts unsolicited mss. Query first. Agented fiction 5%. Reports in 2 weeks on queries; 6 months on mss. Simultaneous and photocopied submissions OK. Accepts computer printout submissions.
Terms: Pays royalties of 10% minimum. Sends galleys to author. Publishes ms 1 year to 15 months after acceptance. Writer's guidelines for SASE or IRC. Free book catalog.

GAY SUNSHINE PRESS AND LEYLAND PUBLICATIONS (IV), Box 40397, San Francisco CA 94140. (415)824-3184. Editor: Winston Leyland. Estab. 1970. Publishes hardcover and paperback originals. Books: natural paper; perfect bound binding; illustrations; average print order: 5,000-10,000.
Needs: Literary, experimental and translations—all gay material only. "We desire fiction on gay themes of *high* literary quality and prefer writers who have already had work published in literary magazines. We also publish erotica—short stories and novels." Recently published *Crystal Boys*, by Pai Hsien-yung (novel).
How to Contact: "Do not send an unsolicited manuscript." Query letter with SASE. Reports in 3 weeks on queries, 2 months on mss.
Terms: Negotiates terms with author. Sends galleys to author. Royalties or outright purchase.
Advice: "We continue to be interested in receiving queries from authors who have manuscripts of high literary quality. We feel it is important that an author know exactly what to expect from our press (promotion, distribution etc.) before a contract is signed. Before submitting a query or manuscript to a particular press, obtain critical feedback from knowledgeable people on your manuscript, e.g. a friend who teaches college English. If you alienate a publisher by submitting a manuscript shoddily prepared/typed, or one needing very extensive re-writing, you will surely not get a second chance with that press."

GOOSE LANE EDITIONS (I, II), 248 Brunswick St., Fredericton, New Brunswick E3B 1G9 Canada. (506)454-8319. General Editor: Peter Thomas. Estab. 1957. Publishes hardcover and paperback originals and hardcover and paperback reprints. Books: illustrations sometimes, average print run: 2,000; first novel print order: 1,500. Averages 12 total titles, 2-4 fiction, each year. Sometimes critiques rejected mss.
Needs: Adventure, contemporary, ethnic, experimental, historical, literary, short story collections. Recently published *A View from the Roof*, by Helen Weinzweig (collected stories); *The Americans are Coming*, by Herb Curtis (first novel); *The Elephant Talks to God*, by Dale Estey, (stories).
How to Contact: Accepts unsolicited mss; complete work, no "samples." Query first. SASE. Reports in 6 weeks. Simultaneous and photocopied submissions OK. Accepts computer printout submissions.
Terms: "*Only mss from Canada considered at this time.*" Pays royalties of 8% minimum; 12% maximum. Average advance: $250, negotiable. Sends galleys to author. Writers guidelines for 9x12 SAE and IRCs.

GRAYWOLF PRESS (III), Box 75006, St. Paul MN 55175. (612)222-8342. Publisher: Scott Walker. Estab. 1974. Growing small press, nonprofit corporation. Publishes hardcover and paperback originals and paperback reprints. Books: acid-free quality paper; offset printing; hardcover and soft binding;

illustrations occasionally; average print order: 3,000-10,000; first novel print order: 2,000-3,000. Averages 12-16 total titles, 6-8 fiction titles each year. Occasionally critiques rejected ms.
Needs: Literary, and short story collections. Published *The Book of Seeing With One's Own Eyes*, Sharon Doubiago; *Blood Line*, David Quammen and *Family: Stories From the Interior*, edited by Geri Giebel Chavis.
How to Contact: Query with SASE. Reports in 2 weeks. Simultaneous and photocopied submissions OK.
Terms: Pays in royalties of 7½% minimum, 10% maximum; negotiates advance and number of author's copies. Sends galleys to author. Writer's guidelines for SASE. Free book catalog.
Advice: Publishing "less fiction, more creative nonfiction, essays, etc."

THE GREEN STREET PRESS (I), Box 1957, Cambridge MA 02238. (508)374-9923. Fiction Editor: Michael Hutcheson. Estab. 1984. Three-person small press with plans to expand. Publishes hardcover and paperback originals and reprints. Books: acid free, high quality paper; average print order: 6,000 copies (paperback); first novel print order: 2,500 copies (hardcover). Plans 2 first novels this year. Averages 10 total titles, all fiction. Occasionally critiques or comments on all rejected mss.
Needs: Contemporary, experimental, literary, regional, short story collections, translations. Published *The Lieutenant*, by André Dubus (reprint); *Into the Silence*, edited by André Dubus (anthology); *The Shallow Grass*, by Tom Horn (reprint).
How to Contact: Accepts unsolicited mss. Submit outline/synopsis and 2 sample chapters with SASE. Reports in 1 month on queries; 4-6 months on mss. Simultaneous and photocopied submissions OK. Accepts computer printout submissions. Accepts electronic submissions via Apple MacIntosh compatible systems.
Terms: Pays royalties of 10% minimum; 15% maximum. Average advance $1,000. Sends galleys to author.
Advice: "I think the most hopeful sign for unpublished fiction writers is the growing acceptance of original paperback publication. The lower financial stakes of this approach may make pubilshers more willing to take a chance with an unpublished writer. The cover letter is a ritualistic form of communication, but an important one. It should be straightforward, honest, and avoid displays of hubris."

GUERNICA EDITIONS (III, IV), 3160 Avenue de Carignan, Montréal, Québec H1N 2Y5 Canada. Editor: Antonio D'Alfonso. Fiction Editor: Umberto Claudio. Estab. 1978. Publishes paperback originals. Books: offset printing; perfect/sewn binding; average print order: 1,000; average first novel print order: 1,000. Plans to publish 1 first novel this year. Publishes 8-10 total titles each year.
Needs: Contemporary, ethnic, literary. Looking for novels about women and ethnic subjects. No unsolicited works. Published *Devour Me Too* by Dacia Mariani; *Talking It Out (the October Crisis)*, by Francis Simard.
How to Contact: Does not accept or return unsolicited mss. Query first. IRC. 100% of fiction is agented. Reports in 6 months. Photocopied submissions OK. Accepts computer printout submissions. Electronic submissions via IBM WordPerfect disks.
Terms: Pays royalty of 10% and 10 author's copies. Book catalog for SAE and $1 postage.
Advice: Publishing "more pocket books."

***MAX HARDY—PUBLISHER (IV)**, Box 28219, Las Vegas NV 89126-2219. (702)368-0379. Contact: Max Hardy. Estab. 1976. Publishes paperback originals. Books: offset printing; perfect binding; illustrations; average print order: 2-3,000; first novel print order: 3,000. Averages 6 total titles each year. Occasionally critiques rejected ms.
Needs: Publishes fiction on bridge only. Published *The Mexican Contract*: by Allan De Serpa (novel); and *Everything's Jake with Me*, by Don Von Elsner (anthology).
How to Contact: Accepts unsolicited mss. Submit complete ms. Simultaneous and photocopied submissions OK.
Terms: Pays in royalties of 10% maximum. "Author pays all expenses; receives 80% of all returns until he recovers 150%—then revert to royalties." Free book catalog.
Advice: "We encourage first novelists. Of our 30+ titles we have 5 novels and 2 anthologies. We consider fiction on bridge only."

‡*HAYPENNY PRESS (I), 211 New St., West Paterson NJ 07424. Estab. 1988. "Small independent publisher with plans to expand." Publishes paperback originals. Books: offset and/or mimeo printing; perfect binding. Published new writers within the last year. Plans 2-4 first novels this year. Averages 2-3 titles (all fiction). Sometimes comments on rejected ms. "No charge for comments . . . *for detailed (separate) critique: $25 (for under 200 pages.)*"

Needs: Contemporary, ethnic, experimental, fantasy, humor/satire, literary, mainstream, military/war, regional, science fiction, short story collections, young adult/teen (10-18 years) easy-to-read and problem novels. No horror, pornography or formula stories. Recently published *Cooper Street*, by P.D. Jordan (Y/A).

How to Contact: Does not accept unsolicited mss. Query first (always!!). Include SASE. Reports in 2 weeks on queries; 1 month on ms. Photocopied submissions OK. Accepts computer printout submissions.

Terms: Pays by "individual arrangement. Cooperative situations possible." Sends galleys to author. Publishes ms up to 1 year after acceptance. Writer's guidelines for #10 SASE and 1 first class stamp.

Advice: Prefer to work with authors who have a specific purpose/market/audience (ie: counselors at runaway shelters; teachers of literacy programs; etc.). The competition in "general" markets is fierce and authors are expected to do all they can to help promote their work. We are open to suggestions/arrangements, if the work merits publication. Y/A writers: project something useful to your teen audience without being "preachy." Others: offbeat, unusual is fine . . . main criteria is to be good/original enough to stand out . . . Please no five-step plots or outlines."

HEART OF THE LAKES PUBLISHING (IV), Box 299, 2989 Lodi Road, Interlaken NY 14847-0299. (607)532-4997. Imprint: Windswept Press, Empire State Books. Editorial Contact Person: Walter Steesy. Estab. 1976. We publish material relating to NY state history and regional studies. Publishes hardcover and paperback originals and hardcover reprints. Books: paper varies; offset printing; perfect and case binding; illustrations; average print order: 1,000; first novel order: 1,000-3,000. Plans 1-2 novels this year. Averages 20-30 titles, 3-5 fiction titles each year. Occasionally critiques or comments on rejected ms.

Needs: Historical, juvenile (5-9 yrs.) historical, regional—New York State. Published new writers within the last year. Recently published *Thistle in Her Hand*, by Diddel; *Towpath*, by Arch Merrill.

How to Contact: Accepts unsolicited mss. Query first or submit outline/synopsis and 1-2 sample chapters. Reports in 1 week on queries. Simultaneous and photocopied submissions OK. Accepts computer printout submissions. Accepts electronic submissions via MS-DOS, ASCII file.

Terms: Pays royalties. Provides 10 author's copies. Sends galleys to author.

Advice: "Windswept Press is a new imprint which includes material of non-New York subject matter. Some of the books under this imprint will be author supported."

***HERITAGE PRESS (II, IV),** Box 18625, Baltimore MD 21216. (301)383-9330. President: Wilbert L. Walker. Estab. 1979. One-man operation, full-time basis; uses contractual staff as needed. Publishes hardcover originals. Books: 60 lb white offset paper; offset printing; sewn hardcover binding; average print order: 2,000; first novel print order: 1,000. Averages 2 total titles, 1-2 fiction titles each year.

Needs: Ethnic (black). Interested in "fiction that presents a balanced portrayal of the black experience in America, from the black perspective. No fiction not dealing with blacks, or which views blacks as inferior." Published *Stalemate at Panmunjon* (the Korean War), and *Servants of All*, by Wilbert L. Walker.

How to Contact: Does not accept unsolicited mss. Query first with SASE. Simultaneous and photocopied submissions OK. Reports in 2 weeks on queries, 2 months on mss. Publishes ms an average of 9 months after acceptance.

Terms: Must return advance if book is not completed or is unacceptable. "*We plan to subsidy publish only those works that meet our standards for approval.* No more than 1 or 2 a year. Payment for publication is based on individual arrangement with author." Book catalog free on request.

Advice: "Write what you know about. No one else can know and feel what it is like to be black in America better than one who has experienced our dichotomy on race." Would like to see new ideas with broad appeal. "First novels must contain previously unexplored areas on the black experience in America. We regard the author/editor relationship as open, one of mutual respect. Editor has final decision, but listens to author's views."

HERMES HOUSE PRESS (II), 39 Adare Place, Northampton MA 01060. (413)584-8402. Imprints include translations. Director: Reuben Mandelblat. Estab. 1980. Small press, few-person operation. Publishes paperback originals and reprints. Books: 70 lb paper; offset printing; paper binding; illustrations; average print order: 1,000; first novel print order: 1,000. Plans 1-2 first novels this year. Averages 2 total titles, 1-2 fiction titles each year. Generally critiques rejected mss.

Needs: Contemporary, experimental, feminist, literary, short story collections, novellas and translations. No sexist, erotica, horror. Recently published *Three Stories*, by R.V. Cassill (short stories), *The Deadly Swarm & Other Stories*, by LaVerne Harrell Clark and *Bella B's fantasy and Other Stories*, by Raymond Jean.

How to Contact: Query first or submit outline/synopsis and 3 sample chapters with SASE. Not currently reading manuscripts. Reports in 3 weeks on queries; 2 months on mss. Photocopied submissions OK. Accepts computer printout submissions. Prefers letter-quality. Publishes ms within 1 year after acceptance.
Terms: Pays in author's copies plus percentage above costs. Sends galleys to author.
Advice: Encourages first novelists. "We regard the author/editor relationship as open communication/free dialogue. Be persistent."

***HOMESTEAD PUBLISHING (I, II)**, Box 227, Moose WY 83012. (406)538-8960. Editor: Carl Schreier. Estab. 1980. Regional publishers for the Rocky Mountains, midsize firm. Publishes hardcover and paperback originals and reprints. Books: natural stock to enamel paper; web, sheet-feed printing; perfect or smythe-sewn binding; b&w or 4-6 color illustrations; average print order: 10,000; first novel print order: 2,000-5,000. Plans 1-2 first novels this year. Averages 8-10 total titles; 1-2 fiction each year. Sometimes critiques rejected mss.
Needs: Historical, juvenile (wildlife, historical), literary, preschool/picture book, short story collection, western, young adult/teen (10-18 years, historical). Looking for "good quality, well written and contemporary" fiction. Published *The Great Plains: A Young Reader's Journal*, by Bullock (children's natural history-adventure).
How to Contact: Accepts unsolicited mss. Query first. SASE. Reports in 1 month. Sends galleys to author. Simultaneous and photocopied submissions OK. Accepts computer printout submissions.
Terms: Pays royalties of 6% minimum; 10% maximum. Provides 6 author's copies. Subsidy publishes "occasionally, depending on project."

‡HYPERION PRESS LIMITED, 300 Wales Ave., Winnipeg Manitoba R2M 2S9 Canada. President: Dr. Marvis Tutiah. Estab. 1977. "Well established small publisher with international distribution." Publishes hardcover and paperback originals. Published new writers within the last year. Plans 1 first novel this year. Averages 11 total titles, 4 fiction titles each year.
Needs: Young adult/teen (10-18 years) historical and spy/adventure. "We need adventure stories for young people." Recently published *The Mysterious Disk*, by Jim Prentice (juvenile adventure); *Sunken Treasure*, by Jim Prentice (juvenile adventure); *The Time Before Dreams*, by Stefan Czernecki and Timothy Rhodes (juvenile tale).
How to Contact: Accepts unsolicited mss. Submit outline/synopsis and sample 3 chapters. SASE. Reports in 1 month on queries; 3 months on mss.
Terms: Pays royalties. Sends galleys to author. Publishes ms 1-2 years after acceptance. Writer's guidelines for 9×4 SAE and 38¢ Canadian or IRC. Book catalog for 9×12 SAE and 76¢ Canadian or IRC.

‡INDEPENDENCE PUBLISHERS INC. (I, II), Box 29905, Atlanta GA 30359. (404)636-7092. Editorial Director: Stanley Beitler. Estab. 1987. Small press. Own printing plant. Publishes hardcover originals. Plans to publish paperback originals, hardcover and paperback reprints in the future. Books: offset, sheetfed printing; case binding; halftone, line illustrations and drawings; first novel print order: 4,500. Published new writers within the last year. Plans 3 total titles, all fiction this year. Rarely critiques rejected ms.
Needs: Contemporary, experimental, fantasy, historical, humor/satire, literary, mainstream, regional, romance, short story collections and translations. Looks for "novels that present the social scene." No horror. Recently published *Appalachian Patterns*, by Bo Ball (short-story collection).
How to Contact: Accepts unsolicited mss. Submit complete ms with cover letter. SASE (IRC) necessary for return of ms. Reports in 2 weeks on queries; 1 month on mss.
Terms: Pays royalties and author's copies. Publishes ms 4 months after acceptance.

INVERTED-A, INC. (II), 401 Forrest Hill, Grand Prairie TX 75051. (214)264-0066. Editors: Amnon or Aya Katz. Estab. 1977. A small press which evolved from publishing technical manuals for other products. "Publishing is a small part of our business." Publishes paperback originals. Books: bond paper; offset printing; illustrations; average print order: 250; first novel print order: 250. Publishes 2 titles a year, in recent years mostly poetry, fiction is now about every other year. Also publishes a periodical *Inverted-A, Horn*, which appears irregularly and is open to very short fiction as well as excerpts from unpublished longer fiction. Comments on rejected mss.
Needs: "We are interested in justice and freedom approached in a positive and romantic perspective." Recently published *The Few Who Count*, by Aya Katz (novel); and *Damned in Hell*, by A.A. Wilson (novella), *Inverted Blake* (collection).
How to Contact: Submit query with sample. SASE. Reports in 6 weeks on queries; 3 months on mss. Simultaneous and photocopied submissions OK. Accepts computer printouts. Accepts electronic submissions via modem or ASCII file on a PC MSDOS diskette. Electronic submission mandatory for final ms of accepted longer work.

Close-up

Austin Wright

Writer

© Art Ranney 1986.

Austin Wright is an award-winning novelist. In 1986, he was one of the first recipients of the $25,000 Whiting Writing Award, which is intended to encourage promising writing talent and to recognize proven writers in the critical stages of their careers. Wright has published three novels, *Camden's Eyes, First Persons,* and *The Morley Mythology* and two books on literary criticism. He is currently putting the finishing touches on his fourth novel.

"I try to write as much as I can as often as I can. During the academic year when I am teaching, I only get to write a couple of days a week." A typical writing day starts after breakfast and will continue until six or seven at night or until he's called to dinner. "Those are the good days when I can do that," Wright says, "I find that on this typical sort of day, I may start out very slowly, spend a lot of time beginning and not getting very far; the steam sort of develops in the afternoon."

Wright does not work in the evening. "I set that up as a rule a few years ago for my health's sake. I used to write late at night, smoking cigarettes, and that was bad for me."

According to Wright, his favorite part of writing is rewriting. He describes it as a three-tiered process. "I go through the chapter and rewrite as I go. When I have a draft of the entire book, I read through the manuscript and make notes. Then I go through it again, rewriting." The final tier is stylistic editing in which he makes sure sentence structure, grammar and form are appropriate to the text.

When rereading the draft, Wright says he tries to imagine somebody else reading his work. He tries to assess whether it reads smoothly, moves well, and is interesting, as well as if it is accomplishing what he intended the work to do.

"Education," Wright tells aspiring writers, "is important. I'm not talking about writing courses. I think those might be useful to some people, but I don't think they are necessary. Reading is necessary, and so is some knowledge of the world—I think a general liberal education. I think an educated person should know something about science." Wright also recommends that writers get responses and criticism from people they respect. This could include an editor or agent, if they have one.

Wright has had positive experiences with the agents who have represented him. "I think an agent helps. They save you a certain amount of tediousness. [They] buffer some of the pain. If you have an agent, it gives you a feeling of security that you perhaps don't have without an agent."

—Judith A. Mills

Terms: We do not pay except for author copies. Sends galleys to author. For current list send SAE and 1 first class stamp.
Advice: "Deal with more than personal problems. Project hope."

INTERTEXT (III), 2633 E. 17th Ave., Anchorage AK 99508. Editor: Sharon Ann Jaeger. Estab. 1982. Independent publisher. Publishes hardcover and paperback originals. Books: pH-neutral paper; offset printing; smythe-sewn and perfect bound binding; illustrations sometimes; occasionally do 4-color covers; average print order: 1,000; first novel print order: 1,000. "We publish writers of excellence and accomplishment only." Averages 1-3 titles each year. No longer able to critique rejected mss. No longer takes on first-timers.
Needs: Literary, short story collections and translations. "We are presently concentrating on poetry, translations and literary criticism, together with selected (and solicited) titles in the fine arts."
How to Contact: Query by first-class mail with sample chapter and SASE. Do not send unsolicited complete mss. Reports in 2 months on queries; 6 months on mss. Simultaneous queries and photocopied submissions OK.
Terms: Pays 10% royalties after all costs of printing, promotion and distribution are met. Sends galleys to author. Writer's guidelines for SASE.
Advice: "A novel has to be very extraordinary indeed – truly compelling, with exquisite craftsmanship and a powerful and poetic style – for us to consider it. Get a variety of experience. Learn about people. Don't be (or at least sound) self-centered. Revise, revise, revise. We are not a market for the beginning writer, but would recommend to new writers to revise ruthlessly, to cut all unnecessary exposition – to make things *happen*, more 'show' than 'tell.' "

‡ISLAND HOUSE (IV), 731 Treat Ave., San Francisco CA 94110. (415)826-7113. Imprints include Cottage Books. Senior Editor: Susan Sullivan. Fiction Editor: Pat Healy. Estab. 1987. "Small Press, four person, full time." Publishes paperback originals. Books: acid free paper; offset printing; perfect binding; average print order: 2-3,000. Published new writers within the last year. Averages 3 total titles, 2 fiction titles each year. Sometimes comments on rejected ms; *$75 charge for critiques*.
Needs: Ethnic, experimental, faction, literary and short story collections. Looking for Irish-Celtic themes and quality. Recently published *The West*, by Ed Stack (short stories).
How to Contact: No unsolicited mss. Query first. Agented fiction 50%. Reports in 2 weeks on queries; 3 months on mss. Simultaneous and photocopied submissions OK. Accepts computer printout submissions.
Terms: Pays royalties of 6% minimum; 10% maximum; offers negotiable advance. Sends galleys to author. Publishes ms 6-9 months after acceptance. Book catalog free.

ITALICA PRESS (IV), #605, 595 Main St., New York NY 10044. (212)935-4230. Publishers: Eileen Gardiner and Ronald G. Musto. Estab. 1985. Small independent publisher. Publishes paperback originals. Books: 50-60 lb natural paper; offset printing; smythe-sewn binding; illustrations; average print order: 1,000. "First time translators published. We would like to see translations of well-known Italian writers in Italy who are not yet translated for an American audience." Publishes 6 total titles each year; 3 fiction titles. Sometimes critiques rejected mss.
Needs: Translations from Italian. Looking for "six novels over next two years – particularly translations of 20th Century Italian literature." Recently published *Woman at War*, by Dacia Maraini and *New Italian Women*, edited by Martha King (short story collection).
How to Contact: Accepts unsolicited mss. Query first. Reports in 3 weeks on queries; 2 months on mss. Simultaneous and photocopied submissions OK. Accepts computer printout submissions. Electronic submissions via Macintosh or IBM-PC disk.
Terms: Pays in royalties of 5-15% and 10 author's copies. Sends pre-publication galleys to author. Book catalog free on request.

JAYELL ENTERPRISES (IV), Box 2616, Dearborn MI 48124. (313)565-9687. President: James L. Limbacher. Estab. 1983. One-person operation on a part-time basis; also produces TV cable programs. Publishes paperback originals. Books: average print order: 500. Averages 1 fiction title each year. Sometimes comments on rejected mss; *$50 charge for critiques*.
Needs: Historical. No "badly written, amateurish works."
How to Contact: Does not accept unsolicited mss. Query first. Reports in 3 weeks on queries; in 1 month on mss. Photocopied submissions OK. Accepts computer printout submissions.
Terms: Pays royalties of 25% minimum. Provides 6 author's copies. Sends galleys to author.
Advice: Publishing "less fiction. Nonfiction sells better."

KAR-BEN COPIES, INC. (II), 6800 Tildenwood La., Rockville MD 20852. (301)984-8733. President: Judye Groner. Estab. 1974. Small publisher specializing in juvenile Judaica. Publishes hardcover and paperback originals. Books: 70-80 lb patina paper; offset printing; perfect and case binding; 2-4 color illustrations; average print order: 5,000-10,000. Averages 8-10 total titles, 6-8 fiction titles each year. Published new writers within the last year.

Needs: Juvenile (3-10 years). Recently published *Rachel and Mischa*, by Steve and Ilene Bayar; *Grandma's Soup*, by Nancy Karkowsky; *Mommy Never Went to Hebrew School*, by Mindy Portnoy.

How to Contact: Accepts unsolicited mss. SASE. Submit outline/synopsis and sample chapters or complete ms with cover letter. SASE. Reports in 1 week on queries; 1 month on mss. Simultaneous and photocopied submissions OK. Accepts computer printouts.

Terms: Pays in royalties of 5% minimum; 10% maximum; average advance: $500; 12 author's copies. Sends galleys to author. Writer's guidelines free for SASE. Book catalog free on request.

KITCHEN TABLE: WOMEN OF COLOR PRESS (II, IV), Box 908, Latham NY 12110. Publisher: Barbara Smith. Estab. 1981. "Independent press with several paid employees, very good distribution." Publishes paperback originals. Books: 50 lb stock paper; offset/web press printing; perfect binding; some b&w graphic elements/designs; average print order: 5,000; first novel print order: 3,000. "All of our books are trade paperbacks, a few of which are bound for libraries." Averages 2 total titles each year; 1 fiction title every two years. Occasionally critiques rejected ms.

Needs: Ethnic, feminist, lesbian, literary, short story collections. Needs for novels include novels by women of color–authors that reflect in some way the experiences of women of color. "We are looking for high quality, politically conscious writing and would particularly like to hear from American Indian women fiction writers." Has published *Cuentos: Stories by Latinas*, edited by Alma Gómez, Cherrie Moraga; Mariana Romo-Carmona (short story anthology with selections in both English and Spanish).

How to Contact: Accepts unsolicited mss. Query first. Submit outline/synopsis and 3 sample chapters. SASE. Reports in 1 month on queries; 6 months on mss. Simultaneous and photocopied submissions OK.

Terms: Pays in royalties of 8% minimum; 10% maximum and 10 author's copies. Sends galleys to author. Book catalog for 2 first class stamps.

Advice: "One of the most common mistakes that our press tries to address is the notion that the first work a writer publishes should be a book as opposed to a submission to a periodical. Periodicals serve as a very valuable apprenticeship for a beginning writer. They should submit work to appropriate literary and other kinds of journals that publish fiction. By appropriate I mean appropriate for the kind of writing they do. Getting published in periodicals gives the writer experience and also creates a 'track record' that may interest the prospective book publisher."

KNIGHTS PRESS (II, IV), Box 454, Pound Ridge NY 10576. (203)969-1699. Publisher: Elizabeth G. Gershman. Estab. 1983. Small press publishing only gay male fiction and non-fiction. Publishes trade paperback originals. Published new writers in the last year. Plans 4 first novels this year. Averages 12 total titles each year.

Needs: "Fiction must have a gay theme (not lesbian or non-gay). We publish on merit, not category." No erotica. Recently published *Boys In the Bars*, by Christopher Davis; *To Indigo Dust*, by Tim Barrus; *Gentle Warriors*, by Geoff Mains.

How to Contact: Accepts unsolicited mss. Query first. SASE. Agented fiction: 25%. Reports in 3 weeks on queries; 3 months on mss. No simultaneous submissions. Photocopied submissions OK. Accepts computer printouts.

Terms: Pays in royalties of 10% minimum; average advance: $500. Sends galleys to author. Writer's guidelines free for #10 SASE and 1 first class stamp. Book catalog free on request, with #10 envelope, SAE, 45¢ stamp.

Advice: "Write about people, places, events you know. Then plot, plot, plot. Story must have a positive gay lifestyle or relationship. Consider that a book costs money to buy and to produce. Would *you* spend your money to read your submission? Would you spend thousands of dollars to produce it? If you wouldn't, neither would the book buyer or the publisher."

KNOLL PUBLISHING CO., INC. (II), 831 W. Washington Blvd., Ft. Wayne IN 46802. (219)426-1926 or (219)422-7774. Publisher: Joseph Laiacona. Estab. 1986. Small, independent, human potential publisher. Publishes paperback originals and reprints. Books: Offset printing; perfect binding; illustrations; average print order: 3,000. Averages 4 total titles, 1 fiction title each year. Sometimes comments on rejected mss.

Needs: Psychic/supernatural/occult, religious/inspirational. Looking for mss on "human potential only."

How to Contact: Does not accept or return unsolicited mss. Submit outline/synopsis with 1 sample chapter. Reports on queries in 2 weeks; on mss in 2 months. Simultaneous and photocopied submissions OK. Accepts computer printouts.

Terms: "Wildly negotiable." Provides 10 author's copies. Sends galleys to author. Book catalog free.

KRUZA KALEIDOSCOPIX, INC. (IV), Box 389, Franklin MA 02038. (508)528-6211. Editor/President: J.A. Kruza. Fiction Editor: R. Burbank. Estab. 1976. Publishes hardcover and paperback originals. Books: 60-80 lb coated paper; offset printing; saddle and perfect binding; illustrations; average print order: 10,000. Averages 12 total titles each year. Sometimes critiques rejected mss.
Needs: Historical (nautical); juvenile (5-9 yrs.) including: animal, lesson teachings about work ethic, historical. "Stories for children, ages 3-7, with problem and characters who work out solution to problem, i.e. work ethic." Published *A Candle For Boo*, by Beth Cox (children's giant story); *The Greedy Dinosaur*, by Terry Barnhill (dino gets stuck in mud); and *The Long Sleep*, by Dorothy L. Blackman (bear loses reading glasses that he must earn back).
How to Contact: Accepts and returns unsolicited mss. Submit complete ms with cover letter. SASE. Reports in 3 weeks on queries; 3 months on mss. Simultaneous and photocopied submissions OK. Accepts computer printout submissions, no dot-matrix.
Terms: *Charges $3 reading fee.* Pays in royalties of 3% minimum; 5% maximum, "or flat fee, depending on strength of story. Length of royalties are usually limited to a specific time, usually 4 to 7 years." Provides 10 author's copies. Writer's guidelines for #10 SAE with 1 first class stamp.

KUBICEK & ASSOCIATES (I,II), Suite 202C, 3701 O St., Box 30269, Lincoln NB 68503-0269. (402)435-4607. President: David Kubicek. Estab. 1988. "We're a small company (3 people) with ambitious plans for expansion over the next few years." Publishes paperback originals. Books: normally 60 lb paper; photo offset printing; usually perfect binding; illustrations (depending on book); average print order: 1,000; first novel print order: 1,000 "unless it's an exceptional novel." Published new writers within the last year. Plans 1 first novel by previously unpublished writers this year. Plans 5 total titles, 3 fiction titles this year. Sometimes critiques rejected mss.
Needs: Fantasy, horror, psychic/supernatural/occult, regional (midwest), science fiction. No romance (the genre—we like to see some romance in our books, when it's done intelligently), pornography, sword and sorcery. Published *The Pelican in the Desert: And Other Stories of the Family Farm*, edited by David Kubicek (anthology of short stories); and *October Dreams*, edited by David Kubicek and Jeff Mason (anthology of horror/supernatural stories).
How to Contact: Accepts unsolicited mss. Query first with outline/synopsis and 1-3 sample chapters. Include social security number with submission. Reports on queries in 3-4 weeks; on mss in 6-8 weeks. Photocopied submissions OK. No dot-matrix computer printouts.
Terms: Pays royalties of 10-15%; at least 10 author's copies; discount on additional copies. Sends galleys to author. Publishes ms 9-18 months after acceptance. Writers guidelines for #10 SAE and 1 first class stamp.
Advice: "Our marketing program is flexible; if we find something we like and think we can sell it, we'll publish it. Our interests range from genre like science fiction to mainstream, but science fiction and horror have the best chance. We like writing that creates a strong mood and evokes an emotional reaction from the readers, writing by writers who enjoy working with the language."

***LIBRA PUBLISHERS, INC. (II)**, 3089C Clairemont Dr., Suite 383, San Diego CA 92117. (619)581-9449. President: William Kroll. Estab. 1960. Small independent publisher. Hardcover and paperback originals. Books: 60 lb offset paper; offset printing; hardcover—smyth sewn binding; paperback—perfect binding; illustrations occasionally; average print order 3,000; first novel print order 1,000+. Plans to publish 3 first novels this year. Averages approximately 15 titles/year; 3-4 fiction titles/year.
Needs: "We consider all categories." Published *All God's Children*, by Alex LaPerchia (inspirational); *Seed of the Divine Fruit*, by Enrico Rinaldi (multi-generational about found of Atlantic City); and *Caveat Emptor*, by William Attias (racist takeover of a city).
How to Contact: Accepts unsolicited mss. Send complete ms with cover letter. SASE. Reports on queries in 1 week; on mss in 2-3 weeks. Simultaneous and photocopied submissions OK. Computer printout submissions OK.
Terms: Pays 10-40% royalties. Send pre-publication galleys to author. Publishes ms an average of 6-12 months after acceptance. Book catalog fro SASE with 5 first class stamps.
Advice: "Libra publishes nonfiction books in all fields, specializing in the behavioral sciences. We also publish two professional journals: *Adolescence* and *Family Therapy*. We have published fiction on a royalty basis but because of the difficulty in marketing works by unknown writers, we are not optimistic about the chances of offering a standard contract. However, we shall contiue to consider fiction in the hope of publishing on a standard basis book that we like and believe have good marketing potential. In addition, our procedure is as follows: Manuscripts we do not consider publishable are returned to the author. When we receive manuscripts which we feel are publishable but are uncertain of the marketability, we suggest that the author continue to try other houses. If they have already done so and are interested in self-publishing, we offer two types of services: (1) we provide editing, proofreading, books and cover design, copyrighting and production of the book; copies are then shipped to the author. (2) We provide these services plus promotion and distribution. In all cases, the problems and risks are spelled out."

LIBRARY RESEARCH ASSOCIATES, INC. (IV), RD. 5, Box 41, Dunderberg Rd., Monroe NY 10950. Imprints include Lloyd-Simone Publishing Co., Willow Tree Press and Criminal Justice Press. Editorial Director: Matilda A. Gocek. Estab. 1968. Publishes hardcover and paperback originals. Books: 50 lb paper; narrow web offset printing; perfect bound hardcover binding; b&w half-tones, line drawings; average print order: 3,500; first novel print order: 1,500. Published 2 new writers within the last year.
Needs: New York State based, fictional biographies or historical events. Recently published *Solarian Chronicles One,* by Michael Bell.
How to Contact: Accepts unsolicited mss. Submit outline/synopsis and sample chapters with SASE. No simultaneous submissions; photocopied submissions OK. Accepts computer printout submissions, prefers letter-quality. Reports in 10 weeks. Publishes ms 12-14 months after acceptance.
Terms: Pays in royalties; no advance. Sends galleys to author. Book catalog for #10 SASE.
Advice: "There is a gradual return to a good story line less dependent upon violence and explicit sex. I am looking to develop our line of Empire State Fiction. Fictionalized biographies based on fact would be welcomed, particularly of women in New York, any period. Prepare clean, double-spaced manuscripts—one-page outline or abstract is most helpful. I want to develop *new authors* so I work willingly with them." Publishing less fiction because it's "hard to generate sales."

LINCOLN SPRINGS PRESS (II), Box 269, Franklin Lakes NJ 07417. Editor: M. Gabriel. Estab. 1987. Small, independent press. Publishes poetry, fiction, photography, high quality. Publishes paperback originals. Books: 65 lb paper; offset printing; perfect binding; average print order: 1,000. "Prefers short stories, but will publish first novels if quality high enough." Averages 4 total titles/year; 2 fiction titles.
Needs: Contemporary, ethnic, experimental, feminist, historical, literary, short story collections. No "romance, Janet Dailey variety." Recently published *Maybe It's My* , by Abigail Stone (novel); *The KGB Solution at Katyn*, by Maurice Shoenbert (memoir).
How to Contact: Accepts unsolicited mss. Query first with 1 sample chapter. SASE. Reports in 2 weeks-3 months. Simultaneous and photocopied submissions OK. Accepts computer printouts.
Terms: Authors receive royalties of 5% minimum; 15% maximum "after all costs met." Provides 10 author's copies. Sends galleys to author. Book catalog for SASE.

LINTEL (II), Box 8609, Roanoke VA 24014. Editorial Director: Walter James Miller. Estab. 1977. Two-person organization on part-time basis. Books: 90% opaque paper; photo offset printing; perfect binding; illustrations; average print order: 1,000; first novel print order: 1,200. Publishes hardcover and paperback originals. Occasionally comments on rejected mss.
Needs: Experimental, short fiction, feminist, gay, lesbian, and regional. Recently published second edition (fourth printing) of *Klytaimnestra Who Stayed at Home*, mythopoeic novel by Nancy Bogen; and *The Mountain,* by Rebecca Rass.
How to Contact: Accepts unsolicited mss. Query with SASE. Simultaneous and photocopied submissions OK. Accepts computer printout submissions. Prefers letter-quality. Reports in 1 month on queries, 2 months on mss. Publishes ms from 6-8 months after acceptance.
Terms: Negotiated. No advance. Sends galleys to author. Free book catalog.
Advice: "Lintel is devoted to the kinds of literary art that will never make The Literary Guild or even the Book-of-the-Month Club: that is, literature concerned with the advancement of literary art. We still look for the innovative work ignored by the commercial presses. We consider any ms on its merits alone. We encourage first novelists. Be innovative, advance the *art* of fiction, but still keep in mind need to reach reader's aspirations as well as your own. Consistent misspelling errors, errors in grammar and syntax can mean only rejection."

LOLLIPOP POWER BOOKS (II), Box 277, Carrboro NC 27510. (919)376-8152. Editors: Judy Hogan, Caroline Wren. Estab. 1970. New children's division of the Carolina Wren Press; publishes non-sexist, multi-racial "alternative" children's books. Publishes paperback originals. Buys juvenile mss with or without illustrations. Averages 1 title (fiction) each year. Average first book run 2,500 copies. Usually critiques rejected ms "unless completely inappropriate submission for our purpose."
Needs: Juvenile. "We are currently looking for well written stories with strong plots which deal with issues of race or sex-role stereotyping or with contemporary family problems, especially divorce. We would like to see ms about a realistic black child or family or ms dealing with handicapped children." Recently published *Brother's Keeper, Sister's Child* by Margaret Stephens; *Love, or a Reasonable Facsimile,* by Gloree Rogers; *The Boy Toy,* by Phyllis Johnson.
How to Contact: Query first for author guidelines and book catalog with SASE. Reports in 2 weeks on queries; 6 weeks on mss. Simultaneous and photocopied submissions OK. Publishes ms from 6 months to 1 year after acceptance.

Terms: Pays royalties of 10%.
Advice: "Know what the publisher's specialty is. Though we want books with a strong message, we also want strong and appealing characters, and plots which children will want to return to again and again."

‡HENDRICK LONG PUBLISHING CO. (IV), Box 25123, Dallas TX 75225. (214)368-4677. Vice President: Joann Long. Estab. 1969. "Independent publisher focusing on Texas material geared primarily to a young audience. (K through high school). Cornerstone of company is a Texas history seventh grade textbook (state adopted)." Publishes hardcover and paperback originals and hardcover reprints. Books: average print order: 2,000 (except textbooks which have a much longer run.) Published new writers within the last year. Averages 8 total titles, 4 fiction titles each year. Sometimes comments on rejected ms.
Needs: Historical, juvenile animal-Texas and historical, regional and young adult/teen (10-18 years) historical. "No material not suitable for junior high/high school audience." Recently published *Great Texas Scare*, by Jones (juvenile and YA); *Davy's Dawg* by Matthews/Hurlburt (juvenile and YA); *Tilli Comes to Texas*, by Oppenheimer (Christmas fantasy).
How to Contact: Accepts unsolicited queries, (but prefer query. Query first or submit outline/synopsis and sample chapters (at least 2—no more than 3). SASE necessary for return of ms. Reports in 2 weeks on queries; 1 month on ms. Photocopied submissions OK. Accepts computer printout submissions.
Terms: Offers negotiable advance. Sends galleys to author. Publishes ms 1 year after acceptance. Writer's guidelines for SASE and $1. Book catalog for $1.

‡LOS HOMBRES PRESS (II,IV), Box 15428, San Diego CA 92115. (619)576-0104. Publisher: James D. Kitchen. Estab. 1989. Small publisher-plan to do 4 books in 1990. Publishes paperback originals. Books: 60# paper; offset printing; perfect binding; average print order: 2,000; first novel print order: 2,000. Published new writers within the last year. Plans 2 first novels this year. Averages 4-5 total titles, 3-4 fiction titles each year. Sometimes comments on rejected mss.
Needs: Gay. "Gay novels including mainstream, literary, science fiction, mystery, fantasy, futuristic, adventure. Open to most categories with a gay theme; short story collections." No men's action, pornography. Recently published *Love Theme with Variations*, by Marsh Cassady (Gay-mainstream); *Silverfinch*, by Pat Colley (gay-futuristic); and *The Search for Sebastion*, by Judston Crown (gay-comedy-adventure).
How to Contact: Accepts unsolicited mss. Query first or submit 3 sample chapters. SASE; include social security number with submission. Agented fiction 50%. Reports in 2 weeks; mss in 2 months. Simultaneous and photocopied submissions OK. Computer printout submissions are acceptable.
Terms: Pays 10-15% royalties and 10 author's copies. Sends galleys to author. Publishes ms 1 year after acceptance. Writer's guidelines for #10 SASE and 1 first class stamp.

LTD. EDITION PRESS (I, II), 4725 Conowingo Rd., Darlington MD 21034. (301)836-3715. Imprint: Penny Paper Novels. Publisher: Fern Smith-Brown. Estab. 1980. "Small publishers, but we are expanding every year." Publishes paperback and hardcover originals and "tabloid size novels distributed through motels, convenience stores and various businesses." Books: Newsprint paper; web offset print; minimal illustrations; average print order: 20,000-100,000 for Penny Paper Novels. Plans 24 first novels this year; "most of our writers are new, having published only short stories." Publishes 30 total titles each year; all fiction. Sometimes critiques rejected ms. Some of our novels are printed in conventional soft cover books for selected distribution.
Needs: Adventure, historical, romance (contemporary, historical), gothics, suspense/mystery, western. Wants to see "fast moving, easy to read novels suitable for men and women from all walks of life. Nothing any member of a family can't read. 30,000-40,000 words preferred. No explicit sex or violence." Recently published *The Marker,* by Leichton D. Brackett; *The Aristocrat and the Urchin,* by Fern Smith-Brown; *Whispering Winds,* by Elizabeth Belland; published fiction by previously unpublished writers within the last year.
How to Contact: Submit complete ms with cover letter. SASE. Reports in 6 weeks. Simultaneous submissions OK. *Ms will not be returned if SASE not included.*
Terms: "We purchase manuscript outright. Amount depends on manuscript and how much editing is required. Differs with each ms and author." Writer's guidelines for #10 SAE and 1 first class stamp. "Book catalog not available but we will send sample of published Penny Paper Novels for perspective writers to peruse if 9×12 SASE and $3 to cover cost is sent."
Advice: "We are an excellent place for new writers to start. We have the readers and we take the time to guide and lend tips. We're a good place to sharpen their craft! Penny Paper Novels are intended for a 'quick read' in a fast-paced society."

LUCKY HEART BOOKS (I), (formerly Salt Lick Press), Subsidiary of Salt Lick Foundation, 1804 E. 38½ St., Austin TX 78722. Imprint: Lucky Heart Books. Editor/Publisher: James Haining. Estab. 1969. Small press with significant work reviews in several national publications. Publishes paperback originals and reprints. Books: offset/bond paper; offset printing; stitch, perfect bound; illustrations; average print order: 500; first novel print order: 500. Sometimes comments on rejected mss.
Needs: Open to all fiction categories.
How to Contact: Accepts unsolicited mss. SASE. 1% of fiction is agented. Reports in 2 weeks on mss. Photocopied submissions OK. Accepts computer printout submissions.
Terms: Pays 10 author's copies. Sends pre-publication galleys to author.

MAINESPRING PRESS (II), Maine Writers Workshop, Box 905, R.F.D, Stonington ME 04681. Also publishes *Letters* Magazine. (207)367-2484. Editor: Helen Nash. Midsize independent publisher. Publishes hardcover and paperback originals. Books: 20 lb paper; photo offset printing; perfect binding; average print order: 2,000-5,000; first novel print order: 3,000. Published new writers within the last year; plans 1 first novel each year. Averages 3 titles, 1 fiction title each year. Average first novel print order 5,000 copies. Always critiques good rejected ms; sometimes charges to critique more than 1 sample chapter. Query first on complete book.
Needs: Contemporary, historical, literary, and science fiction. Recently published *Windfall Poems* and *Born to Die*, by H.G. Woods; *Truth Fairy*, by G. F. Bush.
How to Contact: Accepts unsolicited mss with large SASE. Submit outline/synopsis and first, middle and last chapters to 50 pages. Complete ms on request. Reports in 1 month. No simultaneous submissions; legible photocopied submissions OK. Accepts computer printout submissions, no dot-matrix.
Terms: Pays in usual royalties, 15% maximum. Always cash, not copies, for all rights. Writer's guidelines for SASE.

MELIOR PUBLICATIONS (IV), Division of Futurepast: The History Company, W. 1727 14th Ave., P.O. Box 1905, Spokane WA 99210-1905. (509)455-9617. President: John C. Shideler. Estab. 1986. Small independent press, mostly nonfiction but interested in quality fiction of a historical or regional nature. Books: acid-free book stock; photo offset printing on cut-sheet press; hardcover, smythe-sewn or perfect binding; illustrations sometimes; first novel print order: "probably 2,500." Plans 1 first novel this year. Publishes 4-5 total titles/year; bringing out first fiction title this year.
Needs: Historical, regional. "Well-written historical or regional (Pacific Northwest) works are the only ones we're currently considering. Strong stories get our attention. We especially welcome good women's history and ethnic history, but it has to be a good story, not a soapbox." Published *Fireweed: An American Saga*, by Nellie Burton Picken (historical/regional).
How to Contact: Accepts unsolicited mss. Submit outline/synopsis, 5 sample chapters and cover letter with SASE. Reports on queries in 1 month; on mss in 4-6 months. Simultaneous and photocopied submissions OK. Accepts dot-matrix computer printouts if "readable."
Terms: Royalties negotiated on individual basis. Sends galleys to author. Publishes ms 9 months-1 year after acceptance. Writer's guidelines for #10 SASE. Book catalog for 9×12 envelope and 65¢ postage.
Advice: "We are just bringing out our first fiction—the future depends a great deal on the quality and quantity of submissions. We encourage first novelists if they're willing to put time into rewrites, accept some coaching and editing, and understand that the demands of the marketplace as well as literary value must be part of our decision-making process. We're eager to develop ongoing relationships with writers. We recognize that we can't compete with New York royalties and advances, but feel that the personal attention we give to each and every title more than makes up for this for a first novelist. Do market research—do works of this type do well? What's the audience? Be realistic—we're a small press and probably won't do a first print run of 20,000 and send you to Donahue and Oprah. Above all, write well, with vivid power and imagination—set us on fire."

***METAMORPHOUS PRESS (IV),** 3249 NW 29th Ave., Portland OR 97210. Publisher: David Balding. Fiction Editor: Lori Stephens. Estab. 1982. General trade book publisher and distributor to the trade for other publishers with compatible titles. Publishes hardcover and paperback originals and paperback reprints. Books: white 55 lb paper; sewn, case, perfect or paper binding; average print order: 2,000-5,000; first novel print order: 2,000. Plans 2 first novels this year. Averages 12 total titles, 2 fiction titles each year. Sometimes critiques rejected mss.
Needs: Humor/satire; juvenile (animal, easy-to-read, fantasy, historical, sports, spy/adventure, contemporary); young adult/teen; problem novels. "We look for works that respect the notion that we create our own reality. Works that generally provide the reader tools to gain better control over their personal lives work well for us." Published new writers within the last year.
How to Contact: Accepts unsolicited mss. Query first with outline. SASE. Reports in 3 months on queries; 6 months on mss. Simultaneous and photocopied submissions OK. Accepts computer printout submissions.

Terms: Pays royalties of 10% minimum; 15% maximum. Pays in 10 author's copies. Sends galleys to author. *Subsidy publishes 10% of books.* "Author can increase royalty percent by contributing toward the production cost." Book catalog free on request.
Advice: "Publishing more fiction in an attempt to diversify, but careful to be consistent with statement of purpose. Our editorial staff is a resource to the author. Our policy is to have the author centrally involved to maintain their high energy for their work."

‡*MEY-HOUSE BOOKS (II), Box 794, Stroudsburg PA 18360. (717)646-9556. Editorial contact person: Ted Meyer. Estab. 1983. One-person operation part-time with plans for at least two novels shortly. Publishes hardcover and paperback originals. Averages 1 title/year. Occasionally critiques or comments on rejected ms, "cost varies."
Needs: Adventure, contemporary, ethnic, science fiction. "No gay, erotic or lesbian fiction."
How to Contact: Accepts unsolicited mss. Query first. SASE. Reports in 1 month on queries. Simultaneous, photocopied submissions OK.
Terms: Payment "varies." Sends galleys to author. *Subsidy publishes "on an individual basis."*

MILKWEED EDITIONS, Box 3226, Minneapolis MN 55403. (612)332-3192. Editor: Emilie Buchwald. Estab. 1980—*Milkweed Chronicle*/1984—*Milkweed Editions*. Small press with emphasis on literary and visual arts work. Publishes hardcover and paperback originals. Books: book text quality—acid free paper; offset printing; perfect or hardcover binding; illustrations in all books; average print order: 2,000; first novel print order depends on book. Averages 8 total titles/year. Number of fiction titles "depends on mss."
Needs: Contemporary, experimental, literary. Looking for excellent writing. No romance, mysteries, science fiction. Recently published *Ganado Red*, by Susan Lowell; *Blue Taxis*, by Eileen Drew.
How to Contact: Accepts unsolicited mss. Submit outline/synopsis and 2 sample chapters. SASE. Reports in 4 weeks on queries; 2 months on mss. Simultaneous and photocopied submissions OK. Accepts computer printouts. No dot-matrix. "Please send for guidelines. Must enclose SASE."
Terms: Authors are paid in royalties of 10%; advance is negotiable; 10 author's copies. Sends galleys to author. Book catalog for SASE or IRC and 2 first class stamps.
Advice: "Read good contemporary fiction; find your own voice. Do not send us pornographic work, or work in which violence is done to women or children or men."

MINA PRESS (II), Box 854, Sebastopol CA 95472. (707)829-0854. Fiction Editors: Mei Nakano, Adam David Miller. Estab. 1982. Three-person part-time operation. Publishes hardcover and paperback originals. Books: offset printing; paper binding; average print order: 2,000; first novel print order: 2,500. Plans 3 first books this year. Averages 1-5 total titles each year. Occasionally critiques rejected ms.
Needs: Ethnic, feminist, gay, juvenile (contemporary), lesbian, science fiction, and easy-to-read (teen). "No works that glorify war; no gratuitous violence; nothing racist, sexist, ageist." Published *Riko Rabbit*, by Mei Nakano (folk children's); *Is a Mountain Just a Rock*, by Gregory Uba (early teen initiation); *Quadrille for Tigers*, by Christine Craig (poetry).
How to Contact: Query first. Submit complete ms with SASE. Reports in 3 months. Simultaneous and photocopied submissions OK. Accepts computer printout submissions; prefers letter-quality.
Terms: Pays in royalties of 10% maximum; 10 author's copies; no advance. Sends galleys to author. Writer's guidelines and book catalog for SASE.
Advice: "We regard the author/editor relationship as one of close collaboration on all aspects/phases of publication."

MISTY HILL PRESS (II), 5024 Turner Rd., Sebastopol, CA 95472. (707)823-7437. Managing Editor: Sally S. Karste. Estab. 1985. One person operation on a part-time basis. Publishes paperback originals. Books: illustrations; average print order: 2,000; first novel print order: 500-1,000. Plans 1 first novel this year. Publishes 1 title each year. Sometimes critiques rejected mss; *$15/hour charge for critiques.*
Needs: Juvenile (historical). Looking for "historical fiction for children, well researched for library market." Recently published *Trails to Poosey*, by Olive R. Cook (historical fiction); *Tales Fledgling Homestead*, by Joe Armstrong (nonfiction portraits).
How to Contact: Accepts unsolicited mss. Submit outline/synopsis and sample chapters. Reports within weeks. Simultaneous and photocopied submissions OK. Accepts computer printout submissions, no dot-matrix.
Terms: Pays royalties of 5%. Sends prepublication galleys to author. Writer's guidelines and book catalog for SASE.

***MOSAIC PRESS (II, IV), Fine Miniature Books**, 358 Oliver Rd., Cincinnati OH 45215. (513)761-5977. Publisher: Miriam Irwin. Estab. 1977. Publishes hardcover originals in miniature format. Books: acid-free archival paper; litho or letter press printing; hardbound, cloth, leather or half-leather bind-

WOULD YOU USE THE SAME CALENDAR YEAR AFTER YEAR?

Of course not! If you scheduled your appointments using last year's calendar, you'd risk missing important meetings and deadlines, so you keep up-to-date with a new calendar each year. Just like your calendar, *Novel & Short Story Writer's Market* changes every year, too. Many of the editors move or get promoted, rates of pay increase, and even editorial needs change from the previous year. You can't afford to use an out-of-date book to plan your marketing efforts!

So save yourself the frustration of getting manuscripts returned in the mail, stamped MOVED: ADDRESS UNKNOWN. And of NOT submitting your work to new listings because you don't know they exist. Make sure you have the most current writing and marketing information by ordering *1991 Novel & Short Story Writer's Market* today. All you have to do is complete the attached post card and return it with your payment or charge card information. Order now, and there's one thing that won't change from your *1990 Novel & Short Story Writer's Market* - the price! That's right, we'll send you the 1991 edition for just $18.95. *1991 Novel & Short Story Writer's Market* will be published and ready for shipment in February 1991.

Let an old acquaintance be forgot, and toast the new edition of *Novel & Short Story Writer's Market*. Order today!

(See other side for more helpful writing books)

To order, drop this postpaid card in the mail.

☐ Yes! I want the most current edition of *Novel & Short Story Writer's Market.* Please send me the 1991 edition at the 1990 price - $18.95.* (NOTE: *1991 Novel & Short Story Writer's Market* will be ready for shipment in February 1991.) #10191

Also send me these books to help me get published:

____ (#10111) 1990 Children's Writer's & Illustrator's Market, $15.95,* paper

____ (#10123) On Being a Writer, $19.95,*

____ (#10124) Best Stories from New Writers, $16.95*

*Plus postage and handling: $3.00 for one book, 50c for each additional book. Ohio residents add 5 1/2% sales tax.

☐ Payment enclosed (Slip this card and your payment into an envelope)

☐ Please charge my: ☐ Visa ☐ MasterCard

Account # ______________________ Exp. Date ____________

Signature ______________________

Name ______________________

Address ______________________

City ______________ State ____________ Zip ____________

(This offer expires August 1, 1991)

Writer's Digest Books
1507 Dana Avenue
Cincinnati, OH 45207

Credit card orders call toll-free 1-800-289-0963

5620

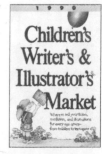

Close-up

Emilie Buchwald

Milkweed Editions

© Judy Olausen.

"People are paying more attention to well-written books that are not necessarily genre fiction," says Emilie Buchwald, editor and co-publisher of Milkweed Editions. "For example, it seems to me more books being picked up by Quality Paperback Book Club include really wonderful literary works."

Buchwald has good reason to be enthusiastic about the increased interest in literary fiction. After all, the trend could mean good things for her own small press, which publishes only literary fiction.

Milkweed Editions evolved from *Milkweed Chronicle*, a literary periodical founded in 1979 by Buchwald and R.W. Scholes. The first book, an anthology about visual arts, came out in 1984. "We began to realize we enjoyed publishing books and realized we could reach a lot of people," says Buchwald. Eventually, publishing books became a fulltime effort and *Milkweed Chronicle* was phased out in 1987. Buchwald says nine books are due to be published in 1990, one more than in 1989.

Since 1988, Milkweed Editions has hosted the Milkweed National Fiction Prize, which is an annual national competition. The first to receive the award, Susan Lowell's *Ganado Red*, was chosen by *Publishers Weekly* as one of the 15 best paperbacks published in 1988.

"People are recognizing that small press has taken on the role of publishing good mid-list writers that major houses can't afford to publish anymore because [the books they write] are not blockbusters. So, we're seeing many really fine authors appearing in small press catalogs," says Buchwald.

According to Buchwald, the key to good writing can be found through engaging in one fundamental act—reading. She suggests writers read several works from any small press they may be interested in submitting to. "Then you'll get an idea what the editor or editors are looking for by what they've published in the past."

Another key to good writing lies in the art of revision, says Buchwald. "Rewriting *is* writing. A writer starts out with a knack or a natural inclination, but unless that person is a genius of great magnitude, it's work and revision from then on. Good writing is a result of working over the manuscript, and then putting it aside and letting yourself forget what you've written. Usually when you write something, you cannot *see* it at all, maybe even for the first month."

When reading submitted manuscripts, Buchwald says she looks for "a distinctive voice, non-derivative, non-imitative. I guess I'm looking for books with what John Gardner called 'life-affirming values.' I don't want anything that's stereotypic, sentimental, religious or overtly propagandist in any way. I want fiction that is grounded in values, that is grounded in place, and that speaks with some authority about the world the writer is creating."

—*Lisa Carpenter*

ing; illustrations; average print order: 2,000. Plans to publish 2 new authors this year. Averages 6 total titles, 1 fiction title each year. Occasionally buys juvenile mss with or without illustrations.
Needs: Comics, historical, humor/satire, literary, regional, religious/inspirational, romance, and young adult (historical, sports). "Our books are short (3,500 words maximum). No fantasy, science fiction or occult." Published *Scrimshaw*, by Carolyn G. Orr.
How to Contact: Accepts unsolicited mss. Query first or submit complete ms. SASE always. Simultaneous and photocopied submissions OK. Accepts computer printout submissions. Reports in 2 weeks on queries; 2 weeks on mss. Publishes ms an average of 2 years after acceptance.
Terms: Pays in outright purchase of $50 and 5 author's copies. "We also do subsidy publishing of private editions. Negotiable arrangements." Book catalog $3. Free writer's guidelines with SASE.
Advice: "We want a good topic, beautifully written, in very few words; no full-length novel submissions. Regarding the author/editor relationship, the writer should trust editor; editor should trust designer. Read the publisher's stated purpose carefully."

MOTHER COURAGE PRESS (II), 1533 Illinois St., Racine WI 53405. (414)634-1047. Executive Editor: Barbara Lindquist. Estab. 1981. Small feminist press. Publishes paperback originals. Books: perfect binding; sometimes illustrations; average print order: 5,000; first novel print order: 5,000. Plans 2 first novels this year. Averages 6 total titles, 2 fiction titles each year.
Needs: Adventure, contemporary, feminist, humor/satire, lesbian, romance (lesbian), science fiction, suspense/mystery. "Need strongly feminist or women oriented, or humanist; nothing written by men." Recently published *News*, by Heather Conrad (political, humanist feminist); and *Night Lights*, by Bonnie Arthur (lesbian romance).
How to Contact: Accepts unsolicited mss. Query first then submit outline/synopsis and 2 sample chapters. SAE. Agented fiction 10%. Reports in 6 weeks on queries; 3 months on mss. Simultaneous and photocopied submissions OK. Accepts computer printout submissions. Accepts electronic submissions via Macintosh.
Terms: Pays in royalties of 10% minimum; 15% maximum. Average advance: $250. Sends galleys to author. Book catalog free on request.
Advice: "Write a good query letter, including, the plot of the novel, main characters, possible markets, etc."

‡MOYER BELL LIMITED, Colonial Hill, RFD #1, Mt. Kisco NY 10549. (914)666-0084. President: Jennifer Moyer. Fiction Editor: Britt Bell. Estab. 1984. "Small publisher established to publish literature, reference and art books." Publishes hardcover and paperback originals and hardcover and paperback reprints. Books: average print order 2,500; first novel print order: 2,500. Averages 14 total titles, 1 fiction title each year. Sometimes comments on rejected ms.
Needs: Serious literary fiction. No genre fiction. Recently published *The Other Garden*, by Francis Wyndham (literary).
How to Contact: Accepts unsolicited mss. Submit outline/synopsis and 2 sample chapters. SASE. Reports in 2 weeks on queries; 2 months on mss. Simultaneous submissions OK. Accepts electronic submissions.
Terms: Pays royalties of 10% minimum. Average advance $1,000. Sends galleys to author. Publishes ms 9-18 months after acceptance. Book catalog free.

THE NAIAD PRESS, INC. (I, II, IV), Box 10543, Tallahassee FL 32302. (904)539-5965. FAX (904)539-9731. Editorial Director: Barbara Grier. Estab. 1973. Books: 55 lb offset paper; sheet-fed offset; perfect binding; illustrations seldom; average print order: 12,000; first novel print order: 12,000. Published new writers within the last year. Publishes 24 total books/year.
Needs: Lesbian fiction, all genres. Recently published *After the Fire,* by Jane Rule; *The Beverly Malibu* (A Kate Delafield Mystery), by Katherine V. Forrest; *Rose Penski,* by Roz Perry; published fiction by previously unpublished writers within the last year.
How to Contact: Query first only. SASE for query, ms. No simultaneous submissions; photocopied submissions OK "but we prefer original mss." Reports in 3 week on queries, 3 months on mss. Publishes ms 1-2 years after acceptance.
Terms: Pays 15% royalties using a standard recovery contract. Occasionally pays 7½% royalties against cover price. "Seldom gives advances and has never seen a first novel worthy of one. Believes authors are investments in their own and the company's future – that the best author is the author that produces a book every 12-18 months forever and knows that there is a *home* for that book." Book catalog for legal-sized SASE.
Advice: "We publish lesbian fiction primarily and prefer honest work (i.e., positive, upbeat lesbian characters). Lesbian content must be accurate . . . a lot of earlier lesbian novels were less than honest. No breast beating or complaining." New imprint will publish reprints and original fiction. "Our fiction titles are becoming increasingly *genre* fiction, which we encourage. Original fiction in paperback is our main field, and its popularity increases. First novels are where the world is . . . really. Don't be a

smart aleck. Send a simple letter, who, what, why, where, when, about yourself and a single page with at most a 2 paragraph precis of your book . . . not how good but WHAT IT IS ABOUT. Remember that no editor has time to waste, and the more accurate your self-description is, the more chance you have of getting a reader who will READ your book. Include telephone numbers, day and evening if possible. Get your homework done, be sure you are sending out the best book you can produce. Publishers are not sitting around waiting to help you write your book. Make it VERY easy for the editor to deal with you. The concise, smart, savvy, self-serving author wins the glass doughnut . . . every time."

THE NAUTICAL & AVIATION PUBLISHING CO. OF AMERICA INC. (II), Suite 314, 101 W. Read St., Baltimore MD 21203. (301)659-0220. Assistant Editor: Kevin Lavey. Fiction Editors: Kevin Lavey, Jan Snouck-Hurgronje. Estab. 1979. Small publisher interested in quality military history and literature. Publishes hardcover originals and reprints. Averages 10 total titles, 1-4 fiction titles each year. Sometimes comments on rejected mss.

Needs: Military/war. Looks for "novels with a strong military history orientation." Published *South to Java*, by Adm. William P. Mack and William Mack, Jr., (historical fiction); *The Captain*, Hartog (reprint); *Greenmantle*, John Buchan (reprint).

How to Contact: Accepts unsolicited mss. Query first or submit complete mss with cover letter, SASE necessary for return of mss. Agented fiction "miniscule." Reports on queries in 2-3 weeks, on mss in 3 weeks. Simultaneous and photocopied submissions OK. Accepts computer printout submissions.

Terms: Pays royalties of 15%. Advance negotiable. After acceptance publishes ms "as quickly as possible – next season." Book catalog free on request.

Advice: Publishing more fiction. Encourages first novelists. "We're interested in good writing – first novel or last novel. Keep it historical, put characters in a historical context. Professionalism counts. Know your subject. *Convince us.*"

NEW DIRECTIONS (I, II), 80 Eighth Ave., New York NY 10011. (212)255-0230. Fiction Editor: Peter Glassgold. Midsize independent publisher with plans to expand. Publishes hardcover and paperback originals and reprints. Average print order: 1,000 hardback; 3,000 paperback. Sometimes critiques rejected ms.

Needs: "Mostly avant-garde; look at everything, including poetry." Published *The Hedgehog*, by H.D.; *A Tree Within*, by Octavio Paz.

How to Contact: Query first with outline/synopsis and sample chapters. Accepts unsolicited mss. SASE. Reports in 6-8 weeks on queries; 3-4 months on mss. Photocopied submissions OK. Accepts computer printout submissions.

Terms: Pays in royalties. Offers advance. Sometimes sends pre-publication galleys to author. Publishes ms at least 1 year after acceptance, "depends on type of book."

Advice: "Try to get published in a literary magazine first to establish a writing reputation and for the experience."

NEW RIVERS PRESS, Suite 910, 420 North 5th St., Minneapolis MN 55401. Editorial Director: C.W. Truesdale. Fiction Editor: C.W. Truesdale. Estab. 1968. Plans 4 fiction titles in 1989.

Needs: Contemporary, literary, experimental, translations. "No popular fantasy/romance. Nothing pious, polemical (unless very good other redeeming qualities). We are interested in only quality literature and always have been (though our concentration in the past has been poetry)."

How to Contact: Query. SASE for query, ms. Photocopied submissions OK. Reports in 2 months on queries, within 2 months of query approval on mss. "No multiple submissions tolerated."

Terms: Pays in 100 author's copies; also pays in royalties; no advance. Minnesota Voices Series pays authors $500 cash plus 15% royalties on list price for second and subsequent printings. Free book catalog.

Advice: "We are not really concerned with trends. We read for quality, which experience has taught can be very eclectic and can come sometimes from out of nowhere. We are interested in publishing short fiction (as well as poetry and translations) because it is and has been a great indigenous American form and is almost completely ignored by the commercial houses. Find a *real* subject, something that belongs to you and not what you think or surmise that you should be doing by current standards and fads."

NEW SEED PRESS (II, IV), Box 9488, Berkeley CA 94709. (415)540-7576. Editor: Helen Chetin. Estab. 1971. Publishes paperback originals in Spanish/English, Chinese/English and English only. Books: 70 lb paper; typeset printing; saddle-stitched binding; b&w line art or halftone. Average print order: 2,000-3,000. Encourages new writers.

Needs: Feminist, ethnic, regional, juvenile (historical, contemporary), and young adult (historical, problem novels, easy-to-read teen). "No adult fiction that is not appropriate for children." Recently published *The Good Bad Wolf,* by Lynn Rosengarten Horowitz; published fiction by previously unpublished writers within the last year.
How to Contact: Query first. SASE always. Simultaneous and photocopied submissions OK. Accepts computer printout submissions. Reports in 2 weeks on queries, 1 month on mss.
Terms: Pays in royalties and by outright purchase. Sends galleys to author. Book catalog for legal-sized SASE.
Advice: "As we are a feminist collective, we discourage writers from sending us 'apolitical animal-type stories' whose intent is to avoid rather than confront issues. We publish children's books free from stereotyping with content that is relative to today's happenings—stories with active female characters who take responsibility for their lives, stories that challenge assumptions about the inferiority of women and Third World peoples."

NEW VICTORIA PUBLISHERS, Box 27, Norwich VT 05055. (802)649-5297. Editor: Claudia Lamperti. Publishes trade paperback originals. Averages 3-4 titles/year.
Needs: Adventure, erotica, ethnic, fantasy, lesbian, historical, humor, feminist, mystery, romance, science fiction and western. Looking for "strong feminist characters, also strong plot and action. We will consider most anything if it is well written and appeals to a lesbian/feminist audience." Recently published *The Names of the Moons of Mars,* by Patricia Roth Schwartz (short fiction); *As the Road Curves,* by Elizabeth Dean.
How to Contact: Submit outline/synopsis and sample chapters. SASE. Reports in 2 weeks on queries; 1 month on mss. Photocopied and disk submissions OK.
Terms: Pays royalties of 10%.
Advice: "We would particularly enjoy a humorous novel."

‡NEWEST PUBLISHERS LTD. (IV), #310, 10359 Whyte Ave., Edmonton, Alberta T6E 1Z9 Canada. General Manager: Eva Radford. Estab. 1977. "Three full time employees work with an editorial board." Publishes paperback originals. Published new writers within the last year. Plans 1 first novel this year. Averages 7 total titles, 2 fiction titles each year. Sometimes offers brief comments on rejected ms.
Needs: Literary. "Our press is most interested in western Canadian literature." Recently published *Winter of the White Wolf*, by Byrna Barclay (literary); *Breathing Water*, by Joan Crate (literary); *Last One Home*, by Fred Stenson (literary).
How to Contact: Accepts unsolicited mss. Query first or submit outline/synopsis and 3 sample chapters. SASE (IRC) necessary for return of manuscript. Reports in 2 weeks on queries; 3 months on mss. Accepts computer printouts, photocopied and electronic submissions.
Terms: Pays royalties of 10% minimum. Sends galleys to author. Publishes ms at least one year after acceptance. Book catalog for 9×12 SASE or IRC.

NIGHT TREE PRESS (II, IV), The Gorge Road, Rt. 46, R.D. 2, Box 140-G, Boonville NY 13309. (315)942-6001. Publisher: Gregg Fedchak. Estab. 1985. "Two people part-time." Paperback originals. Books: 60 lb paper; perfect bound softcover; regional photographs, line drawings, prints; average print order: 1,000 copies; first novel print order: 1,000 copies. Plans 1 first novel this year. Averages 1 total title/year.
Needs: Adventure, historical, humor/satire, literary, regional, short story collections. "Within each category, fiction *must* be strictly regional in nature; the far north country of New York State." Recently published *Lost River*, by Roger Sheffer.
How to Contact: Query first. SASE. Reports in 1-2 months. Simultaneous and photocopied submissions OK. Accepts computer printouts.
Terms: Pays in author's copies; 10% of total press run and/or individual author negotiations. Book listing free on request.
Advice: "We are looking for first novels and short story collections by serious, professional authors who can bring the experience of our region to life. Night Tree wants to be their first break. Unfortunately, we are usually inundated by 'saturation marketers' who obviously can't read this advice—or else ignore it. As a result, we end up with material not pertinent to our regional nature. These amateurs give professional writers a nasty name."

‡OMMATION PRESS (II, IV), 5548 N. Sawyer, Chicago IL 60625. Imprints include *Mati Magazine*, *Ditto Rations Chapbook Series*, *Offset Offshoot Series*, *Salome: A Literary Dance Magazine*, *Dialogues on Dance Series*, Editorial Director: Effie Mihopoulos. Estab. 1975. Rarely comments on rejected mss.
Needs: Contemporary, literary, experimental, feminist, prose poetry. "For the Dialogues on Dance Series, dance-related fiction; for the Offset Offshoot Series, poetry mss, including prose poems." Published *Victims Of The Latest Dance Craze*, by Cornelius Eady (1985 Lamont Selection by Academy of American Poets); *Invisible Mirror*, by Michael Cadnum.

How to Contact: Submit complete ms with SASE. Simultaneous, if so indicated, and photocopied submissions OK. Reports in 1 month.
Terms: Pays 50 author's copies (and $100 honorarium if grant money available). Book catalog for #10 SASE.

‡OUR CHILD PRESS, 800 Maple Glenn Lane, Wayne PA 19087. (215)964-0606. CEO: Carol Hallenbeck. Estab. 1984. Publishes hardcover and paperback originals and hardcover and paperback reprints. Published new writers within the last year. Plans 2 first novels this year. Plans 2 titles, both fiction, this year. Sometimes comments on rejected ms.
Needs: Adventure, contemporary, fantasy, juvenile (5-9 yrs.), preschool/picture book and young adult/teen (10-18 years). Especially interested in book on adoption or learning disabilities. Recently published *Don't Call me Marda*, by Sheila Welch (juvenile).
How to Contact: Does not accept unsolicited mss. Query first. Reports in 2 weeks on queries; 2 months on mss. Simultaneous and photocopied submissions OK. Accepts computer printout submissions.
Terms: Pays royalties of 5% minimum. Publishes ms up to 6 months after acceptance. Book catalog free.

PADRE PRODUCTIONS (II), Box 840, Arroyo Grande CA 93421-0840. (805)473-1947. Imprints include Bear Flag Books, Channel X series, The Press of MacDonald and Reinecke. Editor/Publisher: Lachlan P. MacDonald. Fiction Editor: Mack Sullivan. Estab. 1974. Small independent publisher. Publishes hardcover and paperback originals and paperback reprints. Books: 60 lb book paper; offset printing; hardcover and perfect binding; average print order: 3,000; first novel print order: 3,000. Plans 1 novel per year. Averages 8-12 total titles, 1 fiction title each year. Buys 5% agented fiction. Occasionally critiques rejected ms.
Needs: Contemporary, literary, regional and short story collections. "Overstocked on juveniles." Accepts short stories for Channel X anthology. Juveniles must run 160 pages, for 8-14 year-old readers, both male and female protagonists. No romances, fantasy, sci-fi, or westerns. Published *Chrona*, by Aaron Carob (fantasy); and *Joel in Tananar*, by Robert M. Walton (juvenile fantasy).
How to Contact: Accepts unsolicited mss (include length and subject). Query first with SASE. Reports in 1 month. Simultaneous and photocopied submissions OK. Accepts computer printout submissions, prefers letter-quality. Publishes ms 1-4 years after acceptance.
Terms: Pays in royalties of 6% minimum; 12% maximum. Sends galleys to author. Advance is negotiable. No subsidy publishing; "we package and produce books for self-publishers and small publishers, however." Writer's guidelines and book catalog free for #10 SASE.
Advice: "California-based historical fiction welcome." Published less fiction this year. "We encourage writers of short-short stories."

‡PANDO PUBLICATIONS (II), 540 Longleaf Dr., Roswell GA 30075. (404)587-3363. Editorial Contact Person: Andrew Bernstein. Estab. 1987. "Two person, full-time book publisher." Publishes hardcover and paperback originals. Books: 60 pound paper; perfect bound, smythe sewn or hardcover binding; average print order: 3,000-9,000. Averages 6-10 total titles each year. Rarely comments on rejected mss.
Needs: Adventure, historical, humor/satire, juvenile (animal, easy-to-read, historical, sports, spy/adventure, contemporary), mainstream, military/war, regional, science fiction, suspense/mystery, young adult/teen (easy-to-read, fantasy/science fiction, historical, problem novels, sports, spy/adventure).
How to Contact: Accepts unsolicited mss. Submit outline/synopsis and 3 sample chapters. SASE for ms. Reports in 1 month on queries; 2 months on ms. Simultaneous and photocopied submissions OK. Computer printout submissions are acceptable. Accepts electronic submissions via WordPerfect.
Terms: Pays royalties of 6% minimim; 12½% maximum. Average advance is about ⅓ of royalty of 1st run; negotiable. Sends galleys to author. Publishes ms 6 months after acceptance. Book catalog free on request.
Advice: Would like to see "more children's stories based on myth and legend, current happenings (world events, politics, demogrpahic movements, social problems, ecological concerns, medical problems, growing up in a TV-VCR-cable-computer world, and so on)."

PAPIER-MACHE PRESS (IV), 795 Via Manzana, Watsonville CA 95076. (408)726-2933. Editor/Publisher: Sandra Martz. Estab. 1984. One person operation on a full-time basis. Publishes anthologies and paperback originals. Books: 60-70 lb offset paper; perfect binding; photographs; average print order: 3,000-6,000 copies. Published new writers within the last year. Publishes 4-6 total titles/year; 4-6 fiction/poetry titles/year.

Needs: Contemporary, feminist, short story collections, women's. Recently published fiction by Mary Ann Ashley, Molly Martin, Katharyn Daniels and Ruthann Robson.
How to Contact: Query first. SASE. Reports in 4 weeks on queries; 3 months on mss. Simultaneous and photocopied submissions OK. Accepts computer printouts.
Terms: Standard royalty agreements for novels/fiction collections. Complimentary copies for anthology contributors; honorarium for contributors when anthologies go into second printings.
Advice: "Indicate with your manuscript whether or not you are open to revision suggestions. Always indicate on original submission if this is a simultaneous submission or a previously published work. We can handle either, but only if we know in advance."

‡PAPYRUS PUBLISHERS (III), Box 466, Yonkers NY 10704. (914)664-0840. Editor-in-Chief: Geoffrey Hutchison. Fiction Editor: Jessie Rosé. Estab. London 1946; USA 1982. Small publisher. Publishes hardcover originals and reprints. Audio books; average print order 2,500. Averages 3 total titles each year (all fiction).
Needs: Suspense/Mystery. "No erotica, gay, feminist, children's, spiritual, lesbian, political. Recently published *Wilderness*, by Tony Dawson (suspense); *Curse of the Painted Cats*, by Heather Latimer (romantic suspense); *Louis Wain – King of the Cat Artists 1860-1939*, by Heather Latimer (dramatized biography).
How to Contact: Query first. SASE. Reports on queries in 6 weeks.
Terms: Pays royalties of 10% minimum. Advance varies. Sends galleys to author. Publishes ms 1 year after acceptance. Book catalog for SASE or IRC.

PATH PRESS, INC. (II), Suite 1040, 53 W. Jackson, Chicago IL 60604. (312)663-0167. Editorial Director: Herman C. Gilbert. "Small independent publisher which specializes in books by, for and about Black Americans and Third World Peoples." Averages 6 total titles, 3 fiction titles each year. Occasionally critiques rejected ms.
Needs: Ethnic, historical, sports, and short story collections. Needs for novels include "black or minority-oriented novels of any genre, style or subject." Published *Brown Sky*, by David Covin (a novel of World War II); *Congo Crew*, by William Goodlett (a novel set in Africa during 1960-61); published new writers within the last year.
How to Contact: Accepts unsolicited mss. Query first or submit outline/synopsis and 5 sample chapters with SASE. Reports in 1 month on queries; 2 months on mss. Simultaneous and photocopied submissions OK. Accepts computer printout submissions.
Terms: Pays in royalties.
Advice: "Deal honestly with your subject matter and with your characters. Dig deeply into the motivations of your characters, regardless how painful it might be to you personally."

PAYCOCK PRESS (II), Box 30906, Bethesda MD 20814. (301)656-5146. Imprint: *Gargoyle Magazine*. Editor/Publisher: Richard Peabody, Jr. Estab. 1976. Small independent publisher with international distribution. Publishes paperback originals and reprints. Books: 55 lb natural paper; offset printing; perfect binding; illustrations sometimes; average print order: 1,000; first novel print order: 1,000. Number of titles: 1 in 1988. Encourages new writers. Occasionally comments on rejected mss. "Recently started producing audio tapes of music/spoken-word material."
Needs: Contemporary, literary, experimental, humor/satire and translations. "No tedious AWP résumé-conscious writing or NEA-funded minimalism. We'd be interested in a good first novel that deals with the musical changes of the past few years." Published *The Love Letter Hack*, by Michael Brondoli (contemporary/literary); *Natural History*, by George Myers, Jr. (poems and stories); and a fiction triptych, *Fiction/82*, *Fiction/84* and *Fiction 86*, "which features short stories and novel excerpts by 67 authors. Over 15,000 submissions were considered for those 3 volumes."
How to Contact: Accepts unsolicited mss. Query with SASE. No simultaneous submissions; photocopied submissions OK. Accepts computer printout submissions. Prefers letter-quality. Reports in 1 week on queries, 1 month on mss.
Terms: Pays in author's copies – 10% of print run plus 50% of all sales "after/if we break even on book." Sends galleys to author. No advance.
Advice: "Keep trying. Many good writers simply quit. Many mediocre writers keep writing, eventually get published, and become better writers. If the big magazines won't publish you, try the small magazines, try the local newspaper. Always read your fiction aloud. If you think something is *silly*, no doubt we'd be embarrassed too. Write the kind of stories you'd like to read and can't seem to find. We are more concerned with *how* a novelist says what he/she says, than with *what* he/she says. We are more interested in *right now* than in books about the '50s, '60s, '70s, etc. We are publishing more in anthology format, and encourage first novelists."

PENTAGRAM PRESS (II), 212 N. 2nd St., Minneapolis MN 55401. (612)340-9821. Fiction Editor: Michael Tarachow. Estab. 1974. One-person letterpress shop; presswork, design and distribution are all handled in-house. Publishes hardcover and paperback originals. Books: various handmade and

mouldmade papers; letterpress printing; sewn binding; illustrations; average print order: 123-242. "Fiction *is* seldom published; poetry and typography are the main emphasis." Averages 2-5 total titles, 0-1 fiction title each year.
Needs: Adventure, experimental, literary. "We're committed for next 3 years; writers should *always* query with SASE before sending actual mss." Published *Ninja*, by John Jacob; *The Master*, by Tom Clark; and *A Man in Stir*, by Theodore Enslin.
How to Contact: Query first with SASE. Reports in 1-2 weeks on queries.
Terms: Payment arrangements variable. Book catalog free on request.

PERSEVERANCE PRESS (I, II, IV), Box 384, Menlo Park CA 94026. Editor: Meredith Phillips. Estab. 1979. One-person press publishing only mysteries. Publishes trade paperback originals. Books: 55 lb paper; offset litho printing; perfect binding; average print order: 2,000; first novel print order: 2,000. Plans 1 or 2 first novels this year. Averages 2-3 total titles each year, all fiction. Occasionally critiques rejected ms.
Needs: "Mysteries only, of the old-fashioned sort: whodunits, puzzlers, 'village cozies,' suspense thrillers, etc., with no gratuitous violence, excessive gore, or exploitive sex." No romance novels, historicals, horror, occult. Recently published *Murder Once Done*, by Mary Lou Bennett (first novel) and *The Last Page*, by Bob Fenster.
How to Contact: Accepts unsolicited complete mss "reluctantly." Submit outline/synopsis and 3 sample chapters with SASE. Reports in 1 month. Simultaneous (if noted) and photocopied submissions OK.
Terms: Pays in royalties of 10% (net receipts); 10 author's copies. Sends galleys to author. Writer's guidelines for SASE.
Advice: "We are delighted to find new novelists. We ask for revisions if necessary, and do as much substantive editorial work as required—working with the author till it's right. The quality of material is rising and we are publishing more. We regard the author/editor relationship as open, honest, cooperative, professional."

PERSPECTIVES PRESS (II, IV), Box 90318, Indianapolis IN 46290-0318. (317)872-3055. Publisher: Pat Johnston. Estab. 1981. Small operation expanding to become *the* publisher of fiction and nonfiction materials related to adoption and infertility. Publishes hardcover originals and paperback originals. Books: offset printing; smythe sewn cloth, perfect bound and saddle stitched binding; average print order: 3,000; first novel print order: 2,000. Published new writers within the last year; plans 1 first novel this year. Averages 2-6 total titles, 1 fiction title each year. Critiques or comments on rejected mss.
Needs: Submissions for adults or children but must have adoption or infertility as the theme. Published *The Miracle Seekers*, by Mary Martin Mason.
How to Contact: Query first. SASE. Reports in 2 weeks on queries; 1 month on mss. Simultaneous and photocopied submissions OK. Accepts computer printouts.
Terms: Pays in royalties of 5% minimum; 15% maximum. Advance negotiable. Sends galleys to author. Book catalog for #10 SAE and 45¢ postage.

PIKESTAFF PUBLICATIONS, INC. (I, II), Box 127, Normal IL 61761. (309)452-4831. Imprints include The Pikestaff Press: Pikestaff Fiction Chapbooks; *The Pikestaff Forum*, general literary magazine. Editorial Directors: Robert D. Sutherland and James R. Scrimgeour. Estab. 1977. Small independent publisher with plans to expand gradually. Publishes hardcover and paperback originals. Books: paper varies; offset printing; b&w illustrations; average print order: 500-2,000. "One of the purposes of the press is to encourage new talent." Occasionally comments on rejected mss.
Needs: Contemporary, literary, and experimental. "No slick formula writing written with an eye to the commercial mass market or pure entertainment that does not provide insights into the human condition. Not interested in heroic fantasy (dungeons & dragons, swords & sorcery); science-fiction of the space-opera variety; westerns; mysteries; love-romance; gothic adventure; or pornography (sexploitation)." Published fiction by Constance Pierce and Linnea Johnson.
How to Contact: Query or submit outline/synopsis and sample chapters (1-2 chapters). SASE always. "Anyone may inquire; affirmative responses may submit ms." No simultaneous or photocopied submissions. Accepts computer printout submissions, prefers letter-quality. Reports in 1 month on queries, 3 months on mss. Publishes ms within 1 year after acceptance.
Terms: Negotiates terms with author. Sends galleys to author.
Advice: "Have fictional characters we can really *care* about; we are tired of disembodied characters wandering about in their heads unable to relate to other people or the world about them. Avoid too much TELLING; let the reader participate by leaving something for him or her to do. Yet avoid vagueness, opaqueness, personal or 'private' symbolisms and allusions. Here we regard the relationship between the writer and editor as a cooperative relationship—we are colleagues in getting the book out. The writer has an obligation to do the best self-editing job of which he or she is capable; writers

should not rely on editors to make their books presentable. Don't give up easily; understand your reasons for wanting the work published (personal satisfaction? money? fame? to 'prove' something? to 'be a novelist'? etc.) Ask yourself honestly, Should it be published? What can it provide for a reader that makes it worth part of that reader's *lifetime* to read? Be prepared for shocks and disappointments; study contracts carefully and retain as many rights and as much control over the book's appearance as possible. Be prepared to learn how to be your own best promoter and publicist."

PINEAPPLE PRESS (II), P.O. Drawer 16008, Southside Station, Sarasota FL 34239. (813)952-1085. Executive Editor: June Cussen. Estab. 1982. Small independent trade publisher. Publishes hardcover and paperback originals and paperback reprints. Books: book quality paper; offset printing; smythe sewn hardcover perfect bound paperback binding; illustrations occasionally; average print order: 5,000; first novel print order: 2,000-5,000. Published new writers within the last year. Averages 8-10 total titles each year. Occasionally critiques rejected ms.
Needs: Contemporary, experimental, historical, environmental, regional, how-to and reference. Recently published *Sky Moon*, by T.A. Roberts (novel).
How to Contact: Prefers query, outline or one-page synopsis with sample chapters (including the first) and SASE. Then if requested, submit complete ms with SASE. Reports in 6 weeks. Simultaneous and photocopied submissions OK. Accepts computer printout submissions, prefers letter-quality.
Terms: Pays in royalties of 7½% minimum; 15% maximum. Sends galleys to author. Advance is not usually offered. "Basically, it is an individual agreement with each author depending on the book." Book catalog sent if label and 45¢ stamp enclosed.
Advice: "We publish both Florida regional books and general trade fiction and nonfiction. Quality first novels will be published. We regard the author/editor relationship as a trusting relationship with communication open both ways. Learn all you can about the publishing process and about how to promote your book once it is published."

PIPPIN PRESS. 229 East 85th Street, Gracie Station Box 92, New York NY 10028. (212)288-4920. Publisher: Barbara Francis. Estab. 1987. "Small, independent children's book company, formed by the former editor-in-chief of Prentice Hall's juvenile division." Publishes hardcover originals. Books: 135-150 GSM offset-semi-matte (for picture books) paper; offset, sheet-fed printing; smythe-sewn binding; full color, black and white line illustrations and half tone, b&w and full color photographs. Averages 8-10 titles for first 2 years; will average 10-12. Sometimes comments on rejected mss.
Needs: Juvenile (5-9 yrs. including animal, easy-to-read, fantasy, humorous, spy/adventure). "I am interested in humorous novels for children of about 7-12 and in picture books with the focus on humor."
How to Contact: Accepts unsolicited mss. Query first or submit outline/synopsis and 2 sample chapters. SASE. Reports in 2-3 weeks on queries; 3 months on mss. Simultaneous submissions OK. Accepts computer printout submissions, no dot-matrix.
Terms: Pays royalties. Sends galleys to author. Publication time after ms is accepted "depends on the amount of revision required, type of illustration, etc."

***POCAHONTAS PRESS, INC. (II, IV)**, Manuscript Memories, 2805 Wellesley Court, Blacksburg VA 24060-4126. (703)951-0467. Editorial contact person: Mary C. Holliman. Estab. 1984. "One-person operation on part-time basis, with several part-time colleagues. Subjects not limited, but stories about real people are almost always required. Main intended audience is youth—young adults, ages 10-18." Books 70 lb white offset paper; offset litho printing; perfect binding; illustrations; average print order 3,000-5,000. Averages 4 total titles, 2-3 fiction and 2 poetry titles each year. Usually critiques or comments on rejected mss.
Needs: "Stories based on historical facts about real people." Contemporary, ethnic, historical, sports, regional, translations, western. "I will treat a short story as a book, with illustrations and a translation into Spanish or French and also Chinese someday." No fantasy or horror. Published *From Lions to Lincoln*, by Fran Hartman; and *Mountain Summer*, by Bill Mashburn.
How to Contact: Accepts unsolicited mss. Query first. Reports in 1 month on queries; 1-2 months on manuscripts. Simultaneous, photocopied submissions OK. "If simultaneous, I would need to know up front what other options the author is considering." Accepts computer printout submissions.
Terms: Pays royalties of 10% maximum. $50 advance negotiable. Sends galleys to author. "I will subsidy publish—but expect book and author to meet the same qualifications as a regular author, and will pay royalties on all copies sold as well as pay back the author's investment as books are sold."
Advice: "Get an unbiased, non-friend editor and follow his or her suggestions. Understand that the author *must* be involved in selling the book; if he/she is not willing to help sell, don't expect too much from publisher. Beginning writers seem to think that all they have to do is get the book into bookstores—and they have no conception at all as to how hard that is, and that that's only the *beginning* of selling the book. I'm really looking for long short stories about real people and places, to be published with copious illustrations."

PORCUPINE'S QUILL, INC. (III), 68 Main St., Erin, Ontario, N0B 1T0 Canada. (519)833-9158. Contact: Ann Reatherford. Estab. 1974. Small press. Publishes hardcover and paperback originals. Books: 70 lb Zephyr antique paper; offset on Heidelberg Kord 64 printing; paper, occasional hand hardcover binding; illustrations; average print order: 750; first novel print order: 750. Averages 7 total titles, 4 fiction titles each year.

Needs: Contemporary, fantasy, historical, literary, and young adult/teen (historical). Recently published *A Short Walk in the Rain*, by Hugh Hood.

How to Contact: Accepts unsolicited mss, but prefers query first. Reports in 1 month. Simultaneous and photocopied submissions OK. Accepts computer printout submissions.

Terms: Pays in royalties of 5% minimum; 10% maximum; 10 author's copies. Sends proofs to author. Free book catalog.

‡THE POST-APOLLO PRESS (I), 35 Marie St., Sausalito CA 94965. (415)332-1458. Publisher: Simone Fattal. Estab. 1982. Publishes paperback originals. Book: acid free paper; lithography printing; perfect binding; average print order: 3,000. First novel print order: 3,000. Published new writers within the last year. Averages 2 total titles, 1 fiction title each year. Sometimes comments on rejected ms.

Needs: Feminist, lesbian, literary, short story collections, spiritual and translations. No juvenile, horror, sports or romance. Recently published *Sitt Marie-Rose*, by Etel Adnan; *Home For The Summer*, by Georgina Kleege (psychological thriller).

How to Contact: Send query or complete ms with SASE. Reports in 3 months.

Terms: Pays royalties of 6½% minimum or by individual arrangement. Sends galleys to author. Publishes ms 1½ years after acceptance. Book catalog free.

PRAIRIE JOURNAL PRESS (II, IV), Prairie Journal Trust, Box 997, Station G, Calgory, Alberta T3A 3G2 Canada. Editorial contact person: A. Burke. Estab. 1983. Small-press non-commercial literary publisher. Publishes paperback originals. Books: bond paper; offset printing; stapled binding; b&w line drawings. Average 2 total titles or anthologies/year. Occasionally critiques or comments on rejected ms if requested.

Needs: Experimental. No romance, horror, pulp, erotica, magazine type, children's, adventure, formula, "western." Recently published *Prairie Journal Fiction*, *Prairie Journal Fiction II* (anthologies of short stories) and *Solstice*, (short fiction on the theme of aging).

How to Contact: Accepts unsolicited mss. Query first and send IRCs and $3 for sample copy, then submit 1 or 2 stories. Submit outline/synopsis and 1-2 stories with SASE (IRC). Reports in 2 weeks. Photocopied submissions OK. Accepts computer printout submissions, no dot-matrix.

Terms: Pays 1 author's copy; honorarium depends on grant/award. Book catalog free on request to institutions; SAE with IRC for individuals. "No U.S. stamps!"

Advice: "We wish we had the means to promote more new writers."

THE PRAIRIE PUBLISHING COMPANY, Box 2997, Winnipeg, Manitoba R3C 4B5 Canada. (204)885-6496. Publisher: Ralph Watkins. Estab. 1969. Buys juvenile mss with illustrations. Books: 60 lb high-bulk paper; offset printing; perfect binding; line-drawings illustrations; average print order: 2,000; first novel print order: 2,000.

How to Contact: Query with SASE or IRC. No simultaneous submissions; photocopied submissions OK. Reports in 1 month on queries, 6 weeks on mss. Publishes ms 4-6 months after acceptance.

Terms: Pays 10% in royalties. No advance. Free book catalog.

Advice: "We work on a manuscript with the intensity of a Max Perkins of Charles Scribner's Sons of New York. A clean, well-prepared manuscript can go a long way toward making an editor's job easier. On the other hand, the author should not attempt to anticipate the format of the book, which is a decision for the publisher to make. In order to succeed in today's market, the story must be tight, well written and to the point. Do not be discouraged by rejections."

PRESS GANG PUBLISHERS (II, IV), 603 Powell St., Vancouver, British Columbia V6A 1H2 Canada. (604)253-2537. Estab. 1974. Feminist press, 2 full-time staff, 1 half-time staff. Publishes paperback originals and reprints. Books: paperback paper; offset printing; perfect binding; average print order: 3,500; first novel print order: 2,500. Plans 4 first novels this year. Sometimes critiques rejected mss.

The double dagger before a listing indicates that the listing is new in this edition. New markets are often the most receptive to freelance contributions.

Needs: Contemporary, erotica, ethnic (native women especially), feminist, humor/satire, lesbian, literary, regional (priority), science fiction, short story collections, suspense/mystery. Looking for "feminist, mystery/suspense, short stories." No children's/young adult/teen. Published *Not Vanishing* (poetry/prose) by Native American activist and writer Chrystos.
How to Contact: Accepts unsolicited mss. Query first. SASE (IRC). Reports in 2 weeks on queries; 4-6 weeks on mss. Simultaneous and photocopied submissions OK. Accepts computer printout submissions. Accepts AT compatible discs.
Terms: Pays 10% royalties. Sends galleys to author. Book catalog free on request.

THE PRESS OF MACDONALD AND RENECKE (II,III), Padre Productions, Box 840, Arroyo Grande CA 93420. (805)473-1947. Publisher: Lachlan P. MacDonald. Fiction Editor: Mack Sullivan. Estab. 1974. "Literary imprint of a small independent press." Publishes hardcover and paperback originals. Books: book paper; offset printing; Smyth casebound and perfect binding; illustrations; average print order: 3,000-5,000; first novel print order: 3,500. Publishes fiction by a previously unpublished writer "every 2-3 years." Plans 1 first novel this year. Averages 6 total titles, 1-2 fiction titles each year. Sometimes comments on rejected mss.
Needs: Fantasy, historical, humor/satire, literary, mainstream, short story collections. Currently overstocked. No mystery, suspense, western, religious, military, adventure, romance categories. Published *Chrona*, by Aaron Corob (fantasy); *Joel in Tananar*, by Robert M. Walton (juvenile).
How to Contact: Accepts unsolicited mss. Submit outline/synopsis and sample chapters (1-2). SASE. Agented fiction 5%. Reports on queries in 2 weeks; on mss in 2 months. Simultaneous and photocopied submissions OK.
Terms: Pays in royalties. Sends galleys to author. "Unfortunately, it may be years" before publication after acceptance. Writer's guidelines for SASE. Book catalog for 6×9 SAE.
Advice: Publishing less fiction than in the past. "Buyers prefer big-list promotional titles/videos! Demonstrate a following by documenting publication in literary magazines, general magazines or anthologies."

‡PUCKERBRUSH PRESS (I,II), 76 Main St., Orono ME 04473. (207)581-3832. Publisher/Editor: Constance Hunting. Estab. 1979. One-person operation on part-time basis. Publishes paperback originals. Books: laser printing; perfect binding; sometimes illustrations; average print order: 5,000; first novel print order: 1,000. Published new writers within the last year. Plans 1 first novel this year. Averages 3 total titles, 2 fiction titles each year. Sometimes comments on rejected ms. *If detailed comment, $500.*
Needs: Contemporary, experimental, literary.
How to Contact: Accepts unsolicited mss. Submit complete ms with cover letter. SASE. Reports in 1 week on queries; 2 months on mss.
Terms: Pays royalties of 10%; 10 author's copies. Sends galleys to author. Publishes ms usually 1 year after acceptance. Writer's guidelines for #10 SASE and 1 first class stamp. "I have a book list and flyers."

***PULP PRESS BOOK PUBLISHERS (I)**, Subsidiary of Arsenal Pulp Press Ltd. Imprints include Tillacum Library, Arsenal Editions. 1150 Homer St., Vancouver, British Columbia V6B 2X6 Canada. (604)687-4233. Manager: Brian Lam. Fiction Editor: Linda Field. Estab. 1972. Small literary publisher. Publishes paperback originals. Books: 80 lb paper; offset printing; perfect binding; average print order: 1,000; first novel print order: 750. Published new writers within the past year. Plans 1 first novel this year. Averages 7 total titles, 2-3 fiction titles each year. Sometimes comments on rejected mss.
Needs: Contemporary, feminist, literary, short story collections. "We are looking for well-written literary material, largely regardless of genre. No romance, westerns, thrillers." Recently published *Torque*, by J. Michael Yates (short fiction); *Prelude*, by D.M. Fraser (short fiction); *Starting Small*, by James Dunn (novel).
How to Contact: Accepts unsolicited mss. Query first. Agented fiction 5%. Reports on queries in 2 weeks; on mss in 2 months. Photocopied submissions OK. Accepts computer printout submissions.
Terms: Pays royalties of 15% of net. Average advance: $100. Sends galleys to author. Publishes ms 6 months-1 year after acceptance. Occasionally publishes books on a subsidy basis—0-10%. Book catalog for 9x11½ SAE and 2 IRCs.

***Q.E.D. PRESS OF ANN ARBOR, INC. (I)**, Suite 112, 1008 Island Drive Ct., Ann Arbor MI 48105-2025. (313)994-0371. Imprint: ProForma Books. Fiction Editor: Dan Fox. Estab. 1985. Publishes hardcover and paperback originals. Books: cloth binding; average print order: 1,000; first novel print order:

500. Published new writers within the last year. Plans 2 first novels this year. Publishes 8 titles each year, 2 fiction titles. Sometimes critiques rejected mss.
Needs: Literary. Published *Half Dozen Dutch*, by Tom Broos; *Found Time: An Anti-Novel*, by Mike Gallatin.
How to Contact: Does not accept or return unsolicited mss. Query first or submit outline/synopsis with 1 sample chapter. SASE. Reports on queries in 1 month; on mss in 3 months. Simultaneous and photocopied submissions OK. Accepts computer printouts.
Terms: Pays in royalties of 6-12% and approx. 25 author's copies. Sends galleys to author. Publishes ms 6 months after acceptance. Subsidy publishes 15% of mss.

QUARRY PRESS (I,II), Box 1061, Kingston, Ontario, K7L 4Y5 Canada. (613)548-8429. Managing Editor: Linda Bussière. Estab. 1965. Small independent publisher with plans to expand. Publishes paperback originals. Books: Rolland tint paper; offset printing; perfect binding; illustrations; average print order: 1,200; first novel print order: 1,200. Published new writers within the past year. Plans 1 first novel this year. Averages 12 total titles, 2-4 fiction titles each year. Sometimes comments on rejected mss.
Needs: Experimental, feminist, historical, literary, short story collections. Recently published *Ritual Slaughter,* by Sharon Drache; *Engaged Elsewhere,* edited by Kent Thompson (includes work by Mavis Gallant, Margaret Laurence, Dougles Glover, Ray Smitz, Keath Fraser and others); published fiction by previously unpublished writers within the last year.
How to Contact: Accepts unsolicited mss. Query first. SASE for query and ms. Reports in 4 months. Simultaneous and photocopied submissions OK. Accepts computer printout submissions.
Terms: Pays royalties of 7% minimum; 10% maximum. Advance: negotiable. Provides 5-10 author's copies. Sends galleys to author. Publishes ms 6-8 months after acceptance. Book catalog free on request.
Advice: Publishing more fiction than in the past. Encourages first novelists. Canadian authors only for New Canadian Novelists Series.

***RANGER ASSOCIATES, INC. (II)**, 200 Squirrel Trail, Longwood FL 32779. (407)767-8905. Director of Publications: Sharon M. Lane. Estab. 1979. Small press with plans to expand; presently considers approximately 50 submissions per year, selecting 4-5 for publication. Publishes hardcover and paperback originals and reprints. Books: 50 lb paper; offset printing; perfect binding; illustrations; average print order: 5,000; first novel print order: 3,000. Plans 3-4 first novels this year. Averages 5 total titles, 1 fiction title each year. Usually critiques rejected mss.
Needs: Adventure, historical and war. Accepts short stories from freelancers. Novel needs include military/historical. No erotica. Published *Goodness Gracious*, by Harry Levitt (juvenile); *The Pestilence Plot*, by Betty Patterson (adventure/terrorism); and *A Special Breed of Man*, by Ed Edell (Vietnam war).
How to Contact: Query with SASE. Reports in 6 weeks on queries; 2-3 months on mss. Simultaneous and photocopied submissions OK. Accepts computer printout submissions, prefers letter-quality. Disk submissions OK with IBM or MacIntosh. Prefers hard copy with disk submissions.
Terms: Individual arrangements with authors. Sends galleys to author. Pays in royalties of 5% minimum, 7% maximum; 25 author's copies; honorarium. *Subsidy arrangement:* copyright to author; author agrees to market book; author receives proportion of books related to subsidy, e.g., if author subsidizes at 50% of manufacturing costs, author receives 50% of books. Book catalog for SASE.
Advice: "Rewrite, review, rewrite. Let someone you dislike read your manuscript; rewrite once more before submitting. Query letters reflect on the author—correct grammar, neatness and briefness count. Will publish first novels if good enough. Novelist must be willing to promote his/her own work in every way possible. Small presses cannot afford to publish without *very* active author promotions."

***READ 'N RUN BOOKS (I), Subsidiary of Crumb Elbow Publishing**, Box 294, Rhododendron OR 97049. (503)622-4798. Imprints are Elbow Books, Research Centrex. Publisher: Michael P. Jones. Estab. 1978. Small independent publisher with three on staff. Publishes hardcover and paperback originals and reprints. Books: special order paper; offset printing; "usually a lot" of illustrations; average print order: varies. Published new writers within the last year. Plans 1 first novel this year. Averages 10 titles, 2 fiction titles each year. Sometimes comments on rejected ms; *$75 charge for critiques depending upon length. May be less or more.*
Needs: Adventure, contemporary, ethnic, experimental, fantasy, feminist, historical, horror, humor/satire, juvenile (animal, easy-to-read, fantasy, historical, sports, spy/adventure, contemporary), literary, mainstream, military/war, preschool/picture book, psychic/supernatural/occult, regional, religious/inspirational, romance (contemporary, historical), science fiction, short story collections, spiritual, suspense/mystery, translations, western, young adult/teen (easy-to-read, fantasy/science fiction, historical, problem novels, romance, sports, spy/adventure). Looking for fiction on "historical and wildlife" subjects. "Also, some creative short stories would be nice to see for a change. No pornography."

How to Contact: Accepts unsolicited ms. Query first. Submit outline/synopsis and complete ms with cover letter. SASE. Reports in 2 weeks on queries; 1-2 months on mss. Simultaneous and photocopied submissions OK. Accepts computer printout submissions.
Terms: Provides 5+ author's copies (negotiated). Sends galleys to author. Publishes ms 6-12 months after acceptance. Subsidy publishes two books or more/year. Terms vary from book to book. Writer's guidelines for 45¢ postage. Book catalog for SASE or IRC and $1.25 postage.
Advice: Publishing "more hardcover fiction books based on real-life events. They are in demand by libraries. Submit everything you have—even artwork. Also, if you have ideas for layout, provide those also. If you have an illustrator that you're working with, be sure to get them in touch with us."

RED ALDER BOOKS (IV), Box 2992, Santa Cruz CA 95063. (408)426-7082. Editorial Contact Person: David Steinberg, owner. Imprint: Pan-Erotic Review. Estab. 1974. Small, independent publisher. Publishes hardcover and paperback originals. Books: offset printing, case/perfect binding; some illustrations; average print order: 5,000. Published new writers within the past year. Averages 1 total title, 1 fiction title each year. Sometimes comments on rejected mss.
Needs: "Quality-conscious, provocative erotica only." Erotica, feminist, lesbian, literary, short story collections. "Short stories only." No pornography, cliché sexual stories." Published *Erotic by Nature*, by Steinberg, editor (collection of erotic stories, poems, photographs).
How to Contact: Accepts and returns unsolicited mss. Query first. SASE for query and ms. Reports on queries in 2 weeks; on mss in 4-6 weeks. Simultaneous and photocopied submissions OK. Accepts computer printout submissions.
Terms: Pays royalties of 8% minimum. Sends galleys to author.

RED DEER COLLEGE PRESS (I,IV), Box 5005, Red Deer, Alberta T4N 5H5 Canada. (403)342-3321. Managing Editor: Dennis Johnson. Estab. 1975. Publishes hardcover and paperback originals. Books: offset paper; offset printing; hardcover/perfect binding; average print order: 1,000-4,000; first novel print order 2,500. Plans 1 first novel this year. Averages 8-10 total titles, 1 fiction title each year. Sometimes comments on rejected mss.
Needs: Contemporary, experimental, literary, short story collections. No romance, sci-fi, gay, feminist.
How to Contact: Does not accept unsolicited mss. Query first or submit outline/synopsis and 2 sample chapters. SASE for query and for ms. Agented fiction 10%. Reports in 1 month on queries; in 3 months on mss. Simultaneous and photocopied submissions OK. Accepts computer printout submissions.
Terms: Pays royalties of 8% minimum; 10% maximum. Advance is negotiable. Sends galleys to author. Publishes ms 1 year after acceptance. Book catalog for 8½×11 SASE and IRC.
Advice: "Final manuscripts must be submitted on Mac disk in MS Word. Absolutely *no* unsolicited mss. Query first. Canadian authors only."

‡REFERENCE PRESS (IV), Box 70, Teeswater ON N0G 2S0 Canada. (519)392-6634. Imprints are RP Large Print Books. Editor: Gordon Ripley. Estab. 1982. Small independent Canadian publisher of library reference material, computer software and large print books. Hardcover and paperback originals and hardcover reprints. Books: 70 lb Zepher laid paper; offset printing; casebound, some perfect-bound; average print order: 1,000. Published new writers within the last year. Averages 10 total titles, 4 fiction titles each year. Always comments on rejected mss.
Needs: Sports. Recently published *Canadian Sports Stories* (fiction, anthology); *Dance Me Outside* and *Born Indian*, by W.P. Kinsella (large print).
Terms: Pays in royalties of 10%; 5 author's copies. Writer's guidelines and book catalog free. Accepts unsolicited mss. Accepts electronic submissions.

RE/SEARCH PUBLISHING (I,II), 20 Romolo, Suite B, San Francisco CA 94133. (415)362-1465. Editors: V. Vale and A. Juno. Estab. 1980. Two-person operation, small independent publisher. Publishes paperback originals of non-fiction and paperback reprint classics. Books: 50 lb paper; sewn & stitched binding; photos and other illustrations; average print order: 5,000-7,000. Averages 3-5 total titles per year. Occasionally critiques or comments on rejected ms.
Needs: Experimental, science fiction or *roman noir*. No realism.
How to Contact: Accepts unsolicited mss. Query first. SASE. Reports in 1 month on queries; 1 month on mss. Simultaneous and photocopied submissions OK. Accepts computer printout submissions.
Terms: Pays 8% of press run. Book catalog on request.

Read the Business of Fiction section to learn the correct way to prepare and submit a manuscript.

ROWAN TREE PRESS (II), 124 Chestnut St., Boston MA 02108. (617)523-7627. Editor: Nadya Aisenberg. Fiction Editors: Nadya Aisenberg, Cornelia Veenendaal. Estab. 1980. Small general trade publishing house. Publishes paperback originals and reprints. Books: acid-free, 50-60 lb vellum paper; offset print; perfect binding; illustrations; average print order: 1,500-2,000; first novel print order: 1,500-2,000. Publishes 3 total titles each year; 1 fiction title. Sometimes critiques rejected ms.
Needs: Contemporary literary, biography, travel, memoir, short story collections and suspense/mystery. No political or religious fiction.
How to Contact: Accepts unsolicited mss. Submit complete ms with cover letter. SASE. 10% of fiction is agented. Reports in 2 week on queries; 2 months on mss. Accepts computer printout submissions, no dot-matrix.
Terms: Pays royalties of 7½% and 10 author's copies. Sends pre-publication galleys to author. Book catalog free on request.

‡ST. LUKE'S PRESS, INC. (II), 4210 B.F. Goodrich Blvd., Memphis TN 38118. Managing Director: Phyllis Tickle. Assistant Editor: Barbara Emigh. Estab. 1975. Midsize independent publisher. Part of the Wimmer Companies. Publishes hardcover and paperback originals. Books: offset printing; cloth binding; illustrations sometimes; average print order: 5,000; first novel print order: 3,000. Averages 10 total titles each year.
Needs: "Open." Published fiction by John Osier, Jack Farris, Jackson Collins; published new writers within the last year.
How to Contact: "Discourages" unsolicited mss. Submit complete ms. with SASE. Simultaneous and photocopied submissions OK. Accepts computer printout submissions. Reports in 4-6 weeks on mss.
Terms: Pays "according to circumstances. Sends galleys to author. Individual arrangements with author depending on book, etc."

***SAMISDAT (II)**, Box 129, Richford VT 05476. Imprint: *Samisdat Magazine*. Editor/Publisher: Merritt Clifton. Estab. 1973. Publishes paperback originals. Books: standard bond paper; offset printing; saddle-stitch or square back binding; illustrations sometimes; average print order: 300-500. Encourages new writers. "Over 60% of our titles are first books – about 1 first novel per year." Comments on rejected mss.
Needs: Literary, feminist, gay, lesbian, and regional. Published *An American Love Story*, by Robert Swisher (novel).
How to Contact: Query or submit complete ms. SASE always. Reports in 1 week on queries; time varies on mss.
Terms: No advance. Free book catalog with SASE. "Our author payments for books are a paradox: At this writing, we've published over 200 titles over the past 15 years, about 85% of which have earned the authors a profit. On the other hand, we've relatively seldom issued royalty checks – maybe 20 or 30 in all this time, and all for small amounts. We're also paradoxical in our modus operandi: *Authors cover our cash expenses* (this comes to about a third of the total publishing cost – we're supplying equipment and labor) in exchange for half of the press run, but we make no money from authors, and if we don't promote a book successfully, we still lose." Publishes ms from 2-6 months after acceptance.
Advice: "We do not wish to see *any* book-length ms submissions from anyone who has not already either published in our quarterly magazine, *Samisdat*, or at least subscribed for about a year to find out who we are and what we're doing. We are not a 'market' engaged in handling books as commodities and are equipped to read only about one novel submission per month over and above our magazine submission load. Submissions are getting much slicker, with a lot less guts to them. This is precisely the opposite of what we're after. Read the magazine. Submit stories or poems or chapters to it. When familiar with us, and our subscribers, query about an appropriate book ms. We don't publish books except as special issues of the magazine, and blind submissions stand absolutely no chance of acceptance at all. Go deep. Involve your characters with the outside world, as well as with each other. Use the most compact structure possible, bearing in mind that fiction is essentially drama without a stage. We're much more interested in fiction chapbooks – thematically related groups of 2-3 stories – than in novellas or novels."

SANDPIPER PRESS (IV), Box 286, Brookings OR 97415. (503)469-5588. Owner: Marilyn Reed Riddle. Estab. 1979. One person operation specializing in low-cost large-print 18 pt. books. Publishes paperback originals. Books: 70 lb paper; saddle stitch binding, 80 page maximum; leatherette cover binding; b&w sketches or photos; average print order 1,000; no novels. Averages 1 title every 2 years. Occasionally critiques or comments on rejected mss.
Needs: From Native American "Indian" writers only, *true* visions; from general public writers, unusual quotations, sayings.
How to Contact: Does not accept unsolicited mss. Query first or submit outline/synopsis. SASE. Reports in 1 month on queries; 1 month on mss. Simultaneous and photocopied submissions OK. Accepts computer printout submissions.

Terms: Pays 2 author's copies and $10. Publisher buys true story and owns copyright. Author may buy any number of copies at 40% discount and postage. Book catalog for #10 SAE and 1 first class stamp.
Advice: Send SASE for more information.

‡SATCHELL'S PUBLISHING (II), Adams Press, 3124 5th Ave., Richmond VA 23222. (804)329-6740. President: Alexis Satchell. Fiction Editor: Kim D. Gaines. Estab. 1983. "Midsize independent publisher with plans to expand." Publishes paperback originals. Books: 70 lb wt. paper; typeset printing; saddle stitch, spiral binding, perfect binding; b&w and color illustrations; average print order: 500-250; first novel print order: 500. Plans 20-35 first novels this year. Averages 10 total titles, 3-4 fiction titles each year. Sometimes comments on rejected ms; charges for critiques.
Needs: Adventure, ethnic, faction, fantasy, juvenile (easy-to-read, fantasy), religious/inspirational, romance, spiritual, young adult (fantasy/science fiction). "We will not except obscene novels of any type. We would like to see more poetry-spiritual-text." Recently published *The Calling of Cable*, by Brian Tinsley (spiritual); *Peter Pan Boy*, by Jim Kirby (fiction); and *The Other You*, by Venor Johnson (humor/satire); published new writers within the last year.
How to Contact: Does not accept unsolicited mss. Query first or submit complete ms with cover letter. SASE. Reports in 1 month on mss. Simultaneous and photocopied submissions OK. Accepts computer printout submissions.
Terms: Does not pay. Publishes ms 8-10 weeks after acceptance. Writer's guidelines free.

***SCOJTIA PUBLISHING COMPANY, INC. (II)**, 6457 Wilcox Station, Box 38002, Los Angeles CA 90038. Imprint: The Lion. Managing Editor: Patrique Quintahlen. Estab. 1986. "Small independent publisher plans to expand, ten-member operation on full-time basis." Publishes hardcover and paperback originals and reprints. Books: 50-60 lb weight paper; perfect bound; artists on staff for illustrations; average print order: 1,000-15,000; first novel print order: 1,000. Averages 5 total titles/year; 2 fiction titles/year. Offers editorial/publishing services for a fee. Query for details.
Needs: Adventure, contemporary, ethnic, experimental, fantasy, historical, humor/satire, juvenile (animal, easy-to-read, fantasy, historical, sports, spy/adventure, contemporary), literary, mainstream, preschool/picture book, romance (contemporary, historical), science fiction, suspense/mystery, western, young adult/teen (easy-to-read, fantasy/science fiction, historical, problem novels, romance, sports, spy/adventure). "Looking for contemporary romance novels, science fiction." No horror, gore, erotica, gay, occult, novels. No sexism, racism, or pornography. Recently published *The Boy Who Opened Doors* (novel for intermediate readers 7-14), *The Boy Who Opened Doors* (the musical) and *The Toy And the Boss' Breakfast*, by Prentiss Van Daves.
How to Contact: Accepts unsolicited mss. Query first. Submit outline/synopsis with 3 sample chapters. SASE (IRC). 50% of fiction is agented. Reports in 4 months on queries; in 6 months on mss. Photocopied submissions OK. Accepts computer printout submissions, no dot-matrix. Accepts disk submissions from Macintosh Plus.
Terms: Pays royalties of 7-10%; average advance $1,000-$3,000; advance is negotiable; advance is more for agented ms; 50 author's copies. Sends galleys to author. Subsidy publishes 5% of books each year. Subsidy publishes books of poetry only, 50-150 pages. Subjects: love, psychology, philosophy, new male/female relationships, family. Book catalog for $1.
Advice: "To save time and expense, it is recommended that authors learn as much as possible about not simply their writing craft, but also the very art of publishing. I recommend studying self publishing at some point after the author has completed several works, learning the actual book making process, book design, marketing, sales, distribution, and publishing and the money saving typesetting advantages of today's word processing and computer options. This advice is to speed the 'submission-to-publication' process between author and small press operations. This is valuable in respect to new unpublished authors, but the classical submissions methods of ms to major publishers still remains an important option to the author with a book with commercial value, for literary works of the highest quality small presses are the proven markets for success to the literary author."

SEA FOG PRESS, INC. (II), Box 210056, San Francisco CA 94121-0056. (415)221-8527. President: Rose Evans. Estab. 1984. Small one-person press. Publishes hardcover and paperback originals. Occasionally critiques rejected ms.
Needs: Contemporary, ethnic, feminist, juvenile (animal, historical, contemporary), religious/inspirational, translations, war (anti-war theme) and young adult/teen (historical, problem novels). "We are mainly interested in books that promote reverence for life, including animal welfare, animal rights, disabled achievement and disabled rights, social justice, peace, and reverence for human life." Published *Friends of All Creatures*, by Rose Evans; *The Whale's Tale*, by Deborah Evans Smith (children's).
How to Contact: Accepts unsolicited mss. Query first or submit outline/synopsis and 3 sample chapters with SASE. Reports in 2 weeks on queries. Simultaneous and photocopied submissions OK. Accepts computer printout submissions. Prefers letter-quality.
Terms: Negotiates royalties and advance. Free writer's guidelines and book catalog.

SEAL PRESS (IV), 3131 Western Ave., Seattle WA 98121. (206)283-7844. President: Faith Conlon. Estab. 1976. Publishes hardcover and paperback originals. Books: acid-free paper; offset printing; perfect or cloth binding; average print order: 4,000. Averages 8-10 total titles, including 4-5 fiction, each year. Sometimes critiques rejected ms "very briefly."
Needs: Ethnic, feminist, lesbian, literary, short story collections. "We publish women only. Work must be feminist, non-racist, non-homophobic." Published *Girls, Visions & Everything*, by Sarah Schulman; *Sisters of the Road*, by Barbara Wilson (feminist mystery); and *Two Women in One*, by Nawal El-Saadawi. "A recent development is 'International Women's Crime' (subseries of 'Women in Translation') – a feminist mystery series translated from other languages."
How to Contact: Query first. SASE. Reports in 1-2 months. Accepts "readable" computer printouts.
Terms: "Standard publishing practices; do not wish to disclose specifics." Sends galleys to author. Book catalog for SAE and 45¢ postage.

SECOND CHANCE PRESS AND THE PERMANENT PRESS (II), R.D.#2 Noyac Rd., Sag Harbor NY 11963. (516)725-1101. Editor: Judith Shepard. Estab. 1977. Mid-size, independent publisher. Publishes hardcover originals and reprints. Books: 5½x8½ hardcover and trade paperbacks; average print order: 3,000; first novel print order: 3,000. Plans to publish 3 first novels this year. Averages 12 total titles; 10 fiction titles each year.
Needs: Adventure, contemporary, ethnic, experimental, historical, literary, mainstream, supsense/mystery. "I like novels that have a unique point of view and have a high quality of writing." No gothic, romance, horror, science fiction, pulp. Recently published *1933*, by Philip Metcalfe; *Captain Bennett's Folly,* by Berry Fleming; published new writers within the last year.
How to Contact: Query first. SASE. Agented fiction: 10%. Reports in 2 weeks on queries; 2 months on mss. Simultaneous and photocopied submissions OK. Accepts computer printouts.
Terms: Pays in royalties of 10% minimum; 15% maximum of net sales. Sends galleys to author. Advance to $1,000. Sends galleys to author. Book catalog for $2.
Advice: "Be as thorough in your submissions and covering all bases as you, presumably, have been in writing your book."

SEVEN BUFFALOES PRESS (II), Box 249, Big Timber MT 59011. Editor/Publisher: Art Cuelho. Estab. 1975. Publishes paperback originals. Averages 4-5 total titles each year.
Needs: Contemporary, short story collections, "rural, American Hobo, Okies, American Indian, Southern Appalachia, Arkansas and the Ozarks. Wants farm and ranch based stories." Published *Rig Nine*, by William Rintoul (collection of oilfield short stories).
How to Contact: Query first with SASE. Photocopied submissions OK. Reports in 1 week on queries; 2 weeks on mss.
Terms: Pays in royalties of 10% minimum; 15% on second edition or in author's copies (10% of edition). No advance. Free writer's guidelines and book catalog for SASE.
Advice: "There's too much influence from TV and Hollywood; media writing I call it. We need to get back to the people; to those who built and are still building this nation with sweat, blood, and brains. More people are into it for the money; instead of for the good writing that is still to be cranked out by isolated writers. Remember, I was a writer for 10 years before I became a publisher."

‡THE SHEEP MEADOW PRESS (I,II), Box 1345, Riverdale-on-Hudson NY 10471. (212)549-3365. Editor-in-Chief: George Wen. Estab. 1976. "Small press essentially dealing with poetry, though expanding this year to include fiction." Publishes hardcover and paperback originals. Books: Finch/Mohawk Vellum paper. Averages 10 poetry titles. "We will be starting this year to accept fiction manuscripts." Sometimes comments on rejected ms.
Needs: Adventure, contemporary, ethnic, historical, literary, mainstream, short story collections, suspense/mystery, translations.
How to Contact: Accepts unsolicited mss. Query first. Reports in 1 month on queries; 4-6 weeks on mss. Simultaneous and photocopied submissions OK. Accepts computer printout submissions.
Terms: Pays in royalties and author's copies. Send galleys to author. Publishes ms 6-9 months after acceptance. Writer's guidelines and book catalog free.

‡SHOE TREE PRESS, Box 219, Crozet VA 22932. *Send submissions to* RD2, Box 1162, Hemlock Road, Columbia NJ 07832. (201)496-4441. An Imprint of Betterway Publications Inc. Editor: Joyce McDonald. Estab. 1984. Publishes juvenile hardcover and paperback original and reprints. Books: generally 70 lb vellum paper; offset printing; reinforced binding; and perfect for softcover; occasionally uses illustrations for middle years books; average print order: 5,000. First novel print order: 5,000. Plans 3 novels this year. Averages 5 fiction titles each year. Rarely critiques or comments on rejected mss.

Needs: Young adult, middle years fiction. No formula or genre fiction please. Published *Summer Captive*, by Penny Pollock (young adult); published new writers within the last year.
How to Contact: We no longer accept unsolicited manuscripts. Please query. SASE. Agented fiction 33%. Reports in 2-4 weeks on queries; 10-12 weeks on mss. Simultaneous and photocopied submissions OK. Accepts computer printout submissions.
Terms: Pays in royalties 10% hardcover; 6% softcover. Advance varies and is negotiable. Sends galleys to author.
Advice: "We publish juvenile fiction and nonfiction only. Our primary focus is on historical fiction for middle years and on nonfiction. We do *not* publish picture books. Don't get caught up in trying to follow 'market trends.' Write about what you know, and write it from the heart."

SILVERLEAF PRESS, INC. (I, II), Box 70189, Seattle WA 98107. Editor: Ann Larson. Estab. 1985. Publishes paperback originals. Books: 50 lb book stock; offset printing; perfect binding; no illustrations; average print order: 1,600; first novel print order: 1,600. Plans 1-2 first novels this year. Averages 2 total titles/year; 2 fiction titles/year. Sometimes critiques or comments on rejected mss.
Needs: Feminist, humor/satire, lesbian, short story collections. "Must be feminist or lesbian." Recently published *Three Glasses of Wine Have Been Removed From This Story*, by Marian Michener; published new writers within the last year.
How to Contact: Accepts unsolicited mss. Submit complete ms with cover letter. SASE (IRC). Reports in 2-3 months. Photocopied submissions OK. Accepts computer printout submissions.
Terms: Pays negotiable royalties and advance; author's copies. Sends galleys to author. Book catalog free on request.
Advice: "Try the small presses—they are more likely to give you a chance."

SIMON & PIERRE PUBLISHING COMPANY LIMITED (II), Box 280, Adelaide St. Postal Stn., Toronto, Ontario M5C 2J4 Canada. Imprints includes Bastet Books, Canplay Series, Canadian Theatre History Series, The Canadian Dramatist, and Drama for Life. Contact: Editors. Estab. 1972. Publishes hardcover and paperback originals. Published new writers last year. Books: 55 lb hi bulk web printing; perfect binding; line drawings; average print order 2,000. Averages 10-12 titles/year.
Needs: Contemporary, literary, mystery, spy, historical, humor/satire, juvenile, young adult and translations. No romance, erotica, horror, science fiction, or poetry. Recently published *Across the Bridge*, by Helen Duncan; *The Blackbird's Song*, by Pauline Holdstock; *Brother Sebastian's Little Holiday*, by G.W. Bartram; and *Mizzly Fitch*, by Murra.
How to Contact: Query, submit complete ms, submit outline/synopsis and sample chapter or submit through agent with SASE (Canadian stamps) or IRCs. Simultaneous and photocopied submissions OK. Reports in 1 month on queries, 4 months on mss.
Terms: Pays in royalties; small advance. Sends galleys to author. Free book catalog.
Advice: "We prefer Canadian authors. Include with submissions: professional résumé listing previous publications, detailed outline of proposed work and sample chapters. We publish novelists who are good at proofing themselves and not afraid of being involved in their own marketing, but the fiction must be based on a current topics or themes."

SOHO PRESS, 1 Union Square, New York NY 10003. (212)243-1527. Publisher: Juris Jurjevics. Publishes hardcover and trade paperback originals. Averages 14 titles/year.
Needs: Adventure, ethnic, historical, mainstream, mystery/espionage, suspense. "We do novels that are the very best in their genres." Recently published *His Third, Her Second*, by Paul Estaver; *Straight Through the Night*, by Edward Allen; *Inspector Imanishi Investigates*, by Seicho Matsumoto; published new writers within the last year.
How to Contact: Submit query or complete ms with SASE. Reports in 2 weeks on queries; 1 month on mss. Photocopied and simultaneous submissions OK.
Terms: Pays royalties of 10% minimum; 15% maximum on retail price. For trade paperbacks pays 7½% royalties to 10,000 copies; 10% after. Offers advance. Book catalog free on request.
Advice: "There aren't any tricks (to writing a good query letter)—just say what the book is. Don't analyze the market for it. Don't take writing courses too seriously, and *read* the best people in whatever genre you are working. We are looking for those who have taught themselves or otherwise mastered the craft."

THE SPEECH BIN, INC. (IV), 231 Clarksville Rd., Box 218, Princeton Junction NJ 08550-0218. (609)799-3935. FAX: (609)799-9530. Senior Editor: Jan J. Binney. Estab. 1984. Small independent publisher and major national and international distributor of books and material for speech-language pathologists, audiologists, special educators and caregivers. Publishes hardcover and paperback originals. Averages 6-10 total titles/year. "No fiction at present time, but we are very interested in publishing fiction relevant to our specialties."

Needs: "We are most interested in seeing fiction, including books for children, dealing with individuals experiencing communication disorders, other handicaps, and their families and caregivers, particularly their parents, or family members dealing with individuals who have strokes, physical disability, hearing loss, Alzheimer's and so forth."
How to Contact: Accepts unsolicited mss. Query first. SASE (IRC). 10% of fiction is agented. Reports in 4-6 weeks on queries; 1-3 months on mss. Simultaneous and photocopied submissions OK. Accepts computer printout submissions.
Terms: Pays royalties of 8%+. Sends galleys to author. Writer's guidelines for #10 SASE. Book catalog for 9×12 SAE with 3 first class stamps.
Advice: "We are most interested in publishing fiction about individuals who have speech, hearing and other handicaps."

SPINSTERS/AUNT LUTE BOOK CO. (IV), Box 410687, San Francisco CA 94141. (415)558-9655. Editors: Sherilyn Thomas and Joan Pinkross. Estab. 1978. Moderate size women's publishing company growing steadily. Publishes paperback originals and reprints. Books: 55 lb acid free natural paper; photo offset printing; perfect binding; illustrations when appropriate; average print order: 5,000. Plans 3 first novels this year. Averages 6 total titles, 3-5 fiction titles each year. Occasionally critiques rejected ms.
Needs: Feminist, lesbian. Wants "full-length quality fiction – thoroughly revised novels which display deep characterization, theme and style. We *only* consider books by women. No books by men, or books with sexist, racist or ageist content." Recently published *Singing Softly/Cantando Bajito,* by Carmen de Monteflores; *Bittersweet,* by Nevada Barr; *Coz,* by Marcy Pierrou; published new writers within the last year.
How to Contact: Accepts unsolicited mss. Query or submit outline/synopsis and 3 sample chapters with SASE. Reports in 1 month on queries; 2 months on mss. No simultaneous submissions without specific permission; photocopied submissions OK. Accepts computer printout submissions; prefers letter-quality. Disk submissions OK with Morrow Designs MDII system. Prefers hard copy with disk submission.
Terms: Pays in royalties of 8% minimum, 12% maximum (after 10,000) plus 25 author's copies; unlimited extra copies at 50% discount. Free book catalog.
Advice: "Our recent titles are primarily feminist and/or lesbian. We would publish more fiction if we could get excellent manuscripts. Use writers' groups for critical feedback. Know publisher's market before submitting. Query professionally."

SPIRITUAL FICTION PUBLICATIONS (II, IV), Subsidiary of Garber Communications, Inc., 5 Garber Hill Rd., Blauvelt NY 10913. (914)359-9292. Editor-in-Chief: Bernard J. Garber. Fiction Editor: Patricia Abrams. Midsize publisher. Averages 4-5 titles each year. Average first novel print order 1,000 copies paperback; 300 copies cloth.
Needs: Psychic/supernatural/occult, historical, religious/inspirational. No science fiction. Published *Legend*, by Barry Maher.
How to Contact: Does not accept unsolicited mss. Query first or send 1-2 page outline plus SASE. Reports in 1 month on queries.
Advice: "Read what we have published. We accept first novels if they are good."

***STAR BOOKS, INC.**, 408 Pearson St., Wilson NC 27893. (919)237-1591. President: Irene Burk Harrell. Estab. 1983. "Small but growing" publisher. Publishes paperback originals. Books: offset paper; offset printing; perfect binding. some illustrations; average print order: 1,000; first novel print order: 1,000. Plans 1 first novel this year. Averages 5-6 total titles, 1 fiction title each year. Sometimes comments on rejected mss, "comment no charge; critique $1 per ms page, $25 minimum."
Needs: Religious/inspirational, young adult/teen. "Strongly and specifically Christian." Published *The Bridge*, by Ralph Filicchia (contemporary inner-city); *And Now I See*, by Clyde Bolton (Biblical novel); and *Mory*, by Marie Denison (contemporary).
How to Contact: Accepts unsolicited mss. Submit complete ms with cover letter. SASE for ms. Reports on queries in 2 weeks. Photocopied submissions OK. Accepts computer printout submissions.
Terms: Pays royalties of 10% minimum; 15% maximum. Sends page proofs to author. Publishing of ms after acceptance "depends on our situation." "*Sometimes*, (not always) we need author to buy prepub copies (at 50% off list) to help with first printing costs." Guidelines and book catalog for #10 SAE and 2 first class stamps.
Advice: "Make sure that for us the book is in line with Biblical principles and powerful enough to cause the reader to make an initial commitment of his/her life to Jesus Christ, or if the reader is already a Christian, to strengthen his/her walk with Him."

***STATION HILL PRESS (II, III)**, Barrytown NY 12507. (914)758-5840. Imprints include Open Book, Pulse, Artext, Clinamen Studies and Contemporary Artists Series. Publishers: George Quasha and Susan Quasha. Estab. 1978. Publishes paperback and cloth originals. Averages 10-15 total titles, 5-7 fiction titles each year.
Needs: Contemporary, experimental, literary, translations, and new age. Published *Operas and Plays*, by Gertrude Stein; *Narrative Unbound*, by Donald Ault.
How to Contact: Query first with SASE before sending ms. No unsolicited mss. Reports in 4-6 weeks on queries; 4 months on mss.
Terms: Pays in author's copies (10% of print run) or by standard royalty, depending on the nature of the material. *Occasional subsidy publishing.* "Co-venture arrangements are possible with higher royalty." Book catalog free on request.

STORMLINE PRESS, INC. (I,II, IV), Box 593, Urbana IL 61801. (217)328-2665. Publisher: Raymond Bial. Estab. 1985. Independent literary press. Publishes hardcover and paperback originals. Books: best quality, usually acid-free paper; commercial printing—all graphics in duotone printing; perfect bound and clothbound binding; illustrations photographs and original artwork; average print order: 1,000-1,500; first novel print order: 1,000-1,500. Plans 1 first novel this year. Averages 4-5 total titles; 1 fiction title each year. Occasionally critiques or comments on rejected ms "on serious works only."
Needs: Ethnic, humor/satire, literary, mainstream, short story collections. "Serious literary works only. We are only interested in novels, collections of short stories and novellas that accurately and sensitively portray rural and small town life." No genre fiction, or anything that was written primarily for its commercial value. Recently published *People of Gumption and Other Stories*, by Fran Lehr (short stories).
How to Contact: Accepts mss during November and December only. Query first with SASE. Does not accept unsolicited mss. "We urge that you write for guidelines (enclose SASE)." Reports in 2 weeks on queries. Accepts computer printout submissions.
Terms: Pays royalties of 10% minimum; 15% maximum. Pays 25 author copies. Payment depends on grant/award money. Authors are generally paid 15% royalties once the production costs of the book have been met. Book catalog free on request.
Advice: "We are interested in works of the highest literary quality which also make for enjoyable reading. It is difficult, if not nearly impossible to get book length manuscripts published these days. Of those manuscripts published most are quickly forgotten within a few months or a few years. Only a precious few writers are sufficiently talented to stand the test of time. Therefore, I recommend that you not consider writing unless your work cries to be published and read."

SUNSTONE PRESS (IV), Box 2321, Santa Fe NM 87504-2321. (505)988-4418. Contact: James C. Smith, Jr. Estab. 1971. Midsize publisher. Publishes paperback originals. Plans 2 first novels this year. Averages 16 total titles; 2-3 fiction titles each year. "Sometimes" buys juvenile mss with illustrations. Average first novel print order: 2,000 copies.
Needs: Western. "We have a Southwestern theme emphasis." No science fiction, romance or occult. Published *Apache: The Long Ride Home*, by Grant Gall (Indian/Western); *Border Patrol*, by Cmdr. Alvin E. Moore; and *The Last Narrow Gauge Train Robbery*, by Robert K. Swisher, Jr.; published new writers within the last year.
How to Contact: Accepts unsolicited mss. Query first or submit outline/synopsis and 2 sample chapters with SASE. Reports in 2 weeks. Simultaneous and photocopied submissions OK. Accepts computer printout submissions. Publishes ms 9 months to 1 year after acceptance.
Terms: Pays in royalties, 10% maximum, and 10 author's copies.

TEAL PRESS (II), Box 4098, Santa Fe NM 87502-4098. (505)989-7861. Editor: Robert Jebb. Estab. 1983. Small press publishing 2-4 titles per year. Publishes paperback originals. Books: acid-free paper; offset printing; Smyth-sewn binding; average print order: 1,500.
Needs: Contemporary and literary. Recently published *The Testimony of Mr. Bones,* by Olive Ghiselin (short stories); published new writers within the last year. "Looking for short fiction only, either novellas of around 70 to 100 pages or collections of short stories. No full length novels will be considered. Not interested in science fiction, mysteries, romance or adventure."
How to Contact: Mss without SASE will not be responded to or returned.
Terms: Pays in royalties of 10% minimum.

‡TEXTILE BRIDGE PRESS (II), Subsidiary of Moody Street Irregulars, Inc., Box 157, Clarence Center NY 14032. (716)741-3393. Imprints include The Jack Kerouac Living Writers Reading Series. President/Editor: Joy Walsh. Fiction Editor: Marion Perry. Estab. 1978. "We publish a magazine on and about the work of Jack Kerouac. We also publish book length manuscripts in the spirit of Kerouac when available." Publishes paperback originals. Books: bond paper; offset printing; saddle or perfect binding; average print order: 300-500; first novel print order: 500. Plans 1 first novel this year. Averages

5 total titles each year, 2 fiction titles each year. Sometimes comments on rejected ms; charges for critiques.
Needs: Experimental, literary, short story collections. No romance, gothic. Recently published *Big Ben Hood*, by Emmanual Freed (literary); *Links of the Chain*, by William Harnock (short story collection); and *Walk With Me*, by Dorothy Smith (literary); published new writers within last year.
How to Contact: Accepts unsolicited mss. Submit complete ms with cover letter. SASE. Agented fiction 1%. Reports in 1 week on queries; 1 month on mss. Simultaneous and photocopied submissions OK. Accepts computer printout submissions.
Terms: Pays in author's copies "if run 300, 30 copies/if 500, 50 copies." Sends galleys to author. Publishes ms 1 year after acceptance. Writers guidelines not available. Book catalog free, if available.

THIRD WOMAN PRESS (II), %Chicano-Riqueno Studies, Ballantine 849, Bloomington IN 47401. (812)335-5257. Editorial Assistant: Krystie L. Herndon. Fiction Editor: Norma Alarcon. Estab. 1981. One-person operation on part-time basis. Publishes paperback originals. Book: 5½x8½ inch paper; offset printing; perfect binding; illustrations and photos; average print order 1,000. Publishes 2-3 titles each year; all fiction. Sometimes critiques rejected mss.
Needs: Ethnic, women's. Recently published *Third Woman*, semi-annual journal of literature and the arts focusing on Third World women, primarily Hispanic women; and *My Wicked Wicked Ways*, by Sandra Cisneros (collection of poetry).
How to Contact: Accepts unsolicited mss. Submit complete ms with cover letter. SASE. Reports in 2 months. Simultaneous and photocopied submissions OK. Accepts computer printout submissions.
Terms: Pays in author's copies. Sends pre-publication galleys to author. Book brochures free on request. Offers grants or awards to fiction writers periodically.
Advice: "Read."

THISTLEDOWN PRESS (II, IV), 668 East Place, Saskatoon, Saskatchewan S7J 2Z5 Canada. (306)244-1722. Editor-in-Chief: Paddy O'Rourke. Estab. 1975. Publishes hardcover and paperback originals. Books: quality stock paper; offset printing; Smythe-sewn binding; occasionally illustrations; average print order 1,500-2,000; first novel print order: 1,250-1,500. Plans 1 first novel and 3 collections of stories. Publishes 12 titles/year, 4 or 5 fiction. Occasionally critiques rejected mss.
Needs: Literary, experimental, short story collections and novels. "We *only* want to see Canadian-authored submissions. We will *not* consider multiple submissions."
How to Contact: No unsolicited mss. Query first with SASE. Photocopied submissions OK. Reports in 2 months on queries. Published *Medieval Hour in the Author's Mind*, by Ernest Hekkenan; *The Fungus Garden*, by Brian Brett; *Forms of Captivity and Escape*, by J. J. Steinfeld.
Advice: "We are primarily looking for quality writing that is original and innovative in its perspective and/or use of language. Thistledown would like to receive queries first before submission—perhaps with novel outline, some indication of previous publications, periodicals your work has appeared in. We publish Canadian authors only. We are continuing to publish more fiction and are looking for new fiction writers to add to our list. Familiarize yourself with some of our books before submitting a query or manuscript to the press."

THREE CONTINENTS PRESS (II, IV), 1901 Pennsylvania Ave. N.W., Suite 407, Washington DC 20006. (202)223-2554. Fiction Editor: Donald Herdeck. Estab. 1973. Small independent publisher with expanding list. Publishes hardcover and paperback originals and reprints. Books: library binding; illustrations; average print order: 1,000-1,500; first novel print order: 1,000. Averages 15 total titles, 6-8 fiction titles each year. Average first novel print order: 1,000 copies. Occasionally critiques ("a few sentences") rejected mss.
Needs: "We publish original fiction only by writers from Africa, the Caribbean, the Middle East, Asia and the Pacific. No fiction by writers from North America or Western Europe." Published *Kaidara*, by Mamadou Bah, translated by Daniel Whitman; *Fountain and Tomb* by Naguib Mahfous, translated by James Kennison. Also, short-story collections by established writers.
How to Contact: Query with outline/synopsis and sample pages and SAE, IRC. State "origins (non-Western), education and previous publications." Reports in 1 month on queries; 2 months on mss. Simultaneous and photocopied submissions OK. Computer printout submissions OK.
Terms: "We are not a subsidy publisher, but do a few specialized titles a year with subsidy. In those cases we accept grants or institutional subventions. Foundation or institution receives 20-30 copies of book and at times royalty on first printing. We pay royalties twice yearly (against advance) as a percentage of net paid receipts." Royalties of 5% minimum, 10% maximum; 10 author's copies; offers negotiable advance, $300 average. Depends on grant/award money. Sends galleys to author. Free book catalog.

***TIDE BOOK PUBLISHING COMPANY**, Box 101, York Harbor ME 03911. Subsidiary of Tide Media. President: Rose Safran. Estab. 1979. Independent, small publisher. Publishes paperback originals. Averages 1 title each year. Occasionally critiques rejected mss.

Close-up

Norma Alarcón

Publisher
Third Woman Press

Since its inception in 1980, Third Woman Press has had two major goals: (1) to make the public aware of the work of U.S. Latinas (women of Hispanic descent) and (2) to dispel the feeling of isolation between these writers.

"I chose the name *Third Woman* with the intention of focusing on third world women in a global sense, at least [as the term relates to the] U.S. What it turned out to be was the realization that Latinas didn't have any outlets at all at that time," says Norma Alarcón, Third Woman's founder and publisher. "As writers, we are a minority within a minority. We were so scattered throughout the United States we did not know who the others were."

Each year, Third Woman Press publishes the only journal, *Third Woman,* devoted exclusively to the works of U.S. Latinas. In addition, it publishes two books annually. Past releases include *Speak to Me from Dreams* by Barbara Brinson Curiel, *The Margarita Poems* by Luz María Umpierre-Herrera, and *Chiliagony* by Iris Zavala.

Third Woman accepts manuscripts throughout the year for both the journal and the press. Those wishing to be considered for *Third Woman* should submit their manuscripts by March 31st. Manuscripts received after this date will be considered for the next issue. Alarcón is interested in novels, collections of short stories, scripts or poetry for possible publication. There is no formal submission schedule for the press at this time.

Submissions in both Spanish and English are accepted for the journal. Alarcón says that she will consider bilingual manuscripts for book publication but this depends on length and the author's involvement in distribution. "I have no aversion to Spanish language manuscripts but at this point my philosophy would be that the writer would have to become very involved in helping us identify the outlets for it."

Third Woman acquires First American Rights but negotiates translation rights and additional publication rights. "We have to draw up a contract that is acceptable. I am usually very flexible with that," Alarcón adds.

Alarcón's first consideration when assessing a manuscript is neatness. "After that I like to have well thought-out material with psychological depth and complexity," she says. "I prefer to see the development of female protagonists in all kinds of circumstances and settings and possibilities. This is not to exclude looking at male protagonists, but we tend to go for the females."

Third Woman accepts creative work from Latinas exclusively. Males, however, may submit critical essays which focus on a Latina's work.

Alarcón's advice to Latina writers is to not despair. She believes there are a lot of small presses that look sympathetically on the productions of U.S. Latinas or third world women. She emphasizes they must persevere and find the networks which support their work.

Her goal for the future is to increase the press' circulation. "I think that if our circulation grew and we could start getting other audiences then I could bring in other issues and work in other groups like Asians, for example, or Native Americans, [or] Blacks."

—Judith A. Mills

Needs: Contemporary, feminist, historical, humor/satire, literary, mainstream, regional. Needs women's novels with a social service thrust; contemporary. No gothic, trash.
How to Contact: Query first; submit outline synopsis and 1-2 sample chapters with SASE. Simultaneous submissions OK. Accepts computer printout submissions, prefers letter-quality. Reports in 1 month.
Terms: Pays in 100 author's copies. *Considering cost plus subsidy arrangements*—will advertise.

TIMES EAGLE BOOKS (IV), Box 11735, Portland OR 97211. Fiction Editor: Mark Hurst. Estab. 1971. "Small operation on part-time basis." Specialized publisher limited to contributors from West Coast region. First novel print order: 2,500. Plans 2 first novels this year. Averages 2 titles/year, all fiction.
Needs: Contemporary. "Graphic descriptions of teenage life by West Coast youth, such as Bret Easton Ellis's *Less than Zero*. Recently published *Equator: The Story and the Letters*, by V.O. Blum (erotic/philosophical novel).
How to Contact: Does not accept or return unsolicited mss. Query first in one paragraph. Reports in 2 weeks.
Terms: Pays 10-15% royalties.
Advice: "Times Eagle Books prefers first novelists."

TIPTOE LITERARY SERVICE (IV), Box 206-OH, Naselle WA 98638. (206)484-7722. Publisher: A. Grimm-Richardson. Estab. 1985. Small publisher, books under 75 pages and booklets. Publishes paperback originals. Books: xerographic paper; photocopy print; saddle stitch binding; line drawings/sketches & graphs; average print order: limited 1st edition 250 press run. Plans 1 first novelette this year. Publishes 3 total titles each year; 1 fiction title. Sometimes critiques rejected mss.
Needs: Currently overstocked. Published *Something Fishy at The Panama Canal*, by Meldeau Dampfer (faction); and *Effie's Bytes*, by Lou Lazer (computer science fiction). Has recently published first time author.
How to Contact: Does not accept unsolicited mss. Query first. SASE. No agented fiction. Reports on queries in 3 weeks. Simultaneous and photocopied submissions OK. Accepts computer printout submissions.
Terms: "Private arrangement with local writer associates, usually barter." Book catalog free on request to foreign addresses; otherwise for #10 SAE with 1 first class stamp.
Advice: "Still a 'new' business—plans for a mix of categories, fiction one-third. We will be stressing our Writer Guide pamphlets for the next year."

THE TRANSLATION CENTER (II), 412 Dodge Hall, Columbia University, New York NY 10027. (212)854-2305. Editors: Frank MacShane, William Jay Smith, Lane Dunlop. Estab. 1972. Publishes paperback originals. Books: 6×9; perfect bound; high-quality paper. Averages 2 total titles/year.
Needs: Translations.
How to Contact: Accepts unsolicited ms. Submit complete ms with cover letter and SASE. Photocopied submissions OK. Accepts computer printouts including dot-matrix.
Terms: Pays in 2 translator's copies.

‡TUDOR PUBLISHERS, INC. (II), P.O. Box 3443, Greensboro NC 27402. (919)282-5907. Editor: M.L. Hester. Estab. 1986. Small independent press. Publishes hardcover and paperback originals. Book: offset; Smythe sewn hardcover/trade paperback; occasional illustrations; average print order: 3,000; first novel print order: 1,000-2,000. Plans 1 first novel this year. Averages 5-7 total titles, 1-2 fiction titles each year. Sometimes comments on rejected ms.
Needs: Contemporary, historical, literary, mainstream, regional (Southeast), suspense/mystery, young adult/teen (10-18 years, problem novels). "Especially needs suspense; literary; YA suspense or problem. No romance, western." Recently published *Statutory Murder*, by Dicey Thomas (mystery/suspense); published new writers within the last year.
How to Contact: Accepts unsolicited mss. "Outline and query first, please." Submit outline/synopsis and 3 sample chapters. SASE. Reports on queries in 2 weeks; 6 weeks on mss. Accepts simultaneous, computer printouts and photocopied submissions.
Terms: Pays royalties of 10%. Average advance: $500-1,000. Sends galleys to author. Publishes ms 1 year to 18 months after acceptance. Book catalog for # 10 SASE or IRC and one 1st class stamp.
Advice: "Tell us of any publishing done previously. Send a clear summary or outline of the book with a cover letter. Interested in suspense in both adult and young adult; also literary fiction of high quality. Send only your best work. No romance, science fiction, western; no multigenerational sagas unless of extremely high quality. No horror."

TURNSTONE PRESS (II), 607-100 Arthur St., Winnipeg, Manitoba R3B 1H3 Canada. (204)947-1555. Managing Editor: Marilyn Morton. Books: offset paper; usually photo direct printing; perfect binding; average first novel print order: 2,000. Estab. 1976. Publishes paperback originals. Averages 8 total titles/year. Occasionally critiques rejected ms.

Needs: Experimental and literary. "We will be doing only 2-3 fiction titles a year. Interested in new work exploring new narrative/fiction forms." Recently published *Bone Bird,* by Darlene Barry Quaife; *Older Than Ravens,* by Douglas Reimer; published fiction by previously unpublished writers within the last year.

How to Contact: Send SASE or SAE and IRC. Photocopied submissions OK. Reports in 1 month on queries; 2-4 months on mss.

Terms: "Like most Canadian literary presses, we depend heavily on government grants which are not available for books by nonCanadians. Do some homework before submitting work to make sure your subject matter/genre/writing style falls within the publishers area of interest." Pays in royalties of 10%; 10 (complimentary) author's copies. Book catalog free on request.

ULTRAMARINE PUBLISHING CO., INC. (III), Box 303, Hastings-on-the-Hudson NY 10706. (914)478-2522. Publisher: Christopher P. Stephens. Estab. 1973. Small publisher. "We have 150 titles in print. We also distribute for authors where a major publisher has dropped a title." Encourages new writers. Averages 15 total titles, 12 fiction titles each year. Buys 90% agented fiction. Occasionally critiques rejected ms.

Needs: Experimental, fantasy, mainstream, science fiction, and short story collections. No romance, westerns, mysteries.

How to Contact: Does not accept unsolicited mss. Submit outline/synopsis and 2 sample chapters with SASE. Prefers agented ms. Reports in 6 weeks. Simultaneous, photocopied submissions OK. Accepts computer printout submissions. Publishes ms an average of 8 months after acceptance.

Terms: Pays in royalties of 10% minimum; advance is negotiable. Free book catalog.

***UNIVERSITY EDITIONS (I, II),** 59 Oak Lane, Spring Valley, Huntington WV 25704. Imprint: Aegina Press. Managing Editor: Ira Herman. Estab. 1983. Independent publisher presently expanding. Publishes paperback originals and reprints. Books: 50 lb library-weight paper; litho offset printing; most are perfect bound; illustrations; average print order: 500-1,000; first novel print order: 500-1,000. Plans 10 first novels this year. "We strongly encourage new writers." Averages 20 total titles, approximately 12 fiction titles each year. Often critiques rejected ms.

Needs: Adventure, contemporary, ethnic, experimental, faction, fantasy, feminist, historical, romance, horror, humor/satire, juvenile (all types), literary, mainstream, regional, science fiction, short story collections, translations and war. "Historical, literary, and regional fiction are our main areas of emphasis." Recently published *Circle of Blood,* by Margery La Porte (novel); *Jewish Days,* by Elias Sassoon (short story collection); *Dream Demon,* by Clark Schmidt (novel); published new writers within the last year.

How to Contact: Accepts unsolicited mss. "We depend upon manuscripts that arrive unsolicited." Query or submit outline/synopsis and 3 or more sample chapters or complete ms. "We prefer to see entire manuscripts; we will consider queries and partials as well." SASE for queries, mss. Reports in 1 week on queries; 1 month on mss. Simultaneous and photocopied submissions OK. Accepts computer printout submissions, prefers letter-quality.

Terms: Payment is negotiated individually for each book. Sends galleys to author. Depends upon author and subject. *Subsidy publishes most new titles.*

Advice: "We attempt to encourage and establish new authors. Editorial tastes in fiction are eclectic. We try to be open to any type of fiction that is well written. We are publishing more fiction now that the very large publishers are getting harder to break into. We publish softcovers primarily, in order to keep books affordable. We hope to publish more first novels in 1990."

THE UNIVERSITY OF ARKANSAS PRESS (I), Fayetteville AR 72701. (501)575-3246. Director: Miller Williams. Acquisitions Editor: James Twiggs. Estab. 1980. Small university press. Publishes hardcover and paperback originals. Averages 30 total titles, 2 short fiction titles each year. Average print order 500 cloth and 2,000 paper copies.

Needs: Literary, mainstream, novels and short story collections, and translations. Recently published *Long Blues in a Minor*, by Gerard Herzhaft (novel); *The Blacktop Champion of Ickey Honey and Other Stories*, by Robert Sorrells; *Power Lines and Other Stories*, by Jane Bradley; published fiction by previously unpublished writers within the last year.

How to Contact: Accepts unsolicited mss. Query first with SASE. Simultaneous and photocopied submissions OK "if very clean." Accepts computer printout submissions, no dot-matrix without sample first. Reports in 2 weeks on queries. Publishes ms an average of 1 year after acceptance.

Terms: Pays in royalties of 10%; 10 author's copies. Writer's guidelines and book catalog free for 9x12 SASE.

Advice: "We are looking for fiction written with energy, clarity and economy. Apart from this, we have no predisposition concerning style or subject matter. The University of Arkansas Press does not respond to queries or proposals not accompanied by SASE."

‡UNIVERSITY OF IDAHO PRESS (IV), 16 Brink Hall, University of Idaho, Moscow ID 83843. (208)885-7564. Director: James J. Heaney. Estab. 1972. "Small university press with combined scholarly and regional emphasis." Publishes hardcover and paperback originals and paperback reprints. Averages 7 total titles, 1-2 fiction titles each year. Sometimes comments on rejected ms.

Needs: Regional, short story collections. "We would like to publish some Western fictional works of suitable stylistic competence for a primarily regional market in Idaho and the inland Northwest. No fictionalized memoirs of pioneers, pony express riders, and so on." Recently published *Unearned Pleasures*, by Ursula Hegi (short story collection).

How to Contact: Accepts unsolicited mss. Query first. Reports in 1 month on queries; 4 months on ms. Photocopied submissions OK. Accepts computer printout submissions. Accepts electronic submissions via disk.

Terms: Pays in royalties. "Contracts are always negotiated individually. The small size of the regional fiction market makes less than luxurious terms a necessity for the publisher." Sends galleys to author. Writer's guidelines and book catalog free.

UNIVERSITY OF ILLINOIS PRESS (I), 54 E. Gregory, Champaign IL 61820. (217)333-0950. Senior Editor: Ann Lowry Weir. Estab. 1918. Not-for-profit university press. Publishes clothbound originals. Books: acid free paper; cloth binding; average print order: 1,500-2,000. Number of titles: 4 per year. Encourages new writers who have journal publications. Occasionally comments on rejected mss.

Needs: Contemporary, literary, and experimental. Story collections only. "No novels." Recently published *Man Without Memory*, by Richard Burgin; *The People Down South*, by Cary C. Holladay; *Bodies at Sea*, by Erin McGraw.

How to Contact: Accepts unsolicited mss. Query or submit complete ms. SASE. Simultaneous and photocopied submissions OK. Accepts computer printout submissions. Reports in 1 week on queries, 2-4 months on mss.

Terms: Pays 7½% net of all copies sold. No advance. Free book catalog.

Advice: "We do not publish novels, and we have no outlet for individual short stories. We publish collections of short fiction by authors who've usually established their credentials by being accepted for publication in periodicals, generally literary periodicals."

‡UNIVERSITY OF UTAH PRESS (IV), 101 University Services Bldg., Salt Lake City UT 84112. (801)581-6771. Director: David Catron. Estab. 1949. "Small university press." Publishes hardcover originals. Books: 60# paper; offset printing; sewn binding; average print order: 2,000; first novel print order: 2,000. Plans 2 first novels this year. Averages 25 total titles, 2 fiction titles each year. Sometimes comments on rejected ms.

Needs: Literary, western. Looks for mss on Utah, Western, Mormon. No "historical novels." Recently published *Wake of the General Bliss*, by Lueders; *Keno Runner*, by Kranes; *Benediction*, by Chandler (short stories).

How to Contact: Accepts unsolicited mss. Query first. SASE. Reports in 1-2 weeks on queries; 2 months on mss. Simultaneous and photocopied submissions OK. Accepts computer printout submissions. Accepts electronic submissions.

Terms: Pays 10% royalties. Publishes ms 1 year after acceptance. Writer's guidelines and book catalog free.

Advice: "We particularly want to provide a publishing venue for regional authors whose material tends to be ignored by the large eastern houses."

‡VARDAMAN (I,II), 2720 E. 176 St., Tacoma WA 98445. Editorial Contact Person: Rick Barron. Estab. 1985. One-person operation on part time basis. Publishes paperback originals. Books: perfect binding; average print order: 500; first novel print order: 500. Plans 1 first novel this year. Averages 5 total titles, 5 fiction titles each year.

Needs: Literary, short story collections. Recently published *The Flag*, by R. Baker (short story collection); and *White Buffalo*, by J. Davies (poetry).

How to Contact: Accepts unsolicited mss. Submit complete ms with cover letter. SASE. Reports in 1 month on queries; 2 months on mss.

Terms: Pays in author's copies (10% of press run). Publishes ms 1 year after acceptance.

Advice: "Be yourself. A good writing class can destroy you as a writer. We are looking for writers who have gotten their experience from the world, not from T.V."

W.W. PUBLICATIONS (IV), Subsidiary of A.T.S., Box 373, Highland MI 48031-0373. (313)887-4703. Also publishes *Minas Tirith Evening Star*. Editor: Philip Helms. Estab. 1967. One-man operation on part-time basis. Publishes paperback originals and reprints. Books: typing paper; offset printing; stapled binding; black ink illustrations; average print order: 500+; first novel print order: 500. Averages 1 title (fiction) each year. Occasionally critiques rejected ms.

Needs: Fantasy, science fiction, and young adult/teen (fantasy/science fiction). Novel needs: "Tolkien-related mainly, some fantasy."
How to Contact: Accepts unsolicited mss. Submit complete ms with SASE. Reports in 1 month. Simultaneous and photocopied submissions OK. Accepts computer printout submissions, prefers letter-quality.
Terms: Individual arrangement with author depending on book, etc.; provides 5 author's copies. Free book catalog.
Advice: "We are publishing more fiction and more paperbacks. The author/editor relationship: a friend and helper."

***WATERFRONT PRESS (IV)**, 52 Maple Ave., Maplewood NJ 07040. (201)762-1565. President: Kal Wagenheim. Estab. 1982. Two persons, active part-time small press. Hardcover originals and reprints; paperback originals and reprints. Books: standard trade and textbook formats, illustrations occasionally; average print order: 1,000-1,500; first novel print order: 500-1,000. Averages 4 total titles/year; 1 or 2 fiction titles/year. Occasionally critiques rejected mss.
Needs: Ethnic, translations. "Our main focus is Puerto Rico and Hispanics in the US. We may consider other Caribbean nations." Published *The Labyrinth*, by Enrique A. Laguerre (translation from Spanish of book first published 1959); and *La Charca*, by Manuel Zeno-Gandia (translation from Spanish of 19th century novel).
How to Contact: Does not accept unsolicited mss. Query first or submit outline/synopsis and sample chapters. SASE for query and ms. Reports in 1 month on queries; 2 months on mss. Simultaneous and photocopied submissions OK. Accepts computer printouts.
Terms: Pays in royalties of 10% minimum; 15% maximum; $250-500 advance; advance is negotiable. Sends galleys to author. "On a few occasions, with books of great merit, *we have co-published with author*, who provided part of costs (in cases where our budget did not permit us to proceed quickly with the project)."
Advice: "We will endorse or support grant applications made by writers to foundations, if we believe the work has merit."

WATERMARK PRESS, INC. (I,II,IV), 149 N. Broadway, Suite 201, Wichita KS 67202. (316)263-8951. Editor: Gaylord L. Dold. Estab. 1988. Regional independent publisher, planning to expand. Publishes hardcover originals. "New line in spring, 1989, high quality cover." Plans to publish 2 first novels this year.
Needs: Literary. "We need quality literary manuscripts, short story collections, with a regional theme, novels but no genre work, mystery etc."
How to contact: Accepts unsolicited mss. Query first. Reports on queries in 3 month. Simultaneous and photocopied submissions OK.
Terms: Sends prepublication galleys to author. Publishes ms an average of 1 year after acceptance.
Advice: "We are currently planning to publish four works of fiction for fall 1989. Two of the manuscripts are from new writers who have never before published fiction. These manuscripts were received through previous contacts. We encourage absolutely new writers, established—in fact, the only criterion is the quality of the manuscript itself. No computer printouts."

‡WOMAN IN THE MOON PUBLICATIONS (I,IV), #100, 3601 Crowell Rd., Turlock CA 95380. (209)667-0966. Publisher: Dr. S. Diane A. Bogus. Estab. 1979. "We are a small press with a primary publishing agenda for poetry. We accept short story manuscripts infrequently but are open to them." Publishes paperback originals. Books: 60 lb non-acidic paper; off-set/web press printing; perfect binding preferred, sometimes saddle, smythe sewn; occasionally illustrations; average print order: 1,000. Averages 2-4 total titles each year. Somtimes comments on rejected mss.
Needs: Contemporary, ethnic, fantasy, gay, lesbian, psychic/supernatural/occult, short story collections.
How to Contact: Accepts unsolicited mss. Query first or submit outline/synopsis and sample chapters. SASE for query. Reports in 3 months on queries. Simultaneous submissions OK.
Terms: Pays in author's copies (half of press run). Publishes ms 2 years after acceptance. Writer's guidelines for #10 SASE and 1 first class stamp. Book catalog for 6×9 SASE and 45¢ postage.
Advice: "To the short story writer, write us a real life lesbian gay set of stories. Tell us how life is for a Black person in an enlightened world. Create a possibility, an ideal that humanity can live toward. Write a set of stories that will free, redeem and instruct humanity. We've been publishing poetry and nonfiction directories. We have wanted to do fiction, but have accepted none yet, because our priority is poetry."

THE WOMAN SLEUTH MYSTERY SERIES (II), A specialized series within The Crossing Press, Freedom, CA. Contact series editor directly at 307 W. State St., Ithaca NY 14850. (607)273-4675. Series Editor: Irene Zahava. Publishes paperback originals and reprints. Books: 5x7 inch trade paperbacks; average print order: 5,000-7,500. Publishes 2-4 total titles/year.

Needs: Feminist, lesbian, suspense/mystery. Looking for "mystery novels, written by women, featuring strong female main character(s) – a womansleuth who is either a professional or amateur detective." No romance/mystery, if it's primarily romance. Recently published *Footprints*, by Kelly Bradford; *Clio Browne*, by Dolores Komo; *Shadow Dance*, by Agnes Bushell.
How to Contact: Accepts unsolicited material. Submit detailed outline/synopsis and 3-4 sample chapters. Do not send complete ms. SASE (IRC). Reports in 1 month. Photocopied submissions OK. Accepts computer printout submissions. Also send short stories for forthcoming volumes of *Woman Sleuth Anthology* – open deadline for stories. Subject requirements the same as for novels (see "Needs" above).
Terms: Pays 7-10% royalties on novels; negotiable advance. Sends galleys to author. Book catalog free on request (write to Crossing Press, Box 1048, Freedom CA 95019).
Advice: "Contemporary subjects, settings, characters preferred. Not interested in gothic or romantic subjects/styles. Don't feel you need to 'tack on' romance and/or sexuality if it isn't integral to the plot."

WOMEN'S PRESS (I, II, IV), Suite #204, 229 College St., Toronto, Ontario M5T 1R4 Canada. (416)598-0082. Estab. 1972. Publishes paperback originals. Books: web coat paper; web printing; perfect binding; average print order: 2,000; first novel print order: 1,500. Plans 2 first novels this year. Averages 8 total titles each year. Sometimes "briefly" critiques rejected ms.
Needs: Contemporary, experimental, feminist, historical, juvenile and adolescent (fantasy, historical, contemporary), lesbian, literary, preschool/picture book, short story collections, mysteries, women's and young adult/teen (problem novels). Nothing sexist, pornographic, racist. Recently published *S.P. Likes A.D.*, by Catherine Brett; *Patternmakers*, by Frances Sandy Duncan; *Harriet's Daughter*, by Marlene Nourbese Philip; published fiction by previously unpublished writers within the last year.
How to Contact: Submit complete ms with SAE and "Canadian NB. stamps or a check. Our mandate is to publish Canadian women or landed immigrants." Reports in 3 months. Simultaneous or photocopied submissions OK. Accepts computer printout submissions; prefers letter-quality.
Terms: Pays in royalties of 10% maximum. Sends galleys to author. Advance is negotiable. Free book catalog.
Advice: "We have so far published 4 novels and 2 collections of short stories. Our three adult novels have all been first novels. A translated work of fiction from Québec was published in 1985 and we plan more translations. We encourage first novelists. We edit very carefully. We can sometimes suggest alternative publishers."

‡WOODLEY MEMORIAL PRESS (IV), English Dept., Washburn University, Topeka KS 66621. (913)295-6448. Editor: Robert Lawson. Estab. 1980. "Woodley Memorial Press is a small press organization which publishes book-length poetry and fiction collections by Kansas writers only; by 'Kansas writers' we mean writers who reside in Kansas or have a Kansas connection." Publishes hardcover and paperback originals. Averages varying number of total titles each year. Sometimes comments on rejected ms.
Needs: Contemporary, experimental, literary, mainstream, short story collection. "We do not want to see genre fiction, juvenile, or young adult."
How to Contact: *Charges $5 reading fee*. Accepts unsolicited mss. Submit outline/synopsis and 2 sample chapters. SASE. Reports in 2 weeks on queries; 2 months on mss. Photocopied submissions OK. Accepts computer printout submissions.
Terms: "Terms are individually arranged with author after acceptance of manuscript." Sends galleys to author. Publishes ms one year after acceptance. Writer's guidelines free for #10 SASE and 1 first class stamp. Book catalog for #10 SASE and 2 first class stamps.

WOODSONG GRAPHICS INC. (II), Box 238, New Hope PA 18938. (215)794-8321. Editor: Ellen Bordner. Estab. 1977. "Small publishing firm dedicated to printing quality books and marketing them creatively." Publishes paperback and hardcover originals. Books: standard or coated stock paper; photo offset printing; GBC or standard binding; illustrations; average print order: 5,000; first novel print order; 2,500. Averages 6-8 total titles each year. "Sometimes" buys juvenile mss with illustrations. Occasionally critiques rejected mss.
Needs: Adventure, contemporary, gothic/historical and contemporary romance, historical (general), humor/satire, juvenile (animal, easy-to-read, fantasy, historical, picture book, spy/adventure, contemporary), literary, mainstream, psychic/supernatural/occult, science fiction, suspense/mystery, war, western, and young adult (easy-to-read/teen, fantasy/science fiction, historical, problem novels, spy/adventure). No deviant sex of any kind or pornography.
How to Contact: Accepts unsolicited mss. Query first or submit complete ms. SASE always. Simultaneous and photocopied submissions OK. Accepts computer printout submissions, prefers letter-quality. Reports in 3 weeks on queries, longer on mss. "We do everything possible to get replies out promptly, but do read everything we're sent . . . and that takes time." Publishes ms 6-12 months after acceptance.

Close-up

Irene Zahava

Editor

The Woman Sleuth Mystery Series

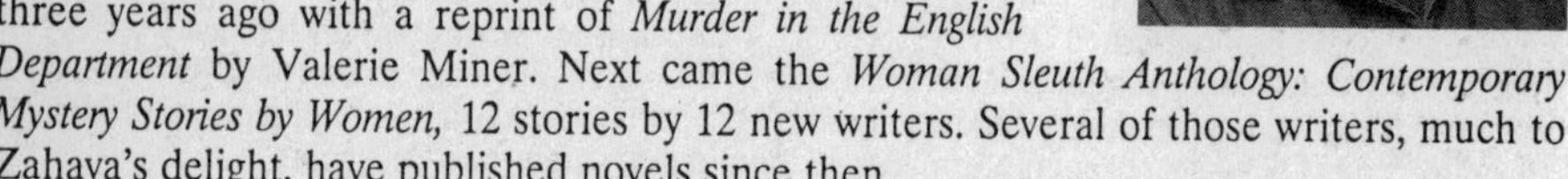

Irene Zahava wants to know whodunit: who has written a well-crafted mystery featuring a female sleuth and some degree of a feminist world view.

She wants to know so much that she and her colleagues at Crossing Press have developed an entire series with such a premise. Woman Sleuth Mystery Series made its debut three years ago with a reprint of *Murder in the English Department* by Valerie Miner. Next came the *Woman Sleuth Anthology: Contemporary Mystery Stories by Women,* 12 stories by 12 new writers. Several of those writers, much to Zahava's delight, have published novels since then.

Zahava's mission is to cultivate women mystery writers, and as a small press editor, she revels in her freedom to do so. "There's not a lot of pressure to publish a certain number of books each season," she explains, "so I can take more time to work with the writer.

"I'm very willing to help lead the writer through the process. In terms of what we publish, it's really a very personal decision. If I like it I'm willing to do endless work."

Unfortunately, she has seen much that falls far short, including a dismaying number of manuscripts with racist overtones and others with plots that do not hang together or characters or settings that seem suprisingly quaint.

"And please," she asserts, "I'm not at all interested in romance or romantic suspense—the type of story with a disinherited heiress. That seems particularly out of place in the late twentieth century." Nor does she insist, as many commercial houses do, on a certain amount of sex to spice the action.

A trend she dislikes is characterizing women as monsters, totally vicious perpetrators of abuse. Another is dealing in a very superficial way with a topical issue—such as AIDS. Zahava is definitely looking for a genuine female slant on the story: "Don't take a male character and turn him into a female, leaving everything else the same," she advises.

Woman Sleuth is very open to nontraditional characters. Three of the protagonists in the latest anthology are over 60, yet decidedly unMarple-ish. Other stories feature lesbians, a middle aged black woman, a policewoman and a rural woman.

Short stories have no length requirements. The most recent anthology included one as brief as two pages, along with novellas, a form she says is hard to place in mystery genre.

In her other life as owner of Smedley's Bookshop in Ithaca, New York, a women's bookstore, she pinpoints the trends among readers. "When I bought the store in 1981, there was no mystery section at all. Within a year I had one shelf and now we have a whole bookcase dedicated to mysteries. It's probably the fastest growing section."

Mystery is fast coming out of the closet, she explains, and more women, including a large number of academics, are viewing the form as literature replete with artful handling of contemporary issues. These are not the shoot-em-up, Raymond Chandler-type stories, she says. They portray a vision of a new world.

—*Carol Lloyd*

Terms: Pays in royalties; negotiates advance. Sends galleys to author. "Arrangements will depend totally on the author and manuscript."
Advice: "If first novels are good, we have no problem with them, and we're always happy to look. Along with queries, send at least a few pages of actual ms text, since quality of writing is more important than topic where fiction is concerned. If you believe in what you've written, stick with it. There is so much good material that we must reject simply because we can't afford to do everything. Others must have the same problem, and it's a matter of being on the right desk on the right day to finally succeed."

WYRICK & COMPANY, 1A Pinckney St., Box 89, Charleston SC 29402. (803)772-0881. Editor-in-Chief: Charles L. Wyrick, Jr. Publishes hardcover and trade paperback originals and reprints. Averages 8-12 titles/year.
Needs: Adventure, ethnic, experimental, humor, mainstream. "We seek exemplary works of fiction, particularly those by southern writers. We welcome submissions by unpublished authors. We are not normally interested in sci-fi, western or romance." Recently published *Things Undone*, by Max Childers; published new writers within the last year.
How to Contact: Submit outline/synopsis with a "clear, concise" cover letter and sample chapters or complete ms. SASE. Reports in 2-3 weeks on queries; 8-10 weeks on mss. Simultaneous and photocopied submissions OK.
Terms: Pays royalties of 8-12% on retail price. Average advance: $250.
Advice: "By publishing quality works of fiction and nonfiction, Wyrick & Company hopes to sell to knowledgeable readers of all ages—those who seek well written, well designed and well produced books of all types. Overemphasis by major houses and the media on blockbusters has created a greater, rather than a lesser, opportunity for small and medium-sized publishers to find and publish tomorrow's great books."

YITH PRESS (I, IV), 1051 Wellington Rd., Lawrence KS 66044. (913)843-4341. Subsidiary: *Eldritch Tales Magazine*. Editor/Publisher: Crispin Burnham. Estab. 1984. One-man operation on part-time basis. Publishes paperback originals and reprints. Books: offset printing; perfect binding; illustrations; average print order: 500-1,000. Averages 1-2 titles each year. Average first novel print order: 500-1,000 (depending pre-publication orders). Occasionally critiques rejected ms.
Needs: Fantasy and horror. Accepts short stories for collections only. Novel needs include "anything in the supernatural horror category." No "mad slasher or sword and sorcery."
How to Contact: Accepts unsolicited mss. Submit complete ms with SASE. Reports in 2 months. Simultaneous and photocopied submissions OK. Accepts computer printout submissions. Prefers letter-quality. Disk submissions OK with MacIntosh II system.
Terms: Individual arrangement with author depending on the book. Sends galleys to author. Pays in royalties of 25% minimum; 35% maximum.
Advice: "Be original, don't try to be the next Lovecraft or Stephen King. Currently, I plan to publish one or two books/year, along with *Eldritch Tales*. The author/editor relationship should be give and take on both sides. I will try *not* to rewrite the author's work. If I feel that it needs some changes then I'll suggest them to the author. We are currently on hold with the book line as we are trying to get *Eldritch Tales* out on a quarterly schedule. Any potential submitter should send a card to inquire as to status."

YORK PRESS, Box 1172, Fredericton, New Brunswick E3B 5C8 Canada. (506)458-8748. Editorial Director: Dr. S. Elkhadem. Estab. 1975. Midsize independent publisher with plans to expand. Publishes hardcover and paperback originals. Publishes in English exclusively. Number of titles: 50 in 1988. Average first novel print order 1,000 copies.
Needs: Contemporary, experimental, and translations by established writers. "No mss written mainly for entertainment, i.e., those without literary or artistic merit." Recently published *Red White & Blue*, by Ben Stoltzfus; *Modern Egyptian Short Stories* and *Three Pioneering Egyptian Novels*, translated and edited by Saad El-Gabalawy; and Michel Butor's *Description of San Marco*, translated by Barbara Mason.
How to Contact: Accepts unsolicited mss, "although an initial query is appreciated." Query with SASE or SAE and IRC. No simultaneous submissions; photocopied submissions OK. Reports in 1 week on queries, 1 month on mss.
Terms: Pays 10% in royalties; no advance. Free book catalog.
Advice: "We are devoted to the promotion of scholarly publications; areas of special interest include general and comparative literature, literary criticism and creative writing of an experimental nature."

ZEPHYR PRESS (I), 13 Robinson St., Somerville MA 02145. Subsidiary of Aspect, Inc. Editors: Ed Hogan, Leora Zeitlin, Hugh Abernethy. Estab. 1980. Publishes hardcover and paperback originals. Books: acid free paper; offset printing; Smythsewn binding; illustrations sometimes; average print order: 1000-1,500; first novel print order: 1,000-1,500. Averages 2 total titles, 1-2 fiction titles each year. *$15 reading fee for all mss submitted*; written critique with all responses.

Needs: Contemporary, ethnic, experimental, feminist/lesbian, gay, historical, humor/satire, literary, mainstream, regional, science fiction, short story collections. "In general we seek fiction or short stories by less-established writers." Published *Two Novels*, by Philip Whalen, and *The St. Veronica Gig Stories*, by Jack Pulaski.

How to Contact: Accepts unsolicited mss. Query first with SASE. Accepts computer printout submissions; prefers letter-quality. Reports in 3-6 weeks on queries.

Terms: Pays in author's copies of 10% of print (1st edition); 20% royalties on publisher's net (subsequent editions, if any). Sends galleys to author by arrangement. "There can be some flexibility of terms, based on mutual arrangements, if desired by author and publisher." Book catalog for SASE.

Advice: "Seek well qualified feedback from press and/or professionally established writers before submitting manuscripts to publishers. We are especially interested in first novels. We encourage first novelists if they truly feel they are ready. We regard the author/editor relationship as one of close cooperation, from editing through promotion."

‡ZOLAND BOOKS, INC. (II), Box 2766, Cambridge MA 02238. (617)864-6252. Publisher: Roland Pease. Estab. 1987. "We are a literary press, publishing poetry, fiction, photography, and other titles of literary interest. We are young and growing." Publishes hardcover and paperback originals. Books: acid-free paper; sewn binding; some with illustrations; average print order: 2,000-5,000. Plans 1 first novel this year. Averages 5-8 total titles, 2-4 fiction titles each year. Sometimes comments on rejected mss.

Needs: Contemporary, experimental, feminist, gay, humor/satire, lesbian, literary, short story collections, translations.

How to Contact: Accepts unsolicited mss. Query first, then send complete ms with cover letter. SASE. Reports in 2 weeks on queries; 6-8 weeks on mss. Photocopied submissions OK. Computer printout submissions are acceptable.

Terms: Pays royalties of 5-10%. Average advance: $500; negotiable (also pays 5 author's copies). Sends galleys to author. Publishes ms 1-2 years after acceptance. Book catalog for #10 SASE and 2 first class stamps.

Foreign Small Press

The following small presses in countries outside the U.S. and Canada will consider novels or short stories in English from North American writers. Most of these markets do not pay. Always include a self-addressed envelope with International Reply Coupons to ensure a response or the return of your manuscript. International Reply Coupons are available at the main branch of your local post office. To save the cost of return postage on your manuscript, you may want to send a copy of your manuscript for the publisher to keep or throw away and enclose a return postcard with one IRC for a reply.

ASHTON SCHOLASTIC LTD., Private Bag 1, Penrose, Auckland New Zealand. Fiction Editor: Penny Scown. Publishes 15 fiction titles annually. "Educational publishing with a focus on books for the teaching of language arts and children's literature for all ages from picture books to teen novels." Pays royalties. "Do not 'write down' to children – write the story you want to tell using the best language – i.e., most appropriate vocabulary, letting the story only dictate the length."

BIBLIOTECA DI NOVA SF, FUTURO, GREAT WORKS OF SF, Perseo Libri srl, Box 1240, I-40100 Bologna Italy. Fiction Editor: Ugo Malaguti. "Science fiction and fantasy; novels and/or collections of stories." Pays 7% royalties on cover price; advance: $800-1,000 on signing contract. Buys Italian book rights; other rights remain with author. "While preferring published writers, we also consider new writers."

EASTERN CARIBBEAN INSTITUTE (ECI) (IV), Box 1338, Frederiksted, Virgin Islands 00841. Editor/President: S.B. Jones-Hendrickson, PhD. Estab. 1982. Small press with plans to expand. Publishes hardcover originals and paperback originals. Regional. Needs for novels include Caribbean issues and settings. No religious. Query with SASE. Reports in 1 week on queries; 1 month for mss.

EXCESS PRESS (IV), 4 Bower St., Maidstone, Kent ME16 8SD England. Subsidiary: *Excess* magazine. Editor: Paul Buck. One-man operation, part-time. Contemporary, sexuality, experimental, language-centered, literary and translations. "If you believe in what you're doing, you'll persevere despite all the odds against you."

FOURTH ESTATE, Classic House, 113 Westbourne Grove, London W2 4UP England. Editorial Director: Giles O'Bryen. Publishes 50 books/year. "Small general publisher. Modern fiction, mostly young writers. Strong storyline but often a new or different way of telling it." Writers paid advance against royalties. "Submit only a synopsis and sample chapter in the first instance."

GMP PUBLISHER LTD., Box 247, London N15 6RW England. Editor: Richard Dipple. Publishes 10 story collections or novels yearly. "Gay publishing house specialising in books for or by gay men, though we do also publish some books of interest to women and/or by women authors. We hope that many of our titles also reach a wider audience." Pays royalties. "We're particularly interested in authors who use a word processor and can supply material on disk. This is particularly true with writers sending in work from abroad."

HARD ECHO PRESS LTD., 171 The Mall, Onehunga AK6 New Zealand. Fiction Editor: Warwick Jordan. Publishes approx. 2-5 fiction titles annually. "Small, independent press. Interested in publishing small editions of novels which are experimental and current in their approach. Am particularly interested in doing handcraft (i.e. letterpress) limited editions for established writers, or publishing work they would prefer to not submit to major publishers, or which their publishers can't handle." Pays 10% royalty on retail sales, paid when publisher receives payment. "Include SASE; must be typed ms; not interested in short stories unless they are particularly brilliant; prefer shorter (100-200 pages) novels."

HEMKUNT, Publishers A-78 Naraina Industrial Area Ph.I, New Delhi India 110028. Managing Director: G.P. Singh. "We would be interested in novels, preferably by authors with a published work. Would like to have distribution rights for US, Canada and UK beside India."

KARNAK HOUSE, 300 Westbourne Park Road, London W11 1EH England. Fiction Editor: Amon Saba Saakana. Publishes 3-4 fiction titles annually. "An Afro-Caribbean publishing company concerned with global literary concerns of the Afrikan community, whether in North and South America, the Caribbean, Afrika or Europe. We rarely pay advances, and if so, very small, but pay a royalty rate of 8-10% on the published price of the book. We look for innovative work in the areas outlined above and work which attempts to express the culture, language, mythology—ethos—of the people. We look for work which tries to break away from standard English as the dominant narrative voice."

KINGSWAY PUBLICATIONS, 1 St. Anne's Road, Eastbourne, E. Sussex BN21 3UN England. Managing Editor: Elizabeth Gibson. Publishes 10-12 fiction titles annually. Publishes "Christian books; children's books. Books on leadership, discipleship, devotional, biography, music, the church, currrent issues from a Christian perspective. A few works of fiction." Payment varies "according to whether writer has an agent or not, and whether we negotiate contract directly or through a US publisher. Submit one sample chapter, double-spaced, typed with adequate margins and a synopsis. Allow 6-8 weeks for response. The writer should understand the international market. Do not send anything on millenium, new age or astrology."

‡MCPHEE GRIBBLE PUBLISHERS, 66 Cecil St., Fitzroy 3065 Victoria, Australia. Contact: Editor. Publishes 12 works of fiction/year. "McPhee Gribble publishes both fiction and general books with no categorical emphasis, though its fiction list is internationally renown (Tim Winton, Rod Jones, Helen Garner, Rodney Hall, Morris Lurie have all been published internationally)." Pays by royalty on recommended retail price. "Authors who do not reside in Australia should be aware that McPhee Gribble will not return unsolicited ms unless covering postage costs are included."

THE MALVERN PUBLISHING CO. LTD., 32 Old Street, Upton-Upon-Severn, Worcs. WR8 OHW England. Fiction Editor: Cintia Stammers. Publishes 12 stories/year. "Full length adult fiction—60,000-80,000 words." Pays in royalties. "No science fiction or fantasy."

MAROVERLAG, Riedingerstrasse 24, D-8900, Augsburg West Germany. Editor: Benno Käsmayr. Publishes 4-6 novels or story collections/year. Publishes "exciting American authors in excellent translations; e.g. Charles Bukowski, Jack Kerouac, William Burroughs, Paul Bowles, Gerald Locklin, Keith Abbott and Gilbert Sorrentino." Writers paid for published fiction. "Please include SAE and postage."

‡MONARCH PUBLICATIONS LIMITED, 1 St. Anne's Road, Eastbourne, E. Sussex, BN21 3UN England. Contact: Managing Editor. Publishes up to 12 novels per year. "We are Christian publishers and therefore only interested in full-length works of fiction with a religious slant. Christian characters and conversions not essential, but a Christian world view on the part of the author is." Pays in advanced royalty and standard royalties based on sales. "Address a synopsis and two sample chapters to the Managing Editor. Please do not send entire manuscripts. International reply coupons are not essential but appreciated. Manuscripts should be typed double-spaced with generous margins. Authors should keep a copy of any material sent. US writers should be aware of barriers created by the use of what is strictly US idiom, and of fiction which is exclusive to the US culture. They should also understand that readers' tastes differ enormously in the UK!"

PROSPICE PUBLISHING (UK) LTD, (formerly Aquila Publishing)Box 18, Buxton, Derbyshire SK17 6YP England. Managing Director/Editor: J.C.R. Green. Estab. 1958. "Small specialists (alternative or 'fringe') publisher of poetry, fiction, etc. Will publish as many first novels as we can afford, but they MUST be good indeed to qualify." Averages 50 total titles; 10 fiction titles each year. Average first novel print order: 500 copies. Pays in royalties of 10% minumum; 15% maximum; "no advance normally. We pay for some short fiction in author's copies, quantity negotiable. We are willing to consider some form of subsidy publishing, with us handling everything from editoral through production to sales and marketing and distribution."

‡RAVAN PRESS (PTY) LTD, Box 31134, Braamfontein, Johannesburg 2017 South Africa. Contact: Manager. Publishes 8 stories/year. "Oppositional, anti-apartheid fiction with a social content, progressive in orientation, for adult and children's market." Pays in royalties.

SETTLE PRESS (WIGMORE), 10 Boyne Terrace Mews, London WII 3LR England. Fiction Editors: Mrs. M. Carter, Mr. D. Settle. Publishes 10+ fiction titles annually. "Political and contemporary thrillers (often with film potential). Books with a strong storyline, from love stories to psychological overtones, animal stories." Writers paid on royalty basis. "Send a synopsis plus information on author. We will consider carefully."

‡THE VANITAS PRESS, Plaatslagarevägen 4 E 1, 22230 Lund Sweden. Fiction Editor: Mr. March Laumer. "One-person full-time operation publishing for prestige, not cash profit motives." Publishes fantasy, historical, satire, mainstream, romance (historical), short story collections. "At present exclusively interested in promising 'Oz' novels. Very actively interested in attracting writers/illustrators who would care to *collaborate* in the creation of 'latter-day' Oz novels."

Other small press

The following small presses appeared in the 1989 edition of *Novel & Short Story Writer's Market* but are not in the 1990 edition. Those presses whose editors did not respond to our request for an update are listed below without further explanation. There are several reasons why a small press did not respond—they may be out of business, for example, or they may be overstocked with submissions. If an explanation was given, it is included next to the listing name. Note that small presses from outside of the U.S. and Canada appear at the end of the list.

Acadia Publishing
Alaska Native Language Center
Androgyne
Ariadne Press
Artifacts Press
Balance Beam Press (not currently publishing)
Bank Street Press
Barn Owl Books
Black Hat Press (no longer publishing fiction)
Black Heron (requested to be removed one year)
Blackberry Books
Blind Beggar Press
Breakwater Books (requested to be deleted)
Cinco Puntos Press (requested to be removed one year)
Conari Press (no longer publishing fiction)
Coyote Love Press
Dancing Bear Productions
The Dragonsbreath Press
Eden Press
Exhile Press
Fiction Collective Inc.
Floricanto Press
Garber Communications
Green Tiger Press
Hickman Systems (no longer publishing fiction)
Lawrence Hill Books (requested to be deleted)
International Marine Publish- ... leted)
Ion Books
The Jewish Publication Society
Liberty Press, Inc.
Loft Press
Magnificat (no longer publishing fiction)
Metis Press (out of business)
Micah Publications (requested to be deleted)
Millers River Publishing Co.
Mogul Books and Filmworks (requested to be deleted)
North Point Press (requested to be deleted)
Owl Creek Press
Peachtree Publishers
Perivale Press (requested to be

Porcé'pic Books
Primal Publishing
Proper Tales Press
S.O.C.O. Publishing (out of business)
St. Johns Publishing (no longer publishing fiction)
Score Publications
Slough Press
Aaron Smirnoff Books
The Smith (requested to be removed one year)
Space and Time
Square One Publishers (in the process of moving)
Still Point Press (no longer publishing fiction)
Studia Hispanica Editors (writers pay all expenses)
Sun and Moon Press (overstocked)
Talon Books Ltd.
Third World Press
Threshold Books
Triple P Publications International (out of business)
Underwood/Miller
Unicorn Publishing House
Véhicule Press
Westgate Press
Windriver Publishing Company
Word Beat Press
Yanaria Press (requested to be removed one year)

Other foreign small press

Albatross Books PTY Ltd.
Arlington Books Publishers Ltd.
Handshake Editions Journeyman
Kawabata Press
Morrigan Publications
New Orchard Editions
Rimu (out of business)
University of Queensland Press
Wolfhound Press

Commercial Publishers

Writers interested in submitting their work to commercial book publishers are finding fewer markets for their work each year. The decade brought many mergers, including Random House's purchase of Crown Books, Robert Maxwell's purchase of Macmillan and most recently the Time-Warner merger, putting some 60 percent of sales revenues for adult books into the hands of the top six publishers. With this consolidation of the market comes increased competition and less willingness on the part of commercial publishers to take risks on new writers or experimental work.

Yet there is some good news. Although there are fewer independent outlets, many publishers have turned to developing new imprints and paperback publishers are no longer just reprint houses. In fact several paperback companies are now not only publishing originals in paper but are also publishing mass market hardcover books.

Competition has been good for writers in one way—publishers are more eager than ever to find 'the next big name' and some talented newcomers are receiving excellent deals.

With the growing success of smaller publishers, some of the larger publishers are even starting to rethink the emphasis on big names and are taking a second look at their mid-list writers. The best news for fiction writers is the growing acceptance of literary fiction and short story collections. The market is strong for children's books and category or genre fiction remains very open to new writers.

Although most publishers will still look at unsolicited fiction, most will give top priority to fiction submitted through an agent. Agents are fast becoming first-readers and busy editors rely on them to screen out unpublishable material. For more about working with an agent see the Literary Agents section. Having an agent will not only help you get a foot in the door, but it may also provide you with a sense of stability no longer found in large publishing companies.

Hardcover houses

Large hardcover publishers are continuing to make big deals with well-known and celebrity authors. Yet as competition for new talent becomes keen, some fortunate newcomers are also walking away with handsome deals. Former construction worker Layne Heath, for example, garnered $300,000 from William Morrow and Avon Books for his first book, *CW2*, and newcomer Marti Leimbach, who sold her first novel to Doubleday, received $150,000.

Although publishers have been paying these large advances for several years now, today they are actually getting more for their money. Mergers have enabled publishers to secure rights to both hardcover and paperback editions, published simultaneously by different subsidiaries of the same company. Publishers are also purchasing more foreign rights, planning to sell to publishers abroad or coming out with their own foreign editions.

Distribution is better than ever for hardcover fiction. Walden Books and B. Dalton offer a combined total of 2,100 outlets. The Book Industry Study Group says one out of every four books is purchased through a nonbookstore outlet. Grocery stores lead the list, but other retail outlets include drug stores, discount stores and a variety of specialty shops.

Wider distribution is only one of several factors leading to a four percent increase in book sales last year. More people are reading fiction than ever and this means there is a strong market for talented, new writers.

Mass market paperbacks

Last year marked the fiftieth anniversary of the "paperback revolution"—the birth of both Pocket Books and American Penguin. Although there were a handful of small paperback book publishers in America before 1939, that was the first year of successful widespread paperback publishing.

In those days, and for many years to follow, paperback publishers were mostly reprint publishers. With the 1980s came a major change, however. Hard and soft deals, a lack of hardcover material available for reprint and increased competition have led many paperback publishers to publish more original fiction.

For years hardcover publishers relied on reprint sales to paperback companies to help offset any losses from poor sales of hardcover books—a sort of hedge. Today more paperback publishers are publishing originals not only in paper but also in mass-market (discounted) hardback. These new mass market editions are actually helping paperback publishers offset costs. Many consumers will purchase hardcovers at a discount, even though the prices are higher than for the paperback editions. So paperback and hardcover publishing has actually come full circle.

Returns continue to be a big problem for most paperback publishers. Publishers of mass market fiction are realizing that "me too" publishing is actually hurting sales. When a certain type of book does well, the tendency for many publishers to try to come out with similar books has led to a saturation of the market and lower overall sales. One way publishers will offset this problem is to publish less of any one type of book, but, on the other hand, they will be more receptive to "something different" from writers.

Trade paperbacks

Trade paperbacks continue to offer excellent opportunities for new writers. Competition is still keen, but the future looks bright for literary fiction in particular. Authors of literary fiction are reporting higher advances.

With more attention being paid to mid-list authors, more originals are being reissued in paperback with new promotion and a new chance to build sales. The market for trade paperbacks is a cautious one, however, with most publishers planning between eight and twelve books in the coming year.

The genres

We've found that many of our more successful writers are those who publish in a particular genre. There is less competition within the field and most genre publishers are eager to see the work of new writers. Genre publishing tends to go in cycles with up and down fluxes in the market normal. This year marks the resurgence of interest in westerns and military fiction. Science fiction, on the other hand, while still doing well, seems to be slowing down a bit. Romance publishers are becoming more cautious about what they buy—some New Age and experimental romance is not doing as well as publishers predicted.

Writers interested in submitting to genre publishers should first become familiar with the field in which they wish to write. Read all the top names, says one publisher, but don't read so much your work is simply imitative. Unlike other types of fiction, most genres provide a strong level of support for writers. Science fiction, horror and mystery groups feature conventions for both fans and writers. The Romance Writers of America and Mystery Writers of America offer their members awards, a newsletter and a network of other writers within the field.

Some trends to look for in particular fields include:

- The growth in popularity of military and adventure fiction. The appeal of these books is their emphasis on the technology of war.

- The focus in science fiction is on hard science. Publishers seem to be moving away from social science based science fiction and discussions of alternate worlds. The emphasis seems to be on the effects of future technology.
- While historical romances continue to be popular, contemporary romances sell very well. Some romance publishers are bringing out longer, more involved works, as well as those designed for a quick read.
- Romance writers in particular are very savvy self-promoters. Many are having their own bookmarks printed for distribution at bookstores. Bookmarks not only list the author's latest book, but also other titles by that author.
- Westerns continue to be a strong market and with the publication this year of *Lonesome Dove* are building a new audience.
- More women than ever are writing detective and mystery fiction. There are more women protagonists and several books are considered feminist mysteries.

Book packagers

This year we've indicated with a square (■)if a listing is that of a book packager. Book packaging has been a common practice for nonfiction publishers for years, but is relatively new to fiction publishers. Book packagers work for publishers and produce books to market to the publishers, not to consumers. These packagers do most production and editorial development for the publisher.

Juvenile and young adult fiction and series adult fiction are sometimes produced by packagers. Writers are hired to write books already developed. They are usually supplied with a "bible" or series outline describing the main characters, setting and the overall story. Sometimes more than one writer will write for the series, but one pseudonym will be used.

Unlike book publishers who pay an advance plus royalties, a book packager usually buys work from the writer for a flat fee. The writer then turns over all rights to the work. Fees can be fairly high, especially for new writers and the opportunity to have publishing experience may offset the sale of all rights for some writers.

Subsidy publishing

Markets listed in this book who offer some subsidy arrangements, but do not publish more than 50 percent of their books under subsidy agreements, are marked with an asterisk (*). For our purposes we consider subsidy any arrangement where the author is asked to pay part or all of the costs for producing the book.

Some publishers feel the financial risks for new writers or experimental works are too high, so they offer marketing and sales help and offer to publish the book for a fee. Writers should consider such an arrangement only after exhausting more conventional publishing routes. Beware of publishers who ask for large sums. To find out if a price is fair, find out exactly how many books will be published and what type of paper and printing will be used. Check with a local printer to find out how much the book would cost if you printed it yourself at the same quantity and quality. If the publisher's fee is considerably higher, you may want to consider carefully if the marketing and distribution offered will be worth the additional cost.

Note that for some university publishers and Canadian publishers books are subsidized by the university or, in the case of Canada, by the government. Writers are not usually asked to pay fees to these publishers, although the term subsidy is sometimes used.

How to submit

Before sending out your manuscript read the Business of Fiction for particulars on mailing and other procedures. For the most part, publishers looking for fiction manuscripts want to see how you write. Querying is fine if you are checking to make sure the publisher is accepting manuscripts and to ask for submission guidelines, but publishers will want to see your work to make a decision on publication.

On the other hand, most do not want to see the entire manuscript. It's best to query first to find out exactly what to send. Many ask for a cover letter and up to three consecutive chapters—preferably the first three chapters.

While you should avoid telling too much of your story in your proposal letter, do spend time crafting it. Make the first few sentences spark the publisher's interest for more. Show you've done your homework by mentioning why you feel your book will fit nicely into the publisher's existing line. Mention any previous publishing credits, but try to keep your letter to one or two pages.

Two ways to obtain publishing credits are to submit shorter pieces or excerpts of your novel to literary magazines and submit material to fiction contests. Both methods help show publishers you are familiar with the editing and publishing process, as well as demonstrate interest in your work.

Check the Category Index to get an idea of possible publishers for your type of work. We've used the following ranking system to help you find appropriate markets for your work.

I *Publisher encourages beginning or unpublished writers to submit work for consideration, and publishes new writers frequently;*
II *Publisher accepts work by established writers and by occasional new writers of unusual talent;*
III *Publisher does not encourage beginning or unagented writers, publishes mainly writers with previous credits;*
IV *Special-interest or regional publisher open only to writers on certain subjects or from certain geographical areas.*

‡ABINGDON PRESS (III), The United Methodist Publishing House, 201 8th Ave. S., Nashville TN 37202. (615)749-6403. Vice President: Neil Alexander. Estab. 1789. Large religious publisher. Publishes hardcover and paperback originals and paperback reprints. Averages 100-120 total titles each year. "We publish no fiction for adults."

Needs: Religious/Bible stories.

How to Contact: Submit outline/synopsis and 2-3 sample chapters with SASE. Accepts unsolicited mss. Reports in 2 weeks. Photocopied submissions OK. Accepts computer printout submissions. Prefers letter-quality. Publishes ms 1-2 years after acceptance.

Terms: Pays in royalties of 2.5% minimum; 15% maximum; average advance $500.

‡ACADEMY CHICAGO PUBLISHERS (I), 213 W. Institute Place, Chicago IL 60610. (312)751-7302. Imprints carrying fiction include Cassandra Editions, Academy Mystery, Academy Travel Classic and Academy Firsts. Editor: Anita Miller. Estab. 1975. Midsize independent publisher. Publishes hardcover and paperback originals and paperback reprints. Books: 55 lb. Glatfelter; mostly sheet fed; perfect, sometimes Smyth-sewn for hardcovers; b&w illustrations; average print order for paperback 5,000; for hardcover 1,500-3,000. Buys 20% agented fiction for reprints only. Average first novel print order 5,000 copies paper, 1,500 copies hardbound. Occasionally comments on rejected mss.

Needs: Mystery, historical, feminist and translations. No experimental, religious, romance or children's. "Mysteries interest us especially." Recently published *In a Dark Wood Wandering*, by Hella S. Haasse; *Loose Connections*, by Sybil Claiborne; and *The Best Horror Stories of Arthur Conan Doyle*, edited by Martin Greenberg.

How to Contact: Accepts unsolicited mss. Query and submit first three chapters with SASE. No simultaneous submissions; photocopied submissions OK. Reports in 2 weeks on queries, 6 weeks on mss. "*No* micro-dot printer. Manuscripts without envelopes will be discarded. *Mailers* are a *must.*" Publishes ms an average of 1 year after acceptance.

Terms: Pays 7-10% in royalties; no advance. Sends galleys to author.

Advice: "We are growing and publishing more of everything. We try to publish one first novel every season. The relationship between novelist and editor should be close; the manuscript is gone over line by line, word by word. An aspiring novelist should submit manuscripts directly to publishers and avoid agents. If the big houses turn it down there are many smaller independent presses which will read everything that comes in a bound manuscript. We do not like to receive postage and label *without* a mailing envelope – it prejudices us against the work from the outset."

ACCENT BOOKS (II), A Division of Accent Publications, Box 15337, Denver CO 80215. (303)988-5300. Executive Editor: Mary B. Nelson. Estab. 1975. Growing midsize independent publisher of Christian books. Publishes paperback originals. Books: type of paper varies; established book printers; average print order varies. Will publish new writers this year. Averages 18-24 total titles, 4-6 fiction titles per year. Occasionally critiques rejected mss.
Needs: "Only Christian books in these categories: contemporary, mystery/romance and frontier romance. We will look at any Christian novel in these areas. All must have strong, evangelical, Christian storylines showing how Christ makes a difference in a person's life." Recently published *In the Foxes' Lair*, by Bea Carlton; *Vow of Silence*, by B.J. Hoff; *Walk in Deep Shadows*, by Sara Mitchell; and *Touch of the Black Widow*, by Bea Carlton.
How to Contact: Does not accept unsolicited mss. Submit outline/synopsis and 3-4 sample chapters with SASE. Reports in 5 weeks on queries, 90 days on mss. Simultaneous submissions and clear photocopied submissions accepted. Accepts computer printout submissions if letter-quality. No dot-matrix.
Terms: Pays royalties. Sends galleys to author. Writer's guidelines for SASE; book catalog for 6x9 SASE with 60¢ postage.
Advice: "We are looking for fiction with a solid evangelical message. The quality of Christian fiction has been improving and people are realizing that important truths as well as clean entertainment can be provided to people hungry for that." "Know the publishing house standards. Be sure to enclose SASE with every submission. Don't take shortcuts. Write it, then re-write it. Be willing to keep re-working the same proposal until it is absolutely tight, top-notch entertainment. Be unique, not trite. Be aware of the world and people around you."

ACE CHARTER BOOKS, Berkley Publishing Group, 200 Madison Ave., New York NY 10016. (212)951-8800. Estab. 1977. Publishes paperback originals and reprints. See Berkley Publishing Group.

APPLE BOOKS, Scholastic, Inc., 730 Broadway, New York NY 10003. (212)505-3000. Senior Editor: Regina Griffin. Children's imprint. See Scholastic Inc.
Needs: "Apple books are generally contemporary. There are no restrictions as to length or subject matter, but all Apple Books are geared toward the capacities and interests of 8-12 year olds." Recently published *Storm Rising*, by Marilyn Singer; *Fifth Grade: Here Comes Trouble*, by Colleen O'Shaugh; and *Fourth Graders Don't Believe in Witches*, by Terri Fields.
How to Contact: Accepts unsolicited mss. Submit outline/synopsis and 3 sample chapters. Reports in 3 weeks on queries; 8 weeks on mss. Single submissions only. Accepts computer printout submissions. Prefers letter-quality.
Terms: Pays an advance against royalties.

ARCHWAY PAPERBACKS, 1230 Avenue of the Americas, New York NY 10020. (212)698-7000. Senior Editor: Patricia MacDonald. Published by Pocket Books. Imprints: Minstrel Books (ages 7-11); and Archway (ages 11 and up). Publishes paperback originals and reprints.
Needs: Young adult (girls' novels, suspense/adventure, thrillers, young readers (short, 80 pages and up), animals, theme – friends, adventure, mystery, family, etc.). Recently published *My Heart Belongs to That Boy*, by Linda Lewis; *Scavenger Hunt*, by Christopher Pike; and the *Fear Street Series*, by R.L. Stine. Published new writers this year.
How to Contact: Submit query first with outline; SASE "mandatory."

ATHENEUM BOOKS FOR CHILDREN (II), Imprint of the Macmillan Children's Book Group, 866 Third Ave., New York NY 10022. (212)702-7894. Editorial Director: Jonathan J. Lanman. Fiction Editors: Gail Paris or Marcia Marshall (especially sf/fantasy). Midsize imprint of large publisher/corporation. Publishes hardcover originals. Books: illustrations for picture books, some illustrated short novels; average print order: 6,000-7,500; first novel print order: 6,000. Averages 70 total titles, 55 fiction titles each year. Very rarely critiques rejected mss.
Needs: Juvenile (animal, fantasy, historical, sports, adventure, contemporary), preschool/picture book, young adult/teen (fantasy/science fiction, historical, problem novels, sports, spy/adventure, mystery). No "paperback romance type" fiction. Published books include *The Good-bye Book*, by Judith

The double dagger before a listing indicates that the listing is new in this edition. New markets are often the most receptive to freelance contributions.

Viorst (3-6, picture book); *Tree by Leaf*, by Cynthia I. Voigt (9-13, pre-teen "problem"); and *Maudie in the Middle*, by Phyllis Reynolds Naylor (7-11, pre-teen illustrated novel).
How to Contact: Accepts unsolicited mss "if novel length; we want outline and 3 sample chapters." SASE. Agented fiction 40%. Reports in 3-4 weeks on queries; 6-8 weeks on mss. Simultaneous submissions OK "if we are so informed"; photocopied submissions OK "if clear and legible." Accepts computer printout submissions.
Terms: Pays in royalties of 10% minimum; 12% maximum. Average advance: $3,000 "along with advance and royalties, authors standardly receive ten free copies of their book and can purchase more at a special discount." Sends galleys to author. Writer's guidelines for #10 SAE and 1 first class stamp. Book catalog for 9x12 SAE and 6 first class stamps.
Advice: "We publish all hardcover originals, occasionally an American edition of a British publication. Our fiction needs have not varied in terms of quantity—of the 60-70 titles we do each year, 50-60 are fiction in different age levels. Our Spring 1989 list consisted of approximately 12 books for those between 3 and 8, one of which was nonfiction; 11 books for ages 7-12 (4 nonfiction); 4 for the 10-14 level (2 nonfiction); and 5 for 10, 11 and up (1 nonfiction). We are less interested in specific topics or subject matter than in overall quality of craftsmanship. First, know your market thoroughly. We publish only children's books, so caring for and *respecting* children is of utmost importance. Also, fad topics are dangerous, as are works you haven't polished to the best of your ability. (Why should we choose a 'jewel in the rough' when we can get a manuscript a professional has polished to be ready for publication.) The juvenile market is not one in which a writer can 'practice' to become an adult writer. In general, be professional. We appreciate the writers who take the time to find out what type of books we publish by visiting the libraries and reading the books. Neatness is a pleasure, too."

AVON BOOKS (II), The Hearst Corporation, 105 Madison Ave., New York NY 10016. (212)481-5600. Imprints include Avon, Camelot and Flare. Estab. 1941. Large paperback publisher. Publishes paperback originals and reprints. Averages 300 titles a year.
Needs: Fantasy, historical romance, mainstream, occult/horror, science fiction, medical thrillers, intrigue, war, western and young adult/teen. No poetry, mystery, short story collections, religious, limited literary or esoteric nonfiction. Recently published *Butterfly*, by Kathryn Harvey; *So Worthy My Love*, by Kathleen Woodiwiss.
How to Contact: Query letters only. SASE to insure response.
Terms: Vary. Book catalog for SASE. Sponsors Flare Novel competition.

BAEN BOOKS (II), 260 5th Ave., New York NY 10001. (212)532-4111. Baen Science Fiction, Baen Fantasy. Publisher and Editor: Jim Baen. Editor: Toni WeisKopf. Consulting Editor: Josepha Sherman. Estab. 1983. Independent publisher; books are distributed by Simon & Schuster. Publishes hardcover and paperback originals and paperback reprints. Published new writers within the last year. Plans 8-12 first novels this year. Averages 60 fiction titles each year. Occasionally critiques rejected mss.
Needs: Fantasy and science fiction. Interested in science fiction novels (generally "hard" science fiction) and fantasy novels "that are not rewrites of last year's bestsellers." Recently published *The Deeds of Paksenarrion*, by Elizabeth Moon (fantasy); *The Man-Kzin Wars II*, by Larry Niven (science fiction); and *Falling Free*, by Lois Bujold (science fiction).
How to Contact: Accepts unsolicited mss. Submit ms or outline/synopsis and 3 consecutive sample chapters with SASE. Reports in 2-3 weeks on partials; 4-8 weeks on mss. Will consider simultaneous submissions, "but grudgingly and not as seriously as exclusives." Accepts letter-quality computer printout submissions.
Terms: Pays in royalties; offers advance. Sends galleys to author. Writer's guidelines for SASE.
Advice: "Keep an eye and a firm hand on the overall story you are telling. Style is important but less important than plot. We like to maintain long-term relationships with authors."

BALLANTINE/EPIPHANY BOOKS (II), 201 E. 50th St., New York NY 10022. (212)751-6200. Division of Random House. Publicist: Carol Fass. Estab. 1983. Imprint includes Ballantine/Epiphany Hardcover. Publishes hardcover and paperback originals and paperback reprints. Books: offset printing; average print order: 30,000. Averages 13 total titles, 20% fiction titles each year. Average first novel print order 30,000 copies.
Needs: Religious/inspirational. "Novels must have inspirational qualities of a Christian nature." No fantasies. No Christian romances. Published *The River Line*, by Charles Morgan; *Poppy*, by Barbara Larriva.
How to Contact: Query; submit outline/synopsis, 3 sample chapters and SASE. Reports in 4-6 weeks. Simultaneous and photocopied submissions OK. Accepts computer printout submissions; prefers letter-quality.

Terms: Offers negotiable advance. Sends galleys to author. Writer's guidelines for #10 SASE. Book catalog for 9x12 SAE and 40¢ postage.
Advice: "Read some novels published by the publishing company to which you intend to submit a manuscript. Find an author you particularly admire and read all of his/her books! Common mistake is to try to describe a lengthy novel in a brief query letter without including a synopsis! It's impossible to assess a novel from a writer's brief description. It also looks amateurish when a writer states that he/her work is copywritten and when he/she states an expected advance. And *never* call an editor to query him/her about your manuscript!"

BALLANTINE BOOKS, 201 E. 50th St., New York NY 10022. Subsidiary of Random House. Senior Editor: Pamela D. Strickler. Publishes originals (general fiction, mass-market, trade paperback and hardcover). Averages over 120 total titles each year.
Needs: Major historical fiction, women's mainstream and general contemporary fiction. Manuscripts can be submitted unsolicited to Pamela D. Strickler. Recently published *Panther In The Sky*, by James Alexander Thom; *Texas Fury*, by Fern Michaels; and *The Hill*, by Leonard B. Scott. Published new writers this year.
How to Contact: Submit outline/synopsis and complete ms. SASE required. Photocopied submissions OK. Reports in 2 months on queries; 4-5 months on mss.
Terms: Pays in royalties and advance.

BANTAM SPECTRA BOOKS/FOUNDATION BOOKS (II, IV), Subsidiary of Bantam Doubleday Dell Publishing Group, 666 5th Ave., New York NY 10103. (212)765-6500. Vice-President and Publisher: Lou Aronica; Executive Editor: Amy Stout. Associate Editor: Betsy Mitchell. Editor: Janna Silverstein. Estab. 1985. Large science fiction, fantasy and speculative fiction line. Publishes hardcover originals and paperback originals and reprint trade paperbacks. Plans to publish 2 first novels in 1989. Averages 66 total titles each year, all fiction.
Needs: Fantasy, literary, science fiction. Needs for novels include novels that attempt to broaden the traditional range of science fiction and fantasy. Strong emphasis on characterization. Especially well written traditional science fiction and fantasy will be considered. No fiction that doesn't have at least some element of speculation or the fantastic. Recently published *Rose of the Prophet*, by Margaret Weis and Tracy Hickman (trilogy); *Prelude to Foundation*, by Isaac Asimov; and *Mona Lisa Overdrive*, by William Gibson.
How to Contact: Query first. "We prefer to see query letters first, including a couple of paragraphs summarizing the story, along with background on the author listing previous writing credits, if any." SASE. Agented fiction 90%. Reports in 3-4 weeks on queries; 6-8 weeks on mss. Photocopied submissions OK. Accepts computer printouts, including dot-matrix, "only very dark and very readable ones."
Terms: Pays in royalties; negotiable advance. Sends galleys to author.
Advice: "With the merging of Bantam with Doubleday and Dell, we have created a hardcover science fiction and fantasy imprint called Foundation with Doubleday. The list presently includes authors such as Isaac Asimov, George Alec Effinger, Lewis Shiner and Sheri S. Tepper.

BANTAM/DOUBLEDAY BOOKS, INC. (II), Division of Bantam Dell Doubleday Publishing Group, 666 5th Ave., New York NY 10103. (212)765-6500. Imprints include Skylark, New Age, Loveswept, Sweet Dreams, Sweet Valley High, Spectra, Bantam New Fiction and Starfire. Estab. 1945. Complete publishing: hard-cover, trade, mass market. Number of titles: Plans 600 for 1990.
Needs: Contemporary, literary, adventure, mystery, spy, historical, western, war, gothic, romance, feminist, gay/lesbian, ethnic, psychic/supernatural, religious/inspirational, science fiction, fantasy, horror, humor/satire, and young adult. Recently published *Bonfire of the Banities*, by Tom Wolfe; *A Brief History of Time* Steven Hawking.
How to Contact: Submit through agent. No unsolicited material accepted. Simultaneous and photocopied submissions OK. Reports on queries as soon as possible.
Terms: Individually negotiated; offers advance.

THE BERKLEY PUBLISHING GROUP (III), Subsidiary of G.P. Putnam's Sons, 200 Madison Ave., New York NY 10016. (212)951-8800. Imprints are Berkley, Jove, Charter, Ace, Pacer. Editor-in-Chief: Leslie Gelbman. Fiction Editors: Natalee Rosenstein, Judith Stern, John Talbot, Melinda Metz, Susan Allison, Beth Fleisher, Ginger Buchanan, Mercer Warriner, Hillary Cige, Jim Morris. Nonfiction: Trish Todd. Large commercial category line. Publishes paperback originals and hardcover and paperback reprints. Books: paperbound printing; perfect binding; average print order: "depends on position

in list." Plans approx. 10 first novels this year. Averages 1,180 total titles, 1,000 fiction titles each year. Sometimes critiques rejected mss.
Needs: Fantasy, horror, humor/satire, literary, mainstream, psychic/supernatural/occult, religious/inspirational, romance (contemporary, historical), science fiction, short story collections (by established authors, but rarely), suspense/mystery, war, western, young adult/teen (problem novels). We are looking for strong horror and contemporary romance/mainstream fiction titles. "Because we are a mass market publishing house, we publish a vast array of genres. We do short story collections, except for the rare collection by an established author." Recently published *Springfancy*, by LaVyrle Spencer (historical romance); *The Cardinal and the Kremlin*, by Tom Clancy (fiction/military); and *Midnight*, by Dean Koontz (horror).
How to Contact: Accepts no unsolicited mss. Submit through agent only. Agented fiction 98%. Reports in 1 month on mss. Simultaneous and photocopied submissions OK. Accepts computer printout submissions.
Terms: Pays royalties of 4% minimum; 10% maximum. Provides 25 author's copies. Writer's guidelines and book catalog not available.
Advice: "Aspiring novelists should keep abreast of the current trends in publishing by reading the New York Times Bestseller Lists, trade magazines for their desired genre and *Publishers Weekly*."

BERKLEY/ACE SCIENCE FICTION (II), Berkley Publishing Group, 200 Madison Ave., New York NY 10016. Editor-in-Chief: Susan Allison. Estab. 1948. Publishes paperback originals and reprints. Number of titles: 10/month. Buys 85-95% agented fiction.
Needs: Science fiction and fantasy. No other genre accepted. No short stories. Published *The Cat Who Walks Through Walls*, by Robert Heinlein; *Neuromancer*, by William Gibson.
How to Contact: Submit outline/synopsis and 3 sample chapters with SASE. No simultaneous submissions; photocopied submissions OK. Reports in 2 months minimum on mss. "Queries answered immediately if SASE enclosed." Publishes ms an average of 18 months after acceptance.
Terms: Standard for the field. Sends galleys to author.
Advice: "Good science fiction and fantasy are almost always written by people who have read and loved a lot of it. We are looking for knowledgeable science or magic, as well as sympathetic characters with recognizable motivation. We need less fantasy and more science fiction. We are looking for solid, well-plotted SF: good action adventure, well-researched hard science with good characterization and books that emphasize characterization without sacrificing plot. In fantasy, again, we are looking for all types of work, from high fantasy to sword and sorcery." Submit fantasy and science fiction to Susan Allison, Ginjer Buchanan and Beth Fleisher.

BETHANY HOUSE PUBLISHERS (II), 6820 Auto Club Rd., Minneapolis MN 55438. (612)829-2500. Fiction lines include: Prairie Love Stories, The Stonewyck Trilogy, The Starlight Trilogy, George MacDonald Classics, Canadian West, The Zion Chronicles. Editorial Director: Carol Johnson. Manuscript Reviews: Sharon Madison. Estab. 1956. Midsize independent religious publisher with plans to expand; publishing in a variety of categories from theological to fiction. Publishes paperback and hardcover originals. Books: type of paper varies; offset printing; average print order: 20,000; first novel print order average: 15,000.
Needs: Religious/inspirational, adventure, mystery, regional, romance (historical and young adult), gothic and juvenile. Published *Love Takes Wing*, by Janette Oke (prairie romance); *Key to Zion*, by Bodie Thoene (historical); *Code of Honor*, by Sandy Dengler (historical).
How to Contact: Query or submit outline/synopsis and 2-3 sample chapters with SASE. Simultaneous and photocopied submissions OK. Accepts computer printout submissions. Prefers letter-quality. No disks. Reports in 1 month on queries, 6 weeks on mss. Publishes ms an average of 1 year after acceptance.
Terms: Pays in royalties. Sends galleys to author. Free book catalog and fiction guidelines with 8½x11 SASE.
Advice: "Prairie romances are *very* strong in our line; next are gothic romances, then historical fiction. We look at everything that is submitted; a first novel has a chance with us, especially if it has series possibilities. We do *not* recommend an agent—this puts an unnecessary barrier between publisher and author (chances for misunderstanding, mistrust). Send queries and proposals around till you have raised some interest; work with the editor to fit it to a publisher's needs."

JOHN F. BLAIR, PUBLISHER (II, IV), 1406 Plaza Dr., Winston-Salem NC 27103. (919)768-1374. President: Margaret Couch. Editor: Stephen Kirk. Estab. 1954. Small independent publisher. Publishes hardcover and paperback originals. Books: acid free paper; offset printing; casebound or softbound;

Read the Business of Fiction section to learn the correct way to prepare and submit a manuscript.

illustrations; average print order 2,500-5,000. Number of titles: 8 in 1989. Encourages new writers. Occasionally comments on rejected mss.

Needs: Contemporary, literary and regional. Generally prefers regional material dealing with southeastern U.S. No confessions or erotica. "We do not limit our consideration of manuscripts to those representing specific genres or styles. Our primary concern is that anything we publish be of high literary quality." Published works include *Being a Boy*, by Paxton Davis (autobiography); and *The Hatterask Incident*, by John D. Randall (novel).

How to Contact: Query or submit with SASE. Simultaneous and photocopied submissions OK. Accepts computer printout submissions. Prefers letter-quality. Reports in 1 month on queries, 3 months on mss. Publishes ms 1-2 years after acceptance. Free book catalog.

Terms: Pays 10% standard royalties, 7% on paperback royalties.

Advice: "We are primarily interested in serious adult novels of high literary quality. Most of our titles have a tie-in with North Carolina or the southeastern United States. Please enclose a cover letter and outline with the manuscript. We prefer to review queries before we are sent complete manuscripts. Queries should include an approximate word count."

BOOKCRAFT, INC., 1848 W. 2300 South, Salt Lake City UT 84119. (801)972-6180. Editorial Manager: Cory H. Maxwell. Publishes hardcover originals. Books: #60 stock paper; sheet-fed and web press; average print order: 5,000-7,000; 3,000 for reprints. Published new writers within the last year. Encourages new writers. "We are always open for creative, fresh ideas."

Needs: Contemporary, historical, western, romance and religious/inspirational. Recently published *Choices*, by Dorothy W. Peterson; *On the Side of the Angels*, by Kristen D. Randle; and *The Falcon Heart*, by Jaroldeen Edwards.

How to Contact: Query, submit outline/synopsis and sample chapters, or submit complete ms with SASE. Photocopied submissions OK. Reports in 2 months on both queries and mss.

Terms: Pays royalties; no advance. Sends galleys to author. Free book catalog and writer's guidelines.

Advice: "Read our fiction. Our market is the membership of The Church of Jesus Christ of Latter-Day Saints (Mormons), and all stories must be related to the background, doctrines or practices of that church. No preaching, but tone should be fresh, positive and motivational. No anti-Mormon works. The amount of fiction we publish has remained the same the last three or four years. We publish little in the way of paperback; given regional nature of our market, it is difficult to price paperbacks competitively."

THOMAS BOUREGY & COMPANY, INC., 401 Lafayette St., New York, NY 10003. Editor: Barbara J. Brett. Imprint: Avalon Books. Publishes hardcover originals. Average print order for all books (including first novels): 2,100. Averages 60 titles/year. Buys very little agented fiction. Recently published *River of Stars*, by Marjorie Everitt (romance); *Mermaids and Magic Words*, by A.R. Provost (career romance); *Nightmare in Morocco*, by Loretta Jackson and Vickie Britton (mystery romance); and *Devil's Canyon Double Cross*, by Clifford Blair (western).

Needs: "Avalon Books publishes wholesome romances, adventures and westerns that are sold to libraries throughout the country. Intended for family reading, our books are read by adults as well as teenagers, and their characters are all adults: The heroines of the romances are all young (early through mid-twenties) single (no divorcees or widows, please!) women, and the heroes of the westerns range in age from late twenties to early thirties. There is no graphic sex in any of our novels; kisses and embraces are as far as our characters go. The heroines of the romances and the heroes of the westerns and adventures should all be looking forward to marriage at the end of the book. Currently, we publish five books a month: two romances, one mystery romance, one career romance and one adventure. All the romances are contemporary; all the westerns are historical. The important action in all our novels takes place over a short period of time, ranging from days to no longer than a year." Books range in length from a minimum of 35,000 words to a maximum of 50,000 words.

How to Contact: Submit the first chapter and a brief, but complete, summary of the book, or submit complete manuscript. Publishes very little agented fiction. Enclose ms-size SASE. Reports in about three months. "Send SASE for a copy of our tip sheet."

Terms: $500 for the first book and $600 thereafter, against the first 3,500 copies sold. (Initial run is 2,100.) A royalty of 10% is paid on any additional sales. The first half of the advance is paid upon signing of the contract; the second within 30 days of publication.

BRADBURY PRESS, INC. (I, II), Affiliate of Macmillan, Inc., 866 3rd Ave., New York NY 10022. (212)702-9809. Editor: Barbara Lalicki. Publishes juvenile hardcover originals. Books: excellent quality paper printing and binding; full color or black-and-white illustrations—depends on what the book needs. Number of titles: 34 in 1989. Encourages new writers. Seldom comments on rejected mss.

Needs: Juvenile and young adult: contemporary, adventure, science fiction. Published *The Riddle and the Rune*, by Grace Chetwin; *Hattie and the Fox*, by Mem Fox; and *Oma and Bobo*, by Amy Schwartz.
How to Contact: Query first on novels. Send complete picture book ms with SASE. Specify simultaneous submissions; photocopied submissions OK. Reports in 3 months on mss.
Terms: Pays royalty based on retail price. Advance negotiable.

BRANDEN PUBLISHING CO. (I, II), Subsidiary of Branden Press, 17 Station St., Box 843, Brookline Village MA 02147. (617)734-2045. Imprint: I.P.L. President: Adolpho Caso. Estab. 1967. Publishes originals and hardcover and paperback originals and reprints. Books: 55-60 lb acid free paper; case or perfect binding; illustrations; average print order: 5,000. Published new writers within the last year. Plans 5 first novels this year. Averages 15 total titles, 5 fiction titles each year.
Needs: Adventure, contemporary, ethnic, historical, literary, mainstream, military/war, romance, short story collections, suspense/mystery and translations. Looking for "contemporary, fast pace, modern society." No porno, experimental or horror. Recently published *Payola!*, by Gerry Cagle; *Miss Emily Martine*, by Lynn Thorsen; *Tales of Suicide*, by Luigi Pirandello; and *The Saving Rain*, by Elsie Webber.
How to Contact: Does not accept unsolicited mss. Query first with vita. SASE. Reports in 1 week on queries. Accepts computer printout submissions.
Terms: Pays royalties of 10% minimum. Advance negotiable. Provides 10 author's copies. Sends galleys to author. Publishes ms "several months" after acceptance. Book catalog for 4x9 SAE with 1 first class stamp.
Advice: "Publishing more fiction because of demand. Do not oversubmit; try single submissions; do not procrastinate if contract is offered."

GEORGE BRAZILLER, INC. (III), 60 Madison Ave., New York NY 10016. (212)889-0909. Literary and Nonfiction Editor: Judith Levin. Estab. 1955. Publishes hardcover originals and paperback reprints. Books: cloth binding; illustrations sometimes; average print order: 4,000. Average first novel print order: 3,000. Buys 10% agented fiction. Averages 25 total titles, 6 fiction titles each year. Occasionally critiques rejected mss.
Needs: Art, feminist, literary, short story collections and translations. Published *Confessions of a Good Arab*, by Yoram Kaniuk (literary); *The Carpanthians*, by Janet Frame (literary); and *A Revolutionary Woman*, by Sheila Fugard.
How to Contact: Query first with SASE. Photocopied submissions OK. Reports in 2 weeks on queries. Publishes ms an average of 1 year after acceptance.
Terms: Negotiates advance. Must return advance if book is not completed or is not acceptable. Sends galleys to author. Free book catalog on request with oversized SASE.

BROADMAN PRESS (II), 127 9th Ave. N., Nashville TN 37234. (615)251-2433. Editorial Director: Harold S. Smith. Religious publisher associated with the Southern Baptist Convention. Publishes hardcover and paperback originals. Books: offset paper stock; offset printing; perfect Smyth sewn binding; illustrations possible; average print order: depends on forecast. Average number of titles: 3/year.
Needs: Adventure, historical, religious/inspirational, humor/satire, juvenile, and young adult. Will accept no other genre. Published: *In Search of a Quiet Place*, by Phyllis C. Gobbell (adult); and *To Make All Things New*, by Caryl Porter.
How to Contact: Query, but decision is not made until ms is reviewed. No simultaneous submissions; photocopied submissions OK. Reports in 2 months on queries and mss.
Terms: Pays 10% in royalties; no advance. Sends galleys to author if requested.
Advice: "We publish very few fiction works, but we encourage first novelists. We encourage a close working relationship with the author to develop the best possible product."

CAMELOT BOOKS (II), Imprint of Avon Books, (Division of the Hearst Corporation), 105 Madison Ave., New York NY 10016. (212)481-5609. Editorial Director: Ellen E. Krieger. Estab. 1961. Publishes paperback originals and reprints for middle-grade juvenile list. Books: 6-10 line drawings in a few of the younger books. No color.
Needs: Juvenile (fantasy—"very selective," contemporary—"selective"). Looking for "contemporary, humorous books about real kids in real-life situations." No "science fiction, animal stories, picture books." Published *Search for Grissi*, by Mary Francis Shura (contemporary fiction); *Count Dracula, Me and Norma D*, by Jessica Hatchigan (contemporary fiction); and *Richard and the Vratch*, by Beatrice Gormley (fantasy, contemporary fiction).
How to Contact: Accepts unsolicited mss. Submit complete ms with cover letter (preferred) or outline/synopsis and 3 sample chapters. Agented fiction 75%. Reports in 3-4 weeks on queries; 6-10 weeks on mss. Simultaneous and photocopied submissions OK. Accepts computer printout submissions.

Terms: Royalties and advance negotiable. Sends galleys to author. Writer's guidelines for #10 SAE and 1 first class stamp. Book catalog for 9x11 SAE and 98¢ postage.

CARROLL & GRAF PUBLISHERS, INC. (III), 260 5th Ave., New York NY 10001. (212)889-8772. Contact: Editor. Estab. 1983. Publishes hardcover and paperback originals and paperback reprints. Plans 5 first novels this year. Averages 80 total titles, 45 fiction titles each year. Average first novel print order 20,000 copies. Occasionally critiques rejected mss.
Needs: Contemporary, erotica, fantasy, science fiction, literary, mainstream and suspense/mystery. No romance.
How to Contact: Does not accept unsolicited mss. Query first or submit outline/synopsis and sample chapters. SASE. Reports in 2 weeks. Photocopied submissions OK. Accepts computer printout submissions, no dot-matrix. Prefers letter-quality.
Terms: Pays in royalties of 6% minimum; 15% maximum; advance negotiable. Sends galleys to author. Free book catalog on request.

***CHILDRENS PRESS (II)**, Division of Regensteiner Publishing Enterprises, Inc., 544 N. Cumberland Ave., Chicago IL 60656. (312)693-0800. Vice President, Editorial: Fran Dyra. Estab. 1946. Publishes hardcover originals. Published new writers within the last year. Averages 125-150 total titles, 40 fiction titles each year.
Needs: Juvenile (easy-to-read, picture books, biographies (historical and contemporary) for middle and Junior high grades.
How to Contact: Query first if long ms (more than 5 ms pages or series idea); or submit outline/synopsis and sample chapters or complete ms with SASE. Simultaneous submissions and photocopied submissions OK. Do not send original artwork. Reports in 3 months.
Terms: Occasionally pays in royalties of 5% minimum; negotiates advance. Generally makes outright purchase of $500 minimum; 6 author's copies. Occasionally subsidy publishes. Offers 25% of sale price for subsidiary rights. Free writer's guidelines; free book catalog on request.
Advice: "Have started trade sales primarily to museums and teacher-supply bookstores. Need authors who can write social studies materials for our Enchantment of the World series (128 page books, 6th-grade reading level). Also need writers for our Cornerstones of Freedom series (48 pages, 4th grade reading level). Looking for action-packed stories for young readers who have second- or third-grade reading skills."

THE CHILD'S WORLD, INC. (II), Box 989, Elgin IL 60121. (708)741-7591. President: Jane Buerger. Estab. 1968. Publishes hardcover and paperback originals. Number of titles: approximately 50/year.
Needs: Supplemental books for school and library market. Juvenile: concept books, sports, animal, spy/adventure, historical, fantasy/science fiction and easy-to-read. "All of our titles are for the juvenile market. Most are only 32 pages." Recently published 5 Alphabet books by Jane Belk Moncure; 4 Great Mysteries, by Janet Riehecky; and 4 Amazing Animal Facts by Janet McDonnell.
How to Contact: Submit complete ms with SASE. Simultaneous and photocopied submissions OK. Reports in 4 months on queries.
Terms: Pays by outright purchase of $400-$700; no advance. Free book catalog.
Advice: "Be persistent. Only submit manuscripts for preschool–grade 2."

CITADEL PRESS (II), Lyle Stuart Inc., 120 Enterprise Ave., Secaucus NJ 07094. (201)866-4199. Vice President: Allan J. Wilson. Estab. 1942. Publishes hardcover and paperback originals and paperback reprints. Averages 65 total titles, 8-10 fiction titles each year. Occasionally critiques rejected mss.
Needs: No religious, romantic or detective. Published *The Rain Maiden*, by Jill M. Phillips and *Human Oddities*, by Martin Monestiere.
How to Contact: Accepts unsolicited mss. Query first with SASE. Reports in 6 weeks on queries; 2 months on mss. Simultaneous and photocopied submissions OK.
Terms: Pays in royalties of 10% minimum; 15% maximum; 12-25 author's copies. Advance is more for agented ms; depends on grant/award money.

CLARION BOOKS (II): A Houghton Mifflin Company, 52 Vanderbilt Ave., New York NY 10017. (212)420-5800. Editor/Publisher: James C. Giblin. Estab. 1965 "as the children's book division of Seabury Press; 1979 as a new children's book imprint of Houghton Mifflin Company." Midsize children's book imprint of a major publishing company. Publishes hardcover originals and paperback reprints from its own backlist. Number of titles: 40 in 1988. Average print order: 6,000-7,000. Published new writers within the last year. Buys 10-15% agented fiction. Comments on rejected mss "only if we're encouraging a revision."
Needs: Juvenile and young adult: adventure, suspense and humorous contemporary stories for ages 8-12 and 10-14; "fresh, personal stories that capture our attention, and that we think young readers would enjoy." Published *Always and Forever Friends*, by C. S. Adler; *Saying Good-bye to Grandma*, by

Jane Resh Thomas; *December Stillness*, by Mary Downing Hahn. Especially interested in humorous stories for ages 8 to 12.
How to Contact: Accepts unsolicited mss. Query on mss of more than 50 pages. SASE. "We like queries to be straightforward—no dramatic teaser openings—and to contain a description of the story, plus any relevant writing credits. It's good if they can be kept to a page, or at most two pages." Reluctantly considers simultaneous submissions; photocopied submissions OK. Accepts computer printout submissions. Reports in 2 weeks on queries, 8 weeks on mss. Publishes ms 1-1½ years after acceptance.
Terms: Pays 5% royalties on picture books; 10% on other books; offers $2,000-$3,500 advances. Writer must return advance if book is not completed or is not acceptable. Free book catalog and guidelines.
Advice: "I really believe that the best novels come out of the author's self-knowledge of his or her own experience and background. Don't send us imitations of other writers' successes. We're always open to first novelists in the hope that they'll become regular contributors to our list. We've noticed a return to lighter stories from the heavier problem novels of recent years. Attend a writer's workshop or critique group in order to study the structure of successful novels." Publishing "more middle grade fiction, less young adult fiction, because paperback originals seem to have covered that market. More paperback reprints from our backlist because bookstores like them."

‡■CLOVERDALE PRESS INC. (II). Imprints include Butterfield Press Inc. and Jeffrey Weiss Group. 96 Morton St., New York NY 10014. (212)727-3370. Senior Editor: Robin Hardy. Estab. 1980. Book packager. Publishes paperback originals. Published new writers within the last year. Plans 2-5 first novels this year. Averages 200 total titles (all fiction). Sometimes comments on rejected ms.
Needs: Adventure, fantasy, historical, horror, military/war, psychic/supernatural/occult, science fiction, suspense/mystery, western, young adult fantasy/science fiction, historical and spy/adventure. No mainstream material. Recently published *Chopper 1*, by Jack Hawkins (Vietnam War series); *Turbo Cowboys*, by Tony Philips (Y/A Fantasy series); and *Hangman*, by Craig Foley (Western series).
How to Contact: Accepts unsolicited mss. Query first and submit outline/synopsis and 2-3 sample chapters (30 pages). Agented fiction 50%. Reports in 2 weeks on queries; 3 months on mss. Simultaneous and photocopied submissions OK. Accepts computer printout submissions.
Terms: Average advance $2,000-$4,000 and 10 author's copies. Publishes ms 6 months after acceptance. Writer's guidelines free.
Advice: "Write to category. Submit 30 pages—if it doesn't happen in 30 pages it's not going to happen."

CONTEMPORARY BOOKS (IV), 180 N. Michigan Ave., Chicago IL 60657. (312)782-9181. Imprint: Congdon & Weed. Associate Publisher: Nancy J. Crossman. Estab. 1977. Mostly nonfiction adult trade publisher. Publishes hardcover and paperback originals and reprints. Recently published *Elements of Chance*, by Louisa Elliott; published new writers within the last year (agented only). Averages 120 total titles, 1-2 fiction titles each year.
How to Contact: Accepts unsolicited mss. Send 2-3 sample chapters. SASE. Reports in 3 weeks on queries; 3 months on mss. Simultaneous and photocopied submissions OK.
Terms: Pays royalties.

CROSSWAY BOOKS (II, IV), Division of Good News Publishers, 9825 W. Roosevelt Rd., Westchester IL 60154. (312)345-7474. Managing Editor: Ted Griffin. Estab. 1938. Midsize independent religious publisher with plans to expand. Publishes paperback originals. Book: illustrations sometimes; average print order 3,000-5,000. Plans 3 first novels this year. Buys 50% agented fiction. Averages 35 total titles, 8-10 fiction titles each year.
Needs: Contemporary, adventure, fantasy, juvenile (fantasy, animal), literary, religious/inspirational, science fiction and young adult (fantasy/science fiction). "All fiction published by Crossway Books must be written from the perspective of historic orthodox Christianity. It need not be *explicitly* Christian, but it must understand and view the world through Christian principle. For example, our books *Taliesin* and *Merlin* take place in a pre-Christian era, but Christian themes (e.g., sin, forgiveness, sacrifice, redemption) are present. We are *eager* to discover and nurture Christian novelists." No sentimental, didactic, "inspirational" religious fiction; heavy-handed allegorical or derivative (of C.S. Lewis or J.R.R. Tolkien) fantasy. Recently published *Merlin* by Stephen R. Lawhead; and *This Present Darkness*, by Frank Peretti.
How to Contact: Send query with synopsis and sample chapters. Accepts computer printout submissions. Prefers letter-quality. Reports in 3 weeks to 4 months on queries. Publishes ms 1-2 years after acceptance.
Terms: Pays in royalties and negotiates advance. Book catalog for 9×12 SAE and $1.25.
Advice: "Publishing a higher quality of writing as we develop a wider reputation for excellent Christian fiction. Christian novelists—you must get your writing *up to standard*. The major reason novels informed by a Christian perspective do not have more presence in the market is because they are inferior.

Close-up

Ellen Steiber
Robin Hardy
Cloverdale Press

Book packagers offer excellent opportunities for writers, especially those who have not been published before, says Ellen Steiber, senior editor for Cloverdale Press. "It's a good place for writers to start and can be a stepping-stone for their career," she says. "We work very closely with our writers, much more closely than do editors at publishing houses."

One reason for the strong editor/writer relationship, she explains, is the nature of book packaging. Publishers buy work from writers after the writing process is completed, but packagers become involved with a book at the concept stage and work closely with the writer through out the development of the book.

Writers should be familiar with differences between packagers and publishers, says Steiber. One major difference is the payment process. Most publishers buy specific rights and pay writers with a combination of an advance plus royalties. Work done for packagers, on the other hand, is considered work-for-hire. The packager owns all rights and the writer is paid a one-time flat fee for the work. In the case of many book series, books are published under one pseudonym and that pseudonym is also the property of the packager.

Steiber admits working with a packager is a tradeoff. Writers give up rights to the work, but in exchange they are paid a competitive fee and first-time authors receive a great deal of support, she says. "We are also very willing to let agents and other publishers know who wrote each of our books and readily give references."

Although Cloverdale publishes some individual books, many are produced as part of a series. "We supply a series 'bible' describing characters, setting and story line . . . but writers must read several books in the series, if they want to write for it."

Since Cloverdale produces series for several different publishers including Lynx, Bantam and Ballantine, each editor is responsible for developing a different line. A series can run from two ore three books to ten or twelve, depending on how well the series sells to publishers. Steiber edits books in Cloverdale's young adult and juvenile series.

Juvenile and young adult series that have done well for Cloverdale include a sports fiction series, a biography series and Nowhere High, a realistic, tough series for high-school age readers. "We are definitely interested in mysteries," says Steiber. "We look for fast-action adventure, science fiction, fantasy, sports and special interest subjects for our juvenile and young adult lines."

Although Cloverdale is open to ideas for individual books and series, writers should not send complete manuscripts, says Steiber. Send the first two chapters of a book or a writing sample, she says.

Robin Hardy, senior editor for Cloverdale's action/adventure lines, asks writers to send him outlines and writing samples of about 30 pages. He handles books for both children (usually boys) and adults.

He's also open to new series ideas, "I may suggest series, but not all our ideas come from in-house." For his lines, Hardy looks for technical expertise, especially knowledge of the military and particularly access to information on warfare and high tech surveillance. "Also snappy dialogue, a good repartee, realistic slang catch my attention."

–Robin Gee

Sad but true. I believe Crossway can successfully publish and market *quality* Christian novelists. Also read John Gardner's *On Moral Fiction*. The market for fantasy/science fiction continues to expand (and genre fiction in general). There are more attempts lately at Christian science fiction and fantasy, though they generally fail from didacticism or from being overly derivative."

T.Y. CROWELL JUNIOR BOOKS (II), 10 E. 53rd St., New York NY 10022. (212)207-7044. See Harper & Row Jr. Books Group.

CROWN PUBLISHERS, INC. (II), 201 E. 50th St., New York NY 10022. (212)572-6190. Imprints include Crown, Harmony Books, Orion Books, Clarkson N. Potter, Inc. Senior Vice President, Editorial: Betta A. Prashker. Crown Executive Editor: James O'Shea Wade. Sr. Editors: Lisa Healy, Barbara Grossman, Editorial Director, Harmony Books: Peter Guzzardi. Executive Editor: Harriet Bell. Editorial Director, Potter: Carol Southern. Executive Editor: Lauren Shakely. Executive Managing Editor: Laurie Stark. Estab. 1936. Large independent publisher of fiction and nonfiction. Publishes hardcover and paperback originals and reprints. Magazine: 50 lb paper; offset printing; hardcover binding; sometimes illustrations; average print order: 15,000. Plans 4 first novels this year. Averages 250 total titles, 20 fiction titles each year. Average first novel print order: 15,000 copies. Occasionally critiques rejected mss.
Needs: Adventure, contemporary, historical, horror, humor/satire, literary, mainstream, romance (historical, contemporary), science fiction, war. Needs for novels: genre. Recently published *If I Never Get Back*, by Darryl Brock; *Jimmy Stewart and His Poems*, by Jimmy Stewart; and *Antiques At Home*, by Barbara Ohrbach.
How to Contact: Query first or submit outline/synopsis and 3 sample chapters; complete mss are returned unread. SASE. Reports in 3-4 months. Photocopied submissions OK.
Terms: Pays advance against royalty; terms vary and are negotiated per book. Book catalog for SASE.

DAW BOOKS, INC. (I, IV), 1633 Broadway, New York NY 10019. Publisher: Donald A. Wollheim. Editor-in-Chief: Betsy Wollheim. Executive Editor: Sheila Gilbert. Estab. 1971. Publishes paperback originals, hardcover reprints and hardcover originals. Books: illustrations sometimes; average print and first novel order vary widely. May publish as many as 6 or more first novels a year. Averages 60 total titles, all fiction, each year. Occasionally critiques rejected mss.
Needs: Fantasy, science fiction and horror only.
How to Contact: Submit complete ms with SASE. Usually reports in 2-3 months on mss, but in special cases may take longer.
Terms: Pays an advance against royalities. Sends galleys to author (if there is time).
Advice: "We strongly encourage new writers. In 1987, we published first novels by six new authors and are currently working with more than a dozen additional new authors whose first novels we plan to publish in 1989 and 1990. We like a close and friendly relationship with authors. We are publishing more fantasy than previously, but we are looking for more *serious* fantasy and especially need science fiction. To unpublished authors: Try to make an educated submission and don't give up."

DEL REY BOOKS, Subsidiary of Ballantine Books, 201 E. 50 St., New York NY 10022. (212)572-2677. Estab. 1977. Publishes hardcover originals and paperback originals and reprints. "In 1989 we published 7 novels by authors who had never published novels before." Plans 6-7 first novels this year. Publishes 120 titles each year, all fiction. Sometimes critiques rejected mss.
Needs: Fantasy and science fiction. Fantasy must have magic as an intrinsic element to the plot. No flying-saucer, Atlantis or occult novels. Recently published *Renegades of Pern*, by Anne McCaffrey (science fiction/hardcover original); *The Diamond Throne*, by David Eddings (fantasy/hardcover original); and *The Metaconcert*, by Julian May (science fiction/paperback reprint).
How to Contact: Accepts unsolicited mss. Submit complete manuscript with cover letter or outline/synopsis and first 3 chapters. Address science fiction to SF editor; fantasy to fantasy editor. Reports in 2 weeks on queries; 10 months on ms. Photocopied submissions OK. Computer printout submissions OK.
Terms: Pays in royalties; "advance is competitive." Sends pre-publication galleys to author. Writer's guidelines for #10 SAE and 1 first class stamp.
Advice: Has been publishing "more fiction and more hardcovers, because the market is there for them. Read a lot of science fiction and fantasy, such as works by Anne McCaffrey, David Eddings, Larry Niven, Arthur C. Clarke, Terry Brooks, Frederik Pohl, Barbara Hambly. When writing, pay particular attention to plotting (and a satisfactory conclusion) and characters (sympathetic and well-rounded) – because those are what readers look for."

DELACORTE/DELL BOOKS FOR YOUNG READERS (II, III, IV), Subsidiary of Doubleday, 666 5th Ave., New York NY 10103. (212)765-6500. New imprint: Young Yearling Books, for readers around 6 years old. Vice President/Editor-in-Chief: George Nicholson. Editor: Michelle Poploff. Large publisher

Close-up

Sheila Gilbert
Executive Editor
Daw Books

"Fantasy must have a logic and consistency within its own world," says Sheila Gilbert, executive editor for Daw Books, a leading publisher of science fiction and fantasy. "Our readers have eagle eyes and are bold about pointing out discrepancies."

The relationship between writers and readers in this field is special. Readers become fans, not only of the genre, but of particular authors. That's why it is important for writers to avoid cheating readers with inconsistencies or unexplainable twists within the plot, says Gilbert.

Although works of fantasy are not based on real life, they must contain the same elements that make all fiction work, she explains. Characters must be well-drawn and plots must be completely thought out.

Daw Books publishes 36 new titles plus a number of reissues each year. "We are very open to work by new writers. In fact, we buy quite a number of manuscripts over the transom. We've had real success with some of the writers whose manuscripts were unsolicited.

"We work with authors very closely and stay with them all the way through the publishing process," she says. "We will also give input on manuscripts we reject, if we think something is very strong." Of course, Daw, like most other publishers, is hampered by the number of manuscripts received. The editors simply do not have the time to comment on all 50 to 100 manuscripts that come in each week. Besides having a consistent internal logic in their work, writers of fantasy and science fiction should also research the genre before submitting manuscripts. "Find out what publishers like and what sells well," she says. "And know your limits. If you are not a technical person, don't try to write a book with a lot of technology in it. We see very little these days that is solid science fiction because the technology is so far ahead, a lot of people just don't have the background for it."

Writers can get a unique sense of the genre by reading science fiction magazines and attending some of the conventions held all over the country each year. "The problem with some of the writers who send us manuscripts is that it is obvious they have not read much in the genre. Their manuscripts are influenced too much by television shows, such as 'Star Trek,' " she says.

Daw Books publishes a lot of books in series, especially trilogies, but "there is no reason why we would not do a single novel,"Gilbert says. "In fact, writers should not think in terms of a series when writing their book—think of the story at hand."

Writers interested in submitting work to Daw Books should send a complete manuscript plus an outline or an outline and sample chapters. Chapters *must* be consecutive, says Gilbert. "Send a short and simple cover letter, but let your material speak for itself."

Since Daw is a small company, she says, she gets involved with all aspects of publishing, but she and the other editors would have it no other way. "Science fiction is our first love, as well as our specialty."

—Robin Gee

specializing in young adult and middle-age fiction. Occasionally critiques or comments on rejected ms.

Needs: Fantasy, juvenile, young adult. "We are looking for quality fiction—all categories possible." No romance of the formula type. Published *Fade*, by Robert Cormier; *Beans on the Roof*, by Betsy Byars; *Cal Cameron by Day, Spiderman by Night*, by Ann Cosum (winner of Delacorte fiction contest).

How to Contact: Query first. Unsolicited manuscripts not accepted. Fiction is agented.

Terms: Pays in royalties; advance is negotiable. Send galleys to author. Book catalog free on request.

Advice: "We are publishing more fiction than in the past. The market is good."

DELL PUBLISHING, 666 Fifth Avenue, New York NY 10103. (212)765-6500. Imprints include Delacorte Press, Delacorte Juvenile, Delta, Dell, Laurel, Laurel-Leaf and Yearling. Estab. 1922. Publishes hardcover and paperback originals and paperback reprints.

Needs: See below for individual imprint requirements.

How to Contact: Reports in 3 months. Photocopied and simultaneous submissions OK. Please adhere strictly to the following procedures: 1. Send *only* a 4-page synopsis or outline with a cover letter stating previous work published or relevant experience. Enclose SASE. 2. *Do not* send ms, sample chapters or artwork. 3. *Do not* register, certify or insure your letter. Dell is comprised of several imprints, each with its own editorial department. Please review carefully the following information and direct your submissions to the appropriate department. Your envelope must be marked: Attention: (One of the following names of imprints), Editorial Department—Proposal.

DELACORTE: Publishes in hardcover; looks for top-notch commercial fiction; historical romance. Recently published *Firefly Summer*, by Maeve Binchy; and *Daddy*, by Danielle Steel. 35 titles/year.

DELTA: Publishes trade paperbacks; will be publishing original fiction; looks for useful, substantial guides (nonfiction). 20 titles/year.

DELL: Publishes mass-market paperbacks; rarely publishes original nonfiction; looks for family sagas, historical romances, sexy modern romances, adventure and suspense thrillers, psychic/supernatural, horror, war novels, fiction and nonfiction. Not currently publishing original mysteries or science fiction. 200 titles/year.

DELACORTE JUVENILE: Publishes in hardcover for children and young adults, grades K-12. 40 titles/year. "We prefer complete mss for fiction."

LAUREL-LEAF: Publishes originals and reprints in paperback for young adults, grades 7-12. 48 titles/year.

YEARLING: Publishes originals and reprints in paperback for children, grades K-6. 75 titles/year.

Terms: Pays 6-15% in royalties; offers advance. Sends galleys to author. Book catalog for 8½x11 SASE plus $1.30 postage (Attention: Customer Service).

Advice: "Don't get your hopes up. Query first only with 4-page synopsis plus SASE. Study the paperback racks in your local drugstore. We encourage first novelists. We also encourage all authors to seek agents."

DEMBNER BOOKS (II), Division of Red Dembner Enterprises, 80 8th Ave., New York NY 10011. Editor: S. Arthur Dembner. Publishes hardcover originals. Books: quality consignment stock paper; sheet and web printing; hardcover binding; illustrations rarely; average print order: 5,000-10,000; first novel print order: 3,000-5,000.

Needs: Mystery/suspense and literary. "We are prepared to publish a limited number of well-written, nonsensational works of fiction." Recently published *The Dividing Line*, by Kjell-Olof Bornemark (a spy thriller); and *Wolf in Sheep's Clothing*, by John R. Riggs.

How to Contact: Submit outline/synopsis and sample chapters with SASE. Simultaneous and legible photocopied submissions OK.

Terms: Offers negotiable advance. Sends galleys to author.

Advice: "Library sales are up; general sales to bookstores are down. Have patience and forbearance. Those who make it big on a first novel are a very not-so-select few. The randomness of publishing success stories is one of the hardest things about being a writer (and editor, I must add)."

DIAL BOOKS FOR YOUNG READERS (II), Subsidiary of Penguin Books U.S.A. Inc., 375 Hudson St., New York NY 10014. (212)725-1818. Imprints include Pied Piper Books, Easy-to-Read Books. Senior Editor: Arthur Levine. Estab. 1961. Trade children's book publisher, "looking for picture book mss and novels." Publishes hardcover originals. Plans 1 first novel this year. Averages 50-60 titles, all fiction. Occasionally critiques or comments on rejected ms.

Needs: Juvenile (1-9 yrs.) including: animal, fantasy, spy/adventure, contemporary and easy-to-read; young adult/teen (10-18 years) including: fantasy/science fiction, literary fiction, sports and spy/adventure. Recently published *Lionel in the Spring*, by Stephen Krensky (easy-to-read); *The Tale of Caliph Stork*, by Lenny Hort (picture book); and *Bailey's Bones*, by Victor Kelleher (novel).

How to Contact: Accepts unsolicited mss. Submit outline/synopsis and sample chapters or complete ms with cover letter. SASE. Agented fiction 50%. Reports in 3-4 weeks on queries. Simultaneous and photocopied submissions OK. Accepts computer printout submissions.
Terms: Pays in royalties. Writer's guidelines free for #10 SAE and 1 first class stamp. Book catalog for 9x12 SAE and $1.92 postage.
Advice: "We are publishing more fiction books than in the past, and we publish only hardcover originals, most of which are fiction. At this time we are particularly interested in both fiction and nonfiction for the middle grades, and innovative picture book manuscripts. We also are looking for easy-to-reads for first and second graders. Plays, collections of games and riddles, and counting and alphabet books are generally discouraged. Before submitting a manuscript to a publisher, it is a good idea to request a catalog to see what the publisher is currently publishing. As the 'Sweet Valley High' phenomenon has loosened its stranglehold on YA fiction, we are seeing more writers able to translate traditional values of literary excellence and contemporary innovation into the genre. Make your cover letters read like jacket flaps—short and compelling. Don't spend a lot of time apologizing for a lack of qualifications. In fact, don't mention them at all unless you have publishing credits, or your background is directly relevant to the story. 'I found this folktale during a return trip to the Tibetan village where I spent the first ten years of my life.' "

DORCHESTER PUBLISHING CO., INC. (II), Leisure Books, 276 Fifth Ave., New York NY 10001. (212)725-8811. Imprint: Leisure Books. Submissions Editor: Carolyn Pittis. Estab. 1982. Publisher of mass market paperbacks. Publishes paperback originals and reprints. Books: photo offset printing; average print order varies. Receptive to first novels. Published new writers within the last year. Averages 150 total titles, mostly fiction. Buys 20% agented fiction.
Needs: Horror, romance (historical, minimum length 90,000 words), science fiction. "At present, Dorchester is looking for historical romance and horror." No juvenile, contemporary romance, gothic or romantic suspense. "Publishes 1 or 2 SF mss/year or occasional nonfiction book, but these are usually agented." Published *Fangs*, by Richard Forsythe (horror); and *Summer Storm*, by Catherine Hart (historical romance).
How to Contact: Query first or submit outline/synopsis and 3 sample chapters with SASE. No unsolicited mss. "*Nothing* will be returned without SASE." Reports in 3 weeks on queries; 6 weeks on mss. Simultaneous and photocopied submissions OK from agents only. Letter-quality computer printouts only. Publishes ms usually within 2 years after acceptance.
Terms: Pays in royalties of 4%. Advance is negotiable. Must return advance (minus 10% which author retains) if book is not completed or is unacceptable. Sends galleys to author.
Advice: "We are concentrating heavily on horror and historical romance. *Learn to spell*! Learn the difference between *its* and *it's*. And most important, don't get discouraged by all those rejection slips—if you're any good, you'll get published sooner or later. We encourage first novelists. Our relationship with authors is 'a limited partnership with limitless possibilities.' "

DOUBLEDAY BOOKS, Division of Bantam Doubleday Dell Publishing Group, 666 Fifth Ave., New York NY 10103. (212)765-6500. Estab. 1897. Publishes hardcover originals.
Needs: Doubleday is not able to consider unsolicited queries, proposals or manuscripts unless submitted through a bona fide literary agent, except that we will consider fiction for science fiction imprints and westerns.
How to Contact: Send copy of complete ms (60,000-80,000 words) to Crime Club Editor, Science Fiction Editor or Western Editor as appropriate. Sufficient postage for return via fourth class mail must accompany ms. Reports in 2-6 months.
Terms: Pays in royalties; offers advance.

DOUBLEDAY CANADA LIMITED (III,IV), 105 Bond St., Toronto, Ontario M5B 1Y3 Canada. (416)340-0777. Imprint: Dell Distributing. Editorial Department: Jill Lambert. Estab. 1936. Large commercial *Canadian* publisher. Publishes hardcover originals (Doubleday) and paperback reprints (Dell). Book: offset or high bulk paper; offset printing; perfect or sewn binding. Plans "one at most" first novels this year. Publishes 20-40 total titles each year, 10-15 fiction titles.
Needs: Mainstream, humor/satire, literary, mysteries, commercial fiction, literary fiction, suspense, science fiction, juvenile. Published *Road to the Top*, by Aird, Novack and Westcott (business); *Death on Prague*; by John Reeves (mystery); *My Father's House*, by Sylvia Fraser (autobiography).
How to Contact: Accepts unsolicited mss. Query or send outline and chapters with cover letter. SASE (IRC) necessary for return of mss. "Please do *not* send SASE with US stamps!" 90% of fiction is agented. Reports on queries in up to 3 weeks; on ms in up to 2 months. Simultaneous and photocopied submissions OK. Accepts computer printout submissions, no dot-matrix.
Terms: Pays standard royalties, negotiable advance and 10 author's copies. Sends prepublication galleys to author.
Advice: "Think about marketability. Research the publishing house you plan to submit your work to."

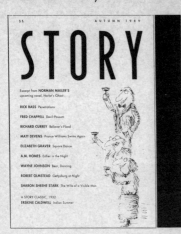

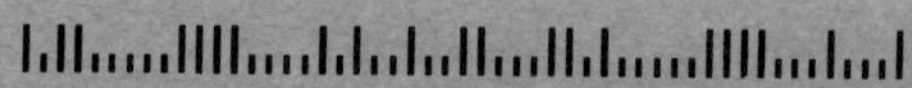

DOUBLEDAY-FOUNDATION BOOKS (II), Subsidiary of Bertelsmann, 666 Fifth Ave., New York NY 10103. (212)492-8971. Editors: Patrick LoBrutto and Lou Aronica. Estab. 1987. Publishes hardcover originals and reprints. Published new writers within the last year. Plans 1 first novel this year. Averages 18 total titles, all fiction each year. Sometimes critiques rejected mss.

Needs: Fantasy, horror, science fiction and short story collections. Needs "SF, fantasy mainly. Horror in very limited amounts. No unimaginative, lousy fiction." Recently published *Prince of the Blood*, by Ray Feist (fantasy); and *Reach*, by Edward Gibson (SF 1st novel).

How to Contact: Accepts unsolicited mss. Query first. SASE. Agented fiction 80-90%. Reports in 2 months. Simultaneous and photocopied submissions OK.

Terms: Pays royalties of 6-10%; offers negotiable advance. Sends galleys to author. Publishes ms within 1½-2 years after acceptance. Writer's guidelines and book catalog free.

EAKIN PRESS (II, IV), Box 90159, Austin TX 78709-0159. (512)288-1771. Imprint: Nortex. Editor: Edwin M. Eakin. Estab. 1978. Publishes hardcover originals. Books: old style (acid free); offset printing; case binding; illustrations; average print order 2,000; first novel print order 5,000. Plans 2 first novels this year. Averages 80 total titles each year.

Needs: Juvenile. Specifically needs historical fiction for school market, juveniles set in Texas for Texas grade schoolers. Recently published *Wall Street Wives*, by Ande Ellen Winkler; *Jericho Day*, by Warren Murphy; and *Blood Red Sun*, by Stephen Mertz. Published new writers within the last year.

How to Contact: Accepts unsolicited mss. First send query or submit outline/synopsis and 2 sample chapters. SASE. Agented fiction 5%. Simultaneous and photocopied submissions OK. Accepts computer printout submissions. Prefers letter quality. Reports in 3 months on queries.

Terms: Pays 10-15% in royalties; average advance: $1,000. Sends galleys to author. Publishes ms 1-1½ years after acceptance. Writers guidelines for #10 SAE and 1 first class stamp. Book catalog for 75¢.

Advice: Juvenile fiction only with strong Texas theme. Just beginning category of adult fiction. We receive around 600 queries or unsolicited mss a year."

PAUL S. ERIKSSON, PUBLISHER (II), 208 Battell Bldg., Middlebury VT 05753. (802)388-7303. Editor: Paul S. Eriksson. Estab. 1960. Publishes hardcover and paperback originals.

Needs: Mainstream. Published *The Headmaster's Papers*, by Richard A. Hawley; and *Norman Rockwell's Greatest Painting*, by Hollis Hodges (novel).

How to Contact: Query first. Photocopied submissions OK. Publishes ms an average of 6 months after acceptance.

Terms: Pays 10-15% in royalties; advance offered if necessary. Free book catalog.

Advice: "Our taste runs to serious fiction."

M. EVANS & CO., INC. (II), 216 E. 49th St., New York NY 10017. (212)688-2810. Contact: Editors. Westerns Editor: Sara Ann Freed. Publishes hardcover and trade paper fiction and nonfiction. Publishes 40-50 titles each year.

Needs: Western, young adult/teen (10-18 years).

How to Contact: Accepts unsolicited mss. Query first with outline/synopsis and 3 sample chapters. SASE. Agented fiction: 100%. Reports on queries in 3-5 weeks. Simultaneous and photocopied submissions OK. Accepts computer printout submissions, no dot-matrix.

Terms: Pays in royalties and offers advance; amounts vary. Sends galleys to author. Publishes ms 6-12 months after acceptance.

FARRAR, STRAUS & GIROUX (II), 19 Union Sq. W., New York NY 10003. Imprints include Michael DiCapua Books, Sunburst Books. Children's Books Publisher: Stephen Roxburgh. Editor-in-Chief: Margaret Ferguson. Number of titles: 40 in 1989. Published new writers within the last year. Buys juvenile mss with illustrations. Buys 50% agented fiction.

Needs: Children's picture books, juvenile novels, nonfiction. Recently published *Valentine & Orson*, by Nancy Ekholm Burkert; *El Guero: A True Adventure Story*, by Elizabeth Borton de Trevino; and *An Acceptable Time*, by Madeleine L'Engle.

How to Contact: Submit outline/synopsis and 3 sample chapters, summary of ms and any pertinent information about author, author's writing, etc. No simultaneous submissions; photocopied submissions OK. Reports in 1 month on queries, 3 months on mss. Publishes ms 18 months to 2 years after acceptance.

Terms: Pays in royalties; offers advance. Free book catalog with 6½×9½ SASE.

Advice: "Study our list before sending something inappropriate. Publishing more hardcovers—our list has expanded."

FAWCETT (I, II, III), Division of Random House/Ballantine, 201 E. 50th St., New York NY 10022. (212)751-2600. Imprints include Ivy, Crest, Gold Medal, Columbine and Juniper. Executive Editor: Barbara Dicks. Editor-in-Chief: Leona Nevler. Estab. 1955. Major publisher of mass market and trade paperbacks. Publishes paperback originals and reprints. Prints 160 titles annually. Encourages new writers. "Always looking for *great* first novels."
Needs: Historical, suspense, occult, adventure, mysteries. Published *The Omega Command*, by John Land; *Mid-town South*, by Christopher O'Brian; *The Incense Tree*, by Jacqueline La Tourette.
How to Contact: Query with SASE. Send outline and sample chapters for adult mass market. If ms is requested, simultaneous and photocopied submissions OK. Accepts computer printout submissions. Prefers letter-quality. Reports in 1 month on queries, 3 months on mss.
Terms: Pays usual advance and royalties.
Advice: "Gold Medal list consists of 5 original paperbacks per month—usually 4 are novels."

FEARON EDUCATION (II), Subsidiary of Simon & Schuster, Supplementary Education Group, 500 Harbor Blvd., Belmont CA 94002. (415)592-7810. Publisher and Editorial Director: Carol Hegarty. Estab. 1954. Special-education publishers with a junior high, high school, and adult basic education audience—publishing program includes high interest/low level fiction and vocational and life skills materials. Publishes paperback originals and reprints. Books: 3 lb book set paper; offset printing; perfect or saddlewired binding, line art illustrations, average print order: 5,000. Published only academic texts in 1989 but plans to publish 30 fiction titles in 1990.
Needs: Adventure, contemporary, ethnic, historical, regional, romance, science fiction, short story collections, suspense/mystery, western, young adult/teen. "Our fiction appears in series of short novellas, aimed at new literates and high school students reading no higher than a fifth-grade level. All are written to specification. It's a hard market to crack without some experience writing at low reading levels. Manuscripts for specific series of fiction are solicited from time to time, and unsolicited manuscripts are accepted occasionally." Recently published *A Question of Freedom*, by Lucy Jane Bledsoe (adventure novella—one of series of eight); *Just for Today*, by Tana Reiff (one novella of series of seven life-issues stories); and *The Everett Eyes*, by Bernard Jackson & Susie Quintanilla (one of twenty in a series of extra-short thrillers).
How to Contact: Submit outline/synopsis and sample chapters. SASE. Reports in 1 month. Simultaneous and photocopied submissions OK.
Terms: Authors usually receive a predetermined project fee. Book catalog for 9x12 SAE with 4 first class stamps.

‡FIELD PUBLICATIONS (II). Subsidiaries include: Weekly Reader Books. 245 Long Hill Road, Middletown CT 06457. Senior Editor: Stephen Fraser. Estab. 1902. Nationwide children's book club using mostly reprints and some original fiction. Publishes hardcover originals and reprints. Books: full color or b&w illustrations; average picture book print order: 100,000; novel print order: 50,000. Plans 2 original books this year. Averages 150 total titles all fiction this year. Comments on rejected ms.
Needs: Juvenile (4-9 yrs.) animal, easy-to-read, fantasy, sports, spy/adventure and contemporary; young/adult/teen (10-14 years) fantasy/science fiction, historical, romance, contemporary, sports and spy/adventure. Especially needs middle grade novels.
How to Contact: Accepts unsolicited mss. Submit complete ms with cover letter. Reports in 2-3 weeks on queries; 1 month on mss. Simultaneous and photocopied submissions OK.
Terms: Pays advance against royalties; provides author's copies. Publishing "varies, maximum 2 years" after acceptance.
Advice: "An important part of the editorial function is discovering and nurturing new writers. Generally, we'd like to see less school-related material and more strongly imaginative or powerfully dramatic material. (Note: If typing is done on a word processor, please proof it. It's very frustrating to read a poorly typed computer printout.)"

FLARE BOOKS (II), Imprint of Avon Books, Div. of the Hearst Corp., 105 Madison Ave., New York NY 10016. (212)481-5609. Editorial Director: Ellen Krieger. Estab. 1981. Small, young adult line. Publishes paperback originals and reprints. Plans 2-3 first novels this year. Averages 30 titles, all fiction each year.
Needs: Young adult (easy-to-read [hi-lo], problem novels, romance, spy/adventure) "very selective." Looking for contemporary fiction. No historical, science fiction/fantasy, heavy problem novels. Published *Breaking Up Is Hard To Do*, by Bruce and Carol Hart; *Maybe By Then I'll Understand*, by Jane McFann; and *Baby Sister*, by Marilyn Sachs (all contemporary).
How to Contact: Accepts unsolicited mss. Submit complete ms with cover letter (preferred) or outline/synopsis and 3 sample chapters. Agented fiction 75%. Reports in 3-4 weeks on queries; 6-10 weeks on mss. Simultaneous and photocopied submissions OK. Accepts computer printout submissions.

Terms: Royalties and advance negotiable. Sends galleys to author. Writer's guidelines for #10 SAE and 1 first class stamp. Book catalog for 9x12 SAE with 98¢ postage. "We run a young adult novel competition each year."

FOUR WINDS PRESS (II), Subsidiary of Macmillan Publishing Co., 866 Third Ave., New York NY 10022. Editor-in-Chief: Cindy Kane. Estab. 1966. A children's trade book imprint. Publishes hardcover originals. Books: 3 piece binding for fiction; 1 piece binding for picture books. Books for children ages 3-12 usually illustrated; average print order 6,000-10,000; first novel print order: 6,000. Published new writers within the last year. Plans 1 first novel this year. Publishes 24 total titles each year, 12 fiction titles. No longer publishing young adult fiction.

Needs: Picture book manuscripts for ages 5-8, especially minimal word mss; middle grade. Recently published *Sarah Bear and Sweet Sidney*, by Nancy Putz (picture book); *Pig and Bear*, by Vit Hořejš (picture book); and *Parchment House*, by Cara Lockhart Smith.

How to Contact: Accepts unsolicited mss. Submit complete ms with cover letter. SASE required. 75% of fiction is agented. Reports in 8 weeks. Photocopied submissions OK. Accepts computer printout submissions. No simultaneous submissions.

Terms: Pays royalties, negotiable advance and author's copies. Book catalogs *not* available. Manuscript guidelines and portfolio guidelines are available on request with #10 SAE and 1 first class stamp.

Advice: "For children's books, study books that are currently being published. Length, vocabulary, subject matter are usually determined by the age group for which the book is intended."

GEMSTONE BOOKS (I, II), Imprint of Dillon Press, 242 Portland Ave. S., Minneapolis MN 55415. (612)333-2691. Fiction Reader: Lisa Erskine. Estab. 1966. "Dillon Press is a juvenile book publisher, both of fiction and educational nonfiction titles." Publishes hardcover and paperback originals. Books: type of paper varies; offset lithography; Smythe and sidesewn binding; illustrations; average print order: 5,000. Averages 40 total titles, 5 fiction titles each year.

Needs: Juvenile (8-14): historical, adventure, contemporary and science fiction/fantasy; juvenile (7-9) 2,000-3,000 words, stories about Hispanics, Asians and Blacks; juvenile (8-11) historical fiction based on actual events. No problem novels. No picture books. Published *Mr. Z and the Time Clock*, by Bonnie Pryor and *A Gift for Tia Rosa*, by Karen Taha.

How to Contact: Accepts unsolicited mss. Prefer complete ms with SASE. Reports in 6 weeks. Simultaneous and photocopied submissions OK. Accepts computer submissions, prefers letter-quality.

Terms: Negotiable. Sends galleys to author. Book catalog for 9x12 SASE with 90¢ postage.

Advice: "We are expanding our fiction imprint, Gemstone Books."

DAVID R. GODINE, PUBLISHER, INC. (I, II), 300 Massachusetts, Boston MA 02115. (617)536-0761. Imprint: Nonpareil Books (trade paperbacks). President: David R. Godine. Editorial Director: William B. Goodman. Manuscript submissions: Julia Hanna. Juvenile ms submissions: Audrey Bryant. Estab. 1970. Books: acid free paper; sewn binding; illustrations; average print order: 4,000-5,000; first novel print order: 3,500-6,500. Small independent publisher (12-person staff). Publishes hardcover and paperback originals and reprints. Comments on rejected mss "only if of particular interest."

Needs: Literary, mystery, collecting, historical, food and wine and juvenile. Recently published *The High Spirits*, by David Huddle; *Out of Mind*, by J. Bernlef; and *A Little Princess*, by Frances Hodgson Burnett.

How to Contact: Accepts unsolicited mss with self-addressed, stamped book envelope. Query with outline/synopsis. "We prefer query letters – include publishing history, complete outline of story and SASE. Do not call to follow up on submission." Simultaneous and photocopied submissions OK. Accepts computer printout submissions; letter-quality only.

Terms: Standard royalties; offers advance. Sends galleys to author. Free book catalog.

Advice: "Keep trying. Remember that every writer now published has been rejected countless times at the beginning."

GOSPEL PUBLISHING HOUSE, Subsidiary of Assemblies of God General Council, 1445 Boonville Ave., Springfield MO 65802-2894. (417)862-2731. Book Editor: Glen Ellard. Publishes hardcover originals, trade-paperback originals and mass-market paperback originals. Averages 18 titles/year.

Needs: Adventure, fantasy, historical, humor, juvenile, mystery, religious and young adult. Published *Mystery at Pier Fourteen*, by Betty Swinford (juvenile Christian); *The Adventures of Heart Longing*, by Julie Klassen (juvenile Christian); and *Grace Comes Home*, by Darlene Stauffer (juvenile Christian).

How to Contact: Query or submit outline/synopsis and sample chapters. Receives approx. 360 queries and mss from writers each year. Agented fiction 10%. 90% of books bought come from first-time authors. Reports in 2 months. Simultaneous submissions OK. Accepts computer printout submissions, no dot-matrix.

Terms: Pays royalties of 10% on retail price. Publishes ms approx. 18 months after acceptance. Book catalog and writer's guidelines free.
Advice: "Gospel Publishing House is owned and operated by the Assemblies of God. Therefore, the doctrinal viewpoint of all books published is required to be compatible with our denominational position."

GROSSET & DUNLAP, INC. (III), A Division of the Putnam & Grosset Group, 200 Madison Ave., 11th Floor, New York NY 10016. Editor-in-Chief: Bernette Ford.
Needs: Juvenile, preschool/picture book. Queries only. "Include such details as length and intended age group and any other information that you think will help us to understand the nature of your material. Be sure to enclose a stamped, self-addressed envelope for our reply. We can no longer review manuscripts that we have not asked to see, and they will be returned unread."

HARCOURT BRACE JOVANOVICH (III), 1250 Sixth Ave., San Diego CA 92101. (619)699-6810. Imprints include HBJ Children's Books and Gulliver Books. Director: Willa Perlman. Senior Editor, HBJ Children's Books: Bonnie V. Ingber. Editors, HBJ Children's Books: Diane D'Andrade and Allyn Johnston. Senior Editors, Gulliver Books: Elinor Williams and Elizabeth Van Doren. Associate Editor, all imprints: Karen Grove. Publishes hardcover originals and paperback reprints. Averages 75 titles/year. Published new writers within the last year.
Needs: Young adult fiction, nonfiction for all ages, picture books for very young children, mystery. Published *Elbert's Bad Word*, by Audrey Wood, illustrated by Don and Audrey Wood; *In the Beginning*, by Virginia Hamilton, illustrated by Barry Moser; *A Sudden Silence*, by Eve Bunting.
How to Contact: Unsolicited mss currently accepted *only* by HBJ Children's Books, not by Gulliver Books, Jane Yolen Books or Voyager Books. Send to "Manuscript Submissions, HBJ Children's Books." SASE. For picture books, send complete ms; for novels, send outline/synopsis and 2-4 sample chapters. Photocopied submissions OK. No simultaneous submissions. No phone calls. Responds in 6-8 weeks.
Terms: Terms vary according to individual books; pays on royalty basis. Writers' guidelines for #10 SASE; catalog for 9×12 SASE.
Advice: "Familiarize yourself with the type of book published by a company before submitting a manuscript; make sure your work is in line with the style of the publishing house. Research the market your work will reach; make yourself familiar with the current children's book field."

HARLEQUIN ENTERPRISES, LTD. (II, IV), 225 Duncan Mill Rd., Don Mills, Ontario M3B 3K9 Canada. (416)445-5860. Imprints include Harlequin Romances, Harlequin Presents, Harlequin American Romances, Superromances, Temptation, Intrigue and Regency, Silhouette, Worldwide Library, Gold Eagle. Managing Editor: Karin Stoecker. Estab. 1949. Publishes paperback originals and reprints. Books: newsprint paper; web printing; perfect binding. Published new writers within the last year. Number of titles: averages 670/year. Buys agented and unagented fiction.
Needs: Romance and heroic adventure. Will accept nothing that is not related to the desired categories.
How to Contact: Send query letter or send outline and first 50 pages (2 or 3 chapters) or submit through agent with IRC and SASE (Canadian). Absolutely no simultaneous submissions; photocopied submissions OK. Reports in 1 month on queries; 2 months on mss. Publishes ms 1-1½ months after acceptance.
Terms: Offers royalties, advance. Must return advance if book is not completed or is unacceptable. Sends galleys to author.
Advice: "The quickest route to success is to follow directions for submissions: query first. We encourage first novelists. Before sending a manuscript, read as many Harlequin titles as you can get your hands on. It's very important to study the style and do your homework first." Authors may send manuscript for Romances and Presents to Karin Stoecker. Superromances: Marsha Zinberg, senior editor; Temptation: Lisa Boyes, senior editor, Regencys: Marmie Charndoff, editor to the Canada address. American Romances and Intrigue: Debra Matteucci, senior editor, Harlequin Books, 300 E. 42 Street, 6th Floor, New York, NY 10017. Silhouette submissions should also be sent to the New York office, attention Karen Solem. Gold Eagle and Worldwide Library query letters should be addressed to Randall Toye, editorial director, at the Canada address. "The relationship between the novelist and editor is regarded highly and treated with professionalism."

HARMONY BOOKS (II), Subsidiary of Crown Publishers, 201 E. 50th St., New York NY 10022. (212)572-6121. Contact: General Editorial Department. Publishes hardcover and paperback originals.
Needs: Literary fiction. Also publishes in serious nonfiction, history, biography, personal growth, media and music fields.
How to Contact: Accepts unsolicited mss. Query first with outline/synopsis and 2-3 sample chapters. SASE. Agented fiction: 75%. Simultaneous and photocopied submissions OK. Accepts computer printouts.

Terms: Pays royalties and advance; amounts negotiable. Sends galleys to authors.

HARPER & ROW JUNIOR BOOKS GROUP (II), 10 E. 53rd St., New York NY 10022. (212)277-7044. Imprints include Harper Junior Books, including Charlotte Zolotow Books; T.Y. Crowell Junior Books; and J.B. Lippincott Junior Books. Publisher: Marilyn Kriney. Editors: Charlotte Zolotow, Nina Ignatowicz, Barbara Fenton, Laura Geringer, Robert O. Warren, Antonia Markiet, David Allender, Joanna Cotler and Pamela D. Hastings. Publishes hardcover originals and paperback reprints. Number of titles: *Harper–Cloth*: 80 in 1989; *Harper–Trophy* (paperback): 74 in 1989; *Crowell*: 29 in 1989; *Lippincott*: 37 in 1989.

Needs: Picture books, easy-to-read, middle-grade, teenage and young adult novels; fiction, fantasy, animal, sports, spy/adventure, historical, science fiction, problem novels and contemporary. Recently published Harper/Charlotte Zolotow Books: *Fell Back*, by M.E. Kerr (ages 12 and up); Harper: *My Daniel*, by Pam conrad (ages 10 and up); Crowell: *Lucie Babbidge's House*, by Sylvia Cassedy (ages 9-12); Lippincotte: *Yours Till Forever*, by David Gifaldi (ages 12 and up).

How to Contact: Query; submit complete ms; submit outline/synopsis and sample chapters; submit through agent. SASE for query, ms. Please identify simultaneous submissions; photocopied submissions OK. Reports in 2-3 months.

Terms: Average 10% in royalties. Royalties on picture books shared with illustrators. Offers advance. Book catalog for self-addressed label.

Advice: "Write from your own experience and the child you once were. Read widely in the field of adult and children's literature. Realize that writing for children is a difficult challenge. Read other young adult novelists as well as adult novelists. Pay attention to styles, approaches, topics. Be willing to rewrite, perhaps many times. We have no rules for subject matter, length or vocabulary but look instead for ideas that are fresh and imaginative. Good writing that involves the reader in a story or subject that has appeal for young readers is also essential. One submission is considered by the four imprints."

HARVEST HOUSE PUBLISHERS (IV), 1075 Arrowsmith, Eugene OR 97402. (503)343-0123. Manuscript Coordinator: LaRae Weikert. Editor-in-Chief: Eileen L. Mason. Estab. 1974. Midsize independent publisher with plans to expand. Publishes hardcover and paperback originals and reprints. Books: 40 lb ground wood paper; offset printing; perfect binding; average print order 10,000; first novel print order: 10,000-15,000. Averages 50 total titles, 4 fiction titles each year.

Needs: Christian living, contemporary issues, humor, Christian preschool/picture books, religious/inspirational and Christian romance (contemporary, historical). Especially seeks inspirational, romance/historical and mystery. Recently published *The Archon Conspiracy*, by Dave Hunt; *Gently Love Beckons*, by June Masters Bacher; *Sweetbriar Spring*, by Brenda Wilber; and *The Christening*, by Roger Elwood.

How to Contact: Accepts unsolicited mss. Query first or submit outline/synopsis and 2 sample chapters with SASE. Reports on queries in 2-8 weeks; on mss in 6-8 weeks. Simultaneous and photocopied submissions OK.

Terms: Pays in royalties of 14-18%; 10 author's copies. Sends galleys to author. Writer's guidelines for SASE. Book catalog for 8½×11 SASE.

‡HEARTFIRE ROMANCE (I), Subsidiary of Zebra Books, 475 Park Ave. So., New York NY 10016. (212)889-2299. Editorial Director: Michael Seidman. Publishes paperback originals and reprints. Publishes 48 fiction titles each year.

Needs: Romance. Recently published *Blood Wings*, by Stephen Gresham; *Lovers' Masquerade*, by Robin St. Thomas; and *Last of the California Girls*, by Pamela Jekel. Ms length ranges from 125,000 to 150,000 words.

How to Contact: Submit short (no more than 3 page) synopsis and first several chapters. SASE. Reports on queries in 6 weeks; on mss in 3 months. Simultaneous and photocopied submissions OK. Accepts computer printout submissions, no dot-matrix.

Terms: Pays royalties and negotiable advance. Writer's guidelines and book catalog free for SASE.

Advice: Send for tip sheet. "Don't use all the fancy fonts available to you; we're not impressed and it often works against you. Don't tell me my business in your cover letter; just give me the basic facts and let your ms sell itself."

HERALD PRESS (II), Division of Mennonite Publishing House, 616 Walnut Ave., Scottdale PA 15683. (412)887-8500. Book Editor: S. David Garber. Denominational publisher with full line of religious books. Publishes hardcover and paperback originals. Books: offset printing; squareback adhesive bound paperback; illustrations in juveniles; average print order: 5,000; first novel print order: 3,500. Published 4 new writers in the last year. Number of fiction titles: 4-6 per year.

Needs: Religious/inspirational, juvenile and young adult. Published *The Splendid Vista*, by Esther Loewen Vogt (adult); and *The Mysterious Passover Visitors*, by Ann Bixby Herold (juvenile).

How to Contact: Accepts unsolicited mss. Query or submit outline/synopsis and 2 sample chapters with SASE. No simultaneous submissions; photocopied submissions OK. Accepts computer printout submissions. Prefers letter-quality. Accepts disk submissions compatible with CP/M. Prefers hard copy with disk submissions. Reports in 4 weeks on queries, 6 weeks on mss.

Terms: Pays 10-15% in royalties; 12 free author's copies; no advance. Sends printouts to author. Book catalog 50¢.

Advice: "We are happy to consider book proposals from Christian authors of adult and juvenile fiction. We like to reflect a Christian response to social issues such as poverty and peacemaking." First novels "no problem if the quality is excellent." Usually publishes original fiction in trade paperback rather than hardcover.

HOLIDAY HOUSE, INC. (I, II), 18 E. 53rd St., New York NY 10022. (212)688-0085. Editor: Margery Cuyler. Estab. 1935. Independent publisher. Books: high quality printing; occasionally reinforced binding; illustrations sometimes. Publishes hardcover originals and paperback reprints. Published new writers within the last year. Number of titles: 48 hardcovers in 1989; 12 paperbacks in 1989.

Needs: Contemporary, literary, adventure, humor and animal stories for young readers—preschool through middle grade. Recently published *Awfully Short for the Fourth Grade*, by Elvira Woodruff; *Glass Slippers Give You Blisters*, by Mary Jane Auch. "We're not in a position to be too encouraging, as our list is tight, but we're always open to good 'family' novels and humor."

How to Contact: "We prefer query letters for novels; complete manuscripts for shorter books and picture books." Simultaneous and photocopied submissions OK as long as a cover letter mentions that other publishers are looking at the same material. Accepts computer printout submissions. Prefers letter-quality. Reports in 1 month on queries, 6-8 weeks on mss.

Terms: Advance and royalties are flexible, depending upon whether the book is illustrated. Sends galleys to author.

Advice: "We have received an increasing number of manuscripts, but the quality has not improved vastly. This appears to be a decade in which publishers are interested in reviving the type of good, solid story that was popular in the '50s. Certainly there's a trend toward humor, family novels, novels with school settings, biographies and historical novels. Problem-type novels and romances seem to be on the wane. We are always open to well-written manuscripts, whether by a published or nonpublished author. Submit only one project at a time."

HOLLOWAY HOUSE PUBLISHING COMPANY (II), 8060 Melrose Ave., Los Angeles CA 90046. (213)653-8060. Imprints include Mankind Books, Melrose Square and Heartline Books. Executive Editor: Raymond Friday Locke. Editors: Peter Stone, Tony Stately. Estab. 1960. Midsize independent publisher of varying interests, publishes black experience books, history, games and gambling books. Publishes paperback originals and reprints. Book: offset printing; paper binding; some illustrations; average print order: 20,000 to 30,000; first novel print order: 15,000. Published new writers within last year. Plans 6 first novels this year. Publishes 30-40 titles each year, 15-25 fiction titles.

Needs: Adventure, contemporary, ethnic, experimental, fantasy, historical, horror, literary, mainstream, romance (historical), science fiction, suspense/mystery, war, western. "We are looking for more 'literary' type books than in the past; books that appeal to young professionals. No books dealing with 'street action' about pimps, whores, dope dealing, prisons, etc." Published *A Mississippi Family*, by Barbara Johnson (fiction); *Diva*, a first novel by the award-winning playright Stanley Bennet Clay; *Secret Music*, by Odie Hawkins (memoirs); also a Jessie Jackson bio, by Eddie Stone.

How to Contact: Accepts unsolicited mss. Submit outlline/synopsis and 3 sample chapters or complete ms with cover letter. SASE. 50% of fiction is agented. Reports in 3 weeks on queries; 2 months on mss. Simultaneous submssions and photocopied submissions OK "if they are legible." Accepts computer printout submissions.

Terms: Pays 5½-8½% royalties, advance of $1,000; more for agented mss and nonfiction. Sometimes sends galleys to author. Writer's guidelines and book catalog for #10 SASE.

Advice: Publishing fewer Heartline Romances "as the contemporary romance market seems to have bottomed out, at least for us. Study the market; we do not publish poetry, short story collections, juvies, etc. but not a week goes by that we don't get at least one submission of each. If you send second-generation copies or dot-matrix check and see if *you* can read it before you expect us to. Neatness, spelling, etc. counts!"

HENRY HOLT & COMPANY (II), 115 W 18th St., 6th Floor, New York NY 10011. (212)886-9200. Imprint includes Owl (paper). Publishes hardcover originals and reprints and paperback originals and reprints. Averages 50-60 total original titles, 20% of total is fiction each year.

Needs: Adventure, contemporary, feminist, historical, humor/satire, juvenile (5-9 years, including animal, easy-to-read, fantasy, historical, sports, spy/adventure and contemporary), literary, mainstream, suspense/mystery, translations and young adult/teen (10-18 years including easy-to-read, fantasy/science fiction, historical, problem novels, romance, sports and spy/adventure). Recently published *Fool's Progress*, by Edward Abbey; *Tracks*, by Louise Erdrich; *Trust*, by George V. Higgins; and *Frank Furbo*, by Wm. Wherton.

How to Contact: Accepts queries; no unsolicited mss. Agented fiction 95%.

Terms: Pays in royalties of 10% minimum; 15% maximum; advance. Sends galleys to author. Book catalog free on request.

■HORIZON PUBLISHERS & DIST., INC. (III, IV), 50 S. 500 West, Box 490, Bountiful UT 84010-0490. (801)295-9451. President: Duane S. Crowther. Estab. 1971. "Midsize independent publisher with in-house printing facilities, staff of 30+." Publishes hardcover and paperback originals and reprints. Books: 60 lb offset paper; hardbound, perfect and saddlestitch binding; illustrations; average print order: 3,000; first novel print order: 3,000. Plans 2 first novels this year. Averages 25-30 total titles; 1-3 fiction titles each year.

Needs: Adventure, historical, humor/satire, juvenile, literary, mainstream, military/war, religious/inspirational, romance (contemporary and historical), science fiction, spiritual and young adult/teen (romance and spy/adventure). "Religious titles are directed only to the LDS (Latter Day Saints) market. General titles are marketed nationwide." Looking for "good quality writing in salable subject areas. Will also consider well-written books on social problems and issues, (divorce, abortion, child abuse, suicide, capital punishment and homosexuality)." Recently published *The Couchman and the Bells*, by Ted C. Hindmarsh.

How to Contact: Accepts unsolicited mss. Query first or submit outline/synopsis and 3 sample chapters or complete ms. SASE. Include social security number with submission. Reports in 2-4 weeks on queries; 10-12 weeks on mss. Simultaneous and photocopied submissions OK if identified as such. Accepts computer printout submissions. Accepts electronic submissions.

Terms: Pays royalties of 6% minimum; 12% maximum. Provides 10 author's copies. Sends page proofs to author. Publishes ms 3-9 months after acceptance. "We are not a subsidy publisher but we do job printing, book production for private authors and book packaging." Writer's guidelines for #10 SAE and 1 first class stamp.

Advice: Encourages "only those first novelists who write very well, with salable subjects. Please avoid the trite themes which are plaguing LDS fiction such as crossing the plains, conversion stories, and struggling courtships that always end in temple marriage. While these themes are important, they have been used so often that they are now frequently perceived as trite and are often ignored by those shopping for new books. In religious fiction we hope to see a process of moral, spiritual, or emotional growth presented. Some type of conflict is definitely essential for good plot development. Watch your vocabulary too—use appropriate words for the age group for which you are writing."

HOUGHTON MIFFLIN COMPANY (III), 2 Park St., Boston MA 02108. (617)725-5000. Subsidiary: Ticknor and Fields Inc. Contact: Fiction Editor. Publishes hardcover and paperback originals and paperback reprints. Averages 150 (includes children's) total titles, 45 fiction titles each year. Buys 70-80% agented fiction.

Needs: Contemporary, literary, mainstream, suspense/mystery. No religious, gothic, occult or westerns. Published *Emperor of the Air*, by Ethan Canin; *Mama Day*, by Gloria Naylor.

How to Contact: Write to Coordinator of Submissions. Query first; submit outline/synopsis with SASE. Simultaneous and photocopied submissions OK, but no default-mode dot matrix. Reports in 1 month on queries; 2 months on mss. Publishes ms an average of 1 year after acceptance.

Terms: Pays in royalties on sliding scale of 10-12-15%; pays advance. Must return advance if book is not completed or is unacceptable.

‡INTERLINK PUBLISHING GROUP, INC. (IV), Imprints include: Interlink Books, Olive Branch Press and Crocodile Books USA. 99 Seventh Ave., Brooklyn NY 11215. (718)797-4292. Publisher: Michel Moushabeck. Fiction Editor: Phyllis Bennis. Estab. 1987. "Midsize independent publisher." Publishes hardcover and paperback originals. Books: 55 lb Warren Sebago Cream white paper; web offset printing; perfect binding; average print order: 5,000; first novel print order: 5,000. Published new writers within the last year. Plans 3-5 first novels this year. Averages 30 total titles, 3-5 fiction titles each year.

Needs: Juvenile (5-9 yrs.), preschool/picture book and translations. Needs adult ficiton—relating to the Middle East, Africa or Latin America; translations accepted. Also needs juvenile (5-9 yrs)—illustrated picture books. Recently published *Wild Thorns*, by Sahar Khalifeh; *Crocodile, Crocodile*, by Peter Nickl, Binette Shroeder (illus.); and *The Elephant's Child*, by Rudyard Kipling, Jan Mogensen (illus.).

How to Contact: Accepts unsolicited mss. Submit outline/synopsis and 2 sample chapters. SASE. Reports in 2 weeks on queries; 3 months on mss. Photocopied submissions OK. Accepts computer printout submissions.
Terms: Pays royalties of 5% minimum; 8% maximum. Sends galleys to author. Publishes ms 1-1½ years.

IRON CROWN ENTERPRISES, INC., 108 Fifth St. SE, Charlottesville VA 22901. (804)295-3918. Editor: John D. Ruemmler. Estab. 1980. "Growing independent publishers of gamebooks expanding into sci fi and fantasy fiction." Publishes paperback originals. Books: offset printing; adhesive paper binding; 4-color covers, 1-color illustrations inside; average print order: 5,000-10,000 (some up to 50,000); first novel print order: 25,000-50,000. Plans 2-10 first novels this year. Averages 45 total titles, 12 fiction titles each year. Sometimes comments on rejected mss.
Needs: Fantasy and science fiction. Published *Murder at The Diogenes Club*, by G. Lientz (interactive mystery); *Return to Deathwater*, by C. Norris (interactive fantasy); and *A Spy in Isengard*, by Terry Amthor (interactive fantasy).
How to Contact: Accepts unsolicited mss. Query first. SASE. Reports in 2-4 weeks on queries; 1-2 months on mss. Simultaneous and photocopied submissions OK. Computer printout submissions OK. Accepts electronic submissions.
Terms: Pays royalties of 2% minimum; 4% maximum. Average advance: $1,000. Provides 25 author's copies. Publishes ms 2-8 months after acceptance. Writer's guidelines for #10 SAE with 1 first class stamp. Book catalog for SASE.
Advice: "We publish only paperback originals, most of it either FRP (gaming) oriented or interactive fiction. We hope to begin publishing paperback originals in fantasy and science fiction in 1990. We still get a lot of letters and manuscripts from writers who have no idea what we're looking for. Take courses and join a club or group if they help to keep you writing. And hang on to your job until you make your first million!"

JAMESON BOOKS (I, II, IV), Jameson Books, Inc., The Frontier Library, 722 Columbus St., Ottawa IL 61350. (815)434-7905. Editor: Jameson G. Campaigne, Jr. Estab. 1986. Publishes hardcover and paperback originals and reprints. Books: free sheet paper; offset printing; average print order: 10,000; first novel print order: 5,000. Plans 6-8 novels this year. Averages 12-16 total titles, 4-8 fiction titles each year. Occasionally critiques or comments on rejected mss.
Needs: Very well-researched western (frontier pre-1850). No romance, sci-fi, mystery, et al. Published *Wister Trace*, by Loren Estelman; *Buckskin Brigades*, by L. Ron Hubbard; *One-Eyed Dream*, by Terry Johnston.
How to Contact: Does not accepted unsolicited mss. Submit outline/synopsis and 3 consecutive sample chapters. SASE. Agented fiction 50%. Reports in 2 weeks on queries; 2-5 months on mss. Simultaneous and photocopied submissions OK. Accepts computer printouts.
Terms: Pays royalties of 5% minimum; 15% maximum. Average advance: $1,500. Sends galleys to author. Book catalog for 6x9 SASE.

JOY STREET BOOKS, 34 Beacon St., Boston MA 02108. (617)227-0730. Imprint of Little, Brown and Co. Children's Books Editor-in-chief: Melanie Kroupa. Publishes hardcover and quality paperback originals. Number of titles: 24 in 1988. Sometimes buys juvenile mss with illustrations.
Needs: General fiction, juvenile: sports, animal, mystery/adventure, realistic contemporary fiction, picture books and easy-to-read. Published *The Arizona Kid*, by Ron Koertge; *The Girl in the Box*, by Ouida Sebestyen; *Alias Madame Doubtfire*, by Anne Fine. Very interested in first novels.
How to Contact: Prefers query letter with sample chapters. SASE. Accepts simultaneous submissions; photocopied submissions OK.
Terms: Pays variable advances and royalties.

ALFRED A. KNOPF (II), 201 E. 50th St., New York NY 10022. Senior Editor: Ashbel Green. Estab. 1915. Publishes hardcover originals. Number of titles: 47 in 1989. Buys 75% agented fiction. Published 16 new writers within the last year.
Needs: Contemporary, literary, mystery and spy. No western, gothic, romance, erotica, religious or science fiction. Recently published *Mile Zero*, by Thomas Sanchez and *Geek Love*, by Katherine Dunn.
How to Contact: Submit complete ms with SASE. Simultaneous and photocopied submissions OK. Reports in 1 month on mss. Publishes ms an average of 1 year after acceptance.
Terms: Pays 10-15% in royalties; offers advance. Must return advance if book is not completed or is unacceptable.
Advice: Publishes book-length fiction of literary merit by known and unknown writers. "Don't submit manuscripts with matrix type."

KNOPF BOOKS FOR YOUNG READERS (II), 201 E. 50th St., New York NY 10022. Subsidiary of Random House, Inc. Editor-in-Chief: Janet Schulman. Publishes hardcover and paperback originals and reprints. New paperback imprints include Dragonfly Books (picture books), Bullseye (middle-grade fiction) and Borzoi Sprinters (Young Adult fiction). Averages 50 total titles, approximately 20 fiction titles each year.
Needs: "High-quality" adventure, contemporary, humor and nonfiction. "Young adult novels, picture books, middle group novels." Recently published *No Star Nights*, by Anna Smucker; *The Boy Who Lost His Face*, by Lewis Sachar.
How to Contact: Query with outline/synopsis and 2 sample chapters with SASE. Simultaneous and photocopied submissions OK. Reports in 6-8 weeks on mss.
Terms: Sends galleys to author.

‡LARKSDALE (II), Subsidiary of Houston Printing & Publishing, Inc. Imprints include Lindahl Books, Harle House, The Linolean Press and Post Oak Press. Suite 190, 10661 Haddington, Houston TX 77043. (713)861-6214. Publisher: James Goodman. Fiction Editor: Charlotte St. John. Estab. 1978. General trade line—national in scope. Publishes hardcover and paperback originals and hardcover and paperback reprints. Books: 60 lb natural Glatfelter paper; web printing; case/perfect binding; illustrations; average print order: 5,000; first novel print order: 2,000. Published new writers within the last year. Plans 4-5 first novels this year. Averages 30 total titles, 2-5 fiction titles each year. Sometimes comments on rejected ms; *charges "nothing if we initiate, $50 fee if requested by author."*
Needs: Humor/satire, juvenile (5-9 yrs.) animal, easy-to-read, literary, mainstream, military/war, religious/inspirational and young adult/teen (10-18 years) easy-to-read, historical, problem novels, romance (young adult) and sports. Recently published *Mending of the Heart*, by Mary Wyche Estes (romance); *Way of the Child*, by Dr. David Patterson (child abuse); and *Angel On The Bridge*, by Kitty Ellis.
How to Contact: Accepts unsolicited mss. Submit complete ms with cover letter. SASE (must include *container, not* just postage). Reports in 4-6 weeks on mss. Simultaneous and photocopied submissions OK. Accepts computer printout submissions.
Terms: Pays royalties of 10% minimum. Provides 10 author's copies. Publishes ms up to 18 months after acceptance.
Advice: (1) Don't be cute; (2) Never make a submission w/o a cover letter; (3) Don't drop names; (4) Don't oversell; (5) The more info on the author, the better.

LEISURE BOOKS (II), A Division of Dorchester Publishing Co., Inc., Suite 1008, 276 Fifth Ave., New York NY 10001. (212)725-8811. Editor: Audrey LaFehr. Address submissions to Audrey LaFehr, Editor. Mass-market paperback publisher—originals and reprints. Books: newsprint paper; offset printing; perfect binding; average print order: variable; first novel print order: variable. Published new writers within the last year. Plans 25 first novels this year. Averages 150 total titles, 145 fiction titles each year. Comments on rejected ms "only if requested ms requires it."
Needs: Techno-thriller, historical, horror, romance (historical), western. Looking for "historical romance (90,000 words), horror novels (80,000 words), western series books." Recently published *Fortune's Lady*, by Patricia Gaffney (romance); *The Sisterhood*, by Florence Stevenson (horror); and *Tough Bullet/The Killers*, by Peter McCurtin.
How to Contact: Accepts unsolicited mss. Query first. SASE. Agented fiction 70%. Reports in 4 weeks on queries; 2 months on mss. Simultaneous and photocopied submissions OK.
Terms: Offers negotiable advance. Payment depends "on category and track record of author." Sends galleys to author. Publishes ms 18 months after acceptance. Writer's guidelines and book catalog for #10 SASE.
Advice: Encourages first novelists "if they are talented and willing to take direction, *and* write the kind of category fiction we publish. The horror market is seriously declining. Too many bad books are being written. We, like other publishers, are cutting back this category. Please include a brief synopsis if sample chapters are requested."

‡LION PUBLISHING CORPORATION (II). Subsidiary of Lion Publishing plc, Oxford, England. 1705 Hubbard Ave., Batavia IL 60510. (312)879-0707. Assistant Editor: Bob Bittner. Estab. 1971 (Oxford offices); 1984 (US). "Christian book publisher publishing books for the *general* market." Publishes hardcover and paperback originals and paperback reprints. Books: average print order 10,000; first-novel print order 7,000-10,000. Plans 1-3 first novels this year. Averages 70-80 total titles, 15-20 fiction titles each year. Sometimes comments on rejected ms.
Needs: Contemporary, fantasy, juvenile fantasy, literary, religious/inspirational, spiritual, young adult/teen fantasy/science fiction, historical, problem novels and spy/adventure. "Because we are a Christian publisher, all books should be written from a Christian perspective." Recently published *Pangur Ban*, by Fay Sampson; *Under the Golden Throne*, by Ralph Batten; and *Sweet 'n' Sour Summer*, by Janice Brown.

How to Contact: Accepts unsolicited mss. Submit complete ms with cover letter. SASE. Agented fiction 5%. Reports in 2 weeks on queries; 1 month on mss. Photocopied submissions OK. Accepts computer printout submissions.
Terms: Pays negotiable royalties. Sends galleys to author. Publishes ms 1 year after acceptance. Writer's guidelines and book catalog free.
Advice: "Seriously study our author guidelines—they're 5 pages of essential information. We're looking for interesting, important stories that show how God can work in the world today—and that applies whether you're exploring the effects of divorce on a teenage girl, retelling the Arthur/Merlin stories, or creating adventure-packed future worlds."

J. B. LIPPINCOTT JUNIOR BOOKS (II), 10 E. 53rd St., New York NY 10022. (212)207-7044. See Harper & Row Junior Books Group.

LITTLE, BROWN & CO. CHILDREN'S BOOKS (II), Trade Division; Children's Books, 34 Beacon St., Boston MA 02108. Editorial Department. Contact: John G. Keller, publisher; Maria Modugno, editor-in-chief; Stephanie Owens Lurie, editor. Books: 70 lb paper; sheet-fed printing; illustrations. Published new writers within the last year. Sometimes buys juvenile mss with illustrations "if by professional artist." Buys 60% agented fiction.
Needs: Middle grade fiction and young adult. Recently published *Dissidents*, by Neal Shusterman; *Eighty-Eight Steps to September*, by Jan Marino.
How to Contact: Will accept unsolicited mss. "Query letters for novels are not necessary."
Terms: Pays on royalty basis. Must return advance if book is not completed or is unacceptable. Sends galleys to author. Publishes ms 1-2 years after acceptance.
Advice: "We are looking for trade books with bookstore appeal. Young adult 'problem' novels are no longer in vogue, but there is now a dearth of good fiction for that age group. We are looking for young children's (ages 3-5) books that might be adapted to unusual toy/book formats. We encourage first novelists. New authors should be aware of what of what is currently being published. I recommend they spend time at the local library familiarizing themselves with new publications."

LITTLE, BROWN AND COMPANY, INC. (II, III), 34 Beacon St., Boston MA 02108. (617)227-0730. Imprints include Little, Brown, Joy Street, Bulfinch Press. Medium-size house. Publishes adult and juvenile hardcover and paperback originals. Averages 100-125 total titles/year. Number of fiction titles varies.
Needs: Open. No science fiction. Recently published *Vineland*, by Thomas Pynchon; *Old Silent*, by Martha Grimes; *The Truth About Lorin Jones*, by Alison Lurie; published new writers within the last year.
How to Contact: Does not accept unsolicited mss. Query editorial department first; "we accept submissions from authors who have published before, in book form, magazines, newspapers or journals. No submissions from unpublished writers." Reports in 4-6 months on queries. Simultaneous and photocopied submissions OK.
Terms: "We publish on a royalty basis, with advance." Writer's guidelines free.

LODESTAR BOOKS (II), An affiliate of Dutton Children's Books; 2 Park Ave., New York NY 10016. (212)725-1818. Editorial Director: Virginia Buckley. Senior Editor: Rosemary Brosnan. Young adult and middle-grade imprint of juvenile department of trade publisher bought by New American Library in 1985. Publishes hardcover fiction for ages 12-17, ages 10-14 and ages 8-12. Books: 50 or 55 lb antique cream paper; offset printing; hardcover binding; illustrations sometimes; average print order: 5,000-6,000; first novel print order 5,000. Nonfiction picture books and a few fiction picture books. Published new writers within the last year. Number of titles: approximately 25-30 annually, 12-15 fiction titles annually. Buys 50% agented fiction.
Needs: Contemporary, humorous, sports, mystery/supernatural, adventure, for middle-grade and young adult. Recently published *The Honorable Prison*, by Lyll Becerra de Jenkins (young adult first novel set in South America); *Beyond Safe Boundaries*, by Margaret Sacks (young adult first novel); and *Park's Quest*, by Katherine Paterson (young adult contemporary).
How to Contact: "Can query, but prefer complete ms." SASE. Simultaneous and photocopied submissions OK. Accepts computer printout submissions. Prefers letter-quality. Reports in 2-4 months. Publishes ms an average of 1 year after acceptance.
Terms: Pays 8-10% in royalties; offers negotiable advance. Sends galleys to author. Free book catalog.
Advice: "We are looking to add to our list more books about black, Hispanic, Native American, and Asian children, in particular. We encourage first novelists. Publishing fewer young adult novels. They are difficult to find and difficult to sell reprint rights. Middle grade does better in terms of subsidiary rights sales."

LOUISIANA STATE UNIVERSITY PRESS (II), French House, Baton Rouge LA 70893. (504)388-6294. Editor-in-Chief: Margaret Fisher Dalrymple. Fiction Editor: Martha Hall. Estab. 1935. University press—medium size. Publishes hardcover originals. Average print order: 1,500-2,500; first novel print order: 2,000. Averages 60 total titles, 4 fiction titles/year.

Needs: Contemporary, literary, mainstream, short story collections. No science fiction and/or juvenile material. Recently published *The Women Who Walk*, by Nancy Huddleston Packer (stories); *Last Things*, by Madison Jones (novel); *Of Memory and Desire*, by Gladys Swan (stories); and *Leechtime*, by Albert Belisle Davis (novel).

How to Contact: Does not accept unsolicited mss. Query first. Reports in 2-3 months on queries and mss. Simultaneous and photocopied submissions OK. No computer printouts.

Terms: Pays in royalties, which vary. Sends pre-publication galleys to the author.

LOVESWEPT (I, II), Bantam Books, 666 5th Ave., New York NY 10103. (212)765-6500. Associate Publisher: Carolyn Nichols. Senior Editor: Susann Brailey. Imprint estab. 1982. Publishes paperback originals. Plans several first novels this year. Averages 72 total titles each year.

Needs: "Contemporary romance, highly sensual, believable primary characters, fresh and vibrant approaches to plot. No gothics, regencies or suspense."

How to Contact: Query with SASE; no unsolicited mss or partial mss. "Query letters should be no more than two to three pages. Content should be a brief description of the plot and the two main characters."

Terms: Pays in royalties of 6%; negotiates advance.

Advice: "Read extensively in the genre. Rewrite, polish, and edit your own work until it is the best it can be—before submitting."

‡■LUCAS/EVANS BOOKS (II), 1123 Broadway, New York NY 10010. (212)929-2583. Editorial Director: Barbara Lucas. Projects Director: Jill Kastner. Estab. 1984. "Book packager—specializes in children's books." Publishes hardcover and paperbook originals. Published new writers within the last year. Plans 1 first novel this year. Averages 17 total titles, 11 or 12, many of which are children's picture books. Sometimes comments on rejected ms; sometimes charge for critiques.

Needs: Juvenile (5-9 yrs.) animal, easy-to-read, fantasy, historical, sports, spy/adventure and contemporary; young adult/teen (10-18 years) easy-to-read, fantasy/science fiction, historical, romance (young adult) and sports and spy/adventure. "Novels are not our specialty. If we come across something really spectacular, we'll try to sell it. Usually publishers handle individual novels themselves." Published *Firebrat*, by Nancy Willard (fantasy); *The Salamander Stone*, by Ann Downer (fantasy); and *Haunted Trail*, by Janet Lorimer (mystery/adventure).

How to Contact: No unsolicited mss. Query first or submit outline/synopsis and 1 or 2 sample chapters. SASE. Agented fiction 15 to 25%. Reports in 2 weeks on queries; 4-6 weeks on mss. Photocopied submissions OK. Accepts computer printout submissions.

Terms: Pays royalties; variable advance. Provides 5-10 author's copies. Sends galleys to author. Writer's guidelines for SASE. Brochure available.

MARGARET K. McELDERRY BOOKS (I, II), Imprint of the Macmillan Children's Book Group, 866 3rd Ave., New York NY 10022. (212)702-7855. Publisher: Margaret K. McElderry. Division estab. at Atheneum Publishers 1971. Publishes hardcover originals. Books: high quality paper; offset printing; cloth and three-piece bindings; illustrations; average print order: 15,000; first novel print order: 6,000. Published new writers within the last year. Number of titles: 23 in 1989. Buys juvenile and young adult mss, agented or non-agented.

Needs: All categories (fiction and nonfiction) for juvenile and young adult: picture books, contemporary, literary, adventure, mystery, science fiction and fantasy. "We will consider any category. Results depend on the quality of the imagination, the artwork and the writing." Recently published *The Sacred Circle of the Hula Hoop*, by Kathy Kennedy Tapp; *Nonstop Nonsense* and *Blood-and-Thunder Adventure on Hurricane Peak*, both by Margaret Mahy; and *Stories From the Big Chair*, by Ruth Wallace-Brodeur.

How to Contact: Accepts unsolicited mss. Prefers complete ms. SASE for queries and mss. Simultaneous submissions OK if so indicated; photocopied submissions must be clear and clean. Accepts computer printout submissions. Prefers letter-quality. Reports in 4 weeks on queries, 8-10 weeks on mss. Publishes ms an average of 1 year after acceptance.

Terms: Pays in royalties; offers advance.

Advice: "Imaginative writing of high quality is always in demand; also picture books that are original and unusual. We are looking especially for nonfiction and for easy-to-read books for beginners. Beginning picture-book writers often assume that texts for the very young must be rhymed. This is a misconception and has been overdone. Picture-book manuscripts written in prose are totally acceptable. We continue to publish for a wide age range."

MACMILLAN CHILDREN'S BOOKS, MacMillan Publishing Co., 866 Third Ave., New York NY 10022. (212)702-4299. Imprints include Four Winds Press, Alladin Books, and Collier Books. Contact: Attention Children's Book Department. Estab. 1919. Large children's trade list which has been expanding. Publishes hardcover originals.
Needs: Juvenile submissions.
How to Contact: Accepts unsolicited mss. Send complete ms with SASE. Reports in 6-8 weeks. No simultaneous submissions; photocopied submissions OK. Accepts computer printout submissions; prefers letter-quality.
Terms: Pays in royalties; negotiates advance. Free book catalog.

MACMILLAN OF CANADA (II), A Division of Canada Publishing Corporation, 29 Birch Ave., Toronto, Ontario M4V 1E2 Canada. (416)963-8830. Editorial Co-ordinator: S. Girvan. Estab. 1905. Publishes hardcover and trade paperback originals and paperback reprints. Published new writers within the last year. Books: average print order: 4,000-5,000; first novel print order: 2,000. Averages 35 total titles, 8-10 fiction titles each year. Rarely comments on rejected mss.
Needs: Literary, mainstream, short story collection and suspense/mystery. Recently published *The Seventh Gate*, by Keith Ross Leckie; *Family News*, by Joan Barfoot; and *An Innocent Bystander*, by H.R. Percy.
How to Contact: Accepts unsolicited mss. Submit outline/synopsis with 2-3 sample chapters. SASE for return of ms. Reports in 1-2 months on mss. Simultaneous and photocopied submissions OK. Accepts computer printout submissions.
Terms: Pays royalties of 8% minimum; 15% maximum; advance negotiable. Provides 10 author's copies. Sends galleys to author. Book catalog for 9×12 SASE.
Advice: Does not encourage first novelists, "but we do consider unsolicited manuscripts."

MACMILLAN PUBLISHING CO., INC. (III), 866 3rd Ave., New York NY 10022. (212)702-2000. Contact: Fiction Editor. Fiction imprints include Collier Books, The Free Press, Bradbury and Schimer. Publishes hardcover and paperback originals and paperback reprints. Recently published *Good Hearts*, by Reynolds Price; *The Mustache*, by Emmanuel Carrére; *Spirit Lost*, by Nancy Thayer.
How to Contact: Submit through agent or brief query.
Terms: Pays in royalties; offers advance. Free book catalog.

MORROW JUNIOR BOOKS (III), 129 W. 56th Street, New York NY 10019. (212)889-3050. Editor-In-Chief: David L. Reuther. Plans 1 first novel this year. Averages 55 total titles each year.
Needs: Juvenile (5-9 years, including animal, easy-to-read, fantasy (little), spy/adventure (very little), preschool/picture book, young adult/teen (10-18 years, including historical, sports). Published new writers within the last year.
How to Contact: Does not accept unsolicited fiction mss.
Terms: Authors paid in royalties. Books published 12-18 months after acceptance. Book catalog free on request.
Advice: "Our list is very full at this time. No unsolicited manuscripts."

‡MULTNOMAH (II, IV), 10209 SE Division, Portland OR 97266. (503)257-0526. Editor: Deena Davis. Estab. 1969. Midsize publisher of religious and inspirational books. Publishes hardcover and paperback originals. Books: average print order: 10,000. Averages 25-35 total titles a year. "We are just getting into publishing fiction and our first books will be for children (8-12 yrs.)." Sometimes comments on rejected ms.
Needs: Juvenile (5-9 yrs.) easy-to-read and fantasy, historical, sports, humorous spy/adventure and contemporary, preschool/picture book, religious/inspirational and spiritual. Young adult/teen (10-18 years), religious/inspirational, fantasy, historical, problem novels, sports and spy/adventure. "We're looking for children's (juvenile) 8-12 yrs. and short chapter books for 7-9 yr. olds—both in series. No adult romance, science fiction."
How to Contact: Accepts unsolicited mss. Submit outline/synopsis and 3 sample chapters. SASE. Simultaneous and photocopied submissions OK. Accepts computer printout submissions.
Terms: Pays royalties of 8-12% net with possible escalation depending on type of children's book, amount of illustrations and stature of author; offers negotiable advance. Provides 15 author's copies. Sends galleys to author. Publishes ms 6-9 months after acceptance. Writer's guidelines free. Book catalog for 9×12 SASE.

THE MYSTERIOUS PRESS (III), 129 W. 56th St., New York NY 10019. (212)765-0923. Imprint: Penzler Books. Publisher: Otto Penzler. Editor-in-Chief: William Malloy. Editors: Sara Ann Freed and Edward Strosser. Estab. 1976. Small independent publisher, publishing only mystery and suspense fiction. Publishes hardcover originals and paperback reprints. Books: hardcover (some Smythe sewn) and paperback binding; illustrations rarely. 76 titles scheduled for 1990. Average first novel print order

Close-up

Kaye Gibbons
Writer

© Sarah Durant.

Kaye Gibbons never thought of herself as a novelist. "I wanted to teach literature and go out like Mr. Chips," the 29-year-old author of the much acclaimed *Ellen Foster* says. While toying with a poem, she explains, "I heard the voice of Ellen Foster. It was so strong that it was frightening. I wrote out 30 pages of it and gave it to Louis Rubin (her professor at the University of North Carolina). All I wanted to know was whether it was art."

Rubin's affirmative was seconded by glowing praise from Eudora Welty and Walker Percy, to whom Rubin sent the passage. Rubin, who is also a publisher with Algonquin Press, then asked her his own question: "Did you know you are a writer?"

"I had never thought of myself as anything other than a mother, a wife, and a part time student," she says. "When he told me, I said, 'I better go home and finish the novel.' " Which she did in six weeks of self-described frenzy.

Gibbons' second book, *A Virtuous Woman*, published in April 1989, experienced a more difficult birth, taking two years and four rewrites before the author felt the story was told in the right way. She mentions the frustration of trying to force the situation. With this book she says she made a common writer's mistake: not being willing to put the story into different characters' voices.

Beginning writers must remember they are storytellers, says Gibbons, and the critical part of telling that story is finding the right voice.

Her third and much longer book, an exploration of the effects of memory on a family's life, has been a more pleasant experience because, she explains, she has been more willing to work with the story. Noting that writing a novel takes a great deal of patience, Gibbons spends a lot of time "waiting for the language. It's ironic, but I'll be finished with this book by the end of the year if I take my time. If I don't take my time, it'll drag on."

Gibbons' advice for aspiring writers is to approach writing from reading. "I think it's mandatory for any writer to read, to have a sense of what is lasting and good."

She writes intuitively, working diligently to please herself. "When I do that, I invariably please others. I think writers should follow what they believe to be true," she says. "It's dangerous to write with publishers in mind." She maintains she can tell when reading the first few pages of a book whether the author wrote it for her or himself or for the public.

Of her response to the overwhelming success of *Ellen Foster* she says, "One side of me, my feeling side, was and is stunned. The thinking side of me said, 'Well, you've read all your life. You've put literature into your brain—what else did you expect to come out?' "

Raised in rural Nash County, North Carolina, she devoured "good literature and bad television, a combination of *Jane Eyre* and 'The Flying Nun.' " She speaks with reverence of the physical qualities of books, their smell and heft. To her, despite her family's lack of money, literature was accessible: "There were no dues; you didn't have to be dressed well.

"I always thought of literature as an entity. In some ways my writing is an unconscious attempt at recalling that and wanting to be a part of it."

—Carol Lloyd

5,000 copies. Critiques "only those rejected writers we wish particularly to encourage."
Needs: Suspense/mystery. Recently published *The Fourth Durango*, by Ross Thomas; *The Bridesmaid*, by Ruth Rendell; *Tomorrow's Crimes*, by Donald E. Westlake; published new writers within the last year.
How to Contact: Agented material only.
Terms: Pays in royalties of 10% minimum; offers negotiable advance. Sends galleys to author. Buys hard and softcover rights. Book catalog for SASE.
Advice: "We have a strong belief in the everlasting interest in and strength of mystery fiction. Don't talk about writing, do it. Don't ride band wagons, create them. Our philosophy about publishing first novels is the same as our philosophy about publishing: the cream rises to the top. We are looking for writers with whom we can have a long term relationship. *Sea of Green*, by Thomas Adcock is a first novel published this year. A good editor is an angel, assisting according to the writer's needs. My job is to see to it that the writer writes the best book he/she is capable of, *not* to have the writer write *my* book. Don't worry, publishing will catch up to you; the cycles continue as they always have. If your work is good, keep it circulating and begin the next one, and keep the faith. Get an agent."

NAVAL INSTITUTE PRESS (II, IV), Book publishing arm of US Naval Institute, Annapolis MD 21402. Fiction Editor: Paul W. Wilderson. Estab. 1873. Nonprofit publisher with area of concentration in naval and maritime subjects. Publishes hardcover originals. Averages 35 total titles each year. Fiction only occasionally. Average first novel print order: 15,000 copies.
Needs: Historical (naval), war (naval aspects) and adventure (naval and maritime). "We are looking for exceptional novels written on a naval or maritime theme." Recently published *Hunt for Red October*, by T. Clancy (naval adventure, contemporary); *Flight of the Intruder*, by Stephen Coonts.
How to Contact: Accepts unsolicited mss. Prefers to receive outline/synopsis and 2 sample chapters. Reports in 8 weeks. Discourages simultaneous submissions. Accepts computer printout submissions; prefers letter-quality.
Terms: Pays in royalties of 14% of net sales minimum; 21% maximum; 6 author's copies; offers negotiable advance. Sends galleys to author. Free writer's guidelines and book catalog.

NEW AMERICAN LIBRARY (III), 1633 Broadway, New York NY 10019. (212)397-8000. Imprints include Onyx, Signet, Mentor, Signet Classic, Plume, Plume Fiction, DAW, Meridian. Contact: Michaela Hamilton, executive editor (hardcover); Arnold Dolin, editor-in-chief, Plume (trade paperback); Maureen Baron, editor-in-chief, Signet/Onyx Books (mass-market). Estab. 1948. Publishes hardcover and paperback originals and paperback reprints.
Needs: "All kinds of commercial and literary fiction, including mainstream, historical, Regency, New Age, western, thriller, science fiction, fantasy, gay. Full length novels and collections." Published *Misery*, by Stephen King; *Small Sacrifices*, by Ann Rule; and *Blood Run*, by Leah Ruth Robinson; published new writers within the last year.
How to Contact: Queries accepted with SASE. "State type of book and past publishing projects." Agented mss only. Simultaneous and photocopied submissions OK. Reports in 3 months.
Terms: Pays in royalties and author's copies; offers advance. Sends galleys to author. Free book catalog.
Advice: "Write the complete manuscript and submit it to an agent or agents."

NEWMARKET PRESS (II), 18 E. 48th St., 15th Floor, New York NY 10017. (212)832-3575. Imprint: Newmarket Medallion (mass-market paperback). Fiction Editor: Teresa Burns. Estab. 1980. Midsize independent publisher with plans to expand. Publishes hardcover and paperback originals. Books: average print order: 15,000.
Needs: "Anything; primarily child care and parenting." No pornography. Published *Stolen Goods*, by Susan Dworkin.
How to Contact: Accepts unsolicited mss. Query first with outline/synopsis. SASE. Most fiction is agented. Reports on queries in 6-10 weeks. Simultaneous and photocopied mss OK. Accepts computer printouts.
Terms: Pays royalties and advance; advance is negotiable. "Almost always" sends galleys to author. Publishes ms "usually 1 or 2 seasons" after acceptance.
Advice: Publishing less fiction than in the past. "Never established as a fiction house." Encourages first novelists "if they show potential and are willing to work at making their writing better. Be aware of what we publish."

W.W. NORTON & COMPANY, INC. (II), 500 5th Ave., New York NY 10110. (212)354-5500. For unsolicited mss contact: Liz Malcolm. Estab. 1924. Midsize independent publisher of trade books and college textbooks. Publishes hardcover originals. Occasionally comments on rejected mss.

Needs: High-quality fiction (preferably literary). No occult, science fiction, religious, gothic, romances, experimental, confession, erotica, psychic/supernatural, fantasy, horror, juvenile or young adult. Published *God's Snake*, by Irini Spanidou (literary); *Agents of Innocence*, by David Ignatius (suspense); published new writers within the last year.
How to Contact: Submit outline/synopsis and sample chapters (of which one is the first). Simultaneous and photocopied submissions OK. Accepts computer printout submissions prefers letter-quality. Reports in 6-8 weeks. Packaging and postage must be enclosed to ensure safe return of materials.
Terms: Graduated royalty scale starting at 7½% or 10% of net invoice price, in addition to 25 author's copies; offers advance. Free book catalog.
Advice: "We will occasionally encourage writers of promise whom we do not immediately publish. We are principally interested in the literary quality of fiction manuscripts. A familiarity with our current list of titles will give you an idea of what we're looking for. Chances are, if your book is good and you have no agent you will eventually succeed; but the road to success will be easier and shorter if you have an agent backing the book. We encourage the submission of first novels."

ORCHARD BOOKS (II, II), Subsidiary of Franklin Watts, Inc., 387 Park Ave. S., New York NY 10016. (212)686-7070. Publisher: Norma Jean Sawacki. Estab. 1986. "Orchard books is a children's trade and library imprint of Franklin Watts, Inc., publishing high quality fiction for the youngest readers through young adult." Publishes hardcover originals. Plans 5 first novels this year. Averages 60 total titles, all fiction titles, each year. Average print order: 7,500. Sometimes critiques rejected ms.
Needs: Fantasy, feminist, historical, juvenile (animal, easy-to-read, fantasy, historical, sports, spy/adventure, contemporary), regional, young adult/teen (easy-to-read, fantasy/science fiction, contemporary, historical, sports, spy/adventure). "We are always interested in new voices, serious or comic, that express insights valuable to children and young adults in original and graceful ways. We are especially interested in novels for the middle grades. And in genre novels that somehow transcend the traditional limits of their specific form." Published *Borrowed Children*, by George Ella Lyon; *The Village by the Sea*, by Paula Fox; *A Thief in the Village*, by James Berry (middle grade); published new writers within the last year.
How to Contact: Accepts unsolicited mss. SASE. Agented fiction 50%. Reports in 1 month on queries; 3 months on mss. Accepts computer printout submissions.
Terms: Pays royalties of 7% minimum; 10% maximum. Advance is negotiable. Provides 10 author's copies. Sends galleys to author. Publishes ms 1-2 years after publication, depending on necessity for illustration. Writer's guidelines for SASE.
Advice: "Our list is about half novels—middle grade to young adult, and half picture books. We are always interested in finding new talent."

PANTHEON BOOKS (III), Subsidiary of Random House, 201 E. 50th St., New York NY 10022. (212)572-2404. Estab. 1950. "Small but well established imprint of well known large house." Publishes hardcover and trade paperback originals and trade paperback reprints. Plans 1-2 first novels this year. Averages 90 total titles, 25 fiction titles each year.
Needs: Pantheon no longer accepts unsolicited fiction. Published *Blue Eyes, Black Hair*, by Marguerite Duras; *A Friend From England*, by Anita Brookner; and *Once in Europa*, by John Berger.
How to Contact: Agented fiction 100%.

PELICAN PUBLISHING COMPANY (IV), Box 189, 1101 Monroe St., Gretna LA 70053. Associate Editor: Dean Shapiro. Executive Editor: James Calhoun. Estab. 1926. Publishes hardcover reprints and originals. Books: hardcover and paperback binding; illustrations sometimes. Published new writers within the last year. Buys juvenile mss with illustrations. Comments on rejected mss "infrequently."
Needs: Juvenile and young adult fiction, especially with a regional focus. "Our adult fiction is *very* limited." Recently published *Belizaire The Cajun*, by Glen Pitre, edited by Dean Shapiro; and *First Steamboat Down the Mississippi*, by George S. Fichter.
How to Contact: Prefers query. May submit complete ms or outline/synopsis and 2-3 sample chapters with SASE. No simultaneous submissions; photocopied submissions only. "Not responsible if writer's only copy is sent." Reports in 4-12 weeks on queries; varies on mss. Publishes ms 12-18 months after acceptance.
Terms: Pays 10% in royalties; 10 free author's copies; advance considered. Sends galleys to author. Catalog of titles and writer's guidelines with SASE.
Advice: "Research the market carefully. Order and look through publishing catalogs to see if your work is consistent with their lists."

PHILOMEL BOOKS (II), 51 Madison Ave., New York NY 10010. (212)951-8700. Subsidiary of The Putnam Publishing Group. Editors: Patricia Lee Gauch, Paula Wiseman. Publishes hardcover originals and paperback reprints. Books: variable paper; offset printing; reinforced bindings; full color illustrations; average print order: 10,000-15,000; first novel print order: 6,000. Averages 30 total titles each

year. "Critiques only if we feel there is some reason to from our point of view."
Needs: Juvenile (animal, nonfiction, historical, picture book, fantasy) and young adult (of more literary variety). "We are not closed to any kind of subject matter, but it must be very well written, fresh and original." Published *A White Romance*, by Virginia Hamilton; *Miracle at Clements Pond*, by Patricia Pendergraft.
How to Contact: Query first with SASE. Accepts computer printout submissions; prefers letter-quality. Reports in 2 weeks on queries; 6 weeks on mss.
Terms: Payment arrangement varies. Sends galleys to author.
Advice: "Philomel is devoted to quality children's and young-adult books. Emphasize beautiful and simple language and make sure your story has substance. We do fiction and nonfiction, picture books and some paperbacks, all of them definitely 'up market.' If they are good enough for Philomel, we publish first novels, but we publish mostly established authors. Do not send unsolicited manuscripts. Don't send 'blind' query letters. Publishing less fiction than in the past."

POCKET BOOKS (II), Division of Simon & Schuster, 1230 Avenue of the Americas, New York NY 10020. (212)698-7000. Imprints include Washington Square Press, Poseidon and Star Trek. Vice President/Editorial Director: William Grose. Publishes paperback and hardcover originals and reprints. Averages 300 titles each year. Buys 90% agented fiction. Sometimes critiques rejected mss.
Needs: Contemporary, literary, faction, adventure, mystery, spy, historical, western, gothic, romance, literary, military/war, mainstream, suspense/mystery, feminist, ethnic, erotica, psychic/supernatural, fantasy, horror and humor/satire. Recently published *Dalva*, by Jim Harrison; *The Wolf's Hour*, by Robert R. McCammon (horror); *A Question of Guilt*, by Frances Fyrield (hardcover); published new writers within the last year.
How to Contact: Query with SASE. No unsolicited mss. Reports in 6 months on queries only. Publishes ms 12-18 months after acceptance.
Terms: Pays in royalties and offers advance. Sends galleys to author. Writer must return advance if book is not completed or is not acceptable. Free book catalog.

POINT BOOKS, Scholastic, Inc., 730 Broadway, New York NY 10003. (212)505-3000. Senior Editor: Regina Griffin. Estab. 1984. Young adult imprint. Publishes paperback originals.
Needs: Young adult/teen (12-18 years). No romance. Published *Fallen Angels*, by Walter Dean Myers; *Born into Light*, by Paul Samuel Jacobs; and *Oh, Brother*, by Johnneice Marshal Wilson.
How to Contact: Query first. SASE.
Advice: "Query letters should describe the genre of the book (mystery, sci-fi, etc.), give a brief plot description, and tell about the writer's background (i.e. have they published anything; taken writing courses, etc.). One common mistake I see is that I get letters that go on and on about the marketing possibilities, but neglect to describe the book at all. That makes me feel I'm dealing with someone who wants to be a 'writer,' but doesn't really take writing seriously enough. We like to publish fiction by previously unpublished writers, if we can. We are expanding our hardcover program and our paperback middle-reader line."

POPULAR LIBRARY (II), Subsidiary of Warner Communications, Inc., 666 5th Ave., 9th Floor, New York NY 10144. (212)484-3145. Executive Editor: Jeanne Tiedge. Large commercial fiction and nonfiction imprint. Publishes paperback originals and reprints. Plans 2 first novels this year. Publishes 60 fiction titles each year.
Needs: True crime, fantasy, horror, mainstream, romance (contemporary, historical), science fiction, military/war and western. Recently published *Fire and Fear: The Inside Story of Mike Tyson*, by Jose-Torres (celebrity bio); *Night Launch*, by Jack Garn; and *Oregon Bride*, by F. Roseanne Bittner.
How to Contact: Does not accept unsolicited mss. Query first. 95% of fiction agented. Reports in 1 month. Photocopied submissions OK "if it's neat." Accepts computer printout submissions.
Terms: Terms vary with author's experience. Author always sees page proofs.

POSEIDON PRESS (II), 1230 Avenue of the Americas, New York NY 10020. (212)698-7290. Distributed by Simon & Schuster. Publisher: Ann E. Patty. Senior Editor: Kathleen Mooney. Estab. 1981. Hardcover and quality trade paper. Books: paper varies; offset printing; illustrations; average print order varies; first novel print order: 5,000-7,500. Averages 20 total titles, 10-12 fiction titles (3 first novels) each year. Does "not critique rejected ms by unsolicited authors unless work merits it."
Needs: General fiction and nonfiction, commercial and literary. Published *Inheritance*, by Judith Michael; and *Bad Behavin*, by Mary Gaitskill.
How to Contact: Query first. No unsolicited manuscripts or sample chapters. Photocopied submissions OK. Reports in 2 months.
Terms: Payment varies, according to content of book.

CLARKSON N. POTTER, INC., 201 E. 50th St., New York NY 10022. (212)572-6121. Distributed by Crown Publishers, Inc. Vice President Editor-in-Chief: Carol Southern.
Needs: Illustrated fiction, biography, humor/satire and juvenile.
How to Contact: Prefers submissions through an agent. Simultaneous and photocopied submissions OK. Accepts computer printout submissions.
Terms: Pays 6-12% in royalties on hardcover; 6-7½% in royalties on paperback; offers $5,000 up in advance.

PRENTICE-HALL BOOKS FOR YOUNG READERS (II), A Division of Simon & Schuster, Inc., Juvenile Publishing Division, 1230 Avenue of the Americas, New York NY 10020. (212)698-7000. Manuscript Coordinator: Rose Lopez. Publishes hardcover originals and paperback originals and reprints. Books: offset printing; illustrations on most titles; average print order: 10,000. Number of titles: 30 hardcover children's books and 15 children's paperbacks/year.
Needs: Juvenile, picture books, humor, mystery, "high-quality middle-grade fiction," and "imaginative nonfiction." Published *Over in the Meadow*, by Paul Galdone (picture book); *Waiter, There's a Fly In My Soup!*, by Charles Keller, illustrations by Lee Lorenz (humor); *Who Let Muddy Boots Into The White House?*, by Robert Quackenbush (biography); published new writers within the last year.
How to Contact: Agented or solicited mss only.
Terms: Pays in royalties; offers advance. Sends galleys to author.

PRESIDIO PRESS (IV), 31 Pamaron Way, Novato CA 94949. (415)883-1373. Editors: Adele Horwitz, Joan Griffin and Robert Tate. Estab. 1976. Small independent general trade—specialist in military. Publishes hardcover originals. Books: 20 lb regular paper, average print order: 5,000. Published new writers within the last year. Publishes at least one military fiction book per list. Averages 15 total titles each year. Critiques or comments on rejected ms.
Needs: Historical with military background, war. Recently published *DefCon One*, by Joe Weber; and *The Fire Dream*, by Frank Leib.
How to Contact: Accepts unsolicited mss. Query first or submit 4 sample chapters. SASE. Reports in 2 weeks on queries; 3 months on mss. Simultaneous and photocopied submissions OK. Accepts computer printouts.
Terms: Pays in royalties of 15% of net minimum; advance: $1,000 average. Sends galleys to author. Book catalog free on request.
Advice: "Think twice before entering any highly competitive genre; don't imitate; do your best. Have faith in your writing and don't let the market disappoint or discourage you."

PRICE STERN SLOAN, INC. (II), 360 N. La Cienega Blvd., Los Angeles CA 90048. (213)657-6100. Subsidiaries/Divisions are Wonder Books, Troubador, Serendipity, Doodle Art and HPBooks. Contact: Editorial Dept. Estab. 1962. Midsize independent, expanding. Publishes hardcover originals, paperback originals and reprints. Books: perfect or saddle-stitched binding; illustrations. Averages 200 total titles each year.
Needs: Humor/satire, juvenile (series, easy-to-read, humor, educational) and adult trade nonfiction. No adult fiction. Published *Shopaholics* (adult trade); *My Grandmother's Cookie Jar* (juvenile fiction); and *How Old Is Old?* (juvenile fiction). Also publishes "self-help, cookbooks, automotive books, photography and gardening."
How to Contact: Query only. Submit outline/synopsis and sample pages. SASE required. Reports in 2 months on queries. Simultaneous and photocopied submissions OK. Accepts computer printouts.
Terms: Terms vary.

G.P. PUTNAM'S SONS (III), The Putnam Publishing Group, 200 Madison Ave., New York NY 10016. (212)576-8900. Imprints include Perigee, Philomel, Platt and Munk, Coward McCann, Grosset and Dunlap Pacer. Publishes hardcover originals.
Needs: Published fiction by Stephen King, Lawrence Sanders, Alice Hoffman; published new writers within the last year.
How to Contact: Does not accept unsolicited mss.

RANDOM HOUSE, INC., 201 E. 50th St., New York NY 10022. (212)751-2600. Imprints include Pantheon Books, Panache Press at Random House, Vintage Books, Times Books, Villard Books and Knopf. Contact: Adult Trade Division. Publishes hardcover and paperback originals. Encourages new writers. Rarely comments on rejected mss.
Needs: Adventure, contemporary, historical, literary, mainstream, short story collections, suspense/mystery. "We publish fiction of the highest standards." Authors include James Michener, Robert Ludlum, Mary Gordon.

How to Contact: Query with SASE. Simultaneous and photocopied submissions OK. Reports in 4-6 weeks on queries, 2 months on mss.
Terms: Payment as per standard minimum book contracts. Free writer's guidelines.
Advice: "Please try to get an agent because of the large volume of manuscripts received, agented work is looked at first."

RESOURCE PUBLICATIONS, INC. (I, IV), Suite 290, 160 E. Virginia St., San Jose CA 95112. (408)286-8505. Book Editor: Kenneth Guentert. Estab. 1973. "Independent book and magazine publisher focusing on imaginative resources for celebration." Publishes paperback originals. Averages 12-14 total titles, 2-3 fiction titles each year.
Needs: Story collections for storytellers, "not short stories in the usual literary sense." No novels. Recently published *Jesus on the Mend: Healing Stories for Ordinary People*, by Andre Papineau; and *The Magic Stone: Stories for Your Faith Journey*, by James Henderschedt.
How to Contact: Query first or submit outline/synopsis and 1 sample chapter with SASE. Reports in 2 weeks on queries; 6 weeks on mss. Photocopied submissions OK "if specified as *not* simultaneous." Accepts computer printout submissions. Prefers letter-quality. Accepts disk submissions compatible with CP/M, IBM system. Prefers hard copy with disk submissions.
Terms: Pays in royalties of 8% minimum, 10% maximum; 10 author's copies. "We do not subsidy publish. *We do require that the author purchase a small portion of the first press run*."

ST. MARTIN'S PRESS, 175 5th Ave., New York NY 10010. (212)674-5151. Imprint: Thomas Dunn. Chairman and CEO: Thomas J. McCormack. President: Roy Gainsburg. Publishes hardcover and paperback reprints and originals.
Needs: Contemporary, literary, experimental, faction, adventure, mystery, spy, historical, war, gothic, romance, confession, feminist, gay, lesbian, ethnic, erotica, psychic/supernatural, religious/inspirational, science fiction, fantasy, horror and humor/satire. No plays, children's literature or short fiction. Published *The Silence of the Lambs*, by Thomas Harris; *Little Saigon*, by T. Jefferson Parker; *The Shell Seekers*, by Rosamunde Pilcher.
How to Contact: Query or submit complete ms with SASE. Simultaneous (if declared as such) and photocopied submissions OK. Reports in 2-3 weeks on queries, 4-6 weeks on mss.
Terms: Pays standard advance and royalties.

ST. PAUL BOOKS AND MEDIA (I), Subsidiary of Daughters of St. Paul, 50 St. Paul's Ave., Jamaica Plain, Boston MA 02130. (617)522-8911. Children's Editor: Sister Anne Joan, fsp. Estab. 1934. Roman Catholic publishing house. Publishes hardcover and paperback originals. Averages 20 total titles, 5 fiction titles each year.
Needs: Juvenile (animal, easy-to-read, fantasy, historical, religion, contemporary), preschool/picture book and young adult/teen (historical, religion, problem novels). All fiction must communicate high moral and family values. "Our fiction needs are entirely in the area of children's literature. We are looking for bedtime stories, historical and contemporary novels for children. Would like to see characters who manifest faith and trust in God." Does not want "characters whose lifestyles are not in conformity with Catholic teachings."
How to Contact: Does not accept unsolicited mss. Query first. SASE. Reports in 2 weeks.
Terms: Pays royalties of 8% minimum; 12% maximum. Provides negotiable number of author's copies. Publishes ms approx. 1 year after acceptance. Writer's guidelines for #10 SAE and 1 first class stamp.
Advice: "There is a dearth of juvenile fiction appropriate for Catholics and other Christians."

SCHOLASTIC, Scholastic, Inc., 730 Broadway, New York NY 10003. (212)505-3000. Publishes a variety of books (hardcovers, paperback originals and reprints) for children and young adults under the following imprints: Scholastic Hardcover: Senior Editor: Regina Griffin. Estab. 1985. A hardcover line of high quality fiction. No multiple submissions. Include SASE.
POINT BOOKS: Senior Editor: Regina Griffin. Estab. 1984. A paperback line of young adult fiction for readers aged 12-up. Most Point novels have contemporary settings, and take as their central characters young adults between the ages of 13-18. No multiple submissions. Scholastic also publishes original paperback books for its school book clubs: Tab Book Club (Teen Age Book Club): Editor: Greg Holch. Especially interested in humorous novels and novels about friendship for readers 12-14.
APPLE BOOKS: Senior Editor: Regina Griffin. Estab. 1981. A paperback line of juvenile fiction for readers aged 8-12. No multiple submissions. include SASE. Executive Editor: Ann Reit. Publishes novels dealing with family, romance and school. Paper and hardcover. Ages 9-11; 12-14.
How to Contact: Query first or submit outline/synopsis and 3 sample chapters with SASE. Simultaneous and photocopied submissions OK. Accepts computer printout submissions.

CHARLES SCRIBNER'S SONS, BOOKS FOR YOUNG READERS, Division of Macmillan Publishing Co., 866 Third Ave., New York NY 10022. (212)702-7885. Editorial Director: Clare Costello. Publishes hardcover originals. Averages 20-25 total titles, 8-13 fiction titles each year.

Needs: Juvenile (animal, easy-to-read, fantasy, historical, picture book, sports, spy/adventure, contemporary, ethnic and science fiction) and young adult (fantasy/science fiction, romance, historical, problem novels, sports and spy/adventure). Published *The Giver*, by Lynn Hall (young adult contemporary fiction); *How Do You Know It's True?*, by David and Marymae Klein (young adult nonfiction); and *Welcome to Grossville*, by Alice Fleming (intermediate contemporary fiction).
How to Contact: Submit complete ms with SASE. Simultaneous and photocopied submissions OK. Reports in 8-10 weeks on mss.
Terms: Free book catalog free on request. Sends galleys to author.

CHARLES SCRIBNER'S SONS (II), Subsidiary of Macmillan, 866 3rd Ave., New York NY 10022. (212)702-2000. Editors: Edward Chase, Susanne Kirk. Publisher and Editor-in-Chief: Robert Stewart. Estab. 1846. Publishes hardcover originals and paperback reprints of its own titles. Number of titles: over 100 last year. Does not comment on rejected mss.
Needs: Contemporary, adventure, mystery, spy, feminist, horror, humor/satire.
How to Contact: Submit outline/synopsis and sample chapter with SASE or submit through agent. "Go to writing workshops. Most important, find an agent." Reports in 2 months on queries. Does not accept unsolicited mss, only queries.
Terms: Pays in royalties; offers advance. Sends galleys to author.

SIERRA CLUB BOOKS, 730 Polk St., San Francisco CA 94109. (415)776-2211. Editor-in-Chief: D. Moses. Estab. 1892. Midsize independent publisher. Publishes hardcover and paperback originals and paperback reprints. Averages 20-25 titles, 1-2 fiction titles each year.
Needs: Contemporary (conservation, environment).
How to Contact: Query only with SASE. "We will only deal with queries; we are not staffed to deal with mss." Simultaneous and photocopied submissions OK. Accepts computer printout submissions; prefers letter-quality. Reports in 6 weeks on queries.
Terms: Pays in royalties. Free book catalog for SASE.
Advice: "Only rarely do we publish fiction. We will consider novels on their quality and on the basis of their relevance to our organization's environmentalist aims."

SILHOUETTE BOOKS (II, IV), 6th Floor, 300 E. 42nd St., New York NY 10017. (212)682-6080. Imprints include Silhouette Romance, Silhouette Special Edition, Silhouette Desire, Silhouette Intimate Moments, Harlequin Historicals; also Silhouette Christmas Stories, Silhouette Summer Sizzlers, Harlequin Historical Christmas Stories. Editorial Manager: Isabel Swift. Senior Editor & Editorial Coordinator (SIM, HH): Leslie J. Wainger. Seniors Editors: (SR) Tara Hughes Gavin, (SD) Lucia Macro, (SSE) Leslie Kazanjian. Editor: Mary Clare Kersten. Associate Editor: Beth de Guzman. Historicals: Editors: Tracy Farrell, Eliza Shallcross. Estab. 1979. Publishes paperback originals. Published 10-20 new writers within the last year. Buys agented and unagented adult romances and young adult fiction. Number of titles: 291/year. Occasionally comments on rejected mss.
Needs: Contemporary romances, adult and young adult, historical romances. Recently published *Ethan*, by Diana Palmer; *Times Change*, by Nora Roberts; *Fire and Rain*, by Elizabeth Lowell.
How to Contact: Submit query letter with brief synopsis and SASE. No unsolicited or simultaneous submissions; photocopied submissions OK. Accepts computer printout submissions. Prefers letter-quality. Publishes ms 9-24 months after acceptance.
Terms: Pays in royalties; offers advance (negotiated on an individual basis). Must return advance if book is not completed or is unacceptable.
Advice: "Study our published books before submitting to make sure that the submission is a potential Silhouette. Added new line of historical romances. Looking for new authors in all lines. Interested in fresh, original ideas and new directions within the romance genre."

SIMON & SCHUSTER, 1230 Avenue of the Americas, New York NY 10020. (212)698-7000. Imprints include Pocket Books, Linden Press.
Needs: General adult fiction, mostly commercial fiction.
How to Contact: Agented material 100%.

GIBBS SMITH, PUBLISHER (II), Box 667, Layton UT 84041. (801)544-9800. Imprints: Peregrine Smith Books. Editorial Director: Madge Baird. Fiction Editor: Steve Chapman. Estab. 1969. Publishes hardcover and paperback originals and reprints. Books: illustrations as needed; average print order 5,000. Publishes 25+ total titles each year, 5-6 fiction titles.
Needs: Adventure, contemporary, experimental, humor/satire, literary, short story collections, translations and nature. Literary works exhibiting the social consciousness of our times. Recently published *Pretend We've Never Met*, by Jonis Agee (short stories); and *The Girl From Cardigan*, by Leslie Norris (short stories).

How to Contact: Query first. SASE. 60% of fiction is agented. Reports in 3 weeks on queries; 10 weeks on mss. Simultaneous and photocopied submissions OK. Accepts computer printout submissions.
Terms: Pays 7-15% royalties. Sends galleys to author. Writer's guidelines for #10 SASE; book catalog for 9x6 SAE and 56¢ postage.
Advice: "Our foremost criteria is the literary merit of the work."

STANDARD PUBLISHING (II, IV), 8121 Hamilton Ave., Cincinnati OH 45231. (513)931-4050. Director: Mark Plunkett. Estab. 1866. Independent religious publisher. Publishes paperback originals and reprints. Books: offset printing; paper binding; b&w line art; average print order: 7,500; first novel print order: 5,000-7,500. Number of titles: averages 18/year. Rarely buys juvenile mss with illustrations. Occasionally comments on rejected mss.
Needs: Religious/inspirational and easy-to-read. "Should have some relation to moral values or Biblical concepts and principles." Katie Hooper Series, by Jane Sorenson; Wheeler Series, by Dan Schantz.
How to Contact: Accepts unsolicited mss. Query or submit outline/synopsis and 2-3 sample chapters with SASE. "Query should include synopsis and general description of perceived market." Accepts computer printout submissions. Prefers letter-quality. Reports in 1 month on queries, 12 weeks on mss. Publishes ms 12-24 months after acceptance.
Terms: Pays varied royalties and by outright purchase; offers varied advance. Sends galleys to author. Free catalog with SASE.
Advice: Publishes fiction with "strong moral and ethical implications." First novels "should be appropriate, fitting into new or existing series. We're dealing more with issues."

STEMMER HOUSE PUBLISHERS, INC. (III), 2627 Caves Rd., Owings Mills MD 21117. (301)363-3690. Imprint includes International Design Library and Victoria and Albert Museum Introductions to the Decorative Arts. Editor: Barbara Holdridge. Estab. 1975. Independent publishing house. Publishes hardcover originals. Books: acid free paper; offset printing; Smythe sewn binding; illustrations occasionally; average print order 3,000-5,000; first novel print order 4,000. Number of titles: averages 20/year, 0-1 fiction titles.
Needs: Literary and historical novels. No fantasy, detective or science fiction. Published *Paradise*, by Dikkon Eberhart (6th century A.D.); *The Fringe of Heaven*, by Margaret Sutherland (contemporary); and *Naked in Deccan*, by Venkatesh Kulkarni (contemporary).
How to Contact: Accepts unsolicited mss. Query first with SASE. Agented fiction: 50%. Simultaneous and photocopied submissions OK if well reproduced. Reports in 2 weeks on queries, 4 weeks on mss, depending on backlog. Publishes ms 1-2 years after acceptance.
Terms: Pays 10% in royalties; offers small advance upon publication. Sends galleys to author. Book catalog free for SASE.
Advice: Publishing "less fiction, since we find little of the quality we require. Trend today seems to be less literate work. Write to be read 50 years from today. Don't tell us how good the novel is. Perfect your grammar and spelling. Most writers seem to have read the latest paperback and swear to write something 'just as good'—but it's most often not even as competent." Interested in "literary quality rather than trendy or genre material. We plan to continue trying to find worthwhile fiction, including first novels, on a long-term basis. Send a cogent query letter, not coy, not a teaser, not self-pitying. We have been overwhelmed with unsolicited, unsuitable submissions and cannot keep up with them. If we cannot cope any better in the future, we will begin returning them unread."

STODDART (III), Subsidiary of General Publishing, 34 Lesmill Rd., Toronto, Ontario M3B 2T6 Canada. (416)445-3333. Managing Editor: Donald G. Bastian. "Largest Canadian-owned publisher in Canada, with a list that features nonfiction primarily." Publishes hardcover and paperback originals and reprints. Plans 2 first novels this year. Averages 50-60 total titles, 8 fiction each year.
Needs: Adventure, suspense/mystery, young adult/teen (10-18 years). Looking for "quality commercial fiction with international potential." Recently published *Other Losses*, by James Bacque; *Rhineland*, by W. Denis and Shelagh Whitaker; *Inventing the Future*, by David Susuki.
How to Contact: Submit outline/synopsis and 2-3 sample chapters. SASE. Agented fiction 50%. Reports in 4-6 weeks on queries; 2-3 months on mss. Simultaneous and photocopied submissions OK. Accepts computer printout submissions, including dot-matrix.
Terms: Pays royalties of 10% minimum; 15% maximum for hardcover. Advance is negotiable. Sends galleys to author. Publishes ms up to 2 years after acceptance.
Advice: "Fiction accounts for about 10% of the list. The amount we do depends on quality and marketability, co-publishing arrangements in US etc., and foreign language sales potential." Encourages first novelists, "but they should be realistic. Don't expect to make a living on it. Presentation is very important. Clear-typed, open spacing. Typos can easily turn readers away from a potentially good book."

SUMMIT BOOKS (II,III), Division of Simon & Schuster, 1230 Avenue of the Americas, New York NY 10020. President and Editor-in-Chief: James Silberman. Estab. 1976. Midsize independent publisher with plans to expand. Publishes hardcover originals. Books: average print order: 3,000-200,000. Plans 1 first novel this year. Averages 30-35 total titles each year.
Needs: Contemporary, feminist, historical (occasionally), satire, literary, mainstream, suspense/mystery, translations.
How to Contact: Does not accept unsolicited mss. Unagented authors should query first. SASE. Agented fiction: 99%. Reports on queries in 8-12 weeks. Simultaneous and photocopied submissions OK. Does not accept dot-matrix computer printouts.
Terms: Pays in royalties and advance; advance is negotiable. Sends galleys to author. Publication time after ms is accepted varies.
Advice: "Our editorial staff is too small to critique writers, and it is sometimes hard to tell exactly what is wrong (or right) with a novel in the time we would have to do it. Get an agent."

TEXAS MONTHLY PRESS (III), Box 1569, Austin TX 78767. (512)476-7085. Subsidiary of Mediatex, Inc. Directors: Cathy Casey Hale and Betsy Williams. Estab. 1978. Publishes hardcover and paperback originals and reprints (60,000 word minimum). Books: 60 lb paper; offset printing; sewn or perfect binding; average first novel print order: 2,500-3,000. Plans 1 first novel this year. Averages 22 total titles, 1 fiction title, each year.
Needs: "Interested in serious fiction of all sorts, particularly novels set in Texas or the Southwest." Published *A Flatland Fable*, by Joe Commer; *Baby Houston*, by June Arnold.
How to Contact: Query first or submit outline/synopsis with SASE. Simultaneous and photocopied submissions OK. Accepts computer printout submissions; prefers letter-quality. Accepts disk submissions compatible with Osborne, Lanier, Xerox, IBM. Prefers hard copy with disk submissions. Reports in 2 weeks on queries; 1 month on mss.
Terms: Pays royalties on net.
Advice: Now publishing fiction reprint series in trade paperback editions.

THORNDIKE PRESS (IV), Subsidiary of Senior Service Corp., Box 159, Thorndike ME 04986. (800)223-6121. Editorial Assistant: Jamie Knobloch. Estab. 1979. Midsize independent publisher, of large print reprints. Publishes hardcover and paperback large print *reprints*. Books: alkaline paper; offset printing; Smythe-sewn library binding; average print order: 4,000. Publishes 132 total titles each year, 80 fiction titles.
Needs: *No fiction that has not been previously published*. Recently published *First Salute*, by Barbara Tuckman; *Temple of My Familiar*, by Alice Walker.
How to Contact: Does not accept unsolicited mss.
Terms: Pays 10% in royalties.

TICKNOR & FIELDS (I, II), Affiliate of Houghton-Mifflin, 52 Vanderbilt Ave., New York NY 10017. (212)420-5800. Estab. 1979. Publishes hardcover originals.
Needs: Open to all categories, but selective list of only 15 titles a year.
How to Contact: Query letters only; no unsolicited mss accepted. No simultaneous submissions (unless very special); photocopied submissions OK. Reports in 2 months on ms.
Terms: Pays standard royalties. Offers advance depending on the book. Free book catalog with SAE and first class stamps.

TOR BOOKS (II), 49 W. 24th St., New York NY 10010. Imprints include Tor Horror, Tor SF, Tor Fantasy and Aerie Books. Editor-in-Chief: Beth Meacham. Managing Editor: Teresa Nielsen Hayden. Estab. 1980. Publishes paperback originals and reprints; also has hardcover trade list of approximately 30 titles a year. Books: 5 point Dombook paper; offset printing; Bursel and perfect binding; few illustrations. Averages 200 total titles, all fiction, each year.
Needs: Fantasy, science fiction, westerns, suspense and mainstream. Recently published *Prentice Alvin*, by Orson Scott Card; *Necroscope*, by Brian Lumley; *Angel Fire*, by Andrew M. Greely; and *Araminta Station*, by Jack Vance.
How to Contact: Agented mss preferred. Buys 90% agented fiction. Photocopied submissions OK. No simultaneous submissions. Address manuscripts to "editorial," *not* to the Managing Editor's office.
Terms: Pays in royalties and advance. Writer must return advance if book is not completed or is unacceptable. Sends galleys to author. Free book catalog on request.

‡TRILLIUM PRESS I, II), Box 209, Monroe NY 10950. (914)783-2999. Vice President: Thomas Holland. Fiction Editor: William Neumann. Estab. 1978. "Independent educational publisher." Publishes hardcover and paperback originals and paperback reprints. Published new writers within the last year. Plans 45 first novels this year. Averages 150 total titles, 70 fiction titles each year.

Needs: Juvenile (5-9 yrs.) animal, easy-to-read, fantasy, historical, sports, spy/adventure and contemporary, young adult/teen (10-18 years) easy-to-read, fantasy/science fiction, historical, problem novels, romance (ya), sports and spy/adventure. Recently published *My Life*, by D.S. Mitchell; *The Man Who Spoke With Jeremiah*, by W. McDonald; and *Anna's Blanket*, by S. Hood.
How to Contact: Accepts unsolicited mss. SASE. Reports in 3 months on mss. Photocopied submissions OK. Accepts computer printouts.
Terms: Negotiated "as appropriate." Sends galleys to author. Writer's guidelines for #10 SAE and 1 first class stamp. Book catalog for 9×12 SAE and 3 first class stamps.

TROLL ASSOCIATES (II), Watermill Press, 100 Corporate Drive, Mahwah NJ 07430. (201)529-4000. Editorial Contact Person: M. Frances. Estab. 1968. Midsize independent publisher. Publishes hardcover originals, paperback originals and reprints. Averages 100-300 total titles each year.
Needs: Adventure, historical, juvenile (5-9 yrs. including: animal, easy-to-read, fantasy), preschool/picture book, young adult/teen (10-18 years) including: easy-to-read, fantasy/science fiction, historical, romance (ya), sports, spy/adventure. Published new writers within the last year.
How to Contact: Accepts and returns unsolicited mss. Query first. Submit outline/synopsis and sample chapters. Reports in 2-3 weeks on queries. Accepts dot-matrix computer printout submissions.
Terms: Pays royalties. Sometimes sends galleys to author. Publishes ms 6-18 months after acceptance.

TSR, INC., Box 756, Lake Geneva WI 53147. (414)248-3625. Imprints include the Dragonlance® series, Forgotten Realms™ series, Buck Rogers® books, TSR™ Books. Contact: Mary Kirchoff, Managing Editor. Estab. 1974. "We publish original paperback novels and "shared world" books. TSR publishes games as well, including the Dungeons & Dragons® role-playing game. Books: standard paperbacks; offset printing; perfect binding; b&w (usually) illustrations; average first novel print order: 75,000. Averages 20-30 titles each year, mostly fiction.
Needs: "We most often publish character-oriented fantasy and science fiction, and some horror. We work with authors who can deal in a serious fashion with the genres we concentrate on and can be creative within the confines of our work-for-hire contracts. Recently published *Tantras*, by Richard Awlinson; *Monkey Station*, by Ardath Mayhar and Ron Fortier; and *Darkness & Light*, by Paul Thompson and Tony Carter.
How to Contact: "TSR seldom accepts unsolicited or unagented manuscripts. Contact with the TSR Book Department should be initiated through an agent or someone we've worked with before. Because most of our books are strongly tied to our other products, we expect our writers to be very familiar with those products."
Terms: Pays royalties of 3%-4% of cover price. Offers advances. Sometimes sends galleys to authors. "Commissioned work, with the exception of our TSR™ Books line, are written as work-for-hire, with TSR, Inc., holding all copyrights.
Advice: "With the huge success of our Dragonlance® series and Forgotten Realms™ books, we expect to be working even more closely with TSR-owned fantasy worlds. Be familiar with our line and have your agent contact us about accepting a proposal."

TYNDALE HOUSE PUBLISHERS (II, IV), 336 Gundersen Dr., Wheaton IL 60187. (312)668-8300. Editor-in-Chief: Dr. Wendell C. Hawley. Estab. 1960. Privately owned religious press. Publishes hardcover and paperback originals and paperback reprints. Plans 6 first novels this year. Averages 87 total titles, 15-20 fiction titles each year. Average first novel print order: 5,000-10,000 copies.
Needs: Religious/inspirational. "We are publishing less fiction."
How to Contact: Accepts unsolicited mss. Submit complete ms. Reports in variable number of weeks. Simultaneous and photocopied submissions OK. Publishes ms an average of 1 year after acceptance.
Terms: Pays in royalties of 10% minimum; negotiable advance. Must return advance if book is not completed or is unacceptable. Sends galleys to author. Free writer's guidelines. Free book catalog on request.

UNIVERSITY OF GEORGIA PRESS (II), Terrell Hall, Athens GA 30602. (404)542-2830. Flannery O'Connor Short Fiction Award Editor: Charles East. Estab. 1938. Midsize university press with editorial program focusing on scholarly nonfiction. Publishes hardcover and paperback originals and reprints.
Needs: Short story collections. No novellas or novels. Published *Silent Retreats*, by Philip F. Deaver; *The Purchase of Order*, by Gail Galloway Adams.
How to Contact: Short story collections are considered only in conjunction with the Flannery O'Connor award competition. Next submission period is June 1-July 31, 1990. *Manuscripts cannot be accepted at any other time. Manuscripts will* not *be returned. Competition information for SASE.*
Terms: The Flannery O'Connor Award carries a $500 cash award plus standard royalties. Free book catalog.

Close-up

Pat Cadigan
Writer

© Arnie Fenner.

Pat Cadigan has always wanted to be a writer. In fact, she says, "I cannot remember not wanting to be a writer." In addition, she has also always been fascinated with science. Thus, science fiction became her logical choice of genre. She started mailing story submissions in 1975, but found the short path to "overnight success" as more of a long, winding road.

In Cadigan's case, persistence paid off. In 1979, four years and roughly a dozen unpublished manuscripts later, she made her first short story sale. In 1986, she sold her first novel, *Mindplayers*. Her second novel, *Synners*, will be out in 1990.

Cadigan is considered a "hard" science fiction writer and deals in great part with the subject of the brain and its relationship with computers. Some of her writing resembles cyberpunk, which also deals with human-computer combinations and the very near future. However, she does not claim to be a pure cyberpunk writer. "Rather than being a *type* of writer, I prefer to pursue whatever story or novel I'm interested in at the moment."

Cadigan attributes the authenticity of her writing to "literally hours of research. If you were to see my office, you'd be confused as to whether I'm taking a heavy course in student writing or completing my residency in neurosurgery!

"Scientific guesses must at least be educated. A certain amount of research needs to be done anytime you're writing science fiction because if you want to write about a planet that has a blue sun as opposed to a sun like ours, there are definitely going to be certain things that are different about the light, climate and everything else. You're going to have to search at least the implications of having a blue sun."

The inclusion and acceptance of women in science fiction is one of the major changes Cadigan cites within the genre. "Basically, science fiction has changed along with today's technology and the status for today's world." Cadigan says that, thanks to the women's movement, more women are moving into traditional male-dominated occupations, including those involving science. Because of this, more women are becoming involved in science fiction.

Before selling her first novel, Cadigan worked a full time job during the day and wrote nights and weekends. "I gave up a lot, but I wanted it badly. A lot of it is psychological. It's not so much the talent that causes someone to make it, but the thick skin. The ability to not take rejection as a crushing blow but to shrug it off and say, 'Well, they didn't like that one—maybe they'll like this one.' "Cadigan also suggests that discouraged writers keep in mind the past plights of now successful writers.

Nevertheless, Cadigan says there are writers who possess inappropriate motives for writing. "Some people do go into writing for the wrong reasons. If you're expecting an immediate affirmation that you are talented and special, you're in for a terrible disappointment."

—Lisa Carpenter

‡*UNIVERSITY OF MINNESOTA PRESS (I, II), 2037 University Ave. SE, Minneapolis MN 55414. (612)624-2516. Senior Editor: Terry Cochran. Estab. 1925. "We are a midsize academic publisher." Publishes hardcover and paperback originals and hardcover and paperback reprints. Books: acid-free paper; offset printing; simultaneous hardcover/paperback binding; b&w, 4-color illustrations and line drawings; average print order: 500 hardcovers; 3,000 paperbacks; first novel print order: 500 hardcovers; 5,000 paperbacks. Averages 55 total titles, 4 fiction titles each year. Sometimes comments on rejected ms; charges for critiques.
Needs: Contemporary, ethnic, experimental, fantasy, feminist, gay, historical, lesbian, literary, science fiction, short story collections and translations. "We are especially interested in submissions from Third-World/minority writers." Recently published *The Stream of Life*, by Clarice Lispector (Brazilian); *The Trickster of Liberty*, by Gerald Vizenor (American Indian); and *Little Mountain*, by Elias Khoury (Lebanese).
How to Contact: Accepts unsolicited mss. Query first. Outline/synopsis and 2 sample chapters. Agented fiction 10%. Reports in 1 month. Simultaneous and photocopied submissions OK. Accepts computer printout submissions. Accepts electronic submissions.
Terms: Pays royalties of 2% minimum; 12% maximum (on list price). Average advance $750-$1,000. Provides 10 author's copies. Subsidy publishes 10%. Book catalog free.
Advice: "We began a fiction series approximately one year ago and plan to continue publishing approximately two new fiction titles per season for the foreseeable future. We are looking for writers with a unique voice that is not usually represented by other U.S. publishers; their number of publications does not enter into our consideration."

***VESTA PUBLICATIONS, LTD (II)**, Box 1641, Cornwall, Ontario K6H 5V6 Canada. (613)932-2135. Editor: Stephen Gill. Estab. 1974. Midsize publisher with plans to expand. Publishes hardcover and paperback originals. Books: bond paper; offset printing; paperback and sewn hardcover binding; illustrations; average print order: 1,200; first novel print order: 1,000. Plans 7 first novels this year. Averages 18 total titles, 5 fiction titles each year. Negotiable charge for critiquing rejected mss.
Needs: Adventure, contemporary, ethnic, experimental, faction, fantasy, feminist, historical, humor/satire, juvenile, literary, mainstream, preschool/picture book, psychic/supernatural/occult, regional, religious/inspirational, romance, science fiction, short story collections, suspense/mystery, translations, war and young adult/teen. Published *Sodom in her Heart*, by Donna Nevling (religious); *The Blessings of a Bird*, by Stephen Gill (juvenile); and *Whistle Stop and Other Stories*, by Ordrach.
How to Contact: Accepts unsolicited mss. Submit complete ms with SASE or SAE and IRC. Reports in 1 month. Simultaneous and photocopied submissions OK. Accepts computer printout submissions. Disk submissions OK with CPM/Kaypro 2 system.
Terms: Pays in royalties of 10% minimum. Sends galleys to author. "For first novel we usually ask authors from outside of Canada to pay half of our printing cost." Free book catalog.

VILLARD BOOKS (II, III), Random House, Inc., 201 E. 50th St., New York NY 10022. (212)572-2720. Editorial Director: Peter Gethers. Fiction Editors: Diane Reverand, Alison Acker, Emily Bestler. Estab. 1983. Imprint specializes in commercial fiction and nonfiction. Publishes hardcover and trade paperback originals. Published new writers within the last year. Plans 2 first novels this year. Averages 30-35 total titles, approx. 10 fiction titles each year. Sometimes critiques rejected mss.
Needs: Strong commercial fiction and nonfiction. Adventure, contemporary, historical, horror, humor/satire, literary, mainstream, romance (contemporary and historical), suspense/mystery. Special interest in mystery, thriller, and literary novels. Recently published *All I Need to Know I Learned in Kindergarten* (inspirational); and *North Dallas After Forty* (commercial fiction).
How to Contact: Does not accept unsolicited mss. Submit outline/synopsis and 1-2 sample chapters to a specific editor. Agented fiction: 95%. Reports in 2-3 weeks. Simultaneous and photocopied submissions OK. Accepts electronic submissions, no dot-matrix.
Terms: "Depends upon contract negotiated." Sends galleys to author. Writer's guidelines for 8½x11 SAE with 1 first class stamp. Book catalog free on request.
Advice: "Most fiction published in hardcover."

WALKER AND COMPANY (II), 720 5th Ave., New York NY 10019. Editors: Jacqueline Johnson, Janet Hutchings, Mary Elizabeth Allen, Sally Paynter, Peter Rubie, Amy Shields, William Thorndike. Midsize independent publisher with plans to expand. Publishes hardcover and paperback originals and reprints. Average first novel print order: 4,000-5,000. Number of titles: averages 250/year. Pub-

The double dagger before a listing indicates that the listing is new in this edition. New markets are often the most receptive to freelance contributions.

lished many new writers within the last year. Occasionally comments on rejected mss.

Needs: Nonfiction, mystery, regency romance, quality male adventure, western and young adult fiction and nonfiction.

How to Contact: Submit outline and chapters as preliminary. Query letter should include "a concise description of the story line, including its outcome, word length of story, writing experience, publishing credits, particular expertise on this subject and in this genre. Common mistakes: sounding unprofessional (i.e. too chatty, too braggardly). Forgetting SASE." Buys 50% agented fiction. Photocopied submissions OK, "but must notify if multiple submissions." Accepts computer printout submissions; must be letter-quality. Reports in 1-2 months. Publishes ms an average of 1 year after acceptance.

Terms: Negotiable (usually advance against royalty). Must return advance if book is not completed or is unacceptable.

Advice: Publishing more fiction than previously, "exclusively hardcover. Manuscripts should be sophisticated. As for mysteries, we are open to all types, including suspense novels. In fact, the line has been renamed Walker Mystery-Suspense. We favor strong plot and compelling action. We are always looking for well written western novels. While we publish some of the traditional 'revenge' westerns, we like to publish historical 'explorations' about any aspect of the West. Character development is most important in all Walker fiction. We have been actively soliciting submissions to all divisions."

WARNER BOOKS (II), Subsidiary of Warner Publishing, Inc., 666 Fifth Ave., New York NY 10103. (212)484-2900. Imprints include Popular Library, Mysterious Press. Contact: Editorial dept. for specific editors. Estab. 1961. Publishes hardcover and paperback originals. Published new writers within the last year. Averages approx. 500 titles/year. Sometimes critiques rejected mss.

Needs: Adventure, contemporary, fantasy, horror, mainstream, preschool/picture book, romance (contemporary, historical, regency), science fiction, suspense/mystery, war, western, "We are continuing to publish romances, mainstream novels, science fiction, men's adventure, etc. No historicals that are not romances, Civil War novels, young adult." Recently published *Red Phoenix*, by Larry Bond (military thriller); *Best Kept Secrets*, by Sandra Brown (commercial women's fiction).

How to Contact: Does not accept unsolicited mss. Query first. Agented fiction 85-90%. Reports in 6-8 weeks on mss. Simultaneous submissions accepted "but we prefer exclusive submissions"; and photocopied submissions "of high quality" OK.

Terms: Varies for each book.

Advice: "Continuing a strong, varied list of fiction titles. We encourage first novelists we feel have potential for more books and whose writing is extremely polished. Be able to explain your work clearly and succinctly in query or cover letter. Read books a publisher has done already—best way to get a feel for publisher's strengths. Read *Publisher's Weekly* to keep in touch with trends and industry news."

‡WASHINGTON SQUARE PRESS (III), Subsidiary of Pocket Books/Simon & Schuster, 1230 Ave. of the Americas, New York NY 10020. Senior Fiction Editor: Stacy Schiff, Assistant Editor: Bryan Oettel. Estab. 1962. Quality imprint of mass-market publisher. Publishes paperback originals and reprints. Recently published *Dalva* and *Sun Dog*, by Jim Harrison (reprints); *The Pigeon*, by Patrick Susskind (reprint); and *Men*, by Margaret Diehl (reprint). Books: trade paperbacks. Averages 26 titles, mostly fiction, each year.

Needs: Literary, high quality novels; serious nonfiction.

How to Contact: Accepts unsolicited mss. Query first. Agented fiction nearly all. Reports in 2 months on queries. Simultaneous and photocopied submissions OK.

WESTERN PRODUCER PRAIRIE BOOKS (II), Subsidiary of Saskatchewan Wheat Pool, 2310 Millar Ave., Box 2500, Saskatoon, Saskatchewan S7K 2C4 Canada. (306)665-3548. Imprint: Concordia International Youth Fiction Series (translations of foreign young adult novels). Editorial Director: Jane McHughen. Estab. 1954. Midsize publisher with plans to expand line of juvenile and young adult fiction. Publishes hardcover and paperback originals and reprints. Books: 60 lb hi-bulk paper; traditional offset printing; perfect bound hardcover and paperback binding; b&w illustrations (if warranted); average print order: 5,000; first novel print order: 3,000. Published new writers within the last year. Plans 1 first novel this year. Averages 20 total titles, 3 fiction titles each year. Sometimes critiques rejected mss.

Needs: Juvenile (historical, sports, contemporary) and young adult/teen (historical, problem novels, sports). Looking for juvenile and young-adult novels appealing to 8 to 14 year olds. Recently published *A Question of Courage*, by Irene Morck; *A Gift of Sky*, by Linda Ghan; *Dog Runner*, by Don Meredith; and *The Ghost of Peppermint Flats and Other Stories*, by Ted Stone.

How to Contact: Accepts unsolicited mss. Submit outline/synopsis and 3-4 sample chapters. SASE. Agented fiction: very little. Reports in 1 month on queries; 2-3 months on mss. Simultaneous (as long as we are notified) and photocopied submissions OK. Accepts computer printout submissions.

Terms: Pays in royalties of 8% minimum; 12.5% maximum. Offers average advance: $1,000. Sends galleys to author. Writer's guidelines and book catalog free on request.
Advice: "Interested in expanding paperback juvenile and young adult fiction list. We have published a greater number of young adult fiction titles, probably because we receive more manuscripts in this area now that we are recognized by authors as a publisher of high-quality young adult fiction."

WESTERN PUBLISHING COMPANY, INC., 850 3rd Ave., New York NY 10022. (212)753-8500. Imprint: Golden Books. Juvenile Editor-in-Chief: Eric Suben. Estab. 1907. High-volume mass market and trade publisher. Publishes hardcover and paperback originals. Number of titles: averages 160/year. Buys 20-30% agented fiction.
Needs: Juvenile: adventure, mystery, humor, sports, animal, easy-to-read picture books, and "a few" nonfiction titles. Published *Little Critter's Bedtime Story*, by Mercer Mayer; *Cyndy Szokeves' Mother Goose Rhymes*; and *Spaghetti Manners*, by Stephanie Calmsenson, illustrated by Lisa MaÇue Karsten.
How to Contact: Send a query letter with a description of the story and SASE. Unsolicited mss are returned unread. Publishes ms an average of 1 year after acceptance.
Terms: Pays by outright purchase or royalty.
Advice: "Read our books to see what we do. Call for appointment if you do illustrations, to show your work. Do not send illustrations. Illustrations are not necessary; if your book is what we are looking for, we can use one of our artists."

ALBERT WHITMAN & COMPANY (II), 5747 W. Howard, Niles IL 60648. (312)647-1358. Senior Editors: Judith Mathews and Abby Levine. Editor-in-Chief: Kathleen Tucker. Estab. 1919. Small independent juvenile publisher. Publishes hardcover originals. Books: paper varies; printing varies; library binding; most books illustrated; average print order: 7,500. Average 20-26 total titles/year. Number of fiction titles varies.
Needs: Juvenile (2-12 years including easy-to-read, fantasy, historical, adventure, contemporary, mysteries, picture-book stories). Primarily interested in picture book manuscripts. Recently published *All About Asthma*, by William Ostrow and Vivian Ostrow; *You Push, I Ride*, by Abby Levine; published new writers within the last year.
How to Contact: Accepts unsolicited mss. Submit outline/synopsis and 1-3 sample chapters; complete ms for picture books. SASE. "Half or more fiction is not agented." Reports in 3 weeks on queries; 2 months on mss. Simultaneous and photocopied submissions OK. ("We prefer to be told.") Accepts computer printouts including dot-matrix.
Terms: Payment varies. Royalties, advance; number of author's copies varies. Some flat fees. Sends galleys to author. Writer's guidelines free for SASE. Book catalog for 9x12 SASE and 85¢ postage.

■**WILDSTAR BOOKS/EMPIRE BOOKS (II, IV)**, Subsidiary of The Holy Grail Co., Inc., 26 Nantucket Pl., Scarsdale NY 10583. (914)961-2965. Vice President: Ralph Leone. Estab. 1986. Packager of Empire Books. Imprint: Wildstar (with Lynx Communications). Publishes paperback originals. Averages 40 fiction titles each year. Sometimes critiques rejected mss.
Needs: Horror, psychic/supernatural/occult, romance (contemporary, historical), suspense/mystery, western. Looking for romance, horror, new age, occult, western, mystery and thriller. Recently published 22-book series *American Regency*; *Wildstar* for Warner Books (romance); 12-book series, *Americans Abroad*, *Empire* for St. Martin's (romance); 18-book series, *Horror, Empire* for Pageant Books (horror).
How to Contact: Accepts unsolicited mss. Query first. SASE. Agented fiction 80%. Reports in 3 weeks on queries; 3 months on mss. Photocopied submissions OK. Accepts computer printout submissions, including dot-matrix.
Terms: Pays in royalties: "depends on deal we make with publisher." Advance negotiable. Provides author's copies. Sends galleys to author. Publishes ms generally within 18 months after acceptance.
Advice: "Short and to the point—not cute or paranoid—is best tone in a query letter."

WILLIAM MORROW AND COMPANY, INC. (II), 105 Madison Ave., New York NY 10016. Imprints include Arbor House, Beech Tree Books, Silver Arrow, Quill, Perigord, Greenwillow Books, Lothrop, Lee & Shepard and Fielding Publications (travel books), and Morrow Junior Books. Publisher, Morrow Adult: James D. Landis. Estab. 1926. Approximately one fourth of books published will be fiction.
Needs: "Morrow accepts only the highest quality submissions" in contemporary, literary, experimental, adventure, mystery, spy, historical, war, romance, feminist, gay/lesbian, science fiction, horror, humor/satire and translations. Juvenile and young adult divisions are separate. Published works by Michael Chabon, William Boyd, Elmore Leonard.

How to Contact: Submit through agent. All unsolicited mss are returned unopened. "We will only accept queries, proposals or mss when submitted through a literary agent." Simultaneous and photocopied submissions OK. Accepts computer printout submissions; prefers letter-quality. Reports in 2-3 months.
Terms: Pays in royalties; offers advance. Sends galleys to author. Free book catalog.
Advice: "The Morrow divisions of Morrow Junior Books, Greenwillow Books, and Lothrop, Lee and Shepard handle juvenile books. We do 5-10 first novels every year and about ¼ titles are fiction. Having an agent helps to find a publisher. Morrow Junior Books not accepting unsolicited mss."

WINSTON-DEREK PUBLISHERS (II), Box 90883, Nashville TN 37209. (615)321-0535, 329-1319. Imprints include Scythe Books. Senior Editor: Marjorie Staton. Estab. 1978. Midsize publisher. Publishes hardcover and paperback originals and reprints. Books: 60 lb old Warren style paper; litho press; perfect and/or sewn binding; illustrations sometimes; average print order: 3,000-5,000 copies; first novel print order: 2,000 copies. Published new writers within the last year. Plans 10 first novels this year. Averages 55-65 total titles, 20 fiction titles each year; "90% of material is from freelance writers; each year we add 15 more titles."
Needs: Gothic, historical, juvenile (historical), psychic, religious/inspirational, and young adult (easy-to-read, historical, romance) and programmed reading material for middle and high school students. "Must be 65,000 words or less. Novels strong with human interest. Characters overcoming a weakness or working through a difficulty. Prefer plots related to a historical event but not necessary. No science fiction, explicit eroticism, minorities in conflict without working out a solution to the problem. Downplay on religious ideal and values." Recently published *Sisters of a Different Dawn*, by Darcy Williamson; *This Side of Tomorrow*, by Janet C. Woolridge; and *Season of Growth*, by Sonia Murray.
How to Contact: Submit outline/synopsis and 3-4 sample chapters with SASE. Simultaneous and photocopied submissions OK. Accepts computer printout submissions. Prefers letter-quality. Reports in 4-6 weeks on queries; 6-8 weeks on mss. Must query first. Do not send complete ms.
Terms: Pays in royalties of 10% minimum, 15% maximum; negotiates advance. Book catalog on request for $1 postage.
Advice: "Stay in the mainstream of writing. The public is reading serene and contemplative literature. Authors should strive for originality and a clear writing style, depicting universal themes which portray character building and are beneficial to mankind. Consider the historical novel; there is always room for one more."

WORLDWIDE LIBRARY (II), Division of Harlequin Books, 225 Duncan Mill Rd., Don Mills, Ontario Canada. (416)445-5860. Imprints are Worldwide Library Science Fiction; Worldwide Library Mysteries; Gold Eagle Books. Senior Editor: Feroze Mohammed. Estab. 1979. Large commercial category line. Publishes paperback originals and reprints. Published new writers within the last year. Averages 60 total titles, all fiction, each year. Sometimes critiques rejected ms.
Needs: Adventure, suspense/mystery. Looking for "men's action-adventure series and writers; mystery; future fiction." Recently published *A Question of Murder*, by Eric Wright (mystery); *Corkscrew*, by Ted Wood; and *Cold Trail*, by Dell Shannon.
How to Contact: Accepts unsolicited mss. Query first or submit outline/synopsis and sample chapters. "Try to establish the category or genre in which your novel fits." SASE. Agented fiction 95%. Reports in 10 weeks on queries; 16 weeks on mss. Simultaneous and photocopied submissions OK. Accepts computer printout submissions.
Terms: Advance and royalties; work for hire. Publishes ms 1-2 years after acceptance.
Advice: "Publishing more fiction, but in very selective areas. As a genre publisher, we are always on the lookout for new talent, especially in the men's adventure area. If you are interested in writing for one of our men's adventure series in the Gold Eagle imprint, study a number of the books in that series before contacting us."

YEARLING (II, III), 666 5th Ave., New York NY 10103. (212)765-6500. See Dell Publishing Co., Inc. Publishes originals and reprints for children grades K-6. Most interested in humorous upbeat novels, mysteries and family stories. 60 titles a year. "Will, regrettably, no longer consider unsolicited material at this time."
Terms: Sends galleys to author.

ZEBRA BOOKS (II), 475 Park Ave. S, New York NY 10016. (212)889-2299. Editorial Director: Michael Seidman. Estab. 1975. Publishes hardcover reprints and paperback originals. Averages 200 total titles/year.

Read the Business of Fiction section to learn the correct way to prepare and submit a manuscript.

Needs: Contemporary, adventure, English-style mysteries, historical, war, gothic, saga, romance, thrillers and horror. No science fiction. Recently published *Missing Beauty*, by Teresa Carpenter; *Kiss of the Night Wind*, by Janelle Taylor; *Stardust*, by Nan Ryan; and *Wolf Time*, by Joe Gores.
How to Contact: Query or submit complete ms or outline/synopsis and sample chapters with SASE. Simultaneous and photocopied submissions OK. Address women's mss to Carin Cohen Ritter and male adventure mss to Michael Seidman. Reports in 3-5 months.
Terms: Pays royalties and advances. Free book catalog.
Advice: "Put aside your literary ideals and be commercial. We like big contemporary women's fiction; glitzy career novels, high-tech espionage and horror. Work fast and on assignment. Keep your cover letter simple and to the point. Too many times, 'cutesy' letters about category or content turn us off some fine mss. We are more involved with family and historical sagas. But please do research. We buy many unsolicited manuscripts, but we're slow readers. Have patience."

CHARLOTTE ZOLOTOW BOOKS (II), 10 E. 53rd St., New York NY 10022. (212)207-7044. "Editor works mainly with authors she has edited over the years." See Harper & Row Junior Books Group.

‡ZONDERVAN, 1415 Lake Dr. SE, Grand Rapids MI 49506. (616)698-6900. Imprints include Academie Books, Broadmoor Books, Cantilever Books, Clarion Classics, Daybreak Books, Francis Asbury Press, Lamplighter Books, Ministry Resources Library, Pyranee Books, Regency Reference Library, Youth Specialties and Zondervan Books. Publishers: Stan Gundry, Scott Bolinder. Estab. 1931. Large evangelical Christian publishing house. Publishes hardcover and paperback originals and reprints, though fiction is generally in paper only. Published new writers in the last year. Averages 120 total titles, 5-10 fiction titles each year. Average first novel: 5,000 copies.
Needs: Adult fiction, (mainstream, biblical, historical, adventure, sci-fi, fantasy, mystery), "Inklings-style" fiction of high literary quality and juvenile fiction (primarily mystery/adventure novels for 8-12-year-olds). Christian relevance necessary in all cases. Will *not* consider collections of short stories or inspirational romances. Recently published *Men of Kent*, by Elizabeth Gibson; *Nightwatch*, by John Leax; and *Morning Morning True*, by Ernest Herndon.
How to Contact: Accepts unsolicited ms. Write for free writer's guidelines first with #10 SASE. Query or submit outline/synopsis and 2 sample chapters. Reports in 4-6 weeks on queries; 3-4 months on mss. Photocopied submissions OK. Accepts computer printout submissions.
Terms: "Standard contract provides for a percentage of the retail price of each copy sold, usually 10-14%."
Advice: "There has been a revival of Christian fiction in last year. The renewed reader interest is exciting. There is great room for improvement of writing quality, however. Send plot outline and one or two sample chapters. Most editors will *not* read entire mss. Your proposal and opening chapter will make or break you."

Foreign Commercial Publishers

The following commercial publishers buy novel and short story manuscripts in English from U.S. and Canadian writers. Query first for submissions guidelines and a catalog, if available. Always include a self-addressed envelope with International Reply Coupons for samples, guidelines and manuscript return. Be sure to include the correct number of IRCs (available from the main branch of your local post office) and an envelope in the appropriate size. To save on the cost of return postage on your manuscript, you may want to send a copy for the publisher to keep along with a return postcard and IRC for reply.

ANGUS & ROBERTSON/COLLINS PUBLISHERS AUSTRALIA, 4 Eden Place, 31 Waterloo Rd., North Ryde, NSW, 2113 (or Box 290, North Ryde). Tel (02)888-4111. FAX: (02)888-9972. Subsidiary imprints: Angus & Robertson, Collins Australia, Imprint, Blacklist. Publishing Director: Lisa Highton. Looking for fiction, poetry and general nonfiction (Australian bias). *No* religion or text books. Send preliminary letter with synopsis of typescript, preferably with sample chapter. Reply in 6-8 weeks. Payment by royalty.

ATMA RAM AND SONS, 1376 Lothian Rd., Kashmere Gate, Delhi 110006 India. Fiction Editor: Ish Kumar Puri. Publishes 30 books/year. Modern themes but not science fiction. Regular royalties are paid on the published prices of the books. "Works of fiction should be in the theme of current affairs, nuclear warfare, romance, etc."

THE BLACKSTAFF PRESS (I), 3 Galway Park, Dundonald BT16 0AN Northern Ireland. Editor: Hilary Parker. Midsize, independent publisher, wide range of subjects. Publishes hardcover and paperback originals and reprints. Contemporary, ethnic (Irish), historical, humor/satire, literary, short story collections, political thrillers and feminist.

‡GRAFTON BOOKS, A Division of Collins Publishing Group, 8 Grafton St., London W1X 3LA United Kingdom. Publishing Directors: John Boothe, Nick Austin. Publishes hardcover and paperback originals and paperback reprints. Adventure, contemporary, erotica, fiction, fantasy, historical, horror, psychic/supernatural/occult, science fiction and war.

‡ROBERT HALE LIMITED (II), Clerkenwell House, 45/47 Clerkenwell Green, London EC1R 0HT England. Publishes hardcover and trade paperback originals and hardcover reprints. Historical, mainstream, romance and western.

***HALLMARK PUBLISHING LTD.**, Gopala Prabhu Rd., Box 3541 Cochin-682 035 India. President: Prof. Dr. M. V. Pylee. Managing and Editorial Director: C. I. Oommen. Publishers of trade paperbacks and educational books. Looking for folktales, adventure, novel and short fiction anthologies. Accepts unsolicited mss, simultaneous and photocopied submissions and computer printouts (prefers letter quality). Reports in 2 months. Pays in royalties of 10% maximum. No advance. "We also produce books for self publishers and small press with marketing and distribution support."

‡HAMISH HAMILTON LTD., 27 Wrights Lane, London W8 5TZ England. Fiction Editors: Andrew Franklin, Peter Straus. General trade publisher quality fiction—literary plus some crime and thrillers. Advance on delivery of accepted book or on accepted commission. Send first chapter with synopsis before submitting whole manuscript.

HEADLINE BOOK PUBLISHING PLC, 79 Great Titchfield St., London W1P 7FN England. Editorial Director: Susan J. Fletcher. Averages approximately 200 titles/year. Mainstream publisher of popular fiction (and nonfiction) in hardcover and mass-market paperback. Pays advance against royalties. "Send a synopsis and *curriculum vita* first, and return postage."

‡HODDER & STOUGHTON PUBLISHERS, 47 Bedford Square, London WC1B 3DP, England, U.K. Imprints: Coronet, NEL, Sceptre. Fiction Editors: Humphrey Price Esq (NEL); Amanda Stewart (Coronet); Roland Philipps (Sceptre). Coronet: intelligent, mainstream romantic fiction; humour; historical novels; Sceptre: literary—fiction and nonfiction; NEL: horror, SF, fantasy, humour, serious nonfiction. "We do not consider short stories." Payment is made "usually by an advance and then final payment on publication." Send a cover letter, synopsis and sample chapters. "If you can't get an agent to represent you, then do make enquiries to the editorial departments first, before sending off complete manuscripts."

MICHAEL JOSEPH LTD., The Penguin Group, 27 Wrights Lane, London W8 5TZ England. Contact: Fiction Editor. General publisher of adult fiction and nonfiction. Publishes hardcover originals and some trade paperback originals and reprints, not mass market. Needs: Adventure, contemporary, historical, humor, literary, mainstream, regional, suspense/mystery and war.

‡THE MACMILLAN COMPANY OF AUSTRALIA (II), 107 Moray St., South Melbourne, Victoria, 3205 Australia. Subsidiary of the Macmillan Publishing Group. Subsidiary includes Sun Books Pty Ltd. Publisher: Teresa Pitt. Publishes hardcover originals and paperback reprints. Averages 50 total lines, 3 fiction titles each year. Needs historical, literary, mainstream. Needs "the usual: Australian up-market quality fiction (novels) that wins literary prizes *and* makes money." No juvenile, science fiction, romances; non-Australian relevance. Query first with SASE; submit outline/synopsis and 2 sample chapters through agent. Reports in 3 weeks on queries; 3 months on mss. Pays as "recommended by Australian Literature Board of Australia Council and Australia Society of Authors scale." Writer's guidelines for SASE. "Give up fiction for nonfiction or develop a hide like a rhino. Read a lot."

MILLS & BOON, Eton House, 18-24 Paradise Road, Richmond, Surrey TW9 1SR England. Publishes 250 fiction titles/year. Modern romantic fiction, historical romances and medical romances. "We are happy to see the whole manuscript or 3 sample chapters and synopsis."

MY WEEKLY STORY LIBRARY, D.C. Thomson and Co., Ltd., 22 Meadowside, Dundee Scotland. Fiction Editor: Mrs. D. Hunter. Publishes 48 35,000-word romantic novels/year. "Cheap paperback story library with full-colour cover. Material should not be violent, controversial or sexually explicit." Writers are paid on acceptance. "Send the opening two chapters and a synopsis."

ORIENT PAPERBACKS, A division of Vision Books Pvt Ltd., Madarsa Rd., Kashmere Gate, Delhi 110 006 India. Editor: Sudhir Malhotra. Publishes 10-15 novels or story collections/year. "We are one of the largest paperback publishers in S.E. Asia and publish English fiction by authors from this part of the world." Pays royalty on copies sold.

‡QUARTET BOOKS LIMITED, 27-29 Goodge Street, London W1P1FD England. Fiction Editor: Stephen Pickles. Publishes 50 stories/year. "Middle East fiction, European classics in translation, original novels." Payment is: advance – half on signature, half on delivery and publication. "Send brief synopsis and sample chapters. *No* romantic fiction, historical fiction, crime or thrillers."

SIDGWICK & JACKSON LTD., 1 Tavistock Chambers Bloomsbury Way, London WC1A 2SG England. Fiction Editor: Oliver Johnson. Publishes 24 titles/year. "Quali-pop, commercial fiction – particularly women's fiction, historical novels, thrillers. No short stories." Pays advance and royalties. "Please send synopsis with manuscript/extract. Please think of potential appeal for the *British* market."

TRANSWORLD PUBLISHERS, 40 Yeo St., Neutral Bay, N.S.W. 2089 Australia. Editor: Jacqueline Kent. "Mass-market fiction with strong plots and characters; some literary fiction under our Black Swan paperback imprint; some children's. Greater interest, at present, in adventure drama/character drama than science fiction or fantasy. Give us a synopsis and sample chapter first. Evaluation normally takes between four and six weeks."

VISION BOOKS PVT LTD., Madarsa Rd., Kashmere Gate, Delhi 110006 India. Fiction Editor: Sudhir Malhotra. Publishes 25 titles/year. "We are a large multilingual publishing house publishing fiction and other trade books." Pays royalties. "A brief synopsis should be submitted initially. Subsequently, upon hearing from the editor, a typescript may be sent."

WALKER BOOKS/JULIA MACRAE BOOKS/NICK HERN BOOKS, 87 Vauxhall Walk, London SE11 5HJ England. Editors: Julia MacRae, Delia Huddy, Nick Hern, Anne Carter, David Lloyd, Wendy Boase, Caroline Royds. Publishes 150 new titles annually. "Walker Books: Children's, board books, picture books, junior fiction, teenage fiction. Julia MacRae Books: picture books, junior fiction, teenage fiction, music and general adult books." Nick Hern Books: theatre, plays and literary books. Writers are paid by royalties. "Walker Books/Julia MacRae Books welcome manuscripts and reply to all letters regarding potential authors. Please send typed manuscripts to the editorial secretary."

WEIDENFELD AND NICOLSON LTD., 91, Clapham High St., London SW4 7TA England. Fiction Editors: Allegra Huston, Malcolm Gerratt. Publishes approx. 30 titles/year. "We are an independent publisher with a well established fiction list. Authors include, or have included, V. Nabokov, J.G. Farrell, Olivia Manning, Edna O'Brien, Margaret Drabble, Richard Powers, John Hersey, Penelope Gilliatt, Charlotte Vale Allen. We publish literary and commercial fiction: sagas, historicals, crime." Pays by advance. Royalties are set against advances. "Send a covering letter, a detailed synopsis and some sample pages such as the first chapter. Do not send the whole typescript unless invited. Please enclose return postage if possible and retain photocopies of all material sent."

THE WOMEN'S PRESS, 34 Great Suton St., London EC1V 0DX England. Publishes approx. 50 titles/year. "Women's fiction, written by women. Centered on women. Theme can be anything – all themes may be women's concern – but we look for political/feminist awareness, originality, wit: fiction of ideas. Includes genre fiction sf, crime, and teenage list *Livewire*." Writers receive royalty, including advance. Writers should ask themselves, "is this a manuscript which would interest a feminist/political press?

Other commercial publishers

The following commercial publishers appeared in the 1989 edition of *Novel and Short Story Writer's Market* but do not appear in the 1990 edition. Those listings that did not respond to our request for an update are listed without further explanation below. There are several reasons why a publisher did not return an update—they could be overstocked, no longer taking fiction or have been recently sold. If a reason for the omission is known, it is included next to the publisher's name. Additional foreign commercial publishers appear at the end of the list.

Antioch Children's Press (no longer open to outside submissions)
Augsburg Publishing House (requested to be deleted)
Avalon Books
Bart Books (out of business)
Blackthorne Publishing (requested to be deleted)
Bogie's Mystery Books (out of business)
Bridge Publishing Inc.
Carolrhoda Books (requested to be deleted)
David C. Cook Publishing (requested to be removed for one year)
Critic's Choice Paperbacks (out of business)
Dodd, Mead and Company (out of business)
Greenleaf Classics, Inc. (out of business)
Harper & Row Publishers (requested to be deleted)
Keepsake (line no longer published)
Mercury House
Modern Publishing
New Readers Press (requested to be removed for one year)
Oddo Publishing Co. (requested to be deleted)
Omeiga Books (out of business)
Pageant Books (out of business)
Paperjacks Books (out of business)
Random House/Juvenile Div. (requested to be deleted)
Richardson & Steirman (out of business)
Seal Books (Toronto) (requested to be deleted)
Second Chance at Love (line no longer published)
Silver Arrow Books (line no longer published)
Starblaze Editions (requested to be deleted)
Lyle Stuart/Irma Heldsman Books (sold)
Sweet Dreams (line no longer published)
TAB Book Club
Viking Penguin Inc. (requested to be removed for one year)
West End Games of Pennsylvania

Other foreign commercial publishers

The Bodley Head (out of business)
Marion Boyars Publishers Inc.
Nioba Uitgevers
Peter Owen Ltd.
Pagoda Books
Pandora Press
Rajpal & Sons
Sphere Books
Virago Press

Contests and Awards

In a way, formal competitions seem to lurk in the shadows of the publishing industry. Even in this book the section dealing with contests and awards is next to last. However, the old cliché' "last but not least" does hold a certain verisimilitude. True, periodicals and publishers are the most likely recipients of your fresh short stories or novels, but these contests should be viewed as a gold mine just waiting to be discovered!

This year we have nearly 300 contests, awards, fellowships and grants in this section. Approximately 60 of these are new listings. As if the prestige of winning one of these competitions isn't enough, the extra "icing on the cake" includes the monetary awards most of them offer. Some offer hundreds, even thousands of dollars.

For those writers considering competitions as an option, keep in mind all are not alike. There are contests for almost every type of fiction, whether it be short stories, novellas or novels.

Many little and literary periodicals consider only those works previously published in their magazines. Therefore, entering a short story contest could be as simple as having a short story published. Other magazines don't necessarily consider previous submissions, but rather solicit entries specifically for the contest and then offer publication as part of the prize. With little and literary publications, the amounts of the financial awards vary. First prize for the *Story Time* Short Story Contest is $15. *Gestalt*, *Greensboro Review* and *Black Ice* offer prizes of $100, $250 and $500 respectively. Of course, more prestigious publications are more likely to offer greater amounts of money. For example, the *Paris Review* awards $1,000 to the recipient of its Aga Khan Prize.

State arts councils and state-affiliated organizations, seeking to promote the literary arts in their state, offer contests, fellowships and grant programs that can run into the thousands of dollars. Pay close attention to the regional citizenship prerequisites required by these type of organizations. Wyoming, Tennessee, Illinois, Idaho, Connecticut, California and Alaska are a few of the states found in this section. University presses and private and literary organizations are also excellent contest sources.

Fellowships, residencies and grants provide money, time and sometimes living accommodations to chosen writers. Compensation packages usually run anywhere from $2,000 to $25,000. Some very elite fellowships can go higher. An example is Princeton's Alfred Hodder fellowship, which offers a total package worth $34,000.

Choosing and submitting

Note the coding scale in this section. Some contests are open to previously unpublished submissions, some to published works only and some to both. If the particular contest accepts previously published writing, be sure to check out the acceptable publication dates. Be aware of competitions that only accept submissions from a nominating body rather than the actual author. Nominating bodies can be teachers, publishers or a contest sponsor's own ad-hoc committee. The type of nominating body varies depending on each contest.

Obtaining a copy of the contest's submission requirements is a must. Chances are there are entry forms to be filled out and entry fees to be paid. For the most part, entry fees range from $5 to $25, more or less. Be wary of entry fees that seem high, especially if they are closely proportional to the actual prize offered (i.e., a $10 fee for a $25 award).

Finally, if submitting outside the United States, remember those International Reply Coupons (IRCs). Otherwise, it's unlikely the manuscript will be returned. SASE's mailed outside the United States are useless to those in foreign countries, even Canada. IRCs are as close as the local post office for 95 cents each.

Coding system for contests and awards

The Roman numeral coding system in this section is different from that used in other parts of the book. A new or unpublished writer is eligible to enter those contests ranked I (and some IVs), while a writer with a published (usually including self-published) book may enter most contests ranked I and II (and again, some IVs). Entrants for contests ranked III must be nominated by someone who is not the writer.

I Contest for unpublished fiction, usually open to both new and experienced writers;
II Contest for published (usually including self-published) fiction, which may be entered by the author;
III Contest for published fiction, which must be nominated by an editor, publisher or other nominating body;
IV Contest limited to residents of a certain region, of a certain age or to writing on certain themes or subjects.

ACT 1 CREATIVITY CENTER FELLOWSHIPS (I), ACTS Institute, Inc., Box 10153, Kansas City MO 64111. (816)753-0208 or (816)753-0383. Contact: Charlotte Plotsky. Award: Residency at the ACT 1 Writers/Artists Colony at the ACT 1 Creativity Center, Lake of the Ozarks, MO. Receives approx. 25 applications/year. Judge: "a professional." Application fee $10. No deadlines—open admissions policy. Send SASE for kit.

***AIM MAGAZINE* SHORT STORY CONTEST (I),** Box 20554, Chicago IL 60619. (312)874-6184. Contact: Ruth Apilado and Mark Boone, publisher and fiction editor. Estab. 1984. Contest likely to be offered annually if money is available. "To encourage and reward good writing in the short story form. The contest is particularly for new writers." Unpublished submissions. Award: $100 plus publication in fall issue. "Judged by *Aim*'s editorial staff." Contest rules for SASE. "We're looking for compelling, well-written stories with lasting social significance." Sample copy $3.50.

ALABAMA STATE COUNCIL ON THE ARTS INDIVIDUAL ARTIST FELLOWSHIP (II, IV), #1 Dexter Ave., Montgomery AL 36130. (205)261-4076. Randy Shoults. "To provide assistance to an individual artist." Annual grant/fellowship. Award: $2,500 and $5,000 grants. Competition receives approximately 30 submissions annually. Judges: independent peer panel. Entry forms or rules for SASE. Deadline: May 1. Two-year Alabama residency required.

ALASKA STATE COUNCIL ON THE ARTS LITERARY ARTS FELLOWSHIPS (I, IV), Alaska State Council on the Arts, 619 Warehouse Ave., #220, Anchorage AK 99501-1682. (907)279-1558. Contact: Christine D'Arcy. "Open-ended grant award, non-matching, to enable creative writers to advance their careers as they see it." Biannual competition for stort stories and novels. Award: $5,000 per writer. Competition receives approx. 45 submissions. Judges: panel of Alaskan writers. Next award offered in October. "Alaskan writers only are eligible to apply."

EDWARD F. ALBEE FOUNDATION FELLOWSHIP (I), Edward F. Albee Foundation, Inc., 14 Harrison St., New York NY 10013. (212)266-2020. Provides one-month residencies for writers and artists at the William Flanagan Memorial Creative Persons Center (better known as "The Barn") in Montauk, on Long Island, New York. 24 residencies per year, June-September. Award for writers of fiction, nonfiction, poetry and plays. Judges: several writers. Applications are accepted from January 1 through April 1. Write for official guidelines.

THE ALBERTA WRITING FOR YOUNG PEOPLE COMPETITION (I, IV), Alberta Culture and Multiculturalism in cooperation with Doubleday Canada Ltd. and Allarcom/Superchannel. 12th Floor, CN Tower, 10004-104 Avenue, Edmonton, Alberta T5J 0K5 Canada. Contact: Ruth Bertelsen Fraser, director. Bienniel award (even years). The competition is designed to direct Alberta's writers to the

The double dagger before a listing indicates that the listing is new in this edition.

challenging world of writing for juveniles. Unpublished submissions. Entry deadline: Dec. 31. The competition brochure and/or further information will be sent upon request. Award: $4,500 prize; an outright award of $2,000 from Alberta Culture and Multiculturalism, a $1,000 advance against royalties from Doubleday Canada Ltd. and a $1,500 12-month option for motion picture/television rights from Allarcom/Superchannel. "We have 2 categories: book mss for young adults (up to age 16) averaging 40,000 words in length; and book mss suitable for younger readers (8-12 years) running between 12,000 and 20,000 words."

THE NELSON ALGREN AWARD FOR SHORT FICTION (I), *Chicago Tribune*, 435 N. Michigan Ave., Chicago IL 60611. (312)222-3232. Annual award. To recognize an outstanding, unpublished short story, minimum 2,500 words; maximum 10,000 words. Awards: $5,000 first prize; three runners-up receive $1,000 awards. Publication of four winning stories in the *Chicago Tribune*. Deadline: Entries are accepted only from November 30-January 1. No entry fee. A poster bearing the rules of the contest will be sent to writers who inquire in writing.

‡*ALLEGHENY REVIEW* AWARDS (I), Box 32, Allegheny College, Meadville PA 16335. Contact: Nancy Williams or Erik Schuckers, editors. Annually. Award for unpublished short stories. U.S. undergraduate students only. Deadline: January 31. SASE for rules.

‡AMBERGRIS FICTION AND POETRY CONTEST (I,IV), *Ambergris* Magazine, Box 29919, Cincinnati OH 45229. Contact: Mark Kissling. Award "to promote and reward excellence in fiction and poetry writing." Annual competition for short stories and poetry. Award: $50 first prize. Competition receives 150-200 mss/contest. Judges: editorial staff. Guidelines for SASE. Deadline is December 1. Previously unpublished submissions. "We give special but not exclusive consideration to works by Ohio writers or about the midwest in general. We prefer works under 5,000 words. Writers may want to review *Ambergris* #5 for results of second annual fiction and poetry contest. Sample for $3."

***AMELIA MAGAZINE* AWARDS (I),** The Reed Smith Fiction Prize; The Willie Lee Martin Short Story Award; The Cassie Wade Short Fiction Award; The Patrick T. T. Bradshaw Fiction Award; and four annual genre awards in science fiction, romance, western and fantasy/horror. 329 "E" St., Bakersfield CA 93303. (805)323-4064. Contact: Frederick A. Raborg, Jr., editor. Estab. 1984. Annually. "To publish the finest fiction possible and reward the writer; to allow good writers to earn some money in small press publication. *Amelia* strives to fill that gap between major circulation magazines and quality university journals." Unpublished submissions. Length: The Reed Smith—3,500-5,000 words; The Willie Lee Martin—3,500-5,000 words, The Cassie Wade—3,500 words; The Patrick T. T. Bradshaw—25,000 words; the genre awards—science fiction, 5,000 words; romance, 3,000 words; western, 5,000 words; fantasy/horror, 5,000 words. Award: "Each prize consists of $200 plus publication and two contributor's copies of issue containing winner's work. The Reed Smith Fiction Prize offers two additional awards of $100 and $50, and publication; Bradshaw Book Award: $300 plus publication, 2 copies. Deadline: The Reed Smith Prize—September 1; The Willie Lee Martin—March 1; The Cassie Wade—June 1; The Patrick T. T. Bradshaw—February 15; Amelia fantasy/horror—February 1; Amelia western—April 1; Amelia romance—October 1; Amelia science fiction—December 15. Entry fee: $5. Bradshaw Award fee: $10. Contest rules for SASE. Looking for "high quality work equal to finest fiction being published today."

***AMERICAN FICTION VOL II* (I),** Birch Lane Press/American Fiction, English Dept., Springfield College, 263 Alden St., Springfield MA 01109. (413)788-3254. Editors: Michael C. White and Alan Davis. To "recognize unpublished stories by both *known* and *unknown* writers." Annual competition for short stories. Award: $1,000 first prize; $500 second; $250 third, publication, 2 copies. Competition received 650 submissions in 1989. Entry fee: $7.50. Deadline: April 1. Guidelines in *AWP Newsletter* and in *Poets and Writers*. Unpublished submissions. 10,000 word limit.

***AMERICAN HEALTH* BODY STORY CONTEST (I),** *American Health* Magazine, 80 Fifth Ave., New York NY 10011. (212)242-2460. Body Story Editor: Erica Franklin. Annual award for unpublished short stories. Award: $2,000 and publication in *American Health*. Receives approximately 700 entries for each award. Judge: Mark Haris. Entry guidelines for SASE. Deadline: September 1. "For the best account—fact or fiction—of an intense physical experience. A detailed story is not enough. We're looking for creative writers who can capture the body's triumphs and trials with imagination, sensitivity, style and humor."

SHERWOOD ANDERSON SHORT FICTION PRIZE (I), *Mid-American Review*, Dept. of English, Bowling Green State University, Bowling Green OH 43403. (419)372-2725. Contact: Robert Early, fiction editor. Award frequency is subject to availability of funds. "To encourage the writer of quality short fiction." Unpublished material. No deadline. No entry fee. "Winners are selected from stories published by the magazine, so submission for publication is the first step."

CHARLES ANGOFF AWARDS (I), *The Literary Review*, Fairleigh Dickinson University, Madison NJ 07940. (201)593-8564. Walter Cummins, editor-in-chief. "To recognize the 4 or 5 best contributions of each volume year." Annual award for short stories, poetry or essays. Cash award. Judges are the *Review*'s editors and advisory board. Prerequisite to consideration: publication in *TLR* during a volume year.

‡*ANTIETAM REVIEW* LITERARY AWARD (I, IV), *Antietam Review*, 82 W. Washington St., Hagerstown MD 21740. (301)791-3125. Contact: Ann B. Knox, editor. Annual award, to encourage and give recognition to excellence in short fiction. Open to writers from Maryland, Pennsylvania, Virginia, West Virginia and Washington DC. "We consider only previously unpublished work. We read manuscripts between October 1 and March 1." Award: $100 plus $100 for the story; the story is printed as lead in the magazine. "We consider all fiction mss sent to *Antietam Review* as entries for the prize. We look for well crafted, serious literary prose fiction under 5,000 words."

ARIZONA AUTHORS' ASSOCIATION ANNUAL LITERARY CONTEST (I), Annual Literary Contest, 3509 E. Shea Blvd., Suite 117, Phoenix AZ 85028. (602)996-9706. Contact: Velma Cooper. Estab. 1981. Annually. "To encourage AAA members and all other writers in the country to discipline themselves to write regularly, steadily for competition and publication." Unpublished submissions. Award: "Cash prizes totalling $1,000 for winners and honorable mentions in short stories, essays and poetry. Winning entries are published in the *Arizona Literary Magazine*." Deadline: July 29. Entry fee: $4 for poetry, $6 for essays and short stories. Contest rules for SASE. Looking for "strong concept; good, effective writing, with emphasis on the subject/story."

ARIZONA COMMISSION ON THE ARTS CREATIVE WRITING FELLOWSHIPS (I,IV), 417 West Roosevelt St., Phoenix AZ 85003. (602)255-5882. Public Information Officer: Tonda Gorton. Fellowships awarded in alternate years to fiction writers and poets. Four awards of $5,000-7,500. Judges: out-of-state writers/editors. Next deadline for fiction writers: 1991. Arizona poets and writers over 18 years of age only.

ASF TRANSLATION PRIZE (I, IV), American-Scandinavian Foundation, 127 E. 73rd St., New York NY 10021. Contact: Publishing office. Estab. 1980. Annual award. Competition includes submissions of poetry, drama, literary prose and fiction translations. To encourage the translation and publication of the best of contemporary Scandinavian poetry and fiction and to make it available to a wider American audience. Submissions must have been previously published in the original Scandinavian language. No previously translated material. Original authors should have been born within past 100 years. Deadline for entry: June 1. Competition rules and entry forms available with SASE. Award: $1,000, a bronze medallion and publication in *Scandinavian Review*.

THE ATHENAEUM LITERARY AWARD (II, IV), The Athenaeum of Philadelphia, 219 S. 6th St., Philadelphia PA 19106. Contact: Literary Award Committee. Annual award. To recognize and encourage outstanding literary achievement in Philadelphia and its vicinity. Submissions must have been published during the preceding year. Deadline: December. Nominations shall be made in writing to the Literary Award Committee by the author, the publisher or a member of the Athenaeum, accompanied by a copy of the book. Judged by committee appointed by Board of Directors. Award: A bronze medal bearing the name of the award, the seal of the Athenaeum, the title of the book, the name of the author and the year. The Athenaeum Literary Award is granted for a work of general literature, not exclusively for fiction. Juvenile fiction is not included.

AVON FLARE YOUNG ADULT NOVEL COMPETITION (I, IV), *Avon Books*, 105 Madison Ave., New York NY 10016. (212)481-5609. Ellen E. Krieger, Editorial Director, Books for Young Readers. "To discover, encourage, and develop young writing talent." Biannual award for novels "about 30,000 to 50,000 words." Award: Publication of the novel under the Avon/Flare imprint for an advance against royalties. Competition receives approximately 400-500 submissions annually. Judges are the Avon editorial staff. Entry forms or rules for SASE. Deadline August 31, 1991. Contest restricted to writers who were no younger than 12 and no older than 18 years of age as of December 31, 1990. With your manuscript include letter with your name, address, telephone number, age and short description of your novel."

AWP AWARD SERIES IN SHORT FICTION (I), The Associated Writing Programs, c/o Old Dominion University, Norfolk VA 23508. Annual award. The AWP Award Series was established in cooperation with several university presses in order to make quality short fiction available to a wide audience. Only book-length manuscripts are eligible. Manuscripts previously published in their entirety, including self-publishing, are not eligible. Submissions dates: manuscripts postmarked between January 1-February 29. Awards judged by distinguished writers in each genre. Contest/award rules and entry forms available for SASE. Award: The winning manuscript in short fiction is published by the University of Missouri Press. Carries a $1,000 honorarium. $10 submission fee with ms.

AWP AWARD SERIES IN THE NOVEL (I), The Associated Writing Programs, c/o Old Dominion University, Norfolk VA 23529-0079. Annual award. The AWP Award Series was established in cooperation with several university presses in order to publish and make fine fiction available to a wide audience. Only book-length manuscripts are eligible. Manuscripts previously published in their entirety, including self-publishing, are not eligible. Submission dates: manuscript postmarked between January 1-February 29. Awards judged by distinguished writers in each genre. Contest/award rules available for SASE. Carries a $1,000 honorarium and publication with a university press. In addition, AWP tries to place mss of finalists with participating presses. $10 submission fee with ms.

‡BANFF WRITING RESIDENCY (I), The Banff Centre for Continuing Education, Box 1020, Banff, Alberta T0L 0C0 Canada. (403)762-6186. Writing residency. Annual competition for short stories, novels, story collections and poetry. Competition receives over 100 applicants for 20 residencies. Judges: Faculty of Writing. Entry fee $35 (Canadian Funds). Guidelines for SASE. Deadline: January 14.

MILDRED L. BATCHELDER AWARD (II), Association for Library Service to Children/American Library Association, 50 E. Huron St., Chicago IL 60611. (312)944-6780. To encourage international exchange of quality children's books by recognizing U.S. publishers of such books in translation. Annual competition for translations. Award: citation. Judge: Mildred L. Batchelder award committee. Guidelines for SASE. Deadline: December. Books should be U.S. trade publications for which children, up to and including age 14 are potential audience.

H.E. BATES SHORT STORY COMPETITION (I), Northampton Borough Council, Bedford Rd., Northampton England. Contact: Leisure Manager. "An arts service." Annual competition for short stories. Award: £100. Competition receives approx. 200 submissions. Entry fee £1.20. Guidelines for SASE. Deadline: August. Word length: 2,000 words.

BELLAGIO CENTER RESIDENCY (I), Rockefeller Foundation, 1133 Avenue of the Americas, New York NY 10036. (212)869-8500. Manager: Susan E. Garfield. Award 4- to 5-week residency in northern Italy for scholars and artists (including writers). Residencies for authors of short stories, novels and story collections. Judges: committee of Foundation officers. Guidelines for SASE. Writers should submit applications 1 year prior to preferred dates. "Competition is most intense for May through September. Each scholar or artist is provided with a private room and a bath, and with a study in which to work. At dinner and over aperitivi, scholars in residence have the opportunity to meet participants in international conferences that are scheduled concurrently. The Foundation does not provide financial assistance to scholars in residence, nor does it contribute ordinarily to travel expenses. Write for application."

GEORGE BENNETT FELLOWSHIP (I), Phillips Exeter Academy, Exeter NH 03833. (603)772-4311. Coordinator, Selection Committee: Charles Pratt. "To provide time and freedom from monetary concerns to a person contemplating or pursuing a career as a professional writer." Annual award for writing residency. Award: A stipend ($5,000 at present), plus room and board for academic year. Competition receives approximately 100 submissions. Judges are a committee of the English department. Entry fee $5. SASE for application form and guidelines. Deadline: December 1.

‡"BEST FIRST PRIVATE EYE NOVEL" CONTEST (I, IV), Private Eye Writers of America, St. Martin's Press and Macmillan London Ltd., Thomas Dunne Books, 175 Fifth Ave., New York NY 10010. To publish a writer's first "private eye" novel. Annual award for novels. Award: Publication of novel by

Read the Business of Fiction section to learn the correct way to prepare and submit a manuscript.

St. Martin's Press in the US and Macmillan London in the UK. Advance: $10,000 against royalties (standard contract). Judges are selected by sponsors. Guidelines for SASE. Deadline: September 30. Unpublished submissions. "Open to any professional or non-professional writer who has never written a 'private eye' novel and who is not under contract with a publisher for the publication of a 'private eye' novel. As used in the rules, private eye novel means: a novel in which the main character is an independent investigator who is not a member of any law enforcement or government agency."

BEST OF BLURBS CONTEST (I), Writer's Refinery, Box 47786, Phoenix AZ 85068-7786. (602)944-5268. President: Libbi Goodman. "Compose a blurb for the back cover of a hypothetical novel. It's the blurb that sells the book, so write in your most dramatic and exciting style. Who knows, you may want to write what's between the covers as well." Annual award for blurbs for novels. Award: Engraved wall plaque/certificate of merit. Judges are a panel of professional writers. Entry forms for SASE. Deadline: September 30. No entry fee.

‡BEST OF HOUSEWIFE-WRITER'S FORUM: SHORT STORY REJECTED BY REDBOOK (OR ANY LARGE MARKET) (I), Housewife-Writer's Forum, P.O. Drawer 1518, Lafayette CA 94549. (415)932-1143. "To find the best short story rejected by a major market. The story need *not* be 'perfect' for the market; it just needs to be a good story." Annual competition for short stories. Award: $20 (1st prize), $10 (2nd prize), $5 (3rd prize). Plus publication of the first place winner, plus more money if proceeds exceed expenses. (See guidelines.) Judges: Deborah and Rob Haeseler, plus volunteers. Entry fee $4 nonsubscribers/$3 subscribers. Guidelines for SASE. Deadline: December 15. Unpublished submissions. Word length: 2,000 word limit. "We also have 6 additional categories in the contest, all separate but with a common deadline." (See guidelines.)

IRMA SIMONTON BLACK CHILDREN'S BOOK AWARD (II), Bank Street College, 610 W. 112th St., New York NY 10025. (212)663-7200, ext. 254. Publications Director: Williams Hooks. Annual award. "To honor the young children's book published in the preceding year judged the most outstanding in text as well as in art. Book must be published the year preceding the May award." Award: Press luncheon at Harvard Club, a scroll and seals by Maurice Sendak for attaching to award book's run. Entry deadline: January 15. No entry fee. "Write to address above. Usually publishers submit books they want considered, but individuals can too. No entries are returned."

***BLACK ICE* MARGARET JONES FICTION AWARD (I)**, *Black Ice*, English Dept. Publications Center, Campus Box 494, Boulder CO 80309-0494. Editor: Ron Sukenick. Associate Editor: Dallas Wiebe. Assistant Editor: Mark Amerika. "Award to recognize best story in each issue of *Black Ice*. Emphasis is on nontraditional fiction." One award per issue. Competition for short stories. Award: $500. Receives approximately 1,500 entries for each award. Judges: The editors. "Stories are to be submitted for publication in *Black Ice*. From the stories published, the prize is awarded."

JAMES TAIT BLACK MEMORIAL PRIZES (III, IV), Department of English Literature, University of Edinburgh, Edinburgh EH8 9JX Scotland. Contact: Professor R.D.S. Jack. "Two prizes are awarded: one for the best work of fiction, one for the best biography or work of that nature, published during the calendar year." Annual competition for short stories, novels and story collections. Award: £1,500 each. Competition receives approx. 100 submissions. Judge: Professor R.D.S. Jack, Chairman, Dept. of English Literature. Guidelines for SASE. Deadline: December 31. Previously published submissions. "Eligible works are those written in English, originating with a British publisher, and first published in Britain in the year of the award. Works should be submitted by publishers."

***THE BLACK WARRIOR REVIEW* LITERARY AWARD (II, III)**, Box 2936, Tuscaloosa AL 35486. (205)348-4518. Editor: Mark Dawson. "Award is to recognize the best fiction published in *BWR* in a volume year." Competition is for short stories and novel chapters. Award: $500. Competition receives approximately 1,500 submissions. Prize awarded by an outside judge. SASE.

BOARDMAN TASKER PRIZE (III, IV), 56 St. Michael's Ave., Bramhall, Stockport, Cheshire SK7 2PL United Kingdom. Contact: Mrs. D. Boardman. "To reward a book which has made an outstanding contribution to mountain literature. A memorial to Peter Boardman and Joe Tasker, who disappeared on Everest in 1982." Award: £1,000. Competition receives approx. 15 submissions. Judges: a panel of 3 judges elected by trustees. Guidelines for SASE. Deadline: August 1. Previously published submissions. Limited to works published or distributed in the UK for the first time between November 1, 1989 and October 31, 1990. Publisher's entry only. "May be fiction, nonfiction, poetry or drama. Not an anthology. The prize is not primarily for fiction though that is not excluded. Subject must be concerned with mountain environment. Previous winners have been books on expeditions, Himalayan experiences, a biography of a mountaineer."

BOOTS ROMANTIC NOVEL OF THE YEAR (II, IV), Dove House Farm, Potter Heigham, Norfolk NR29 5LJ England. Contact: Olga Sinclair, Award Organiser, Romantic Novelists' Association. "To publish good romantic fiction and therefore raise the prestige of the genre." Annual competition for novels. Award £5,000. Competition receives approx. 100 submissions. Judges: a panel of experienced writers. Deadline: September 1-December 15. Previously published submissions. For novels "published in the U.K. only." A modern or historical (before 1950) romantic novel. "Three copies of each entry are required. They may be hardback or paperback. Only novels written in English and published in the U.K. during the relevant year are eligible. Authors must be domiciled in UK or temporarily living abroad whilst in possession of British passport."

***BOSTON GLOBE*-HORN BOOK AWARDS (II)**, *Boston Globe* Newspaper, Horn Book Awards, *Horn Book* Magazine, 14 Beacon St., Boston MA 02108. Annual award. "To honor most outstanding children's fiction, picture and nonfiction books published within the U.S." Previously published material from July 1-June 30 of following year. Award: $500 first prize in each category; silver plate for the 2 honor books in each category. Entry deadline: May 1. No entry fee. Entry forms or rules for SASE.

‡BRANDEIS UNIVERSITY CREATIVE ARTS AWARDS (III), Brandeis University, Gryzmish 201, Waltham MA 02254-9110. (617)736-4400. Special Assistants to the President: Mary R. Anderson and Suzanne Yates. Awards "medal to an established artist in celebration of a lifetime of achievement, and a citation to an individual in an earlier stage of his or her career. From time to time the Creative Arts Awards Commission bestows the Notable Achievement Award, when in the Commission's judgment there is someone whose accomplishments so transcend the normal categories that special recognition is due." Awards are made by internal selection only.

THE F.G. BRESSANI PRIZE (II, IV), Italian Cultural Centre Society, 3075 Slocan Street, Vancouver, B.C. V5M 3E4 Canada. (604)430-3337. Contact: The Literary Committee. Prize "to promote excellence in writing from an ethnic minority viewpoint, to increase appreciation and understanding of Canada's cultural diversity, and to honour an important historical figure F.G. Bressani, the first Italian missionary in Canada." Award granted biannually. Competition for novels and story collections. Award: $500 in prose and poetry categories. Also offers prizes fo $250 each for prose and poetry books written in Italian. (Prizes awarded in cooperation with the Istituto Italiano de Cultura.) Judges: "knowledgeable people in our community." Guidelines for SASE. Deadline: August 1990. Published submissions. Prize "available to Canadian citizens or landed immigrants to Canada. Books must be written from a viewpoint of any of Canada's ethnic minority groups." Books published from July 1, 1988 to June 30, 1990.

BUMBERSHOOT WRITTEN WORKS COMPETITION (I), Seattle's Arts Festival, Box 9750, Seattle WA 98109-0750. (206)622-5123. Contact: Judith Roche. Annual award for short stories. Award: Six awards of $150 for poetry or literary prose. Winners published in Bumbershoot arts magazine, *Ergo*! Judges are professional writers/publishers/literary bookshop managers. Entry forms or rules for SASE. Deadline: mid-April.

BUNTING INSTITUTE FELLOWSHIP (I), Mary Ingraham Bunting Institute of Radcliffe College, 34 Concord Ave., Cambridge MA 02138. (617)495-8212. "Fellowship programs are designed to support women who wish to pursue independent study in academic and professional fields, and in the creative arts. Applications will be judged on the significance and quality of the project proposal, and on the difference the fellowship might make in the applicant's career." Annual award for creative writing. Award: $20,500 for one year. Competition receives 600 total applicant pool. Judges: distinguished academics and professionals from a variety of disciplines. Entry fee $35. Guidelines for SASE. Deadline: October. Previously published or unpublished submissions. "Office or studio space, auditing privileges and access to libraries and other resources of Radcliffe College and Harvard University are provided. Residence in the Boston area and participation in the Institute community are required during the fellowship appointment. Fellows are expected to present their work in progress at public colloquia. Women scholars, professionals, creative writers and musicians, with receipt of doctorate or appropriate terminal degree at least two years prior to appointment, or with equivalent professional experience (i.e., publication, group or solo show) are eligible."

BUSH ARTIST FELLOWSHIPS (I, IV), The Bush Foundation, E-900 First Nat'l Bank Building, St. Paul MN 55101. (612)227-5222. Contact: Sally Dixon, program director. To provide artists of exceptional talent time to work in their chosen art forms. Annual grant. Award: Stipend maximum of $26,000 for 6-18 months, plus a production and travel allowance of $7,000. Competition receives approximately 400 submissions. Judges are writers, critics and editors from outside MN, SD, ND or WI. SASE. Applicants must be at least 25 years old, and Minnesota, South Dakota, North Dakota and Western Wisconsin residents for 12 of 36 months preceding deadline. Students not eligible.

***BYLINE* MAGAZINE LITERARY AWARDS (I,IV)**, Box 130596, Edmond OK 73013. (405)348-3325. Exec. editor/publisher: Marcia Preston. "To encourage our subscribers in striving for high quality writing." Annual award for short stories. Award: $250 cash in each category—fiction and poetry. Judges are published writers not on the *Byline* staff. Entry fee $5 for stories; $2 for poems. Postmark Deadline: December 1. "Entries should be unpublished and not have won money in any previous contest. Winners announced in February issue and published in March issue with photo and short bio. Open to subscribers only."

CALIFORNIA WRITERS' ROUNDTABLE ANNUAL WRITING CONTESTS (I), The Los Angeles Chapter, Women's National Book Association, 11684 Ventura Blvd., Suite 807, Studio City CA 91604-2652. Contact: Lou Carter Keay. Annual competition for short stories. Award: $150 first prize; $75 second prize; $25 third prize. Entry fee $5 to nonmembers of Women's National Book Association. Guidelines for SASE. Deadline: September 30, 1990. Previously unpublished submissions. 3,000 word limit. "Manuscripts must be typed, on standard paper, 8½x11 inches. Margins of one inch on all sides. The title of short story must appear on each page, all pages numbered. Send 3 copies of the short story. Include a small envelope with a card containing the author's name, address and phone number, along with the title of short story. Do not put the name of author on the manuscript itself. If you wish one copy of your manuscript returned, include a SASE."

JOHN W. CAMPBELL MEMORIAL AWARD FOR THE BEST SCIENCE-FICTION NOVEL OF THE YEAR; THEODORE STURGEON MEMORIAL AWARD FOR THE BEST SF SHORT FICTION (II, III), Center for the Study of Science Fiction, English Dept., University of Kansas, Lawrence KS 66045. (913)864-3380. Professor and Director: James Gunn. "To honor the best novel and short science fiction of the year." Annual competition for short stories and novels. Award: Engraved trophy and a certificate. Competition receives approx. 50-100 submissions. Judges: two separate juries. Deadline: May 1. For previously published submissions. "Ordinarily publishers should submit work, but authors have done so when publishers would not. Send for list of jurors."

CANADA COUNCIL GOVERNOR GENERAL'S LITERARY AWARDS (IV), Canada Council, Box 1047, 99 Metcalfe St., Ottawa, Ontario K1P 5V8 Canada. (613)598-4365. Contact: writing and publishing section. "Awards of $10,000 each are given annually to the best English-language and best French-language Canadian work in each of the six categories: children's literature (text and illustration), drama, fiction, poetry, nonfiction and translation."All literary works published by Canadians during the preceding year are considered. Canadian authors, illustrators and translators only.

‡CANADIAN AUTHOR & BOOKMAN STUDENT'S CREATIVE WRITING CONTEST, 121 Avenue Rd., #104, Toronto, Ontario M5R 2G3 Canada. (416)926-8089. "To encourage writing among secondary school students." Annual competition for short stories. Award: $100 plus $100 to the nominating teacher; $500 to pay for undergraduate education to a worthy student enrolled at a college. Receives 100-120 submissions. Judge: Magazine editor. "Must buy copy of magazine to get entry form." Deadline: March. Previously unpublished submissions. Word length: 2,500 words. Writer must be nominated by teacher.

CANADIAN AUTHORS ASSOCIATION LITERARY AWARD (FICTION) (II, IV), Canadian Authors Association, Suite 104, 121 Avenue Road, Toronto M5R 2G3 Ontario, Canada. (416)926-8084. Contact: Executive Director. Annual award. "To honor writing that achieves literary excellence without sacrificing popular appeal." For novels published during the previous calendar year. Award: $5,000 plus silver medal. Entry deadline: December 31. No entry fee. Entry forms or rules for SASE. Restricted to full-length novels. Author must be Canadian or Canadian landed immigrant. CAA also sponsors the Air Canada Award, literary awards as above in poetry, nonfiction and drama, and the Vicky Metcalf Awards for children's literature.

***CANADIAN FICTION MAGAZINE* CONTRIBUTOR'S PRIZE (IV)**, Box 946, Station F, Toronto, Ontario M4Y 2N9 Canada. Contact: Geoffrey Hancock, editor-in-chief. Annual award. To celebrate the best story published by *CFM* in either French or English during the preceding year. Contributors must reside in Canada or be Canadians living abroad. All manuscripts published in *CFM* are eligible. Deadline: August 15. Award: $500, public announcement, photograph. "Looking for contemporary creative writing of the highest possible literary standards."

CANADIAN LIBRARY ASSOCIATION BOOK OF THE YEAR FOR CHILDREN AWARD (III,IV), Canadian Library Association, 200 Elgin Street, Ottawa, Ontario K2P 1L5 Canada. (613)232-9625. To encourage the writing in Canada of good books for children up to and including age 14. Annual competition for short stories and novels for children. Award: a specially designed medal. Competition receives approx. 10-20 submissions/year. Judging: CLA Book of the Year Award Committee. Guidelines for SASE. Deadline Februrary 1, 1989. Book must have been published in Canada during the last year and its author must be Canadian citizen or a landed immigrant. Nominations are generally made by CLA membership—a call for nominations is posted in the Association's newsletter in October. "Although the award is sponsored by the Canadian Library Association, it is the Canadian Association of Children's Librarians (a section of Canadian Association of Public Libraries which in turn is a division of CLA) which staffs the Award Committee, selects the winner and administers the award."

RAYMOND CARVER SHORT STORY CONTEST (I), Dept. of English, Humboldt State University, Arcata CA 95521-4957. Contact: Coordinator. Annual award for previously unpublished short stories. First prize: $500 and publication in *Toyon 90*. Second Prize: $250. For authors living in United States only. Deadline: November. Entry fee $7.50 per story. SASE for rules. Send 2 copies of story; author's name, address, phone number and title of story on separate cover page only. Story must be no more than 25 pages. Title must appear on first page. For notification of receipt of ms, include self-addressed stamped postcard. For Winners List include SASE.

CCL STUDENT WRITING CONTEST (I,IV), Conference on Christianity and Literature. Dept. of English, Seattle Pacific University, Seattle WA 98119. Contact: Daniel Taylor, Dept. of English, Bethel College, 3900 Bethel Drive, St Paul MN 55112. Annual award. "To recognize excellence in undergraduate writing." Unpublished submissions. Award: $75, $50 and $25 awarded in book certificates. Deadline: February 15. Looking for "excellence in artistic achievement and reflection of writer's Christian premises." Contest open to all regularly enrolled undergraduate students. Entries will not be returned. Winners will be announced in summer issue of *Christianity and Literature*.

‡*THE CHATTAHOOCHEE* PRIZE (I), *The Chattahoochee Review*, 2101 Womack Rd., Dunwoody GA 30338. (404)393-3300. Contact: Lamar York, editor. Annual award. Short stories. "Prize winner is selected from contributions throughout the year to the *Chattahoochee Review*." Must be published in the *Review* during the year. No entry fee.

CHILD STUDY CHILDREN'S BOOK AWARD (III, IV), Child Study Children's Book Committee at Bank St. College, 610 W. 112th St., New York NY 10025. Contact: Anita Wilkes Dore, Committee Chair. Annual award. "To honor a book for children or young people which deals realistically with problems in their world. It may concern social, individual and ethical problems." Only books sent by publishers for review are considered. No personal submissions. Books must have been published within current calendar year. Award: Certificate and cash prize.

THE CHILDREN'S BOOK AWARD (II), Federation of Children's Book Groups, 22 Beacon Brow, Bradford W. Yorkshire BD6 3DE England. Award "to promote the publication of good quality books for children." Annual award for short stories, novels, story collections and translations. Award: "portfolio of children's writing and drawings and a magnificent trophy of silver and oak." Competition received 450 submissions in 1988. Judges: thousands of children from all over the United Kingdom. Guidelines for SASE. Deadline: December 31. Published and previously unpublished submissions (first publication in UK). "The book should be suitable for children up to 14 years of age."

THE CHRISTOPHER AWARD (II), The Christophers, 12 E. 48th St., New York NY 10017. Contact: Ms. Peggy Flanagan, awards coordinator. Annual award. "To encourage creative people to continue to produce works which affirm the highest values of the human spirit in adult and children's books." Published submissions only. "Award judged by a grassroots panel and a final panel of experts. Juvenile works are 'children tested.'" Award: Bronze medallion. Examples of books awarded: *Dear Mr. Henshaw*, by Beverly Cleary (ages 8-10); *Sarah, Plain and Tall* by Patricia MacLachlan (ages 10-12).

CINTAS FELLOWSHIP (I, IV), Cintas Foundation/Arts International Program of I.I.E., 809 U.N. Plaza, New York NY 10017. (212)984-5564. Contact: Rebecca A. Sayies. "To foster and encourage the professional development and recognition of talented Cuban creative artists. *Not* intended for furtherance of academic or professional study, nor for research or writings of a scholarly nature." Annual competition for authors of short stories, novels, story collections and poetry. 10 awards of $10,000 each. Fellowship receives approx. 40 literature applicants/year. Judges: selection committees. Guidelines for SASE. Deadline: March 1. Previously published or unpublished submissions. Limited to artists of Cuban lineage *only*. "Awards are given to artists in the following fields: visual arts, literature, music composition and architecture."

CITY OF REGINA WRITING AWARD (I, IV), City of Regina Arts Commission, Saskatchewan Writers Guild, Box 3986, Regina, Saskatchewan S4P 3R9 Canada. (306)757-6310. "To enable a writer to work for 3 months on a specific writing project; to reward merit in writing." Annual competition for short stories, novels and story collections. Award: $3,300. Competition receives approx. 21 submissions.

Judges: selection committee of SWG. Guidelines for SASE. Deadline: March. Unpublished submissions. "Grant available only to residents of Regina for previous year."

COLORADO COUNCIL ON THE ARTS & HUMANITIES CREATIVE FELLOWSHIP (I, II, IV), 770 Pennsylvania Street, Denver CO 80203. (303)866-2617. Director, Individual Artist Programs: Daniel Salazar. To provide both recognition and significant financial support to Colorado's outstanding individual artists and to provide a forum and secure an audience for the promotion of their work. Award presented on rotating basis (in 1992, 1995 and 1998). Award: 8 fellowships of $4,000 each. Competition receives 350 entries/year. Judges: peer panels. Guidelines available for SASE. For either previously published or unpublished manuscripts. Colorado residents only.

COMMONWEALTH CLUB OF CALIFORNIA (II, IV), California Book Awards, 595 Market St., San Francisco CA 94105. (415)543-3353. Contact: Michael J. Brassington, Executive Director. Main contest established in 1931. Annually. Purpose: "To encourage California writers and honor literary merit." Requirements: For books published during the year of the particular contest. Three copies of book and a completed entry form required. Awards: Gold and silver medals. Judged by jury of literary experts. "Write or phone asking for the forms. Either an author or publisher may enter a book. We usually receive over 200 entries."

CONNECTICUT COMMISSION ON THE ARTS ARTIST GRANTS (I, II, IV), 227 Lawrence St., Hartford CT 06106. (203)566-4770. Senior Program Associate: Linda Dente. To support the creation of new work by a creative artist *living in Connecticut*. Biannual competition for the creation or completion of new works in literature, i.e. short stories, novels, story collections, poetry and playwriting. Award: $5,000. Judges: peer professionals (writers, editors). Guidelines available in August. Deadline: January. Writers may send either previously published or unpublished submissions. Writers may submit up to 25 pages of material. Connecticut residents only.

CONNECTICUT WRITERS LEAGUE ANNUAL WRITING CONTEST (I), Box 10536, West Hartford CT 06110. Contact: Ruth Lucas, editor. Estab. 1982. Annual award. "To encourage writers. Winners are published in the annual magazine, *The Connecticut Writer*, produced by the Connecticut Writers League." Unpublished submissions. Award: "Recent prizes were $100 for 1st place in poetry and fiction; 2nd place, $75 each in above categories. A contest committee screens the manuscripts; final selections are made by judges outside the Connecticut Writers League. Interested persons should send for guidelines with SASE in the early spring." Entry fee: $3.

CONSEIL DE LA VIE FRANCAISE EN AMERÍQUE/PRIX CHAMPLAIN (The Champlain Prize) (II, IV), Conseil de la vie française en amérique, 56 rue St-Pierre 3e Étage, Québec, Québec Q1K 4A1 Canada. Prix Champlain estab. 1957. Annual award. To encourage literary work in novel or short story in French by Francophiles living outside Québec and in the US or Canada. "There is no restriction as to the subject matter. If the author lives in Quebec, the subject matter must be related to French-speaking people living outside of Quebec." For previously published or contracted submissions, published no more than 3 years prior to award. Deadline: December 31. Author must furnish 4 examples of work, curriculum vita, address and phone number. Judges: 3 different judges each year. Award: $1,500 in Canadian currency. The prize will be given alternately; one year for fiction, the next for nonfiction. Next fiction award in 1991.

COUNCIL FOR WISCONSIN WRITERS ANNUAL WRITING CONTEST (II, IV), Box 55322, Madison WI 53705. President: Lynn Entine. "To recognize excellence in Wisconsin writing published during the year in 10 categories." Annual competition for short stories and novels. Award: $200-300 for 1st place. Competition receives between 5 and 80 entries, depending on category. Judges: qualified judges from other states. Entry fee $10/member; $15/nonmember. Guidelines for SASE. Previously published submissions. Wisconsin residents only. Official entry form (available in November) required. Deadline: mid-January.

‡CREATIVE ARTIST GRANT (I,IV), Michigan Council for the Arts, 1200 Sixth St., Detroit MI 48226. (313)256-3719. Award "to create new works of art or complete works in progress." Annual competition for short stories, novels, story collections, poetry and nonfiction. Award: up to $10,000. Competition receives approximately 125 submissions. Judges: out-of-state evaluators – different every year. Guidelines for SASE. Deadline April 2. *Michigan residents only.*

CRIME WRITERS' ASSOCIATION AWARDS (III, IV), Box 172, Tring Herts HP23 5LP England. Six awards. Annual award for crime novels. Competition receives varied amount of submissions. Deadline: October 1. Published submissions in UK in current year. Writer must be nominated by UK publishers.

***CROSS-CANADA WRITERS' MAGAZINE* EDITORS' PRIZE (I)**, (formerly WQ Editors' Prize), Box 277, Station F, Toronto, Ontario M4Y 2L7 Canada. Contact: Ted Plantos, editor. Annual award. "To encourage and publicize the best in new Canadian and international fiction writing." Unpublished submissions, under 3,000 words. Award: Over $2,000 in cash and book prizes, plus publication of the 1st and 2nd prize winners in *Cross-Canada Writers' Magazine*. Entry deadline: June 30. Details are announced in Nos. 1 & 2 of annual volume (winter and spring issues). Entry fees are nominal. "Stories must demonstrate excellent handling of characterization, setting, plot and dialogue. Theme and approach must be absorbing and original."

DEEP SOUTH WRITERS CONFERENCE ANNUAL COMPETITION (I), DSWC Inc., English Dept., University of Southwestern Louisiana, Box 44691, Lafayette LA 70504. (318)231-6908. Contact: John Fiero, director. Annual awards. "To encourage aspiring, unpublished writers." Unpublished submissions. Award: Certificates and cash plus possible publication of shorter works. Contest rules for SASE and addition to mailing list. Deadline: July 15.

DELACORTE PRESS ANNUAL PRIZE FOR FIRST YOUNG ADULT NOVEL (I), Delacorte Press, Department BFYR (Books for Young Readers), 666 Fifth Ave., New York NY 10103. (212)765-6500. Contact: Lisa T. Oldenburg, Contest Director. Estab. 1983. Annual award. "To encourage the writing of contemporary young adult fiction." Unpublished submissions; fiction with a contemporary setting in the United States or Canada that will be suitable for ages 12-18. Award: Contract for publication of book; $1,500 cash prize and a $6,000 advance against royalties. Judges are the editors of Delacorte Press Books for Young Readers. Deadline: December 31 (no submissions accepted prior to Labor Day). Contest rules for SASE.

DELAWARE STATE ARTS COUNCIL (I, IV), 820 N. French St., Wilimington DE 19801. (302)571-3540. Barbara R. King, coordinator. "To help further careers of established, emerging and professional artists." Annual award for Delaware residents only. Award: $5,000 for established professional; $2,000 for emerging professional. Judges are out-of-state professionals in each division. Entry forms or rules for SASE. Deadline March 23, 1990.

‡DJERASSI FOUNDATION RESIDENT ARTISTS PROGRAM (I, II), Djerassi Foundation, 2325 Bear Gulch Road, Woodside CA 94062. (415)851-8395. "To provide international working community for mature artists able to work in isolation." Biannual award for short stories, novels, story collections and translations. Award: residency at Foundation. Judges: professional review panel. Guidelines for SASE. Deadline: February 1. Previously published or unpublished submissions.

DORLAND MOUNTAIN ARTS COLONY, INC. (I), Box 6, Temecula CA 92390. (714)676-5039. Contact: Admissions committee. "To provide uninterrupted time for creativity in a natural environment. The Colony is located on a 300-acre nature preserve." Residencies for authors of short stories, novels, translations and story collections. Award: residency for 1-2 months. Judges: admissions committee review panel. $150/month cottage fee requested. Guidelines for SASE. Deadline: March 1 and September 1 annually. "Four to seven residents can be accommodated at one time. Composers, writers and painters live in studio cottages of simple construction, consisting of kitchen, bathroom, living- and work-area. Residents learn to use woodstoves and kerosene lamps for their heat and evening light."

JOHN DOS PASSOS PRIZE FOR LITERATURE (III, IV), Longwood College, Farmville VA 23901. (804)395-2155. "The John Dos Passos Prize for Literature, annually commemorates one of the greatest of 20th-century American authors by honoring other writers in his name." Award: a medal and $1,000 cash. "The winner, announced each fall in ceremonies at the college, is chosen by an independent jury charged especially to seek out American creative writers in the middle stages of their careers—men and women who have established a substantial body of significant publication, and particularly those whose work demonstrates one or more of the following qualities, all characteristics of the art of the man for whom the prize is named: an intense and original exploration of specifically American themes; an experimental tone; and/or writing in a wide range of literature forms." Application for prize is by nomination only.

‡DREAMS & VISIONS: BEST SHORT STORY OF THE YEAR (I, IV), Skysong Press, RR1, Washago, Ontario L0K 2B0 Canada. Contact: Steve Stanton. The "competition serves the dual purpose of rewarding literary excellence among the authors published in Dreams & Visions, and of providing feedback from subscribers as to the type of literature they prefer." Annual award for short stories. Award: $100. "Only the 28 stories published in Dreams & Visions each year are eligible for the award." Judges: subscribers to Dreams & Visions. Guidelines for SASE. Previously unpublished submissions.

EATON LITERARY ASSOCIATES' LITERARY AWARDS PROGRAM (I), Eaton Literary Associates, Box 49795, Sarasota FL 34230. (813)355-4561. Lana L. Bruce, editorial director. Biannual award for short stories and novels. Award: $2,500 for best book-length ms, $500 for best short story. Competition receives approximately 2,000 submissions annually. Judges are 2 staff members in conjunction with an independent agency. Entry forms or rules for SASE. Deadline is March 31 for short stories; August 31 for book-length mss.

EYSTER PRIZES (II), *The New Delta Review*, LSU/Dept. of English, Baton Rouge LA 70803. (504)388-5922. Kathleen Fitzpatrick, editor. "To honor author and teacher Warren Eyster, who has served as advisor to *New Delta Review* predecessors *Manchac* and *Delta*." Annual award for short stories. Award: $50 and 2 free copies of our publication. Competition receives approximately 75 submissions/year. Judges are published authors. Deadline: September 15 for fall, February 15 for spring.

FICTION NETWORK COMPETITION (I), Box 5651, San Francisco CA 94101. (415)391-6610. Jay Schaefer, Editor. "To find quality short fiction and undiscovered writers." Annual award for short stories. Award: $1,500. Competition receives approximately 3,000 submissions. Outside judges. "Requirements (length, entry fee, etc.) change each year; writers must send SASE between April and June for rules, or see Spring issue of *Fiction Network*."

FINE ARTS WORK CENTER IN PROVINCETOWN FELLOWSHIP (I), Box 565, Provincetown MA 02657. (617)487-9960. Contact: Writing Coordinator. "Fellowship is to aid writers who have completed their formal education, but who have yet to firmly establish their careers." Writing residency offered annually. Award: An apartment and stipend, from October 1 to May 1. "We choose 8 fellows out of 400 applicants yearly." Judged by writing committee of the Fine Arts Work Center. Entry fee $20. Entry forms for SASE.

ROBERT L. FISH MEMORIAL AWARD (II), Mystery Writers of America, 236 West 27th St. #600, New York NY 10001-5906. (212)255-7005. Estab. 1984. Annual award. "To encourage new writers in the mystery/detective/suspense short story—and, subsequently, larger work in the genre." Previously published submissions published the year prior to the award. Award: $500. Judged by the MWA committee for best short story of the year in the mystery genre. Deadline: December 1. Looking for "a story with a crime that is central to the plot that is well written and distinctive."

DOROTHY CANFIELD FISHER AWARD (III), Vermont Congress of Parents and Teachers, % Southwest Regional Library, Pierpoint Avenue, Rutland VT 05701. Contact: Betty Lallier, chairperson. Estab. 1957. Annual award. "To encourage Vermont schoolchildren to become enthusiastic and discriminating readers and to honor the memory of one of Vermont's most distinguished and beloved literary figures." Publishers send the committee review copies of books to consider. Only books of the current publishing year can be considered for next year's award. Master list of titles is drawn up in late February or March each year. Children vote each year in the spring and the award is given before the school year ends. Award: illuminated scroll. Submissions must be "written by living American authors, be suitable for children in grades 4-8, and have literary merit. Can be nonfiction also."

FLORIDA ARTS COUNCIL/LITERATURE FELLOWSHIPS (I,IV), Division of Cultural Affairs, Dept. of State, The Capitol, Tallahassee FL 32399-0250. (904)487-2980. Director: Ms. Peyton C. Fearington. "To allow Florida artists time to develop their artistic skills and enhance their careers." Annual award for fiction or poetry. Award: $5,000. Competition receives approximately 100 submissions/year. Judges are review panels made up of individuals with a demonstrated interest in literature. Entry forms for SASE. Entry restricted to practicing, professional writers who are legal residents of Florida and have been living in the state for 12 consecutive months at the time of the deadline.

‡FLORIDA STATE WRITING COMPETITION (I), Florida Freelance Writers Association, Box 9844, Fort Lauderdale FL 33310. (305)485-0795. "To offer additional opportunities for writers to earn income from their stories." Annual competition for short stories and novels. Award: varies from $50-150. Competition receives approx. 300 short stories; 125 novels. Judges: authors, editors and teachers. Entry fee from $5-14. Guidelines for SASE. Deadline: March 15. Unpublished submissions. Literary: 3,000 words maximum; SF/Fantasy: 6,000 words maximum; Genre: 3,000 words maximum; and novel chapter: 5,000 words maximum. "Guidelines are revised each year and subject to change."

‡FOLIO (I), Dept. of Literature, American University, Washington DC 20016. Competition "to recognize outstanding poetry and short fiction submitted to *Folio*." Annual competition for short stories and poetry. Award: $75 in each category, plus a year's subscription. Competition receives 300 submissions. Judges: prominent Washington DC authors. Guidelines for SASE. Deadline: March 1. Previously unpublished submissions. Prefer stories under 3,000 words. "There is no separate submission procedure for the contest. Winners are selected by the judges from work accepted for publication by the editors."

FOUNDATION FOR THE ADVANCEMENT OF CANADIAN LETTERS AUTHOR'S AWARDS (II,IV), In conjunction with Periodical Marketers of Canada (PMC), 20 Toronto St., Ste 400, Toronto, Ontario M5C 2B8 Canada. (416)363-4549. Award Coordinators: Ray Argyle, Marjory Dunstan. "To recognize outstanding Canadian writing and design." Annual award for short stories, novels. 1990 competition judged by an independent panel. Deadline: July 15. "Must be published in a Canadian 'mass market' publication."

‡MILES FRANKLIN LITERARY AWARD (II,IV), Arts Management Pty. Ltd., 56 Kellett St., Potts Point, NSW 2011 Australia. Awards Coordinator: Kate Sraeton. "For the advancement, improvement and betterment of Australian literature." Annual award for novels. Award: AUS $10,000, to the author of the prizewinning novel. Guidelines for SASE. Previously published submissions. "The novel must have been published in the year of competition entry, and must present Australian life in any of its phases."

‡GEORGIA STATE WRITING COMPETITION (I), Georgia Freelance Writers Association. Box 9844, Fort Lauderdale FL 33310. (305)485-0795. To offer additional opportunities for writers to earn income from their stories. Annual competition for short stories. Award from $10-50. Judges: authors, editors and teachers. Entry fee from $5-7. Guidelines for SASE. Deadline: September 15. Unpublished submissions. Word length: 3,000 words maximum. Guidelines are revised each year and subject to change.

‡GESTALT MAGAZINE FICTION AWARD (I,II), Anti-Matter Publishing, Inc., 516 W. Wooster, Bowling Green OH 43402. (419)352-2425. Annual competition for short fiction. Award: $100. Judges: the staff of Gestalt Magazine. Guidelines for SASE. Deadline: December 1. Published or previously unpublished submissions. "Any story, published or unpublished, is acceptable, as long as previously published stories are submitted with permission of right's owner. We want our contest to be as open as possible. We are looking for less traditional fiction, and fiction with a social consciousness."

GOLD MEDALLION BOOK AWARDS (III,IV), Evangelical Christian Publishers Association, Suite 106-B, 950 W. Southern Ave., Tempe AZ 85282. Award to "encourage excellence in evangelical Christian book publishing in 20 categories." Annually. Judges: "at least eight judges for each category chosen from among the ranks of evangelical leaders and book-review editors." Entry fee $75 for ECPA member publishers; $175 for non-member publishers. Deadline December 1, 1990. For books published between 11-1-88 and 12-31-89. Publishers submit entries. Contest breaks down into 20 categories.

GOODMAN FIELDER WATTIE BOOK AWARD (III, IV), Goodman Fielder Wattie Ltd., Book Publishers Association of New Zealand (BPANZ), Box 44146, Auckland 2, New Zealand. Contact: Gerard Reid, executive director. "To recognize excellence in writing and publishing books by New Zealanders. This is not a category award. Fiction/nonfiction/childen's etc. are all included." Award: 1st NZ$18,000; 2nd: NZ$7,000; 3rd: NZ$4,000. Competition receives approx. 80-90 submissions. Judges: panel of 3 selected annually by the BPANZ—1 writer, 1 book trade person and 1 other. Entry fee NZ$65. Guidelines for SASE. Deadline: April 5. "Writer must be New Zealander or resident of New Zealand and its former Pacific territories. Must be submitted by publisher. Fuller details available from BPANZ."

LES GRANDS PRIX DU *JOURNAL DE MONTRÉAL* (I,IV), Union des écrivains Québécois, 1030 rue Cherrier, #510, Montréal, Québec H2L 1H9 Canada. (514)526-6653. "To support the development of the literature of Québec and assure the public recognition of its authors." Annual award for novels and story collections. Award: $1,500 (Canadian). Judges: 5 judges, nominated by the *Journal de Montréal.* Guidelines for SASE. Deadline: June 10. For books published within the 12 months preceding June 1. Writers must have published at least 3 books including the one already submitted and must submit 6 copies of the work to be considered. Write for rules and entry form (in French).

GREAT LAKES COLLEGES ASSOCIATION NEW WRITERS AWARDS (III), Great Lakes Colleges Association, Albion College, Albion MI 49224. Contact: Paul Loakides, Director. Annual award. "To recognize new young writers, promote and encourage interest in good literature." For books published "during the year preceding each year's February 28 deadline for entry, or the following spring." Award judged by critics and writers in residence at Great Lakes Colleges Association colleges and universities. Entry form or rules for SASE. Award: "Invited tour of up to 12 Great Lakes Colleges (usually 7 or 8) with honoraria and expenses paid. Entries in fiction (there is also a poetry section) must be first novels or first volumes of short stories already published, and must be submitted (four copies) *by publishers only*—but this may include privately published books."

GREAT PLAINS STORYTELLING & POETRY READING CONTEST (I,II), Box 438, Walnut IA 51577. (712)366-1136. Contact: Robert Everhart, director. Estab. 1976. Annual award. "To provide an outlet for writers to present not only their works, but also to provide a large audience for their presentation *live* by the writer." Attendance at the event, which takes place annually in Avoca, Iowa, is required. Previously published or unpublished submissions. Award: 1st prize $75; 2nd prize $50; 3rd prize $25; 4th prize $15; and 5th prize $10. Entry deadline: day of contest, which takes place over Labor Day Weekend. Entry fee: $5. Entry forms or rules for SASE.

***THE GREENSBORO REVIEW* LITERARY AWARDS (I)**, Dept. of English, UNC-Greensboro, Greensboro NC 27412. (919)334-5459. Editor: Jim Clark. Annual award. Unpublished submissions. Award: $250. Deadline: September 15. Contest rules for SASE.

***GUARDIAN* CHILDREN'S FICTION AWARD (III, IV)**, The Guardian, 119 Farringdon Rd., London EC1R 3ER England. Contact: Stephanie Nettell, children's books editor. "To recognize an outstanding work of children's fiction – and gain publicity for the field of children's books." Annual competition for fiction. Award: £500. Competition receives approx. 100 submissions. Judges: four eminent children's writers plus children's books editor of the *Guardian*. Deadline: December 31. "British or Commonwealth authors only; published in UK; no picture books. Awarded every March for book published in previous year."

HACKNEY LITERARY AWARDS (I), Birmingham Southern College, Box A-3, Birmingham AL 35254. (205)226-4921. Contact: Special Events Office. Annual award for previously unpublished short stories, poetry and novel. Deadline for submitting a novel – must be postmarked on or before November 24. Deadline for submitting short stories or poetry – must be postmarked on or before December 31. No entry fee. Rules/entry form for SASE.

HAMBIDGE CENTER FOR CREATIVE ARTS AND SCIENCES (I), Box 339, Rabun Gap GA 30568. (404)746-5718. Executive Director: R. Pierotti. Two-week to two-month residencies are offered to writers, visual artists, composers, historians, humanists and scientists. "Center is open from May through October. It is located on 600 acres of quiet woods and streams in north Georgia. Private cottages as well as communal housing available for those who qualify. For application forms send SASE to Executive Director. Once application forms are returned to the Center it takes about 2 months processing time. No deadline."

DRUE HEINZ LITERATURE PRIZE (II), University of Pittsburgh Press, 127 North Bellefield Ave., Pittsburgh PA 15260. (412)624-4110. Annual award. "To support the writer of short fiction at a time when the economics of commercial publishing make it more and more difficult for the serious literary artist working in the short story and novella to find publication." Manuscripts must be unpublished in book form. The award is open to writers who have published a book-length collection of fiction or a minimum of three short stories or novellas in commercial magazines or literary journals of national distribution. Award: $7,500 and publication by the University of Pittsburgh Press. Request complete rules of the competition before submitting a manuscript. Entry deadline: August 31. Submissions will be received only during the months of July and August.

HEMINGWAY DAYS SHORT STORY COMPETITION (I), Hemingway Days Festival, Box 4045, Key West FL 33041. (305)294-4440. "To honor Nobel laureate Ernest Hemingway, who was often pursued during his lifetime by young writers hoping to learn the secrets of his success." Annual competition for short stories. Award: $1000 – 1st; $500 – 2nd; $500 – 3rd. Competition receives approx. 600 submissions. Judges: panel lead by Lorian Hemingway, granddaughter of Ernest Hemingway and journalist based out of Seattle, WA. Entry fee $10/story. Guidelines for SASE. Deadline: July. Unpublished submissions. "Open to anyone so long as the work is unpublished. No longer than 2,500 words."

ERNEST HEMINGWAY FOUNDATION AWARD (II), PEN American Center, 568 Broadway, New York NY 10012. Contact: John Morrone, coordinator of programs. Annual award. "To give beginning writers recognition and encouragement and to stimulate interest in first novels among publishers and readers." Novels must have been published during calendar year under consideration. Deadline: December 31. Entry form or rules for SASE. Award: $7,500. "The Ernest Hemingway Foundation Award is given to an American author of the best first-published book length work of fiction published by an established publishing house in the US each calendar year."

THE O. HENRY AWARDS (III), Doubleday, 666 Fifth Avenue, New York NY 10103. Contact: Sally Arteseros, senior editor. Annual award. To honor the memory of O. Henry with a sampling of outstanding short stories and to make these stories better known to the public. These awards are published by Doubleday in hardcover and by Anchor Books in paperback every spring. Previously published submissions. "All selections are made by the editor of the volume, William Abrahams. No stories may be submitted."

HIGHLIGHTS FOR CHILDREN **(I,IV)**, 803 Church St., Honesdale PA 18431. Editor: Kent L. Brown, Jr. "To honor quality stories (previously unpublished) for young readers." Stories: up to 600 words for beginning readers (to age 8) and 900 words for more advanced readers (ages 9 to 12). No minimum word length. No entry form necessary. To be submitted between January 1 and February 28 to "Fiction Contest" at address above. Three $750 awards. No violence or crime. Non-winning entries returned in June if SASE is included with manuscript. "This year's category is humorous fiction."Write for information.

‡HILAI RESIDENCIES, The Israeli Center for the Creative Arts, 212 B'nei Ephraim St., Maoz Aviv, Tel-Aviv Israel. (03)478704. Two centers for residencies which are international and interdisciplinary – in the Galilee and in the Negev. "To provide tranquil atmosphere for visiting writers and the opportunity to interact with the local community in cultural activities. Provides publicity, organizes and coordinates the meetings and activities with the community. Possibility for a writer and translator to work together to translate a work from Hebrew into English and vice versa." Each residency lasts from one to three months. Award: residency at Hilai Center for up to three months; studio apartment with work and living space. Judges: admission committee. Guidelines for SASE. Deadline ongoing.

THE ALFRED HODDER FELLOWSHIP (II), The Council of the Humanities, Princeton University, 122 E. Pyne, Princeton NJ 08544. "This fellowship is awarded for the pursuit of independent work in the humanities. The recipient is usually a writer or scholar in the early stages of his or her career, a person "with more than ordinary learning" and with "much more than ordinary intellectual and literary gifts." Traditionally, the Hodder Fellow has been a humanist outside of academia. Candidates for the Ph.D. are not eligible. Annual competition for short stories, novels, story collections and translations. Award: $35,000. The Hodder fellow spends an academic year in residence at Princeton working independently. Judges; Princeton Committee on Humanistic studies. Guidelines for SASE. Deadline November 15, 1990. "Applicants must submit a résumé, a sample of previous work (10 page maximum, not returnable), and a project proposal of 2 to 3 pages. Letters of recommendation are not required."

***HONOLULU* MAGAZINE/PARKER PEN COMPANY FICTION CONTEST (I,IV)**, *Honolulu* Magazine, 36 Merchant St., Honolulu HI 96813. (808)524-7400. Brian Nicol, editor. "We do not accept fiction except during our annual contest, at which time we welcome it." Annual award for short stories. Award: $1,000 and publication in the March issue of *Honolulu* Magazine. Competition receives approximately 200 submissions. Judges: panel of well-known writers. Rules for SASE. Deadline: December 9. "Stories must have a Hawaii theme, setting and/or characters. Author should enclose name and address in separate small envelope. Do not put name on story."

‡L. RON HUBBARD'S WRITERS OF THE FUTURE CONTEST (I,IV), P.O. Box 1630, Los Angeles CA 90078. Estab. 1984. Quarterly. "To find, reward and publicize new speculative fiction writers, so that they may more easily attain to professional writing careers." Competition open to new and amateur writers of short stories or novelettes of science fiction or fantasy. Unpublished submissions. Awards: 1st prize, $1,000; 2nd prize, $750; 3rd prize, $500. Annual grand prize $4,000. SASE for contest rules. Contest deadline: September 30, 1990.

‡THE 'HUGO' AWARD (Science Fiction Achievement Award) (III, IV), The World Science Fiction Convention, c/o Howard DeVore, 4705 Weddel St., Dearborn Heights MI 48125. Temporary; address changes each year. "To recognize the best writing in various categories related to science fiction and fantasy." The award is voted on by ballot by the members of the World Science Fiction Convention from previously published material of professional publications. Writers may not nominate their own work. Award: Metal spaceship 15 inches high. "Winning the award almost always results in reprints of the original material and increased payment. Winning a 'Hugo' in the novel category frequently results in additional payment of $10,000-20,000 from future publishers."

‡HUTTON FICTION CONTEST, Hutton Publications, Box 1870, Hayden ID 83835. (208)772-6184. "To encourage beginning short story writers." Granted five times per year; more often if interest warrants for short stories. Award: cash up to $50; publication of winners. Competition receives no more than 50 submissions. Judges: Linda Hutton, editor of Hutton Publications. Entry fee $1-3. (December contest has no fee.) Guidelines for #10 SASE. Deadline: First of March, June, August, November and December. Unpublished submissions.

ILLINOIS ARTS COUNCIL SPECIAL ASSISTANCE GRANT AND ARTIST'S FELLOWSHIP (I,IV), 100 W. Randolph St. (10-500), Chicago IL 60657. (312)814-6750. Communication Arts Coordinator: Alan Leder. "Grant is for project completion or to help defray the costs of attending workshops, seminars or conferences. The fellowships are awarded to Illinois artists of exceptional talent to enable them to pursue their artistic goals. Annually. Grants for up to $1,500 (average is $500). Finalist awards of $500. Fellowships are for set amounts of $15,000, $10,000 and $5,000. Arts Council receives over 200+ fellowship applicants, approx. 30 Special Assistance applicants. Judges: "Grants are evaluated by staff and panel consultants. Fellowships are evaluated by professional out-of-state writers and scholars." Guidelines available, SASE not required. The Special Assistance Grant is an open-deadline program available throughout the year until funds are used up. Fellowship deadline is September 1st each year. Submissions may be either previously published or unpublished. Only Illinois writers are eligible. Fellowship limits submission to 30 pages of fiction or 15 pages of poetry.

ILLINOIS STATE UNIVERSITY NATIONAL FICTION COMPETITION (I), Illinois State University/Fiction Collective, English Dept., Illinois State University, Normal IL 61761. Curtis White, series editor. Annual award for novels, novellas and story collections. Award: publication. Competition receives approximately 150 submissions each year. Judges different each year. Entry fee $10. Entry forms or rules for SASE.

INTERNATIONAL JANUSZ KORCZAK LITERARY COMPETITION (II, IV), Joseph H. and Belle R. Braun Center for Holocaust Studies Anti-Defamation League of B'nai B'rith, 823 United Nations Plaza, New York NY 10017. (212)490-2525. Contact: Dr. Dennis B. Klein, director. For published novels, novellas, translations, short story collections. "Books for or about children which best reflect the humanitarianism and leadership of Janusz Korczak, a Jewish and Polish physician, educator and author." Deadline: inquire.

INTERNATIONAL LITERARY CONTEST (I), Writer's Refinery, Box 47786, Phoenix AZ 85068-7786. Contact: Libbi Goodman, contest director. Annual award for fiction, poetry and essays. Unpublished submissions. Deadline: November 30.

INTERNATIONAL READING ASSOCIATION CHILDREN'S BOOK AWARDS (II), Sponsored by IRA/Institute for Reading Research, 800 Barksdale Rd., Box 8139, Newark DE 19714-8139. (302)731-1600. Annual award. To encourage an author who shows unusual promise in the field of children's books. Two awards will be given for a first or second book in two categories: one for literature for older children, 10-16 years old; one for literature for younger children, 4-10 years old. Submissions must have been published during the calendar year prior to the year in which the award is given. Award: $1,000 stipend. Entry deadline: December 1. No entry fee. Contest/award rules and awards flyer available from IRA. No longer taking applications for 1990 but may inquire about 1991.

IOWA ARTS COUNCIL LITERARY AWARDS (I, IV), Iowa Arts Council, State Capitol Complex, Des Moines IA 50319. (515)281-4451. Director of Partnership Programs: Julie Bailey. Estab. 1984. "To give exposure to Iowa's fine poets and fiction writers." Unpublished submissions by legal residents of Iowa only. Award: 1st prize, $1,000; 2nd prize, $500. Deadline: January 15. Contest rules for SASE.

‡JAB PUBLISHING FICTION CONTEST, Box 4086, Cary NC 27519-4086. (919)460-6668. Competition held when money is available. First place: $100; second place: $50. Competition receives 100-200 short story submissions. Judges: editor/co-publisher. Entry fee: $2. Guidelines for SASE. Deadlines vary. Previously unpublished submissions for most (once or twice each year contests for stories published in our magazine). Length: 4,000 words maximum. Writers may submit their own fiction.

JOSEPH HENRY JACKSON AWARD (I, IV), The San Francisco Foundation, 685 Market St., Suite 910, San Francisco CA 94105. Contact: Kitty Brody, assistant coordinator. Annual competition "to award the author of an unpublished work-in-progress of fiction (novel or short stories), nonfiction or poetry." Unpublished submissions only. Applicant must be resident of northern California or Nevada for 3 consecutive years immediately prior to the deadline date. Age of applicant must be 20 through 35. Deadline: January 15. Entry form and rules available after November 1 for SASE. Award: $2,000 and award certificate.

***JAPANOPHILE* SHORT STORY CONTEST (I, IV),** *Japanophile*, Box 223, Okemos MI 48864. (517)349-1795. Contact: Earl R. Snodgrass, editor. Estab. 1972. Annual award. "To encourage quality writing on Japan-America understanding." Prefers unpublished submissions. Stories should involve Japanese and non-Japanese characters. Award: $100 plus possible publication. Deadline: December 31. Entry fee: $5. Send $4 for sample copy of magazine. Contest rules for SASE.

JAPAN-UNITED STATES FRIENDSHIP COMMISSION PRIZE FOR THE TRANSLATION OF JAPANESE LITERATURE (I, IV), The Donald Keene Center of Japanese Culture, Columbia University, 407 Kent Hall, Columbia University, New York NY 10027. (212)280-5036. Contact: Victoria Lyon-Bestor. "To encourage fine translations of Japanese literature and to award and encourage young translators to develop that craft." Annual competition for translations only. Award: $2,000. Competition receives approx. 10 submissions. Judges: a jury of writers, literary agents, critics and scholar/translators. Guidelines for SASE. Previously published or unpublished submissions. "Translators must be American citizens."

‡THE JANET HEIDINGER KAFKA PRIZE (II,IV), University of Rochester, Susan B. Anthony Center and English Dept., 538 Lattimore Hall, Rochester NY 14627. (716)275-8318. Award for fiction by an American woman. Annual competition for short stories and novels. Award: $1,000. Judges: Kafka Committee. Guidelines for SASE. Deadline: December 31. Recently published submissions. American women only.

***KANSAS QUARTERLY*/KANSAS ARTS COMMISSION AWARDS (I),** *Kansas Quarterly*, 122 Denison Hall, Dept. of English, Kansas State University, Manhattan KS 66506. Contact: Editors. Annual awards. "To reward and recognize the best fiction published in *Kansas Quarterly* during the year from authors anywhere in the US or abroad. Anyone who submits unpublished material which is then accepted for publication becomes eligible for the awards." No deadline; material simply may be submitted for consideration at any time. To submit fiction for consideration, send it in with SASE. Award: Recognition and monetary sums of $250, $200, $100, $50. "Ours are not 'contests'; they are monetary awards and recognition given by persons of national literary stature." Fiction judges recently have included David Bradley, James B. Hall, Annabel Thomas and Mary Morris.

ROBERT F. KENNEDY BOOK AWARDS (II, IV), 1031 31st St., NW, Washington DC 20007. (202)333-1880. Contact: Ms. Caroline Croft. Endowed by Arthur Schlesinger, Jr., from proceeds of his biography, *Robert Kennedy and His Times*. Annual award. "To award the author of a book which most faithfully and forcefully reflects Robert Kennedy's purposes." For books published during the calendar year. Award: $2,500 cash prize awarded in the spring. Looking for "a work of literary merit in fact or fiction that shows compassion for the poor or powerless or those suffering from injustice." Deadline: January 5.

KENTUCKY ARTS COUNCIL, AL SMITH ARTISTS FELLOWSHIPS (I, IV), Berry Hill, Frankfort KY 40601. (502)564-3757. "To encourage and support the professional development of Kentucky artists." Writing fellowships offered every other year in fiction, poetry, playwriting. Award: $5,000. Competition received approximately "110 submissions in 1988 in all writing categories." Judges are out-of-state panelists (writers, editors, playwrights, etc.) of distinction. Open only to Kentucky residents (minimum one year). Entry forms or rules "even without SASE." Next appropriate deadline for writers is July 1, 1990.

LOUISA KERN FUND GRANT (I), University of Washington, Creative Writing, GN-30, Seattle WA 98195. (206)543-9865. "The Louisa Kern Fund has as its 'primary purpose and interest . . . to provide funds and to encourage and assist the training and development of persons interested in the field of literary endeavors and, in particular, the field of creative writing.' In the words of the enabling bequest, 'I wish to make it clear that formal educational training, while desirable, is not required as the sole aim of this trust." Annual competition for short stories, novels and story collections. Award: $2,500. Competition receives approx. 195 submissions. Judges: 3 faculty members (2 in creative writing program and 1 from outside program). Guidelines for SASE. Deadline: April 1. Previously published or unpublished submissions. Preference given to Northwest writers. "Applicants for the grant should send a letter of application by April 1 of the year in which they hope for support. Read guidelines before applying."

AGA KHAN PRIZE (I), Address entry to Aga Khan Prize, *Paris Review*, 541 E. 72nd St., New York NY 10021. Annual award. For the best short story received during the preceding year. Unpublished submissions with SASE. Work should be submitted between May 1-June 1. Award judged by the editors. Award: $1,000 and publication. Unpublished short story (1,000-10,000 words). Translations acceptable.

‡*LANGUAGE BRIDGES* CONTEST, Box 850792, Richardson TX 75086-0792. (214)530-2782. Competition "to disseminate Polish literature and writing in the US." Quarterly competition for short stories, novels, story collections and translations. Award: $25 and a certificate and an announcement in *Language Bridges Quarterly*. Competition receives 10 (all works published in the issue) submissions. Judges: the readers send their votes. Guidelines for SASE. No deadline—ongoing. Previously unpublished submissions. "All works in every issue of *Language Bridges Quarterly* are subject to selection for the award by the readers. But applies *only* to previously unpublished works."

LAWRENCE FELLOWSHIP (I), University of New Mexico, Dept. of English Language and Literature, Albuquerque NM 87131. (505)277-6347. Contact: Prof. Gene Frumkin, chairperson. Annual award. Fellowship for writers of unpublished or previously published fiction, poetry, drama. (June-August residency at D.H. Lawrence Ranch, $2,100 stipend). Deadline: January 31. $10 processing fee. SASE for return of materials. Write for rules, application form.

‡STEPHEN LEACOCK MEDAL FOR HUMOUR (II,IV), Stephen Leacock Associates, Box 854, Orillia, Ontario L3V 6K8 Canada. (705)325-6546. Award "to encourage writing of humour by Canadians." Annual competition for short stories, novels and story collections: Receives 25-40 entries. Award: Stephen Leacock (silver) medal for humour and J.P. Wiser cash award $3,500 (Canadian). Five judges selected across Canada. Entry fee $25 (Canadian). Guidelines for SASE. Deadline December 30. Submissions should have been published in the previous year. Open to Canadian citizens or landed immigrants only.

***LETRAS DE ORO* SPANISH LITERARY PRIZES (I, IV),** American Express and the Graduate School of International Studies, University of Miami, Box 248123, Coral Gables FL 33124. (305)284-3266. "The *Letras de Oro* Spanish Literary Prizes were created in order to reward creative excellence in the Spanish language and to promote Spanish literary production in this country. *Letras de Oro* also serves to recognize the importance of Hispanic culture in the United States." Annual award for novels, story collections, drama, essays and translations of Spanish or Latin American into English. The prizes are $2,500 cash. Deadline: October 12.

LITERARY LIGHTS, SHORT STORY CONTESTS (II), Box 25809, Seattle WA 98125. Contact: Contest Editor. To "encourage and foster new writers." Award granted at completion of each contest for short stories. Award: cash prize and possible publication. Number of entries vary depending on theme of the contest. Entry fee $5. SASE for guidelines. Deadlines: March 15, 1990; May 1, 1990; and September 15, 1990. Unpublished submissions. "Each contest has a theme and maximum word length."

LITERATURE AND BELIEF WRITING CONTEST (I,IV), Center for the Study of Christian Values in Literature, 3134 JKHB, Brigham Young University, Provo UT 84602. (801)378-2304. Director: Jay Fox. Award to "encourage affirmative literature in the Judeo-Christian tradition." Annual competition for short stories. Award $150 (1st place); $100 (2nd place). Competition receives 200-300 entries. Judges: BYU faculty. Guidelines for SASE. Deadline: May 15. Unpublished submissions, up to 25 pages.

LOFT-MCKNIGHT WRITERS AWARDS (I,IV), The Loft, 2301 E. Franklin Ave., Minneapolis MN 55406. (612)341-0431. Susan Broadhead, executive director. "To give Minnesota writers of demonstrated ability an opportunity to work for a concentrated period of time on their writing." Annual award for creative prose. $7,500 per award; four awards. Competition receives approximately 275 submissions/year. Judges are out-of-state judges. Entry forms or rules for SASE. "Applicants must be Minnesota residents and must send for and observe guidelines."

***LOS ANGELES TIMES* BOOK PRIZES (III),** *L.A. Times, Book Review*, Times Mirror Square, Los Angeles CA 90053. Contact: Jack Miles, book editor. Annual award. "To recognize finest books published each year." For books published between August 1 and July 31. Award: $1,000 cash prize plus a handmade, leather-bound version of the winning book. Entry is by nomination; *Times* reviewers nominate. No entry fee.

LOUISIANA LITERARY AWARD (II, IV), Louisiana Library Association (LLA), Box 3058, Baton Rouge LA 70821. (504)342-4928. Contact: Chair, Louisiana Literary Award Committee. Annual award. "To promote interest in books related to Louisiana and to encourage their production." Submissions must have been published during the calendar year prior to presentation of the award. (The award is presented in March or April.) Award: Bronze medallion and $250. Entry deadline: publication by December 31. No entry fee. "All Louisiana-related books which committee members can locate are considered, whether submitted or not. Interested parties may correspond with the committee chair at the address above. All books considered *must* be on subject(s) related to Louisiana or be written by a Louisiana author. Each year, there may be a fiction *and/or* nonfiction award. Most often, however, there is only one award recipient, and he or she is the author of a work of nonfiction."

LYRA SHORT FICTION CONTEST (I), *Lyra, Journal of Poetry and Fiction*, Box 3188, Guttenberg NJ 07093. (201)861-1941. Co-Editor: Lourdes Gil. To encourage emerging writers and to provide a vehicle for publication. Annual competition for short stories. Award: $200, publication in *Lyra*, and 4 copies. Competition receives approx. 120 submissions/year. "Judges alternate; they are also writers." Entry fee $6. Guidelines for SASE. Deadline: June 1. Unpublished submissions. "There are no limits in length, style or topic. They can be written in English, French, Spanish or Italian."

MCDONALD'S LITERARY ACHIEVEMENT AWARDS FOR WRITING ON THE BLACK EXPERIENCE IN AMERICA (I, IV), The Negro Ensemble Company, Box 778, Times Square Station, New York NY 10108. (312)443-8739. Contact: Phyllis Banks (with any phone calls). To offer developing writers a chance to compete for literary awards for writing about the black experience in America. Annual competition for short stories and novels. Award: $2,000 and a trip to New York to participate in a celebrity reading of their work and a literary reception. Guidelines for SASE. Deadline: June 1. Word length: up to 50 pages of a long work or two short works. "Include a biographical statement, including a list of publications, if any, in which your work has appeared."

MACDOWELL COLONY RESIDENCIES (I), The MacDowell Colony, 100 High St., Peterborough NH 03458. (603)924-3886 or (212)966-4860. Admissions Coordinator: Shirley Bewley. "Private studios plus board and room at the MacDowell Colony are provided to competitively selected writers, composers, visual artists and filmmakers, allowing up to 8 weeks of uninterrupted time for creative projects." Colony operates year-round for writers of short stories, novels and story collections, as well as poets and playwrights. Colony helps support costs of residencies for accepted applicants. Colony receives approx. 5-6 applicants for each residency. Judges: panels of professionals in each creative field. Entry fee: $20. Guidelines for SASE. Deadline: April 15 for September-December; September 15 for January-April; January 15 for May-August. Submissions may be either unpublished or previously published. "Open to all professionally qualified writers. See application instructions for length of work sample. Accepted applicants are asked to contribute as much as they are able toward residency costs, but no applicant is rejected for financial reasons. Residencies average 6 weeks. Applications from fiction writers are pooled for review with writers of poetry, plays and nonfiction. Over 200 artists are accepted each year, of whom approx. 90 are writers. The Colony has 31 studios open in summer, 24 in spring and fall, 19 in winter."

THE JOHN H. MCGINNIS MEMORIAL AWARD (I), *Southwest Review*, 6410 Airline Road, Southern Methodist University, Dallas TX 75275. Contact: Elizabeth Mills, managing editor. Biannual award. (One year for fiction and the next for nonfiction). Stories must have been published in the *Southwest Review* within a two-year period prior to the announcement of the award. Award: $1,000. Stories are not submitted directly for the award, but simply for publication in the magazine.

THE ENID MCLEOD LITERARY PRIZE (II, IV), Franco-British Society, Room 636, Linen Hall, 162-168 Regent St., London W1R 5TB England. Executive Secretary: Mrs. Marian Clarke. "To recognize the work of the author published in the UK which in the opinion of the judges has contributed most to Franco-British understanding." Annual competition for short stories, novels and story collections. Award: copy of Enid McLeod's memoirs. Competition receives approx. 6-12 submissions. Judges: Lord Lansdowne (FBS President), Martyn Goff and Terence Kilmartin. Guidelines for SASE. Deadline: December 31. Previously published submissions. "Writers, or their publishers, may submit 4 copies to the London Office. No nominations are necessary."

***MADEMOISELLE* FICTION WRITERS CONTEST (I)**, *Mademoiselle Magazine*, 350 Madison Ave., New York NY 10017. Send entries to Fiction Writers Contest. Each entry must be accompanied by the entry coupon or a 3x5 card with name, age, home address. Award: 1st prize: $2,500 and publication in *Mademoiselle*; 2nd prize: $500 cash. Open to all short story writers, male and female, age 18-30, who have not published fiction in a magazine with a circulation over 25,000. Entries will not be returned.

‡MAGGIE AWARD (I, IV), Georgia Romance Writers, Inc., Box 142, Acworth GA 30101. (404)974-6678. "To encourage and instruct unpublished writers in the romance genre." Annual competition for novels. Award: silver pendant (1st place), certificates (2nd-4th). 4 categories—(50) short contemporary romance; (30) long contemporary, (30) historical, (20) mainstream. Judges: published romance authors. Entry fee $20. Guidelines for SASE. Deadline: July 17. Unpublished submissions. Writers must be members of Romance Writers of America. Entries consist of 3 chapters plus synopsis. "We welcome a variety of fiction types in our mainstream category, since romance has achieved such a broad and sophisticated scope."

‡THE MARTEN BEQUEST AWARD (I, IV), Arts Management Pty. Ltd., 56 Kellett St., Potts Point NSW 2011 Australia. Awards Coordinator: Kate Sraeton. "For the furtherance of culture and the advancement of education in Australia by means of the provision of travelling scholarships as numerous as income will permit, to be awarded to natural born British subjects who have been born in Australia, and awarded to candidates of either sex between the ages of 21 years and 35 years, who shall be adjudged of outstanding ability and promise." Award granted to writers every 2 years (next in 1990). Competition for writers of short stories, novels or story collections. Award: AUS $10,000 payable in two installments of $5,000 per annum. Guidelines for SASE.

‡WALTER RUMSEY MARVIN GRANT (I, IV), Ohioana Library Association, 1105 State Department Building, 65 S. Front St., Columbus OH 43215. (614)466-3831. Contact: Linda Hengst. "To encourage young writers (under age 30)." Biannual competition for short stories. Award: $1,000. Guidelines for SASE. Deadline January 31. Unpublished submissions. Open to unpublished authors born in Ohio or who have lived in Ohio for a minimum of five years. Must be under 30 years of age. Up to six pieces of prose may be submitted.

MARYLAND STATE ARTS COUNCIL FELLOWSHIP (I, IV), 15 West Mulberry St., Baltimore MD 21201. (301)333-8232. Fellowships given to reward artistic excellence and to promote career development. Annual grant for writers of stories, novels, novellas and story collections. Award: $6,000 fellowship or up to $3,000 work-in-progress grants. Competition receives 200 applications for fellowships; 120 for work-in-progress grants annually. Judge: out-of-state selection panel. Further information available for SASE. Applicants must be Maryland residents over 18. Students are not eligible. Writers are required to submit a body of work demonstrating artistic accomplishment and skill.

MASSACHUSETTS ARTISTS FELLOWSHIP PROGRAM (I, IV), Artists Foundation–Artists Fellowship Program, 8 Park Plaza, Boston MA 02116. (617)227-ARTS. Contact: Cathline Brandt, Fellowship Director. Biannual award. "To encourage artists who live and work in Massachusetts." Categories include playwriting, fiction, nonfiction, poetry. Massachusetts residents 18 years of age or older are eligible to apply as long as resident is not enrolled as a student in a degree-granting program in their field. "Specific instructions are detailed in the entry form which is available upon request." Previous publication is not necessary, but any published work must be submitted in typewritten form. Entry forms available upon request. Award: $10,000 for winners; $1,000 for finalists. "Looking for artistic excellence. Work is judged anonymously by a panel of professional working writers and experts in the field who live outside Massachusetts."

THE VICKY METCALF BODY OF WORK AWARD (II, IV), Canadian Authors Association, Suite 104, 121 Avenue Rd., Toronto, Ontario M5R 2G3 Canada. (416)926-8084. Contact: Executive Director. Annual award. "The prize is given solely to stimulate writing for children, written by Canadians, for a *number* of strictly children's books–fiction, nonfiction or even picture books. No set formula." To be considered, a writer must have published at least 4 books. Award: $2,000 for a body of work inspirational to Canadian youth. Entry deadline: December 31. No entry fee. "Nominations may be made by any individual or association by letter *in triplicate* listing the published works of the nominee and providing biographical information. The books are usually considered in regard to their inspirational value for children. Entry forms or rules for SASE."

VICKY METCALF SHORT STORY AWARD (II, IV), Canadian Authors Association, Suite 104, 121 Avenue Rd., Toronto, Ontario M5R 2G3 Canada. (416)926-8084. Contact: Executive Director. "To encourage Canadian writing for children (open only to Canadian citizens)." Submissions must have been published during previous calendar year in Canadian children's magazine or anthology. Award: $1,000 (Canadian). Matching award of $1,000 to editor of winning story if published in a Canadian journal or anthology. Entry deadline: December 31. No entry fee. Entry forms or rules for SASE. Looking for "stories with originality, literary quality for ages 7-17."

MIDLAND AUTHORS' AWARD (II, IV), Society of Midland Authors, 840 E. 87th Ave., Chicago IL 60619. (312)994-7200. Attn: Dempsey Travis. "To honor outstanding works published during the previous year by Midwestern authors." Biannual Summit award for previously published novels or story collections. Award: $400, and plaque and Society of Midland Authors' "Seal" for book jackets. Competition receives approximately 30-50 submissions. Judges are usually members of Society of Midland Authors. Entry forms or rules for SASE. Authors must be residents of IL, IN, IA, KS, MI, MN, MO, NE, OH, SD or WI. Send for entry form.

‡*MILITARY LIFESTYLE* SHORT STORY CONTEST, 1732 Wisconsin Ave. NW, Washington DC 20007. (202)944-4000. "To publish the work of previously unpublished writers; to encourage those of our readers who are military to send us short stories about a lifestyle they know very well." Annual competition for short stories. First Prize: $500; Second Prize: $250; Third Prize: $100. "Also, all three are published in the July/August issue of *Military Lifestyle*." Competition receives 700 submissions. Judges: editorial staff of *Military Lifestyle*. Guidelines for SASE. Deadline: March 31. Previously unpublished submissions. "Any genre, *as long as story features U.S. military servicemembers or their families*. However, science fiction and spy stories would probably have a lesser chance than family drama-type stories. Length: maximum of 2,500 words."

MILKWEED EDITIONS NATIONAL FICTION PRIZE (I), Milkweed Editions, Box 3226, Minneapolis MN 55403. (612)332-3192. Managing Editor: Deborah Keenan. Annual award for three short stories, a short novel or a novella. Award: publication, $3,000 advance against royalties. Received 270 entries for first award; "we expect many more this year and next." Judges: "2 editors at Milkweed narrow it to 10 mss. Then, a final judge—last year, Phillip Lopate. This year, Rosellen Brown." Entry fee $5. Guidelines for SASE. Deadline: October 10. "Please look at *Ganado Red*, by Susan Lowell, our first winning NFP book, or at *Backbone*, by Carol Bly, or *The Country I Come From*, by Maura Stanton—this is the caliber of fiction we are searching for. Catalog available for 2 first class stamps, if people need a sense of our list."

MILLAY COLONY FOR THE ARTS (I), Steepletop, Austerlitz, NY 12017. (518)392-3103. Executive Director: Ann-Ellen Lesser. "The Millay Colony gives residencies to writers, composers and visual artists. Residencies are for one month and usually cover a period from the first to the 28th of each month." Judges: professional artists on admissions committee. Deadline: February 1 (for June-September residencies); May 1 (for October-January residencies); September 1 (for February-May residencies).

THE MILNER AWARD (III), Friends of the Atlanta-Fulton Public Library, 1 Margaret Mitchell Square, Atlanta GA 30303. (404)730-1710. Executive Director: Rennie Davant. Award to a living American author of children's books. Annual competition for novels and story collections. Award: $1,000 honorarium and specially commissioned glass sculpture by Hans Frabel. Judges: children of Atlanta vote during children's book week. Prior winners not eligible. Children vote at will—no list from which to select. Winner must be able to appear personally in Atlanta to receive the award at a formal program.

MIND BOOK OF THE YEAR—THE ALLEN LAND AWARD (II, IV), MIND, 22 Harley St., London W1N 2ED England. Contact: Ms. A. Brackx. "To award a prize to the work of fiction or nonfiction which outstandingly furthers public understanding of the causes, experience or treatment of mental illness." Annual competition for novels and works of nonfiction. Award: £1,000. Competition receives approx. 50-100 submissions. Judges: a panel of judges drawn from MIND's Council of Management. Deadline: December. Previously published submissions. Author's nomination is accepted.

MINNESOTA STATE ARTS BOARD/ARTISTS ASSISTANCE FELLOWSHIP (I, IV), 432 Summit Ave., St. Paul MN 55407. (612)297-2603. Artist Assistance Program Associate: Karen Mueller. "To provide support and recognition to Minnesota's outstanding literary artists." Annual award for fiction, creative nonfiction writers and poets. Award: $6,000. Competition receives approx. 150 submissions/year. Deadline: January. Previously published or unpublished submissions. Send request or call the above number for application guidelines. *Minnesota residents only.*

‡MINNESOTA VOICES PROJECT (IV), New Rivers Press, 420 N. 5th St., #910, Minneapolis MN 55401. Contact: C.W. Truesdale, editor/publisher. Annual award. "To foster and encourage new and emerging regional writers of short fiction, novellas, personal essays and poetry." Requires bibliography of previous publications and residency statement. Awards: $500 to each author published in the series plus "a generous royalty agreement if book goes into second printing." Send request with SASE for guidelines in December. Entry deadline: April 1. No entry fee. Send two copies of each manuscript of 125-200 pages; restricted to writers from Minnesota, Wisconsin, North and South Dakota and Iowa.

MISSISSIPPI ARTS COMMISSION ARTIST FELLOWSHIP GRANT (I, IV), Suite 207, 239 N. Lamar St., Jackson MS 39201. (601)359-6030. Contact: Program Administrator. "To encourage and support the creation of new artwork, and to recognize the contribution that artists of exceptional talent make to the vitality of our environment. Awards are based upon the quality of previously created work." Award granted every 3 years on a rotating basis. Award for writers of short stories, novels and story collections. Grant: up to $5,000. Competition receives 10+ submissions/year. Judging: peer panel. Guidelines for SASE. "The next available grants for creative writing, including fiction, nonfiction and poetry will be in 1990-91." Applicants should request guidelines. Application deadline: March 1. Applicants must be Mississippi residents. "The Mississippi Arts Commission's Art in Education Program contains a creative writing component. For more information, contact the AIE Coordinator. The Mississippi Touring Arts program offers writers the opportunity to give readings and workshops and have the Arts Commission pay part of the fee." For more information, contact the M.T.A. Coordinator.

MISSOURI WRITERS' BIENNAL (I, IV), Suite 105, Missouri Arts Council, 111 N. 7th St., St. Louis MO 63101-2188. (314)444-6845. Award to support and promote Missouri writers. Every 2 years competition for short stories and poetry. Award: $5,000 each to 5 writers. Competition receives approx. 400 submissions. Judges: panel of national judges. Guidelines for SASE. Deadline "approx." July 30. Unpublished submissions. "Writers must have lived in Missouri for at least 2 years immediately preceding submission. Writers *must* request complete written guidelines."

MONTANA ARTS COUNCIL FIRST BOOK AWARD (IV), New York Block, 48 North Last Chance Gulch, Helena MT 59620. (406)444-6430. Director of Artists Services: Julia Smith. Biannual award for publication of a book of poetry or fiction—the best work in Montana. Submissions may be short stories, novellas, story collections or poetry. Award: publication. Competition receives about 35 submissions/year. Judges are professional writers. Entry forms or rules for SASE. Deadline: May 1. Restricted to residents of Montana; not open to degree-seeking students.

MONTANA ARTS COUNCIL INDIVIDUAL ARTIST FELLOWSHIP (IV), New York Block, 48 North Last Chance Gulch, Helena MT 59620. (406)443-4338. Director of Artists Services: Julie Cook. Biannual award of $2,000. Competition receives about 35 submissions/year. 1989 panelists are professional writers. Contest requirements avialable for SASE. Deadline May 1, 1989. Restricted to residents of Montana; not open to degree-seeking students.

MYTHOPOEIC FANTASY AWARD (III), The Mythopoeic Society, Box 6707, Altadena CA 91001. Chair, awards committee: Christine Lowentrout. Annual award for novels. "A statue of a lion is given to the author; magazines and publishers are notified, plus we announce the award in our publications." Judges: members of the Mythopoeic Society who volunteer for the selection committee. Guidelines for SASE. Deadline: February. Fantasy novels only. "Books are nominated by Society members. If an author has published his/her work during the previous year, and is a member of the Society, he/she can nominate his/her own work."

NATIONAL BOOK AWARDS, INC. (III), Fourth Floor, 264 5th Ave., New York NY 10001. (212)685-0261. Executive Director: Neil Baldwin. Assistant: Lucy Logsdon. Annual award to honor distinguished literary achievement in two categories, including fiction. Books published Nov. 1 through Oct. 31 are eligible. Deadline is July 15. Awards judged by panels of critics and writers. November ceremony. Award: $10,000 award to each winner. $1,000 to four runners-up in each category. Selections are submitted by publishers only, or may be called in by judges. A $100 fee is required for entry. Read *Publishers Weekly* for additional information.

NATIONAL BOOK COUNCIL/BANJO AWARDS (III, IV), The Book Printer, National Book Council, Suite 3, 21 Drummond Place, Carlton, Victoria 3053 Australia. "For a book of highest literary merit which makes an outstanding contribution to Australian literature." Annual competition for creative writing. Award: $10,000 each for a work of fiction and nonfiction. Competition receives approx. 100-140 submissions. Judges: 4 judges chosen by the National Book Council. Entry fee $25. Guidelines for SASE. Deadline: mid-December. Previously published submissions. For works "written by Australian citizens and published in Australia during the qualifying period." Books must be nominated by the publisher.

NATIONAL ENDOWMENT FOR THE ARTS FELLOWSHIP (I), Nancy Hanks Center, 1100 Pennsylvania Ave. N.W., Washington DC 20506. (202)682-5732. Program Specialist, Literature Program: Christine Prickett. For fiction contact Susan Campbell. "The mission of the NEA is to foster the excellence, diversity and vitality of the arts in the United States, and to help broaden the availability and appreciation of such excellence, diversity and vitality." The purpose of the fellowship is to enable creative writers "to set aside time for writing, research or travel and generally to advance their careers." Annual award: $20,000. All mss are judged anonymously. Entry forms and guidelines available upon request. Competition open to fiction writers who have published a novel or novella, a collection of stories or at least 5 stories in magazines since 1980. Deadline: March 5.

NATIONAL FOUNDATION FOR ADVANCEMENT IN THE ARTS, ARTS RECOGNITION AND TALENT SEARCH (ARTS) (I, IV), 3915 Biscayne Blvd., Miami FL 33137. (305)573-0490. President: Dr. Grant Beglarian. "To encourage 17- and 18-year-old writers and put them in touch with institutions which offer scholarships." Annual award for short stories, novels, "fiction, essay, poetry, scriptwriting." Award: $3,000, $1,500 and $500 awards. Judges: nationally selected panel. Entry fee $25 by May 15; $35 until October 1. Guidelines for SASE. 17- and 18-year-old writers only.

NATIONAL JEWISH BOOK AWARDS (II, IV), JWB Jewish Book Council, 15 E. 26th St., New York NY 10010. Contact: Paula Gottlieb, director. Annual award. "To promote greater awareness of Jewish-American literary creativity." Previously published submissions in English only by a US or Canadian author/translator. Award judged by authors/scholars. Award: $750 to the author/translator plus citation to publisher. Over 100 entries received for each award. Contest requirements available for SASE. Awards include National Jewish Book Award—Children's Literature, William (Zev) Frank Memorial

Award (for the author of a children's book on a Jewish theme); National Jewish Book Award—Children's Picture Book, Marcia and Louis Posner Award (for the author and illustrator of a children's book on a Jewish theme in which the illustrations are an intrinsic part of the text); National Jewish Book Award—Fiction, William and Janice Epstein Award (for the author of a book of fiction of Jewish interest, either a novel or a collection of short stories); and National Jewish Book Award—Yiddish Literature, The Workmen's Circle Award (for the author of a book of literary merit in the Yiddish language in fiction, poetry, essays and memoirs).

NATIONAL NOVELLA AWARD (I), Arts and Humanities Council of Tulsa, 2210 S. Main St., Tulsa OK 74114. (918)584-3333. Literary Arts Program Coordinator: Elizabeth Thompson. "To provide fiction writers with an opportunity to be awarded for work in a somewhat unrecognized field and to provide a publishing opportunity for a genre that is becoming increasingly important to contemporary literature." Biennial (every other year) award for novellas. Award: $2,500, publication in quality trade paperback and royalties. Judge: nationally recognized fiction writer. Entry fee $10. Guidelines for #10 SASE. Deadline: September 1. Previously unpublished submissions. Word length: 18,000 to 40,000 words.

NATIONAL WRITERS CLUB ANNUAL NOVEL WRITING CONTEST (I), National Writers Club, Suite 620, 1450 S. Havana, Aurora CO 80012. (303)751-7844. Contact: James L. Young, director. Annual award to "recognize and reward outstanding ability and to increase the opportunity for publication." Unpublished submissions, any genre or category. Entry deadline: February 28, 1991. Opens November 1, 1990. Length: 20,000-100,000 words. Award judged by successful writers. Contest/award rules and entry forms available with SASE. Charges $25 entry fee. Award: $500 first prize, $300 second prize; $100 third prize.

NATIONAL WRITERS CLUB ANNUAL SHORT STORY CONTEST (I), National Writers Club, 1450 S. Havana, Aurora CO 80012. (303)751-7844. Contact: James L. Young, director. Annual award. To encourage and recognize writing by freelancers in the short story field. Opens March 1, 1990. All entries must be postmarked by July 1, 1990. Length: No more than 5,000 words. Unpublished submissions. Write for entry form and rule sheet. Charges $10 entry fee. Award: $200 first prize; $100 second prize; $50 third prize.

THE NATIONAL WRITTEN & ILLUSTRATED BY . . . AWARDS CONTEST FOR STUDENTS (I, IV), Landmark Editions, Inc., Box 4469, Kansas City MO 64127. (816)241-4919. Contact: Nan Thatch. "Contest initiated to encourage students to write and illustrate original books and to inspire them to become published authors and illustrators." Annual competition. "Each student whose book is selected for publication will be offered a complete publishing contract. To insure that students benefit from the proceeds, royalties from the sale of their books will be placed in an individual trust fund, set up for each student by his or her parents or legal guardians, at a bank of their choice. Funds may be withdrawn when a student becomes of age, or withdrawn earlier (either in whole or in part) for educational purposes or in case of proof of specific needs due to unusual hardship. Reports of book sales and royalties will be sent to the student and the parents or guardians annually." Winners also receive an all-expense-paid trip to Kansas City to oversee final reproduction phases of their books. Books by students may be entered in one of three age categories: A—6 to 9 years old; B—10 to 13 years old; C—14 to 19 years old. Each book submitted must be both written and illustrated by the same student. Any books that are written by one student and illustrated by another will be automatically disqualified." Book entries must be submitted by a teacher or librarian. Deadline: May 1 of each year. For a free copy of the rules and guidelines, send a #10 SASE envelope to the above address.

NEBULA® AWARDS (III, IV), Science Fiction Writers of America, Inc., Box 4236, W. Columbia SC 29171. Contact: Peter Dennis Pautz, executive secretary. Annual awards for previously published short stories, novels, novellas, novelettes. SF/fantasy only. "No submissions; nominees upon recommendation of members only." Deadline: December 31. "Works are nominated throughout the year by active members of the SFWA."

***NEGATIVE CAPABILITY* SHORT FICTION COMPETITION (I)**, *Negative Capability*, 62 Ridgelawn Dr. E., Mobile AL 36608. (205)343-6163. Contact: Sue Walker. "To promote and publish excellent fiction and to promote the ideals of human rights and dignity." Annual award for short stories. Award: $1,000 best story award. Judge: Leon Driskell. Entry fee $10, "includes copy of journal publishing the award." Guidelines for SASE. Deadline: December 15. Length: 1,500-4,500 words. "Award honors an outstanding author each year, and the award is given his or her name."

THE NENE AWARD (II), School Library Services, Dept. of Education, 641 18th Ave., Honolulu HI 96816. Contact: Linda Reser, chairperson (chairperson changes annually). Annual award. "To help the children of Hawaii become acquainted with the best contemporary writers of fiction for children;

to become aware of the qualities that make a good book; to choose the best rather than the mediocre; and to honor an author whose book has been enjoyed by the children of Hawaii." Award: Koa plaque. Judged by the children of Hawaii. No entry fee.

NEUSTADT INTERNATIONAL PRIZE FOR LITERATURE (III), *World Literature Today*, 110 Monnet Hall, University of Oklahoma, Norman OK 73019. Contact: Dr. Ivar Ivask, director. Biennial award. To recognize distinguished and continuing achievement in fiction, poetry or drama. Awards: $25,000, an eagle feather cast in silver, an award certificate and a special issue of *WLT*. "We are looking for outstanding accomplishment in world literature. The Neustadt Prize is not open to application. Nominations are made only by members of the international jury, which changes for each award. Jury meetings are held in February of even-numbered years. Unsolicited manuscripts, whether published or unpublished, cannot be considered."

‡THE NEW ERA WRITING, ART, PHOTOGRAPHY AND MUSIC CONTEST (I, IV), *New Era Magazine* (LDS Church), 50 E. North Temple, Salt Lake City UT 84150. (801)240-2951. "To encourage young Mormon writers and artists." Annual competition for short stories. Award: Scholarship to Brigham Young University or Ricks College or cash awards. Competition receives approx. 300 submissions. Judges: *New Era* editors. Guidelines for SASE. Deadline: January 3. Unpublished submissions. Contest open only to members of the Church of Jesus Christ of Latter-Day Saints.

NEW HAMPSHIRE STATE COUNCIL ON THE ARTS INDIVIDUAL ARTIST FELLOWSHIP (I, IV), 40 N. Main St., Concord NH 03301-4974. (603)271-2789. Contact: assistant director, Rebecca Lawrence. Fellowship "for career development to professional artists who are legal/permanent residents of the state of New Hampshire." Annual award: up to $2,000. Competition receives 150 entries for 7 awards in all disciplines. Judges: panels of in-state and out-of-state experts (music, theater, dance, literature, film, etc.). Guidelines for SASE. Deadline May 1. Submissions may be either previously published or unpublished. Applicants must be over 18 years of age, not enrolled as full-time students, permanent, legal residents of New Hampshire. Application form required.

NEW JERSEY AUTHOR AWARDS (II, IV), NJIT Alumni Association, New Jersey Institute of Technology, 323 King Blvd., Newark NJ 07102. (201)889-7336. Contact: Dr. Herman A. Estrin, professor of English-Emeritus. Annual award. "To recognize New Jersey writers." Previously published submissions. Award: Citation inscribed with the author's name and the title of his work. Author is an invited guest at the author's luncheon, and a photograph of author receiving the citation is sent to the author's hometown newspaper. Entry deadline: February. No entry fee. Entry forms or rules for SASE.

NEW JERSEY STATE COUNCIL ON THE ARTS PROSE FELLOWSHIP (I, IV), 109 W. State St., CN 306, Trenton NJ 08625. (609)292-6130. Annual award for writers of short stories, novels, story collections. Award: maximum is $15,000; other awards are $8,000 and $5,000. Judges: a peer panel. Guidelines for SASE. Deadline February. For either previously published or unpublished submissions. "Previously published work must be submitted as a manuscript." Applicants must be New Jersey residents. Submit several copies of short fiction, short stories or prose not exceeding 15 pages and no less than 10 pages. For novels in progress, a synopsis and first chapter should be submitted.

NEW LETTERS LITERARY AWARD (I), *New Letters*, UMKC 5216 Rockhill, Kansas City MO 64110. (816)276-1168. Editorial Assistant: Glenda McCrary. Award to "discover and reward good writing." Annual competition for short stories. Award: $750. Competition receives 350 entries/year. Entry Fee $10. Guidelines for SASE. Deadline May 15. Submissions should be unpublished. Length requirement: 5,000 words or less.

NEW YORK FOUNDATION FOR-THE-ARTS FELLOWSHIP (I, IV), New York Foundation for the Arts, #600, 5 Beekman St., New York NY 10038. (212)233-3900. Contact: D. Green. Annual competition for short stories and novels. Award: $7,000. Competition receives approx. 450 submissions. Judges: fiction writers. Call for guidelines (send SASE). Deadline: September 4. Previously published or unpublished submissions. "Applicants must have lived in New York state at least 2 years immediately prior to application deadline."

NEW YORK STATE EDITH WHARTON CITATION OF MERIT (State Author) (III, IV), NYS Writers Institute, Humanities 355, University at Albany/SUNY, Albany NY 12222. (518)442-5620. Contact: Thomas Smith, associate director. Awarded biennially to honor a New York State fiction writer for a lifetime of works of distinction. Fiction writers living in New York State are nominated by an advisory panel. Recipients receive an honorarium of $10,000 and must give two public readings a year, for two years.

JOHN NEWBERY AWARD (III), American Library Association (ALA) Awards and Citations Program, Association for Library Service to Children, 50 E. Huron St., Chicago IL 60611. Annual award. Entry restricted to US citizens-residents. Only books for children published during the preceding year are eligible. Award: Medal.

‡CHARLES H. AND N. MILDRED NILON EXCELLENCE IN MINORITY FICTION AWARD (I, IV), University of Colorado at Boulder and the Fiction Collective Two, English Dept. Publications Center, University of Colorado, Campus Box 494, Boulder CO 80309-0494. "We recognize excellence in new minority fiction." Annual competition for novels; story collections and novellas. Award: $1,000 cash prize; joint publications of mss by CU-Boulder and The Fiction Collective Two. Competition receives approx. 40 submissions. Judges: Three well-known minority writers. Guidelines for SASE. Deadline: November 30. Unpublished submissions. "Only specific recognized U.S. racial and ethnic minorities are eligible. The definitions are in the submission guidelines. The ms must be book length (a minimum of 250 pages)."

THE NOMA AWARD FOR PUBLISHING IN AFRICA (III, IV), ℅ Hans Zeu Associates, P.O. Box 56, Oxford OX1 3EL England. Sponsored by Kodansha Ltd. Administered by *The African Book Publishing Record*. Award "to encourage publications of works by African writers and scholars in Africa, instead of abroad as is still too often the case at present." Annual competition for scholarly or academic, books for children, literature and creative writing, including fiction, drama and poetry. Award: $5,000. Competition receives approx. 100 submissions. Judges: a committee of African scholars and book experts and representatives of the international book community. Chairman: Professor Eldred Jones. Guidelines for SASE. Previously published submissions. Submissions are through publishers only.

NORDMANNS-FORBUNDET TRANSLATION GRANT (II, IV), Nordmann-Forbundet, Rädhusgt 23B, N-0158 Oslo 1 Norway. Contact: Dina Tolfsby, information officer. Annual award for translation of Norwegian poetry or fiction, preferably contemporary. Award: maximum NOK 15,000. Competition receives approx. 10 submissions. Judges: a committee of three members. Deadline March 1. Previously published submissions. "The grants awarded to foreign publishing houses that want to publish Norwegian literature in translation." Payment is made at the time of publication.

NORTH CAROLINA ARTS COUNCIL FELLOWSHIP (IV), 221 E. Lane St., Raleigh NC 27611. (919)733-2111. Contact: Don Linder, Literature Coordinator. Competition "to recognize and encourage North Carolina's finest creative writers." Annual award: $8,000. Competition receives approximately 200 submissions. Judges are a panel of professionals from outside the state. Writers must be over 18 years old, not currently enrolled in degree-granting program on undergraduate or graduate level, and must have been a resident of North Carolina for 1 full year prior to applying. Writers may apply in either poetry or fiction.

NORTHWOOD INSTITUTE ALDEN B. DOW CREATIVITY CENTER FELLOWSHIP (I), Midland MI 48640-2398. (517)832-4478. Carol B. Coppage, director. Annual fellowship: 10-week residency, including travel, housing and food, small stipend and project costs. Competition receives approx. 100 submissions each year. Four awards annually. Judges: board, staff and evaluators. Write or call for entry forms. Deadline: December 31.

‡NUTS TO US!, New Hope Press, 304 S. Denton St., Dothan AL 36301. (205)792-2331. Annual short story competition. Award: $100 (first place) and royalties on books sold. Receives 120 submissions. Judges: Professional writers and poets. $10 entry fee for first submission; $5 for each additional submission. Deadline: July 31, 1990. Previously unpublished fiction. Length: 3,000 words. "Contest open to both new and experienced writers. All manuscripts must be accompanied by SASE."

THE FLANNERY O'CONNOR AWARD FOR SHORT FICTION (I), The University of Georgia Press, Terrell Hall, Athens GA 30602. (404)542-2830. Contact: award coordinator. Annual award, "to recognize outstanding collections of short fiction. Published and unpublished authors are welcome." Award: $1,000 and publication by the University of Georgia Press. Deadline: June 1-July 31. "Manuscripts cannot be accepted at any other time." Entry fee: $10. Contest rules for SASE. Ms will not be returned.

FRANK O'CONNOR FICTION AWARD (I), *Descant*, Dept. of English, Texas Christian University, Fort Worth TX 76129. (817)921-7240. Contact: Betsy Colquitt, editor. Estab. 1979 with *Descant*; earlier awarded through *Quartet*. Annual award. To honor achievement in short fiction. Submissions must be published in the magazine during its current volume. Award: $300 prize. No entry fee. "About 12 to 15 stories are published annually in *Descant*. Winning story is selected from this group."

OHIO ARTS COUNCIL AID TO INDIVIDUAL ARTISTS FELLOWSHIP (I, IV), 727 E. Main St., Columbus OH 43205-1796. (614)466-2613. Susan Dickson, coordinator. "To recognize and support Ohio's outstanding creative artists." Annual grant/fellowship. Award: cash awards of $5,000 or $10,000. Competition receives approx. 200-300 submissions/year. Judges: panel of experts. Contact the OAC office for guidelines. Writers must be residents of Ohio and must not be students.

OHIOANA BOOK AWARD (II, IV), Ohioana Library Association, 1105 Ohio Departments Bldg., 65 S. Front St., Columbus OH 43266-0334. Contact: Linda R. Hengst, director. Annual award (only if the judges believe a book of sufficiently high quality has been submitted). To bring recognition to outstanding books by Ohioans or about Ohio. Criteria: Book written or edited by a native Ohioan or resident of the state for at least 5 years; Two copies of the book MUST be received by the Ohioana Library by December 31 prior to the year the Award is given; Literary quality of the book must be outstanding. Each spring a jury considers all books received since the previous jury. Award judged by a jury, selected from librarians, book reviewers, writers, and other knowledgeable people. No entry forms are needed, but they are available. "We will be glad to answer letters asking specific questions." Award: Certificate and glass sculpture.

‡THE OKANAGAN SHORT FICTION AWARD (I,IV), *Canadian Author & Bookman*, Suite 104, 121 Avenue Rd., Toronto, Ontario M5R 2G3 Canada. Contact: Geoff Hancock, fiction editor. Award offered 4 times a year. To present good fiction "in which the writing surpasses all else" to an appreciative literary readership, and in turn help Canadian writers retain an interest in good fiction. Unpublished submissions. Entries are invited in each issue of our quarterly *CA&B*. Sample copy $5; guidelines printed in the magazine. "Our award regulations stipulate that writers must be Canadian, stories must not have been previously published, and be under 3,000 words. Mss should be typed double-spaced on 8½x11 bond. SASE requested. Award: $125 to each author whose story is accepted for publication. Looking for superior writing ability, stories with good plot, movement, dialogue and characterization. A selection of winning stories has been anthologized as *Pure Fiction: The Okanagan Award Winners*, and is essential reading for prospective contributors."

‡OMMATION PRESS BOOK AWARD (I, II), Ommation Press 5548 N. Sawyer, Chicago IL 60625. (312)539-5745. Annual competition for short stories, novels, story collections and poetry. Award: book publication, $50 and 50 copies of book. Competition receives approx. 60 submissions. Judge: Effie Mihopoulos (editor). Entry fee $8. Guidelines for SASE. Deadline: December 30. Either previously published or unpublished submissions. Submit no more than 50 pages.

‡OPEN VOICE AWARDS (I, II), Westside YMCA – Writer's Voice, 5 W. 63rd St., New York NY 10023. (212)787-6557. Biannual (twice a year) competition for short stories. Award: $50 honorarium and featured reading. Semi-annual deadlines: October 15, April 15. "Submit 10 double-spaced pages in a single genre."

OREGON INDIVIDUAL ARTIST FELLOWSHIP (I,IV), Oregon Arts Commission, 835 Summer St. NE, Salem OR 97301. (503)387-3625. Artist Services Coordinator: Nancy Lindburg. "Award enables professional artists to undertake projects to assist their professional development." Biennial competition for short stories, novels, poetry and story collections. Award: $3,000 and $10,000. (Please note: 8 $3,000 awards and 2 $10,000 Master Fellowship Awards are spread over 5 disciplines – literature, music/opera, media arts, dance and theatre awarded in even-numbered years.) Competition receives approx. 50 entries/year. Judges: professional advisors from outside the state. Guidelines and application available for SASE. Deadline: September 1. Competition limited to Oregon residents.

***THE OTHER SIDE* SHORT FICTION AWARD (I),** 1225 Dandridge St., Fredericksburg VA 22401. (703)371-7416. Mark Olson, editor. "To recognize excellence in short fiction writing among people who have a commitment to Christian faith and an active concern for peace and justice." Annual award for short stories. Award: $250 plus a year's subscription to *The Other Side*. Winning story is published in *The Other Side*. Competition receives approx. 70 submissions/year. Judges are the magazine's editors. Entry forms for SASE. Deadline: May 1.

‡DOBIE PAISANO FELLOWSHIPS (IV), Texas Institute of Letters/University of Texas at Austin, Office of Grad. Studies, University of Texas at Austin, Austin TX 78712. (512)471-7213. Annual award for short stories, novels and story collections. Award: 6 months residence at ranch; $7,200 stipend. Competition receives approx. 100 submissions. Judges: faculty of University of Texas and members of Texas Institute of Letters. Entry fee: $5. Guildelines for SASE. "Open to writers with a Texas connection – native Texans, people living in Texas now or writers whose work focuses on Texas and Southwest." Deadline: January 22.

‡*PAPER BAG* Short, Shorts (I), Paper Bag Press, P.O. Box 268805, Chicago IL 60626-8805. (312)285-7972. Award "to find quality short, short works of fiction (under 500 words)." Annual award for short stories (under 500 words). Award: publication and $25. Competition receives approx. 20 submissions. Judges: editors of *Paper Bag*. Guidelines for SASE. Deadline is ongoing. Unpublished submissions. Nothing over 500 words.

WILLIAM PEDEN PRIZE IN FICTION (I), *The Missouri Review*, 107 Tate Hall, University of Missouri, Columbia MO 65211. (314)882-2339. Contact: Speer Morgan, editor. Annual award. "To honor the best short story published in *The Missouri Review* each year." Submissions are to be previously published in the volume year for which the prize is awarded. Award: $1,000 cash. No deadline entry or entry fee. No rules; all fiction published in *MR* is automatically entered.

‡PEN/BOOK-OF-THE-MONTH CLUB TRANSLATION PRIZE (II, IV), PEN American Center, 568 Broadway, New York NY 10012. (212)334-1660. Awards Coordinator: John Morrone. Award "to recognize the art of the literary translator." Annual competition for translations. Award: $3,000. Deadline: December 31. Previously published submissions within the calendar year. "Translators may be of any nationality, but book must have been published in the U.S. and must be a book-length literary translation." Writer must be nominated by publishers, agents or translators. No application form. Send three copies. "Early submissions are strongly recommended."

THE PEN/FAULKNER AWARD (II, III), c/o The Folger Shakespeare Library, 201 E. Capitol St. SE, Washington DC 20003. (202)544-4600. Attention: Janice Delaney, PEN/Faulkner executive director. Annual award. "To award the most distinguished book-length work of fiction published by an American writer." Published submissions only. Writers and publishers submit four copies of eligible titles published the current year. Deadline for submissions, December 31. No juvenile. Authors must be American citizens or permanent residents of the U.S. Book award judged by three writers chosen by the Trustees of the Award. Award: $7,500 for winner; $2,500 for nominees.

PENNSYLVANIA COUNCIL ON THE ARTS, FELLOWSHIP PROGRAM (I, IV), 216 Finance Bldg. Harrisburg PA 17120. (717)787-6883. Peter M. Carnahan, Literature Program director. Annual awards to provide fellowships for creative writers. Award: up to $6,000. Competition receives approx. 175 submissions for 12 to 15 awards/year. Six judges: three poetry, three fiction, different each year. Guidelines mailed upon request. Deadline: October 1. Applicants must be Pennsylvania residents.

JAMES D. PHELAN AWARD (I,IV), The San Francisco Foundation, 685 Market St., Suite 910, San Francisco CA 94105. Contact: Kitty Brady, assistant coordinator. Annual award "to author of an unpublished work-in-progress of fiction, (novel or short story), nonfictional prose, poetry or drama." Unpublished submissions. Applicant must have been born in the state of California and be 20-35 years old. Entry deadline: January 15. Rules and entry forms available after November 1 for SASE. Award: $2,000 and a certificate.

***PLAYBOY* COLLEGE FICTION CONTEST (I)**, *Playboy* Magazine, 919 North Michigan Ave., Chicago IL 60611. (312)751-8000. Fiction Editor: Alice K. Turner. Award "to foster young writing talent." Annual competition for short stories. Award: $3,000 plus publication in the magazine. Judges: staff. Guidelines available for SASE. Deadline: January 1. Submissions should be unpublished. No age limit; college affiliation required. Stories should be 25 pages or fewer. "Manuscripts are not returned. Results of the contest will be sent via SASE."

***PLOUGHSHARES* DENISE AND MEL COHEN AWARD (III)**, *Ploughshares*, Box 529, Cambridge MA 02139. (617)926-9875. DeWitt Henry, director. The purpose of competition/award is "to highlight outstanding work in each volume of *Ploughshares*." Annual awards for best short story, poem and nonfiction. Award: $300. Judges are coordinating editors. For writers published in *Ploughshares* in the preceding volume year only. No outside applications.

EDGAR ALLAN POE AWARDS (II), Mystery Writers of America, Inc., 236 West 27th St., New York NY 10001. Annual award. To enhance the prestige of the mystery. For manuscripts published during the calendar year. Entry deadline: December 1. Contact above address for specifics. Award: Ceramic bust of Poe. Awards for best mystery novel, best first novel by an American author, best softcover original novel, best short story, best critical/biographical work, best fact crime, best young adult, best juvenile novel, best screenplay, best television feature and best episode in a series.

‡THE RENATO POGGIOLI TRANSLATION AWARD (I, IV), PEN American Center, 568 Broadway, New York NY 10012. (212)334-1660. Awards Coordinator: John Morrone. Award "to encourage beginning and promising translator who is working on a book-length translation from Italian to English." Annual competition for translations. Award: $3,000. Competition receives approx. 30-50 submissions. Judges: A panel of three translators. Guidelines for SASE. Deadline: February 1. Unpublished submissions. "Letters of application should be accompanied by a curriculum vitae, including Italian studies and samples of translation-in-progress."

KATHERINE ANNE PORTER PRIZE FOR FICTION (I), *Nimrod*, Arts and Humanities Council of Tulsa, 2210 S. Main St., Tulsa OK 74114. (918)584-3333. Editor: Francine Ringold. "To award promising young writers and to increase the quality of manuscripts submitted to *Nimrod*." Annual award for short stories. Award: $1,000 first prize; $500 second prize. Receives approx. 650 entries/year. Judge varies each year. Past judges have been Rosellen Brown, Alison Lurie and Gordon Lish, George Garrett. Entry fee: $10. Guidelines for #10 SASE. Deadline for submissions: April 1. Previously unpublished manuscripts. Word length: 7,500 words maximum.

***PRAIRIE SCHOONER* THE LAWRENCE FOUNDATION AWARD (I),** 201 Andrews Hall, University of Nebraska, Lincoln NE 68588-0334. (402)472-1812. Contact: Hilda Raz, editor. Annual award. "The award is given to the author of the best short story published in *Prairie Schooner* during the preceding year." Award $500. "Only short fiction published in *Prairie Schooner* is eligible for consideration."

***PRISM INTERNATIONAL* SHORT FICTION CONTEST (I),** *Prism International*, Dept. of Creative Writing, University of British Columbia, E455-1866 Main Mall, Vancouver, British Columbia V6T 1W5 Canada. (604)228-2514. Contact: Publicity Manager. Award: $2,000 first prize and 5 $200 consolation prizes. Entry fee $10 plus $5 reading fee for each story. SASE for rules/entry forms.

LE PRIX MOLSON DE L'ACADÉMIE CANADIENNE-FRANCAISE (II,IV), Union des écrivains québécois, 1030 rue Cherrier #510, Montréal, Québec H2L 1H9 Canada. (514)526-6653. Prize for a novel in French by a writer from Québec or another province in Canada. Annual award for novels. Award: $5,000 (Canadian). Judges: 5 persons, members of the Académie canadienne française. Guidelines for SASE. Deadline: June 10. Five copies of the work must be submitted. Write for guidelines and entry forms (in French).

‡PUBLISHED SHORT-STORY CONTEST (II), Hutton Publications, P.O. Box 1870, Hayden ID 83835. (208)772-6184. Award "to recognize good literature already published." Annual competition for short stories. Award: cash/subscriptions/books. Competition receives approx. 50-75 submissions. Judge: Linda Hutton, Editor of Hutton Publications. Guidelines for #10 SASE. Deadline: December 1. Previously published submissions.

PULITZER PRIZE IN FICTION (III), Columbia University, Graduate School of Journalism, 702 Journalism Bldg., New York NY 10027. Contact: Robert C. Christopher. Annual award for distinguished fiction *first* published in book form during the year by an American author, preferably dealing with American life. Submit 4 copies of the book, entry form, biography and photo of author and $20 handling fee. Open to American authors. Deadline: Beginning in 1990, books published between January 1 and June 30 must be submitted by July 1. Books published between July 1 and December 31 must be submitted by November 1. Award: $3,000.

PULP PRESS INTERNATIONAL, 3 DAY NOVEL-WRITING COMPETITION (I), Arsenal Pulp Press, 100-1062 Homer St., Vancouver, British Columbia V6B 2W9 Canada. (604)687-4233. Contact: Brian Lam, manager. Contest to write the best novel in 3 days, held every Labor Day weekend. Annually, for unpublished novels. "Prize is publication." Receives approximately 1,000 entries for each award. Judged by Arsenal Pulp Press editorial board. Entry forms for SASE/IRC. Deadline: Friday before Labor Day weekend. "Entrants must register either with Pulp Press or with one of our sponsor bookstores throughout North America, a list of which is available with SASE. Winner is announced October 31."

PURE BRED DOGS/AMERICAN KENNEL GAZETTE (I), 51 Madison Ave., New York NY 10010. (212)696-8331. Executive Editor: Marion Lane. Annual contest for short stories under 2,000 words. Award: Prizes of $500, $350 and $150 for top three entries. Certificate and complimentary one-year subscription for nine honorable mention winners. Top 3 entries published in magazine; all 12 published in separate anthology. Judge: panel. Contest requirements available for SASE. "The *Gazette* sponsors an annual fiction contest for short short stories on some subject relating to pure-bred dogs. Three winning entries are published one per month. Fiction for our magazine needs a slant toward the serious fancier with real insight into the human/dog bond and breed-specific pure-bred behavior."

PUSHCART PRESS EDITORS BOOK AWARD (III), Box 380, Wainscott NY 11975. (516)324-9300. Bill Henderson, president. "Award celebrates an important and unusual book ms that has been overlooked." Award: publication and $1,000. Competition receives approximately 80 submissions/year.

Judged by B. Henderson. Entry forms for SASE. Deadline: August 15. For book-length mss of literary distinction that have made the rounds of commercial publishers without acceptance. Mss may arrive from any source (agent, author, etc.), but must be nominated by an editor.

PUSHCART PRIZE (III), Pushcart Press, Box 380, Wainscott NY 11975. Contact: Bill Henderson, editor. Annual award. To publish and recognize the best of small press literary work. Previously published submissions, short stories, poetry or essays on any subject. Must have been published during the current calendar year. Deadline: October 15. Nomination by small press publishers/editors only. Award: Publication in *Pushcart Prize: Best of the Small Presses*.

***QUARTERLY WEST* NOVELLA COMPETITION (I),** University of Utah, 317 Olpin Union, Salt Lake City UT 84112. Biennial award for novellas. Award: 2 prizes of $300+. Deadline postmarked by December 31. Send SASE for contest rules.

RAGDALE FOUNDATION RESIDENCIES FOR WRITERS AND VISUAL ARTISTS (I), 1260 N. Green Bay Rd., Lake Forest IL 60645. (708)234-1063. Director: Michael Wilkerson. Award "to provide living and work space, as well as uninterrupted time to writers and visual artists for a modest weekly fee ($70/week). Financial assistance is available." The Foundation is open year-round, except for the last two weeks of June and December. Award: includes work and sleeping space, and food for all meals. Residencies for 12 artists and writers for periods of two weeks to two months. Applicants are reviewed by a selection committee composed of professionals in the arts. Guidelines available. Applications should be submitted at least four months in advance, if possible; however, there is no application deadline. Submissions may either be previously published or unpublished.

SIR WALTER RALEIGH AWARD (II, IV), North Carolina Literary and Historical Association, 109 E. Jones St., Raleigh NC 27611. (919)733-7305. Secretary-Treasurer: Jeffrey J. Crow. Award "to promote among the people of North Carolina an interest in their own literature." Annual award for novels. Award: statue of Sir Walter Raleigh. Competition receives approx. 10 entries/year. Judges: University English and history professors. Guidelines for SASE. Book must be published between June 30, 1989 and June 30, 1990. Writer must be a legal or physical resident of North Carolina. Authors or publishers may submit 3 copies of their book to the above address. "(1)Must be an original work published during the twelve months ending June 30 of the year for which the award is given. (2)Its author or authors must have maintained either legal or physical residence, or a combination of both in North Carolina for the three years preceding the close of the contest period."

***RAMBUNCTIOUS REVIEW,* ANNUAL FICTION CONTEST (I),** 1221 W. Pratt, Chicago IL 60626. Contact: Nancy Lennon, co-editor. Annual award. Short stories. Requirements: Typed, double-spaced, maximum 15 pages. SASE for deadline, rules/entry forms.

REGINA MEDAL AWARD (III), Catholic Library Association, 461 W. Lancaster Ave., Haverford PA 19041. Contact: Natalie A. Logan, Executive Director. Annual award. To honor a continued distinguished contribution to children's literature. Award: Silver medal. Award given during Easter week. Selection by a special committee; nominees are suggested by the Catholic Library Association Membership.

RHODE ISLAND STATE ARTS COUNCIL (I,IV), Individual Artist's Fellowship in Literature, 95 Cedar St., Suite 103, Providence RI 02903-1034. (401)277-3880. Contact fellowship program director, Edward Holgate. Annual fellowship. Award: $3,000. Competition receives approximately 50 submissions. In-state panel makes recommendations to an out-of-state judge, who makes the final award. Entry forms for SASE. Deadline: April 1. Artists must be Rhode Island residents and not undergraduate or graduate students.

HAROLD U. RIBALOW PRIZE (II, IV), *Hadassah Magazine*, 50 W. 58th St., New York NY 10019. (212)355-7900. Contact: Alan M. Tigay, Executive Editor. Estab. 1983. Annual award. "For a book of fiction on a Jewish theme. Harold U. Ribalow was a noted writer and editor who devoted his time to the discovery and encouragement of young Jewish writers." Book should have been published the year preceding the award. Award: $500 and excerpt of book in *Hadassah Magazine*. Deadline: December 31.

THE MARY ROBERTS RINEHART FUND (III), *George Mason University*, 4400 University Dr., Fairfax VA 22030. (703)323-2221. Roger Lathbury, director. Biennial award for short stories, novels, novellas and story collections by unpublished writers (that is, writers ineligible to apply for NEA grants). Award: Two grants whose amount varies depending upon income the fund generates. 1989 awards were $950 each. Competition receives approx. 75-100 submissions annually. Entry forms or rules for

SASE. Deadline: November 30. Writers must be nominated by a sponsoring writer or editor.

‡SUMMERFIELD G. ROBERTS AWARD (IV), The Sons of the Republic of Texas, Suite 222, 5942 Abrams Rd., Dallas TX 75231. "Given for the best book or manuscript of biography, essay, fiction, nonfiction, novel, poetry or short story that describes or represents the Republic of Texas, 1836-1846." Annual award of $2,500. Deadline: January 31. "The manuscripts must be written or published during the calendar year for which the award is given. Entries are to be submitted in quintuplicate and will not be returned."

ROBERTS WRITING AWARDS (I), H. G. Roberts Foundation, Box 1868, Pittsburg KS 66762. (316)231-2998. Awards Coordinator: Stephen E. Meats. "To reward and recognize exceptional fiction writers with money and publication." Annual competition for short stories. Award: $500 (first place); $200 (second place); $100 (third place); publication for prize winners and honorable mention receipts. Competition receives approx. 600 submissions. Judges: established fiction writer, different each year. Entry fee $5/story. Guidelines and entry form for SASE. Deadline: September 1. Previously unpublished submissions. "Open to any type of fiction, up to 15 typed pages."

‡ROCKY MOUNTAIN WOMEN'S INSTITUTE ASSOCIATESHIP (I, II), 7150 Montview Blvd., Denver CO 80220. (303)871-6923. "Each year RMWI selects 7 people to become Associates. These are artists, writers and scholars who are given office/studio space, stipend and various supporting services for a 10 month term." Annual competition for short stories, novels, story collections and translations. Competition receives approx. 75 submissions. Judges: a selection committee composed of experts in arts/humanities. Entry fee $5. Guidelines for SASE. Deadline: January 1. Previously published or unpublished submissions. "Since RMWI does not provide residence to Associates, most hail from Denver/Boulder area but there is no geographic restriction."

ROMANCE WRITERS OF AMERICA GOLDEN HEART/GOLDEN MEDALLION AWARDS (I, II, IV), 13700 Veterans Memorial, #315, Houston TX 77014. (713)440-6885. "To recognize best work in romantic fiction in 7 categories by members of RWA, both published and not-published." Annual award for novels. Golden Heart Award: heart and certificate; Golden Medallion Award: etched plaque. Golden Heart award receives 600+ submissions/year; Golden Medallion Award receives 250+ submissions/year. Judges: published writers, editors. Entry fee for Golden Heart is now $20; Golden Medallion fee is $15. Guidelines for SASE. Deadline: November 30. Previously published submissions for Golden Medallion; unpublished for Golden Heart. Categories are "traditional, short and long contemporary, historical, single title (historical and contemporary), young adult."

SACRAMENTO PUBLIC LIBRARY FOCUS ON WRITERS CONTEST (I, IV), 1010 8th St., Sacramento CA 95814. (916)440-5926. Contact: Debbie Runnels. Award "to support and encourage aspiring writers." Annual competition for short stories and novels. Awards: $100 (first place); $50 (second place); $25 (third place). Competition receives approx. 147 short story; 78 novel chapters; 71 children's stories. Judges: local teachers of English, authors and librarians. Entry fee $5/entry. Guidelines for SASE. Deadline February 1. Previously unpublished submissions. Length: 2,500-word short story; 1,000-word story for children. Open to all writers in northern California. Send for guidelines.

‡*SAN JOSE STUDIES* BEST STORY AWARD (I), Bill Casey Memorial Fund, 1 Washington Square, San Jose CA 95192. Contact: Fauneil J. Rinn. Winning author receives a year complimentary subscription to journal, which prints notice of award, and is also considered for the Bill Casey Memorial Award of $100 for the best contribution in each year's volume of *San Jose Studies* in essay, fiction or poetry.

SCHOLASTIC WRITING AWARDS (I, IV), Scholastic Inc., 730 Broadway, New York NY 10003. (212)505-3440. Contact: Director of Awards Program, Chuck Wentzel. To provide opportunity for recognition of young writers. Annual award for short stories. Award: Cash awards, scholarships and grants. Competition receives 22,000 submissions/year. Judges vary each year. Deadline: January 9. Previously unpublished submissions. Contest limited to junior high and senior high school students; grades 7-12. Entry blank must be signed by teacher. "Program is run through school and is only open to students in grades 7 through 12, regularly and currently enrolled in public and non-public schools in the United States and its territories, U.S.-sponsored schools abroad or any schools in Canada."

SCIENCE FICTION WRITERS OF EARTH (SFWoE) SHORT STORY CONTEST (IV), Science Fiction Writers of Earth, Box 121293, Fort Worth TX 76121. (817)451-8674. SFWoE Administrator: Gilbert Gordon Reis. Purpose "to promote the art of science fiction/fantasy short story writing." Annual award for short stories. Award: $100 (1st prize); $50 (2nd prize); $25 (3rd prize). Competition receives approx. 75 submissions/year. Judge: author Edward Bryant. Entry fee: $5 for 1st entry; $2 for additional entries. Guidelines for SASE. Deadline: October 30. Submissions must be unpublished. Stories should be science fiction or fantasy, 2,000-7,500 words. "Although many of our past winners are now published authors, there is still room for improvement. The odds are good for a well written story."

THE SEATON AWARDS (I,IV), *Kansas Quarterly*, 122 Denison Hall, Kansas State University, KS 66506. Annual awards. To reward and recognize the best fiction published in *KQ* during the year from authors native to or resident in Kansas. Submissions must be unpublished. Anyone who submits unpublished material which is then accepted for publication becomes eligible for the awards. No deadline. Material simply may be submitted for consideration at any time with SASE. Award: Recognition and monetary sums of $250, $150, $100 and $50. "Ours are not contests. We give monetary awards and recognition to Kansas writers of national literary stature."

***SEVENTEEN MAGAZINE*/ SMITH CORONA FICTION CONTEST (I,IV),** *Seventeen Magazine*, 850 3rd Ave., New York NY 10022. Contact: Adrian Nicole LeBlanc. To honor best short fiction by a young writer. Rules are found in the November issue. Contest for 13-21 year olds. Deadline: January 31. Submissions judged by a panel of outside readers and *Seventeen*'s editors. Award: $2,000 plus a Smith Corona word processor (first prize); Smith Corona word processor (second prize); Smith Corona electronic typewriter with word processing capabilities (third prize); Smith Corona electronic typewriters for the twenty honorable mention awards.

‡SHORT STORY SCIENCE FICTION/FANTASY COMPETITION (I, IV), Maplecon SF/F Convention (O.F.I.), 2105 Thistle Crescent, Ottawa, Ontario K1H 5P4 Canada. "To offer incentive and encouragement for amateur writers." Annual competition for short stories. Award: certificates and varying prizes. Competition receives approx. 15-20 submissions. Judges: professional authors. Guidelines for SASE. Deadline: May 21. Unpublished submissions. Available to any writer, anywhere, in amateur standing, i.e. has *not* had *more* than 3 short stories published professionally in the SF/F field or not had a novel published in the SF/F field. Maximum word length: 11,000 words. "Name must not appear on ms itself—should be included on a separate sheet. Please include a SASE. Use *Canadian* stamps or IRC's or include *loose* U.S. stamps as trade."

THE SIERRA CLUB AWARD FOR DISTINGUISHED NATURE WRITING, Sierra Club, 730 Polk St., San Francisco CA 94109. (415)776-2211. Contact: James Cohee. Award "to further the American tradition of nature writing and promote environmental consciousness. Award granted occasionally; (this is not an annual award) for fiction and nonfiction that explores the natural environment in human affairs. Award: $20,000 advance, guaranteed. Competition receives approx. 100 submissions in the first year. Judges: a panel appointed by Sierra Club Books; first year: Wallace Stegner and Paul Brooks. SASE for guidelines. No deadline. Unpublished submissions. "Book-length ms, any region; works of literature—we do not consider pictorial books for the award."

W.H. SMITH/BOOKS IN CANADA AWARD FOR FIRST NOVELS (III, IV), Books in Canada, 366 Adelaide St. E, Toronto, Ontario M5A 3X9 Canada. (416)363-5426. Contact: Doris Cowan, editor. Annual award. "To promote and recognize Canadian writing." Award: $5,000. No entry fee. Submissions are made by publishers.

Contest is restricted to first novels in English published in Canada in the previous calendar year.

KAY SNOW CONTEST (I, IV), Willamette Writers, Box 2485, Portland OR 97208. (503)233-1877. Contact: Contest Coordinator. Award "to create a showcase for writers of all fields of literature." Annual competition for short stories; also poetry, nonfiction, juvenile, script and student writers. Award: $100 1st prize in each category except poetry ($75); student ($50). Competition receives approx. 500-1,000 submissions. Judges: Nationally recognized writers and teachers. Entry fee $10-nonmembers; $7-members. Deadline June 30. Previously unpublished submissions. Maximum 1,500 words. "This contest is held in association with our annual conference. Prizes are awarded at the banquet held during the conference in early August." Guidelines for #10 SASE.

SOCIETY OF CHILDREN'S BOOK WRITERS GOLDEN KITE AWARDS (II), Society of Children's Book Writers, Box 296, Mar Vista Station, Los Angeles CA 90066. Contact: Sue Alexander, chairperson. Annual award. "To recognize outstanding works of fiction, nonfiction and picture illustration for children by members of the Society of Children's Book Writers and published in the award year." Published submissions should be submitted from January to December of publication year. Deadline entry: December 15. Rules for SASE. Award: Statuette and plaque. Looking for quality material for children. Individual "must be member of the SCBW to submit books."

SOCIETY OF CHILDREN'S BOOK WRITERS WORK-IN-PROGRESS AWARDS (I,IV), Box 296, Mar Vista, Los Angeles CA 90066. (818)347-2849. Contact: SCBW. Award to "aid children's book writer complete a project." Annual competition for novels. Award: 1st-$1,000; 2nd-$500 (work-in-progress).

1st-$1,000; 2nd-$500 (Judy Blume/SCBW contemporary novel grant). Competition receives approx. 30 submissions. Judges: members of children's book field – editors, authors, etc. Guidelines for SASE. Unpublished submissions. Applicants must be SCBW members.

***SONORA REVIEW* FICTION CONTEST (I)**, Dept. of English, University of Arizona, Tucson AZ 85721. (602)621-8077. Contact: fiction editor. Annual award. "To encourage and support quality short fiction." Unpublished submissions. Award: $150 first prize, plus publication in *Sonora*; $50 second prize, plus publication in *Sonora*. "We accept manuscripts all year, but manuscripts received during the summer (May-August) will not be read until fall." Contest rules for SASE.

SOUTH CAROLINA ARTS COMMISSION AND *THE STATE NEWSPAPER* SOUTH CAROLINA FICTION PROJECT (I,IV), 1800 Gervais St., Columbia SC 29201. (803)734-8696. Steve Lewis, director, Literary Arts Program. The purpose of the award is "to get money to fiction writers and to get their work published and read." Annual award for short stories. Award: $500 cash and publication in *The State Newspaper*. Competition receives approximately 400 submissions for 12 awards (up to 12 stories chosen). Judges are a panel of professional writers and senior writer for *The State Newspaper*. Entry forms or rules for SASE. Deadline November 19. South Carolina residents only.

SOUTH CAROLINA ARTS COMMISSION LITERATURE FELLOWSHIP AND LITERATURE GRANTS (I, IV), 1800 Gervais St., Columbia SC 29201. (803)734-8696. Steve Lewis, director, Literary Arts Program. "The purpose of the fellowships is to give a cash award to two deserving writers (one in poetry, one in creative prose) whose works are of the highest caliber." Award: $7,500 fellowship. Matching grants up to $7,500. Competition receives approximately 40 submissions per fellowship. Judges are out-of-state panel of professional writers and editors for fellowships, and in-state panels and SCAC staff for grants. Entry forms or rules for SASE. Deadline September 15. South Carolina residents only.

SOUTH DAKOTA ARTS COUNCIL, ARTIST FELLOWSHIP (IV), 108 West 11th, Sioux Falls SD 57102. (605)339-6646. Award "to assist artists with career development. Grant can be used for supplies or to set aside time to work, but cannot be used for academic research or formal study toward a degree." Annual competition for writers. Award: $1,000 for emerging artists; $5,000 for established artists. Competition receives approx. 80 submissions. "Grants are awarded on artists' work and *not* on financial need." Judges: panels of in-state and out-of-state experts in each discipline. Guidelines for SASE. Deadline February 1, 1989. Previously published or unpublished submissions. Fellowships are open only to residents of South Dakota. "Writers with specific projects may apply for a Project Grant. They would not be eligible for fellowship grants in that case. Deadline is Feb. 1, 1989 and guidelines are available by writing SDAC."

***THE SOUTHERN REVIEW*/LOUISIANA STATE UNIVERSITY ANNUAL SHORT FICTION AWARD (II)**, *The Southern Review*, 43 Allen Hall, Louisiana State University, Baton Rouge LA 70803. (504)388-5108. Contact: Editors, *The Southern Review*. Annual award. "To encourage publication of good fiction." For a first collection of short stories by an American writer appearing during calendar year. Award: $500 to author. Possible campus reading. Deadline: a month after close of each calendar year. The book of short stories must be released by a U.S. publisher. Two copies to be submitted by publisher or author. Looking for "style, sense of craft, plot, in-depth characters."

SPUR AWARD CONTEST (II, IV), Western Writers of America, Fairgrounds 1753 Victoria, Sheridan WY 82801. Contact: Barb Ketcham, secretary-treasurer. Annual award. To encourage excellence in western writing. Entries are accepted only from the current calendar year for each year's award; that is, books can only be entered in the year they are published. Entry deadline: December 31. Award judged by a panel of experienced authors appointed by the current Spur Awards Chairman. Contest/award rules and entry forms available with SASE. Award: A wooden plaque shaped like a W with a bronze spur attached. "A special Medicine Pipe Bearer Award, is offered in the Best First Western Novel competition. First novels may be entered in both Spur and Medicine Pipe Bearer competition. Books must be of the traditional or historical western theme, set anywhere west of the Mississippi River before the 20th century, ideally from 1850 to 1900." A spur is awarded for Best Historical Fiction, Best Juvenile Fiction and Best Short Fiction works.

***STAND MAGAZINE* SHORT STORY COMPETITION (I)**, *Stand Magazine*, 179 Wingrove Road, Newcastle upon Tyne NE4 9DA England. Biennial award for short stories. Award: 1st prize $1,500; 2nd prize $750; 3rd prize $375; 4th prize $225; 5th prize $150. 1991 judges are Emma Tennant, lan and Corchron Smith. Entry fee $6. Deadline: December 31. Send 2 IRC's and SAE.

WALLACE E. STEGNER FELLOWSHIP (I, IV), Creative Writing Program, Stanford University, Stanford CA 94305-2087. (415)723-2637. Contact: Gay Pierce, program coordinator. Annual award. Five two-year fellowships in fiction ($9,000 stipend plus required tuition or $3,500 annually). For unpublished or previously published fiction writers. Residency required. Deadline: January 1. Entry fee $20.

***STORY TIME* SHORT-STORY CONTEST (I)**, Hutton Publications, Box 1870, Hyden, ID 83835, (208) 772-6184. Contact: Linda Hutton, editor. Estab. 1982. Annual award. "To encourage short-story writers." For previously published submissions. Award: $15 first prize; $10 second prize; $7.50 third prize. Entry deadlines: March 1, June 1, August 1, December 1. Send #10 SASE for entry form and rules. Looking for "tightly written plot and well developed characters."

SUNTORY AWARDS FOR MYSTERY FICTION (I, IV), c/o Dentsu Incorporated, 1-11, Tsukiji, Chuo-Ku, Tokyo 104 Japan. Address work to Steering Committee. Contest for unpublished mystery, suspense, detective or espionage novels. Grand prize: 5 million yen (approximately $38,000); Reader's Choice prize: 1 million yen (approximately $7,600). Judges are four Japanese writers and an American columnist. Entry forms or rules for SASE. No U.S. alcoholic beverage retailers or employees may submit work. Writers should include brief personal history along with manuscript. Manuscripts will not be returned. Deadline: January 31. Manuscripts must be in English or Japanese. Length (English): 40,000-80,000 words.

‡SWG LITERARY AWARDS (I, IV), Saskatchewan Writers Guild, Box 3986, Regina, Saskatchewan S4P 3R9 Canada. (306)757-6310. Award "to recognize excellence in work by Saskatchewan writers." Annual competition for short stories, dramas, humor, poetry, nonfiction, juvenile fiction. Awards: Major awards (3) are $1,000; 3 awards of $100. In 1989 SWG received 118 entries for short fiction. Judges: Writers from outside the Province. Entry fee: $15 for drama (one ms allowed); $4 for other categories (multiple submissions allowed). Guidelines for SASE. Deadline: February 28. Unpublished submissions. Available only to writers living in Saskatchewan.

TENNESSEE ARTS COMMISSION INDIVIDUAL ARTISTS FELLOWSHIP (I,IV), Suite 100, 320 6th Ave. N., Nashville TN 37243-0780. (615)741-1701. Contact: Alice Swanson, director of literary arts. Competition "recognizes outstanding writers in the state." Annual award for fiction in 1991-1992. Award: up to $5,000 ($2,500 minimum). Competition receives approximately 40 submissions. Judges are 2 out-of-state jurors. Entry forms available. Writers must be residents of Tennessee.

‡TEXAS STATE WRITING COMPETITION (I, IV), Texas Freelance Writers Association, Box 9844, Fort Lauderdale FL 33310. (305)485-0795. "To offer additional opportunities for writers to earn income from their stories." Annual competition for short stories. Award: $25-100. Judges: authors, editors, teachers. Entry fee $5-7. Guidelines for SASE. Deadline: June 15. Unpublished submissions. Word length: 3,000 words. "Guidelines are revised each year and subject to change."

THURBER HOUSE RESIDENCIES (II), The Thurber House, 77 Jefferson Ave., Columbus OH 43215. (614)464-1032. Literary Director: Michael J. Rosen. "Four writers/year are chosen as writers-in-residence, one for each quarter." Award for writers of novels and story collections. $5,000 stipend and housing for a quarter in the furnished third-floor apartment of James Thurber's boyhood home. Judges: advisory panel. Guidelines for SASE. Deadline: January 1. "The James Thurber Writer-in-Residence will teach a class in the Creative Writing Program at The Ohio State University in either fiction or poetry, and will offer one public reading and a short workshop for writers in the community. Significant time outside of teaching is reserved for the writer's own work in progress. Candidates should have published at least one book with a major publisher, in any area of fiction, nonfiction or poetry, and should possess some experience in teaching."

TOWSON STATE UNIVERSITY PRIZE FOR LITERATURE (I, IV), Towson State University Foundation, Towson State University, Towson MD 21204. (301)321-2128. Contact: Annette Chappell, dean, College of Liberal Arts. Annual award. Novels or short story collections, previously published. Requirements: writer must not be over 40; must be a Maryland resident. Deadline: May 1. SASE for rules/entry forms.

JOHN TRAIN HUMOR PRIZE (I), *The Paris Review*, 541 E. 72nd St., New York NY 10021. Fiction Editor: George Plimpton. Award for the best previously unpublished work of humorous fiction, nonfiction or poetry. Annual competition for short stories. Award: $1,500 and publication in *The Paris Review*. Guidelines for SASE. Deadline March 31. Submissions should be unpublished. Manuscripts must be less than 10,000 words. No formal application form is required; regular submissions guidelines apply.

TRANSLATION CENTER AWARDS (I, II, IV), The Translation Center, 412 Dodge Hall, Columbia University, New York NY 10027. (212)854-2305. Contact: Award Secretary. Annual awards. "For outstanding translation of a substantial part of a book-length *literary* work." Award: Cash grant (varies). Entry deadline: January 15. No entry fee. Write for application form.

TRANSLATORS ASSOCIATION AWARDS (III, IV), 84 Drayton Gardens, London SW10 9SB England. Scott Moncrieff Prize for best translation into English of 20th century French work; Schlegel Tieck Prize for translations from German; John Florio Prize for translations from Italian into English. Annual competition for translations. Award: Scott Moncrieff Prize: £1,500; Schlegel-Tieck Prize: £2,000; John Florio Prize: £650. Judges: 3 translators. Deadline December 31. Previously published submissions. Awards for translations published in U.K. during year of award. U.K. publishers submit books for consideration.

MARK TWAIN AWARD (III, IV), Missouri Association of School Librarians, P.O. Box 22476, Kansas City MO 647113-2476. Estab. 1970. Annual award. To introduce children to the best of current literature for children and to stimulate reading. Previously published submissions. A committee selects pre-list of the books nominated for the award; statewide reader/selectors review and rate the books, and then children throughout the state vote to choose a winner from the final list. Books must be published two years prior to nomination for the award list. Publishers may send books they wish to nominate for the list to the committee members. Award: A bronze bust of Mark Twain, created by Barbara Shanklin, a Missouri sculptor. 1) Books should be of interest to children in grades 4 through 8; 2) written by an author living in the U.S.; 3) of literary value which may enrich children's personal lives.

UCROSS FOUNDATION/RESIDENCY (I), Residency Program/Ucross Foundation, 2836 U.S. Highway 14-16 East, Clearmont WY 82835. (307)737-2291. Award "to allow artists uninterrupted time to work in their field creatively." Biannual competition for short stories, novels, story collections and translations. Award: time to spend at Ucross to accomplish their works and ideas. Competition receives approx. 150 submissions per session. Judges: three-member selection committee. Guidelines for SASE. Deadline: March 1 and October 1. Previously published or unpublished submissions.

UNIVERSITY OF MISSOURI BREAKTHROUGH SERIES (I), 200 Lewis Hall, Columbia MO 65211. Contact: Susan McGregor Denny, associate director or Janice Smiley, administrative assistant. Biennial competition for authors whose work has not appeared in book form or who are publishing in another media other than the original book publication. Entry fee is $10. Fiction and poetry mss are read only in odd-numbered years. Receives approximately 500 entrants for each award. Competition judged by professional writer or critic. Award: Publication in series. SASE for guidelines.

UTAH ORIGINAL WRITING COMPETITION (I,IV), Utah Arts Council. 617 East South Temple, Salt Lake City UT 84012. (801)533-5895. Literary Arts Coordinator: G. Barnes. "An annual writing competition, now entering its 32nd year." Annual competition for short stories, novels and story collections. Award: varies; last year between $200-$1,000. Competition receives 700 entries. Judges: "published and award-winning judges from across America." Guidelines available, no SASE necessary. Deadline: mid-February. Submissions should be unpublished. *Limited to Utah residents*. "Some limitation on word-length. See guidelines for details."

‡VERMONT COUNCIL ON THE ARTS FELLOWSHIP (I, II, IV), Vermont Council on the Arts, 136 State Street, Montpelier VT 05602. (802)828-3291. "To support creative development." Annual competition for short stories, novels, story collections and translations. Award: $3,500 with $500 Finalist Awards. The VCA awards approximately 17-20 Fellowships annually. There is no pre-determined number of Fellowships by discipline. Judges: a peer panel makes recommendations to the VCA Board of Trustees. Guidelines for SASE after December 1. Deadline: March 15. Previously published and unpublished submissions. Applicants must be legal residents of Vermont and must have lived in VT at least 6 months prior to date of application. Word length: 10-12 pages poetry, 10-20 pages fiction. Applicants may include a synopsis or summary of longer works in addition to submitted excerpts. Applicants must be 18 or older, may not be enrolled as full-time students, and must have submitted all reports on past council grants. Grant money may not be used for foreign travel, tuition applied to academic programs, or purchase of permanent equipment. **Manuscripts should be unsigned and should indicate completion date.

VICTORIAN FELLOWSHIP OF AUSTRALIAN WRITERS ANNUAL NATIONAL LITERARY AWARDS (I, II, IV), 1/317 Barkers Rd., Kew (Melbourne) Victoria 3101 Australia. Contact: J.S. Hamilton, president, Victorian FAW. Sponsors 20 awards for Australian writers, both published and unpublished. Annual competition for shorts stories, novels and story collections. Award varies: largest award is $1,000. Competition receives over 50 entries for books, at least 100 for manuscripts. Judges: writers and critics appointed by the organizer. Guidelines for SASE. Deadline: December 31. Published or previously unpublished submissions, depending on award. Awards offered to Australians (including those living overseas) or residents of Australia. Send for guidelines, but only from October each year.

JAMES F. VICTORIN MEMORIAL AWARD (I,IV), Dialogue Publications, Inc., 3100 Oak Park Ave., Berwyn IL 60402. (312)749-1908. Contact: Bonnie Miller, editor. Annual award. "To recognize the best short story published in *Dialogue* during the previous year." Award: $100. No entry fee. Publication of any story constitutes entry. Only blind or visually handicapped entrants are eligible.

VIRGINIA CENTER FOR THE CREATIVE ARTS RESIDENCY FELLOWSHIP (I), Mt. San Angelo, Sweet Briar VA 24595. (804)946-7236. Director: William Smart. Award to "provide residencies to writers, visual artists and composers in order that they may work without interruption on their own projects. Approximately 250 fellowships awarded annually. Periodic deadlines. Award: 1 to 3 month residencies. Receives 1,000 applications/year. Judges: writers, visual artists and composers established in their fields. Application fee $15. Write for application form.

THE VIRGINIA PRIZE FOR FICTION (I,IV), Virginia Commission for the Arts, 101 N. 14th St., 17th Floor, Richmond VA 23219. (804)225-3132 Voice/TDD. "The Commission has established these awards to support and encourage the work of Virginia's professional writers, and in recognition of exceptional talent. The prizes are intended to assist writers in the creation of new works and to support writers' efforts to advance their careers." Annual competition for novels and story collections (150-page minimum submission). Award: 1st: $10,000; 2nd: $5,000; 3rd: $2,500. Competition receives approx. 130 submissions. Judges: a different out-of-state judge each year. Deadline: March 1. Unpublished submissions (short stories may have been published individually, but the collection unpublished). Virginia residents only. Program administered by Virginia Center for the Creative Arts, Sweet Briar, VA. Funded by VA. Commission for the Arts, a state agency.

‡VOGELSTEIN FOUNDATION GRANTS (II), The Ludwig Vogelstein Foundation, Inç., Box 4924, Brooklyn, NY 11240-4924. Executive Director: Frances Pishny. "A small foundation awarding grants to individuals in the arts and humanities. Criteria are merit and need. No student aid given. Send 9×14 SASE for complete information. Deadline: January 31.

HAROLD D. VURSELL MEMORIAL AWARD (III), American Academy and Institute of Arts and Letters, 633 W. 155th St., New York NY 10032. (212)368-5900. Annual award. "To single out recent writing in book form that merits recognition for the quality of its prose style. It may be given for a work of fiction, biography, history, criticism, belles lettres, memoir, journal or a work of translation." Award: $5,000. Judged by 7-member jury composed of members of the Department of Literature of the American Academy and Institute of Arts and Letters. *No applications accepted.*

EDWARD LEWIS WALLANT MEMORIAL BOOK AWARD (II, IV), 3 Brighton Rd., West Hartford CT 06117. Sponsored by Dr. and Mrs. Irving Waltman. Contact: Mrs. Irving Waltman. Annual award. Memorial to Edward Lewis Wallant, which offers incentive and encouragement to beginning writers, for books published the year before the award is conferred in the spring. Books may be submitted for consideration to Dr. Lothar Kahn, one of the permanent judges. Address: 41 Dayl Drive, Kensington CT 06037. Award: $250 plus award certificate. "Looking for creative work of fiction by an American which has significance for the American Jew. The novel (or collection of short stories) should preferably bear a kinship to the writing of Wallant. The award will seek out the writer who has not yet achieved literary prominence."

‡WASHINGTON PRIZE FOR FICTION (I), 1301 S. Scott St., Arlington VA 22204. (703)920-3771. Larry Kaltman, Director. Award: $300 (1st prize), $200 (2nd prize), $100 (3rd prize). Judges: Isolde Chapin (Washington Independent Writers). Richard Peabody (Gargoyle); Shirley Cochrane (Georgetown University). Entry fee $25. Deadline: November 30. Unpublished submissions. Word length: 75,000 words minimum.

WASHINGTON STATE ARTS COMMISSION ARTIST FELLOWSHIP AWARD (I,IV), 110 9th and Columbia, Olympia WA 97504-4111. (206)753-3860. Arts Program Manager: Karen Kamara Gose. "Unrestricted award to a mid-career artist." Biannual award for writers of short stories, novels and literary criticism. Award: $5,000. Competition receives 50 entries. Judges: peer panel. Guidelines upon request. Deadline: Spring/Summer. Literary arts award made in even-numbered years. Submissions can be either previously published or unpublished. "Applicant must be 5 years out of school in field they're applying to. No emerging artists."

‡WESTERN CANADIAN MAGAZINE AWARDS (II,IV), 3898 Hillcrest Ave., North Vancouver, British Columbia V7R 4B6 Canada. (604)984-7525. "To honour and encourage excellence." Annual competition for short stories (fiction articles in magazines). Award: $500. Entry fee: $15-20 (depending on circulation of magazine). Deadline: January. Previously published submissions (between January and December). "Must be Canadian or have earned immigrant status and the fiction article must have appeared in a publication (magazine) that has its main editorial offices located in the 4 Western provinces, the Yukon or NW territories."

WESTERN HERITAGE AWARDS (II, IV), National Cowboy Hall of Fame, 1700 NE 63rd St., Oklahoma City OK 73111. (405)478-2250. Contact: Dana Sullivan, public relations director. Annual award. "To honor outstanding quality in fiction, nonfiction and art literature." Submissions are to have been published during the previous calendar year. Award: The Wrangler, a replica of a C.M. Russell Bronze. Entry deadline: December 31. No entry fee. Entry forms and rules available November 1 for SASE. Looking for "stories that best capture the spirit of the West."

WESTERN STATES BOOK AWARDS, Western States Arts Federation, 236 Montezuma, Santa Fe NM 87501. (505)988-1166. Contact: Gina Briefs-Elgin, Program Assistance. Estab. 1984. Biannual award. "Recognition for writers living in the West; encouragement of effective production and marketing of quality books published in the West; increase of sales and critical attention." For unpublished manuscripts submitted by publisher. Award: $2,500 for authors; $5,000 for publishers. Write for information on deadline. Contest rules for SASE.

‡WILLIAM ALLEN WHITE CHILDREN'S BOOK AWARD (III), Emporia State University, 1200 Commercial, Emporia KS 66801. Contact: Mary E. Bogan, executive secretary. Estab. 1952. Annual award. To honor the memory of one of the state's most distinguished citizens by encouraging the boys and girls of Kansas to read and enjoy good books. "We do not accept submissions from authors or publishers." Award: bronze medal. The White Award Book Selection Committee looks for excellence of literary quality in fiction, poetry and nonfiction appropriate for 4th through 8th graders. All nominations to the annual White Award master list must be made by a member of the White Award Book Selection Committee.

WHITING WRITER'S AWARDS (III), Mrs. Giles Whiting Foundation, Rm 3500, 30 Rockefeller Pl., New York NY 10112. Director: Dr. Gerald Freund. To encourage the work of emergent writers and to recognize the work of older, proven writers. Annual award for writers of fiction, poetry, nonfiction and plays. Award: $25,000 (10 awards). Writers are submitted by appointed nominators and chosen for awards by an appointed selection committee. Direct applications and informal nominations not accepted by the foundation.

LAURA INGALLS WILDER AWARD (III), American Library Association/Association for Library Service to Children, 50 E. Huron St., Chicago IL 60611. Award offered every 3 years; next year 1992. "To honor a significant body of work for children, for illustration, fiction or nonfiction." Award: bronze medal.

LAURENCE L. WINSHIP BOOK AWARD (III, IV), *The Boston Globe*, Boston MA 02107. (617)929-2649. Contact: Marianne Callahan, public affairs department. Annual award. "To honor *The Globe*'s late editor who did much to encourage young talented New England authors." Previously published submissions from July 1 to July 1 each year. To be submitted by publishers. Award: $2,000. Deadline: June 30. Contest rules for SASE. Book must have some relation to New England—author, theme, plot or locale.

WISCONSIN ARTS BOARD INDIVIDUAL ARTIST PROGRAM (II,IV), 131 W. Wilson St., Suite 301, Madison WI 53703. (608)266-0190. Contact: Matt Radford. Annual award for short stories, poetry, novels, novellas, drama, essay/criticism. Awards: 3 awards of $5,000; 4 awards of $3,500; 6 awards of $1,000. Competition receives approx. 75 submissions. Judges are 3 out-of-state jurors. Entry forms or rules for SASE. Deadline: September 15. Wisconsin residents only. Students are ineligible.

WORLD'S BEST SHORT SHORT STORY CONTEST (I), English Department Writing Program, Florida State University, Tallahassee FL 32306. (904)644-4230. Contact: Jerome Stern, director. Annual award for short-short stories, unpublished, under 250 words. Prize-winning story gets $100 and broadside publication; winner and finalists are published in *Sun Dog: The Southeast Review*. Open to all. Deadline: February 15. SASE for rules.

WRITERS AT WORK FELLOWSHIP COMPETITION (I), Writers At Work, Box 8857, Salt Lake City UT 84108. (801)355-0264. Contact: Steve Wanderli, director. "To award new talent—and in addition to the prizes listed below, winners are invited to attend the Writers at Work Conference (June 12-18) free of charge. Award: first: $500 and publication in *Quarterly West*; second: $200. Competition receives approx. 600 submissions. Judges: preliminary judges *Quarterly West* staff; final judges Francois Camoin, W. D. Wetherell and Peggy Schumaker. Entry fee $6. Guidelines for SASE. Unpublished submissions.

WRITER'S DIGEST ANNUAL WRITING COMPETITION (Short Story Division) (I,II), *Writer's Digest*, 1507 Dana Ave., Cincinnati OH 45207. (513)531-2222. Entry deadline: May 31. All entries must be original, unpublished and not previously submitted to a *Writer's Digest* contest. Length: 2,000 words maximum, one entry only. No acknowledgment will be made of receipt of mss nor will mss be returned. Grand Prize is a trip to New York City with arrangements to meet editors in writer's field. Other awards include electronic typewriters, reference books, plaques and certificates of recognition. Names of grand prize winner and top 100 winners are announced in the October issue of *Writer's Digest*. Top two entries published in booklet ($4.50). Send SASE to *WD* Writing Competition for rules or see January-May issues of *Writer's Digest*.

‡WRITERS GUILD OF ALBERTA LITERARY AWARD (II,IV), Writers Guild of Alberta, 10523-100 Avenue, Edmonton Alberta T5J 0A8 Canada. (403)426-5892. "To recognize, reward and foster writing excellence." Annual competition for novels and story collections. Award: $500 cash, plus leather-bound copy of winning work. Short story competition receives 5-10 submissions; novel competition receives about 20; children's literature category up to 40. Judges: three published writers. Guidelines for SASE. Deadline December 31. Previously published submissions (between January and December). Open to Alberta authors, resident for previous 18 months. Entries must be book-length.

WRITERS' JOURNAL ANNUAL FICTION CONTEST (I), Box 9148, N. St. Paul MN 55109. (612)433-3626. Publisher/Managing Editor: Valerie Hockert. Annual award for short stories. Award: 1st place: $200; 2nd place: $75; 3rd place: $25. Also give honorable mentions. Competition receives approximately 400 submissions/year. Judges are Valerie Hockert, Anne Miller and others. Entry fee $5 each. Maximum of 2 entries/person. Entry forms or rules for SASE. Maximum length is 3,000 words. Two copies of each entry are required – one *without* name or address of writer.

WYOMING COUNCIL ON THE ARTS FRANK NELSON DOUBLEDAY MEMORIAL AWARD (I,IV), 2320 Capitol Ave., Cheyenne WY 82002. (307)777-7742. Contact: literature consultant. To "honor the most promising work by a woman writer." Annual award; no genre restrictions; combined genres acceptable. Award: $1,000 grant. Competition receives 30-40 entries. Judge: A well-known female author (changes each year). Guidelines for SASE. Contact for 1990 deadline. Maximum length for fiction, nonfiction and drama 25 pages; poetry 10 pages. "Writers must have been Wyoming residents for one year prior to entry deadline; must be a woman writer; must not be a full-time student or full-time tenured faculty member."

WYOMING COUNCIL ON THE ARTS, LITERARY FELLOWSHIPS (I, IV), Wyoming Council on the Arts, 2320 Capitol Ave., Cheyenne WY 82002. (307)777-7742. Contact: literature consultant. Award to "honor the most outstanding new work of Wyoming writers – fiction, nonfiction, drama, poetry." Annual competition for short stories, novels, awards, story collections, translations, poetry. Award: 4 awards $25,000 each. Competition receives approx. 120 submissions. Judges: panel of writers selected each year from outside Wyoming. Deadline: Fall. Applicants "must be Wyoming resident for one year prior to application deadline. Must not be a full-time student *or* a full-time tenured faculty member." No genre exclusions; combined genres acceptable. 25 pages double spaced maximum; 10 pages maximum for poetry. Guidelines for SASE. Winners may not apply for 4 years after receiving fellowships.

WYOMING COUNCIL ON THE ARTS NELTJE BLANCHAN MEMORIAL AWARD (I, IV), 2320 Capitol Ave., Cheyenne WY 82002. (307)777-7742. Contact: literature consultant. To "honor best new writing inspired by nature. This does not mean the work need be traditional nature writing. Rather, the view presented should arise from a relationship with the natural world." Annual award, no genre restrictions; combined genres acceptable. Award: $1,000 grant. Competition receives 80 entries. Judge: A well-known writer whose work is informed by nature (changes each year). Guidelines for SASE. Contact for 1990 deadline. Maximum length for fiction, nonfiction and drama 25 pages; poetry 10 pages. "Writers must have been Wyoming residents for one year prior to entry deadline; must not be a full-time student *or* full-time tenured faculty member."

YADDO RESIDENCIES (I, II), Box 395, Saratoga Springs NY 12866-0395. President: Myra Sklarew. To provide undisturbed working time for writers and artists. Award for authors of short stories, novels, translations, story collections. Award: one to two month residency at Yaddo. Judges: advisory committee. Filing fee $20. Guidelines for SASE. Deadlines: January 15 and August 1. "Those qualified for invitation to Yaddo are writers, visual artists and composers who have already published (or exhibited or had performed) work of high artistic merit. Unpublished work may serve as the sole basis for admission, if the judges panels feels that it shows unusual promise."

YOUNG ADULT CANADIAN BOOK AWARD (II, IV), Young Adult Services Interest Group, c/o Saskatoon Public Library, 311 23rd St., E, Saskatoon, Saskatchewan S7K OJ6 Canada. Contact: Nancy E. Black, convener of book award committee. Established 1980 by the Young Adult Caucus of the

Saskatchewan Library Association. Transfered to YASIG 1988. Annual award given when merited. To recognize an outstanding Canadian work of fiction written for young adults. Submissions should have been published during the previous calendar year. Award: Recognition through media press releases; leatherbound copy of book; "usually an author tour." Judged by Young Adult Services Group of the Canadian Library Association.

‡**YOUNG READER'S CHOICE AWARD (III)**, Pacific Northwest Library Association, Graduate School of Library and Information Sciences, FM-3 University of Washington, Seattle WA 98195. (206)543-1897. Contact: Carol A. Doll. Award "to promote reading as an enjoyable activity and to provide children an opportunity to endorse a book they consider an excellent story." Annual award. Award: silver medals. Judges: Children's librarians and teachers nominate; children in grades 4-8 vote for their favorite book on the list. Guidelines for SASE. Deadline: February 1. Previously published submission. Writers must be nominated by children's librarians and teachers.

Other contests

The following contest, grants and awards appeared in the 1989 edition of *Novel & Short Story Writer's Market* but do not appear in the 1990 edition. Those contests, grants and awards that did not respond to our request for an update appear below without further explanation. If a reason for the omission was available, it was included next to the listing name. There are several reasons why a contest may not appear—the contest may not be an annual event, for example, or last year's listing might have resulted in too many unsuitable manuscripts.

Jane Addams Peace Association Children's Book Award
Alberta New Fiction Competition
American Literary Translation Association Gregory Rabassa Prize
Arkansas Arts Council Individual Artist Fellowship
Asted/Prix Marie-ClaireDaveluy
Emily Clark Balch Awards
The Blue Mountain Center
Burnaby Writers Society Annual Competition (not for fiction this year)
Canada Council Awards
Columbia Magazine Editors' Awards
Cotton Boll Short Story Contest
Council for Wisconsin Writers Pauletter Chandler Award (not for fiction this year)
Daly City Poetry and Short Story Contest
Edmonton Journal's Literary Awards
Foster City Annual Writers Contest
Friends of American Writer's Contest
Georgette Heyer Historical Novel Prize
Theodore Christian Hoepfner Award
Hohenberg Award
Idaho Commission on the Arts Awards
Institute for Humane Studies Felix Morley Memorial Prizes
Iowa School of Letters Awards for Short Fiction/The John Simmons Short Fiction Award
McKendree Writers Association Writing Contest
National Book Council/Qantas New Writers Award
The Julian Ocean Literary Award (discontinued)
The Scott O'Dell Award for Historical Fiction
Pacific North West Writers Conference
Pegasus Prize
Pen/Nelson Algren Fiction Award (discontinued)
Philomathean Book Award
The Present Tense/Joel H. Cavior Literary Award
Redbook Short Story Contest (discontinued)
Rockland Center for the Arts Writer-in-Residence
Carl Sandburg Awards
The Seattle Weekly Annual Holiday Short Story Contest
Charlie May Simon Book Award
Southern Arts Literary Prize
Tales of the Old West Westerner Awards (moved, unable to contact)
University of East Anglia Writing Fellowship (too local)
West Virginia Department of Culture and History Arts and Humanities Division, Artist-in-Residence Program
Morton Dauwen Zabel Award

Literary Agents

You've just put the finishing touches on your manuscript, researched the market and compiled a list of publishers you're sure will jump at the chance to publish your book, certain to become a run-away bestseller. Six-figure dreams dance in your head until you discover (after submitting to everybody on your list) not only are publishers not salivating, they won't even look at your work. Manuscripts are returned unopened and violently stamped "No Unsolicited Submissions!"

To many new writers this scenario is becoming all-too familiar. Every year more publishers are closing their doors to unsolicited submissions, not because they are against new writers, but simply as a reaction to market conditions. As more publishers are sold to corporate giants or are merged with other publishers to cut costs, more are losing valuable staff members. Some of the first to go are the front lines of the editorial offices—those first readers and young editors whose job it has been to read through the hundreds of unsolicited manuscripts publishers receive each week. Overwhelmed by the workload, publishers are now looking to literary agents to provide that first screening step.

Who needs an agent and who does not

Writers, especially those whose work is considered mainstream, will want to seriously consider getting an agent. Juvenile book writers and most writers of category fiction may continue to find publishers of these books receptive to unsolicited material, but much of the mainstream fiction published today is agented.

If you are submitting short fiction to literary journals or even commercial magazines, you do not need an agent. Payment for magazine fiction is just not enough to cover the added expense of an agent and most agents will not represent short fiction unless they already handle a writer's novels. If you have a collection of short stories, including many that have been published elsewhere, you may want to query an agent if you are considering marketing your work to a large publisher.

You do not need an agent to approach most small press publishers and, if your work is experimental or has a limited or specialized audience, you may want to send manuscripts to small presses instead of commercial outlets. If you are a new writer, you may also want to try to get published in a literary journal or by a small press before approaching an agent and a larger publisher.

How agents operate

There are no degrees necessary or licenses required to be an agent. In fact, anyone with enough money for an office and a telephone can call themselves an agent. That is why we ask agents in our book a number of detailed questions about how they run their businesses. We want writers to know as much as possible about an agency's operation and fees.

While anyone can call themselves an agent, it takes a certain set of skills to be successful as an agent. A few agents are also lawyers and some lawyers act as agents to some degree, but an understanding of the legal aspects of contracts, as well as their negotiation, is mandatory whether or not an agent has a law degree. Many agents come from editing backgrounds and a working knowledge of the publishing industry is essential. Agents should know about rights and have a good amount of marketing savvy.

Most agents charge an author a standard commission of 10 percent on all advances and royalties earned on domestic sales and 20 percent of foreign sales (often shared with a foreign agent). In recent years some agents' fees have gone as high as 20 percent. Note, too, that several agents also require writers to pay some of the costs of handling their work including photocopying, express mail and phone calls.

Some agents also charge reading fees. A fee of $50 to $100 is not uncommon or unreasonable and the money is often used to reimburse an outside reader. Some agents charge fees and return them if they decide to represent the author. Yet beware of agents who charge several hundred dollars. Reading fees rarely guarantee representation and authors should try non-fee agents first.

Some agents offer criticism services, but many writers tell us critiques by such agents are not detailed. You may get better feedback for less cost through a writers' group or from a writing instructor whose opinion you value.

Agents are not writing teachers or editors—they are "business partners." A good agent has a client's best interest in mind. Agents today provide much of the support and stability once provided by editors. In a recent article agent Richard Balkin described his role as that of an "outfitter and guide. I lead, I teach, I reassure, I watch for hazards, and I look for the streams with the biggest possible fish. No matter what we catch, I've tried my best to make the trip as satisfying and profitable as I could."

Approaching agents

Shop around for your agent. Examine the agents in this book and check the Category Index located just before the Markets Index to find a list of agents who are interested in your type of work. It is better to send queries to agents first, because sending complete manuscripts to several agents is expensive. It is usually acceptable to query more than one agent at a time, but if more than one agent is interested in seeing your work, it is courteous to send manuscripts only to one agent at a time.

Make sure your query letter is as carefully written as your manuscript. If your work can be classified as a particular genre or category, a brief plot description (one or two paragraphs) may be all you need in your query letter. But if your novel is mainstream, you will want to include a detailed outline and one or two sample chapters with your letter.

As with publishers, choose an agent who handles material similar to your own. Many agents who work on the West Coast are experienced in handling scripts and are familiar with the movie business. Many writers feel New York agents have the home field advantage with book publishers, but don't ignore agents in the South or Midwest. With fax machines, express mail and other advances in office technology these days proximity is only a minor consideration.

In addition to checking the Category Index, be sure to read each listing carefully. Note if the agent charges a fee and check the list of "recent sales." This list will give you some idea of the type of work the agent handles. Has the agent you are considering placed books with publishers with which you are familiar? If you have last year's copy of *Novel & Short Story Writer's Market*, check to see if the titles in the Recent Sales subhead have changed from previous years. Agents who sell new fiction titles every year to different publishers are obviously a good bet.

Other sources of information

Literary Agents; How to Get and Work with the Right One for You, by Michael Larson (Writer's Digest Books) contains useful information about working with agents. Also two books that offer insight into publishing from an agent's perspective are *Beyond the Best Seller: A Literary Agent Takes You Inside Publishing*, by Richard Curtis (NAL) and *Writer's Guide to Contract Negotiations* by Richard Balkin (Writer's Digest Books).

For more agent listings see *Literary Agents of North America* (Author Aid/Research Associates International, 340 E. 52nd St., New York NY 10019). This annual directory lists agents by name, region, specialty and size. One way to find successful agents is to look in the Poet's & Writer's annual *Directory of Poets and Fiction Writers* (c/o Poet's & Writers, 201 W. 54th St., New York NY 10019). This directory contains the names and addresses of several well-known authors, but many can only be contacted through their agents. You can find out which agents handle the work of writers you admire.

Some of the agents listed in this section belong to professional organizations. The Independent Literary Agents Association (I.L.L.A.) and the Society of Authors' Representatives (S.A.R.) offer brochures and lists of members for SASE. While membership in these organizations is voluntary, agents who are members are expected to follow the groups' codes of ethics and standards. The I.L.L.A. is located in Suite 1205, 432 Park Ave. S., New York NY 10016. S.A.R. is at 10 S. Portland Ave., Brooklyn NY 11217.

DOMINICK ABEL LITERARY AGENCY, INC., 498 West End Ave., #12C, New York NY 10024. (212)877-0710. Agency estab. 1975. Adult fiction and nonfiction only. Adult fiction specialty: mystery and suspense. Usually obtains new clients via recommendations. Currently represents 75 authors. Occasionally accepts new clients. Query with SASE. Reports to queries in 1 week; to mss in 3 weeks. New/unpublished writers: 10%. Member of I.L.A.A.

Terms: Agent's commission: 10% on domestic sales; 20% on foreign sales. Charges for photocopying expenses, overseas mailing and authors' books.

ACTON AND DYSTEL INC., (formerly Edward J. Acton, Inc.)928 Broadway, New York NY 10010. (212)473-1700. Agent contact: Ed Novak. Agency estab. 1975. Novels. Also reviews nonfiction (50%-50% fiction to nonfiction). Special interests: Commercial works. Usually obtains new clients via author references. Currently represents 100 authors. Presently accepting limited number of new clients. Query first. No unsolicited mss. Responds to queries in 1 month. New/unpublished writers: 10%. Member of I.L.A.A.

Recent Sales: *The Woman*, by Emily Frankel (Putnam); *The Last Kamikaze*, by by M.E. Morris (Random House).

Terms: Agent's commission: 15% on domestic sales; 19% on foreign sales.

LEE ALLAN AGENCY, Box 18617, Milwaukee WI 53218. (414)357-7708; call for our Fax number. Agent contact: Lee A. Matthias. Estab. 1983. Novels and feature film screenplays. Also reviews nonfiction (95%-5% fiction to nonfiction). Special interests: genre fiction, including mystery, thriller, horror, science fiction, western. Usually obtains new clients via "market directory listings, such as *L.M.P.*, *L.A.N.A.*, *Writer's Market*, Writer's Guild List, and various other directories and lists; also recommendations and writer conferences. Currently represents 20 authors. Presently accepting new clients. Send query. Responds to queries in 3-4 weeks; to mss in 4-6 weeks. New/unpublished writers: 80%. Member of WGA; Horror Writers of America. Foreign rights handled by Mildred Hird, NYC.

Recent Sales: *Fire Arrow, The Fire Dream* and *Valley of the Shadow*, by Franklin Allen Leib (Presidio Press); *Barrow*, by John Deakins (New American Library); *Shadowdale* and *Tantras*, by Richard Awlinson (aka Scott Ciencin) (TSR).

Terms: Agent's commission: 10% on domestic sales; higher on foreign sales. 100% of income derived from commission on ms sales. "From new, unpublished writers, we are most interested in material directed toward an established market. If a novel, we prefer fresh, innovative and strong mysteries, thrillers and horror stories. If a feature theatrical-release type screenplay, we prefer low-to medium-budgeted contemporary genre scripts of high quality—no exploitation or trend-followers—written with an immediately compelling, hook-type premise, engaging characters, and a strong point of view. Scripts need to be quite distinctive to get serious consideration. No television material, articles, poetry, or short stories considered. Proper length and format essential. Return postage and/or SASE must accompany all correspondence until we represent the prospective writer. If you do not hear from us soon enough, call during business hours; be a friendly squeaky wheel. Updates when no substantive news is in the offing should be initiated by the author. Otherwise, we'll call when we have something."

‡JAMES ALLEN LITERARY AGENCY, 538 E. Harford St., Milford PA 18337. Agency estab. 1974. Novels. Also reviews nonfiction (90%-10% fiction to nonfiction). Special interests: "genre fiction, especially SF, fantasy, historicals, mysteries, horror and high quality mainstream." Obtains new clients "most happily through recommendation by people whose opinion I respect; secondarily by unsolicited queries." Currently represents 50 authors. Presently accepting hardly any new clients "and *only* if previously published." Query first with descriptive letter, 2-3 page synopsis and SASE. Responds to queries in 1 week; to mss in 3 months. New/unpublished writers: 5%.

Recent Sales: *Mission Tori*, by Johanna M. Bolton (Del Rey Books); *The Gulf*, by David Poyer (St. Martin's Press); *Torments*, by Lisa W. Cantrell (Tor Books).
Terms: Agent's commission: 10% on domestic sales; 20% on dramatic-rights sales; 20% on foreign sales. Charges for extraordinary expenses: "copying of full length mss, intercontinental phone calls on client's behalf—not billed; rather, deducted from future income. I am turning away just about all of the people who approach me; I feel that my list is comfortably full and it takes something really extraordinary to inspire my interest. And absolutely *no* response is given to anyone who queries without a SASE. When I mention commissions on dramatic rights, this reflects that I market film rights to published books that I have sold—I am not representing original screenplays or filmscripts."

MARCIA AMSTERDAM AGENCY, 41 W. 82nd St., New York NY 10024. (212)873-4945. Agency estab. 1969. Novels. Also reviews nonfiction (90%-10% fiction to nonfiction). Special interests: young adult, horror, humor, mainstream, science fiction, romance, men's adventure, mysteries. Usually obtains new clients via recommendations and query letters. Presently accepting new clients. Query with first three sample chapters and outline. Responds to queries in 2 weeks; to mss in 1 month. New/unpublished writers: 80-90%. Member of WGA.
Recent Sales: *Silvercat*, by Kristopher Clark Franklin (Bantam); *Ash Ock*, by Christopher Hinz (St. Martin's); *Black Sun* by Robert Leininger (Avon).
Terms: Agent's commission: 15% on domestic and foreign sales. Charges for legal fees when agreed upon, occasional cable, telex, etc. 100% of income derived from commissions on sales. "If there is no SASE, we do not return queries or submissions."

AUTHORS' MARKETING SERVICES LTD., 217 Degrassi St., Toronto, Ontario M4M 2K8 Canada. (416)463-7200. Agency estab. 1978. Novels. Also reviews nonfiction (60%-40% fiction to nonfiction). Special interests: mainstream, male-adventure/thriller, horror, contemporary, regency. Usually obtains new clients via recommendations, word of mouth and advertising. Currently represents 25 authors. Presently accepting new clients. *Fiction*: We require a query letter first and then, from unpublished authors, the entire manuscript. *Nonfiction*: We require a query letter and then a proposal containing outline and two sample chapters. Responds to queries in 1 week; to mss in 6 weeks. New/unpublished writers: 35%.
Recent Sales: *Warsaw Concerto*, by Dennis Jones (St. Martin's); *With Burning Sorrow*, by Ted Simon (Random House); *Dragon's Play*, by John Pearson (Stoddart).
Terms: Agent's commission: 15% on Canadian/US sales; 20% on foreign sales. Charges $225 to review full mss by unpublished authors. "Fee includes a detailed critique and evaluation, which will indicate the weaknesses of the work, and offer specific suggestions as to how they can be eliminated." 95% of income derived from commission on ms sales; 5% from criticism service.

THE AXELROD AGENCY, INC., Room 5805, 350 Fifth Ave., New York NY 10118. (212)629-5620. Agency estab. 1983. Novels. Also reviews nonfiction (50%-50% fiction to nonfiction). Special interests: mainstream, mysteries. Usually obtains new clients via recommendations from others; at conferences. Currently represents 30 authors. Presently accepting new clients. Query. Responds to queries in 1 week; to mss in 1 month. New/unpublished writers: 20%.
Terms: Agent's commission: 10% on domestic sales; 20% on foreign sales. Charges extra for photocopying expenses. 100% of income derived from commission on ms sales.

BILL BERGER ASSOCIATES, 444 E. 58th St., New York NY 10022. (212)486-9588. Fiction and nonfiction. Query.
Terms: Agent's commission: 10%.

THE BLAKE GROUP LITERARY AGENCY, One Turtle Creek Village, Suite 600, Dallas TX 75219. Director/Agent: Ms. Lee B. Halff. Agency estab. 1979. Novels, novellas, story collections. Also reviews nonfiction (50%-50% fiction to nonfiction). Special interest: general. Usually obtains new clients via recommendations from others and publications. Currently represents 40 authors. Presently accepting new clients. Query first with sample chapters. Responds to queries within 1 month, to mss or chapters in 3 months, "depending on workload." New/unpublished writers: 50%.
Sales: *Captured on Corregdor*, by John M. Wright, Jr. (McFarland & Co.); *Modern Languages for Musicians*, by Julie Yarbrough (Pendragon Press); *Linda Richards* article, by Katherine Kelly (*Cricket* magazine).
Terms: Agent's commission: 10% on domestic sales; 20% on foreign sales. Will read at no charge query letter and two sample chapters. Offers criticism service "if author wants a critique": *$100 for book-length manuscript (400 page maximum); $75 for less than 100 pages*. "Written critique done by a qualified consulting editor." 95% of income derived from commission on ms sales; 5% from criticism service. "No submissions read unless accompanied by a self-addressed, pre-stamped return mailer or envelope."

HARRY BLOOM AGENCY, 16272 Via Embeleso, San Diego CA 92128. (619)487-5531. Agent Contact: Patrice Dale. Estab. 1956. Novels. Also reviews nonfiction (80%-20% fiction to nonfiction). Special interest: mainstream. Usually obtains new clients via recommendations from others. Presently accepting new clients. Send in query. Responds to queries in 2 weeks; to mss in 3-4 weeks. New/unpublished writers: 10%.

Terms: Agent's commission: 10% on domestic sales; 10% on foreign sales. 100% of income derived from commission on ms sales.

REID BOATES LITERARY AGENCY, 44 Mt. Ridge Dr., Wayne NJ 07470. (201)628-7523. Agent nonfiction (15%-85% fiction to nonfiction). Special interests: mainstream, literary and popular. Usually obtains new clients via referral. Currently represents 45 authors. Presently accepting new clients. Query first. Responds to queries in 1 month. New/unpublished writers: 20%.

Recent Sales: *Survival*, nonfiction thriller by Ron Arias (New American Library); *Autobiography of Ava Gardner*, (Bantam).

Terms: Agent's commission: 15% on domestic and movie sales; 20% on foreign sales. Charges for photocopying complete ms. 100% of income derived from commission on ms sales.

BOOK PEDDLERS OF DEEPHAVEN, 18326 Minnetonka Blvd., Deephaven MN 55391. (612)475-3527. Agent contact: Vicki Lansky. Agency estab. 1983. Reviews mainly nonfiction (10%-90% fiction to nonfiction). Usually obtains new clients via recommendations, publicity. Currently represents 25 authors. Accepting few new clients. Query with outline/proposal or outline plus sample chapters and SASE. Responds to queries in 2 weeks. New/unpublished writers: 70%. Member of I.L.A.A.

Sales: *The American-Jewish Baby Name Book*, by Smadar Sidi (Harper and Row); *What You Need to Know About Medicare*, by Mason and Noehgren (NAL).

Terms: Agent's commission: 15% on domestic sales; 20% on foreign sales.

GEORGES BORCHARDT INC., 136 E. 57th St., New York NY 10022. (212)753-5785. Agency estab. 1967. Novels, novellas, short stories, story collections. Also reviews nonfiction (35%-65% fiction to nonfiction). Special interest: literary. Usually obtains new clients via recommendations from others. Currently represents 200 authors. Presently accepting "very few" new clients. Query. No unsolicited mss.

Recent Sales: *Lust and Other Stories*, by Susan Minot (Seymour Lawrence); *Walking the Tightrope*, by Francine du Plessix Gray (Doubleday).

Terms: Agent's commission: 10% on domestic sales; 20% on foreign sales. Charges for photocopying expenses. 100% of income derived from commission on ms sales.

THE BARBARA BOVA LITERARY AGENCY, 207 Sedgwick Rd., West Hartford CT 06107. (203)521-5915. Agent contact: Barbara Bova. Agency estab. 1978. Novels. Also review nonfiction (30%-70% fiction to nonfiction). Special interests: science mysteries, science fiction. Usually obtains new clients via "recommendations from others, occasionally over-the-transom mss." Currently represents 20 authors. Presently accepting new clients. Send query first, don't send mss to read. Responds to queries in 2 weeks; to mss in 2 months. New/unpublished writers: 18%.

Recent Sales: *Alvin Maker*, by Orson Scott Card (St. Martin's); *Peacekeepers*, by Ben Bova (Tor Books); *Stellar Shepherd*, by Kevin Egan (Crown).

Terms: Charges reading fee to unpublished writers. 99.9% of income derived from commission on ms sales; .01% from criticism service. "I do not accept anything without a letter of inquiry first with a self-addressed return envelope included."

BRANDT & BRANDT LITERARY AGENTS, INC., 1501 Broadway, New York NY 10036. (212)840-5760. Agency Contact: Carl Brandt. Agency estab. 1913. Novels, novellas, short stories, story collections, nonfiction. Usually obtains new clients via recommendations by editors and current clients. Currently represents 150 authors. Accepting new clients. Query first. Responds in 1 week. Member of S.A.R.

Terms: Agent's commission: 10% on domestic sales; 20% on foreign sales. 100% of income derived from commissions on ms sales.

RUTH HAGY BROD LITERARY AGENCY, 15 Park Ave., New York NY 10016. (212)683-3232 or 674-0403. Agent contact: Ann Hawwood-Burton. Agency estab. 1977. Novels, story collections. Also reviews nonfiction (60%-40% fiction to nonfiction). Special interests: mainstream, mystery. Usually obtains new clients via solicitation. Presently accepting new clients. Query. Responds to queries in 1-2 weeks; to mss in 1-2 months.

Terms: Agent's commission: 15% on domestic sales. 100% of income derived from commissions on ms sales.

NED BROWN INC., P.O. Box 1044, Malibu CA 90265. Full-length fiction and nonfiction. Send query with SASE. Presently accepting new clients "only if published commercially or recommended by another author, client or publisher."
Terms: Agent's commission: 10%.

CURTIS BROWN, LTD., 10 Astor Pl., New York NY 10003. (212)473-5400. West Coast office: Suite 309, 606 North Largemont Ave., Los Angeles, CA 90004, (213)461-8365; Canadian office: Suite 400, 1235 Bay St., Toronto M5R 3K4 Canada. (416)923-9111. Contact: Perry Knowlton (Chairman/Chief Executive), Peter Ginsberg (President), Emilie Jacobson, Marilyn Marlow, Henry Dunow, Irene Skolnick,Maureen Walters or Clyde Taylor. Fiction and nonfiction (50%-50% fiction to nonfiction). Presently accepting new clients. Query by letter first with SASE. No reading fee. Responds to queries in 2 weeks; to mss in 1 month. Member of S.A.R. and I.L.A.A.
Terms: Charges for special postage (e.g., express mail), telexes, book purchases for subsidiary-rights sales. 100% of income derived from commissions on ms sales.

PEMA BROWNE LTD., 185 E. 85th St., New York NY 10028. (212)369-1925. Agent contact: Pema Browne, Perry J. Browne. Novels. Also reviews nonfiction (60%-40% fiction to nonfiction). Special interests: mass-market romance, thrillers, horror, young adult, picture books, mainstream. Usually obtains new clients via editors, listings, word-of-mouth. Currently represents 40 authors. Presently accepting new clients. Send synopsis plus sample chapters and SASE. Responds to queries in 1 week; to mss in 1 month. New/unpublished writers: 50%. Reading fee for unpublished *book* authors.
Recent Sales: *Extraordinary Perceptions*, by Ron Dee (horror, Dell); *How to Save Big Money When You Lease a Car*, by Michael Flinn (Putnam/Perigee).
Terms: Agent's commission: 15% on domestic sales; 20% on foreign sales. 100% of income derived from commissions on ms sales. "We only review manuscripts not sent out to publishers or other agents."

JANE BUTLER, ART & LITERARY AGENT, 212 Third St., Milford PA 18337. (717)296-2629. Agency estab. 1980. Novels. Also reviews nonfiction (75%-25% fiction to nonfiction). Special interests: science fiction, fantasy, horror, historicals and mystery. Usually obtains new clients by recommendations. Query only, no sample chapters. "NO SASE NO RESPONSE!" Responds to queries in 3 weeks.
Recent Sales: *The Horns of Hattin*, by Judith Tarr (Doubleday Foundation); *Goblin Moon*, by Teresa Edgerton (Berkley Books); *Brother Lowdown*, by Sharon Epperson (St. Martin's).
Terms: Agent's commission: 10% on domestic sales; 20% on foreign sales.

MARIA CARVAINIS AGENCY, INC., 235 West End Ave., New York NY 10023. (212)580-1559. Contact: Maria Carvainis. Agency estab. 1977. Novels, story collections. Also reviews nonfiction (65%-35% fiction to nonfiction). Special interests: general fiction, mainstream, historicals, Regencies, suspense, mysteries, westerns, category romance and young adult novels. Obtains new clients through the recommendations of clients, editors, attendance of conferences and letters of query. Currently represents 60 clients. Accepting new clients. Query with SASE. Responds to queries in 2-3 weeks "if not earlier"; to mss in 4-12 weeks. New/unpublished writers: 15%. Member of Independent Literary Agents Association, Writers Guild of America, The Authors Guild, Romance Writers of America.
Recent Sales: *Mirror Image*, by Sandra Brown; *A Time for Legends*, by Norma Beishir; *Easter Weekend*, by David Bottoms; *Secret Sins*, by Joann Ross.
Terms: Agent's commission: 15% on domestic sales; 20% on foreign sales. 100% of income derived from commissions on ms sales. "I view the project's editorial needs and the author's professional and career development as integral components of the literary agent's role, in addition to the negotiation of intricate contracts and the maintenance of close contact with the New York City publishing industry."

MARTHA CASSELMAN LITERARY AGENCY, Box 342, Calistoga CA 94515-0342. (707)942-4341. Agency estab. 1979. Novels, nonfiction (20%-80% fiction to nonfiction). Special interests: mainstream; food-related books; biography; children's. Usually obtains new clients via referrals from clients and editors. Currently represents 25 authors. Query with outline/proposal. No multiple submissions. No unsolicited mss. Responds to queries in 2-4 weeks. New/unpublished writers: 40-60%. Member of I.L.A.A. "I regret I cannot return long-distance phone queries; send written query, please."
Terms: Agent's commission: 15% on domestic sales; 10% for foreign agent and other sub agents. Charges for copying and overnight mail expenses.

THE LINDA CHESTER LITERARY AGENCY, 265 Coast, La Jolla CA 92037. (619)454-3966. Agent contact: Linda Chester. Estab. originally 1977-1984; reopened 1987. Novels, novellas, short stories and short collections. Also reviews nonfiction (40%-60% fiction to nonfiction). Special interest: mainstream. Usually obtains new clients via recommendations from others, solicitation, at conferences. Currently represents 50 authors. Presently accepting new clients. Send query and outline/proposal first *no sample letters*. Reports on queries in 1 week; on mss in 2-3 weeks. New/unpublished writers: 50%.

Recent Sales: "My agency has been closed for four years and was recently reopened in 1987. I am presently developing fictional writers, and several are on the verge of selling. The following authors, works and publishers are ones I worked with in the past: *The Singer and the Stone*, by John Willet (Houghton Mifflin); *Epidemic 9*, by Richard Lerner (William Morrow & Co.); and *Leaving the Enchanted Forest*, by Stephanie Covington and Linda Beckett (Harper & Row)."

Terms: Agent's commission: 15% on domestic sales; 20% on foreign sales. "I charge a nonrefundable deposit to cover ordinary expenses incurred (phone calls, clerical, etc.)." 99% of income derived from commission on sales; 1% reading fees. "When the agency was in operation between 1977-1984, I mostly handled nonfiction. But since I reopened in 1987, I am trying to develop a strong fiction side to my agency."

CINEMA TALENT INTERNATIONAL, Suite 808, 8033 Sunset Blvd., Hollywood CA 90046. Agent contact: George Kriton. Agency estab. 1979. Motion picture and television scripts and stories. Also reviews nonfiction. Special interests: motion picture and television. Usually obtains new clients via solicitation and recommendations. Currently represents 25 authors. Presently accepting new clients. Send query. Responds to queries in 3 weeks. New/unpublished writers: 35%.

Recent Sales: Motion picture and TV scripts on assignment to my clients.

Terms: Agent's commission: 10% on domestic sales. 100% of income derived from commission on ms sales.

SJ CLARK LITERARY AGENCY, 101 Randall St., San Francisco CA 94131. (415)285-7401. Agent Contact: Sue Clark. Novels. Also reviews nonfiction (75%-25% fiction to nonfiction). Special interests: mystery, psychic, children's. Usually obtains new clients by word of mouth. Represents 15 writers. Presently accepting new clients. Query, then send entire ms. New/unpublished writers: 90%.

Terms: Agent's commission: 15%.

RUTH COHEN, INC., Box 7626, Menlo Park CA 94025. (415)854-2054. Novels. Also reviews nonfiction (60%-40% fiction to nonfiction). Special interests: detective mysteries, juvenile, young adult, historical romance. Usually obtains new clients via recommendations from others; at conferences. Currently represents 70 authors. Presently accepting new clients. Query letter and 10 pages of manuscript. Responds to queries in 2-3 weeks; no unsolicited mss. Member of I.L.A.A.

Sales: *No Way Out* (Harper and Row); *Dear Baby* (Macmillan); *Knaves and Hearts* (Avon).

Terms: Agent's commission: 15% on domestic sales; 20% on foreign sales. Charges for photocopying expenses. 100% of income derived from commissions on ms sales. Writers must include SASE.

HY COHEN LITERARY AGENCY, 111 W. 57th St., New York NY 10019. (212)757-5237. Fiction and nonfiction. Send sample chapters with SASE "if ms is to be returned." Represents approximately 30 writers. Obtains writers via recommendation, conferences, unsolicited mss and queries. New/unpublished writers: 85%.

Terms: Agent's commission: 10%.

COLLIER ASSOCIATES, 2000 Flat Run Rd., Seaman OH 45679. (513)764-1234. Agency estab. 1976. Novels. Also reviews nonfiction. Special interests (adult only): historical romance, detective, SF, fantasy, war. No short stories, articles or poetry. Usually obtains new clients via recommendations and queries. Currently represents 75 authors. Occasionally accepts new clients. Query with outline/proposal or outline plus sample chapters and SASE. Responds to queries in 3-4 weeks; to mss in 6-8 weeks. Member of S.A.R. and I.L.A.A.

Recent Sales: *Death Chain*, by Ken Greenhall (Pocket Books); *Hot Streak*, by Jill Barkin (Berkley).

Terms: Agent's commission: 15% on domestic sales; 20% on foreign sales. Charges for express mail and copies of books ordered from publisher if author approves. 100% of income derived from commissions on mss sales. "This is a small agency run by two people, and it handles authors and contracts dating back to the 1960s from predecessor agencies. So agency is extremely selective in accepting new authors of fiction – at most two or three new clients a year are tried out, including through referrals."

FRANCES COLLIN LITERARY AGENT, (formerly Marie Rodell-Frances Collin Literary Agency), 110 W. 40th St., New York NY 10018. (212)840-8664. Also reviews nonfiction (50%-50% fiction to nonfiction). Special interests: general adult trade books. Query with SASE. Member of S.A.R.

Terms: Agent's commission: 15% on domestic sales; 20% on foreign sales.

COLUMBIA LITERARY ASSOCS., INC., 7902 Nottingham Way, Ellicott City MD 21043. (301)465-1595. Contact: Linda Hayes. Adult novels (mass market). Special interest: mainstream and category, women's fiction. Represents 40-50 writers. Query with publishing credits, synopsis, first chapter and

submission history (pubs/agents). Cannot respond without SASE. Also reviews commercial nonfiction (70%-30% fiction to nonfiction). Writer is billed for specific project expenses (shipping, long distance calls, photocopying). Obtains new clients via referrals and queries. Presently accepting "very few" new clients. Member of I.L.A.A.
Terms: Agent's commission: 15%.
Advice: Does *not* handle short stories or collections, juvenile/young adult books, science fiction/fantasy, poetry, pornography or men's adventure.

‡MOLLY MALONE COOK LITERARY AGENCY, INC., Box 338, Provincetown MA 02657. (508)487-1931. Novels, short story collections. Query. "Queries and/or mss without return postage will not be acknowledged or returned." Also reviews nonfiction (50%-50% fiction to nonfiction).

BILL COOPER ASSOCIATES, INC., Suite 411, 224 West 49th St., New York NY 10019. (212)307-1100. Agency estab. 1964. Novels. Also reviews nonfiction. Special interest: mainstream. Usually obtains new clients via recommendations. Send outline/proposal. Responds to queries in 2 weeks.

ROBERT CORNFIELD LITERARY AGENCY, 145 W. 79th St., New York NY 10024. (212)874-2465. Agent Contact: Robert Cornfield or Jeffrey Essmann. Estab. 1979. Novels. Also reviews nonfiction (30%-70% fiction to nonfiction). Special interests: mainstream. Usually obtains new clients via recommendations from others. Currently represents 60 authors. Presently accepting new clients. Send query with SASE. Responds to queries in 2 weeks; to mss in 1 month. New/unpublished writers: 20%. Member of I.L.A.A.
Recent Sales: *The Journey*, by Indira Ganesan (Knopf); *The Hanged Man*, by Denis Johnson (Farrar Straus); and *Backstreets* by Charles Cross (Harmony).
Terms: Agent's commission: 15% on domestic sales; 20% on foreign sales. 100% of income derived from ms sales.

BONNIE R. CROWN INTERNATIONAL LITERATURE AND ARTS, 50 E. 10th St., New York NY 10003. (212)475-1999. Agency estab. 1976. Novels, novellas, story collections, including translations from Asian languages. Also reviews nonfiction (80%-20% fiction to nonfiction). Special interests: originality of style and tone, mainstream, and anything related to Asia. Usually obtains new clients via recommendation. Currently represents 12 authors. "I am a very small specialized agency." Presently accepting new clients. Send query with SASE for policy. Responds in 2 weeks. New/unpublished writers: 10%.
Recent Sales: *Wings of Stone*, by Linda Casper (Readers International); *The Haiku Handbook*, by William Hisginson (Kodansha International); *Haiku Around the World* (Simon and Schuster).
Terms: Agent's commission: 15% on domestic sales; 20% on foreign sales. "I am particularly interested in any work which has been influenced by some Asian experience, the Asian-American experience, anything cross-cultural."

RICHARD CURTIS ASSOCIATES, INC., 164 E. 64th St., New York NY 10021. (212)371-9481. Agency estab. 1978. Novels, story collections. Also reviews nonfiction (75%-25% fiction to nonfiction). Special interests: genre fiction such as science fiction and fantasy, romance, westerns, male action-adventure, mystery and international thriller. Usually obtains new clients via referrals. Currently represents 100 authors. Presently accepting new clients. Query with outline/proposal. New/unpublished writers: 10%. Member of I.L.A.A.
Recent Sales: *Masquerade*, by Janet Dailey (Little, Brown); *Force of Nature* by Stephen Solomita (Putnam Books); *Carry and Comfort* by Dan Simmons (Dark Harvest Books).
Terms: Agent's commission: 10% on domestic sales; 20% on foreign sales. "Only occasionally do we charge fees, but we have no systematic program." 99% of income derived from commissions on ms sales; less than 1% derived from criticism services.

ELAINE DAVIE LITERARY AGENCY, Village Gate Square, 274 N. Goodman St., Rochester NY 14607. (716)442-0830. President: Elaine Davie. Agency estab. 1986. Novels. Also reviews nonfiction (60%-40% fiction to nonfiction). Special interests: "all types of adult, popular fiction. Both mainstream and category manuscripts are reviewed." No juvenile fiction. "I write several articles each year on 'agenting' for various trade journals. We're always looking for new, talented writers." Currently represents 60 authors. Presently accepting new clients. Query or send outline plus sample chapters. Reports on queries in 2 weeks; on mss in 4 weeks. New/unpublished writers: 30.
Recent Titles: *Perfect Morning*, by Marcia Evanick (Bantam); *City of Glass*, by Paul Bagdon (Dell); *Defiant Captive*, by Christina Skye (Dell).
Terms: Agent's commission: 15% on domestic sales; 20% on foreign sales. 100% of income derived from commission on ms sales. "Our agency specializes in adult fiction and nonfiction by and for women. We are particularly successful in placing genre fiction (romances, historicals, mysteries, sus-

pense, westerns). We welcome queries from non-published writers as well as published authors, and we never charge a fee of any kind."

SANDRA DIJKSTRA LITERARY AGENCY, Box 4500, Del Mar CA 92014. (619)755-3115. Agent contact: Sandra Dijkstra. Associates: Laurie Fox, Katherine Goodwin. Agency estab. 1978. Novels and story collections. Also reviews nonfiction (20%-80% fiction to nonfiction). Special interests: mainstream, literary. Usually obtains new clients via "recommendations from authors, editors, reviewers, booksellers, etc.; conferences; 'over the transom.' " Currently represents 78 authors. Presently accepting new clients selectively. Send query, synopsis and sample chapters plus SASE. Responds to queries in 3-4 weeks; to mss in 5-7 weeks. New/unpublished writers: 30%. Member of I.L.A.A.

Recent Sales: *The Joy Luck Club*, by Amy Tan (Putnam's); *The Horse Latitudes*, by Robert Ferrigno (William Morrow); *A Genuine Monster*, by David Zielinski (Atlantic Monthly Press); *Migrant Souls*, by Arturo Islas (Morrow).

Terms: Agent's commission: 15% on domestic sales; 20% (British) and (translation) on foreign sales. Will critique novels for $1/page on a selective basis, "if we think the ms is ¾ of the way there, we ask the author to re-submit revised version within 6 months and we shall read it at no charge. Extensive assessment of the ms's potential—market, literary, etc. with suggestions for revision and enhancement so that maximum potential can be realized." Charges for postage, Xerox and phone expenses. "We ask an expense fee of $225/year which seems to be average expended." 95% of income derived from commission on ms sales; 5% from criticism service. Payment of evaluation fee does not ensure agency representation. "But we only ask to evaluate those mss which we feel have a true potential."

THE DORESE AGENCY, Suite 210, 1400 Ambassador St., Los Angeles CA 90035. (213)556-0710. Agent contact: Alyss Dorese. Estab. 1979. Novels, story collections. Also reviews nonfiction (50%-50% fiction to nonfiction). Special interest: mainstream. Usually obtains new clients via recommendations from others. Currently represents 35 authors. Presently accepting new clients. Query or send outline/proposal. Responds to queries in 3 weeks; to mss in 3 months. New/unpublished writers: 20%. Member of WGA.

Terms: Agent's commission: 15% on domestic sales; 20% on foreign sales. Charges $75 reading fee to unpublished authors. 95% of income derived from commissions on ms sales; 5% of income derived from criticism service.

DUPREE/MILLER AND ASSOC., INC., 5518 Dyer St., Ste. 3, Dallas TX 75206. (214)692-1388. Agent contact: Jan Miller. Agency estab. 1984. Accepts full-length projects only; no stories or poetry. Also reviews nonfiction (40%-60% fiction to nonfiction). "Prefer proposal format for nonfiction; fiction submissions should include a brief overall synopsis, sample chapters and chapter-by-chapter outline." Responds to queries in 6-8 weeks. New/unpublished writers: 60%.

Recent Sales: *Spud Webb: Flying High*, by Reid Slaughter (Harper & Row); *The Walter Railey Story*, by Mike Shropshire (Doubleday); *Storming Intrepid*, by Payne Harrison (Crown).

Terms: "Minimal handling fee due when contract to represent project is signed." 100% of income derived from commission on ms sales.

ETHAN ELLENBERG LITERARY AGENT/CONSULTANT, 548 Broadway, #5-C, New York NY 10012. (212)431-4554. Agency estab. 1983. Quality fiction and nonfiction. (25%-75% fiction to nonfiction.) Special interests: first novels, thriller, horror, spy, science fiction. Usually obtains new clients via referrals (75%) or solicitations (25%). Currently represents 45 clients. Query. Responds to queries in 10 days; to mss in 21 days. New/unpublished writers: 50%.

Recent Sales: *Two If by Sea*, by Richard Rosenthal (Pocket); *Brack*, by Johnney Quarles (Berkley); *Danary Diary*, by Tom Yarborough (St. Martin's); and *Homicide*, by Charles Sasser (Pocket).

Terms: Agent's commission: 15% on domestic sales. "75% of income derived from commission on ms sales; 25% of my business is derived from selling translations and performance rights. I only take clients I feel I can help, and I will not take a new client lightly. I usually give a quick response. I am actively seeking clients."

NICHOLAS ELLISON, INC., 55 Fifth Ave., New York NY 10003. (212)206-6050. Agency estab. 1984. Novels. Also reviews nonfiction (70%-30% fiction to nonfiction). Special interest: mainstream. Usually obtains new clients via recommendations. Currently represents 70 authors. Presently accepting new clients. Send entire ms. Responds to mss in 1-2 months. New/unpublished writers: 15%.

Recent Sales: *The Gold Coast*, by Nelson DeMille; *To Kill the Potemkin*, by Mark Joseph; *The Secrets of Eva Hathaway*, by Janice Weber; *Family of Spies* by Peter Earley.

Terms: Agent's commission: 15% on domestic sales; 20% on foreign sales. Charges a portion of photocopying expense. 100% of income derived from commissions on ms sales.

Close-up

Sandra Dijkstra
Literary Agent

© Paul A. Longworth.

Literary agent Sandra Dijkstra, says working on the West Coast rather than in New York is actually beneficial because it gives her a different perspective and different contacts. "Being in California just means a longer day. I'm always working on two clocks—New York and California time. But, since most business is done on the phone anyway, it isn't a problem. When an author is hunting for an agent it is the enthusiasm an agent feels for the project, not the geographic locale of the agent, that is critical."

Dijkstra says agents have become more essential than ever because of the growing number of mergers and editors changing houses. "An agent is in there; for the long term and wants to be involved in helping shepherd an author's career, not just to sell one book. But at the same time, we [agents] are all so very busy that most of us want the author to do some proving of themselves beforehand. Credits make a difference. But they don't make *the* difference. If someone with tons of credits comes in but the writing isn't persuasive, then we reluctantly say 'sorry.'

"My philosophy is that when a Sandra Dijkstra envelope comes into a publishing office, I want it opened first. I want the editor to know that the quality assurance is there.

"The reality is that there is an increasing trend toward making agents 'first readers' but convincing an author of that is another thing. They say, 'Oh, we'll deal with this or that when we get a house [publisher]' and I tell them, 'we won't get a house unless we deal with that now.' Again, one of the ways an agent establishes credibility is not to send anything out to a publishing house that is not ready to read."

She says her agency receives about 120 submissions per week, many of them fiction manuscripts. However, they sell more nonfiction (about 75%) than fiction. But she finds fiction more challenging and more rewarding. She sold Amy Tan's first novel, *The Joy Luck Club* to Putnam's after rejecting other enticing offers. Vintage Books acquired reprint rights of the first novel for more than $1.2 million. "Amy Tan's success is inspiring for us all. It tells us that a first book of fiction can break through. It tells us that there's an American reading public for quality books." Another client, Arturo Islas, had his first novel, *The Rain God*, published by a small press publisher. Dijkstra sold the author's second novel, *Migrant Souls*, to William Morrow on the basis of the first novel and a story previously published in the literary journal, *Zzyvva*. "I think that small press has served a function for many writers. I think it's one of the trends in the industry that is very exciting, for example the success of North Point, Algonquin, Gibbs Smith and others which nurture fine writers.

"I do think writers have to be true to their vision and have to let their voice speak from it. An awareness of the business, an awareness of who's writing and publishing, is important, but I would advise against becoming so immersed in all the details of the business end that a writer loses his vision or voice.

"I do hard work out here in the trenches. I became an agent because I thought it would be exciting to find a manuscript and to see it turned into a book. I hope I've created something that will one day become a part of the world's literature."

—*Deborah Cinnamon*

ESTRADA LITERARY AGENCY, 8288 Gilman Dr., #47, La Jolla CA 92037. (619)457-3087. Agent contact: Patricia Estrada. Estab. 1985. Novels. Special interests: mysteries, horror, suspense, romance, other genre fiction. No SF/fantasy, and no YA/children's books. Usually obtains new clients via referrals and recommendations; occasionally at conferences. Currently represents 20 authors. Presently accepting new clients. Query first. No unsolicited mss accepted. Responds to queries in 1-2 weeks; to mss in 4-6 weeks. New/unpublished writers: 50%.
Sales: *To Capture a Rake*, by Valerie Bosna (Berkley); *Man in a Wire Cage*, by Mark Perakh (Critic's Choice); and *Deadly Grounds*, by Patricia Wallace (Zebra).
Terms: Agent's commission: 15% on first novel for previously unpublished writers, reduced to 10% on subsequent books; 15% on foreign sales. Charges $35 one-time-only marketing fee for previously unpublished writers. 95% of income derived from commission on ms sales; .05% from marketing fees. "We are a small agency and offer highly personalized service to our clients, but we are *very* selective. Don't query us until your book is complete, and please submit your very best work in a professional manner. We will work with you to make a good book better, but haven't time for writing clinics."

JOHN FARQUHARSON LTD., 250 W. 57th St., New York NY 10107. (212)245-1993. Agent contact: Deborah Schneider. Agency estab. 1911. Novels. Also reviews nonfiction (50%-50% fiction to nonfiction). Special interests: mainstream, literary, mysteries. Usually obtains new clients via recommendations. Currently represents 125 authors. Presently accepting new clients, but very few. Query. Responds to queries in 1-2 weeks; to mss in 4-6 weeks. Member of S.A.R. and I.L.A.A.
Terms: Agent's commission: 10% on domestic sales; 20% on foreign sales. 100% of income derived from commissions on ms sales.

‡FARWESTERN CONSULTANTS LITERARY AGENCY, Box 47786, Phoenix AZ 85068-7786. (602)861-3546. Agent contact: Elizabeth "Libbi" Goodman. Estab. 1987. Novels and story collections (from established authors only). Also reviews nonfiction (80%-25% fiction to nonfiction). "We specialize in popular fiction (western, mystery, contemporary/historical romance, medical thriller, espionage, horror, occult, fantasy and action/adventure), ethnic fiction/nonfiction and women's fiction. We also handle book-length nonfiction, mainstream, and some literary novels." Usually obtains new clients via writer's conferences, client referral or editor recommendation. Currently represents 38 authors. Presently accepting new clients. Query letters preferred with outline/synopsis. Responds to queries in 1-2 weeks; to mss in 1 week-3 months. New/unpublished writers: 50%.
Recent Sales: *Red Sea, Dead Sea*, by Serita Deborah Stevens (St. Martin's Press); *Judas Guns*, by Howard Pelham (Walker Books); and *A Passage of Seasons*, by Douglas Hirt (Doubleday).
Terms: Agents commission: 15% on domestic sales; 20% on foreign sales. Sometimes charges for photocopying/extraordinary expenses if agreed upon in advance. 100% of income derived from commission on ms sales. "No response, to any correspondence, unless SASE is included with submission. No partials or complete manuscripts unless requested."

MARJE FIELDS—RITA SCOTT, Room 1205, 165 W. 46th St., New York NY 10036. (212)764-5740. Agent Contact: Ray Powers. Agency estab. 1961. Novels. Also reviews nonfiction. Special interests: "All kinds, but we do not represent children's books." Currently represents 40 authors. Presently accepting new clients. Query. Responds to queries in 1 day.
Recent Sales: *Live Free or Die*, by Ernest Hebert (Viking); *Exit Wounds*, by John Westermann (Soho); *Death of a Blue Movie Star*, by Jeff Deaver (Bantam).
Terms: Agent's commission: 15% on domestic sales; 20% on foreign sales.

FRIEDA FISHBEIN LTD., 2556 Hubbard St., Brooklyn NY 11235. (212)247-4398. Contact: Janice Fishbein. Agency estab. 1926. Novels. Also reviews nonfiction: (75%-25% fiction to nonfiction). Special interest: mainstream. Usually obtains new clients via recommendations and referral by staff readers. Currently represents 37 authors. Presently accepting new clients. "Responds to query letters in two weeks. Partial or complete manuscripts are not to be sent with query letter; sends criticism of manuscripts accepted for review in 4-6 weeks."
Sales: *Dr. Death*, by Herb Fisher (Berkley); *French Azilum*, by Jeanne Mackin (St. Martin's Press).
Terms: Agent's commission: 10% on domestic sales; 15% on foreign sales. Charges reading fee for new, unpublished authors—$60 for first 50,000 words, pro-rated thereafter at $1 per thousand. Offers cricitism service. "Analysis (criticism) and summary done by staff reader. If ms found marketable, it is referred to myself or an associate." 75% of income derived from commission on ms sales; 25% from criticism service.

‡FLANNERY, WHITE & STONE, Suite 110, 180 Cook, Denver CO 80206. (303)399-2264. Estab. 1987. Novels, short story collections. Also reviews nonfiction, business, children's literature and screenplays. (50%-50% fiction to nonfiction). Special interests: literary, mainstream, gay novel, women's fiction. Usually obtains new clients via recommendations, some through advertisements in literary journals.

Currently represents 25 authors. Presently accepting new clients. Query, send outline proposal or outline plus 2 sample chapters. Responds to queries in 2 weeks; to mss in 6 weeks. New/unpublished writers: 90%. Member of International Womens Writer's Guild, Society of Children's Literature.
Sales: *I Get on the Bus*, by Reginald McKnight (Little Brown); unnamed collection of short stories, by Reginald McKnight (Little Brown); *The Powwow Highway*, by David Seals (NAL).
Terms: Agent's commission: 15% on domestic sales; 20% on foreign sales. Will critique manuscripts, but sometimes must charge for editing. "All critiques and editing done by published authors." 75% of income derived from commission on ms sales. "Only submit work that is polished to the best of your ability."

THE FOLEY AGENCY, 34 E. 38th St., New York NY 10016. (212)686-6930. Contact: Joan or Joe Foley. Novels and nonfiction (50%-50% fiction to nonfiction). Query first by letter with SASE. No manuscripts. Accepts very few new clients.
Terms: Agent's commission: 10%.

JAY GARON-BROOKE ASSOCIATES, INC., 415 Central Park West, New York NY 10025. (212)866-3654. Contact: Jay Garon. "Mainstream, male and female action, adventure, mainstream romance (contemporary), frontier novels with authentic research, non-category horror novels, generational suspense sagas." Area of specialization: "whatever is selling at a given time; fiction and nonfiction." Query first; no phone calls. No magazine shorts or articles. Represents approximately 110 writers. Presently accepting new clients with credits via queries and recommendations only. New/unpublished writers: queries only.
Terms: Agent's commission: 15% domestic; 30% foreign sales.

MAX GARTENBERG, LITERARY AGENT, 15 W. 44th St., New York NY 10036. (212)860-8451. Contact: Max Gartenberg. Novels. Special interests: mainstream, suspense and mystery novels. Represents 30 writers. Chiefly of nonfiction books. Query. Obtains clients via queries and recommendations from others. Presently accepting few new clients. "Approximately 20% of my sales each year are for new clients, who are rarely, however, unpublished writers."
Terms: Agent's commission: 10%.

GELLES-COLE LITERARY ENTERPRISES, 320 E. 42d St., New York NY 10017. (212)573-9857. Agency estab. 1983. Novels. Also reviews nonfiction (75%-25% fiction to nonfiction). Special interests: mainstream and "relationship" novels. Usually obtains new clients via recommendations from others or at conferences. Currently represents 25 authors. Presently accepting new clients. Query. Responds to queries in 2 weeks; to mss in 3½-4 weeks. New/unpublished writers: 5%.
Recent Sales: *The Seduction*, by Art Bourgeau (Donald Fine Inc.); *Nothing More Than Love*, by Dewanna Pace (Crown/Pageant).
Terms: Agent's commission: 15% on domestic sales; 20% on foreign sales. Charges reading fee: $75-proposal; $100-novel under 250 pages; $150-over 250 pages. Offers criticism service: "This is very varied from project to project. We've charged between $500 and $10,000. The book is completely analyzed and then edited by me." Charges for overseas phone calls, photocopying for multiple submissions, overnight mail expenses. "These two areas of the agency (ms sales and editorial service) are separate—many writers in editorial service come to me from other agents or publishers. I frequently place writers in editorial service with other agents. Usually the literary agency clients are *not* out of the editorial service. In fact there are only two."

‡THE GERSH AGENCY, 222 N. Canyon Dr., Beverly Hills CA 90210. (213)274-6611. Agent Contact: Nancy Nigrosh (formerly Blaylock). Estab. 1962. Novels, novellas, short stories. Also reviews nonfiction (90%-10% fiction to nonfiction). Special interests: "mainstream—convertible to film and television." Usually obtains new clients via professional referrals. Presently accepting new clients. Send entire ms. Responds to ms in 4 weeks. New/unpublished writers: less than 10%.
Recent Sales: *Hot Flashes*, by Barbara Raskin (Weintraub Entertainment); *Donato & Daughter* (Universal); *Libra* by Don Dellio (A&M).
Terms: Agent's commission: 10% on domestic sales. "We strictly deal in *published* manuscripts in terms of potential film or television sales, on a strictly 10% commission—sometimes split with a New York Literary agency—various top agencies.

LUCIANNE S. GOLDBERG LITERARY AGENTS, INC., 255 W. 84th St., New York NY 10024. Estab. 1974. Novels. Also reviews nonfiction (25%-75% fiction to nonfiction). Special interest; mainstream. Usually obtains new clients via recommendations from others. Currently represents 68 writers. Presently accepting new clients. Send sample chapters. New/unpublished writers: 2%.

Recent Sales: *Lovers of the African Night* (Delacorte); *Time Capsule* (Morrow); *Who's Who in Hollywood*, (Facts on File).
Terms: Charges for "long distance, extensive Xerox, express mail." 98% of income derived from commission on ms sales.

GOODMAN ASSOCIATES, 500 West End Ave., New York NY 10024. Contact: Elise Simon Goodman. Agency estab. 1976. General adult fiction and nonfiction. Usually obtains new clients via letters of inquiry, recommendations. Currently represents approximately 100 authors. Presently accepting new clients on a very selective basis. Query with SASE. Responds to queries in 10 days; to mss in 4 weeks. Member of I.L.A.A. (Arnold Goodman is currently president of I.L.A.A.)
Terms: Agent's commission: 15% on domestic sales; 20% on foreign sales. Also bills for certain expenses: faxes, telexes, toll calls, overseas postage, photocopying of mss and proposals, book purchases. 100% of income derived from commissions on ms sales. Does not handle "poetry, sci fi and fantasy, articles, individual stories, or children's or YA material."

‡CHARLOTTE GORDON LITERARY AGENCY, 235 E. 22nd St., New York NY 10010. (212)679-5363. Agent contact: Charlotte Gordon. Estab. 1986. Novels. Also nonfiction (40%-60% fiction to nonfiction). Specializes in "mainstream and literary fiction, mysteries, YA novels." Usually obtains new clients via recommendations. Currently represents 18 authors. Presently accepting new clients. Query. Responds to queries and mss in 3 weeks. New/unpublished writers: 20%.
Recent Sales: *An Almost Perfect Summer*, (Bantam); *The Tarot*, (Paragon House); *What Your Dreams Mean*, (Berkley).
Terms: Agent's commission: 15% on domestic sales; 10% on foreign sales. Charges for photocopying expenses. 95% of income derived from commission on ms sales.

SANFORD J. GREENBURGER ASSOCIATES, 55 5th Ave., New York NY 10003. (212)206-5600. Adult novels only (no short fiction, poetry). Send query letter and detailed description or approximately 50-page sample with synopsis of balance. Also reviews nonfiction (50%-50% fiction to nonfiction). Presently accepting new clients. Interested in new/beginning novelists. Member of I.L.A.A.
Terms: Agent's commission: 15%.

‡CHARLOTTE GUSAY LITERARY AGENCY, 10532 Blythe Ave., Los Angeles CA 90064. (213)559-0831. Agent contact: Charlotte Gusay. Estab. 1988. Novels, novellas and story collections. Also reads nonfiction (50%-50% fiction to nonfiction). No science fiction, fantasy, mysteries *per se*. Usually obtains new clients via recommendations, query letters; sometimes by solicitation. Currently represents 10 authors. Presently accepting new clients. Query. Responds to queries in 6 weeks; to mss in 2-4 months. New/unpublished writers: 65%.
Recent Sales: *Wearing Dad's Head*, by Barry Yourgrau (Peregrine Smith); *Dressing Mary Slowly*, by Gail Wronsky (Peregrine Smith).
Terms: Agent's commission: 15% on domestic sales; 10% on foreign sales. Some basic costs for printing, photocopying and mailing may later be assessed, usually agreed upon between author and agent. 100% of income derived from commission on ms sales.

REECE HALSEY AGENCY, 8733 Sunset Blvd., Los Angeles CA (213)652-2409. Query only with SASE. Also reviews nonfiction ("no set ratio"). Interested in new/beginning novelists, but not presently accepting new clients.
Terms: Agent's commission: 10%.

THE JEFF HERMAN AGENCY, INC., 166 Lexington Ave., New York NY 10016. (212)725-4660. Agent contact: Jeffrey H. Herman. Estab. 1985. Novels. Also reviews nonfiction (25%-75% fiction to nonfiction). Usually obtains new clients via referrals. Currently represents 75 authors. Presently accepting new clients. Send query. Responds to queries in 10 days; to mss in 4 weeks. New/unpublished writers: 25%. Member of I.L.A.A.
Recent Sales: More than 90 titles sold.
Terms: Agent's commission: 15% on domestic sales; 10% on foreign sales. Charges for manuscript/proposal photocopying costs, overseas electronic communications. 100% of income derived from commission on ms sales.

SUSAN HERNER RIGHTS AGENCY, 666 Third Ave. 10th Fl., New York NY 10017. (212)983-5230/1/2. Agent contact: Susan Herner, Sue Yuen. Agency estab. 1986. Novels. Also reviews nonfiction. Special interests: mainstream, romance, mystery, science fiction/fantasy, horror. Usually obtains new clients via referrals, conferences, unsolicited query letters. Currently represents 20 authors. Presently accepting new clients. Send 3-5 sample chapters. Responds to queries in 1-2 weeks; to mss in 6-8 weeks. New/unpublished writers: 75%.

Recent Sales: *Dreamfields*, by Libby Sydes (Dell Publishing); *Stewards*, by Jonn Hohlin (Berkley); *Style Is Not a Size*, by Hara Miarano (Bantam).
Terms: Agent's commission: 15% on domestic sales; 20% on foreign sales. 50% of income derived from commission on ms sales. "Our agency also handles subsidiary rights for middle and small publishing companies and other literary agents and packagers. That income is 50% of our business."

FREDERICK HILL ASSOCIATES, 1842 Union St., San Francisco, CA 94123. (415)921-2910. Agency estab. 1979. Novels. Also reviews nonfiction. Special interests: literary and mainstream fiction. Usually obtains new clients via recommendations from others; solicitation; at conferences. Currently represents 100 authors. Presently accepting new clients. Query.
Terms: Agent's commission: 15% on domestic sales; 20% on foreign sales. 100% of income derived from commissions on ms sales.

ALICE HILTON LITERARY AGENCY, (formerly Warren/Hilton Agency), 13131 Welby Way, Suite B, North Hollywood CA 91606. (818)982-2546. Agent contact: Alice Hilton. Agency estab. 1985. Novels and story collections. "Preliminary query appreciated." Also reviews nonfiction (80%-20% fiction [and films] to nonfiction). Special interests: mainstream, science fiction, romance, quality humor and wit, children's. Usually obtains new clients via *Writer's Market*, *LMP*, other trade publications, referrals. Currently represents 22 clients. Presently accepting new clients. Query or send entire ms. Responds to queries in 2 weeks; to mss in 6 weeks. New/unpublished writers: 60%.
Terms: Agent's commission: 10% on domestic sales; 20% on foreign sales. *Charges reading fee: approx. $150 for 300-page ms.* "Where I am able, I do the evaluating myself, but I use outside readers who are highly qualified in various areas of expertise." 80% of income derived from commission on sales; 20% derived from reading fees. Payment of fees does not ensure agency representation.

YVONNE HUBBS LITERARY AGENCY, Box 342, San Juan Capistrano CA 92693-0342. (714)496-1970. Contact: Yvonne Hubbs. Estab. 1983. Reviews novels. Also reviews nonfiction (80%-20% fiction to nonfiction). Special interests: romance, mainstream, glitz, horror, suspense/intrigue. Usually obtains new clients through references from other writers and at conferences. Presently accepting new clients. Query. Responds to queries in 2 weeks.
Terms: Agent's commission: 15% on domestic sales; 20% on foreign sales. *Charges fee to new writers for full critique* of "basic plot problems, typos, suggestions to improve manuscript. I write the critiques." $50 for 250 pages; $65 for 300 pages. 70% of income derived from commission on ms sales; 30% from criticism service. Payment of fees ensures agency representation "if writer can rewrite for marketability. I operate my business as a doctor/patient or attorney/client set-up. My clients are my best references for new clients."

‡HULL HOUSE LITERARY AGENCY, 240 East 82 St., New York NY 10028. (212)988-0725. Agent contact: David Stewart Hull, President. Lydia Mortimer, Associate. Estab. 1987. Novels. Also reviews nonfiction (50%-50% fiction to nonfiction). Special interests: mainstream commercial fiction. Usually obtains new clients via recommendations. Currently represents 38 authors. Presently accepting new clients. Query. Responds to queries in 1 week; to mss in 1 month. New/unpublished writers: 15%.
Recent Sales: *His Vision of Her*, by G.D. Dess (Harper & Row); *The Pact*, by Sharon Salvato (Berkley); and *A Deep Disturbance*, by Constance Rauch (St. Martin's Press).
Terms: Agent's commission: 15% on domestic sales; 20% on foreign sales. Charges for photocopying expenses. 100% of income derived from commission on ms sales.

SHARON JARVIS & CO., INC., 260 Willard Ave., Staten Island NY 10314. (718)273-1066. Agency estab. 1982. Novels. Also reviews nonfiction (80%-20% fiction to nonfiction). Special interests: "category/genre fiction, esp. science fiction, fantasy, horror, mainstream, nonfiction occult." Usually obtains new clients via conferences and references; mail queries. Currently represents 80 authors. Presently accepting new clients. Send query. Responds to queries immediately; to mss in 2-3 months. New/unpublished writers: 20%. Member of SFWA, WWA, MWA, RWA, I.L.A.A., INFO.
Sales: *Vietnam: Gound Zero* series, by Eric Helm (Gold Eagle); *The Star Trek Interview Book*, by Allan Fasherman (Pocket Books); *Came a Spider*, by Michael Hammonds (Berkley).
Terms: Agent's commission: 15% on domestic sales; 10% on foreign sales; "split 15% for movie/TV." *Charges $50 reading fee for first 3 chapters and outline*; if we request balance of manuscript, there is no further fee; authors can choose to have their entire ms read for $65 instead of chapters." 100% of income derived from commission on ms sales. "Reading fee goes to outside reader." Payment of fees does not ensure agency representation. "Queries should include SASE; partials and manuscripts should include postage and mailing instructions."

ASHER D. JASON ENTERPRISES, INC., 111 Barrow St., New York NY 10014. (212)929-2179. Agency estab. 1983. Novels. Also reviews nonfiction (20%-80% fiction to nonfiction). Special interests: mainstream, suspense/espionage/mystery and romance. Usually obtains new clients via recommendations.

Currently represents 30 authors. Presently accepting new clients. Query with outline plus sample chapters. Responds to queries immediately; to mss in 3 weeks. New/unpublished writers: 35%.
Terms: Agent's commission: 15% on domestic sales; 20% on foreign sales. Charges for photocopying expenses. 100% of income derived from commission on ms sales.

JCA LITERARY AGENCY, INC., 242 West 27th St., New York NY 10001. (212)807-0888. Agent Contact: Jane Cushman, Jeff Gerecke, Tom Cushman, Tony Oathwaite. Agency estab. 1978. Novels. Also reviews nonfiction (60%-40% fiction to nonfiction. Special interests: "literary fiction, thrillers/adventure and mysteries, commercial fiction." Currently represents 100 authors. Presently accepting new clients. Send query. Responds to queries in 2 weeks; to mss in 6 weeks. New/unpublished writers: 10%. Member of S.A.R.
Recent Sales: *The Geography of Desire*, by Robert Boswell (Knopf); *Manifest Destiny*, by Brian Garfield (Otto Denzler Books/Mysterious Press); *Criss Cross*, by Tom Kakonis (St. Martin's Press).
Terms: Agent's commission: 10% on domestic sales; 15/20% on foreign sales. Charges for cost of bound galleys and copies of books to be submitted are deducted from author earnings. 100% of income derived from commission on ms sales.

JET LITERARY ASSOCIATES, INC., 124 E. 84th St., New York NY 10028. (212)879-2578. Agency estab. 1976. Novels. Also reviews nonfiction (40%-60% fiction to nonfiction). "Mainstream only. No children, sci fi or young adult." Usually obtains new clients via recommendation. Currently represents 80 authors. Not presently accepting new clients. Query. Responds to queries in 2 weeks; to mss in 1 month. New/unpublished writers: 5%.
Recent Sales: *When Do Fish Sleep?*, by David Feldman (Harper & Row); *Juice*, by Robert Campbell (Poseidon/Pocket Books); *Age Wave*, by Dr. Ken Dychtwald (Tarcher/Bantam).
Terms: Agent's commission: 15% on domestic sales; 25% on foreign sales. Charges for photocopying long distance phone calls, postage expenses. 100% of income derived from commissions on ms sales.

LARRY KALTMAN LITERARY AGENCY, 1301 S. Scott St., Arlington VA 22204. (703)920-3771. Agent contact: Larry Kaltman. Agency estab. 1984. Novels, novellas. Also reviews nonfiction (75%-25% fiction to nonfiction). Special interest: mainstream. Usually obtains new clients via recommendations from others and solicitation. Currently represents 10 authors. Presently accepting new clients. Responds to queries in 2 weeks; to mss in 2 weeks. New/unpublished writers: 75%.
Sales: *RASTUS on Capitol Hill*, by Samuel Edison (Hunter House).
Terms: Agent's commission: 15% on domestic and foreign sales. *Charges reading fee of $150 for 300 pages*; 50¢ for each additional page. "The author receives an approximately 1,000-word letter commenting on writing style, organization and marketability." 80% of income derived from commissions on ms sales; 20% from criticism service.

KEARNS & ORR ASSOCIATES, Suite 1166, 305 Madison Ave., New York NY 10165. Agency estab. 1987. Novels. Also reviews nonfiction (70%-30% fiction to nonfiction). Special interests: women's fiction (genre and mainstream), mystery/suspense, horror, some science fiction and men's adventure. Lectures nationally and obtains new clients through conferences and recommendations. Currently represents 65-75 writers. Presently accepting new clients, "but selective." Send outline and first three chapters. "For an SASE we will send free guidelines on how to write a synopsis." Responds to manuscript proposals in 6-8 weeks. New/unpublished writers: 50%.
Terms: Agent's commission: 15% on domestic sales. "When I see work I think has potential for me to represent, I will offer suggestions on how to make it more saleable, no fees." 100% of income derived from commissions on ms sales.
Advice: "Don't send out a proposal until it is absolutely your best work. The market is cautious. Writers are competing with better books. Work must be original and executed skillfully."

KIDDE, HOYT & PICARD, 335 E. 51st St., Apt. 1G, New York NY 10022. (212)755-9461. Novels and nonfiction (70%-30% fiction to nonfiction). Special interests: mainstream, literary and romantic fiction. Usually obtains new clients via recommendations from others, solicitations. Currently represents 50 authors. Presently accepting a few new clients. Query. Responds to queries in 1-2 weeks; to mss in 2-4 weeks. Associate member S.A.R. Dramatic Affiliate: Joel Gotler, L.A. Literary Associates. Foreign Rights: A.M. Heath & Co., Ltd., London
Recent Sales: *Timeless Towns*, by J.R. Humphreys, *Love Lies Slain*, by L.L. Blackmur; *Star of the North*, by Helene Lehr.
Terms: Agent's commission: 10% on domestic sales. Charges postage and phone call expenses. 100% of income derived from commissions on ms sales.

DANIEL P. KING, LITERARY AGENT, 5125 N. Cumberland Blvd., Whitefish Bay WI 53217. (414)964-2903; FAX: (414)964-6860; Telex: 724389. Contact: Daniel P. King. Estab. 1974. Novels, novellas, short stories, story collections. Also reviews nonfiction (80%-20% fiction to nonfiction). Special interests:

mystery, crime, science fiction, romance. Usually obtains new clients via conferences, recommendations from present clients. Currently represents 65 authors. Presently accepting new clients. Send query and outline plus 1 or 2 sample chapters. Responds to queries in 10 days; to mss in 2 months. New/unpublished writers: 75%. Member of Association for Authors, Crime Writers' Association.
Recent Sales: *Twice a Victim*, by Cyril Joyce (Pageant); *Widows' Beads*, by Cyril Joyce (Pageant); *Cast a Shadow at Midnight*, by John D'Arcy (Romas Books). *Charges reading fee.* Varies up to $175. Fee charged only to writers without major book or magazine credits. 99% of income derived from commission on ms sales; payment of fees does not ensure agency representation. "We are interested in newer authors and are most impressed by a concise query letter citing any previous credits and a synopsis plus the first and second chapters of the ms. We are very interested in fiction and nonfiction for the European, South American and Japanese markets. Genre fiction is the most salable (mystery, suspense, crime, romance) as well as general nonfiction."

HARVEY KLINGER, INC., 301 W. 53rd St., New York NY 10019. (212)581-7068. Agency estab. 1977. Novels. Also reviews nonfiction (40%-60% fiction to nonfiction). Special interest: mainstream. Usually obtains new clients via referrals from publishers and existing clients. Currently represents 75 authors. Presently accepting new clients. Query with outline/proposal. Responds to queries in 2 weeks; to mss in 6-8 weeks. New/unpublished writers: 15-20%.
Sales: *Green City in the Sun*, by Barbara Wood (Random House); *Butterfly*, by Kathryn Harvey (Villard); *The Final Opus of Leon Solomon*, by Jerome Badanes (Knopf).
Terms: Agent's commission: 15% on domestic sales; 25% on foreign sales.

BARBARA S. KOUTS, LITERARY AGENT, 788 Ninth Ave. 3A, New York NY 10019. (212)265-6003. Agency estab. 1980. Novels. Also reviews nonfiction (50%-50% fiction to nonfiction). Special interests: literary, mainstream, women's and children's novels. Usually obtains new clients via recommendations from others; at conferences; by queries. Currently represents 50 authors. Presently accepting new clients. Query with outline/proposal. Responds to queries in 3 weeks; to mss in 4-8 weeks. New/unpublished writers: 70%.
Sales: *Short and Shivery*, by Robert San Souci (Doubleday); *Bed and Breakfast Across North America*, by Hal Gieseking (Simon & Schuster).
Terms: Agent's commission: 10% on domestic sales; 20% on foreign sales. 100% of income derived from commissions on ms sales.

LUCY KROLL AGENCY, 390 West End Ave., New York NY 10024. Send mss to 2211 Broadway, New York NY 10024. (212)877-0556. Contact: Lucy Kroll or Barbara Hogenson. Novels. Special interest: contemporary. Represents 35 writers (including playwrights and screenwriters). Query. Also reviews nonfiction (50%-50% fiction to nonfiction). Obtains new clients via recommendations from others; queries occasionally. "Not actively seeking new clients, but we take them on occasionally."

PETER LAMPACK AGENCY, INC., Suite 2015, 551 5th Ave., New York NY 10017. (212)687-9106. Agent Contact: Peter Lampack. Agency estab. 1977. Novels, novellas. Also represents nonfiction (60%-40% fiction to nonfiction). Special interests: commercial fiction, especially contemporary relationships, out-of-category male-oriented action adventure, distinguished issue-oriented nonfiction and literary fiction. Usually obtains new clients via recommendations from others. Currently represents 60 authors. Presently accepting new clients. Query—no unsolicited mss. Responds to queries in 2 weeks. New/unpublished writers: 15%.
Recent Sales: *Rightfully Mine*, by Doris Mortman (Bantam); *Dragon*, by Clive Cussler (Simon & Schuster); *Mine*, by Robert McCammon (Pocket Books); *The Glitter and The Gold*, by Fred Mustard Stewart (NAL).
Terms: Agent's commission: 15% on domestic sales; 20% on foreign sales. Author is responsible for supplying all submission copies. 100% of income derived from commissions on ms sales.

THE ROBERT LANTZ/JOY HARRIS LITERARY AGENCY, (formerly The Lantz Office)888 7th Ave., New York NY 10106. (212)586-0200. Contact: Joy Harris. Special interest: mainstream. Also reviews nonfiction (50%-50% fiction to nonfiction). Represents 60 writers. Usually obtains new writers via recommendations and writer's conferences. Presently accepting new clients on limited basis. New/unpublished writers: 10%. Member of S.A.R.

MICHAEL LARSEN/ELIZABETH POMADA LITERARY AGENTS, 1029 Jones St., San Francisco CA 94109. (415)673-0939. Agency estab. 1972. Novels. Also reviews nonfiction. Special interests: mainstream, historical, contemporary, literary, commercial, romance and mysteries. Usually obtains new clients via recommendations from others. Currently represents 100 authors. Presently accepting new clients. Send first 30 pages of completed manuscript and a synopsis with SASE. Responds to queries in 6-8 weeks. New/unpublished writers: 50%. Member of I.L.A.A.

Recent Sales: *Chantal*, by Yvone Lenard (Delacorte); *The Bristling Wood*, by Katharine Kerr (Foundation); *The Gathering of Winds*, by June Lund Shiplett (NAL).
Terms: Agent's commission: 15% on domestic sales; 20% on foreign sales. As agents, we desperately seek good new novelists, who are the lifeblood of the publishing world."

‡THE LAZEAR AGENCY INCORPORATED, Suite 416, 430 First Avenue North, Minneapolis MN 55401. (612)332-8640. Agent contact: Jonathan Lazear, Virginia See, Kathy Erickson, Mary Meehan, Peggy Kelly, Wendy Lazear. Estab. 1984. Novels and story collections. Also reviews nonfiction (40%-60% fiction to nonfiction). Special interests: adult fiction and nonfiction, young adult, mainstream, science fiction, mysteries. Usually obtains new clients via recommendations and solicitations. Currently represents 300+ authors. Presently accepting new clients. Query. Responds to queries in 2 weeks; to mss in 8-10 weeks. New/unpublished writers: 50%. Member of ABA.
Recent Sales: Untitled third novel by Kate Green (Delacorte); *KARI*, by Melody Beattie (Prentice Hall); and an untitled novel by Gary Paulsen (Delacorte).
Terms: Agent's commission: 15% on domestic sales; 20% on foreign sales. Charges for federal express and photocopying expenses. 75% of income derived from ms sales; 25% from motion picture and television sales.

THE L. HARRY LEE LITERARY AGENCY, Box 203, Rocky Point NY 11778. (516)744-1188. Agent contact: Vito Brenna, Lisa Judd, Holli Rovitti, Dawn Dreyer, Ralph Schiano (Sci Fi), Charles Rothery (Humor), Katie Polk (Mainstream). Agency estab. 1979. Novels. Does not review nonfiction. Special interests: mainstream, SF, historical, war, horror, humor, occult, mystery, suspense, modern sexy romance, western, adventure, thrillers, spy and literary works. Usually obtains new clients via recommendations, solicitations, conferences, watering holes. Currently represents 165 authors, 94 are screenwriters or playwrights. Presently accepting new clients. Query. Responds to queries in 3-4 weeks; to mss in 4-6 weeks. New/unpublished writers: 20%. Member of S.A.R., I.L.A.A., WGA, East, Inc.
Recent Sales: *The Gizmo Delicious*, by Holli Rovitti (Dorchester); *The Hermit Kingdom*, by Don Kraus (Dell); *The Tel-Star Conspiracy*, by James G. Kingston (Warner Books); *The Fool's God*, by Richard Shock (Avon).
Terms: Agents commission: 15% on domestic sales; 20% on foreign sales. *Charges $85 reading fee* "for 1st 50 pages; $75 for the rest of the novel regardless of length. That's with a critique." Offers criticism service by "competent associates who have years of experience. Critiques range from 3-6 pages. Plus a marked-up manuscript." Charges fee for "postage, handling (includes phone calls, letters, packaging), file set-up, responses to rejections etc. Copyright forms available. Associates available at all times." 90% of income derived from commissions on mss; 10% from criticism service. "Good story telling essential. Good writing essential. The market is getting tougher and tougher, so you got to be good to sell today."

ELLEN LEVINE LITERARY AGENCY INC., Suite 1205, 432 Park Ave. S, New York NY 10016. (212)889-0620. Agents: Ellen Levine, Diana Finch. Reviews novels and nonfiction (50%-50% fiction to nonfiction). Usually obtains new clients through recommendations from clients and editors. Presently accepting new clients. Query letter first, does not look at unsolicited mss. Responds to queries in 2 weeks; to mss in 4-6 weeks. Member of S.A.R. and I.L.A.A.
Terms: Agent's commision: 10% on domestic sales; 20% on foreign sales.

THE NORMA-LEWIS AGENCY, 521 5th Ave., New York NY 10175. (212)751-4955. Agency estab. 1980. Novels, novellas. Also reviews nonfiction (50%-50% fiction to nonfiction). Special interests: children's, young adult and mainstream adult fiction. Usually obtains new clients via recommendations and listings in directories. Presently accepting new clients. Query. Responds to queries in 2 weeks.
Terms: Agent's commission: 15% on domestic sales; 20% on foreign sales; 15% on Canadian sales. 100% of income derived from commissions on ms sales.

LIGHTHOUSE LITERARY AGENCY, Box 2105, Winter Park FL 32790. Agent contact: Sandy Kangas. Agency estab. 1988. Novel, novellas, story collections. Also reviews nonfiction (71%-29% fiction to nonfiction). Special interests: genre fiction, contemporary, literary, adventure, young adult. Usually obtains new clients via recommendations and professional organizations. Currently represents 68 authors. Presently accepting new clients. Send entire ms if complete; otherwise, send query or proposal package. Responds in 2 weeks. New/unpublished writers: 35%. Member of the Authors Guild.
Recent Sales: *The Draper Solution*, by Galen C. Dukes (Ballantine); *Tooting Your Own Horn*, by D.C. Hill (Fell).
Terms: Agent's commission: 15% on domestic sales; 20% on foreign sales. No charge to review unsolicited mss for acceptance or rejection. *Offers criticism service*: will critique 300/page novel for $300. We promise prompt response to proposals, submissions and analysis requests, whether we offer to represent the author or not. We do not believe in holding up an author's work."

MAXWELL J. LILLIENSTEIN, 7 Rest Ave., Ardsley NY 10502. Agent Contact: Maxwell J. Lillienstein. Agency estab. 1979. Novels. Also reviews nonfiction (80%-20% fiction to nonfiction). Special interests: mainstream, historical romances, fantasy, science fiction. Usually obtains new clients via recommendations from others. Currently represents 6 authors. Presently accepting new clients "only published authors." Send 3 sample chapters. Responds to ms in 30 days.
Terms: Agent's commission: 10% on domestic sales; 10% on foreign sales.

RAY LINCOLN LITERARY AGENCY, 107 B Elkins Park House, 7900 Old York Rd., Elkinspark PA 19117. (215)635-0827. Agency estab. 1974. Novels. Also reviews nonfiction (50%-50% fiction to nonfiction). "I particularly like biographies and popular science." Special interests: "mainstream—contemporary, historical, science fiction, children's—only for ages 8 and upward; mostly young adult; no picture books; no plays; no poetry." Usually obtains new clients by recommendation. Presently accepting new clients. "I prefer a query letter first (with SASE); then if I'm interested I ask for two sample chapters with overview, then on to full ms if promising." Responds to queries in 1-2 weeks; to mss in 3-4 weeks.
Recent Sales: *Silk Road*, by Jeanne Larsen (Henry Holt); *The Incorporation of Eric Chung*, by Steven Lo (Algonquin Books); *Upchuck Summer's Revenge*, by Joel Schwartz (Dell).
Terms: Agent's commission: 15% on domestic sales; 20% on foreign sales. "If I think a ms is very promising and agree to handle it, then I'll make suggestions for changes in order to make it even better. For this there is no fee."

LITERARY/BUSINESS ASSOCIATES, Box 2415, Hollywood CA 90078. (213)465-2630. Contact: Shelley Gross. Agency estab. 1979. Novels, novellas. Also reviews nonfiction (40%-60% fiction to nonfiction). Special interests: mystery, New Age, occult, holistic healing, humor and contemporary, business. Usually obtains new clients via recommendations; solicitations; at conferences. Currently represents 4 authors. Presently accepting new clients. Query with outline/proposal. Responds to queries in 2 weeks; to mss in 4-6 weeks. SASE. New/unpublished writers: 85-90%.
Terms: Agent's commission: 15% on domestic sales; 20% on foreign sales. *Charges $75 evaluation fee* for up to 300-page ms. "Critique includes detailed written letter plus free literary nonfiction or fiction 1-page guide sheet." Charges marketing fee of $50. 60% of income derived from commissions on ms sales; 40% from criticism service. "Marketing fee is refundable after sale has been made."

LOS ANGELES LITERARY ASSOCIATES, 8955 Norma Place, Los Angeles CA 90069. (213)275-6330. Contact: Joel Gotler. Agency estab. 1987. Novels. Also reviews nonficiton (70%-30% fiction to nonfiction). Special interest: mainstream. Usually obtains new clients via recommendations from others. Query. Responds to queries in 2 weeks. "If you send submissions, postage must be included if they are to be returned." New/unpublished writers: 10%.
Recent Sales: *Brain Building*, by Marilyn Vos Savant (Bantam); *Rockets Red Glare*, by Greg Dinallo (St. Martin's Press).
Terms: Commission: 10% minimum on domestic sales but rate varies; 20% on foreign sales.

LOWENSTEIN ASSOCIATES, 121 W. 27th St., New York NY 10001. (212)206-1630. Agent contact: Lori Perkins. Agency estab. 1978. Novels. Also reviews nonfiction (50%-50% fiction to nonfiction). Special interests: horror, thrillers—Lori Perkins; romance—Eileen Fallon; women's fiction—Barbara Lowenstein. Usually obtains new clients via recommendations from clients and published authors, conferences. Currently represents 300 authors. Presently accepting new clients. Send query. Responds to queries in 4 weeks; to mss in 6-8 weeks. New/unpublished writers: 20%. Member of I.L.A.A.
Sales: *The Night of the Weeping Women*, by Lawrence Naumoff (Atlantic Monthly Press); *Revelations*, by Peggy Payne (Simon & Schuster); *Beastmaker*, by James V. Smith, Jr. (Dell). "All first novels."
Terms: Agent's commission: 15% on domestic sales; 20% on foreign sales. 100% of income derived from commission on ms sales.

MARGARET McBRIDE LITERARY AGENCY, Box 8730, La Jolla CA 92038. (619)459-0559. Contact: Winifred Golden, associate; Sheri Douglas, assistant. Fiction and nonfiction for adult mainstream market. Prefers query letter. No unsolicited mss. Member of I.L.A.A.
Terms: Agent's commission: 15%.

DONALD MacCAMPBELL INC., 12 E. 41st St., New York NY 10017. (212)683-5580. Agent Contact: Donald MacCampbell. Agency estab. 1940. Book-length fiction only. Special interests: adult fiction, specializing in the women's market. Usually obtains new clients via recommendations from others. Presently accepting new clients; no unpublished writers. Query with entire ms. Responds to queries in 2 weeks.

Recent Sales: *Kate*, by Joanna McGauran (Pocket Books); *Thunder*, by Lynne Scott-Drennan (Doubleday); *China Silk*, by Florence Hurd (Ballantine).
Terms: Agent's commission: 10% on domestic sales; 20% on foreign sales. 100% of income derived from commissions on ms sales. "This is a small, highly selective agency for professional writers who write full time in the commercial fiction markets."

‡RICHARD P. MCDONOUGH, LITERARY AGENT, 812 Centre St., Box 1950, Boston MA 02130. (617)522-6388. Agent contact: R. McDonough. Novels and story collections. Also reads nonfiction (25%-75% fiction to nonfiction). Special interests: literary. Usually obtains new clients via recommendations. Currently represents 30 authors. Presently accepting new clients. Query with 3 sample chapters. New/unpublished writers: 50%.
Sales: *The Way That Water Enters Stone*, by John Dufresne (Norton).
Terms: Agent's commission: 15% on domestic sales; 15% on foreign. Charges for some extraordinary expenses on sale only. 100% of income derived from commission on ms sales.

JANET WILKENS MANUS LITERARY AGENCY INC., 370 Lexington Ave., New York NY 10017. (212)685-9558. Agency estab. 1981. 50%-50% fiction to nonfiction. Special interests: mainstream, thrillers, mystery, suspense, true crime, horror, children's, psychology, health. Usually obtains new clients via conferences, recommendations from others. Currently represents 35 authors. Presently accepting new clients. Query with 2-3 sample chapters. Responds to queries in 2-3 weeks; to mss in 5-6 weeks. New/unpublished writers: 25%. Member of I.L.A.A.
Recent Sales: *Blood Legacy*, by Prudence Foster; *Loud and Clear*, by Lake Headley and William Hoffman; *The New Mother's Body*, by Paula Siegel.
Terms: Agent's commission: 15% on domestic sales; 20% on foreign sales. 100% of income derived from commissions on ms sales.

DENISE MARCIL LITERARY AGENCY, INC., 685 West End Ave., #9C, New York NY 10025. Agency estab. 1977. Novels. Also reviews nonfiction (65%-35% fiction to nonfiction). Special interests: women's fiction, commercial fiction, horror, psychological suspense. Usually obtains new clients via recommendations from others, conferences, and through query letters. Currently represents 100 authors. Presently accepting few new clients. Query with SASE. Responds to queries in 2 weeks; to mss in 3 months. New/unpublished writers: 80% "were unpublished at the time I began representing them." Member of I.L.A.A.
Recent Sales: *Pearls of Sharah* series, by Fayrene Preston (Bantam); *Betrayals*, by Anne Harrell (Berkley).
Terms: Agent's commission: 15% on domestic sales; 20% on foreign sales. Charges $45 for first three chapters and outlines only if we request material. "If I sell the author's work, I charge for disbursements." 99.9% of income derived from commissions on ms sales; .1% from reading service.

ELAINE MARKSON LITERARY AGENCY, 44 Greenwich Ave., New York NY 10011. (212)243-8480. Query letter first. *Do not* send unsolicited mss. "Authors should write to us (*don't call*) and we will respond." Also reviews nonfiction (about 50%-50% fiction to nonfiction). Presently accepting new clients. ("Very rarely, but we do accept clients if we are very impressed with their potential.") Interested in new/beginning novelists. Member of I.L.A.A.
Terms: Agent's commission: 15%.

‡THE EVAN MARSHALL AGENCY, 228 Watchung Ave., Upper Montclair NJ 07043. (201)744-1661. Agent contacts: Evan Marshall, Anna Szalai. Estab. 1987. Novels. Also reviews nonfiction (50%-50% fiction to nonfiction). Special interests: general adult fiction. Usually obtains new clients via recommendations from current clients and editors; solicitations; writers conferences. Currently represents 100 authors. Presently accepting new clients. Query. Responds to queries in 2 weeks; to mss in 1 month. Member of I.L.A.A.
Terms: Agent's commission: 15% on domestic sales; 20% on foreign sales. 100% of income derived from commission on ms sales.

MAXIMILIAN BECKER, 115 E. 82nd St., New York NY 10028. (212)988-3887. Agent contact: Maximilian Becker and Aleta M. Daley. Agency estab. 1950. Novels. Also reviews nonfiction (75%-25% fiction to nonfiction). Special interests: adventure, mainstream, science fiction, suspense. Usually obtains new clients by recommendations from others. Currently represents 50 authors. Presently accepting new clients. Query. Responds to queries in 1 week; to mss in 2 weeks. 20% of clients are new/unpublished writers.
Sales: *Goering*, by David Irving (William Morrow); *Time to Choose*, by Janine Boissard (Little, Brown); *The Enigma*, by David Kahn (Houghton Mifflin).
Terms: Agent's commission: 15% on domestic sales; 19% on foreign sales. 100% of income is derived from commission on ms sales and film rights.

MEREDITH BERNSTEIN LITERARY AGENCY, Suite 503A, 2112 Broadway, New York NY 10023. (212)799-1007. Agent Contact: Meredith Bernstein. Agency estab. 1981. Novels. Also reviews nonfiction (half fiction and half nonfiction). Usually obtains new clients via recommendations from others, solicitation, at conferences. "Some, I go out and seek, if I have a prospect in mind." Currently represents 75-100 authors. Presently accepting new clients. Query first. Responds to mss within 3 weeks. Member of I.L.A.A.
Recent Sale: *The Know It All's Guide to Life*, (Villard).
Terms: Agent's commission: 15% on domestic sales; 20% on foreign sales. *Charges $45 reading fee to unpublished authors*. Offers criticism service: "My assistant and I collaborate on our suggested ideas."

‡MEWS BOOKS LTD., 20 Bluewater Hill, Westport CT 06880. (203)227-1837. FAX: (203)226-6928. Contact: Fran Pollack, secretary. Novels. Also reviews nonfiction (20% fiction, 20% nonfiction, 50% juvenile, 10% miscellaneous). Special interests: "juvenile (pre-school thru young adult) and adult fiction." Currently represents 35 authors. Presently accepting new clients. Query with outline/proposal with character description and writing sample.
Terms: Agent's commission: 10% on domestic sales for published authors; 15% on domestic sales for unpublished; 20% on foreign sales; $500 minimum commission, if book is published. *Charges $250 circulation fee for new authors* without professional recommendations. Applied against commissions. Charges for direct expenses (photocopying, postage, etc.). No fees unless agency representation.

THE PETER MILLER AGENCY, INC., Box 760, Old Chelsea Sta., New York NY 10011. (212)929-1222. Agent contacts: Peter Miller and Jonathan Blank. Agency estab. 1976. Novels of all kinds. Also reviews nonfiction (40%-60% fiction to nonfiction). "Interested in category fiction, particularly fiction (or nonfiction) which has television and motion picture potential." Usually obtains new clients via referral and reputation as established literary agent for over 15 years. Also writing conferences, and speaking engagements at colleges and universities. Currently represents 50 authors. Presently accepting new clients. Send query. Responds to query quickly; to mss in approximately 3-6 weeks. New/unpublished writers: 40%.
Recent Sales: *Lullaby and Good Night*, by Vincent Bugliosi (NAL); *The Art of Hanna Barbera*, by Ted Sennett (Viking); *Lyndon Larouche and the New American Fascism*, by Dennis King (Doubleday).
Terms: *Charges fee* (refundable out of first monies earned for author) for full-length novels. Will critique 300-page novel for $225 (nonrefundable out of first moneys earned for author). Critiques are 3-5 pages in length and written by the owner, Peter Miller, and a staff of highly qualified editorial consultants. Charges minimal marketing expenses, including photocopies, deliveries, Federal Express, long distance phone calls, and legal fees. 97% of income derived from commission on ms sales; 2-3% from criticism service. Payment of fees does not ensure agency representation. The agency specializes in representing "true-crime projects and all books that have significant television and motion picture potential and is particularly interested in developing agent/client relations. Agency has established relationships with co-agents throughout the world."

HOWARD MORHAIM LITERARY AGENCY, 175 5th Ave., Room #709, New York NY 10010. (212)529-4433. Novels principally. Query. Also reviews nonfiction (70%-30% fiction to nonfiction). Member of I.L.A.A.
Terms: Agent's commission: 15%.

MULTIMEDIA PRODUCT DEVELOPMENT, INC., Suite 724, 410 S. Michigan Ave., Chicago IL 60605. (312)922-3063. Agent Contact: Jane Jordan Browne. Agency estab. 1971. Novels. Also reviews nonfiction (35%-65% fiction to nonfiction). Special interests: mainstream, historical, mystery, science fiction, fantasy and romance. Usually obtains new clients via recommendations, word-of-mouth, conferences. Currently represents 100 authors. Presently accepting new clients. Query. Responds to queries in 5 days; to mss in 1 month. New/unpublished writers: 5%. Member of I.L.A.A.
Recent Sales: *Whippy Bird and Effa Commander*, by Sandra Dallas (Random House); *The Dieter*, by Susan Sussman; *The Fifth Script*, by Ross H. Spencer (Donald I. Fine).
Terms: Agent's commission: 15% on domestic sales; 20% on foreign sales. Charges for photocopying expenses and overseas phone calls. 100% of income derived from commissions on ms sales. "We also review contracts or consult for an hourly fee if someone wants information."

JEAN V. NAGGAR LITERARY AGENCY, INC., 216 E. 75th St., New York NY 10021. (212)794-1082. Agent contacts: Jean Naggar, Teresa Cavanaugh. Novels and nonfiction. Special interests: mainstream fiction (literary and commercial), suspense, science fiction and mystery; no category romances. Query with SASE. No unsolicited mss. Represents 80 writers. Obtains clients via recommendations, solicited mss, queries and writers' conferences. Presently accepting new clients only on a highly selective basis. Interested in some new/beginning novelists. Member of I.L.A.A. and S.A.R.

Terms: Agent's commission: 15% domestic; 20% foreign.

RUTH NATHAN, 242 W. 27th St., Suite 4A, New York NY 10001. (212)685-0808. Agency estab. 1980. Novels. Also reviews nonfiction (20%-80% ficton to nonfiction). Special interests: mainstream, biography, illustrated books on art and decorative arts and show biz. Usually obtains new clients through recommendations, solicitation or at conferences. Currently represents 12 authors. Presently accepting new clients. Send sample chapters. Responds to queries in 4 weeks; to mss in 6-8 weeks. New/unpublished writers: 20%.
Terms: Agent's commission: 15% on domestic sales; 10% on foreign sales.

B.K. NELSON LITERARY AGENCY, Suite 1308A, 303 Fifth Ave., New York NY 10016. (212)899-0637. Agency estab. 1979. Novels. Also reviews nonfiction (10%-90% fiction to nonfiction). Special interest: mainstream. Usually obtains new clients via recommendations by others. Currently represents 12 authors. Presently accepting new clients. Query. Responds to queries in "a few days"; to mss in 2 weeks. New/unpublished writers: 100%.
Recent Sales: *Brecher's Odyssey*, by Gerhard Brecher (Pueblo Press); *Cafe Pierre*, by W. Ware Lynch and Charles Romine (Random House).
Terms: Agent's commission: 15% on domestic sales; 10% on foreign sales. Charges a reading fee of $230 for a completed ms. 99% of income derived from commissions on ms; 1% on criticism service.

THE BETSY NOLAN LITERARY AGENCY, 50 West 29th St., 9W, New York NY 10001. (212)779-0700. Contact: Betsy Nolan. Agency estab. 1982. Novels. Also reviews nonfiction (30%-70% fiction to nonfiction). Special interest: mainstream. Presently accepting new clients. Query with outline/proposal. Responds to queries in 2 weeks; to mss in 6-8 weeks. New/unpublished writers: 50%.
Terms: Agent's commission: 15% on domestic sales; 20% on foreign sales.

NUGENT & ASSOCIATES, INC., 170 10th St. N., Naples FL 33940. (813)262-7562. Agent contact: Ray E. Nugent. Agency estab. 1983. Novels. Also reviews nonfiction (60%-40% fiction to nonfiction). Special interests: "mainstream fiction, particularly historical novels, espionage and mystery/suspense fiction. We do also handle a fairly large amount of nonfiction." Usually obtains new clients via publicity, other writers, writing conferences. Currently represents 44 authors. Presently accepting new clients. Send query and sample chapters and summary along with SASE. Responds to queries in 30 days; to mss in 90 days. New/unpublished writers: 40%.
Recent Sales: *Osteoporosis*, by MacIlwain, et al (John Wiley & Sons); *Disney's World*, by Mosley (Stein & Day); *The 50+ Wellness Program*, (John Wiley & Sons).
Terms: Agent's commission: 15% on domestic sales; 25% on foreign sales. "We charge for all clerical expenses directly associated with the preparation, mailing and materials required for the offering of a client's material. Long distance calls and wires are also billed to the clients." 100% of income derived from commission on ms sales. "On new writers, we request that they deposit in an account with us to offset the clerical expenses as they are incurred. A statement of this account is provided quarterly, and all unused funds in the account are reimbursed to the client in the event the contract is either terminated or the author's first book is sold for publication. The advance payment account is waived after the first book is sold. We only charge our clients for expenses that they would normally incur if they were to attempt to bring their material to market without an agent."

FIFI OSCARD ASSOCIATES, 19 W. 44th St., New York NY 10036. (212)764-1100. Novels. Also reviews nonfiction (50%-50% fiction to nonfiction). Special interests: literary, mainstream. Usually obtains new clients via recommendations. Currently represents over 100 authors. Presently accepting new clients. Query. Responds to queries in 2 weeks; to mss in 2-3 weeks. New/unpublished writers: 10%. Member of S.A.R.
Recent Sales: *TekWar*, by William Shatner (G.P. Putnam's); *Cardinal Numbers*, by Hob Broun (Knopf); *Two Ways to Count to Ten*, by Ruby Dee (Henry Holt); *Beastly Tales*, the 1989 Anthology from Mystery Writers of America (Wynwood Press).
Terms: Agent's commission: 15% on domestic sales; 20% on foreign sales. 100% of income derived from commissions.

RODNEY PELTER, LITERARY AGENT, 129 E. 61st St., New York NY 10021. (212)838-3432. Contact: Rodney Pelter. Fiction and nonfiction. Query with SASE, résumé and first 50 pages. Represents 15-25 writers. Obtains clients via recommendations, unsolicited mss and queries. Presently accepting new clients. New/unpublished writers: "probably a majority."
Terms: Agent's commission: 15% on US book sales.

SIDNEY PORCELAIN AGENCY, Box 1229, Milford PA 18337. (717)296-6420. Agent contact: Sidney Porcelain. Agency estab. 1952. Novels, novellas, short stories. Fiction and nonfiction (75%-25%, fiction to nonfiction). Special interests: novels, mysteries, children's. Usually obtains clients through recom-

mendations; market lists. Currently represents 20 clients. Presently accepting new clients. Query. Responds to queries in a few days; to mss in 2 weeks. New/unpublished writers: 60%. SASE.
Terms: Agent's commission: 10%. "If foreign agent, his fee is separate."

THE AARON M. PRIEST LITERARY AGENCY INC., 122 East 42nd St., New York NY 10168. (212)818-0344. Contact: Aaron Priest, Robert Colgan or Molly Friedrich. Fiction and nonfiction. Presently accepting new clients. Send SASE with ms.
Terms: Agent's commission: 15% (foreign mailing and copying charged to author).

SUSAN ANN PROTTER, LITERARY AGENT, 110 West 40th St., New York NY 10018. (212)840-0480. Agent contact: Susan Ann Protter. Agency estab. 1971. Novels. Fiction and nonfiction (50%-50% fiction to nonfiction). Special interests: contemporary and medical novels, thrillers, mysteries, science fiction and fantasy. Currently represents 45 clients. Presently accepting some new clients. Query. Responds to queries in 2 weeks. New/unpublished writers: 20%. Member of I.L.A.A.
Recent Sales: *The Hollow Earth*, by Rudy Rucker (Morrow/Avon); *Take the "D" Train*, by Frank King (E.P. Dutton); *Strikezone*, by David F. Nighbert (St. Martin's); "Over Flat Mountain," by Terry Bisson (Omni).
Terms: Agent's commission: 15% on domestic sales; 25% on foreign sales. Charges handling charge of $10 on ms submissions (includes sub-agent's commissions). 100% of income derived from commissions on ms sales.

QUICKSILVER BOOKS, INC., 50 Wilson St., Hartsdale NY 10530. (914)946-8748. Agent contact: Bob Silverstein, president. Agency estab. 1973 (as packager); 1987 (as literary agency). Novels. Also reviews nonfiction (50%-50% fiction to nonfiction). Special interests: mainstream, science fiction, mystery/suspense. Usually obtains new clients via recommendations from others, listings in sourcebooks. Currently represents 25 authors. Presently accepting new clients. Send query with outline. Responds to queries in 1 week; to mss in 2-3 weeks. New/unpublished writers: 50%.
Sales: *The Dogs*, by Jerrold Mundis (Berkley); *The Hypnotist*, by Brad Steiger (Berkley); *Coronation*, by W. J. Weatherby (Pocket Books).
Terms: Agent's commissions: 15% on domestic sales; 20% on foreign sales. 100% of income derived from commission on ms sales.

HELEN REES LITERARY AGENCY, 308 Commonwealth Ave., Boston MA 02116. (617)262-2401. Agent contact: Catherine Mahar. Agency estab. 1980. Novels, novellas, short stories, story collections. Also reviews nonfiction (15%-85% fiction to nonfiction). Special interests: mainstream, mystery, suspense, gay, literary. Usually obtains new clients via solicitations, referrals, some through submissions. Currently represents 60 authors. Presently accepting new clients. Query. Responds to queries in 5-10 days; to mss in 2 weeks. Member of I.L.A.A.
Recent Sales: *In The Falcon's Claw*, by Chet Raymo (Viking); *Water From the Moon*, by Lawrence Kinsman (Knights Press); *Ghost Riders*, by Rick Boyer (Ballantine).
Terms: Agent's commission: 15% on domestic sales; 20% on foreign. Charges "reimbursement for expenses (mail, phone, copying)." 100% of income derived from commissions on ms sales.

THE ROBBINS OFFICE, INC., 12th Floor, 866 2nd Ave., New York NY 10017. (212)223-0720. Agency estab. 1978. Novels, story collections. Also reviews nonfiction (25%-75% fiction to nonfiction). Special interests: mainstream hardcover, literary. Usually obtains new clients via recommendations from others. Currently represents 150 authors. Presently accepting new clients. Query. Responds to queries in 2 weeks.
Recent Sales: *When We Get Home*, by Maud Carol Markson (Bantam New Fiction); *Yellow Dogs*, by Donald Zochert (Atlantic Monthly Press).
Terms: Agent's commission: 15%. "Specific expenses incurred in doing business for a client are billed back." 100% of income derived from commissions on ms sales.

THE MITCHELL ROSE LITERARY AGENCY, Suite 410, 799 Broadway, New York NY 10003. (212)418-0747. Agent contact: Mitchell Rose. Agency estab. 1986. Novels, story collections. Also reviews nonfiction (40%-60% fiction to nonfiction). Special interests: commercial fiction, mystery and literary fiction. Usually obtains new clients via recommendations. Currently represents 45 authors. Presently accepting new clients. Query or send outline plus sample chapters. Responds to queries in 3 weeks; to mss in 6 weeks. New/unpublished writers: 20%. Member of Authors Guild.
Sales: *Victorian Tales*, by Michael Patrick Hearn (Pantheon/Random House); *To Laredo*, by Jim Shaffer (St. Martin's); *Chain Reaction*, by Josh Pachter (Alliance Entertainment).
Terms: Agent's commission: 15% on domestic sales; 20% on foreign sales involving a sub-agent. Charges fee for high-volume photocopying, telexes, overseas phone calls. 100% of income derived from commission on mss sales. "For talented writers with promising projects, we can offer extensive editorial guidance when required."

JANE ROTROSEN AGENCY, 318 E. 51st St., New York NY 10022. (212)593-4330. Agents: Andrea Cirillo, Margaret Ruley, Stephanie Laidman. Agency estab. 1973. Reviews novels, novellas, story collections. Also reviews nonfiction (60%-40% fiction to nonfiction). Special interest: commercial fiction. Usually obtains new clients through referrals. Represents 140+ writers. Presently accepting new clients. Query first. Responds to queries in 10 days if SASE included; to mss in 6-8 weeks. Member of I.L.A.A.
Terms: Agent's commission: 15% on domestic sales; 20% on foreign sales (10% to co-agent; 10% to JRA).

RUSSELL & VOLKENING, INC., 50 W. 29th St., Apt. 7E, New York NY 10001. (212)684-6050. Novels, nonfiction. Send query letter with SASE. Member of S.A.R. Agents in all countries.

‡RAPHAEL SAGALYN, INC., LITERARY AGENCY, 1520 New Hampshire Ave., Washington DC 20036. Member of I.L.A.A.

SBC ENTERPRISES, INC., 11 Mabro Dr., Denville NJ 07834-9607, (201)366-3622. Agent contact: Alec Bernard, Eugenia Cohen. Agency estab 1979. Novels and story collections (where bulk are previously published). Also reviews nonfiction (75%-25% fiction to nonfiction). Special interest: mainstream, science projection, espionage. Usually obtains new clients via recommendations, conferences, advertising. Currently represents 25 authors. Presently accepting new clients. Query. Responds "immediately" to queries. New/unpublished writers: 90%.
Sales: *Maximizing Cash Flow*, by Emery Toncré (Wiley); *Action-Step Plan to Owning & Operating Business*, by Toncré (Montclair Press reprint).
Terms: Agent's commission: 15% on domestic sales if advance under $10,000, 10% thereafter; 20% on foreign sales. *Will critique 300-page novel for $2/page reading fee*. 100% of income derived from commission on ms sales.

JACK SCAGNETTI, 5330 Lankershim Blvd. #210, N. Hollywood CA 91601. (818)762-3871. Agency estab. 1974. Novels and scripts. Also reviews nonfiction (40%-60% fiction to nonfiction). Special interest: mainstream. Usually obtains new clients by referrals from other clients or free listings. Currently represents 35 authors. Presently accepting new clients. Query with outline. Responds to queries in 2 weeks; to mss in 4-6 weeks. New/unpublished writers: 75%. Signatory to Writers Guild of America—West.
Recent Sales: *Superstition Gold*, by Melissa Bowesock (Dorchester Publishing); *Successful Car Buying*, by Steve Ross (nonfiction). Script sales: *Family Ties, Women's Penitentiary 3000*.
Terms: Agent's commission: 10% on domestic sales; 15% on foreign sales. No reading fees for screenplays. No reading fees for books unless detailed critique is requested. Offers criticism service: $100 for 400 pages; $125 for 500 pages. Will detail critique 300-page novel for $75. "Experienced readers/analysts write critiques." Charges for one-way postage for multiple submissions. 100% of income derived from commission on ms sales. Payment of fees does not ensure agency representation. "Also handle screenwriters; spend more time reading/selling screenplays than books; represent more screenwriters than authors."

SCHAFFNER AGENCY, INC., 264 5th Ave., New York NY 10001. (212)689-6888. Agency Contact: Timothy Schaffner or Patrick Delahunt. Agency estab: 1948. Novels and story collections. Also reviews nonfiction. Special interest: mainstream, science fiction, fantasy, literary fiction and serious nonfiction. Usually obtains new clients via referrals, conventions and by reading magazine fiction. Currently represents 75 authors. Presently accepting new clients. Query with outline. "No unsolicited manuscripts, please." Responds to queries in 2 weeks; to mss in 4-6 weeks. Member of S.A.R. and I.L.A.A.
Recent Sales: *Life During War Time*, by Lucius Shepard (Bantam Books); *Proud Monster*, by Ian Macmillan (North Point Press); *The Watch*, by Rick Bass (story collections).
Terms: Agent's commission: 15% on domestic sales; 20% on foreign sales. Charges for return postage or $15 if SASE not included. 100% of income derived from commission on ms sales.

SCHLESSINGER-VAN DYCK AGENCY, 2814 PSFS Bldg., 12 S. 12th St., Philadelphia PA 19107. (215)627-4665. Agent contact: Blanche Schlessinger or Barrie Van Dyck. Agency estab. 1987. Novels. Also reviews nonfiction (40%-60% fiction to nonfiction). Usually obtains new clients via recommendations from others. Currently represents 40 clients. Presently accepting new clients. Send query or outline plus sample chapters. Responds to queries in 4-6 weeks; to mss in 4 weeks. New/unpublished writers: 20%.
Sales: *Indecent Proposal*, by Jack Engelhard (Donald I. Fine); *Maggie Among the Seneca* and *The Bread Sister of Sinking Creek*, by Robin Moore (Harper & Row).
Terms: Agent's commission: 15% on domestic sales; 20% on foreign sales. 100% of income derived from commission on sales.

SUSAN SCHULMAN LITERARY AGENCY, INC., 454 West 44th St., New York NY 10036. (212)713-1633. FAX: (212)315-4782. Agent contact: Susan Schulman. Estab. 1978. Novels and short stories. Also reviews nonfiction (50%-50% fiction to nonfiction). Special interests: mainstream, literary fiction and women's stories (genre fiction). Usually obtains new clients via recommendations from current clients. Presently accepting new clients. Send outline plus 3 sample chapters. Responds to queries in 6 days; to ms in 6 weeks. New/unpublished writers: 20%. Member of S.A.R., I.L.A.A.
Recent Sales: *Prayer Devil*, by Christopher Fawles (Ballantine, horror); *Hard Ball*, by Barbara D'Amato (Scribner's, mystery); *17 Martin Street*, by Catherine Hules (St. Martin's, contemporary women's fiction).
Terms: Agent's commission: 15% on domestic sales; 20% foreign sales. Charges $50 reading fee for any length ms. "I do the reading, evaluating and writing myself." Charges for postage and photocopying expenses. 99% of income derived from commission on ms sales; 1% from criticism service.

ARTHUR P. SCHWARTZ, 435 Riverside Dr., New York NY 10025. Branch office: Box 9132, Christchurch 2 New Zealand. Novels only. Area of specialization: commercially oriented fiction (i.e., frank, realistic sex and themes), adult-oriented romantic fiction, mainstream, family sagas, women's historical, contemporary romantic fiction, and science fiction. No "Harlequin" type books. Represents approximately 70 writers. Query. "Do not register, certify or insure; retain original ms for your file. Enclose ms-size SASE." Also reviews nonfiction (33%-66% fiction to nonfiction). Presently accepting new clients. New/unpublished writers, 33%. Member of I.L.A.A.
Terms: Agent's commission: 12½%.

‡LYNN SELIGMAN LITERARY AGENCY, 400 Highland Ave., Upper Montclair NJ 07043. (201)783-3631. Agent contact: Lynn Seligman. Estab. 1985. Novels, short stories and story collections. Also reviews nonfiction (20%-80% fiction to nonfiction). Special interests: women's novel, literary mainstream, fantasy. Usually obtains new clients via recommendations. Currently represents 35 authors. Presently accepting new clients. Query with entire ms or outline/proposal (for nonfiction). Responds to queries in 1-2 weeks; to mss in 2 months. New/unpublished writers: 50%.
Recent Sales: *Everything You've Heard is True*, by Frances Sherwood (Johns Hopkins University Press); *Fly by Night*, by Carol McD. Wallace (St. Martin's Press); and *Tourists*, by Lisa Goldstein (Simon and Schuster).
Terms: Agent's commission: 15% on domestic sales; 25% on foreign sales. Charges for photocopying and unusual mail or transatlantic calls. 100% of income derived from commission on ms sales.

BOBBE SIEGEL AGENCY, 41 West 83rd St., New York NY 10024. (212)877-4985. Associate: Richard Siegel. Agency estab. 1975. Novels. Also reviews nonfiction (45%-55% fiction to nonfiction). Special interests: mainstream, literary, science fiction, mystery, historical, any fiction. "But I do not handle children's books or cookbooks." Usually obtains new clients via "referral from editors and authors I know or whom I represent." Currently represents 60 authors. Presently accepting new clients. Query with letter. Responds to queries in 2-3 weeks; to mss in 6-8 weeks. New/unpublished writers: 30%.
Sales: *The Drowned & The Saved*, by Primo Levi (Summit); *The Lost Souls*, by Anthony Schmitz (Ballantine); *Choke Hold*, by Lew Dykes (Berkley).
Terms: Agent's commission: 15% on domestic sales; 10% on foreign sales. Charges for airmail, overseas phone, photocopy etc. 100% of income derived from commission on ms sales. "I will not read any manuscript or proposal that is not preceded by a letter. Do not send unless I ask to see—and always send with return postage, otherwise material will not be returned."

EVELYN SINGER LITERARY AGENCY INC., Box 594, White Plains NY 10602. Contact: Evelyn Singer. Agency estab. 1951. Novels. Also reviews nonfiction (25%-75% fiction to nonfiction). Special interests: fiction and nonfiction adult and juvenile books. Interested in fiction for general trade departments and suspense or mystery. Usually obtains new clients via recommendations. Currently represents 50-75 writers. Not presently accepting new fiction writers. Query or send outline plus 2-3 sample chapters. New/unpublished writers: 15%. Responds to queries in 2-4 weeks; to mss in 2-6 weeks.
Recent Sales: *Secret Kills*, by William Beechcroft (Dodd, Mead); *Run Baby Run*, by Cruz with Buckingham (Bridge); *Snakes & Other Reptiles*, by Mary Elting (Simon & Schuster).
Terms: Agent's commission: 15% on domestic sales; 20% on foreign sales. Charges for: "Long distance calls; copyright; charges other than local postage, phone and overhead, that are special for a particular property." 100% of income derived from commission on ms sales. "Include bio pertinent to literary background; type double-space (or use letter-quality printer; I cannot read dot matrix) on 8½x11 paper. Do not bind ms. Paginate consecutively. Do not send sample material from a section of the ms; send first part and outline. Include SASE for reply and/or return of material. Write; do not phone."

SINGER MEDIA CORPORATION, 3164 Tyler Ave., Anaheim CA 92801. (714)527-5650. Agent contact: John J. Kearns. Agency estab. 1945. Novels. Also reviews nonfiction (95%-5% fiction to nonfiction). Special interests: contemporary romance, adventure, suspense, mysteries. Usually obtains new clients

via conferences, word of mouth. Presently accepting new clients. Query or send entire ms. Responds to queries by return mail; to mss in 6 weeks. New/unpublished writers: 80%.
Terms: Agent's commission: 15% on domestic sales; 20% on foreign sales. Charges reading fee for unpublished authors; $200 for 300-page novel. "Compilation of readers' reports." Payment of fees does not ensure agency representation.

MICHAEL SNELL LITERARY AGENCY, Box 655, Truro MA 02666. (508)349-3718. Patricia Smith. Estab. 1980. Reviews novels. Also reads nonfiction (20%-80% fiction to nonfiction). Special interests: mystery, suspense, thrillers. Usually obtains news clients through *LMP*, word of mouth, publishers. Currently represents 200 clients. Presently accepting new clients. Send outline/proposal and query. Reports on queries in 1 week; on mss in 2 weeks.
Sales: *Blood Dawn, Blood Moon, Blood Tide*, by Kalish (3-book series) (Harvest/Avon); *The Brothers K*, by Duncan (Doubleday).
Terms: Agent's commission: 15% on domestic and foreign sales. 100% of business is derived from commission on mss sales.

SOUTHERN WRITERS, INC., Suite 1020, 635 Gravier St., New Orleans LA 70130. (504)525-6390. Agent contact: Pamela Ahearn. Agency estab: 1979. Novels and novellas. Also reviews nonfiction (65%-35% fiction to nonfiction). Special interest: fiction with a Southern flavor or background and romances—both contemporary and historical. Usually obtains new clients via recommendations from others, at conferences, and from listings. Currently represents 25-30 authors. Presently accepting new clients. Query. Responds to queries in 2 weeks; to mss in 4 weeks. New/unpublished writers: 35%.
Recent Sales: *Where the Towers Pierce the Sky*, by Marie Goodwin (Macmillan); *My Wicked Enchantress*, by Meagan McKinney (Dell); *The Heart's Haven*, by Jill Barnett (Pocket).
Terms: Agent's commission: 15% on domestic sales; 20% on foreign sales. Foreign Representatives: Abner Stein (UK); Uwe Luserke (Europe). *Charges $175 reading fee to new writer* on 300-page ms. "We charge a reading fee to unpublished authors and to those writing in areas other than that of previous publication." Offers criticism service for $275. Descripton of criticism service: "A letter (3-4 pp. single-spaced) evaluating work on the basis of style, content and marketability, offering constructive advice on this work and pointers for future writing." Charges for office expenses, which are deducted from royalties if book is sold. 65% of income derived from commission on ms sales; 35% from criticism service and reading fees.

‡DAVID M. SPATT, ESQ., 96 Sachem Road, Narragansett RI 02882. (401)789-5686. Estab. 1987. Novels, novellas, short stories. "All fiction, but especially sci-fi, fantasy, horror, mystery and stories with a New England flavor." Usually obtains new clients via recommendations. Currently represents under 10 authors. Presently accepting new clients. Query. Responds to queries in 2 weeks; to mss in 2 months. New/unpublished writers: 50%.
Terms: Agent's commission: 15% on domestic sales; 15% on foreign sales. "Costs which are directly attributed to marketing of the writers work. No general office expenses. This is an arts/entertainment law firm which has recently begun acting as a literary agent for the benefit of its clients, but now is looking to expand with new writers and previously published" writers, especially in the New England area.

F. JOSEPH SPIELER LITERARY AGENCY, 410 W. 24th Street., New York NY 10011. (212)242-7152 or (212)757-4439. Contact: Joseph Spieler. Estab. 1982. Reviews novels, novellas, short stories, story collections. Also reads nonfiction (40% to 50% fiction to nonfiction). Special interests: mainstream, children's, history, economics and contemporary issues, especially those dealing with the environment. Obtains clients through recommendations only. Currently represents 45 clients. Presently accepting new clients. Prefers query, outline/proposal or sample chapters. Reports in 1 week on queries; 3 weeks on mss. 20-30% of clients are new/unpublished writers.
Recent Sales: *Intimacy*, Susan Chace (Random House); *The Age of Miracles*, Catherine MacCoun (Atlantic/Little Brown); and *Growing A Business*, by Paul Hawken (Simon & Schuster).
Terms: Agent's commission: 15% on domestic sales; 20% on foreign. Sometimes charges criticism fee. "Exceptionally rare: done only at writer's request and then only if I feel it would be useful to the writer." Charges for bulk photocopying, long-distance telephone, bulk mailing. 95+% of business derived from commissions on mss sales; less than 1% derived from criticism services. Payment of fee does not guarantee representation.

PHILIP G. SPITZER LITERARY AGENCY, 788 9th Ave., New York NY 10019. (212)265-6003. Agency estab. 1969. Novels and nonfiction (50%-50% fiction to nonfiction). Special interest: quality fiction, suspense fiction. Obtains new clients primarily via recommendation. Currently represents 50 authors. Query. Also reviews nonfiction (50%-50% fiction to nonfiction). Accepting few new clients. Send outline/proposal. Responds to queries in 1 week; to mss in 6 weeks. New/unpublished writers: 25%.

Recent Sales: *Black Cherry Blues*, by James Lee Burke (Little, Brown); *Selected Stories*, by Andre Dubus (Vintage); *Fall From Grace: The Failed Crusade of the Christian Right*, by Michael D'Antonio (Farrar, Straus & Giroux).
Terms: Agent's commission: 10% on domestic sales; 20% on foreign sales. 100% of income derived from commission on ms sales.

LYLE STEELE & CO., LTD., LITERARY AGENTS, 511 E. 73d St., Suite 7, New York NY 10021. (212)288-2981. Agent contact: Lyle Steele. Agency estab. 1984. Novels. Also reviews nonfiction (50%-50% fiction to nonfiction). Special interests: mysteries, horror, particularly continuing series. Currently represents 50 clients. Presently accepting new clients. Query. Responds to queries in 1 week; to mss in 3 weeks. New/unpublished writers: .05%.
Sales: Eileen Fulton's eight book *Take One for Murder* series (Ballantine/Ivy).
Terms: Agent's commission: 10% on domestic sales; 10% on foreign sales (foreign agent also takes 10%). 100% of income derived from commission on mss sales.

STEPPING STONE, 59 West 71st St., New York NY 10023. (212)362-9277. Agent contact: Sarah Jane Freymann. Agency estab. 1974. Novels. Also reviews nonfiction (50%-50% fiction to nonfiction). Special interests: mainstream, self help, women's fiction, women's issues, spiritual themes, psychology, mystery and current events. Currently represents 75 clients. Presently accepting new clients. Query with outline/proposal. Responds to queries in 2 weeks; to mss in 1 month. New/unpublished writers: 10%. Member of I.L.A.A.
Terms: Agent's commission: 15%. 100% of income derived from commission on ms sales.

GLORIA STERN AGENCY, 1230 Park Ave., New York NY 10028. (212)289-7698. Agent contact: Gloria Stern. Agency estab. 1976. Also reviews nonfiction (10%-90% fiction to nonfiction). Represents 35 writers. Not presently accepting new clients unless referred by established writer or editor or previously published. Query with outline plus 1 sample chapter. Member of I.L.A.A.
Terms: Agent's commission: 15% on domestic sales; 20% on foreign sales. "I am sorry that I cannot take any new fiction at the present time. This may change in the future."

CHARLES M. STERN ASSOCIATES, Box 790742, San Antonio TX 78279-0742. (512)349-6141. Agency estab. 1977. Novels, nonfiction and how-to. Special interests: adventure, children's books, mainstream, women's, romance and mystery. Send query with SASE and/or send outline/proposal. Represents approximately 30+ writers. Obtains clients via recommendations and queries. Presently accepting new clients. Interested in new/unpublished novelists/writers. "Selection of new clients is based on quality work."
Terms: Agent's commission: 15%. "Return postage must accompany every query or submission. Phone calls made to authors to discuss their work will be made collect."

‡LARRY STERNIG LITERARY AGENCY, 742 Robertson St., Milwaukee WI 53213. (414)771-7677. Estab. 1950. Also reviews nonfiction (95%-5% fiction to nonfiction). Special interests: mainstream, children's, mystery and science fiction. Usually obtains new clients via recommendations. Currently represents 30 authors. Occasionally accepting new clients. Query. Responds to queries in 1 week; to mss in 2 weeks. New/unpublished writers 5%.
Recent Sales: *Rosie and the Dance of the Dinosaurs*, by Betty Ren Wright (Holiday House); *Prom Dress*, by Lael Littke (Scholastic); and *Little Boxes of Bewilderment*, by Jack Ritchie (St. Martin's, short story collection).
Terms: Agent's commission: 10% on domestic sales; 20% on foreign sales. 100% of income derived from commission on ms sales.

JO STEWART AGENCY, 201 E. 66th St., New York NY 10021. (212)879-1301. Agent contact: Jo Stewart. Agency estab. 1976. Novels. Also reviews nonfiction. Special interest: "all kinds of fiction and nonfiction – young adult fiction." Usually obtains new clients via recommendations of other writers and editors. Presently accepting new clients. Query first or send synopsis plus 2-3 sample chapters. Responds to queries within 2 days, "depends on my schedule and length of manuscript." Member of I.L.A.A.
Terms: Agent's commission: 15% on unpublished writers on domestic sales; 10% on published authors on domestic sales; 20% on foreign sales.

GUNTHER STUHLMANN AUTHOR'S REPRESENTATIVE, Box 276, Becket MA 01223. (413)623-5170. Agent Contact: Barbara Ward. Agency estab. 1954. Fiction and nonfiction books; no sci-fi. Special interest: quality literary fiction. Usually obtains new clients via recommendations. Query with outline and SASE. Responds to queries in 2 weeks.

Sales: *Prisoner's Dilemma*, by Richard Powers (Morrow).
Terms: Agent's commission: 10% on domestic sales; 20% on foreign sales; 15% British Commonwealth. 100% of income derived from commission on ms sales.

H.N. SWANSON, INC., 8523 Sunset Blvd., Los Angeles CA 90069. (213)652-5385. Agent Contact: B.F. Kamsler. Agency estab. 1932. Novels, novellas and story collections. Also reviews nonfiction (90%-10% fiction to nonfiction). Special interests: mainstream, adventure and thrillers. Usually obtains new clients via recommendations from others. Currently represents 125 authors. Presently accepting new clients. Query with outline plus sample chapters. Responds to queries in 1 week; to mss in 4 weeks.
Recent Sales: *You Must Remember This*, by Joyce Carol Oates (E.P. Dutton); *Freaky Deaky*, by Elmore Leonard (Arbor House)
Terms: Agent's commission: 10% on domestic sales; 15% on foreign sales. 100% of income derived from commission on ms sales.

ROSLYN TARG LITERARY AGENCY, INC., 105 W. 13th St., New York NY 10011. (212)206-9390. Agent contact: Roslyn Targ. Estab. 1969. Novels. Also reads nonfiction. Special interest: mainstream. Usually obtains new clients via recommendations from others. Query with SASE, and where sending manuscripts. Responds to mss in 2-3 weeks. Member of S.A.R. and I.L.A.A.
Terms: Agent's commission: 15% on unpublished authors; 10% on published authors; 20% on foreign sales. 100% of income derived from commission on ms sales.

PATRICIA TEAL LITERARY AGENCY, 2036 Vista Del Rosa, Fullerton CA 92631. (714)738-8333. Contact: Patricia Teal. Agency estab. 1978. Novels. Also reviews nonfiction (75%-25% fiction to nonfiction). Special interest: category novels. Usually obtains new clients via recommendations from others, solicitation, at conferences. Currently represents 60 authors. Presently accepting "a few" new clients. Query. Responds to queries in 2 weeks; to mss in 1 month. New/unpublished writers: 50%. Member of I.L.A.A.
Recent Sales: *Bound By Blood*, by June Triglia (NAL); *Rose*, by Jill Marie Landis (Berkley Publishing Group); *Wild Winds*, by Catherine Palmer (Bantam).
Terms: Agent's commission: 10-15% on domestic sales; 20% on foreign sales. "We do not read entire manuscripts, only queries or partials. Would not charge a fee for a book we asked to see." Charges for postage and telephone calls. 100% of income derived from commission on mss sales. "We do not welcome mainstream fiction by unpublished writers except through professional writer referral or through contact at conferences."

THOMPSON TALENT AGENCY, Box 4272, Modesto CA 95352. Agent contact: Sharon Harris, director of literary talent. Agency estab. 1982. Novels, novellas, short stories, story collections. Also reviews nonfiction (60%-40% fiction to nonfiction). Special interests: novels. Presently accepting new clients. Query. Responds to queries in 1 month; to mss in 3 months. New/unpublished writers: 25%. Member of S.A.R., I.L.A.A.
Terms: Agents commission: 10% on domestic sales. Offers criticism service. "Writer must provide all postage expenses. Do not send money, checks or money orders."

SUSAN P. URSTADT INC., 271 Madison Ave., Suite 708, New York NY 10016. Agent contact: Susan P. Urstadt. Agency estab. 1975. Novels. Also reviews nonfiction (30%-70% fiction to nonfiction). Special interest: "thoughtful, quality fiction – commercial, literary and accessible with psychological insight." Usually obtains new clients via recommendations from others. Currently represents 50 authors. Presently accepting new clients. Send outline plus 1 sample chapter and SASE. Responds to queries in 3-4 weeks. New/unpublished writers: 10%. Member of I.L.A.A. "Please do not phone."
Recent Sales: *Miracle of Bohemin*, by Josef Skvovecky (Knopf); *Code Name Kris*, by Carol Matas (Scribners juvenile).
Terms: Agent's commission: 15% on domestic sales; 20% on foreign sales. Charges for photocopying, airmail and foreign postage. 100% of income derived from commission on ms sales.

RALPH M. VICINANZA, LTD., 432 Park Ave., New York NY 10016. (212)725-5133. Agent contact: Chris Lotts. Estab. 1978. Novels. Also reviews nonfiction. Special interests: science fiction, fantasy, thrillers. New clients via recommendations only. Currently represents 50 clients. New/unpublished writer: 10%.
Terms: Agent's commission: 10% on domestic sales; 20% on foreign sales.

MARY JACK WALD ASSOCIATES, INC., 70A Greenwich Ave., New York NY 10011. (212)254-7842. Contact: Mary Jack Wald. Agency estab. 1985 (1983-1985 was Wald-Hardy Associates, Inc.). Novels, "novellas if in or with a short story collection." Also reviews nonfiction (50%-50% fiction to nonfic-

tion). Special interests: mainstream and literary fiction and nonfiction for the adult and juvenile audience. Usually obtains clients via recommendations from others. Currently represents 50 writers. Presently accepting new clients. Responds to queries in 3-4 weeks; to mss in 1-2 months. Member of The Authors Guild, The Society of Children's Book Writers and Authors League of America.

Recent Sales: *On the Wings of the Phoenix*, by Susan Witty (Grove-Weidenfeld); *Scarecrow*, by Richie Tankersley Cusick (Pocket Books); *The Rabbit Club*, by Jan Wahl (HBJ).

Terms: Agent's commission: 15% on domestic sales; 15% on foreign sales.

THE GERRY B. WALLERSTEIN AGENCY, 2315 Powell Ave., Suite 12, Erie PA 16506. (814)833-5511. Contact: Ms. Gerry B. Wallerstein. Agency estab. 1984. Novels, novellas, short stories, story collections for adult market only. Also reads adult nonfiction (25%-75% fiction to nonfiction). Usually obtains new clients through (1) ongoing ad in *Writer's Digest*; (2) recommendations; (3) referrals from existing clients; (4) writers' groups. Currently represents 40 clients. Presently accepting new clients. Query. "Brochure is sent right away; responds to ms in approximately 4 weeks; no ms until writer sees brochure." New/unpublished writers: 25%. Member of Author's Guild and Society of Professional Journalists.

Terms: Agent's commission: 15% on domestic sales; 15% on dramatic sales; 20% on foreign sales. *"I charge a reading/critique fee* (waived for some published writers), which must accompany your material, on the following basis: $50 for each manuscript under 5,000 words; $100 for each manuscript of 5,000 to 20,000 words; $200 for each manuscript 20,000 to 65,000 words; $250 for each manuscript 65,000 to 85,000 words; $300 for each manuscript 85,000 to 105,000 words; $350 for each manuscript 105,000 to 125,000 words. Query for manuscript over 125,000 words. A critique will be provided, including my assessment of the work's marketability. If the work requires revision or editing to make it salable, it will be up to you to do it, if you so decide, based on the advice I give you; I will re-read the revised manuscript without additional charge. Clients charged for copyright applications, photocopying manuscripts, typing manuscripts, legal fees (if required and approved by author), my travel (if approved by author), $20 monthly mail/telephone fee." 50% of income derived from commissions on ms sales; 50% derived from reading fees and criticism services. "Only about 10-15% of the fiction manuscripts I see have marketing potential, and of that percentage perhaps 5% are really likely to sell at all. Quality must be high for today's fiction marketplace."

JOHN A. WARE LITERARY AGENCY, 392 Central Park West, New York NY 10025. (212)866-4733. Agency estab. 1978. Novels and story collections "if individual stories have been placed." Also reviews nonfiction (40%-60% fiction to nonfiction). Special interests: literary, thrillers, mysteries, mainstream. "No romances, men's adventure or science fiction, please." Usually obtains new clients via referrals or at conferences. Currently represents 50 authors. Presently accepting new clients. Please query first. Responds to queries in 2 weeks; to mss in 1 month. New/unpublished writers: 25%.

Recent Sales: *Fires in the Sky*, by Phillip Parotti (Ticknor & Fields); *The Old Way*, by Lucy Taylor (New American Library); *Heathern*, by Jack Womack (Tor).

Terms: Agent's commission: 10% on domestic sales; 20% on foreign sales.

JAMES WARREN LITERARY AGENCY, (formerly Warren/Hilton Agency), 13131 Welby Way, Suite B, North Hollywood CA 91606. (818)982-5423. Agent contacts: James Warren, Romilde-Ann Dicke, Bob Carlson. Agency estab. 1969. Novels, novellas, stories and story collections, "but query first." Also reviews nonfiction (70%-30% fiction to nonfiction). Special interests: mainstream, adventure, gothic, history, historical romance, science fiction, mystery, horror, humor. Usually obtains new clients via *Writer's Market*, *LMP*, other trade publications, referrals. Currently represents 48 clients. Presently accepting new clients. Query or send entire ms. Responds to queries in 1 week; to mss in 1 month. New/unpublished writers: 60%.

Terms: Agent's commission: 10% on domestic sales; 20% on foreign sales. *Charges reading fee*: $150 for 300-page ms typed with pica typeface; $225 or more for ms typed with elite typeface. "On rare occasions we may charge a submission fee if we think the material is excellent but has little chance of publication." 80% of income derived from commission on sales; 20% derived from reading fees. Payment of fees does not ensure agency representation.

WATERSIDE PRODUCTIONS, INC, 832 Camino Del Mar, Del Mar CA 92014. (619)481-8335. Contact: Julie Castiglia, agent, fiction. Novels. Also reviews nonfiction (22%-78% fiction to nonfiction). Special interest: mainstream novels. Usually obtains new clients through recommendations from others. Currently represents 150 authors. Presently accepting new clients. Query, then send outline/proposal. Responds to queries in 2 weeks. New/unpublished writers: 25%.

Recent Sales: *Good Friday*, by Bob Holt (Tab-hardcover, NAL-paperback); *Ashes to Empire*, by Faye Daniels (Paperjacks); *Other Suns Other Worlds*, by Dennis Mammana and Donald McCarthy; *The Art Biz*, by Alice Marquis.

Terms: Agent's commission: 15% on domestic sales; 25% on foreign sales. No initial reading fee. Editorial services for pre-determined fee. Charges for postage and photocopies. 99% of income derived from commission on ms sales; 1% from criticism service. "We are only interested in writers with track records in national magazines, film experience, drama experience or superlative recommendations from known writers or writing teachers."

SANDRA WATT AND ASSOCIATES, Suite 4053, 8033 Sunset Blvd., Los Angeles CA 90046. (213)653-2339. Agent contact: Sandra Watt or Robert Drake. Agency estab. 1977. Novels and some short stories. Special interests: gay fiction, women's fiction, men's action/adventure, mystery, thrillers, New Age, literary fiction, humor, cookbooks and YA. Usually obtains new clients via client referrals and conferences. Currently represents 100+ clients. Presently accepting new clients. Query first. Responds to queries in 1 week; to mss in 8 weeks. Always SASE. New/unpublished writers: 15%. Member I.L.A.A. and Writer's Guild West.

Recent Sales: *Hungry Women*, by Laramie Dunaway (Warner); *Walk on the Wild Side*, by Holly Woodlawn (New American Library); and *Half a Mind*, by Wendy Hornsby (New American Library).

Terms: Agent's commission: 15% on domestic sales and 25% on foreign sales. "We charge an unpublished writer of fiction a $100 marketing fee." 100% of income derived from commission of ms sales.

‡THE WENDY WEIL AGENCY, INC., 747 Third Ave., New York NY 10017. (212)753-2605. Agent contact: Wendy Weil. Estab. 1987. Novels. Also reviews nonfiction (50%-50% fiction to nonfiction). Usually obtains new clients via recommendations from others. Currently represents 75 authors. Not presently accepting new clients. Query. Responds to queries in 2 weeks; to mss in 2 months. New/unpublished writers: 25%. Member of S.A.R.

Recent Sales: *Secret Harmonies*, by Andrea Barrett (Delacorte); *The Summer of the Paymaster*, by Al Nielsen (Norton); *We're Alive*, by Heywood Gould (Morrow).

Terms: Agent's commission: 10% on domestic sales; 20% on foreign sales. Charges for cost of books and galleys. 100% of income derived from commissions on sales.

FRANK WEIMANN ASSOCIATES, (formerly Victoria Management), Suite 1H, 262 Central Park West, New York NY 10024. (212)873-0972. Agent contact: Frank Weimann. Agency estab. 1984. Novels. Also reviews nonfiction (25%-75% fiction to nonfiction). Special interests: how-to, biography and mainstream. Obtains new clients primarily through referrals. Currently represents 25 clients. Presently accepting new clients. Submit sample chapters. Responds in 1 month. New/unpublished writers: 50%.

Recent Sales: *It's Not What You Eat It's What's Eating You*, by Dr. Janet Greeson (Simon & Schuster); *Success Through Better Memory*, by Dr. Eric Bienstock (Putnam); *The Joy of Depression*, by David Rudnitsky (NAL).

Terms: Agent's commission: 15% on domestic sales; 19% on foreign sales. 100% of income derived from commission on ms sales.

CHERRY WEINER LITERARY AGENCY, 28 Kipling Way, Manalapan NJ 07726. (201)446-2096. Agency estab. 1977. Novels, novellas. Also reviews nonfiction (80%-20% fiction to nonfiction). Special interests: mainstream, science fiction, romance. Usually obtains new clients via recommendations from others. Currently represents 40 authors. Query or send outline plus sample chapters. Responds "immediately" to queries; to mss in 4-6 weeks. New/unpublished writers: 15%—not taking without recommendation.

Terms: Agent's commission: 15%. 100% of income derived from commission on ms sales. Sub agents: Germany, Scandinavia, Japan, England, France.

RHODA WEYR AGENCY, 151 Berger St., Brooklyn NY 11217. Novels. Also reviews nonfiction. Query or send outline plus sample chapters. "The query letter should give any relevant information about the author and her/his work, publishing history, etc." Also represents nonfiction (about equal fiction to nonfiction). Presently accepting new clients. Interested in both fiction and nonfiction writers. Member of S.A.R and I.L.A.A. "Send letter/material, etc., with SASE to fit mss."

Terms: Agent's commission: 10% for domestic; 20% foreign.

WIESER & WIESER, 118 East 25th St., New York NY 10010. (212)260-0860. Agent contact: Olga Wieser. Agency estab. 1976. Novels. Also reviews nonfiction (40%-60% fiction to nonfiction). Special interests: mainstream, literary, historical and regency. Usually obtains new clients via recommendations from clients and other professionals. Currently represents 60 authors. Presently accepting new clients. Send outline plus sample chapters. Responds to queries in 1-2 weeks; to mss in 4 weeks.

Recent Sales: *Come Winter*, by Douglas C. Jones (Henry Holt); *Road to Avalon*, by Joan Wolf (NAL hardcover); *Day of the Cheeta*, by Dale Brown (Donald I. Fine, Inc.).

Terms: Agent's commission: 15% on domestic sales; 20% on foreign sales; 15% motion picture rights sale. Offers criticism service. "No fees; if we decide to critique a work, we feel our input will improve the chances for publication." Charges for overseas cables and duplicating manuscript. 100% of income derived from commission on ms sales.

RUTH WRESCHNER, AUTHORS' REPRESENTATIVE, 10 W. 74th St., New York NY 10023. (212)877-2605. Contact: Ruth Wreschner. Agency estab. 1981. Novels. Also reviews nonfiction (15%-85% fiction to nonfiction). Special interests: mainstream, some romantic fiction, mysteries and science fiction. Usually obtains new clients via recommendations from others, solicitation, at conferences and listings. Represents about 40 writers. Send query and outline/proposal. Responds to queries in 2 days; to mss in 2-3 weeks. "Must enclose SASE."

Terms: Agent's commission: 15% on domestic sales; 20% on foreign sales. Charges for photocopy expenses "and when a book has been sold, I withhold certain funds for foreign mailings from the second advance." 100% of income derived from commission on ms sales. "While I avidly review fiction, I sell much more nonfiction. A first novel is very difficult to place, unless it really is superb."

ANN WRIGHT REPRESENTATIVES INC., Suite 2C 136 East 56th St., New York NY 10022. (212)832-0110. Agent contact: Dan Wright, head—literary department. Agency estab. 1962. Novels, novellas, short stories. Special needs: fiction that applies both to publishing and motion pictures/TV. Usually obtains clients via word of mouth, references from film industry. Currently represents 31 clients. Not presently accepting new clients. Query first. Responds to queries in 2 months; to mss in 3+ months. New/unpublished writers: 25%. Member of WGA.

Terms: Agent's commission: 10% on domestic sales; 20% on foreign sales.

WRITERS HOUSE, INC., 21 W. 26th St., New York NY 10010. President: Albert Zuckerman. Novels. Also reviews nonfiction (50%-50% fiction to nonfiction). Usually obtains clients via recommendations. Represents around 120 writers. Presently accepting new clients. Query. Responds to queries in 2 weeks; to mss in 8 weeks. New/unpublished writers. "About 75% when they started with us."

Recent Sales: *Pillars of the Earth*, by Ken Follett; *Garden of Lies*, by Eileen Goudge; *Sweet Revenge*, by Nora Roberts.

Terms: Agent's commission: 15% on domestic sales; 20% on foreign sales. 100% of income derived from commission on ms sales. "We are always on the lookout for skilled and talented writers."

WRITERS' PRODUCTIONS, Box 630, Westport CT 06881. Agent contact: David L. Meth. Agency estab. 1981. "Literary quality fiction; dramatic photo-essay books of exceptional quality on unique subjects; and works of nonfiction that are well researched, carefully planned and thought out, with a high degree of originality. We welcome health and fitness, and family-oriented books. We have a special interest in work by Asian Americans; work about Southeast Asia and the Far East." Usually obtains new clients by "word of mouth, though we read and respond to all work." Presently accepting new clients. Send one-page cover letter plus 30 pages and a SASE for return of ms. Responds to queries in 1 week; to mss in 1 month. New/unpublished writers: 50%.

Recent Sales: *Inspector Imanismi Investigates*, by Matsumoto Seicho (Japan), (Soho Press); *In Malacanang, Even the Toilets Have Chandeliers*, by Kathleen Barnes (Thunder's Mouth Press); *The Day Care Kit*, by Debbie Spaide (Birch Lane Press).

Terms: Agent's commission: 15% on domestic sales; 20% on foreign sales; 20% dramatic sales. SASE must accompany ms for its return and any correspondence. No phone calls please.

MARY YOST ASSOCIATES, 59 E. 54th St., New York NY 10022. (212)980-4988. Contact: Mary Yost. Novels. Special interests: mainstream, women's. Query or send outline plus 50 pages. Also reviews nonfiction (40%-60% fiction to nonfiction). Obtains new clients via recommendations from other clients, editors, a few unsolicited mss. Presently accepting new clients. Member of S.A.R.

Terms: Agent's commission: 15%.

SUSAN ZECKENDORF ASSOCIATES, 171 W. 57th St., New York NY 10019. (212)245-2928. Contact: Susan Zeckendorf. Agency estab. 1979. Novels. Also reviews nonfiction (60%-40% fiction to nonfiction). Special interests: mainstream, thrillers, mysteries, and literary, historical, and commercial women's fiction. Usually obtains new clients via recommendations and solicitation. Represents 45 writers. Presently accepting new clients. Query. Responds to queries in 2 weeks; to solicited mss in 3 weeks. New/unpublished writers: 25%. Member of I.L.A.A.

Recent Sales: *Veil of Secrets*, by Una Mary Parker (NAL); *Making Music*, by Nancy Uscher (St. Martin's Press); *Jermian Martin* by Robert Fowler (St. Martin's Press).
Terms: Agent's commission: 15% on domestic sales; 20% on foreign sales. Charges for photocopying expenses. 100% of income derived from commission on ms sales.

Other literary agents

The following agents appeared in the 1989 edition of *Novel & Short Story Writer's Market* but not in the 1990 edition. Those agents who did not respond to our request for an update appear without further explanation below. Agents do not respond for a variety of reasons—they may be out of business, for example, or they may have received too many inappropriate submissions.

Linda Allen Agency
The Bradley-Goldstein Agency
Ruth Cantor
Diane Cleaver, Inc.
Joyce Cole Literary Agency
Shirley Collier Agency
Athos Demetriou
Anita Diamant: The Writers Workshop
Joseph Elder Agency (temporarily away)
Ann Elmo Agency Inc.
Felicia Eth Literary Representation
Florence Feiler Literary Agency
Flaming Star Literary
The Ricardo Hunter Garcia Agency
Maia Gregory Associates
Alexandria Hatcher Agency
Heacock Literary Agency
HHM Literary Agency
Hintz & Fitzgerald Literary Agency (requested to be deleted)
John Hochmann Books (requested to be removed for one year)
International Creative Management
Peter Livingston Associates
Los Angeles Literary Associates
Gina Maccoby Literary Agency (requested to be deleted)
Kirby McCauley (requested to be deleted)
Helen Merrill Ltd.
Elinor Midlik Associates
William Morris Agency, Inc.
Charles Neighobors
Harold Ober Associates
Peckner Literary Agency
Pickering Associates
Julian Portman & Associates
Sherry Robb Literary Properties
Rosenstone/Wender
Harold Schmidt Literary Agency
Elsye Sommer, Inc.
Phyllis R. Tornetta Literary Agency
Writers World Forum

Glossary

The following words are used differently when applied to writing and publishing than they are when spoken or written in other situations. For more general definitions and terms, check a standard dictionary.

Advance. Payment by a publisher to an author prior to the publication of a book, to be deducted from the author's future royalties.

Adventure. Genre in which an exciting, event-filled plot is the most important aspect, in which the reader's primary goal is to find out what happens next.

All rights. The rights contracted to a publisher permitting a manuscript's use anywhere and in any form, including movie and book-club sales, without additional payment to the writer.

Backlist. A publisher's list of its books that were not published during the current season but which are still in print.

Bimonthly. Every two months.

Biweekly. Every two weeks.

Book auction. Sale of rights (e.g. paperback, movie) by a book publisher to the highest bidder.

Book producer/packager. An organization that plans all elements of a book, from its initial concept to writing and marketing strategies, and then sells the package to a book publisher and/or movie producer.

Category fiction. See Genre.

Chapbook. A booklet of 15-30 pages of fiction or poetry.

Clean copy. Manuscript free of errors, cross-outs and smudges, ready to be typeset for printing.

Cliffhanger. Fictional event in which the reader is left in suspense at the end of a chapter or episode, so that interest in the story's outcome will be sustained.

Clip. Sample, usually from newspaper or magazine, of a writer's published work.

Cloak-and-dagger. A melodramatic, romantic type of fiction dealing with espionage and intrigue.

Collective. A group of writers and editors who work together to publish books, usually collaborating on editing tasks and sharing financial risk.

Commercial. Publishers whose chief concern is with salability, profit and success with a large readership.

Confession. Genre of love story where a sympathetic narrator, usually a female from a blue-collar family, faces and eventually solves an emotional problem with a husband, lover or family members.

Contemporary. Material dealing with popular current trends, themes or topics.

Contributor's copy. Copy of an issue of a magazine or published book sent to an author whose work is included; often the only form of payment from little/literary magazines and small presses.

Co-publishing. An arrangement in which the author and publisher share publication costs and profits.

Copyediting. Editing a manuscript for writing style, grammar, punctuation and factual accuracy.

Copyright. The legal right to exclusive publication, sale or distribution of a literary work.

Cover letter. A brief descriptive letter sent along with a complete manuscript submitted to an editor.

Cyberpunk. Type of science fiction, usually concerned with computer networks and human-computer combinations, involving young, sophisticated protagonists.

Division. An unincorporated branch of a company (e.g. Penguin Books, a division of Viking, Penguin, Inc.).

Dot-matrix printer. Computer printer on which the letters are formed with tiny dots rather than with a single key or other element.

Edition. All copies of a work printed from a single setting of type.

El-hi. Elementary to high school.

Escape literature. Writing, often genre fiction, that allows a reader to forget the realities of life and dwell in fantasies.

Experimental fiction. Fiction that is innovative in subject matter and style; avant-garde, non-formulaic, usually literary material.

Exposition. The portion of the storyline, usually the beginning, where background information about character and setting is related.

Faction. A combination of fact and fiction, depicting both real people under their own names and real people under fictitious names.

Fair use. A provision in the copyright law that says short passages from copyrighted material may be used without infringing on the owner's rights.

Fantasy. Literary work in which the action occurs in a non-existent and unreal world with incredible, imaginary characters.
Fanzine. A noncommercial, small-circulation magazine usually dealing with fantasy, horror or science-fiction literature and art.
First North American serial rights. The right to publish material in a periodical before it appears in book form, for the first time, in the United States or Canada.
Formula. A fixed and conventional method of plot development, which varies little from one book to another in a particular genre.
Galleys. The first typeset version of a manuscript that has not yet been divided into pages.
Genre. A formulaic type of fiction such as romance, western or horror.
Gothic. A genre in which the central character is usually a beautiful young woman and the setting an old mansion or castle, involving a handsome hero and real danger, either natural or supernatural.
Guidelines. A magazine or publishing house's rule sheet for potential contributors.
Honorarium. A small, token payment for published work.
Horror. A genre stressing fear, death and other aspects of the macabre.
Imprint. Name applied to a publisher's specific line of books (e.g. Aerie Books, an imprint of Tor Books).
Interactive fiction. Fiction in book or computer-software format where the reader determines the path the story will take by choosing from several alternatives at the end of each chapter or episode.
International Reply Coupon (IRC). A form purchased at a post office and enclosed with a letter or manuscript to a foreign publisher, to cover return postage costs.
Juvenile. Fiction intended for children 2-12.
Kill fee. A percentage of the agreed-upon purchase price paid to an author for a completed story or book that was assigned but subsequently canceled by the publisher.
Letter-quality printer. Computer printer with a typeface that is identical to that of a good-quality typewriter.
Libel. Written or printed words that defame, malign or damagingly misrepresent a living person.
Literary. The general category of serious, non-formulaic, intelligent fiction, sometimes experimental, that most frequently appears in little magazines.
Literary agent. A person who acts for an author in finding a publisher or arranging contract terms on a literary project.
Mainstream. Traditionally written fiction on subjects or trends that transcend experimental or genre fiction categories.
Manuscript. The author's unpublished copy of a work, usually typewritten, used as the basis for typesetting.
Mass market paperback. Softcover book on a popular subject, usually around 4×7, directed to a general audience and sold in drugstores and groceries as well as in bookstores.
Ms(s). Abbreviation for manuscript(s).
Multiple submission (also simultaneous submission). The practice of sending copies of the same manuscript to several editors or publishers at the same time.
Narration. The account of events in a story's plot as related by the speaker or the voice of the author.
Narrator. The person who tells the story, either someone involved in the action or the voice of the writer.
New Age. A term including categories such as astrology, psychic phenomena, spiritual healing, UFOs, mysticism and other aspects of the occult.
Nom de plume. French for "pen name"; a pseudonym.
Novella (also novelette). A short novel or long story, approximately 7,000-15,000 words.
#10 envelope. 4×9½ envelope, used for queries and other business letters.
Offprint. Copy of a story taken from a magazine before it is bound.
One-time rights. Permission to publish a story in periodical or book form one time only.
Over the transom. Slang for the path of an unsolicited manuscript into the slush pile.
Page rate. A fixed rate paid to an author per published page of fiction.
Payment on acceptance. Payment from the magazine or publishing house as soon as the decision to print a manuscript is made.
Payment on publication. Payment from the publisher after a manuscript is printed.
Pen name. A pseudonym used to conceal a writer's real name.
Periodical. A magazine or journal published at regular intervals – not ordinarily referring to newspapers.
Plot. The carefully devised series of events through which the characters progress in a work of fiction.
Proofreading. Close reading and correction of a manuscript's typographical errors.
Proofs. A typeset version of a manuscript used for correcting errors and making changes, often a photocopy of the galleys.
Proposal. An offer to an editor to write a specific work, usually consisting of an outline of the work and one or two completed chapters.
Prose poem. Short piece of prose with the language and expression of poetry.
Protagonist. The principal or leading character in a literary work.
Public domain. Material that either was never copyrighted or whose copyright term has expired.

Pulp magazine. A periodical printed on inexpensive paper, usually containing lurid, sensational stories or articles.
Purple prose. Ornate writing using exaggerated and excessive literary devices.
Query. A letter written to an editor to elicit interest in a story the writer wants to submit.
Reader. A person hired by a publisher to read unsolicited manuscripts.
Reading fee. An arbitrary amount of money charged by some agents and publishers to read a submitted manuscript.
Regency romance. A genre romance, usually set in England between 1811-1820.
Remainders. Leftover copies of an out-of-print book, sold by the publisher at a reduced price.
Reporting time. The number of weeks or months it takes an editor to report back on an author's query or manuscript.
Reprint rights. Permission to print an already published work whose rights have been sold to another magazine or book publisher.
Roman à clef. French "novel with a key." A novel that represents actual living or historical characters and events in fictionalized form.
Romance. The genre relating accounts of passionate love and fictional heroic achievements.
Royalties. A percentage of the retail price paid to he author for each copy of the book that is sold.
SASE. Self-addressed stamped envelope.
Scene. Unit of dramatic action in which a single point is made or one specific effect is attained.
Science fiction. Genre in which scientific facts and hypotheses form the basis of actions and events.
Second serial rights. Permission for the reprinting of a work in another periodical after its first publication in book or magazine form.
Self publishing. An independent publishing effort where full financial and editorial responsibility for the printing and marketing of a work is taken by its author.
Semimonthly. Twice a month.
Semiweekly. Twice a week.
Sequel. A literary work that continues the narrative of a previous, related story or novel.
Serial rights. The rights given by an author to a publisher to print a piece in one or more periodicals.
Serialized novel. A book-length work of fiction published in sequential issues of a periodical.
Setting. The environment and time period during which the action of a story takes place.
Shelf life. Length of time that a book is sold in a bookstore or other retail outlet.
Short short story. A condensed piece of fiction, usually under 1,000 words.
Simultaneous submission. See Multiple submission.
Slant. A story's particular approach or style, designed to appeal to the readers of a specific magazine.
Slice of life. A presentation of characters in a seemingly mundane situation which offers the reader a flash of illumination about the characters or their situation.
Slick. Popular, commercial, usually non-literary publication. (Name derived from the coated or polished stock on which it is printed.)
Slush pile. A stack of unsolicited manuscripts in the editorial offices of a publisher.
Speculation (or Spec). An editor's agreement to look at an author's manuscript with no promise to purchase.
Subsidiary. An incorporated branch of a company or conglomerate (e.g. Alfred Knopf, Inc., a subsidiary of Random House, Inc.).
Subsidiary rights. All rights other than book publishing rights included in a book contract, such as paperback, book club and movie rights.
Subsidy publisher. A book publisher who charges the author for the cost of typesetting, printing and promoting a book. Also Vanity publisher.
Suspense. A genre of fiction where the plot's primary function is to build a feeling of anticipation and fear in the reader over its possible outcome.
Tabloid. Publication printed on paper about half the size of a regular newspaper page (e.g. *The National Enquirer*).
Tearsheet. Page from a magazine containing a published story.
Theme. The dominant or central idea in a literary work; its message, moral or main thread.
Trade paperback. A softbound volume, usually around 5 × 8, published and designed for the general public, available mainly in bookstores.
Unsolicited manuscript. A story or novel manuscript that an editor did not specifically ask to see.
Vanity publisher. See Subsidy publisher.
Viewpoint. The position or attitude of the first- or third-person narrator or multiple narrators, which determines how a story's action is seen and evaluated.
Western. Genre with a setting in the West, usually between 1860-1890, with a formula plot about cowboys or other aspects of frontier life.
Whodunit. Genre dealing with murder, suspense and the detection of criminals.
Writer's block. The inability to begin or complete work on a writing project.
Young adult. The general classification of books written for readers 12-18.

Category Index

The category index is a good place to begin searching for a market for your fiction.

Below is an alphabetized list of subjects of particular interest to the editors and agents listed in *Novel and Short Story Writer's Market*. The category index is divided into five sections: literary and small circulation magazines, commercial periodicals, small presses, commercial publishers and literary agents.

If you have prepared a manuscript for a children's novel, for example, check the small press, commercial publisher or agents sections under Juvenile. Then look up that publisher or agent you have selected in the Markets Index to find the correct page number. Read the listing *very* carefully.

The category index is a useful—but very general—guide to help you save time as you market your work. The categories are broad, and different editors—especially periodical editors—interpret them differently. For example, the romance fiction desired by *Cosmopolitan* is obviously different from that used by *St. Anthony Messenger*.

Remember too that some periodicals, presses and agents choose not to specify their needs for fiction too exactly, preferring not to be limited by categories. Their specifications may be *quality* fiction only—including literary or mainstream work in all categories. It would be a mistake to use this category index as your *only* guide for choosing markets for your work, especially in the literary and small circulation magazine category. Browse through the book, and order sample copies of the magazines that interest you.

Literary and Small Circulation Magazines

Adventure. Adara; Adroit Expression, The; Amaranth; Amateur Writers Journal; Amelia; Amherst Review, The; Arnazella; Atalantik; Atlantis (British Columbia); Ball State University Forum; Black Jack; Blue Water Review, The; Blueline; Bradley's Fantasy Magazine, Marion Zimmer; Breakthrough!; Bristlecone; Caffe, Il; Carousel Literary Arts Magazine; Chapter One; Chrysalis; Cicada; Cochran's Corner; Cold-Drill Magazine; Couch Potato Journal, The; Cross Timbers Review; Cube Literary Magazine; Dan River Anthology; Dream International/Quarterly; Eldritch Science; Event; F.O.C. Review; Fighting Woman News; First Stories; Galactic Discourse; Garm Lu; Gas; Gateways; Gestalt; Gotta Write Network Litmag; Grasslands Review; Green Mountains Review; Greens Magazine; Hawaii Pacific Review; Hibiscus Magazine; Hippo; Hob-Nob; Innisfree; Jeopardy; Journal of Regional Criticism; Kana; Leading Edge, The; Left-Footed Wombat; Legend; Lighthouse; Little Balkans Review; Llamas Magazine; Long Shot; Macguffin, The; Meal, Ready-To-Eat; Merlyn's Pen; Microcosm; Mind's Eye, The; Minnesota Ink; Mirror-Northern Report, The; Muse's Mill; Negative Capability; New Methods; New Press, The; Nimrod; No Idea Magazine; Ouroboros; P. I. Magazine; Paper Bag, The; Perceptions; Pig Paper, The; Plowman, The; Portable Wall, The; Post, The; Prisoners of the Night; Proof Rock; Pub, The; Queen's Quarterly; Rag Mag; Rambunctious Review; Re Arts and Letters; Read Me; Renegade; Riverwind; Rose Arts Magazine, The; Salome: A Journal of the Performing Arts; Samisdat; San Gabriel Valley Magazine; Scream Magazine; Sensations; Shawnee Silhouette; Shoe Tree; Sneak Preview, The; Solid Copy; Space and Time; SPSM&H; Stamp Axe; Sword of Shahrazad; Tentra Artnet BBS; Thema; Thumbprints; Tucumcari Literary Review; Tyro Magazine; Very Small Magazine, A; Village Idiot, The; Vintage Northwest; Virginia Quarterly Review; Wayside; West Texas Sun, The; Wide Open Magazine; Wisconsin Restaurateur, The; Writers' Bar-B-Q, The; Writers Newsletter

Canada. ACTA Victoriana; Alchemist, The; Alpha Beat Soup; Anglican Magazine, The; Antigonish Review, The; Atavachron and All Our Yesterdays; Atlantis (British Columbia); Atlantis (Nova Scotia); Breakthrough!; Canadian Author & Bookman; Canadian Fiction Magazine; Capilano Review, The; Conspiracy of Silence, The; Cross-Canada Writers' Magazine; Dalhousie Review, The; Descant (Ontario); Dreams & Visions; Event; (F.) Lip; Fiddlehead, The; Fireweed; Garm Lu; Grain; Greens Magazine; Impulse Magazine; Indigo; K; Kola; Legend; Malahat Review, The; Mirror-Northern Report, The; Musicworks; New Quarterly, The; NeWest Review; Pig Paper, The; Plowman, The; Poetry Halifax Dartmouth; Pottersfield Portfolio; Prairie Fire; Prairie Journal of Canadian Literature, The; Prism International; Proem Canada; Quarry; Queen's Quarterly; Raddle Moon, The; Scrivener; Stamp Axe; Sub-Terrain; Tabula Rasa; Tyro Magazine; Wascana Review; West Coast Review; What; Whetstone; White Wall Review, The; Wild East; Writ Magazine; Yak; Zymergy

Comics. Apaeros; Fat Tuesday; Freeway; Lone Star; Naked Man; Processed World; Rag Mag; Sign of the Times; Working Classics

Condensed/Excerpted Novel. After Hours; Alabama Literary Review; Art:Mag; Atalantik; Ball State University Forum; Caffe, Il; Chakra; Chaminade Literary Review; Chapter One; Conspiracy of Silence, The; Cube Literary Magazine; Deviance; darknerve; F.O.C. Review; Fireweed; Garm Lu; Gestalt; Jacaranda Review; Jazziminds Magazine; K; Kenyon Review, The; Language Bridges Quarterly; Limestone: A Literary Journal; Manoa; Mind's Eye, The; Muse's Mill; New Methods; Northland Quarterly; Perceptions; Pub, The; Quimby; Renegade; River Styx; Serendipity; Sneak Preview, The; Stamp Axe; Stone Drum; Story; Sword of Shahrazad; Tandava; Tidewater; Toad Hiway; Tucumcari Literary Review; TV-TS Tapestry Journal; Two-Ton Santa; Tyro Magazine; Union Street Review; Vintage Northwest; West Texas Sun, The; Witness (Michigan); Word & Image; Yak; Zymergy

Confession. Allegheny Review; Amherst Review, The; Apaeros; Art:Mag; Caffe, Il; Columbus Single Scene; Cube Literary Magazine; Dream International/Quarterly; Feminist Baseball; Fireweed; First Stories; Garm Lu; Gas; Haight Ashbury Literary Journal; Hippo; Housewife-Writer's Forum; K; Kana; Long Shot; Mind's Eye, The; New Press, The; Perceptions; Pig Paper, The; Plowman, The; Processed World; Read Me; Shattered Wig Review; SPSM&H; Stamp Axe; Tyro Magazine; Unspeakable Visions of the Individual, The; Very Small Magazine, A; Village Idiot, The; Zero Hour

Contemporary. Abbey; ACM, (Another Chicago Magazine); ACTA Victoriana; Adrift; Adroit Expression, The; Alabama Literary Review; Alaska Quarterly Review; Albany Review, The; Allegheny Review; Amaranth; Amaranth Review, The; Amateur Writers Journal; Ambergris; Amelia; Amherst Review, The; Anglican Magazine, The; Antaeus; Antietam Review; Antigonish Review, The; Antioch Review; Arnazella; Art Brigade; Artemis; Art:Mag; Atalantik; Aura Literary/Arts Review; Azorean Express, The; Ball State University Forum; Bellowing Ark; Beloit Fiction Journal; Black Jack; Black Scholar, The; Black Warrior Review; Blatant Artifice; Bloomsbury Review, The; Blue Water Review, The; Blueline; Boulevard; Bradley's Fantasy Magazine, Marion Zimmer; Bristlecone; Caesura; Caffe, Il; Callaloo; Calliope; Canadian Author & Bookman; Capilano Review, The; Caribbean Writer, The; Carolina Literary Companion, A; Carousel Literary Arts Magazine; Cathedral of Insanity; Central Park; Chapter One; Chariton Review, The; Chattahoochee Review, The; Chelsea; Chiron Review; Choplogic; Chrysalis; Cicada; Cimarron Review; Clockwatch Review; Coe Review, The; Cold-Drill Magazine; Collages and Bricolages; Colorado Review; Colorado-North Review; Columbus Single Scene; Concho River Review; Confrontation; Conspiracy of Silence, The; Cornfield Review; Corona; Crab Creek Review; Crazyquilt; Crescent Review, The; Cube Literary Magazine; Cutting Edge Irregular; Dan River Anthology; Delirium; Descant (Texas); Deviance; Dream International/Quarterly; darknerve; Elephant-Ear, The; Emrys Journal; Epoch Magazine; Event; (F.) Lip; F.O.C. Review; Farmer's Market, The; Fiction; Fine Madness; Fireweed; First Stories; Florida Review, The; Folio: A Literary Journal; Footwork; Gamut, The; Gargoyle Magazine; Garland, The; Garm Lu; Gas; Gestalt; Gettysburg Review, The; Glens Falls Review, The; Gotta Write Network Litmag; Grain; Grasslands Review; Green Mountains Review; Groundswell; Haight Ashbury Literary Journal; Hawaii Pacific Review; Hawaii Review; Hibiscus Magazine; High Plains Literary Review; Hill and Holler; Hippo; Hob-Nob; Hobo Stew Review; Housewife-Writer's Forum; Howling Dog; Indiana Review; Indigo; Inlet; Innisfree; Interim; Jacaranda Review; Jam To-Day; Jazziminds Magazine; Jeopardy; Journal of Regional Criticism; Journal, The; K; Kana; Karamu; Kenyon Review, The; Kingfisher; Lake Effect; Lake Street Review; Laurel Review; Left Curve; Left-Footed Wombat; Lighthouse; Limestone: A Literary Journal; Little Balkans Review; Long Shot; Long Story, The; Lost and Found Times; Louisville Review, The; Macguffin, The; Manoa; Mark; Maryland Review, The; Mati; Meal, Ready-To-Eat; Mind's Eye, The; Minnesota Ink; Mirror-Northern Report, The; Mississippi Review; Mississippi Valley Review; Missouri Review, The; Muse's Mill; Naked Man; Nebraska Review, The; Negative Capability; New Delta Review; New Laurel Review; New Letters Magazine; New Methods; New Orleans Review; New Virginia Review; Nimrod; No Idea Magazine; North Dakota Quarterly; Northern New England Review, The; Northland Quarterly; Northwest Review; NRG; Oak Square; Ohio Review, The; Old Hickory Review; Other Voices; Ouroboros; Oyez Review; Painted Bride Quarterly; Panhandler, The; Paper Bag, The; Partisan Review; Pennsylvania English; Perceptions; Permafrost; Pig Paper, The; Pikestaff Forum, The; Plowman, The; Poetic Liberty; Poetry Magic; Portable Wall, The; Potato Eyes; Pottersfield Portfolio; Prairie Fire; Prairie Journal of Canadian Literature, The; Primavera; Prism International; Prisoners of the Night; Processed World; Proof Rock; Ptolemy/The Browns Mills Review; Puerto Del Sol; Quarterly West; Queen's Quarterly; Quimby; Rag Mag; Rambunctious Review; Re Arts and Letters; Read Me; Reaper, The; Redneck Review of Literature, The; Renegade; Response; River Styx; Riverwind; Rohwedder; Rose Arts Magazine, The; Salome: A Journal of the Performing Arts; Salt Lick Press; Samisdat; San Gabriel

Valley Magazine; San Jose Studies; Santa Monica Review; Scream Magazine; Seattle Review, The; Sensations; Sewanee Review, The; Shattered Wig Review; Shawnee Silhouette; Shoe Tree; Sing Heavenly Muse!; Skylark; Slipstream; Sneak Preview, The; Sojourner; Solid Copy; Soundings East; South Carolina Review; South Dakota Review; Southern California Anthology; Southern Review, The; Sou'Wester; Spectrum (Massachusetts); Spindrift; Spirit That Moves Us, The; SPSM&H; Stamp Axe; Stone Drum; Stories; Story; Stroker Magazine; Struggle; Sword of Shahrazad; Sycamore Review; T.W.I.; Tabula Rasa; Tampa Review, The; Tandava; Tentra Artnet BBS; Texas Review, The; Thema; Tidewater; Toad Hiway; Tramp; Triquarterly; Tucumcari Literary Review; Turnstile; TV-TS Tapestry Journal; Two-Ton Santa; Tyro Magazine; University of Portland Review; Unmuzzled Ox; Unspeakable Visions of the Individual, The; Valley Grapevine; Village Idiot, The; Virginia Quarterly Review; Wayside; West Branch; West Coast Review; West Texas Sun, The; Wide Open Magazine; Widener Review, The; Wild East; Wisconsin Restaurateur, The; Witness (Michigan); Word & Image; Working Classics; Writers' Bar-B-Q, The; Writers' Forum; Writers Newsletter; Wyoming the Hub of the Wheel; Xavier Review; Yak; Yale Review, The; Z Miscellaneous; Zyzzyva

Erotica. Adrift; Alabama Literary Review; Alpha Beat Soup; Amaranth; Amelia; Apaeros; Arnazella; Art Brigade; Art:Mag; Baby Sue; Bad Newz; Blatant Artifice; Bvi-Pacifica Newsletter; Central Park; Chattahoochee Review, The; Cicada; Coe Review, The; Cold-Drill Magazine; Conspiracy of Silence, The; Coydog Review; Crescent Review, The; Desert Sun; Deviance; Dream International/Quarterly; darknerve; Eidos; Erotic Fiction Quarterly; Explorations '90; (F.) Lip; Fat Tuesday; Feminist Baseball; Fireweed; Garm Lu; Gas; Gateways; Gay Chicago Magazine; Haight Ashbury Literary Journal; Hippo; Journal, The; Joyeux Erotique; K; Kiosk; Left-Footed Wombat; Long Shot; Magic Changes; Mind's Eye, The; New Blood Magazine; New Delta Review; Northern New England Review, The; Oak Square; Paper Bag, The; Paper Radio; Pig Paper, The; Prisoners of the Night; Proof Rock; Ptolemy/The Browns Mills Review; Quimby; Rag Mag; Rambunctious Review; Reaper, The; Riverwind; Salt Lick Press; Samisdat; Scream Magazine; Shattered Wig Review; Sign of the Times; Slipstream; Sou'Wester; SPSM&H; Stamp Axe; Starry Nights; Sub-Terrain; Sword of Shahrazad; T.W.I.; Tentra Artnet BBS; Toad Hiway; Tramp; Two-Ton Santa; Unspeakable Visions of the Individual, The; Very Small Magazine, A; Village Idiot, The; Wayside; Writers' Bar-B-Q, The; Yak; Yellow Silk; Zero Hour

Ethnic. ACM, (Another Chicago Magazine); ACTA Victoriana; Adrift; Aegean Review; Alabama Literary Review; Amaranth; Amelia; American Dane; Amherst Review, The; Antietam Review; Arnazella; Art:Mag; Atalantik; Aura Literary/Arts Review; Azorean Express, The; Ball State University Forum; Bella Figura, La; Bilingual Review; Black Jack; Black Scholar, The; Black Warrior Review; Black Writer Magazine; Blatant Artifice; Blue Water Review, The; Bristlecone; Caffe, Il; Callaloo; Caribbean Writer, The; Carolina Literary Companion, A; Carousel Literary Arts Magazine; Central Park; Chakra; Chaminade Literary Review; Chapter One; Cicada; Coe Review, The; Cold-Drill Magazine; Collages and Bricolages; Colorado Review; Concho River Review; Conditions; Conspiracy of Silence, The; Cornfield Review; Coydog Review; Crazyquilt; Crescent Review, The; Cross Timbers Review; Cube Literary Magazine; Dan River Anthology; Deviance; Dream International/Quarterly; Elephant-Ear, The; Epoch Magazine; (F.) Lip; Fireweed; Five Fingers Review; Footwork; Garm Lu; Gestalt; Grasslands Review; Groundswell; Haight Ashbury Literary Journal; Hawaii Pacific Review; Hawaii Review; Hill and Holler; Innisfree; Japanophile; Jeopardy; Jest; Jewish Currents Magazine; Journal of Regional Criticism; Journal, The; Kabbalah Yichud; Kana; Kenyon Review, The; Kola; Lake Street Review; Left Curve; Left-Footed Wombat; Lilith Magazine; Little Balkans Review; Long Shot; Long Story, The; Macguffin, The; Mark; Middle Eastern Dancer; Midland Review; Mind's Eye, The; Miorita, a Journal of Romanian Studies; Mirror-Northern Report, The; Muse's Mill; Musicworks; Negative Capability; New Letters Magazine; New Press, The; Nimrod; North Dakota Quarterly; Northern New England Review, The; Notebook: A Little Magazine; Now and Then; Oak Square; Obsidian II: Black Literature in Review; Oxford Magazine; Painted Bride Quarterly; Panhandler, The; Paper Bag, The; Pennsylvania Review; Permafrost; Plowman, The; Portable Wall, The; Pottersfield Portfolio; Puerto Del Sol; Quimby; Rag Mag; Rambunctious Review; Read Me; Reaper, The; Reconstructionist; Response; River Styx; Riverwind; Rockford Review, The; Rohwedder; Rose Arts Magazine, The; Salt Lick Press; Samisdat; San Jose Studies; Seattle Review, The; Shattered Wig Review; Shooting Star Review; Sing Heavenly Muse!; Skylark; Slipstream; Sojourner; Solid Copy; South Carolina Review; South Dakota Review; Southern California Anthology; Sou'Wester; Spindrift; Spirit That Moves Us, The; Spoofing!; SPSM&H; Stamp Axe; Stories; Struggle; Sword of Shahrazad; Tampa Review, The; Tentra Artnet BBS; Third Woman; Tidewater; Tramp; Tucumcari Literary Review; Tyro Magazine; Union Street Review; Valley Grapevine; Valley Women's Voice; Village Idiot, The; Wayside; Whispering Wind Magazine; Wicazo SA Review, The; Wide Open Magazine; Wild East; Working Classics; Writers' Bar-B-Q, The; Writers' Forum; Wyoming the Hub of the Wheel; Xavier Review; Yak; Z Miscellaneous; Zero Hour

Experimental. ACM, (Another Chicago Magazine); ACTA Victoriana; Adrift; Adroit Expression, The; Aerial; Alabama Literary Review; Alaska Quarterly Review; Albany Review, The; Allegheny Review; Alpha Beat Soup; Alternative Fiction & Poetry; Amaranth; Amelia; American Voice,

The; Amherst Review, The; Antietam Review; Antioch Review; Arnazella; Art Brigade; Artful Dodge; Art:Mag; Asymptotical World, The; Atalantik; Azorean Express, The; Baby Sue; Bad Haircut; Bad Newz; Ball State University Forum; Blue Water Review, The; Bogg; Bottomfish Magazine; Boulevard; Bvi-Pacifica Newsletter; Cache Review; Calliope; Capilano Review, The; Carousel Literary Arts Magazine; Cathedral of Insanity; Ceilidh; Central Park; Chakra; Chaminade Literary Review; Chapter One; Chattahoochee Review, The; Chiron Review; Choplogic; Chrysalis; Cicada; Clockwatch Review; Cold-Drill Magazine; Collages and Bricolages; Colorado Review; Columbus Single Scene; Compost Newsletter; Cornfield Review; Corona; Coydog Review; Crescent Review, The; Cube Literary Magazine; Cutting Edge Irregular; Dan River Anthology; Deathrealm; Delirium; Denver Quarterly; Deviance; Dharma Combat; Dream International/Quarterly; darknerve; Elephant-Ear, The; Eotu; Explorations '90; (F.) Lip; F.O.C. Review; Feminist Baseball; Fiction; Fine Madness; Fireweed; Five Fingers Review; Florida Review, The; Footwork; Gamut, The; Gargoyle Magazine; Gas; Gateways; Georgia Review, The; Gestalt; Gettysburg Review, The; Grain; Grasslands Review; Green Mountains Review; Groundswell; Haight Ashbury Literary Journal; Hawaii Pacific Review; Hawaii Review; Heaven Bone; Hippo; Housewife-Writer's Forum; Howling Dog; Ice River; Impulse Magazine; Indiana Review; Indigo; Inside Joke; Jabberwocky; Jacaranda Review; Jazziminds Magazine; Jeopardy; Jest; Journal of Regional Criticism; Journal, The; K; Kairos; Kana; Kenyon Review, The; Kingfisher; Kiosk; Lake Street Review; Leading Edge, The; Left Curve; Left-Footed Wombat; Limestone: A Literary Journal; Little Balkans Review; Long Shot; Lost and Found Times; Louisville Review, The; Lyra; Macguffin, The; Madison Review, The; Mage, The; Meal, Ready-To-Eat; Merlyn's Pen; Microcosm; Mid-American Review; Midland Review; Mind in Motion; Mind's Eye, The; Minnesota Ink; Minnesota Review, The; Mississippi Review; Muse's Mill; Musicworks; Naked Man; Nebo; Negative Capability; New Blood Magazine; New Delta Review; New Letters Magazine; New Methods; New Moon; New Pathways; New Press, The; New Virginia Review; Night Slivers; Nimrod; No Idea Magazine; North Dakota Quarterly; Northern New England Review, The; Northwest Review; NRG; Oak Square; Ohio Review, The; Old Hickory Review; Open Magazine; Other Voices; Ouroboros; Oxford Magazine; Oyez Review; Painted Bride Quarterly; Panhandler, The; Paper Bag, The; Paper Radio; Partisan Review; Pavor Nocturnus; Pennsylvania Review; Perceptions; Permafrost; Phoebe; Pig Paper, The; Poetry Halifax Dartmouth; Portable Wall, The; Pottersfield Portfolio; Prairie Fire; Prisoners of the Night; Proof Rock; Ptolemy/The Browns Mills Review; Puerto Del Sol; Quarry; Quarry West; Queen's Quarterly; Quimby; Raddle Moon, The; Rag Mag; Rambunctious Review; Re Arts and Letters [REAL]; Reaper, The; Red Cedar Review; Renegade; Response; River Styx; Rockford Review, The; Rohwedder; Rose Arts Magazine, The; Round Table, The; Salt Lick Press; Samisdat; Scream Magazine; Seattle Review, The; Serendipity; Shattered Wig Review; Sign of the Times; Skylark; Slipstream; Sneak Preview, The; Sojourner; Solid Copy; South Dakota Review; Southern California Anthology; Sou'Wester; Spectrum (Massachusetts); Spindrift; SPSM&H; Stamp Axe; Starshore; Sterling Web, The; Story; Strange Plasma; Struggle; Sub-Terrain; Sword of Shahrazad; Sycamore Review; T.W.I.; Tabula Rasa; Tampa Review, The; Tandava; Tentra Artnet BBS; Thema; Thin Ice; Tidewater; Toad Hiway; Tramp; Turnstile; Two AM Magazine2 AM Magazine; Two-Ton Santa; Tyro Magazine; Very Small Magazine, A; Videomania; Village Idiot, The; Wayside; West Coast Review; Whetstone; Wide Open Magazine; Widener Review, The; Wild East; Wisconsin Academy Review; Wisconsin Review; Witness (Michigan); Working Classics; Writers' Bar-B-Q, The; Writers Newsletter; Wyoming the Hub of the Wheel; Xavier Review; Yak; Zero Hour; Zoiks!; Zyzzyva

Fantasy. Adara; Adroit Expression, The; After Hours; Alabama Literary Review; Amateur Writers Journal; Amelia; Amherst Review, The; Argonaut; Arnazella; Art Brigade; Art:Mag; Asymptotical World, The; Atlantis (British Columbia); Ball State University Forum; Beyond Science Fiction & Fantasy; Book of Spells, The; Bradley's Fantasy Magazine, Marion Zimmer; Bristlecone; Bvi-Pacifica Newsletter; Cache Review; Carousel Literary Arts Magazine; Chapter One; Coe Review, The; Cold-Drill Magazine; Columbus Single Scene; Companion in Zeor, A; Compost Newsletter; Cornfield Review; Corona; Couch Potato Journal, The; Crazyquilt; Crescent Review, The; Cube Literary Magazine; Cutting Edge Irregular; Dan River Anthology; Dead Of Night Magazine; Deathrealm; Desert Sun; Deviance; Dream International/Quarterly; Eldritch Science; Encounters Magazine; (F.) Lip; F.O.C. Review; Fat Tuesday; Feminist Baseball; Fighting Woman News; Figment Magazine; Fireweed; First Stories; Galactic Discourse; Garland, The; Gas; Gateways; Golden Isis Magazine; Gotta Write Network Litmag; Grasslands Review; Greens Magazine; Groundswell; Haunts; Hawaii Pacific Review; Heaven Bone; Hibiscus Magazine; Hippo; Hob-Nob; Hor-Tasy; Ice River; Inlet; Innisfree; Inside Joke; Jabberwocky; Jeopardy; Jest; Journal of Regional Criticism; Kana; Kenyon Review, The; Lake Effect; Language Bridges Quarterly; Leading Edge, The; Legend; Lennis, Pablo; Little Balkans Review; Long Shot; Macguffin, The; Mage, The; Magic Changes; Merlyn's Pen; Microcosm; Minas Tirith Evening-Star; Mind in Motion; Mind's Eye, The; Minnesota Ink; Minnesota Review, The; Mirror-Northern Report, The; Mississippi Review; Muse's Mill; Mythic Circle, The; Negative Capability; New Blood Magazine; New Laurel Review; New Moon; New Pathways; New Press, The; No Idea Magazine; Northern New England Review, The; Northern New England Review, The; Nuclear Fiction; Old Hickory Review; Ouroboros; Owlflight; Pandora; Paper Bag, The; Paper Radio; Pavor Nocturnus; Perceptions; Pig

Paper, The; Pléiades Magazine/Philae Magazine; Pottersfield Portfolio; Primavera; Prisoners of the Night; Processed World; Proof Rock; Pub, The; Pulphouse; Quarry; Queen's Quarterly; Quintessential Space Debris; Rag Mag; Rampant Guinea Pig, The; Read Me; Renaissance Fan; Renegade; Resonance; Riverside Quarterly; Rockford Review, The; Rose Arts Magazine, The; Salome: A Journal of the Performing Arts; Samisdat; Science Fiction Randomly; Scream Magazine; Seattle Review, The; Sensations; Serendipity; Shoe Tree; Sing Heavenly Muse!; Skylark; Slipstream; Sojourner; Solid Copy; Southern Humanities Review; Sou'Wester; Space and Time; SPSM&H; Stamp Axe; Starshore; Starsong; Starwind; Sterling Web, The; Stone Drum; Strange Plasma; Sword of Shahrazad; Tabula Rasa; Tampa Review, The; Tandava; Tapestry; Tentra Artnet BBS; Thin Ice; Trajectories; Tramp; Twisted; 2 AM Magazine; Tyro Magazine; Videomania; Village Idiot, The; Vintage Northwest; Wayside; Weirdbook; Wide Open Magazine; Witness (Michigan); Witness (Pennsylvania); Word & Image; Writers' Bar-B-Q, The; Z Miscellaneous

Feminist. ACM, (Another Chicago Magazine); Adara; Adrift; Alabama Literary Review; Alchemist, The; Amaranth; Amelia; Amelia; American Voice, The; Amherst Review, The; Antietam Review; Apaeros; Arnazella; Art Brigade; Art:Mag; Atlantis (Nova Scotia); Aura Literary/Arts Review; Ball State University Forum; Bella Figura, La; Blatant Artifice; Bristlecone; Callaloo; Carousel Literary Arts Magazine; Central Park; Chapter One; Chattahoochee Review, The; Cicada; Coe Review, The; Cold-Drill Magazine; Collages and Bricolages; Compost Newsletter; Conditions; Corona; Coydog Review; Creative Woman, The; Crimson Full Moon, The; Daughters of Sarah; Deviance; darknerve; Earth's Daughters; Elephant-Ear, The; Emrys Journal; Event; (F.) Lip; F.O.C. Review; Farmer's Market, The; Fiction; Fighting Woman News; Five Fingers Review; Galactic Discourse; Gamut, The; Garm Lu; Gestalt; Groundswell; Haight Ashbury Literary Journal; Heresies; Hobo Stew Review; Jam To-Day; Jeopardy; Journal, The; K; Kairos; Kana; Kenyon Review, The; Kiosk; Left-Footed Wombat; Lilith Magazine; Limestone: A Literary Journal; Little Balkans Review; Long Shot; Long Story, The; Mati; Midland Review; Mind's Eye, The; Minnesota Review, The; Mirror-Northern Report, The; Negative Capability; New Moon; North Dakota Quarterly; Northern New England Review, The; Northland Quarterly; Northwest Review; Obsidian II: Black Literature in Review; Open Magazine; Oxford Magazine; Oyez Review; Painted Bride Quarterly; Paper Bag, The; Pennsylvania Review; Perceptions; Permafrost; Portable Wall, The; Pottersfield Portfolio; Primavera; Prisoners of the Night; Quimby; Rag Mag; Rainbow City Express; Rambunctious Review; Re Arts and Letters [REAL]; Read Me; Reaper, The; Red Cedar Review; Renegade; Response; River Styx; Riverwind; Rockford Review, The; Rohwedder; Room of One's Own; Rose Arts Magazine, The; Salome: A Journal of the Performing Arts; Salt Lick Press; Samisdat; Scream Magazine; Seattle Review, The; Shattered Wig Review; Sing Heavenly Muse!; Skylark; Slipstream; Sojourner; Southern California Anthology; Southern Humanities Review; Sou'Wester; Spirit That Moves Us, The; SPSM&H; Struggle; Tentra Artnet BBS; Third Woman; Tidewater; Two-Ton Santa; Valley Women's Voice; Very Small Magazine, A; Videomania; Village Idiot, The; Virginia Quarterly Review; Wayside; Wide Open Magazine; Wild East; Wisconsin Restaurateur, The; Witness (Michigan); Woman of Power; Working Classics; Writers' Bar-B-Q, The; Yak; Zero Hour; Zymergy

Gay. ACM, (Another Chicago Magazine); Adara; Adrift; Alchemist, The; Amaranth; Amelia; American Voice, The; Amherst Review, The; Apaeros; Arnazella; Art Brigade; Art:Mag; Blatant Artifice; Carousel Literary Arts Magazine; Central Park; Chattahoochee Review, The; Coe Review, The; Cold-Drill Magazine; Compost Newsletter; Corona; Coydog Review; Crazyquilt; Deviance; darknerve; Evergreen Chronicles, The; Fag Rag; Feminist Baseball; Five Fingers Review; Galactic Discourse; Garm Lu; Gay Chicago Magazine; Groundswell; Haight Ashbury Literary Journal; Journal, The; Kana; Kenyon Review, The; Kiosk; Left-Footed Wombat; Long Shot; Mind's Eye, The; Minnesota Review, The; Open Magazine; Oxford Magazine; Painted Bride Quarterly; Pennsylvania Review; Permafrost; Pottersfield Portfolio; Primavera; Prisoners of the Night; Quimby; Reaper, The; RFD; River Styx; Rose Arts Magazine, The; Salt Lick Press; Samisdat; Scream Magazine; Seattle Review, The; Sensations; Shattered Wig Review; Sign of the Times; Slipstream; Sou'Wester; Spirit That Moves Us, The; SPSM&H; Tidewater; Tramp; Two-Ton Santa; Village Idiot, The; Wayside; Wide Open Magazine; Working Classics; Writers' Bar-B-Q, The; Yak; Zero Hour

Historical. Adara; Alabama Literary Review; Amaranth; Amelia; Amherst Review, The; Appalachian Heritage; Arnazella; Art:Mag; Atalantik; Ball State University Forum; Black Writer Magazine; Breakthrough!; Bristlecone; Cache Review; Callaloo; Caribbean Writer, The; Carolina Literary Companion, A; Central Park; Chapter One; Chrysalis; Cicada; Cochran's Corner; Concho River Review; Cornfield Review; Crazyquilt; Cross Timbers Review; Dan River Anthology; Daughters of Sarah; Deviance; Dream International/Quarterly; Fireweed; First Stories; Garm Lu; Gestalt; Gettysburg Review, The; Gotta Write Network Litmag; Housewife-Writer's Forum; In-Between; Jest; Journal of Regional Criticism; Kana; Kenyon Review, The; Lake Effect; Language Bridges Quarterly; Left Curve; Legend; Lighthouse; Linington Lineup; Little Balkans Review; Llamas Magazine; Macguffin, The; Merlyn's Pen; Mickle Street Review, The; Midland Review; Mind's Eye, The; Minnesota Review, The; Miorita, a Journal of Romanian Studies; Mirror-Northern Report, The; Mountain Laurel, The; Negative Capability; New Methods; North Dakota Quarterly; Northern New England Review, The; Notebook: A Little Magazine; Ouroboros; Pipe Smoker's Ephemeris, The; Pléiades Magazine/Philae Magazine; Plowman, The; Poetic Liberty; Portable Wall, The; Ptolemy/The Browns Mills Review; Queen's Quarterly; Rambunctious Review; Re Arts and Letters [REAL]; Read Me; Renegade; Response; Riverwind; Rockford Review, The; Rose Arts Magazine, The; Samisdat; Scream Magazine; Seattle Review, The; Sensations; Serendipity; Shawnee Silhouette; Shoe Tree; Sneak Preview, The; Solid Copy; Southern California Anthology; Spectrum (Massachusetts); Spindrift; SPSM&H; Stamp Axe; Struggle; Sword of Shahrazad; Sycamore Review; Tampa Review, The; Tentra Artnet BBS; Thumbprints; Tucumcari Literary Review; TV-TS Tapestry Journal; Tyro Magazine; Village Idiot, The; Vintage Northwest; Wayside; West Texas Sun, The; Wide Open Magazine; Wisconsin Academy Review; Word & Image; Working Classics; Writers' Bar-B-Q, The; Writers Newsletter; Xavier Review

Horror. After Hours; Amaranth; Amateur Writers Journal; Amherst Review, The; Argonaut; Art Brigade; Art:Mag; Asymptotical World, The; Atlantis (British Columbia); Bad Newz; Book of Spells, The; Bvi-Pacifica Newsletter; Cache Review; Carousel Literary Arts Magazine; Chapter One; Cicada; Cochran's Corner; Cold-Drill Magazine; Cube Literary Magazine; Dan River Anthology; Dead Of Night Magazine; Deathrealm; Delirium; Desert Sun; Deviance; Dream International/Quarterly; darknerve; Eldritch Tales; Encounters Magazine; Event; Feminist Baseball; Figment Magazine; Gas; Gestalt; Grasslands Review; Grue Magazine; Haunts; Hawaii Review; Hippo; Horror; Hor-Tasy; Indigo; Jabberwocky; Jest; Journal of Regional Criticism; Left-Footed Wombat; Little Balkans Review; Long Shot; Mage, The; Meal, Ready-To-Eat; Merlyn's Pen; Microcosm; Midland Review; Mind's Eye, The; Miss Lucy Westenra Society of the Undead, The; Muse's Mill; New Blood Magazine; Night Slivers; No Idea Magazine; Nuclear Fiction; Ouroboros; Paper Bag, The; Pavor Nocturnus; Pléiades Magazine/Philae Magazine; Portents; Prisoners of the Night; Pub, The; Pulphouse; Read Me; Renegade; Riverwind; Science Fiction Randomly; Scream Magazine; Seattle Review, The; Sensations; Serendipity; Shoe Tree; Solid Copy; South Carolina Review; Space and Time; SPSM&H; Stamp Axe; Starshore; Starsong; Sterling Web, The; Stories; Sword of Shahrazad; Tabula Rasa; Tapestry; Terror Time Again; Thin Ice; Twisted; 2 AM Magazine; Two-Ton Santa; Tyro Magazine; Var Tufa; Videomania; Wayside; Weirdbook; Wide Open Magazine; Witness (Pennsylvania); Writers' Bar-B-Q, The; Z Miscellaneous

Humor/Satire. ACM, (Another Chicago Magazine); ACTA Victoriana; Adara; After Hours; Alabama Literary Review; Albany Review, The; Allegheny Review; Amateur Writers Journal; Amelia; American Voice, The; Amherst Review, The; Anglican Magazine, The; Arnazella; Art Brigade; Art:Mag; Atalantik; Atrocity; Azorean Express, The; Baby Sue; Bad Haircut; Bad Newz; Ball State University Forum; Big Two-Hearted; Black Jack; Blatant Artifice; Blue Water Review, The; Blueline; Bradley's Fantasy Magazine, Marion Zimmer; Breakthrough!; Bristlecone; Bvi-Pacifica Newsletter; Cache Review; Caffe, Il; Callaloo; Canadian Author & Bookman; Caribbean Writer, The; Carolina Literary Companion, A; Carousel Literary Arts Magazine; Cathedral of Insanity; Chakra; Chaminade Literary Review; Chapter One; Chattahoochee Review, The; Chiron Review; Choplogic; Cicada; Clockwatch Review; Cochran's Corner; Cold-Drill Magazine; Collages and Bricolages; Columbus Single Scene; Companion in Zeor, A; Compost Newsletter; Concho River Review; Corona; Coydog Review; Crab Creek Review; Crazyquilt; Crescent Review, The; Cross Timbers Review; Cube Literary Magazine; Cutting Edge Irregular; Dan River Anthology; Delirium; Desert Sun; Deviance; Dharma Combat; Dream International/Quarterly; darknerve; Eidos; Elephant-Ear, The; Explorations '90; (F.) Lip; F.O.C. Review; Farmer's Market, The; Fat Tuesday; Feminist Baseball; Fiction; Fireweed; First Stories; Five Fingers Review; Freeway; Galactic Discourse; Gamut, The; Gargoyle Magazine; Garland, The; Garm Lu; Gas; Gestalt; Gettysburg Review, The; Gotta Write Network Litmag; Grasslands Review; Green Mountains Review; Greens Magazine; Groundswell; Haight Ashbury Literary Journal; Hawaii Pacific Review; Hawaii Review; Hibiscus Magazine; High Plains Literary Review; Hill and Holler; Hippo; Hob-Nob; Hobo Stew Review; Housewife-Writer's Forum; Howling Dog; In-Between; Indigo; Inlet; Inside Joke; Jabberwocky; Jeopardy; Jest; Journal of Polymorphous Perversity; Journal of Regional Criticism; K; Kana; Kenyon Review, The; Kiosk; Lake Effect; Lake Street Review; Language Bridges Quarterly; Leading Edge, The; Left Curve; Left-Footed Wombat; Lighthouse; Limestone: A Literary Journal; Little Balkans Review; Llamas Magazine; Lone Star; Long Shot; Macguffin, The; Mark; Maryland Review, The; Meal, Ready-To-Eat; Merlyn's Pen; Mind in Motion; Mind's Eye, The; Minnesota Ink; Mirror-Northern Report, The; Mississippi Review; Mountain Laurel, The; Muse's Mill; Naked Man; Nebraska Review, The; New Delta Review; New Letters Magazine; New Press, The; No Idea Magazine; North Dakota Quarterly; Northern New England Review, The; Notebook: A Little Magazine; Oak Square; Other Voices; Ouroboros; Oxford Magazine; P. I. Magazine; P. U.N. (Play on Words); Panhandler, The; Pegasus Review, The; Pencil Press Quarterly; Pennsylvania Review; Permafrost; Pig Paper, The; Pipe Smoker's Ephemeris, The; Poetic Liberty; Poetry Halifax Dartmouth; Poetry Magic; Portable Wall, The; Potato Eyes; Pottersfield Portfolio; Poultry; Primavera; Processed World; Proof Rock; Ptolemy/The Browns Mills Review; Queen's Quarterly; Quimby; Quintessential Space Debris; Rambunctious Review; Read Me; Reaper, The; Red Cedar Review; Renegade; Resonance; Response; River Styx; Riverwind; Rockford Review, The; Rose Arts Magazine, The; Salome: A Journal of the Performing Arts; Samisdat; San Gabriel Valley Magazine; San Jose Studies; Science Fiction Randomly; Scream Magazine; Seattle Review, The; Sensations;

Serendipity; Shattered Wig Review; Shawnee Silhouette; Shoe Tree; Sing Heavenly Muse!; Skylark; Slipstream; Sneak Preview, The; Sojourner; Solid Copy; Southern California Anthology; Southern Humanities Review; Space and Time; Spirit That Moves Us, The; Spoofing!; SPSM&H; Stamp Axe; Starsong; Starwind; Sterling Web, The; Stone Drum; Stories; Stories; Struggle; Sub-Terrain; Sword of Shahrazad; Sycamore Review; T.W.I.; Tabula Rasa; Tampa Review, The; Tentra Artnet BBS; Thema; Thin Ice; Thumbprints; Tidewater; Toad Hiway; Trajectories; Tramp; Tucumcari Literary Review; Turnstile; TV-TS Tapestry Journal; 2 AM Magazine; Two-Ton Santa; Tyro Magazine; Union Street Review; Var Tufa; Very Small Magazine, A; Videomania; Village Idiot, The; Vintage Northwest; Virginia Quarterly Review; Wascana Review; Wayside; West Texas Sun, The; Wide Open Magazine; Wild East; Wisconsin Academy Review; Wisconsin Restaurateur, The; Word & Image; Working Classics; Writers' Bar-B-Q, The; Writers Newsletter; Writing Pursuits; Yak; Z Miscellaneous; Zero Hour; Zoiks!

Juvenile. Atalantik; Black Scholar, The; Brilliant Star; Chapter One; Cochran's Corner; Creative Kids; Day Care and Early Education; Dream International/Quarterly; First Stories; Hob-Nob; In-Between; Lighthouse; Plowman, The; Resonance; Shattered Wig Review; Skylark; Sneak Preview, The; Spoofing!; Two-Ton Santa; Tyro Magazine; Young Voices Magazine

Lesbian. ACM, (Another Chicago Magazine); Adrift; Alchemist, The; Amaranth; Amelia; American Voice, The; Amherst Review, The; Apacros; Arnazella; Art Brigade; Art:Mag; Bella Figura, La; Blatant Artifice; Carousel Literary Arts Magazine; Central Park; Cicada; Coe Review, The; Cold-Drill Magazine; Common Lives/Lesbian Lives; Compost Newsletter; Conditions; Corona; Coydog Review; Crimson Full Moon, The; Deviance; darknerve; Evergreen Chronicles, The; (F.) Lip; Feminist Baseball; Fireweed; Five Fingers Review; Galactic Discourse; Garm Lu; Gay Chicago Magazine; Groundswell; Haight Ashbury Literary Journal; Heresies; Kana; Kenyon Review, The; Kiosk; Left-Footed Wombat; Lilith Magazine; Long Shot; Mind's Eye, The; Minnesota Review, The; Open Magazine; Oxford Magazine; Painted Bride Quarterly; Pennsylvania Review; Permafrost; Pottersfield Portfolio; Primavera; Prisoners of the Night; Reaper, The; River Styx; Room of One's Own; Rose Arts Magazine, The; Salt Lick Press; Samisdat; Scream Magazine; Seattle Review, The; Sensations; Shattered Wig Review; Sign of the Times; Sinister Wisdom; Slipstream; Sojourner; Sou'Wester; Spirit That Moves Us, The; SPSM&H; Tidewater; Tramp; Two-Ton Santa; Valley Women's Voice; Videomania; Village Idiot, The; Visibilities; Wayside; Wide Open Magazine; Working Classics; Writers' Bar-B-Q, The; Yak

Mainstream. ACTA Victoriana; Adroit Expression, The; Albany Review, The; Allegheny Review; Amateur Writers Journal; Amelia; Amherst Review, The; Arnazella; Art:Mag; Atalantik; Ball State University Forum; Bellowing Ark; Beloit Fiction Journal; Black Warrior Review; Bloomsbury Review, The; Blue Water Review, The; Cache Review; Caesura; Caribbean Writer, The; Carolina Literary Companion, A; Chapter One; Chattahoochee Review, The; Chrysalis; Cicada; Clockwatch Review; Cold-Drill Magazine; Collages and Bricolages; Colorado Review; Columbus Single Scene; Coydog Review; Crazyquilt; Crescent Review, The; Cube Literary Magazine; Cutting Edge Irregular; Dan River Anthology; Dream International/Quarterly; darknerve; Eagle's Flight; Emrys Journal; Feminist Baseball; First Stories; Folio: A Literary Journal; Gamut, The; Gas; Gettysburg Review, The; Gotta Write Network Litmag; Grain; Green Mountains Review; Greens Magazine; Groundswell; Haight Ashbury Literary Journal; Hawaii Pacific Review; Hibiscus Magazine; High Plains Literary Review; Hippo; Housewife-Writer's Forum; Howling Dog; Indiana Review; Indigo; Inlet; Innisfree; Jacaranda Review; Jeopardy; Journal of Regional Criticism; K; Kana; Kenyon Review, The; Lake Effect; Lake Street Review; Lighthouse; Limestone: A Literary Journal; Little Balkans Review; Louisiana Literature; Macguffin, The; Manoa; Maryland Review, The; Meal, Ready-To-Eat; Merlyn's Pen; Mind's Eye, The; Minnesota Ink; Mirror-Northern Report, The; Muse's Mill; Naked Man; Nebo; Nebraska Review, The; New Delta Review; New Letters Magazine; New Methods; New Pathways; New Press, The; New Virginia Review; Northern New England Review, The; Northland Quarterly; Oak Square; Old Hickory Review; Ouroboros; Panhandler, The; Paper Bag, The; Pencil Press Quarterly; Pennsylvania English; Phoebe; Plowman, The; Poetic Liberty; Portable Wall, The; Potato Eyes; Pottersfield Portfolio; Proof Rock; Ptolemy/The Browns Mills Review; Puerto Del Sol; Queen's Quarterly; Rag Mag; Rambunctious Review; Read Me; Renegade; River Styx; Riverwind; Round Table, The; Samisdat; Seattle Review, The; Sensations; Serendipity; Shawnee Silhouette; Shoe Tree; Skylark; Slipstream; Sneak Preview, The; Solid Copy; Southern California Anthology; Sou'Wester; Spectrum (Massachusetts); SPSM&H; Stone Drum; Story; Sword of Shahrazad; Sycamore Review; Tabula Rasa; Tampa Review, The; Tentra Artnet BBS; Thema; Thumbprints; Tucumcari Literary Review; Tyro Magazine; Union Street Review; Videomania; Village Idiot, The; West Texas Sun, The; Whetstone; Wide Open Magazine; Widener Review, The; Wisconsin Academy Review; Writers' Bar-B-Q, The; Writers Newsletter; Z Miscellaneous

Novella. Prairie Journal of Canadian Literature, The

Preschool. Chapter One; Cochran's Corner; Corona; Day Care and Early Education; Plowman, The; Two-Ton Santa

Prose Poem. Abbey; ACM, (Another Chicago Magazine); ACTA Victoriana; Adara; Adroit Expression, The; Agni; Alabama Literary Review; Alaska Quarterly Review; Albany Review, The; Alpha Beat Soup; Amaranth; Amelia; Amherst Review, The; Antaeus; Antietam Review; Antigonish Review, The; Apaeros; Argonaut; Arnazella; Artful Dodge; Art:Mag; Bad Haircut; Ball State University Forum; Bella Figura, La; Beloit Fiction Journal; Big Two-Hearted; Black Warrior Review; Black Writer Magazine; Blueline; Bogg; Bottomfish Magazine; Boulevard; Cache Review; Callaloo; Capilano Review, The; Caribbean Writer, The; Carousel Literary Arts Magazine; Ceilidh; Central Park; Chapter One; Clockwatch Review; Cochran's Corner; Collages and Bricolages; Colorado-North Review; Columbia: A Magazine of Poetry & Prose; Companion in Zeor, A; Conditions; Confrontation; Conspiracy of Silence, The; Corona; Couch Potato Journal, The; Coydog Review; Crimson Full Moon, The; Cross-Canada Writers' Magazine; Cube Literary Magazine; Dan River Anthology; Delirium; Deviance; Dream International/Quarterly; darknerve; Eotu; Explorer Magazine; F.O.C. Review; Fat Tuesday; Fine Madness; Fireweed; Five Fingers Review; Folio: A Literary Journal; Galactic Discourse; Gamut, The; Gargoyle Magazine; Gas; Gestalt; Glens Falls Review, The; Gotta Write Network Litmag; Grain; Grasslands Review; Haight Ashbury Literary Journal; Hawaii Review; Hippo; Ice River; In-Between; Jacaranda Review; Jazziminds Magazine; Jeopardy; Jest; Journal, The; Kenyon Review, The; Kiosk; Lake Street Review; Language Bridges Quarterly; Leading Edge, The; Left Curve; Left-Footed Wombat; Lighthouse; Lilith Magazine; Limestone: A Literary Journal; Little Balkans Review; Long Shot; Lost and Found Times; Louisville Review, The; Lyra; Macguffin, The; Madison Review, The; Magic Changes; Meal, Ready-To-Eat; Mid-American Review; Midland Review; Mind in Motion; Mind's Eye, The; Mirror-Northern Report, The; Muse's Mill; Musicworks; Mythic Circle, The; Naked Man; Negative Capability; New Delta Review; New Moon; New Press, The; Nimrod; Now and Then; NRG; Oak Square; Oregon East; Painted Bride Quarterly; Paper Bag, The; Paper Radio; Partisan Review; Pegasus Review, The; Pennsylvania Review; Perceptions; Permafrost; Phoebe; Pig Paper, The; Plowman, The; Poetic Liberty; Poetry Halifax Dartmouth; Poetry Magic; Portable Wall, The; Pottersfield Portfolio; Prairie Fire; Prairie Journal of Canadian Literature, The; Prism International; Prisoners of the Night; Proof Rock; Puerto Del Sol; Quimby; Raddle Moon, The; Rag Mag; Rainbow City Express; Rambunctious Review; Renegade; Response; River Styx; Riverwind; Salome: A Journal of the Performing Arts; Samisdat; Seattle Review, The; Sensations; Serendipity; Shattered Wig Review; Sing Heavenly Muse!; Skylark; Slipstream; Sneak Preview, The; Sojourner; Solid Copy; Soundings East; Spindrift; Spirit That Moves Us, The; Starsong; Struggle; Sword of Shahrazad; T.W.I.; Tabula Rasa; Tampa Review, The; Tandava; Tentra Artnet BBS; Thema; Thumbprints; Tidewater; Toad Hiway; Trajectories; Tramp; Twisted; 2 AM Magazine; Two-Ton Santa; Tyro Magazine; Unmuzzled Ox; Unspeakable Visions of the Individual, The; Valley Women's Voice; Village Idiot, The; Wayside; West Branch; West Coast Review; Willow Springs; Wisconsin Academy Review; Worcester Review, The; Word & Image; Working Classics; Writers Newsletter; Wyoming the Hub of the Wheel; Xavier Review; Yak; Zymergy; Zyzzyva

Psychic/Supernatural/Occult. After Hours; Alchemist, The; Amaranth; Amherst Review, The; Art:Mag; Asymptotical World, The; Atalantik; Bad Newz; Ball State University Forum; Bradley's Fantasy Magazine, Marion Zimmer; Bvi-Pacifica Newsletter; Cathedral of Insanity; Chapter One; Cicada; Coe Review, The; Compost Newsletter; Corona; Crescent Review, The; Crimson Full Moon, The; Cube Literary Magazine; Cutting Edge Irregular; Dan River Anthology; Dead Of Night Magazine; Deathrealm; Deviance; Dharma Combat; Dream International/Quarterly; darknerve; Eldritch Tales; (F.) Lip; Fat Tuesday; Figment Magazine; Galactic Discourse; Gas; Gestalt; Golden Isis Magazine; Grue Magazine; Haunts; Heaven Bone; Hippo; Hob-Nob; Horror; Ice River; Indigo; Inside Joke; Jabberwocky; Jest; Journal of Regional Criticism; Left-Footed Wombat; Lennis, Pablo; Lilith Magazine; Little Balkans Review; Long Shot; Macguffin, The; Microcosm; Midland Review; Mind's Eye, The; Mirror-Northern Report, The; Muse's Mill; Negative Capability; New Blood Magazine; Night Slivers; Ouroboros; Pavor Nocturnus; Perceptions; Pig Paper, The; Prisoners of the Night; Proof Rock; Pub, The; Quimby; Rainbow City Express; Renegade; Rose Arts Magazine, The; San Gabriel Valley Magazine; Scream Magazine; Seattle Review, The; Serendipity; Shattered Wig Review; Solid Copy; Space and Time; Stamp Axe; Starsong; Sterling Web, The; Stone Drum; Sword of Shahrazad; Thema; Thin Ice; Twisted; 2 AM Magazine; Tyro Magazine; Var Tufa; Weirdbook; Wide Open Magazine; Wild East; Witness (Pennsylvania); Writers' Bar-B-Q, The; Zero Hour; Zoiks!

Regional. Abbey; Alabama Literary Review; Amherst Review, The; Appalachian Heritage; Arnazella; Art:Mag; Aura Literary/Arts Review; Azorean Express, The; Big Two-Hearted; Blue Water Review, The; Blueline; Breakthrough!; Bristlecone; Cache Review; Callaloo; Carolina Literary Companion, A; Chapter One; Chattahoochee Review, The; Cicada; Clockwatch Review; Coe Review, The; Cold-Drill Magazine; Concho River Review; Confrontation; Cornfield Review; Corona; Coydog Review; Crescent Review, The; Cross Timbers Review; Cross-Canada Writers' Magazine; Dan River Anthology; Descant (Texas); Elephant-Ear, The; Emrys Journal; Event; Farmer's Market, The; Five Fingers Review; Gamut, The; Garm Lu; Gestalt; Gettysburg Review, The; Glens Falls Review, The; Grasslands Review; Green Mountains Review; Groundswell; Hawaii Pacific Review; Hawaii Review; Heaven Bone; High Plains Literary Review; Hill and Holler; Hippo; Hob-Nob; In-Between; Innisfree; Japanophile; Jeopardy; Journal of Regional Criticism; Journal, The;

Kana; Kennebec; Lake Effect; Left Curve; Left-Footed Wombat; Lighthouse; Limestone: A Literary Journal; Little Balkans Review; Louisiana Literature; Mark; Merlyn's Pen; Middle Eastern Dancer; Midland Review; Mind's Eye, The; Minnesota Ink; Miorita, a Journal of Romanian Studies; Mirror-Northern Report, The; Mountain Laurel, The; Naked Man; Negative Capability; New Methods; NeWest Review; Northern New England Review, The; Northern Review, The; Northland Quarterly; Notebook: A Little Magazine; Now and Then; Oak Square; Oregon East; Oyez Review; Partisan Review; Pennsylvania Review; Phoebe; Plowman, The; Portable Wall, The; Potato Eyes; Pottersfield Portfolio; Prairie Journal of Canadian Literature, The; Quimby; Rag Mag; Re Arts and Letters [REAL]; Red Cedar Review; Response; Riverwind; Rockford Review, The; Rohwedder; Rose Arts Magazine, The; Samisdat; San Jose Studies; Scream Magazine; Seattle Review, The; Sensations; Shattered Wig Review; Shawnee Silhouette; Skylark; Sneak Preview, The; Solid Copy; South Dakota Review; Southern California Anthology; Southern Humanities Review; Sou'Wester; Spindrift; Spoofing!; SPSM&H; Struggle; Sword of Shahrazad; Sycamore Review; Tentra Artnet BBS; Thema; Thumbprints; Tucumcari Literary Review; Turnstile; Tyro Magazine; Washington Review; West Texas Sun, The; Widener Review, The; Wild East; Wind Magazine; Wisconsin Academy Review; Word & Image; Working Classics; Writers' Bar-B-Q, The; Writers' Forum; Writers Newsletter; Writing Pursuits; Wyoming the Hub of the Wheel; Xavier Review; Zyzzyva

Religious/Inspirational. Amateur Writers Journal; Apaeros; Arnazella; Ball State University Forum; Beloit Fiction Journal; Black Writer Magazine; Breakthrough!; Carousel Literary Arts Magazine; Chakra; Chaminade Literary Review; Chapter One; Christian Outlook; Cochran's Corner; Daughters of Sarah; Dreams & Visions; Explorer Magazine; (F.) Lip; Freeway; Garm Lu; Heaven Bone; Hob-Nob; Journal of Regional Criticism; Kabbalah Yichud; Language Bridges Quarterly; Left-Footed Wombat; Lennis, Pablo; Lilith Magazine; Little Balkans Review; Modern Liturgy; New Press, The; North American Voice of Fatima, The; Now and Then; Pegasus Review, The; Perceptions; Plowman, The; Queen of All Hearts; Rainbow City Express; Reformed Journal, The; Renegade; Resonance; Response; Riverwind; Skylark; Solid Copy; Spirit That Moves Us, The; Studia Mystica; Two-Ton Santa; Tyro Magazine; Valley Women's Voice; Vintage Northwest; West Texas Sun, The; Word & Image; Writers Newsletter; Xavier Review

Romance. Adroit Expression, The; Amaranth; Amateur Writers Journal; Amherst Review, The; Apaeros; Atalantik; Aura Literary/Arts Review; Ball State University Forum; Breakthrough!; Carousel Literary Arts Magazine; Chapter One; Cicada; Cochran's Corner; Corona; Couch Potato Journal, The; Dan River Anthology; Delirium; Dream International/Quarterly; Eagle's Flight; Explorer Magazine; Feminist Baseball; First Stories; Gay Chicago Magazine; Gotta Write Network Litmag; Hob-Nob; Housewife-Writer's Forum; Jeopardy; Journal of Regional Criticism; Lighthouse; Merlyn's Pen; Mind's Eye, The; Minnesota Ink; Mirror-Northern Report, The; Muse's Mill; Negative Capability; Northern New England Review, The; Northland Quarterly; Peoplenet; Plowman, The; Post, The; Proof Rock; PSI; Rambunctious Review; Read Me; Renegade; Rose Arts Magazine, The; Salome: A Journal of the Performing Arts; Sensations; Shawnee Silhouette; Sneak Preview, The; SPSM&H; Sword of Shahrazad; Thumbprints; Tyro Magazine; Village Idiot, The; Virginia Quarterly Review; Word & Image; Writers Newsletter

Science Fiction. Abbey; Adara; Alabama Literary Review; Amaranth; Amateur Writers Journal; Amelia; Amherst Review, The; Apaeros; Argonaut; Arnazella; Art Brigade; Art:Mag; Atalantik; Atavachron and All Our Yesterdays; Atlantis (British Columbia); Aura Literary/Arts Review; Ball State University Forum; Beyond Science Fiction & Fantasy; Book of Spells, The; Bvi-Pacifica Newsletter; Cache Review; Callaloo; Carousel Literary Arts Magazine; Ceilidh; Chapter One; Chrysalis; Cicada; Cochran's Corner; Coe Review, The; Cold-Drill Magazine; Collages and Bricolages; Companion in Zeor, A; Compost Newsletter; Cornfield Review; Cosmic Landscapes; Couch Potato Journal, The; Coydog Review; Crazyquilt; Crescent Review, The; Cube Literary Magazine; Cutting Edge Irregular; Dan River Anthology; Deathrealm; Desert Sun; Deviance; Dream International/Quarterly; darknerve; Eldritch Science; Encounters Magazine; Explorer Magazine; (F.) Lip; F.O.C. Review; Fat Tuesday; Feminist Baseball; Figment Magazine; First Stories; Galactic Discourse; Gas; Gateways; Gestalt; Gotta Write Network Litmag; Grasslands Review; Greens Magazine; Hawaii Pacific Review; Hibiscus Magazine; Hippo; Hob-Nob; Ice River; Indigo; Innisfree; Inside Joke; Jabberwocky; Jam To-Day; Jeopardy; Jest; Journal of Regional Criticism; K; Lake Street Review; Leading Edge, The; Left Curve; Left-Footed Wombat; Lennis, Pablo; Letters Magazine; Little Balkans Review; Long Shot; Lyra; Macguffin, The; Mage, The; Magic Changes; Mark; Mati; Merlyn's Pen; Microcosm; Midland Review; Mind in Motion; Mind's Eye, The; Minnesota Ink; Minnesota Review, The; Mirror-Northern Report, The; Muse's Mill; Negative Capability; New Methods; New Moon; New Pathways; Nimrod; No Idea Magazine; Northern New England Review, The; Nuclear Fiction; Other Worlds; Ouroboros; Owlflight; Pandora; Paper Radio; Pavor Nocturnus; Perceptions; Permafrost; Pig Paper, The; Portable Wall, The; Pottersfield Portfolio; Primavera; Prisoners of the Night; Processed World; Pulphouse; Quarry; Queen's Quarterly; Quintessential Space Debris; Re Arts and Letters [REAL]; Read Me; Renaissance Fan; Renegade; Resonance; Riverside Quarterly; Rose Arts Magazine, The; Salome: A Journal of the Performing Arts; Samisdat; Science Fiction Randomly; Scream Magazine; Seattle Review, The; Sensations; Serendipity; Shawnee Silhouette; Shoe Tree; Skylark; Slipstream; Sneak Preview, The; Space and Time; Spindrift; SPSM&H; Stamp Axe; Starshore; Starsong; Starwind; Sterling Web, The; Strange Plasma; Struggle; Tabula Rasa; Tandava; Tentra Artnet BBS; Thema; Toad Hiway; Twisted; 2 AM Magazine; Tyro Magazine; Village Idiot, The; Wayside; Wide Open Magazine; Witness (Pennsylvania); Writers' Bar-B-Q, The; Z Miscellaneous

Senior Citizen/Retirement. Amelia; Carolina Literary Companion, A; Chapter One; Cicada; Corona; Dan River Anthology; Deviance; Dream International/Quarterly; First Stories; Harvest Magazine; Heartland Journal; Kana; Kenyon Review, The; Left-Footed Wombat; Lighthouse; Lilith Magazine; Minnesota Ink; Mirror-Northern Report, The; Negative Capability; Pléiades Magazine/Philae Magazine; Plowman, The; Portable Wall, The; Shattered Wig Review; Sneak Preview, The; Solid Copy; SPSM&H; Struggle; Thumbprints; Tucumcari Literary Review; Two-Ton Santa; Tyro Magazine; Village Idiot, The; Vintage Northwest; Wide Open Magazine; Word & Image

Serialized/Excerpted Novel. Adara; Agni; Alabama Literary Review; American Voice, The; Antaeus; Apaeros; Art Brigade; Art:Mag; Bellowing Ark; Black Jack; Blatant Artifice; Bvi-Pacifica Newsletter; Cache Review; Caffe, Il; Callaloo; Cathedral of Insanity; Ceilidh; Central Park; Coe Review, The; Cold-Drill Magazine; Compost Newsletter; Coydog Review; Crazyquilt; Deviance; Dream International/Quarterly; darknerve; F.O.C. Review; Farmer's Market, The; Garm Lu; Gateways; Gestalt; Gettysburg Review, The; Green Mountains Review; Groundswell; Hob-Nob; Hobo Stew Review; In-Between; Inside Joke; Jabberwocky; K; Kingfisher; Madison Review, The; Mid-American Review; Muse's Mill; Mystery Notebook; New Blood Magazine; New Press, The; New Virginia Review; Northland Quarterly; Now and Then; Oak Square; Other Voices; Phoebe; Pléiades Magazine/Philae Magazine; Prairie Journal of Canadian Literature, The; Pub, The; Puerto Del Sol; Quarry; Read Me; Red Bass; Salome: A Journal of the Performing Arts; Samisdat; Scream Magazine; Seattle Review, The; Serendipity; Shattered Wig Review; Skylark; Solid Copy; South Dakota Review; Southern California Anthology; Spindrift; Tabula Rasa; Tentra Artnet BBS; Trajectories; Tyro Magazine; Unspeakable Visions of the Individual, The; Very Small Magazine, A; Virginia Quarterly Review; West Coast Review; Widener Review, The; Willow Springs; Writ Magazine; Writers' Bar-B-Q, The; Xavier Review

Suspense/Mystery. After Hours; Alabama Literary Review; Amaranth; Amateur Writers Journal; Amelia; Amherst Review, The; Arnazella; Art:Mag; Atalantik; Atlantis (British Columbia); Ball State University Forum; Blue Water Review, The; Bradley's Fantasy Magazine, Marion Zimmer; Breakthrough!; Bristlecone; Bvi-Pacifica Newsletter; Byline; Cache Review; Carolina Literary Companion, A; Carousel Literary Arts Magazine; Chapter One; Chrysalis; Cicada; Cochran's Corner; Cold-Drill Magazine; Columbus Single Scene; Couch Potato Journal, The; Crazyquilt; Crescent Review, The; Cube Literary Magazine; Dan River Anthology; Detective Story Magazine; Deviance; Dream International/Quarterly; Eagle's Flight; F.O.C. Review; First Stories; Folio: A Literary Journal; Galactic Discourse; Gas; Gestalt; Grasslands Review; Greens Magazine; Groundswell; Hawaii Pacific Review; Hibiscus Magazine; Hob-Nob; Housewife-Writer's Forum; In-Between; Innisfree; Left-Footed Wombat; Letters Magazine; Lighthouse; Linington Lineup; Little Balkans Review; Long Shot; Meal, Ready-To-Eat; Merlyn's Pen; Mind's Eye, The; Minnesota Ink; Mirror-Northern Report, The; Muse's Mill; Mystery Notebook; Mystery Time; Negative Capability; New Blood Magazine; No Idea Magazine; Ouroboros; P. I. Magazine; Paper Bag, The; Perceptions; Pléiades Magazine/Philae Magazine; Post, The; Prisoners of the Night; PSI; Pub, The; Quimby; Read Me; Renegade; Rose Arts Magazine, The; Salome: A Journal of the Performing Arts; Samisdat; Scream Magazine; Seattle Review, The; Sensations; Serendipity; Shawnee Silhouette; Shoe Tree; Sing Heavenly Muse!; Skylark; Sneak Preview, The; Solid Copy; SPSM&H; Struggle; Tabula Rasa; Tentra Artnet BBS; Thema; Tucumcari Literary Review; 2 AM Magazine; Tyro Magazine; Village Idiot, The; Vintage Northwest; Wayside; Wide Open Magazine; Witness (Pennsylvania); Writers' Bar-B-Q, The; Writers Newsletter

Sports. Amelia; Beloit Fiction Journal; Blue Water Review, The; Cache Review; Carousel Literary Arts Magazine; Chapter One; Chrysalis; F.O.C. Review; First Stories; Folio: A Literary Journal; Gargoyle Magazine; Hob-Nob; Little Balkans Review; Magic Changes; Meal, Ready-To-Eat; Mind's Eye, The; Mirror-Northern Report, The; Muse's Mill; New Press, The; Now and Then; Portable Wall, The; Riverwind; Samisdat; Skylark; Sneak Preview, The; Solid Copy; Spirit That Moves Us, The; Spitball; Sycamore Review; Tentra Artnet BBS; Thema; Thumbprints; Tyro Magazine; Valley Women's Voice; Wayside; West Texas Sun, The; Witness (Michigan)

Translations. ACM, (Another Chicago Magazine); Adrift; Aerial; Agni; Alabama Literary Review; Alaska Quarterly Review; Albany Review, The; Alternative Fiction & Poetry; Amelia; American Voice, The; Amherst Review, The; Antaeus; Antigonish Review, The; Antioch Review; Arnazella; Art Brigade; Artful Dodge; Art:Mag; Atalantik; Bad Haircut; Ball State University Forum; Bella Figura, La; Blatant Artifice; Cache Review; Caffe, Il; Callaloo; Ceilidh; Central Park; Chakra; Chaminade Literary Review; Chariton Review, The; Chattahoochee Review, The; Chelsea; Cicada; Coe Review, The; Cold-Drill Magazine; Colorado Review; Columbia: A Magazine of Poetry & Prose; Conditions; Confrontation; Conspiracy of Silence, The; Crab Creek Review; Cube

Literary Magazine; Deviance; Dream International/Quarterly; darknerve; (F.) Lip; Fiction; Fighting Woman News; Fine Madness; Fireweed; Folio: A Literary Journal; Footwork; Gamut, The; Gargoyle Magazine; Garm Lu; Gestalt; Green Mountains Review; Groundswell; Hawaii Pacific Review; Hawaii Review; Hobo Stew Review; Jabberwocky; Jacaranda Review; Jazziminds Magazine; Jeopardy; Jest; Jewish Currents Magazine; Kairos; Kana; Kenyon Review, The; Kingfisher; Kiosk; Language Bridges Quarterly; Left Curve; Left-Footed Wombat; Lilith Magazine; Little Balkans Review; Lyra; Macguffin, The; Manoa; Mati; Mid-American Review; Midland Review; Mind's Eye, The; Miorita, a Journal of Romanian Studies; Mirror-Northern Report, The; Mississippi Review; Negative Capability; New Blood Magazine; New Delta Review; New Laurel Review; New Letters Magazine; New Moon; New Orleans Review; New Press, The; Nimrod; Northern New England Review, The; Northwest Review; Oak Square; Open Magazine; Oregon East; Oxford Magazine; Painted Bride Quarterly; Partisan Review; Pennsylvania Review; Phoebe; Plowman, The; Portable Wall, The; Prism International; Proof Rock; Ptolemy/The Browns Mills Review; Puerto Del Sol; Quarry; Quarterly West; Raddle Moon, The; Read Me; Red Bass; Renegade; Response; River Styx; Riverwind; Rohwedder; Rose Arts Magazine, The; Salome: A Journal of the Performing Arts; Samisdat; Seattle Review, The; Shattered Wig Review; Signal, The; South Dakota Review; Sou'Wester; Spindrift; Spirit That Moves Us, The; SPSM&H; Stories; Story; Struggle; Sycamore Review; Tampa Review, The; Tentra Artnet BBS; Third Woman; Toad Hiway; Translation; Triquarterly; Union Street Review; Unmuzzled Ox; Village Idiot, The; Virginia Quarterly Review; West Branch; West Coast Review; Willow Springs; Writ Magazine; Writers' Bar-B-Q, The; Wyoming the Hub of the Wheel; Xavier Review; Zero Hour; Zoiks!

Western. Amelia; Amherst Review, The; Azorean Express, The; Ball State University Forum; Black Jack; Bristlecone; Carousel Literary Arts Magazine; Chapter One; Cold-Drill Magazine; Concho River Review; Cross Timbers Review; Dan River Anthology; Delirium; Dream International/Quarterly; First Stories; Gestalt; Grasslands Review; Hibiscus Magazine; Hippo; Lighthouse; Little Balkans Review; Long Shot; Meal, Ready-To-Eat; Merlyn's Pen; Minnesota Ink; Mirror-Northern Report, The; Muse's Mill; New Methods; Oak Square; Paper Bag, The; Pléiades Magazine/Philae Magazine; Plowman, The; Read Me; Renegade; Riverwind; Samisdat; San Gabriel Valley Magazine; Seattle Review, The; Skylark; Solid Copy; SPSM&H; Sword of Shahrazad; Tentra Artnet BBS; Thema; Tucumcari Literary Review; Valley Grapevine; Village Idiot, The; Wayside; West Texas Sun, The; Wide Open Magazine; Writing Pursuits

Young Adult/Teen. Amateur Writers Journal; Black Scholar, The; Bradley's Fantasy Magazine, Marion Zimmer; Chapter One; Cochran's Corner; Creative Kids; Delirium; Dream International/Quarterly; Feminist Baseball; Gotta Write Network Litmag; Hob-Nob; Hobo Stew Review; Language Bridges Quarterly; Lighthouse; Lilith Magazine; Little Balkans Review; Merlyn's Pen; Minnesota Ink; Muse's Mill; Plowman, The; Proem Canada; Serendipity; Shattered Wig Review; Sneak Preview, The; Spoofing!; Struggle; Tentra Artnet BBS; Tyro Magazine

Commercial Periodicals

Adventure. American Accent Short Story Magazine; Art Times; Bostonia Magazine; Bowbender; Bowhunter Magazine; Boys' Life; Buffalo Spree Magazine; Bugle; Catholic Forester; Cavalier Magazine; Coastal Cruising; Cobblestone; Cosmopolitan Magazine; Crusader Magazine; Dialogue; Equinews: Serving the Horse Industry; Flyfishing News, Views and Reviews; Gent; High Times; Horse Illustrated; Modern Short Stories; North Shore Magazine; Northcoast View; Plain Dealer Magazine, The; Pockets; Prime Times; Radiance; Ranger Rick Magazine; Road King Magazine; Seacoast Life; Senior Life Magazine; Shofar; Sports Afield; Teen Magazine; Teen Power; Touch; Tq (Teenquest); Trailer Boats Magazine

Canada. Atlantic Advocate, The; Atlantic Salmon Journal; Bowbender; Canadian Messenger; Chickadee; Indian Life Magazine; Meridian Magazine; Messenger of the Sacred Heart; North Shore Magazine; Western People

Condensed Novel. Arete; Arizona Coast; Bostonia Magazine; Bugle; Latter-Day Woman Magazine; Northcoast View; Seacoast Life; Senior Life Magazine; Special Report: Fiction; Tattoo Advocate Journal; Tikkun; Virtue; Womens American ORT Reporter

Confession. Computoredge; Jive, Black Confessions, Black Romance, Bronze Thrills; Modern Short Stories

Contemporary. American Accent Short Story Magazine; American Atheist; Arete; Art Times; Atlanta Singles Magazine; Atlantic Monthly; B'nai B'rith International Jewish Monthly, The; Boston Review; Bostonia Magazine; Buffalo Spree Magazine; Catholic Forester; Cosmopolitan Magazine; Dialogue; Family Magazine; First; Good Housekeeping; Harper's Magazine; Ladys Circle; Mademoiselle Magazine; Military Lifestyle; Milwaukee Magazine; Modern Short Stories; Moment Magazine; Naamat Woman; North Shore Magazine; Northcoast View; Northeast; Northwest Magazine; Omni; Other Side, The; Oui Magazine; Plain Dealer Magazine, The; Playboy Magazine; Playgirl Magazine; Pockets; Portland Magazine; Prime Times; Radiance; Saint Anthony Messenger; Saint Joseph's Messenger and Advocate of the Blind; Sassy Magazine; Seacoast Life; Shofar; Tattoo Advocate Journal; Teens Today; Tikkun; Trailer Boats Magazine; Virtue; With Magazine; Womans Day

Erotica. Cavalier Magazine; Contact Advertising; Drummer; First Hand; Fling; Gent; Gentleman's Companion; Guys; Harvey for Loving People; Hustler; Manscape; Modern Short Stories; Northcoast View; Nugget; On Our Backs; Options; Private Letters; Radiance; Swank Magazine; Texas Connection Magazine; Turn-on Letters; Uncensored Letters

Ethnic. American Citizen Italian Press, The; American Dane; Arete; Art Times; Baltimore Jewish Times; B'nai B'rith International Jewish Monthly, The; Boston Review; Bostonia Magazine; Buffalo Spree Magazine; Catholic Forester; Christmas; Detroit Jewish News; Hadassah Magazine; India Currents; Indian Life Magazine; Inside; Jive, Black Confessions, Black Romance, Bronze Thrills; Ladys Circle; Midstream; Moment Magazine; Northcoast View; Other Side, The; Plain Dealer Magazine, The; Pockets; Prime Times; Radiance; Sassy Magazine; Shofar; Special Report: Fiction; Tattoo Advocate Journal; Teens Today; Touch; With Magazine; Womens American ORT Reporter

Experimental. Boston Review; Bostonia Magazine; Bugle; High Times; Modern Short Stories; North Shore Magazine; Northcoast View; Other Side, The; Sassy Magazine

Fantasy. American Accent Short Story Magazine; Art Times; Asimov's Science Fiction Magazine, Isaac; Contact Advertising; Dragon Magazine; High Times; Magazine of Fantasy and Science Fiction; Modern Short Stories; Northcoast View; Northwest Magazine; Omni; On Our Backs; Oui Magazine; Playboy Magazine; Pockets; Radiance; Ranger Rick Magazine; Seacoast Life; Shofar; Tattoo Advocate Journal; Texas Connection Magazine; Tq (Teenquest); Trailer Boats Magazine; Weird Tales; Womans Day; Young American

Feminist. American Atheist; Art Times; Buffalo Spree Magazine; Catholic Forester; Computoredge; Contact Advertising; Mother Jones Magazine; Naamat Woman; Other Side, The; Radiance; Redbook; Sassy Magazine; Special Report: Fiction; Tattoo Advocate Journal; Texas Connection Magazine; Tikkun; Womens American ORT Reporter

Gay. Art Times; Bear; Contact Advertising; Drummer; First Hand; Guide Magazine; Guide, The; Guys; In Touch for Men; Manscape; Mother Jones Magazine; Options; Sassy Magazine; Tattoo Advocate Journal; Texas Connection Magazine; Tikkun

Historical. American Accent Short Story Magazine; American Atheist; American Citizen Italian Press, The; Ann Arbor; Arizona Coast; Art Times; Atlantic Advocate, The; Atlantic Salmon Journal; Beckett Baseball Card Monthly; Bugle; Christmas; Cobblestone; Ladys Circle; Midstream; Modern Short Stories; Moment Magazine; Monroe; Montana Senior Citizens News; North Shore Magazine; Northcoast View; Plain Dealer Magazine, The; Pockets; Portland Magazine; Purpose; Radiance; Senior Life Magazine; Tattoo Advocate Journal; Tikkun

Horror. Bostonia Magazine; Cavalier Magazine; Gent; Modern Short Stories; Northcoast View; Omni; Playboy Magazine; Tattoo Advocate Journal; Weird Tales

Humor/Satire. American Accent Short Story Magazine; American Citizen Italian Press, The; Art Times; Atlanta Singles Magazine; Atlantic Advocate, The; Atlantic Salmon Journal; Balloon Life; Beckett Baseball Card Monthly; Boston Review; Bostonia Magazine; Boys' Life; Buffalo Spree Magazine; Bugle; Catholic Forester; Coastal Cruising; Computoredge; Dialogue; First; Gent; Golf Journal; Harper's Magazine; Horse Illustrated; Ideals Magazine; Ladys Circle; Latter-Day Woman Magazine; Metro Singles Lifestyles; Midstream; Modern Short Stories; North Shore Magazine; Northcoast View; Northwest Magazine; On Our Backs; Other Side, The; Oui Magazine; Outlaw Biker; Plain Dealer Magazine, The; Playboy Magazine; Prime Times; Radiance; Ranger Rick Magazine; Reform Judaism; Road King Magazine; Saint Joseph's Messenger and Advocate of the Blind; Sassy Magazine; Seacoast Life; Senior Life Magazine; Shofar; Singlelife Magazine; Special Report: Fiction; Sports Afield; Tattoo Advocate Journal; Teen Magazine; Teen Power; Teens Today; Texas Connection Magazine; Tikkun; Trailer Boats Magazine; Virtue; Vista; With Magazine; Womens American ORT Reporter; Young American

Juvenile. Associate Reformed Presbyterian, The; Beckett Baseball Card Monthly; Chickadee; Child Life; Children's Digest; Children's Playmate; Clubhouse; Cobblestone; Cricket Magazine; Crusader Magazine; Discoveries; Equinews: Serving the Horse Industry; Faces; Friend Magazine, The; Highlights for Children; Home Altar, The; Humpty Dumpty's Magazine; Jack and Jill; Kid City; Kindergarten Listen; Ladys Circle; Lollipops Magazine; My Friend; Noah's Ark; On the Line; Pennywhistle Press; Pockets; R-A-D-A-R; Ranger Rick Magazine; Shofar; Single Parent, The; Story Friends; Teens Today; Touch; Turtle Magazine for Preschool Kids; Wee Wisdom Magazine; Wonder Time; Young Crusader, The

Lesbian. Art Times; Contact Advertising; Guide, The; Mother Jones Magazine; On Our Backs; Options; Oui Magazine; Tattoo Advocate Journal; Texas Connection Magazine; Tikkun

Mainstream. American Accent Short Story Magazine; American Citizen Italian Press, The; Arete; Art Times; Boston Review; Bostonia Magazine; Catholic Forester; Christmas; Dialogue; First; Gent; Ladys Circle; Latter-Day Woman Magazine; Midstream; Modern Short Stories; North Shore Magazine; Northwest Magazine; Other Side, The; Plain Dealer Magazine, The; Portland Magazine; Radiance; Saint Joseph's Messenger and Advocate of the Blind; Sassy Magazine; Seacoast Life; Tattoo Advocate Journal; Tikkun; With Magazine

Preschool/Picture Book. Radiance; Wee Wisdom Magazine

Prose Poem. Boston Review; Christmas; Church Herald, The; Ideals Magazine; Mature Years; Metro Singles Lifestyles; My Friend; Northwest Magazine; Pennywhistle Press; Radiance; Sassy Magazine; Shofar; Tattoo Advocate Journal; Young American

Psychic/Supernatural/Occult. Modern Short Stories; Northcoast View; Plain Dealer Magazine, The; Tattoo Advocate Journal; Weird Tales

Regional. Aloha; Ann Arbor; Atlantic Advocate, The; Atlantic Salmon Journal; Boston Review; Bostonia Magazine; Catholic Forester; Chesapeake Bay Magazine; Cobblestone; Dialogue; First; Flyfishing News, Views and Reviews; Maine; Milwaukee Magazine; Modern Short Stories; Monroe; North Shore Magazine; Northcoast View; Northeast; Palouse Journal; Plain Dealer Magazine, The; Portland Magazine; Sassy Magazine; Seacoast Life; Special Report: Fiction; Sunday Journal Magazine; Tattoo Advocate Journal; Tq (Teenquest); Washingtonian, The; Western People; Yankee Magazine

Religious/Inspirational. Associate Reformed Presbyterian, The; alive now!; Baltimore Jewish Times; B'nai B'rith International Jewish Monthly, The; Bread; Campus Life Magazine; Canadian Messenger; Christian Living For Senior Highs; Christmas; Church Herald, The; Clubhouse; Crusader Magazine; Detroit Jewish News; Discoveries; Evangel; Family, The; Friend Magazine, The; Hi-Call; Home Altar, The; Home Life; Ideals Magazine; In Touch; Inside; Kindergarten Listen; Ladys Circle; Latter-Day Woman Magazine; Lighted Pathway; Liguorian; Live; Living with Teenagers; Lookout, The; Lutheran Journal, The; Magazine for Christian Youth!; Mature Living; Mature Years; Messenger of the Sacred Heart; Metro Singles Lifestyles; Midstream; Modern Short Stories; Moment Magazine; My Friend; Noah's Ark; Other Side, The; Pockets; Purpose; Reform Judaism; Saint Anthony Messenger; Saint Joseph's Messenger and Advocate of the Blind; Seek; Senior Life Magazine; Shofar; Standard; Straight; Tattoo Advocate Journal; Teen Power; Teens Today; Touch; Tq (Teenquest); Virtue; Vista; With Magazine; Wonder Time; Young Salvationist/Young Soldier

Romance. American Accent Short Story Magazine; Cosmopolitan Magazine; Good Housekeeping; Jive, Black Confessions, Black Romance, Bronze Thrills; Ladys Circle; Metro Singles Lifestyles; Modern Short Stories; Prime Times; Saint Anthony Messenger; Saint Joseph's Messenger and Advocate of the Blind; Tattoo Advocate Journal; Teen Magazine; Teens Today; Tq (Teenquest); Virtue

Science Fiction. Aboriginal Science Fiction; American Accent Short Story Magazine; Analog Science Fiction/Science Fact; Art Times; Asimov's Science Fiction Magazine, Isaac; Boys' Life; Computoredge; Gent; High Times; Magazine of Fantasy and Science Fiction; Modern Short Stories; North Shore Magazine; Northcoast View; Northwest Magazine; Omni; Plain Dealer Magazine, The; Playboy Magazine; Radiance; Ranger Rick Magazine; Seacoast Life; Tattoo Advocate Journal; Tq (Teenquest); Trailer Boats Magazine

Senior Citizen/Retirement. Arizona Coast; Arthritis Today; Catholic Forester; Dialogue; Ladys Circle; Mature Living; Mature Years; Meridian Magazine; Montana Senior Citizens News; Saint Anthony Messenger; Saint Joseph's Messenger and Advocate of the Blind; Seacoast Life; Senior Life Magazine; Vista

Serialized/Excerpted Novel. Analog Science Fiction/Science Fact; Arizona Coast; Boston Review; Bostonia Magazine; Capper's; High Times; Moment Magazine; Seacoast Life; Tattoo Advocate Journal

Sports. Balloon Life; Beckett Baseball Card Monthly; Bike Report; Black Belt; Boston Review; Bowbender; Bowhunter Magazine; Boys' Life; Catholic Forester; Coastal Cruising; Equinews: Serving the Horse Industry; Flyfisher, The; Flyfishing News, Views and Reviews; Hoof Beats; Horse Illustrated; Inside Texas Running; Insights; Modern Short Stories; Plain Dealer Magazine, The; Playboy Magazine; Radiance; Senior Life Magazine; Shofar; Sports Afield; Young American

Suspense/Mystery. American Accent Short Story Magazine; Bostonia Magazine; Boys' Life; Buffalo Spree Magazine; Catholic Forester; Cosmopolitan Magazine; Dialogue; Ellery Queen's Mystery Magazine; Hitchcock's Mystery Magazine, Alfred; Horse Illustrated; Modern Short Stories; North Shore Magazine; Northcoast View; Other Side, The; Oui Magazine; Plain Dealer Magazine, The; Playboy Magazine; Pockets; Portland Magazine; Radiance; Ranger Rick Magazine; Road King Magazine; Seacoast Life; Senior Life Magazine; Shofar; Special Report: Fiction;

Tattoo Advocate Journal; Teen Magazine; Tq (Teenquest); Trailer Boats Magazine; Young American

Translations. American Citizen Italian Press, The; Arete; Boston Review; India Currents; Midstream; Moment Magazine; Northcoast View; Seacoast Life; Shofar; Tikkun; With Magazine

Western. Arizona Coast; Bugle; Modern Short Stories; Montana Senior Citizens News; Playboy Magazine; Road King Magazine; Senior Life Magazine

Young Adult/Teen. American Newspaper Carrier, The; Associate Reformed Presbyterian, The; Beckett Baseball Card Monthly; Boys' Life; Bread; Campus Life Magazine; Christian Living For Senior Highs; Equinews: Serving the Horse Industry; Hi-Call; Insights; Ladys Circle; Lighted Pathway; Magazine for Christian Youth!; Noah's Ark; Northwest Magazine; On the Line; Pennywhistle Press; Radiance; Sassy Magazine; Scholastic Scope; Seventeen; Shofar; Teen Magazine; Teen Power; Teens Today; Vista; Wee Wisdom Magazine; With Magazine; Young Salvationist/Young Soldier

Small Press

Adventure. Aegina Press, Inc.; Alaska Nature Press-Publishers; Ariadne Press; Barlow Press; Bookmakers Guild Inc.; Borealis Press; Bryans & Bryans; Cave Books; Council for Indian Education; Dan River Press; Fasa Corporation; Goose Lane Editions; Mey-House Books; New Victoria Publishers; Night Tree Press; Our Child Press; Pando Publications; Pentagram Press; Ranger Associates, Inc.; Read 'n Run Books; Satchell's Publishing; Scojtia Publishing Company, Inc.; Second Chance Press and the Permanent Press; Sheep Meadow Press, The; Soho Press; University Editions; Woodsong Graphics Inc.; Wyrick & Company

Canada. Arsenal Pulp Press; Black Moss Press; Borealis Press; Canadian Stage and Arts Publications; Coteau Books; Cuff Publications Ltd., Harry; Goose Lane Editions; Guernica Editions; Newest Publishers Ltd.; Porcupine's Quill, Inc.; Prairie Journal Press; Prairie Publishing Company, The; Press Gang Publishers; Pulp Press Book Publishers; Quarry Press; Red Deer College Press; Reference Press; Thistledown Press; Turnstone Press; Women's Press; York Press

Comics. Mosaic Press

Contemporary. Aegina Press, Inc.; Applezaba Press; Ariadne Press; Arsenal Pulp Press; Barlow Press; BkMk Press; Black Tie Press; Books for All Times, Inc.; Borealis Press; Breitenbush Books, Inc.; Bryans & Bryans; Carolina Wren Press; Carpenter Press; Catbird Press; Confluence Press Inc.; Creative Arts Book Co.; Cross-Cultural Communications; Crossing Press, The; Curbstone Press; Dan River Press; Dayspring Press, Inc.; Devonshire Publishing Co.; Esoterica Press; Feminist Press at the City University of New York, The; Four Walls Eight Windows; Goose Lane Editions; Green Street Press, The; Guernica Editions; Haypenny Press; Hermes Hosue Press; Independence Publishers Inc.; Mainespring Press; Mey-House Books; Milkweed Editions; New Rivers Press; Ommation Press; Our Child Press; Padre Productions; Papier-Mache Press; Paycock Press; Pikestaff Publications, Inc.; Pineapple Press; Porcupine's Quill, Inc.; Press Gang Publishers; Puckerbrush Press; Pulp Press Book Publishers; Read 'n Run Books; Red Deer College Press; Scojtia Publishing Company, Inc.; Sea Fog Press, Inc.; Second Chance Press and the Permanent Press; Seven Buffaloes Press; Sheep Meadow Press, The; Station Hill Press; Teal Press; Tide Book Publishing Company; Times Eagle Books; Tudor Publishers, Inc.; University Editions; University of Illinois Press; Woman in the Moon Publications; Women's Press; Woodsong Graphics Inc.; York Press; Zephyr Press; Zoland Books, Inc.

Erotica. Banned Books; Carlton Books; Creative Arts Book Co.; New Victoria Publishers; Press Gang Publishers; Red Alder Books

Ethnic. Arte Publico Press; Bilingual Press/Editorial Bilingüe; BkMk Press; Breitenbush Books, Inc.; Carolina Wren Press; China Books; Clarity Press; Council for Indian Education; Cross-Cultural Communications; Curbstone Press; Eighth Mt. Press, The; Esoterica Press; Feminist Press at the City University of New York, The; Goose Lane Editions; Guernica Editions; Haypenny Press; Heritage Press; Island House; Kitchen Table: Women of Color Press; Mey-House Books; Mina Press; New Seed Press; New Victoria Publishers; Path Press, Inc.; Press Gang Publishers; Read 'n Run Books; Sandpiper Press; Satchell's Publishing; Scojtia Publishing Company, Inc.; Sea Fog Press, Inc.; Seal Press; Second Chance Press and the Permanent Press; Seven Buffaloes Press; Sheep Meadow Press, The; Soho Press; Third Woman Press; University Editions; Waterfront Press; Woman in the Moon Publications; Wyrick & Company; Zephyr Press

Experimental. Aegina Press, Inc.; Applezaba Press; Arsenal Pulp Press; BkMk Press; Black Tie Press; Breitenbush Books, Inc.; Carolina Wren Press; Carpenter Press; Clothespin Fever Press; Cross-Cultural Communications; Dan River Press; Feminist Press at the City University of New York, The; Four Walls Eight Windows; Galileo Press, Ltd., The; Goose Lane Editions; Green Street Press, The; Haypenny Press; Hermes Hosue Press; Independence Publishers Inc.; Island

House; Lintel; Milkweed Editions; New Directions; New Rivers Press; Ommation Press; Paycock Press; Pentagram Press; Pikestaff Publications, Inc.; Pineapple Press; Prairie Journal Press; Puckerbrush Press; Quarry Press; Read 'n Run Books; Red Deer College Press; Re/Search Publishing; Scojtia Publishing Company, Inc.; Second Chance Press and the Permanent Press; Station Hill Press; Textile Bridge Press; Thistledown Press; Turnstone Press; Ultramarine Publishing Co., Inc.; University Editions; University of Illinois Press; Wyrick & Company; York Press; Zephyr Press; Zoland Books, Inc.

Faction. Aegina Press, Inc.; Independence Publishers Inc.; Island House

Fantasy. Aegina Press, Inc.; Ansuda Publications; Applezaba Press; Ariadne Press; Banned Books; Carpenter Press; Dan River Press; Dragon's Den Publishing; Haypenny Press; Independence Publishers Inc.; Kubicek & Associates; New Victoria Publishers; Our Child Press; Porcupine's Quill, Inc.; Press of Macdonald and Reinecke, The; Read 'n Run Books; Satchell's Publishing; Scojtia Publishing Company, Inc.; Ultramarine Publishing Co., Inc.; University Editions; W W. Publications; Woman in the Moon Publications; Yith Press; Yith Press

Feminist. Applezaba Press; Ariadne Press; Calyx Books; Carolina Wren Press; Cleis Press; Clothespin Fever Press; Creative Arts Book Co.; Crossing Press, The; Curbstone Press; Eighth Mt. Press, The; Feminist Press at the City University of New York, The; Hermes Hosue Press; Kitchen Table: Women of Color Press; Lintel; Mina Press; Mother Courage Press; New Seed Press; New Victoria Publishers; Ommation Press; Papier-Mache Press; Post-Apollo Press, The; Press Gang Publishers; Pulp Press Book Publishers; Quarry Press; Read 'n Run Books; Samisdat; Sea Fog Press, Inc.; Seal Press; Silverleaf Press, Inc.; Spinsters/Aunt Lute Book Co.; Third Woman Press; Tide Book Publishing Company; University Editions; Woman Sleuth Mystery Series, The; Women's Press; Zephyr Press; Zoland Books, Inc.

Gay. Applezaba Press; Banned Books; Carolina Wren Press; Crossing Press, The; Curbstone Press; Eighth Mt. Press, The; Feminist Press at the City University of New York, The; Gay Sunshine Press and Leyland Publications; Knights Press; Lintel; Los Hombres Press; Mina Press; Samisdat; Woman in the Moon Publications; Zephyr Press; Zoland Books, Inc.

Historical. Aegina Press, Inc.; Alaska Nature Press-Publishers; Ariadne Press; Barlow Press; BkMk Press; Borealis Press; Breitenbush Books, Inc.; Bryans & Bryans; Council for Indian Education; Creative Arts Book Co.; Cross-Cultural Communications; Dan River Press; Devonshire Publishing Co.; Dragon's Den Publishing; Esoterica Press; Feminist Press at the City University of New York, The; Goose Lane Editions; Heart of the Lakes Publishing; Independence Publishers Inc.; Jayell Enterprises; Kruza Kaleidoscopix, Inc.; Library Research Associates, Inc.; Long Publishing Co., Hendrick; Mainespring Press; Melior Publications; Mosaic Press; New Victoria Publishers; Night Tree Press; Pando Publications; Pineapple Press; Porcupine's Quill, Inc.; Press of Macdonald and Reinecke, The; Quarry Press; Ranger Associates, Inc.; Read 'n Run Books; Scojtia Publishing Company, Inc.; Second Chance Press and the Permanent Press; Sheep Meadow Press, The; Soho Press; Spiritual Fiction Publications; Tide Book Publishing Company; Tudor Publishers, Inc.; University Editions; Woodsong Graphics Inc.; Zephyr Press

Horror. Aegina Press, Inc.; Ansuda Publications; Bryans & Bryans; Dan River Press; Devonshire Publishing Co.; Dragon's Den Publishing; Kubicek & Associates; Read 'n Run Books; University Editions

Humor/Satire. Alaska Nature Press-Publishers; Applezaba Press; Ariadne Press; Banned Books; Barlow Press; Black Moss Press; Bryans & Bryans; Canadian Stage and Arts Publications; Catbird Press; Confluence Press Inc.; Corkscrew Press; Creative with Words Publications; Crosscultural Communications; Dan River Press; Devonshire Publishing Co.; Haypenny Press; Homestead Publishing; Independence Publishers Inc.; Metamorphous Press; Mosaic Press; New Victoria Publishers; Night Tree Press; Pando Publications; Paycock Press; Press Gang Publishers; Press of Macdonald and Reinecke, The; Read 'n Run Books; Scojtia Publishing Company, Inc.; Tide Book Publishing Company; University Editions; Woodsong Graphics Inc.; Wyrick & Company; Zephyr Press; Zoland Books, Inc.

Juvenile. Advocacy Press; Alaska Nature Press-Publishers; Annick Press Ltd.; Black Moss Press; Bookmakers Guild Inc.; Borealis Press; Bright Ring Publishing; Carolina Wren Press; Council for Indian Education; Creative with Words Publications; Cross-Cultural Communications; Double M Press; Esoterica Press; Heart of the Lakes Publishing; Homestead Publishing; Kar-Ben Copies, Inc.; Kruza Kaleidoscopix, Inc.; Lollipop Power Books; Long Publishing Co., Hendrick; Metamorphous Press; Mina Press; Misty Hill Press; New Seed Press; Our Child Press; Pando Publications; Prairie Publishing Company, The; Read 'n Run Books; Satchell's Publishing; Scojtia Publishing Company, Inc.; Sea Fog Press, Inc.; Shoe Tree Press; University Editions; Women's Press; Woodsong Graphics Inc.

Lesbian. Applezaba Press; Banned Books; Calyx Books; Carolina Wren Press; Cleis Press; Clothespin Fever Press; Crossing Press, The; Curbstone Press; Eighth Mt. Press, The; Feminist Press at the City University of New York, The; Kitchen Table: Women of Color Press; Lintel; Mina Press; Mother Courage Press; Naiad Press, Inc., The; New Victoria Publishers; Post-Apollo Press, The; Press Gang Publishers; Rising Tide Press; Samisdat; Seal Press; Silverleaf Press, Inc.; Spinsters/ Aunt Lute Book Co.; Woman in the Moon Publications; Woman Sleuth Mystery Series, The; Zephyr Press; Zoland Books, Inc.

Mainstream. Aegina Press, Inc.; Alaska Nature Press-Publishers; Ansuda Publications; Ariadne Press; Barlow Press; Blood & Guts Press; Bottom Dog Press; Bryans & Bryans; Catbird Press; Confluence Press Inc.; Dan River Press; Daniel and Company, Publishers, John; Devonshire Publishing Co.; Haypenny Press; Independence Publishers Inc.; Pando Publications; Press of Macdonald and Reinecke, The; Read 'n Run Books; Scojtia Publishing Company, Inc.; Second Chance Press and the Permanent Press; Sheep Meadow Press, The; Soho Press; Tide Book Publishing Company; Tudor Publishers, Inc.; Ultramarine Publishing Co., Inc.; University Editions; University of Arkansas Press, The; Woodsong Graphics Inc.; Wyrick & Company; Zephyr Press

Military/War. Dan River Press; Haypenny Press; Nautical & Aviation Publishing Co. of America Inc., The; Pando Publications; Ranger Associates, Inc.; Read 'n Run Books; Sea Fog Press, Inc.

Novella. Galileo Press, Ltd., The; Hermes Hosue Press; Pippin Press; Rising Tide Press; Teal Press

Preschool/Picture Book. Black Moss Press; Bright Ring Publishing; Council for Indian Education; Double M Press; Homestead Publishing; Our Child Press; Read 'n Run Books; Scojtia Publishing Company, Inc.

Prose Poem. Ommation Press

Psychic/Supernatural/Occult. Ansuda Publications; Carolina Wren Press; Dan River Press; Devonshire Publishing Co.; Dragon's Den Publishing; Knoll Publishing Co., Inc.; Kubicek & Associates; Read 'n Run Books; Spiritual Fiction Publications; Woman in the Moon Publications; Woodsong Graphics Inc.

Regional. Aegina Press, Inc.; Alaska Nature Press-Publishers; Barlow Press; Breitenbush Books, Inc.; Carolina Wren Press; Confluence Press Inc.; Council for Indian Education; Creative Arts Book Co.; Cuff Publications Ltd., Harry; Dan River Press; Devonshire Publishing Co.; Feminist Press at the City University of New York, The; Green Street Press, The; Haypenny Press; Heart of the Lakes Publishing; Independence Publishers Inc.; Kubicek & Associates; Library Research Associates, Inc.; Lintel; Long Publishing Co., Hendrick; Melior Publications; Mosaic Press; New Seed Press; Night Tree Press; Padre Productions; Pando Publications; Pineapple Press; Press Gang Publishers; Read 'n Run Books; Samisdat; Seven Buffaloes Press; Three Continents Press; Tide Book Publishing Company; Times Eagle Books; Tudor Publishers, Inc.; University Editions; University of Idaho Press; University of Utah Press; Watermark Press, Inc.; Woodley Memorial Press; Wyrick & Company; Zephyr Press

Religious/Inspirational. Dayspring Press, Inc.; Double M Press; Dragon's Den Publishing; Knoll Publishing Co., Inc.; Mosaic Press; Post-Apollo Press, The; Read 'n Run Books; Satchell's Publishing; Sea Fog Press, Inc.; Spiritual Fiction Publications; Star Books, Inc.

Romance. Bryans & Bryans; Devonshire Publishing Co.; Independence Publishers Inc.; Mosaic Press; New Victoria Publishers; Read 'n Run Books; Satchell's Publishing; Scojtia Publishing Company, Inc.; University Editions; Woodsong Graphics Inc.

Science Fiction. Aegina Press, Inc.; Alaska Nature Press-Publishers; Banned Books; Blood & Guts Press; Carpenter Press; Dan River Press; Dayspring Press, Inc.; Devonshire Publishing Co.; Dragon's Den Publishing; Fasa Corporation; Feminist Press at the City University of New York, The; Haypenny Press; Kubicek & Associates; Mainespring Press; Mey-House Books; Mina Press; New Victoria Publishers; Pando Publications; Press Gang Publishers; Read 'n Run Books; Re/ Search Publishing; Scojtia Publishing Company, Inc.; Ultramarine Publishing Co., Inc.; University Editions; W W. Publications; Woodsong Graphics Inc.; Zephyr Press

Short Story Collections. Aegina Press, Inc.; Alaska Nature Press-Publishers; Ansuda Publications; Applezaba Press; Arsenal Pulp Press; Banned Books; Bilingual Press/Editorial Bilingüe; BkMk Press; Black Moss Press; Bookmakers Guild Inc.; Books for All Times, Inc.; Breitenbush Books, Inc.; Calyx Books; Carolina Wren Press; Clothespin Fever Press; Confluence Press Inc.; Coteau Books; Creative Arts Book Co.; Dan River Press; Daniel and Company, Publishers, John; Dragon's Den Publishing; Ecco Press, The; Eighth Mt. Press, The; Esoterica Press; Feminist Press at the City University of New York, The; Four Walls Eight Windows; Galileo Press, Ltd., The; Goose Lane Editions; Graywolf Press; Green Street Press, The; Haypenny Press; Hermes Hosue Press; Homestead Publishing; Independence Publishers Inc.; Intertext; Island House; Kitchen Table: Women of Color Press; New Rivers Press; Night Tree Press; Padre Productions; Papier-Mache Press; Post-Apollo Press, The; Press Gang Publishers; Press of Macdonald and Reinecke, The; Pulp Press Book Publishers; Quarry Press; Read 'n Run Books; Red Deer College Press; Seal Press; Seven Buffaloes Press; Sheep Meadow Press, The; Teal Press; Textile Bridge Press;

Thistledown Press; Three Continents Press; Ultramarine Publishing Co., Inc.; University Editions; University of Arkansas Press, The; University of Idaho Press; University of Illinois Press; University of Utah Press; Vardaman; Watermark Press, Inc.; Woman in the Moon Publications; Women's Press; Zephyr Press; Zoland Books, Inc.

Sports. Reference Press

Suspense/Mystery. Aegina Press, Inc.; Alaska Nature Press-Publishers; Ansuda Publications; Ariadne Press; Blood and Guts Press; Carlton Books; Cliffhanger Press; Creative Arts Book Co.; Devonshire Publishing Co.; Dragon's Den Publishing; New Victoria Publishers; Pando Publications; Papyrus Publishers; Perseverance Press; Press Gang Publishers; Read 'n Run Books; Scojtia Publishing Company, Inc.; Second Chance Press and the Permanent Press; Sheep Meadow Press, The; Soho Press; Tudor Publishers, Inc.; Woman Sleuth Mystery Series, The; Woodsong Graphics Inc.

Translations. Applezaba Press; Arsenal Pulp Press; Bilingual Press/Editorial Bilingüe; BkMk Press; Calyx Books; Carolina Wren Press; Catbird Press; Cleis Press; Creative Arts Book Co.; Cross-Cultural Communications; Curbstone Press; Esoterica Press; Feminist Press at the City University of New York, The; Four Walls Eight Windows; Green Street Press, The; Hermes Hosue Press; Independence Publishers Inc.; Intertext; Italica Press; New Rivers Press; Paycock Press; Post-Apollo Press, The; Read 'n Run Books; Sea Fog Press, Inc.; Sheep Meadow Press, The; Station Hill Press; Three Continents Press; Translation Center, The; University Editions; University of Arkansas Press, The; Waterfront Press; Women's Press; York Press; Zoland Books, Inc.

Western. Coteau Books; Council for Indian Education; Creative Arts Book Co.; Dan River Press; Homestead Publishing; New Victoria Publishers; Read 'n Run Books; Scojtia Publishing Company, Inc.; Sunstone Press; University of Utah Press; Woodsong Graphics Inc.

Young Adult/Teen. Alaska Nature Press-Publishers; Bookmakers Guild Inc.; Borealis Press; Council for Indian Education; Cross-Cultural Communications; Davenport Publishers, May; Double M Press; Dragon's Den Publishing; Esoterica Press; Haypenny Press; Homestead Publishing; Hyperion Press Limited; Long Publishing Co., Hendrick; Metamorphous Press; Mosaic Press; New Seed Press; Our Child Press; Pando Publications; Pocahontas Press, Inc.; Porcupine's Quill, Inc.; Read 'n Run Books; Satchell's Publishing; Scojtia Publishing Company, Inc.; Sea Fog Press, Inc.; Shoe Tree Press; Star Books, Inc.; Tudor Publishers, Inc.; W W. Publications; Women's Press; Woodsong Graphics Inc.

Commercial Publishers

Adventure. Bantam/Doubleday Books, Inc.; Bethany House Publishers; Bouregy & Company, Inc., Thomas; Branden Publishing Co.; Cloverdale Press Inc.; Crown Publishers, Inc.; Dell Publishing; Fawcett; Fearon Education; Gospel Publishing House; Harlequin Enterprises, Ltd.; Holiday House, Inc.; Holloway House Publishing Company; Holt and Company, Henry; Horizon Publishers and Dist., Inc.; Naval Institute Press; Pocket Books; Random House, Inc.; St. Martin's Press; Scribner's Sons, Charles; Smith, Gibbs, Publisher; Stoddart; Vesta Publications, Ltd; Villard Books; Walker and Company; Warner Books; William Morrow and Company, Inc.; Worldwide Library; Zebra Books; Zondervan

Canada. Doubleday Canada Limited; Harlequin Enterprises, Ltd.; Macmillan of Canada; Stoddart; Worldwide Library

Confession. St. Martin's Press

Contemporary. Ballatine Books; Bantam/Doubleday Books, Inc.; Blair, Publisher, John F.; Bookcraft, Inc.; Branden Publishing Co.; Carroll & Graf Publishers, Inc.; Crown Publishers, Inc.; Dell Publishing; Fearon Education; Harvest House Publishers; Holiday House, Inc.; Holloway House Publishing Company; Holt and Company, Henry; Houghton Mifflin Company; Knopf Alfred A.; Louisiana State University Press; Morrow and Company, Inc., William; Pocket Books; Random House, Inc.; St. Martin's Press; Scribner's Sons, Charles; Sierra Club Books; Smith, Gibbs, Publisher; Summit Books; University of Minnesota Press; Vesta Publications, Ltd; Villard Books; Warner Books; Zebra Books

Erotica. Carroll & Graf Publishers, Inc.; Pocket Books; St. Martin's Press

Ethnic. Bantam/Doubleday Books, Inc.; Branden Publishing Co.; Fearon Education; Holloway House Publishing Company; Pocket Books; Saint Martin's Press; University of Minnesota Press; Vesta Publications, Ltd

Experimental. Holloway House Publishing Company; St. Martin's Press; Smith, Gibbs, Publisher; University of Minnesota Press; Vesta Publications, Ltd; William Morrow and Company, Inc.

Faction. Vesta Publications, Ltd

Fantasy. Avon Books; Baen Books; Bantam Spectra Books/Foundation Books; Bantam/Doubleday Books, Inc.; Berkley/Ace Science Fiction; Carroll & Graf Publishers, Inc.; Cloverdale Press Inc.; Daw Books, Inc.; Del Rey Books; Delacorte/Dell Books for Young Readers; Doubleday-Foundation Books; Gospel Publishing House; Holloway House Publishing Company; Iron Crown Enterprises, Inc.; New American Library; Pocket Books; Popular Library; St. Martin's Press; Tor Books; TSR, Inc.; University of Minnesota Press; Vesta Publications, Ltd; Warner Books; Zondervan

Feminist. Academy Chicago Publishers; Ballatine Books; Bantam/Doubleday Books, Inc.; Braziller, Inc., George; Holt and Company, Henry; Morrow and Company, Inc., William; St. Martin's Press; Scribner's Sons, Charles; Summit Books; University of Minnesota Press; Vesta Publications, Ltd.

Gay. Bantam/Doubleday Books, Inc.; New American Library; St. Martin's Press; University of Minnesota Press; William Morrow and Company, Inc.

Historical. Academy Chicago Publishers; Avon Books; Ballatine Books; Bantam/Doubleday Books, Inc.; Bookcraft, Inc.; Branden Publishing Co.; Broadman Press; Cloverdale Press Inc.; Crown Publishers, Inc.; Dell Publishing; Fawcett; Fearon Education; Godine, Publisher, Inc., David R.; Gospel Publishing House; Harvest House Publishers; Holloway House Publishing Company; Holt and Company, Henry; Horizon Publishers and Dist., Inc.; Leisure Books; Naval Institute Press; New American Library; Pocket Books; Presidio Press; Random House, Inc.; Stemmer House Publishers, Inc.; Summit Books; University of Minnesota Press; Vesta Publications, Ltd; Villard Books; William Morrow and Company, Inc.; Winston Derek Publishers; Zebra Books; Zondervan

Horror. Avon Books; Bantam/Doubleday Books, Inc.; Cloverdale Press Inc.; Crown Publishers, Inc.; Daw Books, Inc.; Dell Publishing; Dorchester Publishing Co., Inc.; Doubleday-Foundation Books; Holloway House Publishing Company; Leisure Books; Morrow and Company, Inc., William; New American Library; Pocket Books; Popular Library; Scribner's Sons, Charles; TSR, Inc.; Villard Books; Walker and Company; Warner Books; Wildstar Books/Empire Books; Zebra Books

Humor/Satire. Bantam/Doubleday Books, Inc.; Broadman Press; Crown Publishers, Inc.; Doubleday Canada Limited; Gospel Publishing House; Harvest House Publishers; Holt and Company, Henry; Horizon Publishers and Dist., Inc.; Larksdale; Morrow and Company, Inc., William; Pocket Books; Potter, Inc., Clarkson N.; Price Stern Sloan, Inc.; St. Martin's Press; Scribner's Sons, Charles; Smith, Gibbs, Publisher; Summit Books; Vesta Publications, Ltd; Villard Books

Juvenile. Ace Charter Books; Atheneum Books for Children; Bethany House Publishers; Bradbury Press, Inc.; Broadman Press; Camelot Books; Childrens Press; Child's World, Inc., The; Clarion Books; Crowell Junior Books, T.Y.; Delacorte/Dell Books for Young Readers; Dell Publishing; Dial Books for Young Readers; Doubleday Canada Limited; Eakin Press; Farrar, Straus & Giroux; Field Publications; Gemstone Books; Godine, Publisher, Inc., David R.; Gospel Publishing House; Grosset and Dunlap, Inc.; Harcourt Brace Jovanovich; Harper & Row Junior Books Group; Herald Press; Holiday House, Inc.; Holt and Company, Henry; Horizon Publishers and Dist., Inc.; Interlink Publishing Group, Inc.; Joy Street Books; Knopf Books for Young Readers; Larksdale; Lion Publishing Corporation; Lippincott Junior Books, J. B.; Little, Brown and Co. Children's Books; Lodestar Books; Lucas/Evans Books; McElderry Books, Margaret K.; Macmillan Children's Books; Morrow Junior Books; Multnomah; Orchard Books; Pantheon Books; Philomel Books; Potter, Inc., Clarkson N.; Prentice-Hall Books for Young Readers; Price Stern Sloan, Inc.; St. Paul Books and Media; Scribner's Sons, Charles, Books for Young Readers; Trillium Press; Troll Associates; Vesta Publications, Ltd; Western Producer Prairie Books; Western Publishing Company, Inc.; Whitman & Company, Albert; Winston Derek Publishers; Yearling; Zolotow Books, Charlotte

Lesbian. Morrow and Company, Inc., William; St. Martin's Press; University of Minnesota Press

Mainstream. Avon Books; Branden Publishing Co.; Carroll & Graf Publishers, Inc.; Crown Publishers, Inc.; Doubleday Canada Limited; Eriksson, Publisher, Paul S.; Holloway House Publishing Company; Holt and Company, Henry; Horizon Publishers and Dist., Inc.; Houghton Mifflin Company; Larksdale; Louisiana State University Press; Macmillan of Canada; Macmillan Pubishing Co., Inc.; Pocket Books; Popular Library; Putnam's Sons, G.P.; Random House, Inc.; Summit Books; Tor Books; Vesta Publications, Ltd; Villard Books; Warner Books; Zondervan

Military/War. Avon Books; Bantam/Doubleday Books, Inc.; Branden Publishing Co.; Cloverdale Press Inc.; Crown Publishers, Inc.; Dell Publishing; Holloway House Publishing Company; Horizon Publishers and Dist., Inc.; Larksdale; Naval Institute Press; Pocket Books; Popular Library; Presidio Press; Vesta Publications, Ltd; Warner Books; Zebra Books

Preschool/Picture Book. Atheneum Books for Children; Farrar, Straus & Giroux; Four Winds Press; Grosset and Dunlap, Inc.; Harcourt Brace Jovanovich; Harper & Row Junior Books Group; Harvest House Publishers; Joy Street Books; Knopf Books for Young Readers; McElderry Books, Margaret K.; Morrow Junior Books; Multnomah; Philomel Books; Prentice-Hall Books for Young Readers; St. Paul Books and Media; Scribner's Sons, Charles, Books for Young Readers; Troll

Associates; Vesta Publications, Ltd; Warner Books; Western Publishing Company, Inc.

Psychic/Supernatural/Occult. Avon Books; Bantam/Doubleday Books, Inc.; Cloverdale Press Inc.; Dell Publishing; Fawcett; Pocket Books; St. Martin's Press; Vesta Publications, Ltd; Wildstar Books/Empire Books; Winston Derek Publishers

Regional. Bethany House Publishers; Blair, Publisher, John F.; Fearon Education; Interlink Publishing Group, Inc.; Texas Monthly Press; Vesta Publications, Ltd

Religious/Inspirational. Abingdon Press; Accent Books; Ballantine/Epiphany Books; Bantam/Doubleday Books, Inc.; Bethany House Publishers; Bookcraft, Inc.; Broadman Press; Crossway Books; Gospel Publishing House; Harvest House Publishers; Herald Press; Horizon Publishers and Dist., Inc.; Larksdale; Lion Publishing Corporation; Multnomah; St. Martin's Press; Tyndale House Publishers; Vesta Publications, Ltd; Winston Derek Publishers; Zondervan

Romance. Bantam/Doubleday Books, Inc.; Bethany House Publishers; Bookcraft, Inc.; Bouregy & Company, Inc., Thomas; Branden Publishing Co.; Crown Publishers, Inc.; Dorchester Publishing Co., Inc.; Fearon Education; Harlequin Enterprises, Ltd.; Harvest House Publishers; Heartfire Romance; Holloway House Publishing Company; Horizon Publishers and Dist., Inc.; Leisure Books; Loveswept; New American Library; Pocket Books; Popular Library; St. Martin's Press; Silhouette Books; Vesta Publications, Ltd; Villard Books; Walker and Company; Warner Books; Wildstar Books/Empire Books; William Morrow and Company, Inc.; Zebra Books

Science Fiction. Avon Books; Baen Books; Bantam Spectra Books/Foundation Books; Bantam/Doubleday Books, Inc.; Berkley/Ace Science Fiction; Carroll & Graf Publishers, Inc.; Cloverdale Press Inc.; Crown Publishers, Inc.; Daw Books, Inc.; Del Rey Books; Dorchester Publishing Co., Inc.; Doubleday Canada Limited; Doubleday-Foundation Books; Fearon Education; Holloway House Publishing Company; Horizon Publishers and Dist., Inc.; Iron Crown Enterprises, Inc.; Morrow and Company, Inc., William; New American Library; Popular Library; St. Martin's Press; Tor Books; TSR, Inc.; University of Minnesota Press; Vesta Publications, Ltd; Warner Books; Zondervan

Short Story Collection. Branden Publishing Co.; Braziller, Inc., George; Doubleday-Foundation Books; Fearon Education; Louisiana State University Press; Macmillan of Canada; Random House, Inc.; Resource Publications, Inc.; Smith, Gibbs, Publisher; University of Georgia Press; University of Minnesota Press; Vesta Publications, Ltd

Suspense/Mystery. Academy Chicago Publishers; Bantam/Doubleday Books, Inc.; Bethany House Publishers; Branden Publishing Co.; Carroll & Graf Publishers, Inc.; Cloverdale Press Inc.; Dell Publishing; Dembner Books; Doubleday Canada Limited; Fawcett; Fearon Education; Godine, Publisher, Inc., David R.; Gospel Publishing House; Holloway House Publishing Company; Holt and Company, Henry; Houghton Mifflin Company; Knopf Alfred A.; Macmillan of Canada; Mysterious Press, The; New American Library; Pocket Books; Random House, Inc.; St. Martin's Press; Scribner's Sons, Charles; Stoddart; Summit Books; Tor Books; Vesta Publications, Ltd; Villard Books; Walker and Company; Warner Books; Wildstar Books/Empire Books; William Morrow and Company, Inc.; Worldwide Library; Zebra Books; Zondervan

Translations. Academy Chicago Publishers; Ace Charter Books; Branden Publishing Co.; Braziller, Inc., George; Holt and Company, Henry; Interlink Publishing Group, Inc.; Morrow and Company, Inc., William; Smith, Gibbs, Publisher; Summit Books; University of Minnesota Press; Vesta Publications, Ltd

Western. Avon Books; Bookcraft, Inc.; Bouregy & Company, Inc., Thomas; Cloverdale Press Inc.; Evans and Co., Inc., M.; Fearon Education; Holloway House Publishing Company; Jameson Books; Leisure Books; New American Library; Popular Library; Tor Books; Walker and Company; Warner Books; Wildstar Books/Empire Books

Young Adult/Teen. Archway Paperbacks; Atheneum Books for Children; Avon Books; Bantam/Doubleday Books, Inc.; Bradbury Press, Inc.; Broadman Press; Clarion Books; Cloverdale Press Inc.; Delacorte/Dell Books for Young Readers; Dell Publishing; Evans and Co., Inc., M.; Fearon Education; Field Publications; Gospel Publishing House; Harcourt Brace Jovanovich; Harper & Row Junior Books Group; Herald Press; Holt and Company, Henry; Horizon Publishers and Dist., Inc.; Knopf Books for Young Readers; Larksdale; Lion Publishing Corporation; Lodestar Books; Lucas/Evans Books; McElderry Books, Margaret K.; Morrow Junior Books; Multnomah; Orchard Books; Pantheon Books; Philomel Books; Point Books; Prentice-Hall Books for Young Readers; St. Paul Books and Media; Scribner's Sons, Charles, Books for Young Readers; Stoddart; Trillium Press; Troll Associates; Vesta Publications, Ltd; Walker and Company; Western Producer Prairie Books; Winston Derek Publishers

Literary Agents

Adventure. Amsterdam Agency, Marcia; Authors' Marketing Services Ltd.; Curtis Associates, Inc., Richard; Farwestern Consultants Literary Agency; Garon-Brooke Associates, Inc., Jay; JCA

Literary Agency, Inc.; Kearns & Orr Associates; Lampack Agency, Inc., Peter; Lee Literary Agency, The L. Harry; Lighthouse Literary Agency; Maximilian Becker; Singer Media Corporation; Stern Associates, Charles M.; Swanson, Inc., H.N.; Warren Literary Agency, James; Watt and Associates, Sandra

Contemporary. Authors' Marketing Services Ltd.; Kroll Agency, Lucy; Lighthouse Literary Agency; Lincoln Literary Agency, Ray; Literary/Business Associates; Protter, Literary Agent, Susan Ann; Schwartz, Arthur P.; Southern Writers, Inc.; Spieler Literary Agency, F. Joseph

Ethnic. Crown International Literature and Arts, Bonnie R.; Farwestern Consultants Literary Agency; Writers' Productions

Fantasy. Allen Literary Agency, James; Butler, Art & Literary Agent, Jane; Collier Associates; Curtis Associates, Inc., Richard; Farwestern Consultants Literary Agency; Herner Rights Agency, Susan; Jarvis & Co., Inc., Sharon; Lillienstein, Maxwell J.; Multimedia Product Development, Inc.; Protter, Literary Agent, Susan Ann; Schaffner Agency, Inc.; Seligman Literary Agency, Lynn; Spatt, Esq., David M.; Vicinanza, Ltd., Ralph M.

Feminist. Flannery, White & Stone

Gay. Flannery, White & Stone; Rees Literary Agency, Helen; Watt and Associates, Sandra

Historical. Allen Literary Agency, James; Butler, Art & Literary Agent, Jane; Carvainis Agency, Inc., Maria; Cohen, Inc., Ruth; Collier Associates; Lee Literary Agency, The L. Harry; Lillienstein, Maxwell J.; Multimedia Product Development, Inc.; Nugent & Associates, Inc.; Schwartz, Arthur P.; Siegel Agency, Bobbe; Southern Writers, Inc.; Spieler Literary Agency, F. Joseph; Warren Literary Agency, James; Wieser & Wieser; Zeckendorf Associates, Susan

Horror. Allan Agency, Lee; Allen Literary Agency, James; Amsterdam Agency, Marcia; Authors' Marketing Services Ltd.; Browne Ltd., Pema; Butler, Art & Literary Agent, Jane; Ellenberg Literary Agent/Consultant, Ethan; Estrada Literary Agency; Farwestern Consultants Literary Agency; Garon-Brooke Associates, Inc., Jay; Herner Rights Agency, Susan; Hubbs Literary Agency, Yvonne; Jarvis & Co., Inc., Sharon; JCA Literary Agency, Inc.; Kearns & Orr Associates; Lee Literary Agency, The L. Harry; Lowenstein Associates; Manus Literary Agency Inc., Janet Wilkens; Protter, Literary Agent, Susan Ann; Snell Literary Agency, Michael; Spatt, Esq., David M.; Swanson, Inc., H.N.; Vicinanza, Ltd., Ralph M.; Ware Literary Agency, John A.; Warren Literary Agency, James; Zeckendorf Associates, Susan

Humor/Satire. Amsterdam Agency, Marcia; Hilton Literary Agency, Alice; Lee Literary Agency, The L. Harry; Lincoln Literary Agency, Ray; Warren Literary Agency, James; Watt and Associates, Sandra

Juvenile. Casselman Literary Agency, Martha; Clark Literary Agency, SJ; Cohen, Inc., Ruth; Hilton Literary Agency, Alice; Kouts, Literary Agent, Barbara S.; Lewis Agency, The Norma; Lincoln Literary Agency, Ray; Manus Literary Agency Inc., Janet Wilkens; Mews Books Ltd.; Porcelain Agency, Sidney; Singer Literary Agency Inc., Evelyn; Spieler Literary Agency, F. Joseph; Stern Associates, Charles M.; Sternig Literary Agency, Larry; Wald Associates, Inc., Mary Jack

Mainstream. Allen Literary Agency, James; Amsterdam Agency, Marcia; Authors' Marketing Services Ltd.; Axelrod Agency, Inc., The; Bloom Agency, Harry; Brod Literary Agency, Ruth Hagy; Browne Ltd., Pema; Carvainis Agency, Inc., Maria; Casselman Literary Agency, Martha; Columbia Literary Assocs., Inc.; Cooper Associates, Inc., Bill; Cornfield Literary Agency, Robert; Crown International Literature and Arts, Bonnie R.; Dijkstra Literary Agency, Sandra; Dorese Agency, The; Ellison, Inc., Nicholas; Farquharson Ltd., John; Fishbein Ltd., Frieda; Flannery, White & Stone; Garon-Brooke Associates, Inc., Jay; Gartenberg, Literary Agent, Max; Gelles-Cole Literary Enterprises; Gersh Agency, The; Goldberg Literary Agents, Inc., Lucianne S.; Gordon Literary Agency, Charlotte; Herner Rights Agency, Susan; Hill Associates, Frederick; Hilton Literary Agency, Alice; Hubbs Literary Agency, Yvonne; Hull House Literary Agency; Jarvis & Co., Inc., Sharon; Jason Enterprises, Inc., Asher D.; Jet Literary Associates, Inc.; Kaltman Literary Agency, Larry; Kidde, Hoyt & Picard; Klinger, Inc., Harvey; Kouts, Literary Agent, Barbara S.; Robert Lantz/Joy Harris Literary Agency, The Robert; Lazear Agency Incorporated, The; Lee Literary Agency, The L. Harry; Lewis Agency, The Norma; Lillienstein, Maxwell J.; Lincoln Literary Agency, Ray; Los Angeles Literary Associates; Manus Literary Agency Inc., Janet Wilkens; Maximilian Becker; McBride Literary Agency, Margaret; Multimedia Product Development, Inc.; Naggar Literary Agency, Inc., Jean V.; Nathan, Ruth; Nelson Literary Agency, B.K.; Nolan Literary Agency, The Betsy; Nugent & Associates, Inc.; Oscard Associates, Fifi; Quicksilver Books, Inc.; Rees Literary Agency, Helen; Robbins Office, Inc., The; SBC Enterprises, Inc.; Scagnetti, Jack; Schaffner Agency, Inc.; Schulman Literary Agency, Inc., Susan; Schwartz, Arthur P.; Seligman Literary Agency, Lynn; Siegel Agency, Bobbe; Spieler Literary Agency, F. Joseph; Stepping Stone; Stern Associates, Charles M.; Sternig Literary Agency, Larry; Swanson, Inc., H.N.; Targ Literary Agency, Inc., Roslyn; Wald Associates, Inc., Mary Jack; Ware Literary Agency, John A.; Warren Literary Agency, James; Waterside Productions, Inc.; Weimann Associates, Frank; Weiner Liter-

Schaffner Agency, Inc.; Schulman Literary Agency, Inc., Susan; Schwartz, Arthur P.; Seligman Literary Agency, Lynn; Siegel Agency, Bobbe; Spieler Literary Agency, F. Joseph; Stepping Stone; Stern Associates, Charles M.; Sternig Literary Agency, Larry; Swanson, Inc., H.N.; Targ Literary Agency, Inc., Roslyn; Wald Associates, Inc., Mary Jack; Ware Literary Agency, John A.; Warren Literary Agency, James; Waterside Productions, Inc.; Weimann Associates, Frank; Weiner Literary Agency, Cherry; Wieser & Wieser; Wreschner, Authors' Representative, Ruth; Yost Associates, Mary

Military/War. Collier Associates; Lee Literary Agency, The L. Harry

Novella. Blake Group Literary Agency, The; Borchardt Inc., Georges; Brandt & Brandt Literary Agents, Inc.; Chester Literary Agency, The Linda; Gusay Literary Agency, Charlotte; King, Literary, Daniel P.; Marshall Agency, The Evan; Thompson Talent Agency; Wald Associates, Inc., Mary Jack; Warren Literary Agency, James

Preschool/Picture Book. Browne Ltd., Pema; Mews Books Ltd.; Sternig Literary Agency, Larry

Psychic/Supernatural/Occult. Clark Literary Agency, SJ; Farwestern Consultants Literary Agency; Jarvis and Co., Inc., Sharon; Lee Literary Agency, The L. Harry; Literarybusiness Associates

Regional. Crown International Literature and Arts, Bonnie R.; Southern Writers, Inc.; Spatt, Esq., David M.; Writers' Productions

Religious/Inspirational. Stepping Stone

Romance. Browne Ltd., Pema; Carvainis Agency, Inc., Maria; Cohen, Inc., Ruth; Collier Associates; Columbia Literary Assocs., Inc.; Curtis Associates, Inc., Richard; Estrada Literary Agency; Farwestern Consultants Literary Agency; Garon-Brooke Associates, Inc., Jay; Herner Rights Agency, Susan; Hilton Literary Agency, Alice; Hubbs Literary Agency, Yvonne; Jason Enterprises, Inc., Asher D.; Kearns And Orr; Kidde, Hoyt & Picard; King, Literary, Daniel P.; Lee Literary Agency, The L. Harry; Lillienstein, Maxwell J.; Lowenstein Associates; Marshall Agency, The Evan; Multimedia Product Development, Inc.; Schwartz, Arthur P.; Singer Media Corporation; Southern Writers, Inc.; Stern Associates, Charles M.; Weiner Literary Agency, Cherry; Wreschner, Authors' Representative, Ruth

Science Fiction. Allan Agency, Lee; Allen Literary Agency, James; Amsterdam Agency, Marcia; Bova Literary Agency, The Barbara; Butler, Art & Literary Agent, Jane; Curtis Associates, Inc., Richard; Ellenberg Literary Agent/Consultant, Ethan; Herner Rights Agency, Susan; Hilton Literary Agency, Alice; Jarvis & Co., Inc., Sharon; Kearns & Orr Associates; King, Literary, Daniel P.; Lazear Agency Incorporated, The; Lillienstein, Maxwell J.; Lincoln Literary Agency, Ray; Maximilian Becker; Multimedia Product Development, Inc.; Naggar Literary Agency, Inc., Jean V.; Protter, Literary Agent, Susan Ann; Quicksilver Books, Inc.; Schaffner Agency, Inc.; Schwartz, Arthur P.; Siegel Agency, Bobbe; Spatt, Esq., David M.; Sternig Literary Agency, Larry; Vicinanza, Ltd., Ralph M.; Warren Literary Agency, James; Weiner Literary Agency, Cherry; Wreschner, Authors' Representative, Ruth

Short Story Collections. Blake Group Literary Agency, The; Borchardt Inc., Georges; Brandt & Brandt Literary Agents, Inc.; Chester Literary Agency, The Linda; Gusay Literary Agency, Charlotte; Hilton Literary Agency, Alice; King, Literary, Daniel P.; Lazear Agency Incorporated, The; Macdonough, Richard P., Literary Agent; Thompson Talent Agency; Wald Associates, Inc., Mary Jack; Warren Literary Agency, James; Watt and Associates, Sandra

Suspense/Mystery. Allan Agency, Lee; Allen Literary Agency, James; Amsterdam Agency, Marcia; Axelrod Agency, Inc., The; Bova Literary Agency, The Barbara; Brod Literary Agency, Ruth Hagy; Butler, Art & Literary Agent, Jane; Carvainis Agency, Inc., Maria; Clark Literary Agency, SJ; Cohen, Inc., Ruth; Collier Associates; Curtis Associates, Inc., Richard; Estrada Literary Agency; Farquharson Ltd., John; Farwestern Consultants Literary Agency; Garon-Brooke Associates, Inc., Jay; Gartenberg, Literary Agent, Max; Gordon Literary Agency, Charlotte; Herner Rights Agency, Susan; Hubbs Literary Agency, Yvonne; Jason Enterprises, Inc., Asher D.; JCA Literary Agency, Inc.; Kearns & Orr Associates; King, Literary, Daniel P.; Lazear Agency Incorporated, The; Lee Literary Agency, The L. Harry; Literary/Business Associates; Manus Literary Agency Inc., Janet Wilkens; Maximilian Becker; Multimedia Product Development, Inc.; Naggar Literary Agency, Inc., Jean V.; Nugent & Associates, Inc.; Porcelain Agency, Sidney; Protter, Literary Agent, Susan Ann; Quicksilver Books, Inc.; Rees Literary Agency, Helen; Rose Literary Agency, The Mitchell; Siegel Agency, Bobbe; Singer Media Corporation; Snell Literary Agency, Michael; Spatt, Esq., David M.; Spitzer Literary Agency, Philip G.; Stern Associates, Charles M.; Sternig Literary Agency, Larry; Ware Literary Agency, John A.; Warren Literary Agency, James; Watt and Associates, Sandra; Wreschner, Authors' Representative, Ruth; Zeckendorf Associates, Susan

Western. Allan Agency, Lee; Carvainis Agency, Inc., Maria; Curtis Associates, Inc., Richard; Farwestern Consultants Literary Agency; Lee Literary Agency, The L. Harry

Young Adult/Teen. Amsterdam Agency, Marcia; Browne Ltd., Pema; Carvainis Agency, Inc., Maria; Cohen, Inc., Ruth; Gordon Literary Agency, Charlotte; Lazear Agency Incorporated, The; Lewis Agency, The Norma; Lighthouse Literary Agency; Lincoln Literary Agency, Ray; Mews Books Ltd.; Stewart Agency, Jo

Markets Index

A

Abbey 118
Abel Literary Agency, Inc., Dominick 544
Abingdon Press 459
Aboriginal Science Fiction 322
Academy Chicago Publishers 459
Accent Books 460
Ace Charter Books 460
ACM, (Another Chicago Magazine) 118
Act One Creativity Center Fellowships 505
ACTA Victoriana 118
Acton and Dystel Inc. 544
Acton, Inc., Edward J. (see Acton and Dystel, Inc. 544).
Acumen 312
Adara 119
Adrift 119
Adroit Expression, The 119
Advocacy Press 394
Aegean Review 119
Aegina Press, Inc. 395
Aerial 120
After Hours 120
Agni 120
Aim Magazine 322
Aim Magazine Short Story Contest 505
Alabama Literary Review 121
Alabama State Council on the Arts Individual Artist Fellowship 505
Alaska Nature Press-Publishers 395
Alaska Quarterly Review 121
Alaska State Council on the Arts Literary Arts Fellowships 505
Albany Review, The 121
Albee Foundation Fellowship, Edward F. 505
Alberta Writing for Young People Competition, The 505
Alchemist, The 122
Aldebaran 122
Algren Award for Short Fiction, The Nelson 506
Allan Agency, Lee 544
Allegheny Review 122
Allegheny Review Awards 506
Allen Literary Agency, James 544
Aloha 322
Alpha Beat Soup 124
Alternative Fiction & Poetry 124
Alyson Publications, Inc. 395
Amaranth 124
Amaranth Review, The 124
Amateur Writers Journal 125
Ambergris 125
Ambergris Fiction and Poetry Contest 506
Ambit 312
Amelia 125
Amelia Magazine Awards 506
American Accent Short Story Magazine 323
American Atheist 323
American Atheist Press 396
American Citizen Italian Press, The 324
American Dane 126
American Dane 324
American Fiction Vol II 506
American Health Body Story Contest 506
American Newspaper Carrier, The 324
American Squaredance 325
American Voice, The 126
Americas Review, The 126
Amherst Review, The 127
Ammonite 312
Amsterdam Agency, Marcia 545
An Seanrvd 312
Analog Science Fiction/Science Fact 325
Anderson Short Fiction Prize, Sherwood 506
Anglican Magazine, The 127
Angoff Awards, Charles 507
Angus & Robertson/Collins Publishers Australia 500
Ann Arbor 325
Annick Press Ltd. 396
Another Chicago Press 396
Another Way 396
Ansuda Publications 397
Antaeus 127
Antietam Review 127
Antietam Review Literary Award 507
Antigonish Review, The 128
Antigruppo 312
Antioch Review 128
Apaeros 128
Appalachian Heritage 129
Apple Books 460
Applezaba Press 397
Aquarius 312
Archway Paperbacks 460
Arete 325
Argonaut 129
Ariadne Press 397
Arizona Authors' Association Annual Literary Contest 507
Arizona Coast 326
Arizona Commission on the Arts Creative Writing Fellowships 507
Arnazella 129
Arsenal Pulp Press 397
Art Brigade 129
Art Times 326
Arte Publico Press 398
Artemis 130
Artful Dodge 130
Arthritis Today 326
Art:Mag 130
ASF Translation Prize 507
Ashton Scholastic Ltd. 452
Asimov's Science Fiction Magazine, Isaac 326
Associate Reformed Presbyterian, The 327
Asymptotical World, The 131
Atalantik 131
Atavachron and All Our Yesterdays 131
Athena Incognito Magazine 132
Athenaeum Literary Award 507
Atheneum Books for Children 460
Atlanta Singles Magazine 327
Atlantic Advocate, The 327
Atlantic Monthly 327
Atlantic Salmon Journal 328
Atlantis (British Columbia) 132
Atlantis (Nova Scotia) 132
Atma Ram and Sons 501
Atrocity 133
Auguries 312
Aura Literary/Arts Review 133
Authors' Marketing Services Ltd. 545
Avon Books 461
Avon Flare Young Adult Novel Competition 507
AWP Award Series in Short Fiction 508
AWP Award Series in the Novel 508
Axe Factory Review 133
Axelrod Agency, Inc., The 545
Azorean Express, The 133

alive now! 322

B

Baby Sue 134
Bad Haircut 134
Bad Newz 134
Baen Books 461
Ball State University Forum 134
Ballantine/Epiphany Books 461
Ballatine Books 462
Balloon Life 328
Baltimore Jewish Times 328
Banff Writing Residency 508
Banned Books 398
Bantam Spectra Books/Foundation Books 462
Bantam/Doubleday Books, Inc. 462
Barlow Press 398
Batchelder Award, Mildred L. 508
Bates Short Story Competition, H.E. 508
Bear 328
Beckett Baseball Card Monthly 329
Beil, Publisher, Inc., Frederic C. 399
Bella Figura, La 135
Bellagio Center Residency 508
Bellingham Review, The 135
Bellowing Ark 135
Beloit Fiction Journal 135
Bennett Fellowship, George 508
Berger Associates, Bill 545
Berkley Publishing Group, The 462
Berkley/Ace Science Fiction 463
Bernstein Literary Agency, Meredith 561
"Best First Private Eye Novel" Contest 508
Best of Blurbs Contest 509
Best of Housewife-Writer's Forum: Short Story Rejected by Redbook (or any large market) 509
Bethany House Publishers 463
Beyond ... Science Fiction & Fantasy 136
Biblioteca Di Nova SF, Futuro, Great Works of SF 452
Big Two-Hearted 136
Bike Report 329
Bilingual Press/Editorial Bilingüe 399
Bilingual Review 136
Bitch 136
BkMk Press 399
Black Belt 329
Black Children's Book Award, Irma Simonton 509
Black Hole Literary Review, The 137
Black Ice Margaret Jones Fiction Award 509
Black Jack 138
Black Memorial Prizes, James Tait 509
Black Moss Press 399
Black River Review 138
Black Scholar, The 138
Black Tie Press 400
Black Warrior Review 139
Black Warrior Review Literary Award, The 509
Black Writer Magazine 139
Blackstaff Press, The 501
Blair, Publisher, John F. 463
Blake Group Literary Agency, The 545
Blatant Artifice 139
Blood & Guts Press 400
Bloom Agency, Harry 546
Bloomsbury Review, The 140
Blue Water Review, The 140
Blueline 140
B'nai B'rith International Jewish Monthly, The 329
Boardman Tasker Prize 509
Boates Literary Agency, Reid 546
Bogg 141
Book of Spells, The 141
Book Peddlers of Deephaven 546
Bookcraft, Inc. 464
Bookmakers Guild Inc. 400
Books for All Times, Inc. 400
Boots Romantic Novel of the Year 510
Borchardt Inc., Georges 546
Borealis Press 401
Boston Globe-Horn Book Awards 510
Boston Review 330
Bostonia Magazine 330
Bottom Dog Press 401
Bottomfish Magazine 141
Boulevard 141
Bouregy & Company, Inc., Thomas 464
Bova Literary Agency, The Barbara 546
Bowbender 330
Bowhunter Magazine 331
Boys' Life 331
Bradbury Press, Inc. 464
Bradley's Fantasy Magazine, Marion Zimmer 142
Brandeis University Creative Arts Awards 510
Branden Publishing Co. 465
Brandt & Brandt Literary Agents, Inc. 546
Brave New Word 312
Braziller, Inc., George 465
Bread 331
Breakthrough! 142
Breitenbush Books, Inc. 401
Bressani Prize, The F.G. 510
Bright Ring Publishing 401
Brilliant Star 142
Bristlecone 143
Broadman Press 465
Brod Literary Agency, Ruth Hagy 546
Brown Inc., Ned 547
Brown, Ltd., Curtis 547
Browne Ltd., Pema 547
Bryans & Bryans 402
Buffalo Spree Magazine 332
Bugle 332
Bumbershoot Written Works Competition 510
Bunting Institute Fellowship 510
Burning Books 402
Bush Artist Fellowships 510
Butler, Art & Literary Agent, Jane 547
Bvi-Pacifica Newsletter 143
Byline 143
Byline Magazine Literary Awards 511

C

Cache Review 144
Cadmus Editions 402
Caesura 144
Caffe, Il 144
California Writers' Roundtable Annual Writing Contests 511
Callaloo 144
Calliope 145
Calyx Books 402
Camelot Books 465
Campbell Memorial Award for the Best Science-Fiction Novel of the Year, John W.; 511
Campus Life Magazine 332
Canada Council Governor General's Literary Awards 511
Canadian Author & Bookman 145
Canadian Author & Bookman Students' Creative Writing Contest 511
Canadian Authors Association Literary Award 511
Canadian Fiction Magazine 145
Canadian Fiction Magazine Contributor's Prize 511
Canadian Library Association Book of the Year for Children Award 511
Canadian Messenger 332
Canadian Stage and Arts Publications 402
Capilano Review, The 146
Capper's 333
Caribbean Writer, The 146
Carlton Books 403
Carolina Literary Companion, A 146
Carolina Quarterly 146
Carolina Wren Press 403

Carousel Literary Arts Magazine 147
Carpenter Press 403
Carroll & Graf Publishers, Inc. 466
Carvainis Agency, Inc., Maria 547
Carver Short Story Contest, Raymond 512
Casselman Literary Agency, Martha 547
Cat Fancy 333
Catbird Press 404
Cathedral of Insanity 147
Catholic Forester 333
Cavalier Magazine 334
Cave Books 404
CCL Student Writing Contest 512
Ceilidh 147
Cencrastus 312
Central Coast Courier 312
Central Park 148
Chakra 148
Chaminade Literary Review 148
Changes 334
Chapter One 149
Chariton Review, The 149
Chattahoochee Prize , The 512
Chattahoochee Review, The 149
Chelsea 149
Chelsea Green Publishing Co. 404
Chesapeake Bay Magazine 334
Chess Life 334
Chester Literary Agency, The Linda 547
Chic 335
Chickadee 335
Child Life 335
Child Study Children's Book Award 512
Child Welfare League of America 404
Children's Book Award, The 512
Children's Digest 335
Children's Playmate 336
Childrens Press 466
Child's World, Inc., The 466
China Books 404
Chips Off the Writer's Block 150
Chiron Review 150
Choplogic 150
Christian Living For Senior Highs 336
Christian Outlook 150
Christmas 336
Christopher Award, The 512
Chrysalis 151
Church Herald, The 336
Church Musician, The 337
Cicada 151
Cimarron Review 151
Cinema Talent International 548
Cintas Fellowship 512
Citadel Press 466
City of Regina Writing Award 512
Clarion Books 466
Clarity Press 405
Clark Literary Agency, SJ 548
Cleis Press 405
Cliffhanger Press 405
Clockwatch Review 152
Clothespin Fever Press 405
Cloverdale Press Inc. 467
Clubhouse 337
Coastal Cruising 337
Cobblestone 338
Cochran's Corner 152
Coe Review, The 152
Cohen, Inc., Ruth 548
Cohen Literary Agency, Hy 548
Cold-Drill Magazine 153
Collages and Bricolages 153
Collier Associates 548
Collin Literary Agent, Frances 548
Colorado Council on the Arts & Humanities Creative Fellowship 513
Colorado Review 153
Colorado-North Review 154
Columbia: A Magazine of Poetry & Prose 154
Columbia Literary Assocs., Inc. 548
Columbus Single Scene 154
Commando 390
Common Lives/Lesbian Lives 155
Commonwealth Club of California 513
Companion in Zeor, A 155
Compost Newsletter 155
Computoredge 338
Concho River Review 156
Conditions 156
Confluence Press Inc. 406
Confrontation 156
Connecticut Commission on the Arts Artist Grants 513
Connecticut Writers League Annual Writing Contest 513
Conseil De La Vie Francaise En Amerique/Prix Champlain (The Champlain Prize) 513
Conspiracy of Silence, The 156
Contact Advertising 338
Contemporary Books 467
Contrast 312
Cook Literary Agency, Inc., Molly Malone 549
Cooper Associates, Inc., Bill 549
Corkscrew Press 406
Cornfield Literary Agency, Robert 549
Cornfield Review 157
Corona 157
Cosmic Landscapes 157
Cosmopolitan Magazine 338
Coteau Books 406
Couch Potato Journal, The 157
Council for Indian Education 406
Council for Wisconsin Writers Annual Writing Contest 513
Country Woman 339
Coydog Review 158
Crab Creek Review 158
Crazyhorse 158
Crazyquilt 159
Creative Artist Grant 513
Creative Arts Book Co. 407
Creative Forum 312
Creative Kids 159
Creative Woman, The 159
Creative with Words Publications 407
Creativity Unlimited Press 407
Crescent Review, The 159
Cricket Magazine 339
Crime Writers' Association Awards 513
Crimson Full Moon, The 160
Cross Timbers Review 160
Cross-Canada Writers' Magazine 160
Cross-Canada Writers' Magazine Editors' Prize 514
Cross-Cultural Communications 407
Crosscurrents 161
Crossing Press, The 408

Can't find a listing? Check pages 318-319 for Other Literary and Small Circulation Magazines, page 392 for Other Commercial Periodicals, pages 454-455 for Other Small Presses, page 503 for Other Commercial Publishers, page 541 for Other Contests or page 572 for Other Agents.

Crossway Books 467
Crowell Junior Books, T.Y. (see Harper & Row Jr. Books) 469
Crown International Literature and Arts, Bonnie R. 549
Crown Publishers, Inc. 469
Crusader Magazine 339
Cube Literary Magazine 161
Cuff Publications Ltd., Harry 408
Curbstone Press 408
Curtis Associates, Inc., Richard 549
Cutbank 161
Cutting Edge Irregular 162

D

Dada Dance Magazine 313
Dalhousie Review, The 162
Dan River Anthology 162
Dan River Press 409
Daniel and Company, Publishers, John 409
darknerve 162
Daughters of Sarah 163
Davenport Publishers, May 409
Davie Literary Agency, Elaine 549
Daw Books, Inc. 469
Dawnwood Press 410
Day Care and Early Education 163
Dayspring Press, Inc. 410
Dead Of Night Magazine 163
Deathrealm 164
Deep South Writers Conference Annual Competition 514
Del Rey Books 469
Delacorte Press Annual Prize for First Young Adult Novel 514
Delacorte/Dell Books for Young Readers 469
Delaware State Arts Council 514
Delirium 164
Dell Publishing 471
Dembner Books 471
Denver Quarterly 164
Descant (Ontario) 165
Descant (Texas) 165
Desert Sun 165
Detective Story Magazine 165
Detroit Jewish News 339
Deviance 166
Devonshire Publishing Co. 410
Dharma Combat 166
Dial Books for Young Readers 471
Dialogue 340
Dijkstra Literary Agency, Sandra 550
Diliman Review 313
Discoveries 340
Djerassi Foundation Resident Artists Program 514
Dog Fancy 340
Dorchester Publishing Co., Inc. 472
Dorese Agency, The 550
Dorland Mountain Arts Colony, Inc. 514
Dos Passos Prize for Literature, John 514
Double M Press 411
Doubleday Books 472
Doubleday Canada Limited 472
Doubleday-Foundation Books 473
Dragon Magazine 340
Dragon's Den Publishing 411
Dream International/Quarterly 166
Dreams & Visions 167
Dreams And Visions: Best Short Story of the Year 514
Drummer 341
Dupree/Miller and Assoc., Inc. 550

E

Eagle's Flight 167
Eakin Press 473
Earth's Daughters 167
Eastern Caribbean Institute 452
Eaton Literary Associates' Literary Awards Program 515
Ecco Press, The 411
Echoes 168
edge magazine 313
Eidos 168
Eighth Mt. Press, The 411
Eldritch Science 168
Eldritch Tales 169
Elephant-Ear, The 169
Ellenberg Literary Agent/Consultant, Ethan 550
Ellery Queen's Mystery Magazine 341
Ellison, Inc., Nicholas 550
Emrys Journal 170
Encounters Magazine 170
Eotu 170
Epoch Magazine 171
Equilibrium Ten 341
Equinews: Serving the Horse Industry 342
Ergo! 171
Eriksson, Publisher, Paul S. 473
Erotic Fiction Quarterly 171
Esoterica Press 411
Estrada Literary Agency 552
Evangel 342
Evans and Co., Inc., M. 473
Event 171
Evergreen Chronicles, The 172
Excess Press 453
Explorations '90 172
Explorer Magazine 172
Eyster Prizes 515

F

(F.) Lip 173
F.O.C. Review 173
Faber and Faber, Inc. 412
Faces 342
Fag Rag 173
Family Magazine 343
Family, The 342
Fantasy Tales 390
Farmer's Market, The 173
Farquharson Ltd., John 552
Farrar, Straus & Giroux 473
Farwestern Consultants Literary Agency 552
Fasa Corporation 412
Fat Tuesday 174
Fawcett 474
Fear 390
Fearon Education 474
Feminist Baseball 174
Feminist Press at the City University of New York, The 412
Fiction 174
Fiction International 175
Fiction Network Competition 515
Fiction Network Magazine 175
Fiddlehead, The 175
Field Publications 474
Fields, Marje—Rita Scott 552
Fighting Woman News 175
Figment Magazine 176
Fine Arts Work Center in Provincetown Fellowship 515
Fine Madness 176
Firebrand Books 412
Fireweed 176
First 343
First Hand 343
First Stories 177
Fish Memorial Award, Robert L. 515
Fishbein Ltd., Frieda 552
Fisher Award, Dorothy Canfield 515
Five Fingers Review 177
Flannery, White & Stone 552
Flare Books 474
Fling 344
Florida Arts Council/Literature Fellowships 515
Florida Review, The 177
Florida State Writing Competition 515
Flyfisher, The 344
Flyfishing News, Views and Reviews 344
Foley Agency, The 553
Folio 515
Folio: A Literary Journal 177
Foolscap 313
Footwork 178
Foresight 313
Formations Magazine 178
Forum 390
Forum Fabulatorum 313
Foundation for the Advance-

ment of Canadian Letters Author's Awards 516
Four Walls Eight Windows 413
Four Winds Press 475
Fourth Estate 453
Frank 313
Franklin Literary Award, Miles 516
Fred, The 313
Freeway 178
Friend Magazine, The 345
Frontiers 178
Futurific Magazine 345

G

Galactic Discourse 179
Galileo Press, Ltd., The 413
Gallery Magazine 345
Gamut, The 179
Gargoyle Magazine 179
Garland, The 180
Garm Lu 180
Garon-Brooke Associates, Inc., Jay 553
Gartenberg, Literary Agent, Max 553
Gas 180
Gateways 181
Gato Tuerto, El 181
Gay Chicago Magazine 181
Gay Sunshine Press and Leyland Publications 413
Gelles-Cole Literary Enterprises 553
Gemstone Books 475
Gent 345
Gentleman's Companion 346
Georgia Review, The 181
Georgia State Writing Competition 516
Gersh Agency, The 553
Gestalt 182
Gestalt Magazine Fiction Award 516
Gettysburg Review, The 183
Glens Falls Review, The 183
Global Tapestry Journal 313
Gmp Publisher Ltd. 453
Godine, Publisher, Inc., David R. 475
Going Down Swinging 313
Gold Medallion Books Awards 516
Goldberg Literary Agents, Inc., Lucianne S. 553
Golden Isis Magazine 183
Golf Journal 346
Good Housekeeping 346
Goodman Associates 554
Goodman Fielder Wattie Book Award 516
Goose Lane Editions 413
Gordon Literary Agency, Charlotte 554
Gospel Publishing House 475
Gotta Write Network Litmag 183
Grafton Books 501
Grain 184
Grands Prix Du *Journal de Montréal*, Les 516
Grasslands Review 184
Graywolf Press 413
Great Lakes Colleges Association New Writers Awards 516
Great Plains Storytelling & Poetry Reading Contest 517
Great River Review 184
Green Mountains Review 184
Green Street Press, The 414
Greenburger Associates, Sanford J. 554
Greens Magazine 185
Greensboro Review 185
Greensboro Review Literary Awards, *The* 517
Grosset and Dunlap, Inc. 476
Groundswell 185
Grue Magazine 186
Guardian Children's Fiction Award 517
Guernica Editions 414
Guide Magazine 347
Guide, The 346
Gusay Literary Agency, Charlotte 554
Guys 347

H

Hackney Literary Awards 517
Hadassah Magazine 347
Haight Ashbury Literary Journal 186
Hale Limited, Robert 501
Hallmark Publishing Ltd. 501
Halsey Agency, Reece 554
Hambidge Center for Creative Arts and Sciences 517
Hamish Hamilton Ltd. 501
Happiness Holding Tank 186
Harcourt Brace Jovanovich 476
Hard Echo Press Ltd. 453
Hardy—Publisher, Max 414
Harlequin Enterprises, Ltd. 476
Harmony Books 476
Harper & Row Junior Books Group 477
Harper's Magazine 347
Harvest House Publishers 477
Harvest Magazine 186
Harvey for Loving People 348
Haunts 187
Hawaii Pacific Review 187
Hawaii Review 187
Haypenny Press 414
Headline Book Publishing PLC 501
Heart of the Lakes Publishing 415
Heartfire Romance 477
Heartland Journal 188
Heaven Bone 188
Hecate 313
Heinz Literature Prize, Drue 517
Hemingway Days Short Story Competition 517
Hemingway Foundation Award, Ernest 517
Hemkunt 453
Henry Awards, The O. 517
Herald Press 477
Heresies 188
Heritage Press 415
Herman Agency, Inc., The Jeff 554
Hermes House Press 415
Herner Rights Agency, Susan 554
Hibiscus Magazine 188
Hi-Call 348
High Plains Literary Review 189
High Times 348
Highlights for Children 348
Highlights for Children 518
Hilai Residencies 518
Hill Associates, Frederick 555
Hill and Holler 189
Hilton Literary Agency, Alice 555
Hippo 189
Hitchcock's Mystery Magazine, Alfred 349
Hob-Nob 190
Hobo Stew Review 190
Hodder and Stoughton Publishers 501

Can't find a listing? Check pages 318-319 for Other Literary and Small Circulation Magazines, page 392 for Other Commercial Periodicals, pages 454-455 for Other Small Presses, page 503 for Other Commercial Publishers, page 541 for Other Contests or page 572 for Other Agents.

Hodder Fellowship, The Alfred 518
Holiday House, Inc. 478
Holloway House Publishing Company 478
Holt & Company, Henry 478
Home Altar, The 349
Home Life 349
Homestead Publishing 416
Honest Ulsterman, The 314
Honolulu Magazine/Parker Pen Company Fiction Contest 518
Hoof Beats 349
Horizon Publishers & Dist., Inc. 479
Horror 191
Horse Illustrated 350
Hor-Tasy 191
Houghton Mifflin Company 479
Housewife-Writer's Forum 191
Howling Dog 192
Hrafnhoh 314
Hubbard's Writers of the Future Contest, L. Ron 518
Hubbs Literary Agency, Yvonne 555
'Hugo' Award (Science Fiction Achievement Award), The 518
Hull House Literary Agency 555
Humpty Dumpty's Magazine 350
Hustler 350
Hutton Fiction Contest 518
Hyperion Press Limited 416

I

Ice River 192
Ideals Magazine 351
Ikarie Xb 314
Illinois Arts Council Special Assistance Grant and Artist's Fellowship 518
Illinois State University National Fiction Competition 519
Illuminations 314
Impulse Magazine 193
In Touch 351
In Touch for Men 351
In-Between 193
Independence Publishers Inc. 416
Independent Review, The 193
India Currents 351
Indian Life Magazine 352
Indian Literature 314
Indiana Review 193
Indigo 194
Inlet 194
Innisfree 194
Inside 352
Inside Joke 194
Inside Texas Running 352
Insights 352
Interim 195
Interlink Publishing Group, Inc. 479
International Janusz Korzak Literary Competition 519
International Literary Contest 519
International Reading Association Children's Book Awards 519
Intertext 418
Interzone 390
Inverted-A Inc. 416
Iowa Arts Council Literary Awards 519
Iowa Woman 195
Ireland's Own 390
Iron Crown Enterprises, Inc. 480
Iron Magazine 314
Island House 418
Israel-Al 391
Italica Press 418

J

Jab Publishing Fiction Contest 519
Jabberwocky 195
Jacaranda Review 196
Jack and Jill 353
Jackie 391
Jackson Award, Joseph Henry 519
Jam To-Day 196
Jameson Books 480
Japanophile 196
Japanophile Short Story Contest 519
Japan-United States Friendship Commission Prize for the Translation of Japanese Literature 519
Jarvis & Co., Inc., Sharon 555
Jason Enterprises, Inc., Asher D. 555
Jayell Enterprises 418
Jazziminds Magazine 197
JCA Literary Agency, Inc. 556
Jeopardy 197
Jest 197
Jet Literary Associates, Inc. 556
Jewish Currents Magazine 197
Jive, Black Confessions, Black Romance, Bronze Thrills 353
Joseph Ltd., Michael 501
Journal of Polymorphous Perversity 198
Journal of Quantum 'Pataphysics 199
Journal of Regional Criticism 199
Journal, The 198
Joy Street Books 480
Joyeux Erotique 199
Juggler's World 353

K

K 200
Kabbalah Yichud 200
Kafka Prize, The Janet Heidinger 520
Kairos 200
Kaleidoscope 201
Kalliope 201
Kaltman Literary Agency, Larry 556
Kana 201
Kansas Quarterly 203
Kansas Quarterly/Kansas Arts Commission Awards 520
Karamu 203
Kar-Ben, Inc. 418
Karnak House 453
Kearns & Orr Associates 556
Kennebec 203
Kennedy Book Awards, Robert F. 520
Kentucky Arts Council, Al Smith Artists Fellowships 520
Kenyon Review, The 203
Kern Fund Grant, Louisa 520
Khan Prize, Aga 520
Kid City 354
Kidde, Hoyt & Picard 556
Kindergarten Listen 354
Kindred Spirit (see Chiron Review 150)
King, Literary, Daniel P. 556
Kingfisher 204
Kingsway Publications 453
Kiosk 204
Kitchen Table: Women of Color Press 419
Klinger, Inc., Harvey 557
Knights Press 419
Knoll Publishing Co., Inc. 419
Knopf, Alfred A. 480
Knopf Books for Young Readers 481
Kola 204
Kouts, Literary Agent, Barbara S. 557
Kroll Agency, Lucy 557
Kruza Kaleidoscopix, Inc. 420
Kubicek & Associates 420

L

La Kancerkliniko 314
Lactuca 205
Ladies' Home Journal 355
Ladys Circle 355
Lake Effect 205
Lake Street Review 205
Lampack Agency, Inc., Peter 557
Landfall/Caxton Press 314
Language Bridges Contest 520
Language Bridges Quarterly 206
Lantz Office, The (see Robert Lantz/Joy Harris Literary Agency 557)

Lantz/Joy Literary Agency, The Robert 557
Larksdale 481
Larsen/Elizabeth Pomada Literary Agents, Michael 557
Latter-Day Woman Magazine 355
Laurel Review 206
Lawrence Fellowship 521
Lazear Agency Incorporated, The 558
Leacock Medal for Humour, Stephen 521
Leading Edge, The 206
Lee Literary Agency, The L. Harry 558
Left Curve 207
Left-Footed Wombat 207
Legend 207
Leisure Books 481
Lennis, Pablo 208
Letras De Oro Spanish Literary Prizes 521
Letters Magazine 208
Levine Literary Agency Inc., Ellen 558
Lewis Agency, The Norma 558
Libra Publishers, Inc. 420
Library Research Associates, Inc. 421
Lighted Pathway 356
Lighthouse 208
Lighthouse Literary Agency 558
Liguorian 356
Lilith Magazine 208
Lillienstein, Maxwell J. 559
Lime Green Bulldozers (and other related species) 209
Limestone: A Literary Journal 209
Lincoln Literary Agency, Ray 559
Lincoln Springs Press 421
Linington Lineup 209
Lintel 421
Lion Publishing Corporation 481
Lippincott Junior Books, J. B. (see Harper & Row Jr. Books) 482
Literary Lights, Short Story Contests 521
Literary Review, The 210
Literary/Business Associates 559
Literature and Belief Writing Contest 521
Little Balkans Review 210
Little, Brown and Co. Children's Books 482
Little, Brown and Company, Inc. 482
Live 356
Living with Teenagers 357
Llamas Magazine 210
Lodestar Books 482
Loft-McKnight Writers Awards 521
Lollipop Power Books 421
Lollipops Magazine 357
London Review of Books 391
Lone Star 210
Long Publishing Co., Hendrick 422
Long Shot 211
Long Story, The 211
Lookout, The 357
Loonfeather 211
Los Angeles Literary Associates 559
Los Angeles Times Book Prizes 521
Los Hombres Press 422
Lost and Found Times 212
Louisiana Literary Award 521
Louisiana Literature 212
Louisiana State University Press 483
Louisville Review, The 212
Loveswept 483
Lowenstein Associates 559
Ltd. Edition Press 422
Lucas/Evans Books 483
Lucky Heart Books 423
Lutheran Journal, The 357
Lyra 212
Lyra Short Fiction Contest 521

M

M.A. Training 357
m needle m. 213
McBride Literary Agency, Margaret 559
McCall's 358
MacCampbell Inc., Donald 559
McDonald's Literary Achievement Awards for Writing on the Black Experience in America 522
Macdonough, Richard P., Literary Agent 560
Macdowell Colony Residencies 522
McElderry Books, Margaret K. 483
McGinnis Memorial Award, The John H. 522
Macguffin, The 213
McCleod Literary Prize, The Enid 522
Macmillan Children's Books 484
Macmillan Company of Australia, The 501
Macmillan of Canada 484
Macmillan Publishing Co., Inc. 484
Mcphee Gribble Publishers 453
Mademoiselle Fiction Writers Contest 522
Mademoiselle Magazine 358
Madison Review, The 213
Magazine for Christian Youth! 358
Magazine of Fantasy and Science Fiction 359
Mage, The 214
Maggie Award 522
Magic Changes 214
Magpie's Nest, The 314
Maine 359
Mainespring Press 423
Malahat Review, The 214
Malvern Publishing Co. Ltd., The 453
Manoa 214
Manscape 359
Manus Literary Agency Inc., Janet Wilkens 560
Manushi 391
Marang 315
Marcil Literary Agency, Inc., Denise 560
Margin 315
Mark 215
Markson Literary Agency, Elaine 560
Maroverlag 453
Marshall Agency, The Evan 560
Marten Bequest Award, The 522
Marvin Grant, Walter Rumsey 523
Maryland Review, The 215
Maryland State Arts Council Fellowship 523
Massachusetts Artists Fellowship Program 523

Can't find a listing? Check pages 318-319 for Other Literary and Small Circulation Magazines, page 392 for Other Commercial Periodicals, pages 454-455 for Other Small Presses, page 503 for Other Commercial Publishers, page 541 for Other Contests or page 572 for Other Agents.

Mati 215
Mature Living 359
Mature Years 360
Maximilian Becker 560
Meal, Ready-To-Eat 216
Meanjin 315
Melior Publications 423
Meridian Magazine 360
Merlyn's Pen 216
Messenger of the Sacred Heart 360
Metamorphous Press 423
Metcalf Body of Work Award, The Vicky 523
Metcalf Short Story Award, Vicky 523
Metro Singles Lifestyles 361
Mews Books Ltd. 561
Mey-House Books 424
Michigan Quarterly Review 216
Mickle Street Review, The 217
Microcosm 217
Mid-American Review 217
Middle Eastern Dancer 217
Midland Author's Award 523
Midland Review 218
Midstream 361
Military Lifestyle 361
Military Lifestyle Short Story Contest 523
Milkweed Editions 424
Milkweed Editions National Fiction Prize 524
Millay Colony for the Arts 524
Miller Agency, Inc., The Peter 561
Mills & Boon 501
Milner Award, The 524
Milwaukee Magazine 362
Mina Press 424
Minas Tirith Evening-Star 218
Mind Book of the Year—the Allen Land Award 524
Mind in Motion 218
Mind's Eye, The 218
Minnesota Ink 219
Minnesota Review, The 219
Minnesota State Arts Board/ Artists Assistance Fellowship 524
Minnesota Voices Project 524
Miorita, a Journal of Romanian Studies 219
Miraculous Medal, The 219
Mirror-Northern Report, The 219
Miss Lucy Westenra Society of the Undead, The 220
Mississippi Arts Commission Artist Fellowship Grant 524
Mississippi Review 220
Mississippi Valley Review 220
Missouri Review, The 220
Missouri Writers' Biennal 524
Misty Hill Press 424
Modern Liturgy 221
Modern Short Stories 362
Modern Woodmen, The 362
Moment Magazine 362
Momentum 315
Monarch Publications Limited 454
Monroe 363
Montana Arts Council First Book Award 525
Montana Arts Council Individual Artist Fellowship 525
Montana Senior Citizens News 363
Morhaim Literary Agency, Howard 561
Morrow and Company, William 498
Morrow Junior Books 484
Mosaic Press 424
Mother Courage Press 426
Mother Jones Magazine 363
Mountain Laurel, The 221
Moyer Bell Limited 426
Multimedia Product Development, Inc. 561
Multnomah 484
Muse, The 315
Muse's Mill 221
Musicworks 222
My Friend 363
My Weekly 391
My Weekly Story Library 502
Mysterious Press, The 484
Mystery Notebook 222
Mystery Time 222
Mythic Circle, The 222
Mythopoeic Fantasy Award 525

N

Naamat Woman 364
Naggar Literary Agency, Inc., Jean V. 561
Naiad Press, Inc., The 426
Naked Man 223
Nathan, Ruth 562
National Book Awards, Inc. 525
National Book Council/Banjo Awards 525
National Endowment for the Arts Fellowship 525
National Foundation for Advancement in the Arts, Arts Recognition and Talent Search (ARTS) 525
National Jewish Book Awards 525
National Lampoon 364
National Novella Award 526
National Writers Club Annual Novel Writing Contest 526
National Writers Club Annual Short Story Contest 526
National Written & Illustrated by . . . Awards for Students, The 526
Nautical & Aviation Publishing Co. of America Inc., The 427
Naval Institute Press 486
Nebo 223
Nebraska Review, The 223
Nebula® Awards 526
Negative Capability 224
Negative Capability Short Fiction Competition 526
Nelson Literary Agency, B.K. 562
Nene Award, The 526
Neustadt International Prize for Literature 527
New American Library 486
New Blood Magazine 224
New Crucible, The 224
New Delta Review 225
New Directions 427
New England Review and Bread Loaf Quarterly 225
New Era Writing, Art, Photography and Music Contest, The 527
New Frontier 225
New Hampshire State Council on the Arts Individual Artist Fellowship 527
New Hope International 315
New Jersey Author Awards 527
New Jersey State Council on the Arts Prose Fellowship 527
New Laurel Review 226
New Letters Literary Award 527
New Letters Magazine 226
New Methods 226
New Mexico Humanities Review 226
New Moon 227
New Orleans Review 227
New Pathways 227
New Press, The 227
New Quarterly, The 228
New Rivers Press 427
New Seed Press 427
New Victoria Publishers 428
New Virginia Review 228
New York Foundation For-The-Arts Fellowship 527
New York State Edith Wharton Citation of Merit 527
New Yorker, The 365
Newbery Award, John 528
Newest Publishers Ltd. 428
NeWest Review 228
Newmarket Press 486
Nieuwe Koekrand 315
Night Slivers 229
Night Tree Press 428
Nilon Excellence in Minority Fiction Award, Charles H. and N. Mildred 528
Nimrod 229
Ninth Decade 315
No Idea Magazine 229
Noah's Ark 365
Nocturnal Lyric, The 230
Nolan Literary Agency, The Betsy 562

Noma Award for Publishing in Africa, The 528
Nordmanns-Forbundet Translation Grant 528
North American Review, The 230
North American Voice of Fatima, The 230
North Carolina Arts Council Fellowship 528
North Dakota Quarterly 230
North Shore Magazine 365
Northcoast View 365
Northeast 366
Northeast Journal 231
Northern New England Review, The 231
Northern Perspective 315
Northern Review, The 231
Northland Quarterly 231
Northwest Magazine 366
Northwest Review 232
Northwood Institute Alden B. Dow Creativity Center Fellowship 528
Norton & Company, Inc., W.W. 486
Notebook: A Little Magazine 232
Nova SF 391
Now and Then 233
NRG 233
Nuclear Fiction 233
Nugent & Associates, Inc. 562
Nugget 366
Nuts To Us! 528

O

Oak Square 233
Obsidian II: Black Literature in Review 234
O'Connor Award for Short Fiction, The Flannery 528
O'Connor Fiction Award, Frank 528
Ohio Arts Council Aid to Individual Artists Fellowship 529
Ohio Review, The 234
Ohioana Book Award 529
Okanagan Short Fiction Award, The 529
Okike 315
Old Hickory Review 234
Old Red Kimono, The 235
Ommation Press 428
Ommation Press Book Award 529
Omni 366
On Our Backs 367
On the Edge 235
On the Line 367
Open Magazine 235
Open Voice Awards 529
Opossum 316
Options 367
Orchard Books 487
Oregon East 235
Oregon Individual Artist Fellowship 529
Orient Paperbacks 502
Oscard Associates, Fifi 562
Other Side Short Fiction Award, The 529
Other Side, The 369
Other Voices 236
Other Worlds 236
Oui Magazine 369
Our Child Press 429
Ouroboros 236
Outlaw Biker 369
Outrider 316
Overseas! 391
Owlflight 237
Oxford Magazine 237
Oyez Review 237

P

P.I. Magazine 238
P.U.N. (Play on Words) 238
Pacific Review 238
Padre Productions 429
Painted Bride Quarterly 238
Paisano Fellowships, Dobie 529
Palouse Journal 369
Pando Publications 429
Pandora 239
Panhandler, The 239
Pantheon Books 487
Panurge 316
Paper Bag Short, Shorts 530
Paper Bag, The 239
Paper Radio 240
Paper-Mache Press 429
Papyrus Publishers 430
Paris Review, The 240
Parting Gifts 240
Partisan Review 240
Path Press, Inc. 430
Pavor Nocturnus 241
Paycock Press 430
Peace and Freedom 316
Peden Prize in Fiction, William 530
Pegasus Review, The 241
Pelican Publishing Company 487
Pelter, Literary Agent, Rodney 562
Pembroke Magazine 241
PEN/Book-of-the-Month Club Translation Prize 530
Pencil Press Quarterly 242
PEN/Faulkner Award, The 530
Pennsylvania Council on the Arts Fellowship Program 530
Pennsylvania English 242
Pennsylvania Review 242
Pennywhistle Press 370
Pentagram Press 430
Peoplenet 242
Perceptions 242
Peregrine 243
Permafrost 243
Perseverance Press 431
Perspectives Press 431
Phelan Award, James D. 530
Philomel Books 487
Phlogiston 316
Phoebe 243
Pig Iron 244
Pig Paper, The 244
Pikestaff Forum, The 244
Pikestaff Publications, Inc. 431
Pillow Talk 370
Pineapple Press 432
Pipe Smoker's Ephemeris, The 245
Pippin Press 432
Plain Dealer Magazine, The 370
Playboy College Fiction Contest 530
Playboy Magazine 370
Playgirl Magazine 370
Pléiades Magazine/Philae Magazine 245
Ploughshares 245
Ploughshares Denise and Mel Cohen Award 530
Plowman, The 246
Pocahontas Press, Inc. 432
Pocket Books 488
Pockets 371
Poe Awards, Edgar Allan 530
Poetic Liberty 246
Poetry Halifax Dartmouth 246
Poetry Magic 247

Can't find a listing? Check pages 318-319 for Other Literary and Small Circulation Magazines, page 392 for Other Commercial Periodicals, pages 454-455 for Other Small Presses, page 503 for Other Commercial Publishers, page 541 for Other Contests or page 572 for Other Agents.

Poggioli Translation Award, The Renato 530
Point Books 488
Popular Library 488
Porcelain Agency, Sidney 562
Porcupine's Quill, Inc. 433
Portable Wall, The 247
Portents 247
Porter Prize for Fiction, Katherine Anne 531
Portland Magazine 371
Portland Review 247
Poseidon Press 488
Post, The 247
Post-Apollo Press, The 433
Potato Eyes 248
Potter, Inc., Clarkson N. 489
Pottersfield Portfolio 248
Poultry 248
Prairie Fire 249
Prairie Journal of Canadian Literature, The 249
Prairie Journal Press 433
Prairie Publishing Company, The 433
Prairie Schooner 249
Prairie Schooner the Lawrence Foundation Award 531
Prentice-Hall Books for Young Readers 489
Presidio Press 489
Press Gang Publishers 433
Press of Macdonald and Renecke, The 434
Price Stern Sloan, Inc. 489
Priest Literary Agency Inc., The Aaron M. 563
Primavera 250
Prime Times 371
Prism International 250
Prism International Short Fiction Contest 531
Prisoners of the Night 251
Private Letters 372
Prix Molson De L'Académie Canadienne-Française, Le 531
Probe 316
Processed World 251
Proem Canada 251
Proof Rock 252
Prospice 316
Prospice Publishing (UK) Ltd. 454
Protter, Literary Agent, Susan Ann 563
PSI 252
Ptolemy/The Browns Mills Review 252
Pub, The 252
Published Short-Story Contest 531
Puckerbrush Press 434
Puerto Del Sol 253
Pulitzer Prize in Fiction 531
Pulp Press Book Publishers 434
Pulp Press International, 3 Day Novel-Writing Competition 531
Pulphouse 253
Pure Bred Dogs/American Kennel Gazette 531
Purpose 372
Pushcart Press Editors Book Award 531
Pushcart Prize 532
Putnam's Sons, G.P. 489

Q

Q.E.D. Press of Ann Arbor, Inc. 434
Quarry 253
Quarry Press 435
Quarry West 254
Quarterly West 254
Quarterly West Novella Competition 532
Quartet Books Limited 502
Queen of All Hearts 254
Queen's Quarterly 254
Quicksilver Books, Inc. 563
Quimby 255
Quintessential Space Debris 255

R

R-A-D-A-R 373
Raddle Moon, The 255
Radiance 373
Rag Mag 255
Ragdale Foundation Residencies for Writers and Visual Artists 532
Rainbow City Express 256
Raleigh Award, Sir Walter 532
Rambunctious Review 256
Rambunctious Review, Annual Fiction Contest 532
Rampant Guinea Pig, The 256
Random House, Inc. 489
R&R Entertainment Digest 391
Ranger Associates, Inc. 435
Ranger Rick Magazine 373
Rashi 316
Ravan Press (Pty) Ltd 454
Re Arts and Letters [REAL] 257
Read Me 257
Read 'n Run Books 435
Reality Magazine 391
Reaper, The 257
Reconstructionist 258
Red Alder Books 436
Red Bass 258
Red Cedar Review 258
Red Deer College Press 436
Redbook 374
Redneck Review of Literature, The 258
Rees Literary Agency, Helen 563
Reference Press 436
Reform Judaism 374
Reformed Journal, The 259
Regina Medal Award 532
Relix Magazine 374
Renaissance Fan 259
Renegade 259
Re/Search Publishing 436
Resonance 260
Resource Publications, Inc. 490
Response 260
RFD 260
Rhode Island State Arts Council 532
Ribalow Prize, Harold U. 532
Rinehart Fund, The Mary Roberts 532
River City 260
River Styx 260
Riverside Quarterly 261
Riverwind 261
Road King Magazine 375
Roanoke Review 261
Robbins Office, Inc., The 563
Roberts Award, Summerfield G. 533
Robert's Writing Awards 533
Rockford Review, The 261
Rocky Mountain Women's Institute Associateship 533
Rodell-Frances Collin Literary Agency, Marie (see Frances Collin, Literary Agent 548)
Rohwedder 262
Romance Writers of America Golden Heart/Golden Medallion Awards 533
Room of One's Own 262
Rose Arts Magazine, The 263
Rose Literary Agency, The Mitchell 563
Rotrosen Agency, Jane 564
Round Table, The 263
Rowan Tree Press 437
Russell & Volkening, Inc. 564

S

Sacramento Public Library Focus on Writers Contest 533
Sagalyn, Inc., Literary Agency, Raphael 564
Saint Anthony Messenger 375
Saint Joseph's Messenger and Advocate of the Blind 375
St. Luke's Press, Inc. 437
St. Martin's Press 490
St. Paul Books and Media 490
Salome: A Journal of the Performing Arts 263
Salt Lick Press 263
Samisdat 264
Samisdat 437
San Gabriel Valley Magazine 264
San Jose Studies 264
San Jose Studies Best Story Award 533
Sandpiper Press 437
Santa Monica Review 265
Sassy Magazine 376
Satchell's Publishing 438

SBC Enterprises, Inc. 564
Scagnetti, Jack 564
Schaffner Agency, Inc. 564
Schlessinger-Van Dyck Agency 564
Scholastic 490
Scholastic Scope 376
Scholastic Writing Awards 533
School Magazine 391
Schulman Literary Agency, Inc., Susan 565
Schwartz, Arthur P. 565
Science Fiction Randomly 265
Science Fiction Writers of Earth (SFWoE) Short Story Contest 533
Scifant 265
Scojtia Publishing Company, Inc. 438
Scream Magazine 265
Scribner's Sons, Charles, Books for Young Readers 490
Scribner's Sons, Charles 491
Scripsi 316
Scrivener 266
Sea Fog Press, Inc. 438
Seacoast Life 376
Seal Press 439
Seaton Awards, The 534
Seattle Review, The 266
Second Chance Press and the Permanent Press 439
Seek 377
Seems 267
Seligman Literary Agency, Lynn 565
Senior Life Magazine 377
Sensations 267
Sequoia 267
Serendipity 267
Settle Press (Wigmore) 454
Seven Buffaloes Press 439
Seventeen 377
Seventeen Magazine/Smith Corona Fiction Contest 534
Sewanee Review, The 268
Shattered Wig Review 268
Shawnee Silhouette 268
Sheep Meadow Press, The 439
Shenandoah: The Washington and Lee University Review 269
Shoe Tree 269
Shoe Tree Press 439
Shofar 378
Shooting Star Review 269
Short Story Science Fiction/Fantasy Competition 534
Sidgwick & Jackson Ltd. 502
Siegel Agency, Bobbe 565
Sierra Club Award for Distinguished Nature Writing, The 534
Sierra Club Books 491
Sign of the Times 269
Signal, The 270
Silhouette Books 491
Silverfish Review 270
Silverleaf Press, Inc. 440
Simon & Pierre Publishing Company Limited 440
Simon & Schuster 491
Sing Heavenly Muse! 270
Singer Literary Agency Inc., Evelyn 565
Singer Media Corporation 565
Single Parent, The 378
Singlelife Magazine 378
Sinister Wisdom 270
Skylark 271
Slipstream 271
Slow Dancer 316
Small Pond Magazine, The 271
Smile 272
Smith, Gibbs, Publisher 491
Smith, W.H./Books in Canada Award for First Novels 534
Sneak Preview, The 272
Snell Literary Agency, Michael 566
Snow Contest, Kay 534
Social Alternatives 317
Society of Children's Book Writers Golden Kite Awards 534
Society of Children's Book Writers Work-In-Progress Awards 534
Soho Press 440
Sojourner 272
Solid Copy 272
Sonora Review 273
Sonora Review Fiction Contest 535
Soundings East 273
South Carolina Arts Commission and The State Newspaper South Carolina Fiction Project 535
South Carolina Arts Commission Literature Fellowship and Literature Grants 535
South Carolina Review 273
South Dakota Arts Council, Artist Fellowship 535
South Dakota Review 274
Southern California Anthology 274
Southern Humanities Review 274
Southern Review, The 275
Southern Review/Louisiana State University Annual Short Fiction Award, The 535
Southern Writers, Inc. 566
Southwest Review 275
Sou'Wester 275
Space and Time 275
Spatt, Esq., David M. 566
Special Report: Fiction 378
Spectrum (California) 276
Spectrum (Massachusetts) 276
Speech Bin, Inc., The 440
Spieler Literary Agency, F. Joseph 566
Spindrift 276
Spinsters/Aunt Lute Book Co. 441
Spirit That Moves Us, The 277
Spiritual Fiction Publications 441
Spitball 277
Spitzer Literary Agency, Philip G. 566
Spoofing! 277
Sports Afield 379
SPSM&H 278
Spur Award Contest 535
Square One 278
Stamp Axe 278
Stand Magazine 317
Stand Magazine Short Story Competition 535
Standard 379
Standard Publishing 492
Star Books, Inc. 441
Star Route Journal 279
Starry Nights 279
Starshore 279
Starsong 280
Starwind 280
Station Hill Press 442
Steele & Co., Ltd., Literary Agents, Lyle 567
Stegner Fellowship, Wallace E. 535
Stemmer House Publishers, Inc. 492
Stepping Stone 567
Sterling Web, The 280

Can't find a listing? Check pages 318-319 for Other Literary and Small Circulation Magazines, page 392 for Other Commercial Periodicals, pages 454-455 for Other Small Presses, page 503 for Other Commercial Publishers, page 541 for Other Contests or page 572 for Other Agents.

Stern Agency, Gloria 567
Stern Associates, Charles M. 567
Sternig Literary Agency, Larry 567
Stewart Agency, Jo 567
Stoddart 492
Stone Drum 281
Stone Soup 281
Stories 281
Stormline Press, Inc. 442
Story 282
Story Friends 380
Story Quarterly 282
Story Time Short-Story Contest 536
Storyette (see First Stories 177)
Straight 380
Strange Plasma 282
Stroker Magazine 282
Struggle 283
Student Lawyer 380
Student, The 380
Studia Mystica 283
Studio: A Journal of Christians Writing 317
Stuhlmann Author's Representative, Gunther 567
Sturgeon Memorial Award for the Best SF Short Fiction (see John W. Campbell Memorial Award 511)
Sub-Terrain 283
Summit Books 493
Sun Dog: The Southeast Review 284
Sun, The 284
Sunday Journal Magazine 381
Sunshine Magazine 381
Sunstone Press 442
Suntory Awards for Mystery Fiction 536
Swank Magazine 381
Swanson, Inc., H.N. 568
SWG Literary Awards 536
Swift Kick 285
Sword of Shahrazad 285
Sycamore Review 285

T

T.W.I.286
Tabula Rasa 286
Tak Ṭak Tak 317
Tampa Review, The 286
Tandava 287
Tapestry 287
Targ Literary Agency, Inc., Roslyn 568
Tattoo Advocate Journal 382
Teal Literary Agency, Patricia 568
Teal Press 442
Tears in the Fence 317
Teen Magazine 382
Teen Power 382
Teens Today 383
Tennessee Arts Commission Individual Artists Fellowship 536
Tentra Artnet BBS 287
Terror Time Again 287
Texas Connection Magazine 383
Texas Monthly Press 493
Texas Review, The 288
Texas State Writing Competition 536
Textile Bridge Press 442
Thema 288
Thin Ice 288
Think for Yourself/Flower Pot Press 317
Third Woman 289
Third Woman Press 443
Thistledown Press 443
Thompson Talent Agency 568
Thorndike Press 493
Three Continents Press 443
Thumbprints 289
Thurber House Residencies 536
Ticknor and Fields 493
Tide Book Publishing Company 443
Tidewater 289
Tikkun 383
Timbuktu 289
Times Eagle Books 445
Tiptoe Literary Service 445
Toad Hiway 290
Today's Guide 391
Together 317
Tor Books 493
Touch 383
Towson State University Prize for Literature 536
Tq (Teenquest) 384
Tradeswomen 290
Trailer Boats Magazine 384
Train Humor Prize, John 536
Trajectories 290
Tramp 291
Translation 291
Translation Center Awards 536
Translation Center, The 445
Translators Association Awards 537
Transworld Publishers 502
Treetop Panorama 291
Trillium Press 493
Triquarterly 291
Troll Associates 494
TSR, Inc. 494
Tucumcari Literary Review 292
Tudor Publishers, Inc. 445
Turn-On Letters 384
Turnstile 292
Turnstone Press 445
Turtle Magazine for Preschool Kids 385
TV-TS Journal 292
Twain Award, Mark 537
Twisted 293
2 AM Magazine 293
Two-Ton Santa 293
Tyndale House Publishers 494
Tyro Magazine 294

U

Ucross Foundation/Residency 537
Ultramarine Publishing Co., Inc. 446
Uncensored Letters 385
Union Street Review 294
US1 Worksheets 295
University Editions 446
University of Arkansas Press, The 446
University of Georgia Press 494
University of Idaho Press 447
University of Illinois Press 447
University of Minnesota Press 496
University of Missouri Breakthrough Series 537
University of Portland Review 294
University of Utah Press 447
Unknowns 294
Unmuzzled Ox 295
Unspeakable Visions of the Individual, The 295
Urstadt Inc., Susan P. 568
Utah Original Writing Competition 537

V

Valley Grapevine 295
Valley Women's Voice 295
Vanitas Press, The 454
Var Tufa 296
Vardaman 447
Verandah 317
Verdict Magazine 296
Vermont Council on the Arts Fellowship 537
Very Small Magazine, A 296
Vesta Publications, Ltd 496
Vicinanza, Ltd., Ralph M. 568
Victoria Management (see Frank Weimann Associates 570)
Victorian Fellowship of Australian Writers Annual National Literary Awards 537
Victorin Memorial Award, James F. 538
Videomania 296
Vigil 317
Village Idiot, The 297
Villard Books 496
Vintage Northwest 297
Virgin Meat Fanzine 297
Virginia Center for the Creative Arts Residency Fellowship 538
Virginia Prize for Fiction, The 538
Virginia Quarterly Review 298
Virtue 385
Visibilities 298
Vision 385

Vision Books Pvt Ltd. 502
Vista 386
Vogelstein Foundation Grants 538
Vursell Memorial Award, Harold D. 538

W

W W. Publications 447
Wald Associates, Inc., Mary Jack 568
Walker and Company 496
Walker Books/Julia Macrae Books/Nick Hern Books 502
Wallant Memorial Book Award, Edward Lewis 538
Wallerstein Agency, The Gerry B. 569
Ware Literary Agency, John A. 569
Warner Books 497
Warren Literary Agency, James 569
Warren/Hilton Agency (see Alice Hilton Literary Agency 555)
Wascana Review 298
Washington Prize for Fiction 538
Washington Review 298
Washington Square Press 497
Washington State Arts Commission Artist Fellowship Award 538
Washingtonian, The 386
Waterfront Press 448
Watermark Press, Inc. 448
Waterside Productions, Inc. 569
Watt and Associates, Sandra 570
Wayside 298
Wee Wisdom Magazine 386
Weidenfeld and Nicolson Ltd. 502
Weil Agency, Inc., The Wendy 570
Weimann Associates, Frank 570
Weiner Literary Agency, Cherry 570
Weird Tales 386
Weirdbook 299
West Branch 299
West Coast Review 299
West Texas Sun, The 300
Westerly 317
Western Canadian Magazine Awards 538
Western Heritage Awards 539
Western People 387
Western Producer Prairie Books 497
Western Publishing Company, Inc. 498
Western States Book Awards 539
Weyr Agency, Rhoda 570
What 300
Whetstone 300
Whiskey Island Magazine 301
Whispering Wind Magazine 301
White Children's Book Award, William Allen 539
White Wall Review, The 301
Whiting Writer's Awards 539
Whitman & Company, Albert 498
Wicazo SA Review, The 301
Wide Open Magazine 302
Widener Review, The 302
Wieser & Wieser 570
Wigwag 387
Wild East 302
Wilder Award, Laura Ingalls 539
Wildstar Books/Empire Books 498
Willow Springs 302
Wind Magazine 303
Winship Book Award, Laurence L. 539
Winston-Derek Publishers 499
Wisconsin Academy Review 303
Wisconsin Arts Board Individual Artist Program 539
Wisconsin Restaurateur, The 303
Wisconsin Review 304
With Magazine 387
Witness (Michigan) 304
Witness (Pennsylvania) 304
Woman in the Moon Publications 448
Woman of Power 304
Woman Sleuth Mystery Series, The 448
Womans Day 388
Woman's Realm 392
Woman's Weekly 392
Womens American ORT Reporter 388
Women's Press 449
Women's Press, The 502
Wonder Time 388
Woodley Memorial Press 449
Woodsong Graphics Inc. 449
Worcester Review, The 305
Word & Image 305
Working Classics 305
Works 317
World's Best Short Short Story Contest 539
Worldwide Library 499
Wreschner, Authors' Representative, Ruth 571
Wright Representatives Inc., Ann 571
Writ Magazine 306
Writers at Work Fellowship Competition 539
Writers' Bar-B-Q, The 306
Writer's Digest Annual Writing Competition (Short Story Division) 540
Writers' Forum 306
Writers Guild of Alberta Literary Award 540
Writers House, Inc. 571
Writer's Journal Annual Fiction Contest 540
Writers Newsletter 307
Writers' Productions 571
Writers' Rendezvous 307
Writers' Rostrum, The 318
Writing 318
Writing Pursuits 307
Wyoming Council on the Arts Frank Nelson Doubleday Memorial Award 540
Wyoming Council on the Arts, Literary Fellowships 540
Wyoming Council on the Arts Neltje Blanchan Memorial Award 540
Wyoming the Hub of the Wheel 308
Wyrick & Company 451

X

Xavier Review 308

Y

Yaddo Residencies 540
Yak 308
Yale Review, The 308
Yankee Magazine 388
Yearling 499
Yellow Silk 309

Can't find a listing? Check pages 318-319 for Other Literary and Small Circulation Magazines, page 392 for Other Commercial Periodicals, pages 454-455 for Other Small Presses, page 503 for Other Commercial Publishers, page 541 for Other Contests or page 572 for Other Agents.

Yith Press 451
York Press 451
Yost Associates, Mary 571
Young Adult Canadian Book Award 540
Young American 389
Young Crusader, The 389
Young Judaean 309
Young Reader's Choice Award 541
Young Salvationist/Young Soldier 389
Young Voices Magazine 309

Z

Z Miscellaneous 310
Zebra Books 499
Zeckendorf Associates, Susan 571
Zephyr Press 451
Zero Hour 310
Zoiks! 310
Zoland Books, Inc. 452
Zolotow Books, Charlotte (see Harper & Row Junior Books) 500
Zondervan 500
Zymergy 311
Zyzzyva 311

Other Books of Interest

Annual Directories
Artist's Market, edited by Susan Conner $19.95
Children's Writer's & Illustrator's Market, edited by Connie Eidenier (paper) $15.95
Humor & Cartoon Markets, edited by Bob Staake (paper) $15.95
Photographer's Market, edited by Sam Marshall $19.95
Poet's Market, by Judson Jerome $18.95
Songwriter's Market, edited by Mark Garvey $18.95
Writer's Market, edited by Glenda Neff $23.95
Fiction Writing Instruction
The Elements of Fiction Writing Series:
Characters & Viewpoint, by Orson Scott Card $13.95
Dialogue, by Lewis Turco $12.95
Plot, by Ansen Dibell $13.95
Revision, by Kit Reed $13.95
Theme & Strategy, by Ronald B. Tobias $13.95
Manuscript Submission, by Scott Edelstein $13.95
The Writer's Digest Genre Writing Series:
How to Write Romances, by Phyllis Taylor Pianka $13.95
How to Write Western Novels, by Matt Braun $13.95
How to Write Action/Adventure Novels, by Michael Newton $13.95
How to Write Mysteries, by Shannon OCork $13.95
The Art & Craft of Novel Writing, by Oakley Hall $16.95
Creating Short Fiction, by Damon Knight (paper) $9.95
Dare to Be a Great Writer: 329 Keys to Powerful Fiction, by Leonard Bishop $15.95
Fiction is Folks: How to Create Unforgettable Characters, by Robert Newton Peck (paper) $8.95
Handbook of Short Story Writing: Vol 1, by Dickson and Smythe (paper) $9.95
Handbook of Short Story Writing: Vol. II, edited by Jean M. Fredette $15.95
How to Write & Sell Your First Novel, by Oscar Collier, with Frances Spatz Leighton (paper) $12.95
How to Write Tales of Horror, Fantasy & Science Fiction, edited by J.N. Williamson $15.95
Mystery Writer's Handbook, by The Mystery Writers of America (paper) $11.95
One Great Way to Write Short Stories, by Ben Nyberg $14.95
Spider Spin Me a Web: Lawrence Block on Writing Fiction, by Lawrence Block $16.95
Storycrafting, by Paul Darcy Boles (paper) $10.95
Writing the Modern Mystery, by Barbara Norville $15.95
Writing the Novel: From Plot to Print, by Lawrence Block (paper) $10.95
Writing Young Adult Novels, by Hadley Irwin & Jeanette Eyerly $14.95
Best Stories from New Writers, edited by Linda Sanders $16.95
Writing Reference
Beginning Writer's Answer Book, edited by Kirk Polking (paper) $13.95
How to Write a Book Proposal, by Michael Larsen $10.95
Make Every Word Count, by Gary Provost (paper) $9.95
12 Keys to Writing Books that Sell, by Kathleen Krull (paper) 12.95
The Writer's Digest Guide to Manuscript Formats, by Dian Dincin Buchman & Seli Groves $16.95
Discovering the Writer Within, by Bruce Ballenger & Barry Lane $16.95
On Being A Writer, edited by Bill Strickland $19.95

To order directly from the publisher, include $3.00 postage and handling for 1 book and 50¢ for each additional book. Allow 30 days for delivery.

Writer's Digest Books, 1507 Dana Avenue, Cincinnati, Ohio 45207
Credit card orders call TOLL-FREE
1-800-289-0963
Prices subject to change without notice.

Write to this same address for information on *Writer's Digest* magazine, Writer's Digest Book Club, Writer's Digest School, and Writer's Digest Criticism Service.

Notes

Notes